Parliament, Inventions and Patents

M000275235

This book is a research guide and bibliography of Parliamentary material, including the Old Scottish Parliament and the Old Irish Parliament, relating to patents and inventions from the early seventeenth century to 1976. It chronicles the entire history of a purely British patent law before the coming into force of the European Patent Convention under the Patents Act 1977. It provides a comprehensive record of every Act, Bill, Parliamentary paper, report, petition and recorded debate or Parliamentary question on patent law during the period.

The work will be an essential resource for scholars and researchers in intellectual property law, the history of technology, and legal and economic history.

Phillip Johnson is Professor of Commercial Law at Cardiff University, UK. His research interests include patent law, public law and legal history. His publications include a leading practitioner text, *The Modern Law of Patents* (LexisNexis), and *Privatised Law Reform: A History of Patent Law through Private Legislation, 1620–1907*.

Parliament, Inventions and Patents

A Research Guide and Bibliography

Phillip Johnson

Routledge
Taylor & Francis Group

LONDON AND NEW YORK

First published 2018 by Routledge

2 Park Square, Milton Park, Abingdon, Oxfordshire OX14 4RN
52 Vanderbilt Avenue, New York, NY 10017

Routledge is an imprint of the Taylor & Francis Group, an informa business

First issued in paperback 2020

Copyright © 2018 Phillip Johnson

The right of Phillip Johnson to be identified as author of this work
has been asserted by him in accordance with sections 77 and 78 of the
Copyright, Designs and Patents Act 1988.

All rights reserved. No part of this book may be reprinted or reproduced or
utilised in any form or by any electronic, mechanical, or other means, now
known or hereafter invented, including photocopying and recording, or in
any information storage or retrieval system, without permission in writing
from the publishers.

Notice:
Product or corporate names may be trademarks or registered trademarks,
and are used only for identification and explanation without intent to
infringe.

British Library Cataloguing-in-Publication Data
A catalogue record for this book is available from the British Library

Library of Congress Cataloging-in-Publication Data
Names: Johnson, Phillip (Phillip Michael), author.
Title: Parliament, inventions and patents : a research guide and
    bibliography / Phillip Johnson.
Description: Abingdon, Oxon ; New York, NY : Routledge, 2018. |
    Includes bibliographical references and index.
Identifiers: LCCN 2017035809| ISBN 9781138572270 (hardback) |
    ISBN 9781351332644 (adobe reader) | ISBN 9781351332637
    (epub) | ISBN 9781351332620 (mobipocket)
Subjects: LCSH: Patent laws and legislation—Great Britain—
    Bibliography. | Patent laws and legislation—Great Britain—Legal
    research. | Patent laws and legislation—Great Britain—Sources.
Classification: LCC KD1361 .J64 2018 | DDC 346.4104/860262—dc23
LC record available at https://lccn.loc.gov/2017035809

ISBN: 978-1-138-57227-0 (hbk)
ISBN: 978-0-367-66679-8 (pbk)

Typeset in Bembo
by Swales & Willis Ltd, Exeter, Devon, UK

Contents

Acknowledgements

This book is the accidental child of my monograph *Privatised Law Reform: A History of Patent Law through Private Legislation, 1620–1907*. It began as a short appendix listing private Acts, and later Bills, relating to patent law and little more. I then added to it a little, and then a little more, including more material about private legislation, and then prizes and so on. Soon it was as long as the monograph and would no longer be an appendix, but a separate work in its own right. As it grew in maturity, it took on a life of its own. If it included private Acts, it would be odd not to include public Acts, if it included rewards paid, why not rewards claimed but refused? What about the vast swath of legislation on the taxation of patents? So its limbs strengthened and extended until it was around three and a half times the size of its parent. And of course, as the child grew, it discovered new things and these were fed back into the parent work. The cataloguing central to this book enabled the monograph from where it came to develop and be much better than it would otherwise have been.

The cataloguing of materials from so many different sources means that I have benefited from assistance from some outstanding archivists and librarians. Whenever I visited the Parliamentary Archive, I would first send very long lists of volumes to consult, and the staff there were unstintingly helpful. Usually, I would collect the book from the desk, find a page, photograph it and return it to the desk and take the next. This meant I was keeping the book for only a minute or two, and repeating this through tens of volumes over a day. The staff at the archive did everything they could to assist. In addition, I have to thank in particular Simon Gough, Rhiannon Compton, Annie Pinder and Richard Ward, who answered my particular questions and made many of the arrangements to enable this to happen.

I made similarly unreasonable requests at the British library, asking to see tens of volumes in one go, and once more the staff we incredibly helpful – in particular Lee Taylor, who helped me work out what was in the collection in the first place. In addition, I would like to thank the librarians at the London School of Economics Library, in particular Daniel Payne, Gemma Read and Emma Pizarro, and those at the Institute of Historical Research including Mette Lund Newlyn, Michael Townsend and Kate Wilcox. I would similarly like to thank the staff at the Birmingham Library and London Metropolitan Archive (Guildhall Library). I would also like to thank Shane Mawe at Trinity College Dublin's library and Erin O'Mahony from the Oireachtas Library.

As always, I received immense help from my regular librarians, as it were, Matthew Davies at Cardiff University, Malcolm Langley at the Queen Mary Intellectual Property Archive and the staff at Lincoln's Inn and Inner Temple libraries. I would also particularly like to thank Philip Baker, who kindly sent me copies of his working documents for *Proceedings in Parliament 1624: The House of Commons*.

Thanks also go to Alison Kirk, my commissioning editor, for her support and willingness to take forward this somewhat unusual project, and George Warburton who has guided it through a very tricky and complicated production.

Most importantly, I have to thank Jo, who put up with me making my "lists" for most of the last two years.

Abbreviations

Journal references

1R	First Reading	Ord	Ordered
2R	Second Reading	Pet	Petition
3R	Third Reading	Pet Ag	Petition against
adj	A particular stage is adjourned or deferred	Pet Fav	Petition in favour
Ag	Agreed	Pres	Presented
Adj 3m	A Bill being adjourned for three months (or six months) is the usual method of a Bill being killed	Proc	Proceed/Proceedings
Amd	Amendment	Prt	Printed
App	Appendix	Re-C'tted	Re-committed
Bill Ord	Bill ordered	Ref	Referred to committee or similar
Brought HC	Bill brought from HC	Rep	Report/Reported
Brought HL	Bill brought from HL	Req	Request
Com/C'tee	Committee	Res	Resolution
Conf	Conference (between House of Lords and House of Commons)	SC	Select Committee/Standing Committee
Cons	Considered/Consideration	SOC	Standing Orders Committee
COS	Committee of Supply	SO cw	Standing Orders complied with
C'tted	Committed	SO ncw	Standing Orders not complied with
CWH	Committee of the Whole House	SpOC	Special Orders Committee
day app	A day is appointed for a particular stage	Sub	Substituted
DisAg	Disagreement (with amendments)	Sums	Summons (e.g. witness summons)
Disc	Discharged	Susp	Suspended
Disp	Dispensed with	V	Vote recorded in the journal
Ex	Examined/Examiner	V&P	Votes and Proceedings
Ex Cert	Examiner's Certificate	w/d	Withdrawn
Ing	Ingrossed/Ingrossment	Wit	Witness
Mem	Memorandum	with Amds	With amendments
NC	New clause	w/o Amds	Without amendments
Obs	Observations		

Offices

Adm	Admiralty	Hom Off	Home Office
A-G	Attorney-General	Hom Sec	Home Secretary
Agric	Agriculture	Ir	Ireland
Air	Air Force	Jr Ld Tr	Junior Lord of the Treasury
Ass	Assistant	LC	Lord Chancellor
Av	Aviation	Ld Ch	Lord Chairman
Bd Control	Board of Control	Ld House	Leader of the House
BoAgric	Board of Agriculture	Par Sec	Parliamentary Secretary
BoEd	Board of Education	PM	Prime Minister
BoT	Board of Trade	PM Gen	Postmaster General
Ch Com	Chief Commissioner	Pr	President
Ch Ex	Chancellor of the Exchequer	Prod	Production
Ch W&M	Chair of Ways and Means	Sc	Science
Ch Whip	Chief Whip	Sec	Secretary
Civ Av	Civil Aviation	S-G	Solicitor-General
Co Av Ship	Companies, Aviation and Shipping	SG Ord	Surveyor-General Ordnance
Col	Colonial Office/Colonies	Soc Ser	Social Services
Def	Defence	SoS	Secretary of State
Dep	Deputy	Supp	Supply
Dept	Department	Sur Ord	Surveyor of Ordnance
DHSS	Department of Health and Social Security	Tech	Technology
Econ Aff	Economic Affairs	T&I	Trade and Industry
Ed	Education	Tr	Treasury
Fin Sec	Financial Secretary	Tr Com Aff	Trade and Commercial Affairs
(Fir) Com Works	(First) Commissioner of Works	Trans	Transport
(Fir) Ld Adm	(First) Lord of the Admiralty	US	Under Secretary of State
FO	Foreign Office	VC Household	Vice Chamberlain of the Household (Whip)
For Sec	Foreign Secretary	VP	Vice President
HC	House of Commons	W&B	Works and Boards
He	Health	War	War Office
HL	House of Lords	w/o Port	Without Portfolio

Introduction

The role of Parliament in the history of patent law and in rewarding inventors is often neglected. This is largely because the granting of patents was an exercise of the royal prerogative and was not fully a creature of statute under recent times. This means that those looking at the history of patent law in the United Kingdom before the nineteenth century have traditionally only considered the turbulent Parliaments towards the end of the reign of James I when the great monopolies were challenged and the Statute of Monopolies enacted,[1] with Boehm and Silberston going so as far as to abdicate any need to consider Parliament for the next two hundred years.[2]

While there are some excellent histories of the earlier period in the development of patent law,[3] these have often stopped before the role of Parliament became significant once more. They cover the long eighteenth century and usually stop at the point where the patent system becomes modern.[4] This has enabled historians to sideline the role of Parliament without necessarily undermining their narrative. Only where there has been a specific attempt to address a Parliamentary matter, such as Parliamentary rewards[5] or the movement to abolish the patent system,[6] has there been a need to look at Parliament.

One of the difficulties historians have faced when considering patents and their role in Parliament is the fact that the Parliamentary materials are Byzantine at times. The absence of adequate Parliamentary reporting until late in the nineteenth century, the complexities of an evolving Parliamentary procedure as well as the difficulty in finding many of the sources can put off all but the most determined. By way of example, the Patents, Designs and Trade Marks Act 1883 was a turning point in the history of patents, as it represented British patent law reaching maturity. This Act was the thirteenth patent Act to be passed since the beginning of the reign of James I. During this same period, there were forty-one failed attempts to legislate for patents, and finding materials about failed Bills is much more difficult than Acts of Parliament. To understand the evolution of patent law and the protection of inventions, it is necessary to discover both the successes and the multitude of failures.

The purpose of this book is to lay bare Parliamentary material until modern times, to enable researchers to unpick and discover new stories, and to facilitate a fuller and more complete history of technology, invention and patent law to be written.[7] Patents have always presented problems to researchers, whether industrial, legal or bibliographical. It was only in the middle of the nineteenth century that patent specifications were enrolled in only one place. Before that time, they could be enrolled in any one of three different offices of the Chancery. This problem was largely, although not completely, addressed by Bennett Woodcroft[8] in the nineteenth century.

He attempted to catalogue all the patents that had been granted between 1617 and 1852,[9] and produced four indexes of patents:[10] an index of the title of patents,[11] a subject matter index,[12] an alphabetical index of patentees[13] and a reference index.[14] While there were a few patents missed by Woodcroft which others have subsequently discovered,[15] his work has made the descriptions of early patented inventions available. Indeed, once Woodcroft began his work at the Office of the Commissioners for Patents,[16] the proper cataloguing

---

1 Harold G Fox, *Monopolies and Patents: A Study of the History of Future of the Patent Monopoly* (Toronto 1947).

2 Klaus Boehm and Aubrey Silberston, *The British Patent System: I. Administration* (Cambridge 1967), p 18.

3 Harry Dutton, *The Patent System and Inventive Activity during the Industrial Revolution 1750–1852* (Manchester 1984); Christine MacLeod, *Inventing the Industrial Revolution: The English Patent System 1660–1800* (Cambridge 1988); Sean Bottomley, *The British Patent System during the Industrial Revolution 1700–1852* (Cambridge 2014).

4 The role of Parliament in the evolution of patent law is discussed in great detail in Phillip Johnson, *Privatised Law Reform: A History of Patent Law through Private Legislation, 1620–1907* (Routledge 2017).

5 Robert Burrell and Catherine Kelly, "Parliamentary Rewards and the Evolution of the Patent System" (2015) 74 *Cam LJ* 423; Robert Burrell and Catherine Kelly, "Public Rewards and Innovation Policy: Lessons from the Eighteenth and Nineteenth Centuries" (2014) 77 *MLR* 858.

6 Fritz Machlup and Edith Penrose, "The Patent Controversy in the Nineteenth Century" (1950) 10 *Journal of Economic History* 1; Moureen Coulter, *Property in Ideas: The Patent Question in Mid-Victorian Britain* (Thomas Jefferson University Press 1991), Ch 3–5 (although she deals with some other topics as well).

7 As Brad Sherman has suggested, a legal history of patent law has "yet to be written": see "Towards an History of Patent Law", in *Intellectual Property in Common Law and Civil Law* (ed Toshiko Takenaka) (Edward Elgar 2013) at p 3.

of patents commenced, which has continued. This means that the subject matter of patents themselves is well documented.

In the 1980s, Peter Hayward sought out every reported decision relating to patents from the Case of Monopolies in 1601 to 1883, when the Official Reports of Patent Cases began to be published. He produced eleven volumes of *Hayward's Patent Cases* containing over eight hundred reported cases. The last volume included various additional tables linking patent numbers to cases, as well a technical index of those litigated patents. While Bottomley has discovered actions before the Courts of Chancery which were unreported[17] and so not included in Hayward's collection, there are also a multitude of reports of patent cases in newspapers, such as *The Times* which did not lead to formal law reports.[18] Nevertheless, Hayward's work, and particularly his indexing and cross-referencing,[19] has made patent cases more accessible. Once the Reports of Patent Cases were published, thereafter digests were published well into the twentieth century.

Thus, the granting of patents and the reporting of patent cases has been well documented. The work of Parliament, however, has received no similar treatment. The purpose of this Research Guide is to fill that gap. The development of patent law, the oversight of the work of the Patent Office, and the awards given to individuals were routinely considered in Parliament over hundreds of years. The aim of this Guide is to identify all the Parliamentary material relating to patents and for supporting inventions,[20] up until the beginning of the 1976–77 Parliamentary Session. This session was chosen as it marks the beginning of a European patent system, under the Patents Act 1977, and the end of the development of a purely British patent system.

In contrast to when Woodcroft and Hayward published their works, the availability of digital resources means that a reproduction of the original material in a series of volumes would be of little assistance to modern researchers. Instead, this volume is a giant bibliography and index to the material.

The Guide is divided into eight parts, and each begins with an introduction to give further details about the material it catalogues.[21] The first part deals with public legislation relating to patents, both Acts and Bills. The second part details private Acts and Bills which have related to patents. The third part covers the old Scottish and Irish Parliaments and their Acts relating to inventions. In the fourth part, there is a list of statutory instruments and rules passed with information about the related parliamentary material. Thereafter, in Part 5, there are detailed the rewards granted by Parliament by way of a specific resolution. Part 6 contains all the various Parliamentary papers and reports into the patent system. The penultimate part lists all the petitions lodged with Parliament relating to patent law and inventions. The final part details questions asked of ministers and mentions of patents and significant mentions of inventions.

---

8   For biographical information, see: John Hewish, *The Indefatigable Mr Woodcroft: The Legacy of Invention* (British Library 1980); Brian Speat, "Bennet Woodcroft – Patent Information Pioneer" (2012) 34 *World Patent Information* 159.

9   Some of the earlier Elizabethan grants have been catalogued by Edward Wyndham Hulme, "The History of the Patent System under the Prerogative and the Common Law" (1896) 12 *LQR* 141 and (1900) 16 *LQR* 44. The entire Elizabethan patent roll has now been calendared, which further assists with finding earlier grants.

10 There is also the *Cradle of Invention: 1617 to 1895* (Finishing Publications), which provides a database of the bibliographic details of each patent during that period.

11 Bennett Woodcroft, *Titles of Patents of Inventions: Chronologically Arranged, 1617–1852* (GE Eyre & W Spottiswoode 1854).

12 Bennett Woodcroft, *Subject-matter index (made from titles only) of patents of invention, 1617–1852* (2nd Ed, GE Eyre & W Spottiswoode 1857).

13 Bennett Woodcroft, *Alphabetical Index of Patentees of Inventions 1617–1852* (Rvsd Ed, Evelyn, Adams and Mackay 1969).

14 Bennett Woodcroft, *Reference index of English patents of invention 1617–1852* (GE Eyre & W Spottiswoode 1862).

15 AA Gomme, *Patents of Invention: Origin and Growth of the Patent System in Britain* (1946); see, more recently, Aurélien Ruellet, *Les privilèges d'invention en France et en Angleteer (ca 1600–ca 1660): base de données proviso ire* (2014), as well as the development of the PRIVILEGES databases as part of the Agence Nationale de la Recherche-funded project *Les privilèges économiques en Europe, XVe–XIXe siècles: étude quantitative et comparative* (led by Dominique Margairaz).

16 The forerunner of the Patent Office; for a history, see John Hewish, *Rooms Near Chancery Lane: The Patent Office under the Commissioners 1852–1883* (British Library 2000).

17 Sean Bottomley, "Patent Cases in the Court of Chancery, 1714–58" (2014) 35 *Journal of Legal History* 27.

18 The author has found well over a hundred cases mentioned in *The Times* which are not included in Hayward's collection. However, these are usually not law reports, but journalistic notes: see Nathaniel Lindley, "History of the Law Reports" (1885) 1 *LQR* 137 at 142.

19 Included in the eleventh volume.

20 This is a slightly amorphous category, and open to far more interpretation.

21 The introductions to Parts 1 and 2 also provide broader information about the nature of Parliamentary material.

Part 1 | Public Acts and Bills

Part 1 contents

Chapter 1: Public patent Acts

Chapter 2: Public Acts with patent provisions

(continued)

(continued)

Chapter 3: Public patent Bills

Introduction

The first part of this work relates to public Acts and Bills. The first chapter includes a "record" for every patent enactment from the Statute of Monopolies in 1624[1] to the last before the beginning of the European system under the Patents Act 1977, namely the Patents and Designs (Renewals, Extensions and Fees) Act 1961. The second chapter includes a record for each other enactment which amends substantive patent law specifically, other than those which make merely consequential amendments. The third chapter includes a record of every patent or similar Bill which has been presented to Parliament over this period. Throughout each chapter, there is a separate record for each enactment and they all follow largely the same pattern. Acts which related to the expansion of the Patent Office buildings are also included in this part despite the fact they were enacted following the private Bill procedure.[2]

---

1 The Statute of Monopolies is sometimes dated 1623 and sometimes 1624. This arises because the New Year moved from 25 March to 1 January in 1752 by reason of the Calendar (New Style) Act 1750. Furthermore, before the Acts of Parliament (Commencement) Act 1793, an Act came into force at the beginning of the Parliamentary session when it was enacted. Accordingly, the Parliamentary session in which the Statute of Monopolies was passed assembled on 12 February 1624 (using modern dating), but at the time this would have been 12 February 1623 (as it was before 25 March). It received Royal Assent on 29 May 1624. Accordingly, at the time it would have been said to be an Act passed in 1623, but using modern dating practice, it would be 1624 either because a modern calendar is used or, mistakenly, it is dated from Royal Assent.

2 For the materials on these Bills, see also the introduction to Part 2.

Reference number and year

Each enactment is assigned a patent unique reference number which begins PUBA, for public Acts, or PUBB, for public Bills. The year of enactment is listed next, which is the legal rather than historical year.[3] The Acts and Bills are chronologically ordered based on regnal year and, in the case of Acts, chapter number and in the case of Bills the date of presentment.

Short title and regnal citation and chapter number

The second entry for each record is the short title of the enactment. The source of the short title varies between enactments. Later enactments usually included a provision in the Act itself giving its short title. However, in respect of earlier enactments there are two sources which have been used. The first is where a short title has been assigned to the Acts by a later enactment[4] (e.g. the Statute of Monopolies). Where there is no statutory authority for the short title, that given in the Chronological Table of the Statutes is used.[5]

Each Act prior to 1963[6] could be cited based on the regnal year it was passed and its chapter number.[7] Thus, the Patent Law Amendment Act 1852 is 16 & 17 Vict. c. 5, which means it is the fifth public Act enacted during the Parliamentary Session held during the sixteenth and seventeenth year of Queen Victoria's reign. In the guide, the chapter is always expressed as "c" whereas the printed statutes usually used "cap" until modern times. Similarly, chapter numbers have been simplified so that in relation to public Acts the numbers are always Arabic style and presented in Roman type. Accordingly, the many variations which have been used over the past four hundred years have not been adopted.[8]

In relation to Bills, the regnal year of the session it was presented is included, although as it was not enacted there is no chapter number. In addition, reference is made to the coding given in Julian Hoppit, *Failed Legislation 1660–1800*,[9] where he lists every Bill (of any sort) which failed before Parliament between the Restoration and 1800 (however, where something was not included in that work – i.e. it was missed – the code FL: NFL is used). There is no additional information to be found in Hoppit's book that is not in this Guide, but as it was used as one of the source materials to identify relevant Bills, the coding is given.

Long title

The long title of an Act was, for many years, the correct way of citing it until it became permissible to cite the regnal year and chapter number as an alternative,[10] and later the short title.[11] The purpose of a long title is to give a general indication of the contents of the Act, and it must be comprehensive as to what it covers.[12] It is relevant in the determination of the scope of a Bill, and so, in simple terms, it is not possible to lead an amendment to a Bill during its passage unless the amendment falls within the scope of the Bill (i.e. its long title).[13]

Table of contents

The next entry in each record is a table of contents. This is made up of each section[14] heading, or side note as they were then called throughout the period. Where there are only a few patent provisions in an enactment, the table of contents only refers to those provisions with a connection to patents. Early enactments did not include side notes, they have been added by subsequent editors; in such cases, the headings used in the text come from Ruffhead's *Statutes at Large* up to 1866 and thereafter the Stationery Office version. Where a heading was not assigned by a previous editor, one has been added editorially in this Guide between square

---

3 See fn 1 above for a more detailed explanation.

4 See in particular, the Short Titles Act 1892 and 1896 and the Statute Law Revision Act 1948.

5 The table of statutes produced by HMSO.

6 When the Parliamentary Numbering and Citation Act 1962, s 1 came into force.

7 In relation to Acts and Ordinances passed during the Interregnum, the reference (A & O Interregnum) with the page number is used: see Charles Firth and Robert Rait, *Acts and Ordinances of the Interregnum, 1642–1660* (HMSO 1911).

8 For a full discussion of the numbering issues see Robert Perceval, "Chapter Six, VI, vi, 6 or 6: The Classification and Recording of Acts" (1949) 13 *Parliamentary Affairs* 506.

9 Julian Hoppit (ed), *Failed Legislation: Extracted from the Commons and Lords Journal* (Hambledon 1997).

10 Interpretation of Acts, 1850, s 3.

11 Interpretation Act 1889, s 35.

12 Daniel Greenberg (ed), *Craies on Legislation* (11th Ed, Sweet and Maxwell 2017), [2.5.9].

13 It is possible to amend the long title: Daniel Greenberg (ed), *Craies on Legislation* (11th Ed, Sweet and Maxwell 2017), [2.5.9] but it is unusual.

14 For Bills, they are clauses, not yet sections.

brackets. In relation to the Bills in Chapter 3, the table of contents is based on the last available version of the Bill before it failed, with the document used being referenced.

Where the enactment is a consolidation Act,[15] the origin of each provision is included in a separate column. This enables readers to trace a provision back to its origin. Thus, for example, s 18 of the Patents and Designs Act 1907 indicates that it originates from s 25 of the Patents, Designs and Trade Marks Act 1883 (along with an amendment made by s 17 of the Patents and Designs (Amendment) Act 1907). The table for s 25 of the 1883 Act shows that its origin is s 4 of the Letters Patent for Inventions Act 1835 (and it also indicates the amendments made by enactments thereafter: namely, the Patents Act 1839 and the Judicial Committee Act 1844). This enables researchers to work back and unpick a statutory provision from its inception.

Journals of the House of Commons and House of Lords

The *House of Commons Journal* (CJ) and *House of Lords Journal* (LJ) are the central reference point for this Guide. The official version of the journal was, until the nineteenth century, the manuscript version, which is still available in the Parliamentary Archive.[16] These manuscript journals were eventually printed by order of the respective Houses, and subsequent volumes for each session have been have been printed ever since.

The content of the journals, and the *Commons Journal* in particular, has varied over time. The first volume of the *Commons Journal* includes not only minutes of the respective incidents, but also an occasional comment and summary of a debate.[17] The eighteenth-century journal is much more detailed than those that came before or after. During this period, the *Commons Journal* included a summary of petitions lodged before the House and well as detailed reports of committees (where full reports were made to the House). As almost all of the original House of Commons material was destroyed in the fire of 1834,[18] the journal record is often all that remains. The *House of Lords Journal* was always in a more abbreviated form than that of the Commons, and by the mid-nineteenth century it became more abbreviated still.

The passage of a Bill and the journals

The passage of a public Bill has remained largely the same from the seventeenth century to the present day. In the House of Commons (but not the Lords), it begins with the House giving leave (or an order) that a Bill maybe introduced. This was followed by the Bill being presented and its First Reading, which soon became a mere formality with just the title of the Bill be read out. In turn, this was followed by the Second Reading, where the principle of the Bill was debated. As a full debate was usual, it was often difficult to find Parliamentary time, and during the nineteenth century the Second Reading of a Bill was often put off again and again. Each adjournment or deferment of a Bill's reading or committee meeting is recorded in the journal, and so is included for each record. The number of adjournments might tell a scholar a few things about the Bill: for instance, how important the Bill was perceived to be by the government or the House. It also provides a timeframe for non-Parliamentary activity to enable scholars to consult relevant non-Parliamentary sources. Where there was a vote, the journal includes the results of the division (but not which members voted which way), and this is indicated in the record by a "V".

Where the House gave the Bill a Second Reading, it would usually, although not always, be committed. Most public Bills, right up until the twentieth century, were usually committed to a Committee of the Whole House (and in the Lords this still remains the case).[19] However, a Bill might sometimes be committed to named persons, or a particular Select or Standing Committee. The committee would then make a report to the whole House of the amendments it made. When the Bill was considered by a Committee of the Whole House, each amendment tabled or considered would be minuted in the journal.[20] Where a committee heard witnesses, any orders for this purpose were also included in the journal. It is therefore sometimes possible to surmise what was debated or a contentious issue even where there was no contemporaneous Parliamentary reporting. Where something was referred to a committee, it was the practice until 1873 (the Commons ceased earlier) to include in the journal all the amendments made by the committee on report. By the late nineteenth century, the reports of Standing Committees were printed as a Parliamentary paper, so this record became less important.

---

15 A consolidation Bill is one introduced with the intention of consolidating several earlier enactments into a single Act. In the later period, they followed a different Parliamentary procedure.

16 For a detailed discussion of the holding, see Maurice Bond, *Guide to the Records of Parliament* (HMSO 1971), p 28–36 (HL) and 207–211 (HC); much of this information is now extracted onto the Portcullis catalogue, but Bond provides the most accessible introduction to the holding.

17 The first volume of the *House of Commons Journal* includes periods when there were two versions by different clerks – so-called second scribes – (in particular, in 1621), so in such cases two sets of page references are included.

18 See generally Caroline Shenton, *The Day Parliament Burned Down* (Oxford 2012).

19 The Patents, Designs and Trade Marks Act 1883 was committed to a Grand Committee for Trade, and this is probably why it passed.

20 This was not the case for the early journals.

Once the report had been considered in the first House, it was the practice until 1849 that the Bill would be Ingrossed. The "Official" Acts of Parliament were these Ingrossments, and any amendments in the second House had to be made to the Ingrossments themselves. On report and Third Reading, where an amendment was made or rejected, this would be recorded in the journal. Once the Bill passed Third Reading in the first House, it was brought to the other House. This was often, although not always, immediately followed by its First Reading. The stages in the second House would be the same as the first, with roughly the same records made in the respective journals. Once the Bill had had its Third Reading in the second House (it passed that House), it would be returned to the first House and any new amendments made to the Bill would be considered. These amendments would be included in the journal, as would any votes on them. Where there was a disagreement on a particular amendment, then the reasons would be provided (again recorded in the journal) and it would be passed back to the other House to either insist on the amendment or not to press it.[21] This process (now called ping-pong) continued until both Houses agreed the final text. The Bill would then go for Royal Assent. The granting of Assent would be the final thing recorded in the journal.

The journal also recorded who presented the Bill (at First Reading) and who reported on the Bill (in the second House, the Bill was not presented again, so only the person who reported on the Bill is recorded). This enables researchers to determine who was interested in a particular reform, and may potentially open up other avenues of research. In addition to these entries, the journal may record petitions lodged in favour of or against the Bill. In the Commons from 1832, these petitions were included in the Reports of the Public Petitions Committee (see Part 7), and from 1850 were no longer minuted in the journal. In the Lords, petitions were always noted in the journal, although they were infrequently lodged.[22]

The record for each public Act and Bill includes every entry from the journal, and in relation to particular events, this record is treated as the definitive source in this Guide. Accordingly, newspapers occasionally reported stages of Bills which did not appear in the journal (usually simply the wrong stage being mentioned in the paper) or reported something happening which was not recorded in the journal. Each entry in the journal is recorded next to the date on which it occurred and what occurred. Where there is something more than a mere minute of an event in the journal (such as the text of proposed amendments), the entry is in **bold**. The page number used is the first page of the relevant entry, although where the journal minutes some proceedings, the entry can continue for some pages. Further, the date recorded is the actual date of the incident, and not the date of the beginning of the sitting day. This means where something happened after midnight (midnight being recorded in the journal), it would be recorded as the date of the early morning.[23] As *Hansard* uses the date at the start of the day's session, this occasionally can cause confusion, as the date might be different in each parts of the record.

Votes and Proceedings/House of Lords minutes

Every sitting day from 1680, the House of Commons has issued the vote bundle, what is usually known as the *Votes and Proceedings*. This usually minutes what happened in the Commons on the previous day's sittings and, eventually from the early nineteenth century, it included details of what was due to happen on the current day. The *Votes and Proceedings* is the basis of the journal, and almost all of its content is transferred to the journal at the end of the session. From 1825, the House of Lords printed the *Minutes of Proceedings* every day, which, like the *Votes and Proceedings*, were eventually turned into the journal. Only occasionally is anything included in the *Votes and Proceedings* which is not also included in the journal. For this reason, no separate entry is made for *Votes and Proceedings* or *Minutes of Proceedings*, but those wishing to consult the vote bundle can use the journal entry to inform them what will be there.

Reports of Parliamentary debates

The reporting of Parliamentary debates can be divided into four periods. Working in reverse, the last period begins in 1909, when both Houses of Parliament took over responsibility for producing the transcript of the debates. Thus, anything which was said on the floor of either House from 1909 is officially recorded in what is properly called the *Official Reports*, but more commonly known as *Hansard*.[24] From this time, there is no better source of what was said in the House. The same approach was adopted for the Standing Committee debates (i.e. on Bills) from 1919.[25] These debates are recorded in a separate series, the *Hansard Standing Committee Debates*.

---

21 This happened with the Letters Patent Amendment Act 1835.
22 The House of Lords formed a Public Petitions Select Committee for only one session (see Part 7 for more details).
23 The journal usually records the date as "13–14 July" in the heading in such instances.
24 The *Official Reports* are usually called the fifth series of *Hansard* (and from 1989, the sixth series began), so this term is used throughout.
25 In the first few years after this practice was adopted, not every Standing Committee had a shorthand writer in attendance, so some Bills were still not recorded (an example is the Air Navigation Act 1920).

The fourth series of *Hansard* began in 1892, and this provides the best record of what is said on the floor of the House from that period. The fourth series was much more detailed than the earlier series, although it was still not contemporaneous. By this stage, it contained far better reports of Parliamentary proceedings than the newspapers. The only exception to this was in relation to Standing Committee debates (which were becoming increasingly common). These were not reported in *Hansard* during this period, so the only record is that in newspapers. The first three series of *Hansard* from 1803 to 1891 gradually improved, but until the 1870s[26] they were almost entirely compiled from various newspaper reports (most commonly *The Times*). This meant many significant debates were not recorded, or were only summarised or minuted in *Hansard*, so there were often better reports in newspapers. Indeed, between 1829 and 1841, the *Mirror of Parliament*, published by John Barrow,[27] was far superior to *Hansard* (although still far from comprehensive). Barrow, like Hansard, found printing the debates was not a profitable venture,[28] and while there were other competitors to *Hansard* at times,[29] none have been found to include any debates relating to patents.

The period before 1803 is covered by various collections of reports, usually derived from earlier newspaper reports of proceedings.[30] In most cases, these were very erratic. The best-known is Debrett's (and later Stockdale's) *Parliamentary Register*, which ran from 1774 to 1812.[31] Other early reports with debates on patents include *Woodfall's Reports* (which after his death became *Woodfall's Parliamentary Diaries*), which ran from 1794 to 1801; the *Senator or Clarendon's Parliamentary Chronicle* ran through two series from 1790 to 1802. Collections earlier than these do not include any debates on patent law[32] except in one instance: there is the discussion of one private petition relating to patent law (Sir Thomas Lombe[33]) mentioned in *Chandler's Commons Debates*[34] and also in *Torbuck's Parliamentary Debates*.[35] Finally, there is Corbett's magisterial *Parliamentary History of England from the Norman conquest, in 1066. To the year 1803*,[36] which is essentially a compilation of numerous earlier sources and is recorded where relevant discussion took place.

In relating to each report, any references to patent legislation are recorded. In many cases there was little recorded in *Hansard* other than a minute that a Parliamentary stage took place, where there is any debate recorded, entries are in bold. When reporting became contemporaneous in 1909, it becomes unnecessary to distinguish between debates and mere minuting, so all entries are in Roman. In the later period, where Parliamentary reporting became adequate, it is recorded where in *Hansard* a specific section or clause is debated. Where the clause number is different from the section number this is made clear. Where a new clause was proposed, but not adopted, or a clause was deleted during the passage of the Bill, the heading for the clause is given and any debate recorded in the same way.

Parliamentary papers

Each record includes a list of the Parliamentary papers connected to the particular Act or Bill. The Parliamentary papers in the eighteenth century were much more disorganised and limited than for the later period.[37] The first attempt to collate these papers was started by Speaker Abbot, and this led to a series being printed in the early nineteenth century by Luke Hansard. These papers were printed and indexed in the *Catalogue of Papers printed by Order of the House of Commons, from the year 1731 to 1800. In the Custody of the Clerk of the Journals* (1807),[38] which included reports on inventions and Bills, so references are provided in the Guide. Luke Hansard also published a collection called the *Reports from the Committees of the House of Commons 1715–1801*[39] (usually called "the First Series") which printed some reports that had not otherwise been printed in the *Commons Journal*. The most complete set of eighteenth-century Parliamentary papers is that produced by Shelia Lambert

26 When Hansard first employed his own reporters.
27 It famously had Charles Dickens as a reporter for a period: John Trewin and Evelyn King, *Printer to the House: The Story of Hansard* (Methuen 1952), p 238.
28 John Trewin and Evelyn King, *Printer to the House: The Story of Hansard* (Methuen 1952), p 238.
29 For a bibliography of such sources, see "Bibliographical Aids to Research" (1933) 10 *Bulletin of the Institute of Historical Research* 171; that list is complemented by Arthur Aspinall, "The Reporting and Publishing of the House of Commons Debates", in *Essays presented to Sir Lewis Namier* (Macmillan 1956), p 227 at 251, fn (a).
30 These have been partially digitised: see www.britishonlinearchives.co.uk.
31 It has been digitised, and is available through ProQuest.
32 Such as *Debrett's Parliamentary Debates* 1743–1774.
33 There is also reference to a public grant to Joanna Stephens.
34 Chandler, *The History and Proceedings of the House of Commons from the Restoration to the Present Time 1660–1743* (London 1742–43).
35 Torbuck, *A Collection of Parliamentary Debates in England from the year M, DC, LXVIII to the present time* (Torbuck 1742).
36 (Hansard 1806–20).
37 For a discussion, see Sheila Lambert, "House of Commons Papers of the Eighteenth Century" (1976) 3 *Government Publications Review* 195; also see Edgar L Erickson, "The Sessional Papers: Last Phase" (1960) 21 *College and Research Libraries* 343.
38 (Reprint: HMSO 1954).
39 (Hansard 1802).

in the 1970s, which has now been digitised. She went through the journal and identified every paper that was ordered to be printed, and then tried to find a copy. Using this resource, she produced what remains the definitive list and collection of these eighteenth-century papers, and references to her collection are included in the Guide.

The House of Commons Parliamentary papers in the nineteenth century are more readily available. These were catalogued by Peter Chadwick in his *House of Commons Parliamentary Papers, 1801–1900: Guide to the Chadwyck-Healey Microfiche Edition*.[40] Each paper is referenced by the session and paper number, and then a volume number and page number in the printed format (e.g. *Report from the Standing Committee on Trade on Patents Bill* (1902 HC Papers 303), Vol 7, p 301).[41] In the nineteenth century, the collection usually includes the various prints of public Bills in the House of Commons, and by the twentieth century, a Bill was usually printed after every Parliamentary stage (e.g. one after committee and one after report) where it had been amended in the previous stage. Later, when Bills were routinely sent to Standing Committees, the minutes of those committees were also printed as a House of Commons paper.[42] An official record of the debates, as discussed above, was much later.

Supplement to the Votes and Proceedings

A member of the House of Commons who wanted to table an amendment to a Bill in committee, on consideration of the report or at Third Reading has to give a notice of amendment to the Public Bill Office. These notices started to be printed in the *Supplement to the Votes and Proceedings*,[43] which was printed for most sitting days in the Commons. Every so often, the notices of amendments were compiled together to form a Marshalled List of Amendments, and this too was included in the Supplement. Originally, these were only printed for significant Bills,[44] but during the early part of the twentieth century they became routine for all public Bills.[45] *Hansard* eventually started publishing all the amendments which were debated, but during the earlier periods, the Supplement is the only record of the proposed amendment (and who proposed it), and later, more significantly, it includes amendments which were not debated (as they were withdrawn due to insufficient time or for any other reason). This means it is possible to see what concerned certain Parliamentarians, even if not Parliament itself.

Unfortunately, the Supplement is held at very few places.[46] The Parliamentary Archive has a complete set before 1939. In the postwar period, the volumes are still held by the House of Commons Library, and in theory at least, it is possible to ask to see them in the Archive reading room.[47] The British Library has an extensive but not complete set. For each record, the dates and pages in the Supplement are listed. For some Bills, this can cover many hundreds of pages. Indeed, in the 1970s the binding changed so that the amendments to one Bill were all paginated together.[48]

House of Lords papers

The House of Lords papers are more complicated than those for the Commons. The pre-1805 papers were collected by William Torrington and were published in the 1970s as the *House of Lords Sessional Papers*.[49] In the period after 1805, the papers form three distinct periods. The first period is before 1835, when the volumes run in one set and references were traditionally given as paper number and year (e.g. 34 of 1818), but for consistency, the modern citation approach is used in this Guide. In the second period, which runs until 1920, there are a series of volumes for each session with a sessional index. From 1920, the House of Lords papers contained less and less material, so the need for an index diminished until each volume just had a table of contents. Where a paper is ordered to be printed by both Houses, it will be given a reference in the House of Lords papers, but usually the collection of Sessional Papers does not actually include the paper itself, rather just a reference

---

40 (Chadwyck-Healey 1991). Some papers have also been published thematically: *British Parliamentary Papers*, Inventions (Irish Academic Press 1972), Vol 1 and 2.

41 The collection has now been digitised, but unfortunately a few things relating to patents have not been digitised accurately, so at the moment it is still sometimes necessary to check the microfiche (or printed) version.

42 Unfortunately, this started after the passage of the Patent Law Amendment Act 1852.

43 The Supplement used to include all sorts of things, but eventually it came to just include these Notices of Amendments.

44 Such as the Patents, Designs and Trade Marks Act 1883.

45 There were some Bills where no amendments were tabled, so nothing was included in the Supplement.

46 It has yet to be digitised.

47 They are held remotely, and the resources for viewing are limited.

48 The only example in this Guide is the Fair Trading Act 1973, and the volume runs to hundreds of pages.

49 F William Torrington, *House of Lords Sessional Papers, 1714–1805* (Oceana 1972–78).

to a page number where it would theoretically be. In this Guide, therefore, there will only be a reference to a House of Lords paper where it is not also included in the House of Commons papers.

As for the House of Commons papers, the Lords papers include the various prints of Bills and some committee reports. A significant difference between the two is that notices of amendments and Marshalled Lists of Amendments are included in the House of Lords papers, rather than separate. Only in the 1970s did this change, when only the Marshalled Lists were included as Parliamentary papers.

Newspaper reports

Throughout the seventeenth century and during much of the eighteenth century, the best source for Parliamentary debates are the diaries of members of Parliament or the clerk's official notes. Indeed, Parliamentary diaries for the 1620s are quite extensive, and there are diaries for the session in 1621[50] when the Bill of Monopolies failed to pass and also for 1624 when the Statute of Monopolies did pass.[51] These diaries are not, however, anything like a system of modern objective Parliamentary reporting, and it is important to remember that diarists may have biases in what they record, how clearly they were listening, whether they were capturing exact phrases or relaying what they heard from witnesses and so forth.[52] While there are some limited reports in newspapers before 1770,[53] it was from that date that newspapers began to routinely report Parliamentary proceedings. Indeed, this was despite the fact that at the time it was still contrary to the rules of the House to do so. Reporters therefore could not make notes and had to rely on their memory. This meant that many newspapers copied from each other, and myths could be propagated between them.[54]

Throughout most of the nineteenth century, newspapers remained the most important source of Parliamentary debate. Eventually, there was a convention that minister's speeches would be recorded in full and about two thirds of other speeches would be recorded. This means that the content of newspapers varied throughout the period and some things were never recorded at all.

The references in this Guide are complied from three digitised collections of newspapers. The first is the *Burnley Collection*,[55] which was put together by Charles Burnley and includes newspapers until the beginning of the nineteenth century. The second collection is the still-growing *British Newspaper Archive*, which is a digitised version of various newspaper collections held by the British Library. The third collection is *The Times* digital archive. The approach in this Guide is to reference the debates on public Bills or grants in London newspapers[56] from 1800 until 1891 (and more widely from the *Burnley Collection*). From 1892, the fourth series of *Hansard* was launched and Parliamentary reporting in newspapers slowly declined. The main exception to this was *The Times*, which continued to report Parliamentary affairs in detail, so references in *The Times* are maintained until 1909. The fifth series of *Hansard* includes a verbatim report of all proceedings on the floor of the House, so there is no need for researchers to consult alternative sources. One exception to this rule is Standing Committee reports, which were not recorded in the official reports until 1919, so newspaper summaries on the proceedings are recorded until this point.

A coding system has been used so that where the newspaper title is in **bold**, the newspaper reports (or purports to report) at least one speaker's actual words. Where it is in *italics*, the report includes some details falling short of a speech, and where it is in Roman type, then the entry is a mention of a procedure being completed only (e.g. "the Patent Law Bill was given a Second Reading").

---

50 Wallace Notestein, Frances Relf and Hartley Simpson, *Commons Debates 1621* (Yale 1935), 7 Vols; Samuel Gardiner, *Notes of the Debates in the House of Lords 1621 (Henry Elsing)* (1871) 103 *Camden Society (Old Series)*.

51 Philip Baker (ed), *Proceedings in Parliament 1624: The House of Commons* (2015), British History Online; Samuel Gardiner (ed), *Notes on the Debates in the House of Lords: Officially taken by Henry Elsing, 1624–1626* (1879) *Camden New Series*, Vol 24.

52 As to these points, see Chris Kyle, "Introduction", in *Parliament, Politics and Elections 1604–1648* (2001) 17 *Camden Fifth Series* 1 at 4–7.

53 See Arthur Aspinall, "The Reporting and Publishing of the House of Commons Debates", in *Essays presented to Sir Lewis Namier* (Macmillan 1956), p, 227; also see Peter Thomas, "The Beginning of Parliamentary Reporting in Newspapers 1768–1774" (1959) 74 *English Historical Review* 623; and John Trewin and Evelyn King, *Printer to the House: The Story of Hansard* (Methuen 1952), Ch 1.

54 This issue was raised in relation to *Donaldson v Beckett* (1774) 4 Burr 2408, 98 ER 257, the leading copyright case of the day, where there has been a lively debate over how their Lordships voted: see Tomas Gomez-Arostegui, "Copyright at Common Law in 1774" (2014) 47 *Connecticut Law Review* 1.

55 The original of which is held by the British Library.

56 For these purposes, "the London papers" means *The Times*, the *Morning Advertiser* (from 1804 to 1872, the period covered by the British Newspaper Archive), the *Morning Chronicle* (from 1800 until 1862, when it ceased publication), the *Morning Post* (1800–1892, when *Hansard* fourth series began); the *(London) Daily News* (from its first publication in 1846 to 1892) and the *(London) Evening Standard* (from its first publication in 1827 to 1892). The last paper was published with a morning and evening edition, but Parliamentary reporting was usually the same in both, so the references are interchangeable. In the earlier periods, the *Globe* (first published in 1824) and the *Public Ledger and Daily Advertiser* (first published in 1805) included extensive Parliamentary reporting, but this declined (particularly in the second paper).

Notes

At the end of each record, where appropriate, a notes section provides additional information about an Act. This might include where there is otherwise unpublished material in the Parliamentary Archive or which can be found in the National Archive[57] catalogue.[58] While the Ingrossment remained the official version of the Bill, the reference to it in the Parliamentary Archive is provided. When Ingrossment ended in 1849, the "official" version became that printed on vellum. However, by this stage printing was widespread and accurate, so references to the vellum version of the Act provide no further information as to amendments.

57 Parliamentary Counsel's papers have been transferred to the National Archive for most, but not all, of the first half of the twentieth century. The remainder are still held by the Office of Parliamentary Counsel, and all are now available under the Thirty Year Rule. Applications need to made to that office to view the material.
58 This includes some material held in other archives.

1 Public patent Acts

Statute of Monopolies 1624

PUBA1	1624
Statute of Monopolies (21 Ja 1. c. 11)	
An Act concerning Monopolies and Dispensations of Penal Laws, and the Forfeitures thereof	

Table of contents

s 1 All Monopolies, &c. shall be void
s 2 Monopolies, &c. shall be tried by the Common Laws of this Realm
s 3 Persons disabled to use Monopolies, &c.
s 4 The Party grieved by Pretext of a Monopoly, &c. shall recover treble Damages and double Costs
s 5 Letters Patents to use new Manufactures, saved
s 6 [Letters Patent for new Inventions after enactment]
s 7 [Letters Patent not be granted where generally inconvenient]
s 8 Warrants granted to Justices, saved
s 9 Charters granted to Corporations, saved
s 10 Letters Patents that concern Printing, Saltpetre, Gunpowder, great Ordnance, Shot, or Offices, saved
s 11 This Act shall not extend to Commissions for Allum Mines
s 12 Nor to the Liberties of Newcastle upon Tyne, nor to Licences of keeping Taverns
s 13 Nor to Letters Patents granted to Sir Robert Mansel, Knt. or to James Maxewell, Esq
s 14 Nor to those granted to Abraham Baker, or Edward Lord Dudley

Journal

House of Commons			House of Lords		
Pres: Sir Edward Coke Rep: John Glanville			Pres: Henry Montagu (Ld Pr) Reps: George Abbott (Archbishop of Canterbury)		
23 Feb 1624	1 CJ 671, 715	Bill brought from last Parl	21 Feb 1624	3 LJ 212	**R Speech**
24 Feb 1624	1 CJ 672, 716	1R	13 Mar 1624	3 LJ 261	1R
26 Feb 1624	1 CJ 674, 719	2R/C'tted	18 Mar 1624	3 LJ 267	2R/C'tted
9 Mar 1624	1 CJ 680, 731	**Rep/Re–C'tted**	2 Apr 1624	3 LJ 286	Com to meet
9 Mar 1624	1 CJ 680, 731	**Rep**	3 Apr 1624	3 LJ 287	Rep/HC Conf proposed
12 Mar 1624	1 CJ 683, 734	3R day app	5 Apr 1624	3 LJ 290	Conf agreed
13 Mar 1624	1 CJ 685, 735	3R	7 Apr 1624	3 LJ 293	Conf day app
7 Apr 1624	1 CJ 757	HL Req Conf	8 Apr 1624	3 LJ 294	Conf adj
8 Apr 1624	1 CJ 758	Conf adj	10 Apr 1624	3 LJ 297	Conf day app
9 Apr 1624	1 CJ 760	HC Req Conf	12 Apr 1624	3 LJ 299	Conf day app
10 Apr 1624	1 CJ 761	HL Conf day app	1 May 1624	3 LJ 335	Conf day app
12 Apr 1624	1 CJ 762	HL Conf adj	3 May 1624	3 LJ 328	Conf adj
12 Apr 1624	1 CJ 763	HL Conf day app	4 May 1624	3 LJ 329	Conf day app
19 Apr 1624	1 CJ 770	**HL Conf Rep**	8 May 1624	3 LJ 362	Conf day app
22 Apr 1624	1 CJ 772	Proviso prop	15 May 1624	3 LJ 386	Conf req renewed
27 Apr 1624	1 CJ 691	C'tted Star Chamber	19 May 1624	3 LJ 391	HC notified of Amds
1 May 1624	1 CJ 696, 781	**Rep Star C/Conf Powers**	20 May 1624	3 LJ 393	**Rep with Amds**
3 May 1624	1 CJ 697, 782	**HL Conf Adj/date app**	21 May 1624	3 LJ 397	Amds 1R and 2R
4 May 1624	1 CJ 698, 783	Adj	22 May 1624	3 LJ 400	3R
8 May 1624	1 CJ 701, 786	HL Agree to expedite Bill	22 May 1624	3 LJ 402	Noted
13 May 1624	1 CJ 703, 788	**Conf Rep**	27 May 1624	3 LJ 412	HC Ag with HL Amds
15 May 1624	1 CJ 704, 789	Conf Ord	29 May 1624	3 LJ 425	Royal Assent
24 May 1624	1 CJ 710, 793	HL Amds/C'tted	2 Nov 1624	3 LJ 427	List of Acts
25 May 1624	1 CJ 711, 794	Provisos Rep and Ag	24 Mar 1626	3 LJ 541	Discussion of proviso
27 May 1624	1 CJ 713, 796	Brought HL			

(continued)

(continued)

Parliamentary debates
Proceedings in Parliament 1624: The House of Commons (ed) Philip Baker (2015), British History Online:
Brought Last Sess (23 Feb): Hawarde, p 147; Holles, f 81; Rich, f 3; Spring, p 9; Earle, f 13v1
1R (24 Feb): Hawarde, p 150; Jervoise, p 5; Lowtherm f 4; Rich, f 5; *Nicholas, f 5*; Spring, p 16; Pym, f 5; Earle, f 14v; D'Ewes, f 58v
2R (26 Feb): Hawarde, p 154; Rich, f 18; *Anon, f 25–25v; Spring, p 32*; Holland, f 4v; Pym, f 8v; Earle, f 30v; D'Ewes, f 16v
Rep (9 Mar): *Hawarde, p 187; Spring, p 95*; **Dyott, f 34–f 37**; **Pym, f 23**; Earle, f 63; *D'Ewes, f 74–f74v*
3R day app (12 Mar): Harwarde, p 205
3R (13 Mar): *Holles, f 99v-100*; Lowther, f 31; *Anon, f 77v; Spring, p 113–114; Holland, f 51–51v; Pym, f 28v; Earle, f 81–82; D'Ewes, f 78v*
Conf Req (7 Apr): Lowther, f 53v; **Nicholas, f 118–118v**; **Spring, p 182**; *Holland, f 83v*; **Pym, f 52v**; *Earle, f 117v*; D'Ewes, f 99v
Conf (8 Apr): Hawarde, p 240; Nicholas, f 124; D'Ewes, f 100v
Conf day app (10 Apr): Holland, f 5; Pym, f 59v
Conf adj (12 Apr): Holland, f 6; Earle, f 131v
Conf Rep (19 Apr): **Pym, f 71v–f 73**; **Earle, f 149–150**; D'Ewes, f 106
Proviso Pres (22 Apr): Hawarde, p 251 and 253; **Nicholas, f 168–169**; **Dyott, f 74 and f 76–78**
Com Star Chamber (27 Apr): Holland, f 51v
Rep Star Chamber (1 May): Dyott, f 118v; *Pym, f 86*
HL Conf adj (3 May); Nicholas, f 224; Pym, f 86; Earle, f 166v
Conf Rep: (13 May): Hawarde, p 287; *Holland, f 87*
HL Amds (24 May); *Spring, p 239; Earle, f 191v*; Dyott, f 157
Proviso Rep (25 May): Dyott, f 161
Samuel Gardiner (ed), *Notes on the Debates in the House of Lords: Officially taken by Henry Elsing, 1624–1626* (1879) 24 Camden Society (New Series)
Rep (3 Apr): Gardiner, p 50
Rep with Amds (20 May): Gardiner, p 97–98
Amds 1R and 2R (21 May): Gardiner, p 98–99
3R (22 May): Gardiner, p 191
Parliamentary papers
No papers printed
Newspaper coverage of debates
N/A
Notes
The short title was the "Statute of Monopolies" without any year (see, e.g., Patents, Designs and Trade Marks Act 1883, s 46 and Sch 3). This being the usual short title was confirmed by the Statute Law Revision Act 1948 (c. 62), s 5 and Sch 2 (it was not mentioned in either the Short Title Act 1892 or 1896).
Archive
Ing: HL/PO/PU/1/1623/21J1n3

Letters Patent for Inventions Act 1835

PUBA2	1835
Letters Patent for Inventions Act 1835 (5 & 6 Will 4. c. 83)	
An Act to amend the Law touching Letters Patent for Inventions	
Table of contents	
s 1 Any Person having obtained Letters Patent for any Inventions may enter a Disclaimer of any Part of his Specification, or a Memorandum of any Alteration therein, which, when filed, to be deemed Part of Such Specification. Caveat may be entered as heretofore. Disclaimer not to affect Actions pending at the Time. Attorney General may require the Party to advertise his Disclaimer	
s 2 Mode of proceeding where Patentee is proved not to be the real inventor, though he believed himself to be so	
s 3 If in any Action or Suit a Verdict or Decree shall pass for the Patentee, the Judge may grant a Certificate, which shall entitle the Patentee, upon a Verdict in his Favour, to receive Treble Costs	
s 4 Mode of proceeding in case of Application for the Prolongation of the Term of a Patent	

s 5 In the case of Action, &c. Notice of Objections to be given
s 6 As to Costs in Actions for infringing Letters Patent
s 7 Penalty for using, unauthorised, the Name of Patentee, &c.

Proposed Clauses

Cl A Publication of the nature of the Inventions for which Letters Patent have been obtained
Cl B Any person purchasing the property of an Invention may obtain letters patent in his own name, with all the privileges of the inventor; Proviso
Cl C What shall be deemed the date of the letters patent
Cl D Attorney General may require the person to alter the title and statement of Inventions
Cl E Persons may sell or transfer rights, or grant licence to others

Journal

House of Commons			House of Lords		
Rep: William Tooke			Pres: Lord Brougham and Vaux Rep: Earl of Shaftesbury (Ld Ch)		
14 Jul 1835	90 CJ 451	Brought HL	3 Jun 1835	67 LJ 183	1R
16 Jul 1835	90 CJ 462	1R	16 Jun 1835	67 LJ 216	2R/C'tted SC
23 Jul 1835	90 CJ 479	2R adj	19 Jun 1835	67 LJ 227	SC Rep/Re-C'tted
29 Jul 1835	90 CJ 494	2R adj	22 Jun 1835	67 LJ 231	HC MP Req Attend C'tte
5 Aug 1835	90 CJ 515	2R adj	8 Jul 1835	67 LJ 282	SC Rep with Amds
11 Aug 1835	90 CJ 531	2R adj	9 Jul 1835	67 LJ 287	CWH
13 Aug 1835	90 CJ 542	2R	10 Jul 1835	67 LJ 290	Rep with Amds/Ing
18 Aug 1835	90 CJ 565	CWH	13 Jul 1835	67 LJ 295	3R with Amds
20 Aug 1835	90 CJ 572	Rep adj	25 Aug 1835	67 LJ 610	HC Agree with Amds
20 Aug 1835	90 CJ 576	Rep adj	1 Sep 1835	67 LJ 662	**HC Amds Cons**
21 Aug 1835	90 CJ 578	Pet for Amd [PET26]	4 Sep 1835	67 LJ 681	**Rep of Reasons Ag**
22 Aug 1835	90 CJ 580	**Rep with Amds**	9 Sep 1835	67 LJ 702	HC Not insisted
24 Aug 1835	90 CJ 584	Pet Ag [PET27]	10 Sep 1835	67 LJ 704	Royal Assent
24 Aug 1835	90 CJ 587	**3R with Amds**			
4 Sep 1835	90 CJ 646	HL Req Conf			
7 Sep 1835	90 CJ 654 – V	Amds not insisted			
10 Sep 1835	90 CJ 661	Royal Assent			

Parliamentary debates

Brought HL: Mirror, 14 Jul 1835, Vol 3, p 1890

1R: Mirror, 15 Jul 1835, Vol 3, p 1942

2R: **HC Deb, 13 Aug 1835, Vol 30(3rd), col 466–471**; **Mirror, 13 Aug 1835, Vol 4, p 2479–2481**

CWH: **Mirror, 18 Aug 1835, Vol 3, p 2594**

Rep adj: Mirror, 19 Aug 1835, Vol 3, p 2622

Pet for Amd: Mirror, 21 Aug 1835, Vol 3, p 2665

Pet Ag: Mirror, 24 Aug 1835, Vol 3, p 2713

3R: HC Deb, 24 Aug 1835, Vol 30(3rd), col 936; Mirror, 24 Aug 1835, Vol 3, p 2725

Conf: **Mirror, 4 Sep 1835, Vol 3, p 2946**

Amds not insisted: HC Deb, 7 Sep 1835, Vol 30(2nd), col 1442; **Mirror, 7 Sep 1835, Vol 3, p 2976–2977**

1R: **HL Deb, 3 Jun 1835, Vol 28(3rd), col 472–477**; **Mirror, 1835, Vol 2, p 1206–1207**

2R: HL Deb, 16 Jun 1835, Vol 28(3rd), col 843; Mirror, 1835, Vol 2, p 1392

Re-C'tted: HL Deb, 19 Jun 1835, Vol 28(3rd), col 891–892; Mirror, 19 Jun 1835, Vol 2, p 1425

HC MP Req Attend C'ttee: Mirror, 22 Jun 1835, Vol 2, p 1461, 1471

SC Rep: Mirror, 8 Jul 1835, Vol 2, p 1764

CWH: Mirror, 9 Jul 1835, Vol 2, p 1790

Rep: Mirror, 10 Jul 1835, Vol 2, p 1816

HC Amds Ag: Mirror, 25 Aug 1835, Vol 3, p 2727

DisAg of HC Amds: **HL Deb, 1 Sep 1835, Vol 30(3rd), col 1186–1188**; **Mirror, 1 Sep 1835, Vol 3, p 2848–2849**

Conf called: Mirror, 4 Sep 1835, Vol 3, p 2927

HC Not insisted: Mirror, 9 Sep 1835, Vol 3, p 2982

Royal Assent: HL Deb, 10 Sep 1835, Vol 30(3rd), col 1449; Mirror, 10 Sep 1835, Vol 3, p 2985

Debates on particular provisions

s 4	HL Deb, 4 1 Sep 1835, Vol 30(3rd), col 1186–1188	Cl E	HC Deb, 13 Aug 1835, Vol 30(3rd), col 469

(continued)

(continued)

Parliamentary papers
Bill to amend the Law touching Letters Patent for Inventions (1835 HL Papers 68), Vol 1, p 197
Bill to amend the Law touching Letters Patent for Inventions (as amended in Committee) (1835 HL Papers 80), Vol 1, p 203
Bill to amend the Law touching Letters Patent for Inventions (as amended on Re-Commitment) (1835 HL Papers 101), Vol 1, p 209
Bill to amend the Law touching Letters Patent for Inventions (1835 HC Papers 396), Vol 3, p 597
Amendments made by the Commons (1835 HL Papers 195), Vol 1, p 215

Newspaper coverage of debates

House of Lords

1R: **The Times, 4 Jun 1835**; **Morning Chronicle, 4 Jun 1835**; **Morning Post, 4 Jun 1835**; **London Courier and Evening Gazette, 4 Jun 1835**; **Evening Mail, 5 Jun 1835**; *Public Ledger and Daily Advertiser, 5 Jun 1835*; *Bell's Weekly Messenger, 7 Jun 1835*; *The Examiner, 7 Jun 1835*

SC Rep: The Times, 20 Jun 1835; Morning Advertiser, 20 Jun 1835; Morning Chronicle, 20 Jun 1835; Morning Post, 20 Jun 1835; Evening Chronicle, 20 Jun 1835; Bell's Weekly Messenger, 21 Jun 1835; The Examiner, 21 Jun 1835; *Mechanics Magazine, Vol 23, p 352*

Mem to Att: Morning Advertiser, 23 Jun 1835

CWH: The Times, 10 Jul 1835; London Evening Standard, 10 Jul 1835; Evening Mail, 10 Jul 1835

Rep: The Times, 11 Jul 1835; Morning Post, 11 Jul 1835; Evening Mail, 13 Jul 1835; London Evening Standard, 11 July 1835

Brought HC: Morning Advertiser, 26 Aug 1835; Morning Post, 26 Aug 1835; Public Ledger and Daily Advertiser, 26 Aug 1835

HC Amds: **The Times, 2 Sep 1835**; **Morning Post, 2 Sep 1835**; **Evening Mail, 2 Sep 1835**; **London Courier and Evening Gazette, 2 Sep 1835**; **London Evening Standard, 2 Sep 1835**; **Evening Chronicle, 3 Sep 1835**; **The Examiner, 6 Sep 1835**; *Morning Advertiser, 2 Sep 1835*

Conf Rep and Amds: **London Courier and Evening Gazette, 5 Sep 1835**; **Bell's New Weekly Messenger, 6 Sep 1835**; **The Examiner, 6 Sep 1835**; *The Times, 5 Sep 1835*; *Morning Advertiser, 5 Sep 1835*; *Morning Chronicle, 5 Sep 1835*; *Bell's Life in London and Sporting Chronicle, 6 Sep 1835*

HC Ag Amd: The Times, 10 Sep 1835; Morning Advertiser, 10 Sep 1835; Public Ledger and Daily Advertiser, 10 Sep 1835; The Evening Chronicle, 10 Sep 1835; London Courier and Evening Gazette, 10 Sep 1835

House of Commons

1R: London Courier and Evening Gazette, 17 Jul 1835

2R: **London Courier and Evening Gazette, 13 Aug 1835**; **The Times, 14 Aug 1835**; **Morning Advertisers, 14 Aug 1835**; **Morning Chronicle, 14 Aug 1835**; **Morning Post, 14 Aug 1835**; **Public Ledger and Daily Advertiser, 14 Aug 1835**; **Evening Mail, 14 Aug 1835**; **Evening Chronicle, 15 Aug 1835**; *Mechanics Magazine, Vol 23, p 384*

CWH: **The Times, 19 Aug 1835**; **Morning Post, 19 Aug 1835**; **Public Ledger and Daily Advertiser, 19 Aug 1835**; **Evening Mail, 19 Aug 1835**; **London Courier and Evening Gazette, 19 Aug 1835**; **Evening Chronicle, 20 Aug 1835**

3R: Morning Post, 25 Aug 1835; London Evening Standard, 25 Aug 1835

HL Conf: **The Times, 7 Sep 1835**; Evening Mail, 7 Sep 1835; Bell's Weekly Messenger, 7 Sep 1835

Amd not insisted: **London Courier and Evening Gazette, 8 Sep 1835**; *Morning Advertiser, 8 Sep 1835*; *The Evening Chronicle, 8 Sep 1835*; Morning Post, 8 Sep 1835; The Times, 9 Sep 1835; The Examiner, 13 Sep 1835

Royal Assent: The Times, 11 Sep 1835; Morning Advertiser, 11 Sep 1835; Evening Mail, 11 Sep 1835

Notes

General

Phillip Johnson (ed) "Report of the Select Committee on the Letters Patent for Inventions Bill 1835" (2017) 7 Queen Mary Journal of Intellectual Property 99 [Transcript of Evidence in HL/PO/JO/10/8/1113]

Archive

Letter to HC for John Heathcoat to attend Com: 22 Jun 1835 [HL/PO/JO/10/8/1099] (No 502)

Minutes of Evidence: Patents for Inventors, 25 Jun 1835 [HL/PO/JO/10/8/1113]

Minutes of Evidence: Patents Amendments Bill, 6 Jul 1835 [HL/PO/JO/10/8/1113]

Report of Reasons for Conf: 4 Sep 1835: [HL/PO/JO/10/8/1108] (No 896)

Ing: HL/PO/PU/1/1835/5&6W4n243

Petitions – see PET26 and PET27

Patents Act 1839

PUBA3	1839

Patents Act 1839 (2 & 3 Vict. c. 67)

An Act to amend an Act of the Fifth and Sixth Years of the Reign of King William the Fourth, intituled An Act to amend the Law touching Letters Patent for Inventions

Table of contents

s 1 [Letters Patent for Inventions Act 1835] 5 & 6 W 4 c 83 Repealing Provision requiring the Application by Petition to be prosecuted with Effect before the Expiration of the Term of the Patent

s 2 Term of Patent Right may be extended in certain Cases through the Application for such Extension not prosecuted with Effect before the Expiration thereof

s 3 Act may be amended, &c. [by an Act passed in this Session]

Journal

House of Commons			House of Lords		
Rep: Robert Rolfe (SG)			Pres: Lord Brougham and Vaux Rep: Earl of Shaftesbury (Ld Ch)		
2 Aug 1839	94 CJ 507	Brought HL	28 Jun 1839	71 LJ 445	1R
7 Aug 1839	94 CJ 527	1R	29 Jul 1839	71 LJ 544	2R/C'ted CWH
9 Aug 1839	94 CJ 536	2R/C'tted CWH	30 Jul 1839	71 LJ 550	C'tee/Rep w/o Amds/Ing
12 Aug 1839	94 CJ 550	CWH	1 Aug 1839	71 LJ 558	3R
13 Aug 1839	94 CJ 553	**Rep with Amds**	17 Aug 1839	71 LJ 615	HC pass with Amds/Amds Ag
14 Aug 1839	94 CJ 554	3R with Amds	24 Aug 1839	71 LJ 637	Royal Assent
20 Aug 1839	94 CJ 567	HL Ag HC Amds			
24 Aug 1839	94 CJ 579	Royal Assent			

Parliamentary debates

Brought HL: Mirror, 2 Aug 1839, Vol 6, p 4617	1R: HL Deb, 28 Jun 1839, Vol 48(3rd), col 1004; Mirror, 28 Jun 1838, Vol 4, p 3423
1R: HC Deb, 7 Aug 1839, Vol 50(3rd), col 1; Mirror, 7 Aug 1839, Vol 6, p 4822	2R: HL Deb, 29 Jul 1839, Vol 49(3rd), col 914; Mirror, 29 Jul 1839, Vol 6, p 4401
2R: HC Deb, 9 Aug 1839, Vol 50(3rd), col 135	Com: Mirror, 30 Jul 1839, Vol 6, p 4473
CWH: Mirror, 12 Aug 1839, Vol 6, p 4962	3R: HL Deb, 1 Aug 1839, Vol 49(3rd), col 1052; Mirror, 1 Aug 1839, Vol 6, p 4552
3R: HC Deb, 14 Aug 1839, Vol 50(3rd), col 262; Mirror, 14 Aug 1839, Vol 6, p 4998	HC pass: Mirror, 17 Aug 1839, Vol 6, p 5075
HL Agree: Mirror, 20 Aug 1839, Vol 6, p 5137	Royal Assent: HL Deb, 24 Aug 1839, Vol 50(3rd), col 587; Mirror, 24 Aug 1839, Vol 6, p 5219

Parliamentary papers

Bill to amend an Act of the Fifth and Sixth Years of the Reign of King William the Fourth, intituled An Act to amend the Law touching Letters Patent for Inventions (1839 HC Papers 506), Vol 4, p 371

Bill to amend an Act of the Fifth and Sixth Years of the Reign of King William the Fourth, intituled An Act to amend the Law touching Letters Patent for Inventions (1839 HL Papers 140), Vol 2, p 497

Newspaper coverage of debates

House of Lords

1R: London Courier and Evening Gazette, 29 Jun 1839

3R: Morning Post, 2 Aug 1839; The Evening Chronicle, 2 Aug 1839; London Courier and Evening Gazette, 2 Aug 1839; London Evening Standard, 2 Aug 1839

House of Commons

2R: The Times, 10 Aug 1839

3R: Morning Advertiser, 15 Aug 1839

Rep: The Times, 14 Aug 1839; Morning Chronicle, 14 Aug 1839

HC pass with Amds: **Morning Advertiser, 19 Aug 1839**; The Times, 19 Aug 1839; Morning Chronicle, 19 Aug 1839; The Evening Chronicle, 19 Aug 1839

Royal Assent: Morning Advertiser, 26 Aug 1839; Evening Mail, 26 Aug 1839

Notes

Archive

Ing: HL/PO/PU/1/1839/2&3V1n239

Protection of Inventions Act 1851

PUBA4	1851

Protection of Inventions Act 1851 (14 & 15 Vict. c. 8)

An Act to extend the Provisions of the Designs Act, 1850, and to give Protection from Piracy to Persons exhibiting new Inventions in the Exhibition of the Works of Industry of all Nations in One thousand eight hundred and fifty-one

Table of contents

s 1 Inventions may be exhibited Without Prejudice to Letters Patent to be Thereafter Granted
s 2 Public Trial of Agricultural or Horticultural Implements not to prejudice Letters Patent
s 3 Certificate of Inventions to be Granted for Provisional Registration
s 4 Certificate of Inventions to be registered
s 5 Description to be preserved, and Inventions to be marked
s 6 Provisional registration to confer same benefits as under the Designs Act 1850
s 7 Letters Patent thereafter granted to be as valid as if Inventions were not Registered or Exhibited
s 8 [Relates to designs]
s 9 The Designs Act 1850 and this Act to be Construed as One Act
s 10 Short Title

Journal

House of Commons			House of Lords		
Rep: Ralph Bernal (Ch W&M)			Pres: Earl Granville Rep: Lord Redesdale (Ld Ch)		
20 Mar 1851	106 CJ 109	Brought HL	21 Feb 1851	83 LJ 37	1R
20 Mar 1851	106 CJ 110	1R	6 Mar 1851	83 LJ 60	2R/C'tted SC
25 Mar 1851	106 CJ 114	2R/C'tted CWH	10 Mar 1851	83 LJ 63	Rep SC/C'tted CWH
26 Mar 1851	106 CJ 118	CWH adj	13 Mar 1851	83 LJ 66	CWH
28 Mar 1851	106 CJ 124	CWH adj	14 Mar 1851	83 LJ 68	CWH
3 Apr 1851	106 CJ 142 – V	CWH/Rep with Amds	17 Mar 1851	83 LJ 71	Rep with Amds
4 Apr 1851	106 CJ 145	Cons	18 Mar 1851	83 LJ 72	3R
7 Apr 1851	106 CJ 149	3R with Amds	24 Mar 1851	83 LJ 79	Rep Req by HC
10 Apr 1851	106 CJ 159	HL Ag HC Amds	25 Mar 1851	83 LJ 79	Rep sent HC
11 Apr 1851	106 CJ 162	Royal Assent	8 Apr 1851	83 LJ 119	HC pass with Amds
			10 Apr 1851	83 LJ 124	**HC Amd Ag**
			11 Apr 1851	83 LJ 128	Royal Assent

Parliamentary debates

1R: HC Deb, 20 Mar 1851, Vol 115(3rd), col 220	Rep: **HL Deb, 17 Mar 1851, Vol 115(3rd), col 1–3**
2R: **HC Deb, 24 Mar 1851, Vol 115(3rd), col 493–494**	3R: HL Deb, 18 Mar 1851, Vol 115(3rd), col 109
Rep: **HC Deb, 3 Apr 1851, Vol 115(3rd), col 1019–1029**	Royal Assent: HL Deb, 11 Apr 1851, Vol 116(3rd), col 1
3R: HC Deb, 7 Apr 1851, Vol 115(3rd), col 111	

Parliamentary papers

Bill to extend the Provisions of the Designs Act, 1850, and to give Protection from Piracy to Persons exhibiting new Inventions in the Exhibition of the Works of Industry of all Nations in One thousand eight hundred and fifty-one (1851 HL Papers 28), Vol 4, p 327

Bill to extend the Provisions of the Designs Act, 1850, and to give Protection from Piracy to Persons exhibiting new Inventions in the Exhibition of the Works of Industry of all Nations in One thousand eight hundred and fifty-one (as amended by Select Committee) (1851 HL Papers 44), Vol 4, p 333

Bill to extend the Provisions of the Designs Act, 1850, and to give Protection from Piracy to Persons exhibiting new Inventions in the Exhibition of the Works of Industry of all Nations in One thousand eight hundred and fifty-one (1851 HC Papers 131), Vol 2, 443

Bill to extend the Provisions of the Designs Act, 1850, and to give Protection from Piracy to Persons exhibiting new Inventions in the Exhibition of the Works of Industry of all Nations in One thousand eight hundred and fifty-one (as amended in Committee) (1851 HC Papers 177), Vol 2, 449

Bill to extend the Provisions of the Designs Act, 1850, and to give Protection from Piracy to Persons exhibiting new Inventions in the Exhibition of the Works of Industry of all Nations in One thousand eight hundred and fifty-one (with amendments made by the House of Commons) (1851 HL Papers 66), Vol 4, p 339

Select Committee of House of Lords to consider Bill, intituled, Act to extend provisions of Designs Act, 1850, and to give Protection from Piracy to Persons exhibiting new Inventions in Exhibition of Works of Industry of all Nations in 1851. Minutes of Evidence (1851 HC Papers 145), Vol 18, p 671

Newspaper coverage of debates
House of Lords
CWH: Morning Advertiser, 8 Mar 1851 (misreport)
Rep/C'tted CWH: *London Daily News, 11 Mar 1851; London Evening Standard, 11 Mar 1851*
CWH: **The Times, 15 Mar 1851; Morning Post, 18 Mar 1851; Evening Mail, 17 Mar 1851; London Daily News, 18 Mar 1851;** *London Evening Standard, 18 Mar 1851*
CWH: **The Times, 18 Mar 1851**
3R: The Times, 19 Mar 1851; Evening Mail, 19 Mar 1851
HC Amds: The Times, 11 Apr 1851; Morning Advertiser, 11 Apr 1851
House of Commons
2R: **The Times, 25 Mar 1881; Morning Advertiser, 25 Mar 1851; Morning Chronicle, 25 Mar 1851; Morning Post, 25 Mar 1851; London Daily News, 25 Mar 1851; London Evening Standard, 25 Mar 1851**
CWH: **The Times, 4 Apr 1851; Morning Advertiser, 4 Apr 1851; Morning Chronicle, 4 Apr 1851; Morning Post, 4 Apr 1851; Evening Mail, 4 Apr 1851; London Daily News, 4 Apr 1851**
3R: The Times, 8 Apr 1851
Royal Assent: Morning Advertiser, 12 Apr 1851; Morning Chronicle, 12 Apr 1851; London Daily News, 12 Apr 1851; Bell's New Weekly Messenger, 13 Apr 1851
Extract of HL Bill: Morning Post, 24 Mar 1851; Bell's Weekly Messenger, 24 Mar 1851; Morning Post, 29 Mar 1851
Summary of Evidence of SC: Morning Chronicle, 24 Mar 1851
Notes
Petitions – see PET168 and PET170 Also see: REP6

Protection of Inventions Act 1852

PUBA5	1852		
Protection of Inventions Act 1852 (15 & 16 Vict. c. 6)			
An Act for extending the Term of the provisional Registration of Inventions under The Protection of Inventions Act, 1851			
Table of contents			
s 1 Provisional Registration under the recited Act [Protection of Inventions Act 1851] to continue in force till 1st Feb. 1853			

Journal

House of Commons			House of Lords		
No report			Pres: Lord Colchester (VP BoT) No report		
29 Mar 1852	107 CJ 131	Brought HL	25 Mar 1852	84 LJ 68	1R
30 Mar 1852	107 CJ 134	1R	26 Mar 1852	84 LJ 73	2R/No Com
2 Apr 1852	107 CJ 143	2R/C'tted CWH/Rep	29 Mar 1852	84 LJ 76	3R
5 Apr 1852	107 CJ 148	3R	6 Apr 1852	84 LJ 92	HC pass w/o Amds
20 Apr 1852	107 CJ 157	Royal Assent	20 Apr 1852	84 LJ 97	Royal Assent

Parliamentary debates

1R: HC Deb, 30 Mar 1852, Vol 120(3rd), col 369	1R: HL Deb, 25 Mar 1852, Vol 120(3rd), col 53
2R: HL Deb, 2 Apr 1852, Vol 120(3rd), col 583	2R: HL Deb, 26 Mar 1852, Vol 120(3rd), col 171
3R: HL Deb, 5 Apr 1852, Vol 120(3rd), col 683	3R: HL Deb, 29 Mar 1852, Vol 120(3rd), col 238
	Royal Assent: HL Deb, 20 Apr 1852, Vol 120(3rd), col 873

Parliamentary papers

Bill for extending the Term of the provisional Registration of Inventions under The Protection of Inventions Act, 1851 (1852 HL Papers 60), Vol 4, p 313
Bill for extending the Term of the provisional Registration of Inventions under the Protection of Inventions Act, 1851 (1852 HC Papers 223), Vol 4, p 149

(continued)

(continued)

Newspaper coverage of debates
House of Lords
2R: The Times, 27 Mar 1852; Morning Advertiser, 27 Mar 1852; Morning Chronicle, 27 Mar 1852; Morning Post, 27 Mar 1852; London Daily News, 27 Mar 1852; London Evening Standard, 27 Mar 1852
3R: Morning Advertiser, 30 Mar 1852; Morning Chronicle, 30 Mar 1852; Morning Post, 30 Mar 1852; London Daily News, 30 Mar 1852
House of Commons
2R: **The Times, 3 Apr 1852; Morning Chronicle, 3 Apr 1852; Morning Post, 3 Apr 1852; London Daily News, 3 Apr 1852; London Evening Standard, 3 Apr 1852**
3R: The Times, 6 Apr 1852; Morning Advertiser, 6 Apr 1852; Morning Chronicle, 6 Apr 1852; London Daily News, 6 Apr 1852; London Evening Standard, 6 Apr 1852
Notes
Petition – PET197

Patent Law Amendment Act 1852

PUBA6	1852
Patent Law Amendment Act 1852 (15 & 16 Vict. c. 83)	
An Act for amending the Law for granting Patents for Inventions	
Table of contents	

s 32 Commissioners to cause Indexes to be made to old Specifications, &c., which may be printed and published
s 33 Specifications, &c. as printed by Queen's Printers to be Evidence
s 34 Register of Patents to be kept
s 35 A Register of Proprietors to be kept at the Office for filing Specifications
s 36 As to Interest in Letters Patent
s 37 Falsification or Forgery of Entries a Misdemeanor
s 38 Entries may be expunged
s 39 Provisions of [Letters Patent for Inventions Act 1835] 5 & 6 W 4. c. 83. and of [Judicial Committee Act 1844] 7 & 8 Vict. c. 69. as to Disclaimers and Memoranda of Alterations to apply to Patents under this Act
s 40 Provisions of [Letters Patent for Inventions Act 1835] 5 & 6 W 4. c. 83, [Patents Act 1839] 2 & 3 Vict. c. 67. and [Judicial Committee Act 1844] 7 & 8 Vict. c. 69. as to Confirmation and Prolongation, to apply to Patents under this Act
s 41 In Actions for Infringement of Letters Patent, Particulars to be delivered, and no Evidence allowed not mentioned therein
s 42 Courts of Common Law may grant Injunction in case of Infringement
s 43 Particulars to be regarded in Taxation of Costs
s 44 Payments and Stamp Duties on Letters Patent to be as in Schedule
s 45 Duties under Management of Commissioners of Inland Revenue
s 46 Fees to be paid to Consolidated Fund
s 47 Not to prevent Payment of Fees to Law Officers in Cases of Opposition, &c.
s 48 Fees and Salaries of Officers
s 49 Salaries and Expenses under this Act to be paid out of Monies provided by Parliament
s 50 Power to Treasury to grant Compensation to Persons affected by this Act
s 51 Account of Salaries, &c. to be laid before Parliament
s 52 As to Patents applied for before Commencement of Act
s 53 As to Letters Patent granted before Commencement of this Act for England, Scotland, or Ireland
s 54 Forms in Schedule may be used
s 55 Interpretation of Terms
s 56 Short Title
s 57 Commencement of Act
Schedule

Journal

House of Commons			House of Lords		
SC Rep: George Alexander Hamilton Stamp Duty Rep: Ralph Bernal (Ch W&M) CWH Rep: Matthew Baines			Pres: Lord Colchester (VP BoT) Rep SC: Lord Colchester (VP BoT) CWH Rep: Lord Redesdale (Ld Ch)		
23 Apr 1852	107 CJ 167	Brought HL	18 Mar 1852	84 LJ 55	1R
30 Apr 1852	107 CJ 179	1R	19 Mar 1852	84 LJ 61	2R/Ref SC
8 May 1852	107 CJ 201	2R adj	22 Mar 1852	84 LJ 64	SC Mem App
15 May 1852	107 CJ 216	2R adj	30 Mar 1852	84 LJ 80	SC Rep
18 May 1852	107 CJ 221	2R adj	5 Apr 1852	84 LJ 89	CWH
20 May 1852	107 CJ 230	2R adj	6 Apr 1852	84 LJ 92	Rep with Amds
22 May 1852	107 CJ 235	2R adj	20 Apr 1852	84 LJ 98	3R
27 May 1852	107 CJ 246	2R/C'tted SC	25 Jun 1852	84 LJ 340	HC pass with Amds
29 May 1852	107 CJ 254	SC Nom	28 Jun 1852	84 LJ 366	**HC DisAg some Amds**
15 Jun 1852	107 CJ 298	Stamp Duty ref to C'tee	30 Jun 1852	84 LJ 425	**HC insist/HL yield**
17 Jun 1852	107 CJ 303	SC Rep/Re-C'tted CWH	1 Jul 1852	84 LJ 429	Royal Assent
18 Jun 1852	107 CJ 309	**C'tee Cons Stamp Duty**			
18 Jun 1852	107 CJ 312	**Rep Stamp Duty**			
19 Jun 1852	107 CJ 314	CWH adj			
21 Jun 1852	107 CJ 319	**CWH/Rep with Amds**			
23 Jun 1852	107 CJ 327	3R			
29 Jun 1852	107 CJ 358	HL Ag Am/DisAg Amds			
29 Jun 1852	107 CJ 359	HL Amds DisAg Reasons			
30 Jun 1852	107 CJ 364	**HL Reasons Cons**			
30 Jun 1852	107 CJ 368	**HC Reasons to Insist**			
1 Jul 1852	107 CJ 370	HL do not Insist DisAg Amds			
1 Jul 1852	107 CJ 373	Royal Assent			

Parliamentary debates

1R: HC Deb, 29 Apr 1852, Vol 120(3rd), col 1315	Pre-Intro: HL Deb, 9 Feb 1852, Vol 119(3rd), col 246–251
2R: HC Deb, 27 May 1852, Vol 121(3rd), col 1221–1234	1R: HL Deb, 18 Mar 1852, Vol 119(3rd), col 1223
Rep: HC Deb, 21 Jun 1852, Vol 122(3rd), col 1202–1203	**2R: HL Deb, 19 Mar 1852, Vol 119(3rd), col 1297–1299**
3R: HC Deb, 23 Jun 1852, Vol 122(3rd), col 1204	CWH: **HL Deb, 5 Apr 1852, Vol 120(3rd), col 682**

(continued)

(continued)

HL Reasons Cons: **HC Deb, 30 Jun 1852, Vol 122(3rd), col 1418**	Rep: HL Deb, 6 Apr 1852, Vol 120(3rd), col 774
	3R: HL Deb, 20 Apr 1852, Vol 120(3rd), col 873
	Amd DisAg: **HL Deb, 28 Jun 1852, Vol 122(3rd), col 1336–1337**
	Royal Assent: HL Deb, 1 Jul 1852, Vol 122(3rd), col 1423

Parliamentary papers

Bill for amending the Law for granting Patents for Inventions (1852 HL Papers 51), Vol 4, p 139

Bill for amending the Law for granting Patents for Inventions (as amended in Select Committee) (1852 HL Papers 74), Vol 4, p 171

Bill for amending the Law for granting Patents for Inventions (as amended in Committee) (1852 HL Papers 81), Vol 4, p 203

Bill for amending the Law for granting Patents for Inventions (1852 HC Papers 299), Vol 4, p 1

Bill for amending the Law for granting Patents for Inventions (as amended by Select Committee) (1852 HC Papers 486), Vol 4, p 33

Bill for amending the Law for granting Patents for Inventions (with amendments of House of Commons marked) (1852 HL Papers 237), Vol 4, p 235

Newspaper coverage of debates

House of Lords

2R: **The Times, 20 Mar 1852; Morning Chronicle, 20 Mar 1852; Morning Post, 20 Mar 1852; London Daily News, 20 Mar 1852**; Morning Advertiser, 20 Mar 1852; London Evening Standard, 20 Mar 1852

CWH: *The Times, 6 Apr 1852; Morning Chronicle, 6 Apr 1852; Morning Post, 6 Apr 1852; London Daily News, 6 Apr 1852; London Evening Standard, 6 Apr 1852*; Morning Advertiser, 6 Apr 1852

Rep: The Times, 7 Apr 1852; Morning Post, 7 Apr 1852; Evening Mail, 7 Apr 1852; London Daily News, 7 Apr 1852

3R: *Evening Mail, 21 Apr 1852*; The Times, 21 Apr 1852; Morning Advertiser, 21 Apr 1852; Morning Chronicle, 21 Apr 1852; Morning Post, 21 Apr 1852

HC DisAg some Amds: **The Times, 29 Jun 1852; Morning Advertiser, 29 Jun 1852; Morning Chronicle, 29 Jun 1852; Morning Post, 29 Jun 1852; London Evening Standard, 29 Jun 1852**; London Daily News, 29 Jun 1852

House of Commons

Suggested Withdrawal: **The Times, 15 May 1852; Morning Advertiser, 15 May 1852; Morning Chronicle, 15 May 1852; Morning Post, 15 May 1852**

2R: **The Times, 28 May 1852; Morning Advertiser, 28 Apr 1852; Morning Chronicle, 28 May 1852; Morning Post, 28 May 1852; Evening Mail, 28 May 1852; London Daily News, 28 May 1852; London Evening Standard, 28 May 1852**

SC App: The Times, 29 May 1852

Stamp Rep: The Times, 19 Jun 1852; Morning Advertiser, 19 Jun 1852; Morning Chronicle, 19 Jun 1852; Morning Post, 19 Jun 1852; London Daily News, 19 Jun 1852; London Evening Standard, 19 Jun 1852

CWH: **The Times, 23 Jun 1852; Morning Chronicle, 23 Jun 1852; Morning Post, 23 Jun 1852; London Daily News, 23 Jul 1852**; Morning Advertiser, 23 Jun 1852; Evening Mail, 23 Jun 1852; London Evening Standard, 23 Jun 1852

3R: Morning Advertiser, 24 Jun 1852; Morning Chronicle, 24 Jun 1852; Morning Post, 24 Jun 1852; London Daily News, 24 Jun 1852; London Evening Standard, 24 Jun 1852

Conf: **Morning Post, 1 Jul 1852**; *Morning Chronicle, 1 Jul 1852*; The Times, 1 Jul 1852; Morning Advertiser, 1 Jul 1852; London Daily News, 1 Jul 1852;

Royal Assent: Morning Advertiser, 2 Jul 1852; Morning Chronicle, 2 Jul 1852; Morning Post, 2 Jul 1852; London Daily News, 2 Jul 1852

Notes

Related debates

Prorogation: **HL Deb, 1 Jul 1852, Vol 122(3rd), col 1424**

Fees: **HL Deb, 16 Nov 1852, Vol 123(3rd), col 181**

Petitions – PET202 to PET215

Patent Law Act 1853 (c. 5)

PUBA7	1853
	Patent Law Act 1853 (16 & 17 Vict. c. 5)
	An Act to substitute Stamp Duties for Fees on passing Letters Patent for Inventions, and to provide for the Purchase for the public Use of certain Indexes of Specifications

Table of contents

s 1 §§ 17, 44, 45, 46, and 53, and Part of Schedule of recited Act [Patent Law Amendment Act 1852] repealed
s 2 Letters Patent to be made subject to Avoidance on Non-payment of Stamp Duties expressed in Schedule to this Act annexed
s 3 Stamp Duties mentioned in the Schedule to this Act to be payable
s 4 As to Payment of Stamp Duties on Letters Patent for England, Scotland, or Ireland respectively
s 5 Duties to be under Management of Commissioners of Inland Revenue
s 6 Who are to provide the proper Stamps for the Purpose
s 7 Conditions of Letters Patent already granted under recited Act to be satisfied by Payment of Stamp Duties, &c. under this Act
s 8 Power to Commissioners to purchase the Indexes of existing Specifications prepared by Mr. Woodcroft
s 9 As to the Word "Duplicate"
s 10 This Act and [Patent Law Amendment Act 1852] 15 & 16 Vict. c. 83. to be construed together
Schedule – Stamp Duties to be paid to which this Act refers

Journal

House of Commons			House of Lords		
Pres: George Alexander Hamilton (Fin Sec Tr) All Reports: John Wilson-Patten (Ch W&M)			No report		
7 Dec 1852	108 CJ 173	Stamp Duty ref C'tee	17 Dec 1852	85 LJ 61	Brought HC/1R
8 Dec 1852	108 CJ 177	**Stamp Duty C'tee**	20 Dec 1852	85 LJ 62	2R/C'tee Neg
8 Dec 1852	108 CJ 178	**Stamp Duty Rep**	23 Dec 1852	85 LJ 64	3R
8 Dec 1852	108 CJ 179	1R	21 Feb 1853	85 LJ 99	Royal Assent
9 Dec 1852	108 CJ 185	**Index purchase ref C'tee**			
11 Dec 1852	108 CJ 188	2R/C'tted CWH			
11 Dec 1852	108 CJ 188	**Index C'tee**			
14 Dec 1852	108 CJ 190	**Rep Index C'tee**			
14 Dec 1852	108 CJ 191	CWH/Rep			
15 Dec 1852	108 CJ 193	Cons			
16 Dec 1852	108 CJ 198	3R			
24 Dec 1852	108 CJ 206	HL pass w/o Amds			
21 Feb 1853	108 CJ 266	Royal Assent			

Parliamentary debates

1R: HC Deb, 8 Dec 1852, Vol 123(3rd), col 1144	2R: HL Deb, 20 Dec 1852, Vol 123(3rd), col 1698
3R: HC Deb, 16 Dec 1852, Vol 123(3rd), col 1569	3R: HL Deb, 23 Dec 1852, Vol 123(3rd), col 1717
	Royal Assent: HL Deb, 21 Feb 1853, Vol 124(3rd), col 335

Parliamentary papers

Bill to substitute Stamp Duties for Fees on passing Letters Patent for Inventions, and to provide for the Purchase for the public Use of certain Indexes of Specifications (1852–53 HC Papers 61), Vol 6, p 505

Bill to substitute Stamp Duties for Fees on passing Letters Patent for Inventions, and to provide for the Purchase for the public Use of certain Indexes of Specifications (1852–53 HL Papers 46), Vol 7, p 431

Newspaper coverage of debates

Reason for introduction: The Times, 17 Nov 1852

House of Commons

COS Res: Morning Advertiser, 8 Dec 1852; Morning Chronicle, 8 Dec 1852; Morning Post, 8 Dec 1852; London Daily News, 8 Dec 1852; London Evening Standard, 8 Dec 1852; The Times, 9 Dec 1852

COS Res Rep: Morning Chronicle, 9 Dec 1852; The Times, 11 Dec 1852

CWH: Morning Chronicle, 14 Dec 1852; Morning Post, 14 Dec 1852; London Daily News, 14 Dec 1852; London Evening Standard, 14 Dec 1852

3R: Morning Advertiser, 17 Dec 1852; Morning Chronicle, 17 Dec 1852; London Daily News, 17 Dec 1852

(continued)

(continued)

House of Lords
2R: Morning Chronicle, 21 Dec 1852; Morning Post, 21 Dec 1852; London Daily News, 21 Dec 1852; London Evening Standard, 21 Dec 1852
3R: The Times, 24 Dec 1852; Morning Advertiser, 24 Dec 1852; Morning Chronicle, 24 Dec 1852; Morning Post, 24 Dec 1852; Evening Mail, 24 Dec 1852; London Evening Standard, 24 Dec 1852
Royal Assent: The Times, 22 Feb 1853; Morning Advertiser, 22 Feb 1853; Morning Chronicle, 22 Feb 1853; Morning Post, 22 Feb 1853; London Evening Standard, 22 Feb 1853

Patent Law Act 1853 (c. 115)

PUBA8	1853
	Patent Law Act 1853 (16 & 17 Vict. c. 115)

An Act to amend certain Provisions of the Patent Law Amendment Act, 1852, in respect of the Transmission of certified Copies of Letters Patent and Specifications to certain Offices in Edinburgh and Dublin, and otherwise to amend the said Act [Copies of Specification Bill]

Table of contents

s 1 Sect. 33. and Part of Sect. 28. of recited Act [Patent Law Amendment Act 1852] repealed
s 2 Copies of Provisional Specifications to be open to Inspection
s 3 Copy of Specification, &c., under Hand of Patentee, &c. to be left
s 4 Copies or Extracts of Letters Patent, &c., to be received in Evidence
s 5 Certified printed Copies of Specifications, &c. under Seal of Commissioners, to be sent to Director of Chancery in Scotland and Court of Chancery in Ireland, which shall be Evidence
s 6 Lord Chancellor, in certain Cases, may seal Letters Patent after the Expiration of provisional Protection
s 7 Removing Doubts as to Provision of [Patent Law Amendment Act 1852] 15 & 16 Vict. c. 83. respecting the making and sealing of new Letters Patent for a further Term
s 8 [Patent Law Amendment Act 1852] 15. & 16 Vict. c. 83. and this Act to be construed as One

Journal

House of Commons			House of Lords		
All Reports: Edward Pleydell-Bouverie (Ch W&M)			Pres: Lord Cranworth LC Rep: Lord Redesdale (Ld Ch)		
23 May 1853	108 CJ 510	Brought HL	8 Mar 1853	85 LJ 117	1R
27 May 1853	108 CJ 520	1R	6 May 1853	85 LJ 237	2R day app
31 May 1853	108 CJ 529	2R adj	9 May 1853	85 LJ 245	2R/C'tted CWH
3 Jun 1853	108 CJ 544	2R adj	10 May 1853	85 LJ 250	CWH/Rep with Amds
9 Jun 1853	108 CJ 563	Pets	12 May 1853	85 LJ 253	Cons
10 Jun 1853	108 CJ 564	2R adj	13 May 1853	85 LJ 272	3R
16 Jun 1853	108 CJ 588	Pets	15 Aug 1853	85 LJ 649	HC pass with Amds
17 Jun 1853	108 CJ 590	2R adj	16 Aug 1853	85 LJ 658	HC Amds Cons day app
18 Jun 1853	108 CJ 595	2R adj	18 Aug 1853	85 LJ 699	**HC Amds Cons/Ag**
21 Jun 1853	108 CJ 600	2R adj	20 Aug 1853	85 LJ 717	Royal Assent
24 Jun 1853	108 CJ 611	2R adj			
28 Jun 1853	108 CJ 624	2R adj			
5 Jul 1853	108 CJ 643	2R adj			
8 Jul 1853	108 CJ 659	2R/C'tted CWH			
12 Jul 1853	108 CJ 672	CWH/Rep/Re-C'tted CWH			
19 Jul 1853	108 CJ 693	CWH adj			
23 Jul 1853	108 CJ 716	CWH adj			
26 Jul 1853	108 CJ 723	CWH adj			
30 Jul 1853	108 CJ 743	CWH adj			
2 Aug 1853	108 CJ 755	CWH adj			
5 Aug 1853	108 CJ 768	CWH/Rep/Re-C'tted CWH			
9 Aug 1853	108 CJ 808	CWH adj			
10 Aug 1853	108 CJ 814	CWH/Rep with Amds			
11 Aug 1853	108 CJ 818	Cons			
12 Aug 1853	108 CJ 821	3R			
19 Aug 1853	108 CJ 840	HL Ag HC Amds			
20 Aug 1853	108 CJ 847	Royal Assent			

Parliamentary debates	
1R: HC Deb, 27 May 1853, Vol 127(3rd), col 706	1R: HL Deb, 8 Mar 1853, Vol 124(3rd), col 1288
2R: HC Deb, 7 Jul 1853, Vol 128(3rd), col 1367	2R: HL Deb, 9 May 1853, Vol 126(3rd), col 1286
CWH: **HC Deb, 11 Jul 1853, Vol 129(3rd), col 85–86**	3R: HL Deb, 13 May 1853, Vol 127(3rd), col 293
3R: HC Deb, 12 Aug 1853, Vol 129(3rd), col 1679	Royal Assent: HL Deb, 20 Aug 1853, Vol 129(3rd), col 1824

Parliamentary papers
Bill to repeal certain Provisions of the Patent Law Amendment Act, 1852, in respect of the Transmission of certified Copies of Letters Patent and Specifications to certain Offices in Edinburgh and Dublin (1852–53 HL Papers 88), Vol 3, p 639
Bill to repeal certain Provisions of the Patent Law Amendment Act, 1852, in respect of the Transmission of certified Copies of Letters Patent and Specifications to certain Offices in Edinburgh and Dublin (as amended in Committee) (1852–53 HL Papers 190), Vol 3, p 641
Bill to amend certain Provisions of the Patent Law Amendment Act, 1852, in respect of the Transmission of certified Copies of Letters Patent and Specifications to certain Offices in Edinburgh and Dublin, and otherwise to amend the said Act (1852–53 HC Papers 527), Vol 1, p 395
Bill to amend certain Provisions of the Patent Law Amendment Act, 1852, in respect of the Transmission of certified Copies of Letters Patent and Specifications to certain Offices in Edinburgh and Dublin, and otherwise to amend the said Act (as amended in Committee) (1852–53 HC Papers 739), Vol 1, p 399
Bill to amend certain Provisions of the Patent Law Amendment Act, 1852, in respect of the Transmission of certified Copies of Letters Patent and Specifications to certain Offices in Edinburgh and Dublin, and otherwise to amend the said Act (as amended in Committee, and on Re-Commitment) (1852–53 HC Papers 874), Vol 1, p 403
Bill to repeal certain Provisions of the Patent Law Amendment Act, 1852, in respect of the Transmission of certified Copies of Letters Patent and Specifications to certain Offices in Edinburgh and Dublin (as amended by the House of Commons) (1852–53 HL Papers 420), Vol 3, p 645

Newspaper coverage of debates
House of Lords
2R: *Morning Post, 10 May 1853*; *London Daily News, 10 May 1853*; The Times, 10 May 1853; Morning Advertiser, 10 May 1853; Morning Chronicle, 10 May 1853; Evening Standard, 10 May 1853
CWH: The Times, 11 May 1853; Morning Chronicle, 11 May 1853; Evening Mail, 11 May 1853
Rep: The Times, 13 May 1853; Morning Advertiser, 13 May 1853; Morning Chronicle, 13 May 1853; Morning Post, 13 May 1853; Evening Mail, 13 May 1853; London Evening Standard, 13 May 1853
3R: The Times, 14 May 1853; Morning Advertiser, 14 May 1853; Morning Chronicle, 14 May 1853; Morning Post, 14 May 1853; London Daily News, 14 May 1853;
HC Amds Cons: Morning Advertiser, 19 Aug 1853; Morning Chronicle, 19 Aug 1853; Morning Post, 19 Aug 1853; London Daily News, 19 Aug 1853
House of Commons
CWH: **Morning Advertiser, 12 Jul 1853**; **Morning Post, 12 Jul 1853**; **London Daily News, 12 Aug 1853**; *London Evening Standard, 12 Jul 1853*; The Times, 12 Jul 1853
CWH: **The Times, 11 Aug 1853**; **Morning Advertiser, 11 Aug 1853**; Morning Chronicle, 11 Aug 1853; Morning Post, 11 Aug 1853; London Daily News, 11 Aug 1853; London Evening Standard, 12 Aug 1853
3R: The Times, 13 Aug 1853; Morning Chronicle, 13 Aug 1853; Morning Post, 13 Aug 1853; London Evening Standard, 13 Aug 1853

Notes
Petitions – PET218 to PET222

Patents for Inventions Act 1859

PUBA9	1859
Patents for Inventions Act 1859 (22 Vict. c. 13)	
An Act to amend the Law concerning Patents for Inventions with respect to Inventions for Improvements in Instruments and Munitions of War	
Table of contents	
s 1 Improvements in Instruments Or Munitions Of War May Be Assigned By Inventors To Secretary of State for War s 2 Foregoing Enactment to Extend to Assignments Already Made	

(continued)

(continued)

s 3 Secretary of State for War may Certify to Commissioners of Patents that the Inventions should be Kept Secret
s 4 Where the Secretary of State for War has so Certified, Petition for Letters Patent, &c. To be Left with the Clerk of the Patents in a Packet under Seal of Secretary of State
s 5 Such Packet to be Kept so Sealed, or under the Seal of the Commissioners
s 6 And to be delivered to Secretary of State, &c.
s 7 And on Expiration of Term to Secretary of State
s 8 Where Secretary of State certifies after Filing of Petition, documents to be Put into a Sealed Packet
s 9 Copy of Specification, &c. Not to be published but otherwise Provisions of Patent Acts to Apply
s 10 No Scire Facias to be Brought
s 11 Benefit of Act may be waived
s 12 Communication of Inventions &c. Not to Prejudice Letters Patent
s 13 Construction of "Secretary of State"

Journal						
House of Commons			**House of Lords**			
Pres: Sir Fitzroy Kelly (A-G) Rep: Henry Fitzroy (Ch W&M)			Rep: Lord Redesdale (Ld Ch)			
22 Mar 1859	114 CJ 125	Bill Ord/1R	31 Mar 1859	91 LJ 147	Brought HC/1R	
24 Mar 1859	114 CJ 131	2R/C'tted CWH	4 Apr 1859	91 LJ 159	2R/C'tted CWH	
26 Mar 1859	114 CJ 135	CWH/Rep with Amds	5 Apr 1859	91 LJ 165	CWH/Rep w/o Amds	
29 Mar 1859	114 CJ 138	Cons	7 Apr 1859	91 LJ 169	3R	
30 Mar 1859	114 CJ 141	3R	8 Apr 1859	91 LJ 171	Royal Assent	
8 Apr 1859	114 CJ 160	HL pass w/o Amds				
8 Apr 1859	114 CJ 160	Royal Assent				

Parliamentary debates

1R: **HC Deb, 21 Mar 1859, Vol 153(3rd), col 482**

2R: HC Deb, 24 Mar 1859, Vol 153(3rd), col 688

3R: HC Deb, 29 Mar 1859, Vol 153(3rd), col 1040

1R: HL Deb, 31 Mar 1859, Vol 153(3rd), col 1149

2R: HL Deb, 4 Apr 1859, Vol 153(3rd), col 1266

3R: HL Deb, 7 Apr 1859, Vol 153(3rd), col 1474

Royal Assent: HL Deb, 8 Apr 1859, Vol 153(3rd), col 1528

Parliamentary papers

Bill to amend the Law concerning Patents for Inventions with respect to Inventions for Improvements in Instruments and Munitions of War (1850 Sess 1 HC Papers 87), Vol 2, p 389

Bill to amend the Law concerning Patents for Inventions with respect to Inventions for Improvements in Instruments and Munitions of War (1850 Sess 1 HL Papers 81), Vol 3, p 11

Newspaper coverage of debates

House of Commons

1R: *The Times, 22 Mar 1859; Morning Advertiser, 22 Mar 1859; Morning Posts, 22 Mar 1859; London Daily News, 22 Mar 1859;* Morning Chronicle, 22 Mar 1859

2R: The Times, 25 Mar 1859; Morning Advertiser, 25 Mar 1859; Morning Chronicle, 25 Mar 1859; Morning Post, 25 Mar 1859; London Daily News, 25 Mar 1859

CWH: The Times, 26 Mar 1859; Morning Post, 26 Mar 1859; London Evening Standard, 26 Mar 1859;

3R: Morning Advertiser, 30 Mar 1859; Morning Chronicle, 30 Mar 1859; Morning Post, 30 Mar 1859; London Daily News, 30 Mar 1859; London Evening Standard, 30 Mar 1859

House of Lords

Cons: The Times, 6 Apr 1859; Morning Advertiser, 6 Apr 1859; Morning Chronicle, 6 Apr 1859; Morning Post, 6 Apr 1859; London Daily News, 6 Apr 1859; London Evening Standards, 6 Apr 1859

3R: The Times, 8 Apr 1859; Morning Chronicle, 8 Apr 1859; Evening Mail, 8 Apr 1859; London Daily News, 8 Apr 1859

Royal Assent: The Times, 8 Apr 1859

Protection of Inventions and Designs Amendment Act 1862

PUBA10	1862
Protection of Inventions and Designs Amendment Act 1862 (25 & 26 Vict. c. 12)	
An Act for the Protection of Inventions and Designs exhibited at the International Exhibition of Industry and Art for the Year One thousand eight hundred and sixty-two	

Table of contents
s 1 Short Title
s 2 Exhibition of new Inventions not to prejudice Patent Rights
s 3 Exhibition of Designs not to prejudice Provisional Registration

Journal					
House of Commons			**House of Lords**		
Rep: William Massey (Ch W&M)			Pres: Earl Granville (Ld Pr) No report		
5 Apr 1862	117 CJ 138	Brought HL	28 Mar 1862	94 LJ 108	1R
8 Apr 1862	117 CJ 142	1R	3 Apr 1862	94 LJ 142	2R/No Com
9 Apr 1862	117 CJ 147	2R/C'tted CWH	4 Apr 1862	94 LJ 147	3R
11 Apr 1862	117 CJ 151	CWH/Rep w/o Amds	29 Apr 1862	94 LJ 169	HC pass w/o Amds
12 Apr 1862	117 CJ 157	3R	29 Apr 1862	94 LJ 170	Royal Assent
29 Apr 1862	117 CJ 164	Royal Assent			

Parliamentary debates	
1R: HC Deb, 7 Apr 1862, Vol 166(3rd), col 635	1R: HL Deb, 28 Mar 1862, Vol 166(3rd), col 231
2R: HC Deb, 9 Apr 1862, Vol 166(3rd), col 715	2R: HL Deb, 3 Apr 1862, Vol 166(3rd), col 430
3R: HC Deb, 11 Apr 1862, Vol 166(3rd), col 855	3R: HL Deb, 4 Apr 1862, Vol 166(3rd), col 532
	Royal Assent: HL Deb, 29 April 1862, Vol 166(3rd), col 1038

Parliamentary papers
Bill for the Protection of Inventions and Designs exhibited at the International Exhibition of Industry and Art for the Year One thousand eight hundred and sixty-two (1862 HL Papers 45), Vol 6, p 609
Bill for the Protection of Inventions and Designs exhibited at the International Exhibition of Industry and Art for the Year One thousand eight hundred and sixty-two (1862 HC Papers 78), Vol 4, p 605

Newspaper coverage of debates
House of Lords
2R: *The Times, 4 Apr 1862*; Morning Advertiser, 4 Apr 1862; Morning Post, 4 Apr 1862; London Daily News, 4 Apr 1862; London Evening Standard, 4 Apr 1862
3R: The Times, 5 Apr 1862; Morning Advertiser, 5 Apr 1862; Morning Post, 5 Apr 1862; London Daily News, 5 Apr 1862; London Evening Standard, 5 Apr 1862
House of Commons
2R: The Times, 10 Apr 1862; Morning Advertiser, 10 Apr 1862; Morning Post, 10 Apr 1862; London Daily News, 10 Apr 1862; London Evening Standard, 10 Apr 1862
CWH: The Times, 11 Apr 1862; Morning Advertiser, 11 Apr 1862; Morning Post, 11 Apr 1862; London Daily News, 11 Apr 1862
3R: The Times, 12 Apr 1862; Morning Advertiser, 12 Apr 1862; London Daily News, 12 Apr 1862
Royal Assent: The Times, 30 Apr 1862

Industrial Exhibitions Act 1865

PUBA11	1865
Industrial Exhibitions Act 1865 (28 & 29 Vict. c. 3)	
An Act for the Protection of Inventions and Designs exhibited at certain Industrial Exhibitions in the United Kingdom	

Table of contents
s 1 Short Title
s 2 Power to Board of Trade to certify that certain Industrial Exhibitions are entitled to the Benefit of this Act
s 3 Exhibition of new Inventions not to prejudice Patent Rights
s 4 Exhibition of Designs not to prejudice Right to Registration

Journal	
House of Commons	**House of Lords**
Pres: Thomas Milner Gibson (Pr BoT) Rep: John Dodson (Ch W&M)	Rep: Lord Redesdale (Ld Ch)

(continued)

(continued)

21 Feb 1865	120 CJ 85	Bill Ord	9 Mar 1865	97 LJ 58	Brought HC/1R
21 Feb 1865	120 CJ 86	1R	14 Mar 1865	97 LJ 67	2R day app
27 Feb 1865	120 CJ 99	2R/C'tted CWH	16 Mar 1865	97 LJ 76	2R/C'tted CWH
2 Mar 1865	120 CJ 106	CWH adj	17 Mar 1865	97 LJ 81	CWH/Rep w/o Amds
3 Mar 1865	120 CJ 110	CWH/Rep with Amds	20 Mar 1865	97 LJ 83	3R
6 Mar 1865	120 CJ 114	Cons	27 Mar 1865	97 LJ 99	Royal Assent
8 Mar 1865	120 CJ 118	3R			
21 Mar 1865	120 CJ 148	HL pass w/o Amds			
27 Mar 1865	120 CJ 163	Royal Assent			

Parliamentary debates	
1R: HC Deb, 21 Feb 1865, Vol 177(3rd), col 490	1R: HL Deb, 9 Mar 1865, Vol 177(3rd), col 1365
2R: HC Deb, 27 Feb 1865, Vol 177(3rd), col 743	2R: HL Deb, 16 Mar 1865, Vol 177(3rd), col 1726
Rep: HC Deb, 3 Mar 1865, Vol 177(3rd), col 1042	Com: HL Deb, 17 Mar 1865, Vol 177(3rd), col 1824
Cons: HC Deb, 6 Mar 1865, Vol 177(3rd), col 1115	3R: HL Deb, 20 Mar 1865, Vol 177(3rd), col 1910

Parliamentary papers
Bill for the Protection of Inventions and Designs exhibited at certain Industrial Exhibitions in the United Kingdom (1865 HC Papers 36), Vol 2, p 157
Bill for the Protection of Inventions and Designs exhibited at certain Industrial Exhibitions in the United Kingdom (1865 HL Papers 28), Vol 3, p 519

Newspaper coverage of debates
House of Commons
Bill Ord: *The Times, 22 Feb 1865; Morning Advertiser, 22 Feb 1865; Morning Post, 22 Feb 1865; London Daily News, 22 Feb 1865; London Evening Standard, 22 Feb 1865*
2R: The Times, 28 Feb 1865; Morning Advertiser, 28 Feb 1865; Morning Post, 28 Feb 1865; London Daily News, 28 Feb 1865
CWH: The Times, 4 Mar 1865; Morning Advertiser, 4 Mar 1865; Morning Post, 4 Mar 1865; London Daily News, 4 Mar 1865; London Evening Standard, 4 Mar 1865
Cons: The Times, 7 Mar 1865; London Daily News, 7 Mar 1865; London Evening Standard, 7 Mar 1865
House of Lords
2R: The Times, 17 Mar 1865; Morning Advertiser, 17 Mar 1865; Morning Post, 17 Mar 1865; London Daily News, 17 Mar 1865; London Evening Standard, 17 Mar 1865
CWH: The Times, 18 Mar 1865; Morning Advertiser, 18 Mar 1865; Morning Post, 18 Mar 1865; London Daily News, 18 Mar 1865; London Evening Standard, 18 Mar 1865
3R: The Times, 21 Mar 1865; Morning Advertiser, 21 Mar 1865; Morning Post, 21 Mar 1865; London Daily News, 21 Mar 1865; London Evening Standard, 21 Mar 1865
Royal Assent: The Times, 28 Mar 1865; Morning Post, 28 Mar 1865; London Daily News, 28 Mar 1865; London Evening Standard, 28 Mar 1865

Protection of Inventions and Designs Amendment Act 1865

PUBA12	1865
Protection of Inventions and Designs Amendment Act 1865 (28 & 29 Vict. c. 6)	
An Act for the Protection of Inventions and Designs exhibited at the Dublin International Exhibition for the Year One thousand eight hundred and sixty-five	

Table of contents
s 1 Short Title
s 2 Exhibition of New Inventions Not to Prejudice Rights to Register the Same
s 3 Exhibition of New Designs Not to Prejudice Rights to Register the Same

Journal	
House of Commons	**House of Lords**
Pres: Sir Robert Peel (Ch Sec Ire) Rep: John Dodson (Ch W&M)	Rep: Lord Redesdale (Ld Ch)

13 Feb 1865	120 CJ 52	Bill Ord	23 Feb 1865	97 LJ 37	Brought HC/1R
13 Feb 1865	120 CJ 53	1R	21 Mar 1865	97 LJ 85	2R day app
17 Feb 1865	120 CJ 75	2R/C'tted CWH	23 Mar 1865	97 LJ 92	2R/Com Neg
20 Feb 1865	120 CJ 81	CWH/Rep w/o Amds	24 Mar 1865	97 LJ 96	3R
21 Feb 1865	120 CJ 86	3R	27 Mar 1865	97 LJ 99	Royal Assent
25 Mar 1865	120 CJ 160	HL pass w/o Amds			
27 Mar 1865	120 CJ 163	Royal Assent			

Parliamentary debates

1R: HC Deb, 13 Feb 1865, Vol 177(3rd), col 203	1R: HL Deb, 23 Feb 1865, Vol 177(3rd), col 580
2R: HC Deb, 17 Feb 1865, Vol 177(3rd), col 318	2R: HL Deb, 23 Mar 1865, Vol 178(3rd), col 68
CWH: HC Deb, 20 Feb 1865, Vol 177(3rd), col 440	3R: HL Deb, 24 Mar 1865, Vol 178(3rd), col 188
3R: HC Deb, 21 Feb 1865, Vol 177(3rd), col 490	

Parliamentary papers

Bill for the Protection of Inventions and Designs exhibited at the Dublin International Exhibition for the Year One thousand eight hundred and sixty-five (1865 HC Papers 17), Vol 1, p 603

Bill for the Protection of Inventions and Designs exhibited at the Dublin International Exhibition for the Year One thousand eight hundred and sixty-five (1865 HL Papers 13), Vol 3, p 373

Newspaper coverage of debates

House of Commons

1R: *The Times, 14 Feb 1865*; *Morning Advertiser, 14 Feb 1865*; *Morning Post, 14 Feb 1865*; London Evening Standard, 14 Feb 1865

2R: The Times, 18 Feb 1865; Morning Advertiser, 18 Feb 1865; Morning Post, 18 Feb 1865; London Daily News, 18 Feb 1865; London Evening Standard, 18 Feb 1865

CWH: The Times, 21 Feb 1865

3R: Morning Advertiser, 22 Feb 1865; Morning Post, 22 Feb 1865; London Daily News, 22 Feb 1865; London Evening Standard, 22 Feb 1865

House of Lords

2R: **Morning Post, 24 Mar 1865**; **London Daily News, 24 Mar 1865**; **London Evening Standard, 24 Mar 1865**; The Times, 24 Mar 1865

3R: The Times, 25 Mar 1865; Morning Post, 25 Mar 1865; London Daily News, 25 Mar 1865; London Evening Standard, 25 Mar 1865

Royal Assent: The Times, 28 Mar 1865; Morning Post, 28 Mar 1865; London Daily News, 28 Mar 1865; London Evening Standard, 28 Mar 1865

Protection of Inventions Act 1870

PUBA13	1870

Protection of Inventions Act 1870 (33 & 34 Vict. c. 27)

An Act for the Protection of Inventions exhibited at International Exhibitions in the United Kingdom

Table of contents

s 1 Short title
s 2 Exhibition of new inventions not to prejudice patent rights
s 3 Exhibition of designs not to prejudice right to registration
s 4 Application of Act to international exhibitions in general

Journal

House of Commons			House of Lords		
Pres: Sir Robert Collier (A-G) Rep: John Dodson (Ch W&M)			Rep: Lord Redesdale (Ld Ch)		
9 Jun 1870	125 CJ 245	Bill Ord/1R	17 Jun 1870	102 LJ 306	Brought HC/1R
11 Jun 1870	125 CJ 247	2R/C'tted CWH	4 Jul 1870	102 LJ 386	2R day app
14 Jun 1870	125 CJ 251	CWH/Rep w/o Amds	5 Jul 1870	102 LJ 397	2R/C'tted CWH
16 Jun 1870	125 CJ 257	3R	7 Jul 1870	102 LJ 403	**Rep with Amds**

(continued)

(continued)

9 Jul 1870	125 CJ 316	HL pass with Amds	8 Jul 1870	102 LJ 415	3R
12 Jul 1870	125 CJ 321	HL Amds day app	12 Jul 1870	102 LJ 425	HC Ag Amds
12 Jul 1870	125 CJ 324	HL Amds Cons	14 Jul 1870	102 LJ 428	Royal Assent
14 Jul 1870	125 CJ 328	Royal Assent			

Parliamentary debates

1R: HC Deb, 9 Jun 1870, Vol 201(3rd), col 1767	1R: HL Deb, 17 Jun 1870, Vol 202(3rd), col 316
2R: HC Deb, 10 Jun 1870, Vol 201(3rd), col 1841	2R: HL Deb, 5 Jul 1870, Vol 202(3rd), col 1428
CWH: HC Deb, 13 Jun 1870, Vol 201(3rd), col 1940	CWH: HL Deb, 7 Jul 1870, Vol 202(3rd), col 1593
3R: HC Deb, 16 Jun 1870, Vol 202(3rd), col 259	3R: HL Deb, 8 Jul 1870, Vol 202(3rd), col 1693
	Royal Assent: HL Deb, 14 Jul 1870, Vol 203(3rd), col 196

Parliamentary papers

Bill for the Protection of Inventions exhibited at International Exhibitions in the United Kingdom (1870 HC Papers 157), Vol 4, p 53

Bill for the Protection of Inventions and Designs exhibited at certain Industrial Exhibitions in the United Kingdom (1870 HL Papers 142), Vol 6, p 567

Amendments to be moved in Committee on Bill by Earl of Lichfield (1870 HL Papers 142a), Vol 6, p 569

Supplement to Votes & Proceedings, 1870 – No amendments

Newspaper coverage of debates

House of Commons

2R: The Times, 11 Jun 1870; Morning Advertiser, 11 Jun 1870; Morning Post, 11 Jun 1870; London Daily News, 11 Jun 1870; London Evening Standard, 11 Jun 1870

CWH: The Times, 14 Jun 1870; Morning Post, 14 Jun 1870; London Evening Standard, 14 Jun 1870

3R: The Times, 17 Jun 1870; Morning Advertiser, 17 Jun 1870; Morning Post, 17 Jun 1870; London Daily News 17 Jun 1870; London Evening Standard, 17 Jun 1870

House of Lords

2R: The Times, 6 Jul 1870; Morning Advertiser, 6 Jul 1870; Morning Post, 6 Jul 1870; London Daily News, 6 Jul 1870; London Evening Standard, 6 Jul 1870

CWH: The Times, 8 Jul 1870; Morning Advertiser, 8 Jul 1870; Morning Post, 8 Jul 1870; London Daily News, 8 Jul 1870; London Evening Standard, 8 Jul 1870

3R: The Times, 9 Jul 1870; Morning Advertiser, 9 Jul 1870; Morning Post, 9 Jul 1870; London Daily News, 9 Jul 1870; London Evening Standard, 9 Jul 1870

Royal Assent: The Times, 15 Jul 1870; Morning Advertiser, 15 Jul 1870; Morning Post, 15 Jul 1870; London Daily News, 15 Jul 1870; London Evening Standard, 15 Jul 1870

Notes

Petition – PET307

Patents, Designs, and Trade Marks Act 1883

PUBA14	1883

Patents, Designs, and Trade Marks Act 1883 (46 & 47 Vict. c. 57)

An Act to amend and consolidate the Law relating to Patents for Inventions, Registration of Designs, and of Trade Marks

Table of contents

	Table of origin
Part I – Preliminary	
s 1 Short title	—
s 2 Division of Act into parts	—
s 3 Commencement of Act	—
Part II – Patents	
s 4 Persons entitled to apply for patent	—
s 5 Application and specification	1852, s 6 and 9
s 6 Reference of application to examiner	—

s 7 Power for Comptroller to refuse application or require amendment	—
s 8 Time for leaving complete specification	—
s 9 Comparison of provisional and complete specification	
s 10 Advertisement on acceptance of complete specification	1852, s 9, 12 and 29; 1853, s 2
s 11 Opposition to grant of patent	1852, s 8, 12 to 14
s 12 Sealing of patent	1852, s 18 to 22
s 13 Date of patent	1852, s 23
s 14 Provisional protection	1852, s 8
s 15 Effect of acceptance of complete specification	1852, s 9
s 16 Extent of patent	1852, s 18
s 17 Term of patent	1853 (c.5), s 2
s 18 Amendment of specification	1835, s 1; 1844, s 5; 1852, s 39
s 19 Power to disclaim part of Inventions during action, &c.	—
s 20 Restriction on recovery of damages	—
s 21 Advertisement of amendment	—
s 22 Power for Board to order grant of licenses	—
s 23 Register of patents	1852, s 34 and 35
s 24 Fees in schedule	1853 (c.5), s 3
s 25 Extension of term of patent on petition to Queen in Council	1835, s 4; 1839, s 2; 1844, s 2 and 3
s 26 Revocation of patent	1852, s 41
s 27 Patent to bind Crown	—
s 28 Hearing with assessor	Judicature Act 1873, s 57; Ord 36, r 2 and 28
s 29 Delivery of particulars	1835, s 5 and 6; 1852, s 41 and 43
s 30 Order for inspection, &c., in action	1852, s 42
s 31 Certificate of validity questioned and costs thereon	1835, s 3; 1852, s 43
s 32 Remedy in case of groundless threats of legal proceedings	—
s 33 Patent for one Inventions only	—
s 34 Patent on application of representative of deceased inventor	—
s 35 Patent to first inventor not invalidated by application in fraud of him	1852, s 10
s 36 Assignment for particular places	1852, s 35
s 37 Loss or destruction of patent	1852, s 22
s 38 Proceedings and costs before law officer	—
s 39 Exhibition at industrial or international exhibition not to prejudice patent rights	1865, s 3; 1870, s 2
s 40 Publication of illustrated journal, indexes, &c.	—
s 41 Patent Museum	—
s 42 Power to require models on payment	—
s 43 Foreign vessels in British waters	1852, s 26
s 44 Assignment to Secretary for War of certain inventions	1859 Act
s 45 Provisions respecting existing patents	—
s 46 Definitions of patent, patentee, and Inventions	1852, s 55
Part III – Designs	
[s 47 to 61 – Designs]	
Part IV – Trade Marks	
[s 62 to 81 – Trade Marks]	
Part V – General	
s 82 Patent Office	—
s 83 Officers and clerks	1852, s 5 to 8 and 49
s 84 Seal of patent office	1852, s 2
s 85 Trust not to be entered in registers	Rule 22
s 86 Refusal to grant patent, &c. in certain cases	—
s 87 Entry of assignments and transmissions in registers	1852, s 34 and 35
s 88 Inspection of and extracts from registers	1853 (c 115), s 4
s 89 Sealed copies to be received in evidence	—
s 90 Rectification of registers by court	TMA 1875, s 3
s 91 Power for Comptroller to correct clerical errors	—
s 92 Alteration of registered mark	

(continued)

(continued)

s 93 Falsification of entries in registers	1852, s 37
s 94 Exercise of discretionary power by Comptroller	—
s 95 Power of Comptroller to take directions of law officers	—
s 96 Certificate of Comptroller to be evidence	1852, s 38
s 97 Applications and notices by post	—
s 98 Provision as to days for leaving documents at office	—
s 99 Declaration by infant, lunatic, &c.	Rule 67
s 100 Transmission of certified printed copies of specifications, &c.	—
s 101 Power for Board of Trade to make general rules for classifying goods and regulating business of patent office	1852, s 3, 29 and 30
s 102 Annual reports of Comptroller	1852, s 3 and 51
s 103 International arrangements for protection of inventions, designs, and trade marks	—
s 104 Provision for colonies and India	—
s 105 Penalty on falsely representing articles to be patented	—
s 106 Penalty on unauthorised assumption of Royal arms	—
s 107 Saving for Courts in Scotland	1852, s 43
s 108 Summary proceedings in Scotland	—
s 109 Proceedings for revocation of patent in Scotland	1852, s 35 and 43
s 110 Reservation of remedies in Ireland	1852, s 29
s 111 General saving for jurisdiction of courts	TMA 1875, s 10
s 112 Isle of Man	—
s 113 Repeal and saving for past operation of repealed enactments, &c.	—
s 114 Former registers to be deemed continued	—
s 115 Saving for existing rules	—
s 116 Saving for prerogative	1852, s 16
s 117 General definitions	—
First Schedule – Forms of Application, &c.	—
Second Schedule – Fees on instruments for obtaining Patents, and Renewal	—
Third Schedule – Enactments repealed	—

Journal

House of Commons			House of Lords		
Pres: Joseph Chamberlain (Pr BoT) Money Res: Sir Arthur Otway Rep: Lyon Playfair (Ch W&M)			Rep: Earl of Selbourne LC		
17 Feb 1883	138 CJ 10	Bill Ord	6 Aug 1883	115 LJ 380	Brought HC/1R
17 Feb 1883	138 CJ 15	1R	9 Aug 1883	115 LJ 390	2R/C'tted CWH
16 Apr 1883	138 CJ 141	2R/C'tted SC on trade	10 Aug 1883	115 LJ 400	**CWH**
17 Apr 1883	138 CJ 145	15 Mem Add to SC	13 Aug 1883	115 LJ 406	Rep with Amd/Re-C'tted CWH
18 Apr 1883	138 CJ 148	Money Res	24 Aug 1883	138 CJ 488	HL Amds Cons
20 Apr 1883	138 CJ 151	Rep Money Res	25 Aug 1883	138 CJ 491	Royal Assent
29 Jun 1883	138 CJ 309	Print Amds Clauses	16 Aug 1883	115 LJ 415	**CWH**
9 Jul 1883	138 CJ 331	SC Rep	20 Aug 1883	115 LJ 428	**CWH/Rep with Amds**
4 Aug 1883	138 CJ 415	**3R**	21 Aug 1883	115 LJ 436	3R
22 Aug 1883	138 CJ 479	HL pass with Amds	23 Aug 1883	115 LJ 448	HC Amds Ag
22 Aug 1883	138 CJ 482 – V	**HL Amds Cons**	25 Aug 1883	115 LJ 453	Royal Assent

Standing Committee on Trade

First Sitting – 29 Jun 1883 [Cl 1 to 7]	*Second Sitting* – 2 Jul 1883 [Cl 7 to 30] – 2 votes
Third Sitting – 6 Jul 1883 [Cl 31 to 49]	*Fourth Sitting* – 9 Jul 1883 [Cl 49 to end] – 3 votes

Parliamentary debates

Ord: HC Deb, 16 Feb 1883, Vol 276(3rd), col 165	1R: HL Deb, 6 Aug 1883, Vol 282(3rd), col 1601
2R: HC Deb, 16 Apr 1883, Vol 278(3rd), col 349–394	2R: **HL Deb, 9 Aug 1883, Vol 282(3rd), col 2034–2036**
Mon Res: HC Deb, 18 Apr 1883, Vol 278(3rd), col 585	CWH: HL Deb, 10 Aug 1883, Vol 283(3rd), col 1
Rep: HC Deb, 9 Jul 1883, Vol 281(3rd), col 766	Rep/Re-C'tted: HL Deb, 13 Aug 1883, Vol 283(3rd), col 210
Comment: **HC Deb, 4 Aug 1883, Vol 282(3rd), col 1539–1540**	CWH: HL Deb, 16 Aug 1883, Vol 283(3rd), col 683
Rep/3R: **HC Deb, 4 Aug 1883, Vol 282(3rd), col 1600**	Rep: HL Deb, 20 Aug 1883, Vol 283(3rd), col 1309
HL Amds Cons: HC Deb, 22 Aug 1883, Vol 283(3rd), col 1710	3R: HL Deb, 21 Aug 1883, Vol 283(3rd), col 1448
	Royal Assent: HL Deb, 25 Aug 1883, Vol 283(3rd), col 1838

Parliamentary papers

Bill to amend and consolidate the law relating to patents for inventions, trade marks and registration of designs (1883 HC Papers 3), Vol 8, p. 301 [includes Memorandum on the Bill]

Bill to amend and consolidate the law relating to patents for inventions, trade marks and registration of designs (as amended in Standing Committee on Trade) (1883 HC Papers 261), Vol 8, p. 355

Bill to amend and consolidate the law relating to patents for inventions, trade marks and registration of designs (1883 HL Papers 179), Vol 7, p 209

Bill to amend and consolidate the law relating to patents for inventions, trade marks and registration of designs (as amended in Committee) (1883 HL Papers 188), Vol 7, p 263

    Amendments to be moved in Committee (on Re-Commitment) by the Lord Chancellor (1883 HL Papers 188a), Vol 7, p 317

    Amendments to be moved in Committee (on Re- Commitment) by the Lord Ker (1883 HL Papers 188b), Vol 7, p 319

    Amendments to be moved on Report by the Lord Chancellor and the Lord Balfour (1883 HL Papers 188d), Vol 7, p 321

Bill to amend and consolidate the law relating to patents for inventions, trade marks and registration of designs (as amended in Committee on Re-Commitment) (1883 HL Papers 201), Vol 7, p 323

House of Lords Amendments (1883 HC Papers 303), Vol 8, p 409

Report from the Standing Committee on Trade, Shipping, and Manufactures, on the Patents for Inventions Bill (1883 HC Papers 247), Vol 14, p 547

Memorials from Chambers of Commerce, Liverpool and Edinburgh relating to Patents for Inventions Bill (1883 HC Papers 246), Vol 64, p 643: Ord: 28 Jun 1883 (138 CJ 305); Pres: 4 Jul 1883 (138 CJ 320); Prt: 6 Jul 1883 (138 CJ 328)

Supplement to Votes & Proceedings, 1883

    18 Apr 1883, p 290–292; 23 Apr 1883, p 420–421; 8 May 1883, p 692; 19 Jun 1883, p 1565–1569; 22 Jun 1883, p 1741; 25 Jun 1883, p 1771–1781; 29 Jun 1883, p 1893–1902; 2 Jul 1883, p 1929–1940; 2 Jul 1883, p 1969–1970; 3 Jul 1883, p 1995–6; 6 Jul 1883, p 2019–2032; 9 Jul 1883, p 2053–2065

Newspaper coverage of debates

House of Commons

1R: The Times, 17 Feb 1883; London Daily News, 17 Feb 1883; London Evening Standard, 17 Feb 1883

2R: **The Times, 17 Apr 1883**; **Morning Post, 17 Apr 1883**; **London Daily News, 17 Apr 1883**; **London Evening Standard, 17 Apr 1883**

Grand Committee (on Trade) – 29 Jun: **London Daily News, 30 Jun 1883**; *Morning Post, 30 Jun 1883*; *London Evening Standard, 30 Jun 1883*

Grand Committee (on Trade) – 2 Jul: **London Daily News, 3 Jul 1883**; *Morning Post, 4 Jul 1883*; *London Evening Standard, 3 Jul 1883*

Grand Committee (on Trade) – 6 Jul: **London Daily News, 7 Jul 1883**; *Morning Post, 7 Jul 1883*; *London Evening Standard, 7 Jul 1883*

Grand Committee (on Trade) – 9 Jul: **London Daily News, 10 Jul 1883**; *Morning Post, 10 Jul 1883*

Rep: The Times, 10 Jul 1883; London Daily News, 10 Jul 1883; London Evening Standard, 10 Jul 1883

3R: **London Daily News, 6 Aug 1883**; The Times, 6 Aug 1883; Morning Post, 6 Aug 1883; London Evening Standard, 6 Aug 1883

HC Amds Cons: **The Times, 23 Aug 1883**; **Morning Post, 23 Aug 1883**; **London Daily News, 23 Aug 1883**; **London Evening Standard, 23 Aug 1883**

House of Lords

1R: Morning Post, 7 Aug 1883; London Daily News, 7 Aug 1883; London Evening Standard, 7 Aug 1883

2R: **The Times, 10 Apr 1883**; **Morning Post, 10 Aug 1883**; **London Daily News, 10 Aug 1883**; **London Evening Standard, 10 Aug 1883**

CWH: The Times, 11 Apr 1883

Rep: The Times, 14 Aug 1883; Morning Post, 14 Aug 1883; London Daily News, 14 Aug 1883; London Evening Standard, 14 Aug 1883

CWH: The Times, 17 Aug 1883; Morning Post, 17 Aug 1883; London Daily News, 17 Aug 1883; London Evening Standard, 17 Aug 1883

Cons: The Times, 21 Aug 1883; Morning Post, 21 Aug 1883; London Daily News, 21 Aug 1883

3R: The Times, 22 Aug 1883; Morning Post, 22 Aug 1883; London Daily News, 22 Aug 1883

HL Amds Ag: The Times, 24 Aug 1883; Morning Post, 24 Aug 1883; London Daily News, 24 Aug 1883

Royal Assent: The Times, 27 Aug 1883; Morning Post, 27 Aug 1883; London Daily News, 27 Aug 1883; London Evening Standard, 27 Aug 1883

Deputation visit BoT: The Times, 30 May 1883

(continued)

(continued)

Notes
Archive
Patents, Designs and Trade Marks Bill 1883 Part 1: National Archive (BT 22/31)
Patents, Designs and Trade Marks Bill 1883 Part 2: National Archive (BT 22/32)
Petitions – PET578 to PET588

Patents, Designs, and Trade Marks (Amendment) Act 1885

PUBA15	1885
Patents, Designs, and Trade Marks (Amendment) Act 1885 (48 & 49 Vict. c. 63)	
An Act to amend the Patents, Designs, and Trade Marks Act 1883	

Table of contents

s 1 Construction and short title

s 2 Amendment of s 5 of [Patents, Designs, and Trade Marks Act 1883] 46 & 47 Vict. c. 57 [Application and specification]

s 3 Amendment of s 8, 9, & 12 of [Patents, Designs, and Trade Marks Act 1883] 46 & 47 Vict. c. 57 [Time for leaving complete specification; Comparison of provisional and complete specification; Sealing of patent]

s 4 Specifications, &c. not to be published unless application accepted

s 5 Power to grant patents to several persons jointly

s 6 Amendment of s 103 of [Patents, Designs, and Trade Marks Act 1883] 46 & 47 Vict. c. 57 [International arrangements for protection of inventions, designs, and trade marks]

Journal

House of Commons			House of Lords		
Pres: Sir Farrer Herschell (S-G) Rep: Charles Ritchie (Sec Adm)			Rep: Lord FitzGerald		
22 Jul 1885	140 CJ 339	Bill Ord	30 Jul 1885	117 LJ 422	Brought HC
22 Jul 1885	140 CJ 340	1R	30 Jul 1885	117 LJ 424	1R
25 Jul 1885	140 CJ 350	2R/C'tted CWH	31 Jul 1885	117 LJ 430	2R/C'tted CWH
28 Jul 1885	140 CJ 356	CWH	3 Aug 1885	117 LJ 434	**CWH/Rep with Amds/3R**
29 Jul 1885	140 CJ 361	CWH/Rep w/o Amds/3R	7 Aug 1885	117 LJ 447	HC Ag Amds
3 Aug 1885	140 CJ 381	HL pass with Amds	14 Aug 1885	117 LJ 471	Royal Assent
7 Aug 1885	140 CJ 396	HL Amds Ag			
14 Aug 1885	140 CJ 416	Royal Assent			

Parliamentary debates

1R: **HC Deb, 21 Jul 1885, Vol 299(3rd), col 1513–1514**	1R: HL Deb, 30 Jul 1885, Vol 300(3rd), col 476
2R: **HC Deb, 24 Jul 1885, Vol 299(3rd), col 1864**	2R: HL Deb, 31 Jul 1885, Vol 300(3rd), col 632
CWH: **HC Deb, 27 Jul 1885, Vol 300(3rd), col 210**	CWH/3R: HL Deb, 3 Aug 1885, Vol 300(3rd), col 812
CWH/3R: HC Deb, 28 Jul 1885, Vol 300(3rd), col 238	Royal Assent: HL Deb, 14 Aug 1885, Vol 301(3rd), col 30

Parliamentary papers

Bill to amend the Patents, Designs, and Trade Marks Act, 1883 (1884–85 HC Papers 240), Vol 4, p 367

Bill to amend the Patents, Designs, and Trade Marks Act 1883 (1884–85 HL Papers 223), Vol 5, p 687

Supplement to Votes & Proceedings, 1884–85 – No amendments

Newspaper coverage of debates

House of Commons

2R: The Times, 25 Jul 1885; London Daily News, 25 Jul 1885

3R: The Times, 29 Jul 1885

House of Lords

2R: The Times, 1 Aug 1885; Morning Post, 1 Aug 1885; London Daily News, 1 Aug 1885

CWH/3R: The Times, 4 Aug 1835; London Daily News, 4 Aug 1885; London Evening Standard, 4 Aug 1885

Royal Assent: The Times, 15 Aug 1885

Patents Act 1886

PUBA16	1886

Patents Act 1886 (49 & 50 Vict. c. 37)

An Act to remove certain doubts respecting the construction of the Patents, Designs, and Trade Marks Act, 1883, so far as respects the drawings by which specifications are required to be accompanied, and as respects exhibitions

Table of contents

Journal

House of Commons			House of Lords		
Rep: Leonard Courtney (Ch W&M)			Pres and Rep: Lord Herschell LC		
17 Jun 1886	141 CJ 283	Brought HL/1R	31 May 1886	118 LJ 238	1R
18 Jun 1886	141 CJ 291	2R/C'tted CWH	4 Jun 1886	118 LJ 263	2R/C'tted CWH
22 Jun 1886	141 CJ 298	CWH/Rep w/o Amds/3R	8 Jun 1886	118 LJ 269	CWH
25 Jun 1886	141 CJ 308	Royal Assent	10 Jun 1886	118 LJ 273	Rep with Amds
			17 Jun 1886	118 LJ 278	3R
			22 Jun 1886	118 LJ 299	HC pass w/o Amds
			25 Jun 1886	118 LJ 323	Royal Assent

Parliamentary debates

1R: HC Deb, 17 Jun 1886, Vol 306(3rd), col 1680	1R: HL Deb, 31 May 1886, Vol 306(3rd), col 449
2R: HC Deb, 18 Jun 1886, Vol 306(3rd), col 1840	2R: **HL Deb, 4 Jun 1886, Vol 306(3rd), col 986 and 997–999**
CWH/3R: HC Deb, 21 Jun 1886, Vol 307(3rd), col 33	CWH: **HL Deb, 8 Jun 1886, Vol 306(3rd), col 1251**
	Rep: HL Deb, 10 Jun 1886, Vol 306(3rd), col 1254
	3R: HL Deb, 17 Jun 1886, Vol 306(3rd), col 1677
	Royal Assent: HL Deb, 25 Jun 1886, Vol 307(3rd), col 276

Parliamentary papers

Bill to remove certain doubts respecting the construction of the Patents, Designs, and Trade Marks Act, 1883, so far as respects the drawings by which specifications are required to be accompanied (1886 HL Papers 133), Vol 6, p 133

Amendments to be moved in Committee by the Lord Chancellor (1886 HL Papers 133a), Vol 6, p 135

Bill to remove certain doubts respecting the construction of the Patents, Designs, and Trade Marks Act, 1883, so far as respects the drawings by which specifications are required to be accompanied, and as respects exhibitions (1886 HC Papers 289), Vol 4, p 433

Supplement to Votes & Proceedings, 1886 – No amendments

Newspaper coverage of debates

House of Lords

2R: **The Times, 5 Jun 1886; London Evening Standard, 5 Jun 1886**; Morning Post, 5 Jun 1886; London Daily News, 5 Jun 1886

CWH: **The Times, 9 Jun 1886; London Evening Standard, 9 Jun 1886**; London Daily News, 9 Jun 1886

Cons: *The Times, 11 Jun 1886*; London Evening Standard, 11 Jun 1886

3R: The Times, 18 Jun 1886; Morning Post, 18 Jun 1886; London Evening Standard, 18 Jun 1886; London Daily News, 18 Jun 1886

House of Commons

2R: The Times, 19 Jun 1886; Morning Post, 19 Jun 1886; London Daily News, 19 Jun 1886

CWH: The Times, 22 Jun 1886; London Daily News, 22 Jun 1886; London Evening Standard, 22 Jun 1886

Royal Assent: The Times, 26 Jun 1886; London Evening Standard, 26 Jun 1886

Patents, Designs, and Trade Marks Act 1888

PUBA17	1888
Patents, Designs, and Trade Marks Act 1888 (51 & 52 Vict. c. 50)	
An Act to amend the Patents, Designs, and Trade Marks Act 1883	

Table of contents

s 1 Register of patent agents
s 2 Amendments of [Patents, Designs, and Trade Marks Act 1883] 46 & 47 Vict. c. 57. – s 7, as to applications
s 3 s 9, as to disclosure of reports of examiners
s 4 s 11, as to opposition to grant of patent
s 5 s 18, as to amended specifications
[s 6 to s 8 relate to designs]
[s 9 to s 20 relate to trade marks]
s 21 s 87, as to entry of assignments, &c.
s 22 s 88, as to inspection
s 23 s 90, as to rectification of register
s 24 s 91, as to correction of errors
s 25 Proceedings of Board of Trade
s 26 Jurisdiction of Lancashire Palatine Court
s 27 Construction of principal Act
s 28 Commencement of Act
s 29 Short title

Journal

House of Commons			House of Lords		
Rep: Leonard Courtney (Ch W&M)			Pres: Earl of Onslow (Par Sec BoT) Rep: Duke of Buckingham and Chandos (Ld Ch)		
24 Jul 1888	143 CJ 392	Brought HL	29 Jun 1888	120 LJ 266	1R
25 Jul 1888	143 CJ 399	1R	3 Jul 1888	120 LJ 272	2R
28 Jul 1888	143 CJ 408	2R adj	5 Jul 1888	120 LJ 278	C'tted CWH
31 Jul 1888	143 CJ 411	2R adj	12 Jul 1888	120 LJ 303	**CWH/Rep with Amds**
1 Aug 1888	143 CJ 415	2R adj	16 Jul 1888	120 LJ 311	Cons day app
1 Aug 1888	143 CJ 417	2R adj	19 Jul 1888	120 LJ 324	**Cons with Amds**
3 Aug 1888	143 CJ 422	2R adj	23 Jul 1888	120 LJ 332	3R
4 Aug 1888	143 CJ 426	2R adj	10 Dec 1888	120 LJ 440	HC pass with Amds
7 Aug 1888	143 CJ 433	2R adj	11 Dec 1888	120 LJ 441	**HC Amds Ag**
8 Aug 1888	143 CJ 437	2R adj	24 Dec 1888	120 LJ 462	Royal Assent
10 Aug 1888	143 CJ 445	2R adj			
10 Aug 1888	143 CJ 453	2R/C'tted CWH			
16 Nov 1888	143 CJ 473	CWH adj			
20 Nov 1888	143 CJ 477	CWH adj			
21 Nov 1888	143 CJ 479	CWH adj			
23 Nov 1888	143 CJ 481	CWH adj			
24 Nov 1888	143 CJ 483	CWH adj			
27 Nov 1888	143 CJ 485	CWH adj			
29 Nov 1888	143 CJ 490	**CWH/Rep with Amds**			
4 Dec 1888	143 CJ 495	Cons day app			
5 Dec 1888	143 CJ 496	Cons adj			
7 Dec 1888	143 CJ 499	Cons/3R			
18 Dec 1888	143 CJ 521	HL Ag HC Amds			
24 Dec 1888	143 CJ 533	Royal Assent			

Parliamentary debates

1R: HC Deb, 25 Jul 1888, Vol 329(3rd), col 431

2R: HC Deb, 10 Aug 1888, Vol 330(3rd), col 361

Com adj: **HC Deb, 19 Nov 1888, Vol 330(3rd), col 1614**

Rep: **HC Deb, 29 Nov 1888, Vol 331(3rd), col 383–386**

Rep adj: **HC Deb, 3 Dec 1888, Vol 331(3rd), col 975**

Rep adj: **HC Deb, 4 Dec 1888, Vol 331(3rd), col 1134**

3R: **HC Deb, 6 Dec 1888, Vol 331(3rd), col 1380**

1R: HL Deb, 29 Jun 1888, Vol 327(3rd), col 1711

2R: HL Deb, 3 Jul 1888, Vol 328(3rd), col 155–156

Com: **HL Deb, 12 Jul 1888, Vol 328(3rd), col 1051–1053**

Rep: HL Deb, 19 Jul 1888, Vol 328(3rd), col 1730

3R: HL Deb, 23 Jul 1888, Vol 329(3rd), col 168

Royal Assent: HL Deb, 24 Dec 1888, Vol 322(3rd), col 1044

Parliamentary papers
Bill to amend the Patents, Designs, and Trade Marks Act, 1883 (1888 HL Papers 193), Vol 7, p 363
Bill to amend and consolidate the Patents, Designs, and Trade Marks Act, 1883 (as proposed to be amended) (1888 HL Papers 193a), Vol 7, p 407
Amendments to be moved in Committee by the Earl of Onslow (1888 HL Papers 193b), Vol 7, p 377
Bill to amend the Patents, Designs, and Trade Marks Act, 1883 (as amended in Committee) (1888 HL Papers 211), Vol 7, p 379
Amendments to be moved on Report by the Earl of Onslow (1888 HL Papers 211a), Vol 7, p 391
Bill to amend the Patents, Designs, and Trade Marks Act, 1883 (as amended on Report) (1888 HL Papers 225), Vol 7, p 393
Bill to amend the Patents, Designs, and Trade Marks Act, 1883 (1888 HC Papers 348), Vol 6, p 21
Commons Amendments (1888 HL Papers 300), Vol 6, p 405
Supplement to Votes & Proceedings, 1888 – No amendments

Newspaper coverage of debates

House of Lords

2R: **The Times, 4 Jul 1888**; **Morning Post, 4 Jul 1888**; **London Daily News, 4 Jul 1888**; **London Evening Standard, 4 Jul 1888**

CWH: **The Times, 13 Jul 1888**; Morning Post, 13 Jul 1888; London Daily News, 13 Jul 1888; London Evening Standard, 13 Jul 1888

3R: The Times, 24 Jul 1888; Morning Post, 24 Jul 1888; London Daily News, 24 Jul 1888; London Evening Standard, 24 Jul 1888

HC Amds: The Times, 12 Dec 1888

House of Commons

2R: *The Times, 11 Aug 1888*; Morning Post, 11 Aug 1888; London Daily News, 11 Aug 1888; London Evening Standard, 11 Aug 1888

CWH adj: **The Times, 20 Nov 1888**

CWH: The Times, 30 Nov 1888; Morning Post, 30 Nov 1888; London Daily News, 30 Nov 1888; London Evening Standard, 30 Nov 1888

Cons: The Times, 7 Dec 1888

Royal Assent: The Times, 25 Dec 1888

Notes

Petitions – PET589 and PET590

Patent Office (Extension) Act 1897

PUBA18	1897
Patent Office (Extension) Act 1897 (60 & 61 Vict. c. xxv)	
An Act for the acquisition of Land for the Extension of the Patent Office, and for purposes connected therewith	
Table of contents	

s 1 Power to purchase land
s 2 Incorporation of Lands Clauses Acts
s 3 Land tax
s 4 Extinction of rights of way and other easements
s 5 Saving for County Council
s 6 Power to enter on lands
s 7 Power of Commissioners to build
s 8 Protection of works of gas, water, and electricity companies
s 9 Provisions as to expenses, &c. of Commissioners
s 10 Penalty for obstructing Commissioners
s 11 Short title

(continued)

(continued)

Journal					
House of Commons			**House of Lords**		
Pres and SC Rep: Aretas Akers-Douglas (Fir Com Works) CWH Rep: James William Lowther (Ch W&M)			Rep: Earl of Pembroke (Ld Steward)		
25 Mar 1897	152 CJ 136	Bill Ord/1R	18 Jun 1897	129 LJ 248	Brought HC
26 Mar 1897	152 CJ 139	Ref to Ex	18 Jun 1897	129 LJ 251	Prt
30 Mar 1897	152 CJ 145	2R adj	21 Jun 1897	129 LJ 253	Ref to Ex
1 Apr 1897	152 CJ 151	Report SO cw	2 Jul 1897	129 LJ 265	Ex Cert
2 Apr 1897	152 CJ 154	2R adj	12 Jul 1897	129 LJ 301	2R/C'tted CWH
5 Apr 1897	152 CJ 161	2R/C'tted SC	13 Jul 1897	129 LJ 307	CWH/Rep with Amds/SC neg
6 Apr 1897	152 CJ 163	Expenses Motion	16 Jul 1897	129 LJ 321	3R
8 Apr 1897	152 CJ 170	SC Mems Nom	6 Aug 1897	129 LJ 407	Royal Assent
13 Apr 1897	152 CJ 179–V	COS			
26 Apr 1897	152 CJ 183	COS Res Ag			
7 May 1897	152 CJ 209	Rep/C'tted CWH			
14 May 1897	152 CJ 226	CWH adj			
18 May 1897	152 CJ 232	CWH adj			
21 May 1897	152 CJ 242	CWH adj			
25 May 1897	152 CJ 250	CWH adj			
1 Jun 1897	152 CJ 269	CWH adj			
4 Jun 1897	152 CJ 286	CWH adj			
4 Jun 1897	152 CJ 290	CWH/Rep w/o Amds/3R			
19 Jun 1897	152 CJ 368	HL pass w/o Amds			
6 Aug 1897	152 CJ 435	Royal Assent			

Parliamentary debates	
Pres/1R: HC Deb, 25 Mar 1897, Vol 47(4th), col 1329	1R: HL Deb, 18 Jun 1897, Vol 50(4th), col 361
2R: **HC Deb, 5 Apr 1897, Vol 48(4th), col 589–590**	2R: HL Deb, 12 Jul 1897, Vol 50(4th), col 1579
Com to rep: HC Deb, 6 Apr 1897, Vol 48(4th), col 638	CWH: HL Deb, 13 Jul 1897, Vol 51(4th), col 3
COS: **HC Deb, 12 Apr 1897, Vol 48(4th), col 1057**	3R: HL Deb, 16 July 1897, Vol 51(4th), col 295
COS Res: **HC Deb, 26 Apr 1897, Vol 48(4th), col 1124**	Royal Assent: HL Deb, 6 Aug 1897, Vol 52(4th), col 508
Rep/3R: HC Deb, 4 Jun 1897, Vol 50(4th), col 281	
List of Acts: HC Deb, 6 Aug 1897, Vol 52(4th), col 532	

Parliamentary papers

Bill for the Acquisition of Land for the Extension of the Patent Office, and for the purposes connected therewith (1897 HL Papers 125), Vol 7, p 125

Bill for Acquisition of Land for Extension of Patent Office (1897 HC Papers 175), Vol 5, p 539

Bill for Acquisition of Land for Extension of Patent Office (as amended in Select Committee) (1897 HC Papers 224), Vol 5, p 547

Report of Select Committee on Patent Office Extension Bill (1897 HC Papers 204), Vol 13, p 101

Newspaper coverage of debates

House of Commons

Money Res: The Times, 13 Apr 1897

2R: **The Times, 6 Apr 1897**

C'ttee: *The Times, 10 May 1897*

3R: The Times, 5 Jun 1897

House of Lords

2R: The Times, 13 Jul 1897

Rep: The Times, 14 Jul 1897

3R: The Times, 17 Jul 1897

Royal Assent: The Times, 7 Aug 1897

Patents Act 1901

PUBA19	1901
Patents Act 1901 (1 Edw 7. c. 18)	
An Act to amend the Law with reference to International Arrangements for Patents	

Table of contents	
s 1 International Arrangements [Priority period charged from 7m to 12m] s 2 Short title, construction and commencement	

Journal	
House of Commons	**House of Lords**
Rep: James William Lowther (Ch W&M)	Pres: Earl of Dudley (Par Sec BoT) Rep: Earl of Morley (Ld Ch)

House of Commons			House of Lords		
2 Aug 1901	156 CJ 367	Brought HL	19 Jul 1901	133 LJ 297	1R
12 Aug 1901	156 CJ 396	1R	29 Jul 1901	133 LJ 329	2R day app
14 Aug 1901	156 CJ 405	2R/C'tted CWH	30 Jul 1901	133 LJ 331	2R adj
14 Aug 1901	156 CJ 411	CWH/Rep w/o Amds/3R	1 Aug 1901	133 LJ 343	2R/C'tted CWH
17 Aug 1901	156 CJ 420	Royal Assent	2 Aug 1901	133 LJ 346	CWH
			2 Aug 1901	133 LJ 347	Rep w/o Amds/3R
			15 Aug 1901	133 LJ 369	HC pass w/o Amds
			17 Aug 1901	133 LJ 382	Royal Assent

Parliamentary debates	
Br HL: HC Deb, 2 Aug 1901, Vol 98(4th), col 1092	1R: HL Deb, 19 Jul 1901, Vol 97(4th), col 959
1R: HC Deb, 12 Aug 1901, Vol 99(4th), col 455	2R: **HL Deb, 1 Aug 1901, Vol 98(4th), col 832–833**
2R: HC Deb, 13 Aug 1901, Vol 99(4th), col 727	CWH/3R: HL Deb, 2 Aug 1901, Vol 98(4th), col 1004–1005
CWH/3R: **HC Deb, 14 Aug 1901, Vol 99(4th), col 859–860**	Royal Assent: HL Deb, 17 Aug 1901, Vol 99(4th), col 1290

Parliamentary papers
Patents Bill (1901 HL Papers 168), Vol 5, p 251
Patents Bill (1901 HC Papers 292), Vol 3, p 595
Supplement to Votes & Proceedings, 1901 – No amendments

Newspaper coverage of debates
House of Lords
2R: **The Times, 2 Aug 1901**
Rep/3R: The Times, 3 Aug 1901
House of Commons
2R/CWH: The Times, 15 Aug 1901
Royal Assent: The Times, 19 Aug 1901

Notes
Archive
Period of Priority for patents under International Convention of 1883: draft Bill: National Archive (BT 209/52)

Patents Act 1902

PUBA20	1902
Patents Act 1902 (2 Edw 7. c. 34)	
An Act to amend the Law with reference to Applications for Patents and Compulsory Licences, and other matters connected therewith	

(continued)

(continued)

Table of contents
s 1 Examination of previous specifications in United Kingdom on applications for patents
s 2 Limitation as to anticipation
s 3 Amendment of law relating to compulsory licences
s 4 Performance of Comptroller's duties
s 5 Short title and construction

<table>
<tr><th colspan="6">Journal</th></tr>
<tr><th colspan="3">House of Commons</th><th colspan="3">House of Lords</th></tr>
<tr><td colspan="3">Pres: Gerald Balfour (Pr BoT)
Rep SC: Lord Edmond Fitzmaurice</td><td colspan="3">Rep: Lord Wolverton (VC Household)</td></tr>
<tr><td>10 Feb 1902</td><td>157 CJ 55</td><td>Bill Ord/1R</td><td>3 Nov 1902</td><td>134 LJ 376</td><td>Brought HC</td></tr>
<tr><td>11 Mar 1902</td><td>157 CJ 102</td><td>2R adj</td><td>3 Nov 1902</td><td>134 LJ 378</td><td>1R</td></tr>
<tr><td>17 Mar 1902</td><td>157 CJ 115</td><td>2R adj</td><td>11 Nov 1902</td><td>134 LJ 380</td><td>2R date app</td></tr>
<tr><td>21 Mar 1902</td><td>157 CJ 123</td><td>2R adj</td><td>17 Nov 1902</td><td>134 LJ 385</td><td>**2R/C'tted CWH**</td></tr>
<tr><td>25 Mar 1902</td><td>157 CJ 130</td><td>2R adj</td><td>20 Nov 1902</td><td>134 LJ 388</td><td>**CWH/SC neg**</td></tr>
<tr><td>18 Apr 1902</td><td>157 CJ 158</td><td>2R adj</td><td>24 Nov 1902</td><td>134 LJ 391</td><td>**Rep with Amds**</td></tr>
<tr><td>22 Apr 1902</td><td>157 CJ 165</td><td>2R adj</td><td>1 Dec 1902</td><td>134 LJ 400</td><td>3R with Amds</td></tr>
<tr><td>6 May 1902</td><td>157 CJ 207</td><td>2R adj</td><td>10 Dec 1902</td><td>134 LJ 413</td><td>HC Ag Amds</td></tr>
<tr><td>6 May 1902</td><td>157 CJ 211</td><td>2R adj</td><td>18 Dec 1902</td><td>134 LJ 446</td><td>Royal Assent</td></tr>
<tr><td>9 May 1902</td><td>157 CJ 216</td><td>2R adj</td><td></td><td></td><td></td></tr>
<tr><td>14 May 1902</td><td>157 CJ 227</td><td>2R adj</td><td></td><td></td><td></td></tr>
<tr><td>15 May 1902</td><td>157 CJ 230</td><td>2R adj</td><td></td><td></td><td></td></tr>
<tr><td>27 May 1902</td><td>157 CJ 238</td><td>2R adj</td><td></td><td></td><td></td></tr>
<tr><td>29 May 1902</td><td>157 CJ 245</td><td>2R adj</td><td></td><td></td><td></td></tr>
<tr><td>3 Jun 1902</td><td>157 CJ 255</td><td>2R adj</td><td></td><td></td><td></td></tr>
<tr><td>10 Jun 1902</td><td>157 CJ 272</td><td>2R adj</td><td></td><td></td><td></td></tr>
<tr><td>12 Jun 1902</td><td>157 CJ 279</td><td>2R adj</td><td></td><td></td><td></td></tr>
<tr><td>17 Jun 1902</td><td>157 CJ 290</td><td>2R adj</td><td></td><td></td><td></td></tr>
<tr><td>18 Jun 1902</td><td>157 CJ 294</td><td>2R adj</td><td></td><td></td><td></td></tr>
<tr><td>24 Jun 1902</td><td>157 CJ 307</td><td>2R adj</td><td></td><td></td><td></td></tr>
<tr><td>25 Jun 1902</td><td>157 CJ 313</td><td>2R adj</td><td></td><td></td><td></td></tr>
<tr><td>26 Jun 1902</td><td>157 CJ 315</td><td>2R adj</td><td></td><td></td><td></td></tr>
<tr><td>27 Jun 1902</td><td>157 CJ 319</td><td>2R adj</td><td></td><td></td><td></td></tr>
<tr><td>1 Jul 1902</td><td>157 CJ 323</td><td>2R adj</td><td></td><td></td><td></td></tr>
<tr><td>1 Jul 1902</td><td>157 CJ 326</td><td>2R adj</td><td></td><td></td><td></td></tr>
<tr><td>4 Jul 1902</td><td>157 CJ 333 – V</td><td>2R/C'tted SC Trade</td><td></td><td></td><td></td></tr>
<tr><td>8 Jul 1902</td><td>157 CJ 340</td><td>Mem added to SC</td><td></td><td></td><td></td></tr>
<tr><td>28 Jul 1902</td><td>157 CJ 389</td><td>SC Rep with Amds</td><td></td><td></td><td></td></tr>
<tr><td>30 Jul 1902</td><td>157 CJ 394</td><td>Cons adj</td><td></td><td></td><td></td></tr>
<tr><td>1 Aug 1902</td><td>157 CJ 405</td><td>Cons adj</td><td></td><td></td><td></td></tr>
<tr><td>1 Aug 1902</td><td>157 CJ 408</td><td>Cons adj</td><td></td><td></td><td></td></tr>
<tr><td>5 Aug 1902</td><td>157 CJ 415</td><td>Cons adj</td><td></td><td></td><td></td></tr>
<tr><td>6 Aug 1902</td><td>157 CJ 422</td><td>Cons adj</td><td></td><td></td><td></td></tr>
<tr><td>7 Aug 1902</td><td>157 CJ 426</td><td>Cons adj</td><td></td><td></td><td></td></tr>
<tr><td>8 Aug 1902</td><td>157 CJ 431</td><td>Cons adj</td><td></td><td></td><td></td></tr>
<tr><td>16 Oct 1902</td><td>157 CJ 438</td><td>Cons adj</td><td></td><td></td><td></td></tr>
<tr><td>17 Oct 1902</td><td>157 CJ 440</td><td>Cons adj</td><td></td><td></td><td></td></tr>
<tr><td>21 Oct 1902</td><td>157 CJ 442</td><td>Cons adj</td><td></td><td></td><td></td></tr>
<tr><td>21 Oct 1902</td><td>157 CJ 444</td><td>**Cons/3R**</td><td></td><td></td><td></td></tr>
<tr><td>1 Dec 1902</td><td>157 CJ 500</td><td>HL pass with Amds</td><td></td><td></td><td></td></tr>
<tr><td>3 Dec 1902</td><td>157 CJ 503</td><td>HL Amds Cons adj</td><td></td><td></td><td></td></tr>
<tr><td>4 Dec 1902</td><td>157 CJ 504</td><td>HL Amds Cons adj</td><td></td><td></td><td></td></tr>
<tr><td>5 Dec 1902</td><td>157 CJ 506</td><td>HL Amds Cons adj</td><td></td><td></td><td></td></tr>
<tr><td>5 Dec 1902</td><td>157 CJ 508</td><td>HL Amds Cons adj</td><td></td><td></td><td></td></tr>
<tr><td>9 Dec 1902</td><td>157 CJ 511</td><td>HL Amds Cons adj</td><td></td><td></td><td></td></tr>
<tr><td>9 Dec 1902</td><td>157 CJ 513</td><td>HL Amds Ag</td><td></td><td></td><td></td></tr>
<tr><td>18 Dec 1902</td><td>157 CJ 525</td><td>Royal Assent</td><td></td><td></td><td></td></tr>
<tr><th colspan="6">Standing Committee on Trade</th></tr>
<tr><td colspan="3">*First Sitting* – 24 Jul 1902 [Cl 1 and 2]</td><td colspan="3">*Second Sitting* – 28 Jul 1902 [Cl 2 to end] – 1 Vote</td></tr>
</table>

Parliamentary debates	
1R: **HC Deb, 10 Feb 1902, Vol 102(4th), col 919–921**	1R: HL Deb, 3 Nov 1902, Vol 113(4th), col 1378
2R: **HC Deb, 4 Jul 1902, Vol 110(4th), col 852–879**	2R: **HL Deb, 17 Nov 1902, Vol 114(4th), col 1099–1103**
Rep: HC Deb, 28 Jul 1902, Vol 111(4th), col 1371	Com: **HL Deb, 20 Nov 1902, Vol 115(4th), col 3**
3R: **HC Deb, 21 Oct 1902, Vol 113(4th), col 441–447**	Rep: HL Deb, 24 Nov 1902, Vol 115(4th), col 226
HL pass with Amds: HC Deb, 1 Dec 1902, Vol 115(4th), col 856	3R: HL Deb, 1 Dec 1902, Vol 115(4th), col 813
HL Amds Ag: HC Deb, 9 Dec 1902, Vol 116(4th), col 500	Royal Assent: HL Deb, 18 Dec 1902, Vol 116(4th), col 1605
Royal Assent: HC Deb, 18 Dec 1902, Vol 116(4th), col 1642	

Debates on particular provisions	
s 2	HC Deb, 21 Oct 1902, Vol 113(4th), col 441

Parliamentary papers

Patents Bill (1902 HC Papers 87), Vol 3, p 641

Patents Bill (as amended in Committee) (1902 HC Papers 288), Vol 3, p 645

Patents Law Bill (1902 HL Papers 180), Vol 6, p 497

    Amendments to be moved in Committee by the Lord Chancellor (1902 HL Papers 180a), Vol 6, p 501

    Amendments to be moved in Committee by Lord Davey (1902 HL Papers 180c), Vol 6, p 503

Patents Law Bill (1902 HL Papers 188), Vol 6, p 505

Lords Amendments (1902 HC Papers 305), Vol 3, p 651

Report from the Standing Committee on Trade on Patents Bill (1902 HC Papers 303), Vol 7, p 301

Supplement to Votes & Proceedings, 1902 – No amendments

Newspaper coverage of debates

House of Commons

1R: **The Times, 11 Feb 1902**

2R: **The Times, 5 Jul 1902**

SC Com: **The Times, 25 Jul 1902**; **London Daily News, 25 Jul 1902**

SC Com: **The Times, 29 Jul 1902**; **London Daily News, 29 Jul 1902**

Cons/3R: **The Times, 22 Oct 1902**

HL Amd Ag: The Times, 10 Dec 1902

House of Lords

Brought HC: The Times, 4 Nov 1902

2R: **The Times, 18 Nov 1902**

CWH: *The Times, 21 Nov 1902*

Rep: The Times, 25 Nov 1902

3R: 2 Dec 1902

Royal Assent: The Times, 19 Dec 1902

Deputation meeting Pr BotT: The Times, 17 Mar 1902; its composition: The Times, 20 Mar 1902; Meeting date appointed: The Times, 24 Mar 1902

Notes

Petitions – PET594 to PET596

Archive

Working of Patent Act 1902: National Archive (BT209/4)

Patent Office Extension Act 1903

PUBA21	1903
Patent Office Extension Act 1903 (3 Edw 7. c. cccxxx)	
An Act for the acquisition of land for the further extension of the Patent Office and for purposes connected therewith	

(continued)

(continued)

Table of contents
s 1 Power to purchase land
s 2 Commissioners not to take certain land
s 3 Incorporation of Land Clauses Act
s 4 Land tax
s 5 Extinction of rights of way and other easements
s 6 Saving for county council
s 7 Saving for Corporation of London
s 8 As to area in front of premises in Furnival Street
s 9 Power to enter on land
s 10 Power of Commissioners to build
s 11 Protection of works of gas water hydraulic power or electricity companys
s 12 Provision as to expenses &c. of Commissioners
s 13 Penalty for obstructing Commissioners
s 14 Short title

Journal

House of Commons			House of Lords		
Pres: Arthur Elliot (Fin Sec Tr) COS Rep: Sir Alexander Acland-Hood (Ch Whip) Rep: Victor Cavendish (Fin Sec Tr)			Rep: Earl of Morley (Ld Ch)		
27 May 1903	158 CJ 209	Bill Ord/1R	5 Aug 1903	135 LJ 304	Brought HC
28 May 1903	158 CJ 213	Ref to Ex	5 Aug 1903	135 LJ 305	1R/Prt/Ref to Ex
9 Jun 1903	158 CJ 218	2R adj	7 Aug 1903	135 LJ 322	Ex Cert
9 Jun 1903	158 CJ 219	Ex Rep SO cw	10 Aug 1903	135 LJ 338	2R
10 Jun 1903	158 CJ 221	2R adj	12 Aug 1903	135 LJ 355	C'tted
11 Jun 1903	158 CJ 224	2R adj	12 Aug 1903	135 LJ 363	Rep w/o Amds/CWH neg
15 Jun 1903	158 CJ 235	2R adj	13 Aug 1903	135 LJ 367	3R
17 Jun 1903	158 CJ 238	2R adj	14 Aug 1903	135 LJ 371	Royal Assent
18 Jun 1903	158 CJ 241	2R adj			
23 Jun 1903	158 CJ 251	2R adj			
24 Jun 1903	158 CJ 255	2R adj			
24 Jun 1903	158 CJ 259	2R/C'tted SC			
25 Jun 1903	158 CJ 261	Royal consent/Res COS			
26 Jun 1903	158 CJ 266	COS adj			
30 Jun 1903	158 CJ 272	COS adj			
1 Jul 1903	158 CJ 279	COS adj			
2 Jul 1903	158 CJ 283	COS adj			
2 Jul 1903	158 CJ 285	COS adj			
3 Jul 1903	158 CJ 287	COS adj			
7 Jul 1903	158 CJ 294	COS adj			
8 Jul 1903	158 CJ 299	COS adj			
9 Jul 1903	158 CJ 302	COS adj			
10 Jul 1903	158 CJ 306	COS adj			
10 Jul 1903	158 CJ 308	COS adj			
14 Jul 1903	158 CJ 316	COS adj			
15 Jul 1903	158 CJ 320	COS adj			
16 Jul 1903	158 CJ 325	COS adj			
21 Jul 1903	158 CJ 336	COS adj			
22 Jul 1903	158 CJ 342	COS adj			
23 Jul 1903	158 CJ 344	**COS Res**			
24 Jul 1903	158 CJ 348	**Rep COS Res**			
27 Jul 1903	158 CJ 355	Mem Add			
31 Jul 1903	158 CJ 375	Mem Disc			
3 Aug 1903	158 CJ 377	SC Rep/C'tted CWH			
4 Aug 1903	158 CJ 383 – V	**CWH**			
4 Aug 1903	158 CJ 384	CWH/Rep w/o Amds/3R			
13 Aug 1903	158 CJ 423	HL pass w/o Amds			
14 Aug 1903	158 CJ 425	Royal Assent			

Parliamentary debates	
SO cw: HC Deb, 9 Jun 1903, Vol 123(4th), col 314	Brought HC: HL Deb, 5 Aug 1903, Vol 126(4th), col 1570
1R: HC Deb, 27 May 1903, Vol 123(4th), col 30	1R: HL Deb, 5 Aug 1903, Vol 126(4th), col 1571

Ex: HC Deb, 28 May 1903, Vol 123(4th), col 98	C'tted: HL Deb, 12 Aug 1903, Vol 127(4th), col 954
SO cw: HC Deb, 9 Jun 1903, Vol 123(4th), col 314	Rep: HL Deb, 12 Aug 1903, Vol 127(4th), col 989
2R: **HC Deb, 24 Jun 1903, Vol 124(4th), col 487–488**	3R: HL Deb, 13 Aug 1903, Vol 127(4th), col 1120
COS: HC Deb, 25 Jun 1903, Vol 124(4th), col 541–542	Royal Assent: HL Deb, 14 Aug 1903, Vol 127(4th), col 1282
COS: HC Deb, 23 Jul 1903, Vol 125(4th), col 1559–1560	
COS Rep: HC Deb, 23 Jul 1903, Vol 126(4th), col 204	
Mems Add: HC Deb, 27 Jul 1903, Vol 126(4th), col 339	
CWH: **HC Deb, 4 Aug 1903, Vol 126(4th), col 1517–1523**	
3R: **HC Deb, 4 Aug 1903, Vol 126(4th), col 1567**	
HL pass: HC Deb, 13 Aug 1903, Vol 127(4th), col 1152	

Debates on particular provisions

Cl 4	HL Deb, 13 Aug 1903, Vol 127(4th), col 1120

Parliamentary papers

Patent Office Extension Bill (1903 HC Papers 225), Vol 3, p 549
Patent Office Extension Bill (as amended in Committee) (1903 HC Papers 308), Vol 3, p 557
Patent Office Extension Bill (1903 HL Papers 193), Vol 6, p 351
Select Committee Patent Office Extension Bill (1903 HC Papers 308), Vol 7, p 523

Newspaper coverage of debates

House of Commons
2R: The Times, 25 Jun 1903
Res COS: The Times, 26 Jun 1903
CWH: **The Times, 5 Aug 1903**

House of Lords
1R: The Times, 6 Aug 1903
2R: The Times, 11 Aug 1903
3R: The Times, 14 Aug 1903

Notes

Archive
Plan: HL/PO/PB/3/plan1903/P5
House Bill: HL/PO/JO/10/10/170 (No 258)
Minute Bill: HL/PO/JO/10/10/156/496

Petition – PET597

Patents and Designs (Amendment) Act 1907

PUBA22	1907
	Patents and Designs (Amendment) Act 1907 (7 Edw 7. c. 28)
	An Act to amend the Law relating to Patents and Designs

Table of contents

s 1 Grant of patents to two or more persons
s 2 Amendment of [Patents, Designs and Trade Marks Act 1883] 46 & 47 Vict. c. 57. s 5
s 3 Deposit of samples in the case of chemical inventions
s 4 Supplementary provisional specifications
s 5 Patents of addition
s 6 Extension of [Patents Act 1902] 2 Edw 7. c. 34. s 1 to specifications published subsequently to application
s 7 Amendment of [Patents Act 1902] 2 Edw 7. c. 34. s 1 (6)
s 8 Power to postdate application in cases of disconformity
s 9 Disconformity
s 10 Grounds of opposition
s 11 Extension of period for sealing patents in certain cases
s 12 Applications for extension of time for payment of fees, &c.
s 13 Amendment of specification by disclaimers

(continued)

(continued)

s 14 Power of Comptroller to revoke patents on certain grounds
s 15 Revocation of patents worked outside the United Kingdom
s 16 Compulsory licences
s 17 Procedure on petitions for extension of term of patent
s 18 Date of patent substituted for patent obtained by fraud
s 19 Repeal of provisions as to procedure
s 20 Time for applications by representatives of deceased inventors
s 21 Secret patents
s 22 Anticipation
s 23 Restoration of lapsed patents
s 24 Avoidance of certain conditions attached to the sale, &c. of patented articles
s 25 Defences to actions for infringement, &c.
s 26 Power to counterclaim for revocation in an action for infringement
s 27 Exemption of innocent infringer from liability for damages
s 28 Provisions as to appeals and references to the court
[ss 29 to 37 relate to designs]
s 38 Rules as to branch offices
s 39 Entries in registers
s 40 Rectification of registers by court
s 41 Correction of clerical errors
s 42 Excluded days
s 43 Penalties for false representations
s 44 Royal Arms
s 45 Evidence before Comptroller
s 46 Costs and security for costs
s 47 Misuse of title of "Patent Office"
s 48 Agents for patents
s 49 Construction
s 50 Application of Act to Scotland
s 51 Short title, commencement, and repeal
Schedule One. Enactments Repealed

Proposed clauses

Cl 25 Disclosure of date and number of patent
Cl 26 Appeal to Law Officers transferred to Court

Journal

House of Commons			House of Lords		
Pres: David Lloyd George (Pr BoT) SC Rep: John Wilson			Rep: Earl of Granard (Ld-in-Wait)		
19 Mar 1907	162 CJ 74	Bill Ord/1R	14 Aug 1907	139 LJ 332	Brought HC
25 Mar 1907	162 CJ 89	2R adj	14 Aug 1907	139 LJ 334	1R
8 Apr 1907	162 CJ 99	2R adj	16 Aug 1907	139 LJ 341	2R adj
9 Apr 1907	162 CJ 101	2R adj	20 Aug 1907	139 LJ 351	2R/C'tted CWH
10 Apr 1907	162 CJ 106	2R adj	23 Aug 1907	139 LJ 379	CWH/SC neg
11 Apr 1907	162 CJ 110	2R adj	26 Aug 1907	139 LJ 393	Rep with Amds/3R
15 Apr 1907	162 CJ 115	2R adj	27 Aug 1907	139 LJ 406	HC Ag Amds
17 Apr 1907	162 CJ 122	2R adj	28 Aug 1907	139 LJ 415	Royal Assent
17 Apr 1907	162 CJ 125	2R/C'tted			
24 Apr 1907	162 CJ 142	Allocated to SC C			
4 Jun 1907	162 CJ 226	SC Rep w/o Amds			
5 Jun 1907	162 CJ 233	Cons adj			
10 Jun 1907	162 CJ 241	Cons adj			
17 Jun 1907	162 CJ 259	Cons adj			
24 Jun 1907	162 CJ 276	Cons adj			
1 Jul 1907	162 CJ 293	Cons adj			
2 Jul 1907	162 CJ 297	Cons adj			
3 Jul 1907	162 CJ 301	Cons adj			
8 Jul 1907	162 CJ 313	Cons adj			
15 Jul 1907	162 CJ 329	Cons adj			
16 Jul 1907	162 CJ 334	Cons adj			
17 Jul 1907	162 CJ 338	Cons adj			
19 Jul 1907	162 CJ 344	Cons adj			

22 Jul 1907	162 CJ 349	Cons adj			
25 Jul 1907	162 CJ 356	Cons adj			
26 Jul 1907	162 CJ 364	Cons adj			
30 Jul 1907	162 CJ 370	Cons adj			
31 Jul 1907	162 CJ 374	Cons adj			
1 Aug 1907	162 CJ 380	Cons adj			
2 Aug 1907	162 CJ 389	Cons adj			
6 Aug 1907	162 CJ 394	Cons adj			
9 Aug 1907	162 CJ 408	**Cons**			
13 Aug 1907	162 CJ 416 – V	**Cons/3R with Amds**			
26 Aug 1907	162 CJ 459	HL pass with Amds			
26 Aug 1907	162 CJ 469	HL Amds day app			
27 Aug 1907	162 CJ 461	HL Amds Ag			
28 Aug 1907	162 CJ 462	Royal Assent			

Standing Committee

First Sitting – 7 May 1907 [Cl 1 to 8] – One vote *Second Sitting* – 9 May 1907 [Cl 9 and 10] – One vote

Third Sitting – 14 May 1907 [Cl 10 to 15] – One vote *Third Sitting* – 28 May 1907 [Cl 16]

Fourth Sitting – 30 May 1907 [Cl 16 to 17] – One vote *Fifth Sitting* – 4 Jun 1907 [Cl 18 to End]

Parliamentary debates

Ord/1R: **HC Deb, 19 Mar 1907, Vol 171(4th), col 683–687** 1R: HL Deb, 14 Aug 1907, Vol 180(4th), col 1273

2R: **HC Deb, 17 Apr 1907, Vol 172(4th), col 1012–1056** 2R: **HL Deb, 20 Aug 1907, Vol 181(4th), col 419–428**

Pet Fav: HC Deb, 25 Apr 1907, Vol 173(4th), col 229 CWH: **HL Deb, 23 Aug 1907, Vol 181(4th), col 1351–1367**

Mems App: HC Deb, 25 Apr 1907, Vol 173(4th), col 293 Rep/3R: **HL Deb, 26 Aug 1907, Vol 182(4th), col 89**

Mems App: HC Deb, 1 May 1907, Vol 173(4th), col 899 Royal Assent: HL Deb, 28 Aug 1907, Vol 182(4th), col 425

Mems App: HC Deb, 2 May 1907, Vol 173(4th), col 1086

Mems App: HC Deb, 6 May 1907, Vol 173(4th), col 1364

Mems App: HC Deb, 8 May 1907, Vol 174(4th), col 244

SC Rep: HC Deb, 4 Jun 1907, Vol 175(4th), col 501–502

Cons: **HC Deb, 9 Aug 1907, Vol 180(4th), col 645–676**

Cons: **HC Deb, 13 Aug 1907, Vol 180(4th), col 1169–1194**

3R: HC Deb, 13 Aug 1907, Vol 180(4th), col 1194

HL pass with Amds: HC Deb, 26 Aug 1907, Vol 182(4th), col 276

HL Amds Ag: **HC Deb, 27 Aug 1907, Vol 182(4th), col 416**

Debates on particular provisions

s 3	HC Deb, 17 Apr 1907, Vol 172(4th), col 1017, 1027, 1043, 1048 (Cl 2); HL Deb, 20 Aug 1907, Vol 181(4th), col 425	s 4	HL Deb, 20 Aug 1907, Vol 181(4th), col 425
s 7	HL Deb, 20 Aug 1907, Vol 181(4th), col 425–427; HL Deb, 23 Aug 1907, Vol 181(4th), col 1351–1356	s 10	HC Deb, 17 Apr 1907, Vol 172(4th), col 1017–1018, 1041, 1043 (Cl 6); HC Deb, 9 Aug 1907, Vol 180(4th), col 658; HL Deb, 23 Aug 1907, Vol 181(4th), col 1356
s 13	HC Deb, 9 Aug 1907, Vol 180(4th), col 659	s 14	HC Deb, 17 Apr 1907, Vol 172(4th), col 1018–1020, 1028, 1041 (Cl 9); HC Deb, 9 Aug 1907, Vol 180(4th), col 659–663
s 15	HC Deb, 17 Apr 1907, Vol 172(4th), col 1016–1017, 1027, 1031–1032, 1036, 1037, 1041, 1044–1045, 1053–1054 (Cl 10); HC Deb, 9 Aug 1907, Vol 180(4th), col 663–668; HL Deb, 20 Aug 1907, Vol 181(4th), col 421–422; HL Deb, 23 Aug 1907, Vol 181(4th), col 1356–1357	s 16	HC Deb, 17 Apr 1907, Vol 172(4th), col 1020–1021, 1024–1025, 1037–1038, 1039, 1046–1047 (Cl 11); HC Deb, 9 Aug 1907, Vol 180(4th), col 668–669
s 17	HC Deb, 9 Aug 1907, Vol 180(4th), col 647–649	s 23	HC Deb, 9 Aug 1907, Vol 180(4th), col 669–670 (Cl 22); HL Deb, 23 Aug 1907, Vol 181(4th), col 1357–1358

(continued)

(continued)

s 24	HC Deb, 17 Apr 1907, Vol 172(4th), col 1020, 1024–1025, 1028–1031, 1039, 1045–1046, 1048–1049, 1052 (Cl 16); HC Deb, 9 Aug 1907, Vol 180(4th), col 670–675 (Cl 23); HC Deb, 13 Aug 1907, Vol 180(4th), col 1169–1180 (Cl 23); HL Deb, 20 Aug 1907, Vol 181(4th), col 422–423, 427; HL Deb, 23 Aug 1907, Vol 181(4th), col 1358–1363	s 26	HC Deb, 9 Aug 1907, Vol 180(4th), col 645 (NC)
s 27	HC Deb, 9 Aug 1907, Vol 180(4th), col 649–658 (NC)	s 28	HC Deb, 17 Apr 1907, Vol 172(4th), col 1020 (Cl 17); HC Deb, 13 Aug 1907, Vol 180(4th), col 1186–1188 (Cl 27); HL Deb, 23 Aug 1907, Vol 181(4th), col 1363–1366
s 47	HC Deb, 13 Aug 1907, Vol 180(4th), col 1190–1194 (Cl 45)	s 50	HL Deb, 23 Aug 1907, Vol 181(4th), col 1367 (NC)

Omitted provisions

Cl 25	Disclosure of date and number of patent HC Deb, 13 Aug 1907, Vol 180(4th), col 1180	Cl 26	Appeal to Law Officers transferred to Court HC Deb, 13 Aug 1907, Vol 180(4th), col 1180–1186

Parliamentary papers

Patents and Designs Bill (1907 HC Papers Bill No 121), Vol 3, p 369

Patents and Designs Bill (as amended by Standing Committee C) (1907 HC Papers 221), Vol 3, p 387

Patents and Designs Bill (1907 HL Papers 174), Vol 5, p 159

    Amendments to be moved in Committee by Lord Granard (1907 HL Papers 174a), Vol 5, p 183

    Amendments to be moved in Committee by Marques of Salisbury (1907 HL Papers 174b), Vol 5, p 187

    Amendments to be moved in Committee by Lord Granard (1907 HL Papers 174c), Vol 5, p 189

Patents and Designs Bill (as amended in Committee) (1907 HL Papers 211), Vol 5, p 193

Lords Amendments to the Patents and Designs Bill (1907 HC Papers 334), Vol 3, p 409

Report by Standing Committee C on the Patents and Designs Bill (1907 HC Papers 177), Vol 7, p 233

Supplement to Votes & Proceedings, 1907

    17 Apr 1907, p 171–173; 18 Apr 1907, p 183–185; 19 Apr 1907, p 193; 24 Apr 1907, p 237–241; 25 Apr 1907, p 245–249; 29 Apr 1907, p 273–291; 2 May 1907, p 305–306; 3 May 1907, p 329–349; 7 May 1907, p 357–377; 7 May 1907, p 391; 9 May 1907, p 397–416; 9 May 1907, p 435–436; 10 May 1907, p 461; 14 May 1907, p 511–529; 15 May 1907, p 575–576; 16 May 1907, p 613–627; 24 May 1907, p 697–700; 28 May 1907, p 723–739; 28 May 1907, p 791–792; 30 May 1907, p 797–813; 30 May 1907, p 839; 4 Jun 1907, p 897–909; 2 Jul 1907, p 1619–1624; 3 Jul 1907, p 1689–1694; 8 Jul 1907, p 1793–1804; 15 Jul 1907, p 1957–1968

Newspaper coverage of debates

House of Commons

Proposed: Note, The Times, 20 Feb 1907

1R: **The Times, 20 Mar 1907**

2R: **The Times, 18 Apr 1907**

Political Note: *The Times, 27 Mar 1907*

S Committee B (7 May): *The Times, 8 May 1907, p 5*

S Committee B (9 May): *The Times, 11 May 1907, p 4*

S Committee B (14 May): *The Times, 15 May 1907, p 4*

S Committee B (28 May): *The Times, 30 May 1907, p 11*

S Committee B (4 Jun): *The Times, 5 Jun 1907, p 17*

Cons: **The Times, 10 Aug 1907 (cont: The Times, 15 Aug 1907)**; Note, The Times, 3 Aug 1907

HL Amd Ag: The Times, 28 Aug 1907

House of Lords

2R: **The Times, 21 Aug 1907**

CWH: The Times, 26 Aug 1907

Rep: The Times, 27 Aug 1907

Royal Assent: The Times, 29 Aug 1907

Notes	
Archive	
Patents and Designs Bill: Representations: National Archive (BT 15/55)	
Report on Committee on Secret Patents: National Archive (BT 15/55)	
Patents Bills (Parliamentary Counsel): National Archive (AM 1/26)	
Petitions – PET599 to PET601	

Patents and Designs Act 1907

PUBA23	1907

Patents and Designs Act 1907 (7 Edw 7. c. 29)
An Act to consolidate the enactments relating to Patents for Inventions and the Registration of Designs and certain enactments relating to Trade Marks

(continued)

(continued)

s 38 Avoidance of certain conditions attached to the sale, &c. of patented articles	1907, s 24
s 39 Costs and security for costs	1907, s 39
s 40 Procedure on appeal to law officer	1883, s 38
s 41 Provisions as to anticipation	1902, s 2; 1907, s 22
s 42 Disconformity	1907, s 9
s 43 Patent on application of representative of deceased inventor	1883, s 34; 1907, s 20
s 44 Loss or destruction of patent	1883, s 37
s 45 Provisions as to exhibitions	1883, s 39; 1888, s 3
s 46 Publication of illustrated journal, indexes, &c.	1883, s 40
s 47 Patent Museum	1883, s 41 and 42
s 48 Foreign vessels in British waters	1883, s 43
	1883, s 82; 1902, s 4; 1907, s 62
Part II – Designs.	
Registration of Designs.	—
[s 49 to s 61 relate to designs]	—
Part III – General.	
Patent Office and Proceedings Threats	—
s 62 Patent Office	1883, s 83
s 63 Officers and clerks	1883, s 84
s 64 Seal of Patent Office	1883, s 84
s 65 Fees	1883, s 24 and 56
s 66 Trust not to be entered in registers	1883, s 85
s 67 Inspection of and extracts from registers	1883, s 88; 1888, s 22
s 68 Privilege of reports of examiners	1883, s 9(5); 1902, s 1(4)
s 69 Prohibition of publication of specification, drawings, &c. where application abandoned, &c.	1885, s 4
s 70 Power for Comptroller to correct clerical errors	1883, s 91; 1888, s 24; 1907, s 41
s 71 Entry of assignments and transmissions in registers	1883, s 87; 1888, s 21; 1907, s 39
s 72 Rectification of registers by court	1883, s 90; 1888, s 23; 1907, s 40
s 73 Exercise of discretionary power by Comptroller	1883, s 94
s 74 Power of Comptroller to take directions of law officers	1883, s 95
s 75 Refusal to grant patent, &c. in certain cases	1883, s 86
s 76 Annual reports of Comptroller	1883, s 102
s 77 Evidence before Comptroller	1907, s 45
s 78 Certificate of Comptroller to be evidence	1883, s 96
s 79 Evidence of documents in Patent Office	1883, s 89
s 80 Transmission of certified printed copies of specifications, &c.	1883, s 100
s 81 Applications and notices by post	1883, s 97
s 82 Excluded days	1883, s 98; 1907, s 42
s 83 Declaration by infant, lunatic, &c.	1883, s 99
s 84 Register of patent agents	1888, s 1
s 85 Agents for patents	1907, s 48
s 86 Power for Board of Trade to make general rules	1883, s 101; 1888, s 1(2); 1907, s 48
s 87 Proceedings of the Board of Trade	1888, s 25
s 88 Provision as to Order in Council	1883, s 104
s 89 Offences	1883, s 93 and 105; 1907, s 47
s 90 Unauthorised assumption of Royal Arms	1883, s 106; 1907, s 44
s 91 International and Colonial arrangements	1883, s 103 and 104; 1885 s 6; 1901, s 1
s 92 Provisions as to "the court"	1907, s 28
s 93 Definitions	1883, s 46, 60, 61 and 117
s 94 Application to Scotland	1883, s 46, 107 108, 109 and 111; 1907, s 94
s 95 Application to Ireland	1883, s 110 and 111
s 96 Isle of Man	1883, s 112
s 97 Saving for prerogative	1883, s 116

s 98 Repeal and savings	1883, s 45; 1902, s 3(11)
s 99 Short title and commencement	—
First Schedule – Fees on Instruments for obtaining Patents and Renewal	1902, s 1(10)
Second Schedule – Enactments Repealed	—

Journal

House of Commons			House of Lords		
Pres: Hudson Kearly (Par Sec BoT) Rep: James Caldwell (Dep Ch W&M)			Rep: Earl of Granard (Ld-in-Waiting)		
18 Apr 1907	162 CJ 128	1R	14 Aug 1907	139 LJ 332	Brought HC
22 Apr 1907	162 CJ 133	2R adj	14 Aug 1907	139 LJ 334	1R
23 Apr 1907	162 CJ 138	2R adj	16 Aug 1907	139 LJ 341	2R adj
24 Apr 1907	162 CJ 140	2R adj	20 Aug 1907	139 LJ 351	2R/C'tted CWH
29 Apr 1907	162 CJ 150	2R adj	23 Aug 1907	139 LJ 381	CWH/SC neg
6 May 1907	162 CJ 167	2R adj	26 Aug 1907	139 LJ 394	Rep with Amds/3R
13 May 1907	162 CJ 187	2R adj	27 Aug 1907	139 LJ 406	HC Ag Amds
23 May 1907	162 CJ 202	2R adj	28 Aug 1907	139 LJ 415	Royal Assent
24 May 1907	162 CJ 204	2R adj			
28 May 1907	162 CJ 208	2R adj			
28 May 1907	162 CJ 212	2R adj			
29 May 1907	162 CJ 216	2R adj			
31 May 1907	162 CJ 221	2R adj			
3 Jun 1907	162 CJ 225	2R adj			
4 Jun 1907	162 CJ 229	2R adj			
5 Jun 1907	162 CJ 233	2R adj			
6 Jun 1907	162 CJ 236	2R adj			
10 Jun 1907	162 CJ 242	2R adj			
11 Jun 1907	162 CJ 246	2R adj			
12 Jun 1907	162 CJ 249	2R adj			
13 Jun 1907	162 CJ 252	2R adj			
17 Jun 1907	162 CJ 260	2R adj			
18 Jun 1907	162 CJ 265	2R adj			
19 Jun 1907	162 CJ 267	2R adj			
21 Jun 1907	162 CJ 272	2R adj			
24 Jun 1907	162 CJ 277	2R adj			
25 Jun 1907	162 CJ 280	2R adj			
26 Jun 1907	162 CJ 284	2R adj			
28 Jun 1907	162 CJ 289	2R adj			
1 Jul 1907	162 CJ 294	2R adj			
2 Jul 1907	162 CJ 298	2R adj			
3 Jul 1907	162 CJ 301	2R adj			
5 Jul 1907	162 CJ 309	2R adj			
8 Jul 1907	162 CJ 313	2R adj			
10 Jul 1907	162 CJ 318	2R adj			
12 Jul 1907	162 CJ 325	2R adj			
15 Jul 1907	162 CJ 330	2R adj			
16 Jul 1907	162 CJ 334	2R adj			
17 Jul 1907	162 CJ 339	2R adj			
19 Jul 1907	162 CJ 344	2R adj			
22 Jul 1907	162 CJ 349	2R adj			
25 Jul 1907	162 CJ 356	2R adj			
26 Jul 1907	162 CJ 365	2R/C'tted CWH			
30 Jul 1907	162 CJ 370	CWH adj			
31 Jul 1907	162 CJ 373	CWH adj			
1 Aug 1907	162 CJ 379	CWH adj			
2 Aug 1907	162 CJ 389	CWH adj			
6 Aug 1907	162 CJ 393	CWH adj			
7 Aug 1907	162 CJ 397	CWH adj			
8 Aug 1907	162 CJ 401	CWH adj			
9 Aug 1907	162 CJ 405	CWH adj			
13 Aug 1907	162 CJ 413	CWH adj			

(continued)

(continued)

14 Aug 1907	162 CJ 417	CWH/Rep w/o Amds/3R			
26 Aug 1907	162 CJ 459	HL pass with Amds			
26 Aug 1907	162 CJ 459	HL Amds Cons day app			
27 Aug 1907	162 CJ 461	HL Amds Ag			
28 Aug 1907	162 CJ 462	Royal Assent			

Parliamentary debates

Brought HL: HC Deb, 14 Apr 1908, Vol 187(4th), col 967

1R: HC Deb, 18 Apr 1907, Vol 172(4th), col 1174

2R: HC Deb, 26 Jul 1907, Vol 179(4th), col 376

CWH: **HC Deb, 13 Aug 1907, Vol 180(4th), col 1194–1200**

Rep/3R: HC Deb, 13 Aug 1907, Vol 180(4th), col 1200

HL Ret: HC Deb, 27 Aug 1907, Vol 182(4th), col 276

HL Amds Ag: **HC Deb, 27 Aug, Vol 182(4th), col 416**

1R: HL Deb, 14 Aug 1907, Vol 180(4th), col 1273

2R: **HL Deb, 20 Aug 1907, Vol 181(4th), col 428–429**

CWH: **HL Deb, 23 Aug 1907, Vol 181(4th), col 1367–1368**

Rep/3R: **HL Deb, 26 Aug 1907, Vol 182(4th), col 89–91**

Royal Assent: HL Deb, 28 Aug 1907, Vol 175(4th), col 474

Parliamentary papers

Patents and Designs (Consolidation) Bill (1907 HC Papers Bill No 165), Vol 3, p 421

Patents and Designs (Consolidation) Bill (1907 HL Papers 175), Vol 5, p 217

    Amendments to be moved in Committee by Lord Granard (1907 HL Papers 175a), Vol 5, p 255

    Amendments to be moved on Report by the Lord Chancellor (1907 HL Papers 175b), Vol 5, p 257

Lords Amendments to the Patents and Designs (Consolidation) Bill (1907 HC Papers Bill No 335), Vol 3, p 461

Standing Committee C. Report on Patents and Designs Bill (1907 HC Papers 177), Vol 7, p 233

Newspaper coverage of debates

House of Commons

1R: Note, The Times, 18 Apr 1907

2R: The Times, 27 Jul 1907

House of Lords

1R: The Times, 15 Aug 1907

2R: The Times, 21 Aug 1907

Rep: The Times, 27 Aug 1907

HC Ag HL Amd: The Times, 28 Aug 1907

Royal Assent: The Times, 29 Aug 1907

Notes

Archives

Working of the Patents and Designs Act 1907: National Archive: (BT 209/8 and 9)

Patents and Designs (Consolidation) Bill 1907: Notes on Clauses: National Archive (BT 209/459)

Patents and Designs (Consolidation) Bill 1907: First Reading: National Archive (BT 209/460)

Patents and Designs (Consolidation) Bill 1907: Committee Stage: National Archive (BT 209/461)

Patents and Designs (Consolidation) Bill 1907: Amendments clauses 1 to 15: National Archive (BT 209/462)

Patents and Designs (Consolidation) Bill 1907: Amendments clauses 16 to end: National Archive (BT 209/463)

Patents and Designs (Consolidation) Bill 1907: Drafts and amendments: National Archive (BT 209/464)

Patents and Designs (Consolidation) Bill 1907: Notes on amendments at report stage in House of Commons: National Archive (BT 209/465)

Patents and Designs (Consolidation) Bill 1907: Consideration by House of Lords: National Archive (BT 209/466)

Patents and Designs (Consolidation) Bill 1907: Representations: National Archive (BT 209/467)

Patents and Designs (Consolidation) Bill 1907: Various prints of Bill: National Archive (BT 209/468)

Patents and Designs (Consolidation) Bill 1907: Press cuttings (BT 209/469)

Patents and Designs Act 1907: Notes on Various Sections (BT209/470)

Patents Bills (Parliamentary Counsel): National Archive AM 1/26

Patents and Designs Act 1908

PUBA24	1908	

Patents and Designs Act 1908 (8 Edw 7. c. 4)

An Act to explain section ninety-two of the Patents and Designs Act, 1907

Table of contents

s 1 Explanation of [Patents and Designs Act 1907] 7 Edw 7 c. 29 s 92 [finality of decision does not apply to revocation petition]
s 2 Short title

Journal					
House of Commons			**House of Lords**		
Rep: Alfred Emmott (Ch W&M)			Pres: Earl of Granard (Ld-in-Wait) Rep: Viscount Cross		
14 Apr 1908	163 CJ 144	Brought HL	10 Feb 1908	140 LJ 37	1R
25 May 1908	163 CJ 208	1R	11 Feb 1908	140 LJ 39	2R day app
26 May 1908	163 CJ 213	2R adj	18 Feb 1908	140 LJ 48	2R/C'tted CWH
27 May 1908	163 CJ 220	2R adj	20 Feb 1908	140 LJ 56	Rep w/o Amds
28 May 1908	163 CJ 223	2R adj	31 Mar 1908	140 LJ Ap iii	Standing Committee
1 Jun 1908	163 CJ 229	2R adj	31 Mar 1908	140 LJ 113	SC Rep w/o Amds
2 Jun 1908	163 CJ 234	2R adj	1 Apr 1908	140 LJ 115	3R
3 Jun 1908	163 CJ 240	2R adj	13 Jul 1908	140 LJ 263	HC pass w/o Amds
4 Jun 1908	163 CJ 241	2R adj	1 Aug 1908	140 LJ 350	Royal Assent
11 Jun 1908	163 CJ 246	2R adj			
12 Jun 1908	163 CJ 248	2R adj			
15 Jun 1908	163 CJ 251	2R adj			
16 Jun 1908	163 CJ 254	2R adj			
17 Jun 1908	163 CJ 259	2R adj			
18 Jun 1908	163 CJ 262	2R adj			
19 Jun 1908	163 CJ 264	2R/C'tted CWH			
22 Jun 1908	163 CJ 267	CWH adj			
23 Jun 1908	163 CJ 271	CWH adj			
24 Jun 1908	163 CJ 275	CWH adj			
25 Jun 1908	163 CJ 279	CWH adj			
29 Jun 1908	163 CJ 287	CWH adj			
1 Jul 1908	163 CJ 291	CWH adj			
1 Jul 1908	163 CJ 295	CWH adj			
2 Jul 1908	163 CJ 298	CWH adj			
3 Jul 1908	163 CJ 301	CWH adj			
7 Jul 1908	163 CJ 305	CWH adj			
7 Jul 1908	163 CJ 310	CWH adj			
8 Jul 1908	163 CJ 313	CWH adj			
10 Jul 1908	163 CJ 318	CWH/Rep w/o Amds/3R			
1 Aug 1908	163 CJ 390	Royal Assent			

Parliamentary debates	
Brought HL: HC Deb, 14 Apr 1908, Vol 187(4th), col 967	1R: HL Deb, 10 Feb 1908, Vol 183(4th), col 1303
1R: HC Deb, 25 May 1908, Vol 189(4th), col 776	2R: **HL Deb, 18 Feb 1908, Vol 184(4th), col 566**
Bus: HC Deb, 16 Jun 1908, Vol 190(4th), col 724	CWH/Rep: HL Deb, 20 Feb 1908, Vol 184(4th), col 942
2R: **HC Deb, 19 Jun 1908, Vol 190(4th), col 1220**	SC Rep: HL Deb, 31 Mar 1908, Vol 187(4th), col 247
CWH/Rep/3R: **HC Deb, 10 Jul 1908, Vol 192(4th), col 265–267**	3R: HL Deb, 1 Apr 1908, Vol 187(4th), col 466
	Royal Assent: HL Deb, 1 Aug 1908, Vol 193(4th), col 2074

Parliamentary papers

Patents and Designs Bill (1908 HL Papers 8), Vol 8, p 235

Patents and Designs Bill (1908 HC Papers 239), Vol 4, p 59

Supplement to Votes & Proceedings, 1908 – No amendments

(continued)

(continued)

Newspaper coverage of debates
House of Lords
1R: **The Times, 11 Feb 1908**
2R: **The Times, 19 Feb 1908**; Notes, The Times, 18 Feb 1908
SC: *The Times, 1 Apr 1908*
Rep: The Times, 21 Feb 1908
3R: The Times, 2 Apr 1908
House of Commons
2R: **The Times, 20 Jun 1908**
CWH: The Times, 11 Jul 1908

Notes
Archive
Patents Bills (Parliamentary Counsel): National Archive AM 1/26

Public Offices (Extension) Act 1908

PUBA25	1908

Public Offices (Extension) Act 1908 (8 Edw 7. c. cxii)

An Act to provide for the acquisition of Land for the extension of certain Public Offices in Westminster and of the Patent Office and for certain other public purposes

Table of contents
s 1 Acquisition of land
s 2 Incorporation of Land Clauses Act
s 3 Power to stop up public thoroughfares
s 4 Land tax
s 5 Extinction of rights of way and other easements
s 6 Power to construct archway over Downing Street
s 7 Power of Commissioners to build
s 8 Provision as to substituted site for new building of Institution of Civil Engineers
s 9 Provision as to costs of repaving Prince's Street
s 10 Protection of works of gas water hydraulic power and electricity companies
s 11 Provisions as to expenses &c. of Commissioners
s 12 Correction of errors &c. in deposited plans and book of references
s 13 Penalty for obstructing Commissioners
s 14 Short title

Journal

House of Commons			House of Lords		
Pres and Rep: Lewis Harcourt (Fir Com Works) CWH Rep: Alfred Emmott (Ch W&M) COS Rep: James Caldwell (Dep Ch W&M)			Rep: Duke of Devonshire Rep CWH: Lord Balfour of Burleigh		
20 Feb 1908	163 CJ 55	1R	22 Jun 1908	140 LJ 215	Brought HC/1R
21 Feb 1908	163 CJ 57	Ref to Ex	30 Jun 1908	140 LJ 232	Ex Cert SO cw
25 Feb 1908	163 CJ 61	SO cw	29 Jun 1908	140 LJ 228	Pet Ag
26 Feb 1908	163 CJ 65	2R adj	1 Jul 1908	140 LJ 236	2R day app
28 Feb 1908	163 CJ 69	2R adj	6 Jul 1908	140 LJ 243	Pet Ag
2 Mar 1908	163 CJ 72	2R adj	6 Jul 1908	140 LJ 245	2R/C'tted
4 Mar 1908	163 CJ 77	2R adj	6 Jul 1908	140 LJ 246	Peer Add
5 Mar 1908	163 CJ 80	2R adj	13 Jul 1908	140 LJ 262	Com adj
9 Mar 1908	163 CJ 84	2R adj	14 Jul 1908	140 LJ 269	Peer sub
10 Mar 1908	163 CJ 86	2R adj	16 Jul 1908	140 LJ 277	Peer sub
11 Mar 1908	163 CJ 90	2R adj	20 Jul 1908	140 LJ 283	Com adj
12 Mar 1908	163 CJ 93	2R adj	27 Jul 1908	140 LJ 308	Rep with Amds/C'tted CWH
16 Mar 1908	163 CJ 98	2R adj	28 Jul 1908	140 LJ 318	CWH/SC neg/3R

17 Mar 1908	163 CJ 102	2R adj	30 Jul 1908	140 LJ 336	HC Ag Amds
19 Mar 1908	163 CJ 107	2R adj	1 Aug 1908	140 LJ 351	Royal Assent
19 Mar 1908	163 CJ 110	2R adj			
24 Mar 1908	163 CJ 115	2R adj			
25 Mar 1908	163 CJ 119	2R adj			
26 Mar 1908	163 CJ 122	2R adj			
31 Mar 1908	163 CJ 127	2R adj			
31 Mar 1908	163 CJ 131	2R adj			
1 Apr 1908	163 CJ 134	2R adj			
2 Apr 1908	163 CJ 138	2R adj			
28 Apr 1908	163 CJ 149	2R adj			
29 Apr 1908	163 CJ 156	2R adj			
30 Apr 1908	163 CJ 158	2R adj			
5 May 1908	163 CJ 162	2R adj			
5 May 1908	163 CJ 165	2R adj			
6 May 1908	163 CJ 169	2R adj			
7 May 1908	163 CJ 171	2R adj			
11 May 1908	163 CJ 176	2R adj			
12 May 1908	163 CJ 179	2R adj			
13 May 1908	163 CJ 182–V	2R/C'tted			
13 May 1908	163 CJ 184	Royal consent			
15 May 1908	163 CJ 189	COS adj			
18 May 1908	163 CJ 192	COS			
19 May 1908	163 CJ 195	SC Mem App			
19 May 1908	163 CJ 196	COS adj			
20 May 1908	163 CJ 199	COS adj			
26 May 1908	163 CJ 209	COS adj			
26 May 1908	163 CJ 214	COS/Rep			
27 May 1908	163 CJ 217	COS Res			
27 May 1908	163 CJ 219	COS Res			
28 May 1908	163 CJ 223	COS Res/Ag			
16 Jun 1908	163 CJ 253	**Rep with Amd/Re–C'tted CWH**			
17 Jun 1908	163 CJ 259	CWH adj			
19 Jun 1908	163 CJ 263	**CWH Rep w/o Amds/3R**			
28 Jul 1908	163 CJ 369	HL pass with Amds			
28 Jul 1908	163 CJ 370	HL Amds Cons day app			
29 Jul 1908	163 CJ 380	HL Amds Ag			
1 Aug 1908	163 CJ 390	Royal Assent			

Petitions

29 Jun 1908	140 LJ 228	1. Lands Improvement Company; 2. Nicholson, Paterson and Freeland
6 Jul 1908	140 LJ 243	Institute of Civil Engineers

Parliamentary debates

1R: HC Deb, 20 Feb 1908, Vol 184(4th), col 1047

Ref Ex: HC Deb, 21 Feb 1908, Vol 184(4th), col 1190

SO cw: HC Deb, 25 Feb 1908, Vol 184(4th), col 1541

2R: **HC Deb, 13 May 1908, Vol 188(4th), col 1176–1203**

COS: HC Deb, 18 May 1908, Vol 188(4th), col 1774

COS Mem: HC Deb, 19 May 1908, Vol 189(4th), col 90

COS/Rep **HC Deb, 26 May 1908, Vol 189(4th), col 1037–1039**

COS Res: **HC Deb, 27 May 1908, Vol 189(4th), col 1185–1188**

COS Res: **HC Deb, 28 May 1908, Vol 189(4th), col 1395–1396**

3R: **HC Deb, 19 Jun 1908, Vol 190(4th), col 1169–1177**

HL pass: HC Deb, 28 Jul 1908, Vol 193(4th), col 1167

SO cw: HL Deb, 30 Jun 1908, Vol 191(4th), col 493

2R: HL Deb, 6 Jul 1908, Vol 191(4th), col 1147

Com App: HL Deb. 13 Jul 1908, Vol 192(4th), col 31

Mem Sub: HL Deb, 14 Jul 1908, Vol 192(4th), col 53

Mem Sub: H: Deb, 16 Jul 1908, Vol 192(4th), col 994

SC adj: HL Deb, 20 Jul 1908, Vol 192(4th), col 133

Rep: HL Deb, 27 Jul 1908, Vol 193(4th), col 705

CWH/3R: HL Deb, 28 Jul 1908, Vol 193(4th), col 1072

Royal Assent: HL Deb, 1 Aug 1908, Vol 193(4th), col 2074

(continued)

(continued)

Parliamentary papers
Public Offices Sites (Extension) Bill (1908 HC Papers 108), Vol 4, p 917
Public Offices Sites (Extension) Bill (As Amended in Committee) (1908 HC Papers 264), Vol 4, p 927
Public Offices Sites (Extension) Bill (1908 HL Papers 103), Vol 8, p 907
Lords Amendments to Public Offices Sites (Extension) Bill (1908 HC Papers 346), Vol 4, p 937
Report of the Select Committee on Public Offices Sites (Extension) Bill, together with proceedings of the committee and minutes of evidence (1908 HC Papers 180), Vol 10, p 991

Newspaper coverage of debates
House of Commons
Notes: The Times, 24 Feb 1908
2R: The Times, 14 May 1908
Re-C'tted: The Times, 20 Jun 1908
SC: *The Times, 17 Jun 1908*
SC: *The Times, 21 Jun 1908*

Public Office (Sites) Act 1912

PUBA26	1912

Public Office (Sites) Act 1912 (2 & 3 Geo 5. c. cx)
An Act to make provision for the acquisition of a Site for Public Offices in Westminster for the acquisition of land for the further extension of the Patent Office and for purposes in connection with the Record Office to amend the Public Offices Sites (Extension) Act 1908 and to make provision for certain other public purposes

Table of contents (provisions relevant to Patent Office)
s 4 Extension of time for compulsory acquisition of land under [Public Offices (Extension) Act 1908] 8 Edw 7, c. cxii

Journal					
House of Commons			**House of Lords**		
Pres: William Wedgwood Benn (Ch Whip)			Rep: Select Committee CWH Rep: Earl of Donoughmore (Ld Ch)		
13 Mar 1912	167 CJ 53	COS Res/1R	10 Jul 1912	144 LJ 187	Brought HC
13 Mar 1912	167 CJ 56	Ref to Ex	10 Jul 1912	144 LJ 191	1R/Ref to Exam
18 Mar 1912	167 CJ 62	Ex Rep SO cw	16 Jul 1912	144 LJ 204	Ex Cert/No SO app
18 Mar 1912	167 CJ 63	2R adj	16 Jul 1912	144 LJ 207	Pet Ag
19 Mar 1912	167 CJ 66	2R adj	17 Jul 1912	144 LJ 207	2R day app
21 Mar 1912	167 CJ 69	2R adj	17 Jul 1912	144 LJ 211	2R/C'tted
22 Mar 1912	167 CJ 72	2R adj	23 Jul 1912	144 LJ 223	Peer sub
25 Mar 1912	167 CJ 77	2R adj	25 Jul 1912	144 LJ 231	Rep w/o Amds/C'tted CWH
27 Mar 1912	167 CJ 85	2R adj	29 Jul 1912	144 LJ 239	CWH/Rep w/o Amds
28 Mar 1912	167 CJ 87	2R adj	30 Jul 1912	144 LJ 242	Royal consent/3R
29 Mar 1912	167 CJ 90	2R adj	7 Aug 1912	144 LJ 258	Royal Assent
1 Apr 1912	167 CJ 92	2R adj			
2 Apr 1912	167 CJ 94	2R adj			
3 Apr 1912	167 CJ 96	2R adj			
10 Apr 1912	167 CJ 97	2R/C'tted SC/Counsel Ord			
12 Apr 1912	167 CJ 101	R Rec'd			
15 Apr 1912	167 CJ 104	COS adj			
16 Apr 1912	167 CJ 106	Mem app			
16 Apr 1912	167 CJ 106	COS adj			
17 Apr 1912	167 CJ 109	COS adj			
18 Apr 1912	167 CJ 111	COS adj			
22 Apr 1912	167 CJ 115	COS adj			
23 Apr 1912	167 CJ 118	COS adj			
25 Apr 1912	167 CJ 124	COS adj			
26 Apr 1912	167 CJ 127	COS adj			

29 Apr 1912	167 CJ 129	COS adj			
30 Apr 1912	167 CJ 132	COS adj			
1 May 1912	167 CJ 134	**COS**			
3 May 1912	167 CJ 140	COS Rep adj			
6 May 1912	167 CJ 142	COS Rep adj			
7 May 1912	167 CJ 145	COS Rep adj			
8 May 1912	167 CJ 148	COS Rep adj			
9 May 1912	167 CJ 151	COS Rep adj			
13 May 1912	167 CJ 156	**COS Rep**			
14 May 1912	167 CJ 160	Adj			
15 May 1912	167 CJ 164	**COS Rep Cons**			
17 May 1912	167 CJ 170	COS Rep adj			
20 May 1912	167 CJ 175	COS Rep adj			
21 May 1912	167 CJ 178	COS Rep adj			
5 Jun 1912	167 CJ 188	COS Rep adj			
6 Jun 1912	167 CJ 191	COS Rep adj			
7 Jun 1912	167 CJ 193	**COS Res Ag**			
27 Jun 1912	167 CJ 238	Pet Ag Ord			
4 Jul 1912	167 CJ 253	Rep with Amds/C'tted CWH			
8 Jul 1912	167 CJ 258	CWH adj			
9 Jul 1912	167 CJ 260 – V	**CWH/Rep**/3R			
30 Jul 1912	167 CJ 316	HL pass w/o Amds			
7 Aug 1912	167 CJ 344	Royal Assent			

Parliamentary debates	
1R: HC Deb, 13 Mar 1912, Vol 35(5th), col 1111–1112	Brought HC: HL Deb, 10 Jul 1912, Vol 12(5th), col 383
Ex Rep: HC Deb, 18 Mar 1912, Vol 35(5th), col 1503	1R: HL Deb, 10 Jul 1912, Vol 12(5th), col 402
2R: HC Deb, 10 Apr 1912, Vol 36(5th), col 1349–1360	Cert: HL Deb, 16 Jul 1912, Vol 12(5th), col 495
R Rec: HC Deb, 12 Apr 1912, Vol 36(5th), col 1522	2R: HL Deb, 17 Jul 1912, Vol 12(5th), col 530
COS: HC Deb, 1 May 1912, Vol 37(5th), col 1948	Peer sub: HL Deb, 23 Jul 1912, Vol 12(5th), col 615
COS Rep: HC Deb, 13 May 1912, Vol 38(5th), col 911–912	SC Rep/Re-C'tted: HL Deb, 25 Jul 1912, Vol 12(5th), col 709
COS Res Ag: HC Deb, 7 Jun 1912, Vol 39(5th), col 487	CWH/Rep: HL Deb, 29 Jul 1912, Vol 12(5th), col 752
Rep: HC Deb, 4 Jul 1912, Vol 40(5th), col 1296	3R: HL Deb, 30 Jul 1912, Vol 12(5th), col 767
CWH/3R: HC Deb, 9 Jul 1912, Vol 40(5th), col 1782–1831	Royal Assent: HL Deb, 7 Aug 1912, Vol 12(5th), col 808
Royal Assent: HC Deb, 7 Aug 1912, Vol 41(5th), col 3290	

Parliamentary papers
Public Office (Sites) Bill (1912 HC Papers 79), Vol 4, p 785
Public Office (Sites) Bill (1912 HC Papers 272), Vol 4, p 797
Public Office (Sites) Bill (1912 HL Papers 106) Vol 7, p 433
Report of Select Committee on Public Office (Sites) Bill (1912 HC Papers 204), Vol 9, p 175

Patents and Designs Act 1914

PUBA27	1914	
Patents and Designs Act 1914 (4 & 5 Geo 5. c. 18)		
An Act to amend section ninety-one of the Patents and Designs Act, 1907		
Table of contents		
s 1 Amendment of s 91 [Patents and Designs Act 1907] 7 Edw 7 c 29 [agent and assignee may claim priority] s 2 Short title		
Journal		
House of Commons	**House of Lords**	
Pres: John Robertson (Par Sec BoT) Rep: Sir David Brymar Jones	Rep: Earl of Donoughmore (Ld Ch)	

(continued)

(continued)

17 Mar 1914	169 CJ 84	Bill Ord/1R	22 Jul 1914	146 LJ 325	Brought HC
24 Mar 1914	169 CJ 99	2R adj	22 Jul 1914	146 LJ 326	1R
31 Mar 1914	169 CJ 110	2R adj	3 Aug 1914	146 LJ 355	2R day app
31 Mar 1914	169 CJ 115	2R adj	4 Aug 1914	146 LJ 364	2R/C'tted CWH
1 Apr 1914	169 CJ 117	2R adj	5 Aug 1914	146 LJ 368	CWH/Rep w/o Amds
2 Apr 1914	169 CJ 121	2R adj	6 Aug 1914	146 LJ 376	3R
6 Apr 1914	169 CJ 125	2R adj	7 Aug 1914	146 LJ 389	Royal Assent
7 Apr 1914	169 CJ 131	2R adj			
14 Apr 1914	169 CJ 136	2R adj			
15 Apr 1914	169 CJ 140	2R adj			
16 Apr 1914	169 CJ 142	2R adj			
20 Apr 1914	169 CJ 147	2R adj			
21 Apr 1914	169 CJ 150	2R adj			
22 Apr 1914	169 CJ 156	2R adj			
27 Apr 1914	169 CJ 163	2R adj			
28 Apr 1914	169 CJ 166	2R adj			
29 Apr 1914	169 CJ 172	2R adj			
30 Apr 1914	169 CJ 174	2R adj			
5 May 1914	169 CJ 184	2R/C'tted SC			
6 May 1914	169 CJ 189	Assigned SC C			
15 Jun 1914	169 CJ 263	Mems dis			
15 Jun 1914	169 CJ 263	15 Mem app			
16 Jun 1914	169 CJ 268	Mem dis			
18 Jun 1914	169 CJ 275	SC Rep w/o Amds			
23 Jun 1914	169 CJ 284	Cons adj			
24 Jun 1914	169 CJ 289	Cons adj			
29 Jun 1914	169 CJ 299	Cons adj			
1 Jul 1914	169 CJ 308	Cons adj			
2 Jul 1914	169 CJ 313	Cons adj			
8 Jul 1914	169 CJ 324	Cons adj			
8 Jul 1914	169 CJ 333	Cons adj			
9 Jul 1914	169 CJ 337	Cons adj			
13 Jul 1914	169 CJ 344	Cons adj			
15 Jul 1914	169 CJ 349	Cons adj			
15 Jul 1914	169 CJ 354	Cons adj			
17 Jul 1914	169 CJ 362	Cons adj			
20 Jul 1914	169 CJ 368	Cons adj			
21 Jul 1914	169 CJ 372	3R			
7 Aug 1914	169 CJ 429	HL pass w/o Amds			
7 Aug 1914	169 CJ 434	Royal Assent			

Parliamentary debates

1R: HC Deb, 18 Mar 1914, Vol 59(5th), col 1896	1R: HL Deb, 22 Jul 1914, Vol 17(5th), col 102
2R: HC Deb, 5 May 1914, Vol 62(5th), col 249	2R: HL Deb, 4 Aug 1914, Vol 17(5th), col 370
Mem app: HC Deb, 16 Jun 1914, Vol 63(5th), col 955	CWH/Rep: HL Deb, 5 Aug 1914, Vol 17(5th), col 398
Rep: HC Deb, 18 Jun 1914, Vol 63(5th), col 1291	3R: HL Deb, 6 Aug 1914, Vol 17(5th), col 440
Cons/3R: HC Deb, 21 Jul 1914, Vol 65(5th), col 410	Royal Assent: HL Deb, 7 Aug 1914, Vol 17(5th), col 471
Royal Assent: HC Deb, 7 Aug 1914, Vol 65(5th), col 2190	

Parliamentary papers

Patents and Designs Bill (1914 HC Papers 126), Vol 5, p 257

Patents and Designs Bill (1914 HL Papers 189), Vol 7, p 521

Report from Standing Committee C on Patents and Designs Bill (1914 HC Papers 285), Vol 10, p 1

Supplement to Votes & Proceedings, 1914 – No amendments

Notes

Archive

Patents and Designs Bill 1914: National Archive (BT 209/483)

Patents, Designs, and Trade Marks (Temporary Rules) Act 1914

PUBA28	1914

Patents, Designs, and Trade Marks (Temporary Rules) Act 1914 (4 & 5 Geo 5. c. 27)

An Act to extend the powers of the Board of Trade during the continuance of the present hostilities to make Rules under the Patents and Designs Act, 1907, and the Trade Marks Act, 1905

Table of contents

s 1 Extension of power to make rules [Rules to suspend/licence enemy patents]
s 2 Short title
s 3 Duration

Journal

House of Commons			House of Lords		
Pres: Walter Runciman (Pr BoT) Rep: Donald Maclean (Dep Ch W&M)			No report		
7 Aug 1914	169 CJ 433	Bill Ord/1R	7 Aug 1914	146 LJ 386	Brought HC/1R/SO 39 susp
7 Aug 1914	169 CJ 433	2R/CWH/Rep w/o Amds/3R	7 Aug 1914	146 LJ 386	2R/Com neg/3R
7 Aug 1914	169 CJ 435	HL pass w/o Amds	7 Aug 1914	146 LJ 389	Royal Assent
7 Aug 1914	169 CJ 434	Royal Assent			

Parliamentary debates

1R/2R/3R: HC Deb, 7 Aug 1914, Vol 65(5th), col 2187	1R/2R/3R: HL Deb, 7 Aug 1914, Vol 17(5th), col 470
Royal Assent: HC Deb, 7 Aug 1914, Vol 65(5th), col 2190	Royal Assent: HL Deb, 7 Aug 1914, Vol 17(5th), col 471

Parliamentary papers

Patents, Designs, and Trade Marks (Temporary Rules) Bill (1914 HC Papers 368), Vol 5, p 261

Patents, Designs, and Trade Marks (Temporary Rules) Bill (1914 HL Papers 250), Vol 7, p 525

Supplement to Votes & Proceedings, 1914 – No amendments

Patents, Designs, and Trade Marks Temporary Rules (Amendment) Act 1914

PUBA29	1914

Patents, Designs, and Trade Marks Temporary Rules (Amendment) Act 1914 (4 & 5 Geo 5. c. 73)

An Act to amend the Patents, Designs, and Trade Marks (Temporary Rules) Act, 1914

Table of contents

s 1 Extension of powers to make temporary rules [extending to other intellectual property rights]
s 2 Short title

Journal

House of Commons			House of Lords		
Pres: Walter Runciman (Pr BoT) Rep: John Henry Whitley (Ch W&M)			No report		
25 Aug 1914	169 CJ 443	1R	28 Aug 1914	146 LJ 406	Brought HC/1R
26 Aug 1914	169 CJ 446	2R adj	28 Aug 1914	146 LJ 406	2R/C'tee neg/3R
27 Aug 1914	169 CJ 449	2R/CWH/Rep w/o Amds/3R	28 Aug 1914	146 LJ 408	Royal Assent
28 Aug 1914	169 CJ 451	HL pass w/o Amds			
28 Aug 1914	169 CJ 452	Royal Assent			

Parliamentary debates

1R: HC Deb, 25 Aug 1914, Vol 66(5th), col 28	1R/2R/3R: HL Deb, 28 Aug 1914, Vol 17(5th), col 553
2R/CWH/3R: HC Deb, 27 Aug 1914, Vol 66(5th), col 218–219	Royal Assent: HL Deb, 28 Aug 1914, Vol 17(5th), col 558
Royal Assent: HC Deb, 28 Aug 1914, Vol 66(5th), col 343	

(continued)

(continued)

Parliamentary papers
Patents, Designs, and Trade Marks Temporary Rules (Amendment) Bill (1914 HC Papers 386), Vol 5, p 265
Patents, Designs, and Trade Marks Temporary Rules (Amendment) Bill (1914 HL Papers 277), Vol 7, p 529
Supplement to Votes & Proceedings, 1914 – No amendments

Patents and Designs Act (Partial Suspension) Act 1915

PUBA30	1915
	Patents and Designs Act (Partial Suspension) Act 1915 (5 & 6 Geo 5. c. 85)

An Act to suspend the operation of section twenty-seven of the Patents and Designs Act, 1907, during the continuance of the present war, and for a period of six months thereafter

Table of contents
s 1 Suspension of 7 Edw 7 c 29 s 27 [Revocation of patent worked outside United Kingdom] s 2 Short title

Journal					
House of Commons			**House of Lords**		
Pres: Ernst Pretyman (Pr BoT) Rep: John Henry Whitley (Ch W&M)			No report		
10 Nov 1915	170 CJ 281	1R	22 Nov 1915	147 LJ 327	Brought HC/1R
11 Nov 1915	170 CJ 283	2R adj	23 Nov 1915	147 LJ 329	2R/Com neg/3R
15 Nov 1915	170 CJ 284	2R adj	23 Nov 1915	147 LJ 331	Royal Assent
16 Nov 1915	170 CJ 285	2R adj			
17 Nov 1915	170 CJ 287	2R adj			
18 Nov 1915	170 CJ 288	2R/CWH/Rep w/o Amds/3R			
23 Nov 1915	170 CJ 292	HL pass w/o Amds			
23 Nov 1915	170 CJ 293	Royal Assent			

Parliamentary debates	
1R: HC Deb, 10 Nov 1915, Vol 75(5th), col 1191	1R: HL Deb, 22 Nov 1915, Vol 20(5th), col 419
2R/CWH/3R: HC Deb, 18 Nov 1915, Vol 75(5th), col 2139–2142	2R/3R: HL Deb, 23 Nov 1915, Vol 20(5th), col 421–422
	Royal Assent: HL Deb, 23 Nov 1915, Vol 20(5th), col 444

Parliamentary papers
Patents and Designs (Partial Suspension) Bill (1914–16 HC Papers 155), Vol 3, p 257
Patents and Designs (Partial Suspension) Bill (1914–16 HL Papers 173), Vol 6, p 7
Supplement to Votes & Proceedings, 1914–16 – No amendments

Patents and Designs Act 1919

PUBA31	1919
	Patents and Designs Act 1919 (9 & 10 Geo 5. c. 80)
	An Act to amend the Patents and Designs Acts

Table of contents
s 1 Provisions for the prevention of abuse of monopoly rights s 2 Provision as to patents indorsed "licences of right" s 3 Enforcement of order for grant of licence s 4 Amendment of s 11 of principal Act [Patents and Designs Act 1907] as to opposition to grant of patent s 5 Amendment of s 12 of principal Act as to grant and sealing of patents s 6 Term of patent s 7 Amendment of s 18 of principal Act as to extension of term of patent s 8 Right of Crown to use patented inventions s 9 Power of court to grant relief in respect of particular claims

s 10 Amendment of s 34 of principal Act as to actions for infringement
s 11 Chemical produces and substances intended for food or medicine
s 12 Costs and security for costs
s 13 Amendment of s 41 (2) of principal Act as to anticipation
[s 14 Cancellation of registration of designs]
[s 15 Registration of designs to bind the Crown]
s 16 Registration of assignments, &c.
s 17 Amendment of s 75 of principal Act as to refusal to grant patents, &c.
s 18 Registration of patent agents
s 19 Definitions
s 20 Minor amendments of principal Act
s 21 Construction printing, and repeal
s 22 Short title and commencement
Schedule One – Minor Amendments of Principal Act

Proposed clauses

NC Amendment of s 38 of the Patents and Designs Act 1907
NC National service

Journal

House of Commons			House of Lords		
Pres: Sir Auckland Geddes (Pr BoT) Rep: No details			Rep: Lord Birkenhead LC		
15 Jul 1919	174 CJ 229	1R	11 Aug 1919	151 LJ 363	Brought HC/1R
17 Jul 1919	174 CJ 234	2R adj	14 Aug 1919	151 LJ 380	2R adj
28 Jul 1919	174 CJ 256	2R (adj motion)	7 Nov 1919	151 LJ 427	2R day app
29 Jul 1919	174 CJ 263	C'tted SC D	12 Nov 1919	151 LJ 436	2R/C'tted CWH
31 Jul 1919	174 CJ 272	Transferred to SC C	27 Nov 1919	151 LJ 465	CWH day app
6 Aug 1919	174 CJ 285	Rep with Amds	1 Dec 1919	151 LJ 468	CWH adj
8 Aug 1919	174 CJ 290	Cons adj	4 Dec 1919	151 LJ 499– V	**CWH**
8 Aug 1919	174 CJ 293	**Cons/3R**	8 Dec 1919	151 LJ 510	Report adj
16 Dec 1919	174 CJ 412	HL pass with Amds	11 Dec 1919	151 LJ 521	**Rep with Amds/Cons Amds**
18 Dec 1919	174 CJ 418	**HL Amds Ag with F. Amds**			
18 Dec 1919	174 CJ 420	HL Ag Further Amds	15 Dec 1919	151 LJ 533	**3R with Amds**
23 Dec 1919	174 CJ 428	Royal Assent	18 Dec 1919	151 LJ 554	HC pass with Amds
			18 Dec 1919	151 LJ 559	**HC Amds Ag**
			23 Dec 1919	151 LJ 573	Royal Assent

Parliamentary debates

1R: HC Deb, 15 Jul 1919, Vol 118(5th), col 219

2R: HC Deb, 28 Jul 1919, Vol 118(5th), col 1841–1868

SC C Deb, 6 Aug 1919, col 1–52

Rep: HC Deb, 6 Aug 1919, Vol 119(5th), col 371

Con/3R: HC Deb, 8 Aug 1919, Vol 119(5th), col 752–776

HL Amds: HC Deb, 17 Dec 1919, Vol 123(5th), col 597–609

Royal Assent: HC Deb, 28 Dec 1919, Vol 123(5th), col 1301

1R: HL Deb, 11 Aug 1919, Vol 36(5th), col 661

2R: HL Deb, 14 Aug 1919, Vol 36(5th), col 880–882

2R: HL Deb, 12 Nov 1919, Vol 37(5th), col 221–239

Com: HL Deb, 4 Dec 1919, Vol 37(5th), col 602–671

Rep: HL Deb, 11 Dec 1919, Vol 37(5th), col 936–640

3R: HL Deb, 15 Dec 1919, Vol 38(5th), col 88–89

HC Amds: HL Deb, 18 Dec 1919, Vol 38(5th), col 369

HC Amds: HL Deb, 18 Dec 1919, Vol 38(5th), col 437

Royal Assent: HL Deb, 23 Dec 1919, Vol 38(5th), col 538

Debates on particular provisions

s 1	HC Deb, 28 Jul 1919, Vol 118(5th), col 1841–1842, 1843–1847, 1850–1856, 1859, 1866–1867; SC C Deb, 6 Aug 1919, col 3–25 (V); HC Deb, 8 Aug 1919, Vol 119(5th), col 769–771; HL Deb, 12 Nov 1919, Vol 37(5th), col 221, 226–227, 238–239; HL Deb, 4 Dec 1919, Vol 37(5th), col 602–633; HL Deb, 11 Dec 1919, Vol 37(5th), col 936–937; HC Deb, 17 Dec 1919, Vol 123(5th), col 597–598	s 2	HC Deb, 28 Jul 1919, Vol 118(5th), col, 1841, 1843; SC C Deb, 6 Aug 1919, col 25–26; HL Deb, 12 Nov 1919, Vol 37(5th), col 223–224; HL Deb, 4 Dec 1919, Vol 37(5th), col 633–635; HL Deb, 11 Dec 1919, Vol 37(5th), col 937; HC Deb, 17 Dec 1919, Vol 123(5th), col 598–599
s 4	HL Deb, 4 Dec 1919, Vol 37(5th), col 635–637; HC Deb, 17 Dec 1919, Vol 123(5th), col 599–600	s 5	SC C Deb, 6 Aug 1919, col 26–27

(continued)

(continued)

s 6	HC Deb, 28 Jul 1919, Vol 118(5th), col 1842; SC C Deb, 6 Aug 1919, col 27–32; HL Deb, 12 Nov 1919, Vol 37(5th), col 224–225; HL Deb, 4 Dec 1919, Vol 37(5th), col 638–647	s 7	HC Deb, 28 Jul 1919, Vol 118(5th), col 1865–1866; HL Deb, 12 Nov 1919, Vol 37(5th), col 224–225; HL Deb, 11 Dec 1919, Vol 37(5th), col 938–939; HC Deb, 17 Dec 1919, Vol 123(5th), col 600–601
s 8	HC Deb, 28 Jul 1919, Vol 118(5th), col 1842, 1850–1851, 1863; SC C Deb, 6 Aug 1919, col 32–36; HC Deb, 8 Aug 1919, Vol 119(5th), col 771–773; HL Deb, 4 Dec 1919, Vol 37(5th), col 653–657; HC Deb, 17 Dec 1919, Vol 123(5th), col 601–604	s 9	HL Deb, 4 Dec 1919, Vol 37(5th), col 657–658; HC Deb, 17 Dec 1919, Vol 123(5th), col 604
s 11	HC Deb, 28 Jul 1919, Vol 118(5th), col 1860; SC C Deb, 6 Aug 1919, col 36–39; HL Deb, 4 Dec 1919, Vol 37(5th), col 658–659; HC Deb, 17 Dec 1919, Vol 123(5th), col 604	s 13	HL Deb, 4 Dec 1919, Vol 37(5th), col 659–660; HC Deb, 17 Dec 1919, Vol 123(5th), col 604–605
s 18	HC Deb, 28 Jul 1919, Vol 118(5th), col 1843; SC C Deb, 6 Aug 1919, col 39–40; HC Deb, 8 Aug 1919, Vol 119(5th), col 773–776; HL Deb, 4 Dec 1919, Vol 37(5th), col 661–664; HC Deb, 17 Dec 1919, Vol 123(5th), col 606–607	s 19	SC C Deb, 6 Aug 1919, col 40–42
s 22	SC C Deb, 6 Aug 1919, col 42–44; HL Deb, 4 Dec 1919, Vol 37(5th), col 664–665; HC Deb, 17 Dec 1919, Vol 123(5th), col 607	Sch	SC C Deb, 6 Aug 1919, col 44–50; HL Deb, 4 Dec 1919, Vol 37(5th), col 665–671; HC Deb, 17 Dec 1919, Vol 123(5th), col 607–609

Proposed clauses			
NC	Amendment of s 38 of the Patents and Designs Act 1907 HC Deb, 8 Aug 1919, Vol 119(5th), col 752–769	NC	National service HL Deb, 4 Dec 1919, Vol 37(5th), col 647–653

Parliamentary papers

Bills and amendments

Patents and Designs Bill (1919 HC Papers 131), Vol 2, p 559

Patents and Designs Bill (1919 HL Papers 177), Vol 6, p 239

  Amendments to be moved in Committee by Lord Queenborough (1919 HL Papers 177a), Vol 6, p 263

  Amendments to be moved in Committee by Lord Emmott (1919 HL Papers 177b), Vol 6, p 265

  Amendments to be moved in Committee by Lord Parmoor (1919 HL Papers 177c), Vol 6, p 267

  Amendments to be moved in Committee by Lord Parmoor (1919 HL Papers 177d), Vol 6, p 269

  Amendments to be moved in Committee by Lord Emmott (1919 HL Papers 177e), Vol 6, p 271

  Amendments to be moved in Committee by the Lord Chancellor (1919 HL Papers 177f), Vol 6, p 273

  Marshalled List of Amendments to be moved in Committee (1919 HL Papers 177**), Vol 6, p 277

  Second Marshalled List of Amendments to be moved in Committee (1919 HL Papers 177††), Vol 6, p 287

  Third List of Amendments to be moved in Committee (1919 HL Papers 177‡‡), Vol 6, p 299

Patents and Designs Bill (as amended in Committee) (1919 HL Papers 244), Vol 6, p 311

  Amendments to be moved on Report by Lord Moulton (1919 HL Papers 244a), Vol 6, p 335

  Amendments to be moved on Report by the Lord Chancellor (1919 HL Papers 244a), p 337

Patents and Designs Bill (as amended on Report) (1919 HL Papers 260), Vol 6, p 339

Patents and Designs Bill (as amended in Third Reading) (1919 HL Papers 272), Vol 6, p 365

Lords Amendments (1919 HC Papers 243), Vol 2, p 583

Report of Standing Committee C on Patents and Designs Bill (1919 HC Papers 161), Vol 6, p 1

Supplement to Votes & Proceedings – Not printed in 1919

Notes

Archive

Bill to Amend Patents and Designs Act 1907: Response from Reconstruction Committee (BT 209/488)

Bill to Amend Patents and Designs Act 1907: Advisory Committee on Commercial Intelligence: extract from minutes of meeting held to discuss proposed amendments (BT 209/489)

Replies from those who received draft copies of Bill: National Archive (BT 209/490)

Comments by Federation of British Industry: National Archive (BT 209/491)

Amended Copies of the Bill: National Archive (BT 209/492)

Patents and Designs Bill 1919: Correspondence after first reading: National Archive (BT 209/493)

Patents and Designs Bill 1917 and Trade Marks Bill 1917: Deputations from London Chamber of Commerce: National Archive (BT 209/494)

Patents and Designs Bill 1919: Miscellaneous Papers: National Archive (BT 209/495)

Patents and Designs Bill 1919: Correspondence after first reading: National Archive (BT 209/496)

Patents and Designs Bill 1919: Amendments to s 7: National Archive (BT 209/497)

Patents and Designs Bill 1919: Request by Ministry of Munitions of War: National Archive (BT 209/498)

Patents and Designs Bill 1919: Request by Admiralty for an Order: National Archive (BT 209/499)

Patents and Designs Bill: Cabinet Conclusions: National Archive (CAB 24/82/91)

Patents and Designs Bill Committee Minutes: Institute of Mechanical Engineers Archive (CMB 2/10)

Patents and Designs Bill 1919: Lord Chancellors Department National Archive (LCO 2/437)

Patents Rules 1920, renewal fees: Bill for Amendment of Patents and Designs Act 1907; term extended from 14 to 16 years: National Archive (BT 209/94)

Patents and Designs (Convention) Act 1928

PUBA32	1928
	Patents and Designs (Convention) Act 1928 (18 & 19 Geo 5. c. 3)

An Act to make such amendments of the Patents and Designs Acts, 1907 and 1919, as are necessary to be given to a Convention for the Protection of Industrial Property

Table of contents

s 1 Amendments of ss 7, 8 and 11 of the [Patents and Designs Act 1907] principal Act [Investigation of previous specifications in United Kingdom on applications for patents; Investigation of specifications published subsequently to application; Opposition to grant of patent]
s 2 Amendments of s 27 of the principal Act [Revocation of patents worked outside the United Kingdom]
s 3 Special provisions as to vessels, aircraft and land vehicles
s 4 Amendment of s 91 of principal Act [International and Colonial arrangements]
s 5 Short title, construction and printing

Journal

House of Commons			House of Lords		
Pres: Sir Philip Cunliffe-Lister (Pr BoT) and Herbert Williams (Par Sec BoT) Rep: James Hope (Ch W&M)			Rep: Earl of Donoughmore (Ld Ch)		
10 Feb 1928	183 CJ 17	1R	29 Feb 1928	160 LJ 45	Brought HC/1R
21 Feb 1928	183 CJ 33	2R/C'tted CWH	1 Mar 1928	160 LJ 47	2R day app
23 Feb 1928	183 CJ 36	CWH	7 Mar 1928	160 LJ 53	2R/C'tted CWH
28 Feb 1928	183 CJ 44	Rep w/o Amds/3R	13 Mar 1928	160 LJ 59	CWH adj
21 Mar 1928	183 CJ 78	HL pass w/o Amds	14 Mar 1928	160 LJ 60–V	**CWH/Rep w/o Amds**
28 Mar 1928	183 CJ 91	Royal Assent	15 Mar 1928	160 LJ 62	Paper Presented (Cmd 3057)
			20 Mar 1928	160 LJ 69	3R
			28 Mar 1928	160 LJ 82	Royal Assent

Parliamentary debates

1R: HC Deb, 10 Feb 1928, Vol 213(5th), col 405	1R: HL Deb, 29 Feb 1928, Vol 70(5th), col 287
2R: HC Deb, 21 Feb 1928, Vol 213(5th), col 1528–1532	2R: HL Deb, 7 Mar 1928, Vol 70(5th), col 403–406
CWH/3R: HC Deb, 28 Feb 1928, Vol 214(5th), col 360	CWH adj: HL Deb, 13 Mar 1928, Vol 70(5th), col 430
HL pass: HC Deb, 21 Mar 1928, Vol 215(5th), col 383	CWH: HL Deb, 14 Mar 1928, Vol 70(5th), col 450–464
Royal Assent: HC Deb, 28 Mar 1928, Vol 215(5th), col 1227	3R day app: HL Deb, 14 Mar 1928, Vol 70(5th), col 465
	3R: HL Deb, 20 Mar 1928, Vol 70(5th), col 513
	Royal Assent: HL Deb, 28 Mar 1928, Vol 70(5th), col 692

(continued)

(continued)

Debates on particular provisions			
s 1	HC Deb, 21 Feb 1928, Vol 213(5th), col 1529; HL Deb, 7 Mar 1928, Vol 70(5th), col 404–406; HL Deb, 14 Mar 1928, Vol 70(5th), col 451–456	s 2	HC Deb, 21 Feb 1928, Vol 213(5th), col 1529
s 3	HC Deb, 21 Feb 1928, Vol 213(5th), col 1529; HL Deb, 7 Mar 1928, Vol 70(5th), col 404	s 4	HC Deb, 21 Feb 1928, Vol 213(5th), col 1529–1530
s 5	HC Deb, 21 Feb 1928, Vol 213(5th), col 1530, 1531–1532; HL Deb, 7 Mar 1928, Vol 70(5th), col 406		

Parliamentary papers
Patents and Designs (Convention) Bill (1928 HC Papers 26), Vol 4, p 27
Patents and Designs (Convention) Bill (1928 HL Papers 8), Vol 3
Amendment Moved in Committee by Lord Parmoor (1928 HL Papers 8a), Vol 3
Patents and Designs (Convention) Bill, Provisions as proposed to be amended 1928 (1928 Cmd 3057) Vol 19, p 867: 15 Mar 1928 (183 CJ 68; 160 LJ 62)
Supplement to Votes & Proceedings, 1928 – No amendments

Notes
Archive
Patents and Designs (Convention) Bill 1928: House of Commons: National Archive (BT 209/717)
Patents and Designs Bill: Cabinet Minutes: National Archive (CAB 23/57/6)
Patents and Designs Bill: Cabinet Minutes: National Archive (CAB 23/57/3)

Patents and Designs Act 1932

PUBA33	1932
Patents and Designs Act 1932 (22 & 23 Geo 5. c. 32)	
An Act to amend the Patents and Designs Acts, 1907 to 1928	

Table of contents
s 1 Provisional protection
s 2 Amendments of s 7 of [Patents and Designs Act 1907] principal Act and provision as to anticipation in documents other than British specifications
s 3 Grounds for revocation of patent
s 4 Provisions as to unfair exercise of process patent
s 5 Power of court in infringement action as regards relief in respect of particular claims in patents
s 6 Remedy in case of groundless threats of legal proceedings
s 7 Power to give direction as to development of patents jointly owned
s 8 Subject matter of patents for chemical products and substances intended for food or medicine
s 9 Amendment of s 50 of principal Act
s 10 Period of secrecy as regards designs
s 11 Amendments of s 75 of principal Act as to frivolous applications and applications for patents for illegal inventions
s 12 Tribunal for appeals from the Comptroller
s 13 Minor amendments of principal Act
s 14 Construction and printing
s 15 Short title and commencement
Schedule One – Minor Amendments of Principal Act

Proposed clause
NC Unfair exercise of process patent

Journal	
House of Commons	**House of Lords**
Rep: Sir William Jenkins Money Res Rep: Stanley Baldwin	Pre: Lord Templeman (Ld-in-Wait) Rep: Earl of Onslow (Ld Ch)

12 May 1932	187 CJ 197	Brought HL	21 Apr 1932	164 LJ 147	1R
25 May 1932	187 CJ 207	1R	26 Apr 1932	164 LJ 154	2R/C'tted CWH
7 Jun 1932	187 CJ 230	2R/Money Res	10 May 1932	164 LJ 176	**CWH/Rep w/o Amds**
8 Jun 1932	187 CJ 232	Money Res Rep	12 May 1932	164 LJ 184	**3R with Amds**
8 Jun 1932	187 CJ 233	C'tted SC A	27 Jun 1932	164 LJ 248	HC Ret with Amds
16 Jun 1932	187 CJ 243	Rep with Amds	28 Jun 1932	164 LJ 253	HC Amds to be Cons
24 Jun 1932	187 CJ 258	Cons/3R	30 Jun 1932	164 LJ 270	**HC Amds Cons**
1 Jul 1932	187 CJ 271	HL Ag Amds	12 Jul 1932	164 LJ 303	Royal Assent
12 Jul 1932	187 CJ 297	Royal Assent			

Parliamentary debates

Brought HL: HC Deb, 12 May 1932, Vol 265(5th), col 2091

1R: HC Deb, 25 May 1932, Vol 266(5th), col 371

2R: HC Deb, 7 Jun 1932, Vol 266(5th), col 1890–1904

Money: HC Deb, 7 Jun 1932, Vol 266(5th), col 1904

Money Res: HC Deb, 8 Jun 1932, Vol 266(5th), col 2076

Mem Add: HC Deb, 10 Jun 1932, Vol 266(5th), col 2263

Chair App: HC Deb, 14 Jun 1932, Vol 267(5th), col 197

SC: SC A Deb, 16 Jun 1932, col 941–972

Rep: HC Deb, 16 Jun 1932, Vol 267(5th), col 530

Cons/3R: HC Deb, 24 Jun 1932, Vol 267(5th), col 1434–1442

HL Ag Amds: HC Deb, 1 Jul 1932, Vol 267(5th), col 2130

Royal Assent: HC Deb, 12 Jul 1932, Vol 268(5th), col 1166

1R: HL Deb, 21 Apr 1932, Vol 84(5th), col 118

2R: HL Deb, 26 Apr 1932, Vol 84(5th), col 196–201

Com: HL Deb, 10 May 1932, Vol 84(5th), col 345–351

3R: HL Deb, 12 May 1932, Vol 84(5th), col 427

HC pass: HL Deb, 27 Jun 1932, Vol 85(5th), col 195

HC Amds: HL Deb, 30 Jun 1932, Vol 85(5th), col 484

Royal Assent: HL Deb, 12 Jul 1932, Vol 85(5th), col 686

Debates on particular provisions

s 1	SC Deb A, 16 Jun 1932, col 941	s 2	HC Deb, 7 Jun 1932, Vol 266(5th), col 1892; SC Deb A, 16 Jun 1932, col 941–947; HL Deb, 26 Apr 1932, Vol 84(5th), col 198–199
s 3	SC Deb A, 16 Jun 1932, col 947–950; HC Deb, 24 Jun 1932, Vol 267(5th), col 1434–1435	s 4	SC Deb A, 16 Jun 1932, col 950–951; HC Deb, 24 Jun 1932, Vol 267(5th), col 1435–1436
s 5	HC Deb, 24 Jun 1932, Vol 267(5th), col 1436–1439	s 6	SC Deb A, 16 Jun 1932, col 951–952;
s 7	N/A	s 8	SC Deb A, 16 Jun 1932, col 952–953; HC Deb, 24 Jun 1932, Vol 267(5th), col 1439
s 9	SC Deb A, 16 Jun 1932, col 954	s 10	N/A
s 11	HL Deb, 26 Apr 1932, Vol 84 (5th), col 199	s 12	SC Deb A, 16 Jun 1932, col 954–956; HL Deb, 26 Apr 1932, Vol 84 (5th), col 199
s 13	SC Deb A, 16 Jun 1932, col 956	s 14	HL Deb, 26 Apr 1932, Vol 84 (5th), col 198
Sch	SC Deb A, 16 Jun 1932, col 957–970; HL Deb, 10 May 1932, Vol 84(5th), col 345–351; HC Deb, 24 Jun 1932, Vol 267(5th), col 1440–1442; HL Deb, 26 Apr 1932, Vol 84 (5th), col 345–351		

Proposed clause

| NC | Unfair exercise of process patent: SC A Deb, 16 Jun 1932, col 970 |

Parliamentary papers

Patents and Designs Bill (1932 HL Papers 51), Vol 2

Amendment to be Moved in Committee by Lord Marks (1932 HL Papers 51a), Vol 2

(continued)

(continued)

Patents and Designs Bill (1931–32 HC Papers 87), Vol 3, p 113
Patents and Designs Bill (as amended in Committee) (1931–32 HC Papers 100), Vol 3, p 141
Commons Amendments (1932 HL Papers 117), Vol 2
Report of Standing Committee A on the Patents and Designs Bill (1931–32 HC Papers 89), Vol 5, p 117
Memorandum on the Patents and Designs Bill (1931–32 Cmd 4067), Vol 20, p 693: 26 Apr 1932 (187 CJ 168; 164 LJ 153)
Patents and Designs Bill: Memorandum explaining the financial resolution (1931–32 Cmd 4096), Vol 20, p 757: 7 Jun 1932 (187 CJ 228; 164 LJ 207)
Supplement to Votes & Proceedings, 1932   8 Jun 1932, p 1243; 13 Jun 1932, p 1275–1277; 14 Jun 1932, p 1279–1284; 16 Jun 1932, p 1285–1290

Notes
Archives
Draft Bill to deal with Recommendations of the Sargent Committee: National Archive (BT 209/19)
Bill to amend Patents and Designs Act 1907–28: National Archive (BT 209/92)
Patents and Designs Bill 1932: Notes on Clauses and Amendments (BT 209/521)
Patents and Designs Bill 1932: Notes and Memoranda: National Archive (BT 209/522)
Patents and Designs Bill 1932: Views on Interested Bodies: National Archive (BT 209/523)
Patents and Designs Bill: Cabinet Conclusions: National Archive (CAB 23/71/5)
Medical Research Council: Medical Inventions and Discoveries: Remuneration and Reward: Patents and Designs Bill 1932: National Archive (MH 58/260)
Patents and Designs Act and the Practice of the Patent Office: Report of Departmental Committee: National Archive (LCO 2/1192)

Patents &c. (International Conventions) Act 1938

PUBA34	1938
	Patents &c. (International Conventions) Act 1938 (1 & 2 Geo 6. c. 29)

An Act to give effect to an International Convention for the Protection of Industrial Property and to amend the provisions of the Patents and Designs Acts, 1907 to 1932, relating to matters affected by the said Convention; and to give effect to an International Agreement regarding false indications of origin on goods and to amend the provisions of the Merchandise Marks Acts, 1887 to 1926, relating to matters affected by the said Agreement

Table of contents
s 1 Mention of inventor as such in patent
s 2 Term in case of new patents
s 3 No revocation until two years after first compulsory licence
s 4 Construction of s (2) of s 91 of Patents and Designs Act [1907]
s 5 Elements of inventions not formally claimed in Convention country
s 6 Appeal from Comptroller's refusal of application under s 91 of Patents and Designs Act [1907]
s 7 Repeal of proviso \(b) to s \(4) of s 91 of Patents and Designs Act [1907]
s 8 Certain applications abroad equivalent to regular national applications
s 9 Orders in Council as to Convention countries
[s 10 Amendment of s 5 of Merchandise Marks Act 1887]
s 11 Consequential and minor amendments of the Patents and Designs Act [1907]
s 12 Short title, citation, construction, printing and commencement
Schedule One – Consequential and minor amendments of Patents and Designs Act [1907]

Journal					
House of Commons			**House of Lords**		
Rep: Douglas Clifton Brown (Dep Ch W&M)			Pres: Lord Templemore (Ld-in-Wait) Rep: Earl of Onslow (Ld Ch)		
10 Feb 1938	193 CJ 100	Brought HL	7 Dec 1937	170 LJ 37	1R
15 Feb 1938	193 CJ 108	1R	14 Dec 1937	170 LJ 43	2R/C'tted CWH
8 Apr 1938	193 CJ 202	2R	1 Feb 1938	170 LJ 62	**CWH/Rep with Amd**
12 Apr 1938	193 CJ 208	C'tted SC A	8 Feb 1938	170 LJ 73	**Cons with Amd**
10 May 1938	193 CJ 248	Rep with Amds	10 Feb 1938	170 LJ 76	**3R with Amd**
19 May 1938	193 CJ 266	**3R with Amds**	23 May 1938	170 LJ 206	HC Ret with Amd
26 May 1938	193 CJ 275	HL Ag Amds	26 May 1938	170 LJ 229	**HC Amd Cons**
26 May 1938	193 CJ 276	Royal Assent	26 May 1938	170 LJ 234	Royal Assent

Parliamentary debates	
Brought HL: HC Deb, 10 Feb 1938, Vol 331(5th), col 1269–1270	1R: HL Deb, 7 Dec 1937, Vol 107(5th), col 351
1R: HC Deb, 15 Feb 1938, Vol 331(5th), col 1714	2R: HL Deb, 14 Dec 1937, Vol 107(5th), col 466–479
2R: HC Deb, 8 Apr 1938, Vol 334(5th), col 714–730	Com: HL Deb, 1 Feb 1938, Vol 107(5th), col 565–570
Mem add: HC Deb, 28 Apr 1838, Vol 335(5th), col 315	Rep: HL Deb, 8 Feb 1938, Vol 107(5th), col 616–618
SC: SC A Deb, 10 May 1938, col 785–806	3R: HL Deb, 10 Feb 1938, Vol 107(5th), col 643
Rep: HC Deb, 10 May 1938, Vol 335(5th), col 1426	HC pass with Amds: HL Deb, 23 May 1938, Vol 109(5th), col 286
Cons/3R: HC Deb, 19 May 1938, Vol 336(5th), col 701–703	HC Amds Ag: HL Deb, 26 May 1938, Vol 109(5th), col 598–602
HL Ag Amds: HC Deb, 26 May 1938, Vol 336(5th), col 1398	Royal Assent: HL Deb, 26 May 1938, Vol 109(5th), col 663
Royal Assent: HC Deb, 26 May 1938, Vol 336(5th), col 1489	

Debates on particular provisions			
s 1	HL Deb, 8 Feb 1938, Vol 107(5th), col 616–617; SC A Deb, 10 May 1938, col 785–791; HL Deb, 26 May 1938, Vol 109(5th), col 599–600	s 3	SC A Deb, 10 May 1938, col 791–802; HL Deb, 26 May 1938, Vol 109(5th), col 600–601
s 4	HC Deb, 19 May 1938, Vol 336(5th), col 701–702	s 5	SC A Deb, 10 May 1938, col 802
s 6	SC A Deb, 10 May 1938, col 802; HL Deb, 26 May 1938, Vol 109(5th), col 601	Sch	SC A Deb, 10 May 1938, col 804; HC Deb, 19 May 1938, Vol 336(5th), col 703; HL Deb, 26 May 1938, Vol 109(5th), col 601–602

Parliamentary papers
Patents &c. (International Conventions) Bill (1938 HL Papers 19), Vol 3
Amendments to be Moved in Committee by Lord Templemore (1938 HL Papers 19a), Vol 3
Patents &c. (International Conventions) Bill (as amended in Committee) (1938 HL Papers 30), Vol 3
Amendments to be moved on Report by Lord Templemore (1938 HL Papers 30a), Vol 3
Patents &c. (International Conventions) Bill (as amended on Report) (1938 HL Papers 33), Vol 3
Patents &c. (International Conventions) Bill (1938 HC Papers 84), Vol 4, p 37
Patents &c. (International Conventions) Bill (as amended in Committee) (1938 HC Papers 141), Vol 4, p 53
Commons Amendments (1938 HL Papers 108), Vol 3
Report of Standing Committee A on the Patents &c. (International Conventions) Bill (1937–38 HC Papers 115), Vol 7, p 565
Supplement to Votes & Proceedings, 1938
3 May 1938, p 1337–1340; 6 May 1938, p 1393–1397; 10 May 1938, p 1399–1403

Notes
Archive
Patents and Designs (International Conventions) Bill: Cabinet Conclusions: National Archive (CAB 24/272/10 and CAB 23/90A/3 and CAB 23/90A/6; also see CAB 26/21 and 22)
Patents and Designs (International Conventions) Bill and Patents and Designs (Limits of Time Bill) 1939: Arrangement of Clauses, amendments, and memoranda: National Archive (BT 103/75)

Patents and Designs (Limits of Time) Act 1939

PUBA35	1939
Patents and Designs (Limits of Time) Act 1939 (2 & 3 Geo 6. c. 32)	
An Act to amend certain provisions of the Patents and Designs Acts, 1907 to 1938, relating to time limits	

(continued)

(continued)

Table of contents
s 1 Time for leaving complete specification
s 2 Time within which application must be in order and for acceptance of complete specification
s 3 Amendments as to various time limits
s 4 Provisions as to failure to comply with certain time limits of the principal Act [Patents and Designs Act 1907]
s 5 Short title, citation, interpretation and printing

Journal

House of Commons			House of Lords		
Rep: Sir Cyril Entwhistle			Pre: Lord Templemore (Gov Ch Whip) Rep: Earl of Onslow (Ld Ch)		
21 Mar 1939	194 CJ 139	Brought HL	21 Feb 1939	171 LJ 83	1R
24 Mar 1939	194 CJ 147	1R	7 Mar 1939	171 LJ 101	2R/C'tted CWH
20 Apr 1939	194 CJ 180	2R	14 Mar 1939	171 LJ 111	**CWH/Rep with Amds**
21 Apr 1939	194 CJ 182	C'tted SC A	16 Mar 1939	171 LJ 115	Cons
13 Jun 1939	194 CJ 279	Transferred to SC C	21 Mar 1939	171 LJ 120	3R
20 Jun 1939	194 CJ 293	Rep with Amds	4 Jul 1939	171 LJ 291	HC pass with Amds
3 Jul 1939	194 CJ 318	3R	11 Jul 1939	171 LJ 309	**HC Amd Cons**
11 Jul 1939	194 CJ 335	HL Ag Amds	13 Jul 1939	171 LJ 316	Royal Assent
13 Jul 1939	194 CJ 344	Royal Assent			

Parliamentary debates

Brought HL: HC Deb, 21 Mar 1939, Vol 345(5th), col 1126	1R: HL Deb, 21 Feb 1939, Vol 111(5th), col 848
1R: HC Deb, 24 Mar 1939, Vol 345(5th), col 1596	2R: HL Deb, 7 Mar 1939, Vol 112(5th), col 28–30
2R: HC Deb, 20 Apr 1939, Vol 346(5th), col 641–644	Com: HL Deb, 14 Mar 1939, Vol 112(5th), col 185–186
Mem add: HC Deb, 2 May 1939 Vol 346(5th), col 1702	Rep: HL Deb, 16 Mar 1939, Vol 112(5th), col 295
Mem add: HC Deb, 13 Jun 1939, Vol 348(5th), col 1118–1119	3R: HL Deb, 21 Mar 1939, Vol 112(5th), col 366
SC: SC C Deb, 20 Jun 1939, col 813–820	HC pass: HL Deb, 4 Jul 1939, Vol 113(5th), col 913
Rep: HC Deb, 20 Jun 1939, Vol 348(5th), col 2022–2023	HC Amds Ag: HL Deb, 11 Jul 1939, Vol 114(5th), col 49–50
Cons/3R: HC Deb, 3 Jul 1939, Vol 349(5th), col 1079	Royal Assent: HL Deb, 13 Jul 1939, Vol 114(5th), col 172
HL Ag Amds: HC Deb, 11 Jul 1939, Vol 349(5th), col 2074	
Royal Assent: HC Deb, 13 Jul 1939, Vol 349(5th), col 2481	

Debates on particular provisions

s 1	HC Deb, 20 Apr 1939, Vol 346(5th), col 642	s 2	HL Deb, 7 Mar 1939, Vol 112(5th), col 29–30; HL Deb, 14 Mar 1939, Vol 112(5th), col 186; HC Deb, 20 Apr 1939, Vol 346(5th), col 641–642; SC C Deb, 20 Jun 1939, col 813–814
s 3	HL Deb, 14 Mar 1939, Vol 112(5th), col 186; HC Deb, 20 Apr 1939, Vol 346(5th), col 643	s 4	HC Deb, 20 Apr 1939, Vol 346(5th), col 643
s 5	SC C Deb, 20 Jun 1939, col 814–820		

Parliamentary papers

Patents and Designs (Limits of Time) Bill (1939 HL Papers 37), Vol 3

   Amendments to be Moved in Committee by Lord Templemore (1939 HL Papers 37a), Vol 3

Patents and Designs (Limits of Time) Bill (as amended in Committee) (1939 HL Papers 47), Vol 3

Patents and Designs (Limits of Time) Bill (1938–39 HC Papers 98), Vol 4, p 819

Patents and Designs (Limits of Time) Bill (as amended in Committee) (1938–39 HC Papers 161), Vol 4, p 829

Commons Amendments (1939 HL Papers 144), Vol 3

Report of Standing Committee C on the Patents and Designs (Limits of Time) (1938–39 HC Papers 136), Vol 8, p 291

Supplement to Votes & Proceedings, 1938–9

   15 May 1939, p 1181; 16 Jun 1939, p 1571; 20 Jun 1939, p 1583

Notes
Archive
Patents and Designs (International Conventions) Bill and Patents and Designs (Limits of Time Bill) 1939: Arrangement of Clauses, amendments, and memoranda: National Archive (BT 103/75)
Correspondence on drafting Patents and Designs (Limit of Time) Bill: National Archive (BT 209/371)
Patents and Designs Act – Amendment of Statutory Time Limits: Cabinet Conclusions: National Archives (CAB 23/94/7) (also see CAB 26/24)
Patents and Designs (Limits of Time) Bill: Cabinet Conclusions: National Archives (CAB 23/97/7)

Patents, Designs, Copyright and Trade Marks (Emergency) Act 1939

PUBA36	1939
Patents, Designs, Copyright and Trade Marks (Emergency) Act 1939 (2 & 3 Geo 6. c. 107)	
An Act to make such special provision with respect to patents, registered designs, copyright and trade marks, as is expedient to meet any emergency which may arise as a result of war	

Table of contents

s 1 Provisions as to existing licences under patents, designs and copyright of enemies and enemy subjects, and as to contracts relating thereto
s 2 Power of Comptroller to grant licences under patents, designs or copyright of enemies and enemy subjects
[s 3 Power of Comptroller to suspend trade mark rights of an enemy or an enemy subject]
s 4 Effect of war on grant of patents and registration of designs and trade marks
[s 5 Effect of war on international arrangements as to copyright]
s 6 Power of Comptroller to extend time limits having regard to war circumstances
s 7 Evidence relating to nationality and place of residence, and decisions relating to enemy character
s 8 Persons to be heard before making of orders
s 9 Rules and fees
s 10 Interpretation
s 11 Short title, commencement and extent

Journal

House of Commons			House of Lords		
Pres: Oliver Stanley (Pr BoT) Rep: Douglas Clifton Brown (Dep Ch W&M)			No report		
7 Sep 1939	194 CJ 425	1R	15 Sep 1939	171 LJ 403	Brought HC/1R
13 Sep 1939	194 CJ 428	2R/C'tted CWH	20 Sep 1939	171 LJ 405	2R/C'tted CWH
14 Sep 1939	194 CJ 429	CWH/Rep with Amds/3R	21 Sep 1939	171 LJ 407	CWH neg/3R
21 Sep 1939	194 CJ 432	HL pass w/o Amds	21 Sep 1939	171 LJ 408	Royal Assent
21 Sep 1939	194 CJ 432	Royal Assent			

Parliamentary debates

1R: HC Deb, 7 Sep 1939, Vol 351(5th), col 588–589	1R: HL Deb, 15 Sep 1939, Vol 114(5th), col 1079
2R: HC Deb, 13 Sep 1939, Vol 351(5th), col 742–744	2R: HL Deb, 20 Sep 1939, Vol 114(5th), col 1100–1107
CWH/Rep/3R: HC Deb, 14 May 1939, Vol 351(5th), col 797–799	3R/Royal Assent: HL Deb, 21 Sep 1939, Vol 114(5th), col 1120
HL pass w/o Amds: HC Deb, 21 Sep 1939, Vol 351(5th), col 1071	
Royal Assent: HC Deb, 21 Sep 1939, Vol 351(5th), col 1092	

Parliamentary papers

Patents, Designs, Copyright and Trade Marks (Emergency) Bill (1938–39 HC Papers 270), Vol 4, p 839

Patents, Designs, Copyright and Trade Marks (Emergency) Bill (1938–39 HL Papers 214), Vol 3

Supplement to Votes & Proceedings, 1938–39 – No amendments

(continued)

(continued)

Notes
Archive
Patents, Designs, Copyright and Trade Marks (Emergency) Act 1939: Cabinet Conclusions: National Archive (CAB 75/5/15)
Stamp Duty: Patents, Designs, Copyright and Trade Marks (Emergency) Bill 1939: National Archive (IR 40/5786)
Patents, Designs, Copyright and Trade Marks (Emergency Legislation) Amendment of s 2 and 3: National Archive (BT 103/66)

Patents and Designs Act 1942

PUBA37	1942

Patents and Designs Act 1942 (5 & 6 Geo 6. c. 6)
An Act to amend the Patents and Designs Acts, 1907 to 1939, as respects the extension of the term of a patent where the patentee has suffered loss by reason of hostilities, as respects the right of the Crown to use inventions and designs, and as respects arrangements with other countries relating to inventions and designs

Table of contents
s 1 Amendments as to extension of patents where loss by reason of hostilities
s 2 Amendments as to right of Crown to use inventions
s 3 Arrangements with other countries
s 4 Short title, citation, printing and interpretation

Journal					
House of Commons			**House of Lords**		
Rep: Patrick Munro (Par Sec Tr)			Pres: Lord Templemore (Gov Ch Whip) Rep: Earl of Onslow (Ld Ch)		
10 Dec 1941	197 CJ 23	Brought HL	25 Nov 1941	174 LJ 13	1R
11 Dec 1941	197 CJ 25	1R	2 Dec 1941	174 LJ 16	2R/C'tted CWH
20 Jan 1942	197 CJ 36	2R/Money Res/C'tted CWH	9 Dec 1941	174 LJ 22	CWH/Rep w/o Amds
3 Feb 1942	197 CJ 42	Money Res Rep/CWH	10 Dec 1941	174 LJ 24	**3R with Amds**
10 Feb 1942	197 CJ 48	Rep with Amds/3R	10 Feb 1942	174 LJ 55	HC pass with Amds/Ag
25 Feb 1942	197 CJ 55	HL Ag Amds	26 Feb 1942	174 LJ 67	Royal Assent
26 Feb 1942	197 CJ 56	Royal Assent			

Parliamentary debates	
1R: HC Deb, 11 Dec 1941, Vol 376(5th), col 1700	1R: HL Deb, 25 Nov 1941, Vol 121(5th), col 73
2R: HC Deb, 20 Jan 1942, Vol 377(5th), col 302–306	2R: HL Deb, 2 Dec 1941, Vol 121(5th), col 143–145
CWH: HC Deb, 3 Feb 1942, Vol 377(5th), col 1119–1120	CWH: HL Deb, 9 Dec 1941, Vol 121(5th), col 203
Cons/3R: HC Deb, 10 Feb 1942, Vol 377(5th), col 1472	3R: HL Deb, 10 Dec 1941, Vol 121(5th), col 241
HL Ag Amds: HC Deb, 25 Feb 1942, Vol 378(5th), col 216	HC Amds Ag: HL Deb, 10 Feb 1942, Vol 121(5th), col 748
Royal Assent: HC Deb, 26 Feb 1942, Vol 378(5th), col 407	Royal Assent: HL Deb, 26 Feb 1942, Vol 122(5th), col 77

Parliamentary papers
Patents and Designs Bill (1941–42 HL Papers 2), Vol 1
Patents and Designs Bill (1941–42 HC Papers 8), Vol 1, p 395
Supplement to Votes & Proceedings, 1941–42 – No amendments

Notes
Archive materials
Amendment of s 18 of Patents and Designs Bill: Extension of term of patents: National Archive (BT 209/185)
Draft Bill Patents and Designs Act 1941: Ministry of Aviation: National Archive (AVIA 15/2403)
Admiralty and Inventions: Suggestions for changes to Patents and Designs Act: National Archive (ADM 1/11768)
Draft Bill for making certain amendment in and additions to Patents and Designs Act 1907: Cabinet Conclusion: National Archive (CAB 75/12/101)

Patents and Designs Act 1946

PUBA38	1946

Patents and Designs Act 1946 (9 & 10 Geo 6. c. 44)

An Act to amend the Patents and Designs Acts, 1907 to 1942, and the Patents, Designs, Copyright and Trade Marks (Emergency) Act, 1939, in respect of matters arising out of hostilities or the communication of inventions and designs in accordance with agreements or arrangements with other countries

Table of contents
s 1 Application to Comptroller for extension of term of patents where loss arises by reason of hostilities
s 2 Protection of inventions and designs communicated under agreements or arrangements with other countries
s 3 Revocation of patents for inventions worked in war-time by or on behalf of Government departments
s 4 Inventions and designs made in Germany or Japan
s 5 Power of Comptroller to publish specifications etc., accompanying abandoned German or Japanese applications
s 6 Amendment of enactments providing for extension of time
s 7 Interpretation
s 8 Short title, citation, extent and printing

Journal

House of Commons			**House of Lords**		
Rep: Thomas Burden			Pres and Rep: Lord Pakenham (Ld-in-Wait)		
26 Feb 1946	201 CJ 165	Brought HL	24 Jan 1946	178 LJ 150	1R
27 Feb 1946	201 CJ 166	1R	5 Feb 1946	178 LJ 162	2R/C'tted CWH
11 Mar 1946	201 CJ 182	2R/C'tted	6 Feb 1946	178 LJ 165	CWH date
12 Mar 1946	201 CJ 183	C'tted SC B	14 Feb 1946	178 LJ 177	**CWH**
26 Mar 1946	201 CJ 202	Rep with Amds	21 Feb 1946	178 LJ 187	**Rep with Amds**
5 Apr 1946	201 CJ 217	3R	26 Feb 1946	178 LJ 192	3R
15 Apr 1946	201 CJ 228	Royal Assent	9 Apr 1946	178 LJ 241	HC pass with Amds/Ag
			15 Apr 1946	178 LJ 253	Royal Assent

Parliamentary debates

Brought HL: 1R: HC Deb, 26 Feb 1946, Vol 419(5th), col 1754	1R: HL Deb, 24 Jan 1946, Vol 138(5th), col 1089
1R: HC Deb, 27 Feb 1946, Vol 419(5th), col 1934	2R: HL Deb, 5 Feb 1946, Vol 139(5th), col 197–216
2R: HC Deb, 11 Mar 1946, Vol 420(5th), col 873–886	CWH: HL Deb, 14 Feb 1946, Vol 139(5th), col 567–580
SC: SC B Deb, 26 Mar 1946, col 963–970	Rep: HL Deb, 21 Feb 1946, Vol 139(5th), col 846–851
Cons/3R: HC Deb, 5 Apr 1946, Vol 421(5th), col 1513	3R: HL Deb, 26 Feb 1946, Vol 139(5th), col 890
Royal Assent: HC Deb, 15 Apr 1946, Vol 421(5th), col 2377	HC Ag Amds: HL Deb, 9 Apr 1946, Vol 140(5th), col 639
	Royal Assent: HL Deb, 15 Apr 1946, Vol 140(5th), col 777

Debates on particular provisions

s 1	HL Deb, 5 Feb 1946, Vol 139(5th), col 198–202, 205, 211–212; HC Deb, 11 Mar 1946, Vol 420(5th), col 874, 877, 879, 880–882; SC B Deb, 26 Mar 1946, col 965–970	s 2	HL Deb, 5 Feb 1946, Vol 139(5th), col 202–203, 206–207; HC Deb, 11 Mar 1946, Vol 420(5th), col 874–875, 879
s 3	HL Deb, 5 Feb 1946, Vol 139(5th), col 202–204; HC Deb, 11 Mar 1946, Vol 420(5th), col 875	s 4	HL Deb, 5 Feb 1946, Vol 139(5th), col 204, 205–206, 207–209, 209–210, 215; HL Deb, 14 Feb 1946, Vol 139(5th), col 567–580; HC Deb, 11 Mar 1946, Vol 420(5th), col 876–877
s 5	HL Deb, 5 Feb 1946, Vol 139(5th), col 204; HC Deb, 11 Mar 1946, Vol 420(5th), col 877 and 884–885	s 6	HL Deb, 5 Feb 1946, Vol 139(5th), col 204; HC Deb, 11 Mar 1946, Vol 420(5th), col 877 and 884–885

Parliamentary papers

Patents and Designs Bill (1946 HL Papers 40), Vol 3
Amendments to be Moved in Committee by Viscount Swinton (1946 HL Papers 40a), Vol 3

(continued)

Amendments to be Moved in Committee by Lord Pakenham (1946 HL Papers 40b), Vol 3

Marshalled List of Amendments to be Moved in Committee (1946 HL Papers 40**), Vol 3

Patents and Designs Bill (1946 HL Papers 52), Vol 3

Amendments to be Moved on Report by Lord Pakenham (1946 HL Papers 40a), Vol 3 (Paper Mis-numbered)

Amendment to be Moved on Report by Viscount Swinton (1946 HL Papers 52b), Vol 3

Marshalled List of Amendments to be Moved on Report (1946 HL Papers 52**), Vol 3

Patents and Designs Bill (1945–46 HC Papers 86), Vol 4, p 107

Report of Standing Committee B on the Patents and Designs Bill (1945–46 HC Papers 109), Vol 8, p 497

Supplement to Votes & Proceedings, 1941–42 – No amendments

Notes
Archive
Patents and Designs (Amendment) Bill 1946: Notes on amendments, clauses and memoranda: National Archive (BT 103/269)
Patents C'ttee: First interim report Patents and Designs Bill 1946: National Archive (BT 209/923)

Patents and Designs Act 1949

PUBA39	1949
	Patents and Designs Act 1949 (12, 13 & 14 Geo 6. c. 62)
	An Act to amend the enactments relating to Patents and Designs and to provide for the appointment of an additional puisne judge of the High Court

Table of contents

s 1 Application for patent assignee
s 2 Amendments relating to specifications
s 3 Date and term of patent
s 4 Priority date of claims of complete specification
s 5 Publication of matter described in provisional specification or priority document
s 6 Additional powers of Comptroller in relation to applications
s 7 Additional grounds of opposition to grant of patent
s 8 Amendment of patent granted to deceased applicant
s 9 Extension of term of patent
s 10 Patents of addition
s 11 Substitution of applicants, etc.
s 12 Restoration of lapsed application for patents
s 13 Voluntary indorsement of patents
s 14 Revocation of patent by court
s 15 Repeal of [Patents and Designs Act 1907] principal Act, s 27 and 38A(3)
s 16 Compulsory licences
s 17 Provisions as to licences under s 16
s 18 Exercise of powers on applications under s 16
s 19 Indorsement of patent on application of Government department
s 20 Inventions relating to food or medicine, etc.
s 21 Revocation of patent
s 22 Procedure and evidence on application under s 16 to 21
s 23 Appeal and references to arbitrator
s 24 Supplementary provisions as to orders under s 16 to 21
s 25 Repeal of principal Act, s 29
s 26 Effect of patent as against Crown
s 27 Use of patented inventions for services of the Crown
s 28 Rights of third parties in respect of use for services of the Crown
s 29 Reference of disputes as to use for Services of the Crown
s 30 Special provisions as to Crown user during emergency
s 31 Provisions for ensuring secrecy in respect of inventions relevant for defence purposes
s 32 Amendment of Atomic Energy Act, 1946, section 12
s 33 Appointment of scientific advisers
s 34 Order for account in action for infringement

s 35 Proceedings by licensee for infringement
s 36 Threats of legal proceedings, and additional power to make declaration as to non-infringement
s 37 Reference to Comptroller of disputes as to infringement
s 38 Co-ownership of patents
s 39 Disputes as to inventions made by employees
s 40 Claims for chemical substances
[ss 41 to 44 relate to designs]
s 45 Registration of assignments, etc.
s 46 Preparation of documents by patent agents
s 47 Appeals from decisions of the Comptroller
s 48 Appeals from decisions of the Comptroller in Scottish cases
s 49 Increase of number of judges of High Court
s 50 Interpretation and construction
s 51 Amendments, repeals and transitional provisions
s 52 Application to Northern Ireland
s 53 Short title and commencement
Schedule One – Minor and consequential amendments of principal Act
Schedule Two – Provisions of principal Act repealed
Schedule Three – Transitional Provisions

Proposed clause

NC Agents for patents
NC Additions to principal Act, s 85

Journal

House of Commons			House of Lords		
Money Res Rep: Robert Taylor SC Rep: Gordon Touche CWH Rep: James Milner (Ch W&M)			Pres and Rep: Lord Lucas of Chilworth (Cap Yeo Guard)		
2 Jun 1949	204 CJ 268	Brought HL/1R	8 Mar 1949	181 LJ 132	1R
29 Jun 1949	204 CJ 286	2R/C'tted/Money Res	8 Mar 1949	181 LJ 132	Draft Bill (consolidation)
30 Jun 1949	204 CJ 288	Sent to SC D	29 Mar 1949	181 LJ 158	2R/C'tted CWH
4 Jul 1849	204 CJ 291	Rep Money Res	31 Mar 1949	181 LJ 167	CWH day app
14 Jul 1949	204 CJ 311	Rep with Amds	10 May 1949	181 LJ 212	**CWH**
18 Jul 1949	204 CJ 315	Money Res (No2)	16 May 1949	181 LJ 222	**CWH**
22 Jul 1949	204 CJ 326	CWH/Money R/Rep with Amds/3R	30 May 1949	181 LJ 244	**Rep with Amds**
			2 Jun 1949	181 LJ 257	**3R**
27 Jul 1949	204 CJ 341	HL Ag Amds	25 Jul 1949	181 LJ 342	HC pass with Amds
30 Jul 1949	204 CJ 352	Royal Assent	26 Jul 1949	181 LJ 345	HC Amds day app
			27 Jul 1949	181 LJ 352	**HC Amds Ag**
			30 Jul 1949	181 LJ 364	Royal Assent

Parliamentary debates

2R/Mon Res: HC Deb, 29 Jun 1949, Vol 466(5th), col 1408–1439

Money Res: HC Deb, 4 Jul 1949, Vol 466(5th), col 1923

SC D Deb, 7 Jul 1949, Vol 3, col 595–636

SC D Deb, 12 Jul 1949, Vol 3, col 637–690

SC D Deb, 14 Jul 1949, Vol 3, col 691–726

Money Com 2: HC Deb, 18 Jul 1949, Vol 467(5th), col 1102

Mon/Cons/Re-C'tted: HC Deb, 22 Jul 1949, Vol 467(5th), col 1709–1736

R cons/3R: HC Deb, 22 Jul 1949, Vol 467(5th), col 1740

Royal Assent: HC Deb, 30 Jul 1949, Vol 467(5th), col 2941

1R: HL Deb, 8 Mar 1949, Vol 161(5th), col 176

2R: HL Deb, 29 Mar 1949, Vol 161(5th), col 752–784

CWH: HL Deb, 10 May 1949, Vol 162(5th), col 426–493

CWH: HL Deb, 16 May 1949, Vol 162(5th), col 651–719

Rep: HL Deb, 30 May 1949, Vol 162(5th), col 1203–1233

3R: HL Deb, 2 Jun 1949, Vol 162(5th), col 1369–1375

HC pass with Amds: HL Deb, 25 Jul 1949, Vol 164(5th), col 480

HC Amds Ag: HL Deb, 27 Jul 1949, Vol 164(5th), col 569–581

Royal Assent: HL Deb, 30 Jul 1949, Vol 164(5th), col 704

Debates on particular provisions

s 1	HL Deb, 29 Mar 1949, Vol 161(5th), col 755; HL Deb, 10 May 1949, Vol 162(5th) col 426; SC D Deb, 7 Jul 1949, Vol 3, col 597–599; HL Deb, 27 Jul 1949, Vol 164(5th), col 570	s 2	HL Deb, 29 Mar 1949, Vol 161(5th), col 755; SC D Deb, 7 Jul 1949, Vol 3, col 599–600

(continued)

(continued)

s 3	HL Deb, 29 Mar 1949, Vol 161(5th), col 755; HC Deb, 29 Jun 1949, Vol 466(5th), col 1411	s 4	HL Deb, 29 Mar 1949, Vol 161(5th), col 755; HL Deb, 10 May 1949, Vol 162(5th), col 426–430; HC Deb, 29 Jun 1949, Vol 466(5th), col 1411; SC D Deb, 7 Jul 1949, Vol 3, col 600–605; HL Deb, 27 Jul 1949, Vol 164(5th), col 570
s 5	HL Deb, 10 May 1949, Vol 162(5th) col 430–431 (NC)	s 6	HL Deb, 29 Mar 1949, Vol 161(5th), col 756; HL Deb, 10 May 1949, Vol 162(5th) col 431–439 (Cl 5); HC Deb, 29 Jun 1949, Vol 466(5th), col 1428–1429; SC D Deb, 7 Jul 1949, Vol 3, col 605–618; HC Deb, 22 Jul 1949, Vol 467(5th), col 1712–1720; HL Deb, 27 Jul 1949, Vol 164(5th), col 570–572
s 7	HL Deb, 29 Mar 1949, Vol 161(5th), col 778–781 (Cl 6); HL Deb, 10 May 1949, Vol 162(5th) col 439–441 (Cl 6); SC D Deb, 7 Jul 1949, Vol 3, col 618–621; HL Deb, 27 Jul 1949, Vol 164(5th), col 572	s 8	N/A
s 9	HL Deb, 10 May 1949, Vol 162(5th) col 441–442 (Cl 8)	s 10	HL Deb, 10 May 1949, Vol 162(5th) col 442–443 (Cl 9); SC D Deb, 7 Jul 1949, Vol 3, col 621–622; HC Deb, 22 Jul 1949, Vol 467(5th), col 1720–1721; HL Deb, 27 Jul 1949, Vol 164(5th), col 572
s 11	N/A	s 12	SC D Deb, 7 Jul 1949, Vol 3, col 622; HL Deb, 27 Jul 1949, Vol 164(5th), 572
s 13	HL Deb, 10 May 1949, Vol 162(5th) col 443–444 (Cl 12)	s 14	HL Deb, 10 May 1949, Vol 162(5th) col 444–451 (Cl 13); HC Deb, 29 Jun 1949, Vol 466(5th), col 1438; SC D Deb, 7 Jul 1949, Vol 3, col 623–626; HC Deb, 22 Jul 1949, Vol 467(5th), col 1721; HL Deb, 27 Jul 1949, Vol 164(5th), 572–573
s 15	N/A	s 16	HL Deb, 29 Mar 1949, Vol 161(5th), col 768–771, 782–783 (Cl 15); HL Deb, 10 May 1949, Vol 162(5th) col 451–467 (Cl 15); HC Deb, 29 Jun 1949, Vol 466(5th), col 1412; HC Deb, 29 Jun 1949, Vol 466(5th), col 1420–1428; HC Deb, 29 Jun 1949, Vol 466(5th), col 1437–1438; SC D Deb, 7 Jul 1949, Vol 3, col 626–636; HC Deb, 22 Jul 1949, Vol 467(5th), col 1721–1727
s 17	HL Deb, 10 May 1949, Vol 162(5th) col 467–468 (Cl 16)	s 18	HL Deb, 29 Mar 1949, Vol 161(5th), col 783; HL Deb, 10 May 1949, Vol 162(5th) col 468–469 (Cl 17)
s 19	HL Deb, 29 Mar 1949, Vol 161(5th), col 757–758, 771–773 (Cl 18); HL Deb, 10 May 1949, Vol 162(5th) col 469–493 (Cl 18); HL Deb, 16 May 1949, Vol 162(5th), col 651–656 (Cl 18); HC Deb, 29 Jun 1949, Vol 466(5th), col 1412–1413; HC Deb, 29 Jun 1949, Vol 466(5th), col 1437–1438; SC D Deb, 12 Jul 1949, Vol 3, col 637–659(V); HL Deb, 27 Jul 1949, Vol 164(5th), col 573–574	s 20	SC D Deb, 12 Jul 1949, Vol 3, col 659–662
s 21	N/A	s 22	HL Deb, 29 Mar 1949, Vol 161(5th), col 758, 773–774 (Cl 21); HL Deb, 16 May 1949, Vol 162(5th), col 656–662 (Cl 21); SC D Deb, 12 Jul 1949, Vol 3, col 662

s 23	N/A	s 24	N/A
s 25	N/A	s 26	N/A
s 27	HL Deb, 29 Mar 1949, Vol 161(5th), col 759–760 (Cl 26); HL Deb, 16 May 1949, Vol 162(5th), col 662–672 (Cl 26); HC Deb, 29 Jun 1949, Vol 466(5th), col 1429–1430	s 28	HL Deb, 29 Mar 1949, Vol 161(5th), col 758–759 (Cl 27); HL Deb, 16 May 1949, Vol 162(5th), col 673–684 (Cl 27); SC D Deb, 12 Jul 1949, Vol 3, col 663–667; HC Deb, 29 Jun 1949, Vol 466(5th), col 1429–1430
s 29	N/A	s 30	HL Deb, 29 Mar 1949, Vol 161(5th), col, 775–777; HL Deb, 16 May 1949, Vol 162(5th), col 684–686 (Cl 29); SC D Deb, 12 Jul 1949, Vol 3, col 667–677; HC Deb, 22 Jul 1949, Vol 467(5th), col 1727–1730
s 31	HL Deb, 16 May 1949, Vol 162(5th), col 686–696(Cl 30); HC Deb, 29 Jun 1949, Vol 466(5th), col 1413–1414; SC D Deb, 12 Jul 1949, Vol 3, col 677–679	s 32	SC D Deb, 12 Jul 1949, Vol 3, col 679
s 33	HL Deb, 29 Mar 1949, Vol 161(5th), col 761–762 (Cl 32); HC Deb, 29 Jun 1949, Vol 466(5th), col 1414; SC D Deb, 12 Jul 1949, Vol 3, col 679–680	s 34	SC D Deb, 12 Jul 1949, Vol 3, col 680–681; HC Deb, 22 Jul 1949, Vol 467(5th), col 1730; HL Deb, 27 Jul 1949, Vol 164(5th), col 574–575
s 35	HL Deb, 16 May 1949, Vol 162(5th), col 696 (Cl 35); HC Deb, 22 Jul 1949, Vol 467(5th), col 1730; HL Deb, 27 Jul 1949, Vol 164(5th), col 575	s 36	HL Deb, 29 Mar 1949, Vol 161(5th), col 762; HL Deb, 16 May 1949, Vol 162(5th), col 696–699 (Cl 35); HC Deb, 29 Jun 1949, Vol 466(5th), col 1414; SC D Deb, 12 Jul 1949, Vol 3, col 681–682
s 37	HL Deb, 29 Mar 1949, Vol 161(5th), col 762; SC D Deb, 12 Jul 1949, Vol 3, col 683; HC Deb, 29 Jun 1949, Vol 466(5th), col 1414	s 38	SC D Deb, 12 Jul 1949, Vol 3, col 683–685; HC Deb, 22 Jul 1949, Vol 467(5th), col 1730–1731; HL Deb, 27 Jul 1949, Vol 164(5th), col 575
s 39	HL Deb, 16 May 1949, Vol 162(5th), col 699–700 (Cl 38); HL Deb, 2 Jun 1949, Vol 162(5th), col 1373–1375; HC Deb, 29 Jun 1949, Vol 466(5th), col 1414; HC Deb, 29 Jun 1949, Vol 466(5th), col 1432–1433	s 40–46	N/A
s 47	HL Deb, 16 May 1949, Vol 162(5th), col 706; HL Deb, 2 Jun 1949, Vol 162(5th), col 1370–1373; HC Deb, 29 Jun 1949, Vol 466(5th), col 1414; SC D Deb, 12 Jul 1949, Vol 3, col 686; HL Deb, 27 Jul 1949, Vol 164(5th), col 575–576	s 48	SC D Deb, 12 Jul 1949, Vol 3, col 686–688; HC Deb, 22 Jul 1949, Vol 467(5th), col 1709–1710; HL Deb, 27 Jul 1949, Vol 164(5th), col 576–567
s 49	HL Deb, 29 Mar 1949, Vol 161(5th), col 761, 766–768; HL Deb, 16 May 1949, Vol 162(5th), col 706 (Cl 47); HC Deb, 29 Jun 1949, Vol 466(5th), col 1414–1415 (Cl 48)	s 50–51	N/A
s 52	SC D Deb, 12 Jul 1949, Vol 3, col 688–690	Sch 1	HL Deb, 16 May 1949, Vol 162(5th), col 706–718; SC D Deb, 14 Jul 1949, Vol 3, col 706–722; HC Deb, 22 Jul 1949, Vol 467(5th), col 1731–1736; HL Deb, 27 Jul 1949, Vol 164(5th), col 577–581
Sch 2	SC D Deb, 14 Jul 1949, Vol 3, col 722–724; HL Deb, 27 Jul 1949, Vol 164(5th), col 581	Sch 3	HL Deb, 16 May 1949, Vol 162(5th), col 718–719; HL Deb, 27 Jul 1949, Vol 164(5th), col 581
Proposed clauses			
NC	Agents for patents – withdrawn SC D Deb, 14 Jul 1949, Vol 3, col 691–699	NC	Addition to principal act s 85 [patents agents] – withdrawn SC D Deb, 14 Jul 1949, Vol 3, col 699–706; HC Deb, 22 Jul 1949, Vol 467(5th), col 1710–1712

(continued)

(continued)

Parliamentary papers
Draft Bills to Consolidate the enactments relating to Patents and the enactments relating to registered designs as proposed to be amended by the Patents and Designs Bill 1949 (1948–49 Cmd 7645): 8 Mar 1949 (204 CJ 143; 181 LJ 132)
Patents and Designs Bill (1949 HL Papers 56), Vol 3 [includes Explanatory Memorandum]
Amendments to be Moved in Committee by Lord Lucas (1949 HL Papers 56a), Vol 3
Amendments to be Moved in Committee by Viscount Simon, Viscount Swinton and the Earl of Munster (1949 HL Papers 56b), Vol 3
Amendments to be Moved in Committee by Lord Lucas and Viscount Simon (1949 HL Papers 56c), 1949 Vol 3
Amendments to be Moved in Committee by Lord Lucas (1949 HL Papers 56d), 1949 Vol 3
Amendment to be Moved in Committee by Lord Lucas (1949 HL Papers 56e), 1949 Vol 3
Marshalled List of Amendments to be Moved in Committee (1949 HL Papers 56**), 1949 Vol 3
Second Marshalled List of Amendments to be Moved in Committee (1949 HL Papers 56‡), Vol 3
Patents and Designs Bill (as amended in Committee) (1949 HL Papers 95), Vol 3
Amendments to be Moved on Report by Lord Lucas and Viscount Simon (1949 HL Papers 95a), Vol 3
Marshalled List of Amendments to be Moved on Report (1949 HL Papers 95**), 1949 Vol 3
Patents and Designs Bill (as amended on Report) (1949 HL Papers 107), 1949 Vol 3
Patents and Designs Bill (HC Papers 153), Vol 4, p 761
Patents and Designs Bill (as amended in Committee) (HC Papers 170), Vol 4, p 833
Commons Amendments (References to Bill No 107) (1949 HL Papers 165), 1949 Vol 3
Report of Standing Committee D on the Patents and Designs Bill (1948–49 HC Papers 215), Vol 10, p 285
Supplement to Votes & Proceedings, 1948–9
1 Jul 1949, p 2791–2792; 4 Jul 1949, p 2811; 5 Jul 1949, p 2859– 2866; 7 Jul 1949, p 2869–2876; 7 Jul 1949, p 2891; 12 Jul 1949, p 2911–2916; 14 Jul 1949, p 2939–2943; 19 Jul 1949, p 3035–3037; 20 Jul 1949, p 3039–3044; 22 Jul 1949, p 3045–3050
Notes
Archive
First interim report: signed copy and arrangements for publication: National Archive (BT 306/64)
Atomic Energy Act 1946 and Patents and Designs Bill 1949: National Archive (AB 16/4428)
Atomic Energy Act 1946 and Patents and Designs Bill 1949: National Archive (AB 16/2681)
Patents and Designs Act: Second interim and final report of Departmental Committee with recommendations: National Archive (LCO 2/4060)
Patents and Designs Bill in relation to Monopolies and Restrictive Practice: National Archive (BT 209/376)
Bill to amend the Law relating to Patents and Designs: National Archive (BT 103/298)
Patents and Designs Consolidation Bills. 1949 Notes on Clauses: National Archive (BT 103/299)
Patent and Designs Bill: Second Reading and Committee Stage, House of Lords: National Archive (BT 103/300)
Patent and Designs Bill: Notes on Clauses (House of Lords): National Archive (BT 103/301)
Patents and Designs Bill: Correspondence; jurisdiction of Scottish Courts: National Archive (BT 209/372)
Patent and Designs Bill: Observations: National Archive (BT 209/373)
Patents and Designs Bill: Correspondence; jurisdiction of Scottish Courts: National Archive (BT 209/374)
Patents and Designs Bill: Treatment of Scottish cases: National Archive (BT 209/375)
Patents and Designs Bill in relation to Monopolies and Restrictive Practices: National Archive (BT 209/376)
Patent and Designs Bill: Clauses 4 and 9: National Archive (BT 209/377)
Patents and Designs Bill: Houses of Lords Consideration of Commons' amendments: National Archive (BT 209/378)
Patents and Designs Bill: Correspondence with Ministry of Supply and Admiralty: National Archive (BT 209/379)
Prohibition on publication of secret applications: National Archive (BT 209/380)
Patent and Designs Bill 1949: HM Treasury Bill Papers: National Archive (T 225/132)
Proceeding and memoranda up to including introduction in House of Lord: National Archive (BT 209/525)
Drafting: correspondence with Parliamentary Counsel: National Archive (BT 209/526 and BT 209/527)
Patent and Designs Bill: Correspondence and Representations after Publication: National Archive (BT 209/528)
Patent and Designs Bill: House of Lords stage: National Archive (BT 209/529)
Patent and Designs Bill: House of Lords stage: National Archive (BT 209/530)

Patent and Designs Bill: House of Commons stage: National Archive (BT 209/531)

Patents and Designs Bill 1949: Correspondence: National Archive (LCO 2/4061)

Patents and Designs Bill 1949: Ministry of Aviation: National Archive (AVIA 49/183)

Patents Rules 1949: National Archive (BT 103/297)

Prolongation of patents (s 24 of Patents Act 1949): National Archive (BT 209/39)

Patents Act 1949

PUBA40	1949
Patents Act 1949 (12, 13 & 14 Geo 6. c. 87)	
An Act to consolidate certain enactments relating to patents	
Table of contents	

(continued)

(continued)

s 45 Supplementary provisions	1907, s 83A, 27(3)(a); 1949, s 24, Sch 1
s 46 Use of patented inventions for services of the Crown	1949, s 27
s 47 Rights of third parties in respect of Crown use	1949, s 28
s 48 Reference of disputes as to Crown use	1949, s 29
s 49 Special provisions as to Crown use during emergency	1949, s 30
s 50 Previous publication	1907, s 15, 41, 45; 1949, Sch 1
s 51 Previous communication, display or working	30(12), 45
s 52 Use and publication after provisional specification or foreign application	1907, s 42
s 53 Priority date in case of obtaining	1907, s 15(2) and (3); 1949, Sch 1
s 54 Co-ownership of patents	1949, s 38; Sch 1
s 55 Power of Comptroller to give directions to co-owners	1949, s 38(2) to (5)
s 56 Disputes as to inventions made by employees	1949, s 39
s 57 Avoidance of certain restrictive conditions	1907, s 38(1), (4) and (5); 1949, Sch 1
s 58 Determination of certain contracts	1907, s 38(2), (5); 1949, Sch 1
s 59 Restrictions on recovery of damages for infringement	1907, s 17(3), 23, 33; 1949, Sch 1
s 60 Order for account in action for infringement	1949, s 34
s 61 Counterclaim for revocation in action for infringement	1907, s 32
s 62 Relief for infringement of partially valid specification	1907, s 32A; 1949, Sch 1
s 63 Proceedings for infringement by exclusive licensee	1949, s 35
s 64 Certificate of contested validity of specification	1907, s 35; 1949, Sch 1
s 65 Remedy for groundless threats of infringement proceedings	1907, s 36(1); 1949, s 36(1), Sch 1
s 66 Power of court to make declaration as to non-infringement	1949, s 36(2)
s 67 Reference to Comptroller of disputes as to infringement	1949, s 37
s 68 Orders in Council as to convention countries	1907, s 91A; 1949, Sch 1
s 69 Supplementary provisions as to convention applications	1907, s 91(5)
s 70 Special provisions as to vessels, aircraft and land vehicles	1907, s 48
s 71 Extension of time for certain convention applications	1907, s 91B; 1949, Sch 1
s 72 Protection of inventions communicated under international agreements	1907, s 91C; 1949, Sch 1
s 73 Register of patents	1907, s 28, 66, 67; 1949, Sch 1
s 74 Registration of assignments, etc	1907, s 28(4), 71 ; 1949, s 45, Sch 1
s 75 Rectification of register	1907, s 72; 1949, Sch 1
s 76 Power to correct clerical errors, etc.	1907, s 70; 1949, Sch 1
s 77 Evidence of entries, documents etc.	1907, s 78, 79
s 78 Requests for information as to patent or patent application	1907, s 44A
s 79 Restriction upon publication of specifications, etc	1907, s 68, 69(1); 1949, Sch 1
s 80 Loss or destruction of patent	1907, s 44
s 81 Exercise of discretionary powers of Comptroller	1907, s 73; 1949, Sch 1
s 82 Costs and security for costs	1907, s 73A; 1949, Sch 1
s 83 Evidence before Comptroller	1907, s 77; 1949, Sch 1
s 84 The Court	1907, s 31(1), 92(2); 1949, s 33, Sch 1
s 85 The Appeal Tribunal	1907, s 92A; 1949, s 47
s 86 Appeals from decisions of the Comptroller in Scottish cases	1949, s 48, Sch 1
s 87 Appeals to Court of Appeal and Court of Session	1907, s 92(2); 1949; s 48
s 88 Restrictions on practice as patent agent	1907, s 84; 1949, Sch 1
s 89 Power of Comptroller to refuse to deal with certain agents	1907, s 85; 1949, Sch 1
s 90 Falsification of register, etc	1907, s 89(1)
s 91 Unauthorised claim of patent rights	1907, s 89(2), (3) and (5)
s 92 Unauthorised assumption of Royal Arms	1907, s 90
s 93 Offences by companies	1907, s 84(2); 1949, Sch 1
s 94 General power of Board of Trade to make rules, etc	1907, s 46, 86(1); 1949, Sch 1
s 95 Provisions as to rules and Orders	1907, s 86(3), 88, 91D(1); 1946, 1(2) and 5(2); 1949, Sch 1
s 96 Proceedings of Board of Trade	1907, s 87; 1949, Sch 1
s 97 Service of notices, etc., by post	1907, s 81
s 98 Hours of business and excluded days	1907, s 82; 1949, Sch 1
s 99 Fees	1907, s 65
s 100 Annual report of Comptroller	1907, s 76
s 101 Interpretation	1907, s 4, 84(4), 92(1), 93; 1949, Sch 1
s 102 Saving for Royal prerogative, etc	1907, s 97; 1949, 26
s 103 Application to Scotland	1907, s 94; 1949, Sch 1

s 104 Application to Northern Ireland	1907, s 95; 1949, s 52
s 105 Isle of Man	1907, s 96
s 106 Repeals, transitional provisions and amendment	1949, s 32, 51
s 107 Short title and commencement	—
First Schedule – Maximum Fees	—
Second Schedule – Enactments Repealed	—
Third Schedule – Transitional Provisions	1949, Sch 3; 1938, s 2(2)

Journal

House of Commons			House of Lords		
Rep: James Milner (Ch W&M)			Pres and Rep: Lord Jowitt LC		
3 Nov 1949	204 CJ 389	JC Report	30 Jul 1949	181 LJ 365	1R
23 Nov 1949	204 CJ 408	Brought HL/1R	19 Oct 1949	181 LJ 382	2R day app
9 Dec 1949	204 CJ 431	2R/C'tted CWH	25 Oct 1949	181 LJ 388	2R/Ref JC
12 Dec 1949	204 CJ 432	CWH/Rep w/o Amds/3R	3 Nov 1949	181 LJ 408	JC Rep with Amds
16 Dec 1949	204 CJ 445	Royal Assent	9 Nov 1949	181 LJ 425	CWH day app
			17 Nov 1949	181 LJ 447	**CWH**
			22 Nov 1949	181 LJ 455	Rep with Amds
			23 Nov 1949	181 LJ 460	3R
			13 Dec 1949	181 LJ 505	HC pass w/o Amds
			15 Dec 1949	181 LJ 517	Royal Assent

Parliamentary debates

2R: HC Deb, 9 Dec 1949, Vol 470(5th), col 2292	1R: HL Deb, 30 Jul 1949, Vol 164(5th), col 705
CWH/Rep/3R: HC Deb, 12 Dec 1949, Vol 470(5th), col 2365	2R: HL Deb, 25 Oct 1949, Vol 164(5th), col 1096–1097
	Rep from JC: HL Deb, 3 Nov 1949, Vol 165(5th), col 203
Royal Assent: HC Deb, 16 Dec 1949, Vol 470(5th), col 3056	CWH: HL Deb, 17 Nov 1949, Vol 165(5th), col 808
	Rep: HL Deb, 22 Nov 1949, Vol 165(5th), col 921
	3R: HL Deb, 23 Nov 1949, Vol 165(5th), col 956
	HC pass: HL Deb, 13 Dec 1949, Vol 165(5th), col 1516
	Royal Assent: HL Deb, 16 Dec 1949, Vol 165(5th), col 1668

Parliamentary papers

Report of the Joint Committee on Patents Bill Consolidation (1948–49 HC Papers 270), Vol 6, p 849

Patents Bill (1948–49 HL Papers 171), Vol 3

> Amendment Made by the Joint Committee on Consolidation Bills (1949 HL Papers 171a), Vol 3

> Amendments Made by the Joint Committee on Consolidation Bills (1949 HL Papers 171b), Vol 3

Patents Bill (1948–49 HC Papers 211), Vol 4, p 677

Draft Bills to consolidate the Enactments relating to Patents and the Enacting relating to Register Designs as proposed to be amended by the Patents and Designs Bill 1949 (1948–49 Cmd 7645), Vol 29, p 959: 8 Mar 1949 (204 CJ 143; 181 LJ 132)

Supplement to Votes & Proceedings, 1948–49 – No amendments

Notes

Archive

Patents Bill 1949 and Registered Designs Bill 1949: Bill papers; correspondence on public use of Patent Office: National Archive (T228/251)

Patents Act 1957

PUBA41	1957
Patents Act 1957 (5 & 6 Eliz 2. c. 13)	
An Act to provide for extending time limits for certain purposes relating to applications for patents; to validate extensions of time under section six of the Patents, Designs, Copyright and Trade Marks (Emergency) Act, 1939, in connection with such applications in so far as any such extensions may have been invalid; and for purposes connected with the matters aforesaid	

(continued)

(continued)

Table of contents
s 1 Time limits under s 12 and 13 of Patents Act, 1949
s 2 Provisions as to pending applications
s 3 Extension of time under s 6 of Patents, Designs, Copyright and Trade Marks (Emergency) Act, 1939
s 4 Interpretation
s 5 Short title, citation, extent and commencement

Journal

House of Commons			House of Lords		
SC Rep: Horace King			Pre: Lord Mancroft (Min w/o Port) Rep: Earl of Drogheda (Ld Ch)		
6 Dec 1956	212 CJ 41	Brought HL/1R	14 Nov 1956	189 LJ 13	1R
18 Dec 1956	212 CJ 52	2R	22 Nov 1956	189 LJ 21	2R/CWH
19 Dec 1956	212 CJ 55	C'tted SC B	4 Dec 1956	189 LJ 30	**CWH/Rep w/o Amds**
31 Jan 1956	212 CJ 73	Rep w/o Amds	6 Dec 1956	189 LJ 35	3R
20 Feb 1956	212 CJ 102	Cons/3R	21 Feb 1957	189 LJ 96	HC pass with Amds
5 Mar 1957	212 CJ 117	HL pass w/o Amds	5 Mar 1957	189 LJ 108	**HC Amds Ag**
21 Mar 1957	212 CJ 142	Royal Assent	21 Mar 1957	189 LJ 127	Royal Assent

Parliamentary debates

2R: HC Deb, 18 Dec 1956, Vol 562(5th), col 1212–1219	1R: HL Deb, 14 Nov 1956, Vol 200(5th), col 299
SC: SC B Deb, 31 Jan 1957, Vol 2, col 1–30	2R: HL Deb, 22 Nov 1956, Vol 200(5th), col 529–536
Cons/3R: HC Deb, 20 Feb 1957, Vol 565(5th), col 525–527	CWH/Rep: HL Deb, 4 Dec 1956, Vol 200(5th), col 727–740
Royal Assent: HC Deb, 21 Mar 1957, Vol 567(5th), col 584	3R: HL Deb, 6 Dec 1956, Vol 200(5th), col 811–813
	HC pass: HL Deb, 21 Feb 1957, Vol 201(5th), col 1165
	HC Amd Ag: HL Deb, 5 Mar 1957, Vol 202(5th), col 210–214
	Royal Assent: HL Deb, 21 Mar 1957, Vol 202(5th), col 726

Debates on particular provisions

s 1	HL Deb, 4 Dec 1956, Vol 200(5th), col 727–740; SC B Deb, 31 Jan 1957, Vol 2, col 3–30; HC Deb, 20 Feb 1958, Vol 565(5th), col 525–526	s 2	HC Deb, 20 Feb 1958, Vol 565(5th), col 527

Parliamentary papers

Patents Bill (1956–57 HL Papers 4), Vol 2 [includes Explanatory Memorandum]

    Amendments to be Moved in Committee by Lord Cawley (1956 HL Papers 4a), Vol 2

Patents Bill (1956–57 HC Papers 36), Vol 3, p 311

Commons Amendments (1956 HL Papers 40), Vol 2

Standing Committee B on the Patents Bill (1956–57 HC Papers 70), Vol 7, p 611

Supplement to Votes & Proceedings, 1956–57

    29 Jan 1957, p 331; 31 Jan 1957, p 345; 18 Feb 1957, p 569; 20 Feb 1957, p 575

Notes

Archive

Patents Act 1957: House of Commons and Lords stages: Departmental papers (BT 281/12)

Preparatory Papers Patents Bill: National Archive (BT 209/604)

Drafting of Bill: National Archive (BT 209/605)

House of Lords Stages: National Archive (BT 209/606)

House of Commons Stages: National Archive (BT 209/607)

Discussion of CIPA Memo on the Bill: National Archive (BT 209/608)

Memorandum of CIPA on Bill: National Archive (BT 209/609)

Defence Contracts Act 1958

PUBA42	1958

Defence Contracts Act 1958 (6 & 7 Eliz 2. c. 38)
An Act to amend three enactments authorising the use of patented inventions and registered designs for the services of the Crown in respect of articles required for defence and similar purposes by the Governments of allied or associated countries or the United Nations; to make permanent provision with respect to the use for defence and similar purposes of other technical information protected by contractual arrangements; to repeal certain emergency provisions relating to inventions and designs; and for purposes connected with the matters aforesaid

Table of contents
s 1 Amendments of statutory provisions for use of patented inventions and registered designs for services of the Crown s 2 Provision for use of other technical information by Crown contractors for production and supply of defence materials s 3 Procedure in connection with authorisations under s 2 s 4 Payments for use and determination of disputes s 5 Expenses s 6 Interpretation, etc. s 7 Repeal and transitional provisions s 8 Citation, construction, commencement and extent

Proposed clauses
NC Power to require information relating to inventions or designs

Journal					
House of Commons			**House of Lords**		
Pres: Sir David Eccles (Pr BoT) Rep: Henry Hynd Money Rep: Gerald Wills			Rep: Lord Terrington (Dep Ld Ch)		
25 Nov 1957	213 CJ 33	1R	1 May 1957	190 LJ 160	Brought HC/1R
12 Dec 1957	213 CJ 51	Money Res/2R/C'tted SC	21 May 1957	190 LJ 186	2R date app
13 Dec 1957	213 CJ 52	C'tted SC A	17 Jun 1957	190 LJ 207	2R/C'tted CWH
18 Dec 1958	213 CJ 59	Money Res Rep	30 Jun 1957	190 LJ 228	CWH/Rep w/o Amds
28 Mar 1958	213 CJ 148	Transferred to SC E	3 Jul 1957	190 LJ 241	3R
16 Apr 1958	213 CJ 162	Rep with Amds	7 Jul 1957	190 LJ 245	Royal Assent
30 Apr 1958	213 CJ 186	Cons/3R			
3 Jul 1958	213 CJ 254	HL Agree w/o Amds			
7 Jul 1958	213 CJ 258	Royal Assent			

Parliamentary debates	
1R: HC Deb, 25 Nov 1957, Vol 578(5th), col 807	Brought HC/1R: HL Deb, 1 May 1958, Vol 208(5th), col 1180
2R: HC Deb, 12 Dec 1957, Vol 579(5th), col 1447–1539	2R: HL Deb, 17 Jun 1958, Vol 209(5th), col 986–1001
Res Rep: HC Deb, 18 Dec 1957, Vol 580(5th), col 568	CWH: HL Deb, 30 Jun 1958, Vol 210(5th), col 383
SC: SC E Deb, 16 Apr 1958, col 1–52	3R: HL Deb, 3 Jul 1958, Vol 210(5th), col 610
Cons/3R: HC Deb, 30 Apr 1958, Vol 587(5th), col 519–523	Royal Assent: HL Deb, 7 Jul 1958, Vol 210(5th), col 657
Royal Assent: HC Deb, 7 Jul 1958, Vol 591(5th), col 63	

Debates on particular provisions			
s 1	SC E Deb, 16 Apr 1958, col 3–20	s 2	SC E Deb, 16 Apr 1958, col 20–32
s 3	SC E Deb, 16 Apr 1958, col 32–33	s 4–5	N/A
s 6	SC E Deb, 16 Apr 1958, 33–36		

Proposed clauses	
NC	(Power to require information relating to inventions or designs –not accepted) SC E Deb, 16 Apr 1958, col 36–51

(continued)

(continued)

Parliamentary papers
Report of the Committee of Enquiry on the Powers of the Crown to Authorise the Use of Unpatented Inventions and Unregistered Designs in connection with Defence Contracts (1955–56 Cmd 9788), Vol 14, p 187: 20 Jun 1956 (211 CJ 338; 118 LJ 334) (Howitt Committee: see REP23)
Defence Contracts Bill (1957–58 HC Papers 37), Vol 1, p 423
Defence Contracts Bill (as amended in Committee) (1957–58 HC Papers 100), Vol 1, p 435
Defence Contracts Bill (1957–58 HL Papers 79), Vol 1 [Memorandum]
Report of Standing Committee E on the Defence Contracts Bill (1957–58 HC Papers 163), Vol 4, p 821
Supplement to Votes & Proceedings, 1955–56
1 Apr 1958, p 1390; 11 Apr 1958, p 1475–1477; 14 Apr 1958, p 1515–1518; 16 Apr 1958, p 1537–1540

Notes
Archive
Defence Contracts Bill 1958: National Archive (BT 209/610)
Defence Contracts Bill 1958: House of Commons stage: National Archive (BT 209/611)
Defence Contracts Bill 1958: House of Lords stage: National Archive (BT 209/612)

Patents and Designs (Renewals, Extensions and Fees) Act 1961

PUBA43	1961
	Patents and Designs (Renewals, Extensions and Fees) Act 1961 (9 & 10 Eliz 2. c. 25)

An Act to extend to six months the period of grace for the payment of renewal fees for patents and the payment of fees for the extension of the period of copyright in registered designs, to provide a like period of grace for the making of applications for such extension, to validate certain extensions of the said period of copyright, and to provide for amending provisions of the Patents Act, 1949, relating to fees

Table of contents
s 1 Period of grace for payment of fees and for applications
s 2 Patent fees
s 3 Short title and citation

Journal

House of Commons			House of Lords		
Rep: William Anstruther-Gray (Dep Ch W&M)			Pres: Earl of Dundee (Min w/o Port) Rep: Lord Merthyr (Ld Ch)		
6 Dec 1960	216 CJ 46	Brought HL	1 Nov 1960	193 LJ 6	1R
7 Dec 1960	216 CJ 47	1R	2 Nov 1960	193 LJ 9	2R day app
12 Dec 1960	216 CJ 52	2R/C'tted CWH	15 Nov 1960	193 LJ 21	2R/C'tted CWH
2 Jun 1961	216 CJ 243	CWH/Rep w/o Amds/3R	29 Nov 1960	193 LJ 38	**CWH/Rep w/o Amd**
22 Jun 1961	216 CJ 266	Royal Assent	6 Dec 1960	193 LJ 46	**Cons/3R**
			5 Jun 1961	193 LJ 269	HC pass w/o Amds
			22 Jun 1961	193 LJ 309	Royal Assent

Parliamentary debates

2R: HC Deb, 12 Dec 1960, Vol 632(5th), col 111–1125	1R: HL Deb, 1 Nov 1960, Vol 226(5th), col 26
CWH/Rep/3R/3R: HC Deb, 2 Jun 1961, Vol 641(5th), col 616	2R: HL Deb, 15 Nov 1960, Vol 226(5th), col 525–542
Royal Assent: HC Deb, 22 Jun 1961, Vol 642(5th), col 1739	Com: HL Deb, 29 Nov 1960, Vol 226(5th), col 1021–1042
	Rep/3R: HL Deb, 6 Dec 1960, Vol 227(5th), col 48–58
	HC Ret: HL Deb, 5 Jun 1961, Vol 231(5th), col 966
	Royal Assent: HL Deb, 22 Jun 1961, Vol 232(5th), col 777

Parliamentary papers
Patents and Designs (Renewals, Extensions and Fees) Bill (1960 HL Papers 2), Vol 2
Amendments to be Moved in Committee by Lord Silkin and Lord Chorley (1960 HL Papers 2a), Vol 2
Amendment to be Moved in Committee by Lord Cawley (1960 HL Papers 2b), Vol 2
Amendment to be Moved in Committee by Lord Douglas of Barloch (1960 HL Papers 2c), Vol 2
Amendment to be Moved on Report by Lord Silkin (1960 HL Papers 2d), Vol 2
Marshalled List of Amendments to be Moved in Committee (1960 HL Papers 2**), Vol 2
Marshalled List of Amendments to be Moved on Report (1960 HL Papers 2††), Vol 2
Revised Marshalled List of Amendments to be Moved on Report (1960 HL Papers 2‡‡), Vol 2
Patents and Designs (Renewals, Extensions and Fees) Bill (1960–61 HC Papers 45), Vol 2, p 945
Supplement to Votes & Proceedings, 1960–61 – No amendments
Notes
Archive
Patents and Designs (Renewals, Extensions and fees) Bill 1960: House of Commons Committee and House of Lords Second Reading: National Archive (BT 103/926)
Patents and Designs (Renewals, Extensions and fees) Bill 1960: House of Commons stages and departmental papers: National Archive (BT 281/35)
Patents and Designs (Renewals, Extensions and fees) Bill 1960: Preparatory papers: National Archive (BT 209/613)
Patents and Designs (Renewals, Extensions and fees) Bill 1960: House of Lords stage: National Archive (BT 209/614)
Patents and Designs (Renewals, Extensions and fees) Bill 1960: House of commons stage: National Archive (BT 209/615)
Patents (Fees Amendment) Order 1961: National Archive (BT 209/616)

2 Public Acts with patent provisions

Judicial Committee Act 1844

PUBA44	1844
Judicial Committee Act 1844 (7 & 8 Vict. c. 69)	
An Act for amending an Act passed in the Fourth Year of the Reign of His late Majesty, intituled An Act for the better Administration of Justice in His Majesty's Privy Council; and to extend its Jurisdiction and Powers	

Table of contents

[s 1 Her Majesty may allow appeals from the colonies to be heard by the Privy Council]
s 2 On Petition, Her Majesty may grant an Extension of Patent Term in certain Cases
s 3 Her Majesty may grant a lesser Term than that prayed
s 4 As to Extension of Term where Patentees have assigned their Patent Rights
s 5 Disclaimer and Memorandum of Alteration under [Letters Patent for Inventions Act 1835] 5 & 6 W 4. c. 83. may be made notwithstanding original Patentee may have assigned his Patent Right
s 6 Disclaimer and Memorandum of Alteration already made to be deemed valid
s 7 New Letters Patent granted under [Letters Patent for Inventions Act 1835] 5 & 6 W 4. to Assignees before passing of this Act declared valid

Journal

House of Commons			House of Lords		
Rep: Thomas Greene (Ch W&M)			Pres: Lord Brougham and Vaux Rep: Lord Lyndhurst LC		
5 Jul 1844	99 CJ 472	Brought HL	4 Mar 1844	76 LJ 49	1R
9 Jul 1844	99 CJ 479	1R	8 Mar 1844	76 LJ 58	2R/C'tted SC
15 Jul 1844	99 CJ 501	2R adj	11 Mar 1844	76 LJ 60	SC Members App
20 Jul 1844	99 CJ 524	2R/C'tted CWH	14 Mar 1844	76 LJ 71	Print SC Evidence
23 Jul 1844	99 CJ 529	CWH adj	25 Mar 1844	76 LJ 98	Witness Sworn
25 Jul 1844	99 CJ 538	CWH adj	3 Jun 1844	76 LJ 317	Divorce issue for Bill
26 Jul 1844	99 CJ 550	CWH	25 Jun 1844	76 LJ421	SC Rep with Amds
29 Jul 1844	99 CJ 555	**Rep with Amds**	1 Jul 1844	76 LJ 453	CWH
30 Jul 1844	99 CJ 559	3R	2 Jul 1844	76 LJ 460	CWH/Rep with Amds
1 Aug 1844	99 CJ 570	HL Ag Amds	4 Jul 1844	76 LJ 469	3R with Amds
6 Aug 1844	99 CJ 614	Royal Assent	30 Jul 1844	76 LJ 623	HC pass with Amds/Ag
			6 Aug 1844	76 LJ 656	Royal Assent

Parliamentary debates

1R: HC Deb, 9 Jul 1844, Vol 76(3rd), col 530	1R: HL Deb, 4 Mar 1844, Vol 73(3rd), col 487
2R: HC Deb, 19 Jul 1844, Vol 76(3rd), col 1073	2R: **HL Deb, 8 Mar 1844, Vol 73(3rd), col 691–720**
Rep: HC Deb, 29 Jul 1844, Vol 76(3rd), col 1509	CWH: **HL Deb, 11 Mar 1844, Vol 73(3rd), col 796–797**
3R: HC Deb, 30 Jul 1844, Vol 76(3rd), col 1560	CWH: **HL Deb, 1 Jul 1844, Vol 76(3rd), col 121–122**
	3R: HL Deb, 4 Jul 1844, Vol 76(3rd), col 294
	Royal Assent: HL Deb, 6 Aug 1844, Vol 76(3rd), col 1786

Parliamentary papers

Bill for amending an Act passed in the Fourth Year of the Reign of His late Majesty, intituled An Act for the better Administration of Justice in His Majesty's Privy Council; and to extend its Jurisdiction and Powers (1844 HL Papers 27), Vol 5, p 531

Bill (as amended in Select Committee) for amending an Act passed in the Fourth Year of the Reign of His late Majesty, intituled An Act for the better Administration of Justice in His Majesty's Privy Council; and to extend its Jurisdiction and Powers (1844 HL Papers 162), Vol 5, p 537

Bill (as amended in Committee) for amending an Act passed in the Fourth Year of the Reign of His late Majesty, intituled An Act for the better Administration of Justice in His Majesty's Privy Council; and to extend its Jurisdiction and Powers (1844 HL Papers 168), Vol 5, p 545

Bill for amending an Act passed in the Fourth Year of the Reign of His late Majesty, intituled An Act for the better Administration of Justice in His Majesty's Privy Council; and to extend its Jurisdiction and Powers (1844 HC Papers 464), Vol 4, p 377

Report of Select Committee of House of Lords appointed to consider of the Bill intitled An Act for amending an Act passed in the Fourth Year of the Reign of His late Majesty, intituled An Act for the better Administration of Justice in His Majesty's Privy Council; and to extend its Jurisdiction and Powers with Minutes of Evidence (1844 HL Papers 34), Vol 19, p 323 [REP4]

Newspaper coverage of debates

House of Lords

Intention to introduce (9 Feb): **The Times, 10 Feb 1844**

1R: *Morning Advertiser, 5 Mar 1844; Morning Chronicle, 5 Mar 1844; Morning Post, 5 Mar 1844; London Evening Standard, 5 Mar 1844; Bell's New Weekly Messenger, 10 Mar 1844;* The Times, 5 Mar 1844

2R: **The Times, 9 Mar 1844; Morning Advertiser, 9 Mar 1844; Morning Chronicle, 9 Mar 1844; Morning Post, 9 Mar 1844; London Evening Standard, 9 Mar 1844**

Com Rep: **The Times, 12 Mar 1844; Morning Advertiser, 12 Mar 1844; Morning Chronicle, 12 Mar 1844; Morning Post, 12 Mar 1844; London Evening Standard, 12 Mar 1844**

CWH: **The Times, 2 Jul 1844; Morning Chronicle, 2 Jul 1844; Morning Post, 2 Jul 1844; London Evening Standard, 2 Jul 1844; Evening Chronicle, 3 Jul 1844; Evening Mail, 3 Jul 1844**

Rep: *The Times, 3 Jul 1844; Evening Mail, 3 Jul 1844;* Morning Advertiser, 3 Jul 1844; Morning Chronicle, 3 Jul 1844; London Evening Standard, 3 Jul 1844

3R: *The Times, 5 Jul 1844; Bell's Weekly Messenger, 6 Jul 1844;* Morning Advertiser, 5 Jul 1844; Morning Chronicle, 5 Jul 1844; Morning Post, 5 Jul 1844; Evening Chronicle, 5 Jul 1844; London Evening Standard, 5 Jul 1844

House of Commons

2R: **The Times, 20 Jul 1844; Morning Advertiser, 20 Jul 1844; Morning Chronicle, 20 Jul 1844; Morning Post, 20 Jul 1844; London Evening Standard, 20 Jul 1844**

CWH: **The Times, 27 Jul 1844; Morning Advertiser, 27 Jul 1844; Morning Chronicle, 27 Jul 1844; Morning Post, 27 Jul 1844; London Evening Standard, 27 Jul 1844**

Rep: **Morning Advertiser, 30 Jul 1844;** Morning Post, 30 Jul 1844; London Evening Standard, 30 Jul 1844

3R: *Evening Mail, 31 Jul 1844;* The Times, 31 Jul 1844; Morning Advertiser, 31 Jul 1844; Morning Chronicle, 31 Jul 1844; Morning Post, 31 Jul 1844

Royal Assent: The Times, 7 Aug 1844; Morning Chronicle, 7 Aug 1844; Morning Post, 7 Aug 1844; Evening Chronicle, 7 Aug 1844; Evening Mail, 7 Aug 1844; London Evening Standard, 7 Aug 1844

Notes

Mention prior to introduction: HL Deb, 19 Feb 1844, Vol 72(3rd), col 1098–1103

Petitions: PET131 and PET132

Related legislation

In the same year, Lord Brougham proposed a similar Bill: see PUBB19

Court of Chancery Offices Act 1848

PUBA45	1848

Court of Chancery Offices Act 1848 (11 & 12 Vict. c. 94)

An Act to regulate certain Offices in the Petty Bag in the High Court of Chancery, the Practice of the Common-Law Side of that Court, and the Enrolment Office of the said Court

Table of contents (patent provisions only)

s 14 Specifications and Disclaimers enrolled under 5 & 6 W 4. c. 83. [Letters Patent for Inventions Act 1835] to be enrolled in the Enrolment Office only

Journal

House of Commons			House of Lords		
Pres: Sir John Romilly (S-G) Rep: Ralph Bernal (Ch W&M)			Rep: Earl of Shaftesbury (Ld Ch)		
8 Aug 1848	103 CJ 888	Bill Ord/1R	18 Aug 1848	80 LJ 803	Brought HC/1R
11 Aug 1848	103 CJ 908	2R/C'tted	24 Aug 1848	80 LJ 817	2R/C'tted CWH
15 Aug 1848	103 CJ 925	Rep with Amds	25 Aug 1848	80 LJ 820	CWH/Rep
17 Aug 1848	103 CJ 940	Cons	28 Aug 1848	80 LJ 825	3R
18 Aug 1848	103 CJ 944	3R	31 Aug 1848	80 LJ 838	Royal Assent
29 Aug 1848	103 CJ 988	HL pass w/o Amds			
31 Aug 1848	103 CJ 997	Royal Assent			

(continued)

(continued)

Parliamentary debates	
1R: HC Deb, 8 Aug 1848, Vol 100(3rd), col 1163	1R: HL Deb, 18 Aug 1848, Vol 101(3rd), col 235
2R: HC Deb, 10 Aug 1848, Vol 101(3rd), col 54	2R: HL Deb, 24 Aug 1848, Vol 101(3rd), col 465
Rep: HC Deb, 14 Aug 1848, Vol 101(3rd), col 126	CWH: HL Deb, 25 Aug 1848, Vol 101(3rd), col 514
3R: HC Deb, 18 Aug 1848, Vol 101(3rd), col 259	3R: HL Deb, 28 Aug 1848, Vol 101(3rd), col 568
	Royal Assent: HL Deb, 31 Aug 1848, Vol 101(3rd), col 726

Parliamentary papers
Bill to regulate certain Offices in the Petty Bag in the High Court of Chancery, the Practice of the Common-Law Side of that Court, and the Enrolment Office of the said Court (1847–48 HL Papers 327), Vol 5, p 611
Bill to regulate certain Offices in the Petty Bag in the High Court of Chancery, the Practice of the Common-Law Side of that Court, and the Enrolment Office of the said Court (1847–48 HC Papers 605), Vol 5, p 55
Bill (as amended by Committee) to regulate certain Offices in the Petty Bag in the High Court of Chancery, the Practice of the Common-Law Side of that Court, and the Enrolment Office of the said Court (1847–48 HC Papers 605), Vol 5, p 73

Newspaper coverage of debates

House of Commons

1R: The Times, 8 Aug 1848; Morning Advertiser, 8 Aug 1848; Morning Chronicle, 8 Aug 1848; Morning Post, 8 Aug 1848; London Evening Standard, 9 Aug 1848

2R: The Times, 11 Aug 1848; London Daily News, 11 Aug 1848

Rep: Morning Advertiser, 15 Aug 1848

Cons: *Morning Post, 18 Aug* 1848; The Times, 18 Aug 1848; Morning Advertiser, 18 Aug 1848; London Evening Standard, 17 Aug 1848

3R: The Times, 19 Aug 1848; Morning Advertiser, 19 Aug 1848; Morning Chronicle, 19 Aug 1848; Morning Post, 19 Aug 1848; Evening Mail, 21 Aug 1848; London Evening Standard, 18 Aug 1848

House of Lords

2R: The Times, 25 Aug 1848; Morning Advertiser, 25 Aug 1848; Evening Mail, 25 Aug 1848; London Evening Standard, 25 Aug 1848

CWH: The Times, 26 Aug 1848; Morning Chronicle, 26 Aug 1848; Morning Post, 26 Aug 1848; London Daily News, 26 Aug 1848; London Evening Standard, 26 Aug 1848

3R: The Times, 29 Aug 1848; Morning Advertiser, 29 Aug 1848; Morning Chronicle, 29 Aug 1848; Morning Post, 29 Aug 1848; London Evening Standard, 29 Aug 1848

Royal Assent: The Times, 1 Sep 1848; Morning Advertiser, 1 Sep 1848; Morning Chronicle, 1 Sep 1848; Morning Post, 1 Sep 1848; Evening Mail, 1 Sep 1848; London Evening Standard, 1 Sep 1838

Petty Bag Act 1849

PUBA46	1849

Petty Bag Act 1849 (12 & 13 Vict. c. 9)
An Act to amend an Act to regulate certain Offices in the Petty Bag in the High Court of Chancery, the Practice of the Common-Law Side of that Court, and the Enrolment Office of the said Court

Table of contents (patent provisions only)
s 15 Specifications [for inventions] to be enrolled in the Enrolment Office

Journal					
House of Commons			**House of Lords**		
Pres: Sir John Romilly (S-G) Rep: Ralph Bernal (Ch W&M)			Rep: Earl of Shaftesbury (Ld Ch)		
10 Jul 1849	104 CJ 473	Bill Ord	19 Jul 1849	81 LJ 453	Brought HC
10 Jul 1849	104 CJ 474	1R	19 Jul 1849	81 LJ 454	1R
13 Jul 1849	104 CJ 485	2R/C'tted CWH	20 Jul 1849	81 LJ 460	2R day app
13 Jul 1849	104 CJ 492	CWH/Rep	23 Jul 1849	81 LJ 468	2R/C'tted CWH
16 Jul 1849	104 CJ 495	Cons	24 Jul 1849	81 LJ 481	**Rep with Amds**
17 Jul 1849	104 CJ 505	3R with Amds (s 15)	27 Jul 1849	81 LJ 522	3R
28 Jul 1849	104 CJ 608	HL pass with Amds	31 Jul 1849	81 LJ 590	HC Ag HL Amds

28 Jul 1849	104 CJ 610	HL Amds Cons day app	1 Aug 1849	81 LJ 601	Royal Assent
31 Jul 1849	104 CJ 619	**HL Amds Cons/Ag**			
1 Aug 1849	104 CJ 626	Royal Assent			

Parliamentary debates

Ord/1R: HC Deb, 9 Jul 1849, Vol 107(3rd), col 2	1R: HL Deb, 19 Jul 1849, Vol 107(3rd), col 554
2R: HC Deb, 12 Jul 1849, Vol 107(3rd), col 211	2R: HL Deb, 23 Jul 1849, Vol 107(3rd), col 817
CWH: HC Deb, 13 Jul 1849, Vol 107(3rd), col 324	Rep: HL Deb, 24 Jul 1849, Vol 107(3rd), col 878
3R: HC Deb, 17 Jul 1849, Vol 107(3rd), col 466	3R: HL Deb, 27 Jul 1849, Vol 107(3rd), col 1016
	Royal Assent: HL Deb, 1 Aug 1849, Vol 107(3rd), col 1156

Parliamentary papers
Bill to amend an Act to regulate certain Offices in the Petty Bag in the High Court of Chancery, the Practice of the Common-Law Side of that Court, and the Enrolment Office of the said Court (1849 HC Papers 479), Vol 4, p 507
Bill to amend an Act to regulate certain Offices in the Petty Bag in the High Court of Chancery, the Practice of the Common-Law Side of that Court, and the Enrolment Office of the said Court (1849 HL Papers 238), Vol 6, p 153

Newspaper coverage of debates

House of Commons

1R: Morning Post, 10 Jul 1849; London Daily News, 10 Jul 1849

2R: London Daily News, 13 Jul 1849

CWH: **Morning Post, 14 Jul 1849**; The Times, 14 Jul 1849; Morning Advertiser, 14 Jul 1849; Morning Chronicle, 14 Jul 1849; London Daily News, 13 Jul 1849

Cons: Evening Mail, 16 Jul 1849

3R: The Times, 18 Jul 1849; Morning Advertiser, 18 Jul 1849; Morning Chronicle, 18 Jul 1849; Morning Post, 18 Jul 1849; Evening Mail, 18 Jul 1849; London Daily News, 18 July 1849; London Evening Standard, 18 Jul 1849

HL Amd Ag: The Times, 1 Aug 1849; Morning Post, 1 Aug 1849; London Daily News, 1 Aug 1849; London Evening Standard, 1 Aug 1849

House of Lords

2R: The Times, 24 Jul 1849; Morning Advertiser, 24 Jul 1849; Morning Chronicle, 24 Jul 1849; London Daily News, 24 Jul 1849; London Evening Standard, 24 Jul 1849;

CWH/Rep: **The Times, 25 Jul 1849**; **Morning Chronicle, 25 Jul 1849**; **London Evening Standard, 25 Jul 1849**; Morning Advertiser, 25 Jul 1849; Evening Mail, 25 Jul 1849

3R: The Times, 28 Jul 1849; Morning Advertiser, 28 Jul 1849; Morning Chronicle, 28 Jul 1849; Morning Post, 28 Jul 1849; Evening Mail, 28 Jul 1849; London Daily News, 28 Jul 1849; London Evening Standard, 28 Jul 1849

Royal Assent: The Times, 2 Aug 1849; Morning Post, 2 Aug 1849; London Daily News, 2 Aug 1849

Revenue, Friendly Societies, and National Debt Act 1882

PUBA47	1882

Revenue, Friendly Societies, and National Debt Act 1882 (45 & 46 Vict. c. 72)
An Act for amending the Laws relating to Customs and Inland Revenue, and Postage and other Stamps, and for making further provision respecting the National Debt and charges payable out of the public revenue or by the Commissioners for the Reduction of the National Debt; and for other purposes

Table of contents (patent provisions only)
s 16 The stamp duties granted in respect of letters patent for inventions, and on the certificate of registration of a design, to be deemed public office fees and not stamp duties

Journal					
House of Commons			**House of Lords**		
Pres: Leonard Courtney (Fin Sec Tr) Rep Lyon Playfair (Ch W&M)			No report		
2 Aug 1882	137 CJ 424	Bill Ord/1R	15 Aug 1882	114 LJ 419	Brought HC
4 Aug 1882	137 CJ 432	2R/C'tted CWH	15 Aug 1882	114 LJ 420	1R
4 Aug 1882	137 CJ 433	Ref Money Res	16 Aug 1882	114 LJ 424	2R/Com neg

(continued)

5 Aug 1882	137 CJ 439	**Res Com**	17 Aug 1882	114 LJ 429	Royal consent/3R
5 Aug 1882	137 CJ 443	**Res Rep**	18 Aug 1882	114 LJ 433	Royal Assent
8 Aug 1882	137 CJ 447	**CWH/Rep**			
9 Aug 1882	137 CJ 455	Cons adj			
9 Aug 1882	137 CJ 459	Cons adj			
11 Aug 1882	137 CJ 465	Cons adj			
12 Aug 1882	137 CJ 472	Cons adj			
15 Aug 1882	137 CJ 478	Cons/3R			
17 Aug 1882	137 CJ 487	HL pass w/o Amds			
18 Aug 1882	137 CJ 488	Royal Assent			

Parliamentary debates	
1R: HC Deb, 1 Aug 1882, Vol 273(3rd), col 368	1R: HL Deb, 15 Aug 1882, Vol 273(3rd), col 1795
2R: HC Deb, 3 Aug 1882, Vol 273(3rd), col 581	2R: HL Deb, 16 Aug 1882, Vol 273(3rd), col 1921
Res: HC Deb, 4 Aug 1882, Vol 273(3rd), col 743	3R: HL Deb, 17 Aug 1882, Vol 273(3rd), col 1968
Res Rep: HC Deb, 4 Aug 1882, Vol 273(3rd), col 890–891	Royal Assent: HL Deb, 18 Aug 1882, Vol 273(3rd), col 2051
Rep: HC Deb, 7 Aug 1882, Vol 273(3rd), col 952	
3R: HC Deb, 14 Aug 1882, Vol 273(3rd), col 1674, 1783–1788	

Parliamentary papers
Bill for amending the Laws relating to Customs and Inland Revenue, and Postage and other Stamps, and for making further provision respecting the National Debt and charges payable out of the public revenue or by the Commissioners for the Reduction of the National Debt; and for other purposes (1882 HC Papers 260), Vol 6, p 49
Bill for amending the Laws relating to Customs and Inland Revenue, and Postage and other Stamps, and for making further provision respecting the National Debt and charges payable out of the public revenue or by the Commissioners for the Reduction of the National Debt; and for other purposes (1882 HL Papers 257), Vol 6, p 35
Supplement to Votes & Proceedings, 1882 – No amendments

Newspaper coverage of debates
House of Commons
1R: The Times, 3 Aug 1882
2R: The Times, 4 Aug 1882
CWH: The Times, 8 Aug 1882
3R: The Times, 15 Aug 1882
House of Lords
2R: The Times, 17 Aug 1882; Morning Post, 17 Aug 1882; London Daily News, 17 Aug 1882; London Evening Standard, 17 Aug 1882
3R: The Times, 18 Aug 1882; Morning Post, 18 Aug 1882; London Daily News, 18 Aug 1882; London Evening Standard, 18 Aug 1882
Royal Assent: The Times, 19 Aug 1882; Morning Post, 19 Aug 1882; London Daily News, 19 Aug 1882; London Evening Standard, 19 Aug 1882

Finance Act 1907

PUBA48	1907	
Finance Act 1907 (7 Edw 7. c. 13)		
An Act to grant certain duties of Customs and Inland Revenue, to alter other duties, and to amend the Law relating to Customs and Inland Revenue and the National Debt, and to make other provisions for the financial arrangements of the year		
Table of contents (patent provisions only)		
s 25 Payment of tax on patent royalties by deduction.		
Journal		
House of Commons		**House of Lords**
Pres: Herbert Asquith (Ch Ex) Rep: Alfred Emmott (Ch W&M)		No report

1 May 1907	162 CJ 159	Bill Ord	31 Jul 1907	139 LJ 286	Brought HC
8 May 1907	162 CJ 173	**Res**	31 Jul 1907	139 LJ 287	1R
8 May 1907	162 CJ 174	1R	7 Aug 1907	139 LJ 305	2R/Not C'tted
13 May 1907	162 CJ 185	2R adj	8 Aug 1907	139 LJ 310	3R
13 May 1907	162 CJ 186	2R	9 Aug 1907	139 LJ 314	Royal Assent
14 May 1907	162 CJ 191 – V	2R/C'tted CWH			
15 May 1907	162 CJ 194	CWH adj			
23 May 1907	162 CJ 202	CWH adj			
28 May 1907	162 CJ 208	CWH adj			
3 Jun 1907	162 CJ 224	CWH adj			
10 Jun 1907	162 CJ 241	CWH adj			
17 Jun 1907	162 CJ 259	CWH adj			
24 Jun 1907	162 CJ 276	CWH adj			
1 Jul 1907	162 CJ 292 – V	**CWH**			
2 Jul 1907	162 CJ 296	**CWH**			
2 Jul 1907	162 CJ 297 – V	**CWH**			
3 Jul 1907	162 CJ 300 – V	**CWH**			
8 Jul 1907	162 CJ 313	CWH adj			
9 Jul 1907	162 CJ 316	**CWH**			
10 Jul 1907	162 CJ 318	CWH adj			
11 Jul 1907	162 CJ 322	**CWH/Rep with Amds**			
15 Jul 1907	162 CJ 329	Cons			
16 Jul 1907	162 CJ 332	**Cons with Amds**			
16 Jul 1907	162 CJ 333	**Cons with Amds**			
22 Jul 1907	162 CJ 349	3R adj			
30 Jul 1907	162 CJ 370	3R adj			
30 Jul 1907	162 CJ 372 – V	3R			
8 Aug 1907	162 CJ 402	HL pass w/o Amds			
9 Aug 1907	162 CJ 406	Royal Assent			

Parliamentary debates

Ord: HC Deb, 1 May 1907, Vol 173(4th), col 991	1R: HL Deb, 31 Jul 1907, Vol 179(4th), col 932
1R: HC Deb, 8 May 1907, Vol 174(4th), col 277–278	2R: HL Deb, 7 Aug 1907, Vol 180(4th), col 16–52
2R: HC Deb, 13 May 1907, Vol 174(4th), col 651–701 and 717–732	3R: HL Deb, 8 Aug 1907, Vol 180(4th), col 285
2R: HC Deb, 14 May 1907, Vol 174(4th), col 805–871	Royal Assent: HL Deb, 9 Aug 1907, Vol 180(4th), col 485
CWH: HC Deb, 1 Jul 1907, Vol 177(4th), col 378–440	
CWH: HC Deb, 2 Jul 1907, Vol 177(4th), col 629–648	
CWH: HC Deb, 3 Jul 1907, Vol 177(4th), col 724–812	
CWH: HC Deb, 9 Jul 1907, Vol 177(4th), col 1449–1536	
Rep: HC Deb, 11 Jul 1907, Vol 178(4th), col 157–191	
Cons: HC Deb, 16 Jul 1907, Vol 178(4th), col 550–601 and 631–648	
3R: HC Deb, 30 Jul 1907, Vol 179(4th), col 786–835	

Debates on particular provisions

s 25	HC Deb, 13 May 1907, Vol 174(4th), col 660–661; HC Deb, 3 Jul 1907, Vol 177(4th), col 804–805

Parliamentary papers

Finance Bill (1907 HC Papers 190), Vol 2, p 223

Finance Bill (as amended in Committee and on Re-Committal) (1907 HC Papers 275), Vol 2, p 241

Finance Bill (as amended in Committee and on Re-Committal and on Report) (1907 HC Papers 288), Vol 2, p 261

Finance Bill (1907 HL Papers 144), Vol 4, p 41

Supplement to Votes & Proceedings, 1907

    27 May 1907, p 683–688; 3 Jun 1907, p 863–871; 10 Jun 1907, p 1019–1027; 17 Jun 1907, p 1179–1189; 24 Jun 1907, p 1341–1352; 1 Jul 1907, p 1525–1538; 2 Jul 1907, p 1605–1617; 3 Jul 1907, p 1677–1687; 8 Jul 1907, p 1785–1791; 9 Jul 1907, p 1811–1817; 10 Jul 1907, p 1871–1875; 11 Jul 1907, p 1891–1895

(continued)

(continued)

Newspaper coverage of debates (patent provisions only)
House of Commons
2R: **The Times, 15 May 1907**
CWH: **The Times, 4 Jul 1907**

White Phosphorus Matches Prohibition Act 1908

PUBA49	1908

White Phosphorus Matches Prohibition Act 1908 (8 Edw 7. c. 42)
An Act to prohibit the Manufacture, Sale, and Importation of Matches made with White Phosphorus, and for other purposes in connection therewith

Table of contents (patent provisions only)

s 4 Compulsory licence to use patents

Journal

House of Commons			House of Lords		
Pres: Herbert Gladstone (Hom Sec) Rep: Eugene Wason			Rep: Earl Beauchamp (Ld Stew)		
30 Jul 1908	163 CJ 384	1R	7 Dec 1908	140 LJ 458	Brought HC
12 Oct 1908	163 CJ 397	2R adj	7 Dec 1908	140 LJ 459	1R
13 Oct 1908	163 CJ 400	2R adj	8 Dec 1908	140 LJ 462	2R/C'tted CWH
14 Oct 1908	163 CJ 402	2R adj	14 Dec 1908	140 LJ 471	CWH/Rep w/o Amds
15 Oct 1908	163 CJ 403	2R adj	15 Dec 1908	140 LJ 478	3R
16 Oct 1908	163 CJ 405	2R adj	21 Dec 1908	140 LJ 504	Royal Assent
19 Oct 1908	163 CJ 407	2R/C'tted SC			
22 Oct 1908	163 CJ 414	Assigned SC A			
29 Oct 1908	163 CJ 420	Mem app			
30 Oct 1908	163 CJ 423	Mem app			
2 Nov 1908	163 CJ 424	Mem app			
5 Nov 1908	163 CJ 430	Mem disc/app			
24 Nov 1908	163 CJ 457	Mem disc/app			
25 Nov 1908	163 CJ 460	Rep with Amds			
26 Nov 1908	163 CJ 462	Cons adj			
27 Nov 1908	163 CJ 466	Cons adj			
1 Dec 1908	163 CJ 468	Cons adj			
1 Dec 1908	163 CJ 470	Cons adj			
2 Dec 1908	163 CJ 473	Cons adj			
3 Dec 1908	163 CJ 474	**Cons/3R**			
16 Dec 1908	163 CJ 505	HL pass w/o Amds			
21 Dec 1908	163 CJ 514	Royal Assent			

Parliamentary debates

1R: HC Deb, 30 Jul 1908, Vol 193(4th), col 1774	1R: HL Deb, 7 Dec 1908, Vol 198(4th), col 5
2R: HC Deb, 19 Oct 1908, Vol 194(4th), col 832–833	2R: HL Deb, 8 Dec 1908, Vol 198(4th), col 205–206
Cons/3R: HC Deb, 3 Dec 1908, Vol 194(4th), col 1746–1754	CWH/Rep: HL Deb, 14 Dec 1908, Vol 198(4th), col 1108
	3R: HL Deb, 15 Dec 1908, Vol 198(4th), col 1540
	Royal Assent: HL Deb, 21 Dec 1908, Vol 198(4th), col 2346

Debates on particular provisions

s 4	HC Deb, 19 Oct 1908, Vol 194(4th), col 832–833; HC Deb, 3 Dec 1908, Vol 194(4th), col 1748, 1750; HL Deb, 8 Dec 1908, Vol 198(4th), col 206

Parliamentary papers

White Phosphorus Matches Prohibition Bill (1908 HL Papers 238), Vol 9, p 809

White Phosphorus Matches Prohibition Bill (1908 HC Papers 351), Vol 5, p 951

White Phosphorus Matches Prohibition Bill (as amended by Standing Committee A) (1908 HC Papers 383), Vol 5, p 957

Report from Standing Committee A on the White Phosphorous Matches Prohibition Bill (1908 HC Papers 337), Vol 10, p 1291	
Supplement to Votes & Proceedings, 1908 – No amendments	
Implements: International Convention respecting the Prohibition of the Use of White (Yellow) Phosphorus in the Manufacture of Matches (1909 Cd 4530), 1909 Treaty Series 4, Vol 105, p 263: 2 Mar 1909 (164 CJ 34; 141 LJ 40)	
Newspaper coverage of debates (patent provisions only)	
House of Commons	
Cons: **The Times, 4 Dec 1908**	

Trading with the Enemy Amendment Act 1916

PUBA50	1916
Trading with the Enemy Amendment Act 1916 (5 & 6 Geo 5. c. 105)	
An Act to amend the Trading with the Enemy Acts	

Table of contents (patent provisions only)

s 6 Right of custodian to have enemy patent granted to him

Journal

House of Commons			House of Lords		
Pres: Sir George Cave (S-G) Rep: John Whitley (Ch W&M)			Rep: Earl of Donoughmore (Ld Ch)		
18 Jan 1916	170 CJ 337	Bill Ord/1R	25 Jan 1916	147 LJ 383	Brought HC/1R
20 Jan 1916	170 CJ 342	2R adj	26 Jan 1916	147 LJ 386	**2R//CWH/Rep with Amds/3R**
20 Jan 1916	170 CJ 344	2R adj	27 Jan 1916	147 LJ 388	HC Ag Amds
21 Jan 1916	170 CJ 345	2R/C'tted CWH	27 Jan 1916	147 LJ 391	Royal Assent
24 Jan 1916	170 CJ 347	CWH adj			
25 Jan 1916	170 CJ 348	**CWH/Rep with Amds**			
25 Jan 1916	170 CJ 350	3R			
26 Jan 1916	170 CJ 351	HL pass with Amds			
27 Jan 1916	170 CJ 352	HL Amds Ag			
27 Jan 1916	170 CJ 353	Royal Assent			

Parliamentary debates

1R: HC Deb, 18 Jan 1916, Vol 78(5th), col 180	1R: HL Deb, 25 Jan 1916, Vol 20(5th), col 1024
2R: HC Deb, 21 Jan 1916, Vol 78(5th), col 771–837	2R/CWH/3R: HL Deb, 26 Jan 1916, Vol 20(5th), col 1078–1090
CWH/3R: HC Deb, 25 Jan 1916, Vol 78(5), col 1079–1192	Royal Assent: HL Deb, 27 Jan 1916, Vol 20(5th), col 1109
HL Amds: HC Deb, 26 Jan 1916, Vol 78(5), col 1266–1267	
HL Amds Ag: HC Deb, 27 Jan 1916, Vol 78(5), col 1459–1464	
Royal Assent: HC Deb, 27 Jan 1916, Vol 78(5), col 1464	

Particular debates on patent provisions

s 6	HC Deb, 21 Jan 1916, Vol 78(5th), col 776–777, 801–803, 814–820, 829–835; HC Deb, 25 Jan 1916, Vol 78(5th), col 150–157

Parliamentary papers

Trading with the Enemy Amendment (No 2) Bill (1914–16 HC Papers 179), Vol 3, p 489

Trading with the Enemy Amendment Bill (1914–16 HL Papers 88), Vol 3, p 813

    Amendment to be moved in Committee by Lord Tenterden (1914–16 HL Papers 88a), Vol 3, p 827

Lords Amendments to the Trading with the Enemy (Amendment) (No 2) Bill (1914–16 HC Papers 184), Vol 3, p 499

Supplement to Votes & Proceedings, 1914–16

    25 Jan 1916, p 833–841

Notes

Archive

Enemy patents vested in Public Trustee: Trading with Enemy (Amendment) (No 2) Bill: National Archive (BT 209/119)

Trading with the Enemy Amendment Act 1918

PUBA51			1918		
Trading with the Enemy Amendment Act 1918 (8 & 9 Geo 5. c. 31)					
An Act to amend the enactments relating to Trading with the Enemy, and to extend temporarily certain of those enactments to the carrying on of banking business after the termination of the present war					
Table of contents (patent provisions only)					
s 8 Extension of power to vest property in custodian					
Journal					
House of Commons			**House of Lords**		
Presented: Sir Albert Stanley (Pr BoT) Rep: John Whitley (Ch W&M)			Rep: Earl of Donoughmore (Ld Ch)		
19 Jul 1918	173 CJ 170	Bill Ord/1R	26 Jul 1918	150 LJ 202	Brought HC/1R
22 Jul 1918	173 CJ 173	2R adj	31 Jul 1918	150 LJ 216	2R/C'tted
23 Jul 1918	173 CJ 175	2R/C'tted CWH	5 Aug 1918	150 LJ 230–V	**CWH/Rep w/o Amds/3R**
24 Jul 1918	173 CJ 179	CWH adj	8 Aug 1918	150 LJ 240	Royal Assent
25 Jul 1918	173 CJ 182	CWH adj			
26 Jul 1918	173 CJ 183	Proc not interrupted SO 183			
26 Jul 1918	173 CJ 183	**CWH/Rep with Amds/3R**			
5 Aug 1918	173 CJ 201	HL pass with Amds			
8 Aug 1918	173 CJ 208	Royal Assent			
Parliamentary debates					
1R: HC Deb, 19 Jul 1918, Vol 108(5th), col 1340			1R: HL Deb, 26 Jul 1918, Vol 30(5th), col 1207		
2R: HC Deb, 23 Jul 1918, Vol 108(5th), col 1700–1738			2R: HL Deb, 31 Jul 1918, Vol 31(5th), col 244		
CWH/Rep/3R: HC Deb, 26 Jul 1918, Vol 108(5th), col 2172–2216			CWH/Rep/3R: HL Deb, 5 Aug 1918, Vol 31(5th), col 489–494		
Royal Assent: HC Deb, 8 Aug 1918, Vol 109(5th), col 1559			Royal Assent: HL Deb, 8 Aug 1918, Vol 31(5th), col 680		
Debates on particular provisions					
s 8	HC Deb, 26 Jul 1918, Vol 108(5), col 2211–2212				
Parliamentary papers					
Trading with the Enemy Amendment Bill (1918 HC Papers 72), Vol 2, p 617					
Trading with the Enemy Amendment Bill (1918 HL Papers 124), Vol 3, p 705					
Amendments to be moved in Committee by Marquis of Lansdown (1918 HL Papers 124a), Vol 3, p 709					
Trading with the Enemy Amendment Bill (Amended in Committee) (1918 HL Papers 130), Vol 3, p 711					
Supplement to Votes & Proceedings – Not printed in 1918					

Income Tax Act 1918

PUBA52	1918
Income Tax Act 1918 (8 & 9 Geo 5. c. 40)	
An Act to Consolidate the Enactments relating to Income Tax	
Table of contents (patents provision)	
Schedule D, par 3(m) Schedule E, par 19 and 21	
Journal	
House of Commons	**House of Lords**
Rep: John Whitley (Ch W&M)	Presented: Lord Finlay Rep: Earl of Donoughmore (Ld Ch)

5 Mar 1918	173 CJ 27	HL Bill ref JC Cons	19 Feb 1918	150 LJ 19	1R
24 Jul 1918	173 CJ 177	JC Rep	20 Feb 1918	150 LJ 23	2R adj
30 Jul 1918	173 CJ 187	Brought HL/1R	28 Feb 1918	150 LJ 30	2R
31 Jul 1918	173 CJ 196	2R adj	5 Mar 1918	150 LJ 33	Ref JC Cons
1 Aug 1918	173 CJ 198	2R adj	24 Apr 1918	150 LJ 85	Pet for Amds
6 Aug 1918	173 CJ 204	2R/**CWH**/Rep with Amds/3R	24 Jul 1918	150 LJ 195	C'tted CWH
8 Aug 1918	173 CJ 207	HL Ag Amds	29 Jul 1918	150 LJ 205	SO 39 cons
8 Aug 1918	173 CJ 208	Royal Assent	30 Jul 1918	150 LJ 207	CWH/Rep with Amds/3R
			7 Aug 1918	150 LJ 235	**HC pass with Amds/Ag**
			8 Aug 1918	150 LJ 240	Royal Assent

Parliamentary debates	
1R: HC Deb, 30 Jul 1918, Vol 109(5th), col 243	1R: HL Deb, 19 Feb 1918, Vol 29(5th), col 38
2R/CWH/3R: HC Deb, 6 Aug 1918, Vol 109(5th), col 1307–1315	2R: HL Deb, 28 Feb 1918, Vol 29(5th), col 177–186
	CWH/3R: HL Deb, 30 Jul 1918, Vol 31(5th), col 53–59
Royal Assent: HC Deb, 8 Aug 1918, Vol 109(5th), col 1559	HC Amds: HL Deb, 7 Aug 1918, Vol 31(5th), col 621–622
	Royal Assent: HL Deb, 8 Aug 1918, Vol 31(5th), col 681

Parliamentary papers
Income Tax Bill (1917–18 HL Papers 1), Vol 2, p 771
Income Tax Bill (1918 HC Papers 80), Vol 1, p 573
Report from Joint Committee on Income Tax Bill (1918 HC Papers 95), Vol 4, p 1
Supplement to Votes & Proceedings – Not printed in 1918

Air Navigation Act 1920

PUBA53	1920				
Air Navigation Act 1920 (10 & 11 Geo 5. c. 80)					
An Act to enable effect to be given to a Convention for regulating air Navigation, and to make further provision for the control and regulation of aviation					
Table of contents (patent provisions only)					
s 13 Infringement of patents					
Journal					
House of Commons			**House of Lords**		
Rep: Sir William Pearce			Pres and Rep: Earl Vane (US Air)		
25 Jun 1920	175 CJ 241	Brought HL/1R	4 May 1920	152 LJ 145	1R
9 Aug 1920	175 CJ 373	2R/C'tted	11 May 1920	152 LJ 162	2R/C'tted CWH
10 Aug 1920	175 CJ 376	Assigned SC A	9 Jun 1920	152 LJ 204	CWH
20 Oct 1920	175 CJ 392	Mem Add	14 Jun 1920	152 LJ 209	Rep adj
21 Oct 1920	175 CJ 393	Ref COS	22 Jun 1920	152 LJ 229	**Rep with Amds/More Amds**
21 Oct 1920	175 CJ 394	COS adj	24 Jun 1920	152 LJ 238	**3R with Amds**
22 Oct 1920	175 CJ 396	Money Res	21 Dec 1920	152 LJ 584	HC pass with Amds
25 Oct 1920	175 CJ 397	Rep Money Res	22 Dec 1920	152 LJ 587	**HC Amds Ag**
4 Nov 1920	175 CJ 413	Rep with Amds	23 Dec 1920	152 LJ 598	Royal Assent
20 Dec 1920	175 CJ 501	**Cons/3R with Amds**			
23 Dec 1920	175 CJ 512	HL Ag Amds			
23 Dec 1920	175 CJ 516	Royal Assent			
Parliamentary debates					
Brought HL: HC Deb, 25 Jun 1920, Vol 130(5th), col 2547			1R: HL Deb, 4 May 1920, Vol 40(5th), col 59		
2R: HC Deb, 9 Aug 1920, Vol 133, Vol 133(5th), col 172–181			2R: HL Deb, 11 May 1920, Vol 40(5th), col 223–234		
			CWH: HL Deb, 9 Jun 1920, Vol 40(5th), col 534–551		
Mem Add: HC Deb, 20 Oct 1920, Vol 133(5th), col 922			Rep adj: HL Deb, 10 Jun 1920, Vol 40(5th), col 590		
Money Res: HC Deb, 20 Oct 1920, Vol 133(5th), col 1040			Rep: HL Deb, 22 Jun 1920, Vol 40(5th), col 734–735		
Ch App: HC Deb, 21 Oct 1920, Vol 133(5th), col 1087			3R: HL Deb, 24 Jun 1920, Vol 40(5th), col 842–843		
Money Res: HC Deb, 22 Oct 1920, Vol 133(5th), col 1292			HC pass: HL Deb, 21 Dec 1920, Vol 39(5th), col 820		

(continued)

(continued)

No SC Debate recorded Rep: HC Deb, 4 Nov 1920, Vol 134(5th), col 577–578 Cons/3R: HC Deb, 20 Dec 1920, Vol 136(5th), col 1458–1479 HL Ag Amd: HC Deb, 23 Dec 1920, Vol 136(5th), col 2126	HC Amd Ag: HL Deb, 22 Dec 1920, Vol 39(5th), col 874–876

Debate on particular provisions	
s 13	HL Deb, 11 May 1920, Vol 40(5th), col 232; HL Deb, 9 Jun 1920, Vol 40(5th), col 547–548

Parliamentary papers

Air Navigation Bill (1920 HL Papers 38), Vol 3, p 413

    Amendments to be moved in Committee by the Lord Montagu of Beaulien (1920 HL Papers 38a), Vol 3, p 429

    Amendments to be moved in Committee by the Earl Vane (1920 HL Papers 38b), Vol 3, p 431

    Marshalled List of Amendments to be moved in Committee (1920 HL Papers 38**), Vol 3, 433

Air Navigation Bill (as amended in Committee) (1920 HL Papers 70), Vol 3, p 437

    Amendments to be moved on Report by the Earl Vane (1920 HL Papers 70a), Vol 3, p 453

Air Navigation Bill (as amended on Report) (1920 HL Papers 86), Vol 3, p 437

Air Navigation Bill (1920 HC Papers 150), Vol 1, p 139

Air Navigation Bill (as amended by Standing Committee E) (1920 HC Papers 225), Vol 1, p 153

Commons Amendments (1920 HL Papers 254), Vol 3, p 471

Report from Standing Committee A on the Air Navigation Bill (1920 HC Papers 205), Vol 6, p 555

Air Navigation Bill, Memorandum on financial clauses (1920 Cmd 792), Vol 30, p 197: 28 Jun 1920 (175 CJ 243; Not LJ)

Supplement to Votes & Proceedings, 1920

    10 Aug 1920, p 1797; 21 Oct 1920, p 1897; 2 Nov 1920, p 2091–2092; 4 Nov 1920, p 2093–2094

Notes

Committee Home: Air Navigation Bill 1920: Minutes of Meetings and Reports: Ministry of Aviation: National Archive (AVIA 2/1739)

Finance Act 1927

PUBA54	1927

Finance Act 1927 (17 & 18 Geo 5. c. 10)

An Act to grant certain duties of Customs and Inland Revenue (including Excise), to alter other duties, and to amend the law relating to Customs and Inland Revenue (including Excise) and the National Debt, and to make further provision in connection with finance

Table of contents (patent provisions only)
s 39 Provisions with respect to income tax chargeable by way of deduction s 55 Relief from capital and transfer stamp duty in case of reconstructions or amalgamations of companies

Journal					
House of Commons			**House of Lords**		
Pres: Winston Churchill (Ch Ex) Rep: Edward FitzRoy (Dep Ch W&M)			No report		
28 Apr 1927	182 CJ 136	Bill Ord/1R	25 Jul 1927	159 LJ 237	Brought HC/1R
19 May 1927	182 CJ 170 – V	2R / C'tted CWH	26 Jul 1927	159 LJ 245	2R/Com neg
28 Jun 1927	182 CJ 226	**CWH**	27 Jul 1927	159 LJ 248	3R
30 Jun 1927	182 CJ 233	**CWH**	29 Jul 1927	159 LJ 255	Royal Assent
4 Jul 1927	182 CJ 238	**CWH**			
5 Jul 1927	182 CJ 243	**CWH**			
7 Jul 1927	182 CJ 248	**CWH/Rep with Amds**			
18 Jul 1927	182 CJ 270	**Cons**			
19 Jul 1927	182 CJ 276	**Cons**			
22 Jul 1927	182 CJ 284	**3R**			
27 Jul 1927	182 CJ 298	HL pass w/o Amds			
29 Jul 1927	182 CJ 308	Royal Assent			

Parliamentary Debates	
1R: HC Deb, 28 Apr 1927, Vol 205(5th), col 1169	1R: HL Deb, 25 Jul 1927, Vol 68(5th), col 809
2R: HC Deb, 19 May 1927, Vol 206(5th), col 1403–1515	2R: HL Deb, 26 Jul 1927, Vol 68(5th), col 881–923
CWH: HC Deb, 28 Jun 1927, Vol 208(5th), col 229–378	3R: HL Deb, 27 Jul 1927, Vol 68(5th), col 940
CWH: HC Deb, 30 Jun 1927, Vol 208(5th), col 597–798	Royal Assent: HL Deb, 29 Jul 1927, Vol 68(5th), col 962
CWH: HC Deb, 4 Jul 1927, Vol 208(5th), col 879–1064	
CWH: HC Deb, 5 Jul 1927, Vol 208(5th), col 1103–1234	
CWH: HC Deb, 7 Jul 1927, Vol 208(5th), col 1447–1529	
CWH: HC Deb, 7 Jul 1927, Vol 208(5th), col 1531–1609	
Cons: HC Deb, 18 Jul 1927, Vol 209(5th), col 43–199	
Cons: HC Deb, 19 Jul 1927, Vol 209(5th), col 337–378	
3R: HC Deb, 22 Jul 1927, Vol 209(5th), col 725–744	
Royal Assent: HC Deb, 29 Jul 1927, Vol 209(5th), col 1703	

Parliamentary papers
Finance Bill (1926–27 HC Papers 104), Vol 2, p 325
Finance Bill (as amended in Committee) (1926–27 HC Papers 131), Vol 2, p 377
Finance Bill (1926–27 HL Papers 108), Vol 2
Supplement to Votes & Proceedings, 1926–27
13 Jun 1927, p 1207–1218; 16 Jun 1927, p 1317–1320; 23 Jun 1927, p 1143–1462; 24 Jun 1927, p 1465–1467; 28 Jun 1927, p 1475–1496; 28 Jun 1927, p 1523–1531; 30 Jun 1927, p 1525–1558; 30 Jun 1927, p 1599–1606; 4 Jul 1927, p 1611–1633; 5 Jul 1927, p 1641–1653; 7 Jul 1927, p 1703–1712; 18 Jul 1927, p 1823–1834; 19 Jul 1927, p 1845–1848

Notes
Archive
Parliamentary Counsel Papers: Finance Bill 1927: Volume 1, 2 & 3: National Archive (AM 6/18, AM 6/19 and AM 6/20)

Finance Act 1930

PUBA55	1927					
Finance Act 1930 (20 & 21 Geo 5. c. 28)						
An Act to grant certain duties of Customs and Inland Revenue (including Excise), to alter other duties, and to amend the law relating to Customs and Inland Revenue (including Excise) and the National Debt, and to make further provision in connection with finance						

Table of contents (patent provisions only)

s 12 Deduction of tax
s 39 Provisions with respect to income tax chargeable by way of deduction
s 55 Relief from capital and transfer stamp duty in case of reconstructions or amalgamations of companies

Proposed clauses

NC Earned income relief in respect of royalties received by inventors
Cl 29 Estate duty

Journal

House of Commons			House of Lords		
Pres: Frederick Pethick-Lawrence (Fin Sec Tr) Rep: Robert Young (Ch W&M)			No report		
6 May 1930	185 CJ 327	1R	28 Jul 1930	162 LJ 522	Brought HC/1R
20 May 1930	185 CJ 352 – V	**2R/C'tted CWH**	29 Jul 1930	162 LJ 529	2R/Com neg/3R
27 May 1930	185 CJ 363 – V	**CWH**	1 Aug 1930	162 LJ 556	Royal Assent
3 Jun 1930	185 CJ 376 – V	**CWH**			
5 Jun 1930	185 CJ 386 – V	**CWH**			
17 Jun 1930	185 CJ 390 – V	**CWH**			
19 Jun 1930	185 CJ 397 – V	**CWH**			
23 Jun 1930	185 CJ 401 – V	**CWH**			

(continued)

(continued)

25 Jun 1930	185 CJ 408 – V	**CWH**			
1 Jul 1930	185 CJ 419 – V	**CWH**			
2 Jul 1930	185 CJ 421 – V	**CWH**			
3 Jul 1930	185 CJ 425 – V	**CWH**			
7 Jul 1930	185 CJ 429 – V	**CWH**			
9 Jul 1930	185 CJ 435 – V	**CWH/Rep with Amds**			
15 Jul 1930	185 CJ 448 – V	**Correct Div Nos**			
17 Jul 1930	185 CJ 454 – V	**Re–C'tted w/d**			
22 Jul 1930	185 CJ 463 – V	**Cons**			
25 Jul 1930	185 CJ 475 – V	**3R**			
30 Jul 1930	185 CJ 496	HL pass w/o Amds			
1 Aug 1930	185 CJ 509	Royal Assent			

Parliamentary debates

1R: HC Deb, 6 May 1930, Vol 238(5th), col 905–906	1R: HL Deb, 28 Jul 1930, Vol 78(5th), col 918
2R: HC Deb, 20 May 1930, Vol 239(5th), col 227–368	2R/Com neg/3R: HL Deb, 29 Jul 1930, Vol 78(5th), col 986–995
CWH: HC Deb, 27 May 1930, Vol 239(5th), col 1011–1264	Royal Assent: HL Deb, 1 Aug 1930, Vol 78(5th), col 1208
CWH: HC Deb, 3 Jun 1930, Vol 239(5th), col 1985–2126	
CWH: HC Deb, 5 Jun 1930, Vol 239(5th), col 2415–2536	
CWH: HC Deb, 17 Jun 1930, Vol 240(5th), col 55–370	
CWH: HC Deb, 19 Jun 1930, Vol 240(5th), col 601–738	
CWH: HC Deb, 23 Jun 1930, Vol 240(5th), col 823–939	
CWH: HC Deb, 25 Jun 1930, Vol 240(5th), col 1183–1312	
CWH: HC Deb, 1 Jul 1930, Vol 240(5th), col 1797–1930	
CWH: HC Deb, 2 Jul 1930, Vol 240(5th), col 1983–2114	
CWH: HC Deb, 3 Jul 1930, Vol 240(5th), col 2167–2308	
CWH: HC Deb, 7 Jul 1930, Vol 241(5th), col 59–122, 151–206	
CWH: HC Deb, 9 Jul 1930, Vol 241(5th), col 459–545	
Cons: HC Deb, 17 Jul 1930, Vol 241(5th), col 1499–1622	
Cons: HC Deb, 22 Jul 1930, Vol 241(5th), col 1965–2077	
3R: HC Deb, 25 Jul 1930, Vol 241(5th), col 2569–2655	
HL pass: HC Deb, 30 Jul 1930, Vol 242(5th), col 505	
Royal Assent: HC Deb, 1 Aug 1930, Vol 242(5th), col 1013	

Debate on particular provisions

s 12	HC Deb, 5 Jun 1930, Vol 239(5th), col 2447–2479

Proposed clauses

NC (w/d)	Earned income relief in respect of royalties received by inventors - clause w/d HC Deb, 17 Jul 1930, Vol 241(5th), col 1521–1526	Cl 29	Estate Duty HC Deb, 1 Jul 1930, Vol 240(5th), col 1864–1865, 1810–1811, 1856–1857, 1862–1865; HC Deb, 22 Jul 1930, Vol 241(5th), col 2005–2009

Parliamentary papers

Finance Bill (1929–30 HC Papers 184), Vol 1, p 809

Finance Bill (as amended in Committee) (1929–30 HC Papers 230), Vol 1, p 857

Finance Bill (1929–30 HL Papers 204), Vol 2

Supplement to Votes & Proceedings, 1929–30

> 20 May 1930, p 1915–1918; 22 May 1930, p 1973–1976; 23 May 1930, p 1979–1989; 27 May 1930, p 1993–2006; 27 May 1930, p 2041–2044; 29 May 1930, p 2089–2093; 2 Jun 1930, p 2101–2122; 3 Jun 1930, p 2135–2164; 5 Jun 1930, p 2225–2255; 5 Jun 1930, p 2257–2261; 17 Jun 1930, p 2275–2306; 17 Jun 1930, p 2323–2326; 19 Jun 1930, p 2369–2405; 23 Jun 1930, p 2411–2451; 25 Jun 1930, p 2491–2531; 30 Jun 1930, p 2585–2624; 1 Jul 1939, p 2637–2678; 2 Jul 1930, p 2713–52; 3 Jul 1930, p 2761–2789; 3 Jul 1930, p 2817–2820; 7 Jul 1930, p 2859–2880; 7 Jul 1930, p 2925–2927; 9 Jul 1930, p 2941–2951; 15 Jul 1930, p 3057–3061; 15 Jul 1930, p 3093–3194; 17 Jul 1930, p 3109–3130; 22 Jul 1930, p 3185–3194

Notes

Archive

Parliamentary Counsel Papers: Finance Bill 1930: Vol 1, 2 & 3: National Archive (AM 6/24, AM 6/25 and AM 6/26)

Finance Act 1935

PUBA56	1935
Finance Act 1935 (25 & 26 Geo 5. c. 24)	

An Act to grant certain duties of Customs and Inland Revenue (including Excise), to alter other duties, and to amend the law relating to Customs and Inland Revenue (including Excise) and the National Debt, and to make further provision in connection with finance

Table of contents (patent provisions only)

s 10 Valuation of goods for purpose of ad valorem duties

Journal

House of Commons			House of Lords		
Pres: Neville Chamberlain (Ch Ex) Rep: Robert Bourne (Dep Ch W&M)			No report		
1 May 1935	190 CJ 185	1R	5 Jul 1935	167 LJ 279	Brought HC/1R
21 May 1935	190 CJ 213 – V	**2R/C'tted CWH**	9 Jul 1935	167 LJ 290	2R/Com neg
18 Jun 1935	190 CJ 244 – V	**CWH**	10 Jul 1935	167 LJ 298	3R
19 Jun 1935	190 CJ 247 – V	**CWH**	10 Jul 1935	167 LJ 302	Royal Assent
24 Jun 1935	190 CJ 253 – V	**CWH/Rep with Amds**			
27 Jun 1935	190 CJ 266	Cons			
5 Jul 1935	190 CJ 278 – V	**Royal consent/3R**			
10 Jul 1935	190 CJ 285	HL pass w/o Amds			
10 Jul 1935	190 CJ 286	Royal Assent			

Parliamentary debates

1R: HC Deb, 1 May 1935, Vol 301(5th), col 519	1R: HL Deb, 5 Jul 1935, Vol 97(5th), col 1332
2R: HC Deb, 21 May 1935, Vol 302(5th), col 187–316	2R/Com Neg: HL Deb, 9 Jul 1935, Vol 98(5th), col 95–104
CWH: HC Deb, 18 Jun 1935, Vol 303(5th), col 187–334	3R: HL Deb, 10 Jul 1935, Vol 98(5th), col 191
CWH: HC Deb, 19 Jun 1935, Vol 303(5th), col 375–519	Royal Assent: HL Deb, 10 Jul 1935, Vol 98(5th), col 245
CWH: HC Deb, 24 Jun 1935, Vol 303(5th), col 823–919	
Rep: HC Deb, 1 Jul 1935, Vol 303(5th), col 1539–1670	
Royal consent: HC Deb, 5 Jul 1935, Vol 303(5th), col 2139	
3R: HC Deb, 5 Jul 1935, Vol 303(5th), col 2139–2224	
HL pass: HC Deb, 10 Jul 1935, Vol 304(5th), col 331	
Royal Assent: HC Deb, 10 Jul 1935, Vol 304(5th), col 376	

Debates on particular provisions

s 10	HC Deb, 18 Jun 1935, Vol 303(5th), col 297–319

Parliamentary papers

Finance Bill (1934–35 HL Papers 114), Vol 1

Finance Bill (1934–35 HC Papers 85), Vol 1, p 463

Finance Bill (as amended in Committee and on Report) (1934–35 HC Papers 90) Vol 1, p 495

Supplement to Votes & Proceedings, 1934–35

    21 May 1935, p 2337–2345; 5 Jun 1935, p 2517–2530; 6 Jun 1935, p 2351–2536; 18 Jun 1935, p 2543–2560; 19 Jun 1935, p 2561–2575; 24 Jun 1935, p 2577–2587; 27 Jun 1935, p 2607–2613; 1 Jul 1935, p 2629–2636

Notes

Archive

Parliamentary Counsel Papers: Finance Bill 1935: Vol 1 & 2: National Archive (AM 6/36 & AM 6/37)

Finance (No 2) Act 1940

PUBA57	1940
Finance (No 2) Act 1940 (3 & 4 Geo 6. c. 48)	

An Act to increase certain duties of customs and excise; to increase the standard rate of income tax for the year 1940–41 and the higher rates of income tax for the year 1939–40; to make certain amendments in the enactments relating to income tax, national defence contribution and excess profits tax; to increase the rates of estate duty; to impose a purchase tax; and for purposes connected with the matters aforesaid

(continued)

(continued)

Table of contents (patent provisions only)
Sch 8 Purchase Tax (Determination of wholesale value), par 3

Journal

House of Commons			House of Lords		
Pres: Harry Crookshank (Fin Sec Tr) Rep: Dennis Herbert (Ch W&M)			No report		
31 Jul 1940	195 CJ 217	1R	20 Aug 1940	172 LJ 221	Brought HC/1R
6 Aug 1940	195 CJ 220	2R/C'tted CWH	21 Aug 1940	172 LJ 223	2R/Com neg/3R
8 Aug 1940	195 CJ 223	CWH	22 Aug 1940	172 LJ 225	Royal Assent
13 Aug 1940	195 CJ 225 – V	**CWH/Rep with Amds**			
15 Aug 1940	195 CJ 228	Cons/3R			
21 Aug 1940	195 CJ 231	HL pass w/o Amds			
22 Aug 1940	195 CJ 233	Royal Assent			

Parliamentary debates

1R: HC Deb, 31 Jul 1940, Vol 363(5th), col 1306	Brought HL: HL Deb, 20 Aug 1940, Vol 117(5th), col 271
2R: HC Deb, 6 Aug 1940, Vol 364(5th), col 38–176	2R/3R: HL Deb, 21 Aug 1940, Vol 117(5th), col 319–350
CWH: HC Deb, 8 Aug 1940, Vol 364(5th), col 428–576	Royal Assent: HL Deb, 22 Aug 1940, Vol 117(5th), col 363
CWH: HC Deb, 13 Aug 1940, Vol 364(5th), col 613–752	
Rep/3R: HC Deb, 15 Aug 1940, Vol 364(5th), col 970–1085	
HL pass: HC Deb, 21 Aug 1940, Vol 364(5th), col 1314	
Royal Assent: HC Deb, 22 Aug 1940, Vol 364(5th), col 1475	

Parliamentary papers

Finance Bill (No 2) (1939–40 HC Papers 77, Vol 2, p 225

Finance Bill (No 2) (1939–40 HC Papers 81), Vol 2, p 279

Finance Bill (No 2) (1939–40 HL Papers 75), Vol 1

Supplement to Votes & Proceedings, 1940

> 6 Aug 1940, p 107–109; 8 Aug 1940, p 111–120; 8 Aug 1940, p 121–127; 13 Aug 1940, p 129–135; 15 Aug 1940, p 137–139

Notes

Archive

Parliamentary Counsel Papers: Finance Bill (No 2) 1940: Vol 1, 2 & 3: National Archive (AM 6/49 & AM 6/50)

Income Tax Act 1945

PUBA58	1945
Income Tax Act 1945 (8 & 9 Geo 6. c. 32)	
An Act to amend the law relating to income tax in certain respects	

Table of contents (patent provisions only)
Part V s 35 Annual allowances for capital expenditure on purchase of patent rights s 36 Effect of lapse of patent right, sales, etc. s 37 Charges on capital sums received for sale of patent rights s 38 Patent rights sold before appointed day s 39 Relief for expenses s 40 Patent income to be earned income in certain cases s 41 Spreading of income payment over several years s 42 When a person is to be treated as a trader s 43 Interpretation of Part V, etc. s 59 Special provisions as to certain sales s 64 Interpretation of certain references to expenditure, etc. Sch 2 Effect of Deaths, Windings Up and Partnership Changes on Certain Charges in respect of Patent Rights

Journal					
House of Commons			**House of Lords**		
Pres: Sir John Anderson (Ch Ex) Rep: Charles Williams (Dep Ch W&M)			No report		
14 Feb 1945	200 CJ 52	1R	4 Jun 1945	177 LJ 131	Brought HC/1R
14 Mar 1945	200 CJ 75	2R/C'tted CWH	7 Jun 1945	177 LJ 139	2R/Com neg/3R
27 Apr 1945	200 CJ 109	**CWH**	15 Jun 1945	177 LJ 152	Royal Assent
15 May 1945	200 CJ 128	**CWH/Rep with Amds**			
4 Jun 1945	200 CJ 146	**Cons/3R**			
7 Jun 1945	200 CJ 154	HL pass w/o Amds			
15 Jun 1945	200 CJ 169	Royal Assent			

Parliamentary debates	
1R: HC Deb, 14 Feb 1945, Vol 408(5th), col 233	1R: HL Deb, 3 Jun 1945, Vol 136(5th), col 364
2R: HC Deb, 14 Mar 1945, Vol 409(5th), col 257–340	2R/3R: HL Deb, 7 Jun 1945, Vol 136(5th), col 497–507
CWH: HC Deb, 27 Apr 1945, Vol 410(5th), col 1113–1197	Royal Assent: HL Deb, 15 Jun 1945, Vol 136(5th), col 649
CWH: HC Deb, 15 May 1945, Vol 410(5th), col 2311–2426	
CWH: HC Deb, 4 Jun 1945, Vol 411(5th), col 586–600	
HL pass: HC Deb, 7 Jun 1945, Vol 411(5th), col 1076	
Royal Assent: HC Deb, 15 Jun 1945, Vol 411(5th), col 1904	

Debates on particular provisions	
Part V	HC Deb, HC Deb, 14 Mar 1945, Vol 409(5th), col 298–299, 327, 337–338

Parliamentary papers
Income Tax Bill (1944–45 HC Papers 27), Vol 1, p 517
Income Tax Bill (as amended in Committee) (1944–45 HC Papers 54), Vol 1, p 583
Income Tax Bill (1944–45 HL Papers 42), Vol 1
Supplement to Votes & Proceedings, 1944–45
20 Apr 1945, p 783–796; 24 Apr 1945, p 807–824; 25 Apr 1945, p 833–852; 27 Apr 1945, p 855–875; 3 May 1945, p 953–970; 8 May 1945, p 983–1000; 15 May 1945, p 1059–1077

Notes
Archive
Parliamentary Counsel Papers: Income Tax Bill 1945: Vol 1, 2 & 3: National Archive (AM 1/349, AM 1/350 & AM 1/351)

Atomic Energy Act 1946

PUBA59	1946		
Atomic Energy Act 1946 (9 & 10 Geo 6. c. 80)			
An Act to provide for the development of atomic energy and the control of such development and for purposes connected therewith			
Table of contents (patent provisions only)			
s 12 Special provisions as to inventions			

Journal					
House of Commons			**House of Lords**		
Pres: John Wilmot (Min Air Prod) Money Res: Robert Taylor (Dep Ch Wh) CWH Rep: James Milner (Ch W&M)			Rep: Earl of Drogheda (Ld Ch)		
1 May 1946	201 CJ 240	1R	11 Oct 1946	178 LJ 417	Brought HC/1R
8 Oct 1946	201 CJ 377	2R/C'tted CWH/Money Res	15 Oct 1946	178 LJ 421	2R day app
11 Oct 1946	201 CJ 382	**Money Res Rep**	23 Oct 1946	178 LJ 438	2R/C'tted CWH
11 Oct 1946	201 CJ 382	**CWH/Rep with Amds/3R**	29 Oct 1946	178 LJ 449	**CWH/Rep with Amds**
31 Oct 1946	201 CJ 399	HL pass with Amds	31 Oct 1946	178 LJ 454	3R
4 Nov 1946	201 CJ 404	HL Amds Ag	5 Nov 1946	178 LJ 456	HC Ag Amds
6 Nov 1946	201 CJ 407	Royal Assent	6 Nov 1946	178 LJ 460	Royal Assent

(continued)

(continued)

Parliamentary debates	
2R: HC Deb, 8 Oct 1946, Vol 427(5th), col 43–98, 133–146	Brought HC: HL Deb, 11 Oct 1946, Vol 143(5th), col 161
CWH/3R: HC Deb, 11 Oct 1946, Vol 427(5th), col 495–571	2R: HL Deb, 23 Oct 1946, Vol 143(5th), col 569–590
Royal Assent: HC Deb, 6 Dec 1946, Vol 428(5th), col 1399	3R: HL Deb, 31 Oct 1946, Vol 143(5th), col 952
	Royal Assent: HL Deb, 6 Nov 1946, Vol 143(5th), col 1067

Debates on particular provisions	
s 12	HC Deb, 8 Oct 1946, Vol 427(5th), col 48; HC Deb, 11 Oct 1946, Vol 427(5th), col 552–555; HL Deb, 29 Oct 1946, Vol 143(5th), col 815–818

Parliamentary papers
Atomic Energy Bill (1945–46 HC Papers 113), Vol 1, p 157
Atomic Energy Bill (1946 HL Papers 136), Vol 1
Amendments to be moved in Committee by Viscount Addison (1946 HL Papers 136a), Vol 1
Lords Amendments to Atomic Energy Bill (1945–46 HC Papers 169), Vol 1, p 181
Supplement to Votes & Proceedings, 1945–6
11 Oct 1946, p 2893–2896

Air Navigation Act 1947

PUBA60	1947

Air Navigation Act 1947 (10 & 11 Geo 6. c. 18)
An Act to provide for giving effect to a Convention on International Civil Aviation signed at Chicago on the seventh day of December, nineteen hundred and forty-four, and to make further provision for the regulation of air navigation; to provide for giving effect to certain provisions of an Interim Agreement on International Civil Aviation so signed; and for purposes connected with the matters aforesaid

Table of contents (patent provisions only)
s 3 Exemption of aircraft and parts thereof from seizure on patent claims

Journal					
House of Commons			**House of Lords**		
Money Rep: Robert Taylor (Dep Ch Whip) CWH Rep: Hubert Beaumont (Dep Ch W&M)			Pres: Lord Nathan (Min Civ Av) Rep: Earl of Drogheda (Ld Ch)		
12 Feb 1947	202 CJ 94	Brought HL/1R	10 Dec 1946	179 LJ 32	1R
21 Feb 1947	202 CJ 108	**2R/Money/C'tted CWH**	19 Dec 1946	179 LJ 45	2R/C'tted CWH
14 Mar 1947	202 CJ 138	**CWH/Rep with Amds/3R**	30 Jan 1947	179 LJ 68	**CWH/Rep with Amds**
24 Mar 1947	202 CJ 149	HL Ag Amds	6 Feb 1947	179 LJ 77	**Cons with Amds**
27 Mar 1947	202 CJ 154	Royal Assent	11 Feb 1947	179 LJ 80	**3R with Amds**
			18 Mar 1947	179 LJ 140	HC pass with Amds
			24 Mar 1947	179 LJ 150	**HC Amds Ag**
			27 Mar 1947	179 LJ 171	Royal Assent

Parliamentary debates	
2R: HC Deb, 21 Feb 1947, Vol 433(5th), col 1585–1626	1R: HL Deb, 10 Dec 1946, Vol 144(5th), col 709
CWH/3R: HC Deb, 14 Mar 1947, Vol 434(5th), col 1709–1753	2R: HL Deb, 19 Dec 1946, Vol 144(5th), col 1136–1164
Royal Assent: HC Deb, 27 Mar 1947, Vol 435(5th), col 1454	CWH: HL Deb, 30 Jan 1947, Vol 145(5th), col 310–344
	Cons: HL Deb, 6 Feb 1947, Vol 145(5th), col 466–470
	3R: HL Deb, 11 Feb 1947, Vol 145(5th), col 556
	Royal Assent: HL Deb, 27 Mar 1947, Vol 146(5th), col 912

Debates on particular provisions	
s 3	HC Deb, 21 Feb 1947, Vol 433(5th), col 1591

Parliamentary papers
Air Navigation Bill (1946–47 HL Papers 15), Vol 1
Air Navigation Bill (1946–47 HC Papers 38), Vol 1, p 527
Supplement to Votes & Proceedings, 1946–47 – No amendments

Crown Proceedings Act 1947

PUBA61	1947

Crown Proceedings Act 1947 (10 & 11 Geo 6. c. 44)

An Act to amend the law relating to the civil liabilities and rights of the Crown and to civil proceedings by and against the Crown, to amend the law relating to the civil liabilities of persons other than the Crown in certain cases involving the affairs or property of the Crown, and for purposes connected with the matters aforesaid

Table of contents (patent provisions only)

s 3 Infringement of intellectual property rights

Journal

House of Commons			House of Lords		
Money Rep: Michael Stewart CWH: Hubert Beaumont (Dep Ch W&M)			Pres: Lord Jowitt LC Rep: Earl of Drogheda (Ld Ch)		
31 Mar 1947	202 CJ 157	Brought HL	13 Feb 1947	179 LJ 87	1R
1 Apr 1947	202 CJ 159	1R	19 Feb 1947	179 LJ 98	2R day app
4 Jul 1947	202 CJ 295	2R/Royal consent/C'tted CWH/ Money Res	4 Mar 1947	179 LJ 119	Royal consent/2R/C'tted CWH
			13 Mar 1947	179 LJ 135	**CWH**
11 Jul 1947	202 CJ 306	**Res Ag/CWH**	14 Mar 1947	179 LJ 138	Cons adj
25 Jul 1947	202 CJ 330	**CWH/Rep with Amds/3R**	24 Mar 1947	179 LJ 149	**Cons with Amds**
31 Jul 1947	202 CJ 339	HL Ag Amds	26 Mar 1947	179 LJ 169	3R adj
31 Jul 1947	202 CJ 340	Royal Assent	31 Mar 1947	179 LJ 175	**3R with Amds**
			28 Jul 1947	179 LJ 427	HC pass with Amds
			31 Jul 1947	179 LJ 460	**HC Amds Ag**
			31 Jul 1947	179 LJ 465	Royal Assent

Parliamentary debates

2R: HC Deb, 4 Apr 1947, Vol 439(5th), col 1675–1753	1R: HL Deb, 13 Feb 1947, Vol 145(5th), col 617
CWH: HC Deb, 11 Jul 1947, Vol 439(5th) col 2607–2657	2R: HL Deb, 4 Mar 1947, Vol 146(5th), col 60–93
CWH/3R: HC Deb, 25 Jul 1947, Vol 440(5th), col 1779–1796	CWH: HL Deb, 13 Mar 1947, Vol 146(5th), col 60–93
Royal Assent: HC Deb, 31 Jul 1947, Vol 441(5th), col 683	Cons: HL Deb, 24 Mar 1947, Vol 146(5th), col 655–664
	3R: HL Deb, 31 Mar 1947, Vol 146(5th) col 923–933
	HC Amds Ag: HL Deb, 31 Jul 1947, Vol 151(5th), col 847–856
	Royal Assent: HL Deb, 31 Jul 1947, Vol 151(5th), col 925–926

Debates on particular provisions

s 3 (and related)	HL Deb, 4 Mar 1946, Vol 146(5th), col 67; HL Deb, 13 Mar 1947, Vol 146(5th), col 367–369

Parliamentary papers

Crown Proceedings Bill (1946–47 HL Papers 32), Vol 1

Amendments to be Moved in Committee by the Marquess of Reading (1946–47 HL Papers 32a), Vol 1

Amendments to be Moved in Committee by the Lord Chancellor, the Lord Llewellin, The Lord Simonds, the Lord Normand and the Earl of Munster (1946–47 HL Papers 32b), Vol 1

Marshalled List of Amendments (1946–47 HL Papers 32**), Vol 1

(continued)

(continued)

Crown Proceedings Bill (as amended in Committee) (1946–47 HL Papers 42), Vol 1
Amendments to be moved on Report by the Lord Chancellor and the Viscount Simon (1946–47 HL Papers 42a), Vol 1
Amendment to be moved on Report by the Lord Simonds (1946–47 HL Papers 42b), Vol 1
Marshalled List of Amendments to be Moved on Report (1946–47 HL Papers 42**), Vol 1
Crown Proceedings Bill (as amended on Report) (1946–47 HL Papers 46), Vol 1
Crown Proceedings Bill (1946–47 HC Papers 58), Vol 1, p 949
Commons Amendments (1946–47 HL Papers 116), Vol 1
Supplement to Votes & Proceedings, 1946–47
7 Jul 1947, p 4333–4335; 8 Jul 1947, p 4373–4376; 9 Jul 1947, p 4385–4391; 11 Jul 1047, p 4393–4399

Finance Act 1947

PUBA62	1947					
	Finance Act 1947 (10 & 11 Geo 6. c. 35)					

An Act to grant certain duties, to alter other duties, and to amend the law relating to the National Debt, the Public Revenue and Savings Banks and to make further provision in connection with Finance

Table of contents (patent provisions only)
Sch 7 Income tax in relation to assets transferred under Coal Industry Nationalisation Act, 1946 (Patent Rights), par 10 Sch 8 Computation of profits, etc., for purposes of the profits tax

Journal					
House of Commons			**House of Lords**		
Pres: William Glenvil Hall (Fin Sec Tr) Money Rep: Robert Taylor (Dep Ch Wh) CWH Rep: Hubert Beaumont (Dep Ch W&M)			No report		
17 Apr 1947	202 CJ 174	Money Res	21 Jul 1947	179 LJ 405	Brought HC/1R
24 Apr 1947	202 CJ 189	**Money Rep/1R**	24 Jul 1947	179 LJ 423	2R/Com neg
19 May 1947	202 CJ 232 – V	2R/C'tted CWH	30 Jul 1947	179 LJ 455	3R
9 Jun 1947	202 CJ 254	CWH Instruction	31 Jul 1947	179 LJ 465	Royal Assent
10 Jun 1947	202 CJ 255 – V	**CWH**			
11 Jun 1947	202 CJ 257 – V	**CWH**			
16 Jun 1947	202 CJ 264 – V	**CWH**			
17 Jun 1947	202 CJ 266 – V	**CWH**			
25 Jun 1947	202 CJ 283	**Instructions to C'tee**			
3 Jul 1947	202 CJ 293	**Instructions to C'tee**			
9 Jul 1947	202 CJ 302 – V	**Rep with Amds/Re–Ct CWH**			
16 Jul 1947	202 CJ 311 – V	**Rep with Amds**			
18 Jul 1947	202 CJ 317	3R			
30 Jul 1947	202 CJ 337	HL pass w/o Amds			
31 Jul 1947	202 CJ 340	Royal Assent			

Parliamentary debates	
1R: HC Deb, 23 Apr 1947, Vol 436(5th), col 1203–1205	1R: HL Deb, 21 Jul 1947, Vol 151(5th), col 1
2R: HC Deb, 19 May 1947, Vol 437(5th), col 2011–2138	2R: HL Deb, 24 Jul 1947, Vol 151(5th), col 362–402
CWH: HC Deb, 10 Jun 1947, Vol 438(5th), col 883–1028	3R: HL Deb, 30 Jul 1947, Vol 151(5th), col 747
CWH: HC Deb, 11 Jun 1947, Vol 438(5th), col 1076–1312	Royal Assent: HL Deb, 31 Jul 1947, Vol 151(5th), col 925
CWH: HC Deb, 16 Jun 1947, Vol 438(5th), col 1594–1751	
CWH: HC Deb, 17 Jun 1947, Vol 438(5th), col 1793–1822	
CWH: HC Deb, 17 Jun 1947, Vol 438(5th), col 1921–1968	
Re-Ct: Com: HC Deb, 9 Jul 1947, Vol 439(5th), col 2215–2398	
Rep: HC Deb, 16 Jul 1947, Vol 440(5th), col 399–552	
3R: HC Deb, 18 Jul 1947, Vol 440(5th), col 734–757, 757–808	
Royal Assent: HC Deb, 31 Jul 1947, Vol 441(5th), col 683	

Parliamentary papers
Finance Bill (1946–47 HC Papers 64), Vol 2, p 437
Finance Bill (as amended in Committee) (1946–47 HC Papers 88), Vol 2, p 533
Finance Bill (1946–47 HL Papers 111), Vol 2
Supplement to Votes & Proceedings, 1946–47
22 May 1947, p 3295–3301; 30 May 1947, p 3365–3368; 3 Jun 1947, p 3435–3438; 5 Jun 1947, p 3485–3509; 6 Jun 1947, p 3517–3557; 10 Jun 1947, p 3601–3644; 11 Jun 1947, p 3679–3710; 16 Jun 1947, p 3747–3768; 17 Jun 1947, p 3773–3787; 18 Jun 1947, p 3873–3876; 26 Jun 1947, p 4063–4065; 27 Jun 1947, p 4079–4084; 30 Jun 1947, p 4103–4110; 1 Jul 1947, p 4117–4146; 2 Jul 1947, p 4217–4221; 3 Jul 1947, p 4225–4227; 7 Jul 1947, p 4297–4331; 9 Jul 1947, p 4337–4372; 16 Jul 1947, p 4407–4435

Development of Inventions Act 1948

PUBA63	1948
	Development of Inventions Act 1948 (10 & 11 Geo 6. c. 60)

An Act to establish a national corporation for securing the development and exploitation of inventions; to authorise advances to the corporation out of the Consolidated Fund and, in respect of certain services, payments to the corporation out of moneys provided by Parliament; and for matters connected therewith

Table of contents

s 1 The National Research Development Corporation
s 2 Constitution of Corporation
s 3 Balancing of accounts of Corporation
s 4 Powers of Board of Trade as to exercise of functions of Corporation
s 5 Power of Government departments to meet Corporation's losses on services provided for departments
s 6 Temporary borrowing powers of Corporation
s 7 Power of Board of Trade to make advances to Corporation
s 8 Repayment of, and interest on, advances under last foregoing section
s 9 Establishment of reserve
s 10 Accounts and audit
s 11 Issues out of the Consolidated Fund
s 12 Application of, and accounting for, receipts of Board of Trade
s 13 Exercise of powers of Board of Trade
s 14 Short title
Schedule Provisions relating to Constitution, etc., of Corporation

Journal

House of Commons			House of Lords		
Money Rep: Charles Simmons (Ass Whip) SC Rep: Herbert Butcher			Pres: Viscount Hall (Fir Ld Adm) Rep: Earl of Drogheda (Ld Ch)		
11 May 1948	203 CJ 270	Brought HL	13 Apr 1948	180 LJ 203	1R
11 May 1948	203 CJ 271	1R	29 Apr 1948	180 LJ 230	2R/C'tted CWH
11 Jun 1948	203 CJ 312	Money Res/2R/C'tted	6 May 1948	180 LJ 242	**CWH/Rep with Amds**
15 Jun 1948	203 CJ 317	Assigned SC C	11 May 1948	180 LJ 248	**Cons with Amds/3R**
17 Jun 1948	203 CJ 320	Money Res Ag	19 Jul 1948	180 LJ 402	HC pass with Amds
17 Jun 1948	203 CJ 321	Chair App	27 Jul 1948	180 LJ 421	**HC Amds Ag**
21 Jun 1948	203 CJ 323	Mem App	30 Jul 1948	180 LJ 431	Royal Assent
30 Jun 1948	203 CJ 339	Rep with Amds			
16 Jul 1948	203 CJ 362	Cons/3R			
27 Jul 1948	203 CJ 383	HL Ag Amds			
30 Jul 1948	203 CJ 393	Royal Assent			

Parliamentary debates

2R: HC Deb, 11 Jun 1948, Vol 451(5th), col 2676–2745	1R: HL Deb, 13 Apr 1948, Vol 155(5th), col 1
Money Res HC Deb, 17 Jun 1948, Vol 452(5th), col 808–809	2R: HL Deb, 29 Apr 1948, Vol 155(5th), col 591–597
SC Deb C, 30 Jun 1948, Vol 3, col 331–374	CWH: HL Deb, 6 May 1948, Vol 155(5th), col 685–690
Cons/3R: HC Deb, 16 Jul 1948, Vol 453(5th), col 1637–1650	Cons/3R: HL Deb, 11 May 1948, Vol 155(5th), col 753–754
	Royal Assent: HL Deb, 30 Jul 1948, Vol 157(5th), col 1337

(continued)

(continued)

Parliamentary papers
Development of Inventions Bill (1948 HL Papers 65), Vol 2
Amendment to be moved in Committee (1948 HL Papers 65a), Vol 2
Amendments to be moved in Committee by the Viscounts Maugham and Swinton and the Lord Teynham (1948 HL Papers 65b), Vol 2
Amendment to be moved on Report [sic] by the Viscount Hall (1948 HL Papers 65c), Vol 2
Development of Inventions Bill (1947–48 HC Papers 95), Vol 2, p 315
Development of Inventions Bill (as amended in Committee) (1947–48 HC Papers 122), Vol 2, p 329
Commons Amendments (1948 HL Papers 140), Vol 2
Standing Committee C. Minutes of proceedings on the Development of Inventions Bill (1947–48 HC Papers 178), Vol 6, p 167
Supplement to Votes & Proceedings, 1947–48   24 Jun 1948, p 3803–3804; 25 Jun 1948, p 3815–3817; 28 Jun 1948, p 3827–3830; 30 Jun 1948, p 3839–3842

Civil Aviation Act 1949

PUBA64	1949

Civil Aviation Act 1949 (12 & 13 Geo 5. c. 67)
An Act to consolidate the enactments relating to civil aviation, other than the Carriage by Air Act, 1932, and other than the enactments relating to the constitution and functions of the Airways Corporations

Table of contents (patent provisions only)
S 53 Exemption of aircraft and parts thereof from seizure on patent claims [Origin: Air Navigation Act 1947, s 3] Sch 8 Patent Claims against Aircraft not protected under Chicago Convention

Journal

House of Commons			House of Lords		
Rep: James Milner (Ch WM)			Pres: Viscount Jowitt LC Rep: Earl of Drogheda (Ld Ch)		
30 Jun 1949	204 CJ 288	Rep JC Cons	23 Jun 1949	181 LJ 272	1R
14 Jul 1949	204 CJ 311	Brought HL	28 Jun 1949	181 LJ 278	2R/Ref JC Cons
15 Jul 1949	204 CJ 313	1R	30 Jun 1949	181 LJ 286	Rep with Amds/Re-C'tted CWH
21 Oct 1949	204 CJ 371	2R/C'tted CWH			
28 Oct 1949	204 CJ 383	CWH/Rep w/o Amds/3R	6 Jul 1949	181 LJ 304	CWH with Amds
24 Nov 1949	204 CJ 410	Royal Assent	14 Jul 1949	181 LJ 318	**Rep with Amds/3R**
			1 Nov 1949	181 LJ 403	HC pass w/o Amds
			24 Nov 1949	181 LJ 472	Royal Assent

Parliamentary debates

2R: HC Deb, 21 Oct 1949, Vol 468(5th), col 964	1R: HL Deb, 23 Jun 1949, Vol 163(5th), col 226
CWH/3R: HC Deb, 28 Oct 1949, Vol 468(5th), col 1729	2R: HL Deb, 28 Jun 1949, Vol 163(5th), col 353
Royal Assent: HC Deb, 24 Nov 1949, Vol 470(5th), col 578	Rep: HL Deb, 30 Jun 1949, Vol 163(5th), col 744
	Cons/3R: HL Deb, 14 Jul 1949, Vol 163(5th), col 1360
	HC pass: HL Deb, 1 Nov 1949, Vol 165(5th), col 20
	Royal Assent: HL Deb, 24 Nov 1949, Vol 165(5th), col 1007

Parliamentary papers

Civil Aviation Bill (1948–49 HL Papers 120), Vol 1
Amendment made by the Joint Committee on Consolidation Bills (1948–49 HL Papers 120a), Vol 1
Civil Aviation Bill (1948–49 HC Papers 174), Vol 1, p 397
Fourth Report by Joint Committee on Consolidation Bills upon Civil Aviation Bill (1948–49 HC Papers 200 and 200–I), Vol 6, p 763 and 765
Supplement to Votes & Proceedings, 1948–49 – No amendments

Finance Act 1951

PUBA65	1951
	Finance Act 1951 (14 & 15 Geo 6. c. 43)

An Act to grant certain duties, to alter other duties, and to amend the law with respect to the National Debt (including the Sinking Funds therefor), Customs and Inland Revenue (including Excise)

Table of contents (patent provisions)

Sch 2 Value of Imported Goods

Journal

House of Commons			House of Lords		
Pres: Douglas Jay (Fin Sec Tr) Rep: Charles MacAndrew (Dep Ch W&M)			No report		
16 Apr 1951	206 CJ 173	Money Res	4 Jul 1951	183 LJ 223	Brought HC/1R
18 Apr 1951	206 CJ 183	Rep Money Res	17 Jul 1941	183 LJ 243	2R/Com neg
18 Apr 1951	206 CJ 184	Bill Ord/1R	24 Jul 1951	183 LJ 251	3R
8 May 1951	206 CJ 208	2R/C'tted CWH	1 Aug 1951	183 LJ 276	Royal Assent
5 Jun 1951	206 CJ 228 – V	**CWH**			
6 Jun 1951	206 CJ 229 – V	**CWH**			
7 Jun 1951	206 CJ 230 – V	**CWH**			
11 Jun 1951	206 CJ 234 – V	**CWH**			
13 Jun 1951	206 CJ 240 – V	**CWH**			
14 Jun 1951	206 CJ 242 – V	**CWH**			
18 Jun 1951	206 CJ 244 – V	**CWH**			
19 Jun 1951	206 CJ 247 – V	**Rep with Amds**			
28 Jun 1951	206 CJ 260 – V	**Cons**			
2 Jul 1951	206 CJ 264 – V	**Cons**			
3 Jul 1951	206 CJ 268	3R			
24 Jul 1951	206 CJ 298	HL pass w/o Amds			
1 Aug 1951	206 CJ 318	Royal Assent			

Parliamentary debates

1R: HC Deb, 18 Apr 1951, Vol 486(5th), col 1842

2R: HC Deb, 8 May 1951, Vol 487(5th), col 1765–1912

CWH: HC Deb, 5 Jun 1951, Vol 488(5th), col 811–967

CWH: HC Deb, 6 Jun 1951, Vol 488(5th), col 1021–1179

CWH: HC Deb, 7 Jun 1951, Vol 488(5th), col 1235–1625

CWH: HC Deb, 11 Jun 1951, Vol 488(5th), col 1677–2258

CWH: HC Deb, 13 Jun 1951, Vol 488(5th), col 2325–2471

CWH: HC Deb, 14 Jun 1951, Vol 488(5th), col 2526–2575

CWH: HC Deb, 18 Jun 1951, Vol 489(5th), col 53–200

CWH: HC Deb, 19 Jun 1951, Vol 489(5th), col 255–477

Cons: HC Deb, 28 Jun 1951, Vol 489(5th), col 1588–1751

Cons: HC Deb, 2 Jul 1951, Vol 489(5th), col 1907–2105

3R: HC Deb, 3 Jul 1951, Vol 489(5th), col 2149–2200, 2200–2226

Royal Assent: HC Deb, 1 Aug 1951, Vol 491(5th), col 1501

1R: HL Deb, 4 Jul 1951, Vol 172(5th), col 578

2R/Com neg: HL Deb, 17 Jul 1951, Vol 172(5th), col 912–957

3R: HL Deb, 24 Jul 1951, Vol 172(5th), col 1155

Royal Assent: HL Deb, 1 Aug 1951, Vol 173(5th), col 209

Parliamentary papers

Finance Bill (1950–51 HC Papers 94), Vol 1, p 515

Finance Bill (as amended in Committee) (1950–51 HC Papers 122), Vol 1, p 571

Finance Bill (1950–51 HL Papers 99), Vol 1

Supplement to Votes & Proceedings, 1948–49

8 May 1951, p 921–922; 9 May 1951, p 923–924; 10 May 1951, p 939–940; 25 May 1951, p 947–948; 28 May 1951, p 957; 29 May 1951, p 967–975; 30 May 1951, p 1015–1018; 31 May 1951 p 1025–1031; 1 Jun 1951, p 1957–1082; 5 Jun 1951, p 1097–1133; 6 Jun 1951, p 1143–1181; 7 Jun 1951, p 1189–1231; 11 Jun 1951, p 1235–1276; 11 Jun 1951, p 1297–1338; 14 Jun 1951, p 1355–1394; 18 Jun 1951, p 1399–1428; 19 Jun 1951, p 1475–1490; 20 Jun 1951, p 1527–1530; 21 Jun 1951, p 1531–1533; 22 Jun 1951, p 1547–1556; 25 Jun 1951, p 1583–1600; 26 Jun 1951, p 1611–1633; 28 Jun 1951, p 1669–1693; 2 Jul 1951 p 1703–1717

Income Tax Act 1952

PUBA66	1952
	Income Tax Act 1952 (15 & 16 Geo 6 & 1 Eliz 2. c. 10)

An Act to consolidate certain of the enactments relating to income tax, including certain enactments relating also to other taxes

Table of contents (patent provisions only)

s 2 Effect of charge of income tax at a standard rate and at higher rates
s 137 General rules as to deductions not allowable
s 139 Patent and other fees, etc.
s 169 Payments out of profits or gains already taxed
s 170 Payments not made out of profits or gains already taxed
s 180 Mining rents, mining royalties, etc.
s 199 Explanation of income tax deductions to be annexed to dividend warrants, etc.
s 316 Annual allowances for capital expenditure on purchase of patent rights
s 317 Effect of lapse of patent rights, sales, etc.
s 318 Charges on capital sums received for sale of patent rights
s 319 Patent rights sold before appointed day
s 320 Relief for expenses
s 321 When a person is to be treated as a trader
s 322 Interpretation of Chapter V, etc.
s 330 Interpretation of certain references to expenditure, etc.
s 345 Amount of assessment under s 170 of this Act to be allowed as a loss for certain purposes
s 472 Spreading of patent royalties over several years
s 491 Under-deductions from payments made before passing of annual Act
s 525 Meaning of "earned, income"
Thirteenth Schedule – Effect of deaths, windings up and partnership changes on certain charges in respect of patent rights
Fourteenth Schedule – Special provisions as to operation of Parts X and XI in relation to certain sales
Twenty-Second Schedule – Income tax in relation to assets transferred under the Coal Industry Nationalisation Act, 1946 (Patent Rights), par 11 to 13

Journal

House of Commons			House of Lords		
Rep: Sir Charles MacAndrew (Ch W&M)			Pres: Lord Simonds LC Rep: Earl of Drogheda (Ld Ch)		
29 Jan 1952	207 CJ 79	Rep from JC Con	6 Nov 1951	184 LJ 21	1R
5 Feb 1952	207 CJ 87	Brought HL/1R	21 Nov 1951	184 LJ 35	2R day app
19 Feb 1952	207 CJ 98	2R/C'tted CWH	22 Nov 1951	184 LJ 36	2R/C'tted JC Cons
25 Feb 1952	207 CJ 107	CWH/Rep w/o Amds/3R	29 Jan 1952	184 LJ 61	Rep with Amd/Re-C'tted CWH
28 Feb 1952	207 CJ 114	Royal Assent	5 Feb 1952	184 LJ 76	CWH/Rep with Amds/3R
			26 Feb 1952	184 LJ 101	HC pass w/o Amds
			28 Feb 1952	184 LJ 107	Royal Assent

Parliamentary debates

2R: HC Deb, 19 Feb 1952, Vol 496(5th), col 65–81

CWH/Rep/3R: HC Deb, 25 Feb 1952, Vol 496(5th), col 888–891

Royal Assent: HC Deb, 28 Feb 1952, Vol 496(5th), col 1503

1R: HL Deb, 6 Nov 1951, Vol 174(5th), col 20

2R: HL Deb, 22 Nov 1951, Vol 174(5th), col 505

Rep: HL Deb, 29 Jan 1952, Vol 174(5th), col 946

CWH: HL Deb, 5 Feb 1952, Vol 174(5th), col 1060–1064

HC pass: HL Deb, 26 Feb 1952, Vol 175(5th), col 293

Royal Assent: HL Deb, 28 Feb 1952, Vol 175(5th), col 415

Parliamentary papers

Income Tax Bill (1951–52 HL Papers 1), Vol 2

   Amendments made by the Joint Committee on Consolidation Bills (1951–52 HL Papers 1a), Vol 2

Income Tax Bill (as amended by Joint Committee) (1951–52 HL Papers 18), Vol 2

Income Tax (1951–52 HC Papers 51), Vol 2, p 551

First Report of Joint Committee on the Income Tax Bill (1951–52 HC Papers 62 and 62–I), Vol 5, p 37 and 39

Supplement to Votes & Proceedings, 1951–52 – No amendments

Finance Act 1952

PUBA67	1927
Finance Act 1952 (15 & 16 Geo 6 & 1 Eliz 2 c. 33)	
An Act to grant certain duties, to alter other duties, and to amend the law relating to the National Debt and the Public Revenue, and to make further provision in connection with Finance	
Table of contents (patent provisions only)	
s 23 Fees and expenses in connection with unsuccessful applications for patents s 24 Amendments as to allowances, etc., in respect of machinery or plant and patent rights Sch 6 Income Tax: Capital Allowances Sch 10 Excess Profits Levy: Ascertainment of Undistributed Profits or Over-distribution of Profits for an Accounting Period Sch 11 Excess Profits Levy: Effect of Certain Transfers of Going Concerns	
Proposed clauses	
Cl 39 Computation of Profit and Losses for excess profits	

Journal

House of Commons			House of Lords		
Pres: John Boyd-Carpenter (Fin Sec Tr) Rep: Sir Charles MacAndrew (Ch W&M)			No report		
11 Mar 1952	207 CJ 132	**Money Res**	1 Jul 1952	184 LJ 227	Brought HC/1R
13 Mar 1952	207 CJ 138	Money Res	8 Jul 1952	184 LJ 235	2R/Com neg
17 Mar 1952	207 CJ 142	Rep Money Res	9 Jul 1952	184 LJ 237	3R
20 Mar 1952	207 CJ 156	Bill Ord/1R	9 Jul 1952	184 LJ 238	Royal Assent
7 Apr 1952	207 CJ 185 – V	**2R/C'tted CWH**			
30 Apr 1952	207 CJ 209	**CWH**			
6 May 1952	207 CJ 217 – V	**CWH**			
7 May 1952	207 CJ 221	CWH adj			
8 May 1952	207 CJ 222 – V	**CWH**			
12 May 1952	207 CJ 225 – V	**CWH**			
13 May 1952	207 CJ 228 – V	**CWH**			
19 May 1952	207 CJ 236 – V	**CWH**			
20 May 1952	207 CJ 240 – V	**CWH**			
22 May 1952	207 CJ 243 – V	**CWH**			
26 May 1952	207 CJ 248 – V	**CWH**			
27 May 1952	207 CJ 251 – V	**CWH**			
28 May 1952	207 CJ 253 – V	**Rep with Amds**			
17 Jun 1952	207 CJ 269 – V	**Cons**			
18 Jun 1952	207 CJ 271 – V	**Cons**			
26 Jun 1952	207 CJ 286	3R			
9 Jul 1952	207 CJ 306	HL pass w/o Amds			
9 Jul 1952	207 CJ 307	Royal Assent			

Parliamentary debates

Money Res: HC Deb, 11 Mar 1952, Vol 497(5th), col 1319	1R: HL Deb, 1 Jul 1952, Vol 177(5th), col 520
1R: HC Deb, 20 Mar 1952, Vol 497(5th), col 2585	2R: HL Deb, 8 Jul 1952, Vol 177(5th), col 836–922
2R: HC Deb, 7 Apr 1952, Vol 498(5th), col 2295–2446	3R: HL Deb, 9 Jul 1952, Vol 177(5th), col 924
CWH: HC Deb, 30 Apr 1952, Vol 499(5th), col 1458–1505, 1506–1613	Royal Assent: HL Deb, 9 Jul 1952, Vol 177(5th), col 984
CWH: HC Deb, 6 May 1952, Vol 500(5th), col 199–341	
CWH: HC Deb, 8 May 1952, Vol 500(5th), col 561–711	
CWH: HC Deb, 12 May 1952, Vol 500(5th), col 867–1025	
CWH: HC Deb, 13 May 1952, Vol 500(5th), col 1123–1396	
CWH: HC Deb, 19 May 1952, Vol 501(5th), col 37–198	
CWH: HC Deb, 20 May 1952, Vol 501(5th), col 276–431	
CWH: HC Deb, 22 May 1952, Vol 501(5th), col 678–830	
CWH: HC Deb, 26 May 1952, Vol 501(5th), col 943–1122	
CWH: HC Deb, 27 May 1952, Vol 501(5th), col 1160–1316	

(continued)

(continued)

CWH: HC Deb, 28 May 1952, Vol 501(5th), col 1373–1626
R'Ctted/CWH/Rep: HC Deb, 17 Jun 1952, Vol 502(5th), col 1000–1160
Rep: HC Deb, 18 Jun 1952, Vol 502(5th), col 1207–1516
House Business: HC Deb, 19 Jun 1952, Vol 502(5th), col 1557
3R: HC Deb, 26 Jun 1952, Vol 502(5th), col 2444–2486, 2487–2524
Royal Assent: HC Deb, 9 Jul 1952, Vol 503(5th), col 1363

Debates on particular provisions			
s 21	HC Deb, 7 Apr 1952, Vol 498(5th), col 2297; HL Deb, 8 Jul 1952, Vol 177(5th), col 838–839	s 24	HC Deb, 19 May 1952, Vol 501(5th), col 175–177 (Cl 21)

Proposed clause	
Cl 39	Computation of Profit and Losses for excess profits HC Deb, 22 May 1952, Vol 501(5th), col 808–819; HC Deb, 26 May 1952, Vol 501(5th), col 1052–1054

Parliamentary papers
Finance Bill (1951–52 HC Papers 68), Vol 2, p 7
Finance Bill (as amended in Committee) (1951–52 HC Papers 110), Vol 2, p 135
Finance Bill (as amended in Committee, Re-Committal and Report) (1951–52 HC Papers 117), Vol 2, p 279
Finance Bill (1951–52 HL Papers 91), Vol 1
Supplement to Votes & Proceedings, 1948–49
9 Apr 1952, p 407–410; 10 Apr 1952, p 411; 18 Apr 1952, p 415–417; 21 Apr 1952, p 425–428; 22 Apr 1952, p 431–434; 23 Apr 1952, p 453–472b; 24 Apr 1952, p 477–488; 25 Apr 1952, p 489–526; 28 Apr 1952, p 537–588; 30 Apr 1952, p 595–668; 1 May 1952, p 675–682; 2 May 1952, p 689–757; 6 May 1952, p 767–836; 6 May 1952, 843–848; 8 May 1952, p 861–948; 12 May 1952, p 959–1033; 13 May 1952, p 1075–1148; 13 May 1952, 1159–1161; 15 May 1952, p 1175–1240; 19 May 1952, p 1241–1307; 22 May 1952, p 1417–1488; 26 May 1952, p 1491–1546; 27 May 1952, 1553–1590; 28 May 1952, p 1597–1624; 29 May 1952, p 1631–1634; 6 Jun 1952, p 1641–1642; 10 Jun 1952, p 1651–1666; 11 Jun 1952, p 1675–1677; 12 Jun 1952, p 1687–1716; 13 Jun 1952, p 1727–1764; 17 Jun 1952, p 1767–1806; 18 Jun 1952, p 1809–1834

Customs and Excise Act 1952

PUBA68	1952
Customs and Excise Act 1952 (15 & 16 Geo 6 & 1 Eliz 2. c. 44)	

An Act to consolidate with amendments certain enactments relating to customs and excise and to extend certain provisions of those enactments to any other matter in relation to which the Commissioners of Customs and Excise are for the time being required in pursuance of any enactment to perform any duties

Table of contents (patent provisions only)
Sch 6 Value of Imported Goods

Journal					
House of Commons			**House of Lords**		
Pres: Richard (Rab) Butler (Ch Ex) Rep: Rhys Hopkins Morris			Rep: Earl of Drogheda (Ld Ch)		
30 Jan 1952	207 CJ 81	1R	20 Feb 1952	184 LJ 96	Ref JC Cons
19 Feb 1952	207 CJ 98	**2R/Money/C'tted JC**	21 Feb 1952	184 LJ 98	HC Mess Ag
21 Feb 1952	207 CJ 103	HL Ag Ref JC	26 Feb 1952	184 LJ 101	HC Mess Com App
25 Feb 1952	207 CJ 107	Rep Money Res	28 Feb 1952	184 LJ 107	Com named
25 Feb 1952	207 CJ 108	**C'tted JC Cons**	4 Mar 1952	184 LJ 108	HC Mess Ag
25 Mar 1952	207 CJ 166	Rep with Amds/Re-C't CWH	5 Mar 1952	184 LJ 114	Evidence Pres
15 Jul 1952	207 CJ 317	CWH/Rep with Amds/3R	25 Mar 1952	184 LJ 138	JC Rep
24 Jul 1952	207 CJ 332	HL pass w/o Amds	16 Jul 1952	184 LJ 251	Brought HC/1R
1 Aug 1952	207 CJ 352	Royal Assent	21 Jul 1952	184 LJ 255	2R/C'tted CWH
			24 Jul 1952	184 LJ 264	CWH/Rep w/o Amds/3R
			1 Aug 1952	184 LJ 283	Royal Assent

Parliamentary debates	
1R: HC Deb, 30 Jan 1952, Vol 495(5th), col 206	1R HL Deb, 16 Jul 1952, Vol 177(5th), col 1167
2R: HC Deb, 19 Feb 1952, Vol 496(5th), col 82–142	2R: HL Deb, 21 Jul 1952, Vol 178(5th), col 2–10
Money Res: HC Deb, 25 Feb 1952, Vol 496(5th), col 894–895	3R: HL Deb, 24 Jul 1952, Vol 178(5th), col 246
CWH/Rep/3R: HC Deb, 15 Jul 1952, Vol 503(5th), col 2045–2049	Royal Assent: HL Deb, 1 Aug 1952, Vol 178(5th), col 613

Parliamentary papers
Customs and Excise Bill (1951–52 HC Papers 44), Vol 1, p 349
Customs and Excise Bill (as amended by Joint Committee) (1951–52 HC Papers 72), Vol 1, p 605
Customs and Excise Bill (1951–52 HL Papers 107), Vol 1
Report of Select Committee of House of Lords and House of Commons to consider Customs and Excise Bill with Minutes (1951–52 HC Papers 137), Vol 5, p 203
Report on draft Customs and Excise Bill (C 8453), Vol 10, p 1183: 30 Jan 1952 (207 CJ 80; 184 LJ 69)
Supplement to Votes & Proceedings, 1951–52   21 Apr 1952, p 413–414

Monopolies and Restrictive Practices Commission Act 1953

PUBA69	1953

Monopolies and Restrictive Practices Commission Act 1953 (1 & 2 Eliz 2. c. 51)
An Act to make provision for a chairman and deputy chairmen of the Monopolies and Restrictive Practices Commission, and for the tenure of office and superannuation benefits of the chairman and deputy chairmen thereof; to enable functions of the Commission to be exercised by groups of its members; and for purposes connected with the matters aforesaid

Table of contents (patent provisions only)

s 2 and Sch 2, par 1 [Patents Act 1949, s 40 and 43 apply to report of Monopolies and Restrictive Practices Commission Reports]

Journal

House of Commons			House of Lords		
Pres: Peter Thorneycroft (Pr BoT) Rep: Sir Cedric Drewe (Dep Ch Wh)			Rep: Earl of Drogheda (Ld Ch)		
1 Jul 1953	208 CJ 257	Bill Ord/1R	21 Jul 1953	185 LJ 250	Brought HC/1R
11 Jul 1953	208 CJ 270	2R/C'tted CWH	21 Jul 1953	185 LJ 251	2R day app
17 Jul 1953	208 CJ 277	CWH/Rep with Amds/3R	27 Jul 1953	185 LJ 257	2R/C'tted CWH
22 Oct 1953	208 CJ 312	HL pass with Amds	20 Oct 1953	185 LJ 282	**CWH**
27 Oct 1953	208 CJ 317	HL Amds Ag	20 Oct 1953	185 LJ 282	**Rep with Amds**
29 Oct 1953	208 CJ 320	Royal Assent	21 Oct 1953	185 LJ 285	**Cons with Amds**
			22 Oct 1953	185 LJ 286	3R
			28 Oct 1953	185 LJ 291	HC Ag Amds
			29 Oct 1953	185 LJ 293	Royal Assent

Parliamentary debates

1R: HC Deb, 1 Jul 1953, Vol 517(5th), col 406	1R: HL Deb, 21 Jul 1953, Vol 183(5th), col 665
2R: HC Deb, 10 Jul 1953, Vol 517(5th), col 1590–1668	2R: HL Deb, 27 Jul 1953, Vol 183(5th), col 884–893, 889–907
CWH/Rep/3R: HC Deb, 17 Jul 1953, Vol 517(5th), col 2388–2462	CWH: HL Deb, 20 Oct 1953, Vol 183(5th), col 1246–1259
HL Amds Ag: HC Deb, 27 Oct 1953, Vol 518(5th), col 2749–2753	Rep: HL Deb, 21 Oct 1953, Vol 183(5th), col 1312
Royal Assent: HC Deb, 29 Oct 1953, Vol 518(5th), col 2945	3R: HL Deb, 22 Oct 1953, Vol 183(5th), col 1314
	HC Ag Amds: HL Deb, 28 Oct 1953, Vol 183(5th), col 1419
	Royal Assent: HL Deb, 29 Oct 1953, Vol 183(5th), col 1461

(continued)

(continued)

Parliamentary papers
Monopolies and Restrictive Practices Commission Bill (1953 HC Papers 101), Vol 2, p 259 [includes Explanatory Memorandum]
Monopolies and Restrictive Practices Commission Bill (1953 HL Papers 116), Vol 2 [includes Explanatory Memorandum]
Amendments to be Moved in Committee by Viscount Woolton (1953 HL Papers 116a), Vol 2
Amendments to be Moved in Committee by Lord Silkin (1953 HL Papers 116b), Vol 2
Marshalled List of Amendments be Moved in Committee (1953 HL Papers 116**), Vol 2
Monopolies and Restrictive Practices Commission Bill (As Amended in Committee) (1953 HL Papers 123), Vol 2
Amendments to be Moved on Report by Lord Silkin (1953 HL Papers 123a), Vol 2
Lords Amendments to the Monopolies and Restrictive Practices Commission Bill (1952–53 HC Papers 115), Vol 2, p 217
Supplement to Votes & Proceedings, 1951–52
13 Jul 1952, p 1967; 15 Jul 1952, p 1977–1981; 17 Jul 1952, p 1983–1988

Enemy Property Act 1953

PUBA70	1953

Enemy Property Act 1953 (1 & 2 Eliz 2. c. 52)
An Act to make provision as respects things done, in relation to enemy property or property treated as enemy property, in excess of the powers conferred by the law relating to trading with the enemy, and as respects income from moneys invested by custodians of enemy property; as respects copyrights, rights in inventions and designs, and other rights in or in connection with which German enemy interests subsisted, or were properly treated as subsisting, during the period of the war with Germany, as respects property allocated by way of reparation from Germany and as respects other property seized from Germany; and for purposes connected with the matters aforesaid

Table of contents (patent provisions only)
s 7 Infringements of patents and registered designs
s 8 Crown use of patented inventions and registered designs
s 9 Disclosure of information about inventions, etc., in breach of contract
s 12 Meaning of "German enemy" and "German enemy interest"
s 13 Interpretation of Part II

Journal					
House of Commons			**House of Lords**		
Rep: Sir Charles MacAndrew (Ch W&M)			Pres: Lord Mancroft (Ld Wait) Rep: Earl of Drogheda (Ld Ch)		
13 Jul 1953	208 CJ 271	Brought HL/1R	17 Mar 1953	185 LJ 116	1R
24 Jul 1953	208 CJ 288	2R/C'tted CWH	12 May 1953	185 LJ 181	2R/C'tted CWH
20 Oct 1953	208 CJ 310	**CWH/Rep with Amds**	9 Jun 1953	185 LJ 200	CWH day app
23 Oct 1953	208 CJ 313	Cons/**3R with Amds**	18 Jun 1953	185 LJ 210	**CWH/Rep with Amds**
27 Oct 1953	208 CJ 317	HL Ag Amds	23 Jun 1953	185 LJ 215	Rep adj
29 Oct 1953	208 CJ 320	Royal Assent	9 Jul 1953	185 LJ 236	**Cons with Amds**
			13 Jul 1953	185 LJ 240	**3R with Amds**
			23 Oct 1953	185 LJ 287	HC pass with Amds
			27 Oct 1953	185 LJ 290	**HL Amds Ag**
			29 Oct 1953	185 LJ 293	Royal Assent

Parliamentary debates	
2R: HC Deb, 24 Jul 1953, Vol 518(5th), col 789–815	1R: HL Deb, 17 Mar 1953, Vol 181(5th), col 1–2
CWH: HC Deb, 20 Oct 1953, Vol 518(5th), col 1818–1869	2R: HL Deb, 12 May 1953, Vol 182(5th), col 395–420
Rep/3R: HC Deb, 23 Oct 1953, Vol 518(5th), col 2298–2311	CWH: HL Deb, 18 Jun 1953, Vol 182(5th), col 1063–1148
Royal Assent: HC Deb, 29 Oct 1953, Vol 518(5th), col 2945	Rep: HL Deb, 9 Jul 1953, Vol 183(5th), col 430–444, 448–458
	3R: HL Deb, 13 Jul 1953, Vol 183(5th), col 583–588
	HC pass: HL Deb, 23 Oct 1953, Vol 183(5th), col 1367
	HC Amds Ag: HL Deb, 27 Oct 1953, Vol 183(5th), col 1393–1396
	Royal Assent: HL Deb, 29 Oct 1953, Vol 183(5th), col 1461

Debates on particular provisions			
s 7	HL Deb, 12 May 1953, Vol 182(5th), col 403–404, 409–410, 419–420; HL Deb, 18 Jun 1953, Vol 182(5th), col 1112; HC Deb, 24 Jul 1953, Vol 518(5th), col 795–796	s 8	HL Deb, 12 May 1953, Vol 182(5th), col 404; HL Deb, 18 Jun 1953, Vol 182(5th), col 1112; HC Deb, 20 Oct 1953, Vol 518(5th), col 1848–1849
s 9	HL Deb, 12 May 1953, Vol 182(5th), col 403–404; HL Deb, 12 May 1953, Vol 182(5th), col 404 and 410; HL Deb, 18 Jun 1953, Vol 182(5th), col 1113–1115; HL Deb, 9 Jul 1953, Vol 183(5th), col 442–444	s 12	HL Deb, 18 Jun 1953, Vol 182(5th), col 1121–1124; HC Deb, 20 Oct 1953, Vol 518(5th), col 1854–1863; HC Deb, 23 Oct 1953, Vol 518(5th), col 2304–2311
s 13	HL Deb, 18 Jun 1953, Vol 182(5th), col 1124–1127; HL Deb, 9 Jul 1953, Vol 183(5th), col 448–458		

Parliamentary papers
Enemy Property Bill (1953 HL Papers 37), Vol 1 [includes Explanatory Memorandum]
Amendments to be moved in Committee by Lord Mancroft (1953 HL Papers 37a), Vol 1
Amendments to be moved in Committee by Lord Lucas and Lord Chorley (1953 HL Papers 37b), Vol 1
Amendments to be moved in Committee by Lord Silkin (1953 HL Papers 37c), Vol 1
Amendments to be moved in Committee by Lord Silkin (1953 HL Papers 37d) (in substitution of 1953 HL Papers 37c), Vol 1
Marshalled List of Amendments to be Moved in Committee (1957 HL Papers 37**), Vol 1
Enemy Property Bill (as amended in Committee) (1953 HL Papers 89), Vol 1
Amendments to be moved in Report by Lord Mancroft (1953 HL Papers 89a), Vol 1
Amendments to be moved in Report by Lord Lucas and Lord Mancroft (1953 HL Papers 89b), Vol 1
Amendments to be moved in Report by Lord Chorley (1953 HL Papers 89c), Vol 1
Marshalled List of Amendments to be Moved on Report (1957 HL Papers 89**), Vol 1
Enemy Property Bill (as amended on Report) (1953 HL Papers 105), Vol 1
Enemy Property Bill (1952–53 HC Papers 107), Vol 1, p 351
Enemy Property Bill (as amended in Committee) (1952–53 HC Papers 114), Vol 1, p 375
Commons Amendments (1953 HL Papers 127), Vol 1
Supplement to Votes & Proceedings, 1952–53
14 Oct 1953, p 2017–2020; 20 Oct 1953, p 2021–2024; 21 Oct 1953, p 2025; 22 Oct 1953, p 2027–2028

Food and Drugs Amendment Act 1954

PUBA71	1953				
Food and Drugs Amendment Act 1954 (2 & 3 Eliz 2. c. 67)					
An Act to amend the Food and Drugs Act, 1938, and the Food and Drugs (Milk, Dairies and Artificial Cream) Act, 1950, and for purposes connected therewith					
Table of contents (patent provisions only)					
s 4 Power of Ministers to obtain particulars of certain food ingredients					
Journal					
House of Commons			**House of Lords**		
Rep: Sir Charles MacAndrew (Ch W&M)			Pres: Viscount Woolton Rep: Earl of Drogheda (Ld Ch)		
30 Mar 1954	209 CJ 150	Brought HL/1R	10 Nov 1953	186 LJ 10	1R
23 Jul 1954	209 CJ 293	2R/C'tted CWH/Money Res	24 Nov 1953	186 LJ 24	2R/C'tted CWH
26 Oct 1954	209 CJ 325	**CWH**	8 Dec 1953	186 LJ 42	CWH adj

(continued)

(continued)

27 Oct 1954	209 CJ 327	**CWH**	14 Dec 1953	186 LJ 49	CWH adj
3 Nov 1954	209 CJ 333 – V	**CWH**	20 Jan 1954	186 LJ 64	**CWH/Rep**
11 Nov 1954	209 CJ 344	**Rep with Amds**	16 Feb 1954	186 LJ 90	**Cons/Re-C'tted CWH**
11 Nov 1954	209 CJ 344	**Re-C'tted CWH**	18 Mar 1954	186 LJ 126	Re-C'tted disc
11 Nov 1954	209 CJ 344 – V	**CWH/Rep with Amds/ Cons/3R**	30 Mar 1954	186 LJ 141	**3R**
			15 Nov 1954	186 LJ 395	HC Ret with Amds
22 Nov 1954	209 CJ 353	HL Ag Amds	22 Nov 1954	186 LJ 406	**HC Amds Agreed**
25 Nov 1954	209 CJ 373	Royal Assent	25 Nov 1954	186 LJ 420	Royal Assent

Parliamentary debates

House Business: HC Deb, 27 May 1954, Vol 528(5th), col 614

House Business: HC Deb, 12 Jul 1954, Vol 530(5th), col 10–13

2R: HC Deb, 23 Jul 1954, Vol 530(5th), col 1753–1840

Com: HC Deb, 26 Oct 1954, Vol 531(5th), col 1769–1890

Com: HC Deb, 27 Oct 1954, Vol 531(5th), col 1938–2060

CWH/Rep: HC Deb, 3 Nov 1954, Vol 532(5th), col 383–474

Re-Ct/CWH/Rep/3R: HC Deb, 11 Nov 1954, Vol 532(5th), col 1408–1530

Royal Assent: HC Deb, 25 Nov 1954, Vol 533(5th), col 1393

1R: HL Deb, 10 Nov 1953, Vol 184(5th), col 193

2R: HL Deb, 24 Nov 1953, Vol 184(5th), col 480–510

CWH adj: HL Deb, 8 Dec 1953, Vol 184(5th), col 1106

CWH: HL Deb, 20 Jan 1954, Vol 185(5th), col 300–315, 319–378

Cons: HL Deb, 16 Feb 1954, Vol 185(5th), col 883–921

3R: HL Deb, 30 Mar 1954, Vol 186(5th), col 862–870

HC pass: HL Deb, 15 Nov 1954, Vol 189(5th), col 1484

HL Amds Cons: HL Deb, 22 Nov 1954, Vol 189(5th), col 1683–1749

Royal Assent: HL Deb, 25 Nov 1954, Vol 189(5th), col 1964

Debates on particular provisions

s 4	HC Deb, 26 Oct 1954, Vol 531(5th), col 1853–1859

Parliamentary papers

Food and Drugs Amendment Bill (1954 HL Papers 5), Vol 2

Amendment to be Moved in Committee by Viscount Bledisloe (1954 HL Papers 5a), Vol 2

Amendment to be Moved in Committee by Viscount Bledisloe (1954 HL Papers 5b), Vol 2

Amendments to be Moved in Committee by Viscount Woolton, Lord Balfour of Inchrye, Viscount Long and Viscount Hudson (1954 HL Papers 5c), Vol 2

Amendment to be Moved in Committee by Viscount Woolton, Viscount Hudson, Lord Silkin, Lord Douglas of Barloch (1954 HL Papers 5d), Vol 2

Amendment to be Moved in Committee by Viscount Woolton and Lord Balfour of Inchrye (1954 HL Papers 5e), Vol 2

Marshalled List of Amendments to be Moved in Committee (1954 HL Papers 5**), Vol 2

Amendment to be Moved in Committee by Viscount Woolton (1954 HL Papers 5f), Vol 2

Amendment to be Moved in Committee by Lord Douglas of Barloch (1954 HL Papers 5g), Vol 2

Revised Marshalled List of Amendments to be Moved in Committee (including previously unprinted amendments) (1954 HL Papers 5††), Vol 2

Revised Marshalled List of Amendments to be Moved in Committee (including previously unprinted amendments) (1954 HL Papers 5‡‡), Vol 2

Food and Drugs Amendment Bill (as amended in Committee) (1954 HL Papers 33), Vol 2

Amendments to be Moved on Report by Lord Douglas of Barloch (1954 HL Papers 33a), Vol 2

Amendments to be Moved on Report by Lord Burden (1954 HL Papers 33b), Vol 2

Amendments to be Moved on Report by Viscount Woolton (1954 HL Papers 33c), Vol 2

Amendments to be Moved on Report by Viscount Woolton and Lord Merthyr (1954 HL Papers 33d), Vol 2

Amendment to be Moved on Report by Lord Waleran (1954 HL Papers 33e), Vol 2

Marshalled List of Amendment to be Moved on Report (including previously unprinted amendments) (1954 HL Papers 33**), Vol 2

Revised Marshalled List of Amendment to be Moved on Report (including previously unprinted amendment) (1954 HL Papers 33††), Vol 2

Food and Drugs Amendment Bill (as amended on Report) (1954 HL Papers 51), Vol 2	

Amendment to be Moved in Committee (on Re-Committal) by Lord Saltoun (1954 HL Papers 51a), Vol 2

Amendment to be Moved in Committee (on Re-Committal) by Lord Teviot (1954 HL Papers 51b), Vol 2

Amendment to be Moved on Third Reading by Lord Waleran (1954 HL Papers 51c), Vol 2

Amendments to be Moved on Third Reading by Viscount Woolton (1954 HL Papers 51d), Vol 2

Marshalled List of Amendments to be Moved on Third Reading (1954 HL Papers 51**), Vol 2

Food and Drugs Amendment (1953–54 HC Papers 88), Vol 1, p 781

Food and Drugs Amendment (as amended in Committee) (1953–54 HC Papers 157), Vol 1, p 827

Commons Amendments (1954 HL Papers 175), Vol 2

Supplement to Votes & Proceedings, 1953–54

28 Jul 1954, p 3842; 30 Sep 1954, p 3859–3860; 7 Oct 1954, p 3861–3854; 15 Oct 1954, p 3881–3882; 19 Oct 1954, p 3905–3912; 20 Oct 1954, p 3913–3916; 21 Oct 1954, p 3917–3924; 22 Oct 1954, p 3925–3946; 26 Oct 1954, p 3947–3970; 27 Oct 1954, p 3973–3990; 28 Oct 1954, p 3994; 1 Nov 1954, p 4000; 3 Nov 1954, p 4001–4015; 4 Nov 1954, p 4041; 5 Nov 1954, p 4043–4049; 8 Nov 1954, p 4057–4058; 9 Nov 1954, p 4069–4062; 11 Nov 1954, p 4083–4096

Notes

Related non-patent questions

Q: HC Deb, 14 Apr 1954, Vol 526(5th), col 1116–1117

Q: HC Deb, 5 Jul 1954, Vol 529(5th), col 1786–1788

Development of Inventions Act 1954

PUBA72	1954

Development of Inventions Act 1954 (2 & 3 Eliz 2. c. 20)

An Act to extend to ten years the period during which advances may be made to the National Research Development Corporation out of the Consolidated Fund and during which the Board of Trade may with the approval of the Treasury waive payments by way of interest on such advances; to make further provision as to the functions of the Corporation relating to research; and otherwise to amend the Development of Inventions Act, 1948

Table of contents

s 1 Extension of period for making advances to National Research Development Corporation and for waiving interest on such advances
s 2 Functions of Corporation relating to research
s 3 Minor amendments of principal Act
s 4 Short title, interpretation, construction and citation

Journal

House of Commons			House of Lords		
Pres: Peter Thorneycroft (Pr BoT) Money Rep: Donald Kaberry CWH Rep: Sir Charles MacAndrew (Ch W&M)			Rep: Earl of Drogheda (Ld Ch)		
10 Dec 1953	209 CJ 49	1R	2 Feb 1954	186 LJ 77	Brought HC/1R
26 Jan 1954	209 CJ 69	Money Res/2R/C'tted CWH	16 Feb 1954	186 LJ 92	2R/C'tted CWH
1 Feb 1954	209 CJ 74	Res Rep	2 Mar 1954	186 LJ 111	**CWH/Rep with Amds**
1 Feb 1954	209 CJ 75	CWH/Rep w/o Amds/3R	4 Mar 1954	186 LJ 115	Cons
9 Mar 1954	209 CJ 120	HL pass with Amds	9 Mar 1954	186 LJ 117	3R
16 Mar 1954	209 CJ 129	HL Amds Ag	17 Mar 1954	186 LJ 125	HC Ag Amds
18 Mar 1954	209 CJ 133	Royal Assent	18 Mar 1954	186 LJ 128	Royal Assent

Parliamentary debates

1R: HC Deb, 10 Dec 1953, Vol 521(5th), col 2192	Br HC/1R: HL Deb, 2 Feb 1954, Vol 185(5th), col 594
2R: HC Deb, 26 Jan 1954, Vol 522(5th), col 1623–1654	2R: HL Deb, 16 Feb 1954, Vol 185(5th), col 921–933
CWH/3R: HC Deb, 1 Feb 1954, Vol 523(5th), col 161–163	CWH: HL Deb, 2 Mar 1954, Vol 186(5th), col 4–6

(continued)

(continued)

	Cons: HL Deb, 4 Mar 1954, Vol 186(5th), col 176
	3R: HL Deb, 9 Mar 1954, Vol 186(5th), col 224
	Royal Assent: HL Deb, 18 Mar 1954, Vol 186(5th), col 526

Parliamentary papers
Development of Inventions Bill (1953–54 HC Papers 47), Vol 1, p 337
Development of Inventions Bill (1953–54 HL Papers 38), Vol 1
Amendment to be Moved in Committee by the Lord Mancroft (1953–54 HL Papers 38a), Vol 1
Development of Inventions Bill (as amended in Committee) (1953–54 HL Papers 61), Vol 1
Lords Amendments to the Development of Inventions Bill (1953–54 HC Papers 78), Vol 1, p 343
Supplement to Votes & Proceedings, 1952–53 – No amendments

Food and Drugs Act 1955

PUBA73	1955
	Food and Drugs Act 1955 (2 & 3 Eliz 2. c. 67)

An Act to consolidate the Food and Drugs Act, 1938, the Food and Drugs (Milk, Dairies and Artificial Cream) Act, 1950, and the Food and Drugs Amendment Act, 1954, together with certain other enactments amending and supplementing Part V of the said Act of 1938 in relation to slaughterhouses and knackers' yards

Table of contents (patent provisions only)

s 5 Power of Ministers to obtain particulars of certain food ingredients

Journal

House of Commons			House of Lords		
Rep: Sir Charles MacAndrew (Ch W&M)			Pres: Viscount Kilmuir LC Rep: Earl of Drogheda (Ld Ch)		
12 Jul 1955	211 CJ 67	Rep JC Cons	22 Jun 1955	188 LJ 37	1R
3 Nov 1955	211 CJ 112	Brought HL	28 Jun 1955	188 LJ 43	2R/Ref JC Cons
4 Nov 1955	211 CJ 114	1R	13 Jul 1955	188 LJ 60	Rep/C'tted CWH
14 Nov 1955	211 CJ 123	2R/C'tted CWH	26 Jul 1953	188 LJ 81	CWH adj
22 Nov 1955	211 CJ 132	CWH/Rep with Amds/3R	25 Oct 1953	188 LJ 100	**CWH/Rep with Amds**
22 Nov 1955	211 CJ 134	Royal Assent	27 Oct 1953	188 LJ 105	Cons
			3 Nov 1953	188 LJ 113	3R
			22 Nov 1953	188 LJ 126	HC HC pass with Amds/Ag
			22 Nov 1953	188 LJ 127	Royal Assent

Parliamentary debates

2R: HC Deb, 14 Nov 1955, Vol 546(5th), col 46	1R: HL Deb, 22 Jun 1955, Vol 193(5th), col 252
CWH/Rep/3R: HC Deb, 21 Nov 1955, Vol 546(5th), col 1218	2R: HL Deb, 28 Jun 1955, Vol 193(5th), col 344–345
Royal Assent: HC Deb, 22 Nov 1955, Vol 546(5th), col 1306	Rep JC: HL Deb, 13 Jul 1955, Vol 193(5th), col 758
	CWH on Re-Ct: HL Deb, 25 Oct 1955, Vol 194(5th), col 12
	Rep: HL Deb, 27 Oct 1955, Vol 194(5th), col 74
	3R: HL Deb, 3 Nov 1955, Vol 194(5th), col 293–294
	HC pass: HL Deb, 22 Nov 1955, Vol 194(5th), col 679
	Royal Assent: HL Deb, 22 Nov 1955, Vol 194(5th), col 732

Parliamentary papers

Foods and Drugs Bill (1955 HL Papers 5), Vol 2
Amendments made by the Joint Committee on Consolidation Bills (1955 HL Papers 5a), Vol 2
Foods and Drugs Bill (as amended by Joint Committee) (1955 HL Papers 22), Vol 2
Amendment to be moved in Committee (on Re-Committal) by Lord Chancellor (1955 HL Papers 22a), Vol 2
Food and Drugs Bill (as amended on Committee on Re-Committal) (1955 HL Papers 34, Vol 34)
Food and Drug Bill (1955–56 HC Papers 47), Vol 2, p 355
Second Report of the Joint Committee on Consolidation Bills on the Food and Drugs Bill (1955–56 HC Papers 38 and 38–I), Vol 6, p 251 and p 253
Supplement to Votes & Proceedings, 1955–56 – No amendments

Food and Drugs (Scotland) Act 1956

PUBA74	1956
	Food and Drugs (Scotland) Act 1956 (4 & 5 Eliz 2. c. 30)

An Act to amend and consolidate certain enactments in Scotland relating to food and drugs, and for purposes connected therewith

Table of contents (patent provisions only)

s 5 Power of Ministers to obtain particulars of certain food ingredients

Journal

House of Commons			House of Lords		
Pres: James Stuart (SoS Scot) SC Rep: William Ansturther-Gray			Rep: Earl of Drogheda (Ld Ch)		
10 Jun 1955	211 CJ 21	1R	9 Feb 1956	188 LJ 202	Brought HC/1R
14 Jun 1955	211 CJ 25	Certified as Scot only	14 Feb 1956	188 LJ 206	2R day app
20 Jun 1955	211 CJ 31	Ref SC Scot	1 Mar 1956	188 LJ 235	2R/C'tted CWH
5 Jul 1955	211 CJ 51	2R day app	13 Mar 1956	188 LJ 245	CWH/Rep w/o Amds
6 Jul 1955	211 CJ 56	2R deemed/C'tted Scot SC	14 Mar 1956	188 LJ 246	3R
29 Nov 1955	211 CJ 139	Rep with Amds	15 Mar 1956	188 LJ 250	Royal Assent
8 Feb 1956	211 CJ 183	Royal consent/3R			
14 Mar 1956	211 CJ 224	HL pass w/o Amds			
15 Mar 1956	211 CJ 227	Royal Assent			

Parliamentary debates

1R: HC Deb, 10 Jun 1955, Vol 542(5th), col 142	Br HC/1R: HL Deb, 9 Feb 1956, Vol 195(5th), col 846
Motion to ref to SSC: HC Deb, 20 Jun 1955, Vol 542(5th), col 1078–1079	2R: HL Deb, 1 Mar 1956, Vol 196(5th), col 66–73
Principle: SC Scot, 28 Jun 1955, col 1–52	CWH: HL Deb, 13 Mar 1956, Vol 196(5th), col 310
Principle: SC Scot, 5 Jul 1955, col 53–96	3R: HL Deb, 14 Mar 1956, Vol 196(5th), col 444
Deemed 2R/C'tted: HC Deb, 6 Jul 1955, Vol 543(5th), col 1260	Royal Assent: HL Deb, 15 Mar 1956, Vol 196(5th), col 494
Money Res: HC Deb, 12 Jul 1955, Vol 543(5th), col 1891	
SC Scot, 1st Sit, 12 Jul 1955, col 1–52	
Res Rep: HC Deb, 13 Jul 1955, Vol 543(5th), col 2069	
SC Scot, 2nd Sit, 14 Jul 1955, col 53–98	
SC Scot, 3rd Sit, 19 Jul 1955, col 99–142	
SC Scot, 4th Sit, 21 Jul 1955, col 143–190	
SC Scot, 5th Sit, 26 Jul 1955, col 191–238	
SC Scot, 6th Sit, 1 Nov 1955, col 239–284	
SC Scot, 7th Sit, 3 Nov 1955, col 285–330	
SC Scot, 8th Sit, 8 Nov 1955, col 331–378	
SC Scot, 9th Sit, 10 Nov 1955, col 379–424	
SC Scot, 10th Sit, 15 Nov 1955, col 425–472	
SC Scot, 11th Sit, 17 Nov 1955, col 473–520	
SC Scot, 12th Sit, 22 Nov 1955, col 521–568	
SC Scot, 13th Sit, 24 Nov 1955, col 569–616	
SC Scot, 14th Sit, 29 Nov 1955, col 617–644	
Rep/3R: HC Deb, 8 Feb 1956, Vol 548(5th), col 1677–1734	
Royal Assent: HC Deb, 15 Mar 1956, Vol 550(5th), col 599	

Debates on particular provisions

s 5 & 6	SC Scot, 1st Sit, 12 Jul 1955, col 47

Parliamentary papers

Food and Drugs (Scotland) Bill (1955–56 HC Papers 3), Vol 2, p 475

Scottish Standing Committee. Minutes of Proceedings on the Foods and Drugs (Scotland) Bill (Principle) (1955–56 HC Papers 111), Vol 9, p 7

(continued)

(continued)

Scottish Standing Committee. Minutes of Proceedings on the Foods and Drugs (Scotland) Bill (Committee Stage) (1955–56 HC Papers 111), Vol 9, p 11

Food and Drugs (Scotland) Bill (as amended in Committee) (1955–56 HC Papers 78), Vol 2, p 529

Food and Drugs (Scotland) Bill (1955 HL Papers 73), Vol 2

Supplement to Votes & Proceedings, 1955–56

> 6 Jul 1955, p 151–154; 7 Jul 1955, p 157; 8 Jul 1955, p 159–163; 12 Jul 1955, p 171–175; 14 Jul 1955, p 185–189; 19 Jul 1955, p 227–230; 19 Jul 1955, p 232; 21 Jul 1955, p 245–247; 21 Jul 1955, p 249–250; 26 Jul 1955, p 269–273; 26 Oct 1955, p 317; 27 Oct 1955, p 321–325; 28 Oct 1955, p 329–330; 1 Nov 1955, p 349–354; 1 Nov 1955, p 358; 3 Nov 1955, p 379–385; 3 Nov 1955, p 391; 8 Nov 1955, p 411–416; 8 Nov 1955, p 429; 10 Nov 1955, p 441–445; 10 Nov 1955, p 458; 11 Nov 1955, p 478; 15 Nov. 1955, p 503–506; 17 Nov 1955, p 579–582; 22 Nov 1955, p 623–625; 22 Nov 1955, p 651; 24 Nov 1955, p 689–691; 29 Nov 1955, p 733–734; 6 Feb 1956, p 1311–1314; 8 Feb 1956, p 1321–1324

Restrictive Trade Practices Act 1956

PUBA75	1956

Restrictive Trade Practices Act 1956 (4 & 5 Eliz 2. c. 68)

An Act to provide for the registration and judicial investigation of certain restrictive trading agreements, and for the prohibition of such agreements when found contrary to the public interest; to prohibit the collective enforcement of conditions regulating the resale price of goods, and to make further provision for the individual enforcement of such conditions by legal proceedings; to amend the Monopolies and Restrictive Practices Acts, 1948 and 1953; to provide for the appointment of additional judges of the High Court and of the Court of Session; and for other purposes connected with the matters aforesaid

Table of contents (patent provisions only)

s 8 Excepted agreements [patent licences]

Journal

House of Commons			House of Lords		
Pres: Peter. Thorneycroft (Pr BoT); Richard (Rab) Butler (Ch Ex) and Derek Walker-Smith (Par Sec BoT) CWH Rep: Henry Hynd			Rep: Viscount Kilmuir LC		
15 Feb 1956	211 CJ 192	1R	15 Jun 1956	188 LJ 330	Brought HC/1R
6 Mar 1956	211 CJ 216	2R/C'tted CWH	26 Jun 1956	188 LJ 349	2R/C'tted CWH
11 Apr 1956	211 CJ 255	**CWH**	11 Jul 1956	188 LJ 384 – V	**CWH**
12 Apr 1956	211 CJ 258	**CWH**	12 Jul 1956	188 LJ 389 – V	**CWH**
26 Apr 1956	211 CJ 279	**CWH**	24 Jul 1956	188 LJ 415 – V	**Rep with Amds**
1 May 1956	211 CJ 284	**CWH**	26 Jul 1956	188 LJ 422	**3R**
2 May 1956	211 CJ 287	**CWH**	31 Jul 1956	188 LJ 426	HC Ag Amds
3 May 1956	211 CJ 290	**CWH**	2 Aug 1956	188 LJ 431	Royal Assent
8 May 1956	211 CJ 293	**CWH**			
17 May 1956	211 CJ 305	Rep with Amds/Re-C'tted			
13 Jun 1956	211 CJ 330	**CWH**			
14 Jun 1956	211 CJ 333	**CWH**			
14 Jun 1956	211 CJ 334	3R			
26 Jul 1956	211 CJ 386	HL pass with Amds			
30 Jul 1956	211 CJ 396	HL Amds Ag			
2 Aug 1956	211 CJ 406	Royal Assent			

Parliamentary debates

1R: HC Deb, 15 Feb 1956, Vol 548(5th), col 2368	1R: HL Deb, 15 Jun 1956, Vol 197(5th), col 1039
2R: HC Deb, 6 Mar 1956, Vol 549(5th), col 1927–2050	2R: HL Deb, 26 Jun 1956, Vol 198(5th), col 9–88
CWH: HC Deb, 11 Apr 1956. Vol 551(5th), col 223–345	CWH: HL Deb, 11 Jul 1956, Vol 198(5th), col 852–995
CWH: HC Deb, 12 Apr 1956, Vol 551(5th), col 399–550	CWH: HL Deb, 12 Jul 1956, Vol 198(5th), col 1001–1029, 1032–1033
CWH: HC Deb, 26 Apr 1956, Vol 551(5th), col 1976–2124	
Proceedings exempt from SO: CWH: HC Deb, 12 Apr 1956, Vol 551(5th), col 394–398	Rep: HL Deb, 24 Jul 1956, Vol 199(5th), col 105–115, 121–198
CWH: HC Deb, 1 May 1956, Vol 552(5th), col 215–346	3R: HL Deb, 26 Jul 1956, Vol 199(5th), col 327–350

CWH: HC Deb, 2 May 1956, Vol 552(5th), col 398–553	HC pass: HL Deb, 31 Jul 1956, Vol 199(5th), col 422
CWH: HC Deb, 3 May 1956, Vol 552(5th), col 599–749	Royal Assent: HL Deb, 2 Aug 1956, Vol 199(5th), col 561
CWH: HC Deb, 8 May 1956, Vol 552(5th), col 1013–1186	
CWH/Rep: HC Deb, 17 May 1956, Vol 552(5th), col 2255–2318	
Re-C'tted/Rep/Cons: HC Deb, 13 Jun 1956, Vol 554(5th), col 584–722	
Rep/3R: HC Deb, 14 Jun 1956, Vol 554(5th), col 784–903	
HL Amds Ag: HC Deb, 30 Jul 1956, Vol 557(5th), col 929–994	
Royal Assent: HC Deb, 2 Aug 1956, Vol 557(5th), col 1644	

Debate on particular provisions	
s 8	HC Deb, 12 Apr 1956, Vol 551(5th), col 414, 426–430, 436, 443–444, 453–454, 463; HC Deb, 26 Apr 1956, Vol 551(5th), col 2099–2124; HC Deb, 1 May 1956, Vol 552(5th), col 215–258; HC Deb, 2 May 1956, Vol 552(5th), col 415, 453, 530; HC Deb, 13 Jun 1956, Vol 554(5th), col 659–701(Cl 6); HL Deb, 11 Jul 1956, Vol 198(5th), col 872–889 (Cl 7); HL Deb, 24 Jul 1956, Vol 199(5th), col 113–115 and 121–127; HC Deb, 30 Jul 1956, Vol 557(5th), col 937–945(Cl 7)

Parliamentary papers

Restrictive Trade Practices Bill (1955–56 HC Papers 99), Vol 3, p 239

Restrictive Trade Practices Bill (as amended in Committee) (1955–56 HC Papers 141), Vol 3, p 271

Restrictive Trade Practices Bill (1956 HL Papers 141), Vol 3 [includes Explanatory Memorandum]

  Amendment to be Moved in Committee by Lord Amwell (1956 HL Papers 141a), Vol 3

  Amendment to be Moved in Committee by Lord Dovercourt (1956 HL Papers 141b), Vol 3

  Amendments to be Moved in Committee by Lord Grantchester (1956 HL Papers 141c), Vol 3

  Amendments to be Moved in Committee by Lord Lucas (1956 HL Papers 141d), Vol 3

  Amendments to be Moved in Committee by the Lord Chancellor (1956 HL Papers 141e), Vol 3

  Amendments to be Moved in Committee by Viscount Alexander, Lord Lucas and Lord Williams (1956 HL Papers 141f), Vol 3

  Amendment to be Moved in Committee by the Lord Chancellor (1956 HL Papers 141g), Vol 3

  Amendments to be Moved in Committee by Lord Jessel, Lord Baillieu, Lord McCorquodale and Lord Gridley (1956 HL Papers 141h), Vol 3

  Marshalled List of Amendments to be Moved in Committee (1956 HL Papers 141**), Vol 3

  Revised Marshalled List of Amendments to be Moved in Committee (1956 HL Papers 141††), Vol 3

  Second Marshalled List of Amendments to be Moved in Committee (1956 HL Papers 141‡‡), Vol 3

Restrictive Trade Practices Bill (as amended in Committee) (1956 HL Papers 158), Vol 3

  Amendments to be Moved on Report by Viscount Alexander, Lord Lucas and Lord Williams (1956 HL Papers 158a), Vol 3

  Amendments to be Moved on Report by Lord Baillieu (1956 HL Papers 158b), Vol 3

  Amendments to be Moved on Report by Viscount Alexander, Lord Lucas and Lord Williams (1956 HL Papers 158c), Vol 3

  Amendments to be Moved on Report by the Lord Chancellor (1956 HL Papers 158d), Vol 3

  Marshalled List of Amendments to be Moved on Report (1956 HL Papers 158**), Vol 3

  Revised Marshalled List of Amendments to be Moved on Report (1956 HL Papers 158††), Vol 3

Restrictive Trade Practices Bill (as amended on Report) (1956 HL Papers 171), Vol 3

  Amendments to be Moved on Third Reading by Lord Baillieu (1956 HL Papers 171a), Vol 3

  Amendments to be Moved on Third Reading by the Lord Chancellor (1956 HL Papers 171b), Vol 3

  Marshalled List of Amendments to be Moved on Third Reading (1956 HL Papers 171**), Vol 3

Restrictive Trade Practices Bill (as amended on Third Reading) (1956 HL Papers 172), Vol 3

Lords Amendments to the Restrictive Trade Practices Bill (1955–56 HC Papers 169), Vol 3, p 303

Supplement to Votes & Proceedings, 1955–56

  13 Mar 1956, p 1997–1998; 16 Mar 1956, p 2063–2069; 19 Mar 1956, p 2115–2123; 20 Mar 1956, p 2139–2141; 21 Mar 1956, p 2189–2203; 23 Mar 1956, p 2219; 26 Mar 1956, p 2247–2281; 27 Mar 1956, p 2312; 28 Mar 1956, p 2315–2318; 29 Mar 1956, p 2339–2377; 6 Apr 1956, p 2393–2432; 9 Apr 1956, p 2443; 11 Apr 1956, p 2465–2508; 12 Apr 1956, p 2535–2576; 18 Apr 1956, p 2677–2679; 19 Apr 1956, p 2681; 23 Apr 1956, p 2709; 24 Apr 1956, p 2735–2778; 26 Apr 1956, p 2793–2837; 26 Apr 1956, p 2841–2842; 1 May 1956, p 2885–2925; 2 May 1956, p 2943–2979; 3 May 1956, p 2995–3022; 8 May 1956, p 3033–3050; 10 May 1956, p 3115; 15 May 1956, p 3132; 17 May 1956, p 3133–3142; 1 Jun 1956, p 3307–3308; 5 Jun 1956, p 3351–3357; 6 Jun 1956, p 3395–3396; 7 Jun 1956, p 3405–3410; 8 Jun 1956, p 3443–3457; 11 Jun 1956, p 3471–3485; 13 Jun 1956, p 3521–3535; 14 Jun 1956, p 3549–3554

Finance Act 1958

PUBA76	1927

Finance Act 1958 (6 & 7 Eliz 2. c. 56)
An Act to grant certain duties, to alter other duties, and to amend the law relating to the National Debt and the Public Revenue, and to make further provision in connection with Finance.

Table of contents (patent provisions only)

Sch 5 Statutory Fees and Contributions eligible for Deduction under Section Sixteen

Journal

House of Commons			House of Lords		
Pres: Jocelyn Simon (Fin Sec Tr) Money Rep: Hendrie Oakshott CWH Rep: Gordon Touche (Dep Ch W&M)			No report		
17 Apr 1958	213 CJ 164	Money Res	21 Jul 1958	190 LJ 280	Brought HC/1R
23 Apr 1958	213 CJ 174	Rep of Money Res	29 Jul 1958	190 LJ 298	2R/C'tted neg
23 Apr 1958	213 CJ 174	Bill Ord/1R	30 Jul 1958	190 LJ 301	3R
12 May 1958	213 CJ 201 – V	**2R/C'tted CWH**	1 Aug 1958	190 LJ 310	Royal Assent
19 May 1958	213 CJ 211 – V	**CWH**			
20 May 1958	213 CJ 213 – V	**CWH**			
21 May 1958	213 CJ 215 – V	**CWH**			
11 Jun 1958	213 CJ 223 – V	**CWH**			
12 Jun 1958	213 CJ 224 – V	**CWH**			
17 Jun 1958	213 CJ 231 – V	**CWH**			
18 Jun 1958	213 CJ 234 – V	**CWH**			
1 Jul 1958	213 CJ 250 – V	**CWH**			
2 Jul 1958	213 CJ 252 – V	**CWH/Rep with Amds**			
15 Jul 1958	213 CJ 268 – V	**Cons**			
18 Jul 1958	213 CJ 275	3R			
30 Jul 1958	213 CJ 300	HL pass w/o Amds			
1 Aug 1958	213 CJ 306	Royal Assent			

Parliamentary debates

1R: HC Deb, 23 Apr 1958, Vol 586(5th), col 968

2R: HC Deb, 12 May 1958, Vol 588(5th), col 31–162

CWH: HC Deb, 19 May 1958, Vol 588(5th), col 894–1040

CWH: HC Deb, 20 May 1958, Vol 588(5th), col 1101–1248

CWH: HC Deb, 21 May 1958, Vol 588(5th), col 1310–1459

CWH: HC Deb, 11 Jun 1958, Vol 589(5th), col 223–380

CWH: HC Deb, 12 Jun 1958, Vol 589(5th), col 417–537

CWH: HC Deb, 17 Jun 1958, Vol 589(5th), col 903–1054

CWH: HC Deb, 18 Jun 1958, Vol 589(5th), col 1115–1182

CWH: HC Deb, 1 Jul 1958, Vol 590(5th), col 1077–1286

CWH/Rep: HC Deb, 2 Jul 1958, Vol 590(5th), col 1337–1543

Cons: HC Deb, 15 Jul 1958, Vol 591(5th), col 1024–1182

3R: HC Deb, 18 Jul 1958, Vol 591(5th), col 1584–1642

Royal Assent: HC Deb, 1 Aug 1958, Vol 592(5th), col 1791

1R: HL Deb, 21 Jul 1958, Vol 211(5th), col 6

2R: HL Deb, 29 Jul 1958, Vol 211(5th), col 386–448

3R: HL Deb, 30 Jul 1958, Vol 211(5th), col 486–488

Royal Assent: HL Deb, 1 Aug 1958, Vol 211(5th), col 656

Parliamentary papers

Finance Bill (1957–58 HC Papers 104), Vol 1, p 789

Finance Bill (as amended in Committee) (1957–58 HC Papers 142), Vol 1, p 853

Finance Bill (as amended in Committee, on Re-Committal and Report) (1957–58 HC Papers 148), Vol 1, p 919

Finance Bill (1957–58 HL Papers 158), Vol 1

Supplement to Votes & Proceedings, 1956–57

12 May 1958, p 2175–2193; 13 May 1958, p 2223–2233; 14 May 1958, p 2271–2309; 15 May 1958, p 2321–2363; 19 May 1958, p 2365–2408; 20 May 1958, p 2437–2492; 21 May 1958, p 2511–2565; 21 May 1958, p 2579–2581; 22 May 1958, p 2595; 23 May 1958, p 2597–2598; 6 Jun 1958, p 2599–2652; 9 Jun 1958, p 2670; 11 Jun 1958, p 2681–2736; 12 Jun 1958, p 2745–2793; 13 Jun 1958, p 2849–2851; 17 Jun 1958, p 2859–2953; 18 Jun 1958, p 2956; 19 Jun 1958, p 2957; 20 Jun 1958, p 2971; 23 Jun 1958, p 2991; 25 Jun 1958, p 2997–2998; 26 Jun 1958, p 3005–3006; 27 Jun 1958, p 3009–3053; 1 Jul 1958, p 3061–3105; 2 Jul 1958, p 3113–3147; 3 Jul 1958, p 3157; 4 Jul 1958, p 3167; 7 Jul 1958, p 3179–3180; 8 Jul 1958, p 3197–3203; 9 Jul 1958, p 3215–3217; 10 Jul 1958, p 3229–3233; 11 Jul 1958, p 3241–3260; 15 Jul 1958, p 3277–3298

Development of Inventions Act 1958

PUBA77	1958		
	Development of Inventions Act 1958 (7 & 8 Eliz 2. c. 3)		

An Act to extend the period during which advances may be made to the National Research Development Corporation out of the Consolidated Fund and to increase the limit on such advances

Table of contents

s 1 Extension of period for making advances to National Research Development Corporation and increase of limit on such advances
s 2 Short title and citation

Journal

House of Commons			House of Lords		
Pres: Sir David Eccles (Pr BoT) Money Res: Robin Chicester-Clark CWH Rep: Gordon Touche (Dep Ch W&M)			No report		
5 Nov 1958	214 CJ 16	1R	26 Nov 1958	191 LJ 38	Brought HC/1R
14 Nov 1958	214 CJ 28	Money/2R/C/tted CWH	4 Dec 1958	191 LJ 52	2R/Com neg
25 Nov 1958	214 CJ 41	Res Rep/CWH/Rep w/o Amds/3R	9 Dec 1958	191 LJ 57	3R
9 Dec 1958	214 CJ 53	HL pass w/o Amds	18 Dec 1958	191 LJ 75	Royal Assent
18 Dec 1958	214 CJ 67	Royal Assent			

Parliamentary debates

1R: HC Deb, 5 Nov 1958, Vol 594(5th), col 950	1R: HL Deb, 26 Nov 1958, Vol 212(5th), col 842
2R: HC Deb, 14 Nov 1958, Vol 595(5th), col 725–743	2R: HL Deb, 4 Dec 1958, Vol 212(5th), col 1225–1229
CWH/3R: HC Deb, 25 Nov 1958, Vol 596(5th), col 315	3R: HL Deb, 9 Dec 1958, Vol 213(5th), col 162
Royal Assent: HC Deb, 18 Dec 1958, Vol 597(5th), col 1361	Royal Assent: HL Deb, 18 Dec 1958, Vol 213(5th), col 467

Parliamentary papers

Development of Inventions Bill (1958–59 HC Papers 9), Vol 1, p 489

Development of Inventions Bill (1958–59 HL Papers 19), Vol 1

Supplement to Votes & Proceedings, 1958–59 – No amendments

Finance Act 1962

PUBA78	1962		
	Finance Act 1962 (10 & 11 Eliz 2. c. 44)		

An Act to grant certain duties, to alter other duties, and to amend the law relating to the National Debt and the Public Revenue, and to make further provision in connection with Finance

Table of contents (patent provisions only)

s 11 Chargeable assets

Journal

House of Commons			House of Lords		
Pres: Sir Edward Boyle (Fin Sec Tr) Rep: Sir William Anstruther-Gray (Dep Ch W&M)			No report		
16 Apr 1962	217 CJ 202	Money Res/Bill Ord/1R	9 Jul 1962	194 LJ 320	Brought HC/1R
3 May 1962	217 CJ 217	2R/C'tted CWH	16 Jul 1962	194 LJ 339	2R adj
15 May 1962	217 CJ 231 – V	**CWH**	30 Jul 1962	194 LJ 367	2R/Com neg/3R
16 May 1962	217 CJ 233 – V	**CWH**	1 Aug 1962	194 LJ 387	Royal Assent
21 May 1962	217 CJ 239 – V	**CWH**			
22 May 1962	217 CJ 241 – V	**CWH**			
23 May 1962	217 CJ 243 – V	**CWH**			
29 May 1962	217 CJ 249 – V	**CWH**			
30 May 1962	217 CJ 251 – V	**CWH**			
5 Jun 1962	217 CJ 257 – V	**CWH/Rep with Amds**			

(continued)

(continued)

2 Jul 1962	217 CJ 270 – V	**Re–C'tted/Cons**			
3 Jul 1962	217 CJ 274 – V	**Re–C'tted/Cos**			
6 Jul 1962	217 CJ 280	3R			
30 Jul 1962	217 CJ 318	HL pass w/o Amds			
1 Aug 1962	217 CJ 321	Royal Assent			

Parliamentary debates

2R: HC Deb, 3 May 1962, Vol 658(5th), col 1217–1350	1R: HL Deb, 9 Jul 1962, Vol 242(5th), col 4
CWH: HC Deb, 15 May 1962, Vol 659(5th), col 1156–1289	2R/Com neg/3R: HL Deb, 30 Jul 1962, Vol 243(5th), col 4–33, 39–103
CWH: HC Deb, 16 May 1962, Vol 659(5th), col 1359–1500	Royal Assent: HL Deb, 1 Aug 1962, Vol 243(5th), col 351–352
CWH: HC Deb, 21 May 1962, Vol 660(5th), col 34–180	
CWH: HC Deb, 23 May 1962, Vol 660(5th), col 438–630	
CWH: HC Deb, 29 May 1962, Vol 660(5th), col 1173–1319	
CWH: HC Deb, 30 May 1962, Vol 660(5th), col 1366–1547	
CWH/Rep: HC Deb, 5 Jun 1962, Vol 661(5th), col 246–424	
Cons: HC Deb, 2 Jul 1962, Vol 662(5th), col 43–241	
Cons: HC Deb, 3 Jul 1962, Vol 662(5th), col 295–336, 337–510	
3R: HC Deb, 6 Jul 1962, Vol 662(5th), col 847–901	
Royal Assent: HC Deb, 1 Aug 1962, Vol 664(5th), col 677	

Debates on particular provisions

s 11	HC Deb, 2 Jul 1962, Vol 658(5th), col 85–113 (Cl 10)

Parliamentary papers

Finance Bill (1961–62 HL Papers 113), Vol 1

Finance Bill (1961–62 HC Papers 96), Vol 2, p 1

Finance Bill (as amended in Committee) (1961–62 HC Papers 121), Vol 2, p 81

Finance Bill (as amended in Committee, on Re-Committal and Report) (1961–62 HC Papers 128), Vol 2, p 161

Supplement to Votes & Proceedings, 1961–62

> 3 May 1962, p 1981–1994; 4 May 1962, p 2003; 7 May 1962, p 2028; 8 May 1962, p 2032; 9 May 1962, p 2079–2100; 10 May 1962, p 2107–2133; 11 May 1962, p 2135–2161; 15 May 1962, p 2201–2229; 16 May 1962, p 2237–2270; 16 May 1992, p 2305–2306; 17 May 1962, p 2331–2364; 21 May 1962, p 2367–2401; 22 May 1962, p 2451–2486; 23 May 1962, p 2491–2520; 23 May 1962, p 2571–2574; 24 May 1962, p 2575; 25 May 1962, p 2587–2615; 29 May 1962, p 2665–2694; 30 May 1962, p 2701–2725; 30 May 1962, p 2747; 5 Jun 1962, p 2831–2848; 5 Jun 1962, p 2897–2900; 7 Jun 1962, p 2949–2950; 8 Jun 1962, p 2953–2959; 22 Jun 1962, p 2973–2981; 25 Jun 1962, p 3033; 26 Jun 1962, p 3035–3059; 27 Jun 1962, p 3115–3174; 2 Jul 1962, p 3179; 3210; 3 Jul 1962, p 3251–3275

Purchase Tax Act 1963

PUBA79	1963

Purchase Tax Act 1963 (c. 9)

An Act to consolidate the enactments relating to purchase tax

Table of contents (patent provisions only)

Sch 2 Determination of Wholesale Value, par 3

Journal

House of Commons			House of Lords		
Rep: Sir William Anstruther-Gray (Ch W&M)			Pres: Lord Dilhorne LC Rep: Lord Merthyr (Ld Ch)		
13 Feb 1963	218 CJ 104	Rep JC Cons	29 Jan 1963	195 LJ 105	1R
19 Feb 1963	218 CJ 108	Brought HL/1R	5 Feb 1963	195 LJ 115	2R/Ref JC Cons
28 Feb 1963	218 CJ 124	2R/C'tted CWH	13 Feb 1963	195 LJ 130	Rep JC w/o Amds/C'tted CWH
5 Mar 1963	218 CJ 128	CWH/Rep w/o Amds//3R	18 Feb 1963	195 LJ 141	CWH/Rep w/o Amds
28 Mar 1963	218 CJ 162	Royal Assent	19 Feb 1963	195 LJ 143	3R
			6 Mar 1963	195 LJ 170	HC pass w/o Amds
			28 Mar 1963	195 LJ 200	Royal Assent

Parliamentary debates	
2R: HC Deb, 28 Feb 1963, Vol 672(5th), col 1580	1R: HL Deb, 29 Jan 1963, Vol 246(5th), col 252
CWH/Rep/3R: HC Deb, 5 Mar 1963, Vol 673(5th), col 351	2R: HL Deb, 5 Feb 1963, Vol 246(5th), col 493–494
Royal Assent: HC Deb, 28 Mar 1963, Vol 674(5th), col 1591	Rep JC: HL Deb, 13 Feb 1963, Vol 246(5th), col 1058
	Rep CWH: HL Deb, 18 Feb 1963, Vol 246(5th), col 1155
	3R: HL Deb, 19 Feb 1963, Vol 246(5th), col 1248
	HC pass: HL Deb, 6 Mar 1963, Vol 247(5th), col 409
	Royal Assent: HL Deb, 28 Mar 1963, Vol 248(5th), col 322
Parliamentary papers	
Purchase Tax Bill (1962–63 HL Papers 35), Vol 3	
Purchase Tax Bill (1962–63 HC Papers 71), Vol 3, p 73	
Supplement to Votes & Proceedings, 1962–63 – No amendments	

Resale Prices Act 1964

PUBA80	1961

Resale Prices Act 1964 (c. 58)
An Act to restrict the maintenance by contractual and other means of minimum resale prices in respect of goods supplied for resale in the United Kingdom; and for purposes connected therewith
Table of contents (patent provisions only)
s 1 Avoidance of conditions for maintaining resale prices [applies to patented articles]

Journal					
House of Commons			**House of Lords**		
Pres: Edward Heath (SoS Tr) Rep: Sir William Anstruther-Gray (Ch W&M)			Rep: Earl of Drogheda (Ld Ch)		
25 Feb 1964	219 CJ 123	Bill Ord/1R	14 May 1964	196 LJ ???	Brought HC
10 Mar 1964	219 CJ 142 – V	2R/C'ted CWH	2 Jun 1964	196 LJ 278	1R
23 Mar 1964	219 CJ 171 – V	**CWH**	9 Jun 1964	196 LJ 300	2R/C'tted CWH
24 Mar 1964	219 CJ 174 – V	**CWH**	18 Jun 1964	196 LJ 314 – V	**CWH**
25 Mar 1964	219 CJ 177 – V	**CWH**	22 Jun 1964	196 LJ 318 – V	**CWH**
25 Mar 1964	219 CJ 178 – V	**CWH**	23 Jun 1964	196 LJ 321 – V	**CWH**
8 Apr 1964	219 CJ 185 – V	**CWH**	2 Jul 1964	196 LJ 343 – V	**CWH/Rep with Amds**
8 Apr 1964	219 CJ 186 – V	**CWH**	9 Jul 1964	196 LJ 368	3R
21 Apr 1964	219 CJ 209 – V	**CWH**	16 Jul 1964	196 LJ 383	HC Ag Amds
22 Apr 1964	219 CJ 211 – V	**CWH**	16 Jul 1964	196 LJ 386	Royal Assent
23 Apr 1964	219 CJ 213 – V	**CWH**			
23 Apr 1964	219 CJ 214	Rep with Amds			
12 May 1964	219 CJ 234 – V	**Cons with Amds**			
13 May 1964	219 CJ 237	Cons/3R			
9 Jul 1964	219 CJ 292	HL pass with Amds			
15 Jul 1964	219 CJ 300	HL Amds Ag			
16 Jul 1964	219 CJ 302	Royal Assent			

Parliamentary debates	
1R: HC Deb, 25 Feb 1964, Vol 690(5th), col 240	Brought HC/1R: HL Deb, 2 Jun 1964, Vol 258(5th), col 379
2R: HC Deb, 10 Mar 1964, Vol 691(5th), col 255–382	2R: HL Deb, 9 Jun 1964, Vol 258(5th), col 782–800 and 804–874
CWH: HC Deb, 23 Mar 1964, Vol 692(5th), col 42–206	
CWH: HC Deb, 24 Mar 1964, Vol 692(5th), col 264–424	CWH: HL Deb, 18 Jun 1964, Vol 258(5th), col 1293–1363

(continued)

(continued)

CWH: HC Deb, 25 Mar 1964, Vol 692(5th), col 481–519, 520–600, 601–616 CWH: HC Deb, 8 Apr 1964, Vol 692(5th), col 1021–1141, 1042–1169 CWH: HC Deb, 21 Apr 1964, Vol 693(5th), col 1112–1228, 1239–1262 CWH: HC Deb, 22 Apr 1964, Vol 693(5th), col 1312–1466 CWH/Rep: HC Deb, 23 Apr 1964, Vol 693(5th), col 1515–1680 Cons: HC Deb, 12 May 1964, Vol 695(5th), col 241–383 Cons: HC Deb, 13 May 1964, Vol 695(5th), col 429–566 HL Amds Ag: HC Deb, 15 Jul 1964, Vol 698(5th), col 1287–1300 Royal Assent: HC Deb, 16 Jul 1964, Vol 698(5th), col 1498	CWH: HL Deb, 22 Jun 1964, Vol 259(5th), col 33-82 CWH/Rep: HL Deb, 2 Jul 1964, Vol 259(5th), col 722-752 3R: HL Deb, 9 Jul 1964, Vol 259(5th), col 1094-1100 HC Ag Amds: HL Deb, 16 Jul 1964, Vol 260(5th), col 394 Royal Assent: HL Deb, 16 Jul 1964, Vol 260(5th), col 435

Debates on particular provisions	
s 1	HC Deb, 23 Mar 1964, Vol 692(5th), col 42–206; HC Deb, 24 Mar 1964, Vol 692(5th), col 264–424; HL Deb, 9 Jun 1964, Vol 258(5th), col 786–787, 835 and 855; HC Deb, 12 May 1964, Vol 695(5th), col 283–317; HL Deb, 18 Jun 1964, Vol 258(5th), col 1293–1335

Parliamentary papers

Resale Price Bill (1963–64 HC Papers 94), Vol 3, p 487

Resale Price Bill (as amended in Committee) (1963–64 HC Papers 132), Vol 3, p 507

Lords Amendments to the Resale Prices Bill (1963–64 HC Papers 186), Vol 3, p 523

Resale Prices Bill (1964 HL Papers 138), Vol 4 [Explanatory Memorandum]

> Amendments to be Moved in Committee by the Lord Chancellor (1964 HL Papers 138a), Vol 4

> Amendments to be Moved in Committee by Lord Conesford, Viscount Colville of Culross and Lord Lindgren (1964 HL Papers 138b), Vol 4

> Amendments to be Moved in Committee by Lord Conesford, Viscount Colville of Culross and Lord Lindgren (1964 HL Papers 138c), Vol 4

> Amendments to be Moved in Committee (1964 HL Papers 138d), Vol 4

> Amendments to be Moved in Committee by Viscount Hanworth, Lord Jessel, Lord Mabane, Viscount Massereene and Ferrard, Lord Sinclair of Cleeve, Lord Stonham, Lord Coleraine (1964 HL Papers 138e), Vol 4

> Amendments to be Moved in Committee by the Lord Shepard, Lord Silkin and Lord Shackleton (1964 HL Papers 138f), Vol 4

> Amendments to be Moved in Committee by the Lord Shepard, Lord Silkin, Lord Shackleton, Lord Stonham, Lord Lindgrem and Lord Champion (1964 HL Papers 138g), Vol 4

> Amendments to be Moved in Committee by the Lord Conesford and Viscount Colville of Culross (1964 HL Papers 138h) (in substitution of Clause 5 previously published), Vol 4

> Amendments to be Moved in Committee by the Lord Chancellor (Supplementary to the Marshalled List) (1964 HL Papers 138i) (in substitution of Nos 43 and 45 in Marshalled List), Vol 4

> Amendments to be Moved in Committee by Lord Tangley and Lord Airedale (Supplementary to the Marshalled List) (1964 HL Papers 138j), Vol 4

> Marshalled List of Amendments to be Moved in Committee (1964 HL Papers 138**), Vol 4

> Second Marshalled List of Amendments to be Moved in Committee (1964 HL Papers 138††), Vol 4

> Third Marshalled List of Amendments to be Moved in Committee (1964 HL Papers 138‡‡), Vol 4

Resale Prices Bill (as amended In Committee) (1964 HL Papers 154), Vol 4

> Amendments to be Moved on Report by the Lord Chancellor (1964 HL Papers 154a), Vol 4

> Amendments to be Moved on Report by Lord Stonham, Lord Robertson of Oakridge and Lord Sinclair of Cleeve (1964 HL Papers 154b), Vol 4

> Amendments to be Moved on Report by Lord Shackleton, Lord Shepherd and Lord Chorley (1964 HL Papers 154c), Vol 4

> Marshalled List of Amendments to be Moved on Report (1964 HL Papers 154**), Vol 4

Resale Prices Bill (as amended on Report) (1964 HL Papers 174), Vol 4

Supplement to Votes & Proceedings, 1963–64

10 Mar 1964, p 1541–1546; 11 Mar 1964, p 1591–1598; 12 Mar 1964, p 1599–1603; 13 Mar 1964, p 1631– 1648; 16 Mar 1964, p 1681–1692; 17 Mar 1964, p 1701–1704; 18 Mar 1964, p 1745–1751; 19 Mar 1964, p 1765–1818; 23 Mar 1964, p 1825–1872; 24 Mar 1964, p 1923–1971; 25 Mar 1964, p 1983–2028; 8 Apr 1964, p 2121–2166; 16 Apr 1964, p 2334; 21 Apr 1964, p 2359–2398; 22 Apr 1964, p 2415–2450; 23 Apr 1964, p 2467–2495; 4 May 1964, p 2579; 5 May 1964, p 2593–2595; 6 May 1964, p 2597–2599; 7 May 1964, p 2609–2617; 8 May 1964, p 2647–2657; 12 May 1964, p 2659–2669; 13 May 1964, p 2701–2706

Development of Inventions Act 1965

PUBA81	1965

Development of Inventions Act 1965 (c. 21)

An Act to amend the Development of Inventions Acts 1948 to 1958

Table of contents

s 1 Exchequer advances to Corporation
s 2 Remission of liability to repay advance where the advance is represented by an asset with a written-down value
s 3 Exchequer payments to meet interest due from Corporation
s 4 Projects carried out by Corporation in response to representations by a Government department
s 5 Disposal of excess revenue
s 6 Increase in membership of Corporation
s 7 Minor amendments
s 8 Interpretation
s 9 Powers of Parliament of Northern Ireland
s 10 Citation, repeals and commencement
Schedule – Repeals

Journal

House of Commons			House of Lords		
Pres and Money Res: Frank Cousins (Min Tech) Rep SC: Sir Barnet Janner			Rep: Lord Merthyr (Ld Ch)		
5 Feb 1965	220 CJ 125	1R	29 Apr 1965	197 LJ 268	Brought HC/1R
18 Feb 1965	220 CJ 140	Money Res/2R/C'tted	13 May 1965	197 LJ 287 – V	2R/C'tted CWH
19 Feb 1965	220 CJ 142	Assigned SC D	27 May 1965	197 LJ 313	CWH/Rep w/o Amds
22 Feb 1965	220 CJ 143	**Rep Money Res**	1 Jun 1965	197 LJ 320	3R
8 Apr 1965	220 CJ 220	Rep with Amds	2 Jun 1965	197 LJ 325	Royal Assent
28 Apr 1965	220 CJ 246	Cons/3R			
1 Jun 1965	220 CJ 295	HL pass w/o Amds			
2 Jun 1965	220 CJ 298	Royal Assent			

Parliamentary debates

1R: HC Deb, 5 Feb 1965, Vol 705(5th), col 1395	Br HC/1R: HL Deb, 29 Apr 1965, Vol 265(5th), col 718
2R: HC Deb, 18 Feb 1965, Vol 706(5th), col 1373–1426	2R: HL Deb, 13 May 1965, Vol 266(5th), col 261–268
Res: HC Deb, 22 Feb 1965, Vol 707(5th), col 189–190	CWH: HL Deb, 27 May 1965, Vol 266(5th), col 958–963
Cons/3R: HC Deb, 28 Apr 1965, Vol 711(5th), col 550–563	3R: HL Deb, 1 Jun 1965, Vol 266(5th), col 1089
Royal Assent: HC Deb, 2 Jun 1965, Vol 713(5th), col 1772	Royal Assent: HL Deb, 2 Jun 1965, Vol 266(5th), col 1558

Parliamentary papers

Development of Inventions Bill (1964–65 HC Papers 75), Vol 1, p 695 [Explanatory Memorandum]

Development of Inventions Bill (as amended by Standing Committee D) (1964–65 HC Papers 126), Vol 1, p 707

Development of Inventions Bill (1964–65 HL Papers 100), Vol 1 [Explanatory Memorandum]

Standing Committee D Minutes of Proceedings on the Development of Inventions Bill (1964–65 HC Papers 165), Vol 5, p 1069

Supplement to Votes & Proceedings, 1964–65

22 Mar 1965, p 997; 24 Mar 1965, p 1033; 6 Apr 1965, p 1161–1163

Finance Act 1965

PUBA82	1927	
	Finance Act 1965 (c. 25)	
	An Act to grant certain duties, to alter other duties, and to amend the law relating to the National Debt and the Public Revenue, and to make further provision in connection with Finance	

Table of contents (patent provisions only)

s 43 Residence and location of assets
Sch 14 Adaptation of System of Capital Allowances

Journal

House of Commons			House of Lords		
Pres: Niall MacDermot (Fin Sec Tr) / Money Res (No 1): Alan Fitch / Money Res (No 2): Brian O'Malley / Money Res (No 3): John Diamond / CWH Rep: Sir Samuel Storey (Dep Ch W&M)			No report		
12 Apr 1965	220 CJ 223 – V	Money Res (No 1)	16 Jul 1965	197 LJ 397	Brought HC
13 Apr 1965	220 CJ 232	Rep Res No 1	19 Jul 1965	197 LJ 399	1R
13 Apr 1965	220 CJ 233	Bill Ord/1R	4 Aug 1965	197 LJ 447	2R/Com neg/3R
10 May 1965	220 CJ 259 – V	**2R/C'tted CWH**	5 Aug 1965	197 LJ 450	Royal Assent
17 May 1965	220 CJ 267 – V	**CWH**			
19 May 1965	220 CJ 272 – V	**CWH**			
20 May 1965	220 CJ 274 – V	**CWH**			
24 May 1965	220 CJ 278 – V	**CWH**			
25 May 1965	220 CJ 280 – V	**CWH**			
26 May 1965	220 CJ 284 – V	**CWH**			
27 May 1965	220 CJ 288 – V	**CWH**			
31 May 1965	220 CJ 291 – V	**CWH**			
2 Jun 1965	220 CJ 298 – V	**CWH**			
3 Jun 1965	220 CJ 300 – V	**CWH**			
3 Jun 1965	220 CJ 302 – V	**Money Res (No 2)**			
15 Jun 1965	220 CJ 306 – V	**CWH**			
15 Jun 1965	220 CJ 307	Money Res Rep (No 2)			
16 Jun 1965	220 CJ 309 – V	**CWH**			
21 Jun 1965	220 CJ 317 – V	**CWH**			
22 Jun 1965	220 CJ 321 – V	**CWH**			
23 Jun 1965	220 CJ 326 – V	**CWH**			
24 Jun 1965	220 CJ 327 – V	**CWH/Rep**			
1 Jul 1965	220 CJ 340	Money Res (No 3)			
5 Jul 1965	220 CJ 344	CWH/Cons			
6 Jul 1965	220 CJ 346 – V	**Cons**			
7 Jul 1965	220 CJ 349 – V	**Cons**			
8 Jul 1965	220 CJ 351 – V	**Cons**			
12 Jul 1965	220 CJ 359 – V	**Cons**			
15 Jul 1965	220 CJ 368 – V	**3R**			
15 Jul 1965	220 CJ 369 – V	**3R**			
4 Aug 1965	220 CJ 409	HL pass w/o Amds			
5 Aug 1965	220 CJ 411	Royal Assent			

Parliamentary debates

1R: HC Deb, 12 Apr 1965, Vol 710(5th), col 1093–1094

2R: HC Deb, 10 Apr 1965, Vol 710(5th), col 44–172

CWH: HC Deb, 17 May 1965, Vol 712(5th), col 1013–1168

CWH: HC Deb, 19 May 1965, Vol 712(5th), col 1461–1590

CWH: HC Deb, 20 May 1965, Vol 712(5th), col 1673–1913

CWH: HC Deb, 24 May 1965, Vol 713(5th), col 34–199

CWH: HC Deb, 25 May 1965, Vol 713(5th), col 243–519

CWH: HC Deb, 26 May 1965, Vol 713(5th), col 621–791

CWH: HC Deb, 27 May 1965, Vol 713(5th), col 847–1021

1R: HL Deb, 8 Dec 1964, Vol 262(5th), col 85

2R: HL Deb, 9 Dec 1964, Vol 262(5th), col 92–104 and 111–222

3R: HL Deb, 15 Dec 1964, Vol 262(5th), col 367

Royal Assent: HL Deb, 17 Dec 1964, Vol 262(5th), col 590

CWH: HC Deb, 31 May 1965, Vol 713(5th), col 1177–1468	
CWH: HC Deb, 2 Jun 1965, Vol 713(5th), col 1722–1772	
CWH: HC Deb, 3 Jun 1965, Vol 713(5th), col 1977–2126	
Money: HC Deb, 3 Jun 1965, Vol 713(5th), col 2123	
CWH: HC Deb, 15 Jun 1965, Vol 714(5th), col 259–406	
CWH: HC Deb, 15 Jun 1965, Vol 714(5th), col 406	
CWH: HC Deb, 16 Jun 1965, Vol 714(5th), col 453–860	
CWH: HC Deb, 21 Jun 1965, Vol 714(5th), col 1203–1432	
CWH: HC Deb, 22 Jun 1965, Vol 714(5th), col 1477–1715	
CWH: HC Deb, 23 Jun 1965, Vol 714(5th), col 1768–1904	
CWH: HC Deb, 24 Jun 1965, Vol 714(5th), col 1962–2103	
Mon Res: HC Deb, 1 Jul 1965, Vol 715(5th), col 971	
CWH/Rep: HC Deb, 5 Jul 1965, Vol 715(5th), col 1204–1318	
Cons: HC Deb, 6 Jul 1965, Vol 715(5th), col 1369–1558	
Cons: HC Deb, 7 Jul 1965, Vol 715(5th), col 1594–1755	
Cons: HC Deb, 8 Jul 1965, Vol 715(5th), col 1833–1972	
Cons: HC Deb, 12 Jul 1965, Vol 716(5th), col 40–240	
3R: HC Deb, 15 Jul 1965, Vol 716(5th), col 794–928	
Royal Assent: HC Deb, 5 Aug 1965, Vol 717(5th), col 1968	

Debates on particular provisions	
s 43	HC Deb, 31 May 1965, Vol 713(5th), col 1368 (Cl 39)

Parliamentary papers
Finance (No 2) Bill (1964–65 HC Papers 128), Vol 2, p 93
Finance (No 2) Bill (as amended in Committee) (1964–65 HC Papers 156–I and II), Vol 2, p 325 and 429
Finance Bill (1964–65 HL Papers 14), Vol 1
Supplement to Votes & Proceedings, 1964–65
10 May 1965, p 1615–1618; 11 May 1965, p 1655–1656; 12 May 1965, p 1709–1718; 13 May 1965, p 1723–1745; 17 May 1965, p 1753–1777; 17 May 1965, p 1827–1832; 19 May 1965, p 1873–1922; 20 May 1965, p 1955–2015; 20 May 1965, p 2029–2088; 24 May 1965, p 2107–2170; 25 May 1965, p 2217–2295; 26 May 1965, p 2323–2399; 27 May 1965, p 2441–2518; 27 May 1965, p 2519–2532; 31 May 1965, p 2543–2624; 31 May 1965, p 2665–2670; 2 Jun 1965, p 2701–2773; 3 Jun 1965, p 2809–2884; 3 Jun 1965, p 2891–2897; 4 Jun 1965, p 2901; 11 Jun 1965, p 2909–2987; 15 Jun 1965, p 3027–3111; 16 Jun 1965, p 3133–3219; 16 Jun 1965, p 3301–3302; 17 Jun 1965, p 3305–3377; 21 Jun 1965, p 3391–3467; 22 Jun 1965, p 3469–3538; 24 Jun 1965, p 3579–3628; 24 Jun 1965, p 3683–3704; 25 Jun 1965, p 3789–3795; 29 Jun 1965, p 3909–3921; 30 Jun 1965, p 3935–3968; 1 Jul 1965, p 3989–4040; 5 Jul 1965, p 4053–4145; 6 Jul 1965, p 4149–4241; 7 Jul 1965, p 4247–4329; 8 Jul 1965, p 4331–4394; 8 Jul 1965, p 4395–4396; 12 Jul 1965, p 4403–4442

Development of Inventions Act 1967

PUBA83	1967	
Development of Inventions Act 1967 (c. 32)		
An Act to consolidate the Development of Inventions Act 1948, the Development of Inventions Act 1954 and the Development of Inventions Act 1965		
Table of contents		
		Table of origin
s 1 Constitution		1948, s 1(1), s 2(2)–(3) 1965, s 6(1) SI 1965/125, art 2
s 2 Functions		1948, s 1(1), (2), (3) and (4) 1954, s 2(1), (2) and (3) 1965, s 7(3) and (4)

(continued)

(continued)

s 3 General directions	1948, s 4(1)
	1965, s 7(1)
s 4 Matters requiring Ministerial approval	1948, s 4(2)
	1954, s 2(4)
	SI 1959/1826
	SI 1964/490
s 5 Financial duty	1948, s 3
	1965, s 5(1) and (2)
s 6 Temporary borrowing	1948, s 6
s 7 Exchequer advances	1948, s 7(1), (2), 8(1), (2), (3) and 12(1)
	1965, s 1(1) and (3)
s 8 Remission of liability to repay advances	1965, s 2 (except (7) and (8))
s 9 Relief from interest on advances	1965, s 3
s 10 Establishment of reserve	1948, s 9
s 11 Projects sponsored by Government departments	1965, s 4
s 12 Accounts and audit	1948, s 10
	1954, s 3(2) and (3)
	1965, s 1(5) to (7), 7(2)
s 13 Information and annual report	1948, s 4(3) to (5)
	1965, s 2(7) and (8)
s 14 Powers of Parliament of Northern Ireland	1965, s 9
s 15 Short title, interpretation, repeals, savings and commencement	1948, s 1(2) and 1(3) part
	1954, s 4(3)
	1965, s 8(1)
Schedule – The National Research Development Corporation	1948, Sch

Journal

House of Commons			House of Lords		
Rep: Sydney Irving (Dep Ch W&M)			Pres: Lord Gardier LC Rep: Earl of Listowel (Ld Ch)		
22 Mar 1967	222 CJ 407	Rep JC Cons	20 Oct 1966	199 LJ 215	1R
25 Apr 1967	222 CJ 454	Brought HL	1 Nov 1966	199 LJ 228	Ref JC Cons
26 Apr 1967	222 CJ 458	1R	22 Mar 1967	199 LJ 471	Rep JC with Amds/Re-C'tted CWH
8 May 1967	222 CJ 473	2R/C'tted CWH	17 Apr 1967	199 LJ 492	CWH day fixed
10 May 1967	222 CJ 477	CWH/Rep w/o Amds/3R	18 Apr 1967	199 LJ 495	CWH adj
10 May 1967	222 CJ 479	Royal Assent	20 Apr 1967	199 LJ 499	CWH/Rep w/o Amds
			25 Apr 1967	199 LJ 505	3R
			10 May 1967	199 LJ 531	HC pass w/o Amds
			10 May 1967	199 LJ 532	Royal Assent

Parliamentary debates

2R: HC Deb, 8 May 1967, Vol 746(5th), col 1010–1013	1R: HL Deb, 20 Oct 1966, Vol 277(5th), col 122
CWH/3R: HC Deb, 10 May 1967, Vol 746(5th), col 1450–1452	Ref JC: HL Deb, 1 Nov 1966, Vol 277(5th), col 568
	JC Rep/C'tted: HL Deb, 22 Mar 1967, Vol 281(5th), col 842
Royal Assent: HC Deb, 10 May 1967, Vol 746(5th), col 1553	CWH: HL Deb, 20 Apr 1967, Vol 282(5th), col 337
	3R: HL Deb, 25 Apr 1967, Vol 282(5th), col 439–440
	HC pass: HL Deb, 10 May 1967, Vol 282(5th), col 1488
	Royal Assent: HL Deb, 10 May 1967, Vol 282(5th), col 1489

Parliamentary papers

Development of Inventions Bill (1966–67 HL Papers 96), Vol 2

    Amendment made by the Joint Committee on Consolidation Bill (1966–67 HL Papers 96a), Vol 2

Development of Inventions Bill (as amended in Joint Committee) (1966–67 HL Papers 209), Vol 2

Development of Inventions Bill (1966–67 HC Papers 245), Vol 2, p 579

Health Services and Public Health Act 1968

PUBA84	1968
	Health Services and Public Health Act 1968 (c 46)

An Act to amend the National Health Service Act 1946 and the National Health Service (Scotland) Act 1947 and make other amendments connected with the national health service; to make amendments connected with local authorities' services under the National Assistance Act 1948; to amend the law relating to notifiable diseases and food poisoning; to amend the Nurseries and Child-Minders Regulation Act 1948; to amend the law relating to food and drugs; to enable assistance to be given to certain voluntary organisations; to enable the Minister of Health and Secretary of State to purchase goods for supply to certain authorities; to make other amendments in the law relating to the public health; and for purposes connected with the matters aforesaid

Table of contents (patent provisions only)

s 59 Extension of power of user by Crown of patented inventions to user for certain health services

Journal

House of Commons			House of Lords		
Pres: Kenneth Robinson (Min Health) SC Rep: Victor Yates			Rep: Earl of Listowel (Ld Ch)		
22 Nov 1967	223 CJ 31	Pres/1R	2 Apr 1968	200 LJ 228	From HC/1R
7 Dec 1967	223 CJ 49	2R/C'tted	9 Apr 1968	200 LJ 245	Ord Varied
8 Dec 1967	223 CJ 51	Assigned to SC D	23 Apr 1968	200 LJ 264	2R/C'tted CWH
29 Feb 1968	223 CJ 132	Rep with Amds	14 May 1968	200 LJ 314	**CWH**/Rep with Amds
1 Apr 1968	223 CJ 190	Cons/3R	27 May 1968	200 LJ 345	**Cons with Amds**
13 Jun 1968	223 CJ 292	HL Ag with Amds	13 Jun 1968	200 LJ 367	3R
10 Jul 1968	223 CJ 340	**HL Amds Ag/Further Amds**	11 Jul 1968	200 LJ 471	HC Ag Amd/DisAg Amd
16 Jul 1968	223 CJ 344	HL Ag Further Amds	16 Jul 1968	200 LJ 481	**HC Amd Ag**
26 Jul 1968	223 CJ 367	Royal Assent	26 Jul 1968	200 LJ 553	Royal Assent

Parliamentary debates

1R: HC Deb, 22 Nov 1967, Vol 754(5th), col 1313	1R: HL Deb, 2 Apr 1968, Vol 290(5th), col 1195
2R: HC Deb, 7 Dec 1967, Vol 755(5th), col 1679–1803	2R: HL Deb, 23 Apr 1968, Vol 291(5th), col 551–619
SC D, 1st Sit, 23 Jan 1968, Vol 5, col 1–46	CWH: HL Deb, 14 May 1968, Vol 292(5th), col 255–322
SC D, 2nd Sit, 25 Jan 1968, Vol 5, col 47–94	Rep: HL Deb, 27 May 1968, Vol 292(5th), col 960–995
SC D, 3rd Sit, 30 Jan 1968, Vol 5, col 95–140	3R: HL Deb, 13 Jun 1968, Vol 293(5th), col 216
SC D, 4th Sit, 1 Feb 1968, Vol 5, col 141–188	HC pass: HL Deb, 11 Jul 1968, Vol 294(5th), col 1086
SC D, 5th Sit, 6 Feb 1968, Vol 5, col 189–232	HC Amds Cons: HL Deb, 16 Jul 1968, Vol 295(5th), col 243–253
SC D, 6th Sit, 8 Feb 1968, Vol 5, col 233–276	Royal Assent: HL Deb, 26 Jul 1968, Vol 295(5th), col 1461
SC D, 7th Sit, 13 Feb 1968, Vol 5, col 277–322	
SC D, 8th Sit, 15 Feb 1968, Vol 5, col 323–374	
SC D, 9th Sit, 20 Feb 1968, Vol 5, col 375–424	
SC D, 10th Sit, 22 Feb 1968, Vol 5, col 425–476	
SC D, 11th Sit, 27 Feb 1968, Vol 5, col 477–524	
SC D, 12th Sit, 29 Feb 1968, Vol 5, col 525–572	
Cons: HC Deb, 1 Apr 1968, Vol 762(5th), col 50–146	
HL Ag Amds: HC Deb, 10 Jul 1968, Vol 768(5th), col 651–704	
Royal Assent: HL Amds: HC Deb, 26 Jul 1968, Vol 769(5th), col 1241	

Debates on particular provisions

s 29	HC Deb, 1 Apr 1968, Vol 762(5th), col 79–107; HL Deb, 23 Apr 1968, Vol 291(5th), col 564–565; HL Deb, 14 May 1968, Vol 292(5th), col 267–307; HL Deb, 27 May 1968, Vol 292(5th), col 960–995; HL Deb, 16 Jul 1968, Vol 295(5th), col 244 and 246–253; HC Deb, 10 Jul 1968, Vol 768(5th), col 651–693

(continued)

(continued)

Parliamentary papers
Health Services and Public Health Bill (1968 HL Papers 93), Vol 2 [Explanatory Memorandum]
Amendment to be Moved in Committee by Lord Ogmore (1968 HL Papers 93a), Vol 2
Amendment to be Moved in Committee by Lord Newton, Baroness Brooke of Ystradfellte and Lord Sandford (1968 HL Papers 93b), Vol 2
Amendments to be Moved in Committee by Lord Newton, Lord Sandford and Baroness Brooke of Ystradfellte (1968 HL Papers 93c), Vol 2
Amendment to be Moved in Committee by Lord Newton, Baroness Brooke of Ystradfellte and Lord Sandford (1968 HL Papers 93d), Vol 2
Amendments to be Moved in Committee by Lord Newton, Lord Sandford and Baroness Brooke of Ystradfellte (1968 HL Papers 93e), Vol 2
Amendments to be Moved in Committee by Baroness Phillips (1968 HL Papers 93f), Vol 2
Amendment to be Moved in Committee by Lord Newton, Lord Sandford and Baroness Brooke of Ystradfellte (1968 HL Papers 93g), Vol 2
Amendment to be Moved in Committee by Lord Brock (1968 HL Papers 93h), Vol 2
Marshalled List of Amendments to be Moved in Committee (1968 HL Papers 93–I), Vol 2
Health Services and Public Health Bill (as amended in Committee) (1968 HL Papers 123), Vol 2
Amendment to be Moved on Report by Lord Ogmore (1968 HL Papers 123a), Vol 2
Amendments to be Moved on Report by Baroness Phillips (1968 HL Papers 123b), Vol 2
Marshalled List of Amendments to be Moved on Report (1968 HL Papers 123–I), Vol 2
Health Services and Public Health Bill (as amended on Report) (1968 HL Papers 138), Vol 2
Health Services and Public Health Bill (1967–68 HC Papers 12), Vol 2, p 745
Health Services and Public Health Bill (as amended by Standing Committee D) (1967–68 HC Papers 96), Vol 2, p 821
Lords Amendments to the Health Services and Public Health Bill (1967–68 HC Papers 176), Vol 2, p 891 Commons Amendments to the Bill Instead of Words Left Out by One of the Lords Amendments, Commons Consequential Amendment to the Bill, and Commons Amendment to One of the Lords Amendments (1968 HL Papers 174), Vol 2
Standing Committee D. Minutes of Proceedings on Health Services and Public Health Bill (1967–68 HC Papers 145), Vol 12, p 115
Supplement to Votes & Proceedings, 1967–68
8 Dec 1957, p 295; 12 Jan 1957, p 487; 17 Jan 1968, p 565–566; 19 Jan 1968, p 839–842; 23 Jan 1968, p 843–847; 23 Jan 1968, p 1027–1028; 25 Jan 1968, p 1039–1044; 26 Jan 1968, p 1137; 30 Jan 1968, p 1309–1315; 30 Jan 1968, p 1427–1428; 1 Feb 1968, p 1487–1492; 1 Feb 1968, p 1557; 6 Feb 1968, p 1749–1753; 6 Feb 1968, p 1919–1920; 8 Feb 1968, p 1965–1970; 8 Feb 1968, p 2061–2064; 13 Feb 1968, p 2267–2273; 13 Feb 1968, p 2435–2436; 15 Feb 1968, p 2481–2486; 19 Feb 1968, p 2821–2826; 20 Feb 1968, p 2985–2988; 22 Feb 1968, p 3041–3048; 22 Feb 1968, p 3097; 23 Feb 1968, p 3116; 27 Feb 1968, p 3339–3345; 27 Feb 1968, p 3455–3456; 29 Feb 1968, p 3487–3492; 15 Mar 1968, p 4533; 21 Mar 1968, p 5055–5057; 25 Mar 1968, p 5339–5342; 28 Mar 1968, p 5535–5543; 1 Apr 1968, p 5583–5591; 8 Jul 1968, p 12,077–12,078; 10 Jul 1968, p 12,091
Notes
Archives
Request by Association of the British Pharmaceutical Industry for repeal of s 41: National Archive (BT 209/431)

Finance Act 1968

PUBA85	1968
	Finance Act 1968 (c. 44)
	An Act to grant certain duties, to alter other duties, and to amend the law relating to the National Debt and the Public Revenue, and to make further provision in connection with Finance

Table of contents (patent provisions only)
s 42 Investment income
s 46 Relief where income attributable to period of years was received in 1967–68

Journal					
House of Commons			**House of Lords**		
Pres: Harod Lever (Fin Sec Tr) CWH Rep: Sir Eric Fletcher (Ch W&M)			No report		
25 Mar 1968	223 CJ 180	Money Res	5 Jul 1968	200 LJ 444	1R
25 Mar 1968	223 CJ 181	Bill Ord/1R	17 Jul 1968	200 LJ 485	2R/Com neg/3R
24 Apr 1968	223 CJ 216 – V	**2R/C'tted**	26 Jul 1968	200 LJ 553	Royal Assent
24 Apr 1968	223 CJ 217	Assigned to SC A			
13 Jun 1968	223 CJ 291	**Rep with Amds**			
18 Jun 1968	223 CJ 298 – V	**Re–C'tted CWH/CWH**			
19 Jun 1968	223 CJ 301 – V	**CWH**			
20 Jun 1968	223 CJ 303 – V	**CWH**			
1 Jul 1968	223 CJ 324 – V	**Cons**			
2 Jul 1968	223 CJ 326 – V	**Cons**			
3 Jul 1968	223 CJ 328 – V	**Cons**			
4 Jul 1968	223 CJ 330 – V	**Cons/3R**			
17 Jul 1968	223 CJ 346	HL pass w/o Amds			
26 Jul 1968	223 CJ 367	Royal Assent			

Parliamentary debates

1R: HC Deb, 25 Mar 1968, Vol 761(5th), col 1078

2R: HC Deb, 24 Apr 1968, Vol 763(5th), col 250–412

CWH: HC Deb, 18 Jun 1968, Vol 766(5th), col 921–1063

CWH: HC Deb, 19 Jun 1968, Vol 766(5th), col 1116–1245

CWH: HC Deb, 20 Jun 1968, Vol 766(5th), col 1329–1381

Cons: HC Deb, 1 Jul 1968, Vol 767(5th), col 1156–1244

Cons: HC Deb, 2 Jul 1968, Vol 767(5th), col 1235–1468

Cons: HC Deb, 3 Jul 1968, Vol 767(5th), col 1504–1651

Cons/3R: HC Deb, 4 Jul 1968, Vol 767(5th), col 1706–1858

Royal Assent: HC Deb, 26 Jul 1968, Vol 769(5th), col 1241

1R: HL Deb, 5 Jul 1968, Vol 294(5th), col 557

2R: HL Deb, 17 Jul 1968, Vol 295(5th), col 304–333 and 342–408

Com neg/3R: HL Deb, 17 Jul 1968, Vol 295(5th), col 408

Royal Assent: HL Deb, 26 Jul 1968, Vol 295(5th), col 1461

Parliamentary papers

Finance Bill (1967–68 HC Papers 111), Vol 2, p 1

Finance Bill (as amended by Standing Committee A) (1967–68 HC Papers 171 and 171–I), Vol 2, p 117 and 221

Finance Bill (1967–68 HL Papers 163), Vol 2

Standing Committee A. Minutes of Proceedings on Finance Bill (1967–68 HC Papers 283), Vol 12, p 1

Supplement to Votes & Proceedings, 1967–68

24 Apr 1968, p 6905–6916; 26 Apr 1968, p 6941–6955; 29 Apr 1968, p 7121–7142; 1 May 1968, p 7219–7242; 2 May 1968, p 7311–7348; 2 May 1968, p 7407–7448; 6 May 1968, p 7481–7529; 6 May 1968, p 7671–7681; 8 May 1968, p 7755–7808; 8 May 1968, p 7889–7900; 9 May 1968, p 7961–8028; 13 May 1968, p 8039–8108; 13 May 1968, p 8213–8219; 15 May 1968, p 8249–8327; 15 May 1968, p 8457–8461

Civil Evidence Act 1968

PUBA86	1968	
Civil Evidence Act 1968 (c. 64)		
An Act to amend the law of evidence in relation to civil proceedings, and in respect of the privilege against self-incrimination to make corresponding amendments in relation to statutory powers of inspection or investigation		
Table of contents (patent provisions only)		
s 15 Privilege for certain communications relating to patent proceedings		
Journal		
House of Commons		**House of Lords**
SC Rep: Victor Yates		Pres: Lord Gardiner LC Rep: Earl of Listowel (Ld Ch)

(continued)

(continued)

21 Mar 1968	223 CJ 168	Brought HL/1R	19 Dec 1967	200 LJ 89	1R
8 Apr 1968	223 CJ 201	Ref to 2R C'tee	8 Feb 1968	200 LJ 142	2R/C'tted CWH
24 Apr 1968	223 CJ 216	Rep should be 2R	22 Feb 1968	200 LJ 160	**CWH**/Rep with Amds
30 Apr 1968	223 CJ 226	2R/C'tted	7 Mar 1968	200 LJ 185	**Cons with Amds**
1 May 1968	223 CJ 227	Assigned SC G	21 Mar 1968	200 LJ 206	**3R with Amds**
11 Jun 1968	223 CJ 288	Transferred to SC E	24 Jul 1968	200 LJ 527	HC Ag with Amds
20 Jun 1968	223 CJ 303	Rep with Amds	16 Oct 1968	200 LJ 648	**HC Amd Ag**
23 Jul 1968	223 CJ 357	3R with Amds	25 Oct 1968	200 LJ 667	Royal Assent
16 Oct 1968	223 CJ 380	HL Ag Amds			
25 Oct 1968	223 CJ 405	Royal Assent			

Parliamentary debates

Ref 2R C: HC Deb, 8 Apr 1968, Vol 762(5th), col 956

2R Com: HC Deb, 24 Apr 1968, Vol 763(5th), col 423–450

2R: HC Deb, 30 Apr 1968, Vol 763(5th), col 1047

SC E Deb, 20 Jun 1968, Vol 6, col 1–46

Rep/3R: HC Deb, 23 Jul 1968, Vol 769(5th), col 439–462

Royal Assent: HC Deb, 25 Oct 1968, Vol 770(5th), col 1729

1R: HL Deb, 19 Dec 1967, Vol 287(5th), col 1365

2R: HL Deb, 8 Feb 1968, Vol 288(5th), col 1339–1364

CWH/Rep: HL Deb, 22 Feb 1968, Vol 289(5th), col 636–685

Rep: HL Deb, 7 Mar 1968, Vol 289(5th), col 1454–1479

3R: HL Deb, 21 Mar 1968, Vol 290(5th), col 681–689

HC pass: HL Deb, 24 Jul 1968, Vol 295(5th), col 1048

HC Amds Ag: HL Deb, 16 Oct 1968, Vol 296(5th), col 1357–1363

Royal Assent: HL Deb, 25 Oct 1968, Vol 296(5th), col 1607

Debates on particular provisions

s 15	HC Deb, 24 Apr 1968, Vol 763(5th), col 432; HC Deb, 23 Jul 1968, Vol 769(5th), col 456–462; HL Deb, Vol 288(5th), col 1348

Parliamentary papers

Civil Evidence Bill (1967 HL Papers 36), Vol 1

    Amendments to be Moved in Committee by the Lord Chancellor (1967 HL Papers 36a), Vol 1

    Amendments to be Moved in Committee by Viscount Colville of Culross (1967 HL Papers 36b), Vol 1

    Marshalled List of Amendments to be Moved in Committee (1967 HL Papers 36**), Vol 1

Civil Evidence Bill (as amended in Committee) (1967 HL Papers 68), Vol 1

    Amendments to be Moved on Report by the Lord Chancellor (1967 HL Papers 68a), Vol 1

    Amendments to be Moved on Report by Viscount Colville of Culross (1967 HL Papers 68b), Vol 1

    Marshalled List of Amendments to be Moved on Report (1967 HL Papers 68**), Vol 1

Civil Evidence Bill (as amended on Report) (1967 HL Papers 75), Vol 1

    Amendments to be Moved on Third Reading by the Lord Chancellor (1967 HL Papers 75a), Vol 1

    Marshalled List of Amendments to be Moved on Third Reading (1967 HL Papers 75**), Vol 1

Civil Evidence Bill (1967–68 HC Papers 114), Vol 1, p 409

Civil Evidence Bill (as amended in Standing Committee E) (1967–68 HC Papers, Bill 183), Vol 1, p 437

Commons Amendments (1967 HL Papers 186), Vol 1

Second Reading Committee. Minutes of proceedings on the Civil Evidence Bill [Lords] (1967–68 HC Papers 222), Vol 7, p 29

Standing Committee E. Minutes of proceedings on the Civil Evidence Bill [Lords] (1967–68 HC Papers 292), Vol 7, p 33

Law Reform Committee, Sixteenth Report (1967–68 Cmnd 3472), Vol 25, p 3472, [25]: 5 Dec 1967 (223 CJ 44; 200 LJ 59)

Supplement to Votes & Proceedings, 1967–68

    10 May 1968, p 8033; 24 May 1968, p 9387; 11 Jun 1968, p 10,433–10,434; 12 Jun 1968; 18 Jun 1968, p 10,841–10,843; 20 Jun 1968, p 10,997–10,999; 25 Jun 1968, p 11,333; 2 Jul 1968, p 11,923; 4 Jul 1968, p 12,003; 10 Jul 1968, p 12,113; 15 Jul 1968, p 12,127–12,128; 17 Jul 1968, p 12,159–12,160; 19 Jul 1968, p 12,221–12,222; 23 Jul 1968, p 12,223–12,224

Finance Act 1969

PUBA87	1969
Finance Act 1969 (c. 32)	
An Act to grant certain duties, to alter other duties, and to amend the law relating to the National Debt and the Public Revenue, and to make further provision in connection with Finance	

Table of contents (patent provisions only)					
Sch 20 Consolidation Amendments					

Journal

House of Commons			House of Lords		
Pres: Harold Lever (Fin Sec Tr) CWH Rep: Maurice Miller SC Rep: John Jennings			No report		
22 Apr 1969	224 CJ 216	1R	18 Jul 1969	201 LJ 370	Brought HC/1R
6 May 1969	224 CJ 240 – V	**2R/C'tted SC &CWH**	24 Jul 1969	201 LJ 409	2R/Com neg/3R
7 May 1969	224 CJ 243	Sent to SC F	25 Jul 1969	201 LJ 413	Royal Assent
13 May 1969	224 CJ 253 – V	**CWH**			
14 May 1969	224 CJ 256 – V	**CWH**			
14 May 1969	224 CJ 257 – V	**CWH**			
20 May 1969	224 CJ 268 – V	**CWH**			
21 May 1969	224 CJ 270 – V	**CWH/Rep with Amds**			
26 Jun 1969	224 CJ 308	SC Rep with Amds			
15 Jul 1969	224 CJ 334 – V	**Cons**			
16 Jul 1969	224 CJ 336 – V	**Cons**			
17 Jul 1969	224 CJ 340 – V	**Cons**			
18 Jul 1969	224 CJ 343	3R			
24 Jul 1969	224 CJ 360	HL pass w/o Amds			
25 Jul 1969	224 CJ 363	Royal Assent			

Parliamentary debates

1R: HC Deb, 22 Apr 1969, Vol 782(5th), col 210–212

2R: HC Deb, 6 May 1969, Vol 783(5th), col 289–415

CWH: HC Deb, 13 May 1969, Vol 783(5th), col 1228–1362

CWH: HC Deb, 14 May 1969, Vol 783(5th), col 1425–1555

CWH: HC Deb, 20 May 1969, Vol 784(5th), col 256–391

CWH: HC Deb, 21 May 1969, Vol 784(5th), col 460–614

SC F Deb, 1st Sit, 11 Jun 1969, Vol 5, col 1–137

SC F Deb, 2nd Sit, 16 Jun 1969, Vol 5, col 138–266

SC F Deb, 3rd Sit, 18 Jun 1969, Vol 5, col 267–318

SC F Deb, 4th Sit, 18 Jun 1969, Vol 5, col 319–508

SC F Deb, 5th Sit, 23 Jun 1969, Vol 5, col 509–632

SC F Deb, 6th Sit, 24 Jun 1969, Vol 5, col 633–762

SC F Deb, 7th Sit, 25 Jun 1969, Vol 5, col 763–814

SC F Deb, 8th Sit, 26 Jun 1969, Vol 5, col 815–872

CWH: HC Deb, 15 Jul 1969, Vol 787(5th), col 409–410 and 425–578

CWH: HC Deb, 16 Jul 1969, Vol 787(5th), col 622–852

CWH: HC Deb, 17 Jul 1969, Vol 787(5th), col 897–1075

3R: HC Deb, 18 Jul 1969, Vol 787(5th), col 1097–1166

Royal Assent: HC Deb, 25 Jul 1969, Vol 787(5th), col 2280

1R: HL Deb, 18 Jul 1969, Vol 304(5th), col 647

2R/3R: HL Deb, 24 Jul 1969, Vol 304(5th), col 1164–1166

Royal Assent: HL Deb, 25 Jul 1969, Vol 304(5th), col 1202

Parliamentary papers

Finance Bill (1968–69 HC Papers 140), Vol 2, p 259

Finance Bill (as amended in Committee and Standing Committee F) (1968–69 HC Papers 185), Vol 2, p 457

Finance Bill (1968–69 HL Papers 151), Vol 2

Standing Committee F. Minutes of Proceedings (1968–69 HC Papers 323), Vol 15, p 11

(continued)

(continued)

Supplement to Votes & Proceedings, 1968–69
6 May 1969, p 4265–4272; 6 May 1969, p 4273–4275; 7 May 1969, p 4353; 8 May 1969, p 4377; 8 May 1969, p 4379–4388; 9 May 1969, p 4429–4439; 13 May 1969, p 4489–4503; 12 May 1969, p 4513–4516; 14 May 1969, p 4537–4553; 14 May 1969, p 4577; 14 May 1969, p 4579–4581; 15 May 1969, p 4619–4624; 15 May 1969, p 4631; 16 May 1969, p 4651; 16 May 1969, p 4653–4672; 20 May 1969, p 4721–4740; 19 May 1969, p 4773–4788; 19 May 1969, p 4791–4802; 20 May 1969, p 4805–4807; 22 May 1969, p 4937–4967; 23 May 1969, p 4975; 5 Jun 1969, p 5015–5059; 9 Jun 1969, p 5159–5231; 11 Jun 1969, p 5247–5331; 16 Jun 1969, p 5423–5501; 16 Jun 1969, p 5503–5505; 16 Jun 1969, p 5547–5560; 18 Jun 1969, p 5603–5692; 19 Jun 1969, p 5739–5741; 23 Jun 1969, p 5781–5857; 24 Jun 1969, p 5951–5601; 25 Jun 1969, p 6015–6062; 26 Jun 1969, p 6097–6119; 30 Jun 1969, p 6189–6190; 1 Jul 1969, p 6199; 2 Jul 1969, p 6221; 3 Jul 1969, p 6223–6238; 7 Jul 1969, p 6401–6408; 8 Jul 1969, p 6431–6485; 10 Jul 1969, p 6509–6574; 11 Jul 1969, p 6619–6702; 15 Jul 1969, p 6715–6804; 16 Jul 1969, p 6813–6891; 17 Jul 1969, p 6903–6956

Administration of Justice Act 1969

PUBA88	1969

Administration of Justice Act 1969 (c. 58)
An Act to increase the jurisdiction of county courts and to amend the County Courts Act 1959; to make further provision for appeals from the High Court (whether in England and Wales or in Northern Ireland) to the House of Lords; to enable wills and codicils to be made for mentally disordered persons; to make provision for interim payments to be made where proceedings are pending, and for conferring powers to be exercisable by the court before the commencement of an action, and to make further provision with respect to interest on damages; to enable any jurisdiction of the High Court to be assigned to two or more Divisions concurrently; to enable the Appeal Tribunals under the Patents Act 1949 and the Registered Designs Act 1949 to consist of two or more judges; to change the title and qualification of clerks to registrars of the Chancery Division; to make further provision with respect to miscellaneous matters, that is to say, certain employments in the offices of the Supreme Court, records of grants of probate and grants of administration and the making of second and subsequent grants, admission as a public notary, pension rights and related matters in connection with certain judicial offices, and the stipend and fees of the Chancellor of the County Palatine of Durham; to extend the legislative power of the Parliament of Northern Ireland with respect to grand juries and indictments; and for purposes connected with the matters aforesaid

Table of contents (patent provisions only)
s 24 Appeal Tribunals under Patents Act 1949 and Registered Designs Act 1949
s 35 (Sch 1) Enactments Amended [Patents Act 1949]

Journal					
House of Commons			**House of Lords**		
SC Rep: Harold Gurden			Pres: Lord Gardiner LC Rep: Earl of Listowel (Ld Ch)		
17 Dec 1968	224 CJ 72	Brought HL/1R	31 Oct 1968	201 LJ 11	1R
5 Feb 1969	224 CJ 104	2R/C'tted	12 Nov 1968	201 LJ 22	2R/C'tted CWH
6 Feb 1969	224 CJ 107	Assigned to SC B	3 Dec 1968	201 LJ 48	**CWH/Rep with Amds**
25 Mar 1969	224 CJ 175	Transferred to SC D	12 Dec 1968	201 LJ 64	**Cons with Amds**
24 Apr 1969	224 CJ 221	**Rep with Amds**	17 Dec 1968	201 LJ 68	**3R with Amds**
20 Oct 1969	224 CJ 384	R Assent/Cons/3R	21 Oct 1969	201 LJ 449	**HC Ag Amds**
21 Oct 1969	224 CJ 387	HL pass with Amds/Ag	22 Oct 1969	201 LJ 461	Royal Assent
22 Oct 1969	224 CJ 388	Royal Assent			

Parliamentary debates	
2R: HC Deb, 4 Feb 1969, Vol 795(5th), col 445–507	1R: HL Deb, 31 Oct 1968, Vol 297(5th), col 31–2
SC D Deb, 1st Sit, 15 Apr 1969, Vol 3, col 1–42	2R: HL Deb, 12 Nov 1968, Vol 297(5th), col 433–449, 458–494
SC D Deb, 2nd Sit, 17 Apr 1969, Vol 3, col 43–80	CWH: HL Deb, 3 Dec 1968, Vol 298(5th), col 48–83
SC D Deb, 3rd Sit, 22 Apr 1969, Vol 3, col 81–120	Rep: HL Deb, 3 Dec 1968, Vol 298(5th), col 83
SC D Deb, 4th Sit, 24 Apr 1969, Vol 3, col 121–150	Rep: HL Deb, 12 Dec 1968, Vol 298(5th), col 661–669
Cons/3R: HC Deb, 20 Oct 1969, Vol 788(5th), col 767–824	3R: HL Deb, 17 Dec 1968, Vol 298(5th), col 708–712
Royal Assent: HC Deb, 22 Oct 1969, Vol 788(5th), col 1131	HC Ag Amds: HL Deb, 21 Oct 1969, Vol 304(5th), col 1614–1627
	Royal Assent: HL Deb, 22 Oct 1969, Vol 298(5th), col 1712

Debates on particular provisions	
s 24 and Sch	SC D Deb, 4th Sit, 24 Apr 1969, Vol 3, col 141–147

Administration of Justice Bill (1968–69 HL Papers 7), Vol 1 [includes Explanatory Memorandum]

    Amendments to be moved in Committee by Viscount Dilhorne, Lord Denning and Lord Diplock (1968–69 HL Papers 7a), Vol 1

    Amendments to be moved in Committee by Lord Airedale (1968–69 HL Papers 7b), Vol 1

    Amendments to be moved in Committee by Viscount Colville of Culross (1968–69 HL Papers 7c), Vol 1

    Amendments to be moved in Committee by the Lord Chancellor (1968–69 HL Papers 7d), Vol 1

    Marshalled Lists of Amendments to be Moved in Committee (1968–69 HL Papers 7–I), Vol 1

Administration of Justice Bill (as amended in Committee) (1968–69 HL Papers 17), Vol 1

    Amendments to be moved on Report by the Lord Chancellor (1968–69 HL Papers 17a), Vol 1

    Amendments to be moved on Report by the Lord Chancellor (1968–69 HL Papers 17b), Vol 1

    Marshalled Lists of Amendments to be Moved on Report (1968–69 HL Papers 17–I), Vol 1

Administration of Justice Bill (as amended on Report) (1968–69 HL Papers 22), Vol 1

    Amendments to be moved on Third Reading by the Lord Chancellor (1968–69 HL Papers 22a), Vol 1

Administration of Justice (1968–69 HC Papers 60), Vol 143, Vol 1, p 13

Administration of Justice (as amended in Standing Committee D) (1968–69 HC Papers 143), Vol 143, Vol 1, p 45

Standing Committee D. Minutes of Proceedings on the Administration of Justice Bill (1968–69 HC Papers 253), Vol 5, p 681

Supplement to Votes & Proceedings, 1968–69

    6 Feb 1969, p 885; 7 Feb 1969, p 917; 11 Feb 1969, p 1025; 27 Mar 1969, p 2747; 31 Mar 1969, p 2917–2920; 11 Apr 1969, p 3041–3046; 15 Apr 1969, p 3143–3149; 15 Apr 1969, p 3193; 22 Apr 1969, p 3349–3353; 24 Apr 1969, p 3563–3567; 20 Oct 1969, p 7047–7050

Administration of Justice Act 1970

PUBA89	1970

Administrative of Justice Act 1970 (c. 31)
An Act to make further provision about the courts (including assizes), their business, jurisdiction and procedure; to enable a High Court judge to accept appointment as arbitrator or umpire under an arbitration agreement; to amend the law respecting the enforcement of debt and other liabilities; to amend section 106 of the Rent Act 1968; and for miscellaneous purposes connected with the administration of justice
Table of contents (patent provisions only)
s 10 Temporary additional judges [to Patent Appeals Tribunal]

Journal					
House of Commons			**House of Lords**		
SC Rep: Sir Ronald Russell			Pres: Lord Gardiner LC Rep: Earl of Listowel (Ld Ch)		
27 Jan 1970	225 CJ 123	Brought HL/1R	20 Nov 1969	202 LJ 41	1R
4 Feb 1970	225 CJ 141	2R/Money Res/C'tted	4 Dec 1969	202 LJ 65	2R/C'tted CWH
5 Feb 1970	225 CJ 145	Assigned SC A	15 Dec 1969	202 LJ 80	**CWH/Rep with Amds**
2 Mar 1970	225 CJ 188	Tran'f to SC G	20 Jan 1970	202 LJ 102	**Cons with Amds**
21 Apr 1970	225 CJ 278	Rep with Amds	27 Jan 1970	202 LJ 117	**Royal consent/3R with Amds**
4 May 1970	225 CJ 305 – V	**Cons with Amds**	15 May 1970	202 LJ 310	HC pass with Amds
14 May 1970	225 CJ 333	**Cons with Amds**	19 May 1970	202 LJ 317	**HC Amds Ag**
14 May 1970	225 CJ 334	**Royal consent/3R with Amds**	28 May 1970	202 LJ 338	HC notified Amds missing
			28 May 1970	202 LJ 339	**HL Ag further Amds**
28 May 1970	225 CJ 358	HL Ag Amds	29 May 1970	202 LJ 349	Royal Assent
28 May 1970	225 CJ 358	HL Request Return			
28 May 1970	225 CJ 358	HL Ret Bill			
28 May 1970	225 CJ 358	HL Req Ag Missing Amd			
28 May 1970	225 CJ 359	HL Ag Missing Amds			
29 May 1970	225 CJ 364	Royal Assent			

(continued)

(continued)

Parliamentary debates
2R: HC Deb, 4 Feb 1970, Vol 795(5th), col 445–508   1R: HL Deb, 20 Nov 1969, Vol 305(5th), col 1070

2R: HC Deb, 4 Feb 1970, Vol 795(5th), col 445–508	1R: HL Deb, 20 Nov 1969, Vol 305(5th), col 1070
SC G Deb, 1st Sit, 17 Mar 1970, Vol 5, col 1–46	2R: HL Deb, 4 Dec 1969, Vol 306(5th), col 196–262
SC G Deb, 2nd Sit, 19 Mar 1970, Vol 5, col 47–92	CWH: HL Deb, 15 Dec 1969, Vol 306(5th), col 869–924
SC G Deb, 3rd Sit, 24 Mar 1970, Vol 5, col 93–136	Cons: HL Deb, 20 Jan 1970, Vol 307(5th), col 13–61
SC G Deb, 4th Sit, 7 Apr 1970, Vol 5, col 137–184	3R: HL Deb, 27 Jan 1970, Vol 307(5th), col 266–289
SC G Deb, 5th Sit, 9 Apr 1970, Vol 5, col 185–232	HC Amds: HL Deb, 19 May 1970, Vol 310(5th), col 991–1040
SC G Deb, 6th Sit, 14 Apr 1970, Vol 5, col 233–276	HC pass: HL Deb, 28 May 1970, Vol 310(5th), col 1176, 1179–1180
SC G Deb, 7th Sit, 16 Apr 1970, Vol 5, col 277–324	Royal Assent: HL Deb, 29 May 1970, Vol 310(5th), col 1238
SC G Deb, 8th Sit, 21 Apr 1970, Vol 5, col 325–368	
Cons: HC Deb, 4 May 1970, Vol 801(5th), col 105–168	
Cons/3R: HC Deb, 14 May 1970, Vol 801(5th), col 1603–1646	
Royal Assent: HC Deb, 29 May 1970, Vol 801(5th), col 2130	

Debates on particular provisions	
s 10	SC G Deb, 8th Sit, 21 Apr 1970, Vol 5, col 357–358

Parliamentary papers
Administration of Justice Bill (1969–70 HL Papers 14), Vol 1 [Explanatory Memorandum]

Administration of Justice Bill (1969–70 HL Papers 14), Vol 1 [Explanatory Memorandum]

    Marshalled List of Amendments to be Moved in Committee (1969–70 HL Papers 14–I), Vol 1

Administration of Justice Bill (as amended in Committee) (1969–70 HL Papers 33), Vol 1

    Marshalled List of Amendments to be Moved on Report (1969–70 HL Papers 33–I), Vol 1

    Revised Marshalled List of Amendments to be Moved on Report (1969–70 HL Papers 33–II), Vol 1

Administration of Justice Bill (as amended on Report) (1969–70 HL Papers 38), Vol 1

    Marshalled List of Amendments to be Moved on Third Reading (1969–70 HL Papers 38–I), Vol 1

Administration of Justice Bill (1969–70 HC Papers 85), Vol 1, p 5

Administration of Justice Bill (as amended in Standing Committee G) (1969–70 HC Papers 149), 1, p 87

Commons Amendments (1969–70 HL Papers, 122), Vol 1

Further Commons Amendments (1969–70 HL Papers, 130), Vol 1

Standing Committee G, Minutes of Proceedings on the Administration of Justice Bill (1969–70), Vol 1, p 71

Supplement to Votes & Proceedings, 1968–69

    26 Feb 1970, p 1515–1519; 2 Mar 1970, p 1633; 5 Mar 1970, p 1767–1768; 9 Mar 1970, p 1907; 11 Mar 1970, p 2043–2045; 12 Mar 1970, p 2059–2060; 13 Mar 1970, p 2081–2093; 17 Mar 1970, p 2151–2164; 19 Mar 1970, p 2305–2318; 24 Mar 1979, p 2517–2530; 7 Apr 1970, p 2665–2678; 9 Apr 1970, p 2769–2780; 14 Apr 1970, p 2857–2867; 16 Apr 1970, p 2941–2949; 23 Apr 1970, p 3299; 27 Apr 1970, p 3373; 28 Apr 1970, p 3439–3442; 29 Apr 1970, p 3521–3524; 30 Apr 1970, p 3539–3549; 4 May 1970, p 3551–3561; 12 May 1970, p 4051–4059; 14 May 1970, p 4081–4089

Income and Corporation Taxes Act 1970

PUBA90	1970

PUBA90	1970
Income and Corporation Taxes Act 1970 (c. 10)	
An Act to consolidate certain of the enactments relating to income tax and corporation tax, including certain enactments relating also to other taxes	

Table of contents (patent and know–how provisions only)	
	Table of origin
	IT Income Tax Act CA Capital Allowance Act ITM Income Tax Allowance Act FA Finance Act

Patents	IT 1952, s 316
s 378 Writing-down allowances for capital expenditure on purchase of patent rights	FA 1965, SCh 14, par 2 and 20
	CA 1968, Sch 12
s 379 Effect of lapses of patent rights, sales, etc	IT 1952, s 317
	FA 1965, Sch 14, par 2 and 20
s 380 Taxation as income of capital sums received for sale of patent rights	IT 1952, s 318
	FA 1952, Sch 6, par 17
	FA 1958, Sch 6, par 2
	FA 1965, Sch 14, par 21
	ITM 1964, Sch 2
s 381 Capital sums: death, winding up or partnership change	IT 1952, Sch 13, par 1 to 3
	FA 1952, Sch 6, par 5
	FA 1965, Sch 14, par 2
s 382 Relief for expenses	IT 1952, s 320
	FA 1952, s 23
	FA 1965, Sch 14, par 2
s 383 Patent income to be earned income in certain cases	IT 1952, s 525(2)(d)
s 384 Spreading of patent royalties over several years	IT 1952, s 472
	ITM 1964, Sch 2
	FA 1969, Sch 20, par 17
s 385 Manner of making allowances and charges	IT 1952, s 321
	FA 1965, Sch 14, par 2(4) to (7)
	CA 1968, s 71, Sch 12, par 3(2)
Know-how (income tax, corporation tax and capital gains tax)	
s 386 Dealings in know-how	FA 1968, s 21
Supplemental	
s 387 Application of Capital Allowances Act 1968	CA 1968, Sch 12, par 3
	FA 1968 s 21(9)
s 388 Interpretation of provisions about patents	IT 1952, s 322
	FA 1965, Sch 14, par 2
	FA 1952, Sch 6, par 16

Journal

House of Commons			House of Lords		
Rep: Sydney Irvine (Ch W&M)			Pres: Lord Gardiner LC Rep: Earl of Listowel (Ld Ch)		
18 Feb1970	225 CJ 167	Rep JC Cons	20 Jan 1970	202 LJ 102	1R
4 Mar 1970	225 CJ 192	Brought HL/1R	27 Jan 1970	202 LJ 120	2R/Ref JC Cons
9 Mar 1970	225 CJ 198	2R/C'tted CWH	18 Feb 1970	202 LJ 152	**Rep with Amds/C'tted CWH**
10 Mar 1970	225 CJ 202	CWH/Rep w/o Amds/3R	4 Mar 1970	202 LJ 172	CWH/Rep w/o Amds/3R
12 Mar 1970	225 CJ 209	Royal Assent	11 Mar 1970	202 LJ 181	HC pass w/o Amds
			12 Mar 1970	202 LJ 183	Royal Assent

Parliamentary debates

2R: HC Deb, 9 Mar 1970, Vol 797(5th), col 1051–1055	1R: HL Deb, 20 Jan 1970, Vol 307(5th), col 5
CWH/Rep/3R: HC Deb, 10 Mar 1970, Vol 797(5th), col 1297	2R: HL Deb, 27 Jan 1970, Vol 307(5th), col 290–293
	JC Rep/C'tted: H: Deb, 18 Feb 307(5th), col 1278
Royal Assent: HC Deb, 12 Mar 1970, Vol 797(5th), col 1531	CWH: HL Deb, 4 Mar 1970, Vol 308(5th), col 331–332
	HC pass: HL Deb, 11 Mar 1970, Vol 308(5th), col 886
	Royal Assent: HL Deb, 12 Mar 1970, Vol 308(5th), col 889

Parliamentary papers

Income and Corporation Tax (1969–70 HC Papers 114), Vol 2, p 351

Income and Corporation Tax (1969–70 HL Papers 37), Vol 2

   Amendments made by the Joint Committee on Consolidation Bills (1969–70 HL Papers 37a), Vol 2

Supplement to Votes & Proceedings, 1972–73 – No amendments

Courts Act 1971

PUBA91	1971

Courts Act 1971 (c. 23)
An Act to make further provision as respects the Supreme Court and county courts, judges and juries, to establish a Crown Court as part of the Supreme Court to try indictments and exercise certain other jurisdiction, to abolish courts of assize and certain other courts and to deal with their jurisdiction and other consequential matters, and to amend in other respects the law about courts and court proceedings

Table of contents (patent provisions only)

s 46 Patent appeals

Journal

House of Commons			House of Lords		
SC Rep: Joyce Butler			Pres: Lord Hailsham LC Rep: No record		
17 Dec 1970	226 CJ 179	Brought HL/1R	10 Nov 1970	203 LJ 119	1R
14 Jan 1971	226 CJ 194	2R/C'tted	19 Nov 1970	203 LJ 139	2R/C'tted CWH
20 Jan 1971	226 CJ 206	Assigned SC A	3 Dec 1970	203 LJ 160 – V	**CWH**
4 Mar 1971	226 CJ 304	Rep with Amds	8 Dec 1970	203 LJ 170	**CWH/Rep with Amds**
7 Apr 1971	226 CJ 377	**Cons/3R with Amds**	17 Dec 1970	203 LJ 197	**Cons/3R with Amds**
22 Apr 1971	226 CJ 394	HL Ag Amds	8 Apr 1971	203 LJ 366	HC pass with Amds
12 May 1971	226 CJ 432	Royal Assent	22 Apr 1971	203 LJ 379	**HC Amds Ag**
			12 May 1971	203 LJ 458	Royal Assent

Parliamentary debates

Money Res: HC Deb, 14 Jan 1971, Vol 809(5th), col 364

2R: HC Deb, 14 Jan 1971, Vol 809(5th), col 272–364

SC A Deb, 1st Sit, 28 Jan 1971, Vol 1, col 1–48

SC A Deb, 2nd Sit, 2 Feb 1971, Vol 1, col 49–96

SC A Deb, 3rd Sit, 4 Feb 1971, Vol 1, col 97–144

SC A Deb, 4th Sit, 9 Feb 1971, Vol 1, col 145–190

SC A Deb, 5th Sit, 11 Feb 1971, Vol 1, col 191–234

SC A Deb, 6th Sit, 2 Feb 1971, Vol 1, col 235–280

SC A Deb, 7th Sit, 2 Feb 1971, Vol 1, col 281–328

SC A Deb, 8th Sit, 23 Feb 1971, Vol 1, col 329–376

SC A Deb, 9th Sit, 25 Feb 1971, Vol 1, col 377–424

SC A Deb, 10th Sit, 2 Mar 1971, Vol 1, col 425–474

SC A Deb, 11th Sit, 4 Mar 1971, Vol 1, col 475–526

Cons/3R: HC Deb, 7 Apr 1971, Vol 815(5th), col 501–596

Royal Assent: HC Deb, 12 May 1971, Vol 817(5th), col 383

1R: HL Deb, 10 Nov 1970, Vol 312(5th), col 602–603

2R: HL Deb, 19 Nov 1970, Vol 312(5th), col 1245–1267, 1271–1322

CWH: HL Deb, 3 Dec 1970, Vol 313(5th), col 648–741

CWH: HL Deb, 8 Dec 1970, Vol 313(5th), col 874–926

Cons: HL Deb, 17 Dec 1970, Vol 313(5th), col 1531–1550, 1554–1599

3R: HL Deb, 17 Dec 1970, Vol 313(5th), col 1599–1600

HC pass: HL Deb, 8 Apr 1971, Vol 317(5th), col 518

HC Amds Ag: HL Deb, 22 Apr 1971, Vol 317(5th), col 822–864

Royal Assent: HL Deb, 12 May 1971, Vol 318(5th), col 1067

Debates on particular provisions

s 46	HL Deb, 19 Nov 1970, Vol 312(5th), col 1253 (Cl 45); HC Deb, 14 Jan 1971, Vol 809(5th) col 277–278; SC A, 9th Sit, 25 Feb 1971, Vol 1, col 421; HC Deb, 7 April 1971, Vol 815(5th), col 579–580

Parliamentary papers

Courts Bill (1970–71 HL Papers 26), Vol 1

    Amendments to be Moved in Committee by Lord Airdale (1970–71 HL Papers 26a), Vol 1

    Amendment to be Moved in Committee by Lord Merthyr and Lord Royle (1970–71 HL Papers 26b), Vol 1

    Amendment to be Moved in Committee by Lord Parker of Waddington (1970–71 HL Papers 26c), Vol 1

    Amendments to be Moved in Committee by Lord Goodman (1970–71 HL Papers 26d), Vol 1

    Amendments to be Moved in Committee by Lord Ilford and Lord Milverton (1970–71 HL Papers 26e), Vol 1

    Amendments to be Moved in Committee by Lord Gardiner (1970–71 HL Papers 26f), Vol 1

    Amendments to be Moved in Committee by the Lord Chancellor (1970–71 HL Papers 26g), Vol 1

Amendments to be Moved in Committee by the Lord Chancellor (1970–71 HL Papers 26h), Vol 1

Amendment to be Moved in Committee by the Lord Chancellor (1970–71 HL Papers 26i), Vol 1

Marshalled List of Amendments to be Moved in Committee (1970–71 HL Papers 26–I), Vol 1

Revised Marshalled List of Amendments to be Moved in Committee (1970–71 HL Papers 26–II), Vol 1

Second Marshalled List of Amendments to be Moved in Committee (1970–71 HL Papers 26–III), Vol 1

Courts Bill (as amended in Committee) (1970–71 HL Papers 55), Vol 1

Amendments to be Moved on Report by the Lord Gardiner, Lord Royle and Lord Merthyr (1970–71 HL Papers 55a), Vol 1

Amendment to be Moved on Report by Viscount Dilhorne (1970–71 HL Papers 55b), Vol 1

Amendments to be Moved on Report by the Lord Chancellor (1970–71 HL Papers 55c), Vol 1

Amendment to be Moved on Report by Lord Parker of Waddington (1970–71 HL Papers 55d), Vol 1

Amendment to be Moved on Report by Lord Tangley and Lord Goodman (1970–71 HL Papers 55e), Vol 1

Amendment to be Moved on Report by Viscount Dilhorne (1970–71 HL Papers 55f), Vol 1

Marshalled List of Amendments to be Moved on Report (1970–71 HL Papers 55–I), Vol 1

Courts Bill (1970–71 HC Papers 85), Vol 2, p 1

Courts Bill (as amended in Standing Committee A) (1970–71 HC Papers 124), Vol 2, p 133

Commons Amendments (1970–71 HL Papers 136), Vol 1

Standing Committee A. Minutes of proceedings on the Courts Bill [Lords] (HC Papers 306), Vol 2, p 113

Supplement to Votes & Proceedings, 1970–71

19 Jan 1971, p 749–754; 21 Jan 1971, p 811; 25 Jan 1971, p 913–925; 26 Jan 1971, p 939–966; 28 Jan 1971, p 1047–1074a; 2 Feb 1971, p 1257–1284; 4 Feb 1971, p 1343–1369; 9 Feb 1971, p 1465–1490; 9 Feb 1971, p 1605–1606; 11 Feb 1971, p 1613–1638; 16 Feb 1971, p 1669–1694; 16 Feb 1971, p 1777; 18 Feb 1971, p 1785–1808; 18 Feb 1971, p 1825; 23 Feb 1971, p 1895–1917; 23 Feb 1971, p 1969; 25 Feb 1971, p 1989–2009; 26 Feb 1971, p 2019–2037; 2 Mar 1971, p 2053–2072; 2 Mar 1971, p 2093; 4 Mar 1971, p 2109–2124; 24 Mar 1971, p 2891–2892; 31 Mar 1971, p 2945–2948; 31 Mar 1971, p 2973; 1 Apr 1971, p 2981; 5 Apr 1971, p 3019–3033; 7 Apr 1971, p 3045–3060

Also see: Royal Commission on Assizes and Quarter Sessions (Beeching Report) 1968–69 HC Papers (Cmnd 4153), Vol 28, p 433 (no mention of Patents Court in the report): 13 Oct 1968 (224 CJ 365; 201 LJ 423)

Finance Act 1971

PUBA92	1971
Finance Act 1971 (c. 68)	
An Act to grant certain duties, to alter other duties, and to amend the law relating to the National Debt and the Public Revenue, and to make further provision in connection with Finance	
Table of contents (patent provisions only)	
Sch 6 Amendments consequential on new method of charging tax (par 3)	
Journal	

House of Commons			House of Lords		
Pres: Patrick Jenkin (Par Sec Tr) Rep CWH: Joan Quennell Rep SC F: Sir Myer Galpern			No report		
5 Apr 1971	226 CJ 372	1R	8 Jul 1971	203 LJ 651	Brought HC/1R
28 Apr 1971	226 CJ 404	2R/C'tted CWH and SC F	21 Jul 1971	203 LJ 714	2R/Com neg
11 May 1971	226 CJ 429	**CWH**	28 Jul 1971	203 LJ 732	3R
12 May 1971	226 CJ 432	**CWH**	5 Aug 1971	203 LJ 777	Royal Assent
12 May 1971	226 CJ 434	Clauses C'tted SC F			
18 May 1971	226 CJ 442	**CWH**			
20 May 1971	226 CJ 448	CWH			
20 May 1971	226 CJ 449	Rep CWH with Amds			
22 Jun 1971	226 CJ 498	Rep SC F with Amds			
5 Jul 1971	226 CJ 521	Cons			

(continued)

(continued)

6 Jul 1971	226 CJ 524	**Cons**			
7 Jul 1971	226 CJ 528	Cons			
7 Jul 1971	226 CJ 528	3R			
28 Jul 1971	226 CJ 568	HL pass w/o Amds			
5 Aug 1971	226 CJ 593	Royal Assent			

Parliamentary debates	
1R: HC Deb, 5 Apr 1971, Vol 815(5th), col 180	1R: HL Deb, 8 Jul 1971, Vol 321(5th), col 1126
2R: HC Deb, 28 Apr 1971, Vol 815(5th), col 438–570	2R: HL Deb, 21 Jul 1971, Vol 322(5th), col 1110
CWH: HC Deb, 11 May 1971, Vol 817(5th), col 216–336	3R: HL Deb, 28 Jul 1971, Vol 323(5th), col 406
CWH: HC Deb, 12 May 1971, Vol 817(5th), col 395–518	Royal Assent: HL Deb, 5 Aug 1971, Vol 323(5th), col 1272
CWH: HC Deb, 18 May 1971, Vol 817(5th), col 1085–1229	
SC H Deb, 1st Sit, 24 May 1971, Vol 5, col 1–86	
SC H Deb, 2nd Sit, 26 May 1971, Vol 5, col 87–262	
SC H Deb, 3rd Sit, 9 Jun 1971, Vol 5, col 263–418	
SC H Deb, 4th Sit, 14 Jun 1971, Vol 5, col 419–542	
SC H Deb, 5th Sit, 15 Jun 1971, Vol 5, col 533–614	
SC H Deb, 6th Sit, 16 Jun 1971, Vol 5, col 615–788	
SC H Deb, 7th Sit, 21 Jun 1971, Vol 5, col 789–946	
CWH/Rep: HC Deb, 20 May 1971, Vol 817(5th), col 1557–1654	
Cons: HC Deb, 5 Jul 1971, Vol 820(5th), col 935–1091	
Cons: HC Deb, 6 Jul 1971, Vol 820(5th), col 1128–1298	
Cons/3R: HC Deb, 7 Jul 1971, Vol 820(5th), col 1349–1378	
Royal Assent: HC Deb, 5 Aug 1971, Vol 822(5th), col 1900	

Parliamentary papers
Finance Bill (1970–71 HC Papers 148), Vol 2, p 553
Finance Bill (1970–71 HC Papers 193), Vol 2, p 707
Finance Bill (1970–71 HL Papers 199), Vol 1
Standing Committee H. Minutes of Proceedings on the Finance Bill (1970–71 HC Papers 457), Vol 2, p 679
Supplement to Votes & Proceedings, 1970–71
CWH (and Report &c.)
28 Apr 1971, p 3419; 3 May 1971, p 3507–3508; 5 May 1971, p 3585–3586; 6 May 1971, p 3625–3627; 7 May 1971, p 3645–3647; 11 May 1971, p 3655–3657; 12 May 1971, p 3727–3729; 12 May 1971, p 3825; 13 May 1971, p 3833–3834; 18 May 1971, p 3859–3862; 20 May 1971, p 3985–3986; 22 Jun 1971, p 4961–4963; 23 Jun 1971, p 4995; 24 Jun 1971, p 5011–5016; 25 Jun 1971, p 5039–5040; 28 Jun 1971, p 5069–5072; 29 Jun 1971, p 5079–5107; 30 Jun 1071, p 5117–5120; 1 Jul 1971, p 5123–5162; 5 Jul 1971, p 5169–5210; 6 Jul 1971, p 5217–5249; 7 Jul 1971, p 5261–5276
Standing Committee H
3 May 1971, p 3509–3510; 4 May 1971, p 3529–3530; 5 May 1971, p 3587–3588; 6 May 1971, p 3621–3624; 7 May 1971, p 3653; 10 May 1971, p 3723; 11 May 1971, p 3751; 12 May 1971, p 3827; 13 May 1971, p 3841; 14 May 1971, p 3847–3857; 17 May 1971, p 3941–3946; 18 May 1971, p 3979–3982; 19 May 1971, p 4057–4126; 24 May 1971, p 4133–4170; 24 May 1971, p 4235–4242; 26 May 1971, p 4243–4285; 26 May 1971, p 4333–4334; 27 May 1971, p 4341–4344; 7 Jun 1971, p 4357–4360; 9 Jun 1971, p 4363–4407; 9 Jun 1971, p 4457–4468; 10 Jun 1971, p 4479–4528; 14 Jun 1971, p 4553–4604; 15 Jun 1971, p 4667–4719; 16 Jun 1971, p 4753–4804; 16 Jun 1971, p 4859; 17 Jun 1971, p 4869; 21 Jun 1971, p 4883–4926

Fair Trading Act 1973

PUBA93	1973
Fair Trading Act 1973 (c. 41)	
An Act to provide for the appointment of a Director General of Fair Trading and of a Consumer Protection Advisory Committee, and to confer on the Director General and the Committee so appointed, on the Secretary of State,	

on the Restrictive Practices Court and on certain other courts new functions for the protection of consumers; to make provision, in substitution for the Monopolies and Restrictive Practices (Inquiry and Control) Act 1948 and the Monopolies and Mergers Act 1965, for the matters dealt with in those Acts and related matters, including restrictive labour practices; to amend the Restrictive Trade Practices Act 1956 and the Restrictive Trade Practices Act 1968, to make provision for extending the said Act of 1956 to agreements relating to services, and to transfer to the Director General of Fair Trading the functions of the Registrar of Restrictive Trading Agreements; to make provision with respect to pyramid selling and similar trading schemes; to make new provision in place of section 30(2) to (4) of the Trade Descriptions Act 1968; and for purposes connected with those matters

Table of contents (patent provisions only)

Journal

House of Commons			House of Lords		
Pres: Peter Walker (SoS Tr) Rep: Bryant Godman Irvine (Dep Ch W&M)			Rep: Earl of Listowel (Ld Ch)		
30 Nov 1972	228 CJ 58	1R	21 May 1972	205 LJ 381	Brought HC/1R
13 Dec 1972	228 CJ 76	2R/C'tted SC	5 Jun 1972	205 LJ 394	2R/C'tted CWH
20 Dec 1972	228 CJ 92	Assigned SC B	15 Jun 1972	205 LJ 437	**CWH**
12 Apr 1972	228 CJ 259	Rep with Amds	21 Jun 1972	205 LJ 479	**CWH**
16 May 1972	228 CJ 320	Cons adj	21 Jun 1972	205 LJ 482	**CWH**
16 May 1972	228 CJ 320	Cons	25 Jun 1972	205 LJ 506	**CWH**/Rep with Amds
17 May 1972	228 CJ 324	Cons/3R	9 Jul 1972	205 LJ 577–V	**Cons with Amds**
12 Jul 1972	228 CJ 423	HL Ag with Amds	12 Jul 1972	205 LJ 596	3R
18 Jul 1972	228 CJ 434	HL Amds Ag	19 Jul 1972	205 LJ 626	HC Ag Am
25 Jul 1972	228 CJ 455	Royal Assent	25 Jul 1972	205 LJ 680	Royal Assent

Parliamentary debates

1R: HC Deb, 30 Nov 1972, Vol 847(5th), col 644

2R: HC Deb, 13 Dec 1972, Vol 848(5th), col 453–578

SC B, 1st Sit, 25 Jan 1973, Vol 2, col 1–52

SC B, 2nd Sit, 30 Jan 1973, Vol 2, col 53–102

SC B, 3rd Sit, 1 Feb 1973, Vol 2, col 103–154

SC B, 4th Sit, 6 Feb 1973, Vol 2, col 155–200

SC B, 5th Sit, 8 Feb 1973, Vol 2, col 201–246

SC B, 6th Sit, 13 Feb 1973, Vol 2, col 247–296

SC B, 7th Sit, 15 Feb 1973, Vol 2, col 297–346

SC B, 8th Sit, 20 Feb 1973, Vol 2, col 347–396

SC B, 9th Sit, 22 Feb 1973, Vol 2, col 397–444

SC B, 10th Sit, 27 Feb 1973, Vol 2, col 445–496

SC B, 11th Sit, 1 Mar 1973, Vol 2, col 497–540

SC B, 12th Sit, 6 Mar 1973, Vol 2, col 541–586

SC B, 13th Sit, 8 Mar 1973, Vol 2, col 587–634

SC B, 14th Sit, 13 Mar 1973, Vol 2, col 635–684

SC B, 15th Sit, 15 Mar 1973, Vol 2, col 685–730

SC B, 16th Sit, 20 Mar 1973, Vol 2, col 731–780

SC B, 17th Sit, 22 Mar 1973, Vol 2, col 781–828

SC B, 18th Sit, 27 Mar 1973, Vol 2, col 829–882

SC B, 19th Sit, 27 Mar 1973, Vol 2, col 883–924

SC B, 20th Sit, 29 Mar 1973, Vol 2, col 925–970

SC B, 21st Sit, 3 Apr 1973, Vol 2, col 971–1018

Brought HC/1R: HL Deb, 21 May 1972, Vol 342(5th), col 1009

2R: HL Deb, 5 Jun 1972, Vol 343(5th), col 44–96

Motion: HL Deb, 15 Jun 1972, Vol 343(5th), col 980–983

CWH: HL Deb, 21 Jun 1972, Vol 343(5th), col 1472–1542, 1545–1572

CWH: HL Deb, 25 Jun 1972, Vol 343(5th), col 1808–1831

Cons: HL Deb, 25 Jun 1972, Vol 343(5th), col 1831

Cons: HL Deb, 9 Jul 1972, Vol 344(5th), col 544–615

3R: HL Deb, 12 Jul 1972, Vol 343(5th), col 902–903

Royal Assent: HL Deb, 25 Jul 1972, Vol 343(5th), col 1829

(continued)

(continued)

SC B, 22nd Sit, 3 Apr 1973, Vol 2, col 1019–1088	
SC B, 23rd Sit, 5 Apr 1973, Vol 2, col 1089–1132	
SC B, 24th Sit, 10 Apr 1973, Vol 2, col 1133–1182	
SC B, 25th Sit, 10 Apr 1973, Vol 2, col 1183–1306	
SC B, 26th Sit, 12 Apr 1973, Vol 2, col 1307–1356	
Cons: HC Deb, 16 May 1973, Vol 856(5th), col 1516–1666	
Cons: HC Deb, 17 May 1973, Vol 856(5th), col 1720–1839	
HL Amds Ag: HC Deb, 18 Jul 1973, Vol 860(5th), col 625–670	
Royal Assent: HC Deb, 25 Jul 1973, Vol 860(5th), col 1677	

Debates on particular provisions	
s 101	SC B Deb, 23rd Sit, 5 Apr 1973, Vol 2, col 1121–1124 (Cl 93); HC Deb, 18 Jul, Vol 860(5), col 636–637 (Cl 98)
s 126	SC B Deb, 24th Sit, 10 Apr 1973, Vol 2, col 1174 (Cl 111–112L)

Parliamentary papers

Fair Trading Bill (1972–73 HC Papers 36), Vol 2, p 1

Fair Trading Bill (As Amended by Standing Committee B) (1972–73 HC Papers 112), Vol 2, p 209

Standing Committee B Minutes of Proceedings on Fair Trading Bill (1972–73 HC Papers 224), Vol 2, p 141

Fair Trading Bill (1973 HL Papers 123), Vol 1

   Amendments to be Moved in Committee by Lord Diamond, Baroness Phillips, Lord Hoy and Lord Sainsbury (1973 HL Papers 123a), Vol 1

   Amendments to be Moved in Committee by Lord Drumalbyn (1973 HL Papers 123b), Vol 1

   Amendments to be Moved in Committee by Lord Drumalbyn (1973 HL Papers 123c), Vol 1

   Amendment to be Moved in Committee by Baroness Burton of Coventry (1973 HL Papers 123d), Vol 1

   Amendments to be Moved in Committee by Lord Drumalbyn (1973 HL Papers 123e), Vol 1

   Amendments to be Moved in Committee by Lord Drumalbyn (1973 HL Papers 123f), Vol 1

   Amendments to be Moved in Committee by Lord Drumalbyn (1973 HL Papers 123g), Vol 1

   Amendments to be Moved in Committee by Lord Airedale (1973 HL Papers 123h), Vol 1

   Marshalled List of Amendments to be Moved in Committee (1973 HL Papers 123–I), Vol 1

Fair Trading Bill (as amended in Committee) (1973 HL Papers 149), Vol 1

   Amendment to be Moved on Report by Lord Stow Hill (1973 HL Papers 149a), Vol 1

   Amendment to be Moved on Report by Baroness Phillips and Lord Hanworth (1973 HL Papers 149b), Vol 1

   Amendments to be Moved on Report by Lord Jacques, Baroness Phillips, Lord Diamond and Lord Sainsbury (1973 HL Papers 149c), Vol 1

   Amendment to be Moved on Report by Baroness Phillips and Lord Hanworth (1973 HL Papers 149d), Vol 1

   Amendments to be Moved on Report by Lord Drumalbyn and Earl of Limerick (1973 HL Papers 149e), Vol 1

   Amendment to be Moved on Report by Baroness Burton of Coventry (1973 HL Papers 149f), Vol 1

   Amendment to be Moved on Report by Lord Airedale (1973 HL Papers 149g), Vol 1

   Amendments to be Moved on Report by Lord Drumalbyn and Earl of Limerick (1973 HL Papers 149h), Vol 1

   Marshalled List of Amendments to be Moved on Report (1973 HL Papers 149–I), Vol 1

Lords Amendments to Fair Trading Bill (1972–73 HC Papers 191), Vol 2, p 337

Supplement to Votes & Proceedings, 1972–3

Standing Committee B

   9 Jan 1973, p 21–22; 22 Jan 1973, p 23–24; 23 Jan 1973, p 25–30; 25 Jan 1973, p 31–37; 25 Jan 1973, p 39–41; 26 Jan 1973, p 43; 30 Jan 1973, p 45–54; 30 Jan 1973, p 55–58; 1 Feb 1973, p 59–71; 1 Feb 1973, p 73–74; 6 Feb 1973, p 75–90; 6 Feb 1973, p 91–99; 8 Feb 1973, p 101–126; 15 Feb 1973, p 127–130; 13 Feb 1973, p 131–158; 13 Feb 1973, p 159–160; 15 Feb 1973, p 161–200; 15 Feb 1973, p 201–202; 20 Feb 1973, p 203–255; 20 Feb 1973, p 257–258; 22 Feb 1973, p 259–312; 23 Feb 1973, p 313; 27 Feb 1973, p 315–372; 1 Mar 1973, p 373–428; 1 Mar 1973, p 429; 6 Mar 1973, p 431–484; 8 Mar 1973, p 485–537; 8 Mar 1973, p 539; 9 Mar 1973, p 541; 13 Mar 1973, p 543–598; 13 Mar 1973, p 599; 15 Mar 1973, p 601–660; 20 Mar 1973, p 661–719; 22 Mar 1973, p 721–779; 22 Mar 1973, p 781–787; 27 Mar 1973, p 789–847; 27 Mar 1973, p 849–852; 29 Mar 1973, p 853–908; 30 Mar 1973, p 909–911; 3 Apr 1973, p 913–969; 3 Apr 1973, p 971–972; 5 Apr 1973, p 973–1018; 5 Apr 1973, p 1019; 10 Apr 1973, p 1021–1058; 12 Apr 1973, p 1059–1072

Report (Whole House)

   9 May 1973, p 627–629; 10 May 1973, p 641–650; 11 May 1973, p 655–656; 14 May 1973, p 659–680; 16 May 1973, p 681–702; 17 May 1973, p 703–714

Restrictive Trade Practices Act 1976

PUBA94	1976
Restrictive Trade Practices Act 1976 (c. 34)	
An Act to consolidate the enactments relating to restrictive trade practices	
Table of contents (patent provisions only)	
s 28 and Sch 3 Excepted Agreements [Known how and Patent licences and agreements]	

Journal

House of Commons			House of Lords		
Rep: Thomas Cox (Wh)			Pres: Lord Elwyn-Jones LC Rep: Earl of Listowel (Ld Ch)		
25 Feb 1976	232 CJ 169	JC Con Rep	4 Feb 1976	209 LJ 152	1R
6 Jul 1976	232 CJ 430	Brought HL/1R	16 Feb 1976	209 LJ 171	2R/Ref JC Cons
12 Jul 1976	232 CJ 445	2R/C'tted CWH/Rep w/o	26 Feb 1976	209 LJ 196	Rep with JC/Re-C'tted CWH
		Amds/3R	24 Jun 1976	209 LJ 509	CWH/Rep with Amds
22 Jul 1976	232 CJ 484	Royal Assent	6 Jul 1976	209 LJ 543	3R
			13 Jul 1976	209 LJ 597	HC pass w/o Amds
			22 Jul 1976	209 LJ 627	Royal Assent

Parliamentary debates

2R/3R: HC Deb, 12 Jul 1976, Vol 915(5th), col 321	1R: HL Deb, 4 Feb 1976, Vol 367(5th), col 1295
Royal Assent: HC Deb, 22 Jul 1976, Vol 915(5th), col 2065	2R: HL Deb, 16 Feb 1976, Vol 368(5th), col 311–312
	Rep: HL Deb, 26 Feb 1976, Vol 368(5th), col 890
	CWH: HL Deb, 24 Jun 1976, Vol 372(5th), col 433–436
	Cons: HL Deb, 1 Jul 1976, Vol 372(5th), col 872
	3R: HL Deb, 6 Jul 1976, Vol 372(5th), col 1142
	Royal Assent: HL Deb, 22 Jul 1976, Vol 373(5th), col 1004

Parliamentary papers

Restrictive Trade Practices Bill (1976 HL Papers 78), Vol 6

Restrictive Trade Practices Bill (as amended by the Joint Committee on Consolidation Bills) (1976 HL Papers 104), Vol 6
    Marshalled List of Amendments to be Moved in Committee (on Re-Committal) (1976 HL Papers 104–I), Vol 6

Restrictive Trade Practices Bill (as amended in Committee on Re-Committal) (1976 HL Papers 241), Vol 6

Restrictive Trade Practices Bill (1975–76 HC Papers 190), Vol 7, p 1

Fourth Report of the Joint Committee on Consolidation Bills being a report upon the Restrictive Trade Practices Bill (1975–76 HC Papers 218) Minutes of Evidence (1975–76 HC Papers 218) Vol 7, p 77 and 79

Resale Prices Act 1976

PUBA95	1976
Resale Prices Act 1976 (c. 53)	
An Act to consolidate those provisions of the Resale Prices Act 1964 still having effect, Part II of the Restrictive Trade Practices Act 1956, and related enactments; and to repeal the provisions of the Resale Prices Act 1964 and the Restrictive Trade Practices Act 1968 which have ceased to have any effect	
Table of contents (patent provisions only)	
s 10 Patented articles under s 9 [Minimum resale prices maintained by contract or agreement]	

Journal

House of Commons			House of Lords		
Rep: Thomas Cox (Wh)			Pres: Lord Elwyn-Jones LC Rep: Joint Committee		
30 Jun 1976	232 CJ 418	Rep JC Cons	14 Jun 1976	209 LJ 466	1R
11 Oct 1976	232 CJ 529	Brought HL/1R	24 Jun 1976	209 LJ 509	2R/Ref JC Cons
18 Oct 1976	232 CJ 555	2R/C'tted CWH/3R	30 Jun 1976	209 LJ 531	Rep JC/C'tted CWH
26 Oct 1976	232 CJ 575	Royal Assent	5 Oct 1976	209 LJ 731	Ord Re-C'tted Disc

(continued)

(continued)

			7 Oct 1976	209 LJ 744	3R
			19 Oct 1976	209 LJ 797	HC pass w/o Amds
			26 Oct 1976	209 LJ 832	Royal Assent

Parliamentary debates

2R/3R: HC Deb, 18 Oct 1976, Vol 917(5th), col 1078	1R: HL Deb, 14 Jun 1976, Vol 371(5th), col 919
Royal Assent: HC Deb, 26 Oct 1976, Vol 918(5th), col 286	2R: HL Deb, 24 Jun 1976, Vol 372(5th), col 436–437
	Re-C'tted: HL Deb, 30 Jun 1976, Vol 371(5th), col 862
	Ord disc: HL Deb, 5 Oct 1976, Vol 374(5th), col 1085
	3R: HL Deb, 7 Oct 1976, Vol 371(5th), col 1498
	HC pass: HL Deb, 19 Oct 1976, Vol 374(5th), col 1267
	Royal Assent: HL Deb, 26 Oct 1976, Vol 374(5th), col 317

Parliamentary papers

Resale Prices Bill (1976 HL Papers 217), Vol 6

Resale Prices Bill (as amended by the Joint Committee on Consolidation Bills) (1976 HL Papers 254), Vol 6

Resale Prices Bill (1975–76) HC Papers 228), Vol 6, p 793

Twelfth Report of the Joint Committee on Consolidation Bills being a Report on the Resale Prices Bill (1975–76 HC Papers 549) Minutes of Evidence (1975–76 HC Papers 549–I), Vol 6, p 817 and 819

Supplement to Votes & Proceedings, 1975–76 – No amendments

3   Public patent Bills

Bill to Explain Letters Patents 1601

PUBB1	1601
	Bill to Explain Letters Patents 1601 (43 Eliz 1)

Bill for the Explanation of the Common Law in certain Cases of Letters Patent

Table of contents

No details survive

Journal

House of Commons			House of Lords
Pres: Lawrence Hide			
20 Nov 1601	No CJ	**1R**	*Never considered by House of Lords*

Parliamentary debates

1R: Simonds d'Ewes, Journals of All the Parliaments During the Reign of Queen Elizabeth (John Starky, London 1682), p 644–648; Heywood Townsend, Historical Collections or An exact Account of the Proceedings of the Four Last Parliaments of Queen Elizabeth (The George: Fleet Street London 1680), p 230–235; Corbett's Parliamentary History, Vol 1, col 923–933

Parliamentary papers

None

Penal and Monopolies Bill 1606

PUBB2	1606
	Penal and Monopolies Bill 1606 (4 Ja 1)

Bill for the better execution of penal statutes and restraint of monopolies

Table of contents

[Cl 1 Any grant of a monopoly or any grant authorising a person to do an act prohibited by a penal statute is void under the common law of the Realm; although the same grant continues in Statutes general or non-obstante the same penal statute or any of them]
[Cl 2 Any grant of the sums paid or forfeiture to a person under a penal statute be void]
[Cl 3 Any warrant authorising the grant of Letters or Warrants to avoid a penal statute to pay £100 to be recovered as a debt in the courts]

Journal

House of Commons			House of Lords		
Pres: Lawrence Hide					
21 Jan 1606	1 CJ 257	1R	17 Apr 1606	2 LJ 416	Brought HC/1R
22 Jan 1606	1 CJ 258	2R/C'tted	1 May 1606	2 LJ 422	2R
25 Jan 1606	1 CJ 260	Com adj			
15 Feb 1606	1 CJ 268	Com day app			
4 Mar 1606	1 CJ 277	Com day app			
27 Mar 1606	1 CJ 290	Com			
17 Apr 1606	1 CJ 299	3R			

Parliamentary debates

None

(continued)

(continued)

Parliamentary papers
None
Notes
Ing: Fourth Report of the Royal Commission on Historical Manuscripts (1873 C 857), Vol 25, Pt 1, p 1 at p 118 [HL/PO/JO/10/2/1E]

Welsh Butter Bill 1621

PUBB3	1621
	Welsh Butter Bill 1621 (18 Ja 1)

Bill to enable all and every of his Majesty's Subjects, within this Realm of England, and Dominions of Wales, to transport Welsh Butter out of the said Dominion of Wales in any foreign Realm, in Aminity with his Majesty, at such Times, as Butter in Wales shall not exceed the Prices of 3d the Pound, in Summer Season, and 4d the Pound, in the Winter Season

Table of contents

[Cl 1 Monopoly granted for transporting and selling butter in Wales and Monmouth to cease after 30 days from the end of Present Parliament]

Journal

House of Commons			House of Lords		
Rep: (John) Glanville			Rep: George Abbott (Archbishop of Canterbury)		
5 Mar 1621	1 CJ 537	1R	26 May 1621	3 LJ 135	Brought HC
10 Mar 1621	1 CJ 549	2R/C'tted CWH	1 Dec 1621	3 LJ 177	1R
15 Mar 1621	1 CJ 556	Counsel Welsh Butter Heard	7 Dec 1621	3 LJ 185	2R/C'tted
26 Mar 1621	1 CJ 575	CWH/Rep with Amds/Re-C'tt	7 Dec 1621	3 LJ 185	Rep with Amds
27 Apr 1621	1 CJ 593	Rep with Amds/Ing	8 Dec 1621	3 LJ 185	3R
25 May 1621	1 CJ 627	3R			
10 Dec 1621	1 CJ 661	HL pass with Amds			

Parliamentary debates

Wallace Notestein, Frances Relf and Hartley Simpson, *Commons Debates 1621* (Yale 1935):

Vol 2: X's Journal; Vol 3: Barrington's Diary; Vol 4: Pym's Diary; Vol 5: Belasye Diary, Smyth's Diary, Wentworths Diary, Rich's Notes; Vol 6: Holland''s Diary, Z Diary, Book of Committee, Howard's Diary; Horn Collection (B's diary); Minnesota Manuscript

1R: X, p 162; Pym, p 124; Smyth, p 270; Holland, p 28

2R: *X, p 204*; *Pym, p 142–143*; Smyth, p 287

Rep/Re-C'tted: X, p 267 n 37; Pym, p 198; Smyth, p 322

Rep/Ing: X, p 326; Pym, p 265; Holland, p 103

3R: X, p 389; Barrington, p 305; *Pym, p 371*; Smyth, p 383; Holland, p 168

Sent to HL: X, p 394; Pym, p 379; Smyth, p 385; Holland, p 171

HL Amds: X, p 508, n 3

Comments (31 May 1621): *Belasyse, p 190*; Barrington, p 375

Proclamation: Barrington, p 416 n 25

Parliamentary papers

None

Notes

The Bill

Wallace Notestein, Frances Relf and Hartley Simpson, *Commons Debates 1621* (Yale 1935), Vol 7, p 108–110

The Grant to Edward Celston et al, p 468–469

Archive

Patent (20 Feb 1618/9): *Third Report of the Royal Commission on Historical Manuscripts* (1872 C 673), Vol 33, p 337 at p 16 [HL/PO/JO/10/2/1F]

Bill (26 May 1621): *Third Report of the Royal Commission on Historical Manuscripts* (1872 C 673), Vol 33, p 337 at p 24 [HL/PO/JO/10/1/18]

Bill on Monopolies 1621

PUBB4	1621
	Bill on Monopolies 1621 (18 Ja 1)

Bill concerning [against patentees of] monopolyes and dispensations, with [and forfeiture of] penal law

Table of contents

[Cl 1 All Monopolies, &c. shall be void]
[Cl 2 Monopolies, &c. shall be tried by the Common Laws of this Realm]
[Cl 3 Persons disabled to use Monopolies, &c.]
[Cl 4 The Party grieved by Pretext of a Monopoly, &c. shall recover treble Damages and double Cost]
[Cl 5 Letters Patents to use new Manufactures, saved]
[Cl 6 Letters Patent for new Inventions after enactment; Letters Patent not be granted where generally inconvenient]
[Cl 7 Patents for printing Bible or Book of Common prayer not affected by Act]
[Cl 8 All patents for printing books which last for 16 years not affected by Act]
[Cl 9 Nothing affecting grants by Parliament]
[Cl 10 Saltpetre and making iron or allum not affected]
[Cl 11Charters granted to Corporations, saved]
[Cl 12 Grant to Earl of Nottingham not affected if not prejudicial]

Journal					
House of Commons			**House of Lords**		
Rep: (John) Glanville			Rep: George Abbott (Archbishop of Canterbury)		
16 Feb 1621	1 CJ 523	Condemnation of Monopolies	18 May 1621	3 LJ 128	1R
12 Mar 1621	1 CJ 549	Ord	25 May 1621	3 LJ 132	2R day app
12 Mar 1621	1 CJ 551	1R	28 May 1621	3 LJ 137	2R/C'tted
14 Mar 1621	1 CJ 553	**2R**/C'tted Privy Council in HC	24 Nov 1621	3 LJ 168	C'tee to meet
18 Mar 1621	1 CJ 563	Rep day app	27 Nov 1621	3 LJ 172	Lords added
19 Mar 1621	1 CJ 564	**Rep/Re–C'tted**	1 Dec 1621	3 LJ 177	3R – rejected
26 Mar 1621	1 CJ 575	**Rep from Re–C'tt**	1 Dec 1621	3 LJ 177	New Bill
8 May 1621	1 CJ 612	Query Proviso to Bill	7 Dec 1621	3 LJ 185	C'tee to meet (New Bill)
12 May 1621	1 CJ 619	3R	8 Dec 1621	3 LJ 187	Peers add
10 Dec 1621	1 CJ 661	HL Conf Request	10 Dec 1621	3 LJ 188	**Rep on Heads of Bill**
14 Dec 1621	1 CJ 663	Progress of Bill	8 Feb 1622	3 LJ 204	Notes on Bills
15 Dec 1621	1 CJ 664	**Progress of Bill**			
17 Dec 1621	1 CJ 667	Progress of Bill			

Parliamentary debates

House of Commons

Wallace Notestein, Frances Relf and Hartley Simpson, *Commons Debates 1621* (Yale 1935):

Vol 2: X's Journal; Vol 3: Barrington's Diary; Vol 4: Pym's Diary; Vol 5: Belasye Diary, Smyth's Diary, Wentworths Diary, Rich's Notes; Vol 6: Holland's Diary, Z Diary, Book of Committee, Howard's Diary; Horn Collection (B's diary); Minnesota Manuscript

Proceedings and Debates of the House of Commons in 1620 and 1621 (Oxford 1764) (Nicholas)

Prop (5 Mar 1621): **X, p 167–168**; *Pym, p 124*; Belasyse, p 25; Holland, p 31; Nicholas, Vol 1, p 122

Re-C'tted HL (8 Mar 1621): X, p 194; *Holland, p 44*; Howard, p 309

1R (12 Mar 1621): X, p 210; Pym, p 147; Belasyse, p 26, n 10; Smyth, p 289–290; Holland, p 56 n 18; Nicholas, Vol 1, p 145

2R (14 Mar 1621): **X, p 218–219**; *Pym, p 153*; *Belasyse, p 38*; Smyth, p 296; *Holland, p 61–62*; Nicholas, Vol 1, p 155

C'ttee (15 Mar 1621): *Pym, p 160*

Rep day app (19 Mar 1621): Smyth, p 309, n 6

Rep/Re-Ctt'ed (20 Mar 1621): **Pym, p 173**; Smyth, p 312; Nicholas, Vol 1, p 199–200

Rep (26 Mar 1621): X, p 266, n 33 and 267; **Pym, p 197–198**; Smyth, p 322

Unwanted provisos (8 May 1621): X, p 354; **Barrington, p 198–200**; **Pym, p 318**; Nicholas, Vol 2, p 40–41

3R (12 May 1621): **Barrington, p 235–236**; **Pym, p 333–334**; Belasyse, p 161; Smyth, p 373; Holland, p 153; Nicholas, Vol 2, p 62

Sent HL (12 May 1621): Barrington, p 236; Pym, p 334; Smyth, p 373

(continued)

(continued)

Almost ready (26 Nov 1621): X, p 450; Barrington, p 456; Pym, p 439; Smyth, p 404; Z, p 198; Howard, p 320; Nicholas, Vol 2, p 214–215

HL Req Conf (10 Dec 1621): **X, p 508–509**; Smyth, p 413; Z, p 230; Nicholas, Vol 2, p 301–303

HL Rej (10 Dec 1621): X, p 509; Smyth, p 413

HL Sent Msg (13 Dec 1621): Z, p 236

HL Req Conf (14 Dec 1621): X, p 519; Nicholas, Vol 2, p 328

HL Rej (14 Dec 1621): X, p 521

HL Req Conf (15 Dec 1621): X, p 522

HL Rej (15 Dec 1621): X, p 522; *Z, p 239*; Nicholas, Vol 2, p 335–336

HL Req Conf: X, p 532; Z, p 243

Royal Assent desired: Barrington, Vol 3, p 333; X's Journal, Vol 2, p 400

House of Lords

Samuel Gardiner, *Notes of the Debates in the House of Lords official taken by Henry Elsing, Clerk of the Parliaments, 1621 (1871)* 103 Camden Society (Old Series)

HC Req pass of Bill (28 Nov 1621): Gardiner, p 97

3R/Neg (1 Dec 1621): Gardiner, p 102–105

Com to draft new Bill (3 Dec 1621): Gardiner, p 106

Parliamentary papers
None
Notes

Text of Bill: Samuel Gardiner, *Notes of the Debates of the Houses of Lords officially taken by Henry Elsing, Clerk of the Parliaments*, 1621 (Camden Society 1871), Vol 103, p 151 to 155

Text of Bill: *Historical Manuscripts Commission, Third Report* (C 673), Vol 33, p 337 at p 23 [HL/PO/JO/10/1/17A]

3 Dec 1621: Draft of Report of Lord Keeper on the Bill: Historical Manuscripts Commission, Third Report (C 673), Vol 33, p 337 at p 25 [HL/PO/JO/10/1/19]

10 Dec 1621: Draft of Proceedings: Historic Manuscripts Commission, Third Report (C 673), Vol 33, p 337 at p 25 [HL/PO/JO/10/1/19]

Wallace Notestein, Frances Relf and Hartley Simpson, *Commons Debates 1621* (Yale 1935), Vol 7

    Concering a Proviso for Iron, p 165

Bill to Confirm Patent Grants 1621

PUBB5	1621		
Bill to Confirm Patent Grants 1621 (18 Ja 1)			
Bill for the Confirmation of Grants made to the King's Majesty, and of Letters Patent made by his Highness to others			
Table of contents			
No details			
Journal			
House of Commons		**House of Lords**	
Pres: Sir Henry Poole			
25 Apr 1621	1 CJ 590 – V	**1R**	*Never considered by House of Lords*
Parliamentary debates			

Wallace Notestein, Frances Relf and Hartley Simpson, *Commons Debates 1621* (Yale 1935):

    Vol 2: X's Journal; Vol 3: Barrington's Diary; Vol 4: Pym's Diary; Vol 5: Belasye Diary, Smyth's Diary, Wentworths Diary, Rich's Notes; Vol 6: Holland''s Diary, Z Diary, Book of Committee, Howard's Diary; Horn Collection (B's diary); Minnesota Manuscript

Proceedings and Debates of the House of Commons in 1620 and 1621 (Oxford 1764) (Nicholas)

1R: X, p 258; *Barrington, p 77–78*; Belasyse, p 96; Smyth, p 348; Holland, p 97; *Nicholas, Vol 1, p 314*

Parliamentary papers
None

Rights of Patentees Bill 1793

PUBB6	1793
	Rights of Patentees Bill 1793 (33 Geo 3)
	Bill for Securing the Rights of Patentees, in Certain Cases, from The Encouragement of Foreigners

Table of contents

[Cl 1 Where a petition for Letters patent represents that it would be prejudicial to the Patentee and injurious to the Trade of the Kingdom, if a description was inrolled it may be delivered to the Lord Chancellor instead]

[Cl 2 Specification inspected by Two Person under oath of secrecy; those persons shall point out any amendments to perfect the description; Specification thereunder held under seal which may be broken only under order of Lord Chancellor or Master in Chancery]

[Cl 3 Lord Chancellor to set fees under the Act; security for fees may be taken from Patentee]

[Cl 4 First Lord Commissioner acts when Lord Chancellorship vacant; saving for current method of granting patents]

Journal

House of Commons			House of Lords		
Pres:Scrope Bernard Rep: Henry Hobart					
9 May 1793	48 CJ 761	Bill Ord	3 Jun 1793	39 LJ 718	1R
10 May 1793	48 CJ 766	1R	6 Jun 1793	39 LJ 725	2R/C'tted CWH
16 May 1793	48 CJ 785	2R/C'tted CWH	7 Jun 1793	39 LJ 735	CWH adj
27 May 1793	48 CJ 807	CWH adj	10 Jun 1793	39 LJ 739	CWH adj 3m
28 May 1793	48 CJ 815	CWH/Rep with Amds			
30 May 1793	48 CJ 821	Cons			
3 Jun 1793	48 CJ 831	3R			

Parliamentary debates

None

Parliamentary papers

Catalogue of Papers printed by Order of the House of Commons, from the year 1731 to 1800. In the Custody of the Clerk of the Journals (1807) (Reprint: HMSO 1954): Patentees securing their rights from the encroachment of foreigners, 1793, Vol 23, No 670

A Bill, Intituled An Act for securing the Rights of Patentees, in certain Cases, from the Encroachments of Foreigners (House of Lords Sessional Papers, Vol 1)

A Bill, Intituled An Act for securing the Rights of Patentees, in certain Cases, from the Encroachments of Foreigners (House of Commons Sessional Papers, Vol 86)

Newspaper coverage of debates

House of Commons

Bill Ord: The Times, 10 May 1793

CWH Adj: The Times, 28 May 1793

Notes

Archive

Ing: HL/PO/JO/10/2/66

Letters Patent Specification Bill 1820

PUBB7	1820
	Letters Patent Specification Bill 1820 (1 Geo 4)
	Bill to prevent the inconvenience arising from the facility of procuring copies of specification enrolled by Grantees of Letters Patent for the sole working and vending of new manufactures within this Realm

Table of contents

[Cl 1] Persons to whom Letters Patent are granted, shall within the time limited for the inrolment of the Specification of such Letters Patent, produce before person to be appointed for that purpose, the Specification so to be inrolled; And no such Specification shall be inrolled without a certificate from such persons that the inventions is new, and may be prepared by following the directions of such Specifications

(continued)

(continued)

[Cl 2] Regulations to be observed by the persons to be appointed to grant such Certificates

[Cl 3] After the examination of the Specifications, such persons are to deliver them, sealed up, to the Officer of the Court, who is not to open the same except by an order of Court, or from the Law Officers of the Crown

[Cl 4] Register to be kept of all Patents granted and inrolled, under certain regulations

[Cl 5] Patentees apprehensive of infringements on their rights, may petition the law officers of the Crown, before any new Patent is granted for similar inventions

[Cl 6] In certain cases the law officers of the Crown may direct Specifications to be examined

[Cl 7] Persons appointed to make such inspections to be paid by the Grantee

[Cl 8] Copies of Specifications for English Patents allowed to be used and deposited, within limited periods, for Irish and Scotch Patents

[Cl 9] Specifications may be opened and inspected by orders of the Judges of His Majesty's Courts in Ireland and Scotland

[Cl 10] Specifications of Patents for Ireland and Scotland to be kept sealed, except in certain cases

[Cl 11] A Register of Patents to be kept in Ireland and Scotland

[Cl 12] Specifications deposited under this Act, to be held sufficient performance of the Proviso in the Letters Patent

Journal			
House of Commons			**House of Lords**
Pres: Henry Wrottesley			
14 Jun 1820	75 CJ 312	Bill Ord	*Never considered by House of Lords*
24 Jun 1820	75 CJ 352	1R	
27 Jun 1820	75 CJ 362	2R adj	
29 Jun 1820	75 CJ 368	2R adj	
4 Jul 1820	75 CJ 399	2R adj	
5 Jul 1820	75 CJ 402	2R adj	

Parliamentary debates
Bill Ord: **HC Deb, 14 Jun 1820, Vol 1(2nd), col 1052–1053**

Parliamentary papers
Bill to prevent the inconvenience arising from the facility of procuring copies of specifications inrolled by grantees of letters patent, for the sole working and vending of new manufactures within this realm (1820 HC Papers 184), Vol 1, p 285

Newspaper coverage of debates
House of Commons
Delay introduction: The Times, 26 May 1820
Bill Ord: *The Times, 15 Jun 1820; Morning Chronicle, 15 Jun 1820; Evening Mail, 16 Jun 1820*
2R def: Morning Post, 6 Jul 1820; Public Ledger and Daily Advertiser, 6 Jul 1820

Patents Bill 1820

PUBB8	1820
Patents Bill 1820 (1 Geo 4)	
Bill for the protection of persons applying for Patents for inventions	
Table of contents	

[Cl 1] Commissioners to be appointed by the Lord Chancellor

[Cl 2] Mode of summoning the Commissioners for executing the Act; Form of application for Summons

[Cl 3] Commissioners to meet on Summons; and grant a Warrant of Experiment; Form of Warrant of Experiment

[Cl 4] Date of Warrant to decide priority of Claims

[Cl 5] Summoning Witnesses and administering Oaths

[Cl 6] Time mentioned in Warrant may be extended

[Cl 7] At the end of the term granted by Warrant on Experiment, Certificate may be granted; Form of Certificate

[Cl 8] Petition to be presented within a certain time

[Cl 9] Specification to be enrolled within a certain time

[Cl 10] For ascertaining Infringement; Form of Certificate

[Cl 11] Specification to be examined and reported on; Form of Report

[Cl 12] For amending Errors in Specifications

[Cl 13] Respecting Copies of Specifications

[Cl 14] Patents may be granted to Purchasers of Inventions; Form of Affidavit

[Cl 15] Allowing Appeal

[Cl 16] Commissioner's Fees

[Cl 17] Warrants, &c. to be on a Stamp
[Cl 18] Clerk to be appointed. Books kept; Clerk's Fees; Room to be provided for Commissioners Meetings; List of Patents to be kept; Books to Evidence
[Cl 19] Commissioner's Oath

Journal			
House of Commons			**House of Lords**
Pres: John Curwen			
21 Jun 1820	75 CJ 338	Bill Ord	*Never considered by House of Lords*
22 Jun 1820	75 CJ 343	1R	
6 Jul 1820	75 CJ 413	2R adj	

Parliamentary debates
None

Parliamentary papers
Bill for the protection of persons applying for patents for inventions (1820 HC Papers 181), Vol 1, p 277

Newspaper coverage of debates
House of Commons
Bill Ord: The Times, 22 Jun 1820; Public Ledger and Daily Advertiser, 22 Jun 1820
1R: Morning Chronicle, 23 Jun 1820; Evening Mail, 23 Jun 1820

Notes
A similar Bill, albeit with some changes, was introduced in the following sessions: PUBB9

Patentees Protection Bill 1821

PUBB9	1821
Patentees Protection Bill 1821 (1 & 2 Geo 4)	
Bill for the encouragement of Philosophical and Mechanical Experiment, and for the protection of Patentees in their rights	

Table of contents
[Cl 1] Commissioners to be appointed by the Lord Chancellor
[Cl 2] Mode of summoning the Commissioners for executing the Act; Form of application for Summons
[Cl 3] Commissioners to meet on Summons; and grant a Warrant of Experiment; Form of Warrant of Experiment
[Cl 4] Date of Warrant to decide priority of Claims
[Cl 5] Summoning Witnesses and administering Oaths
[Cl 6] At the end of the term granted by Warrant on Experiment, Certificate may be granted; Form of Certificate
[Cl 7] Petition to be presented within a certain time
[Cl 8] Specification to be enrolled within a certain time
[Cl 9] Specification to be examined and reported on; Form of Report
[Cl 10] Patents may be granted to Purchasers of Inventions; Form of Affidavit
[Cl 11] Commissioner's Fees
[Cl 12] Warrants, &c. to be on a Stamp
[Cl 13] Clerk to be appointed: Books kept; Clerk's Fees; Room to be provided for Commissioners Meetings; List of Patents to be kept; Books to Evidence
[Cl 14] Commissioner's Oath
[Cl 15] Inventor's Deposit Money
[Cl 16] Receipt

Journal			
House of Commons			**House of Lords**
Pres: John Curwen			
6 Feb 1821	76 CJ 40	Bill Ord	*Never considered by House of Lords*
8 Feb 1821	76 CJ 51	1R	
22 Feb 1821	76 CJ 101	2R adj	

Parliamentary debates
None

(continued)

(continued)

Parliamentary papers
Bill for the encouragement of philosophical and mechanical experiment, and for the protection of patentees in their rights (1821, HC Papers 17) 1821, Vol 1, p 21
Newspaper coverage of debates
House of Commons
Bill Ord: *The Times, 7 Feb 1821; Morning Chronicle, 7 Feb 1821; Morning Post, 7 Feb 1821*; Public Ledger and Daily Advertiser, 7 Feb 1821
1R: The Times, 9 Feb 1821; Morning Chronicle, 9 Feb 1821; Evening Mail, 9 Feb 1821
2R: **Morning Post, 23 Feb 1821**; **Public Ledger and Daily Advertiser, 23 Feb 1821**; *The Times, 23 Feb 1821*; *Globe, 23 Feb 1821; Morning Chronicle, 23 Feb 1821*
Notes
A similar Bill was introduced in the previous sessions: PUBB8

Letters Patents Bill 1833

PUBB10	1833
Letters Patents Bill 1833 (3 & 4 Will 4)	
Bill to explain and amend the Laws respecting Letters Patent	
Table of contents (as introduced: 1833 HC Papers 34)	

[Cl 1] Empowers the King to grant Patents for Seven Years and Fourteen Years
[Cl 2] Who shall become Patentees
[Cl 3] Patentee may sell his Right
[Cl 4] What shall be the Subject of Patents
[Cl 5] Patent not to become void inconsequence of the same having been used in an imperfect state
[Cl 6] May deposit Models
[Cl 7] May put in "Secondary Specifications" to remedy Defects, or for Improvements
[Cl 8] Stamp Duty
[Cl 9] If a Specification is bad in Law, another shall be inrolled
[Cl 10] Judge or Court may amendment Matters of form
[Cl 11] The practice of obtaining Patents [may specify if seeking Scottish and Irish patent in petition]
[Cl 12] A preparatory Description of Inventions to be made
[Cl 13] Specification to be referred to the Attorney General, who is to report thereupon
[Cl 13] Empowering Lord Chancellor to affix Great Seal to Letters Patent
[Cl 14] As to Caveats
[Cl 15] Examiners to assist the Attorney General
[Cl 16] Attorney General to direct what Costs shall be paid to Examiners
[Cl 17] The Price of Patents
[Cl 18] Places at which Fees are to be paid
[Cl 19] Patents for Scotland and Ireland, after a Patent has been obtained in England
[Cl 20] Patents for Scotland and Ireland, before a Patent has been obtained for England
[Cl 21] Person in Ireland obtaining Letters Patent in Ireland, may obtain Certificate and vice versa
[Cl 22] Unlimited Transfer of Patents [to any number of persons]
[Cl 22] Extension of the Time granted in the Patent [Prolongation]
[Cl 23] Proceedings at Law to uphold the Patent
[Cl 24] Defendant may plead the General Issue
[Cl 25] Venue may be changed
[Cl 26] Jurors to be skilled in the Arts and Science
[Cl 27] Defendant against whom a Verdict shall pass, to pay Treble Damages
[Cl 28] Costs
[Cl 29] Proceedings to cancel the Patent
[Cl 30] If Patentee obtain a Verdict, Court to grant a Certificate [of validity]
[Cl 31] This Act to apply to Scotland and Ireland, and the protecting Enactments to be retrospective
[Cl 32] Act to extend to Scotland and Ireland

Table of contents (after Bill divided: 1833 HC Papers 496)

[Cl 1] Person introducing Foreign Inventions to be deemed Inventors
[Cl 2] What shall be Subject of Patents
[Cl 3] Patent not to become void in consequence of the subject of it having been previously used in an imperfect state

[Cl 4] Patent bad in part not bad in the whole
[Cl 5] Patent void if Specification fraudulently defective; Amendment of Specification
[Cl 6] Stamps for amended Specifications; Inrolment
[Cl 7] Judge may amend Matters of Form
[Cl 7] Title to a Patent to contain an Outline or Sketch of Inventions
[Cl 8] Patent to take effect from the Day of presenting Petition for it
[Cl 9] Transfers of Patents and Licences
[Cl 10] Proceedings at Law respecting the Patent
[Cl 11] The Defendant may plead the General Issue
[Cl 12] Jurors may examine Specification and Drawings Two Days before Trial
[Cl 13] Act to take effect from the time of passing
[Cl 14] Act not to apply to infringement of Letters patent [in pending proceedings]
[Cl 15] Property in Patterns accrued to Inventors for a limited time
[Cl 16] Provisions in recited Acts to extent to all new Patterns to which they may be applicable
[Cl 17] Costs
[Cl 18] Act to extend to Scotland and Ireland

Journal					
House of Commons			**House of Lords**		
Pres: Henry Lyton Bulwer Rep: Richard Godson					
19 Feb 1833	88 CJ 72	Bill Ord	17 Jul 1833	65 LJ 504	Brought HC/1R
28 Feb 1833	88 CJ 130	1R	15 Aug 1833	65 LJ 585	2R adj 6m
7 Mar 1833	88 CJ 145	2R day app			
28 Mar 1833	88 CJ 231	Pet in Fav [PET17]			
23Apr 1833	88 CJ 297	2R/C'tted			
7 May 1833	88 CJ 358	Mem Add			
22 May 1833	88 CJ 421	Mem Add			
27 Jun 1833	88 CJ 528	Rep with Amds/Re-C'tted			
1 Jul 1833	88 CJ 535	Pet Ag [PET19]			
2 Jul 1833	88 CJ 536	CWH adj			
4 Jul 1833	88 CJ 545	**CWH**			
9 Jul 1833	88 CJ 558	CWH adj			
9 Jul 1833	88 CJ 559	Rep with Amds/Bill Div			
11 Jul 1833	88 CJ 564	Cons adj			
11 Jul 1833	88 CJ 565	Cons/Ing			
13 Jul 1833	88 CJ 570	3R adj			
16 Jul 1833	88 CJ 575	**3R adj**			
16 Jul 1833	88 CJ 577	**3R**			
17 Jul 1833	88 CJ 579	3R			

Parliamentary debates

Ord: **HC Deb, 19 Feb 1833, Vol 15(3rd), col 974–988; Mirror, 19 Feb 1833, Vol 1, p 325–329**

1R: Mirror, 28 Feb 1833, Vol 1, p 453

Pet: Mirror, 28 Mar 1833, Vol 2, p 1047

2R/C'tted: Mirror, 22 Apr 1833, Vol 2, p 1375

Rep: Mirror, 27 Jun 1833, Vol 3, p 2587

Pet: Mirror, 1 Jul 1833, Vol 3, p 2645

CWH: Mirror, 3 Jul 1833, Vol 3, p 2731 (Bill divided)

Rep: **HC Deb, 9 Jul 1833, Vol 19(3rd), col 382–384; Mirror, 9 Jul 1833, Vol 3, p 2863–2864**

Cons: Mirror, 11 Jul 1833, Vol 3, p 2941

3R adj: Mirror, 13 Jul 1833, Vol 3, p 2986

3R: **Mirror, 15 Jul 1833, Vol 3, p 3012**

3R: **Mirror, 16 Jul 1833, Vol 3, p 3019**; HC Deb, 16 Jul 1833, Vol 19(3rd), col 638

3R: Mirror, 16 Jul 1833, Vol 3, p 3040

1R: Mirror, 17 Jul 1833, Vol 3, p 3041

2R adj: **HL Deb, 9 Aug 1833, Vol 20(3rd), col 440–441; Mirror, 9 Aug 1833, Vol 3, p 3641**

2R adj 6m: Mirror, 15 Aug 1833, Vol 3, p 3812

(continued)

(continued)

Parliamentary papers
Bill to explain and amend the laws respecting Letters patent for inventions (1833 HC Papers 34), Vol 3, p 169
Bill to explain and amend the laws respecting Letters patent for inventions (as amended in Committee) (1833 HC Papers 496), Vol 3, p 177
Clauses Proposed to be added by Mr Jervis (1833 HC Papers 0.75), Vol 3, p 187
Bill to amend the laws respecting Letters Patent, and to secure the Property therein to Inventors, and to secure the Property in new Patterns (1833 HL Papers 135), Vol 305, p 235
Newspaper coverage of debates
House of Commons
Bill Ord: **Morning Advertiser, 20 Feb 1833**; **Morning Chronicle, 20 Feb 1833**; **Morning Post, 20 Feb 1833**; **Public Ledger and Daily Advertiser, 20 Feb 1833**; **London Courier and Evening Gazette, 20 Feb 1833**; **London Evening Standard, 20 Feb 1833**; *The Times, 20 Feb 1833*
2R: London Journal and Repertory of Patents (1833), Vol 2, p 255–257
Rep: *The Times, 28 Jun 1833; Morning Advertiser, 28 Jun 1833; Morning Chronicle, 28 Jun 1833; Morning Post, 28 Jun 1833; London Evening Standard, 28 Jun 1833;* Evening Mail, 28 Jun 1833; London Courier and Evening Gazette, 28 Jun 1833
CWH/REP: **Morning Advertiser, 10 Jul 1833**; **Morning Chronicle, 10 Jul 1833**; **Morning Post, 10 Jul 1833**; **London Evening Standard, 10 Jul 1833**; **Public Ledger and Daily Advertiser, 10 Jul 1833**; *The Times, 10 Jul 1833; London Courier and Evening Gazette, 10 Jul 1833*
Cons: *Morning Advertiser, 12 Jul 1833; Public Ledger and Daily Advertiser, 12 Jul 1833; Evening Mail, 12 Jul 1833; London Courier and Evening Gazette, 12 Jul 1833; London Evening Standard, 12 Jul 1833;* The Times, 12 Jul 1833; Morning Chronicle, 12 Jul 1833; Morning Post, 12 Jul 1833
3R: *Morning Advertiser, 17 Jul 1833; Morning Chronicle, 17 Jul 1833; Morning Post, 17 Jul 1833; Public Ledger and Daily Advertiser, 17 Jul 1833; London Courier and Evening Gazette, 17 Jul 1833; London Evening Standard, 17 Jul 1833; Evening Mail, 17 Jul 1833;* The Times, 17 Jul 1833
House of Lords
Postpone: **The Times, 10 Aug 1833**; **Morning Advertiser, 10 Aug 1833**; **Morning Chronicle, 10 Aug 1833**; **Morning Post, 10 Aug 1833**; **Public Ledger and Daily Advertiser, 10 Aug 1833**; **London Courier and Evening Gazette, 10 Aug 1833**; **London Evening Standard, 10 Aug 1833**
Notes
Petitions – PET17 and PET19

Letters Patent Expenses Bill 1833

PUBB11	1833
Letters Patent Expenses Bill 1833 (3 & 4 Will 4)	
Bill to further amend the Laws Respecting Letters Patent for Inventions, and to settle the Practice and lessen the Expense of obtaining the same	
Table of contents	
[Cl 1] Empowers the King to grant Patents for Seven Years and Fourteen Years [Cl 2] One Patent for the Three Kingdoms and the Colonies [Cl 3] Who shall become Patentees [Cl 4] May deposit models [Cl 5] As to caveats [Cl 6] The Price of Patents [Cl 7] His Majesty's Sign Manual no longer necessary [Cl 8] Costs [Cl 9] Act to extend to Scotland and Ireland	

Journal			
House of Commons			**House of Lords**
9 Jul 1833	88 CJ 559	Rep (Bill divided)	*Never considered by House of Lords*
11 Jul 1833	88 CJ 564	CWH adj	
11 Jul 1833	88 CJ 565	CWH adj 6m	

Parliamentary debates	
Rep: Mirror, 9 Jul 1833, Vol 3, p 2864 CWH adj: **Mirror, 11 Jul 1833, Vol 3, p 2941**	

Parliamentary papers
Bill to explain and amend the laws respecting Letters patent for inventions (as amended in Committee) (1833 HC Papers 497), Vol 3, p 183

Newspaper coverage of debates
House of Commons
Rep: **Morning Advertiser, 10 Jul 1833**; **Morning Chronicle, 10 Jul 1833**; **Morning Post, 10 Jul 1833**; **London Evening Standard, 10 Jul 1833**; **Public Ledger and Daily Advertiser, 10 Jul 1833**; *The Times, 10 Jul 1833*; *London Courier and Evening Gazette, 10 Jul 1833*
Cons adj 6m: *The Times, 12 Jul 1833*; *Morning Advertiser, 12 Jul 1833*; *Public Ledger and Daily Advertiser, 12 Jul 1833*; *Evening Mail, 12 Jul 1833*; *London Courier and Evening Gazette, 12 Jul 1833*; *London Evening Standard, 12 Jul 1833*

Patent for Inventions Bill 1836

PUBB12	1836

Patent for Inventions Bill 1836 (6 & 7 Will 4)

Bill to amend the law relating to Letters Patent for Inventions, and for the better encouragement of the Arts of Manufactures

Table of contents
Cl 1 Acts repealed: [Designing and Printing of Linens, etc. Act 1787] 27 Geo 3, c 38; [Designing and Printing of Linens, etc. Act 1789] 29 Geo 3, c 19; [Excises Duties Act 1794] 34 Geo 3, c. 33; [Letters Patent for Inventions Act 1835] 5 & 6 W 4, c 83 partly repealed Cl 2 That a person having obtained Letters Patent for England, Scotland or Ireland may, on payment of the usual Fees, have them extended to the other Kingdoms, by enrolling a copy of the Specification in the usual manner Cl 3 All Stamps on Letters Patent reduced to 2l: 1l on the Petition, and 1l on the Specification Cl 4 Warrant of a Chief Justice or Chief Baron substituted in lieu of the King's Signature Cl 5 Application to Chief Justices of King's Bench and Commons Pleas for their signatures to a Bill Cl 6 Signature of Lord Chief Justice to have same validity as the Signature of His Majesty was affixed Cl 7 Letters Patent to bear date from Petition Cl 8 Power of inspecting Shops &c., of Parties suspected of infringement Cl 9 Judge may direct that the Engineer shall be accompanied by the Under-Sheriff of the County Cl 10 For defraying Expenses of Inspection Cl 11 Power to extend term of Patent to Fourteen Years [further term of 14 years] Cl 12 In case of Action, &c. notice of Objections to be given Cl 13 Property in new Design secured to Inventor or Proprietor for Twelve calendar Months Cl 14 Appointment of Commissioners or Registrars Cl 15 Commissioners or Registrars to receive Deposit of Models, &c. for Exhibition; on payment of 10l; and give Certificate of License to Depositor Cl 16 Penalty for using unauthorized the subject matter of a License; or counterfeiting Proprietor's mark &c.; Holder of Licenses not to be exempt in consequence of infringement of a Patent; Subject matter of License not to be capable of being afterwards patented; or licensed a second time Cl 17 Application of Monies to be received by Registrars

Journal			
House of Commons			**House of Lords**
Pres: William Mackinnon and John Hardy			
14 Jun 1836	91 CJ 475	Bill Ord	*Never considered by House of Lords*
21 Jun 1836	91 CJ 526	1R	
28 Jun 1836	91 CJ 571	2R adj	
7 Jul 1836	91 CJ 634	2R adj	
14 Jul 1836	91 CJ 662	2R adj	
21 Jul 1836	91 CJ 684	Pet Fav [PET40]	
21 Jul 1836	91 C J 685	2R adj	
28 Jul 1836	91 CJ 709	Pet Fav [PET41]	

(continued)

(continued)

29 Jul 1836	91 CJ 713	2R adj	
10 Aug 1836	91 CJ 775	Pet Fav [PET43]	
11 Aug 1836	91 CJ 777	2R adj	
17 Aug 1836	91 CJ 823	Pet Fav [PET45]	
17 Aug 1836	91 CJ 825	2R adj	

Parliamentary debates	
1R: Mirror, 20 Jun 1836, Vol 2, p 1979	
2R adj: Mirror, 27 Jun 1836, Vol 2, p 2109	
2R adj: Mirror, 7 Jul 1836, Vol 3, p 2260	
2R adj: Mirror, 14 Jul 1836, Vol 3, p 2367	
Pet: Mirror, 21 Jul 1836, Vol 3, p 2480	
2R adj: **Mirror, 28 Jul 1836, Vol 3, p 2586**	
Pet: Mirror, 10 Aug 1836, Vol 3, p 2818	
2R adj: HC Deb, 10 Aug 1836, Vol 35(3rd), col 1057; Mirror, 10 Aug 1836, Vol 3, p 2838	
Pet: Mirror, 17 Aug 1836, Vol 3, p 2938	
2R adj: Mirror, 17 Aug 1836, Vol 3, p 2940	

Parliamentary papers
Bill to amend the law relating to letters patent for inventions, and for the better encouragement of the arts and manufactures (1836 HC Papers 348), Vol 4, p. 513

Newspaper coverage of debates
House of Commons
1R: London Courier and Evening Gazette, 21 Jun 1836
2R adj: **The Times, 29 Jul 1836; Morning Advertiser, 29 Jul 1836; Morning Chronicle, 29 Jul 1836; Morning Post, 29 Jul 1836; Public Ledger and Daily Advertiser, 29 Jul 1836; Evening Chronicle, 29 Jul 1836; Evening Mail, 29 Jul 1836; London Evening Standard, 29 Jul 1836**
2R adj: **The Times, 11 Aug 1836; Morning Advertiser, 11 Aug 1836; Morning Post, 11 Aug 1836; Public Ledger and Daily Advertiser, 11 Aug 1836; Evening Chronicle, 12 Aug 1836; Evening Mail, 12 Aug 1836; London Evening Standard, 11 Aug 1836;** *Morning Chronicle, 11 Aug 1836*

Notes
Petitions – PET32, PET40, PET41, PET43 and PET45

Patents for Inventions Bill 1837

PUBB13	1837
Patents for Inventions Bill 1837 (7 Will 4)	
Bill to amend the practice relating to Letters patent for inventions, and for the better encouragement of the Arts and Manufacturer	

Table of contents
Cl 1 Appointment of Board of Commissioners to carry this Act into execution; Commissioners to be appointed during good behaviour
Cl 2 Style of Commissioners, who may sit as a Board to carry this Act into execution, with power to summon; and examine Witnesses, and call for production of Papers on Oath, or to substitute Declaration upon Oath
Cl 3 To have a common seal; Rules sealed to be received as Evidence
Cl 4 Appointment of one Principal Secretary and Two Registrars of Board
Cl 5 Commissioners to have power to appoint inferior Officers; Salaries to be regulated by Commissioners of Treasury
Cl 6 Commissioners to take an Oath
Cl 7 Power of Commissioners to hear and determine all matters relating to Letters Patent for Inventions hitherto heard by Attorney and Solicitor General; Powers of Commissioners not to interfere with the Jurisdiction of the Judicial Committee of Privy Council or Courts at Westminster
Cl 8 Powers of Attorney and Solicitor General to cease, and to be transferred to Commissioners
Cl 9 Method to be used in obtaining Letters Patent; Commissioners to publish objects of Petition in London Gazette, and appoint a day for hearing all objections to grant of Letters Patent; Parties to attend Commissioners by themselves or their Agents to support and oppose grant of Letters Patent; Commissioners if they shall think the prayer of Petition ought to be granted, to make out a Draft or Bill of Letters; Secretary of State to return Draft or Bill with His Majesty's Sign Manual, to Commissioners; Commissioners to make out Letters Patent, and send same with Draft or Bill to Lord Chancellor; Authority to Lord Chancellor to affix Great Seal to Letters Patent, and return same to Commissioners

Cl 10 Repeal of so much of [Letters Patent for Inventions Act 1835] Act 5 and 6 W 4 as relates to entering Disclaimer and Memorandum of Alteration

Cl 11 Practice in entering Disclaimers; To apply to Commissioners for leave to enter a Memorandum with Registrar

Cl 12 Commissioners to publish application for leave to disclaim; Commissioners to fix a time for hearing Parties support and opposition to such entry; Memorandum filed with Registrar to be deemed part of Letters Patent or Specification; Provided in all Suits then pending, original Letters Patent, &c., alone be given in Evidence

Cl 13 Stamps on Letters Patent and Specifications reduced to 10l

Cl 14 Letters Patent to bear date from filing of Petition; provided that the specification shall be duly enrolled; and provided that the term of the Letters Patent shall bear date from the sealing

Cl 15 Letters Patent to extent to Great Britain, Ireland, and the Colonies, except when specially limited

Cl 16 Property in new design secured to Inventor or Proprietor for Twelve calendar Months

Cl 17 Person availing themselves of this Act, to deposit a Facsimile, Model or Specimen of their Inventions with Commissioners

Cl 18 Commissioners to find some suitable place for exposing Models, &c. to public Inspection

Cl 19 Persons depositing Models, &c. to pay the Sums mentioned in Schedule to Act; Entitled to a Certificate sealed by Commissioners

Cl 20 Persons imitating subject-matter of License, without consent of Person having license, or mark "Licensed" on same, to be liable to a Penalty of 50 l for every Offence; Certificate not to exempt Persons from liability for infringement of Patents; Subject-matter of License not to be afterwards subject of Letters Patent; not to be capable of a second License

Cl 21 Fees respecting Letters Patent to cease; No Fees payable for any thing to be done under this Act, save as set forth in Schedule or general Order of Commissioners

Cl 22 Secretary of Commissioners to receive Fees in Schedule set forth, and also all other Sums payable under this Act, and to pay same into Bank of England once a Week to credit of Commissioners; Monies in Bank subject to Orders of Commissioners, or as directed by this Act

Cl 23 Salaries of Offices under this Act

Cl 24 Penalty to Officers for taking Fees, or for acting as Patent Agent

Cl 25 Commissioners to form and issue general Orders, and for affixing the Fees not hereby settled; General Orders not to be valid, except sanction by Lord Chancellor

Cl 26 Compensation to be awarded to Persons injured by the operation of this Act; Commissioners of Treasury to take into account whether any Office under this Act is held by Person claiming Compensation; Commissioners of Treasury to award Compensation; Commissioners of Treasury to signify amount of Compensations to Commissioners of Patents, who shall thereupon order same to be paid out of Monies standing to account of said Commissioners; Rates of Compensation to be laid before Parliament

Cl 27 Monies standing to account of Commissioners chargeable, first, with Compensation secondly, with Salaries of Officers, and Expenses and Surplus to be carried over to Consolidated Fund

Cl 28 Act may be altered by this Session

Cl 29 Act to come into operation as to appointment of Officers on passing, as to other matters, First of January one thousand eight hundred and Thirty-eight

Schedule of Fees

Journal			
House of Commons			**House of Lords**
Pres: William Mackinnon and Edward Baines			
14 Feb 1837	92 CJ 46	Bill Ord	*Never considered by House of Lords*
15 Feb 1837	92 CJ 50	1R	
2 Mar 1837	92 CJ 101	2R adj	
8 Mar 1837	92 CJ 139	Pet Fav [PET46]	
10 Mar 1837	92 CJ 152	Pet Fav [PET47]	
12 Apr 1837	92 CJ 254	2R adj	
15 Apr 1837	92 CJ 266	2R adj	
26 Apr 1837	92 CJ 302	2R adj	
1 Jun 1837	92 CJ 425	2R adj	
5 Jun 1837	92 CJ 435	Pet Fav [PET52 to PET54]	
22 Jun 1837	92 CJ 494	2R adj	
Parliamentary debates			
Bill Ord: **HC Deb, 14 Feb 1837, Vol 36(3rd), col 554–558; Mirror, 14 Feb 1837, Vol 1, p 175–178**			
1R: HC Deb, 15 Feb 1837, Vol 36(3rd), col 567; Mirror, 15 Feb 1837, Vol 1, p 185			
Pet: Mirror, 8 Mar 1837, Vol 1, p 512			
Pet: Mirror, 10 Mar 1837, Vol 1, p 570			
2R adj: **Mirror, 12 Apr 1837, Vol 2, p 965**			

(continued)

(continued)

2R adj: Mirror, 14 Apr 1837, Vol 2, p 1031	
2R adj: Mirror, 26 Apr 1837, Vol 2, p 1222	
2R adj: Mirror, 1 Jun 1837, Vol 3, p 1666	
Pet: Mirror, 5 Jun 1837, Vol 3, p 1702	

Parliamentary papers
Bill to amend the practice relating to Letters patent for inventions, and for the better encouragement of the Arts and Manufacturer (1837 HC Papers 40), Vol 3, p 315

Newspaper coverage of debates
House of Commons
Bill Ord: **The Times, 15 Feb 1837; Morning Advertiser, 15 Feb 1837; Morning Chronicle, 15 Feb 1837; Morning Post, 15 Feb 1837; Public Ledger and Daily Advertiser, 15 Feb 1837; Evening Chronicle, 15 Feb 1837; London Courier and Evening Gazette, 15 Feb 1837; London Evening Standard, 15 Feb 1837**
1R: London Courier and Evening, 16 Feb 1837
2R adj: **Morning Post, 13, Apr 1837**; Morning Advertiser, 13 Apr 1837; Public Ledger and Daily Advertiser, 13 Apr 1837

Notes
Petitions – PET46, PET47 and PET52 to PET54
A similar Bill was introduced in the next session (PUBB16) and the one thereafter (PUBB17)

Patents for Inventions Bill 1837

PUBB14	1837
Patents for Inventions Bill 1837 (1 & 2 Vict)	
Bill to amend the Law of Patents, and to secure to Individuals the Benefit of their Inventions	

Table of contents
No details

Journal			
House of Commons			**House of Lords**
Pres: William Mackinnon and Edward Baines			
29 Nov 1837	93 CJ 75	Bill Ord	*Never considered by House of Lords*
13 Dec 1837	93 CJ 197	Ord Disc	

Parliamentary debates	
Bill Ord: Mirror, 29 Nov 1837, Vol 1, p 238	
Ord Disc: Mirror, 13 Dec 1837, Vol 1, p 704	

Parliamentary papers
None

Newspaper coverage of debates
House of Commons
Ord: *Evening Mail, 1 Dec 1837*; The Times, 30 Nov 1837; Morning Advertiser, 30 Nov 1837; Morning Chronicle, 30 Nov 1837; Morning Post, 30 Nov 1837; Public Ledger and Daily Advertiser, 30 Nov 1837; London Courier and Evening Gazette, 30 Nov 1837; London Evening Standard, 30 Nov 1837
Disc: *The Times, 14 Dec 1837*; Morning Advertiser, 14 Dec 1837; Morning Post, 14 Dec 1837; Public Ledger and Daily Advertiser, 14 Dec 1837; London Courier and Evening Gazette, 14 Dec 1837; London Evening Standard, 14 Dec 1837

Patents for Inventions Bill (No 2) 1837

PUBB15	1837
Patents for Inventions Bill (No 2) 1837 (1 & 2 Vict)	
Bill for amending the Law and Practice relating to Letters Patent for Inventions	

Table of contents	
No details	
Journal	
House of Commons	**House of Lords**
13 Dec 1837	93 CJ 197	Bill Ord	*Never considered by House of Lords*

Parliamentary debates	
Bill Ord: Mirror, 13 Dec 1837, Vol 1, p 704	
Parliamentary papers	
None	
Newspaper coverage of debates	
Bill Ord: *The Times, 14 Dec 1837*	

Patterns and Inventions Bill 1838

PUBB16	1838
Patterns and Inventions Bill 1838 (1 & 2 Vict)	
Bill for the better Encouragement of the Arts and Manufactures, and securing to Individuals the Benefit of their Inventions for a limited Time	

Table of contents
Cl 1 Repeal of certain Acts [Designing and Printing of Linens, etc, Act 1789; Designing and Printing of Linens, etc, Act 1789; Linens, etc. Act 1794] 27, 29 & 34 G 3, relative to Linens, &c.
Cl 2 Property in new Design, secured to Inventor or Proprietor for Twelve calendar Months
Cl 3 Persons availing themselves of this Act, to deposit a Fac-simile, Model or Specimens of their Inventions with Commissioners
Cl 4 Commissioners to find some suitable piace for exposing Models, &c. to public Inspection
Cl 5 Persons depositing Models, &c. to pay 10l; Entitled to a Certificate sealed by Commissioners
Cl 6 Persons imitating subject-matter of Licenses, without consent of person having License, or mark "Licensed" on same, to be liable to a penalty of 50l for every offence; Certificate not to exempt persons from liability for infringement of Patents; Subject-matter of License not to be afterwards subject of Letters Patent; not to be capable of second License
Cl 7 Proviso that the persons who were protected by the Acts hereby repealed, shall still be entitled to the benefit of said Acts, if they think fit
Cl 8 Appointment of Board of Commissioners to carry this Act into execution; Commissioners to be appointed during good behaviour
Cl 9 Style of Commissioners, who may sit as a Board to carry this Act into execution, with power to summon and examine Witnesses, and call for production of papers on Oath, or to substitute a Declaration upon Oath
Cl 10 To have a common seal; Rules sealed to be received as Evidence
Cl 11 Commissioners to appoint Officers; Salaries to be regulated by Commissioners of Treasury
Cl 12 Commissioner to take an Oath
Cl 13 Secretary of Commissioners to receive Fees, and also all other sums payable under this Act, and to pay same into Bank of England once a week, to credit of Commissioners; Monies in Bank, subject to orders of Commissioners, or as directed by this Act
Cl 14 Salaries of Officers under this Act
Cl 15 Penalty on Officers taking Fees
Cl 16 Commissioners to make Rules; General Orders not to be valid, except sanctions by Lord Chancellor
Cl 17 Monies standing to account of Commissioners, chargeable first with Compensation, secondly with Salaries of Officers and Expenses, and Surplus to be carried over to the Consolidated Funds
Cl 18 Act may be altered this Session
Cl 19 Act to come into operation as to appointment of Officers on passing, as to other matters 1st of January 1839

Journal			
House of Commons			**House of Lords**
Pres: William Mackinnon and Edward Baines			
13 Dec 1837	93 CJ 197	Bill Ord	*Never considered by House of Lords*
23 Dec 1837	93 CJ 226	1R	
25 Jan 1838	93 CJ 236	2R adj	

(continued)

(continued)

26 Jan 1838	93 CJ 237	Pet Fav [PET57]	
29 Jan 1838	93 CJ 239	Pets Fav [PET58 and PET59]	
2 Feb 1838	93 CJ 242	Pet Fav [PET60]	
7 Feb 1838	93 CJ 253	Pets Fav [PET62 and PET63]	
7 Feb 1838	93 CJ 255	2R adj	
21 Feb 1838	93 CJ 296	Pets Fav [PET64 to PET67]	
23 Feb 1838	93 CJ 300	2R adj	
28 Feb 1838	93 CJ 316	Pet Ag [PET69]	
7 Mar 1838	93 CJ 340	2R adj	
21 Mar 1838	93 CJ 381	2R adj	
28 Mar 1838	93 CJ 410	2R adj	
9 Apr 1838	93 CJ 442	Pet Fav [PET72]	
11 Apr 1838	93 CJ 457	2R adj	
16 May 1838	93 CJ 526	2R adj	
31 May 1838	93 CJ 569	2R adj	
1 Jun 1838	93 CJ 578	2R adj	
12 Jun 1838	93 CJ 601	Pet Fav [PET74 and PET75]	
15 Jun 1838	93 CJ 612	Pet Fav [PET76]	

Parliamentary debates	
Ord: **Mirror, 13 Dec 1837, Vol 1, p 704**	
1R: Mirror, 23 Dec 1837, Vol 2, p 1074	
2R adj: Mirror, 25 Jan 1837, Vol 2, p 1377	
2R adj: Mirror, 7 Feb 1838, Vol 2, p 1631	
2R adj: Mirror, 22 Feb 1838, Vol 3, p 2103	
2R adj: Mirror, 7 Mar 1838, Vol 3, p 2465	
2R adj: Mirror, 21 Mar 1838, Vol 4, p 2912	
2R adj: Mirror, 28 Mar 1838, Vol 4, p 3131	
2R adj: **Mirror, 11 Apr 1838, Vol 5, p 3511–3512**	
2R adj: Mirror, 16 May 1838, Vol 5, p 4081	
2R adj: Mirror, 31 Mar 1838, Vol 6, p 4484	
2R adj: Mirror, 1 Jun 1838, Vol 6, p 4535	

Parliamentary papers
Bill for the better Encouragement of the Arts and Manufactures, and securing to Individuals the Benefit of their Inventions for a limited Time (1837–38 HC Papers 71), Vol 1, p 27

Newspaper coverage of debates
House of Commons
Bill Ord: Morning Advertiser, 14 Dec 1837 (editorial with quotations: 15 Dec 1837); Morning Post, 14 Dec 1837; Public Ledger and Daily Advertiser, 14 Dec 1837; London Courier and Evening Gazette, 14 Dec 1837; London Evening Standard, 14 Dec 1837
2R adj: The Times, 8 Feb 1838; Morning Advertiser, 8 Feb 1838; Morning Post, 8 Feb 1838; London Evening Standard, 8 Feb 1838
2R adj: **Morning Advertiser, 12 Apr 1838**; **Morning Post, 12 Apr 1838**; *The Times, 12 Apr 1838*; *Morning Chronicle, 12 Apr 1838*; *London Evening Standard, 12 Apr 1838*; London Courier and Evening Gazette, 12 Apr 1838
Pet: Morning Post, 13 Jun 1838; London Evening Standard, 13 Jun 1838
Pet: Morning Chronicle, 16 Jun 1838; Morning Post, 16 Jun 1838

Notes
Petitions – PET57 to PET60; PET62 to PET67; PET69; PET72; PET74 to PET76
A similar Bill was introduced in the next session (PUBB17)

Patterns and Inventions Bill 1839

PUBB17	1839
Patterns and Inventions Bill 1839 (2 & 3 Vict)	
Bill for better encouragement of arts and manufactures, and securing to individuals the benefit of their inventions for a limited time	

Table of contents

Cl 1 Repeal of certain Acts [Designing and Printing of Linens, etc, Act 1789; Designing and Printing of Linens, etc, Act 1789; Linens, etc. Act 1794] 27, 29 & 34 G 3, relative to Linens, &c.

Cl 2 Property in new Design, secured to Inventor or Proprietor for Twelve calendar Months

Cl 3 Persons availing themselves of this Act, to deposit a Fac-simile, Model or Specimen of their Inventions with Commissioners

Cl 4 Commissioners to find some suitable place for exposing Models, &c. to public Inspection

Cl 5 Persons deposing Models, &c. to pay 10l; Entitled to a Certificate sealed by Commissioners

Cl 6 Persons imitating subject-matter of License, without consent of Person having license, or mark "Licensed" on same, to be liable to a Penalty of 50l for every Offence; Certificate not to exempt Persons from liability for infringement of Patents; Subject-matter of License not to be afterwards subject of Letters Patent; not to be capable of a second License

Cl 7 Proviso that the persons who were protected by the Acts hereby repealed, shall still be entitled to the benefit of the said Acts, if they think fit

Cl 8 Appointment of Board of Commissioners to carry this Act into execution; Commissioner to be appointed during good behaviour

Cl 9 Style of Commissioners, who may sit as a Board to carry this Act into execution, with power to summon and examine Witnesses, and all for production of papers on Oath, or to substitute a Declaration upon Oath

Cl 10 To have a common seal; Rules sealed, to be received as Evidence

Cl 11 Commissioners to appoint Officers; Salaries to be regulation by Commissioners of Treasury

Cl 12 Commissioner to take an Oath

Cl 13 Secretary of Commissioners to receive Fees, and also all other sums payable under this Act, and to pay same into Bank of England once a week, to credit of Commissioners; Monies in Bank, subject to orders of Commissioners, or as directed by this Act

Cl 14 Salaries of Officers under this Act

Cl 15 Penalty on Officers taking Fees

Cl 16 Commissioners to Make Rules; General Orders not to be valid, except sanctioned by Lord Chancellor

Cl 17 Monies standing to account of Commissioners, chargeable first with Compensation, secondly with Salaries of Officers and Expenses, and Surplus to be carried over to the Consolidated Fund

Cl 18 Act may be altered this Session

Cl 19 Act to come into operation as to appointment of Officers on passing, as to other matters 1st of January [1840]

Journal	
House of Commons	**House of Lords**
Pres: William Mackinnon and Edward Baines	

			House of Lords
19 Feb 1839	94 CJ 39	Bill Ord	*Never considered by House of Lords*
19 Feb 1839	94 CJ 39	1R	
27 Feb 1839	94 CJ 64	2R adj	
7 Mar 1839	94 CJ 89	2R adj	
20 Mar 1839	94 CJ 135	2R adj	
11 Apr 1839	94 CJ 173	2R adj	
24 Apr 1839	94 CJ 218	2R adj	
7 May 1839	94 CJ 257	2R adj	
15 May 1839	94 CJ 272	2R adj	
30 May 1839	94 CJ 284	2R adj	
5 Jun 1839	94 CJ 310	2R adj	
19 Jun 1839	94 CJ 363	2R adj	
27 Jun 1839	94 CJ 386	2R adj	
3 Jul 1839	94 CJ 405	2R adj	
11 Jul 1839	94 CJ 427	2R adj 3m	

Parliamentary debates	

Ord/1R: Mirror, 19 Feb 1839, Vol 1, p 411

Obs: **Mirror, 27 Feb 1839, Vol 1, p 562–563**

2R adj: Mirror, 27 Feb 1839, Vol 1, p 577

2R adj: Mirror, 7 Mar 1839, Vol 1, p 914

2R adj: Mirror, 20 Mar 1839, Vol 2, p 1420

2R adj: Mirror, 11 Apr 1839, Vol 2, p 1662

2R adj: Mirror, 24 Apr 1839, Vol 3, p 2052

2R adj: Mirror, 7 May 1839, Vol 3, p 2392

2R adj: Mirror, 15 May 1839, Vol 3, p 2451

2R adj: Mirror, 30 May 1839, Vol 3, p 2525

(continued)

(continued)

2R adj: Mirror, 5 Jun 1839, Vol 4, p 2723	
2R adj: Mirror, 19 Jun 1839, Vol 4, p 3131	
2R adj: Mirror, 27 Jun 1839, Vol 4, p 3393	
2R adj: Mirror, 3 Jul 1839, Vol 5, p 3578	
2R adj 3m: Mirror, 11 Jul 1839, Vol 5, p 3812	
Parliamentary papers	
Bill for the better Encouragement of the Arts and Manufactures, and securing to Individuals the Benefit of their Inventions for a limited Time (1839 HC Papers 31), Vol 4, p 363	
Newspaper coverage of debates	
House of Commons	
Ord/1R: London Courier and Evening Gazette, 20 Feb 1839	
Obs: **The Times, 28 Feb 1839; Morning Advertiser, 28 Feb 1839; Morning Chronicle, 28 Feb 1839; London Evening Standard, 28 Feb 1839**	

Letters Patent Act Amendment Bill 1843

PUBB18	1843		
Letters Patent Act Amendment Bill 1843 (6 & 7 Vict)			
Bill to amend an Act passed in the Sixth Year of the Reign of His late Majesty King William the Fourth, intuled An Act to amend the Law touching Letters Patent for Inventions			
Table of contents			
s 1 Objections to Patents may be made and proved other than those which Notice shall have been given			
Journal			
House of Commons	**House of Lords**		
	Pres: Lord Brougham and Vaux		
Never considered by House of Commons	1 Jun 1843	75 LJ 362	Bill Ord/1R
Parliamentary debates			
	1R: HL Deb, 1 Jun 1843, Vol 69(3rd), col 1221		
Parliamentary papers			
Bill to amend an Act passed in the Sixth Year of the Reign of His late Majesty King William the Fourth, intuled An Act to amend the Law touching Letters Patent for Inventions (1843 HL Papers 130), Vol 3, p 7			
Newspaper coverage of debates			
None			

Letters Patent Act Amendment Bill 1844

PUBB19	1844		
Letters Patent Act Amendment Bill 1844 (7 & 8 Vict)			
Bill for further amending the Law touching Patents for Inventions			
Table of contents			
s 1 On Petition to either House of Parliament Her Majesty may grant an Extension of Patent Term in certain cases [beyond 7 years] s 2 Her Majesty may grant Extension for lesser Term than that prayed s 3 Act may be repealed, &c.			
Journal			
House of Commons	**House of Lords**		
	Pres: Lord Brougham and Vaux		
Never considered by House of Commons	19 Feb 1844	76 LJ 34	Bill Ord/1R

Parliamentary debates	
	1R: HL Deb, 19 Feb 1844, Vol 72(3rd), col 1097
Parliamentary papers	
Bill for further amending the Law touching Patents for Inventions (1844 HL Papers 17), Vol 4, p 565	
Newspaper coverage of debates	
House of Lords	
1R: **The Times, 20 Feb 1844; Morning Advertiser, 20 Feb 1844; Morning Chronicle, 20 Feb 1844; Morning Post, 20 Feb 1844; London Evening Standard, 20 Feb 1844**	
Notes	
The Bill did not progress as it was superseded by the Judicial Committee Act 1844 (which had similar, but broader, subject matter): see PUBA44	

Patent Law Amendment Bill 1851

PUBB20	1851
	Patent Law Amendment Bill 1851 (14 & 15 Vict)
	Bill further to amend the Law touching Letters Patent for Inventions

Table of contents
Cl 1 Letters Patent to be issued as after mentioned
Cl 2 Certain Persons constituted Commissioners, of whom Three may act
Cl 3 Commissioners to make Rules and Orders, and appoint Clerks, &c.
Cl 4 The Date of Delivery of the Petition to be recorded, and Letters Patent may be sealed and bear Date as such Day
Cl 5 Petition for Letters Patent to be referred and reported upon
Cl 6 On Report, Commissioners to cause a Warrant for Sign Manual to be made
Cl 7 On Receipt of Warrant, Lord Chancellor to issue Letters Patent of like Force as heretofore
Cl 8 Letters Patent to be made subject to Avoidance on Non-fulfilment of certain Conditions
Cl 9 Specifications and Drawings to be preserved
Cl 10 Enrolments, &c. may be removed to Office directed by Commissioners; Seal of Office may be varied
Cl 11 Copies of Specifications to be open to Inspection
Cl 12 Specifications, &c. to be printed and published, and printed Copies to be Evidence
Cl 13 Patentees may, with Leave of Commissioners, enter Disclaimers and Memoranda of Alterations, which shall be deemed Part of Letters Patent
Cl 14 Disclaimers, &c. entered and certified, to be valid notwithstanding Want of Concurrence of Co-Patentees
Cl 15 Certain Provisions of [Letters Patent for Inventions Act 1835] 5 & 6 W 4 c. 83, [Patents Act 1839] 2 & 3 Vict. c. 67, and [Judicial Committee Act 1844] 7 & 8 Vict. c. 69. to apply to Letters Patent granted under this Act
Cl 16 In Actions for Infringement of Letters Patent, Particulars to be delivered in, and no Evidence allowed not mentioned therein
Cl 17 Particulars to be regarded in Taxation of Costs
Cl 18 Payment and Stamp Duties to be as in Schedule
Cl 19 Providing for Compensation of Persons affected by this Act
Cl 20 Interpretation of Terms
Cl 21 Short Title
Cl 22 Commencement of Act

Journal			
House of Commons	**House of Lords**		
	Pres: Lord Brougham and Vaux		
Never considered by House of Commons	24 Mar 1851	83 LJ 78	1R
	4 Apr 1851	83 LJ 114	Pet to ref to SC [PET175]
	11 Apr 1851	83 LJ 130	2R/C'tted SC
	14 Apr 1851	83 LJ 137	Evid Print
	1 May 1851	83 LJ 142	Com adj
	27 May 1851	83 LJ 217	MP Sum
	30 May 1851	83 LJ 223	Pet to Amd [PET178]
	16 Jun 1851	83 LJ 253	Pet to Amd [PET179]
	16 Jun 1851	83 LJ 253	MP Sum
	23 Jun 1851	83 LJ 274	SC Rep/Bill Not to Proc
	30 Jun 1851	83 LJ 299	HC Req SC Rep
	1 Jul 1851	83 LJ 304	Rep Print

(continued)

(continued)

Parliamentary debates	
	1R: HL Deb, 24 Mar 1851, Vol 115(3rd), col 422
	2R: HL Deb, 11 Apr 1851, Vol 116(3rd), col 1
Parliamentary papers	
Bill to further to amend the Law touching Letters Patent for Inventions (1851 HL Papers 52), Vol 5, p 359	
Report of Select Committee of House of Lords to consider Bills for Amendment of Law touching Letters Patent for Inventions (1851 HL Papers 77), Vol 18, p 35; (1851 HC Papers 486), Vol 18, p 233	
Newspaper coverage of debates	
2R: The Times, 12 Apr 1851; Morning Advertiser, 12 Apr 1851; Morning Chronicle, 12 Apr 1851; Morning Post, 12 Apr 1851; London Daily News, 12 Apr 1851; London Evening Standard, 12 Apr 1851	
Notes	
This Bill, along with PUBB21 and PUBB22, were considered by the same Select Committee *Petitions* – PET175, PET178 to PET179	

Patent Law Amendment (No 2) Bill 1851

PUBB21	1851
Patent Law Amendment (No 2) Bill 1851 (14 & 15 Vict)	
Bill for the further Amendment of the Law touching Letters Patent for Inventions	
Table of contents	

Cl 1 Constitution of Commissioners, of whom Three may act, the Lord Chancellor or Master of the Rolls being One
Cl 2 Commissioner's may make Rules; Rules to be laid before Parliament
Cl 3 Commissioners may appoint Clerks, &c.
Cl 4 A Statement describing Nature of the Inventions to be left with the Petition for Grant of Letters Patent
Cl 5 Letters Patent may be dated as the Day of Presenting Petition, or of subsequent Day
Cl 6 Report of Attorney or Solicitor General to be accompanied by Statement of Nature of Inventions, and, if necessary by an amended Statement
Cl 7 No Letters Patent to be granted unless sued out within Three Months after Report on Petition
Cl 8 A Warrant under Royal Sign Manual, countersigned by Secretary of State, to be sufficient Authority for sealing Letters Patent
Cl 9 Letters Patent so issued may extend to the whole of the United Kingdom
Cl 10 Letters Patent to be made subject to Avoidance on Non-fulfilment of certain Conditions
Cl 11 Letters Patent for Scotland or Ireland only may be issued as heretofore
C 12 The Use of Publication abroad, &c. of any Inventions to have the like Effect on Letters Patent as Use or Publication in the United Kingdom
Cl 13 On Deposit or Filing of Provisional Specification, Inventor to be entitled for a limited Time to the like Privileges as under Letters Patent
Cl 14 Certain Provisions of [Letters Patent for Inventions Act 1836] 5 & 6 W 4. c. 83, [Patents Act 1839] 2 & 3 Vict. c. 67., and [Judicial Committee Act 1844] 7 & 8 Vict. c. 69. to apply to Letters Patent granted under this Act
Cl 15 Master of the Rolls may cause Indices to existing Specification &c. to be prepared, and also Copies of such Specifications to be made
Cl 16 Enrolments, &c. may be removed to any Office or Place appointed by Commissioners
Cl 17 Commissioners to prove a Seal for such Office or Place of Deposit; and Documents sealed therewith to be received in Evidence without Production of the Original
Cl 18 Payments and Stamp Duties on account of Letters Patent, &c. to be according to the Schedule of this Act
Cl 19 Compensation for Fees and Enrolments, &c. abolished or interfered with by this Act
Cl 20 Interpretation of Terms
Cl 21 Short Title of Act
Cl 22 Commencement of Act
Schedule

Journal	
House of Commons	**House of Lords**
	Pres: Earl Granville (VP BoT)

Never considered by House of Commons	10 Apr 1851	83 LJ 125	1R
	11 Apr 1851	83 LJ 130	2R/C'tted SC
	14 Apr 1851	83 LJ 137	Ev Pr
	1 May 1851	83 LJ 142	C'tee adj
	27 May 1851	83 LJ 217	MP Sum
	30 May 1851	83 LJ 223	Pet to Amd [PET178]
	16 Jun 1851	83 LJ 253	Pet to Amd [PET179]
	16 Jun 1851	83 LJ 253	MP Sum
	23 Jun 1851	83 LJ 274	SC Rep/Bill Not to Proc
	27 Jun 1851	83 LJ 294	Lack of oath of witness
	30 Jun 1851	83 LJ 299	HC Req SC Rep
	1 Jul 1851	83 LJ 304	Rep Pr

Parliamentary debates
1R: HL Deb, 10 Apr 1851, Vol 115(3rd), col 1349
2R: HL Deb, 11 Apr 1851, Vol 116(3rd), col 1

Parliamentary papers
Bill for the further Amendment of the Law touching Letters Patent for Inventions (1851 HL Papers 69), Vol 5, p 371
Report of Select Committee of House of Lords to consider Bills for Amendment of Law touching Letters Patent for Inventions (1851 HL Papers 77), Vol 18, p 35; (1851 HC Papers 486), Vol 18, p 233

Newspaper coverage of debates
House of Lords
Pat Law delay: **Morning Chronicle, 5 Apr 1851**; **London Daily News, 5 Apr 1851**
1R: Morning Advertiser, 11 Apr 1851
2R: The Times, 12 Apr 1851; Morning Advertiser, 12 Apr 1851; Morning Chronicle, 12 Apr 1851; Morning Post, 12 Apr 1851; London Daily News, 12 Apr 1851; London Evening Standard, 12 Apr 1851

Notes
This Bill, along with PUBB20 and PUBB22, were considered by the same Select Committee
Petitions – PET178 and PET179

Patent Law Amendment (No 3) Bill 1851

PUBB22	1851
Patent Law Amendment (No 3) Bill 1851 (HL)/Patent Law Amendment Bill (HC) (14 & 15 Vict)	
Bill for the further amendment of the law touching Letters Patent for Inventions	
Table of contents (1851 HL Papers 316)	

Cl 1 Her Majesty empowered to grant Letters Patent as after mentioned
Cl 2 Constitution of Commissioners, of whom Three may act, the Lord Chancellor or Master of the Rolls being One
Cl 3 Seal of Commissioners
Cl 4 Commissioners to appoint Examiners, make Rules and Regulations, and report annually to Parliament
Cl 5 Treasury to provide Officers
Cl 6 Treasury to appoint Officers, except such as the Commissioners are authorized to appoint
Cl 7 Petition and Declaration to be accompanied with a Provisional Specification
Cl 8 Every Application to be referred to One of the Law Officers
Cl 9 Provisional Protection for limited Period from the Day of presenting Petition
Cl 10 Inventor may deposit, in lieu of a Provisional Specification, a complete Specification, such Deposit to confer for a limited Time the like Rights as Letters Patent
Cl 11 Letters Patent granted to the First Inventor not to be invalidated by Protection obtained in Fraud
Cl 12 Commissioners to advertise Protection
Cl 13 Application for Letters Patent to be advertised, and Examiner to report on Inventions to Law Officer
Cl 14 Law Officer to refer Specification and Objections to an Examiner for his Report
Cl 15 Appeal to Law Officer; Power to give Costs
Cl 16 Warrant of Law Officer for sealing of Patent
Cl 17 Letters Patent to be made subject to Avoidance on Non-fulfilment of certain Conditions
Cl 18 Letters Patent for the whole of the United Kingdom, the Channel Islands, and the Isle of Man to be issued under the Seal of the Commissioners

(continued)

(continued)

Cl 19 Letters Patent not to be issued after Three Months from Date of Warrant
Cl 20 Nor after Expiration of Protection given by this Act
Cl 21 If Letters Patent be destroyed or lost, another Letters Patent may be issued
Cl 22 Letters Patent may be dated as of the Day of the Application
Cl 23 Letters Patent where ante-dated to be of the same Validity as if sealed on the Day of the Date
Cl 24 Existing Letters Patent extended to Scotland or Ireland
Cl 25 The Use of Inventions abroad to have the like Effect on Letters Patent as Use or Publication in United Kingdom, &c.
Cl 26 Specifications to be required to be filed in the Office of the Commissioners
Cl 27 Specifications and Drawings to be filed; extra Copies of Drawings to be left
Cl 28 Copies of Specification to be open to Inspection
Cl 29 Specifications and other Documents to be printed and published
Cl 30 Enrolments, &c. may be removed to the Office of the Commissioners
Cl 31 Commissioners to cause Indices to old Specifications, &c. to be made, printed and published
Cl 32 Printed Copies to be Evidence
Cl 33 Register of Patents to be kept
Cl 34 Register of Proprietors to be kept
Cl 35 Making false Entry in Register of Proprietors a Misdemeanour
Cl 36 Entries may be expunged and varied
Cl 37 Provisions of [Letters Patent for Inventions Act 1835] 5 & 6 W 4, c 83 [Judicial Committee Act 1844] 7 & 8 Vict. c. 69 as to Disclaimers and Memoranda of Alterations, to apply to Patents under this Act
Cl 38 Provisions of [Letters Patent for Inventions Act 1835] 5 & 6 W 4. c. 83, [Patents Act 1839] 2 & 3 Vict. c. 67, and [Judicial Committee Act 1844] 7 & 8 Vict. c. 69 as to Confirmation and Prolongation; to apply to Patents under this Act
Cl 39 In Actions for Infringements, Particulars of the Breaches, and of Grounds of Invalidity, to be delivered
Cl 40 Particulars to be expressed in Taxation for Costs
Cl 41 Courts of Common Law may grant Injunction in case of Infringement
Cl 42 Payments and Stamp Duties on Letters Patent to be as in Schedule
Cl 43 Duties to be under Management of Commissioners of Inland Revenue
Cl 44 All Monies received to be paid into Consolidated Fund
Cl 45 Nothing in this Act to prevent Payment of Fees to Law Officers in Cases of Appeals
Cl 46 Fees and Salaries of Officers
Cl 47 Sums for defraying Salaries and Expenses under this Act to be paid out of Monies to be provided by Parliament
Cl 48 Accounts to be kept and audited
Cl 49 Compensation to Persons affected by this Act
Cl 50 Account of Salaries, &c. to be laid before Parliament
Cl 51 Act not to extend to Letters Patent on Applications before passing of this Act
Cl 52 Letters Patent for Scotland or Ireland
Cl 53 Forms in Schedule may be used
Cl 54 Interpretation of Terms
Cl 55 Short Title of Act
First Schedule Fees to be Paid
Second Schedule Stamp Duties to be Paid
Third Schedule Forms

Clauses originally included in Bill, but not in version returned from Commons

Cl A Specification may be left with Petition and Declaration
Cl B Invention may be used without Prejudice to subsequent Letters Patent
Cl C Three Transcripts of Letters Patent to be issued for passing under the respective Seals
Cl D Use of Inventions abroad to have the like Effect on Letters Patent as Use or Publication in the United Kingdom
Cl E Indices to be made; Specification to be printed and published; gratuitous Copies of Specifications to Libraries and Inventors
Cl F Period of provisional Protection may be extended

Journal					
House of Commons			**House of Lords**		
Rep: Charles Shaw-Lefevre (Speaker)			Pres: Earl Granville (VP BoT) Rep: Lord Redesdale (Ld Ch)		
4 Jul 1851	106 CJ 335	Brought HL	23 Jun 1851	83 LJ 275	1R
8 Jul 1851	106 CJ 343	1R	24 Jun 1851	83 LJ 281	Pet in Fav [PET181]
9 Jul 1851	106 CJ 346	2R adj	26 Jun 1851	83 LJ 283	2R/C'tted CWH
15 Jul 1851	106 CJ 363	2R adj	1 Jul 1851	83 LJ 307	CWH/Rep w/o Amds
19 Jul 1851	106 CJ 376	2R adj	3 Jul 1851	83 LJ 323	3R
22 Jul 1851	106 CJ 385	2R adj	7 Aug 1851	83 LJ 507	HC pass with Amds
25 Jul 1851	106 CJ 397	**Stamp Duties Res**	7 Aug 1851	83 LJ 508	HC Amds Cons/Adj 3m

25 Jul 1851	106 CJ 401	2R/C'tted				
26 Jul 1851	106 CJ 402	**Cons Stamp Duty Res**				
26 Jul 1851	106 CJ 404	**Res Stamp Duty**				
29 Jul 1851	106 CJ 414	Rep with Amds/Re-C'tted				
1 Aug 1851	106 CJ 423	CWH adj				
4 Aug 1851	106 CJ 429	CWH adj		⸱		
4 Aug 1851	106 CJ 429	**CWH**				
5 Aug 1851	106 CJ 433	**CWH**				
6 Aug 1851	106 CJ 436	**CWH/Rep with Amds**				
7 Aug 1851	106 CJ 443	Cons/3R				

Parliamentary debates

1R: HC Deb, 7 Jul 1851, Vol 118(3rd), col 286	1R: HL Deb, 23 Jun 1851, Vol 117(3rd), col 1069
2R: HC Deb, 25 Jul 1851, Vol 118(3rd), col 1534–1548	2R: HL Deb, 26 Jun 1851, Vol 117(3rd), col 1245
CWH: HC Deb, 4 Aug 1851, Vol 118(3rd), col 1848–1856	Rep: HL Deb, 1 Jul 1851, Vol 118(3rd), col 1 and 5–21
CWH: HC Deb, 5 Aug 1851, Vol 118(3rd), col 1895–1903	3R: HL Deb, 3 Jul 1851, Vol 118(3rd), col 124
CWH: HC Deb, 6 Aug 1851, Vol 118(3rd), col 1912–1926	HC pass with Amds: HL Deb, 7 Aug 1851, Vol 118(3rd), col 1933–1934
3R: HC Deb, 7 Aug 1851, Vol 118(3rd), col 1937–1939	

Parliamentary papers

Bill for the further amendment of the law touching letters patent for inventions (1851 HL Papers 167), Vol 5, p 383

Bill for the further amendment of the law touching letters patent for inventions (as amended on Report) (1851 HL Papers 192), Vol 5, p 411

Bill for the further amendment of the law touching letters patent for inventions (1851 HC Papers 502), Vol 5, p 63

Bill for the further amendment of the law touching letters patent for inventions (as amended in Committee) (1851 HC Papers 612), Vol 5, p 91

Bill for the further amendment of the law touching letters patent for inventions (marked to show amendments of House of Commons) (1851 HL Papers 316), Vol 5, p 439

Report of Select Committee of House of Lords to consider Bills for Amendment of Law touching Letters Patent for Inventions (1851 HL Papers 77), Vol 18, p 35; (1851 HC Papers 486), Vol 18, p 233

Newspaper coverage of debates

House of Lords

Pet: Morning Advertiser, 25 Jun 1851; Morning Chronicle, 25 Jun 1851; Morning Post, 25 Jun 1851; Evening Mail, 25 Jun 1851; London Daily News, 25 Jun 1851; London Evening Standard, 25 Jun 1851

2R: Morning Chronicle, 27 Jun 1851; Morning Post, 27 Jun 1851; London Daily News, 27 Jun 1851; London Evening Standard, 27 Jun 1851

CWH: **The Times, 2 Jul 1851**; **Morning Advertiser, 2 Jul 1851**; **Morning Chronicle, 2 Jul 1851**; **Morning Post, 2 Jul 1851**; **Evening Mail, 2 Jul 1851**; **London Daily News, 2 Jul 1851**; *London Evening Standard, 2 Jul 1851*

3R: The Times, 4 Jul 1851; Morning Advertiser, 4 Jul 1851; Morning Chronicle, 4 Jul 1851; Morning Post, 4 Jul 1851; Evening Mail 4 Jul 1851; London Daily News, 4 Jul 1851; London Evening Standard, 4 Jul 1851

HC Amds: **Morning Advertiser, 8 Aug 1851**; **Morning Chronicle, 8 Aug 1851**; **Morning Post, 8 Aug 1851**; **London Daily News, 8 Aug 1851**; **London Evening Standard, 8 Aug 1851**

House of Commons

2R: **The Times, 26 Jul 1851**; **Morning Advertiser, 26 Jul 1851**; **Morning Chronicle, 26 Jul 1851**; **Morning Post, 26 Jul 1851**; **Evening Mail, 28 Jul 1851**; **London Daily News, 26 Jul 1851**; **London Evening Standard, 26 Jul 1851**

Res: **Morning Chronicle, 28 Jul 1851**; *The Times, 28 Jul 1851*; Morning Post, 28 Jul 1851; Evening Mail, 28 Jul 1851; London Daily News, 28 Jul 1851; London Evening Standard, 28 Jul 1851

CWH: **The Times, 31 Jul 1851**; **Morning Advertiser, 31 Jul 1851**; **Morning Chronicle, 31 Jul 1851**; **Morning Post, 31 Jul 1851**; **London Daily News, 31 Jul 1851**

CWH adj: The Times, 1 Aug 1851; Morning Chronicle, 1 Aug 1851; Morning Post, 1 Aug 1851; Evening Mail, 1 Aug 1851; London Daily News, 1 Aug 1851

CWH adj: The Times, 2 Aug 1851; Morning Advertiser, 2 Aug 1851

CWH: **The Times, 5 Aug 1851**; **Morning Advertiser, 5 Aug 1851**; **Morning Chronicle, 5 Aug 1851**; **Morning Post, 5 Aug 1851**; **Evening Mail, 5 Aug 1851**; **London Daily News, 5 Aug 1851**; **London Evening Standard, 5 Aug 1851**

CWH: **The Times, 6 Aug 1851**; **Morning Advertiser, 6 Aug 1851**; **Morning Chronicle, 6 Aug 1851**; **Morning Post, 6 Aug 1851**; **London Daily News, 6 Aug 1851**; **London Evening Standard, 6 Aug 1851**

(continued)

(continued)

CWH: **Morning Advertiser, 7 Aug 1851; Morning Chronicle, 7 Aug 1851; Morning Post, 7 Aug 1851; Evening Mail, 8 Aug 1851; London Daily News, 7 Aug 1851; London Evening Standard, 7 Aug 1851;** The Times, 7 Aug 1851
3R: **The Times, 8 Aug 1851; Morning Advertiser, 8 Aug 1851; Morning Chronicle, 8 Aug 1851; Morning Post, 8 Aug 1851; London Daily News, 8 Aug 1851;** London Evening Standard. 8 Aug 1851

Notes
Petitions – PET180, PET181 and PET185 to PET196
This Bill, along with PUBB20 and PUBB21, was considered by the same Select Committee

Patent Law Amendment Bill 1852

PUBB23	1852
Patent Law Amendment Bill 1852 (16 & 17 Vict.)	
Bill for the further Amendment of the Law touching Letters Patent for Inventions	
Table of contents	

Cl 1 Her Majesty empowered to grant Letters Patent as after mentioned
Cl 2 Constitution of Commissioners, of whom Three may act, the Lord Chancellor or Master of the Rolls being One
Cl 3 Seal of Commissioners
Cl 4 Commissioners to appoint Examiners, make Rules and Regulations, and report annually to Parliament
Cl 5 Treasury to provide Officers
Cl 6 Commissioners, with the Consent of the Treasury, to appoint Officers, except such as the Commissioners are authorized to appoint
Cl 7 Petition and Declaration to be accompanied with a Provisional Specification
Cl 8 Provisional Protection for limited Period from the Day of presenting Petition
Cl 9 Inventor provisionally registered under the Protection of Inventions Act, 1851, to be protected under this Act
Cl 10 Commissioners to advertise Protection, and Objections to be delivered
Cl 11 Appeal to Law Officer against provisional Protection
Cl 12 Letters Patent grant to the First Inventor and to be invalidated by Protection obtained in Fraud
Cl 13 Examiners to report on Inventions
Cl 14 Appeal to Law Officer against Report
Cl 15 Power of Law Officer to give Costs
Cl 16 Warrant of Law Officer for sealing of Patent
Cl 17 Appeal to Lord Chancellor against Decision of Law Officer
Cl 18 Letters Patent to be made subject to Avoidance on Non-fulfilment of certain Conditions
Cl 19 Letters Patent for the whole of the United Kingdom, the Channel Islands, and the Isle of Man to be issued under the Great Seal
Cl 20 Her Majesty empowered by Order in Council to authorise Letters Patent to be granted for the Colonies
Cl 21 Letters Patent not to be issued unless granted and Application made to seal the Patent within Six months from the Application
Cl 22 Letters Patent for inventions registered under the Protection of Inventions Act not to be issued after the Expiration of provisional Protection
Cl 23 If Letters Patent be destroyed or lost, other Letters Patent may be issued
Cl 24 Letters Patent may be dated as of the Day of the Application
Cl 25 Letters Patent for Inventions provisionally registered may be dated of any Day during such provisional Protection
Cl 26 Letters Patent where ante-dated to be of the same Validity as if sealed on the Day of the Date
Cl 27 Existing Letters Patent extended to England, Scotland or Ireland
Cl 28 Specifications to be required to be filed in the Office of the Commissioners
Cl 29 Specifications and Drawings to be filed; extra Copies of Drawings to be left
Cl 30 Copies of Specification and Indexes to be open to Inspection
Cl 31 Specifications and other Documents to be printed and published
Cl 32 Enrolments, &c. may be removed to the Office of the Commissioners
Cl 33 Commissioners to cause Indices to old Specifications, &c. to be made, printed and published
Cl 34 Printed Copies to be Evidence
Cl 35 Register of Patents to be kept
Cl 36 Register of Proprietors to be kept
Cl 37 Making false Entry in Register of Proprietors a Misdemeanour
Cl 38 Entries may be expunged and varied
Cl 39 Provisions of [Letters Patent for Inventions Act 1835] 5 & 6 W 4, c 83 [Judicial Committee Act 1844], 7 & 8 Vict. c 69 as to Disclaimers and Memoranda of Alterations, to apply to Patents under this Act

Cl 40 Provisions of [Letters Patent for Inventions Act 1835] 5 & 6 W 4, c 83 [Patents Act 1839], 2 & 3 Vict. c 67 [Judicial Committee Act 1844], 7 & 8 Vict. c 69 as to Confirmation and Prolongation; to apply to Patents under this Act
Cl 41 In Actions for Infringements, Particulars of the Breaches, and of Grounds of Invalidity, to be delivered
Cl 42 Courts of Common Law may grant Injunction in case of Infringement
Cl 43 Particulars to be regarded in Taxation for Costs
Cl 44 Writs of Scire facias to repeal Patent made under Warrant
Cl 45 Payments and Stamp Duties on Letters Patent to be as in Schedule
Cl 46 Duties to be under Management of Commissioners of Inland Revenue
Cl 47 All Monies received to be paid into Consolidated Fund
Cl 48 Nothing in this Act to prevent Payment of Fees to Law Officers in Cases of Appeals
Cl 49 Fees and Salaries of Officers
Cl 50 Sums for defraying Salaries and Expenses under this Act to be paid out of Monies to be provided by Parliament
Cl 51 Accounts to be kept and audited
Cl 52 Compensation to Persons affected by this Act
Cl 53 Account of Salaries, &c. to be laid before Parliament
Cl 54 Act not to extend to Letters Patent on Applications before passing of this Act
Cl 55 Letters Patent for England, Scotland or Ireland
Cl 56 Forms in Schedule may be used
Cl 57 Interpretation of Terms
Cl 58 Short Title of Act
Schedule

Journal

House of Commons	House of Lords		
	Pres: Lord Brougham and Vaux		
Never considered by House of Commons	13 Feb 1852	84 LJ 22	1R
	19 Mar 1852	84 LJ 62	Ref to SC
	22 Mar 1852	84 LJ 63	Order ref to SC Disc
	22 Mar 1852	84 LJ 63	2R/Ref to SC
	30 Mar 1852	84 LJ 80	Rep SC/Not expedient to Proc

Parliamentary debates

1R: HL Deb, 13 Feb 1852, Vol 119(3rd), col 476

2R: HL Deb, 22 Mar 1852, Vol 119(3rd), col 1404

Parliamentary papers

Bill for the further Amendment of the Law touching Letters Patent for Inventions (1852 HL Papers 23), Vol 4, p 107

Newspaper coverage of debates

House of Commons

1R: **Morning Chronicle, 14 Feb 1852**; **Morning Post, 14 Feb 1852**; **London Daily News, 14 Feb 1852**; *The Times, 14 Feb 1852*; London Evening Standard, 14 Feb 1852

Comment: **The Times, 17 Feb 1852**; **Morning Advertiser, 17 Feb 1852**; **Morning Post, 17 Feb 1852**; **London Daily News, 17 Feb 1852**; *Morning Chronicle, 17 Feb 1852*

Protection of Inventions Bill 1853

PUBB24	1853
Protection of Inventions Bill 1853 (16 & 17 Vict)	
Bill to extend the provisions of the Designs Act 1850, and to give Protection from Piracy to Persons exhibiting new Inventions at the Great Industrial Exhibition of 1853 [Designs Act Extension]	

Table of contents (HL Bill brought HC)

s 1 New Inventions may be exhibited without Prejudice to Letters Patent to be thereafter granted. Inventions to be provisionally registered, and not to be used before granting of Letter Patent
s 2 A public Trial of agricultural or horticultural Implements, under the Direction of the Committee of Exhibition of 1853, not to prejudice Letters Patent
s 3 Certificate of Inventions to be granted for Provisional Registration and to be registered
s 6 Provisional Registration to confer the same Benefits as under the Designs Act 1850
s 7 Letters Patent thereafter granted to be valid as if Inventions were not registered or exhibited

(continued)

(continued)

s 8 Proprietors of new Designs exhibited to be entitled to Benefits of Designs Act, although such Designs have been previously published elsewhere than in the United Kingdom
s 9 The Designs Act 1850, and this Act to be construed as One
s 10 Short Title of Act

Journal					
House of Commons			**House of Lords**		
Pres: Lord Naas and Joseph Napier					
14 Dec 1852	108 CJ 191	Bill Ord/1R	10 Mar 1853	85 LJ 119	Brought HC/1R
20 Dec 1852	108 CJ 205	2R adj	11 Mar 1853	85 LJ 122	2R day app
16 Feb 1853	108 CJ 250	2R/C'tted CWH	14 Mar 1853	85 LJ 123	2R adj
17 Feb 1853	108 CJ 255	CWH/Rep with Amds	15 Mar 1853	85 LJ 127	2R adj sine die
19 Feb 1853	108 CJ 260	Cons adj			
25 Feb 1853	108 CJ 289	Cons adj			
28 Feb 1853	108 CJ 296	Cons adj			
8 Mar 1853	108 CJ 316	Cons adj			
8 Mar 1853	108 CJ 319	3R			

Parliamentary debates	
1R: HC Deb, 13 Dec 1852, Vol 123(3rd), col 1315	1R: HL Deb, 10 Mar 1853, Vol 124(3rd), col 1362
2R: HC Deb, 16 Feb 1853, Vol 124(3rd), col 153	
3R: HC Deb, 8 Mar 1853, Vol 124(3rd), col 1290	

Parliamentary papers
Bill to extend the provisions of the Designs Act, 1850, and to give Protection from Piracy to Persons exhibiting new Inventions in Great Industrial Exhibition of 1853 (1852–53 HC Papers 71), Vol 3, p 5
Bill to extend the provisions of the Designs Act 1850, and to give Protection from Piracy to Persons exhibiting new Inventions at the Great Industrial Exhibition of 1853 (1852–53 HL Papers 89), Vol 4, p 581

Newspaper coverage of debates

House of Commons

1R: The Times, 14 Dec 1852; Morning Chronicle, 14 Dec 1852; Morning Post, 14 Dec 1852; London Daily News, 14 Dec 1852; London Evening Standard, 14 Dec 1852; Evening Mail, 15 Dec 1852

2R: The Times, 17 Feb 1853; Morning Advertiser, 17 Feb 1853; Morning Chronicle, 17 Feb 1853; Morning Post, 17 Feb 1853; London Daily News, 17 Feb 1853; Evening Mail, 18 Feb 1853

CWH: The Times, 1853; Morning Advertiser, 18 Feb 1853; Morning Chronicle, 18 Feb 1853; Morning Post, 18 Feb 1853; London Daily News, 18 Feb 1853; London Evening Standard, 18 Feb 1853

3R: The Times, 9 Mar 1853; Morning Advertiser, 9 Mar 1853; Morning Chronicle, 9 Mar 1853; Morning Post, 9 Mar 1853; Evening Mail, 9 Mar 1853; London Daily News, 9 Mar 1853; London Evening Standard, 9 Mar 1853

House of Lords

2R adj: The Times, 16 Mar 1853; Morning Advertiser, 16 Mar 1853; Morning Post, 16 Mar 1853; London Daily News, 16 Mar 1853 (all misrep at 2R); London Evening Standard, 16 Mar 1853 (misrep)

Notes
The need for this Bill was superseded by the Patent Law Amendment Act 1852 (PUBA6)

Letters Patent for Inventions Bill 1854

PUBB25	1854
Letters Patent for Inventions Bill 1854 (17 & 18 Vict)	
Bill to enable the Lord Chancellor, in certain cases, to extend the Time for sealing Letters Patent for Inventions and filing Specifications, for a more extended Time from the expiration of the Term of Provisional Protection	

Table of contents
Cl 1 Time extended for sealing Letters Patent for Inventions
Cl 2 Recited Act and this Act to be considered as One Act

Journal	
House of Commons	**House of Lords**
Pres: Apsley Pellatt and George Muntz	

29 Jun 1854	109 CJ 349	Bill Ord/1R	*Never considered by House of Lords*
5 Jul 1854	109 CJ 367	2R adj	
12 Jul 1854	109 CJ 387	2R adj	
14 Jul 1854	109 CJ 395	2R adj	
17 Jul 1854	109 CJ 405	Bill w/d	

Parliamentary debates
1R: HC Deb, 29 Jun 1854, Vol 134(3rd), col 868

Parliamentary papers
Bill to enable Lord Chancellor to extend Time for sealing Letters Patent for Inventions and filing Specifications from Expiration of Term of Provisional Protection (1854 HC Papers 165) Vol 3, p 457

Newspaper coverage of debates
House of Commons
1R: The Times, 30 Jun 1854; Morning Advertiser, 30 Jun 1854; Morning Chronicle, 30 Jun 1854; Morning Post, 30 Jun 1854; Evening Mail, 30 Jun 1854; London Daily News, 30 Jun 1854; London Evening Standard, 30 Jun 1854.
Bill w/d: *The Times, 18 Jul 1854; Morning Post, 18 Jul 1854*; Morning Advertiser, 18 Jul 1854 (misrep); Morning Chronicle, 18 Jul 1854

Patent Law Amendment Bill 1858

PUBB26	1858

Patent Law Amendment Bill 1858 (21 & 22 Vict)
Bill to amend the Patent Law Amendment Act (1852)

Table of contents
Cl 1 In lieu of Stamp Duties now received the Sums specified in the Schedule to be levied in respect of Letters Patent, &c. Cl 2 Second Application for Letters Patent to be valid if made before Expiration of the first Provisional Protection Cl 3 Acts to be construed together Schedule [of Fees]

Journal	
House of Commons	**House of Lords**

Pres: Thomas Duncombe			*Never considered by House of Lords*
21 Apr 1858	113 CJ 127	Bill Ord/1R	
12 May 1858	113 CJ 170	2R adj 6m	

Parliamentary debates
1R: HC Deb, 21 Apr 1858, Vol 149(3rd), col 1424
2R adj: **HC Deb, 12 May 1858, Vol 150(3rd), col 516–520**

Parliamentary papers
Bill to amend the Patent Law Amendment Act (1852) (1857–58 HC Papers 54), Vol 4, p 1

Newspaper coverage of debates
House of Commons
1R: The Times, 22 Apr 1858; Morning Advertiser, 22 Apr 1858; Morning Chronicle, 22 Apr 1858; Morning Post, 22 Apr 1858; London Daily News, 22 Apr 1858; London Evening Standard, 22 Apr 1858
2R: **The Times, 13 May 1858; Morning Chronicle, 13 May 1858; London Daily News, 13 May 1858; London Evening Standard, 13 May 1858**; *Morning Advertiser, 13 May 1858; Morning Post, 13 May 1858*

International Patent Rights Bill 1858

PUBB27	1858

International Patent Rights Bill 1858 (21 & 22 Vict)
Bill to make provision to secure international patent right

(continued)

(continued)

Table of contents
Cl 1 Her Majesty by Order in Council may apply the Provisions of this Act to Inventions patented in a Foreign State (named in the Order)
Cl 2 On Application to the Patent Office a Foreign Patent and Specification may be filed
Cl 3 The Foreign Patent and Specification to be filed in the Office
Cl 4 Certificate to be granted to the Person interested in the Inventions to have Effect of Letters Patent; [Patent Law Amendment Act 1852] 15 & 16 Vict c. 83
Cl 5 Term of Protection under the Certificate
Cl 6 No Order in Council to have any Effect, unless its states that reciprocal Protection is secured
Cl 7 Orders in Council to be laid before Parliament
Cl 8 Orders in Council may be revoked
Cl 9 Orders in Council to be published in Gazette and to have same Effect as this Act
Cl 10 Power to Commissioners to make Rules and Regulations, which shall be laid before Parliament
Cl 11 Commissioners to make Tables of Fees

Journal					
House of Commons			**House of Lords**		
Pres: William Vessey-Fitzgerald, Joseph Henley and Gathorne Hardy Rep: George Hamilton					
23 Jul 1858	113 CJ 343	Bill Ord/1R	28 Jul 1858	90 LJ 478	Brought HC/1R
26 Jul 1858	113 CJ 347	2R/C'tted CWH			
27 Jul 1858	113 CJ 349	CWH			
27 Jul 1858	113 CJ 352	Rep/3R			

Parliamentary debates	
1R: HC Deb, 23 Jul 1858, Vol 151(3rd), col 2020	1R: HL Deb, 28 Jul 1958, Vol 151(3rd), col 2241
2R: HC Deb, 26 Jul 1858, Vol 151(3rd), col 2105	

Parliamentary papers
Bill to make provisions to secure International Patent Right (1857–58 HC Papers 235), Vol 2, p 587
Bill to make provisions to secure International Patent Right (1857–58 HL Papers 276), Vol 4, p 297

Newspaper coverage of debates
House of Commons
1R: The Times, 24 Jul 1858; Morning Chronicle, 24 Jul 1858; Morning Post, 24 Jul 1858 (misreported as Int Copyright of Designs Bill); London Evening Standard, 24 Jul 1858
2R: The Times, 27 Jul 1858; Morning Advertiser, 27 Jul 1858; Morning Chronicle, 27 Jul 1858; Morning Post, 27 Jul 1858; London Daily News, 27 Jul 1858; London Evening Standard, 27 Jul 1858
Rep/3R: The Times, 28 Jul 1858; Morning Advertiser, 28 Jul 1858; Morning Chronicle, 28 Jul 1858; Morning Post, 28 Jul 1858; London Daily News, 28 Jul 1858; London Evening Standard, 28 Jul 1858

Patents for Inventions Bill 1871

PUBB28	1871
Patents for Inventions Bill 1871 (34 & 35 Vict)	
Bill to amend the law relating to patents for inventions	
Table of contents	
Cl 1 Title of Act	
Cl 2 Appointment of Special Commissioners	
Cl 3 Salaries of Special Commissioners	
Cl 4 Power and duties of law officers to be vested in Special Commissioners	
Cl 5 Mode of proceedings before Special Commissioners	
Cl 6 Rules to be made by Special Commissioners	
Cl 7 Right of appeal from Special Commissioners	
Cl 8 Proceedings to obtain an indefeasible patent	

Cl 9 Right to show cause against an indefensible patent
Cl 10 Registration of indefensible patents
Cl 11 Register to be kept of indefeasible patents
Cl 12 References in patent suits may be made to Special Commissioners
Cl 13 Compulsory grant of licenses
Cl 14 Compensation to law officers for loss of fees
Cl 15 Stamp duties to be paid on letters patent
Cl 16 This Act to be construed with Act of 1852 [Patent Law Amendment Act 1852]
Schedules of Stamp Duties under this Act

Journal			
House of Commons			**House of Lords**
Pres: John Hinde Palmer			
7 Mar 1871	126 CJ 76	Bill Ord/1R	*Never considered by House of Lords*
18 Mar 1871	126 CJ 92	2R adj	
31 Mar 1871	126 CJ 121	2R adj	
28 Jun 1871	126 CJ 299	2R adj	
5 Jul 1871	126 CJ 317	2R adj	
26 Jul 1871	126 CJ 371	2R adj	
2 Aug 1871	126 CJ 390	Bill w/d	

Parliamentary debates	
Ord/1R: HC Deb, 7 Mar 1871, Vol 204(3rd), col 1559	
Bill w/d: HC Deb, 2 Aug 1871, Vol 208(3rd), col 694	

Parliamentary papers
Bill to amend the law relating to patents for inventions (1871 HC Papers 65), Vol 4, p 419

Newspaper coverage of debates
House of Commons
1R: The Times, 8 Mar 1871; Morning Post, 8 Mar 1871
Bill w/d: The Times, 3 Aug 1871; Morning Post, 3 Aug 1871; London Daily News, 3 Aug 1871

Patents for Inventions Bill 1875

PUBB29	1875
Patents for Inventions Bill 1875 (38 & 39 Vict)	
Bill for consolidating, with Amendments, the Acts relating to Letters Patent for Inventions	

Table of contents (1875 HC Papers 133)	
	Table of origin
Cl 1 Short title	1852, s 56
Cl 2 Commencement of Act	1852, s 57
Cl 3 Repeal of enactments in Schedule	—
Cl 4 Interpretation	1852, s 55
Cl 5 Commissioners of Patents	1852, s 1
Cl 6 Examiners and Assistant Examiners of Patents	—
Cl 7 Referees for Patents	—
Cl 8 Filing of application and specification, and of notice of opposition	1852, s 6, 9, 11 and 12
Cl 9 Provisional protection	1852, s 8
Cl 10 Reference to examiner	—
Cl 11 Report of examiner	—
Cl 12 Association of referee or referees with examiner	—
Cl 13 Reference to and report by law officer	1852, s 8
Cl 14 Notice to proceed	1852, s 12
Cl 15 Preparation of patent and warrant	1852, s 15 and 18
Cl 16 Petition against sealing	—

(continued)

(continued)

Cl 17 Time for sealing	1852, s 19, 20 and 23
Cl 18 Extent of patent	1852, s 18
Cl 19 Power for Lord Chancellor to extend time in certain cases	—
Cl 20 Conditions of patent for foreign inventions	1852, s 25
Cl 21 Foreign vessels in British waters	1852, s 26
Cl 22 Amendment of specification	1835, s 1; 1844, s 5; 1852, s 8 and 39
Cl 23 Petition for revocation instead of scire facias	—
Cl 24 Assignment for part of United Kingdom	1852, s 35
Cl 25 Register of assignment and licences	1852, s 35
Cl 26 Correction of register	1852, s 38
Cl 27 Patent revocable if not used or licences not given	—
Cl 28 Prolongation of patent	1835, s4; 1839, s 2; 1844, s 2–4
Cl 29 Protection of inventions at exhibitions	1865, s 2 and 3; 1870, s 2 and 4
Cl 30 Patent to first inventor not invalidated by application in fraud of him	1852, s 10
Cl 31 Falsification of entries in register	1852, s 37
Cl 32 Penalty for unauthorized use of name of patentee, mark of word patent	1835, s 7
Cl 33 False declaration misdemeanour	1852, s 6 and Sch
Cl 34 Patent to bind Crown	—
Cl 35 Costs of opposition	1852, s 14
Cl 36 Hearing of petitions	—
Cl 37 Dismissal of petition for want of interest	—
Cl 38 No appeal on petition	—
Cl 39 Costs on petition	—
Cl 40 Particulars on petitions, declarations, &c.	1835, s 5; 1852, s 41
Cl 41 Costs in actions for infringement	1835, s 3 and 6; 1852, s 43
Cl 42 Power for court of law to grant injunction, &c.	1852, s 42
Cl 43 Attendance of expert	—
Cl 44 Power for Lord Chancellor to make general orders	—
Cl 45 Seal of Commissioners	1852, s 2
Cl 46 Sealed copies to be received in evidence	1853 (c. 115), s 4
Cl 47 (Cl A) Officers, clerks, and officers	1852, s 4, 5 and 48
Cl 48 General duties of examiners	—
Cl 49 Power for Commissioners to make general rules regulating details, business of office, &c.	1852, s 3, 29, 30, 32 and 34
Cl 50 Annual report of Commissioners	1852, s 3 and 51
Cl 51 Quorum of Commissioners	1852, s 1
Cl B Stamp duties in Schedule	1853 (c. 5), s 3
Cl C Periodical payment of stamp duties	1853 (c. 5), s 2
Cl 52 Costs of opposition	1852, s 14
Cl 53 Saving for courts [Scotland]	1852, s 43
Cl 54 Proceedings for revocation of patent [Scotland]	1852, s 35 and 43
Cl 55 Recovery of penalty for unauthorized use of name, &c. [Scotland]	1835, s 7
Cl 56 Reservation of remedies [Ireland]	1852, s 29
Cl 57 Saving for effect of repeal and for rights accrued, existing patents, pending applications, &c.	—
Cl 58 Commissioners under former Acts to be deemed continued, &c.	—
Cl 59 Saving for powers of Lord Chancellor	1852, s 15
Cl 60 Reservation of powers to Crown	1852, s 16
Cl 61 Saving for prerogative	1852, s 16
First Schedule – Enactments repealed	
Second Schedule – Stamp Duties	

Journal					
House of Commons			**House of Lords**		
			Pres and Rep: Lord Cairns LC		
15 Apr 1875	130 CJ 145	Brought HL	12 Feb 1875	107 LJ 24	1R
21 Apr 1875	130 CJ 158	1R	26 Feb 1875	107 LJ 45	2R/C'tted CWH
27 Apr 1875	130 CJ 170	2R adj	11 Mar 1875	107 LJ 63	**CWH/Rep with Amds**
4 May 1875	130 CJ 187	2R adj	18 Mar 1875	107 LJ 80	Cons adj
11 May 1875	130 CJ 204	2R adj	8 Apr 1875	107 LJ 89	Rep with Amds
13 May 1875	130 CJ 216	2R adj	13 Apr 1875	107 LJ 98	**R Cons/3R with Amds**
21 May 1875	130 CJ 220	2R adj	24 Jun 1875	107 LJ 290	Pet for Amds
28 May 1875	130 CJ 237	2R adj	2 Jul 1875	107 LJ 318	Pet for Amds
4 Jun 1875	130 CJ 257	2R adj			
11 Jun 1875	130 CJ 270	2R adj			
18 Jun 1875	130 CJ 285	2R adj			
25 Jun 1875	130 CJ 301	2R adj			
2 Jul 1875	130 CJ 321	2R adj			
6 Jul 1875	130 CJ 331	2R adj			
13 Jul 1875	130 CJ 350	2R adj			
23 Jul 1875	130 CJ 379	Ord Disc/Bill w/d			

Parliamentary debates

1R: HC Deb, 20 Apr 1875, Vol 223(3rd), col 1279	R Speech: HL Deb, 5 Feb 1875, Vol 222(3rd), col 33–34
W/D: HC Deb, 22 Jul 1875, Vol 225(3rd), col 1808	1R: **HL Deb, 12 Feb 1875, Vol 222(3rd), col 241–268**
	2R: HL Deb, 26 Feb 1875, Vol 222(3rd), col 916
	CWH: **HL Deb, 11 Mar 1875, Vol 222(3rd), col 1595–1602**
	Rep: HL Deb, 8 Apr 1875, Vol 223(3rd), col 490
	3R: HL Deb, 13 Apr 1875, Vol 223(3rd), col 765

Parliamentary papers

Bill for consolidating, with Amendments, the Acts relating to Letters Patent for Inventions (1875 HL Papers 15), Vol 6, p 237

   Amendments to be moved in Committee by the Marquess of Lansdowne (1875 HL Papers 15a), Vol 6, p 259

   Amendments to be moved in Committee by the Lord Chancellor (1875 HL Papers 15b), Vol 6, p 261

Bill for consolidating, with Amendments, the Acts relating to Letters Patent for Inventions (as amended in Committee) (1875 HL Papers 36), Vol 6, p 265

   Amendments proposed on Report by the Lord Chancellor (1875 HL Papers 36a), Vol 6, p 289

   Amendments proposed on Third Reading by the Lord Chancellor (1875 HL Papers 36b), Vol 6, p 293

Bill for consolidating, with Amendments, the Acts relating to Letters Patent for Inventions (1875 HC Papers 133), Vol 6, p 491

Newspaper coverage of debates

House of Lords

1R: **The Times, 13 Feb 1875; Morning Post, 13 Feb 1875; London Daily News, 13 Feb 1875; London Evening Standard, 13 Feb 1875**

2R: **The Times, 27 Feb 1875; Morning Post, 27 Feb 1875; London Daily News, 27 Feb 1875; London Evening Standard, 27 Feb 1875**

CWH: **The Times, 12 Mar 1875; Morning Post, 12 Mar 1875; London Daily News, 12 Mar 1875; London Evening Standard, 12 Mar 1875**

Rep: The Times, 9 Apr 1875; Morning Post, 9 Apr 1875; London Daily News, 9 Apr 1875; London Evening Standard, 9 Apr 1875

(continued)

(continued)

3R: The Times, 14 Apr 1875; Morning Post, 14 Apr 1875; London Daily News, 14 Apr 1875; London Evening Standard, 14 Apr 1875
House of Commons
Amds Prop: *The Times, 22 May 1875; Morning Post, 22 May 1875; London Daily News, 22 May 1875; London Evening Standard, 22 May 1875*
Bill w/d: The Times, 23 Jul 1875; Morning Post, 23 Jul 1875; London Evening Standard, 23 Jul 1875

Notes
There are clauses labelled Clause A to C in the version of the Bill as replicated above.
Petitions – PET316 to PET320; PET322 to PET355; PET357 to PET363; PET365, PET366 and PET368 to PET373
This was essentially the same Bill as presented in the next two sessions: PUBB30 and PUBB31

Patents for Inventions Bill 1876

PUBB30	1876
	Patents for Inventions Bill 1876 (39 & 40 Vict)
	Bill for consolidating, with Amendments, the Acts relating to Letters Patent for Inventions

Table of contents (1876 HC Papers 137)	
	Table of origin
Cl 1 Short title	1852, s 56
Cl 2 Commencement of Act	1852, s 57
Cl 3 Repeal of enactments in Schedule	—
Cl 4 Interpretation	1852, s 55
Cl 5 Commissioners of Patents	1852, s 1
Cl 6 Examiners and Assistant Examiners of Patents	—
Cl 7 Filing of application and specification, and of notice of opposition	1852, s 6, 9, 11 and 12
Cl 8 Provisional protection	1852, s 8
Cl 9 Reference to examiner	—
Cl 10 Report of examiner	—
Cl 11 Reference to and report by law officer	1852, s 8
Cl 12 Notice to proceed	1852, s 12
Cl 13 Preparation of patent and warrant	1852, s 15 and 18
Cl 14 Petition against sealing	—
Cl 15 Time for sealing	1852, s 19, 20 and 23
Cl 16 Sealing, extent and duration of patent	1852, s 18
Cl 17 Power for Lord Chancellor to extend time in certain cases	1852, s 20; 1853 (c. 115), s 6
Cl 18 Certificate of renewal to be taken out at end of third and seventh year	1853 (c. 5), s 2
Cl 19 Conditions of patents for foreign and colonial inventions	1852, s 25
Cl 20 Foreign vessels in British waters	1852, s 26
Cl 21 Amendment of specification	1835, s 1; 1844, s 5; 1852, s 8 and 39
Cl 22 Petition for revocation instead of scire facias	—
Cl 23 Assignment for part of United Kingdom	1852, s 35
Cl 24 Register of proprietors	1852, s 35
Cl 25 Correction of register	1852, s 38
Cl 26 Patent revocable if not used or licences not given	—
Cl 27 Protection of inventions at exhibitions	1865, s 2 and 3; 1870, s 2 and 4

Cl 28 Patent to first inventor not invalidated by application in fraud of him	1852, s 10
Cl 29 Falsification of entries in register	1852, s 37
Cl 30 Penalty for unauthorized use of name of patentee, mark of word patent, &c.	1835, s 7
Cl 31 False declaration misdemeanour	1852, s 6 and Sch
Cl 32 Patent to bind Crown	—
Cl 33 Costs of opposition	1852, s 14
Cl 34 Hearing of petitions	—
Cl 35 Dismissal of petition for want of interest	—
Cl 36 No appeal on petition	—
Cl 37 Costs on petition	—
Cl 38 Particulars on petitions, declarations, &c.	1835, s 5; 1852, s 41
Cl 39 Costs in actions for infringement	1835, s 3 and 6; 1852, s 43
Cl 40 Power for court of law to grant injunction, &c.	1852, s 42
Cl 41 Attendance of expert	—
Cl 42 Power for Lord Chancellor to make general orders	—
Cl 43 Seal of Commissioners	1852, s 2
Cl 44 Sealed copies to be received in evidence	1853 (c 115), s 4
Cl A Offices	1852, s 4
Cl 45 Clerks, and officers	1852, s 5 and 48
Cl 46 General duties of examiners and assistants	—
Cl 47 Power for Commissioners to make general rules regulating details, business of office, &c.	1852, s 3, 29, 30, 32 and 34
Cl 48 Annual report of Commissioners	1852, s 3 and 51
Cl 59 Quorum of Commissioners	1852, s 1
Cl B Stamp duties in Schedule	1853, c.5, s 3
Cl 50 Costs of opposition [Scotland]	1852, s 14
Cl 51 Saving for courts [Scotland]	1852, s 43
Cl 52 Proceedings for revocation of patent [Scotland]	1852, s 35 and 43
Cl 53 Recovery of penalty for unauthorized use of name, &c. [Scotland]	1835, s 7
Cl 54 Reservation of remedies [Ireland]	1852, s 29
Cl 55 Saving for effect of repeal and for rights accrued, existing patents, pending applications, &c.	—
Cl 56 Commissioners under former Acts to be deemed continued, &c.	—
Cl 57 Extension to existing patents of provisions respecting renewal	—
Cl 58 Saving for powers of Lord Chancellor	1852, s 15
Cl 59 Reservation of powers to Crown	1852, s 16
Cl 60 Saving for prerogative	1852, s 16
First Schedule – Enactment repealed	—
Second Schedule – Stamp Duties	—

House of Commons			House of Lords		
			Pres and Rep: Lord Cairns LC		
30 Mar 1876	131 CJ 128	Brought HL	22 Feb 1876	108 LJ 38	1R
26 Apr 1876	131 CJ 162	1R	6 Mar 1876	108 LJ 62	2R adj
5 May 1876	131 CJ 178	2R adj	14 Mar 1876	108 LJ 74	2R/C'tted CWH
12 May 1876	131 CJ 191	2R adj	21 Mar 1876	108 LJ 83	**CWH**
19 May 1876	131 CJ 205	2R adj	27 Mar 1876	108 LJ 96	Rep with Amds
26 May 1876	131 CJ 221	2R adj	28 Mar 1876	108 LJ 98	**3R with Amd**
2 Jun 1876	131 CJ 241	2R adj			
16 Jun 1876	131 CJ 263	2R adj			
23 Jun 1876	131 CJ 279	2R adj			
30 Jun 1876	131 CJ 295	2R adj			
7 Jul 1876	131 CJ 313	2R adj			
11 Jul 1876	131 CJ 321	2R adj			
18 Jul 1876	131 CJ 343	2R adj			
25 Jul 1876	131 CJ 363	Bill w/d			

(continued)

(continued)

Parliamentary debates	
1R: HC Deb, 26 Apr 1876, Vol 228(3rd), col 1658	**1R: HL Deb, 22 Feb 1876, Vol 227(3rd), col 663–664**
Bill w/d: HC Deb, 24 Jul 1876, Vol 230(3rd), col 1808	**2R: HL Deb, 14 Mar 1876, Vol 227(3rd), col 1944–1946**
	CWH: HL Deb, 21 Mar 1876, Vol 228(3rd), col 345
	Rep: HL Deb, 27 Mar 1876, Vol 228(3rd), col 598
	3R: HL Deb, 28 Mar 1876, Vol 228(3rd), col 689

Parliamentary papers
Bill for consolidating, with Amendments, the Acts relating to Letters Patent for Inventions (1876 HL Papers 15), Vol 5, p 483
Bill for consolidating, with Amendments, the Acts relating to Letters Patent for Inventions (as amended in Committee) (1876 HL Papers 38), Vol 5, p 507
Bill for consolidating, with Amendments, the Acts relating to Letters Patent for Inventions (1876 HC Papers 137), Vol 5, p 461

Newspaper coverage of debates
House of Lords
1R: **The Times, 23 Feb 1876**; **Morning Post, 23 Feb 1876**; **London Evening Standard, 23 Feb 1876**; *London Daily News, 23 Feb 1876*
2R: **The Times, 15 Mar 1876**; **London Daily News, 15 Mar 1876**; **London Evening Standard, 15 Mar 1876**; *Morning Post, 15 Mar 1876*
CWH: *Morning Post, 22 Mar 1876*; *London Daily News, 22 Mar 1876*; The Times, 22 Mar 1876; London Evening Standard, 22 Mar 1876
3R: Morning Post, 29 Mar 1876; London Evening Standard, 29 Mar 1876; London Daily News, 29 Mar 1876

Notes
Petitions – PET378, PET382 to PET403 and PET405 to PET419 and PET421
This was essentially the same Bill as presented in the former session PUBB29 and the next PUBB31

Patents for Inventions Bill 1877

PUBB31	1877
Patents for Inventions Bill 1877 (40 & 41 Vict)	
Bill for consolidating, with amendments, the Acts relating to Letters Patent for Inventions	

Table of contents	
	Table of origin
Cl 1 Short title	1852, s 56
Cl 2 Commencement of Act	1852, s 57
Cl 3 Repeal of enactments in Schedule	—
Cl 4 Interpretation	1852, s 55
Cl 5 Commissioners of Patents	1852, s 1
Cl 6 Examiners and Assistant Examiners of Patents	—
Cl 7 Filing of application and specification, and of notice of opposition	1852, s 6, 9, 11 and 12
Cl 8 Provisional protection	1852, s 8
Cl 9 Reference to and report by law officer	—
Cl 10 Complete Specification	—
Cl 11 Publication of complete speciation and other documents	—
Cl 12 Further reference to and report by examiner	—
Cl 13 Reference to and report by law officer	1852, s 8
Cl 14 Notice to proceed	1852, s 12

Cl 15 Warrant for sealing	1852, s 15 and 18
Cl 16 Petition for sealing	—
Cl 17 Petition against sealing	—
Cl 18 Time for sealing	1852, s 19, 20 and 23
Cl 19 Sealing and extent of patent	1852, s 18
Cl 20 Duration of Patent; Certificate of renewal at end of third, seventh, and fourteenth year	1853 (c. 5), s 2
Cl 21 Patent to bind Crown	—
Cl 22 Patent revocable if not used or licences not given	—
Cl 23 Conditions of patents for foreign and colonial inventions	1852, s 25
Cl 24 Amendment of specification	1835, s 1; 1844, s 5; 1852, s 8 and 39
Cl 25 Petition for revocation instead of scire facias	—
Cl 26 Assignment for part of United Kingdom	1852, s 35
Cl 27 Register of proprietors	1852, s 35
Cl 28 Correction of register	1852, s 38
Cl 29 Protection of inventions at exhibitions	1865, s 2 and 3; 1870, s 2 and 4
Cl 30 Foreign vessels in British water	1852, s 26
Cl 31 Patent to first inventor not invalidated by application in fraud of him	1852, s 10
Cl 32 Falsification of entries in register	1852, s 37
Cl 33 Penalty for unauthorized use of name of patentee, mark of word patent, &c.	1835, s 7
Cl 34 False declaration misdemeanour	1852, s 6 and Sch
Cl 35 Nomination of examiner	—
Cl 36 Power for law officer to administer oaths, &c.	—
Cl 37 Costs of opposition	1852, s 14
Cl 38 Power for Lord Chancellor to extend time in certain cases	1853 (c. 115), s 6
Cl 39 Hearing of petitions	—
Cl 40 Dismissal of petition for want of interest	—
Cl 41 No appeal on petition	—
Cl 42 Costs on petition	—
Cl 43 Particulars on petitions and in actions	1835, s 5; 1852, s 41
Cl 44 Costs in actions for infringement	1835, s 3 and 6; 1852, s 43
Cl 45 Power for court in action for infringement	1852, s 42
Cl 46 Attendance of expert	—
Cl 47 Power for Lord Chancellor to make general orders	—
Cl 48 Seal of Commissioners	1852, s 2
Cl 49 Sealed copies to be received in evidence	1853 (c. 115), s 4
Cl 50 Offices	1852, s 4
Cl 51 Clerks, officers, &c.	1852, s 5 and 48
Cl 52 General duties of examiners and assistants	—
Cl 53 Power for Commissioners to make general rules regulating details, business of office, &c.	1852, s 3, 13, 29, 30, 32 and 34
Cl 54 Annual report of Commissioners	1852, s 3 and 51
Cl 55 Quorum of Commissioners	1852, s 1
Cl 56 Stamp duties in Schedule	1853 (c. 5), s 3
Cl 57 Costs of opposition [Scotland]	1852, s 14
Cl 58 Saving for courts [Scotland]	1852, s 43
Cl 59 Proceedings for revocation of patent [Scotland]	1852, s 35 and 43
Cl 60 Recovery of penalty for unauthorized use of name, &c. [Scotland]	1835, s 7
Cl 61 Reservation of remedies [Ireland]	1852, s 29
Cl 62 Saving for effect of repeal and for rights accrued, existing patents, pending applications, &c.	—
Cl 63 Commissioners under former Acts to be deemed continued, &c.	—
Cl 64 Extension to existing patents of provisions respecting renewal	—
Cl 65 Provision for foreign and colonial patents taken before commencement of Act	—
Cl 66 Saving for powers of Lord Chancellor	1852, s 15

(continued)

(continued)

Cl 67 Reservation of powers to Crown	1852, s 16
Cl 68 Saving for prerogative	1852, s 16
First Schedule – Enactments repealed	—
Second Schedule – Stamp Duties	—

Journal

House of Commons			House of Lords
Pres: Sir John Holker (A-G), William Watson (Ld Adv) and David Plunket (SG Ir)			*Never considered by House of Lords*
12 Feb 1877	132 CJ 30	Bill Ord	
13 Feb 1877	132 CJ 31	1R	
22 Feb 1877	132 CJ 59	2R adj	
2 Mar 1877	132 CJ 75	2R adj	
9 Mar 1877	132 CJ 87	2R adj	
16 Mar 1877	132 CJ 101	2R adj	
23 Mar 1877	132 CJ 114	2R adj	
10 Apr 1877	132 CJ 140	2R adj	
17 Apr 1877	132 CJ 157	2R adj	
23 Apr 1877	132 CJ 173	2R adj	
1 May 1877	132 CJ 189	2R adj	
11 May 1877	132 CJ 212	2R adj	
18 May 1877	132 CJ 236	2R adj	
5 Jun 1877	132 CJ 248	2R adj	
12 Jun 1877	132 CJ 265	2R adj	
19 Jun 1877	132 CJ 281	2R adj	
26 Jun 1877	132 CJ 297	2R adj	
4 Jul 1877	132 CJ 317	2R adj	
10 Jul 1877	132 CJ 329	2R adj	
17 Jul 1877	132 CJ 346	2R adj	
20 Jul 1877	132 CJ 357	Bill w/d	

Parliamentary debates

Leave/1R: **HC Deb, 12 Feb 1877, Vol 232(3rd), col 217–234**

Bill w/d: HC Deb, 19 Jul 1877, Vol 235(3rd), col 1512

Parliamentary papers

Bill for consolidating Acts relating to Letters Patent for Inventions (1877 HC Papers 64), Vol 4, p 359

Newspaper coverage of debates

House of Commons

1R: **The Times, 13 Feb 1877; Morning Post, 13 Feb 1877; London Daily News, 13 Feb 1877; London Evening Standard, 13 Feb 1877**

Bill W/D: The Times, 20 Jul 1877; Morning Post, 20 Jul 1877; London Daily News, 20 Jul 1877; London Evening Stannard, 20 Jul 1877

Notes

Petitions – PET424 to PET452; PET454 to PET456

This was essentially the same Bill as presented in the former two sessions: PUBB29 and PUBB30

Patent Law Amendment Bill 1878

PUBB32	1878
Patent Law Amendment Bill 1878 (41 & 42 Vict)	
Bill for the amendment of the patent laws	

Table of contents

Cl 1 Commencement of Act
Cl 2 Duration of new Letters Patent
Cl 3 Application of Act to existing Letters Patent
Cl 4 Duties payable for Letters Patent
Cl 5 Short title
Schedule of Stamp Duties

Journal	
House of Commons	**House of Lords**
Pres: George Anderson, Anthony Mundella, James Dalrymple-Horn-Elphinstone and Alexander Brown	

13 Mar 1878	133 CJ 109	Bill Ord/1R	*Never considered by House of Lords*
14 Mar 1878	133 CJ 112	2R adj	
15 May 1878	133 CJ 220	2R adj	
4 Jun 1878	133 CJ 269	2R adj	
15 Jun 1878	133 CJ 290	2R adj	
2 Jul 1878	133 CJ 322	2R adj	
5 Jul 1878	133 CJ 336	2R adj	
9 Jul 1878	133 CJ 340	2R adj	
10 Jul 1878	133 CJ 347	2R adj	
11 Jul 1878	133 CJ 350	2R adj	
13 Jul 1878	133 CJ 353	2R adj	
17 Jul 1878	133 CJ 361	2R adj	
23 Jul 1878	133 CJ 375	2R adj	
24 Jul 1878	133 CJ 377	2R adj	

Parliamentary debates

Ord/1R: HC Deb, 13 Mar 1878, Vol 238(3rd), col 1274

Parliamentary papers

Bill for amendment of the patent laws (1878 HC Papers 127), Vol 5, p 387.

Newspaper coverage of debates

House of Commons

1R: The Times, 14 Mar 1878; Morning Post, 14 Mar 1878; London Daily News, 14 Mar 1878; London Evening Standard, 14 Mar 1878

Notes

Petitions – PET457 to PET497

This was the first of three times this Bill was introduced: see PUBB33 and PUBB35; they introduced slightly longer Bills thereafter, starting with PUBB36

Patent for Inventions Bill 1879

PUBB33	1879
	Patent for Inventions Bill 1879 (42 & 43 Vict)
	Bill to amend the Patents for Inventions Laws

Table of contents

Cl 1 Commencement of Act
Cl 2 Duration of new Letters Patent
Cl 3 Application of Act to existing Letters Patent
Cl 4 Duties payable for Letters Patent
Cl 5 Short title
Schedule of Stamp Duties

Journal	
House of Commons	**House of Lords**
Pres: George Anderson, Anthony Mundella, James Dalrymple-Horn-Elphinstone and Alexander Brown	

(continued)

(continued)

10 Dec 1878	134 CJ 16	Bill Ord	*Never considered by House of Lords*
10 Dec 1878	134 CJ 17	1R	
5 Mar 1879	134 CJ 76	2R adj	
7 Mar 1879	134 CJ 80	2R adj	
8 Mar 1879	134 CJ 82	2R adj	
11 Mar 1879	134 CJ 86	2R adj	
14 Mar 1879	134 CJ 93	2R adj	
18 Mar 1879	134 CJ 98	2R adj	
21 Mar 1879	134 CJ 106	2R adj	
22 Mar 1879	134 CJ 110	2R adj	
25 Mar 1879	134 CJ 114	2R adj	
26 Mar 1879	134 CJ 118	2R adj	
28 Mar 1879	134 CJ 122	2R adj	
29 Mar 1879	134 CJ 124	2R adj	
4 Apr 1879	134 CJ 133	2R adj	
5 Apr 1879	134 CJ 138	2R adj	
22 Apr 1879	134 CJ 153	2R adj	
26 Apr 1879	134 CJ 163	2R adj	
2 May 1879	134 CJ 174	2R adj	
9 May 1879	134 CJ 190	2R adj	
13 May 1879	134 CJ 199	2R adj	
23 May 1879	134 CJ 237	2R adj	
27 May 1879	134 CJ 249	2R adj	
13 Jun 1879	134 CJ 266	2R adj	
27 Jun 1879	134 CJ 297	2R adj	
1 Jul 1879	134 CJ 306	2R adj	
8 Jul 1879	134 CJ 325	2R adj	
11 Jul 1879	134 CJ 335	2R adj	

Parliamentary debates	
Ord/1R: HC Deb, 10 Dec 1878, Vol 243(3rd), col 622	

Parliamentary papers
Bill to amend Patents for Inventions Laws (1878–79 HC Papers 55), Vol 5, p 71

Newspaper coverage of debates
House of Commons
1R: The Times, 11 Dec 1878; Morning Post, 11 Dec 1878

Notes
Petitions – PET498 to PET509 (it is not clear whether it is this Bill or the next one for some of these petitions)
This was the second of three times this Bill was introduced: see PUBB32 and PUBB35; they introduced slightly longer Bills thereafter, starting with PUBB36

Patents for Inventions (No 2) Bill 1879

PUBB34	1879		
Patents for Inventions (No 2) Bill 1879 (42 & 43 Vict)			
Bill to consolidate, with amendments, the Acts relating to Letters Patent for Inventions			
Table of contents			
		Table of origin	
Cl 1 Short title		1852, s 56	
Cl 2 Commencement of Act		1852, s 57	
Cl 3 Repeal of enactments in Schedule		—	
Cl 4 Interpretation		1852, s 55	
Cl 5 Commissioners of Patents		1852, s 1	
Cl 6 Filing of application and specification, and of notice of opposition		1852, s 6, 9, 11 and 12	
Cl 7 Provisional protection		1852, s 8	

Cl 8 Complete Specification	1852, s 9
Cl 9 Publication of complete specification and other documents	1852, s 9
Cl 10 On opposition reference to and report by law officer	1852, s 8
Cl 11 Notice to proceed	1852, s 12
Cl 12 Warrant for sealing	1852, s 15 and 18
Cl 13 Petition for sealing	—
Cl 14 Petition against sealing	
Cl 15 Time for sealing; date; extent of patent	1852, s 18,19, 20 and 23
Cl 16 Duration of Patent; certificate of renewal	1853 (c. 5), s 2
Cl 17 Amendment of specification	1835, s 1; 1844, s 5; 1852, s 8 and 39
Cl 18 Patent to bind Crown	—
Cl 19 Patent revocable if not used or licences not given	—
Cl 20 Assignment for part of United Kingdom	1852, s 35
Cl 21 Register of proprietors	1852, s 35
Cl 22 Correction of register	1852, s 38
Cl 23 Petition for revocation instead of scire facias	—
Cl 24 Conditions of patents for imported inventions	1852, s 25
Cl 25 Foreign vessels in British water	1852, s 26
Cl 26 Patent to first inventor not invalidated by application in fraud of him	1852, s 10
Cl 27 Falsification of entries in register	1852, s 37
Cl 28 Penalty for unauthorized use of name of patentee, mark of word patent, &c.	1835, s 7
Cl 29 False declaration misdemeanour	1852, s 6 and Sch
Cl 30 Power for law officer to administer oaths, &c.	—
Cl 31 Costs of opposition	1852, s 14
Cl 32 Power for Lord Chancellor to extend time in certain cases	1852, s 20; 1853 (c. 115), s 6
Cl 33 Procedure on petitions	—
Cl 34 Particulars on petitions and in actions	1835, s 3, 5 and 6; 1852, s 41 and 43
Cl 35 Power for court in action for infringement	1852, s 42
Cl 36 Attendance of expert	—
Cl 37 Certificate of validity questioned, and costs thereupon	1835, s 3; 1852, s 43
Cl 38 Remuneration of expert	1852, s 8
Cl 39 Power for Lord Chancellor to make general orders	—
Cl 40 Seal of Commissioners	1852, s 2
Cl 41 Sealed copies to be received in evidence	1853 ,c 115, s 4
Cl 42 Offices	1852, s 4
Cl 43 Officers and clerks	1852, s 5 and 48
Cl 44 Power for Commissioners to make general rules regulating details, business of officers &c.	1852, s 3, 13, 29, 30, 32 and 34
Cl 45 Annual report of Commissioners	1852, s 3 and 51
Cl 46 Quorum of Commissioners	1852, s 1
Cl 47 Stamp duties in Schedule	1853 (c. 5), s 3
Cl 48 Costs of opposition [Scotland]	1852, s 14
Cl 49 Saving for courts [Scotland]	1852, s 43
Cl 50 Proceedings for revocation of patent [Scotland]	1852, s 35 and 43
Cl 51 Recovery of penalty for unauthorized use of name, &c. [Scotland]	1835, s 7
Cl 52 Reservation of remedies [Ireland]	1852, s 29
Cl 53 Provisions respecting existing patents, &c.	—
Cl 54 Exceptions from repeal as regards existing patents, &c.	1852, s 36
Cl 55 Former Commissioners to be deemed continued	1852, s 1
Cl 56 Former registers to be deemed continued	—
Cl 57 Saving for powers of Lord Chancellor	1852, s 15
Cl 58 Reservation of powers to Crown	1852, s 16
Cl 59 Saving for prerogative	1852, s 16
First Schedule – Enactments repealed	—
Second Schedule – Stamp Duties	—

Journal

House of Commons	House of Lords
Pres: Sir John Holker (A-G), Sir Hardinge Giffard (S-G) and Richard Cross (Hom Sec).	

(continued)

(continued)

18 Feb 1879	134 CJ 43	Bill Ord/1R	*Never considered by House of Lords*
27 Feb 1879	134 CJ 60	2R adj	
28 Feb 1879	134 CJ 67	2R adj	
4 Mar 1879	134 CJ 74	2R adj	
7 Mar 1879	134 CJ 79	2R adj	
8 Mar 1879	134 CJ 82	2R adj	
11 Mar 1879	134 CJ 86	2R adj	
14 Mar 1879	134 CJ 93	2R adj	
18 Mar 1879	134 CJ 98	2R adj	
21 Mar 1879	134 CJ 106	2R adj	
22 Mar 1879	134 CJ 108	2R adj	
25 Mar 1879	134 CJ 114	2R adj	
26 Mar 1879	134 CJ 118	2R adj	
28 Mar 1879	134 CJ 122	2R adj	
29 Mar 1879	134 CJ 124	2R adj	
4 Apr 1879	134 CJ 133	2R adj	
5 Apr 1879	134 CJ 137	2R adj	
22 Apr 1879	134 CJ 152	2R adj	
29 Apr 1879	134 CJ 165	2R adj	
9 May 1879	134 CJ 189	2R adj	
23 May 1879	134 CJ 236	2R adj	
13 Jun 1879	134 CJ 265	2R adj	
21 Jun 1879	134 CJ 286	2R adj	
1 Jul 1879	134 CJ 306	2R adj	
11 Jul 1879	134 CJ 334	2R adj	
15 Jul 1879	134 CJ 344	2R Disc/Bill With	

Parliamentary debates
Ord/1R: HC Deb, 17 Feb 1879, Vol 243(3rd), col 1392
Bill w/d: HC Deb, 14 Jul 1879, Vol 248(3rd), col 297

Parliamentary papers
Bill to consolidate, with amendments, the Acts relating to Letters Patent for Inventions (1878–79 HC Papers 77), Vol 5, p 75 [includes Memorandum explaining basis and reason for changes to the law]

Newspaper coverage of debates
House of Commons
Ord: The Times, 18 Feb 1879; Morning Post, 18 Feb 1879
Bill w/d: Morning Post, 15 Jul 1879; London Daily News, 15 Jul 1879; London Evening Standard, 15 Jul 1879; Pall Mall Gazette, 15 Jul 1879

Notes
Petitions – PET498 to PET503 and PET505 to PET509 (it is not clear whether it is the last Bill or this one for some of these petitions)
This Bill is similar, with some moderate variations, to Bills as presented in the former sessions (PUBB29, PUBB30 and PUBB31)

Patents for Inventions Bill (Session 1) 1880

PUBB35	1880
Patents for Inventions Bill (Session 1) 1880 (43 & 44 Vict)	
Bill to amend the Law of Patents for Inventions	
Table of contents	

Table of contents
Cl 1 Commencement of Act
Cl 2 Appointment of Paid Commissioners
Cl 3 Salaries of paid Commissioners

Cl 4 Duties of paid Commissioners
Cl 5 Duration of new Letters Patent
Cl 6 Application of Act to existing Letters Patent
Cl 7 Duties payable for Letters Patent
Cl 8 Short title
Schedule of Stamp Duties

Journal			
House of Commons			**House of Lords**
Pres: George Anderson, Anthony Mundella, James Dalrymple-Horn-Elphinstone and Alexander Brown			
25 Feb 1880	135 CJ 63	Bill Ord/1R	*Never considered by House of Lords*
10 Mar 1880	135 CJ 92	2R w/d	

Parliamentary debates	
Ord/1R: HC Deb, 25 Feb 1880, Vol 250(3rd), col 1427	
2R: **HC Deb, 10 Mar 1880, Vol 251(3rd), col 742–752**	

Parliamentary papers
Bill to amend Law relating to Patents for Inventions (1880 Sess 1 HC Papers 92), Vol 5, p 547

Newspaper coverage of debates
House of Commons
1R: The Times, 26 Feb 1880; Morning Post, 26 Feb 1880; London Daily News, 26 Feb 1880; London Evening Standard, 26 Feb 1880
2R w/d: **The Times, 11 Mar 1880**; **Morning Post, 11 Mar 1880**; **London Daily News, 11 Mar 1880**; **London Evening Standard, 11 Mar 1880**

Notes
This was the third of three times this Bill was introduced: see PUBB32 and PUBB33; they introduced slightly longer Bills thereafter, starting with PUBB36

Patents for Inventions Bill (Session 2) 1880

PUBB36	1880
Patents for Inventions Bill (Session 2) 1880 (43 & 44 Vict)	
Bill to amend the law relating to Patents for Inventions	

Table of contents
Cl 1 Commencement of Act
Cl 2 Appointment of Paid Commissioners
Cl 3 Salaries of paid Commissioners
Cl 4 Duties of paid Commissioners
Cl 5 Duration of new Letters Patent
Cl 6 Application of Act to existing Letters Patent
Cl 7 Terms of grace for payment
Cl 8 Duties payable for Letters Patent
Cl 9 Extended provisional protection
Cl 10 Subsequent improvements may be added to an existing patent for half fees
Cl 11 Patent rights good against Crown, but may be used for public service on terms to be agreed on
Cl 12 Public servants, except those in Patent Office, may become patentees
Cl 13 Short title
Schedule of Stamp Duties
Schedule of Fines for Postponed Payments

Journal	
House of Commons	**House of Lords**
Pres: George Anderson, Alexander Brown, John Hinde Palmer and Henry Broadhurst	

(continued)

(continued)

25 May 1880	135 CJ 152	Bill Ord	*Never considered by House of Lords*
25 May 1880	135 CJ 153	1R	
9 Jun 1880	135 CJ 188	2R adj	
12 Jun 1880	135 CJ 200	2R adj	
16 Jun 1880	135 CJ 215	2R adj	
23 Jun 1880	135 CJ 237	2R adj	
30 Jun 1880	135 CJ 262	2R adj	
2 Jul 1880	135 CJ 268	2R adj	
10 Jul 1880	135 CJ 292	2R adj	

Parliamentary debate	
Ord/1R: HC Deb, 24 May 1880, Vol 252(3rd), col 425	

Parliamentary papers
Bill to amend Law relating to Patents for Inventions (1880 Sess 2 HC Papers 184), Vol 5, p 551

Newspaper coverage of debate
House of Commons
2R adj: **The Times, 16 Jun 1881**; **Morning Post, 16 Jun 1881**; **London Daily News, 16 Jun 1881**; **London Evening Standard, 16 Jun 1881**; **Pall Mall Gazette, 16 Jun 1881**

Notes
Petitions – PET512 to PET556
This is an extended version of Bills which had previously been introduced by George Anderson (the last of which, see PUBB35); this Bill was introduced three further times (PUBB37, PUBB38 and PUBB41)

Patents for Inventions Bill 1881

PUBB37	1881
Patents for Inventions Bill 1881 (44 & 45 Vict)	
Bill for the amendment of the law as to Patents for Inventions	

Table of contents
Cl 1 Commencement of Act
Cl 2 Appointment of Paid Commissioners
Cl 3 Salaries of paid Commissioners
Cl 4 Duties of paid Commissioners
Cl 5 Duration of new Letters Patent
Cl 6 Application of Act to existing Letters Patent
Cl 7 Terms of grace for payment
Cl 8 Duties payable for Letters Patent
Cl 9 Extended provisional protection
Cl 10 Subsequent improvements may be added to an existing patent for half fees
Cl 11 Patent rights good against Crown, but may be used for public service on terms to be agreed on
Cl 12 Public servants, except those in Patent Office, may become patentees
Cl 13 Short title
Schedule of Stamp Duties
Schedule of Fines for Postponed Payments

Journal			
House of Commons			**House of Lords**
Pres: George Anderson, Alexander Brown, John Hinde Palmer and Henry Broadhurst			
8 Jan 1881	136 CJ 12	Bill Ord	*Never considered by House of Lords*
8 Jan 1881	136 CJ 14	1R	
27 Apr 1881	136 CJ 199	2R adj	
4 May 1881	136 CJ 212	2R adj	
11 May 1881	136 CJ 229	2R adj	
17 May 1881	136 CJ 240	2R adj	

18 May 1881	136 CJ 244	2R adj	
15 Jun 1881	136 CJ 302	2R/C'tted CWH	
29 Jun 1881	136 CJ 334	CWH adj	
6 Jul 1881	136 CJ 350	CWH adj	
13 Jul 1881	136 CJ 371	CWH adj	
19 Jul 1881	136 CJ 384	CWH adj	
22 Jul 1881	136 CJ 394	CWH adj	
27 Jul 1881	136 CJ 410	CWH adj	

Parliamentary debates	
Ord/1R: HC Deb, 7 Jan 1881, Vol 257(3rd), col 277	
2R: **HC Deb, 15 Jun 1883, Vol 262(3rd), col 570–613**	

Parliamentary papers
Bill for the amendment of the law as to Patents for Inventions (1881 HC Papers 15), Vol 4, p 369

Newspaper coverage of debates
House of Commons
2R: **The Times, 16 Jun 1881**

Notes
Petitions – PET557 to PET570
This Bill was the second of four times the Bill was introduced: see PUBB36, PUBB38 and PUBB41

Patents for Inventions Bill 1882

PUBB38	1882
	Patents for Inventions Bill 1882 (45 & 46 Vict)
	Bill to amend the Law relating to Patents for Inventions

Table of contents
Cl 1 Commencement of Act
Cl 2 Appointment of Paid Commissioners
Cl 3 Salaries of paid Commissioners
Cl 4 Duties of paid Commissioners
Cl 5 Duration of new Letters Patent
Cl 6 Application of Act to existing Letters Patent
Cl 7 Terms of grace for payment
Cl 8 Duties payable for Letters Patent
Cl 9 Extended provisional protection
Cl 10 Subsequent improvements may be added to an existing patent for half fees
Cl 11 Patent rights good against Crown, but may be used for public service on terms to be agreed on
Cl 12 Public servants, except those in Patent Office, may become patentees
Cl 13 Short title
Schedule of Stamp Duties
Schedule of Fines for Postponed Payments

Journal	
House of Commons	**House of Lords**
Pres: George Anderson, Alexander Brown, John Hinde Palmer and Henry Broadhurst	

			House of Lords
15 Feb 1882	137 CJ 48	Bill Ord/1R	*Never considered by House of Lords*
24 May 1882	137 CJ 229	2R adj	
13 Jun 1882	137 CJ 273	2R adj	
21 Jun 1882	137 CJ 291	2R adj	
24 Jun 1882	137 CJ 301	2R adj	
30 Jun 1882	137 CJ 320	2R adj	
8 Jul 1882	137 CJ 346	2R adj	
19 Jul 1882	137 CJ 376	2R adj	
26 Jul 1882	137 CJ 402	2R disc/Bill w/d	

(continued)

(continued)

Parliamentary debates	
Ord/1R: HC Deb, 15 Feb 1882, Vol 266(3rd), col 764	
Bill w/d: HC Deb, 25 Jul 1882, Vol 272(3rd), col 1682	

Parliamentary papers
Bill for the amendment of the law as to Patents for Inventions (1882 HC Papers 72), Vol 5, p 239

Newspaper coverage of debates
House of Commons
1R: The Times, 16 Feb 1882; Morning Post, 16 Feb 1882
Bill w/d: The Times, 26 Jul 1882

Notes
This Bill was the third of four times the Bill was introduced: see PUBB36, PUBB37 and PUBB41

Patents for Inventions (No 2) Bill 1882

PUBB39	1882
	Patents for Inventions (No 2) Bill 1882 (45 & 46 Vict)
	Bill to amend the Law relating to Patents

Table of contents

	Table of origin	1879 Bill
Cl 1 Short title, extent, and commencement of Act	1852, s 56 & 57	1 & 2
Cl 2 Repeal of scheduled enactments and rules	—	3
Cl 3 Interpretation of terms	1852, s 55	4
Cl 4 Patents excepted from Statute of Monopolies	—	—
Cl 5 Subject matter for which a patent may be granted	1852, s 55	4
Cl 6 To whom a patent may be granted	—	24
Cl 7 Case of inventions patented abroad	1852, s 25	24
Cl 8 Establishment of Board of Commissioners for Patents	1852, s 1 & 2	5 & 40
Cl 9 Examiners of patents	—	—
Cl 10 Lodging application and provisional specification	1852, s 6, 9, 11 & 12	6
Cl 11 Provisional protection	1852, s 8	7
Cl 12 Reference to and report by examiner	—	—
Cl 13 Complete specification	1852, s 9	8
Cl 14 Applicant may lodge complete specification in the first instance	1852, s 9	—
Cl 15 Further reference to and report by Examiner	—	9
Cl 16 Publication of complete specification and effect thereof	—	—
Cl 17 Opposition to grant of patent	1852, s 8	10
Cl 18 Sealing of patent	1852, s 15 & 18	12, 13, 14 & 15
Cl 19 Date and time for sealing patent	1852, s 20, 23 & 24	15
Cl 20 Duration of patent	—	16
Cl 21 Extent of patent	1852, s 18	15
Cl 22 Certificate of renewal of patent	—	—
Cl 23 Proceedings for obtaining of specification	1852, s 8 & 39	17
Cl 24 Application for prolongation of patent	—	—
Cl 25 Power of Commissioners to grant prolongation	—	—
Cl 26 Stamp duties in Schedule	1852, s 44	—
Cl 27 Patent to bind Crown subject to provision for naval and military service	—	18
Cl 28 Assignment for part of United Kingdom	1852, s 35	20
Cl 29 Order of Commissioners for grant of licences in certain events	—	19
Cl 30 Register of patents	1852, s 34	21
Cl 31 Register of proprietors	1852, s 35	21
Cl 32 Inspection of registers	1852, s 34	44
Cl 33 Correction of registers	—	22
Cl 34 Abolition of *scire facias*	—	23
Cl 35 Proceedings for revocation of patents	—	23

Cl 36 New patents on revocation for fraud	—	—
Cl 37 Foreign vessels in British waters	1852, s 26	25
Cl 38 Protection of inventions from consequences of public use at exhibitions	—	—
Cl 39 Patent to true inventor not invalidated by application in fraud of him	1852, s 10	26
Cl 40 Falsification of entries in registers	1852, s 37	27
Cl 41 Penalty for unauthorised use of name of patentee, of word patent, &c.	—	28
Cl 42 False declaration a misdemeanour	1852, s 6	29
Cl 43 Power for Commissioners to extend time in certain cases	1852, s 20	32
Cl 44 Costs of opposition	1852, s 14	31
Cl 45 Particulars on opposition or petition for revocation	1852, s 41 & 43	34
Cl 46 Assistance of expert	—	38 & 39
Cl 47 Patent Office	1852, s 4	42
Cl 48 Remuneration of Commissioners and of Examiners	—	—
Cl 49 Officers and clerks	1852, s 3	43 & 44
Cl 50 Duties of Commissioners as to publication of *Patents Journal* and other matters	1852, s 5 & 48	44
Cl 51 General rules for management of Patent Office and business of Commissioners	1852, s 3	—
Cl 52 Rules to laid before Parliament	1852, s 3	—
Cl 53 Copies of documents admissible in evidence	—	41
Cl 54 Annual report of Commissioners	1852, s 3 & 51	45
Cl 55 Quorum of Commissioners	1852, s 1	46
Cl 56 Occasional appointment of Examiner to act as Commissioner	—	—
Cl 57 Delivery of particulars	1852, s 41 & 43	34
Cl 58 Certain pleases in actions for infringements abolished	—	—
Cl 59 Pleas that Inventions is not new	—	—
Cl 60 Order for inspection, &c. in action	1852, s 42	39
Cl 61 Certificate of validity questioned and costs thereon	1852, s 43	37
Cl 62 Security for costs in case of endorsed patent	—	—
Cl 63 Duty of Commissioners to act as assessors on request of court or judge	—	—
Cl 64 Reference to Commissioners of cases triable by referee	—	—
Cl 65 Duty of Commissioners to act as arbitrators	—	—
Cl 66 General rules as to arbitrations	—	—
Cl 67 General Powers of Commissioners	—	44
Cl 68 Power of Commissioners and Examiners to administer oaths	—	—
Cl 69 Enforcement of orders of Commissioners	—	—
Cl 70 Evidence of documents	—	—
Cl 71 Collection of fees	—	—
Cl 72 Notices, how to be given	—	—
Cl 73 Existing patents	1852, s 52 & 53	53
Cl 74 Existing registers	—	56
Cl 75 Pending applications	1852, s 52 & 53	53
Cl 76 Transfer of property, &c. of existing Commissioners	—	55
Cl 77 Savings from repeal	—	54
Cl 78 Transfer of power of existing Commissioners in relation to trade marks and copyright of designs	—	—
Cl 79 Recovery of penalties [Scotland]	—	51
Cl 80 Payment of costs by Commissioners [Scotland]	—	48
Cl 81 Saving for courts [Scotland]	1852, s 43	49
Cl 82 Proceedings for revocation of patent [Scotland]	1852, s 35 & 43	50
Cl 83 Reservation of remedies [Ireland]	1852, s 29	52
Cl 84 Reservation of powers to Crown	1852, s 16	58
Cl 85 Saving for prerogative	1852, s 16	59
First Schedule – Acts repealed	—	—
Second Schedule – Form of Letters Patent	—	—
Third Schedule – Stamp Duties	—	—

(continued)

(continued)

Journal	
House of Commons	**House of Lords**
Pres: Sir John Lubbock, William Henry Smith and John Compton Lawrence	

House of Commons			House of Lords
15 Mar 1882	137 CJ 104	Bill Ord/1R	*Never considered by House of Lords*
17 Apr 1882	137 CJ 141	2R adj	
29 Apr 1882	137 CJ 168	2R/C'tted CWH	
23 May 1882	137 CJ 222	CWH adj	
16 Jun 1882	137 CJ 278	CWH adj	
6 Jul 1882	137 CJ 339	CWH adj	

Parliamentary debates
Bill Ord/1R: HC Deb, 15 Mar 1882, Vol 267(3rd), col 984
2R: **HC Deb, 28 Apr 1882, Vol 268(3rd), col 1785**

Parliamentary papers
Bill to amend the Law relating to Patents (1882 HC Papers 104), Vol 5, p 245

Newspaper coverage of debates
House of Commons
1R: The Times, 16 Mar 1882; Morning Post, 16 Feb 1882
2R: *The Times, 29 Apr 1882*

Notes
Petitions – PET572 to PET577
The same Bill was introduced in the following session: PUBB40

Patents for Inventions (No 2) Bill 1883

PUBB40	1883
Patents for Inventions (No 2) Bill 1883 (46 & 47 Vict)	
Bill to amend the Law relating to Patents	

Table of contents		
	Table of origin	**1879 Bill**
Cl 1 Short title, extent, and commencement of Act	1852, s 56 & 57	1 & 2
Cl 2 Repeal of scheduled enactments and rules	—	3
Cl 3 Interpretation of terms	1852, s 55	4
Cl 4 Patents excepted from Statute of Monopolies	—	—
Cl 5 Subject matter for which a patent may be granted	1852, s 55	4
Cl 6 To whom a patent may be granted	—	24
Cl 7 Case of inventions patented abroad	1852, s 25	24
Cl 8 Establishment of Board of Commissioners for Patents	1852, s 1 & 2	5 & 40
Cl 9 Examiners of patents	—	
Cl 10 Lodging application and provisional specification	1852, s 6, 9, 11 & 12	6
Cl 11 Provisional protection	1852, s 8	7
Cl 12 Reference to and report by examiner	—	—
Cl 13 Complete specification	1852, s 9	8
Cl 14 Applicant may lodge complete specification in the first instance	1852, s 9	—
Cl 15 Further reference to and report by Examiner	—	9
Cl 16 Publication of complete specification and effect thereof	—	—
Cl 17 Opposition to grant of patent	1852, s 8	10
Cl 18 Sealing of patent	1852, s 15 & 18	12, 13, 14 & 15
Cl 19 Date and time for sealing patent	1852, s 20, 23 & 24	15
Cl 20 Duration of patent	—	16
Cl 21 Extent of patent	1852, s 18	15
Cl 22 Certificate of renewal of patent	—	—
Cl 23 Proceedings for obtaining of specification	1852, s 8 & 39	17

Cl 24 Application for prolongation of patent	—	—
Cl 25 Power of Commissioners to grant prolongation	—	—
Cl 26 Stamp duties in Schedule	1852, s 44	—
Cl 27 Patent to bind Crown subject to provision for naval and military service	—	18
Cl 28 Assignment for part of United Kingdom	1852, s 35	20
Cl 29 Order of Commissioners for grant of licences in certain events	—	19
Cl 30 Register of patents	1852, s 34	21
Cl 31 Register of proprietors	1852, s 35	21
Cl 32 Inspection of registers	1852, s 34	44
Cl 33 Correction of registers	—	22
Cl 34 Abolition of *scire facias*	—	23
Cl 35 Proceedings for revocation of patents	—	23
Cl 36 New patents on revocation for fraud	—	—
Cl 37 Foreign vessels in British waters	1852, s 26	25
Cl 38 Protection of inventions from consequences of public use at exhibitions	—	—
Cl 39 Patent to true inventor not invalidated by application in fraud of him	1852, s 10	26
Cl 40 Falsification of entries in registers	1852, s 37	27
Cl 41 Penalty for unauthorised use of name of patentee, of word patent, &c.	—	28
Cl 42 False declaration a misdemeanour	1852, s 6	29
Cl 43 Power for Commissioners to extend time in certain cases	1852, s 20	32
Cl 44 Costs of opposition	1852, s 14	31
Cl 45 Particulars on opposition or petition for revocation	1852, s 41 & 43	34
Cl 46 Assistance of expert	—	38 & 39
Cl 47 Patent Office	1852, s 4	42
Cl 48 Remuneration of Commissioners and of Examiners	—	—
Cl 49 Officers and clerks	1852, s 3	43 & 44
Cl 50 Duties of Commissioners as to publication of *Patents Journal* and other matters	1852, s 5 & 48	44
Cl 51 General rules for management of Patent Office and business of Commissioners	1852, s 3	—
Cl 52 Rules to laid before Parliament	1852, s 3	—
Cl 53 Copies of documents admissible in evidence	—	41
Cl 54 Annual report of Commissioners	1852, s 3 & 51	45
Cl 55 Quorum of Commissioners	1852, s 1	46
Cl 56 Occasional appointment of Examiner to act as Commissioner	—	—
Cl 57 Delivery of particulars	1852, s 41 & 43	34
Cl 58 Certain pleases in actions for infringements abolished	—	—
Cl 59 Please that inventions is not new	—	—
Cl 60 Order for inspection, &c. in action	1852, s 42	39
Cl 61 Certificate of validity questioned and costs thereon	1852, s 43	37
Cl 62 Security for costs in case of endorsed patent	—	—
Cl 63 Duty of Commissioners to act as assessors on request of court or judge	—	—
Cl 64 Reference to Commissioners of cases triable by referee	—	—
Cl 65 Duty of Commissioners to act as arbitrators	—	—
Cl 66 General rules as to arbitrations	—	—
Cl 67 General Powers of Commissioners	—	44
Cl 68 Power of Commissioners and Examiners to administer oaths	—	—
Cl 69 Enforcement of orders of Commissioners	—	—
Cl 70 Evidence of documents	—	—
Cl 71 Collection of fees	—	—
Cl 72 Notices, how to be given	—	—
Cl 73 Existing patents	1852, s 52 & 53	53
Cl 74 Existing registers	—	56
Cl 75 Pending applications	1852, s 52 & 53	53
Cl 76 Transfer of property, &c. of existing Commissioners	—	55
Cl 77 Savings from repeal	—	54
Cl 78 Transfer of power of existing Commissioners in relation to trade marks and copyright of designs	—	—

(continued)

(continued)

Cl 79 Recovery of penalties [Scotland]	—	51
Cl 80 Payment of costs by Commissioners [Scotland]	—	48
Cl 81 Saving for courts [Scotland]	1852, s 43	49
Cl 82 Proceedings for revocation of patent [Scotland]	1852, s 35 & 43	50
Cl 83 Reservation of remedies [Ireland]	1852, s 29	52
Cl 84 Reservation of powers to Crown	1852, s 16	58
Cl 85 Saving for prerogative	1852, s 16	59
First Schedule – Acts repealed	—	—
Second Schedule – Form of Letters Patent	—	—
Third Schedule – Stamp Duties	—	—

Journal	
House of Commons	**House of Lords**
Pres: Sir John Lubbock, William Henry Smith and John Compton Lawrence	

House of Commons			House of Lords
17 Feb 1883	138 CJ 13	Bill Ord	*Never considered by House of Lords*
17 Feb 1883	138 CJ 18	1R	
27 Feb 1883	138 CJ 55	2R/C'tted CWH	
7 Mar 1883	138 CJ 72	CWH adj	
14 Mar 1883	138 CJ 90	CWH adj	
20 Mar 1883	138 CJ 103	CWH adj	
17 Apr 1883	138 CJ 143	CWH adj	
25 Apr 1883	138 CJ 162	CWH adj	
27 Apr 1883	138 CJ 165	CWH adj	
28 Apr 1883	138 CJ 168	CWH adj	
28 May 1883	138 CJ 221	CWH adj	
8 Jun 1883	138 CJ 258	CWH adj	
26 Jun 1883	138 CJ 300	CWH adj	
30 Jun 1883	138 CJ 312	CWH adj	
10 Jul 1883	138 CJ 336	CWH adj	
20 Jul 1883	138 CJ 367	CWH adj	
25 Jul 1883	138 CJ 385	CWH Disc	

Parliamentary debates	
Ord/1R: HC Deb, 16 Feb 1883, Vol 276(3rd), col 268	
2R: **HC Deb, 27 Feb 1883, Vol 276(3rd), col 1095–1096**	
Bill w/d: HC Deb, 25 Jul 1883, Vol 282(3rd), col 422	

Parliamentary papers
Bill to amend the law relating to patents (1883 HC Papers 83), Vol 8, p 417

Newspaper coverage of debates
House of Commons
1R: Pall Mall Gazette, 17 Feb 1883
2R: **The Times, 28 Feb 1883**; Morning Post, 28 Feb 1883; London Evening Standard, 28 Feb 1883

Notes
The same Bill was introduced in the previous session: PUBB39

Patents for Inventions (No 3) Bill 1883

PUBB41	1883
Patents for Inventions (No 3) Bill 1883 (46 & 47 Vict)	
Bill for the amendment of the Laws relating to Patents for Inventions	

Table of contents
Cl 1 Commencement of Act
Cl 2 Appointment of Paid Commissioners
Cl 3 Salaries of paid Commissioners
Cl 4 Duties of paid Commissioners
Cl 5 Duration of new Letters Patent
Cl 6 Application of Act to existing Letters Patent
Cl 7 Terms of grace for payment
Cl 8 Duties payable for Letters Patent
Cl 9 Extended provisional protection
Cl 10 Subsequent improvements may be added to an existing patent for half fees
Cl 11 Patent rights good against Crown, but may be used for public service on terms to be agreed on
Cl 12 Public servants, except those in Patent Office, may become patentees
Cl 13 Short title
Schedule of Stamp Duties
Schedule of Fines for Postponed Payments

Journal

House of Commons			House of Lords
Pres: George Anderson, Alexander Brown, John Hinde Palmer and Henry Broadhurst			
22 Feb 1883	138 CJ 42	Bill Ord/1R	*Never considered by House of Lords*
27 Feb 1883	138 CJ 55	2R/C'tted CWH	
7 Mar 1883	138 CJ 73	CWH adj	
14 Mar 1883	138 CJ 90	CWH adj	
11 Apr 1883	138 CJ 131	CWH	
9 May 1883	138 CJ 192	CWH adj	
11 May 1883	138 CJ 205	CWH adj	
20 Jun 1883	138 CJ 288	CWH adj	
4 Jul 1883	138 CJ 321	CWH adj	
18 Jul 1883	138 CJ 362	CWH adj	
1 Aug 1883	138 CJ 407	Ord Disc/Bill w/d	

Parliamentary debates

1R: HC Deb, 21 Feb 1883, Vol 276(3rd), col 565	
2R: HC Deb, 27 Feb 1883, Vol 276(3rd), col 1096–1097	
CWH: HC Deb, 10 Apr 1883, Vol 277(3rd), col 2052	
Bill w/d: HC Deb, 1 Aug 1883, Vol 282(3rd), col 1219	

Parliamentary papers

Bill for the amendment of the Laws relating to Patents for Inventions (1883 HC Papers 99), Vol 8, p 451

Newspaper coverage of debates

House of Commons
2R: The Times, 28 Feb 1883
CWH: The Times, 11 Apr 1883

Notes

This Bill was the fourth and final time the Bill was introduced: see PUBB36, PUBB37 and PUBB38

Patent Agents Bill 1894

PUBB42	1894
	Patent Agents Bill 1894 (57 & 58 Vict)
	Bill to amend the law relating to Patent Agents

(continued)

(continued)

Table of contents
Cl 1 Short title
Cl 2 Interpretation of Terms
Cl 3 Incorporation
Cl 4 The council to keep a roll of patent agents
Cl 5 Persons entitled to have their name on the roll and register
Cl 6 A register to be kept at the Patent Office
Cl 7 Certificate of enrolment
Cl 8 Enrolment fee
Cl 9 Provision for ensuring that only fit and proper persons are admitted by examination to practise at patent agents
Cl 10 Annual fee for continued enrolment
Cl 11 Procedure for striking name off the roll in the event of professional misconduct
Cl 12 Reference to court of a resolution to remove a name or not to examine an application for examination
Cl 13 Re-entry of a name on the roll and register
Cl 14 Penalty for illegally acting as a patent agent
Cl 15 The institute, the society and the committee may be incorporate with the body by this Act created
Cl 16 The council
Cl 17 Bylaws
Cl 18 First election of council and officers
Cl 19 Amendment of byelaws
Cl 20 Bylaws not to fix minimum fees or to prevent patent agents from advertising or from carrying on other business
Cl 21 Repeal of [Patents, Designs, and Trade Marks Act 1888] 51 & 52 Vict c 50, s 1 as and from 1 June 1895 and saving clause
Cl 22 Provision for varying first council and adapting byelaws in the event of amalgamation under section fifteen of this Act
Schedule

Journal	
House of Commons	**House of Lords**
Pres: Alban Gibbs, Sir Reginald Hanson, William Frederick Smith, Henry Kimber, Robert Farquharson, Augustine Birrell and Sir Albert Rollit Rep: Thomas Bolton	

16 Mar 1894	149 CJ 23	Bill Ord	*Never considered by House of Lords*
16 Mar 1894	149 CJ 27	1R	
4 Apr 1894	149 CJ 55	2R/C'tted SC	
21 Apr 1894	149 CJ 91	Three quorum	
25 Jul 1894	149 CJ 319	Rep/Re-C'tted CWH	

Parliamentary debates	
Ord/1R: HC Deb, 16 Mar 1894, Vol 22(4th), col 451	
2R: HC Deb, 4 Apr 1894, Vol 22(4th), col 1373–1376	
Rep: HC Deb, 25 Jul 1894, Vol 27(4th), col 95	

Parliamentary papers
Bill to amend the law relating to Patent Agents (1894 HC Papers 18), Vol 7, p 309 [includes Memorandum]
Special report from the Select Committee on the Patent Agents Bill (1894 HC Papers 235), Vol 14, p 247 [report also dealt with Patent Agents Registration Bill: PUBB43]
Supplement to Votes & Proceedings, 1894 – No amendments

Newspaper coverage of debates
House of Commons
1R: The Times, 17 Mar 1894
2R: The Times, 5 Apr 1894

Notes
Petitions – PET591 and PET592

Patent Agents Registration Bill 1894

PUBB43	1894
Patent Agents Registration Bill 1894 (57 & 58 Vict)	
Bill to provide for the Registration of Patent Agents	

Table of contents (1894 HC Papers 334)
Cl 1 Short title Cl 2 Interpretation Cl 3 Statutory Committee; future transfer of power of Statutory Committee to Council of Institute Cl 4 Penalty on unregistered persons using the title of "patent agent, &c." Cl 5 Institution of prosecutions Cl 6 Qualifications necessary for registration Cl 7 Registration of qualified persons Cl 8 Refusal of registrar to register Cl 9 Appeal from Statutory Committee and therefrom to Court Cl 10 Contents and form of register and other provisions as to register Cl 11 Alterations in register; removal of name from register on request or death Cl 12 Discipline Cl 13 Proceeding of Statutory Committee Cl 14 Power of Court to order removal and restoration of name to register Cl 15 Examination Cl 16 Fees for examinations Cl 17 Cancellation of existing Board of Trade rules Cl 18 Taxation of patent agents charges Cl 19 Appointment and duties of registrar Cl 20 Application of fess Cl 21 Penalty of wilful falsification of register Cl 22 Penalty for obtaining registration by false representation Cl 23 Recovery of penalties Cl 24 Rules by Lord Chancellor Cl 25 Charter Cl 26 Committee of election and admission of fellows Cl 27 Proceedings of committee of election Cl 28 Existing register Cl 29 Exceptions Schedule – Form of register

Journal			
House of Commons			**House of Lords**
Pres: Cornelius Warmington, David Thomas and Edmund Byrne			
4 Apr 1894	149 CJ 55	Bill Ord	*Never considered by House of Lords*
4 Apr 1894	149 CJ 56	1R	
10 Apr 1894	149 CJ 63	2R adj	
11 Apr 1894	149 CJ 66	2R adj	
11 Apr 1894	149 CJ 68	2R/C'tted SC	
25 Jul 1894	149 CJ 319	Rep/Re-C'tted CWH	
27 Jul 1894	149 CJ 325	CWH disc	
7 Aug 1894	149 CJ 352	Bill w/d	

(continued)

(continued)

Parliamentary debates	
Ord/1R: **HC Deb, 4 Apr 1894, Vol 22(4th), col 1373–1376**	
2R: HC Deb, 11 Apr 1894, Vol 23(4th), col 171	
SC Nom: HC Deb, 20 Apr 1894, Vol 23(4th), col 1068	
Rep: HC Deb, 25 Jul 1894, Vol 27(4th), col 952	

Parliamentary papers
Bill to provide for the Registration of Patent Agents (1894 HC Papers 143), Vol 7, p 323 [includes Memorandum]
Bill to provide for the Registration of Patent Agents (as amended in Committee) (1894 HC Papers 334), Vol 7, p 339
Special report from the Select Committee on the Patent Agents Bill (1894 HC Papers 235), Vol 14, p 247 [report also dealt with Patent Agents Bill: PUBB42]
Supplement to Votes & Proceedings, 1894 – No amendments

Newspaper coverage of debates
House of Commons
2R: The Times, 12 Apr 1894
Com: *The Times, 25 Jul 1894*
Bill w/d: The Times, 7 Aug 1894

Notes
Petitions – PET591 and PET592

Patents, Designs and Trade Marks (1883 to 1888) Amendment Bill 1895

PUBB44	1895
Patents, Designs and Trade Marks (1883 to 1888) Amendment Bill 1895 (58 & 59 Vict)	
Bill to Amend the Patents, Designs, and Trade Marks Acts, 1883 to 1888	

Table of contents
Cl 1 Letters Patent not to be invalidated by unintentional prior publication
Cl 2 Supplementary provisional specifications
Cl 3 Disconformity
Cl 4 Amendment of [Patents, Designs and Trade Marks Act 1883] 46 & 47 Vict c 57, s 11 [Opposition period]
Cl 5 Anticipation of ancient date
Cl 6 Amendment of [Patents, Designs, and Trade Marks (Amendment) Act 1885] 48 & 49 Vict c 63, s 4 [prior publication]
Cl 7 Amendment of [Patents, Designs, and Trade Marks (Amendment) Act 1885] 48 & 49 Vict c 63, s 8 [period extended to nine months]
Cl 8 Disclaimer
Cl 9 Right to put disclaimed specification in evidence
Cl 10 Procedure in action for continuing infringement
Cl 11 Short title and construction

Journal			
House of Commons			**House of Lords**
Pres: John Moulton, Sir Richard Webster, Sir William Houldsworth, Sir Albert Rollit, Richard Haldane and Edward Blake			
2 Apr 1895	150 CJ 129	Bill Ord/1R	*Never considered by House of Lords*
9 Apr 1895	150 CJ 142	2R adj	
30 Apr 1895	150 CJ 166	2R adj	
14 May 1895	150 CJ 202	2R adj	
28 May 1895	150 CJ 243	2R adj	
18 Jun 1895	150 CJ 283	2R adj	

Parliamentary debates	
Ord/1R: HC Deb, 1 Apr 1895, Vol 32(4th), col 700	

Parliamentary papers
Bill to Amend the Patents, Designs, and Trade Marks Acts, 1883 to 1888 (1895 HC Papers 189), Vol 5, p 387 [includes Explanatory Memorandum]

Newspaper coverage of debates
House of Commons
1R: The Times, 2 Apr 1895

Notes
Archive
Patents, Designs and Trade Marks Act (1883 to 1888) Amendment Bill 189: National Archive (BT 13/25)
Patents, Designs and Trade Marks Act (1883 to 1888) Amendment Bill: Papers read before Society of Patents Agents: National Archive (BT 209/447)
Patents, Designs and Trade Marks Act (1883 to 1888) Amendment Bill: Chief Examiner's Notes: National Archive (BT 209/448)
Petition – PET593

Patents, Designs and Trade Marks (Registration of Patent Agents) Bill 1905

PUBB45	1905

Patents, Designs and Trade Marks (Registration of Patent Agents) Bill 1905 (5 Edw 7)

Bill to amend the Law relating to Patent Agents

Table of contents
Cl 1 Interpretation Cl 2 Penalty on unregistered persons using the title of "patent agent", &c. Cl 3 Short title

Journal

House of Commons	House of Lords		
	Pres: Lord Coleridge		
Never considered by House of Commons	23 Mar 1905	137 LJ 76	1R
	6 Apr 1905	137 LJ 102	2R day app
	10 Apr 1905	137 LJ 108	2R/C'tted CWH
	13 Apr 1905	137 LJ 116	Ord for CWH disc
	18 Jul 1905	137 LJ 261	Pet Patent Ag [PET598]/Ref SC

Parliamentary debates	
	1R: HL Deb, 23 Mar 1905, Vol 143(4th), col 923
	2R: **HL Deb, 10 Apr 1905, Vol 144(4th), col 963 and 969–971**
	Pet ref C'ttee: HL Deb, 18 Jul 1905, Vol 149(4th), col 1019

Parliamentary papers
Patents, Designs and Trade Marks (Registration of Patent Agents) Bill (1905 HL Papers 36), Vol 6, p 553 [includes Explanatory Memorandum]
Amendments to be moved in Committee by the Lord Coleridge (1905 HL Papers 36a), Vol 6, p 557

Newspaper coverage of debates
House of Lords
2R: *The Times, 11 Apr 1905*

Notes
Petition – PET598

Patents, Designs and Trade Marks (Registration of Patent Agents) Bill 1906

PUBB46	1906
	Patents, Designs and Trade Marks (Registration of Patent Agents) Bill 1906 (6 Edw 7)
	Bill to amend the Law relating to Patent Agents

Table of contents

Cl 1 Interpretation
Cl 2 Penalty on unregistered persons using the title of "patent agent", &c.
Cl 3 Exceptions
Cl 4 Definition clause
Cl 5 Short title

Journal

House of Commons			House of Lords		
			Pres: Lord Coleridge SC Rep: Viscount Cross CWH Rep: Lord Coleridge		
29 May 1906	161 CJ 222	Brought HL	13 Mar 1906	138 LJ 85	1R
11 Jun 1906	161 CJ 233	1R	26 Mar 1906	138 LJ 102	2R/C'tted CWH
13 Jun 1906	161 CJ 242	2R adj	27 Mar 1906	138 LJ 105	Rep with Amds/C'tted SC Standing Committee
19 Jun 1906	161 CJ 262	2R adj	8 May 1906	138 LJ Ap iv	Standing Committee
20 Jun 1906	161 CJ 264	2R adj	8 May 1906	138 LJ 150	**SC Rep with Amds**
21 Jun 1906	161 CJ 268	2R adj	22 May 1906	138 LJ 176	Cons date app
25 Jun 1906	161 CJ 276	2R adj	28 May 1906	138 LJ 185	**Cons with Amds**
27 Jun 1906	161 CJ 281	2R adj	29 May 1906	138 LJ 194	3R
3 Jul 1906	161 CJ 300	2R adj			
12 Jul 1906	161 CJ 331	2R adj			

Parliamentary debates

1R: HC Deb, 11 Jun 1906, Vol 158(4th), col 707	1R: HL Deb, 13 Mar 1906, Vol 153(4th), col 1066
	2R: **HL Deb, 26 Mar 1906, Vol 154(4th), col 808–809**
	CWH/Rep: HL Deb, 27 Mar 1906, Vol 154(4th), col 992
	Rep SC: HL Deb, 8 May 1906, Vol 156(4th), col 1104
	Rep: **HL Deb, 28 May 1906, Vol 158(4th), col 9–14**
	3R: HL Deb, 29 May 1906, Vol 158(4th), col 247

Parliamentary papers

Patents, Designs and Trade Marks (Registration of Patent Agents) Bill (1906 HL Papers 30) [includes Explanatory Memorandum], Vol 7, p 415

Patents, Designs and Trade Marks (Registration of Patent Agents) Bill (as amended by Standing Committee) (1906 HL Papers 77), Vol 7, p 419

  Amendments to be moved on Report by the Lord Granard (1906 HL Papers 77a), Vol 7, p 423

  Amendments to be moved on Report by the Lord Granard (1906 HL Papers 77b), Vol 7, p 425

  Amendments to be moved on Report by the Lord Coleridge (1906 HL Papers 77c), Vol 7, p 427

Patents, Designs and Trade Marks (Registration of Patent Agents) Bill (as amended on Report) (1906 HL Papers 102), Vol 7, p 429

Patents, Designs and Trade Marks (Registration of Patent Agents) Bill (1906 HC Papers 248), Vol 4, p 377

Newspaper coverage of debates

House of Lords

2R: **The Times, 27 Mar 1906**

Rep: The Times, 28 Mar 1906

Cons: **The Times, 29 May 1906**

3R: The Times, 30 May 1906

Notes
Archive
Patents, Designs and Trade Marks (Registration of Patents Agent) Bill 1906: National Archive (BT 209/452)
Patents, Designs and Trade Marks (Patents Agent) 1906: National Archive (BT 13/40)

Patents Bill 1906

PUBB47	1906
Patents Bill 1906 (6 Edw 7)	
Bill to amend the law relating to patents	

Table of contents
Cl 1 Representation of articles as "patented" Cl 2 Notice by reference to patent Cl 3 Misuse of name "Patent Office" Cl 4 Short title and construction Cl 5 Commencement

Journal			
House of Commons			**House of Lords**
Pres: James Dundas White			
16 May 1906	161 CJ 188	Bill Ord/1R	*Never considered by House of Lords*
15 Jun 1906	161 CJ 250	2R adj	
6 Jul 1906	161 CJ 315	2R adj	
9 Jul 1906	161 CJ 323	2R adj	

Parliamentary debates	
1R: HC Deb, 16 May 1906, Vol 157(4th), col 499–500	

Parliamentary papers
Patents Bill (1906 HC Papers 212), Vol 4, p 371

Newspaper coverage of debates
1R: The Times, 17 May 1906
2R adj: The Times, 19 Jun 1908

Notes
Archive
Patent Law Amendment Bill 1906: non-working of patents in UK: National Archive (BT 209/89)

Patents and Designs (No 2) Bill 1907

PUBB48	1907
Patents and Designs (No 2) Bill 1907 (7 Edw 7)	
Bill to amend the law relating to Patents and Designs	

Table of contents
Cl 1 Grant of patents to inventors only Cl 2 Marking of articles as "patented" Cl 3 Notice by reference to patent Cl 4 Limitation of injunctions and interdicts Cl 5 Marking of designs as "registered" Cl 6 Short title and construction Cl 7 Commencement

(continued)

(continued)

Journal			
House of Commons			**House of Lords**
Pres: James Dundas White			
11 Apr 1907	162 CJ 109	Bill Ord/1R	*Never considered by House of Lords*
29 Apr 1907	162 CJ 151	2R adj	
10 May 1907	162 CJ 182	2R adj	
7 Jun 1907	162 CJ 237	2R adj	
Parliamentary debates			
1R: HC Deb, 11 Apr 1907, Vol 172(4th), col 394			
Parliamentary papers			
Patents and Designs (No 2) Bill (1907 HC Papers 151), Vol 3, p 413			

Patents and Designs Bill 1917

PUBB49	1917
Patents and Designs Bill 1917 (7 & 8 Geo 5)	
Bill to amend the Patents and Designs, 1907	

Table of contents
Cl 1 Provisions for the protection of abuse of monopoly rights
Cl 2 Provision as to patents indorsed "licences of right"
Cl 3 Enforcement of order for grant of licence
Cl 4 Amendment of s 11 of principal Act [Patents and Designs Act 1907] as to the opposition to grant of patent
Cl 5 Amendment of s 12 of the principal Act as to the grant and sealing of patents
Cl 6 Term of patent
Cl 7 Amendment of s 18 of principal Act as to extension of term of patent
Cl 8 Power of court to grant relief in respect of particular claims
Cl 9 Amendment of s 34 of principal Act as to actions for infringement
Cl 10 Repeal of s 38(4) of principal Act
Cl 11 Articles for food or medical purposes
Cl 12 Costs and security for costs
Cl 13 Amendment of s 41(2) of principal Act as to anticipation
Cl 14 Cancellation of registration of designs
Cl 15 Registration of assignments, &c.
Cl 16 Amendment of s 75 of principal Act as to refusal to grant patents, &c.
Cl 17 Registration of patent agents
Cl 18 Definitions
Cl 19 Minor amendments of principal Act
Cl 20 Construction, printing and repeal
Cl 21 Short title
Schedule – Minor Amendments of Principal Act

Journal			
House of Commons			**House of Lords**
Pres: Sir Albert Stanley (Pr BoT)			
19 Nov 1917	172 CJ 245	1R	*Never considered by House of Lords*
20 Nov 1917	172 CJ 248	2R adj	
21 Nov 1917	172 CJ 249	2R adj	
26 Nov 1917	172 CJ 255	2R adj	
3 Dec 1917	172 CJ 266	2R adj	
10 Dec 1917	172 CJ 274	2R adj	
17 Dec 1917	172 CJ 281	2R adj	
20 Dec 1917	172 CJ 284	2R adj	
14 Jan 1918	172 CJ 286	2R adj	
21 Jan 1918	172 CJ 294	2R adj	
28 Jan 1918	172 CJ 302	2R adj	
5 Feb 1918	172 CJ 316	2R adj	

Parliamentary debates	
1R: HC Deb, 19 Nov 1917, Vol 99(5th), col 867	

Parliamentary papers
Patents and Designs Bill (1917–18 HC Papers 106), Vol 2, p 257

Notes
Archive
Advisory Committee on Commercial Intelligence: extract from minutes held to discussed proposed amendments to legislation: National Archive (BT 209/489)
Replies from those who received draft copies of Bill (BT 209/490)
Patents and Designs Bill to Amend Patents and Designs Act 1907. Comments by Federation of British Industries (BT 209/491)
Patents and Designs Bill to Amend Patents and Designs Act 1907. Amended Copies: National Archive (BT 209/492)
Patents and Designs Bill to Amend Patents and Designs Act 1907: Responses from Reconstruction C'ttee: National Archive (BT 209/488)
Patents and Designs Bill to Amend Patents and Designs Act 1907. Correspondence following first reading: National Archive (BT 209/493)
Patents and Designs Bill: Deputations from London Chamber of Commerce and Federation of British Industry: National Archive (BT 209/494)
Draft Bill to amend Patents and Designs Act 1907 and Trade Marks Act 1905: National Archive (BT 209/90)
Draft Bill to amend Patents and Designs Act 1907 and Trade Marks Act 1905: comments and criticisms: National Archive (BT 209/91)
Memorandum: Patents and Designs Bill: Cabinet Conclusions: National Archive (CAB 24/23/34)
Memorandum: Patents and Designs Bill: Cabinet Conclusions: National Archive (CAB 23/4/20)
Patents and Designs Bill Committee Minutes: Institute of Mechanical Engineers Archive (CMB 2/10)

Patents and Designs Bill 1934

PUBB50	1934		
Patents and Designs Bill 1934 (24 & 25 Geo 5)			
Bill to amend the law related to patents and designs by providing for the protection of employee inventors			
Table of contents			
Cl 1 Protection of employee inventors Cl 2 Short title and commencement			
Journal			
House of Commons		**House of Lords**	
Pres: John Wilmot, Charles Brown, Frederick Seymour Cocks, Rhys Davies, Neil Maclean and Alexander West Russell			
12 Jun 1934	189 CJ 229	Bill Ord/1R	*Never considered by House of Lords*
Parliamentary debates			
Ord/1R: **HC Deb, 12 Jun 1934, Vol 290(5th), col 1534–1536**			
Parliamentary papers			
Patents and Designs Bill 1934 (1933–34 HC Papers 136), Vol 3, p 423			

Inventions and Designs (Crown Use) Bill 1953

PUBB51	1953
Inventions and Designs (Crown Use) Bill 1953 (2 & 3 Eliz 2)	

(continued)

(continued)

Bill to make further provision as to the use from the services of the Crown of patented inventions and registered designs; to make permanent provision for the use of the purpose aforesaid of other inventions and designs and for the disclosure of industrial information required by the Crown for defence purposes; and for purposes connected with the matters aforesaid

Table of contents
Cl 1 Extension of powers of Crown to use patented inventions and registered designs Cl 2 Crown use of other inventions, designs etc. Cl 3 Power of Minister of Supply and Admiralty to require disclosure of industrial information Cl 4 Enforcement of directions under s 3 Cl 5 References of disputes as to payments under this Act Cl 6 Interpretation Cl 7 Expenses Cl 8 Short title, commencement, extent and repeal

Journal			
House of Commons	**House of Lords**		
	Pres: Lord Mancroft		
Never considered by House of Commons	10 Nov 1953	186 LJ 10	1R
	1 Dec 1953	186 LJ 32	2R deb adj sine die

Parliamentary debates	
	1R: HL Deb, 10 Nov 1953, Vol 184(5th), col 194
	2R: **HL Deb, 1 Dec 1953, Vol 184(5th), col 768–783**

Parliamentary papers
Inventions and Designs (Crown Use) Bill (1953 HL Papers 8), Vol 1 [includes Explanatory Memorandum]

Patents (Employees' Inventions) Bill 1965

PUBB52	1965
Patents (Employees' Inventions) Bill 1965	
Bill to amend the law governing rights in respect of inventions made by employees	

Table of contents
Cl 1 Rights in inventions made by employees Cl 2 Citation, interpretation and extent

Journal					
House of Commons			**House of Lords**		
			Pres: Lord Rhodes Rep: Lord Merthyr (Ld Ch)		
15 Jun 1965	220 CJ 306	Brought HL	14 Apr 1965	197 LJ 255	1R
16 Jun 1965	220 CJ 309	1R	27 Apr 1965	197 LJ 263	**2R/C'tted CWH**
23 Jul 1965	220 CJ 382	2R	11 May 1965	197 LJ 278	**CWH**
27 Jul 1965	220 CJ 388	2R/C'tted CWH	1 Jun 1965	197 LJ 317	**Rep w/o Amds/Cons**
			15 Jun 1965	197 LJ 333	**3R**

Parliamentary debates	
Bus: HC Deb, 24 June 1965, Vol 714(5th), col 1946	1R: HL Deb, 14 Apr 1965, Vol 265(5th), col 397
2R: HC Deb, 23 Jul 1965, Vol 716(5th), col 2227–2234	2R: HL Deb, 27 Apr 1965, Vol 265(5th), col 506–516
2R: HC Deb, 27 Jul 1965, Vol 717(5th), col 422–430	CWH/Rep: HL Deb, 11 May 1965, Vol 266(5th), col 12–55
	Rep: HL Deb, 1 Jun 1965, Vol 266(5th), col 1029–1051
	3R: HL Deb, 15 Jun 1965, Vol 267(5th), col 88–93

Parliamentary papers
Patents (Employees' Inventions) Bill (1964–65 HL Papers 94), Vol 3
Amendments to be moved in Committee by Lord Drumalbyn and Lord Cawley (1964–65 HL Papers 94a), Vol 3
Amendment to be moved on Report by Lord Rhodes (1964–65 HL Papers 94b), Vol 3
Amendments to be moved on Report by Lord Cawley and Lord Drumalbyn (1964–65 HL Papers 94c), Vol 3
Marshalled List of Amendments to be Moved in Committee (1964–65 HL Papers 94**), Vol 3
Marshalled List of Amendments to be Moved on Report (1964–65 HL Papers 94††), Vol 3
Patents (Employees' Inventions) Bill (as amended on Report) (1964–65 HL Papers 133), Vol 3
Marshalled List of Amendments to be Moved on Third Reading (1964–65 HL Papers 133**), Vol 3
Patents (Employees' Inventions) Bill (Brought from HL) (1964–65 HC Papers 161), Vol 3, p 861
When it failed
Instructions to Parliamentary Counsel: Departmental Papers: National Archive (BT 103/1118)

Part 2 contents

Chapter 1: Private Acts

(continued)

(continued)

Chapter 2: Private Bills and notices

(continued)

(continued)

Chapter 3: Standing Orders

Introduction

The work of Parliament in the eighteenth and nineteenth century included a substantial volume of private business. In simple terms, a private Act of Parliament allowed a person (and only that person) to do something which would otherwise be unlawful. This might be excepting them from the maximum term of a patent (e.g. a private Act to prolong the term of a patent) or from the restriction on more than twelve people owning a patent (e.g. one of the many company formation acts during the second quarter of the nineteenth century). Private Acts were started[1] by petition,[2] which would be referred to a committee, and later to examiners,[3] to

---

1 It was possible to start it by motion before 1685, when this was forbidden: 9 CJ 719 (26 May 1685).
2 Where the petition was lodged in the House of Commons but ordered to originate in the Lords, there was no record of the petition being read in the journals.

approve a Bill being introduced.[4] If a Bill was introduced, it went through the same process as public Acts so that it had a First and then Second Reading before being committed, reported and then moving to a Third Reading. However, it was possible for other people to petition Parliament to object to the Bill, at which point evidence would be heard before committees.

General structure

The general structure of records for private Bills follows the same basic structure as public Acts.[5] Thus, it begins with the year and the unique reference number, beginning PRVA for Acts and PRVB for Bills or notices. It is then followed by the short title (either that assigned by the Act itself or from the Chronological Table of Statutes as the case may be) and then the long title. This is then followed by the table of contents of the Private Act, Bill or notice, which in appropriate cases includes the relevant patent provisions only. Where necessary, the table of contents will be reconstructed as far as possible from the notice. The details of the underlying patent are then set out. This is followed by the journal entries setting out the particular stages and orders relating to the Bill. In addition, where petitions were lodged by opponents (or supporters), these are listed below the other journal entries with the name of the opponent and in square brackets the key points of the opposition.

In the unusual case where there are Parliamentary debates recorded in *Hansard* or similar on the Bill, these too are included. This is followed by the details of any Parliamentary papers (such as where there is a report of a Select Committee on a particular Bill). In contrast to public Bills, published Parliamentary papers are rare in relation to private Bills. After these papers, there are details of the *Gazette* notice related to the Bill, and then details of any debates in newspapers. In the eighteenth century, private Bills were often debated on the floor of the House and were covered in newspaper reports of proceedings. In contrast to public Bills, mentions in regional newspapers are included as well.[6] As the nineteenth century progressed, the reports on private Bills became more and more uncommon. Eventually, it became the case that papers did not report on private Bills beyond a mention that the Bill had passed certain stages.

The Archive section in the record includes the details held about the Bill in the Parliamentary Archive. This is followed by the Notes section, which includes details of any cases heard relating to the patent (found in *Hayward's Patent Cases* (HPC) and then the Official Reports of Patent Cases (RPC)). In each case, where the Act is included in Woodcroft's Collection of Patents, the number is given.

Patents

The private Acts included in Part 2 are those which relate to particular patents.[7] In respect of each private Act, the patent number is provided. In the period 1617-1852,[8] the numbers used are those assigned by Bennett Woodcroft in his collection of patents.[9] In addition, the title of the invention (based on that assigned by Woodcroft in his *Alphabetical Index*) and the inventor or inventors is recorded immediately afterwards in square brackets. In the period before 1852, it was necessary for patentees to get separate patents for England, Scotland and Ireland. Some, but not many, of the private Bills relate to Scots and Irish patents instead of, or as well as, the English patent. While there are some indexes to these patents,[10] these are based on the dates above. Accordingly, the date of the Irish or Scottish patent is recorded in curly brackets. In relation to United Kingdom patents granted after 1852, a number was assigned by the Commissioners (and later Comptroller)

3   The House of Commons introduced examiners in 1846, and the Lords in 1854.

4   In the early period, the committee considered whether the petition was prima facie expedient: see Thomas Sherwood, *A Treatise upon the Proceedings to be Adopted by Members in Conducting Private Bills* (Private 1828), p 7. Later, it just checked compliance with Standing Orders.

5   See Introduction to Part 1.

6   In contrast to the London papers, these have not been systematically searched (i.e. searched the day after events which are usually reported – meaning stages which are not usually reported may be omitted). The regional papers are entirely dependent on optical character recognition in the online archives. This means there are likely to be many more gaps and omissions.

7   Acts where a company is simply empowered to take a patent licence are not included as they are just spelling out the corporate powers (and therefore not specific).

8   One or two are omitted from that collection (by oversight), and the patent roll numbers are included in those cases.

9   See Introduction in Bennett Woodcroft, *Alpabetical Index of Patentees of Inventions 1617-1852* (Rsvd Ed, Evelyn Adams & Mackay 1969), at p v–viii. There is one instance of a patent mentioned in a record which is missed from this collection, so the patent roll citation is given.

10 In the CD-ROM collection *The Cradle of Invention* (Finishing Publishing); also see Sean Bottomley, "Patenting in England, Scotland and Ireland during the Industrial Revolution, 1700-1852" (2014) 54 *Explorations in Economic History* 48.

of Patents. This number and the formal title of the invention along with the inventor are included for each record. Indeed, later private Acts usually included the text of the patent grant (not the specification) as a Schedule to the Act.

Notices

The first Standing Orders for posting notices in relation to patent term extension were adopted by the House of Commons in 1798.[11] This required three notices to be published in the *London Gazette*, and where it affected Scotland, in Scottish newspapers.[12] Upon the Union with Ireland, the requirement was extended to the *Dublin Gazette* and the *Scottish Gazette*. A general rule requiring notices for most classes of private Bills was adopted in 1837,[13] and from that point, three notices needed to be published in the respective gazette where that part of the United Kingdom was affected. The rule remained the same until 1847,[14] when it was relaxed to require only one notice in each relevant gazette.

While there were many private Bills which only related to English patents prior to 1852 (and so notices were only required in the *London Gazette*), after the unified patent was introduced by the Patent Law Amendment Act 1852, every private Bill relating to patents had to have a notice in all three gazettes. Accordingly, for each Act the relevant gazette notices are included, specifying the date of the issue of the gazette, the issue number of the gazette and the page number. The *London Gazette* and *Edinburgh Gazette* have now been digitised, so are easily accessible online.[15] This is not yet the case for the *Dublin Gazette*. There appears to be only one complete set of the *Dublin Gazette* in existence,[16] which is held by the Oireachtas Library in Leinster House.[17] From the mid-1840s there are more or less complete sets held by the British Library and the Institute of Historical Research, University of London. The British Library also hold some years between 1800 and the 1820s, and Trinity College Dublin holds most of the 1830s (except 1838). Using a combination of these sources, it has been possible to identify all the relevant notices.

In 1889, the House of Lords added a new notice requirement,[18] namely a notice had to be posted in the Comptroller's Journal that an application to restore a patent was to be made. Accordingly, from that time the references in the journal are also included.[19]

Archive

While sessional papers were published on private Bills, this was a rarity. Accordingly, those seeking to undertake research into a particular Bill need to visit the Parliamentary Archive. The details of the papers held by the Parliamentary Archive for each Bill are provided in the Archive section. There are extensive records in relation to private Bills generally,[20] but patent Bills form a small part of that collection, and usually an uncontentious one. This means the papers available are more restricted. There is one very important thing which must be borne in mind: the fire in 1834 destroyed almost all the records of the House of Commons, so there are no archival records relating to private Bills in the Commons before that time. In relation to patents Bills, the following records exist.

House, minute and Ingrossed Bills

A Bill introduced into the House of Lords would have a "paper Bill" before 1849, and these have usually survived.[21] However, most patent-related Bills were introduced in the House of Commons, so no such records exist.[22] From 1849, the "paper Bill" became the "House Bill", and where a "House Bill" survives in the

11 53 CJ 524; 1 May 1798.
12 From 1800, and the Union with Ireland, where an Irish patent is affected, a notice has to be included in the *Dublin Gazette*.
13 92 CJ 638; 13 Jul 1837.
14 102 CJ 880; 15 Jul 1847.
15 www.thegazette.co.uk.
16 It has started to be digitised, but at the time of writing had got as far as 1800. It is also available in the *Burnley Collection of Newspapers* during this early period. However, no patent notices were posted before 1800, so it is of little help.
17 See Joseph Hammond, "The Dublin Gazette: 1705-1922" (1953) 13 *Dublin Historical Record* 108.
18 SO 8A (121 LJ 340; 6 Aug 1889).
19 Notices were sometimes placed in that journal before it was required by Standing Orders, but references to these are not included.
20 See Maurice Bond, *Guide to the Records of Parliament* (HMSO 1971), p 70-92 and 227-231.
21 Maurice Bond, *Guide to the Records of Parliament* (HMSO 1971), p 65.
22 While there are some printed private Bills held in the Parliamentary Archive, these are usually no more than the basis of the Private Acts collection (and there do not appear to be any patent Bills in the collection, which runs until 1849: Maurice Bond, *Guide to the Records of Parliament* (HMSO 1971), p 84).

archive, it is included in this section. Before 1849, after the Third Reading in the first House, the Bill would have been Ingrossed. The Ingrossment had the amendments of the second House directly written onto it (and these were in turn agreed by the first House). Over the relevant period, all patent Ingrossments survive in the Parliamentary Archive, so the reference to the Ingrossment is recorded. Furthermore, Bills which passed the House of Commons but were defeated in the Lords survive in Ingrossed form in the archive, so it is possible to know the text of the Bill which was being debated.

House of Lords committee books

The House of Lords committee books[23] run from the Restoration until well after the last private patent Bill (1907). These books were originally used by all committees, so they include a variety of material. Every private Bill,[24] except those heard by a Committee of the Whole House, will include an entry in the book. The books are in manuscript (usually legible, requiring no palaeography skills), most volumes have pencil page numbers and all books are arranged chronologically. In the Guide, the record for each committee book includes the dates and pages of each sitting of the relevant committee. The material included in the committee book relevant to a particular Bill can range from half a page to half a dozen pages, although longer entries were sometimes no more than reciting the preamble to the Bill.

From 1836, the committee minute book was divided into four series:[25] one dealing with Estate Bills, one with opposed Bills, one with unopposed Bills and one dealing with the Standing Orders Committee. The opposed and unopposed Bill minute books are largely a continuation of the early minute book (although the information in relation to unopposed Bills declined). As before, the dates and page numbers are recorded for each Bill. As the nineteenth century progressed, the material recorded in the Standing Orders minute books included more original material, such as petitions, certificates of non-compliance with standing orders and witness statements. Accordingly, where more than minutes of proceedings are included in the committee books, this is recorded in square brackets after the date and page number.

House of Lords main papers

Most documents laid before the House of Lords are collected in the House of Lords main papers.[26] This might include reports from Select Committees, reports from examiners, and minutes of evidence heard before the whole House. Where, if any, relevant material exists, it is referenced in the Archive section with a short description.

House of Commons

The House of Commons papers relating to private Bills are far more limited. There is nothing before 1834. The minutes of the Unopposed Bill Committee[27] begin in 1841, but there is a hiatus after this session until 1851. The minutes of this committee usually include only an entry of a few lines for each Bill setting out the agent, the date and whether it was approved. In each case, the page number and date are included in the record entry. Where a Bill was opposed, there are the minutes of the Opposed Bill Committee, which are similarly short, but will indicate the witnesses called and similar procedural matters.[28]

Evidence in relation to opposed Bills

Where evidence was heard from witnesses, a shorthand note would be made and then it would be transcribed into books of evidence. For some Bills, this evidence can run to over a hundred pages; although only a few patent Bills were so opposed.[29] In relation to each book of evidence, the names of the witnesses heard are included in square brackets in the Guide.

---

23   HL/PO/CO/1/.
24   Except, strangely, Thomas Savery's Patent Act 1699.
25   Under the same reference for all series: HL/PO/CO/1/.
26   Usually, HL/PO/10/.
27   Under reference: HC/CL/WM/UB/1/.
28   Under reference: HC/CL/PB/1/.
29   Under reference: HL/PO/PB/5/66 (and the Evidence Book numbers are included as well).

Miscellaneous papers

There is an assortment of other papers, which can include examiners' certificates, petitions, amendment sheets and so forth. These are included when archived.

National and regional archives

Any records in the National Archive which relate to a particular private Bill have been included. There are some private Bills where papers are held in archives other than the Parliamentary and National Archive. These have not been systematically searched, although where they are included in a search of the National Archive catalogue, they have been recorded.[30]

Standing Orders

The regulation of business before the Houses of Parliament was made more certain by the adoption of Standing Orders.[31] The details of these are included in Chapter 3. In relation to private Bills, Standing Orders began to be passed during the seventeenth century, but they covered a few very limited aspects of procedure. Over time, the number increased until there was a code of nearly three hundred orders governing private Bills. These orders regulated procedure (such as what must be lodged and when), but they could also, indirectly, regulate substance (e.g. a Third Reading will not be given to a Bill for a particular reason).

While there were many Standing Orders regulating private business before the House of Commons, there were only four Standing Orders directly connected with private Bills for patents. Each of these records includes the text of each version of the Standing Order (while they retained the same general purpose, many changed slightly over the years), the reference to the Parliamentary paper where that change was first published, and any reference to debates in *Hansard*, the journal or in newspapers. As the number assigned to a Standing Order varied over the years (sometimes almost every year), the number of the relevant Standing Order for each session is given. Finally, there is a Notes section for further information. The House of Lords Standing Orders follow the same pattern as House of Commons Standing Orders. The Standing Orders in the House of Lords, however, were more extensive in relation to patents, in that there were nine different orders passed.

---

30 In relation to Hornblower's Bill 1792, the papers from the Birmingham library archive were individually inspected as well.
31 See, generally, O Cyprian Williams, *The Historical Development of Private Bill Procedure and Standing Orders in the House of Commons* (2 Vols, HMSO 1948).

1 Private Acts

Censure Act 1621

PRVA1	1621
Censure Act 1621 (18 Ja 1. c. i)	

An Act containing the Censure given in Parliament against Sir Giles Mompesson, Sir Francis Mitchell, Francis Viscount Saint Albane Lord Chancellor of England, and Edward Flood

Judgments against Sir Gyles Mompesson and Sir Francis Michell (other judgments do not relate to patents)

"And so his Lordship pronounced the Judgement of the Lords against the said Sir Gyles Mompesson, in hæc verba:

"The Lords Spiritual and Temporal of this High Court of Parliament do Award and Adjudge:

1. That Sir Gyles Mompesson shall stand, and be from henceforth, degraded of the Order of Knighthood, with Reservation of the Dignity of his Wife and Children; and the Ceremonies of Degradation to be performed, by Direction of the Earl Marshal's Court, whensoever he shall be taken
2. And that he shall stand perpetually in Degree of a Person out-lawed for Misdemeanour and Trespass
3. And that his Testimony be received in no Court; and that he shall be of no Assize, Inquisition, or Jury
4. And that he shall be excepted out of all General Pardons to be hereafter granted
5. And that he shall be imprisoned during his Life
6. And that he shall not approach within Twelve Miles of the Courts of the King or Prince, nor of the King's High Courts, usually holden at Westminster
7. And that the King's Majesty shall have the Profits of his Lands for Life; and shall have all his Goods and Chattels as forfeited; and that he shall undergo Fine and Ransom, which their Lordships assess at Ten Thousand Pounds
8. And that he shall be disabled to hold or receive any Office under the King or for the Common Wealth
9. And Lastly, that he be ever held an Infamous Person." [26 Mar 1621 (3 LJ 72)]

"And therefore the Lords Spiritual and Temporal of this great and High Court of Parliament do award and adjudge:
Judgment against Sir Francis Michell

1. That the said Sir Frauncis Michell shall stand, and be from henceforth, degraded of the Order of Knighthood, with Reservation of the Dignity of his now Wife and Children; and the Ceremonies of Degradation to be performed by Direction of this Court to the Earl Marshal's Court
2. That he shall be imprisoned, during the King's Pleasure, in Finsbury Gaol, in the same Chamber there, where he provided for others; The Tower, where he now remains, being a Prison too worthy of him
3. That he shall undergo the Fine of a Thousand Pounds
4. That he shall be disabled to hold or receive any Office under the King, or for the Common-wealth." [4 May 1621 (3 LJ 109)]

Relevant patents	
Assorted dates	Wallace Notestein, Frances Relf and Hartley Simpson, *Commons Debates 1621* (Yale 1935), Vol 7 Alehouse Grant, p 311–322 Concealments, p 346–347 Gold and Silver Thread Patent, p 364–370 Inns Patent: p 379–387 Alehouse petitions, p 553–555

Journal

House of Commons			House of Lords		
27 Feb 1621	1 CJ 530	**Grievance Com – Mompesson**	3 Mar 1621	3 LJ 33	**Mompesson Escape Conf**
28 Feb 1621	1 CJ 531	**Grievance Com – Mompesson**	5 Mar 1621	3 LJ 34	Conf Mompesson
1 Mar 1621	1 CJ 533	Rep Grievance Com – Mompesson	5 Mar 1621	3 LJ 34	**Proclamation Mompesson**
1 Mar 1621	1 CJ 533	**Next stages for Mompesson**	5 Mar 1621	3 LJ 35	**Mompesson warrant issued**
2 Mar 1621	1 CJ 534	Rep Grievance Com – Mompesson	5 Mar 1621	3 LJ 36	**Search in Mompesson house**
3 Mar 1621	1 CJ 535	Mompesson escape	6 Mar 1621	3 LJ 38	**HC reqests Mompesson papers**
3 Mar 1621	1 CJ 535	**Re: Mompesson escape**	6 Mar 1621	3 LJ 38	Papers delivered to HC
3 Mar 1621	1 CJ 536	**Warrant for Mompesson**	12 Mar 1621	3 LJ 42	Rep on HC Conf
5 Mar 1621	1 CJ 538	**Grievance C'tee – Michell**	15 Mar 1621	3 LJ 45	**Grievances set out**

(continued)

(continued)

5 Mar 1621	1 CJ 539	**Search Ord**	16 Mar 1621	3 LJ 48	**Grievance Com**
6 Mar 1621	1 CJ 540	**Mompesson papers Ord**	17 Mar 1621	3 LJ 50	Wits Sums
6 Mar 1621	1 CJ 540	HL message Mompesson papers	19 Mar 1621	3 LJ 51	Wits Ex
6 Mar 1621	1 CJ 540	**Impeach Mompesson**	20 Mar 1621	3 LJ 56	Wit sworn
6 Mar 1621	1 CJ 544	Mompesson warrant concealment	22 Mar 1621	3 LJ 62	**Com findings against**
13 Mar 1621	1 CJ 552	HL message Mompesson Proc			**Mompesson**
16 Mar 1621	1 CJ 556	Letter from Mompesson	23 Mar 1621	3 LJ 67	Wits sworn
20 Mar 1621	1 CJ 564	Ord Michell refused	26 Mar 1621	3 LJ 68	**King's Speech**
26 Mar 1621	1 CJ 575	**Judgment against Mompesson**	26 Mar 1621	3 LJ 70	**HL findings against**
27 Mar 1621	1 CJ 576	Mompesson debts not lost			**Mompesson**
27 Apr 1621	1 CJ 595	HL Michell judgment adj	26 Mar 1621	3 LJ 71	HC demand judgment
4 May 1621	1 CJ 608	HL Michell judgment	26 Mar 1621	3 LJ 72	Mompesson judgment
			27 Mar 1621	3 LJ 73	Thanks for judgment
			26 Apr 1621	3 LJ 89	**Charges Michell and response**
			27 Apr 1621	3 LJ 94	Michell judgment date app
			27 Apr 1621	3 LJ 95	Michell judgment adj
			4 May 1621	3 LJ 108	Michell charges read
			4 May 1621	3 LJ 108	HC demand Michell judgment
			4 May 1621	3 LJ 109	**Michell judgment**
			26 May 1621	3 LJ 135	Enrolled as Act

Parliamentary debates

Wallace Notestein, Frances Relf and Hartley Simpson, *Commons Debates 1621* (Yale 1935):

Vol 2: X's Journal; Vol 3: Barrington's Diary; Vol 4: Pym's Diary; Vol 5: Belasye Diary, Smyth's Diary, Wentworths Diary, Rich's Notes; Vol 6: Holland''s Diary, Z Diary, Book of Committee, Howard's Diary; Horn Collection (B's diary); Minnesota Manuscript

Proceedings and Debates of the House of Commons in 1620 and 1621 (Oxford 1764) (Nicholas)

19 Feb 1621 (Mitchell questioned): Book of Committee, p 253. n 30

19 Feb 1621 (Grand C'tee): **Pym, p 78–81**; Smyth, p 257–258; **Wentworth, p 475–476**; **Book of Committee, p 249–253**; **Nicholas, Vol 1, p 63–66**

20 Feb 1621 (Mompesson Ex on Inns): **X, p 108–111**; Pym, p 82; **Wentworth, p 477–481**; **Book of Committee, p 254–257**; *Howard, p 300–301*; **Nicholas, Vol 1, p 69–72**

20 Feb 1621 (Case Rep): **X, p 112–115**; Wentworth, p 480–481; **Horn Collection (B), p 377**; **Nicholas, Vol 1, p 67 and 73**

20 Feb 1621 (Ord for Impeachment): Book of Orders, p 452

21 Feb 1621 (Rep on Mompesson Inns; alehouses Ex): **Pym, p 84–87**; **Wentworth, p 483**; Howard, p 284; **Book of Committee, p 260–261**; **Nicholas, Vol 1, p 75–77**

22 Feb 1621 (Mitchell Ex): *Pym, p 91–92*; Book of Committee, p 263–264; Howard, p 286

22 Feb 1621 (Rep on Alehouses): X, p 123; **Nicholas, Vol 1, p 78–79**

23 Feb 1621 (Mitchell Pet and sanction): **X, p 127–128**; *Pym, p 94*; Minnesota Manuscript, p 431; **Nicholas, Vol 1, p 82–85**

23 Feb 1621 (Mitchell punishment): **X, p 130–132**; Pym, p 94; **Wentworth, p 485–486**; Holland, p 4–5; Howard, p 286–287; Book of Orders, p 453–454

23 Feb 1621 (Power to punish Mitchell): **Pym, p 111–112**; *Smyth, p 260*; *Howard, p 356*; Minnesota Manuscript, p 431

24 Feb 1621 (Pet by Mompesson): X, p 134; *Pym, p 99*; Holland, p 7; Howard, p 301; Nicholas, Vol 1, p 89

24 Feb 1621 (Rep on Inns/Power to punish): *Wentworth. p 488–489*; Rich, p 523; Horn Collection, p 378

26 Feb 1621 (Mompesson Ex on Inns): Pym, p 107; **Rich, p 519–521**; **Holland, p 12–13**; **Book of Committee, p 268–270**; **Nicholas, Vol 1, p 100–101**

27 Feb 1621 (Inns Rep/Punishing Mompesson): **X, p 145–147**; **Pym, p 110–112**; *Smyth, p 260–261*; **Rich, p 522–523**; *Holland, p 14–15*; *Howard, p 301*; *Belasyse, p 15*; **Nicholas, Vol 1, p 102–104**

28 Feb 1621 (Committee to Impeach): *Barrington, p 137*; *Rich, p 531*; *Howard, p 302*; Nicholas, Vol 1, p 109

28 Feb 1621 (Mompesson Ex): **X, p 148–150**; Pym, p 116–117; Smyth, p 264; *Holland, p 19–20*; Howard, p 301–302

1 Mar 1621 (Impeachment Com): X, p 151, n 8; Belasyse, p 17; Smyth, p 266; Holland, p 22 and n 2; Horn Collection, p 379; **Nicholas, Vol 1, p 112–113**

2 Mar 1621 (Form of message to HL): Pym, p 119; *Belasyse, p 19*; Smyth, p 268; Holland, p 23; Nicholas, Vol 1, p 114

2 Mar 1621 (Gold Thread Com): **Pym, p 121–122**; Holland, p 25–26

3 Mar 1621 (Mompesson escape): **X, p 157–162**; *Pym, p 122–123*; **Belasyse, p 21–23**; *Smyth, p 269–270*; Nicholas, Vol 1, p 117–118

3 Mar 1621 (Com to hear Gold Thread): Smyth, p 269; **Nicholas, Vol 1, p 117–118**

5 Mar 1621 (Rep on Gold Thread; Mompesson grounds to impeach): **X, p 163–167** and n 25; Pym, p 124; **Belasyse, p 24**; **Smyth, p 271–272**; *Holland, p 29–30*; Howard, p 304–305 and 309–311; **Nicholas, Vol 1, p 120–123**

6 Mar 1621 (Mompesson patent called in/Mitchell papers seized and searched): Pym, p 125; Belasyse, p 28 and 30 n 13 and 16; Smyth, p 274; Holland, p 32; Howard, p 302–303

6 Mar 1621 (Rep Gold Thread): **Pym, p 126–128**; **Belasyse, p 29–31**; Smyth, p 274; **Holland, p 32–33**; Horn Collection, p 378–379

6 Mar 1621 (How to prosecute Mompesson/HL Req Mompesson papers): X, p 170; *Pym, p 126*; Smyth, p 274; Holland, p 32; Horn Collection, p 305; Nicholas, Vol 1, p 123 and 127

6 Mar 1621 (Concealment Rep): Belasyse, p 31; **Smyth, p 274–275**; **Holland, p 33–34**

6 Mar 1621 (Michell Ex): **X, p 172–173**; Pym, p 129; **Belasyse, p 31–32**; **Smyth, p 275–277**; **Holland, p 34–35**; **Nicholas, Vol 1, p 128–129**

7 Mar 1621 (Law for inns prepared, Gold Thread and concealments condemned): **X, p 174–176**; Pym, p 130–131; *Smyth, p 278–279*; Holland, p 36; Minnesota Manuscript, p 432; **Nicholas, Vol 1, p 131–132**

8 Mar 1621 (Rehearse impeach Mompesson): **X, p 179–199**; **Pym, p 134–137**; **Belasyse, p 32–33**; **Smyth, p 280–282**; *Holland, p 38–39*; **Nicholas, Vol 1, p 135–139**

8 Mar 1621 (Michell denounced to HL): Holland, p 41–42; Howard, p 306

9 Mar 1621 (Responsibility of referees/Summary of evidence): **X, p 199–202**; **Pym, p 138–140**; **Smyth, p 283–285**; Holland, p 45–51; **Nicholas, Vol 1, p 139–140**

10 Mar 1621 (HL Second Conf): **X, p 204–205**; **Smyth, p 287–288**; *Holland, p 52*; Horn Collection, p 382–383

10 Mar 1621 (Review of evidence): **Nicholas, Vol 1, p 141–142**

12 Mar 1621 (HL Second Conf Rep/HL Req Third Conf): X, p 209–210; Pym, p 146 and147; Smyth, p 289; Holland's Notes, Vol 6, p 56

13 Mar 1621 (Third Conf with HL): **X, p 211–212**; **Pym, p 149**; **Smyth, p 293–294**; Horn Collection, p 381–382; Nicholas, Vol 1, p 150

14 Mar 1621 (Mitchell and Mompesson written declarations): **X, p 220–221**; Smyth, p 296; Holland, p 62; Nicholas, Vol 1, p 155–157

15 Mar 1621 (Declaration and final arguments Mompesson): **X, p 227–231**; **Pym, p 157–158**; Belasyse, p 41–43; **Smyth, p 300–301**; *Holland, p 66*; Horn Collection, p 382

16 Mar 1621 (Should MPs testify in HL): **X, p 232–235**; **Pym, p 162–164**; **Belasyse, p 45–48**; *Smyth, p 302–303*; **Holland, p 69–71**; **Nicholas, Vol 1, p 176–178**

17 Mar 1621 (Message from HL): Nicholas, Vol 1, p 183

22 Mar 1621 (Custody of Mompesson/HL promise sentence): X, p 258; Pym, p 184; Belasyse, p 63–64

26 Mar 1621 (Mompesson judgment): **X, p 267–269**; **Pym, p 200–201**; Belasyse, p 68; *Smyth, p 323–324*; *Holland, p 86*; Horn Collection, p 384; Nicholas, Vol 1, p 228–229

27 Mar 1621 (Mompesson concealment condemned, delayed by R): X, p 272; Pym, p 205 and 207; Belasyse, p 71; Nicholas, Vol 1, p 230–231

27 Apr 1621 (HL Mompesson adj sentence): Smyth, p 353; Nicholas, Vol 1, p 341

28 Apr 1621 (Alehouse Patent investigated): Holland, p 111

4 May 1621 (Michell judgment): X, p 346–347; **Barrington, p 170–171**; **Pym, p 305–306**; *Belasyse, p 143*; *Smyth, p 366–367*; Holland, p 138; Horn Collection, p 403; **Nicholas, Vol 2, p 23–24**

11 May 1621 (Alehouse Rep): Barrington, p 224–226; *Pym, p 328–329*; Holland, p 150–152; Nicholas, Vol 2, p 52–57

House of Lords

Samuel Gardiner, *Notes of the Debates in the House of Lords officially taken by Henry Elsing, Clerk of the Parliaments, 1621 (1871)* (1870) 103 Camden Society (Old Series)

Frances Relf, *Notes of the Debates in the House of Lords 1621* (1929) 42 Camden Society (3rd)

Hastings Journal of Parliament of 1621 (1953) 83 Camden Society (3rd)

10 Mar 1621 (King's Speech on Mompesson): Relf, p13; **Hastings, p 24–31**

12 Mar 1621 (Demand Mompesson's patent): Relf, p 19

15 Mar 1621 (How to deal with dispute): **Relf, p 24–25**

22 Mar 1621 (Declaration and procedure against Mompesson): **Relf, p 32–35;** Gardiner, p 129

22 Mar 1621 (No to Cons Michell): **Relf, p 35–36;** Gardiner, p 131

23 Mar 1621 (Mompesson offences set out): Relf, p 37; Gardiner, p 133

26 Mar 1621 (Procedure against Mompesson and sentence): **Relf, p 40–48;** Gardiner, p 133

27 Mar 1621 (Royal thanks for Mompesson sentence and proclamation): **Relf, p 49–51**

(continued)

(continued)

17 Apr 1621 (Procs against Mitchell): Gardiner, p 1

26 Apr 1621 (Mitchell brought in and questioned): **Gardiner, p 24–27**

27 Apr 1621 (Mitchell ready for sentence, but adj): **Gardiner, p 36–39**

4 May 1621 (Judgment Mitchell): Gardiner, **p 64–65**

Corbett's Parliamentary History

20 Feb 1621: **1 Parliamentary History, col 1192–1194**

3 Mar 1621: **1 Parliamentary History, col 1198–2000**

6 Mar 1621: **1 Parliamentary History, col 1201**

15 Mar 1621: **1 Parliamentary History, col 1204–1208**

26 Mar 1621: **1 Parliamentary History, col 1224–1228** (King's Speech)

26 Mar 1621: **1 Parliamentary History, col 1224–1228**

26 Apr 1621: **1 Parliamentary History, col 1242–1243**

Parliamentary papers and cases

See Archives notes below

Archives

Third Report of Royal Commission on Historical Manuscripts (1872 C 673), Vol 33, p 337:

3 Mar 1617 – Mompesson's Letters Patent for Inns (p 15) [HL/PO/JO/10/3/176/1]

19 Mar 1617 – Mompesson Granting Share of Inn's Income (p 15) [HL/PO/JO/10/2/1F]

22 Apr 1618 – Warrant of Arrest [of Patrickson and Whiting] issued to Michell (p 16) [HL/PO/JO/10/1/10]

2 Jun 1618 – Warrant of Arrest [of More] issued to Michell (p 16) [HL/PO/JO/10/1/10]

6 Jun 1618 – Warrant for discharge of More and others from Prison from Michell (p 16) [HL/PO/JO/10/1/10]

9 Dec 1618 – Grant to Mompesson for Inns (p 16) [HL/PO/JO/10/2/1F]

29 Apr 1619 – Summons from Mompesson and Michell re Gold Thread infringements (p 16) [HL/PO/JO/10/1/10]

15 May 1619 – Duplicate of Mompesson Accounts (p 16) [HL/PO/JO/10/2/2A]

9 Aug 1619 – Warrant signed by Michell [for Henshawe and others to appear] (p 16) [HL/PO/JO/10/1/10]

1619 – Grievance of Michael Seller regarding imprisonment by Mompesson (p 16) [HL/PO/JO/10/1/10]

19 Jan 1620 –Orders signed by Mompesson and Michell regarding Gold and Silver Thread (p 16) [HL/PO/JO/10/1/10]

2 Mar 1620 – Warrant signed by Mompesson to summon Patrickson and Durrell (p 17) [HL/PO/JO/10/1/10]

16 May 1620 – Warrant signed by Mompesson and Michell to summon Eaton (p 17) [HL/PO/JO/10/1/10]

4 Jun 1620 – Warrant by Mompesson and Michell to seize Gold and Silver thread through customs (p 17) [HL/PO/JO/10/1/10]

7 Jul 1620 – Concealments Book seized from Mompesson (p 17) [HL/PO/JO/10/1/10]

26 Jul 1620 – Warrant signed by Mompesson for Patrickson (p 17) [HL/PO/JO/10/1/10]

28 Jul 1620 – Warrant signed by Mompesson for Blechienden (p 17) [HL/PO/JO/10/1/10]

16 Aug 1620 – Warrant signed by Mompesson to release certain gold and silver thread from customs (p 17) [HL/PO/JO/10/1/10]

29 Sep 1620 – Bond given to Mompesson and Michell by Deard (p 17) [HL/PO/JO/10/1/10]

14 Oct 1620 – Warrant signed by Mompesson for Lambard (p 17) [HL/PO/JO/10/1/10]

23 Oct 1620 – Warrant signed by Mompesson and Michell for certain papers from customs (p 17) [HL/PO/JO/10/1/13]

3 Nov 1620 – Summons from Mompesson and Mitchell to Parker (p 17) [HL/PO/JO/10/1/13]

14 Dec 1620 – Register of Commissioners of Patents for Gold and Silver Thread (p 17) [HL/PO/JO/10/1/13]

1 Mar 1621 – Request from Mompesson to set charges down in writing (p 18) [HL/PO/JO/10/1/14]

3 Mar 1621 – Warrant for search of Mompessons (p 19) [HL/PO/JO/10/1/14] [HL/PO/JO/10/1/14]

3 Mar 1621 – Proclamation regarding Mompesson (p 19) [HL/PO/JO/10/1/14]

16 Mar 1621 – Depositions regarding Gold and Silver Thread (p 20) [HL/PO/JO/10/1/15]

17 Mar 1621 – Deposition of Robert More regarding Gold and Silver Thread (p 20) [HL/PO/JO/10/1/15]

23 Mar 1621 – Collection of charges against Mompesson (p 20) [HL/PO/JO/10/1/16]

23 Mar 1621 – Examination of Thomas Norton on Gold and Silver Thread (p 21) [HL/PO/JO/10/1/16]

30 Mar 1621 – Proclamation against Mompesson (p 21) [HL/PO/JO/10/1/16] and [HL/PO/JO/10/1/17]

4 Apr 1621 – Proceedings against Mompesson (p 21) [HL/PO/JO/10/1/16]

18 Apr 1621 – Sir Randolph Crew's brief of charges against Michell (p 21) [HL/PO/JO/10/1/17]

26 Apr 1621 – Draft of charges against Michell (p 22) [HL/PO/JO/10/1/17]
28 May 1621 – Writ of Certiorari for record of proceedings against Mompesson et al (p 24) [HL/PO/JO/10/1/8] and [HL/PO/JO/10/1/18]
1621 – Grievances of Agents of Commissions of Gold and Silver Thread (p 26) [HL/PO/JO/10/1/21]
1621 – Particulars of Charges to be paid to Mompesson (p 26) [HL/PO/JO/10/1/21]
1621 – Order to take money out of Chest from Mompesson (p 26) [HL/PO/JO/10/1/21]
1621 – Memorandum of Goods seized related to Mompesson and Michell (p 26) [HL/PO/JO/10/1/21]
Fourth Report of Royal Commission on Historical Manuscripts (1873 C 857), Vol 35, p 1
26 Mar 1621 – Sentence against Mompesson (at p 121) [HL/PO/JO/10/13/7]
15 Mar 1621 – Declaration of Grievance of House of Commons against Mompesson [HL/PO/JO/10/14/3]
Manuscripts of the House of Lords, New Series (HMSO 1962), Vol 11, p 141 [HL/PO/JO/10/14/3]
Memorandum of proceedings in House of Lords, concerning proceedings against Lord Chancellor and Sir Giles Mompesson [Braye Manuscripts (Parliamentary Archives): BRY/47/25] (also see BRY/51, pp 126–248]
Notes
Reported cases
Proceedings in Parliament Against Sir Giles Mompesson (1621) 2 State Trials 1119
Proceedings in Parliament Against Sir Francis Michell (1621) 2 State Trials 1131
There was no actual enactment enrolled for this "Statute", but the judgment is held on the Chancery Roll in the National Archives: C 65/186

Heron's Fish-curing Patent Void Act 1623

PRVA2	1624
	Heron's Fish-curing Patent Void Act 1623 (21 Ja. c. xi)
	An Act for Confirmation of a Judgement given for His Majesty in a Scire Facias in the Time of this Session of Parliament against H. Heron, and for a declaration of the Letters Patents, therein mentioned, to be void

Table of contents
[s 1] Letters Patent Aug 17 Jac I to Henry Heron, for curing Fish in Devonshire and Cornwall for 31 Years; Scire facias in Chancery in Easter Term 19 Jac I to revoked said Letters Patent; Judgement for revoking same, on Default of Appearance by the Patentee; the said Judgment confirmed

Relevant patent	
5 Aug 1619	For salting, drying and packing of fish in Devon and Cornwall [Henry Heron](1619) (STC 8609) [EEBO]

Journal					
House of Commons			**House of Lords**		
Rep: William Noye			Rep: Earl of Mountgomery		
4 May 1624	1 CJ 698, 783	1R/2R/C'tted	20 Apr 1624	3 LJ 313	1R/2R/C'tted
5 May 1624	1 CJ 698, 783	Rep w/o Amds/3R	29 Apr 1624	3 LJ 327	Rep w/o Amds
			1 May 1624	3 LJ 329	Delivery of patent
			4 May 1624	3 LJ 339	3R

Parliamentary debates
Proceedings in Parliament 1624: The House of Commons (ed) Philip Baker (2015), British History Online
1R/2R (4 May): Hawarde, p 281; Nicholas, f 190; Holland, f 76; Dyott, f 124 and 125; Pym, f 87v
Rep/3R (5 May): Hawarde, p 283; Nicholas, f 191–191v; Holland, f 77v; Pym, f 88

Parliamentary papers and cases
Wallace Notestein, Frances Relf and Hartley Simpson, *Commons Debates 1621* (Yale 1935), Vol 7
Text of patent, p 359–360

Archives
Letters Patent (19 Aug 1619): Third Report of the Royal Commission on Historical Manuscripts (1872 C 673), Vol 33, p 337 at p 116 [HL/PO/JO/10/2/2A]
Ing: HL/PO/PU/1/1623/21J1n11

(continued)

(continued)

Notes
General
The text is not included in Statutes of Large, but it is in Ruffhead's Statutes of the Realm, Vol IV, p.1219
The Act was repealed by the Statute Law Revision Act 1948

Delicques and Fancault's Ordinance 1643

PRVA3	1643

Delicques and Fancault's Ordinance 1643 (A&O Interregnum, p 263)

Ordinance Concerning an Engine for the Recovery of things out of the sea, contrived by Delicques and Fancault

Table of contents
[s 1 Dominicke Petit, Peter Deliques, and Claudius Fancault, and their Associates, for 7 years, to use any new Engine, or Invention, for the drawing up of any such Ships, Lading, and Cannon; and to obtain one Moiety for all things drawned up invention] [s 2 Petit, Deliques, and Fancault to make true entry of ships drawn up on forfeit of Moiety] [s 3 No other person shall use such invention created by Petit, Deliques and Fancault during period of 7 years] [s 4 Provided invention only put into use where the Committee of the Admiralty directs]

Relevant patent
None

Journal					
House of Commons			**House of Lords**		
17 Aug 1643	3 CJ 209	Pet	26 Aug 1643	6 LJ 198	**Passed Ord**
21 Aug 1643	3 CJ 213	Read/Passed			

Parliamentary debates
None

Parliamentary papers and cases
None

Archives
None

Notes
Order Supporting Ordnance: 4 Jun 1645 (7 LJ 407)

Petty's Ordinance 1648

PRVA4	1648

Petty's Ordinance 1648 (Not in A&O Interregnum)

Ordinance for Wm. Petty, Inventor of an Instrument to double and multiply Writing, to have the Benefit of his said Invention for Fourteen Years

Table of contents
[s 1 William Petty and his assigns shall have the sole Benefit of his Invention to double and multiple writing for 14 years; any person using the invention within his licence will forfeit 100l] [s 2 Solicitor General to prepare a Bill containing His Majesty's Grant to William Petty and the Commissioners of the Great Seal shall seal it]

Relevant patent
None

Journal					
House of Commons			**House of Lords**		
6 Mar 1648	5 CJ 481	Passed	25 Feb 1648	10 LJ 78	Passed
			8 Mar 1648	10 LJ 101	**Ordinance**

Parliamentary debates
None
Parliamentary papers and cases
None
Archives
Pet of Wm Petty (25 Feb): Seventh Report of Historic Manuscripts Commission (1879 C 2340), Vol 40, p 1 at p 11 [HL/PO/ JO/10/1/254]

Manby's Patent Act 1650

PRVA5	1650		
Manby's Patent Act 1650 (A&O Interregnum, p 490)			
An Act for George Manby to prohibit any to make use of his Invention for the boyling of all sorts of Liquors for fourteen years			
Table of contents			
s 1 George Manby to enjoy the sole use of his invention in boyling liquors, for fourteen years s 2 The forfeiture for making use of said invention s 3 Indemnity to Justices and other officers			
Relevant patent			
None			
Journal			
House of Commons			**House of Lords**
Pres: Sir Arthur Heslerigge Rep: Augustine Garland			
4 Feb 1650	6 CJ 357	Pet/1R	Enacted after: An Act for Abolishing the House of Peers 1649 (A&O Interregnum, p 24)
30 Mar 1650	6 CJ 389	2R/C'tted/Pet Ag	
22 Aug 1650	6 CJ 457	**Rep with Amds**	
6 Nov 1650	6 CJ 491	3R adj	
27 Nov 1650	6 CJ 502	3R	
Petitions			
30 Mar 1650	6 CJ 389	Thousands interested in Making Salt in North of England	
Parliamentary debates			
None			
Parliamentary papers and cases			
None			
Archives			
None			

Buck's Patent Act 1651

PRVA6	1651
Buck's Patent Act 1651 (A&O Interregnum, p 509)	
An Act concerning the new Invention of Melting down Iron, and other Metals, with Stone-Coals, and other Metals with Stone-Coals without Charking thereof	
Table of contents	
s 1 Jeremy Buck to make use of his new invention for melting iron, &c. for fourteen years s 2 Other ways of melting iron not prohibited s 3 The forfeiture of those that offered against this Act s 4 Buck, after seven years, to take Apprentices	

(continued)

(continued)

Relevant patent
None

Journal	
House of Commons	**House of Lords**

Pres: No details				
Rep: Henry Marten				

26 Dec 1650	6 CJ 515	1R	Enacted after:	
22 Jan 1651	6 CJ 527	2R/C'tted (14 years)	An Act for Abolishing the House of Peers 1649 (A&O	
21 Feb 1651	6 CJ 538	Rep Adj	Interregnum, p 24)	
27 Feb 1651	6 CJ 543	Rep with Amds (7 years)		
2 Apr 1651	6 CJ 555	3R/Passed		

Parliamentary debates
None

Parliamentary papers and cases
None

Archives
None

Notes
The length of the exclusive right is unclear. It was 14 years at 2R, but the journal indicates it was changed to 7 years at Report, but the A&O Interregnum version has it at 14 years.

Marquis of Worcester's Act 1663

PRVA7	1663
Marquis of Worcester's Act 1663 (15 Cha 2. c. xv)	
To enable Edward, Marquis of Worcester, to receive the benefit of a water commanding engine invented by him, a tenth part of which is appropriated for the King's Majesty, his heirs and successors	

Table of contents
[s 1 To receive and enjoy to use invention for 99 years]
[s 2 One Tenth of profits to His Majesty; first payment feast of St Michael the Archangel [29 September] 1663]
[s 3 Any person using the invention without consent lawful of Marquis of Worcester with a warrant from LCJ or two JPs to enter into place where works are located; and a right to proceed against such person and seize the engine]
[s 4 Such person to forfeit £5 for every hour of use; one third to His Majesty; one third to Informer; and one third to Marquis of Worcester]
[s 5 Not to prejudice any existing water works]
[s 6 Nothing in Act shall hinder any person from using any Invention other than that of Marquis of Worcester]
[s 7 Model by Marquis of Worcester be given to Lord Treasurer or Commissioners of Treasury on or before 29 September 1663; to be put in exchequer and kept there]

Relevant patent
None

Journal					
House of Commons			**House of Lords**		
Rep: Edward Hungerford			Pres: No details		
			Rep: Earl of Northampton		
2 Apr 1663	8 CJ 464	Brought HL	16 Mar 1663	11 LJ 493	1R
3 Apr 1663	8 CJ 464	1R	19 Mar 1663	11 LJ 494	2R/C'tted
4 Apr 1663	8 CJ 465	2R/C'tted	28 Mar 1663	11 LJ 499	Rep with Amds
13 Apr 1663	8 CJ 470	**Rep with Amds/Re-C'tted**	30 Mar 1663	11 LJ 501	Re-C'tted/Rep with Amds
5 May 1663	8 CJ 475	**Rep with Amds/Ing/3R**	31 Mar 1663	11 LJ 502	3R
12 May 1663	8 CJ 480	HL Ag Amds	2 Apr 1663	11 LJ 504	Sent to HC
3 June 1663	8 CJ 497	Royal Assent	8 May 1663	11 LJ 519	HC pass with Amds/Ag
			3 Jun 1663	11 LJ 533	Royal Assent

Parliamentary debates
None
Parliamentary papers and cases
None
Archives
C'tee Minutes: 21 Mar 1663 (p 300–301); 24 Mar 1663 (p 302); 26 Mar 1663 (p 303); 26 Mar 1663 (p 304–305); 28 Mar 1663 (p 314–315): HL/PO/CO/1/1
Seventh Report of the Historic Manuscripts Commission (1879 C 2340), Vol 40, p 1
16 Mar 1663 – Ingrossment, p 168 [HL/PO/PB/1/1663/15C2n29]
Notes
The Act is printed in: An exact and true definition of the most stupendious water-commanding engine, invented by the Right Honourable (and deservedly to be praised and admired) Edward Somerset, Lord Marquess of Worcester (1663) (Wing W3532A)

Howard and Watson's Act 1670

PRVA8	1670		
Howard and Watson's Act 1670 (22 & 23 Cha 2. c. vii)			
Granting Sir Philip Howard and Francis Watson sole use of an invention for the benefit of shipping			
Table of contents			
[s 1 Sir Philip Howard and Francis Watson &c. have sole use of manufacture for 25 years from 1 Jan 1670 within England and Ireland; does not apply to material made before 1 Jan 1665; use without consent forfeit £100 (one moiety to suitor and other to the King)] [s 2 In every such action plaintiff shall recover treble costs] [s 3 Philip Howard and Francis Watson enter in Court of Exchequer the said manufacturer within three months from 1 Feb 1670 else Act void] [s 4 Act only extends to the use of the invention on ships and shipping]			

Relevant patent	
23 Mar 1668 (No 158) Act (No 158*)	Liquor, for colouring ships also for graining and colouring wood, stone &c. [Sir Philip Howard and Francis Watson]

Journal					
House of Commons			**House of Lords**		
Pres: No details First Rep: Sir Thomas Higgons Second Rep: Sir John Birkenhead			Rep: Earl of Dorset		
7 Nov 1670	9 CJ 160	1R	20 Dec 1670	12 J 394	Brought HC
10 Nov 1670	9 CJ 161	2R/C'tted	29 Dec 1670	12 LJ 396	1R
24 Nov 1670	9 CJ 170	Rep adj	4 Jan 1671	12 LJ 397	2R/C'tted
25 Nov 1670	9 CJ 170	Rep with Amds/Re-C'tted	16 Jan 1671	12 LJ 405	Rep/Re-C'tted
26 Nov 1670	9 CJ 172	Mem add	15 Feb 1671	12 LJ 430	Rep with Amds/3R
14 Dec 1670	9 CJ 183	Rep with Amds/Ing	4 Mar 1671	12 LJ 443	HC Ag Amds
20 Dec 1670	9 CJ 186	3R	6 Mar 1671	12 LJ 446	Royal Assent
16 Feb 1671	9 CJ 202	HL pass with Amds			
25 Feb 1671	9 CJ 209	HL Amds Ag			
6 Mar 1671	9 CJ 214	Royal Assent			
Parliamentary debates					
Rep with Amds: Basil Henning (ed), *The Parliamentary Diary of Sir Edward Dering, 1670–1670* (New Haven 1940), p 12–13					
Parliamentary papers and cases					
None					

(continued)

(continued)

Archives
C'tee Minutes: 10 and 11 Jan 1671 (p 400); 12 Jan 1671 (p 401); 19 Jan 1671 (p 405): HL/PO/CO/1/2   Ing: HL/PO/PB/1/1670/22&23C2n15

Notes
Related case   Howard and Watson (1667), 11 HPC App; 1 HPC 128n

White Paper Company Act 1689

PRVA9	1689
White Paper Company Act 1689 (2 Will & Mar. c. xvi)	
For encouraging the manufacture of white paper	

Table of contents
[s 1 The Letters Patent allowing incorporation to be treated as if enacted; save the clauses on oaths mentioned in the Letters patent; save the Power to break doors and enter and search]
[s 2 Privileges and immunities of Letters Patent extended for 14 years from end of present session of Parliament]
[s 3 During 14 year term, no person shall put in practice the art or manufacture of making white paper]
[s 4 Governor and Company shall lay books open at its Warehouse for subscribers until 29 September 1690; subscribers to pay £50]
[s 5 Books closed on 29 September 1690; within 20 days General Meeting to be held; Governor, Deputy Governor, Treasurer &c. to be elected at meeting]
[s 6 Assignment of shares good where entered in book and witnessed by two persons]
[s 7 From 20 June 1691 no person shall directly or indirect transport or send to foreign parts any rag, calves parts, waterspoilt parchment, shavings or tippings, or glover's tippings; upon risk of forfeit; one moiety to the informer the other to the Company]
[s 8 During the 14 year term, the company shall not make any paper for value of 4s or under; lawful for any other person to make such paper or brown paper]
[s 9 Company shall take lease from Dean and Canons of Windsor for Mills]
[s 10 Nothing in Act to prejudice rights of Dame Thedodosia Ivy Alias Brian]
[s 11 Governor or Deputy Government with any three Assistants may administer oaths in relation to appointing people to office]

Relevant patent	
21 Jan 1675 (No 178)	Making white paper for writing and printing [Inventor: Eustace Burneby] [Nathaniel Bladen – 1682; Christopher Jackson – 1684; John Briscoe – 1685; Nicholas Dupin, Adam de Cardonell and Elias de Grunch – 1686]

Journal					
House of Commons			**House of Lords**		
Rep: Sir Thomas Littleton			Rep: Earl of Rochester		
28 Mar 1690	10 CJ 358	Pet	14 May 1690	14 LJ 497	Brought HC/1R/Pet Ag
29 Mar 1690	10 CJ 359	Pres	15 May 1690	14 LJ 499	2R and Pet Ag
31 Mar 1690	10 CJ 360	1R	16 May 1690	14 LJ 500	Pet Ag
3 Apr 1690	10 CJ 365	2R/C'tted	17 May 1690	14 LJ 501	CWH/C'tted SC
3 Apr 1690	10 CJ 366	**Pet Ag**	19 May 1690	14 LJ 502	Rep w/o Amds/3R
5 Apr 1690	10 CJ 369	Mem added	20 May 1690	14 LJ 504	Royal Assent
9 Apr 1690	10 CJ 372	**Pet Ag**			
15 Apr 1690	10 CJ 379	**Pet Ag**			
25 Apr 1690	10 CJ 389	**Pet Ag**			
2 May 1690	10 CJ 397	Rep with Amds/Ing			
7 May 1690	10 CJ 406	Hear Counsel			
9 May 1690	10 CJ 409	Counsel heard			
13 May 1690	10 CJ 412	**Amds Op /3R**			
19 May 1690	10 CJ 421	HL pass w/o Amds			
20 May 1690	10 CJ 422	Royal Assent			

Petitions against the Bill		
3 Apr 1690	10 CJ 366	George Hagar [owner of patent who would be disrupted by Bill; against]
3 Apr 1690	10 CJ 366	Paper Makers [ruined if Bill passed; against]
9 Apr 1690	10 CJ 372	Paper Makers of Kent and Surrey [Grant of Act will ruin them; against]
9 Apr 1690	10 CJ 372	Dean and Canon of Winsor [Loss of rent from paper mill; against]
15 Apr 1690	10 CJ 379	Lady Theodosia Ivy [Bought white papers patents not yet expire; to be heard]
25 Apr 1690	10 CJ 389	Paper sellers in London [Grant of Act will ruin them; against]
14 May 1690	14 LJ 497	Mayor, Aldermen &c. of Chipping Wycombe [Against]
15 May 1690	14 LJ 499	Ancient Papermakers [Against]
15 May 1690	14 LJ 499	Dean of Winsor [Against]

Parliamentary debates
Royal Assent: Chandler, *The History and Proceedings of the House of Commons*, Vol 2, p 374–384

Parliamentary papers and cases
(1) The Case of the White-Paper Makers (Wing C1052)
(2) Case of the Governour and Company of White Paper Makers (BL Harl 5942)
(3) Case of Many hundred paper-makers and owners of paper mills (CSP Dom 1700–1702, p 552–553)
(4) Case and Circumstances of Paper Making in England truly stated And by the Paper Sellers (Wing C487)
(5) An Addition to the Case of the Paper Sellers (BL Cup 645, b. 11)
(6) Objections against the Paper-Bill Answered (BrSides By6 1689)
(7) Some Considerations humberly offered to this Present Parliament by the Ancient Paper-makers (Broadside Collection Yale)
(8) Untitled Pet (BL Cup 645 b.11)
(9) Reasons humbly offered to this honourable house, against receiving any more petitions (BL Harl 5942(2))
(10) The humble reply of the Company of White Paper Makers, in Answer to a printed paper, Intitled Mr Johnson's Case (Yale BrSides By6 1699)
(11) The Case of the Company or White Paper Makers (Second Case) (BL Cup 645, b 11; Yale BrSides By6 1689)
Documents are also available in WJ Cameron, *The Company of White Paper-Makers of England 1686–1696* (Auckland 1964), except document (3)

Archives
C'tee Minutes: 15 May 1690 [HL/PO/CO/1/4] (no page number)
Ing: HL/PO/PB/1/1689/2W&Mn25 [not otherwise printed]
Thirteenth Report of the Historical Manuscripts Commission (1892 C 6822), Appendix Part V, Vol 45, p 583
15 May 1690 – Petition of Chipping Wycombe (No 272) (p 74) [HL/PO/JO/10/1/423/272]

London, Orphans Act 1694

PRVA10	1694
London, Orphans Act 1694 (5 & 6 Will & Mar. c. x)	
An Act for the Relief of the Orphans and other Creditors of the City of London	

Table of contents (patent provisions only)
s 5 Lights granted [to Convex Lights Company] for 21 Years for 600l yearly s28 S. Hutchinson paying a Share in the Lights, to have the same Benefits as others

Relevant patent	
27 Feb 1684 (No 232)	New experiment for the great and durable increase of light by means of extraordinary glasses and lamps, for the great improvement of ship lanterns, lighthouses, dispersing of lights in mines, and other uses where light and heat are required [Edward Wyndus]

Journal	
House of Commons	**House of Lords**
Pres: No details Rep: Henry Goldwell	Rep: Gilbert Burnet (Bishop of Salisbury)

(continued)

(continued)

30 Nov 1693	11 CJ 14	Pet/Ref CWH	12 Mar 1694	15 LJ 391	Brought HC/1R
5 Dec 1693	11 CJ 20	CWH adj	15 Mar 1694	15 LJ 394	2R day app
13 Dec 1693	11 CJ 30	Pet	17 Mar 1694	15 LJ 394	2R/C'tted CWH/Pet Ag
15 Dec 1693	11 CJ32	CWH adj	20 Mar 1694	15 LJ 398	CWH
19 Dec 1693	11 CJ 35	Pet	21 Mar 1694	15 LJ 399	CWH/3R
23 Dec 1693	11 CJ 40	Pet	23 Mar 1694	15 LJ 502	Royal Assent
29 Dec 1693	11 CJ 42	CWH adj			
3 Jan 1694	11 CJ 46	CWH adj			
8 Jan 1694	11 CJ 50	CWH adj			
16 Jan 1694	11 CJ 61	CWH adj			
23 Jan 1694	11 CJ 64	CWH adj			
27 Jan 1694	11 CJ 72	CWH adj			
2 Feb 1694	11 CJ 78	CWH adj			
6 Feb 1694	11 CJ 81	CWH adj			
9 Feb 1694	11 CJ 90	CWH adj			
12 Feb 1694	11 CJ 91	Pet			
15 Feb 1694	11 CJ 96	CWH			
16 Feb 1694	11 CJ 98	Pet			
17 Feb 1694	11 CJ 98	Rep			
22 Feb 1694	11 CJ 102	1R			
22 Feb 1694	11 CJ 102	Pet			
23 Feb 1694	11 CJ 106	Pet			
24 Feb 1694	11 CJ 107	2R			
24 Feb 1694	11 CJ 107	Pet			
26 Feb 1694	11 CJ 109	Pets			
26 Feb 1694	11 CJ 109	List of debtors Ord			
2 Mar 1694	11 CJ 115	List of debtors Pres			
3 Mar 1694	11 CJ 116	**Hutchinson Pet**			
3 Mar 1694	11 CJ 116	**CWH**			
7 Mar 1694	11 CJ 121– V	**Re-C'tted**			
8 Mar 1694	11 CJ 122 – V	**CWH/Rep with Amds/**Ing			
12 Mar 1694	11 CJ 125	3R			
22 Mar 1694	11 CJ 135	HL pass w/o Amds			
23 Mar 1694	11 CJ 136	Royal Assent			

Petitions

13 Dec 1693	11 CJ 30	William and Henry Goodwyn [City of London debt unpaid]
19 Dec 1693	11 CJ 35	Frances Bradbury, Ellen Pank, and Grace Bell [City of London debt unpaid]
23 Dec 1693	11 CJ 40	Lady Anne Dowager Rockingham [City of London debt unpaid]
12 Feb 1694	11 CJ 91	Distressed Orphans of the City of London
16 Feb 1694	11 CJ 98	Ann Wright [City of London debt unpaid]
22 Feb 1694	11 CJ 102	Edward and Ann Northey [City of London debt unpaid]
23 Feb 1694	11 CJ 106	Sir Edmund King [City of London debt unpaid]
24 Feb 1694	11 CJ 107	Merchants of the City of London [Wine duty]
26 Feb 1694	11 CJ 109	John Harvey &c. [City of London debt unpaid]
26 Feb 1694	11 CJ 109	Elisha Patching and Patience Dod [Need provision in Act]
3 Mar 1694	11 CJ 116	Samuel Hutchinson [Provision for inventor of Convex Lights]

Parliamentary debates

None

Parliamentary papers and cases

None

Archives

Manuscripts of the House of Lords, New Series, Vol 1, 1693–95 (HMSO 1900):

17 Mar 1694: Petition of Merchants in the City of London, p 372 (No 822) [HL/PO/JO/10/1/465/822]

17 Mar 1694: Petition of Samuel Hutchinson and Arthur Moore, p 373 (No 822) [HL/PO/JO/10/1/465/822]

17 Mar 1694: Petition of John Reeve and Edward Windus, p 373 (No 822) [HL/PO/JO/10/1/465/822]

2 Apr 1694: Petition of Samuel Hutchison regarding arrest, p 373–374 (No 822) [HL/PO/JO/10/1/465/822]

3 Apr 1694: Petition (and evidence) of Armstrong apologising for arresting Hutchinson, p 541–547 (No 926) [HL/PO/JO/10/1/475/926]

Walcot's Patent Act 1694

PRVA11	1694

Walcot's Patent Act 1694 (6 & 7 Will & Mar. c. xxiv)

An Act for the making of salt Water fresh

Table of contents
[s 1 William Walcot &c. to have 31 years from 10 Apr 1895 to have exclusive rights over his invention and improvements in his Majesty's Dominions and Ireland and His Majesty's Ships; and that no other person shall use without licence] [s 2 Any infringement under pain of forfeiture and treble value of the whole profit; one third part to His Majesty; one third part to informer and one third part to William Walcot] [s 3 Walcot can obtain a warrant for the better discovery of offences]

Relevant patent	
28 Oct 1675 (No 184)	Purifying corrupted water, and making sea water fresh, clear, and wholesome [William Walcot]

Journal					
House of Commons			**House of Lords**		
Rep: Sir Thomas Littleton			Pres: No details Rep: Earl of Bridgewater		
16 Mar 1695	11 CJ 274	Brought HL	21 Feb 1695	15 LJ 501	1R
23 Mar 1695	11 CJ 280	1R	27 Feb 1695	15 LJ 508	2R/C'tted
26 Mar 1695	11 CJ 282	2R/C'tted	14 Mar 1695	15 LJ 518	Rep with Amds/Ing
1 Apr 1695	11 CJ 288	**Rep with Amds/3R**	16 Mar 1695	15 LJ 520	3R
3 Apr 1695	11 CJ 291	HL Ag Amds	2 Apr 1695	15 LJ 529	HL Ag Amds
22 Apr 1695	11 CJ 314	Royal Assent	22 Apr 1695	15 LJ 562	Royal Assent

Parliamentary debates
None

Parliamentary papers and cases
Walcot, The Case of Mr Walcot (1694) (Wing W285B)
Walcot, An Answer to Mr. Fitz-Gerald's state of the case concerning the patent of making salt water fresh (16 Jan 1695) (Wing W285A) [includes a copy of Fitz-Gerald's Case]

Archives
Amended Bill (21 Feb 1695): HL/PO/JO/10/1/474/910
C'tee Minutes: 6 Mar 1695 (p 290); 13 Mar 1695 (p 292–293): HL/PO/CO/1/5
Ing (21 Feb 1695): *House of Lords Manuscripts* (New Series), Vol 1, p 512 (No 910) [HL/PO/PB/1/1694/6&7W&Mn40]

Notes
Related case
Walcot's Patent (1675), 11 HPC App
Printed version of the Act
H. Walcot, Sea-water made fresh and wholsome. Objections against the use thereof removed, and the advantages prov'd to be very great (Parker 1702), p 8 (ESTC T113420)

Lustrings Act 1697

PRVA12	1697

Lustrings Act 1697 (9 Will 3. c. xliii)

An Act for the better Encouragement of the Royal Lustring Company, and the more effectual preventing the fraudulent Importation of Lustrings and Alamodes

Table of contents
s 1 No foreign Alamodes or Lustrings to be imported in England, &c., but in the Port of London, &c.; Licence to be taken for importing the same s 2 Commissioners to seal Alamodes, &c. imported; and keep an Entry thereof; Alamodes, &c. brought into any other Port forfeited, and to be sold, and exported again [Lustrings Act 1696] 8 & 9 W 3. c. 36

(continued)

(continued)

s 3 Penalty on Person importing Alamodes, &c. contrary to this Act

s 4 Officers in the King's Service taking on board or importing Alamodes, &c. made incapable of the King's Service, &c.; Reward to Mariner or other making Discovery

s 5 Penalty on Person altering or counterfeiting the Seal or Mark of the Custom House, or Royal Lustring Company, or buying or selling Alamodes, &c., concealed; Person authorized may go into any Shop, Warehouse, &c. not marked; In case of Resistance may break open Doors, &c.; Justices of Peace to grant Warrant to Searcher, &c.; In case of Dispute Proof to lie on Importer, &c.

s 6 Officers to aid in Execution of this Act; Penalty on Officer conniving at fraudulent Importation of Alamodes, &c.

s 7 Offenders, &c. to forfeit double for every Offence

s 8 How Offenders shall be prosecuted, &c.

s 9 How Penalties and Forfeiture are to be recover and divided

s 10 Before Claims entered, Persons to give Security for answering the Penalties &c.

s 11 General Act; Person sued may plead the General Issue; Treble Costs

s 12 Action to brought in two Years after Offence committed

s 13 Royal Lustring Company and their Successors to be a Body Corporate, &c. and enjoy all Liberties, Privileges, &c. mentioned in the Letters Patent

s 14 Company to have the sole Use and Benefit of making Alamodes, &c. for fourteen Years

s 15 Company may import 17 Bails of Silk from Amsterdam, paying the Duties

Relevant patent

4 Nov 1688 (No 261) Act (No 261*)	Making, dressing, and instrating black plain silks, called alamodes, ranforsees, and lustestrings [Paulo Cloudsley; Peter Duclen; William Sherrard]

Journal

House of Commons			**House of Lords**		
Pres and Rep: Sir Rowland Gwyn			Rep: Henry Compton (Bishop of London)		
18 Feb 1698	12 CJ 117	**Pet**	15 Jun 1698	16 LJ 317	Brought HC
10 Mar 1698	12 CJ 151	**Pet Rep**	16 Jun 1698	16 LJ 319	1R
22 Mar 1698	12 CJ 169	Wit prevaricating	21 Jun 1698	16 LJ 324	2R/Com CWH
15 Apr 1698	12 CJ 207	Pet adj	23 Jun 1698	16 LJ 326	Pet Ag
16 Apr 1698	12 CJ 210	**Pet Rep**	29 Jun 1698	16 LJ 333	CWH/Rep with Amds/3R
19 Apr 1698	12 CJ 239	Cons adj	30 Jun 1698	16 LJ 334	HC Ag Amd
20 Apr 1698	12 CJ 241	**Cons of Pet Rep**	5 Jul 1698	16 LJ 343	Royal Assent
11 May 1698	12 CJ 266	Prt Rep			
12 May 1698	12 CJ 267	Bill Ord			
13 May 1698	12 CJ 268	Bill Pres			
17 May 1698	12 CJ 273	1R			
19 May 1698	12 CJ 277	2R/C'tted CWH			
20 May 1698	12 CJ 279	Cons Res			
27 May 1698	12 CJ 287	Clause accepted			
1 Jun 1698	12 CJ 294 – V	**Rep with Amds/Cons**			
2 Jun 1698	12 CJ 298	Cons/Ing			
13 Jun 1698	12 CJ 310	**3R**			
30 Jun 1698	12 CJ 336	**HL Ag Amds**			
5 Jul 1698	12 CJ 343	Royal Assent			

Petitions

23 Jun 1698	16 LJ 326	Richard Yorke, Richard Briscoe and other shopkeepers within this Kingdom [Against]

Parliamentary debates

None

Parliamentary papers and cases

Report of the Committee of the House of Commons to whom the Petition of the Lustring Company of England was referred (1698) (E2705 Wing)

Archives

Pets Ag (23 Jun 1698): *House of Lords Manuscripts* (New Series), Vol 3, p 256 (No 1307) [HL/PO/JO/10/1/509/1307]

Ing: HL/PO/PU/1/1697/9&10W3n79

Notes

Related Acts

Lustrings Act 1696 (8 & 9 Will 3. c. xxxvi); Royal Lustring Company Act 1706 (6 Ann. c. xx)

Thomas Savery's Patent Act 1699

PRVA13	1699
Thomas Savery's Patent Act 1699 (10 Will 3. c. xxxi)	
Encouraging Thomas Savery's invention for raising water and relating to all sorts of mill work	

Table of contents
[s 1 Thomas Savoy may use and erect the Invention and receive the benefits for the remainder of the 14 year term and for further term of 21 years] [s 2 No person may use the invention during the period and all pipes and utensils may be taken by means and authorities as mentioned in the Letters patent]

Relevant patent	
25 Jul 1698 (No 356) Act (No 356*)	Raising water by impellent force of fire [Thomas Savery]

Journal					
House of Commons			**House of Lords**		
Rep: Francis Scobell			Rep: Lord Ferrers		
6 Apr 1699	12 CJ 635	Brought HL	20 Mar 1699	16 LJ 407	1R
14 Apr 1699	12 CJ 641	1R	31 Mar 1699	16 LJ 429	2R/C'tted
18 Apr 1699	12 CJ 650	2R/C'tted	3 Apr 1699	16 LJ 431	Rep w/o Amds/Ing
20 Apr 1699	12 CJ 654	Mem Add	4 Apr 1699	16 LJ 434	3R
25 Apr 1699	12 CJ 664	Rep w/o Amds/3R	25 Apr 1699	16 LJ 450	HC pass w/o Amds
4 May 1699	12 CJ 688	Royal Assent	4 May 1699	16 LJ 465	Royal Assent

Parliamentary debates
None

Parliamentary papers and cases
None

Archives
Ing (20 Mar 1699): House of Lords Manuscripts (New Series), Vol 3, p 384 (No 1412) [HL/PO/PB/1/1698/10&11W3n61] Amended Draft of the Act: HL/PO/JO/10/1/517/1412

Notes
No record in the House of Lords Committee Books

Lombe's Silk Engines Act 1731

PRVA14	1732
Lombe's Silk Engines Act 1731 (5 Geo 2. c. viii)	
An Act for providing a Recompence for Sir Thomas Lombe, for discovering and introducing the Arts of making and working the three Capital Italian Engines for making Organzine Silk, and for preserving the Invention for the Benefit of this Kingdom	

Table of contents
s 1 14,000l to be paid to Sir T. Lombe by the Crown s 2 In case of his allowing a perfect Model to be taken of his new invented Engines

Original Bill
[Cl 1 Letters Patent extended by [blank] years] [Cl 2 Sir Thomas Lombe will not communicate invention to foreigners; or destroy certain mills] [Cl 3 Extended term will be voided if payment of [blank] is not made by Sir Thomas Lombe] [Cl 4 By payment of [blank] to Sir Thomas Lombe by Parliament the grant can be avoided] [Cl 5 Where Parliament redeems licence, Sir Thomas Lombe may make samples or patterns of the parts of the machine; and directions as to how to make the machine] [Cl 6 Upon failure to provide model, [blank]] [Cl 7 Notice signed by Speaker of Commons sufficient for purposes of the Act] [Cl 8 Nothing affects privileges of the Company of Silk Throwers]

(continued)

(continued)

9 Sep 1718 (No 422) Act (No 422*)	Engine to wind the finest raw silk [Thomas Lombe]

Journal

House of Commons			House of Lords		
Pres and Rep: Micajah Perry			Rep: Lord De La Warr		
1 Feb 1732	21 CJ 782	**Pet (term extension)**	23 Mar 1731	24 LJ 63	Brought HC
11 Feb 1732	21 CJ 795	**Pet Rep**	24 Mar 1731	24 LJ 65	1R
14 Feb 1732	21 CJ 798	Bill Ord	27 Mar 1732	24 LJ 67	2R/C'tted
15 Feb 1732	21 CJ 801	Ord Produce Patent	30 Mar 1732	24 LJ 73	Rep w/o Amds
18 Feb 1732	21 CJ 804	Patent Pr	31 Mar 1732	24 LJ 77	3R
21 Feb 1732	21 CJ 806	Lombe Appears	3 Apr 1732	24 LJ 79	Royal Assent
6 Mar 1732	21 CJ 832	1R			
9 Mar 1732	21 CJ 840	**Pet Ag**			
10 Mar 1732	21 CJ 842	**Pet Ag**			
14 Mar 1732	21 CJ 846	2R/R Con/Money Res/C'tted			
20 Mar 1732	21 CJ 855	COS/CWH			
21 Mar 1732	21 CJ 856	Rep with Amds/Ing			
22 Mar 1732	21 CJ 858	Cons			
23 Mar 1732	21 CJ 859	3R			
27 Mar 1732	21 CJ 865	Patent Returned			
3 Apr 1732	21 CJ 876	Royal Assent			

Petitions

9 Mar 1732	21 CJ 840	Manufacturers of Mohair and Yarn &c. of Manchester [prejudice from patent term extension]
9 Mar 1732	21 CJ 840	Manufacturers of Mohair and Yarn &c. of Macclesfield [prejudice from patent term extension]
9 Mar 1732	21 CJ 840	Manufacturers of Mohair and Yarn &c. of Stafford [prejudice from patent term extension]
9 Mar 1832	21 CJ 840	Manufacturers of Mohair and Yarn &c. of Chester [prejudice from patent term extension]
10 Mar 1732	21 CJ 842	Manufacturers of Mohair and Yarn &c. of Blackburn [prejudice from patent term extension]

Parliamentary debates

Pet: **Chandler, The History and Proceedings of the House of Commons: Vol 7, p 140; Torbuck, A Collection of the Parliamentary debates in England from the Year MDCLXVIII to the present time (1741), Vol 10, pp 101–109; 8 Parliamentary History, col 924–929**

Mention (historic): Chandler, History and the Proceedings of the House of Commons, Vol 10, p 275

Mention (historic): **HC Deb, 10 Jun 1842, Vol 63(3rd), col 1459–1460**

Parliamentary papers and cases

(1) The Case of the Silk Throwers Company (Harper's Bill papers: see Sheila Lambert, *Bills and Acts: Legislative Procedure in Eighteenth Century England* (Cambridge 1971))

(2) The Case of the Manufacturers of Wollen, Linnen, Mohair and Cotton in the Towns of Manchester &c. (Harper)

(3) A Brief State of the Case relating to the Machine erected at Derby for making Italian Organizine Silk (Harper)

(4) Original Bill for Term Extension (2 versions), 1732 (Harper)

Newspaper coverage of debates

Pet: **Historical Register (1732), Vol 17, p 281–284; The Gentleman's Magazine, Vol 2(No 21), Sep 1732, p 940; The Gentleman's Magazine, Vol 2(No 22), Oct 1732, p 985–986**

Royal Assent: London Evening Post, 1–4 April 1732; Daily Journal, 4 April 1732; Daily Post, 4 April 1732; Grub Street Journal, 6 April 1732; Fog's Weekly Journal, 8 April 1732; Read's Weekly Journal or British Gazetteer, 8 April 1732; Universal Spectator and Weekly Journal, 8 April 1732

Warrant for payment issued: Grub Street Journal, 13 April 1732; London Journal, 15 April 1732

Archives

Model (previously at Tower of London): Science Museum, SCM – Textiles Machinery Ob No: 1857–290/3

C'tee Minutes: 30 Mar 1732 (p 210): HL/PO/CO/1/10

Ing: HL/PO/PB/1/1731/5G2n12

Notes
Related cases
Lombes Patent (1720) 11 HPC App
Printed Acts
It should be noted that the version in Webster's Patent Cases, p 38 is a paraphrase of the Act
Related Acts
The Act was repealed by the Statute Law Revision Act 1948
Other records
There is an entry at PRZA1 relating to this Act

Byrom's Shorthand Act 1741

PRVA15	1741

Byrom's Shorthand Act 1741 (15 Geo 2. c. xxiii)

An Act for securing to John Byrom, Master of Arts, the sole Right of publishing, for a certain Term of Years, the Art and Method of Short-hand invented by him

Table of contents
s 1 [John Byrom to have exclusive right to method of shorthand for 21 years] This Act to commence from June 24, 1742 for 21 years s 2 Penalty on Persons offending against this Act s 3 Publick Act

Relevant patent
None

Journal					
House of Commons			**House of Lords**		
Pres and Rep: Sir Thomas Drury			Rep: Earl of Moray		
15 Mar 1742	24 CJ 127	**Pet**	13 May 1742	26 LJ 119	Brought HC /1R
22 Mar 1742	24 CJ 139	**Pet Rep**/Bill Ord	14 May 1742	26 LJ 122	2R/C'tted
12 Apr 1742	24 CJ 176	1R	20 May 1742	26 LJ 125	Rep w/o Amds
27 Apr 1742	24 CJ 186	2R/C'tted	24 May 1742	26 LJ 129	3R
5 May 1742	24 CJ 212	Rep with Amds/Ing	16 Jun 1742	26 LJ 145	Royal Assent
7 May 1742	24 CJ 218	3R			
24 May 1742	24 CJ 249	HL pass w/o Amds			
16 Jun 1742	24 CJ 277	Royal Assent			

Parliamentary debates
None

Parliamentary papers and cases
Catalogue of Papers printed by Order of the House of Commons, from the year 1731 to 1800. In the Custody of the Clerk of the Journals (1807) (Reprint: HMSO 1954): Byrom's Patent for Teaching Shorthand, Vol 1, No 7

Newspaper coverage of debates
None

Archives
C'tee Minutes: 19 May 1742 (p 31): HL/PO/CO/1/12 Ing: HL/PO/PB/1/1741/15G2n44

Notes
The Act was repealed by the Statute Law Revision Act 1948

Elwick's Patent Act 1742

PRVA16	1742
	Elwick's Patent Act 1742 (16 Geo 2. c. xxv)

An Act Vesting in John Elwick the sole property of an engine for making stone pipes and enlarging the term granted by letters patent for that purpose

Table of contents

[s 1 Letters Patent extended for a term of 14 years from expiry of current Letters Patent]
[s 2 Saving for John Tuite, Charles Fleetwood and Richard Roundell]

Relevant patent

21 Nov 1734 (No 549) Act (No 549*)	Engine for making stone water-pipes [John Tuite]

Journal

House of Commons			House of Lords		
Rep: Velters Cornewell			Pet Rep: Earl of Warwick Pres: Lord Raymond Bill Rep: Lord Willoughby of Packham		
3 Mar 1743	24 CJ 447	Brought HL	21 Jan 1743	26 LJ 189	Pet
4 Mar 1743	24 CJ 449	1R	1 Feb 1743	26 LJ 195	Pet Rep
8 Mar 1743	24 CJ 458	2R/C'tted	15 Feb 1743	26 LJ 206	1R
15 Mar 1743	24 CJ 464	Mem add	21 Feb 1743	26 LJ 210	2R/C'tted
17 Mar 1743	24 CJ 467	Rep w/o Amds/Ing	25 Feb 1743	26 LJ 217	Rep with Amds
22 Mar 1743	24 CJ 469	3R	3 Mar 1743	26 LJ 224	3R
22 Mar 1743	24 CJ 470	Royal Assent	22 Mar 1743	26 LJ 240	HC pass w/o Amds
			11 Mar 1743	26 LJ 242	Royal Assent

Parliamentary debates

None

Parliamentary papers and cases

None

Newspaper coverage of debates

None

Archives

House Bill (and petition): 15 Feb 1743: HL/PO/JO/10/6/507

House Bill: 15 Feb 1743: HL/PO/JO/10/3/240/6

C'tee Minutes: 25 Feb 1743 (p 59): HL/PO/CO/1/12

Ing: HL/PO/PB/1/1741/16G2n48

Pownoll's Patent Act 1749

PRVA17	1749
	Pownoll's Patent Act 1749 (23 Geo 2. c. xxxiii)

An Act for Securing the sole property, benefit and Advantage of an Engine invented by Israel Pownoll deceased for raising Ballast, Sullage, and Sand, and for removing Banks, Shelves, and Shoals, in Rivers and Harbours; to the Children of the said Israel Pownoll, for a certain Term of Years

Table of contents

[s 1 The Benefits of the Patent to be enjoyed by Philemon Pownoll, Israel Pownoll, the son, Jacob Pickering, and Elizabeth his wife for 14 years from 1 Aug 1750]

Relevant patent

3 Apr 1712 (No 391) Act (No 391*)	Machine for taking up ballast, sullage, sand, &c; useful in cleansing rivers, harbours, &c [Israel Pownall] {includes Ireland}

Journal					
House of Commons			**House of Lords**		
Pres and Rep: Andrew Wilkinson			Rep: Joseph Wilcocks (Bishop of Rochester)		
18 Jan 1750	25 CJ 938	**Pet/Ref C'tee**	14 Mar 1750	27 LJ 424	Brought HC/1R
31 Jan 1750	25 CJ 970	**Pet Rep**	16 Mar 1750	27 LJ 427	2R/C'tted
8 Feb 1750	25 CJ 981	Bill Ord	22 Mar 1750	27 LJ 432	Rep w/o Amds
20 Feb 1750	25 CJ 1006	1R	23 Mar 1750	27 LJ 433	3R
27 Feb 1750	25 CJ 1019	2R/C'tted	12 Apr 1750	27 J 462	Royal Assent
9 Mar 1750	25 CJ 1040	Rep with Amds/Ing			
12 Mar 1750	25 CJ 1046	3R			
27 Mar 1750	25 CJ 1093	HL pass w/o Amds			
12 Apr 1750	25 CJ 1116	Royal Assent			
Parliamentary debates					
None					
Parliamentary papers and cases					
None					
Newspaper coverage of debates					
Description: **The Gentleman's Magazine, Vol 22, Jan 1752, p 24–25**					
Archives					
C'tee Minutes: 21 Mar 1850 (3 pages – no page numbers): HL/PO/CO/1/13					
Ing: HL/PO/PB/1/1749/23G2n73					

Meinzies' Patent Act 1750

PRVA18	1750
Meinzies' Patent Act 1750 (24 Geo 2. c. xxviii)	

An Act for vesting, for a certain Term of Years, in Michael Meinzies, Esquire, his Executors, Administrators, and Assigns, the Sole Property of a Machine, by him invented, for conveying of Coals, from the Places where they are dug to the Heaps at the Mouths of the Pits; and, in some Cases, from the Heaps to the Straits, or Places where they are put on board Ships, or Keels	
Table of contents	
[s 1 Letters Patent extended for a term of 14 years from expiry of current Letters Patent]	
9 Feb 1750 (No 653) Act (No 653*)	Machine for carrying coals from the coal walls to the bottom of the shaft, and from the mouth of the shaft to the heaps, and for other purposes [Michael Meinzies]

Journal					
House of Commons			**House of Lords**		
Pres and Rep: William Grant (Lord Advocate)			Rep: Earl of Findlater		
5 Mar 1751	26 CJ 90	**Pet/Ref C'tee**	8 May 1751	27 LJ 554	Brought HC/1R
25 Mar 1751	26 CJ 148	**Pet Rep**	9 May 1751	27 LJ 555	2R/C'tted
17 Apr 1751	26 CJ 174	1R	14 May 1751	27 LJ 561	Rep w/o Amds
25 Apr 1751	26 CJ 185	2R/C'tted	15 May 1751	27 LJ 563	3R
6 May 1751	26 CJ 216	Rep w/o Amds/Ing	22 May 1751	27 LJ 575	Royal Assent
8 May 1751	26 CJ 221	3R			
16 May 1751	26 CJ 235	HL pass w/o Amds			
22 May 1751	26 CJ 264	Royal Assent			
Parliamentary debates					
None					
Parliamentary papers and cases					
None					
Newspaper coverage of debates					
None					
Archives					
C'tee Minutes: 14 May 1751 (1 page – no page number): HL/PO/CO/1/13					
Ing: HL/PO/PB/1/1750/24G2n67					

Porcelain Patent Act 1775

PRVA19	1775

Porcelain Patent Act 1775 (15 Geo 3. c. liii)

An Act for enlarging the Term of Letters Patent, granted by his present Majesty to William Cookworthy of Plymouth, Chymist, for the sole Use and Exercise of a Discovery of certain Materials for making Porcelain, in order to enable Richard Champion of Bristol, Merchant, (to whom the said Letters Patent have been assigned) to carry the said Discovery into effectual Execution for the Benefit of the Publick

Table of contents

s 1 All the Powers, Privileges, &c contained in the before-recited Letters Patent, by this Act granted to Richard Champion, his Executors, &c, with a further Term of 14 Years

s 2 Specifications of the Mixture and Proportions of the Raw Materials to be inrolled in the Court of Chancery within 4 months, otherwise this Act to be void

s 3 No Potter, &c hindered from using the same in different Proportions

s 4 Publick Act

Relevant patent

17 Mar 1768 (No 898) Act (No 1096*)	Making porcelain from moorstone, growan, and grown clay [William Cooksworthy]

Journal

House of Commons			House of Lords		
Pres and Rep: Fredrick Montagu			Rep: Lord Scarsdale		
22 Feb 1775	35 CJ 138	**Pet/Ref C'tee**	18 May 1775	34 LJ 461	Brought HC/1R
28 Apr 1775	35 CJ 328	**Pet Rep**	19 May 1775	34 LJ 464	Pet Ag
1 May 1775	35 CJ 334	1R	19 May 1775	34 LJ 464	Wit Sums
5 May 1775	35 CJ 351	2R/C'tted	22 May 1775	34 LJ 473	2R (no Counsel appeared)
10 May 1775	35 CJ 364	**Pet Ag**	25 May 1775	34 LJ 478	**Rep with Amds**
11 May 1775	35 CJ 369	**Pet Ag**	25 May 1775	34 LJ 479	3R
15 May 1775	35 CJ 375 – V	**Rep with Amds**	25 May 1775	34 LJ 479	HC Ag Amds
16 May 1775	35 CJ 378	Pet Ag	26 May 1775	34 LJ 481	Royal Assent
16 May 1775	35 CJ 379	Wit Sums			
17 May 1775	35 CJ 382 – V	**Rep with Amds**/Ing			
18 May 1775	35 CJ 383 – V	**3R**			
25 May 1775	35 CJ 393	HL pass with Amds			
26 May 1775	35 CJ 395	Royal Assent			

Petitions

10 May 1775	35 CJ 364	Manufactures of Earthenware of Stafford [Patent extended injurious]
11 May 1775	35 CJ 369	Potters and Dealers in Earthenware [Patent extended injurious]
16 May 1775	35 CJ 378	Merchants of Liverpool [Patent extended injurious]
19 May 1775	34 LJ 464	Stafford Earthenware Manufacturers [injurious to the petitioners and the public in general]

Parliamentary debates

None

Parliamentary papers and cases

(1) Papers relative to Mr. Champion's application to Parliament, for the extension of the term of a patent (1775) (JISC)

(2) Llewellynn Jewitt, *The Wedgwoods: Being a Life of Josiah Wedgwood* (London: Virtue Bros 1865)

   (a) Memorial of Josiah Wedgewood relative to Mr Champion's Application for a Bill to prolong his patent to make porcelain (p. 237)

   (b) A reply to Mr Wedgewood's Memorial relative to Mr Champion's Application for a Bill to prolong his patent to make porcelain (p 238)

   (c) Remarks upon Mr Champion's Reply to Mr Wedgewood's Memorial on behalf of himself and the Potters in Stafford (p243) (extract)

   (d) Reasons why the extension of the term of Mr Cooksworthy's Patent

   (e) Parliament, would be injurious to many landowners, to the manufacturers of Earthenware, and to public (p 246)

   (f) Case of the manufacturers of Earthenware in Staffordshire (p 247)

(3) Champion's Reply to Wedgewood Memorial: see Hugh Owen, *Two Centuries of Ceramic Art in Bristol* (Gloucester: John Bellows 1873), p 122

Newspaper coverage of debates
House of Commons
2R: Gazetteer and New Daily Advertiser, 6 May 1775; Middlesex Journal and Evening Advertiser, 6 May 1775
Com: **Morning Post and Daily Advertiser, 12 May 1775**; Middlesex Journal and Evening Advertiser, 13 May 1775; Gazetteer and New Daily Advertiser, 16 May 1775; Bath Chronicle and Weekly Gazette, 18 May 1775
Pet Ag: Middlesex Journal and Evening Advertiser, 16–18 May 1775
Rep: London Chronicle, 16 May 1775; Gazetteer and New St. James's Chronicle, 18 May 1775; Craftsman or Say's Weekly Journal, 20 May 1775; Hampshire Chronicle, 22 May 1775
3R: St. James's Chronicle or the British Evening Post, 18–20 May 1775
Royal Assent: Daily Advertiser, 26 May 1775; Gazetteer and New Daily Advertiser, 27 May 1775; Public Advertiser, 27 May 1775; London Evening Post, 27 May 1775; St. James's Chronicle, 27 May 1775; Craftsman or Say's Weekly Journal, 27 May 1775; Oxford Journal, 27 May 1775; Hampshire Chronicle, 29 May 1775; Salisbury and Winchester Journal, 29 May 1775; Manchester Mercury, 30 May 1775; Leeds Intelligencer, 30 May 1775; Caledonian Mercury, 31 May 1775
Archives
C'tee Minutes: 23 May 1775 (p 230–232): HL/PO/CO/1/21
Wit Sums (John Bolton): HL/PO/JO/10/7/477
Ing: HL/PO/PU/1/1775/15G3n159
Notes
Richard Champion petitioned Parliament to incorporate his porcelain business in 1782: 38 CJ 696 (7 Feb 1782). The petition did not progress
Repealed
Statute Law Repeals Act 1986

James Watt's Fire Engines Patent Act 1775

PRVA20	1775
James Watt's Fire Engines Patent Act 1775 (15 Geo 3. c. lxi)	

An Act for vesting in James Watt, Engineer, his Executors, Administrators, and Assigns, the sole Use and Property of certain Steam Engines, commonly called Fire Engines, of his Invention, described in the said Act, throughout his Majesty's Dominions, for a limited Time
Table of contents
s 1 Sole Privilege of making, &c said Engine, vested in James Watt, his Executors, &c for 25 Years
s 2 This Act not to extend to hinder any Person from making or using any Fire Engine, &c. which is not the present Invention of the said James Watt
s 3 Proviso [Objections against patent can be made against Act]
s 4 The Privileges granted by this Act not to be transferred to more than 5 Persons; on Penalty of forfeiting the same
s 5 Publick Act

Relevant patent	
5 Jan 1769 (No 913) Act (913*)	Consumption of fuel in steam engines [James Watt] {extends to colonies}

Journal					
House of Commons			**House of Lords**		
Pres and Rep: Lord Guernsey			Rep: Earl Marchmont		
23 Feb 1775	35 CJ 142	**Pet/Ref C'tee**	27 Apr 1775	34 LJ 416	Brought HC/1R
3 Mar 1775	35 CJ 168	**Pet Rep**	28 Apr 1775	34 LJ 421	2R
9 Mar 1775	35 CJ 185	1R	1 May 1775	34 LJ 422	Rep w/o Amds
13 Mar 1775	35 CJ 191	2R/C'tted	2 May 1775	34 LJ 427	3R
20 Mar 1775	35 CJ 207	**Pet Ag**	22 May 1775	34 LJ 470	Royal Assent
30 Mar 1775	35 CJ 242	Rep adj			
7 Apr 1775	35 CJ 280	Rep with Amds/Re-C'tted			
25 Apr 1775	35 CJ 313	**Rep with Amd**/Ing			
26 Apr 1775	35 CJ 315	3R			

(continued)

(continued)

3 May 1775	35 CJ 343	HL pass w/o Amds			
22 May 1775	35 CJ 387	Royal Assent			

Petitions

20 Mar 1775	35 CJ 207	William Pengree (for William Blakey) [Watt copied Blakey's invention]

Parliamentary debates
Minutes of Parliamentary Committee on Watt's Engine Bill, 1775 – Transcript as Document No 16 in James Watt and the Steam Revolution: A Documentary History (Ed Eric Robinson and A.E. Musson) (Adams and Dart 1969), p 69

Parliamentary papers and cases
None

Newspaper coverage of debates

House of Commons

Rep adj: Morning Chronicle and London Advertiser, 31 Mar 1775; Caledonian Mercury, 3 Apr 1775

Rep with Amds: **Middlesex Journal and Evening Advertiser, 6–8 Apr 1775**; Caledonian Mercury, 12 Apr 1775; Hibernian Journal, 17 Apr 1775; Caledonian Mercury, 12 Apr 1775

Com rep: Gazetteer and New Daily Advertiser, 26 Apr 1775; Morning Chronicle and London Advertiser, 26 Apr 1775; London Chronicle, 27 Apr 1775; Middlesex Journal and Evening Advertiser, 27 Apr 1775; St. James's Chronicle, 27 Apr 1775; Craftsman or Say's Weekly Journal, April 29, 1775; Caledonian Mercury, 29 Apr 1775; Stamford Mercury, 4 May 1775; Hibernian Journal, 17 Apr 1775; Stamford Mercury, 4 May 1775

House of Lords

1R: Morning Chronicle and London Advertiser, 28 April 1775; General Evening Post, 29 April 1775; Caledonian Mercury, 1 May 1775

2R: London Evening Post, 29 April 1775

Rep: Morning Chronicle and London Advertiser, 2 May 1775; General Evening Post, 2 May 1775; London Evening Post, 2 May 1775

3R: Daily Advertiser, 3 May 1775; Morning Chronicle and London Advertiser, 3 May 1775; London Evening Post, 4 May 1775

Royal Assent: Salisbury and Winchester Journal, 29 May 1775

Archives
C'tee Minutes: 1 May 1775 (p 172–173): HL/PO/CO/1/21
Ing: HL/PO/PU/1/15G3n83

Notes

Related cases

Boulton and Watt v Bull (1795) (Com Pl) 1 HPC 369; 1 CPC 117; 126 ER 651; *Boulton and Watt v Bull* (LC) (1796) 1 CPC 155; 3 Ves J 140 (30 ER 937); 1 Ves J Supp 345 (34 ER 820); *Hornblower v Boulton and Watt* (KB) (1799) 1 HPC 397, 8 TR 95 (101 ER 1285); 1 CPC 156

Repealed by

Statute Law Revision Act 1948

Elizabeth Taylor's Patent Act 1776

PRVA21	1776
Elizabeth Taylor's Patent Act 1776 (16 Geo 3. c. xviii)	
An Act for enlarging the Term of Letters Patent granted by his present Majesty to Elizabeth Taylor, of the Town of Southampton, Widow, for the sole Use and Exercise of certain Engines, Tools, Instruments, and other Apparatus, for making Blocks, Sheavers, and Pins, used in the Rigging of Ships	
Table of contents	
s 1 All the Powers, Privileges, &c, contained in the before-recited Letters Patent, by this Act granted to Walter Taylor, his Executors, &c for a further Term of 14 Years s 2 Specification of Improvement to be inrolled in the Court of Chancery within four months, otherwise this Act to be void s 3 Walter Taylor to grant Licences, &c on certain Conditions s 4 Public Act	

Relevant patent	
6 Dec 1762 (No 782) Act (No 1139*)	Set of engines, tools, instruments and other apparatus, for making blocks, shivers, and pins [Elizabeth Taylor]

Journal

House of Commons			House of Lords		
Pres and Rep: Sir Charles Whitworth			Rep: Lord Say and Sele		
15 Feb 1776	35 CJ 559	**Pet/Ref Com**	18 Mar 1776	34 LJ 598	Brought HC
23 Feb 1776	35 CJ 593	**Rep Pet**	19 Mar 1776	34 LJ 600	1R
27 Feb 1776	35 CJ 599	1R	20 Mar 1776	34 LJ 603	2R/C'tted
6 Mar 1776	35 CJ 633	2R/C'tted	22 Mar 1776	34 LJ 607	Rep w/o Amds
14 Mar 1776	35 CJ 653	Rep with Amds/Ing	22 Mar 1776	34 LJ 608	3R
15 Mar 1776	35 CJ 658	3R	25 Mar 1776	34 LJ 612	Royal Assent
22 Mar 1776	35 CJ 677	HL pass w/o Amds			
25 Mar 1776	35 CJ 679	Royal Assent			

Parliamentary debates

None

Parliamentary papers and cases

2R (6 Mar): Daily Advertiser, 20 Mar 1776

Newspaper coverage of debates

None

Archives

C'tee Minutes: 22 Mar 1776 (p 311–315): HL/PO/CO/1/21

Ing: HL/PO/PU/1/1776/16G3n27

Notes

Repealed by

Statute Law Revision Act 1948

Liardet's Cement Patent Act 1776

PRVA22	1776
Liardet's Cement Patent Act 1776 (16 Geo 3. c. xxix)	

An Act for vesting in John Liardet, Clerk, his Executors, Administrators, and Assigns, the sole Use and Property of a certain Composition or Cement of his Invention, throughout his Majesty's Kingdom of Great Britain, and in the Colonies and Plantations abroad, for a limited Time

Table of contents

s 1 The sole Privilege of making and vending the Cement vested in John Liardet, his Executors, &c, for eighteen years; Penalty on other Person making Cement without Licence &c
s 2 John Liardet not to sell his Cement dearer than certain Prices mentioned
s 3 This Act not to hinder the making any Composition which is not the Invention of John Liardet, &c
s 4 [Objections against patent can be made against Act]
s 5 If John Liardet &c, shall transfer the Privilege of making Cement to more than 5 Persons, &c; or shall do any Thing contrary to the recited Act of 6 Geo I [the Bubble Act]; then this Act to become Void
s 6 John Liardet &c, to cause a Specification of the Nature of his Invention to be inrolled in Chancery, within 4 Months, or to lose the Benefit of this Act
s 7 Public Act

Relevant patent

3 Apr 1773 (No 1040) Act (No 1134*)	Cement for building purposes; grease for frictions, for preserving steel and iron, and for other uses [John Lairdet] {extends to colonies}

Journal

House of Commons	House of Lords
Pres and Rep: (John) St John	Rep: Lord Scarsdale Second Rep: Lord Cathcart

(continued)

(continued)

12 Feb 1776	35 CJ 546	**Pet/Ref C'tee**	18 Mar 1776	34 LJ 598	Brought HC
27 Feb 1776	35 CJ 600	**Pet Rep**	19 Mar 1776	34 LJ 600	1R
29 Feb 1776	35 CJ 605	1R	20 Mar 1776	34 LJ 602	2R/C'tted
4 Mar 1776	35 CJ 626	2R/C'tted	28 Mar 1776	34 LJ 620	**Rep with Amds**
12 Mar 1776	35 CJ 649	Rep with Amds/Ing	1 Apr 1776	34 LJ 629	Re-C'tted
14 Mar 1776	35 CJ 654	3R	3 Apr 1776	34 LJ 636	**Rep with Amds/3R**
18 Apr 1776	35 CJ 702	HL pass with Amds	25 Apr 1776	34 LJ 675	HC Ag Amds
25 Apr 1776	35 CJ 721	**HL Amds Ag**	13 May 1776	34 LJ 715	Royal Assent
13 May 1776	35 CJ 782	Royal Assent			

Parliamentary debates
None

Parliamentary papers and cases
None

Newspaper coverage of debates

House of Lords

1R: Morning Chronicle and London Advertiser, 19 Mar 1776

2R: Daily Advertiser, 20 Mar 1776

Rep: General Evening Post, 28–30 Mar 1776; Morning Chronicle and London Advertiser, 29 Mar 1776

Re-C'tted: **Middlesex Journal and Evening Advertiser, 30 Mar–2 Apr 1776**; **Morning Post and Daily Advertiser, 2 Apr 1776**; *General Evening Post, 30 Mar–2 Apr 1776*; *Lloyd's Evening Post, 1–3 Apr 1776*; *Morning Chronicle and London Advertiser, 2 Apr 1776*; *Kentish Gazette, 6 Apr 1776*; *Hampshire Chronicle, 8 Apr 1776*

3R: General Evening Post, 2–4 Apr 1776; Daily Advertiser, 5 Apr 1776; Craftsman or Say's Weekly Journal, 6 Apr 1776

Rep of business: Morning Post and Daily Advertiser, 1 Apr 1776

Royal Assent: London Gazette, 11–14 May 1776; London Evening Post, 11–14 May 1776; Daily Advertiser, 13 May 1776; Norfolk Chronicle, 18 May 1776; Stamford Mercury, 16 May 1776

Archives

C'tee Minutes: 25 Mar 1776 (p 319–323); 2 Apr 1776 (p 345–348): HL/PO/CO/1/21

C'tee Rep: 28 Mar 1776: HL/PO/JO/10/7/498

Ing: HL/PO/PU/1/1776/16G3n103

Notes

Repealed by

Statute Law Revision Act 1948

Hartley's Patent (Fire Prevention) Act 1776

PRVA23	1777
Hartley's Patent (Fire Prevention) Act 1776 (17 Geo 3. c. vi)	
An Act for vesting in David Hartley Esquire, his Executors, Administrators, and Assigns, the sole Use and Property of a certain Method by him invented of securing Buildings against the Calamities of Fire, throughout his Majesty's Dominions, for a limited Time.	

Table of contents

s 1 The sole Privilege of making and vending the aforesaid Invention vested in David Hartley, &c for thirty-one Years; Penalty on person making or imitating the same
s 2 Exception, in favour his Majesty's Dockyards, &c
s 3 Certain Restrictions laid on David Hartley, &c, on the Breach whereof this Act become void
s 4 [Objections against patent can be made against Act]
s 5 Clause for regulation the Price of Fire Plates
s 6 Public Act

Relevant patent	
1 Apr 1773 (No 1037)	Securing buildings and ships from accidents by fire [David Hartley]

Journal					
House of Commons			House of Lords		
Pres and Rep: Sir George Saville			Rep: Lord Scarsdale		
12 Nov 1776	36 CJ 30	**Pet/Ref Com**	27 Nov 1776	35 LJ 29	Brought HC/1R
14 Nov 1776	36 CJ 33	**Pet Rep**	28 Nov 1776	35 LJ 30	2R/C'tted CWH
15 Nov 1776	36 CJ 33	1R	23 Jan 1777	35LJ 35	CWH adj
19 Nov 1776	36 CJ 45	2R/C'tted	6 Feb 1777	35 LJ 44	**Rep with Amds**
26 Nov 1776	36 CJ 57	Rep with Amds/Ing	7 Feb 1777	35 LJ 47	**3R**
27 Nov 1776	36 CJ 59	3R	11 Feb 1777	35 LJ 50	HC Amds Ag
7 Feb 1777	36 CJ 136	**HL Amds Ag**	3 Mar 1777	35 LJ 82	Royal Assent
3 Mar 1777	36 CJ 238	Royal Assent			

Parliamentary debates

None

Parliamentary papers and cases

None

Newspaper coverage of debates

House of Commons

Pre-lodging: Leeds Intelligencer, 3 Dec 1776

Pet: **General Evening Post, 12–14 Nov 1776**; *St. James's Chronicle, 12–14 Nov 1776; Morning Post and Daily Advertiser, 13 Nov 1776; Lloyd's Evening Post, 13–15 Nov 1776; London Packet or New Lloyd's Evening Post, 13–15 Nov 1776; Daily Advertiser, 14 Nov 1776;* Morning Chronicle and London Advertiser, 13 Nov 1776; Derby Mercury, 15 Nov 1776

Pet Rep**:** *General Evening Post, 14–16 Nov 1776; London Chronicle, 14–16 Nov 1776; Gazetteer and New Daily Advertiser, 15 Nov 1776; Morning Post and Daily Advertiser, 15 Nov 1776; Daily Advertiser, 15 Nov 1776; Morning Chronicle and London Advertiser, 15 Nov 1776; New Morning Post or General Advertiser, 15 Nov 1776;* Lloyd's Evening Post 13–15 Nov 1776; London Evening Post, 14–16 Nov 1776

2R: London Packet or New Lloyd's Evening Post, 18–20 Nov 1776

Bill Rep**:** London Chronicle, 21–23 Nov 1776; Lloyd's Evening Post, 22–25 Nov 1776

3R: Gazetteer and New Daily Advertiser, 28 Nov 1776

House of Lords

1R: Lloyd's Evening Post, 27–29 Nov 1776; London Chronicle, 26–28 Nov 1776; St. James's Chronicle or the British Evening Post, 26–28 Nov 1776; Daily Advertiser, 28 Nov 1776; Morning Chronicle and London Advertiser, 28 Nov 1776; New Morning Post or General Advertiser, 28 Nov 1776; Gazetteer and New Daily Advertiser, 28 Nov 1776

2R: **General Evening Post, 28–30 Nov 1776**; *London Chronicle, 28–30 Nov 1776;* St. James's Chronicle or the British Evening Post, 28–30 Nov 1776; Daily Advertiser, 29 Nov 1776; Morning Post and Daily Advertiser, 29 Nov 1776

Rep: Gazetteer and New Daily Advertiser, 7 Feb 1777

3R: *London Chronicle, 6–8 Feb 1777;* London Evening Post, 6–8 Feb 1777; Morning Post and Daily Advertiser, 8 Feb 1777

Rep with Amds: Morning Chronicle and London Advertiser, 12 Feb 1777

Royal Assent: General Evening Post, 1–4 March 1777; Daily Advertiser, 3 Mar 1777; Gazetteer and New Daily Advertiser, 4 Mar 1777; Westminster Journal and London Political Miscellany 8 Mar 1777

Implementation: *General Evening Post, 29 Mar- 1 Apr 1777; St. James's Chronicle or the British Evening Post, 29 Mar–1 Apr 1777*

Archives

C'tee Minutes: 4 Feb 1777 (p 7–12 – V): HL/PO/CO/1/22

Rep of C'tee: 6 Feb 1777: HL/PO/JO/10/7/517

Ing: HL/PO/PU/1/1776/17G3n16

Notes

Repealed by

Statute Law Revision Act 1948

Bancroft's Patent Act 1785

PRVA24	1785

Bancroft's Patent Act 1785 (25 Geo 3. c. xxxviii)
An Act for vesting in Edward Bancroft, Doctor in Physick, his Executors, Administrators, and Assigns, the sole Property of his Invention or Discovery of the Use and Application of certain Vegetables for Dying, Staining, Printing and Painting certain valuable Colours, throughout that Part of his Majesty's Kingdom of Great Britain called England, the Dominion of Wales, and Town of Berwick upon Tweed, for a limited Time

Table of contents
s 1 The sole Privilege of making and vending the Invention vested in Edward Bancroft, his Executors, etc. for 14 Years; Penalty on other persons using the Invention without Licence etc.   s 2 This Act not to hinder the using any Invention which is not the Invention or Application of Edward Bancroft, &c.   s 3 If Edward Bancroft, &c, shall transfer the Privilege of his Invention to more than Five Persons, &c; or shall do any Thing contrary to the recited Act 6 Geo Cap 18 [Bubble Act]; then this Act to become void   s 4 Edward Bancroft, &c, to cause a Specification of the Nature of his [Improved] Invention to be inrolled in Chancery within Four Months; or to lose the Benefit of this Act   s 5 Publick Act

Relevant patent	
23 Oct 1775 (No 1103) Act (No 1496*)	Use of certain vegetables for dyeing, staining, printing, painting or otherwise colouring, wool, hair, fur, silk, hemp, cotton, linen, skins, leather, paper, and wood [Edward Bancroft]

Journal

House of Commons			House of Lords		
Pres and Rep: William Eden			Rep: Lord Scarsdale		
8 Mar 1785	40 CJ 613	**Pet/Ref C'tee**	11 May 1785	37 LJ 267	Brought HC/1R
21 Mar 1785	40 CJ 752	**Pet Rep**	12 May 1785	37 LJ 277	2R/C'tted
8 Apr 1785	40 CJ 822	Rep read/Bill Ord	24 May 1785	37 LJ 278	Rep w/o Amds
15 Apr 1785	40 CJ 852	Re-title Bill	25 May 1785	37 LJ 281	3R
20 Apr 1785	40 CJ 867	1R	13 Jun 1785	37 LJ 310	Royal Assent
25 Apr 1785	40 CJ 885	2R/C'tted			
2 May 1785	40 CJ 919	Rep with Amds/Ing			
4 May 1785	40 CJ 931	3R			
27 May 1785	40 CJ 1024	HL pass w/o Amd			
13 Jun 1785	40 CJ 1067	Royal Assent			

Parliamentary debates
None

Parliamentary papers and cases
None

Newspaper coverage of debates

House of Commons

1R: Morning Chronicle and London Advertiser, 21 April 1785

Rep: Whitehall Evening Post, 3–5 May 1785

3R: Morning Chronicle and London Advertiser, 5 May 1785

House of Lords

1R: Morning Chronicle and London Advertiser, 12 May 1785

2R: General Evening Post, 12–14 May 1785; Whitehall Evening Post, 12–14 May 1785; The Times, 13 May 1785; Gazetteer and New Daily Advertiser, 13 May 1785

3R: Morning Chronicle and London Advertiser, 26 May 1785

Royal Assent: Whitehall Evening Post, 14–16 June 1785; Public Advertiser, 18 June 1785

Archives

C'tee Minutes: 24 May 1785 (p 142–143): HL/PO/CO/1/29

Ing: HL/PO/PU/1/1785/25G3n88

Notes
Related case
Bancroft v Warden (1786) 11 HPC App
Repealed by
Statute Law Revision Act 1948

Lord Dundonald's Patent (Tar, Pitch, etc.) Act 1785

PRVA25	1785
Lord Dundonald's Patent (Tar, Pitch, etc.) Act 1785 (25 Geo 3. c. xlii)	
An Act for vesting in Archibald Earl of Dundonald, his Executors, Administrators, and Assigns, the sole Use and Property of a Method of extracting or making Tar, Pitch, Essential Oils, Volatile Alkali, Mineral Acids, Salts, and Cinders, from Pit Coal, throughout his Majesty's Dominions, for a limited Time.	

Table of contents

s 1 Sole Privilege of making Tar, Pitch, &c from Pit Coal, vesting the Earl of Dundonald for 20 Years
s 2 Act not to extent to hinder any Person from making Tar, Pitch, &c which is not the Invention of the Earl of Dundonald
s 3 Proviso [Objections against patent can be made against Act]
s 4 The Privileges granted by this Act not to be transferred to more than Five Persons
s 5 Publick Act

Relevant patent

30 Apr 1781 (No 1291) Act (No 1291*)	Extracting tar, pitch, essential-oils, volatile-alkali, mineral-acides, salts, and cinders, from pit-coal [Archibald Dundonald, Earl of] {Scottish patent: 27 Feb 1781}

Journal

House of Commons			House of Lords		
Pres and Rep: Sir Adam Ferguson			Rep: Lord Scarsdale		
4 Mar 1785	40 CJ 586	**Pet/Ref Com**	27 May 1785	37 LJ 282	Brought and 1R
14 Mar 1785	40 CJ 633	**Pet Rep**	31 May 1785	37 LJ 286	2R/C'tted
16 Mar 1785	40 CJ 642	1R	2 Jun 1785	37 LJ 292	Rep with Amds
29 Apr 1785	40 CJ 915	2R/C'tted	6 Jun 1785	37 LJ 297	3R
23 May 1785	40 CJ 1006 – V	**Rep with Amds**/Ing	13 Jun 1785	37 LJ 310	Royal Assent
25 May 1785	40 CJ 1013	3R			
7 Jun 1785	40 CJ 1052	HL pass w/o Amds			
13 Jun 1785	40 CJ 1065	Royal Assent			

Parliamentary debates

Rep: Parliamentary Register, 23 May 1785, Vol 18, p 354

Parliamentary papers and cases

None

Newspaper coverage of debates

House of Commons

Pet Rep: Morning Chronicle and London Advertiser, 15 Mar 1785; London Chronicle, 15–17 Mar 1785; Caledonian Mercury, 19 Mar 1785

2R: **The Times, 30 Apr 1785**; **Morning Chronicle and London Advertiser, 30 Apr 1785**; *London Chronicle, 28–30 Apr 1785*; *Morning Post and Daily Advertiser, 30 Apr 1785*; *General Advertiser, 30 Apr 1785*; Derby Mercury, 28 Apr 1785; General Evening Post, 28–30 Apr 1785; Whitehall Evening Post, 28–30 Apr 1785; Morning Herald and Daily Advertiser, 30 Apr 1785 (misrep); Reading Mercury, 30 Apr 1785 (misrep); Caledonian Mercury, 4 May 1785

Rep: **The Times, 24 May 1785**; General Evening Post, 21–24 May 1785; Whitehall Evening Post, 21–24 May 1785; Morning Chronicle and London Advertiser, 24 May 1785; Morning Herald and Daily Advertiser, 24 May 1785; Morning Post and Daily Advertiser, 24 May 1785; Public Advertiser, 24 May 1785; Whitehall Evening Post, 24–26 May 1785; Chelmsford Chronicle, 27 May 1785; Cumberland Pacquet and Ware's Whitehaven Advertiser, 31 May 1785

3R: Caledonian Mercury, 30 May 1785

(continued)

(continued)

House of Lords
1R: Morning Chronicle and London Advertiser, 28 May 1785; Morning Herald and Daily Advertiser, 28 May 1785; Public Advertiser, 28 May 1785; Whitehall Evening Post, 26–28 May 1785; Reading Mercury, 30 May 1785
2R: **The Scots Magazine, 1 Jun 1785**; *Newcastle Courant, 28 May 1785*; *Caledonian Mercury, 28 May 1785*; *Hampshire Chronicle, 30 May 1785*
3R: Morning Chronicle and London Advertiser, 7 Jun 1785; Whitehall Evening Post, 7–9 Jun 1785; Caledonian Mercury, 11 Jun 1785; Leeds Intelligencer, 14 Jun 1785
Royal Assent: Public Advertiser, 14 Jun 1785; Bath Chronicle and Weekly Gazette, 16 Jun 1785; Hereford Journal, 16 Jun 1785; Cumberland Pacquet, and Ware's Whitehaven Advertiser, 21 Jun 1785
Celebrations: Morning Chronicle and London Advertiser, 2 July 1785

Archives
C'tee Minutes: 1 Jun 1785 (p 161–163): HL/PO/CO/1/29
Ing: HL/PO/PU/1/1785/25G3n87

Notes
Repealed by
Statute Law Revision Act 1948

Turner's Patent Act 1792

PRVA26	1792
Turner's Patent Act 1792 (32 Geo 3. c. lxxii)	
An Act for vesting in James Turner, his Executors, Administrators, and Assigns, the sole Use and Property of a certain Yellow Colour, of his Invention, throughout that Part of Great Britain called England, the Dominion of Wales, and Town of Berwick upon Tweed, for a limited Time	

Table of contents
s 1 The sole Privilege of making and vending the Invention vested in Mr Turner his Executors, &c for eleven Years
s 2 Mr Turner not to sell the Colour at more than five Guineas the Hundred Weight
s 3 This Act not to hinder the using any Invention which is not the Invention of Mr Turner
s 4 Objections against this Yellow Colour being a new Invention, &c
s 5 The Invention not to become the Property of more than five Persons, &c; 6 Geo I, c 18 [Bubble Act]
s 6 Publick Act

Relevant patent	
26 Feb 1781 (No 1281)	Producing a yellow colour for painting in oil or water; making white lead, and separating mineral-alkali from common salt, all in one single process [James Turner]

Journal					
House of Commons			**House of Lords**		
Pres and Rep: Sir George Jackson			Rep: Lord Rawdon		
15 Feb 1792	47 CJ 389	**Pet/Ref Com**	27 Mar 1792	39 LJ 332	Brought HC
27 Feb 1792	47 CJ 440	**Pet Rep**	28 Mar 1792	39 LJ 334	1R
5 Mar 1792	47 CJ 479	1R	7 May 1792	39 LJ 396	2R/C'tted
9 Mar 1792	47 CJ 527	2R/C'tted	15 May 1792	39 LJ 422	Rep w/o Amds
21 Mar 1792	47 CJ 580	Rep with Amds/Ing	7 Jun 1792	39 LJ 468	**3R with Amds**
26 Mar 1792	47 CJ 590	3R	12 Jun 1792	39 LJ 485	HC Ag Amds
8 Jun 1792	47 CJ 1068	**HL pass with Amds/Ag**	15 Jun 1792	39 LJ 490	Royal Assent
15 Jun 1792	47 CJ 1090	Royal Assent			

Parliamentary debates
3R: Senator, 7 Jun 1792, Vol 5, p 1013
HC Ag Amds: Senator, 12 Jun 1792, Vol 5, p 1037
Royal Assent: Senator, 15 Jun 1792, Vol 5, p 1058

Parliamentary papers and cases
None

Newspaper coverage of debates
House of Lords
Brought HC: Kentish Gazette, 3 Apr 1792
3R: *The Times, 8 Jun 1792*; *Morning Herald, 8 Jun 1792*; St. James's Chronicle or the British Evening Post, 7–9 Jun 1792; Morning Chronicle, 8 Jun 1792 (misrep); Star, 8 Jun 1792 (misrep)
HL pass: The Times, 9 Jun 1792
Royal Assent: London Chronicle, 14–16 Jun 1792; Diary or Woodfall's Register, 15 Jun 1792; Lloyd's Evening Post, 15–18 Jun 1792; The Times, 16 Jun 1792; Public Advertiser, 16 Jun 1792; Stamford Mercury, 22 June 1792
Archives
C'tee Minutes: 15 May 1792 (p 265–267): HL/PO/CO/1/36
Amendments: 7 Jun 1792: HL/PO/JO/10/7/924
Ing: HL/PO/PU/1/1792/32G3n225
Notes
Repealed by
Statute Law Revision Act 1948

Booth's Patent Act 1792

PRVA27	1792
Booth's Patent Act 1792 (32 Geo 3. c. lxxiii)	
An Act for more effectually securing to Joseph Booth, and to the Publick, the Benefit of a certain Invention or Discovery therein mentioned, for which he hath obtained Letters Patent under the Great Seal of Great Britain	

Table of contents
s 1 Specification instead of being inrolled, to be delivered to the Lord High Chancellor
s 2 Packet inclosing the Specification, not to be removed from the Place where it shall be deposited, but by Order of the Chancellor
s 3 Delivery of the Specification under this Act to be deemed a Compliance with the Proviso in the Patent
s 4 Delivery of Specification agreeable to this Act to be deemed a Compliance with the Proviso in any further Patent
s 5 Publick Act

Relevant patents	
23 Jan 1792 (No 1846)	Apparatus and chemical compositions, for the purpose of making woollen cloths, linens, and various other fabrics [Joseph Booth] {Scottish patent: 27 Jan 1792}
12 Jun 1792 (No 1888) Act (No 1888*)	Apparatus and chemical compositions, for the purpose of making woollen cloths, linens, and various other fabrics [Joseph Booth] [s 4 Application]

Journal					
House of Commons			**House of Lords**		
Pres and Rep: Scrope Bernard			Rep: Earl of Lauderdale		
5 Mar 1792	47 CJ 499	**Pet/Ref Com**	3 May 1792	39 LJ 392	Brought HC
16 Mar 1792	47 CJ 559	**Pet Rep**	4 May 1792	39 LJ 394	1R
30 Mar 1792	47 CJ 626	1R	25 May 1792	39 LJ 446	2R/C'tted
3 Apr 1792	47 CJ 680	2R/C'tted	7 Jun 1792	39 LJ 468	**Rep with Amds**
23 Apr 1792	47 CJ 721	Rep with Amds/Ing	11 Jun 1792	39 LJ 483	3R
3 May 1792	47 CJ 763	3R	12 Jun 1792	39 LJ 485	HC Ag Amds
12 Jun 1792	47 CJ 1075	**HL pass with Amds**	15 Jun 1792	39 LJ 490	Royal Assent
12 Jun 1792	47 CJ 1088	HL Amds Ag			
15 Jun 1792	47 CJ 1090	Royal Assent			

Parliamentary debates
Royal Assent: Senator, 15 Jun 1792, Vol 5, p 1058
Parliamentary papers and cases
None

(continued)

(continued)

Newspaper coverage of debates
House of Commons
Pet Rep: Diary or Woodfall's Register, 17 Mar 1792
1R: Diary or Woodfall's Register, 31 Mar 1792; Kentish Gazette, 3 April 1792
3R: The Times, 4 May 1792; Diary or Woodfall's Register, 4 May 1792
HL pass: London Chronicle, 29–31 May 1792; Evening Mail, 11–13 Jun 1792; Lloyd's Evening Post, 11–13 Jun 1792; Diary or Woodfall's Register, 13 Jun 1792
HL Amds Ag: The Times, 13 Jun 1792
House of Lords
2R: Diary or Woodfall's Register, 26 May 1792
Royal Assent: London Chronicle, 14–16 Jun 1792; Diary or Woodfall's Register, 15 Jun 1792; Lloyd's Evening Post, 15–18 Jun 1792; Public Advertiser, 16 Jun 1792

Archives
C'tee Minutes: 31 May 1792 (p 327); 1 Jun 1792 (p 338); 5 Jun 1792 (p 348); 6 Jun 1792 (p 350); 7 Jun 1792 (p 353–355): HL/PO/CO/1/36
Ing: HL/PO/PU/1/1792/32G3n226

Notes
Repealed by
Statute Law Revision Act 1948

New Method of Tanning Act 1794

PRVA28	1794

New Method of Tanning Act 1794 (34 Geo 3. c. lxiii)
An Act for allowing the exercise of an Invention of a new Method of Tanning Hides and Skins [Samuel Ashton's Patent]

Table of contents
s 1 Nothing in any Act to prevent Samuel Ashton from tanning Hides and Skins in the Manner mentioned in his Letters Patent, &c
s 2 Public Act

Relevant patent	
16 Jan 1794 (No 1977) Act (No 1977*)	Tanning hides and skins [Samuel Ashton]

Journal					
House of Commons			**House of Lords**		
Pres and Rep: William Wilberforce			Rep: John Warren (Bishop of Bangor)		
28 Apr 1794	49 CJ 492	**Pet/Ref Com**	15 May 1794	40 LJ 182	Brought HC/1R
2 May 1794	49 CJ 542	**Pet Rep**	19 May 1794	40 LJ 189	2R/C'tted CWH
2 May 1794	49 CJ 543	1R	20 May 1794	40 LJ 201	CWH/Rep w/o Amds
5 May 1794	49 CJ 554	2R/C'tted	21 May 1794	40 LJ 201	3R
6 May 1794	49 CJ 555	Rep with Amds/Ing	23 May 1794	40 LJ 210	Royal Assent
9 May 1794	49 CJ 578	**3R with Amds**			
22 May 1794	49 CJ 620	HL pass w/o Amds			
23 May 1794	49 CJ 623	Royal Assent			

Parliamentary debates
None

Parliamentary papers and cases
None

Newspaper coverage of debates
Royal Assent: Hereford Journal, 28 May 1794; Caledonian Mercury, 29 May 1794; Stamford Mercury, 30 May 1794

Archives
Ing: HL/PO/PU/1/1794/34G3n167

Conway's Patent Kiln Act 1795

PRVA29	1795

Conway's Patent Kiln Act 1795 (35 Geo 3. c. lxviii)

An Act for vesting, for a certain term of Years, in the Right Honourable Henry Seymour Conway, his Executor, Administrators, and Assigns, the sole Property of a Kiln or Oven, by him invented, for burning lime, and for the use of Distillers and Brewers, and for other beneficial purposes

Table of contents

s 1 Sole Privilege of making and vending the Invention vested in the Right Hon. H.S. Conway, his Executors, &c. for 20 Years
s 2 Act not to hinder the using any Invention, which was not the Invention of H.S. Conway
s 3 Privileges not to be transferred to more than Five Persons, &c.
s 4 Publick Act

Relevant patent

1 Jan 1782 (No 1310)	Kilns and ovens for distilling and brewing purposes [Henry Conway] {Scottish patent: 10 Nov 1786}

Journal

House of Commons			House of Lords		
Pres and Rep: Lord Fredrick Campbell			Rep: Lord Rawden		
5 Feb 1795	50 CJ 144	**Pet/Ref Com**	30 Apr 1795	40 LJ 407	Brought HC/1R
18 Mar 1795	50 CJ 335	**Pet Rep**	1 May 1795	40 LJ 411	2R/C'tted CWH
1 Apr 1795	50 CJ 402	1R	12 May 1795	40 LJ 433 – V	**CWH/C'tted**
9 Apr 1795	50 CJ 405	2R/C'tted	15 May 1795	40 LJ 438	Rep w/o Amds
28 Apr 1795	50 CJ 477	Rep with Amds/Ing	18 May 1795	40 LJ 443	3R
30 Apr 1795	50 CJ 489	3R	19 May 1795	40 LJ 447	Royal Assent
19 May 1795	50 CJ 542	HL pass w/o Amds			
19 May 1795	50 CJ 545	Royal Assent			

Parliamentary debates

Pet: Senator, 5 Feb 1795, Vol 11, p 464

Rep: Senator, 28 Apr 1795, Vol 12, p 947

3R: Senator, 30 Apr 1795, Vol 12, p 955

C'tted: **Parliamentary Register, 12 May 1795, Vol 42, p 506–507; Senator, 12 May 1795, Vol 12, p 1024–1025; Woodfall, 12 May 1795, Vol 3, p 202–213**

Parliamentary papers and cases

None

Newspaper coverage of debates

House of Commons

Pet: The Times, 6 Feb 1795 (mis rep); Star, 6 Feb 1795; True Briton, 6 Feb 1795

Pet Rep: Sun, 19 Mar 1795

2R: Whitehall Evening Post, 9–11 Apr 1795; The Times, 10 Apr 1795; Star, 10 Apr 1795; True Briton, 10 Apr 1795

Rep: Lloyd's Evening Post, 27–29 Apr 1795; Sun, 29 Apr 1795

3R: Lloyd's Evening Post, 29 Apr–1 May 1795; Sun, 29 Apr 1795; Whitehall Evening Post, 30 Apr–2 May 1795; St. James's Chronicle or the British Evening Post, 30 Apr–2 May 1795; The Times, 1 May 1795

House of Lords

CWH (but usually misrep as 2R): **Whitehall Evening Post, 12–14 May 1795; Oracle and Public Advertiser, 13 May 1795; Star, 13 May 1795; True Briton, 13 May 1795;** *London Packet or New Lloyd's Evening Post, 11–13 May 1795; Morning Post and Fashionable World, 13 May 1795; Stamford Mercury, 15 May 1795; Caledonian Mercury, 16 May 1795;* London Packet or New Lloyd's Evening Post, 11–13 May 1795

3R: Whitehall Evening Post, 16–19 May 1795; London Packet or New Lloyd's Evening Post, 18–20 May 1795; E. Johnson's British Gazette and Sunday Monitor, 24 May 1795

Royal Assent: St. James's Chronicle or the British Evening Post, 19–21 May 1795; Caledonian Mercury, 23 May 1795

(continued)

(continued)

Archives
C'tee Minutes: 15 May 1795 (p 318–321): HL/PO/CO/1/39
Ing: HL/PO/PU/1/1795/35G3n146

Notes
Repealed by
Statute Law Revision Act 1948

East India Company Act 1796

PRVA30	1795
East India Company Act 1796 (36 Geo 3. c. cxx)	

An Act for enabling the East India Company to perform an Engagement entered into by them, with William Sabatier Gentleman, respecting the Importation of Cotton from the East Indies [Sabatier's Invention]

Table of contents
s 1 The [East India] Company empowered to deduct the Percentages, and pay them to Mr Sabatier [for use of his invention]
s 2 Mr Sabatier to deliver to the Company, a Specification of the Bales retained according to his Method
s 3 Commencement and Continuance of the Act
s 4 Publick Act

Relevant patent	
4 Jul 1796 (No 2125)	Retaining cotton, tobacco, hemp, flax, hops, hay and other articles in nearly the same compass into which they can be compressed by machinery, without being liable to any material expansion after being removed from such machinery [William Sabatier]

Journal					
House of Commons			**House of Lords**		
Pres and Rep: John Blackburne Rep: Thomas Stanley			Rep: Lord Walsingham (Ld Ch)		
2 Feb 1796	51 CJ 272	**Pet**	12 May 1796	40 LJ 732	Brought HC/1R
11 Feb 1796	51 CJ 382	**Pet Rep**/Leave	13 May 1796	40 LJ 734	2R/C'tted
12 Feb 1796	51 CJ 385	1R	14 May 1796	40 LJ 745	Rep w/o Amds
17 Feb 1796	51 CJ 406	2R/C'tted	16 May 1796	40 LJ 747	3R
10 May 1796	51 CJ 693	Rep with Amds/Ing	18 May 1796	40 LJ 753	Royal Assent
12 May 1796	51 CJ 762	3R			
18 May 1796	51 CJ 789	HL pass w/o Amds			
18 May 1796	51 CJ 791	Royal Assent			

Parliamentary debates
Pet: Senator, 2 Feb 1796, Vol 14, p 935

Parliamentary papers and cases
None

Newspaper coverage of debates
House of Commons
1R: The Times, 13 Feb 1796
2R: The Times, 18 Feb 1796

Archives
C'tee Minutes: 14 May 1796 (p 262–263): HL/PO/CO/1/40
Ing: HL/PO/PU/1/1796/36G3n248

Koops Papermaking Patent Act 1801

PRVA31	1801	
Koops Papermaking Patent Act 1801 (41 Geo 3. c. cxxv)		

An Act for enabling Matthias Koops Gentleman, to assign the Benefit of an Invention of making Paper from Straw and other Substances, to a greater Number of Persons than is at present limited by the Letters Patent granted to the said Matthias Koops

Table of contents

s 1 Authorizing Mr Koops to assign the Letters Patent to any Number of Persons, not exceeding Sixty
s 2 Publick Act

Relevant patent

17 Feb 1801 (No 2481)	Manufacturing paper from straw, hay, thistles, waste and refuse of hemp and flax, and different kinds of wood and bark [Matthias Koops] {Scottish patent: 17 Apr 1801; Irish patent: 22 Jan 1801}

Journal

House of Commons			House of Lords		
Pres and Rep: Sir William Elford			Rep: Lord Walsingham (Ld Ch)		
16 Mar 1801	56 CJ 173	**First Pet**	2 Jun 1801	43 LJ 229	Brought HC/1R
20 Mar 1801	56 CJ 204	**Second Pet/Ref Com**	3 Jun 1801	43 LJ 233	2R/C'tted CWH
4 May 1801	56 CJ 347	**Pet Rep**	5 Jun 1801	43 LJ 238	Ord to Req HC Rep
7 May 1801	56 CJ 372	Cons adj	5 Jun 1801	43 LJ 238	CWH adj
8 May 1801	56 CJ 384	Cons adj	8 Jun 1801	43 LJ 239	Rep Req of HC
11 May 1801	56 CJ 390	Cons adj	10 Jun 1801	43 LJ 253	Rep Rec
12 May 1801	56 CJ 399	Rep read/Bill Ord	10 Jun 1801	43 LJ 255	CWH adj
13 May 1801	56 CJ 402	1R	12 Jun 1801	43 LJ 262	CWH adj
19 May 1801	56 CJ 439	2R/C'tted	15 Jun 1801	43 LJ 271	CWH adj
1 Jun 1801	56 CJ 482	Rep with Amds	16 Jun 1801	43 LJ 287	CWH adj
2 Jun 1801	56 CJ 489	3R	19 Jun 1801	43 LJ 301	Pet from Koops
8 Jun 1801	56 CJ 516	HL Req Rep	22 Jun 1801	43 LJ 322	CWH adj
10 Jun 1801	56 CJ 530	Rep sent HL	23 Jun 1801	43 LJ 338	Rep w/o Amds
24 Jun 1801	56 CJ 628	HL pass w/o Amds	24 Jun 1801	43 LJ 343	3R
27 Jun 1801	56 CJ 640	Royal Assent	27 Jun 1801	43 LJ 367	Royal Assent

Representation

No information

Parliamentary debates

House of Commons

Pet: *Parliamentary Register*, 16 Mar 1801, Vol 14, p 394–395; Senator (2d), 16 Mar 1801, Vol 1, p 481 (Coops); Woodfall, 16 Mar 1801, Vol 1, p 390

Pet: Senator (2d), 20 Mar 1801, Vol 1, p 632

Bill Ord: Parliamentary Register, 12 May 1801, Vol 14, p 260; Senator (2d), 12 May 1801, Vol 2, p 1070; Woodfall, 12 May 1801, Vol 2, p 133

1R: Senator (2d), 13 May 1801, Vol 2, p 1079; Woodfall, 13 May 1801, Vol 2, p 341

3R: Senator (2d), 2 Jun 1801, Vol 2, p 1234; Woodfall, 2 Jun 1801, Vol 2, p 469

House of Lords

Rep: Senator (2d), 23 Jun 1801, Vol 2, p 1521; Woodfall, 23 Jun 1801, Vol 2, p 726

Parliamentary papers and cases

Report on Mr Koops' Petition, respecting his invention for making paper from various refuse materials (1801) (HC Papers 55), Vol 3, p 127 [witnesses: John Hunter, Samuel Lister, William Tate and Elias Carpenter]

Gazette notices

Not required by SO

(continued)

Newspaper coverage of debates
House of Commons
Pet: The Times, 17 Mar 1801; Morning Chronicle, 17 Mar 1801; E. Johnson's British Gazette and Sunday Monitor, 22 Mar 1801
Pet Rep: *Hampshire Chronicle, 18 May 1801*; Kentish Weekly Post or Canterbury Journal, 15 May 1801
Bill Ord: *Caledonian Mercury, 18 May 1801*; *Derby Mercury, 21 May 1801*; Bury and Norwich Post, 20 May 1801
1R: The Times, 14 Mar 1801; Salisbury and Winchester Journal, 18 May 1801
2R: Kentish Weekly Post or Canterbury Journal, 5 Jun 1801; Carlisle Journal, 6 Jun 1801; Derby Mercury, 11 Jun 1801
Rep: Derby Mercury, 11 Jun 1801; Bury and Norwich Post, 1 Jul 1801
House of Lords
2R: *Morning Chronicle, 16–17 Jun 1801*; The Times, 17 Jun 1801; Bell's Weekly Messenger, 21 Jun 1801; Hampshire Telegraph, 22 Jun 1801
CWH: *Morning Chronicle, 24 Jun 1801*; Hampshire Telegraph, 29 Jun 1801
Royal Assent: Bury and Norwich Post, 1 Jul 1801; Leeds Intelligencer, 6 Jul 1801; Cumberland Pacquet, and Ware's Whitehaven Advertiser, 7 Jul 1801
Archives
Motion for Message to HC: 5 Jun 1801: HL/PO/JO/10/8/23
Reps of HC C'tee: 10 Jun 1801: HL/PO/JO/19/8/23
Bill and Evidence [No record of evidence in Lords]: 16 Jun 1801: HL/PO/JO/10/8/24
Pet in support: 19 Jun 1801: HL/PO/10/8/24
Lords Evidence in C'tee: 23 Jun 1801: HL/PO/10/8/24
Ing: HL/PO/PB/1/1801/41G3n319
Notes
There was a failed Bill to achieve the same purpose (and a secret specification) a year earlier: PRVB54

Cartwright's Woolcombing Machinery Act 1801

PRVA32	1801
	Cartwright's Woolcombing Machinery Act 1801 (41 Geo 3. c. cxxxiii)

An Act for vesting for a limited Time in the Reverend Edmund Cartwright Clerk, Master of Arts, his Executors, Administrators, and Assigns, the sole Property in certain Machinery by him invented for Woolcombing
Table of contents
s 1 The sole Right to all his Machines and Inventions, so far as they relate to the Benefits of Woolcombing vest in Mr Cartwright, &c. for a certain Time [14 years from passing Act]
s 2 Mr Cartwright to inrol other Specifications of Inventions with respect to Woolcombing
s 3 To enable Person to sell Woolcombing Machinery not of the invention of Edmund Cartwright
s 4 The Right to Invention not to be transferred to more than a certain number of Persons at one Time, nor any Persons as a Body Corporate
s 5 Claims of Mr Cartwright's Creditors, &c to remain in Force
s 6 Not to affect Mr Toplis's Letters Patent
s 7 Agreements not to be voided
s 8 Objections against Patents, competent against this Act except the Term
s 9 Publick Act

Relevant patents	
27 Apr 1790 (No 1747)	Machinery for dressing, heckling, combing, and preparing hemp, flax, wool, hair, silk and cotton [Edmund Cartwright] {Scottish patent: 23 Dec 1790}
11 Dec 1791 (No 1787)	Machinery for dressing, heckling, combing, and preparing hemp, flax, wool, hair, silk and cotton [Edmund Cartwright]
15 May 1792 (No 1876) Act (No 2524*)	Machinery for manufacturing wool, hemp, flax, silk, hair, and cotton, into yarn, twist, cords, ropes and cables, and until perfected in the loom, and cut for raising a pile [Edmund Cartwright]

Journal					
House of Commons			**House of Lords**		
Pres and Rep: Walter Spencer Stanhope			Rep: Lord Walsingham (Ld Ch)		
17 Mar 1801	56 CJ 178	**Pet/Ref Com**	5 Jun 1801	43 LJ 236	Brought HC /1R
13 Apr 1801	56 CJ 271	**Rep Pet**	9 Jun 1801	43 LJ 247	2R day app
8 May 1801	56 CJ 378	Bill Ord	12 Jun 1801	43 LJ 264	2R/C'tted CWH
11 May 1801	56 CJ 389	1R	17 Jun 1801	43 LJ 290	CWH adj
15 May 1801	56 CJ 415	2R/C'tted	24 Jun 1801	43 LJ 345	CWH adj
15 May 1801	56 CJ 417	**Pet Ag**	25 Jun 1801	43 LJ 354	CWH
22 May 1801	56 CJ 456	**Pet Ag**	26 Jun 1801	43 LJ 358	Rep with Amds
27 May 1801	56 CJ 463	**Rep/Re-C'tted**	27 Jun 1801	43 LJ 369	3R
2 Jun 1801	56 CJ 486	**Rep with Amds/Ing**	29 Jun 1801	43 LJ 374	HC Ag Amd
5 Jun 1801	56 CJ 506	3R	2 Jul 1801	43 LJ 387	Royal Assent
28 Jun 1801	56 CJ 643	HL pass with Amds			
29 Jun 1801	56 CJ 644	**HL Amds Ag**			
2 Jul 1801	56 CJ 665	Royal Assent			

Petitions

15 May 1801	56 CJ 417	William Toplis [owner of competing patent who had consent order to allow both parties to work]
22 May 1801	56 CJ 456	John Adams (manufacturer) [deprived of use of invention]

Representation

Herbert Brace

Parliamentary debates

House of Commons

3R: Woodfall, 5 Jun 1801, Vol 2, p 494

House of Lords

CWH: Senator (2d), 25 Jun 1801, Vol 2, p 1535-1536

Parliamentary papers and cases

Catalogue of Papers printed by Order of the House of Commons, from the year 1731 to 1800. In the Custody of the Clerk of the Journals (1807) (Reprint: HMSO 1954): Weaver's Petition, 1799/1800, Vol 28, No 170

Gazette notices

London Gazette: 20 Sept 1800 (Iss: 15,295, p 1091); 23 Sept 1800 (Iss: 15,296, p 1103); 27 Sept 1800 (Iss: 15,297, p 1119)

Newspaper coverage of debates

House of Commons

Bill Ord: Caledonian Mercury, 11 May 1801

1R: Caledonian Mercury, 14 May 181

Pet Ag: Caledonian Mercury, 18 May 1801

House of Lords

CWH adj: Hampshire Telegraph, 22 Jun 1801; Bury and Norwich Post 24 Jun 1801

Evidence presented/C'tee: *Exeter Flying Post, 2 Jul 1801; Hampshire (Portsmouth) Telegraph, 29 Jun 1801; Salisbury and Winchester Journal, 29 Jun 1801*; London Courier and Evening Gazette, 26 Jun 1801; Hampshire Chronicle, 29 Jun 1801

Archives

Evidence on Bill [witnesses include John Vasman]: HL/PO/JO/10/8/24

Letter from Charles Dashwood to Sir Edmund Hartopp requesting his support to the petition of Edmund Cartwright for the extension of his combing machine (18 Mar 1800): Leicestershire, Leicester and Rutland Record Office: 10D72/621

Notes concerning the application of Mr Edmund Cartwright to extend his patent rights for a longer term and a petition by Mr John Adams opposing the same [intended for use in a Parliamentary speech]: Leicestershire, Leicester and Rutland, Record Office Archives: 10D72/645

Private Acts of Parliament relating to the inventions, and other papers, 1790–1801: Gloucestershire Archives: D1245/CF2

Ing: HL/PO/PB/1/1801/41G3n362

Notes

Related cases

Cartwright v Amatt (1799) (CP) 1 HPC 411; 1 CPC 173; 2 B & P 43 (126 ER 1145); *Cartwright v Amatt* (1800) (CP) 11 East 107 (103 ER 945); *Cartwright v Eamer* (1800) (LC) 1 HPC 415; 14 Ves J 131 (33 ER 470); *Cartwright v Toplis* (1800) 1 HPC 417

Fourdriniers' Paper–Making Machine Act 1807

PRVA33	1807
	Fourdriniers' Paper-Making Machine Act 1807 (47 Geo 3 Sess 2. c. cxxxi)

An Act for prolonging the Term of certain Letters Patent assigned to Henry Fourdrinier and Sealy Fourdrinier, for the Invention of making paper by machinery

Table of contents

s 1 The sole Right to the Improved Machines vested in Messrs Fourdrinier and Mr Gamble for a certain time [15 years, being an extension of 7 years on the original term]

s 2 Certain Rates may be taken from Persons to whom Licences shall be granted for using the Machines

s 3 Not more than the said Rates to be paid

s 4 The Act not to hinder the using any Invention different from those described in Mr Gamble's Specifications

s 5 Specification of Machine to be inrolled

s 6 Objections to the Validity of the Patent not to be affected by this Act

s 7 Inventions not to become Property of more than Five Persons, &c; [Bubble Act] 4 Geo I, c. 13

s 8 Publick Act

Relevant patents

20 Apr 1801 (No 2487)	Machine for making paper in single sheets without seam or joinings [John Gamble] {Scottish patent: 20 January 1802; Irish patent: 22 Jul 1801}
7 Jun 1803 (No 2708)	Machine for making paper in single sheets without seam or joinings [John Gamble] {Scottish patent: 18 Oct 1803; Irish patent: 13 Feb 1804}
14 Aug 1807 (No 3068*)	Machine for making paper in single sheets without seam or joinings, &c. (inrolled under s 5) [Henry Fourdrinier and Sealy Fourdrinier and John Gamble]

Journal

House of Commons			House of Lords		
Pet Rep: Richard Bennett Pet (Renewed) Rep: Stephen Lushington Pet (Re-Pres): William Lygon Pres and Rep: Stephen Lushington			Rep: Lord Redesdale		
26 Feb 1807	62 CJ 169	**Pet/Ref Com**	21 Jul 1807	46 LJ 277	Brought from HC/1R
11 Mar 1807	62 CJ 228	**Rep SO ncw**	23 Jul 1807	46 LJ 290	2R day app
13 Mar 1807	62 CJ 237	Rep read/Re-C'tted	24 Jul 1807	46 LJ 295	2R adj
17 Mar 1807	62 CJ 248	**Rep SO ncw**	29 Jul 1807	46 LJ 319	2R/C'tted
18 Mar 1807	62 CJ 250	Leave to publish notices	10 Aug 1807	46 LJ 376	Prt Evidence
17 Apr 1807	62 CJ 335	**Renewed Pet/Ref Com**	10 Aug 1807	46 LJ 377	**Rep with Amds**
23 Apr 1807	62 CJ 356	**Pet Rep/Leave**	11 Aug 1807	46 LJ 379	3R day app
29 Jun 1807	62 CJ 587	**Pet Re-Pres**	12 Aug 1807	46 LJ 384	**3R with Amd**
2 Jul 1807	62 CJ 615	**Pet Ret/Leave**	13 Aug 1807	46 LJ 395	HC Ag Amds
3 Jul 1807	62 CJ 621	1R	14 Aug 1807	46 LJ 397	Royal Assent
7 Jul 1807	62 CJ 642	2R/C'tted			
18 Jul 1807	62 CJ 737	Rep with Amds/Re-C'tted			
20 Jul 1807	62 CJ 744	Rep with Amds/Ing			
21 Jul 1807	62 CJ 752	3R			
13 Aug 1807	62 CJ 838	HL pass with Amds			
13 Aug 1807	62 CJ 842	**HL Amds Ag**			
14 Aug 1807	62 CJ 848	Royal Assent			

Representation

Solicitor: A & J Weston

Parliamentary debates

None

Parliamentary papers and cases

Minutes of Evidence taken before Lords Committee to whom Bill for prolonging term of Letters Patent assigned to Messers Fourdrinier was referred (1807 HL Papers 36), Vol 14, p 331

Report from the Select Committee on Fourdrinier's Patent (1837 HC Papers 351), Vol 20, p 35 [this includes a discussion of the proceedings on the 1807 Act]

Gazette notices

London Gazette, 24 Mar 1807 (Iss: 16,013, p 380); 28 Mar 1807 (Iss: 16,014, p 396); 31 Mar 1807 (Iss: 16,015, p 412)

Dublin Gazette, 28–31 Mar 1807 (Iss: 8040, p 303); 31 Mar–2 Apr 1807 (Iss: 8041, p 315); 2–4 Apr 1807 (Iss: 8042, p 324)

Newspaper coverage of debates
House of Commons
Leave: Public Ledger and Daily Advertiser, 24 Apr 1807; Lancaster Gazette and General Advertiser, 2 May 1807
House of Lords
2R: *Morning Chronicle, 30 Jul 1807*
Royal Assent: Morning Post, 15 Aug 1807

Archives
C'tee Minutes: 3 Aug 1807 (p 355–356); 5 Aug 1807 (p 371–372); 8 Aug 1807 (p 401); 10 Aug 1807 (p 413–416) [witnesses: John Abbott; Bryan Donkin; John Hall; John Hayes Joseph Liddell; Charles Martindale; John Phipps; Lewis Smith; George Stafford; James Swann]: HL/PO/CO/1/53 [all printed]
Ing: HL/PO/PB/1/1807/47G3s2n270

Notes
Related cases
Bloxam v Elsee (1825) (NP) 1 HPC 879; 1 WPC 132n; 1 CPC 434; 1 C & P 558 (171 ER 1316); Ry & Moo 187 (171 ER 989); *Bloxam v Elsee* (1827) (KB) 1 CPC 440; 6 B & C 169 (108 ER 415); 2 C & P Ad vi (172 ER 293)
Related Bills
There were two further attempts to revive and extend the patent, and eventually a prize was awarded: PRVB74, PRVB85 and PRZA42

Johns Patent Tessera Act 1810

PRVA34	1810
	Johns Patent Tessera Act 1810 (50 Geo 3. c. lxxv)

An Act to amend an Act of the Fourteenth Year of His present Majesty, for the better Regulation of Buildings and Party Walls, and for the more effectually preventing Mischiefs by Fire within the Cities of London and Westminster, by permitting John's Patent Tessera to be used in the Covering of Houses and Buildings within the Places therein mentioned

Table of contents
s 1 Permitting Tessera to be used in the Covering of Buildings within the Bills of Mortality [ie the area covered by the Fire Prevention (Metropolis) Act 1774]
s 2 Tessera to be used, not to contain more than a certain Proportion of Bituminous Substance
s 3 Permitting Persons using Composition as Tessera, for the Tessera to be used by the Act
s 4 Public Act

Relevant patent	
22 Dec 1806 (No 2996) Act (No 2996*)	Compositions; mode of making the same, for covering and facing houses and for other purposes [Ambrose Bowden Johns]

Journal					
House of Commons			**House of Lords**		
Pres and Rep: William Mellish			Rep: Lord Walsingham (Ld Ch)		
9 Feb 1810	65 CJ 60	**Pet/Ref Com**	12 Apr 1810	47 LJ 587	Brought HC/1R
16 Feb 1810	65 CJ 99	Pet Rep	16 Apr 1810	47 LJ 597	2R/C'tted
15 Mar 1810	65 CJ 180	1R	3 May 1810	47 LJ 618	Rep w/o Amds
20 Mar 1810	65 CJ 199	2R/C'tted	4 May 1810	47 LJ 620	3R
10 Apr 1810	65 CJ 273	Rep w/o Amds/Ing	18 May 1810	47 LJ 667	Royal Assent
11 Apr 1810	65 CJ 278	3R			
4 May 1810	65 CJ 329	HL pass w/o Amds			
18 May 1810	65 CJ 379	Royal Assent			

Representation
No information

Parliamentary debates
None

Parliamentary papers and cases
None

(continued)

(continued)

Gazette notices
Not required by SO

Newspaper coverage of debates
None

Archives
C'tee Minutes: 7 Apr 1810 (p 195–196); 2 May 1810 (p 225); 3 May 1810 (p 229): HL/PO/CO/1/56 Ing: HL/PO/PB/1/1810/50G3n131

Notes
There was a related unsuccessful Bill: PRVB62

Lee's Hemp and Flax Preparation Invention Act 1813

PRVA35	1813
Lee's Hemp and Flax Preparation Invention Act 1813 (53 Geo 3. c. clxxix)	
An Act for securing to James Lee, and the Public, the Benefit of his Invention of certain new Methods of preparing Hemp and Flax, by enabling him to lodge the Specification under certain Restrictions	

Table of contents
s 1 Specification to be deposited under Seal for a certain Period, instead of being inrolled
s 2 Regulations as to the Custody and Use of the Specification, previous to Inrolment
s 3 Specification to be delivered in Scotland and Ireland
s 4 Specifications to be produced in Scotland and Ireland when necessary
s 5 Specification to be inrolled after the Expiration of Seven Years
s 6 The Delivery of the Specification, according to this Act, to be deemed a Compliance with the Proviso in the Letters Patent requiring Inrolment
s 7 Docquet of the Patent and Title of the Act to be entered on Specification Rolls
s 8 Letters Patent to become void, in Default of inroling the Specification
s 9 Public Act

Relevant patent	
9 Jun 1812 (No 3574)	Preparing hemp and flax for various uses, by which also other vegetable substances may be made applicable to many purposes for which hemp and flax are now used [James Lee] {Scottish patent: 8 Aug 1812; Irish patent: 14 Aug 1812}

Journal					
House of Commons			**House of Lords**		
Pres and Pet Rep: Thomas Courtenay Bill Rep: William Courtenay			Rep: Lord Walsingham (Ld Ch)		
17 Dec 1812	68 CJ 84	**Pet/Ref Com**	28 Apr 1813	49 LJ 310	Brought HC/1R
11 Feb 1813	68 CJ 147	All voices	25 May 1813	49 LJ 437	2R/C'tted
1 Mar 1813	68 CJ 251	Pet Rep/Prt	26 May 1813	49 LJ 444	All voices
5 Mar 1813	68 CJ 276	Bill Ord	2 Jun 1813	49 LJ 471	Rep with Amds
8 Mar 1813	68 CJ 283	1R	18 Jun 1813	49 LJ 509	3R
22 Mar 1813	68 CJ 336	2R/C'tted All voices	1 Jul 1813	49 LJ 554	HC Ag Amds
9 Apr 1813	68 CJ 396	Rep with Amds/Ing	2 Jul 1813	49 LJ 560	Royal Assent
14 Apr 1813	68 CJ 414	3R with Amds			
21 Jun 1813	68 CJ 586	HL pass with Amds			
28 Jun 1813	68 CJ 614	**HL Amds Ag**			
2 July 1813	68 CJ 630	Royal Assent			

Representation
No information

Parliamentary debates
None

Parliamentary papers and cases
Report on Mr. Lee's patent petition (1812–13 HC Papers 67), Vol 3, p 393

Gazette notices
Not required by SO

Newspaper coverage of debates
House of Commons
2R: *The Times, 22 Mar 1813*; *Morning Chronicle, 23 Mar 1813*; *Morning Post, 23 Mar 1813*
House of Lords
1R: The Times, 29 Apr 1813
2R: **The Times, 26 May 1813**; *Morning Post, 26 May 1813*

Archives
C'tee Minutes: 20 May 1813 (p 504–511); 1 Jun 1813 (p 538–540): HL/PO/CO/1/59
Bill with Amds: 28 Apr 1813: HL/PO/JO/10/8/304
Ing: HL/PO/PB/1/1813/53G3n346

Notes
Another attempt was made to keep a specification secret by Lee (along with incorporation), the Bill failed in the Lords: see PRVB65

Langton's Profits (Wood Seasoning Invention) Act 1829

PRVA36	1829

Langton's Profits (Wood Seasoning Invention) Act 1829 (10 Geo 4. c. cxxxv)

An Act for vesting and securing to John Stephen Langton of the Parish of Langton juxta Putney in the County of Lincoln, Esquire, his Executors, administrators, and Assigns, certain Profits and Emoluments for a limited Time

Table of contents
s 1 Profits [in invention] vested in Mr Langton for 21 Years; Liberty to all Person to use the Invention; Payment for the same
s 2 Vessels containing Timber to be closed and secured; Attendances on opening the same; Attendances how dispensed with; Payment for Attendances; Penalty for Mr Langton's Non-attendance
s 3 Timber to be sorted; Account of Value of Timber to be rendered; Proceeding in case of disputed Value
s 4 Mr Langton to have Access to Apparatus; Provision in case Apparatus set up without Notice
s 5 This Act not to extend to other Methods of seasoning Timber; not to His Majesty's Service. Provision for a certain Quantity of Timber to be used
s 6 Remedy in case of Non-payment of Percentage or Penalty; Power to stop Apparatus
s 7 Power of Appeal to remove Proceedings
s 8 Deeds to be registered
s 9 Public Act

Relevant patent	
11 Aug 1825 (No 5236)	Seasoning timber and other wood [Stephen Langton] {Irish patent: 14 June 1826}

Journal					
House of Commons			**House of Lords**		
Pres and Rep: Thomas Greene			Rep: Earl of Shaftesbury (Ld Ch)		
14 Apr 1829	84 CJ 229	Pet	22 May 1829	61 LJ 494	Brought HC/1R/Ref SC
15 Apr 1829	84 CJ 231	Leave to Pres Pet	25 May 1829	61 LJ 500	SC All Voice
28 Apr 1829	84 CJ 241	Pet Rep/Ref SOC	28 May 1829	61 LJ 522	SC Rep
5 May 1829	84 CJ 263	SO Disp	2 Jun 1829	61 LJ 536	2R/C'tted
6 May 1829	84 CJ 267	Bill Ord	4 Jun 1829	61 LJ 545	Rep w/o Amds
7 May 1829	84 CJ 269	1R	5 Jun 1829	61 LJ 555	**3R with Amds**
11 May 1829	84 CJ 280	2R/C'tted	6 Jun 1829	61 LJ 559	HC pass with Amds
21 May 1829	84 CJ 324	Rep with Amds/Ing	19 Jun 1829	61 LJ 588	Royal Assent
22 May 1829	84 CJ 329	3R			
5 Jun 1829	84 CJ 383	HL pass with Amds			
6 Jun 1829	84 CJ 389	HL Amds Ag			
19 Jun 1829	84 CJ 400	Royal Assent			

Parliamentary debates	
Pet: Mirror, 15 Apr 1829, Vol 2, 1323	Brought HC: Mirror, 22 May 1829, Vol 3, p 1804
Rep Pet: Mirror, 28 Apr 1829, Vol 2, p 1344	All voices: Mirror, 25 May 1829, Vol 3, p 1833
Leave: Mirror, 6 May 1829, Vol 2, p 1460	Rep SC: Mirror, 28 May 1829, Vol 3, p 1895

(continued)

(continued)

1R: Mirror, 7 May 1829, Vol 2, p 1467	2R: Mirror, 2 Jun 1829, Vol 3, p 1955
2R: Mirror, 11 May 1829, Vol 3, p 1541	Rep: Mirror, 4 Jun 1829, Vol 3, p 2014
Rep: Mirror, 21 May 1829, Vol 3, p 1769	3R: Mirror, 5 Jun 1829, Vol 3, p 2046
3R: Mirror, 22 May 1829, Vol 3, p 1810	Royal Assent: Mirror, 19 Jun 1829, Vol 3, p 2117
HL Amds Ag: Mirror, 5 Jun 1829, Vol 3, p 2080	

Representation
No information

Parliamentary papers and cases
Minutes of Evidence taken before Committee to whom Langton's Bill was referred (1829 HL Papers 82), Vol 162, p 223 [witnesses: Charles Street; Mark Isambard Brunel (Civil Engineer); John Donkin (Engineer); Rev George Street; James Courthope Peache (Timber Merchant); John Thurston (Billiard Table marker)]

Gazette notices
None

Newspaper coverage of debates
None

Archives
SC Rep: 28 May 1829: HL/PO/JO/10/8/852 (No 447)
Order to appoint Chair: 25 May 1829: HL/PO/JO/10/8/851 (No 428)
C'tee Minutes: 3 Jun 1829 (p 443–444): HL/PO/CO/1/84
Amds to Bill: 5 Jun 1829: HL/PO/JO/10/8/853 (No 489)
Ing: HL/PO/PB/1/1831/1&2W4n12

Notes
The Act was amended by Langton's Profits Act 1831: PRVA38

Hollingrake Letters Patent Act 1830

PRVA37	1830
Hollingrake Letters Patent Act 1830 (11 Geo 4 & 1 Will 4. c. lxxx)	

An Act for prolonging the Term of certain Letters Patent granted to James Hollingrake for an improved Method of manufacturing Copper or other Metal Rollers, and of casting and forming Metallic Substances into various Forms, with improved Closeness and Soundness of Texture

Table of contents
s 1 Vesting Advantages of Patent in Mr Hollingrake for a limited period [9 years from Acts passing]
s 2 For Protecting of Mr Hollingrake against Infringement of Patent
s 3 Objections to the Validity of the Patents not to be affected by this Act
s 4 Inventions not to become the Property of more than Five Persons
s 5 Proviso as to supply His Majesty's Service
s 6 Not to prejudice Estate of S Davenport and R Fayle
s 7 Public Act

Relevant patent	
7 Aug 1818 (No 4287)	Manufacturing copper or other metal rollers for calico-printing [James Hollingrake]
15 May 1819 (No 4371)	Making and working a manufacture for applying the method of casting metallic substances into various forms, with improved closeness and soundness in texture [James Hollingrake]

Journal					
House of Commons			**House of Lords**		
Pres and Rep: Lord Stanley			Rep: Earl of Shaftesbury (Ld Ch)		
19 Feb 1830	85 CJ 77	**Pet**	11 May 1830	62 LJ 365	Brought HC
4 Mar 1830	85 CJ 130	Pet Rep	11 May 1830	62 LJ 366	1R/Ref SC
8 Mar 1830	85 CJ 145	1R	12 May 1830	62 LJ 380	SC All voice
8 Apr 1830	85 CJ 281	Pet Ag	12 May 1830	62 LJ 383	SC Rep
28 Apr 1830	85 CJ 342	2R/C'tted	14 May 1830	62 LJ 402	2R/C'tted

10 May 1830	85 CJ 393	Rep with Amds/Ing	17 May 1830	62 LJ 428	SC Rep ref'd to C'tee
11 May 1830	85 CJ 401	3R	17 May 1830	62 LJ 456	**Rep with Amds**
25 May 1830	85 CJ 473	HL pass with Amds	21 May 1830	62 LJ 479	Ord SO 173 cons
26 May 1830	85 CJ 478	**HL Amds Ag**	24 May 1830	60 LJ 502	SO 173 Disp/3R
29 May 1830	85 CJ 500	Royal Assent	26 May 1830	60 LJ 547	HC Ag Amds
			29 May 1830	60 LJ 576	Royal Assent

Petition

8 Apr 1830	85 CJ 281	Robert Fayle and Matthew Fayle

Representation

Solicitor: William Norris

Parliamentary debates

Pet: Mirror, 19 Feb 1830, Vol 1, p 295	Brought HC: Mirror, 11 May 1830, Vol 2, p 1620
Pet Rep: Mirror, 4 Mar 1830, Vol 1, p 536	Rep SC: Mirror, 12 May 1830, Vol 2, p 1663
1R: Mirror, 8 Mar 1830, Vol 1, p 593	2R: Mirror, 14 May 1830, Vol 2, p 1724
Pet Ag: Mirror, 8 Apr 1830, Vol 2, p 1299	SC Rep ref: Mirror, 17 May 1830, Vol 2, p 1759
2R: Mirror, 28 Apr 1830, Vol 2, p 1377	Ord SO 173 Cons: Mirror, 21 May 1830, Vol 2, p 1866
Rep: Mirror, 10 May 1830, Vol 2, p 1596	SO 173 Disp/3R: Mirror, 24 May 1830, Vol 2, p 1907
3R: Mirror, 11 May 1830, Vol 2, p 1626	Royal Assent: Mirror, 29 May 1830, Vol 3, p 2066
HL Amds Ag: Mirror, 26 May 1830, Vol 2, p 1989	

Representation

Solicitor and Agent: William Norris

Parliamentary papers and cases

None

Gazette notices

London Gazette, 25 Sep 1829 (Iss: 18,614, p. 1767); 2 Oct 1829 (Iss: 18,616, p. 1808); 6 Oct 1829 (Iss: 18,617, p. 1830)

Newspaper coverage of debates

Royal Assent: The Times, 31 May 1830; Morning Chronicle, 31 May 1830; London Courier and Evening Gazette, 31 May 1830; London Evening Standard, 31 May 1830

Archives

Ref SC: 11 May 1830: HL/PO/JO/10/8/890 (No 492)

Minutes of Evidence: 12 May 1830 [witnesses: George Birbeck; Alexander Galloway; James Hollingrake; Rupert Ingleby; William Norris; Thomas Sherwood; Edmund Turell]: HL/PO/JO/10/8/913

C'tee Minutes: 17 May 1830 (p 293–295): HL/PO/CO/1/86

Rep and Amds: 17 May 1830: HL/PO/JO/10/8/892 (No 535)

Ing: HL/PO/PB/1/1830/11G4&1W4n114

Langton's Profits Act 1831

PRVA38	1831
Langton's Profits Act 1831 (1 & 2 Will 4. c. vi)	
An Act to amend an Act for vesting and securing to John Stephen Langton Esquire certain Profits and Emoluments for a limited Time	

Table of contents

s 1 Repeal of Provision restricting the Time for launching 500 Tons of Shipping
s 2 If amount be not launched within 3 Year of passing this Act, Powers to cease
s 3 What Timber shall be deemed to have been seasoned according to Mr Langton's Method
s 4 Proof of Requisites of Act having been complied with
s 5 Where Oaths are directed to be administered, Justices to have the Power of administering such Oaths
s 6 Public Act

Relevant patent

None, but see PRVA36

(continued)

(continued)

Journal					
House of Commons			**House of Lords**		
Pres and Rep: Sir William Ingilby			Rep: Earl of Shaftesbury (Ld Ch)		
27 Jun 1831	86 CJ 570	**Pet**	19 Jul 1831	63 LJ 833	Brought HC/1R
28 Jun 1831	86 CJ 579	Pet Rep	19 Jul 1831	63 LJ 833	Ref SC under SO 198
1 Jul 1831	86 CJ 598	1R	21 Jul 1831	63 LJ 839	SC Rep
5 Jul 1831	86 CJ 614	2R/C'tted	22 Jul 1831	63 LJ 841	2R/C'tted
15 Jul 1831	86 CJ 658	Rep with Amds/Ing	25 Jul 1831	63 LJ 847	Rep w/o Amds
19 Jul 1831	86 CJ 672	3R	26 Jul 1831	63 LJ 867	3R
27 Jul 1831	86 CJ 703	HL pass w/o Amds	30 Jul 1831	63 LJ 880	Royal Assent
30 Jul 1831	86 CJ 712	Royal Assent			

Parliamentary debates	
Pet: Mirror, 27 Jun 1831, Vol 1, p 134	Brought HC: Mirror, 19 Jul 1831, Vol 1, p 660
Rep: Mirror, 28 Jun 1831, Vol 1, p 170	Rep SC: Mirror, 21 Jul 1831, Vol 1, p 723
1R: Mirror, 1 Jul 1831, Vol 1, p 253	2R: Mirror, 22 Jull 1831, Vol 1, p 758
2R: Mirror, 5 Jul 1831, Vol 1, p 325	Rep: Mirror, 25 Jul 1831, Vol 1, p 791
Rep: Mirror, 15 Jul 1831, Vol 1, p 594	3R: Mirror, 26 Jul 1831, Vol 1, p 833
3R: Mirror, 19 Jul 1831, Vol 1, p 667	Royal Assent: Mirror, 30 Jul 1831, Vol 1, p 955

Representation
No information

Parliamentary papers and cases
None

Gazette notices
Not required by SO

Newspaper coverage of debates
None

Archives
SC Rep: 21 Jul 1831: HL/PO/JO/10/8/945 (No 790)
C'tee Minutes: 25 Jul 1831 (p 132–133): HL/PO/CO/1/88
Ing: HL/PO/PB/1/1831/1&2W4n12

Bernhardt's Warming and Ventilation of Buildings Company Act 1836

PRVA39	1836
Bernhardt's Warming and Ventilation of Buildings Company Act 1836 (6 & 7 Will 4. c. xxvi)	

An Act for enabling Franz Anton Bernhardt to assign to a Company, and for enabling them to purchase and carry into effect the Purposes of a Patent granted to him for warming and ventilating Buildings, and for other Purposes [Bernhardt's Patent]

Table of contents (patent provisions only)
s 2 Purposes for which the Company is established [for the Purpose of purchasing Letters Patent]
s 3 Empowering the Company to purchase and Mr Bernhardt to sell, his Patent
s 4 Property in the Patent &c., to vest in the Company
s 5 After Transfer of Patent the Company may licence any Person to use the Discovery

Relevant patent	
4 Dec 1834 (No 6726)	A System for warming and ventilating Buildings and purifying the Smoke in Buildings [Franz Anton Bernhardt]

Journal	
House of Commons	**House of Lords**
Pres and Pet Rep: George Finch Bill Rep: Viscount Sandon	Rep: Earl of Shaftesbury (Ld Ch)

19 Feb 1836	91 CJ 58	Pet	12 Jul 1836	68 LJ 627	Brought HC/1R
25 Mar 1836	91 CJ 208	Pet Rep	14 Jul 1836	68 LJ 666	2R/C'tted
28 Mar 1836	91 CJ 217	Bill Ord/1R	15 Jul 1836	68 LJ 670	Rep w/o Amd
20 May 1836	91 CJ 397	2R/C'tted	18 Jul 1836	68 LJ 686	3R
6 Jun 1836	91 CJ 428	Rep with Amds/Ing	28 Jul 1836	68 LJ 756	Royal Assent
28 Jun 1836	91 CJ 575	Cons			
11 Jul 1836	91 CJ 642	3R			
18 Jul 1836	91 CJ 676	HL pass w/o Amds			
28 Jul 1836	91 CJ 710	Royal Assent			

Parliamentary debates	
Pet: Mirror, 19 Feb 1836, Vol 1, p 224	Brought HC: Mirror, 12 Jul 1836, Vol 3, p 2326
Rep: Mirror, 25 Mar 1836, Vol 1, p 786	Rep: Mirror, 15 Jul 1836, Vol 3, p 2390
Bill Ord: Mirror, 28 Mar 1836, Vol 1, p 808	3R: Mirror, 18 Jul 1836, Vol 3, p 2417
2R: Mirror, 20 May 1836, Vol 2, p 1570	Royal Assent: Mirror, 28 Jul 1836, Vol 3, p 2580
Rep: Mirror, 6 Jun 1836, Vol 2, p 1719	
Cons: Mirror, 28 Jun 1836, Vol 2, p 2117	
3R: Mirror, 11 Jul 1836, Vol 3, p 2307	

Representation
No information

Parliamentary papers and cases
None

Gazette notices
Not required by SO

Newspaper coverage of debates

House of Commons

2R: London Courier and Evening Gazette, 21 May 1836; North Devon Journal, 26 May 1836

House of Lords

2R: London Courier and Evening Gazette, 15 Jul 1836; Caledonian Mercury, 18 Jul 1836

3R: London Courier and Evening Gazette, 19 Jul 1836

Royal Assent: London Evening Standard, 28 Jul 1836; Globe, 29 Jul 1836; Saunders's News Letter, 1 Aug 1836

Archives

C'tee Minutes: 15 Jul 1836 (p 425): HL/PO/CO/1/95

Ing: HL/PO/PB/1/1836/6&7W4n221

Anti-Dry Rot Company (Letters Patent) Act 1836

PRVA40	1836
Anti-Dry Rot Company (Letters Patent) Act 1836 (6 & 7 Will 4. c. xxvi)	
An Act to enable John Howard Kyan to assign to a Company certain Letters Patent [Kyan's Patent]	
Table of contents (patent provisions only)	

s 2 Purposes of the Company [to obtain and work John Howard Kyan's patents]
s 3 John Howard Kyan may assign the Letters Patent to or in Trust from the Company
s 4 Company after Assignment, to have all the Rights and respective Patents
s 5 And enabled to grant Licences for the Use of the said Discoveries

Relevant patents	
31 Mar 1832 (No 6253)	A New Mode of Preserving Certain Vegetable Substances from Decay [John Howard Kyan]
22 Sep 1832 (No 6309)	An Improved Mode of preserving Paper, Canvass, Cloth, and Cordage for Ships, and other Uses, and the raw Materials of Hemp, Flax, or Cotton from which the same may wholly or in part be made [John Howard Kyan] {Scottish patent: 1 Aug 1832; colonies patent: 11 Feb 1836}

(continued)

(continued)

Journal					
House of Commons			**House of Lords**		
Pres: Richard Alsager Rep: William Hughes Hughes			Rep: Earl of Shaftesbury (Ld Ch)		
17 Feb 1836	91 CJ 44	Pet	19 Apr 1836	68 LJ 125	Brought HC/1R
18 Feb 1836	91 CJ 52	Pet Rep	21 Apr 1836	68 LJ 131	2R/C'tted
14 Mar 1836	91 CJ 139	1R	25 Apr 1836	68 LJ 143	Rep w/o Amds
18 Mar 1836	91 CJ 151	2R/C'tted	26 Apr 1836	68 LJ 151	3R
18 Apr 1836	91 CJ 260	Rep with Amds/Ing	19 May 1836	68 LJ 227	Royal Assent
19 Apr 1836	91 CJ 265	3R			
3 May 1836	91 CJ 316	HL pass w/o Amds			
19 May 1836	91 CJ 392	Royal Assent			

Representation
Solicitor: Winburn and Collett
Solicitor: Porter & Nelson

Parliamentary debates	
Pet: Mirror, 17 Feb 1836, Vol 1, p 177	Brought HC/1R: Mirror, 19 Apr 1836, Vol 1, p 1033
Pet Rep: Mirror, 18 Feb 1836, Vol 1, p 196	2R: Mirror, 21 Apr 1836, Vol 1, p 1083
1R: Mirror, 14 Mar 1836, Vol 1, p 611	Rep: Mirror, 25 Apr 1836, Vol 2, p 1146
2R: Mirror, 18 Mar 1836, Vol 1, p 676	3R: Mirror, 26 Apr 1836, Vol 2, p 1165
Rep: Mirror, 18 Apr 1836, Vol 1, p 1018	Royal Assent: Mirror, 19 May 1836, Vol 2, p 1549
3R: Mirror, 19 Apr 1836, Vol 1, p 1039	

Parliamentary papers and cases
Report from Admiralty Committee on Mr Kyan's Patent for Prevention of Dry Rot (1835 HC Papers 367), Vol 48, p 910

Gazette notices
London Gazette: 17 Nov 1835 (Iss: 19,325, p 2128); 20 Nov 1835 (Iss: 19,326, p 2156); 24 Nov 1835 (Iss: 19,327, p 2193)
Edinburgh Gazette: 17 Nov 1835 (Iss: 4434, p 290); 20 Nov 1835 (Iss: 4435, p 291); 24 Nov 1835 (Iss: 4 436, p 293)
Dublin Gazette: 19 Nov 1835 (Iss: 12,622, p 650); 21 Nov 1835 (Iss: 12,623, p 654); 24 Nov 1835 (Iss: 12,624, p 658)

Newspaper coverage of debates
House of Commons
2R: London Courier and Evening Gazette, 19 Mar 1836
Rep: The Pilot, 20 Apr 1836; Dublin Morning Register. 21 Apr 1836
Royal Assent: Bell's Weekly Messenger, 22 May 1836; Bell's Life in London and Sporting Chronicle. 22 May 1836; Hertford Mercury and Reformer, 24 May 1836

Archives
C'tee Minutes: 22 Apr 1836 (p 65–66); 25 Apr 1836 (p 69): HL/PO/CO/1/95
Ing: HL/PO/PB/1/1836/6&7W4n70

Notes
Petition to use process in Naval Timber: 28 Jul 1834 (89 CJ 531)
Related debates
Petition to use process in Naval Timber: **HC Deb, 28 Jul 1834, Vol 25 (3rd), col 617–620; The Times, 29 Jul 1834**
Use of Kyan's Patent: **Mirror, 6 Aug 1838, Vol 8, p 117–118; The Times, 7 Aug 1838**

London Caoutchouc Company Act 1837

PRVA41	1837
London Caoutchouc Company Act 1837 (7 Will 4 & 1 Vict. c. cxxxii)	
An Act for forming and regulating the London Caoutchouc Company, and to enable the said Company to purchase certain Letters Patent	

Table of contents (patent provision only)
s 17 The Company may purchase Patents or Licenses without causing Forfeiture
s 18 After Assignment &c. Property in Patents or Licences vests in the Company
s 19 Power to grant Licences

Relevant patents

1 Dec 1831 (No 6193)	Manufacture of cables, ropes, whale-fishing and other lines, lath and rigger-bands, bags and purses [Robert William Sievier]
17 Jan 1833 (No 6366)	Manufacture of elastic goods or fabrics [Robert William Sievier]
23 May 1831 (No 6114)	Manufacture of smallwares [Joshua Westhead]
24 Sep 1835 (No 6896)	Manufactures of smallwares; arrangements of machinery for covering or forming a case around wire, cord, gut thread or other substances to render the same appliance to various [Joshua Westhead]
16 Feb 1836 (No 7004)	Cutting caoutchouc, india-rubber, leather, hides, and similar substances, to render them applicable to various purposes [Joshua Westhead]

Journal

House of Commons			House of Lords		
Pres: William Hughes Hughes Rep: Thomas Duncombe			Rep: Lord Redesdale		
13 Mar 1837	92 CJ 160	Pet for Bill/Ref SC	21 Jun 1837	69 LJ 491	Brought HC/1R
18 Mar 1837	92 CJ 187	Rep/Bill Ord/1R	30 Jun 1837	69 LJ 506	Pet Ag
22 Mar 1837	92 CJ 205	2R/C'tted	1 Jul 1837	69 LJ 514	2R/C'tted
18 Apr 1837	92 CJ 271	Pet Ag/Counsel Ord	3 Jul 1837	69 LJ 518	Pet Fav
5 Jun 1837	92 CJ 433	Rep with Amds/Ing	5 Jul 1837	69 LJ 544	Pet Fav
7 Jun 1837	92 CJ 442	Pr by parties	7 Jul 1837	69 LJ 558	Pet Ag
14 Jun 1837	92 CJ 470	3R adj	10 Jul 1837	69 LJ 572	**Rep with Amds**
22 Jun 1837	92 CJ 490	3R adj	11 Jul 1837	69 LJ 581	3R
23 Jun 1837	92 CJ 495	Pet Ag	13 Jul 1837	69 LJ 615	HC Ag Amds
23 Jun 1837	92 CJ 496 – V	3R adj	15 Jul 1837	69 LJ 645	Royal Assent
28 Jun 1837	92 CJ 519	Pet Ag × 2			
28 Jun 1837	92 CJ 519 – V	3R			
12 Jul 1837	92 CJ 620	HL pass with Amds			
13 Jul 1837	92 CJ 630	**HL Amds Ag**			
15 Jul 1837	92 CJ 662	Royal Assent			

Petitions

18 Apr 1837	92 CJ 271	Charles Keene and Others [Against]
23 Jun 1837	92 CJ 495	Thomas Forster [Against]
28 Jun 1837	92 CJ 519	Inhabitants of Lambeth [Against]
28 Jun 1837	92 CJ 519	Charles Keene and Others [Against]
30 Jul 1837	69 LJ 506	Manufacturers and Dealers in Caoutchouc [Against]
3 Jul 1837	69 LJ 518	Inhabitants of London [Against]
5 Jul 1837	69 LJ 544	1. Merchants and Importers of Caoutchouc; 2. And of Indian Rubber [Against]
7 Jul 1837	69 LJ 558	Manufacturers and Dealers of Products Incorporating Caoutchouc [Against]

Parliamentary debates

Pet: Mirror, 14 Feb 1837, Vol 1, p 166	1R: Mirror, 29 Jun 1837, Vol 3, p 2034
Pet Rep: Mirror, 13 Mar 1837, Vol 1, p 607	Pet Ag: Mirror, 30 Jun 1837, Vol 3, p 2056
1R: Mirror, 18 Mar 1837, Vol 1, p 756	2R: Mirror, 1 Jul 1837, Vol 3, p 2085
2R: Mirror, 22 Mar 1837, Vol 1, p 794	Pet Ag: Mirror, 3 Jul 1837, Vol 3, p 2091
Pet Ag: Mirror, 18 Apr 1837, Vol 2, p 1069	Pet fav: Mirror, 5 Jul 1837, Vol 3, p 2136
Rep: Mirror, 5 Jun 1937, Vol 3, p 1701	Pet Ag: Mirror, 7 Jul 1837, Vol 3, p 2162
3R adj: **Mirror, 7 Jun 1837, Vol 3, p 1733**	Rep: Mirror, 10 Jul 1837, Vol 3, p 2172
3R adj: **Mirror, 14 Jun 1837, Vol 3, p 1852–1854**	3R: Mirror, 11 Jul 1837, Vol 3, p 2185
3R adj: Mirror, 22 Jun 1837, Vol 3, p 1936	HC Ag Amds: Mirror, 13 Jul 1837, Vol 3, p 2207
3R adj: **Mirror, 23 Jun 1837, Vol 3, p 1949–1950**	Royal Assent: Mirror, 15 Jul 1837, Vol 3, p 2228

(continued)

(continued)

3R: **Mirror, 28 Jun 1837, Vol 3, p 2024–2025**	
HL pass: Mirror, 12 Jul 1837, Vol 3, p 2204	
HL Amds Ag: Mirror, 13 Jul 1837, Vol 3, p 2212	

Representation
No information
Parliamentary papers and cases
None
Gazette notices
Not required by SO
Newspaper coverage of debates

House of Commons

Pet: London Courier and Evening Gazette, 18 Feb 1837

Rep: London Courier and Evening Gazette, 14 Mar 1837; Oxford Journal, 18 Mar 1837

2R: Globe, 23 Mar 1837; Morning Chronicle, 23 Mar 1837; Evening Chronicle, 24 Mar 1837; London Courier and Evening Gazette, 23 Mar 1837; Oxford Chronicle and Reading Gazette, 25 Mar 1837

Pet Ag: Public Ledge and Daily Advertiser, 19 Apr 1837; London Evening Standard, 19 Apr 1837; Roscommon Journal, 29 Apr 1837

Rep: London Courier and Evening Gazette, 6 Jun 1837

3R: *The Times, 8 Jun 1837; Globe, 8 Jun 1837; Morning Advertiser, 8 Jun 1837; Morning Chronicle, 8 Jun 1837; Morning Post, 8 Jun 1837; Public Ledger and Daily Advertiser, 8 Jun 1837; London Courier and Evening Gazette, 8 Jun 1837; London Evening Standard, 8 Jun 1837; Evening Chronicle, 9 Jun 1837;* Carlisle Journal, 10 Jun 1837; Bell's New Weekly Messenger, 11 Jun 1837; Sherbourne Mercury, 12 Jun 1837

3R adj: **The Times, 15 Jun 1837; Globe, 15 Jun 1837; Morning Advertiser, 15 Jun 1837; Morning Post, 15 Jun 1837; Public Ledger and Daily Advertiser, 15 Jun 1837; London Courier and Evening Gazette, 15 Jun 1837; Oxford Chronicle and Reading Gazette, 17 Jun 1837;** *Bedfordshire Mercury, 17 Jun 1837; Gloucester Journal, 17 Jun 1837; Hereford Times, 17 Jun 1837; Reading Mercury, 17 Jun 1837; Saunders's News-Letter, 17 Jun 1837; Waterford Chronicle, 17 Jun 1837; Windsor and Eton Express, 17 Jun 1837; York Herald, 17 Jun 1837; Bell's New Weekly Messenger, 18 Jun 1837; Bell's Life in London and Sporting Chronicle, 18 Jun 1837; Sherborne Mercury, 19 Jun 1837; Bury and Norwich Post, 21 Jun 1837;* John O'Groats Journal, 23 Jun 1837; North Devon Journal, 22 Jun 1837; South Eastern Gazette, 20 Jun 1837

3R adj: **Morning Chronicle, 20 Jun 1837;** *Morning Post, 20 Jun 1837*

3R adj: *Globe, 23 Jun 1837; Morning Advertiser, 23 Jun 1837; Morning Chronicle, 23 Jun 1837; Morning Post, 23 Jun 1837; Evening Chronicle, 23 Jun 1837; Public Ledger and Daily Advertiser, 23 Jun 1837; London Evening Standard, 23 Jun 1837; Aris's Birmingham Gazette, 26 Jun 1837; Freeman's Journal, 26 Jun 1837; North Wales Chronicle, 27 Jun 1837; Derby Mercury, 28 Jun 1837; Hereford Journal, 28 Jun 1837; Perthshire Advertiser, 29 Jun 1837; Waterford Mail, 28 Jun 1837; Wolverhampton Chronicle and Staffordshire Advertiser, 28 Jun 1837; Worcester Journal, 29 Jun 1837; Lemington Spa, 1 Jul 1837;* Chester Chronicle, 23 Jun 1837; West Kent Guardian, 24 Jun 1837; Bell's New Weekly Messenger, 25 Jun 1837; Dublin Evening Packet and Correspondent, 27 Jun 1837

3R: **The Times, 24 Jun 1837; Globe, 24 Jun 1837; Morning Advertiser, 24 Jun 1837; Morning Chronicle, 24 Jun 1837; Morning Post, 24 Jun 1837; London Courier and Evening Gazette, 24 Jun 1837; London Evening Standard, 24 Jun 1837; Public Ledger and Daily Advertiser, 24 Jun 1837;** *Chester Chronicle, 30 Jun 1837; Coventry Standard, 30 Jun 1837; Stamford Mercury, 30 Jun 1837; Berkshire Chronicle, 1 Jul 1837; Bolton Chronicle 1 Jul 1837; Cardiff and Merthyr Guardian, 1 Jul 1837; Derbyshire Courier, 1 Jul 1837; Huntingdon, Bedford and Peterbourgh Gazette, 1 Jul 1837; Manchester Courier and Lancashire General Advertiser, 1 Jul 1837; Staffordshire Advertiser, 1 Jul 1837; Warwick and Warwickshire Advertiser, 1 Jul 1837; West Kent Guardian, 1 Jul 1837; Westmorland Gazette, 1 Jul 1837; York Herald, 1 Jul 1837; Yorkshire Gazette, 1 Jul 1837;* Dublin Evening Packet and Correspondent, 1 Jul 1837; Gloucester Journal, 1 Jul 1837; Liverpool Mail, 1 Jul 1837; Oxford Chronicle and Reading Gazette, 1 Jul 1837; Roscommon & Letrim Gazette, 1 Jul 1837; Saunders's Newsletter, 1 Jul 1837

Pet Ag: *Brighton Patriot, 27 Jun 1837*

Pet Ag pass: **The Times, 29 Jun 1837; Globe, 29 Jun 1837; Morning Advertiser, 29 Jun 1837; Morning Chronicle, 29 Jun 1837; Morning Post, 29 Jun 1837; Public Ledger and Daily Advertiser, 29 Jun 1837; London Courier and Evening Gazette, 29 Jun 1837; London Evening Standard, 29 Jun 1837;** Aris's Birmingham Gazette, 3 Jul 1837; Sherbourne Mercury, 3 Jul 1837; Kentish Gazette, 4 Jul 1837; Kentish Weekly Post, 4 Jul 1837; South Eastern Gazette, 4 Jul 1837; Blackburn Standard, 5 Jul 1837; Hereford Journal, 5 Jul 1837; Waterford Mail, 5 Jul 1837; Wolverhampton Chronicle and Staffordshire Advertiser, 5 Jul 1837; Bath Chronicle and Weekly Gazette, 6 Jul 1837; Dorset County Chronicle, 6 Jul 1837; Gore's Liverpool General Advertiser, 6 Jul 1837; Durham Chronicle, 7 Jul 1837; Roscommon & Leitrim Gazette, 8 Jul 1837

HL Amds Ag: The Times, 14 Jul 1837; Globe, 14 Jul 1837; Morning Advertiser, 14 Jul 1837; Morning Chronicle, 14 Jul 1837; Morning Post, 14 Jul 1837; Public Ledger and Daily Advertiser, 14 Jul 1837; London Courier and Evening Gazette, 14 Jul 1837; London Evening Standard, 14 Jul 1837; Bell's Weekly Messenger, 16 Jul 1837; Aris's Birmingham Gazette, 17 Jul 1837; Bell's Weekly Messenger, 17 Jul 1837; Sherborne Mercury, 17 Jul 1837; County Chronicle, Surrey Herald and Weekly Advertiser, 18 Jul 1837; Inverness Courier, 19 Jul 1837; Derby Mercury, 19 Jul 1837

House of Lords

Brought HC: London Courier and Evening Gazette, 30 Jun 1837

Pets: Globe, 6 Jul 1837; London Evening Standard, 6 Jul 1837; Evening Chronicle, 7 Jul 1837

Royal Assent: The Times, 17 Jul 1837; Globe, 17 Jul 1837; Morning Advertiser, 17 Jul 1837; Morning Chronicle, 17 Jul 1837; Morning Post, 17 Jul 1837; Public Ledger and Daily Advertiser, 17 Jul 1837; London Courier and Evening Gazette, 17 Jul 1837; London Evening Standard, 17 Jul 1837; Cheltenham Chronicle, 20 Jul 1837; Newry Telegraph, 20 Jul 1837; Worcester Journal, 20 Jul 1837; Royal Cornwall Gazette, 21 Jul 1837; Bolton Chronicle, 22 Jul 1837; Bristol Mercury, 22 Jul 1837; Cambridge Chronicle and Journal, 22 Jul 1837; Gloucestershire Chronicle, 22 Jul 1837; Huntingdon, Bedford and Peterbourgh Gazette, 22 Jul 1837; Leeds Intelligencer, 22 Jul 1837; Leeds Mercury, 22 Jul 1837; Norwich Mercury, 22 Jul 1837; Preston Chronicle, 22 Jul 1837; Warwick and Warwickshire Advertiser, 22 Jul 1837; Waterford Mail, 22 Jul 1837; Yorkshire Gazette, 22 Jul 1837; Sherborne Mercury, 24 Jul 1837; Clonmel Herald, 26 Jul 1837

Archives
C'tee Minutes: 6 Jul 1837 (p 410–413); 7 Jul 1837 (p 438–439); 10 Jul 1837 (p 465–466): HL/PO/CO/1/97
Opposed Bill Evidence (1837), Vol 7 [witnesses: William Hindmarch; Charles Keene; Alexander Macdougall; Nerbeke; Christopher Nickells; Talbot; Thomas White; John Astill; Austin; Miles Berry; William Carpmael]: HL/PO/PB/5/3/7
Ing: HL/PO/PB/1/1837/7W4&1Vn254

Notes
Related cases
Cornish v Keene (1835) (NP) 2 HPC 481; 1 WPC 497; 2 PC 314; *Cornish v Keene* (1836) (CP) 1 WPC 512; 2 CPC 371; *Cornish v Keene* (1837) (CP) 1 WPC 513; 2 CPC 371; 3 Bing NC 570 (132 ER 530); *Cornish v Keene* (1837) (MR) 1 Jur 235; *Cornish v Keene* (1837) (Ex Ch) 1 WPC 519n; *Cornish v Keene* (1839) (MR) 14 Lon J 336; *London Caoutchouc v Bedells* (1840) (MR) 3 HPC 653; 15 Lon J 123; *London Caoutchoc v Carpenter* (1842)(MR) 4 HPC 357, 18 RA 382; *Westhead v Keene* (1838) (MR) 3 HPC 315; 2 WPC 36n; 2 CPC 425, 434; 1 Beav 287 (48 ER 950); *Westhead v Keene* (1839) (MR) 2 CPC 434

Patent Dry Gas Meter Company Act 1837

PRVA42	1837		
Patent Dry Gas Meter Company Act 1837 (7 Will 4 & 1 Vict. c. xiii)			
An Act for forming and regulating a Company to be called "The Patent Dry Gas Meter Company," and to enable the said Company to purchase certain Letters Patent [Berry and Paterson's Patent]			
Table of contents (patent provisions only)			
s 2 Purposes of Company [purchasing and working several Letters Patent] s 3 Patents may be assigned to the Company without causing a Forfeiture s 4 After Assignment the Property in the Patents to vest in the Company s 5 Power to grant Licences			
Relevant patent			
19 Mar 1833 (No 6398)	Making or constructing gasometers [Miles Berry] {Scottish patent: 9 Dec 1836}		

Journal					
House of Commons			**House of Lords**		
Pet Rep: John Evelyn Denison Pres and Rep: William Hughes Hughes			Rep: Earl of Shaftesbury (Ld Ch)		
13 Feb 1837	92 CJ 39	**Pet**	16 Mar 1837	69 LJ 122	Brought HC/1R
21 Feb 1837	92 CJ 71	Pet Rep	18 Mar 1837	69 LJ 129	2R/C'tted
25 Feb 1837	92 CJ 85	1R	11 Apr 1837	69 LJ 179	**Rep with Amd**
1 Mar 1837	92 CJ 100	2R/C'tted	13 Apr 1837	69 LJ 181	3R
13 Mar 1837	92 CJ 161	Rep with Amds/Ing	18 Apr 1837	69 LJ 203	**HC Amds Ag**
14 Mar 1837	92 CJ 166	3R	21 Apr 1837	69 LJ 219	Royal Assent

(continued)

(continued)

13 Apr 1837	92 CJ 259	HL pass with Amds			
17 Apr 1837	92 CJ 269	**HL Amds Ag**			
21 Apr 1837	92 CJ 281	Royal Assent			

Representation

Solicitor: C.H Steadman

Parliamentary debates

Pet: Mirror, 13 Feb 1837, Vol 1, p 139	Br HC/1R: Mirror, 16 Mar 1837, Vol 1, p 698
Rep: Mirror, 21 Feb 1837, Vol 1, p 257	2R: Mirror, 18 Mar 1837, Vol 1, p 755
1R: Mirror, 24 Feb 1837, Vol 1, p 346	Rep: Mirror, 11 Apr 1837, Vol 2, p 926
2R: Mirror, 1 Mar 1837, Vol 1, p 395	3R: Mirror, 13 Apr 1837, Vol 2, p 979
Rep: Mirror, 13 Mar 1837, Vol 1, p 607	HC pass: Mirror, 18 Apr 1837, Vol 2, p 1067
3R: Mirror, 14 Mar 1837, Vol 1, p 639	Royal Assent: Mirror, 21 Apr 1837, Vol 2, p 1135
HL Amds Ag: Mirror, 17 Apr 1837, Vol 2, p 1036	

Parliamentary papers and cases

None

Gazette notices

London Gazette: 22 Nov 1836 (Iss: 19,439, p 2181); 25 Nov 1836 (Iss: 19,441, p 2307); 28 Nov 1836 (Iss: 19,443, p 2425)

Newspaper coverage of debates

House of Commons

2R: Morning Post, 2 Mar 1837; Public Ledger and Daily Advertiser, 2 Mar 1837; Westmorland Gazette, 11 Mar 1837

3R: Morning Post, 15 Mar 1837; London Courier and Evening Gazette, 15 Mar 1837; Leamington Spa Courier, 18 Mar 1837; West Kent Guardian, 18 Mar 1837; Bell's New Weekly Messenger, 19 Mar 1837

House of Lords

1R: London Courier and Evening Gazette, 17 Mar 1837

3R: London Courier and Evening Gazette, 14 Apr 1837

Royal Assent: London Courier and Evening Gazette, 22 Apr 1837

Archives

C'tee Minutes: 22 Mar 1837 (p 45); 6 Apr 1837 (p 46–49); 10 Apr 1837 (p 49–51): HL/PO/CO/1/97

Ing: HL/PO/PB/1/1837/7W4&1V1n32

India Steam Ship Company Act 1838

PRVA43	1838
India Steam Ship Company Act 1838 (1 & 2 Vict. c. xcvii)	
An Act for forming and regulating a Company, to be called "The India Steam Ship Company," and to enable the said Company to purchase certain Letters	

Table of contents (patent provisions only)

s 2 Objects of Company [to purchase and work letters patent]
s 3 J. Stephens and A. Manning may assign the Letters Patent to or in trust for the Company
s 4 Company after Assignment to have all the Rights and respective Patents
s 5 And enabled to grant Licences for the Use of the said Invention

Relevant patents

14 Apr 1831 (No 6106)	Apparatus rendered applicable to steam engines [Thomas Brunton] {extends to colonies; Irish patent: 1 Nov 1831}
13 Jul 1836 (No 7145)	Steam Boilers [Elisha Haydon Collier] {Scottish patent: 7 Jul 1836}

Journal					
House of Commons			**House of Lords**		
Rep: Thomas Greene SOC Rep: Charles Shaw Lefevre Pres: William Ormsby Gore Bill Rep: Charles Wood			Rep: Earl of Shaftesbury (Ld Ch)		
31 May 1838	93 CJ 569	**Pet**	16 Jul 1838	70 LJ 539	Brought HC/1R
7 Jun 1838	93 CJ 584	Pet Rep/Bill Ord	19 Jul 1838	70 LJ 579	2R/C'tted
18 Jun 1838	93 CJ 621	SOC Rep	26 Jul 1838	70 LJ 623	Rep w/o Amds
20 Jun 1838	93 CJ 627	1R	27 Jul 1838	70 LJ 631	3R
27 Jun 1838	93 CJ 660	2R	31 Jul 1838	70 LJ 647	Royal Assent
10 Jul 1838	93 CJ 692	Rep with Amds			
13 Jul 1838	93 CJ 702	Cons/Ing			
14 Jul 1838	93 CJ 705	3R			
28 Jul 1838	93 CJ 765	HL pass w/o Amds			
31 Jul 1838	93 CJ 773	Royal Assent			

Representation

Solicitor: Thomas Jones Maws

Parliamentary debates

Pet: Mirror, 31 May 1838, Vol 6, p 4482	Brought HC/1R: Mirror, 16 Jul 1838, Vol 7, p 5516
Pet Rep: Mirror, 7 Jun 1838, Vol 6, p 4582	2R: Mirror, 19 Jul 1838, Vol 7, p 5605
Bill Ord: Mirror, 18 Jun 1838, Vol 6, p 4843	Wit At: Mirror, 24 Jul 1838, Vol 7, p 5753
1R: Mirror, 20 Jun 1838, Vol 6, p 4907	Rep: Mirror, 26 Jul 1838, Vol 7, p 5801
2R: Mirror, 27 Jun 1838, Vol 6, p 5146	3R: Mirror, 27 Jul 1838, Vol 7, p 5854
Rep: Mirror, 10 Jul 1838, Vol 7, p 5419	HL pass: Mirror, 28 Jul 1838, Vol 7, p 5897
Cons: Mirror, 13 Jul 1838, Vol 7, p 5490	Royal Assent: Mirror, 31 Jul 1838, Vol 7, p 5967
3R: Mirror, 14 Jul 1838, Vol 7, p 5506	

Parliamentary papers and cases

None

Gazette notices

London Gazette: 8 Jun 1838 (Iss: 19,624, p 1312); 12 Jun 1838 (Iss: 19,625, p 1342); 15 Jun 1838
(Iss: 19,626, p 1364); 19 Jun 1838 (Iss: 19,627, p 1388)

Newspaper coverage of debates

House of Commons

SO cw: Morning Post, 19 Jun 1838

1R: London Courier and Evening Gazette, 21 Jun 1838; Bristol Mercury, 23 Jun 1838; Exeter Flying Post, 28 Jun 1838;
Enniskillen Chronicle and Erne Packet, 28 Jun 1838

2R: Morning Post, 28 Jun 1838; Leeds Times, 30 Jun 1838; Durham County Advertiser, 6 Jul 1838; Westmorland
Gazette, 7 Jul 1838

3R: Morning Advertiser, 14 Jul 1838; Morning Chronicle, 14 Jul 1838; Morning Post, 14 Jul 1838; London Courier
and Evening Gazette, 14 Jul 1838; London Evening Standard, 14 Jul 1838; The Examiner, 14 Jul 1838; Bell's Weekly
Messenger, 15 Jul 1838; Evening Chronicle, 16 Jul 1838; The Pilot, 16 Jul 1838; Tipperary Free Press, 18 Jul 1838; Fife
Herald, 19 Jul 1838; Perthshire Advertiser, 18 Jul 1838; Cheltenham Chronicle, 19 Jul 1838; North Devon Journal, 19 Jul
1838; Wiltshire Independent, 19 Jul 1838; Durham Chronicle, 20 Jul 1838; Lincolnshire Chronicle, 20 Jul 1838; Leicester
Journal, 20 Jul 1838; Durham County Advertiser, 20 Jul 1838; Londonderry Sentinel, 21 Jul 1838; Bristol Mercury, 21 Jul
1838; Monmouthshire Merlin, 21 Jul 1838; Bolton Chronicle; Northern Star and Leeds General Advertiser, 21 Jul 1838;
Monmouthshire Beacon, 21 Jul 1838; Gloucester Journal, 21 Jul 1838; Yorkshire Gazette, 21 Jul 1838; Bucks Gazette,
21 Jul 1838; Silurian, 21 Jul 1838; Oxford University and City Herald, 21 Jul 1838; Preston Chronicle, 21 Jul 1838; Bucks
Herald, 21 Jul 1838; Derbyshire Courier, 21 Jul 1838; Clonmel Herald, 21 Jul 1838; Gloucestershire Chronicle, 21 Jul 1838;
Leamington Spa Courier, 21 Jul 1838; Manchester Courier, 21 Jul 1838; Leeds Times, 21 Jul 1838; Newcastle Journal,
21 Jul 1838; Northampton Mercury, 21 Jul 1838; Berwick Advertiser, 21 Jul 1838; Westmorland Gazette, 21 Jul 1838;
Western Times, 21 Jul 1838; Carlisle Journal, 21 Jul 1838; The Champion, 22 Jul 1838; Sherborne Mercury, 23 Jul 1838

(continued)

(continued)

House of Lords

1R: Morning Chronicle, 17 Jul 1838; Morning Post, 17 Jul 1838; London Courier and Evening Gazette, 17 Jul 1838; Dublin Evening Register, 17 Jul 1838; Windsor and Eton Express, 21 Jul 1838; Warder and Dublin Weekly Mail, 21 Jul 1838

2R: London Courier and Evening Gazette, 20 Jul 1838

3R: London Courier and Evening Gazette, 28 Jul 1838

Royal Assent: Morning Post, 2 Aug 1838; Stamford Mercury, 3 Aug 1838; Hull Advertiser and Exchange Gazette, 3 Aug 1838; Liverpool Mercury, 3 Aug 1838; Chester Chronicle, 3 Aug 1838; Belfast Commercial Chronicle, 4 Aug 1838; Leeds Intelligencer, 4 Aug 1838; Bristol Mercury, 4 Aug 1838; Northampton Mercury, 4 Aug 1838; Leeds Times, 4 Aug 1838; Sherborne Mercury, 6 Aug 1838; Belfast News-Letter, 7 Aug 1838; Derry Journal, 7 Aug 1838; Inverness Courier, 8 Aug 1838; Derby Mercury, 8 Aug 1838; Enniskillen Chronicle and Erne Packet, 9 Aug 1838

Archives

C'tee Minutes: 23 Jul 1838 (p 266); 24 Jul 1838 (p 267–272): HL/PO/CO/1/100

Wit Sums: HL/PO/JO/10/8/1244 (No 930)

Ing: HL/PO/PB/1/1838/1&2V1n206

Colonial Patent Sugar Company Act 1838

PRVA44	1838
Colonial Patent Sugar Company Act 1838 (1 & 2 Vict. c. cii)	
An Act for forming and establishing "The Colonial Patent Sugar Company," and to enable the said Company to purchase certain Letters Patent	

Table of contents (patent provisions only)

s 2 Purposes of Company [to purchase letters patent and work the invention]
s 3 Company not to exercise the Invention or carry on Business in Great Britain
s 4 Charles Terry and William Parker may assign the Letters Patent to or in Trust for the Company; Company after Assignment, to have all Rights in the Letters Patent
s 5 Company may grant Licences

Relevant patent

26 Jun 1833 (No 6442)	Making and refining sugars [Charles Terry and William Parker] {Scottish patent: 16 Jul 1833}

Journal

House of Commons			House of Lords		
Rep: Charles Shaw-Lefevre Pres: Joseph Pease Bill Rep: William Holmes			Rep: Earl of Shaftesbury (Ld Ch)		
8 May 1838	93 CJ 496	Pet to Pet Late	30 Jul 1838	70 CJ 641	Brought HC/1R
14 May 1838	93 CJ 515	Rep/Leave	2 Aug 1838	70 CJ 654	2R/C'tted
6 Jun 1838	93 CJ 580	Pet	9 Aug 1838	70 CJ 706	Rep w/o Amds
18 Jun 1838	93 CJ 621	Pet Rep	10 Aug 1838	70 CJ 709	3R
22 Jun 1838	93 CJ 643	Bill Ord/1R	14 Aug 1838	70 CJ 729	Royal Assent
17 Jul 1838	93 CJ 713	2R day app			
18 Jul 1838	93 CJ 717	2R/C'tted			
28 Jul 1838	93 CJ 764	Rep with Amds/Ing			
30 Jul 1838	93 CJ 767	3R			
13 Aug 1838	93 CJ 871	HL pass w/o Amds			
14 Aug 1838	93 CJ 873	Royal Assent			

Representation

No information

Parliamentary debates

Pet: Mirror, 8 May 1838, Vol 5, p 3838	Brought HC/1R: Mirror, 30 Jul 1838, Vol 7, p 5905
Pet Lev: Mirror, 14 May 1838, Vol 5, p 3971	2R: Mirror, 2 Aug 1838, Vol 7, p 5994
Pet Bill: Mirror, 6 Jun 1838, Vol 6, p 4536	Rep: Mirror, 9 Aug 1838, Vol 8, p 6172
Pet Rep: Mirror, 18 Jun 1838, Vol 6, p 4843	3R: Mirror, 10 Aug 1838, Vol 8, p 6183

1R: Mirror, 22 Jun 1838, Vol 6, p 5013 2R day app: Mirror, 17 Jul 1838, Vol 7, p 5574 2R: Mirror, 18 Jul 1838, Vol 7, p 5590 Pet Ag: Mirror, 23 Jul 1838, Vol 7, p 5719 Pet Ag: Mirror, 25 Jul 1838, Vol 7, p 5792 Rep: Mirror, 28 Jul 1838, Vol 7, p 5897 3R: Mirror, 30 Jul 1838, Vol 7, p 5926	HL pass: Mirror, 13 Aug 1838, Vol 8, p 6220 Royal Assent: Mirror, 14 Aug 1838, Vol 8, p 6224

Parliamentary papers and cases

None

Gazette notices

Not required by SO

Newspaper coverage of debates

House of Commons

1R: The Times, 23 Jun 1838; Morning Advertiser, 23 Jun 1838; Morning Post, 23 Jun 1838; London Courier and Evening Gazette, 23 Jun 1838; London Evening Standard, 23 Jun 1838; London Dispatch, 24 Jun 1838; Evening Mail, 25 Jun 1838; Belfast Commercial Chronicle, 27 Jun 1838; Cheltenham Chronicle, 28 Jun 1838; North Devon Journal, 28 Jun 1838; Durham County Advertiser, 29 Jun 1838; Newcastle Courant, 29 Jun 1838; Stamford Mercury, 29 Jun 1838; Buck Herald, 30 Jun 1838; Cardiff and Merthyr Guardian, 30 Jun 1838; Derbyshire Courier, 30 Jun 1838; Monmouthshire Merlin, 30 Jun 1838; Sheffield Independent, 30 Jun 1838; Monmouthshire Beacon, 30 Jun 1838; Hereford Times, 30 Jun 1838; Norwich Mercury, 30 Jun 1838; Westmorland Gazette, 30 Jun 1838

2R: The Times, 19 Jul 1838

House of Lords

1R: The Times, 1 Aug 1838

Royal Assent: The Times, 15 Aug 1838

Archives

C'tee Minutes: 2 Aug 1838 (p 273–274); 3 Aug 1838 (p 286–287): HL/PO/CO/1/100

Ing: HL/PO/PB/1/1838/1&2V1n257

London Patent White Lead Company Act 1839

PRVA45	1839
	London Patent White Lead Company Act 1839 (2 & 3 Vict. c. lxxxiii)

An Act for forming and establishing "The London Patent White Lead Company," and to enable the said Company to purchase certain Letters Patent

Table of contents (patent provisions only)

s 2 Purposes of the Company [purchasing and working letters patent]
s 3 The Letters Patent may be assigned to or in Trust for the Company; Company after Assignment to have all the Rights in the Letters Patent
s 4 Company may grant Licences

Relevant patent

11 Dec 1833 (No 6520)	Improvements in making or producing the Pigment commonly known by the Name of White Lead or Carbonate of Lead [John Baptiste Constantine Torassa, Paul Isaac Muston and Henry Walker Wood] {Scottish patent: 23 Dec 1833; Irish patent: 24 May 1844}
11 Oct 1838 (No 7830)	Improved Process for manufacturing Carbonate of Lead, commonly called White Lead [John Woolrich] {Scottish patent: 17 Apr 1839; Irish patent: 20 Jun 1839}

Journal

House of Commons	House of Lords
Rep: Thomas Greene Second Rep: Charles Shaw Lefevre Pres: William Mackinnon Bill Rep: Philip Howard	Rep: Earl of Shaftesbury (Ld Ch)

(continued)

(continued)

22 Feb 1839	94 CJ 51	Pet (not proc)	7 Jun 1839	71 LJ 360	Brought HC/1R
8 Mar 1839	94 CJ 90	Pet	11 Jun 1839	71 LJ 371	2R/C'tted
12 Mar 1839	94 CJ 100	Pet Rep	28 Jun 1839	71 LJ 446	**Rep with Amds**
12 Mar 1839	94 CJ 101	Pet	1 Jul 1839	71 LJ 452	3R
27 Mar 1839	94 CJ 153	Pet Rep	4 Jul 1839	71 LJ 463	HC Ag Amds
27 Mar 1839	94 CJ 155	1R	19 Jul 1839	71 LJ 510	Royal Assent
13 May 1839	94 CJ 259	2R/C'tted (Middlesex List)			
3 Jun 1839	94 CJ 299	Rep with Amds/Ing			
6 Jun 1839	94 CJ 311	3R			
1 Jul 1839	94 CJ 397	HL pass with Amds			
3 Jul 1839	94 CJ 402	**HL Amds Ag**			
14 Jul 1839	94 CJ 461	Royal Assent			

Representation

Solicitor: Few, Hamilton and Few

Parliamentary debates

Leave: Mirror, 8 Mar 1839, Vol 2, p 925

Rep: Mirror, 12 Mar 1839, Vol 2, p 1048

1R: Mirror, 27 Mar 1839, Vol 2, p 1592

Ord: Mirror, 27 Mar 1839, Vol 2, p 1593

2R: Mirror, 13 May 1839, Vol 3, p 2402

Rep: Mirror 3 Jun 1839, Vol 3, p 2660

3R: Mirror 6 Jun 1839, Vol 4, p 2734

Amds Ag: Mirror, 3 Jul 1839, Vol 5, p 3554

Royal Assent: Mirror, 19 Jul 1839, Vol 5, p 4078

1R: Mirror, 7 Jun 1839, Vol 4, p 2760

2R: Mirror, 11 Jun 1839, Vol 4 p 2837

Wit Ord: Mirror, 25 Jun 1839, Vol 4, p 3296

Rep: Mirror, 28 Jun 1839, Vol 4, p 3423

3R: Mirror, 1 Jul 1839, Vol 4, p 3479

HC pass: Mirror, 4 Jul 1839, Vol 5, p 3580

Royal Assent: Mirror, 19 Jul 1839, Vol 5, p 4069

Parliamentary papers and cases

None

Gazette notices

London Gazette: 2 Nov 1838 (Iss: 19,669, p 2381); 9 Nov 1838 (Iss: 19,671, p 2450); 14 Nov 1838 (Iss: 19,673, p 2509)

Newspaper coverage of debates

House of Commons

1R: London Courier and Evening Gazette, 28 Mar 1839

2R: London Courier and Evening Gazette, 14 May 1839

3R: London Courier and Evening Gazette, 7 Jun 1839

House of Lords

1R: London Courier and Evening Gazette, 8 Jun 1839

2R: London Courier and Evening Gazette, 12 Jun 1839

3R: London Courier and Evening Gazette, 2 Jul 1839

Royal Assent: London Courier and Evening Gazette, 20 Jul 1839

Archives

Opposed Bill Minutes: 29 May 1839 (1 page – no page number): HC/CL/PB/1/1

C'tee Minutes: 13 Jun 1839 (p 182); 25 Jun 1839 (p 231–235); 28 Jun 1839 (p 241–242): HL/PO/CO/1/104

Amendments: 28 Jun 1839: HL/PO/JO/10/8/1285 (No 673)

Sums (David Drew): 25 Jun 1839: HL/PO/JO/10/8/1285 (No 649)

Ing: HL/PO/PB/1/1839/2&3V1n157

General Filtration and Dye Extract Company Act 1839

PRVA46	1839
General Filtration and Dye Extract Company Act 1839 (2 & 3 Vict. c. lxxxiv)	
An Act for forming and regulating a Company to be called "The General Filtration and Dye Extract Company;" and to enable the said Company to purchase certain Letters Patent	

Tables of contents (patent provisions only)

s 2 Purposes of the Company [purchasing and working Letters patent]
s 3 Patentees may assign Letters Patent to the Company without Forfeiture
s 4 Company may grant Licences

Relevant patents

14 Jun 1838 (No 7690)	Improvement in clarifying Water and other Liquids [George Price] {Scottish patent: 29 Oct 1838; Irish patent: 27 Jun 1839}
1 Dec 1838 (No 7889)	Improvements in Apparatus and Materials employed in filtering and clarifying Waters and other Liquids [William Pontifex] {Scottish patent: 6 Dec 1838; Irish patent: 20 Jun 1839}
11 Feb 1839 (No 7964)	New Mode of obtaining Dye Colours, Tannin and Acids from Vegetable Substances [Charles Gabriel Baron du Suarce; William Pontifex] {Scottish patent: 2 Feb 1839}

Journal

House of Commons			House of Lords		
Pet Rep: Charles Shaw Lefevre Pres: William Hutt Bill Rep: Philip Howard			Rep: Earl of Shaftesbury (Ld Ch)		
22 Feb 1839	94 CJ 51	Pet	7 Jun 1839	71 LJ 360	Brought HC/1R
12 Mar 1839	94 CJ 101	Pet Rep	11 Jun 1839	71 LJ 371	2R/C'tted
14 Mar 1839	94 CJ 112	Bill Ord	9 Jul 1839	71 LJ 479	**Rep with Amds**
18 Mar 1839	94 CJ 126	1R	11 Jul 1839	71 LJ 482	**3R with Amds**
13 May 1839	94 CJ 260	2R (Middlesex List)	12 Jul 1839	71 LJ 493	HC concurrence
3 Jun 1839	94 CJ 299	Rep with Amds/Ing	19 Jul 1839	71 LJ 510	Royal Assent
6 Jun 1839	94 CJ 310	3R			
11 Jul 1839	94 CJ 430	HL pass with Amds			
12 Jul 1839	94 CJ 436	**HL Amds Ag**			
19 Jul 1839	94 CJ 461	Royal Assent			

Representation

Solicitor: Few, Hamilton and Few

Parliamentary debates

Bill Ord: Mirror, 14 Mar 1839, Vol 2, p 1198

1R: Mirror, 18 Mar 1839, Vol 2, p 1316

2R: Mirror, 13 May 1839, Vol 3, p 2402

Rep: Mirror 3 Jun 1839, Vol 3, p 2660

3R: Mirror 6 Jun 1839, Vol 4, p 2734

HC pass: Mirror, 11 Jul 1839, Vol 5, p 3869

Amds Agr: Mirror, 12 Jul 1839, Vol 5, p 3876

Royal Assent: Mirror, 19 Jul 1839, Vol 5, p 4078

1R: Mirror, 7 Jun 1839, Vol 4, p 2760

2R: Mirror, 11 Jun 1839, Vol 4 p 2837

Rep: Mirror, 9 Jul 1839, Vol 5, p 3766

3R: Mirror, 11 Jul 1839, Vol 5, p 3814

HC Ag Amds: Mirror, 11 Jul 1839, Vol 5, p 3827

Royal Assent: Mirror, 19 Jul 1839, Vol 5, p 4069

Parliamentary papers and cases

None

Gazette notices

London Gazette: 2 Nov 1838 (Iss: 19,669, p 2381); 9 Nov 1838 (Iss: 19,671, p 2450); 14 Nov 1838 (Iss: 19,673, p 2508)

Newspaper coverage of debates

House of Commons

Pet: London Courier and Evening Gazette, 23 Feb 1839

1R: London Courier and Evening Gazette, 28 Mar 1839

(continued)

(continued)

2R: London Courier and Evening Gazette, 14 May 1839
3R: London Courier and Evening Gazette, 7 Jun 1839
HL Amd Ag: Morning Post, 13 Jul 1839
House of Lords
1R: London Courier and Evening Gazette, 8 Jun 1839
2R: London Courier and Evening Gazette, 12 Jun 1839
3R: London Courier and Evening Gazette, 12 Jul 1839
Royal Assent: Morning Advertiser, 20 Jul 1839; London Courier and Evening Gazette, 20 Jul 1839; London Evening Standard, 20 Jul 1839

Archives
C'tee Minutes: 13 Jun 1839 (p 180); 8 Jul 1839 (p 254–260): HL/PO/CO/1/104
Ing: HL/PO/PB/1/1839/2&3V1n158

Notes
Related cases
Needham v Oxley (1863) (VC) 8 HPC 331

Ship Propeller Company Act 1839

PRVA47	1839
Ship Propeller Company Act 1839 (2 & 3 Vict. c. xciii)	
An Act for forming and regulating a Company to be called "The Ship Propeller Company," and to enable the said Company to purchase certain Letters Patent	

Table of contents (patent provisions only)
s 2 Purposes of the Company [purchasing and working Letters patent]
s 3 Patentees may assign Letters Patent to the Company without Forfeiture
s 4 Company may grant Licences

Relevant patent	
31 May 1836 (No 7104)	Propeller for steam and other vessels [Francis Pettit Smith] {Scottish patent: 4 Jun 1836; Irish patent: 3 Sep 1836}

Journal

House of Commons			House of Lords		
Pet Rep: Sir John Yarde Buller Pres: Sir Charles Style Bill Rep: Thomas Law Hodges			Rep: Earl of Shaftesbury (Ld Ch)		
20 Feb 1839	94 CJ 42	Pet (abandoned)	8 Jul 1839	71 LJ 474	Brought HC/1R
31 May 1839	94 CJ 286	Pet	11 Jul 1839	71 LJ 482	2R/C'tted
10 Jun 1839	94 CJ 326	Pet Rep/Bill Ord	15 Jul 1839	71 LJ 497	**Rep with Amds**
11 Jun 1839	94 CJ 328	1R	16 Jul 1839	71 LJ 502	3R
19 Jun 1839	94 CJ 361	Pet Ag	22 Jul 1839	71 LJ 518	HC Ag Amds
24 Jun 1839	94 CJ 372 – V	2R/C'tted (W Kent)	29 Jul 1839	71 LJ 543	Royal Assent
28 Jun 1839	94 CJ 388	Pet Ag			
5 Jul 1839	94 CJ 412	Rep with Amds/Ing			
8 Jul 1839	94 CJ 416	3R			
18 Jul 1839	94 CJ 458	HL pass with Amds			
19 Jul 1839	94 CJ 462	**HL Amds Ag**			
29 Jul 1839	94 CJ 487	Royal Assent			

Petitions		
19 Jun 1839	94 CJ 361	Bennet Woodcraft and Robert Gardner
28 Jun 1839	94 CJ 372	Bennet Woodcraft

Representation
Solicitor: Few, Hamilton and Few

Parliamentary debates	
Pet (Abd): Mirror, 20 Feb 1839, Vol 1, p 413	1R: HL Deb, 8 Jul 1839, Vol 49(3rd), col 1; Mirror, 8 Jul 1839, Vol 5, p 3723
Pet: Mirror, 31 May 1839, Vol 3, p 2574	2R: Mirror, 2 Jul 1839, Vol 5, p 3814
Ord: Mirror, 10 Jun 1839, Vol 4, p 2805	Rep: Mirror, 15 Jul 1839, Vol 5, p 3925
1R: Mirror, 11 Jun 1839, Vol 4, p 2844	3R: Mirror, 16 Jul 1839, Vol 5, p 3966
Pet Ag: Mirror, 19 Jun 1839, Vol 4, p 3094	Amds Ag: Mirror, 19 Jul 1839, Vol 5, p 4081
2R: **Mirror, 24 Jun 1839, Vol 4, p 3256–3257**	Ret HC: Mirror, 22 Jul 1839, Vol 5, p 4136
Pet Ag: Mirror, 28 Jun 1839, Vol 4, p 3455	Royal Assent: Mirror, 29 Jul 1839, Vol 6, p 4401
Rep: Mirror, 5 Jul 1839, Vol 5, p 3664	
3R: Mirror, 8 Jul 1839, Vol 5, p 3725	
Royal Assent: Mirror, 29 Jul 1839, Vol 6, p 4401 and 4418	

Parliamentary papers and cases
None

Gazette notices
London Gazette: 2 Nov 1838 (Iss: 19,669, p 2381); 9 Nov 1838 (Iss: 19,671, p 2450); 14 Nov 1838 (Iss: 19,673, p 2508)

Newspaper coverage of debates
House of Commons
Pet Ag: Morning Post, 20 Jun 1839; London Evening Standard, 20 Jun 1839
2R: **Morning Post, 25 Jun 1839**; *Evening Mail, 26 Jun 1839*; *Bell's New Weekly Messenger, 30 Jun 1839*; *The Era, 30 Jun 1839*; Morning Advertiser, 25 Jun 1839; The Charter, 30 Jun 1839; The Operative, 30 Jun 1839; London Dispatch, 30 Jun 1839
Rep: The Era, 7 Jul 1839
3R: The Times, 9 Jul 1839; Morning Advertiser, 9 Jul 1839; Evening Mail, 10 Jul 1839; London Courier and Evening Gazette, 9 Jul 1839; London Evening Standard, 9 Jul 1839
House of Lords
2R: London Courier and Evening Gazette, 12 Jul 1839
Royal Assent: Morning Chronicle, 30 Jul 1839; Morning Post, 30 Jul 1839; London Courier and Evening Gazette, 30 Jul 1839

Archives
Minutes Opposed Bill C'tee: 3 Jul 1839 (3 pages – no page numbers): HC/CL/PB/1/1
C'tee Minutes: 12 Jul 1839 (p 267–269): HL/PO/CO/1/104
Ing: HL/PO/PB/1/1839/2&3V1n185

Notes
Related cases
Back v Rennie (1843) (VC) 4 HPC 645; 23 Lon J 466; *Back v Steinman* (1846) (NP) 4 HPC 645; *Smith's Patent* (1850) (PC) 6 HPC 183, 7 Moo PCC 133 (13 ER 830); *Lowe v Penn* (1848) 5 HPC 655; *R v Lowe* (1850) 5 HPC 717

Marquis of Tweeddale's Patents Act 1840

PRVA48	1840
Marquis of Tweeddale's Patents Act 1840 (3 & 4 Vict. c. xxx)	
An Act to authorize the Transfer to more than Twelve Persons of certain Patents granted to the Marquis of Tweeddale relating to the Manufacture of Drain-tiles, Bricks, and other Articles, and for the Establishment of a Company for carrying out the Objects of the said Patents [Tweeddale Brick Company]	
Table of contents (patent provisions only)	
s 1 Patents may be assigned to more than Twelve Persons without causing a Forfeiture s 2 After Assignment the Property in the Patents to vest in the Company s 4 Purposes of the Company [purchasing and working Letters patent] s 5 Power to grant Licences	

(continued)

(continued)

Relevant patent	
9 Dec 1836 (No 7253)	Making Tiles for draining; also, house-tiles, flat-roofing tiles, and bricks [George, Marquis of Tweeddale] {Scottish patent: 24 Sep 1836; Irish patent: 26 Nov 1836}

Journal

House of Commons			House of Lords		
Pet Rep: Robert Palmer Pres: Sir Samual Crompton Rep: William Hayter			Rep: Earl of Shaftesbury (Ld Ch)		
30 Jan 1840	95 CJ 41	Pet	10 Mar 1840	72 LJ 105	Brought HC/1R
13 Feb 1840	95 CJ 79	Pet Rep/Bill Ord	13 Mar 1840	72 LJ 107	2R/C'tted
14 Feb 1840	95 CJ 84	1R	31 Mar 1840	72 LJ 166	**Rep with Amds**
25 Feb 1840	95 CJ 114	2R/C'tted (E Somerset)	3 Apr 1840	72 LJ 178	3R
9 Mar 1840	95 CJ 156	Rep with Amds	9 Apr 1840	72 LJ 202	HC Ag Amds
10 Mar 1840	95 CJ 161	3R	14 Apr 1840	72 LJ 232	Royal Assent
6 Apr 1840	95 CJ 257	HL pass with Amds			
7 Apr 1840	95 CJ 259	**HL Amds Ag**			
14 Apr 1840	95 CJ 280	Royal Assent			

Representation

Agent: Swain, Stevens & Co

Parliamentary debates

Pet: Mirror, 30 Jan 1840, Vol 1, p 502	1R; Mirror, 10 Mar 1840, Vol 2, p 1664
Pet Rep: Mirror, 13 Feb 1840, Vol 2, p 942	2R: Mirror, 13 Mar 1840, Vol 2, p 1715
1R: Mirror, 14 Feb 1840, Vol 2, p 991	Rep: Mirror, 31 Mar 1840, Vol 3, p 2103
2R: Mirror, 25 Feb 1840, Vol 2, p 1255	3R: Mirror, 3 Apr 1840, Vol 3, p 2261
Rep: Mirror, 9 Mar 1840, Vol 2, p 1626	HL Ag Amds: Mirror, 9 Apr 1840, Vol 3, p 2471
3R: Mirror, 10 Mar 1840, Vol 2, p 1669	Royal Assent: Mirror, 14 Apr 1840, Vol 3, p 2644
HL pass: Mirror, 6 Apr 1840, Vol 3, p 2333	
Amds Ag: Mirror, 7 Apr 1840, Vol 3, p 2384	
Royal Assent: Mirror, 14 Apr 1840, Vol 3, p 2654	
List of Acts: HC Deb, 11 Aug 1840, Vol 55(3rd), col 141	

Parliamentary papers and cases

None

Gazette notices

London Gazette: 29 Oct 1839 (Iss: 19,783, p 2018); 5 Nov 1839 (Iss: 19,786, p 2093); 12 Nov 1839 (Iss: 19,788, p 2150)

Edinburgh Gazette: 29 Oct 1839 (Iss: 4847, p 272); 1 Nov 1839 (Iss: 4848, p 278); 8 Nov 1839 (Iss: 4850, p 295); 15 Nov 1839 (Iss: 4852, p 307)

Dublin Gazette: 5 Nov 1839 (Iss: 13,091, p 604); 8 Nov 1839 (Iss: 13,092, p 611); 12 Nov 1839 (Iss: 13,093, p 622)

Newspaper coverage of debates

House of Commons

Rep/Ing: Morning Post, 10 Mar 1840

Royal Assent: Morning Chronicle, 15 Apr 1840; Morning Post, 15 Apr 1840

Archives

C'tee Minutes: 17 Mar 1840 (p 57); 27 Mar 1840 (p 85–89): HL/PO/CO/1/108

Bill Amds: HL/PO/JO/10/8/1318

Ing: HL/PO/PB/1/1840/3&4V1n30

General Salvage Company Act 1840

PRVA49	1840
General Salvage Company Act 1840 (3 & 4 Vict. c. cxv)	
An Act for forming and establishing a Company to be called "The General Salvage Company" and for enabling the said Company to purchase certain Letters Patent [Austin's Patent]	

Table of contents (patent provisions only)	
s 2 Purposes of the Company [purchasing and working letters patent] s 3 Company empowered to purchase certain Letters Patent s 4 After Transfer of Patents the Company may grant Licences	

Relevant patents	
12 May 1837 (No 7372)	Raising sunken Vessels and other Bodies [Edward Austin]
3 Oct 1839 (No 8231)	Constructing Vessels for containing air, applicable to the purpose of raising bodies in or under water; fasteid such vehicles to chains or other apparatus for raising or lifting such bodies [William Henry Burke]

Journal

House of Commons			House of Lords		
Pet Rep: Thomas Greene Pres: William Hayter Rep and Rep Re-C'tted: George Palmer			Rep: Earl of Shaftsbury (Ld Ch)		
31 Jan 1840	95 CJ 48	Pet	29 Jun 1840	72 LJ 441	Brought HC/1R
6 Mar 1840	95 CJ 150	Pet Rep/Bill Ord	2 Jul 1840	72 LJ 451	2R/C'tted
10 Mar 1840	95 CJ 161	Ord Disc/New Ord	7 Jul 1840	72 LJ 474	Rep w/o Amds
10 Mar 1840	95 CJ 161	1R	9 Jul 1840	72 LJ 479	3R
16 May 1840	95 CJ 342	2R/C'tted (Middlesex)	23 Jul 1840	72 LJ 539	Royal Assent
29 May 1840	95 CJ 382	**Pet Ag**			
2 Jun 1840	95 CJ 398	**Pet Fav and Ag**			
2 Jun 1840	95 CJ 398	Rep with Amds/Re-C'tted			
5 Jun 1840	95 CJ 408	Re-C'tted Disc/Re-C'tted			
23 Jun 1840	95 CJ 455	C'tte revived			
25 Jun 1840	95 CJ 458	Rep with Amds/Ing			
26 Jun 1840	95 CJ 464	3R			
9 Jul 1840	95 CJ 505	HL pass w/o Amds			
23 Jul 1840	95 CJ 560	Royal Assent			

Petitions

29 May 1840	95 CJ 382	Edward Austin [alleging promoters trying to suppress invention]
2 Jun 1840	95 CJ 398	John Waton [in favour]
2 Jun 1840	95 CJ 398	Edward Austin [Against]

Representation

No information

Parliamentary debates

Pet: Mirror, 31 Jan 1840, Vol 1, p 555

Ord: Mirror, 6 Mar 1840, Vol 2, p 1576

1R: Mirror, 10 Mar 1840, Vol2, p 1668

Ord Disc: Mirror, 10 Mar 1840, Vol 2, p 1669

2R: Mirror, 15 May 1840, Vol 4, p 3029

Pet Ag (Inventor): Mirror, 29 May 1840, Vol 4, p 3398

Pet: Mirror, 2 Jun 1840, Vol 4, p 3491

Re-C'tted: Mirror, 5 Jun 1840, Vol 4, p 3581

Com Rev: Mirror, 23 Jun 1840, Vol 5, p 3968

Rep: Mirror, 25 Jun 1840, Vol 5, p 4012

3R: Mirror, 26 Jun 1840, Vol 5, p 4047

HL pass: Mirror, 9 Jul 1840, Vol 5, p 4422

Royal Assent: Mirror, 23 Jul 1840, Vol 6, p 4816

List of Acts: HC Deb, 11 Aug 1840, Vol 55(3rd), col 141

1R: Mirror, 29 Jun 1840, Vol 5, p 4075

2R: Mirror, 2 Jun 1840, Vol 5, p 4213

Rep: Mirror, 7 Jun 1840, Vol 5, p 4342

3R: Mirror, 9 Jul 1840, Vol 5, p 4409

Royal Assent: Mirror, 23 Jul 1840, Vol 6, p 4790

(continued)

(continued)

Parliamentary papers and cases
None
Gazette notices
London Gazette: 8 Nov 1839 (Iss: 19,787, p 2122); 16 Nov 1839 (Iss: 19,790, p 2263); 23 Nov 1839 (Iss: 19,794, p 2399)
Newspaper coverage of debates
House of Commons
Re-Ctted: London Evening Standard, 3 Jun 1840
3R: The Examiner, 28 Jun 1840
Royal Assent: London Evening Standard, 24 Jul 1840
Archives
Unopposed Bill C'tee Minutes: 3 Jul 1840 (p 339); 6 Jul 1840 (p 345–347): HL/PO/CO/1/108
Ing: HL/PO/PB/1/1840/3&4V1n179

Edinburgh Silk Yarn Company Act 1840

PRVA50	1840
Edinburgh Silk Yarn Company Act 1840 (3 & 4 Vict. c. xcvii)	
An Act for establishing and regulating a Company, to be called "The Edinburgh Silk Yarn Company;" and to enable the said Company to purchase certain Letters Patent	

Table of contents (patent provisions only)
s 2 Purposes of the Company [purchasing and working Letters patent] s 3 Patents may be assigned to the Company without causing a Forfeiture s 4 After Assignment the Property in the patents to vest in the Company s 5 Power to grant Licences

Relevant patent	
26 Mar 1838 (No 7600)	Preparing and spinning silk-waste, wool, flax, and other fibrous substances; discharging the gum from silks, raw and manufactured [Michael Wheelwright Ivison] {Scottish patent: 12 Dec 1837}

Journal

House of Commons			House of Lords		
Pet Rep: Thomas Greene Pres: Richard Bethall Bill Rep: Henry Handley			Rep: Earl of Shaftesbury (Ld Ch)		
28 Jan 1840	95 CJ 32	Pet	2 Jun 1840	72 LJ 358	Brought HC/1R
14 Feb 1840	95 CJ 84	Pet Rep/Bill Ord	5 Jun 1840	72 LJ 372	2R/C'tted
6 Mar 1840	95 CJ 151	1R	18 Jun 1840	72 LJ 413	**Rep with Amds**
26 Mar 1840	95 CJ 213	2R/C'tted (S Scotland)	19 Jun 1840	72 LJ 415	3R
1 Jun 1840	95 CJ 390	Rep with Amds/Ing	23 Jun 1840	72 LJ 426	HC Ag Amds
2 Jun 1840	95 CJ 398	3R	3 Jul 1840	72 LJ 459	Royal Assent
22 Jun 1840	95 CJ 453	HL pass with Amds			
23 Jun 1840	95 CJ 346	**HL Amds Ag**			
3 Jul 1840	95 CJ 480	Royal Assent			

Representation
Solicitor: Crowder and Maynard

Parliamentary debates	
Pet: Mirror, 28 Jan 1840, Vol 1, p 401	1R: Mirror, 2 Jun 1840, Vol 4, p 3477
Ord: Mirror, 14 Feb 1840, Vol 2, p 991	2R: Mirror, 5 Jun 1840, Vol 4, p 3577
1R: Mirror, 6 Mar 1840, Vol 2, p 1575	Rep: Mirror, 18 Jun 1840, Vol 5, p 3829
2R: Mirror, 26 Mar 1840, Vol 3, p 1971	3R: Mirror, 19 Jun 1840, Vol 5, p 3859
Rep: Mirror, 1 Jun 1840, Vol 4, p 3449	HC Ag Amds: Mirror, 23 Jun 1840, Vol 5, p 3959
3R: Mirror, 2 Jun 1840, Vol 4, p 3491	Royal Assent: Mirror, 3 Jul 1840, Vol 5, p 4261

HL pass: Mirror, 22 Jun 1840, Vol 5, p 3925	
Amds Ag: Mirror, 23 Jun 1840, Vol 5, p 3974	
List of Acts: HC Deb, 11 Aug 1840, Vol 55(3rd), col 141	

Parliamentary papers and cases

None

Gazette notices

London Gazette: 15 Nov 1839 (Iss: 19,789, p 2211); 23 Nov 1839 (Iss: 19,794, p 2407); 27 Nov 1839 (Iss: 19,797, p 2462)
Edinburgh Gazette: 15 Nov 1839 (Iss: 4852, p 307); 22 Nov 1839 (Iss: 4854, p 319); 29 Nov 1839 (Iss: 4856, p 329)

Newspaper coverage of debates

House of Commons
Pet: Caledonian Mercury, 1 Feb 1840
Ref SC: The Scotsman, 8 Feb 1840
Pet Rep: Caledonian Mercury, 20 Feb 1840
1R: The Scotsman 11 Mar 1840; Caledonian Mercury, 12 Mar 1840
2R: *Caledonian Mercury, 28 Mar 1840 and 30 Mar 1840; Falmouth Express and Colonial Journal, 28 Mar 1840;* Morning Advertiser, 27 Mar 1840; Morning Post, 27 Mar 1840
Rep: Morning Post, 2 Jun 1840; The Scotsman, 6 Jun 1840; Inverness Courier, 10 Jun 1849
3R: Morning Post, 3 Jun 1840; London Evening Standard, 3 Jun 1840; Caledonian Mercury, 6 Jun 1840; The Scotsman, 6 Jun 1840; Worcester Journal, 4 Jun 1840; Oxford Journal, 6 Jun 1840; Bell's New Weekly Messenger, 7 Jun 1840; Worcester Journal, 25 Jun 1840
HL Amds Ag: Caledonian Mercury, 27 Jun 1840; Staffordshire Advertiser, 27 Jun 1840; Staffordshire Gazette and County Standard, 27 Jun 1840
Royal Assent: Reading Mercury, 4 Jul 1840; Dublin Monitor, 7 Jul 1840; Stamford Mercury, 10 Jul 1840; Carlisle Patriot, 11 Jul 1840; Westmorland Gazette, 11 Jul 1840

Archives

Unopposed Bill C'tee Minutes: 11 Jun 1840 (p 261); 12 Jun 1840 (p 275–277); 16 Jun 1840 (p 292–293): HL/PO/CO/1/108
Bill (18 Jun 1840): HL/PO/JO/10/8/134 (No 686)
Ing: HL/PO/PB/1/1840/3&4V1n97

Kollmann's Railway Locomotive and Carriage Improvement Company Act 1840

PRVA51	1840
Kollmann's Railway Locomotive and Carriage Improvement Company Act 1840 (3 & 4 Vict. c. xcviii)	
An Act for forming a Company to be called "Kollmann's Railway Locomotive and Carriage Improvement Company," and for enabling the said Company to purchase certain Letters Patent [Kollmann's Patent]	

Table of contents (patent provisions only)

s 2 Company may purchase Letters Patent
s 3 After Purchase the Letters Patent to vest in the Company
s 4 Company may grant Licences to use Inventions

Relevant patents

23 Apr 1836 (No 7069)	Railways and other locomotive- carriages [George Augustus Kollmann]
17 Aug 1839 (No 8200)	Railway; locomotive and other carriages [George Augustus Kollmann]

Journal

House of Commons	House of Lords
Pet Rep: Thomas Greene Pres: Henry Boldero Bill Rep: James Bell	Rep: Earl of Shaftesbury (Ld Ch)

(continued)

(continued)

31 Jan 1840	95 CJ 48	Pet	1 Jun 1840	72 LJ 349	Brought HC/1R
6 Mar 1840	95 CJ 150	Pet Rep	4 Jun 1840	72 LJ 371	2R/C'tted
9 Mar 1840	95 CJ 156	Pet Rep Cons/Bill Ord	22 Jun 1840	72 LJ 422	Rep w/o Amds
10 Mar 1840	95 CJ 161	1R	23 Jun 1840	72 LJ 424	3R
15 May 1840	95 CJ 338	2R/C'tted (N Wilts)	3 Jul 1840	72 LJ 459	Royal Assent
29 May 1840	95 CJ 384	Rep with Amds/Ing			
1 Jun 1840	95 CJ 387	3R			
23 Jun 1840	95 CJ 456	HL pass w/o Amds			
3 Jul 1840	95 CJ 480	Royal Assent			

Representation
No details

Parliamentary debates	
Pet: Mirror, 31 Jan 1840, Vol 1, p 555	1R: Mirror, 1 Jun 1840, Vol 4, p 3436
Rep Pet: Mirror, 6 Mar 1840, Vol 2, p 1576	2R: Mirror, 4 Jun 1840, Vol 4, p 3539
Rep/Ord: Mirror, 9 Mar 1840, Vol 2, p 1624	Rep: Mirror, 22 Jun 1840, Vol 4, p 3914
1R: Mirror, 10 Mar 1840, Vol 2, p 1669	3R: Mirror, 23 Jun 1840, Vol 5, p 3959
2R: Mirror, 15 May 1840, Vol 4, p 3029	Royal Assent: Mirror, 3 Jul 1840, Vol 5, p 4261
Rep: Mirror, 29 May 1840, Vol 4, p 3398	
3R: Mirror, 1 Jun 1840, Vol 4, p 3449	
List of Acts: HC Deb, 11 Aug 1840, Vol 55(3rd), col 141	

Parliamentary papers and cases
None

Gazette notices
London Gazette: 8 Nov 1839 (Iss: 19,787, p 2122); 16 Nov 1839 (Iss: 19,790, p 2263); 23 Nov 1839 (Iss: 19,794, p 2399)

Newspaper coverage of debates
House of Commons
2R: The Examiner, 17 May 1840; North Devon Journal, 21 May 1840; Bristol Mercury, 23 May 1840; Carlisle Journal, 23 May 1840; Derry Journal, 26 Jun 1840; Northampton Mercury, 23 May 1840
Royal Assent: Dublin Monitor, 7 Jul 1840; Stamford Mercury, 10 Jul 1840; Westmorland Gazette, 11 Jul 1840; Carlisle Patriot, 11 Jul 1840

Archives
Unopposed Bill C'tee Minutes: 12 Jun 1840 (p 277–279); 22 Jun 1840 (p 304) HL/PO/CO/1/108
Bill (1 Jun 1840): HL/PO/JO/19/8/1332 (No 596)
Ing: HL/PO/PB/1/1840/3&4V1n98

Patent Rolling and Compressing Iron Company Act 1841

PRVA52	1841
Patent Rolling and Compressing Iron Company Act 1841 (4 & 5 Vict. c. lxxxix)	
An Act to enable "The Patent Rolling and Compressing Iron Company" to purchase certain Letters Patent, and to sue and be sued	

Table of contents (patent sections only)
s 3 Patents may be assigned to the Company without causing a Forfeiture
s 4 Power to grant Licences

Relevant patent	
24 Apr 1838 (No 7623)	Machinery for manufacturing pins, bolts, nails, and rivets; applicable to various purposes [Francis Pope] {Scottish patent: 13 Jul 1838}
22 May 1839 (No 8074)	Rolling Iron [James Vardy]

Journal					
House of Commons			**House of Lords**		
Pres: Henry Fitzroy Rep: Ralph Bernal (Ch W&M)			Rep: Earl of Shaftesbury (Ld Ch)		
26 Mar 1841	96 CJ 170	Pet/Bill Ord	11 May 1841	73 LJ 285	Brought HC/1R
30 Mar 1841	96 CJ 180	1R	14 May 1841	73 LJ 301	2R/C'tted
5 Apr 1841	96 CJ 198	2R/C'tted	25 May 1841	73 LJ 345	Rep w/o Amds
10 May 1841	96 CJ 283	Rep with Amds/Ing	27 May 1841	73 LJ 352	3R
11 May 1841	96 CJ 288	3R	21 Jun 1841	73 LJ 543	Royal Assent
27 May 1841	96 CJ 352	HL pass w/o Amds			
21 Jun 1841	96 CJ 449	Royal Assent			

Representation

Solicitor: Thomas Hanson Peile
Agent: RB Mosse

Parliamentary debates

Ord: Mirror, 26 Mar 1841, Vol 2, p 1031

1R: Mirror, 30 Mar 1841, Vol 2, p 1096

2R: Mirror, 5 Apr 1841, Vol 2, p 1192

Rep: Mirror, 10 May 1841, Vol 2, p 1562

3R: Mirror, 11 May 1841, Vol 2, p 1607

HL Ag: Mirror 27 May 1841, Vol 3, p 1932

List of Acts: HC Deb, 22 Jun 1841, Vol 58(3rd), col 1598

1R: Mirror, 11 May 1841, Vol 2, p 1600

2R: Mirror, 14 May 1841, Vol 3, p 1706

Rep: Mirror, 25 May 1841, Vol 3, p 1880

3R: Mirror, 27 May 1841, Vol 3, p 1922

Royal Assent: Mirror, 21 Jun 1841, Vol 3, p 2368

Parliamentary papers and cases

None

Gazette notices

London Gazette: 21 Nov 1840 (Iss: 19,918, p 2736); 25 Nov 1840 (Iss: 19,921, p 2812);
30 Nov 1840 (Iss: 19,924, p 2895)

Newspaper coverage of debates

House of Commons

3R: Leamington Spa, 15 May 1841; Monmouthshire Beacon, 15 May 1841; The Era, 16 May 1841; Sherborne Mercury, 17 May 1841

Royal Assent: London Evening Standard, 22 Jun 1841; Stamford Mercury, 25 Jun 1841; Bucks Gazette, 26 Jun 1841; Oxford Chronicle, 26 Jun 1841; Sherborne Mercury, 28 Jun 1841

Archives

Unopposed Bill C'tee Minutes: 6 May 1841 (p 76): HC/CL/WM/UB/1/1

Unopposed Bill C'tee Minutes: 18 May 1840 (p 224–227): HL/PO/CO/1/112

Ing: HL/PO/PB/1/1840/4&5V1n139

Stead's Patent Wooden Paving Company Act 1841

PRVA53	1841
Stead's Patent Wooden Paving Company Act 1841 (4 & 5 Vict. c. xci)	
An Act for forming and establishing Stead's Patent Wooden Paving Company; and to enable the said Company to purchase certain Letters Patent, and for confirming the same	
Table of contents (patent sections only)	

s 3 Mr Stead may assign the Letters Patent to or in Trust for the Company; Company after Assignment, to have all Rights in Letters Patent
s 4 Company may grant Licences
s 31 Rectifying Mistake in first-recited Letters Patent

(continued)

(continued)

Relevant patents	
19 May 1838 (No 7645)	Making or paving streets, ways, roads, courts and bridges, with timber or wooden blocks [David Stead]
23 Apr 1839 (No 8041)	Making or paving streets, ways, roads, paths, courts and bridges, with timber or wooden blocks [David Stead]

Journal

House of Commons			House of Lords		
Pet Rep: Robert Palmer Pres: Henry Warburton Rep: Ralph Bernal (Ch W&M)			Rep: Earl of Shaftesbury (Ld Ch)		
12 Feb 1841	96 CJ 46	Pet	4 Jun 1841	73 LJ 414	Brought HC/1R
25 Feb 1841	96 CJ 79	Rep/Bill Ord	8 Jun 1841	73 LJ 443	2R/C'tted
19 Mar 1841	96 CJ 148	1R	14 Jun 1841	73 LJ 492	Rep w/o Amds
26 Apr 1841	96 CJ 231	2R/C'tted	15 Jun 1841	73 LJ 496	3R
3 Jun 1841	96 CJ 365	Rep with Amds/Ing	21 Jun 1841	73 LJ 544	Royal Assent
4 Jun 1841	96 CJ 372	3R			
15 Jun 1841	96 CJ 426	HL pass w/o Amds			
21 Jun 1841	96 CJ 449	Royal Assent			

Representation

Solicitor: Roy, Blunt, Duncan and Johnston

Parliamentary debates

Pet: Mirror, 12 Feb 1841, Vol 1, p 217	1R: Mirror, 4 Jun 1841, Vol 3, p 2075
Ord: Mirror, 25 Feb 1841, Vol 1, p 401	2R: Mirror, 8 Jun 1841, Vol 3, p 2180
1R: Mirror, 19 Mar 1841, Vol 2, p 872	Rep: Mirror, 14 Jun 1841, Vol 3, p 2291
2R: Mirror, 26 Apr 1841, Vol 2, p 1298	3R: Mirror, 15 Jun 1841, Vol 3, p 2310
Rep: Mirror, 3 Jun 1841, Vol 3, p 2053	Royal Assent: Mirror, 21 Jun 1841, Vol 3, p 2368
3R: Mirror, 4 Jun 1841, Vol 3, p 2083	
HL Ag: Mirror, 15 Jun 1841, Vol 3, p 2323	
List of Acts: HC Deb, 22 Jun 1841, Vol 58(3rd), col 1598	

Parliamentary papers and cases

None

Gazette notices

London Gazette: 14 Nov 1840 (Iss: 19,914, p 2574); 20 Nov 1840 (Iss: 19,917, p 2690); 25 Nov 1840 (Iss: 19,921, p 2802)

Newspaper coverage of debates

House of Commons

Rep: Morning Advertiser, 4 Jun 1841; Morning Post, 4 Jun 1841

3R: Morning Post, 5 Jun 1841

Royal Assent: Morning Advertiser, 22 Jun 1841; Morning Chronicle, 22 Jun 1841; Morning Post, 22 Jun 1841; London Evening Standard, 22 Jun 1841; Evening Chronicle, 23 Jun 1841; Worcester Journal, 24 Jun 1841; Stamford Mercury, 25 Jun 1841; Bucks Gazette, 26 Jun 1841; Oxford Chronicle and Reading Gazette, 26 Jun 1841; South Wales General Advertiser, 26 Jun 1841; Reading Mercury, 26 Jun 1841; Windsor and Eton Express, 26 Jun 1841; Sherborne Mercury, 28 Jun 1841

Archives

Unopposed Bill C'tee Minutes: 27 May 1841 (p 111): HC/CL/WM/UB/1/1

Unopposed Bill C'tee Minutes: 9 Jun 1841 (p 328); 10 Jun 1841 (p 353–355): 14 Jun 1841 (p 397–399): HL/PO/CO/1/112

Ing: HL/PO/PB/1/1840/4&5V1n91

Notes

Related cases

Stead v Anderson (1846) (NP) 4 HPC 789; 2 WPC 147; 4 CB 813 (136 ER 727); *Stead v Anderson* (1847) (CP) 2 WPC 151; 4 CB 806 (136 ER 724); *Stead v Carey* (1844) (VC) 4 HPC 767; 3 RA 59; *Stead v Carey* (1845) (CP) 1 CB 496 (135 ER 634); *Stead v Williams* (1843) (NP) 4 HPC 729; 2 WPC 123; *Stead v Williams* (1844) (CP) 4 HPC 729; 2 WPC 137; 7 M & G 818 (135 ER 332); *Stead v Williams* (1848) (CP) 5 CB 528 (136 ER 985); *Stead's Patent* (1846) (PC) 4 HPC 783; 2 WPC 143

Metropolitan Patent Wood Paving Company Act 1842

PRVA54	1842
Metropolitan Patent Wood Paving Company Act 1842 (5 Vic Sess 2, c. lxxxv)	
For Regulating Legal Proceedings by or against the Metropolitan Patent Wood Paving Company, and for granting certain Powers thereto	

Table of contents (patent sections only)

s 1 Formation of the Company
s 2 Power for Company to purchase or take licence
s 3 Power for company to grant Licences
s 4 Company may purchase Letters Patent
s 5 Power for Company to grant Licences
s 34 Act not to affect Validity of prior Patents for Wood paving

Relevant patents

27 Jun 1839 (No 8135)	Forms of materials and substances used for building and paving; their combination for such purposes [Richard Hodgson]

Journal

Pet Rep: Joseph Strutt Pres: John Hardy Bill Rep: Lord Seymour	Rep: Earl of Shaftesbury (Ld Ch)

House of Commons			House of Lords		
25 Feb 1842	97 CJ 67	Pet /Ref SC	7 Jun 1842	74 LJ 305	Brought HC/1R
14 Mar 1842	97 CJ 111	Rep/Bill Ord	10 Jun 1842	74 LJ 316	2R/C'tted
15 Mar 1842	97 CJ 116	1R	16 Jun 1842	74 LJ 336	**Rep with Amds**
29 Mar 1842	97 CJ 238	Bill w/d	17 Jun 1842	74 LJ 339	3R
29 Mar 1842	97 CJ 238	Rep Pet//New Bill Ord	21 Jun 1842	74 LJ 350	HC Ag Amds
4 May 1842	97 CJ 253	1R	22 Jun 1842	74 LJ 357	Royal Assent
9 May 1842	97 CJ 265	2R/C'tted			
3 Jun 1842	97 CJ 334	Rep with Amds/Ing			
7 Jun 1842	97 CJ 344	3R			
17 Jun 1842	97 CJ 397	HL pass with Amds			
20 Jun 1842	97 CJ 402	**HL Amds Ag**			
22 Jun 1842	97 CJ 412	Royal Assent			

Representation

R Prosser Jr (Board Member)

Parliamentary debates

1R: HC Deb, 4 May 1842, Vol 63(3rd), col 94	Royal Assent: HL Deb, 22 Jun 1842, Vol 64(3rd), col 422
2R: HC Deb, 9 May 1842, Vol 63(3rd), col 268	
Rep: HC Deb, 3 Jun 1842, Vol 63(3rd), col 1152	
3R: HC Deb, 6 Jun 1842, Vol 63(3rd), col 1238	

Parliamentary papers and cases

None

Gazette notices

London Gazette: 5 Nov 1841 (Iss: 20,034, p 2725); 13 Nov 1841 (Iss: 20,038, p 2822); 17 Nov 1840 (Iss: 20,040, p 2886)

Newspaper coverage of debates

House of Commons

2R: The Times, 10 May 1842; Morning Advertiser, 10 May 1842; Morning Chronicle, 10 May 1842; Morning Post, 10 May 1842; London Evening Standard, 10 May 1842; Dublin Morning Register, 11 May 1842; Newry Telegraph, 12 May 1842; Worcester Journal, 12 May 1842; Downpatrick Recorder, 14 May 1842; Illustrated London News, 14 May 1842; Northern Standard, 14 May 1842; Yorkshire Gazette, 14 May 1842; Windsor and Eton, 14 May 1842; Dublin Evening Packet and Correspondent, 23 Jun 1842; Worcester Journal, 23 Jun 1842

HL Amds Ag: The Times, 21 Jun 1842; Morning Post, 21 Jun 1842; London Evening Standard, 21 Jun 1842

Royal Assent: Morning Advertiser, 23 Jun 1842; Morning Chronicle, 23 Jun 1842; Morning Post, 23 Jun 1842; London Evening Standard, 23 Jun 1842; Dublin Monitor, 24 Jun 1842; Essex Standard, 24 Jun 1842; Freeman's Journal, 24 Jun 1842; Belfast Commercial Chronicle, 25 Jun 1842; Bedfordshire Mercury, 25 Jun 1842; Cambridge Chronicle, 25 Jun 1842; Leamington Spa Courier, 25 Jun 1842; Northern Standard, 25 Jun 1842; Preston Chronicle, 25 Jun 1842; Bell's New Weekly Messenger, 26 Jun 1842; Bell's Weekly Messenger, 27 Jun 1842; Tipperary Free Press, 29 Jun 1842; Enniskillen Chronicle and Erne Packet, 30 Jun 1842; John O'Groats Journal, 1 Jul 1842

(continued)

(continued)

Archives
Unopposed Bill C'tee Minutes: 14 Jun 1842 (p 244–246); 16 Jun 1842 (p 260–261): HL/PO/CO/1/116
Bill (7 Jun 1842): HL/PO/JO/10/8/1404 (No 583a)
Bill (16 Jun 1842): HL/PO/JO/10/8/1408 (No 652a)
Opposed Bill Evidence (1842), Vol 8 [witnesses: Harrison; Prosser; Burton and unnamed (Parliamentary Agents)]: HC/CL/PB/2/8/8

Notes
Related cases
Parkin v Harrison (1840)(VC), 3 HPC 717; 2 CPC 677

Electric Telegraph Company's Act 1846

PRVA55	1846
	Electric Telegraph Company's Act 1846 (9 & 10 Vict. c. xliv)
	An Act for forming and regulating The Electric Telegraph Company, and to enable the said Company to work certain Letters Patents

Table of contents (patent provisions only)
s 4 Company formed for the Purpose of working the Patents, but subject to the Provisions hereinafter contained
s 27 Patents may be assigned to the Company without causing a Forfeiture
s 28 Patents for Improvements may also be assigned
s 29 Assignments to be valid not cause a Forfeiture
s 30 After Assignment the Patents and Privileges to vest in and be exercised by the Company, freed from the Conditions against assignment to more than 12 Persons
s 31 Licence may be granted to the Company without causing a Forfeiture
s 32 Confirmations and Prolongations may be granted to the Company
s 33 Disclaimers may be made under the Seal of the Company [Letters Patent for Inventions Act 1835] 5 & 6 W 4 c. 83
s 34 Power to Company to grant Licences

Relevant patents	
12 Jun 1837 (No 7390)	Giving signals and sounding alarum in distant places, by means of electric-currents transmitted through metallic-circuits [Charles Wheatstone and William Fothergill Cooke] {Scottish patent: 12 Dec 1837; Irish patent: 23 Apr 1838}
18 Apr 1838 (No 7614)	Giving signals and sounding alarum in distant places, by means of electric-currents transmitted through metallic-circuits [William Fothergill Cooke]
21 Jan 1840 (No 8345)	Giving signals and sounding alarum in distant places, by means of electric-currents transmitted through metallic-circuits [Charles Wheatstone and William Fothergill Cooke] {extends to Crown dependencies and colonies} {Scottish patent: 21 Aug 1840; Irish patent: 27 Oct 1840}
7 Jul 1841 (No 9022)	Producing, regulating, and applying electric-currents [Charles Wheatstone]
8 Sep 1842 (No 9465)	Apparatus for transmitting electricity; applicable to apparatus for giving signals and sounding alarums at distant places, by means of electric-currents [William Fothergill Cooke]
6 May 1845 (No 10,655)	Electric-telegraphs and apparatus relating thereto; in part applicable to other Purposes [Charles Wheatstone and William Fothergill Cooke] {extends to Crown dependencies and colonies} {Scottish patent: 3 Jul 1845; Irish patent: 22 Oct 1846}

Journal					
House of Commons			**House of Lords**		
Pres: Joseph Brotherton Rep: Henry Boldero Rep Re-C't: Benjamin Hawes			SO Rep: Earl of Shaftesbury (Ld Ch) Rep: Duke of Bedford		
4 Feb 1846	101 CJ 48	Pet	12 May 1846	78 LJ 392	Brought HC/1R
17 Feb 1846	101 CJ 155	Bill Ord	15 May 1846	78 LJ 407	2R/Ref SOC
18 Feb 1846	101 CJ 162	1R	22 May 1846	78 LJ 454	SOC Rep/Leave
2 Mar 1846	101 CJ 229	2R/C'tted	25 May 1846	78 LJ 461	C'tted SC
3 Mar 1846	101 CJ 245	Pet Ag	26 May 1846	78 LJ 492	SC Named

26 Mar 1846	101 CJ 411	Rep with Amds	8 Jun 1846	78 LJ 539	Rep w/o Amds
1 Apr 1846	101 CJ 450	Cons adj	15 Jun 1846	78 LJ 607	3R
6 Apr 1846	101 CJ 482	Cons adj	18 Jun 1846	78 LJ 641	Royal Assent
21 Apr 1846	101 CJ 519	Cons adj			
27 Apr 1846	101 CJ 567	Cons/Re-C'tted			
4 May 1846	101 CJ 620	Rep with Amds			
8 May 1846	101 CJ 657	Cons			
12 May 1846	101 CJ 680	3R			
18 Jun 1846	101 CJ 894	Royal Assent			
25 Jun 1846	101 CJ 947	HL pass w/o Amds			

Petitions		
3 Mar 1846	101 CJ 245	Alexander Bain

Representation

Solicitor: Pearce, Phillips and Winkworth
Agent: Wilson and Harrison

Parliamentary debates

None

Parliamentary papers and cases

None

Gazette notices

London Gazette: 8 Nov 1845 (Iss: 20,528, p 3549); 15 Nov 1845 (Iss: 20,534, p 4629); 17 Nov 1845 (Iss: 20,535, p 4909)

Edinburgh Gazette: 14 Nov 1845 (Iss: 5483, p 568); 21 Nov 1845 (Iss: 5485, p 672); 28 Nov 1845 (Iss: 5487, p 740)

Dublin Gazette: 7 Nov 1845 (Iss: 13,729, p 668); 14 Nov 1845 (Iss: 13,731, p 727); 21 Nov 1845 (Iss: 13,734, p 1023)

Newspaper coverage of debates

House of Commons

SO cw: London Evening Standard, 17 Feb 1846; Morning Post, 18 February 1846; Exeter and Plymouth Gazette, 21 Feb 1846; Leeds Intelligencer, 21 Feb 1846; Blackburn, 25 Feb 1846

SO Disp: The Times, 14 Mar 1846

2R: The Times, 3 Mar 1846; Globe, 3 Mar 1846; Morning Post, 3 Mar 1846; London Evening Standard, 3 Mar 1846; York Herald, 7 Mar 1846; Reading Mercury, 7 Mar 1846

Rep: Evening Chronicle, 27 Mar 1846; London Daily News, 27 Mar 1846; Reading Mercury, 28 Mar 1846

Cons adj: London Evening Standard, 1 Apr 1846; Morning Post, 2 Apr 1846; Hull Advertiser and Exchange Gazette, 3 Apr 1846; Hull Packet, 3 Apr 1846

Cons adj: **Globe, 6 Apr 1846**; **The Times, 7 Apr 1846**; **Morning Chronicle, 7 Apr 1846**; **Morning Post, 7 Apr 1846**; **London Daily News, 7 Apr 1846**; **London Evening Standard,7 Apr 1846**; *Newry Telegraph, 9 Apr 1846*; *Belfast Commercial Chronicle, 11 Apr 1846*; *Downpatrick Recorder, 11 Apr 1846*; *Enniskillen Chronicle and Erne Packet, 13 Apr 1846*; *Armagh Guardian, 14 Apr 1846*

Cons: The Times, 9 May 1846

Rep/Re-Ct: Globe, 27 Apr 1846; Globe, 28 Apr 1846; Morning Post, 28 Apr 1846; York Herald, 2 May 1846

Rep: Globe, 4 May 1846; Globe, 5 May 1846; Morning Advertiser, 5 May 1846; Morning Chronicle, 5 May 1846; Morning Post, 5 May 1846; London Evening Standard, 5 May 1846

Cons: Globe, 8 May 1846; London Evening Standard, 9 May 1846; Leeds Intelligencer, 9 May 1846; Bell's Weekly Messenger, 9 May 1846; Evening Chronicle, 11 May 1846; Bell's Weekly Messenger, 11 May 1846

3R: Globe, 12 May 1846; The Times, 13 May 1846; Morning Advertiser, 13 May 1846; Morning Post, 13 May 1846; London Daily News, 13 May 1846; London Evening Standard, 13 May 1846; Dublin Evening Packet and Correspondent, 14 May 1846; Worcester Journal, 14 May 1846; Lincolnshire Chronicle, 15 May 1846; Liverpool Mercury, 15 May 1846; Manchester Times, 15 May 1846; Royal Cornwall Gazette, 15 May 1846; Londonderry Sentinel, 16 May 1846; Norwich Mercury, 16 May 1846; Leeds Intelligencer, 16 May 1846; Aris's Birmingham Gazette, 18 May 1846

House of Lords

1R: London Daily News, 14 May 1846

2R: London Daily News, 18 May 1846; Bell's Weekly Messenger, 18 May 1846

C'tee: *York Herald, 6 Jun 1846*; Morning Advertiser, 6 Jun 1846

Royal Assent: The Times 19 Jun 1846; Globe, 19 Jun 1846; Morning Advertiser, 19 Jun 1846; Morning Chronicle, 19 Jun 1846; Morning Post, 19 Jun 1846; London Daily News, 19 Jun 1846; London Evening Standard, 19 Jun 1846; Dublin Evening Packet and Correspondent, 20 Jun 1846; Leeds Intelligencer, 20 Jun 1846; Saunders's News-Letter, 20 Jun 1846; Bell's New Weekly Messenger, 21 Jun 1846; Enniskillen Chronicle and Erne Packet, 22 Jun 1846; Dublin Evening Mail, 22 Jun 1846; Downpatrick Recorder, 27 Jun 1846

(continued)

(continued)

Archives
Minutes Opposed Bill C'tee: 19 Mar 1846 (p 41–47); 20 Mar 1846 (p 48); 23 Mar 1846 (p 49); 24 Mar 1846 (p 50–51); 1 May 1846 (p 52): HC/CL/PB/1/6
SOC Minutes: 19 May 1846 (p 493–494): HL/PO/CO/1/135
SOC Rep: HL/PO/JO/10/8/1569 (No 845)
Rep to form SC: HL/PO/JO/10/8/1570 (No 888)
Wit to Attend: HL/PO/JO/10/8/1572 (No 932a)
Opposed Bill Evidence (1846), Vol 12 [witnesses: Alexander Bain; William Cooke; John Cooper; Edward Cowper; Alfred Deacon; John Finlaison; Maj-Gen Pasley; Robert Wilson; Henry Young;]: HL/CL/PB/2/12/12
Opposed Bill Evidence (1846), Vol 100 [no witnesses identified]: HC/CL/PB/2/12/100

Notes
Related cases
Cooke & Wheatstone's Patent (1851) (PC) 6 HPC 281; 38 Lon J 223; *Electric Telegraph Co v Brett* (1850) (NP) 6 HPC 285; 36 Lon J 130; *Electric Telegraph Co v Brett* (1851) (CP) 10 CB 838 (138 ER 331); *Electric Telegraph Co v Nott* (1847) (VC) 5 HPC 421; 11 Jur 273; *Electric Telegraph Co v Nott* (1847) (LC) 2 Coop 41 (47 ER 1040); *Electric Telegraph Co v Nott* (1847) (CP) 4 CB 462 (136 ER 587)

Claridge's Patent Asphalt Company Act 1847

PRVA56	1847		
Claridge's Patent Asphalt Company Act 1847(10 & 11 Vict. c. xxxv)			
An Act for regulating legal Proceedings by or against "Claridge's Patent Asphalte Company," and for granting certain Powers thereto			
Table of contents (patent provisions only)			
s 1 Power for Company to take or purchase Licences s 2 Company may take or purchase Letters Patent or any of them s 3 Company may grant Licences			
Relevant patent			
25 Nov 1837 (No 7489)	Mastic cement, applicable to paving and road-making, covering buildings, and various other purposes [Richard Tappin Claridge] {Scottish patent: 27 Mar 1838; Irish patent: 23 Apr 1838}		
Journal			
House of Commons		**House of Lords**	
Pres: Joseph Brotherton Rep: Thomas Greene (Ch W&M)		Rep: Earl of Shaftesbury (Ld Ch)	

22 Feb 1847	102 CJ 134	Pet/Bill Ord	6 May 1847	79 LJ 184	Brought HC/1R
23 Feb 1847	102 CJ 140	1R	10 May 1847	79 LJ 193	2R/C'tted
19 Mar 1847	102 CJ 263	2R/C'tted	17 May 1847	79 LJ 218	**Rep with Amds**
29 Apr 1847	102 CJ 427	Rep with Amds/Ing	18 May 1847	79 LJ 231	3R
5 May 1847	102 CJ 480	3R	3 Jun 1847	79 LJ 288	HC Ag Amd
19 May 1847	102 CJ 543	HL pass with Amds	8 Jun 1847	79 LJ 316	Royal Assent
1 Jun 1847	102 CJ 603	**HL Amds Cons**			
8 Jun 1847	102 CJ 635	Royal Assent			

Representation
Solicitor: Hodgson and Burton

Parliamentary debates
None

Parliamentary papers and cases
None

Gazette notices
London Gazette: 7 Nov 1846 (Iss: 20,658, p 3946); 14 Nov 1846 (Iss: 20,665, p 4478); 18 Nov 1846 (Iss: 20,668, p 4798); 28 Nov 1846 (Iss: 20,677, p 5672)
Edinburgh Gazette: 17 Nov 1846 (Iss: 5591, p 555); 24 Nov 1846 (Iss: 5593, p 636); 30 Nov 1846 (Iss: 5595, p 705)
Dublin Gazette: 13 Nov 1846 (Iss: 13,844, p 1229); 17 Nov 1846 (Iss: 13,846, p 1295); 27 Nov 1846 (Iss: 13,849, p 1359)

Newspaper coverage of debates
House of Commons
SO cw: Globe, 19 Feb 1847
2R: Globe, 19 Mar 1847; The Times, 20 Mar 1847; Globe, 20 Mar 1847; Morning Post, 20 Mar 1847; London Daily News, 20 Mar 1847; London Evening Standard, 20 Mar 1847; Downpatrick Recorder, 27 Mar 1847; Sherbourne Mercury, 27 Mar 1847
Rep: The Times, 30 Apr 1847; Globe, 30 Apr 1847; Morning Advertiser, 30 Apr 1847; Morning Post, 30 Apr 1847; Evening Chronicle, 30 Apr 1847; London Daily News, 30 Apr 1847; London Evening Standard, 30 Apr 1847
3R: Globe, 5 May 1847; London Evening Standard, 5 May 1847; Morning Advertiser, 6 May 1847; Morning Post, 6 May 1847; London Daily News, 6 May 1847; Liverpool Mercury, 7 May 1847
HL pass with Amds: Globe, 21 May 1847; The Times, 22 May 1847; Globe, 22 May 1847; Morning Post, 22 May 1847; London Evening Standard, 22 May 1847; Bell's New Weekly Messenger, 23 May 1847
HL Amds Ag: The Times, 2 Jun 1847; Morning Post, 2 Jun 1847
Royal Assent: London Daily News, 9 Jun 1847; London Evening Standard, 9 Jun 1847

Archives
Unopposed C'tee Minutes: 14 May 1847 (p 92–95): HL/PO/CO/1/140

Notes
Related Cases:
Claridge v Latrade (1840) (NP) 3 HPC 529; 15 Lon J 451; *Claridge's Patent* (1851) (PC) 6 HPC 277; 7 Moo PCC 394 (13 ER 932)
Aborted Bills
There appears to be a Bill to regulate the company (but no mention of patents) proposed for the earlier session: London Gazette: 7 Nov 1845 (Iss: 20,527, p 3467); 10 Nov 1845 (Iss: 20,529, p 3660); 17 Nov 1845 (Iss: 20,535, p 4849)

Timber Preserving Company's Act 1847

PRVA57	1847
Timber Preserving Company's Act 1847 (10 & 11 Vict. c. ccxcvi)	
An Act for forming and regulating "The Timber-preserving Company;" and to enable the said Company to purchase and work certain Letters Patents. [Payne's Patent Assignment]	

Table of contents (patent provisions only)
s 3 Company incorporated for the Purposes of working the Patents, but subject to the Provisions hereinafter contained
s 25 Patents may be assigned to the Company
s 26 Assignments, &c not to cause a Forfeiture
s 27 After Assignment the Patents and Privileges to vest in and be exercised by Company freed from the Conditions against Assignment to more than Twelve Persons
s 28 License may be granted to Company without causing a Forfeiture

Relevant patents	
9 Jul 1841 (No 9025)	Preserving vegetable matters where metallic and earthy solutions are employed [Charles Payne] {extended to Crown dependencies and colonies}
29 Jun 1846 (No 11,265)	Preserving vegetable matters [Charles Payne] {extended to Crown dependencies and colonies}

Journal	
House of Commons	**House of Lords**
Pres: John Masterman Rep: Thomas Greene (Ch W&M)	Rep: Earl of Shaftesbury (Ld Ch)

(continued)

(continued)

22 Feb 1847	102 CJ 135	Pet/Bill Ord	1 Jun 1847	79 LJ 265	Brought from HC/1R
18 Mar 1847	102 CJ 258	1R	4 Jun 1847	79 LJ 292	2R/C'tted
23 Apr 1847	102 CJ 401	2R/C'tted	11 Jun 1847	79 LJ 350	**Rep with Amds**
17 May 1847	102 CJ 531	Rep with Amds	14 Jun 1847	79 LJ 357	3R
21 May 1847	102 CJ 553	Cons/Ing	16 Jul 1847	79 LJ 752	HC Ag Amds
31 May 1847	102 CJ 585	3R	22 Jul 1847	79 LJ 796	Royal Assent
14 Jun 1847	102 CJ 674	HL pass with Amds			
9 Jul 1847	102 CJ 839	**HL Amds Cons**			
22 Jul 1847	102 CJ 954	Royal Assent			

Representation

Solicitor: Macdougall & Co

Parliamentary debates

None

Parliamentary papers and cases

1847–48 Returns of the number of private bills introduced, and brought from the House of Lords, and of acts passed, in 1847–48; of private and railway bills treated as opposed by the Committee of Selection; and of unopposed private and railway bills referred to the Committee of Ways and Means (1847–48 HC Papers 739), Vol 51, p 1 at 9 [entry that Bill unopposed]

Gazette notices

London Gazette: 14 Nov 1846 (Iss: 20,665, p 4396); 21 Nov 1846 (Iss: 20,671, p 4924); 28 Nov 1846 (Iss: 20,677, p 5502)

Newspaper coverage of debates

House of Commons

2R: Globe, 23 Apr 1847; Globe, 24 Apr 1847; Morning Advertiser, 24 Apr 1847; London Daily News, 24 Apr 1847; Hull Packet, 30 Apr 1847; Downpatrick Recorder, 1 May 1847

Rep (not in CJ): Globe, 13 May 1847; The Times, 14 May 1847; Globe, 14 May 1847; Morning Post, 14 May 1847; Evening Chronicle, 14 May 1847; London Daily News, 14 May 1847; Bolton Chronicle, 15 May 1847

Rep: Globe, 17 May 1847; The Times, 18 May 1847; Globe, 18 May 1847; Morning Post, 18 May 1847; London Daily News, 18 May 1847; London Evening Standard, 18 May 1837; Evening Chronicle, 19 May 1847

Cons: Globe, 21 May 1847; The Times, 22 May 1847; Globe, 22 May 1847; Morning Post, 22 May 1847; London Evening Standard, 22 May 1847; Evening Chronicle, 24 May 1847

3R: Globe, 31 May 1847; The Times, 1 Jun 1847; Globe, 1 Jun 1847; Morning Post, 1 Jun 1847; London Daily News, 1 Jun 1847; London Evening Standard, 1 Jun 1847

HL Amds: The Times, 10 Jul 1847; Morning Post, 10 Jul 1847; London Evening Standard, 10 Jul 1847

Royal Assent: The Times, 23 Jul 1847; Morning Post, 23 Jul 1847; London Daily News, 23 Jul 1847; London Evening Standard, 23 Jul 1847; Liverpool Mercury, 23 Jul 1847

Archives

Bill (11 Jun 1847): HL/PO/JO/10/8/1641 (No 834)

Minutes Opposed Bill C'tee: 3 Jul 1839 (3 pages – no page numbers): HC/CL/PB/1/1

C'tee Minutes: 10 Jun 1847 (p 202–203): HL/PO/CO/1/140

Notes

Related cases

Payne v Banner (1846) (LC) 5 HPC 335; 15 LJ Ch 227; *Payne's Patent* (1854) (PC) 7 HPC 91

Price's Patent Candle Company's Act 1848

PRVA58	1848
Prices Patent Candle Company's Act 1848 (11 & 12 Vict. c. xx)	

An Act for the Incorporation, Establishment, and Regulation of "Price's Patent Candle Company," and for enabling the said Company to purchase and work Letters Patent

Table of contents (patent provisions only)

s 29 Recited Patents may be assigned to the Company
s 30 Assignments to be valid and not cause a Forfeiture
s 31 After Assignment, the Patents and Privileges to vest in an be exercised by the Company, free from the Conditions against Assignment to more than Twelve Persons
s 32 Licences may be granted to the Company without occasioning a Forfeiture

s 33 Confirmation and Prolongation may be granted to the Company
s 34 Disclaimers may be made under the Seal of the Company
s 35 Power of Company to grant Licences

15 Sep 1836 (No 7184)	Operating under certain vegetable and animal Substances in the process of manufacturing candles therefrom [John Fredrick William Hempel and Henry Blundell] {Scottish patent: 7 Dec 1837; Irish patent: 20 Dec 1837}
26 Oct 1837 (No 7451)	Preparation of palm-oil for use in woollen manufactures, for lubricating of machinery, and other purposes [Miles Berry] {extended to colonies}
29 Sept 1842 (No 9479)	Treating certain animal matters to obtain products applicable to the making of candles, and to other purposes [William Smith] {extended to Channel Islands and colonies}
8 Nov 1842 (No 9510)	Treating an unctuous substance to obtain products therefrom for manufacturing candles, and for other purposes [William Coley Jones] {extended to Crown dependencies and colonies; Scottish patent: 7 Dec 1842: Irish patent: 29 Dec 1842}
8 Dec 1842 (No 9542)	Operating on certain organic bodies to obtain products therefrom for manufacturing candles, and other purposes [William Coley Jones and George Fergusson Wilson] {extended to Channel Islands and colonies; Scottish patent: 7 Dec 1842; Irish patent: 13 Dec 1842}
16 Nov 1843 (No 9944)	Manufacture of candles; apparatus for and processes of treating fatty and other substance for making candles and for other Uses [George Gwynee and George Fergusson Wilson] {extended to Channel Islands and colonies; Scottish patent: 29 Dec 1843; Irish patent: 15 Feb 1844}
28 Dec 1843 (No 10,000)	Manufacture of candles; treating fatty and oily matters to obtain products for the manufacture of candles and for other uses [George Gwynee and George Fergusson Wilson] {extended to Channel Islands and colonies}
20 May 1844 (No 10,191)	Treating certain fatty or oily matters; manufacture of candles and soap [George Gwynee and George Fergusson Wilson] {extended to Channel Islands and colonies; Scottish patent: 22 Jul 1844; Irish patent: 21 Oct 1844}
29 Aug 1844 (No 10,294)	Treating fatty and oily matters; manufacture of candles [James Pillans Wilson] {extended to Channel Islands and colonies; Scottish patent: 4 Sep 1844}
9 Sep 1844 (No 10,306)	Treating fatty and oily matters; manufacture of candles [James Pillans Wilson] {extended to Channel Islands and colonies}
29 Oct 1844 (No 10,365)	Manufacture of night-lights [George Gwynee, George Fergusson Wilson and James Pillans Wilson] {extended to Channel Islands and colonies; Scottish patent: 11 Nov 1844; Irish patent: 26 Nov 1844}
31 Oct 1844 (No 10,371)	Treating fatty and oily matters; and making candles [George Gwynee, George Fergusson Wilson and James Pillans Wilson] {extended to Channel Islands and colonies}
12 Dec 1844 (No 10,435)	Treating fatty and oily matters, manufacture of candles [George Gwynee, George Fergusson Wilson and James Pillans Wilson] {extended to Channel Islands and colonies}
13 Mar 1845 (No 10,551)	Manufacture of candles when palm-oil is used [George Gwynee, George Fergusson Wilson and James Pillans Wilson] {extended to Channel Islands and colonies}
10 May 1845 (No 10,664)	Treating certain inflammable matters, manufacture of candles and soap [George Gwynee, George Fergusson Wilson and James Pillans Wilson] {extended to Channel Islands and colonies}
10 Oct 1845 (No 10,870)	Manufacture of Soap [George Gwynee, George Fergusson Wilson and James Pillans Wilson] {extended to Channel Islands and colonies}
27 Oct 1845 (No 10,899)	Manufacture of candles [Samuel Childs] {extended to Channel Islands and colonies; Scottish patent: 10 Dec 1845}
20 Dec 1845 (No 11,008)	Treating inflammable matters, manufacture of candles [George Gwynee, George Fergusson Wilson and James Pillans Wilson] {extended to Channel Islands and colonies}
1 Dec 1846 (No 11,470)	Processes of and Apparatus for treating fatty and oily matters; and manufacturing candles and night lights [George Fergusson Wilson and John Jackson] {extended to Channel Islands and colonies; Scottish patent: 24 Dec 1846; Irish patent: 17 Feb 1847}
23 Mar 1847 (No 11,633)	Production of light manufacture or preparation of materials applicable thereto [George Fergusson Wilson] {extended to Channel Islands and colonies; Scottish patent: 6 Apr 1847; Irish patent: 4 Jun 1847}

(continued)

(continued)

Journal					
House of Commons			**House of Lords**		
Pres: William Cripps Rep: Lord Hotham			Rep: Earl of Shaftesbury (Ld Ch)		
3 Feb 1848	103 CJ 141	Pet/Bill Ord	19 Apr 1848	80 LJ 203	Brought HC
4 Feb 1848	103 CJ 164	1R	19 Apr 1848	80 LJ 204	1R/Ref SOC
14 Feb 1848	103 CJ 214	2R/C'tted	9 May 1848	80 LJ 250	SOC Rep/Leave
22 Feb 1848	103 CJ 251	Pet Ag × 2	15 May 1848	80 LJ 266	2R/C'tted
10 Apr 1848	103 CJ 431	Rep with Amds	23 May 1848	80 LJ 306	**Rep with Amds**
14 Apr 1848	103 CJ 444	Cons/Ing	30 May 1848	80 LJ 319	3R
18 Apr 1848	103 CJ 455	3R	2 Jun 1848	80 LJ 332	HC Ag Amds
30 May 1848	103 CJ 579	HL pass with Amds	9 Jun 1848	80 LJ 365	Royal Assent
1 Jun 1848	103 CJ 583	**HL Amds Cons**			
9 Jun 1848	103 CJ 615	Royal Assent			

Petitions		
22 Feb 1848	103 CJ 251	Charles Humphrey
22 Feb 1848	103 CJ 251	Warren Stormes Hall and Others

Representation

Solicitor: Wilson and Harrison

Parliamentary debates

None

Parliamentary papers and cases

None

Gazette notices

London Gazette: 17 Nov 1847 (Iss: 20,794, p 4136)
Edinburgh Gazette: 16 Nov 1847 (Iss: 5697, p 580)
Dublin Gazette: 12 Nov 1847 (Iss: 13,969, p 1258)

Newspaper coverage of debates

House of Commons

Dep to BoT: Globe, 12 Feb 1848; Morning Advertiser, 12 Feb 1848; Morning Chronicle, 12 Feb 1848; Morning Post, 12 Feb 1848

2R: The Times, 15 Feb 1848; Morning Advertiser, 15 Feb 1848; London Daily News, 15 Feb 1848; Greenock Advertiser, 18 Fen 1848

Com nom: Morning Chronicle, 22 Mar 1848; Morning Post, 22 Mar 1848

Rep: London Evening Standard, 14 Apr 1848

3R: The Times, 19 Apr 1848; Globe, 19 Apr 1848; Evening Mail, 19 Apr 1848; London Evening Standard, 19 Apr 1848; Caledonian Mercury, 20 Apr 1848; Bell's Weekly Messenger, 24 Apr 1848

HL Amds: London Evening Standard, 2 Jun 1848; London Daily News, 2 Jun 1848

Royal Assent: The Times, 10 Jun 1848; Globe, 10 Jun 1848; Morning Chronicle, 10 Jun 1848; Morning Post, 10 Jun 1848; London Evening Standard, 10 Jun 1848; Caledonian Mercury, 12 Jun 1848; Dublin Evening Mail, 12 Jun 1848; Hull Packet, 16 Jun 1848

Archives

Minutes Opposed Bill C'tee: 31 Mar 1848 (p 297); 3 Apr 1848 (p 299); 4 Apr 1848 (p 301); 5 Apr 1848 (p 305–306); 7 Apr 1848 (p 307–311): HC/CL/PB/1/8

SOC Minutes: 9 May 1848 (p 22–23): HL/PO/CO/1/147

SOC Rep: HL/PO/JO/10/8/1673 (No 500)

Unopposed Bill C'tee Minutes: 18 Mar 1848 (p 51–54); 19 May 1848 (p 57–58); HL/PO/CO/1/145

Bill (19 Apr 1848): HL/PO/JO/10/8/1670 (No 440)

Opposed Bill Evidence (1847–48), Vol 12 [witnesses: Edward Beach; John Bristow; William Carpmael; John Cooper; Matthew Davies; Warren Hales; Warren Hales Jr; William Hawes; William Hawes; William Hayward; Charles Humpey; William Hutton; Willian Jackson; Benjamin Lancaster; William Marchant; Robert Penny; Scott Alexander; Thomas Sturge; Robert Wilson]: HC/CL/PB/2/15/12

Notes

There was a further Act to acquire patents in 1851 (PRVA66)

Patent Galvanized Iron Company's Enabling Act 1848

PRVA59	1848
	Patent Galvanized Iron Company's Enabling Act 1848 (11 & 12 Vict. c. xlvii)
	An Act for enabling "The Patent Galvanized Iron Company" to purchase and work certain Letters Patent

Table of contents (patent provisions only)

s 6 Recited Patents may be assigned to the Company
s 7 Other Patent may be assigned to the Company
s 8 Assignments of Patents not to cause Forfeiture
s 9 After Assignments Patent's Rights may be exercised by the Company
s 10 Power for Company to grant Licences
s 11 Licences may be granted to the Company without causing Forfeiture
s 12 Disclaimers may be made under the Seal of the Company

Relevant patents

29 Apr 1837 (No 7355)	Coating iron and copper for the prevention of oxidation [Henry William Craufurd]
5 May 1838 (No 7635)	Preventing the oxydation of metals [Pierre Fontainmemoreau, Le Comte de Armand]

Journal

House of Commons			House of Lords		
Pres: James Clay Rep: Lord Hotham			Rep: Earl of Shaftsbury (Ld Ch)		
7 Feb 1848	103 CJ 177	Pet/Bill Ord	11 May 1848	80 LJ 252	Brought HC/1R/Ref SOC
8 Feb 1848	103 CJ 189	1R	18 May 1848	80 LJ 286	SOC Rep/Leave
21 Feb 1848	103 CJ 239	2R/C'tted	23 May 1848	80 LJ 302	2R/C'tted
1 Mar 1848	103 CJ 280	Pet Ag	9 Jun 1848	80 LJ 369	**Rep with Amds**
31 Mar 1848	103 CJ 395	Rep with Amds	15 Jun 1848	80 LJ 376	3R
17 Apr 1848	103 CJ 448	Cons/Ing	19 Jun 1848	80 LJ 391	HC Ag Amds
9 May 1848	103 CJ 495	3R	30 Jun 1848	80 LJ 461	Royal Assent
15 Jun 1848	103 CJ 621	HL pass with Amds			
19 Jun 1848	103 CJ 628	**HL Amds Cons adj**			
19 Jun 1848	103 CJ 628	**HL Amds Cons**			
30 Jun 1848	103 CJ 672	Royal Assent			

Petition

1 Mar 1848	103 CJ 280	Henry Patteson

Representation

Solicitor: Goodwin, Partridge, Williams and Edwards

Parliamentary debates

None

Parliamentary papers and cases

None

Gazette notices

London Gazette: 13 Nov 1847 (Iss: 20,792, p 4079)

Newspaper coverage of debates

House of Commons

Com nom: The Times, 22 Feb 1848; Morning Chronicle, 22 Mar 1848; Morning Post, 22 Mar 1848

2R: The Times, 22 Feb 1848; Globe, 22 Feb 1848; Morning Chronicle, 22 Feb 1848; London Daily News, 22 Feb 1848; London Evening Standard, 22 Feb 1848; Aris's Birmingham Gazette, 28 Feb 1848

Pet Ag: Morning Advertiser, 2 Mar 1848; Morning Chronicle, 2 Mar 1848; Morning Post, 2 Mar 1848; London Daily News, 2 Mar 1848; Wolverhampton Chronicle and Staffordshire Advertiser, 8 Mar 1848

Pets W/D: Morning Advertiser, 25 Mar 1848; Birmingham Journal, 25 Mar 1848

Rep: London Daily News, 18 Apr 1848

(continued)

(continued)

3R: The Times, 10 May 1848; Morning Advertiser, 10 May 1848; Morning Chronicle, 10 May 1848; London Evening Standard, 10 May 1848; Caledonian Mercury, 11 May 1848; Reading Mercury, 13 May 1848; Wolverhampton Chronicle and Staffordshire Advertiser, 17 May 1848

HL Amd Cons: Morning Chronicle, 20 Jun 1848; London Daily News, 20 Jun 1848; London Evening Standard, 20 Jun 1848; Caledonian Mercury, 22 Jun 1848; Aris's Birmingham Gazette, 26 Jun 1848

Royal Assent: The Times, 1 Jul 1848; Globe, 1 Jul 1848; Morning Advertiser, 1 Jul 1848; Morning Chronicle, 1 Jul 1848; Morning Post, 1 Jul 1848; London Evening Standard, 1 Jul 1848; Bell's Life in London and Sporting Chronicle, 2 Jul 1848; Aris's Birmingham Gazette, 3 Jul 1848; Wolverhampton Chronicle and Staffordshire Advertiser, 5 Jul 1848; Eddowes's Journal, 5 Jul 1848

Archives
Minutes Opposed Bill C'tee: Feb 28 and Mar 1 (p 293–295): HC/CL/PB/1/8
SOC Minutes: 16 May 1847 (p 33–34): HL/PO/CO/1/147
Unopposed Bill C'tee Minutes: 25 May 1848 (p 78); 30 May 1848 (p 86–88); 2 Jun 1848 (p 91–93); 8 Jun 1848 (p 99): HL/PO/CO/1/145
Opposed Bill Evidence (1847–48), Vol 12 [witnesses: Samuel Fry; Charles Jones (Solicitor); William Malins; Morewood (Petitioner); Rogers (Petitioner); unnamed]: HC/CL/PB/2/15/12

Notes
Related cases
Patteson v Holland (1844) (VC) 4 HPC 999; 24 Lon J 457; *Patteron v Holland* (1845) (CP) Hind 293
Related Act
Galvanized Iron Company's Dissolution Act 1848 (11 & 12 Vict. c. ciii)

Low's Patent Copper Company Act 1848

PRVA60	1848

Low's Patent Copper Company Act 1848 (11 & 12 Vict. c. cv)
An Act to enable Low's Patent Copper Company to work certain Letters Patent [Low's Patent]

Table of contents (patent provisions only)
s 1 Patent may be assigned to the Company without causing a Forfeiture
s 2 Patents for Improvements may also be assigned
s 3 Assignments to be valid, and not cause a Forfeiture; After Assignment, the Patents and Privileges to be freed from the Conditions against Assignment to more than Twelve Persons
s 4 Licences may be granted to the Company without causing a Forfeiture
s 5 Disclaimers may be made under the Seal of the Company [Letters Patent for Inventions Act 1835] 5 & 6 W 4. c. 83; [Judicial Committee Act 1844] 7 & 8 Vict. c. 69
s 6 Power to grant Licences

Relevant patent	
4 Nov 1847 (No 11,939)	Manufacture of zinc, copper, tin, and other metals [Charles Low]

Journal					
House of Commons			**House of Lords**		
Pres: John Masterman Rep: Ralph Bernal (Ch W&M)			Rep: Earl of Shaftesbury (Ld Ch)		
3 Feb 1848	103 CJ 145	Pet/Bill Ord	8 Jun 1848	80 LJ 357	Brought HC/1R/Ref SOC
7 Feb 1848	103 CJ 178	1R	19 Jun 1848	80 LJ 388	SOC Rep/Leave
18 Feb 1848	103 CJ 232	2R/C'tted	26 Jun 1848	80 LJ 419	2R/C'tted
23 May 1848	103 CJ 550	**Rep with Amds**	30 Jun 1848	80 LJ 456	Rep w/o Amds
30 May 1848	103 CJ 575	Cons/Ing	4 Jul 1848	80 LJ 479	3R
7 Jun 1848	103 CJ 601	3R	22 Jul 1848	80 LJ 633	Royal Assent
4 Jul 1848	103 CJ 682	HL pass w/o Amds			
22 Jul 1848	103 CJ 769	Royal Assent			

Representation
Solicitor: Prile and Son

Parliamentary debates
None
Parliamentary papers and cases
None
Gazette notices
London Gazette: 27 Nov 1847 (Iss: 20,800, p 4429)
Newspaper coverage of debates

House of Commons

2R: The Times, 19 Feb 1848; Globe, 19 Feb 1848; Morning Chronicle, 19 Feb 1848; London Daily News, 19 Feb 1848; London Evening Standard, 19 Feb 1848; Evening Mail, 21 Feb 1848

Rep: The Times, 31 May 1848; Morning Chronicle, 31 May 1848; London Daily News, 31 May 1848; London Evening Standard, 31 May 1848

3R: Morning Post, 8 Jun 1848; London Daily News, 8 Jun 1848

Royal Assent: The Times, 24 Jul 1848; Morning Chronicle, 24 Jul 1848; Morning Post, 24 Jul 1848; Evening Mail, 24 July 1848; London Daily News, 24 Jul 1848; Carlisle Post, 29 Jul 1848

Archives

SOC Minutes: 16 Jun 1848 (p 140): HL/PO/CO/1/147

SOC Rep: HL/PO/JO/10/8/1681 (No 802)

Unopposed Bill C'tee Minutes: 29 Jun 1848 (p 146–147): HL/PO/CO/1/145

Timber Preserving Company's Extension Act 1848

PRVA61	1848
Timber Preserving Company's Extension Act 1848 (11 & 12 Vict. c. cxlix)	
An Act to enable "The Timber Preserving Company" to purchase and work certain Letters Patent, and for confirming the same [Payne's Patent]	

Table of contents (patent provisions only)

s 15 Assignment of Letters Patent [for Scotland and Ireland]
s 16 Letters Patent to continue valid notwithstanding the Assignment
s 17 Company may enjoy Patents free from Conditions against Assignment
s 18 Company may buy up Licences granted to other Persons
s 19 Company may grant Licences
s 20 Enrolment of certain Specifications of Inventions not to be deemed Publications of the same

Relevant patents	
Scots and Irish only	Improvements in preserving vegetable Matters where metallic and earthy Solutions are employed [Charles Payne] {Scottish patent: 13 Mar 1843; Irish patent: 12 Aug 1843} Improvements in preserving vegetable Matters [Charles Payne] {Scottish patent: 30 Dec 1846; Irish patent: 27 Feb 1847}

Journal					
House of Commons			**House of Lords**		
Pres: James Clay Rep: Ralph Bernal (Ch W&M)			Rep: Earl of Shaftesbury (Ld Ch)		
7 Feb 1848	103 CJ 178	Pet/Bill Ord	30 May 1848	80 LJ 321	Brought HC/1R/Ref SOC
8 Feb 1848	103 CJ 189	1R	6 Jun 1848	80 LJ 347	SOC Rep/Leave
18 Feb 1848	103 CJ 232	2R/C'tted	15 Jun 1848	80 LJ 375	2R/C'tted
17 May 1848	103 CJ 527	Rep with Amds	13 Jul 1848	80 LJ 563	**Rep with Amds**
23 May 1848	103 CJ 552	Cons/Ing	18 Jul 1848	80 LJ 592	3R
29 May 1848	103 CJ 569	3R	25 Jul 1848	80 LJ 680	HC Ag Amds
20 Jul 1848	103 CJ 755	HL pass with Amds	14 Aug 1848	80 LJ 789	Royal Assent
22 Jul 1848	103 CJ 767	HL Amds Cons adj			
24 Jul 1848	103 CJ 774	**HL Amds Cons**			
14 Aug 1848	103 CJ 920	Royal Assent			

(continued)

(continued)

Representation
Solicitor: Goodwin, Partridge, Williams & Edwards
Parliamentary debates
None
Parliamentary papers and cases
None
Gazette notices
London Gazette: 13 Nov 1847 (Iss: 20,792, p 4063) Edinburgh Gazette: 16 Nov 1847 (Iss: 5697, p 598) Dublin Gazette: 12 Nov 1847 (Iss: 13,969, p 1257)
Newspaper coverage of debates

House of Commons

2R: The Times, 19 Feb 1848; Globe, 19 Feb 1848; London Evening Standard, 19 Feb 1848; Evening Mail, 21 Feb 1848

Rep: London Daily News, 24 May 1848; London Evening Standard, 24 May 1848

3R: London Daily News, 30 May 1848;

Royal Assent: The Times, 15 Aug 1848; Morning Chronicle, 15 Aug 1848; Morning Post, 15 Aug 1848; London Daily News, 15 Aug 1848; London Evening Standard, 15 Aug 1848

Archives
Bill (30 May 1848): HL/PO/JO/10/8/1676 (No 629)
SOC Minutes: 5 Jun 1848 (p 97): HL/PO/CO/1/147
SOC Rep: HL/PO/JO/10/8/1677 (No 708)
Unopposed Bill C'tee Minutes: 23 Jun 1848 (p 136–138); 27 Jun 1848 (p 143); 30 Jun 1848 (p 148); 11 Jul 1848 (p 205–207): HL/PO/CO/1/145

Westhead's Patent Act 1849

PRVA62	1849
Westhead's Patent Act 1849 (12 & 13 Vict. c. xlix)	
An Act for rendering valid certain Letters Patent granted to Joshua Procter Westhead of Manchester, Manufacturer	

Table of contents
s 1 Letters Patent confirmed [specification inroled 13 December, deadline 8 December 1848] s 2 Public Act

Relevant patent	
8 Jun 1848 (No 12,179)	Manufacturing fur into fabrics [Joshua Procter Westhead]

Journal

House of Commons			House of Lords		
Pres: John Wilson Pattern Rep: Ralph Bernal (Ch W&M)			Reps: Earl of Shaftesbury (Ld Ch)		
26 Mar 1849	104 CJ 174	Pet for Bill	15 Jun 1849	81 LJ 300	Brought HC/1R/Ref SOC
3 Apr 1849	104 CJ 197	Leave granted	21 Jun 1849	81 LJ 340	SOC Rep/Leave
19 Apr 1849	104 CJ 214	**Pet for further time**	26 Jun 1849	81 LJ 355	2R/C'tted
23 Apr 1849	104 CJ 223	Leave to deposit forthwith	29 Jun 1849	81 LJ 371	**Rep w/o Amd**
2 May 1849	104 CJ 255	Ex Rep ref SOC	6 Jul 1849	81 LJ 404	3R
2 May 1849	104 CJ 256	Pet to SOC	13 Jul 1849	81 LJ 431	Royal Assent
4 May 1849	104 CJ 263	Rep SO Disp			
4 May 1849	104 CJ 265	Bill Ord			
7 May 1849	104 CJ 268	1R			
14 May 1849	104 CJ 290	2R/C'tted			
5 Jun 1849	104 CJ 357	**Rep with Amds**			
11 Jun 1849	104 CJ 372	Cons/Ing			
14 Jun 1849	104 CJ 386	3R			
6 Jul 1849	104 CJ 465	HL pass w/o Ands			
13 Jul 1849	104 CJ 490	Royal Assent			

Representation
Solicitor: Goodwin, Partridge, Williams and Edwards
Parliamentary debates
None
Parliamentary papers and cases
None
Gazette notices
London Gazette: 8 May 1849 (Iss: 20,976, p 1532)
Newspaper coverage of debates

House of Commons

2R: The Times, 15 May 1849; Morning Post, 15 May 1849; London Daily News, 15 May 1849

Cons: The Times, 12 Jun 1849; Morning Advertiser, 12 Jun 1849; Morning Post,12 Jun 1849; London Daily News, 12 Jun 1849; London Evening Standard, 12 Jun 1849

3R: Morning Advertiser, 15 Jun 1849; Morning Post, 15 Jun 1849; Evening Mail, 15 Jun 1849; London Daily News, 15 Jun 1849; London Evening Standard, 15 Jun 1849

House of Lords

Rep: The Times, 1 Jul 1848

3R: London Daily News, 7 Jul 1849

Royal Assent: The Times, 14 Jul 1849; Morning Chronicle, 14 Jul 1849; Morning Post, 14 Jul 1849; London Daily News, 14 Jul 1849; London Evening Standard, 14 Jul 1849; Dublin Evening Mail, 16 Jul 1849

Archives
SOC Minutes: 19 Jun 1849 (p 144–145): HL/PO/CO/1/152
Unopposed Bill C'tee Minutes: 28 Jun 1849 (p 164–165): HL/PO/CO/1/155

British Electric Telegraph Company's Act 1850

PRVA63	1850
British Electric Telegraph Company's Act 1850 (13 & 14 Vict. c. lxxxvi)	
An Act for forming and regulating the British Electric Telegraph Company, and to enable the said Company to work certain Letters Patent	

Table of contents (patent provisions only)
s 4 Company formed for the Purposes of working the Patents, but subject to the Provisions herein contained

s 28 Patents may be assigned to the Company without causing a Forfeiture
s 29 Patents for Improvements may also be assigned
s 30 Assignments to be valid, and not cause a Forfeiture
s 31 After the Assignment, the Patents and Privileges to vest in and be exercised by the Company, freed from the Conditions against Assignment to more than 12 Persons
s 32 Licences may be granted to the Company without causing a Forfeiture
s 33 This Act not to give Validity to Patents
s 36 Confirmations and Prolongations may be granted to the Company
s 37 Disclaimers may be made under the Seal of the Company [Letters Patent for Inventions Act 1835] 5 & 6 W 4 c. 83
s 38 Power to Company to grant Licences

Relevant patent	
25 Jan 1848 (No 12,039)	Electric-telegraphs [Edward Highton and Henry Highton] {Scottish patent: 31 Jul 1848; Irish patent: 8 Nov 1848}

Journal	
House of Commons	**House of Lords**
Pres: James Farrer	Rep: Earl of Shaftesbury (Ld Ch)
Rep: George Cornwall Legh	

(continued)

(continued)

8 Feb 1850	105 CJ 42	Pet/Bill Ord	17 Jun 1850	82 LJ 220	Brought HC/1R/Ref SOC
11 Feb 1850	105 CJ 50	1R	24 Jun 1850	82 LJ 240	SOC Rep/Leave
22 Feb 1850	105 CJ 90 – V	2R/C'tted	25 Jun 1850	82 LJ 246	Pet Ag
5 Jun 1850	105 CJ 400	Rep with Amds	27 Jun 1850	82 LJ 252	Pet Fav
10 Jun 1850	105 CJ 413	Cons	28 Jun 1850	82 LJ 255	2R/C'tted
14 Jun 1850	105 CJ 434	3R	2 Jul 1850	82 LJ 269	Pet Fav
23 Jul 1850	105 CJ 556	HL pass w/o Amds	4 Jul 1850	82 LJ 272	SC app
29 Jul 1850	105 CJ 580	Royal Assent	5 Jul 1850	82 LJ 276	Pet Fav /Ref SC
			8 Jul 1850	82 LJ 281	Pet Fav /Ref SC
			9 Jul 1850	82 LJ 293	SC Rep as to adj
			11 Jul 1850	82 LJ 303	Pet Fav
			11 Jul 1850	82 LJ 305	SC Rep as to adj
			15 Jul 1850	82 LJ 332	Rep SC w/o Amd
			22 Jul 1850	82 LJ 365	3R
			29 Jul 1850	82 LJ 390	Royal Assent

Petitions

25 Jun 1850	82 LJ 246	Electric Telegraph Company [Against]
27 Jun 1850	82 LJ 252	Liverpool Stock Exchange [Favour]
2 Jul 1850	82 LJ 269	Manchester Commercial Association [Favour]
5 Jul 1850	82 LJ 276	Numerous Bankers and Local Councils in favour (23 petitions)
8 Jul 1850	82 LJ 281	1. London Stock Exchange; 2. Glasgow Merchants and Bankers [Favour]
11 Jul 1850	82 LJ 303	Birkenhead Docks [Favour]

Representation

Solicitor: Bell, Steward and Lloyd

Parliamentary debates

2R: HC Deb, 22 Feb 1850, Vol 108 (3rd), col 1286 List of Acts: HC Deb, 15 Aug 1850, Vol 113 (3rd), col 1078	

Parliamentary papers and cases

None

Gazette notices

London Gazette: 23 Nov 1849 (Iss: 21,040, p 3559)
Edinburgh Gazette: 23 Nov 1849 (Iss: 5913, p 1143)
Dublin Gazette: 12 Nov 1847 (Iss: 13,969, p 1019)

Newspaper coverage of debates

House of Commons

SO cw: Morning Chronicle, 8 Feb 1850; Morning Post, 8 Feb 1850; London Evening Standard, 8 Feb 1850; Birmingham Journal, 9 Feb 1850; Bell's Weekly Messenger, 9 Feb 1850; Glasgow Herald, 11 Feb 1850; Bell's Weekly Messenger, 11 Feb 1850; Greenock Advertiser, 12 Feb 1850; Western Courier, 14 Feb 1850; Montrose, Arbroath and Brechin Review, 15 Feb 1850

2R: **The Times, 23 Feb 1850; The Globe, 23 Feb 1850; Morning Advertiser, 23 Feb 1850; Morning Chronicle, 23 Feb 1850; London Daily News, 23 Feb 1850; Shipping and Mercantile News, 23 Feb 1850; Bell's New Weekly Messenger, 24 Feb 1850; Lloyd's Weekly Newspaper, 24 Feb 1850; Evening Mail, 25 Feb 1850; Nottinghamshire Guardian, 28 Feb 1850; Hull Packet, 1 Mar 1850; Bolton Chronicle, 2 Mar 1850; Monmouthshire Beacon, 2 Mar 1850;** *Morning Post, 23 Feb 1850; John Bull, 23 Feb 1850; Evening Mail, 25 Feb 1850; Hull Packet, 1 Mar 1850; Bolton Chronicle, 2 Mar 1850;* Reading Mercury, 23 Feb 1850; Glasgow Hearld, 25 Feb 1850; Banbury Guardian, 28 Feb 1850; North and South Shields Gazette, 1 Mar 1850; Nottingham Guardian, 28 Feb 1850; Royal Cornwall Gazette, 1 Mar 1850

Com: *Morning Chronicle, 17 May 1850; Morning Post, 17 May 1850; Aberdeen Press and Journal, 22 May 1850; Worcestershire Chronicle, 22 May 1850; North and South Shields Gazette, 24 May 1850; Leeds Intelligencer, 25 May 1850; Staffordshire Advertiser, 25 May 1850; Aris's Birmingham Gazette, 27 May 1850*

Cons: London Daily News, 11 Jun 1850; London Evening Standard, 11 Jun 1850

3R: The Times, 15 Jun 1850; Globe, 15 Jun 1850; Morning Advertiser, 15 Jun 1850; Morning Chronicle, 15 Jun 1850; Morning Post, 15 Jun 1850; London Daily News, 15 Jun 1850; Reading Mercury, 15 Jun 1850; Bell's New Weekly Messenger, 16 Jun 1850; Aris's Birmingham Gazette, 17 Jun 1850; Bell's Weekly Messenger, 17 Jun 1850; Blackburn Standard, 19 Jun 1850; Cheltenham Chronicle, 20 Jun 1850; Exeter Flying Post, 20 Jun 1850; Nottinghamshire Guardian, 20 Jun 1850; Coventry Herald, 21 Jun 1850; Bristol Mercury, 22 Jun 1850; Derbyshire Courier, 22 Jun 1850; Exeter and Plymouth Gazette, 22 Jun 1850; Leeds Intelligencer, 22 Jun 1850; Yorkshire Gazette, 22 Jun 1850; Greenock Advertiser, 25 Jun 1850; The Scotsman, 26 Jun 1850; Banbury Guardian, 27 Jun 1850; Northampton Mercury, 29 Jun 1850; Hereford Times, 29 Jun 1850

House of Lords

Rep: *London Daily News, 13 Jul 1850; London Evening Standard, 13 Jul 1850; Bell's Weekly Messenger, 13 Jul 1850; Liverpool Mercury, 16 Jul 1850; Montrose, Arbroath and Brechin Review, 19 Jul 1850; Hampshire Chronicle, 20 Jul 1850; Newcastle Journal, 20 Jul 1850; North Wales Chronicle, 20 Jul 1850; Manchester Courier, 20 Jul 1850; Staffordshire Advertiser, 20 Jul 1850*

3R: *London Daily News, 23 Jul 1850*

Royal Assent: *Globe, 29 Jul 1850; The Times, 30 Jul 1850; Globe, 30 Jul 1850; Morning Advertiser, 30 Jul 1850; Morning Post, 30 Jul 1850; London Evening Standard, 30 Jul 1850; Chelmsford Chronicle, 2 Aug 1850; Durham Chronicle, 2 Aug 1850; Essex Standard, 2 Aug 1850; Glasgow Herald, 2 Aug 1850; North and South Shields, 2 Aug 1850; Illustrated London News, 3 Aug 1850; Dundalk Democrat and People's Journal, 3 Aug 1850; Gloucester Journal, 3 Aug 1850; Manchester Courier, 3 Aug 1850; Newcastle Journal, 3 Aug 1850; Sheffield Independent, 3 Aug 1850; Staffordshire Advertiser, 3 Aug 1850; Weekly Freeman's Journal, 3 Aug 1850; Aris's Birmingham Gazette, 5 Aug 1850; Leicester Chronicle, 10 Aug 1850; Leicestershire Mercury, 10 Aug 1850*

Archives
SOC Minutes: 21 Jun 1850 (p 158–159): HL/PO/CO/1/157
SOC Rep: HL/PO/JO/10/9/25 (No 586)
Rep from C'tee to Form SC: HL/PO/JO/10/9/27 (No 648)
Opposed Bill C'tee Minutes: 16 May 1850 (p 182–184); 3 Jun 1850 (p 185); 4 Jun 1850 (p 186)
Opposed Bill C'tee Minutes: 8 Jul 1850 (p 100 and 126–128): HL/PO/CO/1/156
Opposed Bill Evidence (1850), Vol 3 [witnesses: Edward Highton; Benjamin Lay; Alexander Shand]: HL/PO/PB/5/16/3
Opposed Bill Evidence (1850), Vol 32 [witnesses: John Cooper; Theodore George; James Hamilton; Henry Hatcher; Benjamin Lay; James Macgregor; Thomas Mander; John Swift; Charles Walker]: HC/CL/PB/2/18/32
House Bill: HL/PO/JO/10/9/35

Notes
Repealed and amended by British Electric Telegraph Company's Act 1853 (16 & 17 Vict. c. clix) (also a failed repeal Bill in 1852)

Timber Preserving Company's Amendment Act 1850

PRVA64	1850
	Timber Preserving Company's Amendment Act 1850 (13 & 14 Vict. c. lxxxix)

An Act for extending and amending the Powers of the Timber Preserving Company's Acts; and to enable the Company to buy, improve, and sell Substances to be preserved, and to work Mills and Machinery

Table of contents (patent provisions only)
s 3 Assignment of Letters Patent s 4 Patents for Improvements may also be assigned s 5 Letters Patent to continue valid notwithstanding the Assignment s 6 Company may enjoy Patents free from Conditions against Assignment s 7 Company may purchase Licences

Relevant patents	
19 Dec 1837 (No 7511)	Mode of preserving certain animal and vegetable substances from decay [Joshua John Lloyd Margary] {Scottish patent: 30 Mar 1838; Irish patent: 23 Jul 1838}
11 Jul 1838 (No 7731)	Rendering wood, cork, leather, wovern and felted fabrics, ropes, stones, and plasters or compositions, more durable, less pervious to water, or less flammable [John Bethell]
21 Aug 1838 (No 12,250)	Preserving animal and vegetable substances, also stone, chalk, and plaster, from decay [John Bethell]

Journal					
House of Commons			House of Lords		
Pres: Thomas Thornley Rep: Ralph Bernal (Ch W&M)			Rep: Earl of Shaftesbury (Ld Ch)		
13 Feb 1850	105 CJ 64	Pet/Bill Ord	1 Jul 1850	82 LJ 262	Brought HC/1R
14 Feb 1850	105 CJ 67	1R	8 Jul 1850	82 LJ 281	SOC Rep/Leave
25 Feb 1850	105 CJ 94	2R/C'tted	12 Jul 1850	82 LJ 310	2R/C'tted
17 Jun 1850	105 CJ 438	Rep with Amds	19 Jul 1850	82 LJ 349	**Rep with Amds**

(continued)

(continued)

28 Jun 1850	105 CJ 468	3R	22 Jul 1850	82 LJ 365	3R
23 Jul 1850	105 CJ 556	HL pass with Amds	26 Jul 1850	82 LJ 385	HC Ag Amds
26 Jul 1850	105 CJ 568	HL Amds Ag	29 Jul 1850	82 LJ 390	Royal Assent
29 Jul 1850	105 CJ 580	Royal Assent			

Representation

Solicitor: Goodwin, Partridge, Williams and Edwards

Parliamentary debates

List of Acts: HC Deb, 15 Aug 1850, Vol 113(3rd), col 1078

Parliamentary papers and cases

None

Gazette notices

London Gazette: 27 Nov 1849 (Iss: 21,041, p 3600)

Edinburgh Gazette: 23 Nov 1849 (Iss: 5913, p 1143)

Dublin Gazette: 23 Nov 1849 (Iss: 14,248, p 1022)

Newspaper coverage of debates

House of Commons

2R: Morning Advertiser, 26 Feb 1850; Morning Chronicle, 26 Feb 1850; Morning Post, 26 Feb 1850; London Daily News, 26 Feb 1850

Cons: Morning Post, 25 Jun 1850; London Daily News, 25 Jun 1850

3R: Globe, 28 Jun 1850; Morning Chronicle, 28 Jun 1850; Morning Post 28 Jun 1850; Evening Mail, 28 Jun 1850; London Daily News, 28 Jun 1850; London Evening Standard, 28 Jun 1850; Reading Mercury, 29 Jun 1850; Bell's New Weekly Messenger, 30 Jun 1850; Bell's Weekly Messenger, 1 Jul 1850; Banbury Guardian, 4 Jul 1850

3R: London Daily News, 23 Jul 1850

HL Amds: London Evening Standard, 26 Jul 1850; Morning Advertiser, 27 Jul 1850; Morning Post, 27 Jul 1850; The Examiner, 27 Jul 1850

Royal Assent: The Times, 30 Jul 1850; Morning Advertiser, 30 Jul 1850; Morning Chronicle, 30 Jul 1850; Morning Post, 30 Jul 1850; London Daily News, 30 Jul 1850; London Evening Standard, 30 Jul 1850; North and South Shields, 2 Aug 1850; Illustrated London News, 3 Aug 1850

Archives

House Bill: HL/PO/JO/10/9/41

Bill Amds: HL/PO/JO/10/9/29 (No 736)

SOC Minutes: 5 Jul 1850 (p 187–188): HL/PO/CO/1/157

SOC Rep: HL/PO/JO/10/9/27 (No 662)

Unopposed Bill C'tee Minutes: 16 Jul 1850 (p 236–238): HL/PO/CO/1/155

Laird's Patent Act 1851

PRVA65	1851

Laird's Patent Act 1851 (14 & 15 Vict. c. v)
An Act for rendering valid certain Letters Patent granted to John Laird of Birkenhead, Shipbuilder

Table of contents

s 1 Letters Patent confirmed [specification filed late, 11 Jan, deadline 10 Jan 1844]
s 2 Saving of Rights

Relevant patent

10 Jul 1843 (No 9830)	Construction of steam and other vessels [John Laird]

Journal					
House of Commons			**House of Lords**		
Pres: Joseph Brotherton Rep: Ralph Bernal (Ch W&M)			Rep: Lord Redesdale (Ld Ch)		
5 Feb 1851	106 CJ 8	Pet/Leave	28 Mar 1851	83 LJ 88	Brought HC/1R/Ref SOC
6 Feb 1851	106 CJ 19	1R	4 Apr 1851	83 LJ 112	SOC Rep/Leave
11 Feb 1851	106 CJ 37	2R/C'tted	10 Apr 1851	83 LJ 124	2R/C'tted
18 Mar 1851	106 CJ 105	Rep with Amds	14 Apr 1851	83 LJ 137	Rep w/o Amds
24 Mar 1851	106 CJ 112	Cons	2 May 1851	83 LJ 144	3R
27 Mar 1851	106 CJ 119	3R	20 May 1851	83 LJ 192	Royal Assent
2 Apr 1851	106 CJ 195	HL pass w/o Amds			
20 May 1851	106 CJ 234	Royal Assent			

Representation
No information

Parliamentary debates
None

Parliamentary papers and cases
None

Gazette notices
London Gazette: 29 Nov 1850 (Iss: 21,158, p 3278)

Newspaper coverage of debates

House of Commons

2R: Globe, 12 Feb 1851; Morning Advertiser, 12 Feb 1851; Morning Post, 12 Feb 1851; London Daily News, 12 Feb 1851; Liverpool Mercury, 15 Feb 1851

Cons: Morning post, 25 Mar 1851; London Daily News, 25 Mar 1851

3R: The Times, 28 Mar 1851; Morning Advertiser, 28 Mar 1851; Morning Post, 28 Mar 1851; London Daily News, 28 Mar 1851; London Evening Standard, 28 Mar 1851; Bell's New Weekly Messenger, 30 Mar 1851; Bell's Weekly Messenger, 31 Mar 1851

Archives

House Bill: HL/PO/JO/10/9/76

SOC Minutes: 4 Apr 1851 (p 9): HL/PO/CO/1/162

SOC Rep: HL/PO/JO/10/9/50 (No 250)

Unopposed Bill C'tee Minutes: 11 Apr 1851 (p 8): HL/PO/CO/1/160

Notes

Related cases

Laird v Crippen (1852)(VC) 6 HPC 549; 19 RA 109

Price's Patent Candle Company's Amendment Act 1851

PRVA66	1851
Price's Patent Candle Company's Amendment Act 1851 (14 & 15 Vict. c. li)	
An Act for extending the Powers of Price's Patent Candle Company in relation to Letters Patent for Inventions applicable to their Undertaking	
Table of contents	
s 1 Company enabled to become Assignees of Patents applicable to their Undertaking; Powers of recited Act extended to this Act s 2 Seal of the Company alone to validate Disclaimers, &c.	

(continued)

(continued)

Relevant patents	
25 Jan 1848 (No 12,040)	Treating and manufacturing certain fatty or oily matters; manufacture of candles and night lights [George Fergusson Wilson] {extended to Channel Islands and colonies; Scottish patent: 3 Feb 1848; Irish patent: 11 May 1848}
28 Feb 1849 (No 12,501)	Separating more liquid from the more solid parts of fatty and oily matters; separating the same from foreign matters [George Fergusson Wilson] {extended to Channel Islands and colonies; Scottish patent: 13 Mar 1849; Irish patent: 12 Sep 1849}
14 Mar 1849 (No 12,512)	Manufacture of candles and night-lights [George Fergusson Wilson] {extended to Channel Islands and colonies; Scottish patent: 13 Mar 1849}

Journal

House of Commons			House of Lords		
Pres: William Beresford Rep: Sir Harry Verney			Rep: Lord Redesdale (Ld Ch)		
5 Feb 1851	106 CJ 9	Pet/Leave	30 May 1851	83 LJ 220	Brought HC/1R/Ref SC
6 Feb 1851	106 CJ 19	1R	5 Jun 1851	83 LJ 243	SOC Rep/Leave
11 Feb 1851	106 CJ 37	2R/C'tted	17 Jun 1851	83 LJ 255	2R/C'tted
20 Feb 1851	106 CJ 235	Rep with Amds	19 Jun 1851	83 LJ 263	Rep w/o Amds
26 Feb 1851	106 CJ 246	Cons	24 Jun 1851	83 LJ 277	3R
29 Feb 1851	106 CJ 252	3R	3 Jul 1851	83 LJ 318	Royal Assent
26 Jun 1851	106 CJ 311	HL pass w/o Amds			
3 Jul 1851	106 CJ 331	Royal Assent			

Representation

Solicitor: William, Harrison and Bristow

Parliamentary debates

None

Parliamentary papers and cases

None

Gazette notices

London Gazette: 29 Nov 1850 (Iss: 21,158, p 3270)

Edinburgh Gazette: 26 Nov 1850 (Iss: 6204, p 1007)

Dublin Gazette: 26 Nov 1850 (Iss: 14,370, p 895)

Newspaper coverage of debates

House of Commons

2R: Morning Post, 12 Feb 1851; London Daily News, 12 Feb 1851

Cons: Globe, 27 May 1851; Morning Post, 27 May 1851; London Daily News, 27 May 1852

3R: The Times, 30 May 1851; Morning Advertiser, 30 May 1851; Morning Chronicle, 30 May 1851; Morning Post, 30 May 1851; London Daily News, 30 May 1851; Reading Mercury, 31 May 1851; Bell's Weekly Messenger, 2 Jun 1851; Dundee, Perth and Cupar Advertiser, 3 Jun 1851

Royal Assent: The Times, 4 Jul 1851; Globe, 4 Jul 1851; Morning Advertiser, 4 Jul 1851; Morning Chronicle, 4 Jul 1851; Morning Post, 4 Jul 1851; Evening Mail, 4 Jul 1851; London Daily News, 4 Jul 1851

Archives

Minutes Opposed Bill C'tee: 19 May 1851 (p 235–237); 20 May 1851 (p 237–239): HC/CL/PB/1/11

SOC Minutes: 5 Jun 1851 (p 160–161): HL/PO/CO/1/162

SOC Rep: HL/PO/JO/10/9/57 (No 513)

Unopposed Bill C'tee Minutes: 19 Jun 1851 (p 113–115): HL/PO/CO/1/160

Opposed Bill Evidence (1851), Vol 37 and 38 [witnesses: J Browing; Warren Hall; Charles Ogelby; J Sherwood]: HC/CL/PB/2/19/37 and 38

House Bill: HL/PO/JO/10/9/78

Notes

The company obtained an earlier Act for the same purpose: see PRVA58

Magnetic Telegraph Company's Act 1851

PRVA67	1851
Magnetic Telegraph Company's Act 1851 (14 & 15 Vict. c. cxviii)	
An Act for incorporating the Magnetic Telegraph Company, and to enable the said Company to work certain Letters Patent	

Table of contents (patent provisions only)

s 4 Company formed for the Purposes of working the Patents, but subject to the Provisions herein-after-contained
s 23 Patents may be assigned to the Company without causing a Forfeiture
s 24 Patents for Improvements may also be assigned
s 25 Assignments to be valid, and not cause a Forfeiture
s 26 After the Assignments, the Patents, &c to vest in the Company, freed from the Conditions against Assignment to more than Twelve Persons
s 27 Licences may be granted to the Company without causing a Forfeiture
s 28 This Act not to give greater Validity to Patents
s 29 Confirmations and Prolongations may be granted to the Company
s 30 Disclaimers may be made under the Seal of the Company [Letters Patent for Inventions Act 1835] 5 & 6 W 4 c 83
s 31 Power to Company to grant Licences

Relevant patent

10 Aug 1848 (No 12,236)	Telegraphic communication; apparatus connected therewith; partly applicable to moving other machinery [David George Foster and William Thomas Henley] {Scottish patent: 23 Jan 1850; Irish patent: 18 Jan 1851}

Journal

House of Commons			House of Lords		
Pres: Joseph Brotherton Rep: Thomas Greene			Reps: Lord Redesdale (Ld Ch)		
18 Feb 1851	106 CJ 59	Pet/Leave	23 Jun 1851	83 LJ 271	Brought HC/1R/Ref SOC
24 Feb 1851	106 CJ 75	Ord Disc/Pet to Proc	27 Jun 1851	83 LJ 296	Rep SOC/Leave
11 Mar 1851	106 CJ 95	SOC Rep/SO 151 Disp	3 Jul 1851	83 LJ 314	2R/C'tted
14 Mar 1851	106 CJ 99	SOC Rep/Leave	14 Jul 1851	83 LJ 370	**Rep with Amds**
18 Mar 1851	106 CJ 105	1R	21 Jul 1851	83 LJ 396	**3R with Amds**
31 Mar 1851	106 CJ 131	2R/C'tted	28 Jul 1851	83 LJ 441	HC Ag Amds
4 Jun 1851	106 CJ 265	Rep with Amds	1 Aug 1851	83 LJ 471	Royal Assent
13 Jun 1851	106 CJ 280	Cons			
20 Jun 1851	106 CJ 297	3R			
22 Jul 1851	106 CJ 386	HL pass with Amds			
25 Jul 1851	106 CJ 398	HL Amds Ag			
1 Aug 1851	106 CJ 425	Royal Assent			

Representation

No information

Parliamentary debates

None

Parliamentary papers and cases

None

Gazette notices

London Gazette: 26 Nov 1850 (Iss: 21,157, p 3208)
Edinburgh Gazette: 26 Nov 1850 (Iss: 6024, p. 1009)
Dublin Gazette: 26 Nov 1850 (Iss: 14,370, p 894)

Newspaper coverage of debates

House of Commons

SO rep: Globe, 13 Feb 1851; Morning Advertiser, 13 Feb 1851; Morning Chronicle, 13 Feb 1852; London Daily News, 13 Mar 1851; Caledonian Mercury, 17 Feb 1851

2R: Globe, 1 Apr 1851; Morning Chronicle, 1 Apr 1851; Morning Post, 1 Apr 1851; London Daily News, 1 Apr 1851; London Evening Standard, 1 Apr 1851; Dundalk Democrat and People's Journal, 5 Apr 1851

Ref SC: Morning Advertiser, 22 Apr 1851; London Daily News, 22 Apr 1852; Caledonian Mercury, 24 Apr 1851; Leicestershire Mercury, 26 Apr 1851; Newry Telegraph, 1 May 1851

(continued)

(continued)

Com: Morning Advertiser, 30 May 1851; London Daily News, 30 May 1851
Com: Globe, 3 Jun 1851; Morning Advertiser, 3 Jun 1851; London Daily News, 3 Jun 1851; London Evening Standard, 3 Jun 1851; Cork Constitution, 5 Jun 1851; Dundee, Perth and Cupar Advertiser, 6 Jun 1851; Huddersfield Chronicle, 7 Jun 1851; Staffordshire Advertiser, 7 Jun 1851; Yorkshire Gazette, 7 Jun 1851; Belfast News-Letter, 9 Jun 1851; Brechin Advertiser, 10 Jun 1851; Aberdeen Press and Journal, 11 Jun 1851; Worcestershire Chronicle, 11 Jun 1851; Durham Chronicle, 13 Jun 1851; Dublin Evening Packet and Correspondent, 14 Jun 1851; Cumberland Pacquet, 17 Jun 1851
Cons: Globe, 13 Jun 1851; Globe, 14 Jun 1851; Morning Post, 14 Jun 1851; London Daily News, 14 Jun 1851; London Evening Standard, 14 Jun 1852; Reading Mercury, 14 Jun 1851; Bell's Weekly Messenger, 14 Jun 1851; The Era, 15 Jun 1851; Caledonian Mercury, 16 Jun 1851; Bell's Weekly Messenger, 16 Jun 1851; Northern Whig, 17 Jun 1851; Dundee Courier, 18 Jun 1851; Stamford Mercury, 20 Jun 1851; Staffordshire Advertiser, 21 Jun 1851; Oxford Chronicle and Reading Gazette, 21 Jun 1851
3R: The Times, 21 Jun 1851; Globe, 21 Jun 1851; Morning Advertiser, 21 Jun 1851; Morning Chronicle, 21 Jun 1851; Morning Post, 21 Jun 1851; London Daily News, 21 Jun 1851; London Evening Standard, 21 Jun 1851; The Era, 22 Jun 1851; Caledonian Mercury, 23 Jun 1851; Northern Whig, 24 Jun 1851; Edinburgh Evening Courant, 24 Jun 1851; Worcester Journal, 26 Jun 1851; Aberdeen Herald and General Advertiser, 28 Jun 1851; Kendal Mercury, 28 Jun 1851
HL Amds: Globe, 25 Jul 1851; Morning Advertiser, 26 Jul 1851; Morning Post, 26 Jul 1851; London Daily News, 26 Jul 1851; London Evening Standard, 25 Jul 1851; Aberdeen Herald and General Advertiser, 2 Aug 1851; Tralee Chronicle, 2 Aug 1851; Kendal Mercury, 2 Aug 1851
Royal Assent: The Times, 2 Aug 1851; Globe, 2 Aug 1851; Morning Advertiser, 2 Aug 1851; Morning Post, 2 Aug 1851; Evening Mail, 4 Aug 1851; Dublin Evening Packet and Correspondent, 5 Aug 1851; Limerick Reporter, 5 Aug 1851; Northern Whig, 5 Aug 1851; Newcastle Courant, 8 Aug 1851; Armagh Guardian, 9 Aug 1851

Archives
House Bill: HL/PO/JO/10/9/77
Amended Bill (21 Jul): HL/PO/JO/10/9/61 (No 788)
Opposed Bill C'tee: 29 May 1851 (p 287); 2 Jun 1851 (p 296): HC/CL/PB/1/11
Opposed Bill Evidence (1851), Vol 42 [witness: William Henley]: HC/CL/PB/2/19/42
SOC Minutes: 27 Jun 1851 (p 225): HL/PO/CO/1/162
Unopposed Bill C'tee Minutes: 14 Jul 1851 (p 206–208): HL/PO/CO/1/160

European and American Electric Printing Telegraph Company's Act 1851

PRVA68	1851
European and American Electric Printing Telegraph Company's Act 1851 (14 & 15 Vict. c. cxxxv)	
An Act for incorporating the European and American Electric Printing American Printing Telegraph Company, and enabling them to work certain Letters Patent	

Table of contents (patent provisions only)
s 4 Company incorporated for the Purpose of working the Patents
s 27 Patents may be assigned to the Company without causing a Forfeiture
s 28 Patents for Improvements may also be assigned
s 29 Assignments to be valid and not cause a Forfeiture
s 30 After the Assignment, the Patents and Privileged to vest in and be exercised by the Company freed from the Conditions against Assignment to more than Twelve People
s 31 Licences may be granted to the Company without causing a Forfeiture
s 32 This Act not to give Validity to Patents
s 33 Confirmations and Prolongations may be granted to the Company
s 34 Disclaimers may be made under the Seal of the Company, [Letters Patent for Inventions Act 1835] 5 & 6 W 4. c. 83
s 35 Power to Company to grant Licences

Relevant patents	
13 Nov 1845 (No 10,939)	Printed Communications made by electric-telegraphs [Jacob Brett] {Scots patent: 27 Aug 1845}
8 Feb 1848 (No 12, 054)	Electric, printing and other telegraphs [Jacob Brett] {extended to some colonies; Scots patent: 27 Dec 1845; Irish patent – application pending}

Journal					
House of Commons			**House of Lords**		
Pres: Sir Charles Burrell Rep: Thomas Greene			Rep: Lord Redesdale (Ld Ch)		
17 Feb 1851	106 CJ 52	Pet/Leave	17 Jun 1851	83 LJ 257	Brought HC/1R/Ref SOC
18 Feb 1851	106 CJ 59	1R	26 Jun 1851	83 LJ 291	SOC Rep/Leave
28 Feb 1851	106 CJ 80	2R/C'tted	1 Jul 1851	83 LJ 306	2R/C'tted
4 Jun 1851	106 CJ 265	Rep with Amds	7 Jul 1851	83 LJ 332	Instruction to C'tee
12 Jun 1851	106 CJ 276	Cons	28 Jul 1851	83 LJ 438	**Rep with Amds**
16 Jun 1851	106 CJ 283	3R	30 Jul 1851	83 LJ 456	3R
2 Aug 1851	106 CJ 426	HL pass with Amds/Ag	4 Aug 1851	83 LJ 479	HC Ag Amds
7 Aug 1851	106 CJ 445	Royal Assent	7 Aug 1851	83 LJ 506	Royal Assent

Representation

Solicitor: Edwards and Radcliffe

Parliamentary debates

None

Parliamentary papers and cases

None

Gazette notices

London Gazette: 26 Nov 1850 (Iss: 21,157, p 3206)

Newspaper coverage of debates

SO cw: Globe, 13 Feb 1851; Morning Advertiser, 13 Feb 1851; Morning Chronicle, 13 Feb 1852; London Daily News, 13 Mar 1851; Caledonian Mercury, 17 Feb 1851

1R: Caledonian Mercury, 24 Feb 1851

2R: Globe, 1 Mar 1851; Morning Chronicle, 1 Mar 1851; Greenock Advertiser, 4 Mar 1851; Newry Telegraph, 6 Mar 1851

Ref SC: Morning Advertiser, 22 Apr 1851; London Daily News, 22 Apr 1852; Caledonian Mercury, 24 Apr 1851; Leicestershire Mercury, 26 Apr 1851; Newry Telegraph, 1 May 1851

Com: Morning Advertiser, 30 May 1851; London Daily News, 30 May 1851

Com: Globe, 3 Jun 1851; Morning Advertiser, 3 Jun 1851; London Daily News, 3 Jun 1851; London Evening Standard, 3 Jun 1851; Cork Constitution, 5 Jun 1851; Dundee, Perth and Cupar Advertiser, 6 Jun 1851; Huddersfield Chronicle, 7 Jun 1851; Staffordshire Advertiser, 7 Jun 1851; Yorkshire Gazette, 7 Jun 1851; Belfast News-Letter, 9 Jun 1851; Brechin Advertiser, 10 Jun 1851; Aberdeen Press and Journal, 11 Jun 1851; Worcestershire Chronicle, 11 Jun 1851; Durham Chronicle, 13 Jun 1851; Dublin Evening Packet and Correspondent, 14 Jun 1851; Cumberland Pacquet, 17 Jun 1851

Cons: Globe, 13 Jun 1851; Morning Advertiser, 13 Jun 1851; Morning Post, 13 Jun 1851; London Daily News, 13 Jun 1851; Belfast Mercury, 17 Jun 1851

3R: Globe, 17 Jun 1851; Morning Post, 17 Jun 1851; Evening Freeman, 17 Jun 1851; London Daily News, 17 Jun 1851; London Evening Standard, 17 Jun 1851; Freeman's Journal, 18 Jun 1851; Dublin Evening Mail, 18 Jun 1851; Cork Examiner, 20 Jun 1851; Londonderry Sentinel, 20 Jun 1851; Shrewsbury Chronicle, 20 Jun 1851; Dublin Weekly Nation, 21 Jun 1851; Weekly Freeman's Journal, 21 Jun 1851; Kilkenny Journal, 21 Jun 1851

HL Amds: London Evening Standard, 2 Aug 1851; Morning Post, 4 Aug 1851; Caledonian Mercury, 4 Aug 1851; Glasgow Herald, 4 Aug 1851; Cumberland Pacquet, 5 Aug 1851; Derby Mercury, 6 Aug 1851; Kerry Evening Post, 6 Aug 1851; Perthshire Advertiser, 7 Aug 1851; Fife Herald, 7 Aug 1851; Londonderry Standard, 7 Aug 1851; Falkirk Herald, 7 Aug 1851; Gore's Liverpool General Advertiser, 7 Aug 1851; Elgin Courier, 8 Aug 1851; Armagh Guardian, 9 Aug 1851

Royal Assent: Morning Chronicle, 8 Aug 1851; Bristol Mercury, 9 Aug 1851; Glasgow Gazette, 9 Aug 1851; Essex Herald, 12 Aug 1851; Chelmsford Chronicle, 15 Aug 1851

Archives

House Bill: HL/PO/JO/10/9/74

Bill Amds: HL/PO/JO/10/9/62 (No 837)

Instructions to Com: HL/PO/JO/10/9/60 (No 695)

Opposed Bill C'tee: 29 May 1851 (p 287); 2 Jun 1851 (p 294–295): HC/CL/PB/1/11

Opposed Bill Evidence (1851), Vol 42 [witness: Jacob Brett]: HC/CL/PB/2/19/42

SOC Minutes: 26 Jun 1851 (p 209–210): HL/PO/CO/1/162

SOC Rep: HL/PO/JO/10/9/59 (No 614)

Unopposed Bill C'tee Minutes: 3 Jul 1851 (p 174); 8 Jul 1851 (p 192); 18 Jul 1851 (p 213); 21 Jul 1851 (p 216); 28 Jul 1851 (p 228–231): HL/PO/CO/1/160

United Kingdom Electric Telegraph Company's Act 1851

PRVA69	1851

United Kingdom Electric Telegraph Company's Act 1851 (14 & 15 Vict., c. cxxxvii)

An Act for enabling the United Kingdom Electric Telegraph Company to work and purchase certain Letters Patent

Table of contents (patent provisions only)

s 5 Patents may be assigned to the Company without causing a Forfeiture
s 6 Patents for Improvements may also be assigned
s 7 Assignments to be valid and not cause a Forfeiture
s 8 Licences may be granted to the Company without causing a Forfeiture
s 9 This Act may not give Validity in Patents
s 10 Provision as to sealing of Letters Patent for Ireland and Scotland
s 11 Confirmation and Prolongations may be granted to the Company
s 12 Disclaimers may be made under the Seal of the Company [Letters Patent for Inventions Act 1835] 5 & 6 W 4, c. 83
s 13 Power to Company to grant Licences

Relevant patents

16 Jan 1850 (No 13,352)	Electric-telegraphs; applications of electric currents for deflecting magnets, or producing electro-magnets [Thomas Allan]

Journal

House of Commons			House of Lords		
Pres: William Fagan Rep: Thomas Greene			Rep: Lord Redesdale (Ld Ch)		
11 Feb 1851	106 CJ 34	Pet/Leave	17 Jul 1851	83 LJ 384	Brought HC/1R/Ref SOC
12 Feb 1851	106 CJ 42	1R	22 Jul 1851	83 LJ 408	Rep SOC/Leave
17 Feb 1851	106 CJ 54	2R/C'tted	28 Jul 1851	83 LJ 436	2R/C'tted
5 Jun 1851	106 CJ 266	Rep with Amds	29 Jul 1851	83 LJ 452	**Rep with Amds**
13 Jun 1851	106 CJ 280	Cons	30 Jul 1851	83 LJ 456	3R
16 Jul 1851	106 CJ 367	3R with Amd	4 Aug 1851	83 LJ 479	HC Ag Amds
30 Jul 1851	106 CJ 415	HL pass with Amds	7 Aug 1851	83 LJ 506	Royal Assent
1 Aug 1851	106 CJ 421	HL Amds Cons day app			
2 Aug 1851	106 CJ 426	HL Amds Ag			
7 Aug 1851	106 CJ 445	Royal Assent			

Representation

Solicitor: Fry and Hold

Parliamentary debates

None

Parliamentary papers and cases

None

Gazette notices

London Gazette: 29 Nov 1850 (Iss: 21,158, p 3278)

Newspaper coverage of debates

House of Commons

2R: Morning Advertiser, 18 Feb 1851; Morning Post, 18 Feb 1851; London Evening Standard, 18 Feb 1851; Falkirk Herald, 20 Feb 1851; Belfast News-Letter, 21 Feb 1852; Westmeath Independent, 22 Feb 1851; Roscommon & Leitrim, 22 Feb 1851

Ref SC: Morning Advertiser, 22 Apr 1851; London Daily News, 22 Apr 1852; Caledonian Mercury, 24 Apr 1851; Leicestershire Mercury, 26 Apr 1851; Newry Telegraph, 1 May 1851

Com: Morning Advertiser, 30 May 1851; London Daily News, 30 May 1851

Com: Globe, 3 Jun 1851; Morning Advertiser, 3 Jun 1851; London Daily News, 3 Jun 1851; London Evening Standard, 3 Jun 1851; Cork Constitution, 5 Jun 1851; Dundee, Perth and Cupar Advertiser, 6 Jun 1851; Huddersfield Chronicle, 7 Jun 1851; Staffordshire Advertiser, 7 Jun 1851; Yorkshire Gazette, 7 Jun 1851; Belfast News-Letter, 9 Jun 1851; Brechin Advertiser, 10 Jun 1851; Aberdeen Press and Journal, 11 Jun 1851; Worcestershire Chronicle, 11 Jun 1851; Durham Chronicle, 13 Jun 1851; Dublin Evening Packet and Correspondent, 14 Jun 1851; Cumberland Pacquet, 17 Jun 1851

Cons : Globe, 14 Jun 1851; Morning Advertiser, 14 Jun 1851; Morning Post, 14 Jun 1851; London Daily News, 14 Jun 1851; London Evening Standard, 14 Jun 1851; Bell's Weekly Messenger, 14 Jun 1851; The Era, 15 Jun 1851; Bell's Weekly Messenger, 1 Jun 1851; Northern Whig, 17 Jun 1851; Dundee Courier, 18 Jun 1851; Stamford Mercury, 20 Jun 1851; Staffordshire Advertiser, 21 Jun 1851

3R: Globe, 16 Jul 1851; London Evening Standard, 16 Jul 1851; The Times, 17 Jul 1851; Morning Advertiser, 17 Jul 1851; Morning Chronicle, 17 Jul 1852; Morning Post, 17 Jul 1851; London Daily News, 17 Jul 1851; Dublin Evening Packet and Correspondent, 17 Jul 1851; Belfast News-Letter, 18 Jul 1851; Carlisle Journal, 18 Jul 1851; Glasgow Herald, 18 Jul 1851; Newcastle Courant, 18 Jul 1851; Armagh Guardian, 19 Jul 1851; Belfast Mercury, 19 Jul 151; Exeter and Plymouth Gazette, 19 Jul 1851; Hampshire Advertiser, 19 Jul 1851; Ipswich Journal, 19 Jul 1851; Leeds Intelligencer, 19 Jul 1851; Newcastle Journal, 19 Jul 1851; Newry Telegraph, 19 Jul 1851; Reading Mercury, 19 Jul 1851; Yorkshire Gazette, 19 Jul 1851; Leeds Times, 19 Jul 1851; Dublin Weekly Nation, 19 Jul 1851; Aris's Birmingham Gazette, 21 Jul 1851; Bell's Weekly Messenger, 21 Jul 1851; Dumfries and Galloway Standard, 23 Jul 1851; Falkirk Herald, 24 Jul 1851; Londonderry Standard, 24 Jul 1851

Hl Amds: London Evening Standard, 2 Aug 1851; Morning Post, 4 Aug 1851; Glasgow Herald, 4 Aug 1851; Caledonian Mercury, 4 Aug 1851; Cumberland Pacquet, 5 Aug 1851; Derby Mercury, 6 Aug 1851; Kerry Evening Post, 6 Aug 1851; Falkirk Herald, 7 Aug 1851; Fife Herald, 7 Aug 1851; Gore's Liverpool General Advertiser, 7 Aug 1851; Londonderry Standard, 7 Aug 1851; Perthshire Advertiser, 7 Aug 1851; Elgin Courier, 8 Aug 1851; Armagh Guardian, 9 Aug 1851

House of Lords

Com: Morning Advertiser, 30 Jul 1851; Caledonian Mercury, 31 Jul 1851

Royal Assent: Morning Chronicle, 8 Aug 1851; Bristol Mercury, 9 Aug 1851; Glasgow Gazette, 9 Aug 1851; Essex Herald, 12 Aug 1851; Chelmsford Chronicle, 15 Aug 1851

Archives
House Bill: HL/PO/JO/10/9/81
Opposed Bill C'tee: 29 May 1851 (p 287–291); 2 Jun 1851 (p 292–293): HC/CL/PB/1/11
Bill Amds: HL/PO/JO/10/9/62 (No 863)
SOC Minutes: 22 Jul 1851 (p 279–280): HL/PO/CO/1/162
Unopposed Bill C'tee Minutes: 29 Jul 1851 (p 246–248): HL/PO/CO/1/160
Opposed Bill Evidence (1851), Vol 42 [witnesses: Frederick Holt; Thomas Allen]: HC/CL/PB2/19/42

Patent Solid Sewage Manure Company's Act 1852

PRVA70	1852
	Patent Solid Sewage Manure Company's Act 1852 (15 & 16 Vict. c. ii)

An Act for the Incorporation, Establishment, and Regulation of the "Patent Solid Sewage Manure Company," and for enabling the said Company to purchase and work Letters Patent

Table of contents (patent provisions only)
s 21 Patents may be assigned to the Company
s 22 Patents not to be invalidated by the Assignment
s 23 Patents may be held by the Company
s 24 Licences may be granted to the Company
s 25 Power to grant to Company Compensation, &c of Letters Patent, &c
s 26 Disclaimers may be made under the Seal of Company
s 27 Act not to give to certain Letters Patent any greater Validity than they would otherwise have possessed
s 28 Power to Company to grant Licences

Relevant patent	
24 Feb 1851 (No 13,526)	Manufacture of manure; machinery to be used therein [Thomas Wicksteed] {Scottish patent: 19 Feb 1851; Irish patent: 26 Feb 1851}

Journal					
House of Commons			**House of Lords**		
Pres and Rep: Joseph Brotherton			Rep: Lord Redesdale (Ld Ch)		
10 Feb 1852	107 CJ 31	Pet/Leave	25 Mar 1852	84 LJ 68	Brought HC/1R
11 Feb 1852	107 CJ 34	1R	30 Mar 1852	84 LJ 79	SOC Rep/Leave
16 Feb 1852	107 CJ 49	2R/C'tted	5 Apr 1852	84 LJ 88	2R/C'tted
16 Mar 1852	107 CJ 94	Rep with Amds	6 Apr 1852	84 LJ 90	**Rep with Amds**
22 Mar 1852	107 CJ 106	Cons	20 Apr 1852	84 LJ 98	3R
25 Mar 1852	107 CJ 120	3R	29 Apr 1852	84 LJ 112	HC Ag Amds
24 Apr 1852	107 CJ 167	HL pass with Amds	3 May 1852	84 LJ 121	Royal Assent
28 Apr 1852	107 CJ 174	HL Amds Ag			
3 May 1852	107 CJ 184	Royal Assent			

(continued)

(continued)

Representation
Solicitor: Wilson, Harrison and Bristow
Parliamentary debates
None
Parliamentary papers and cases
None
Gazette notices
London Gazette: 28 Nov 1851 (Iss: 21,268, p 3330) Edinburgh Gazette: 28 Nov 1851 (Iss: 6129, p 1102) Dublin Gazette: 18 Nov 1851 (Iss: 14,478, p 966)
Newspaper coverage of debates
House of Commons SO cw: Morning Advertiser, 10 Feb 1852; London Daily News, 10 Feb 1852 2R: Morning Advertiser, 17 Feb 1852; Morning Chronicle, 17 Feb 1852; Morning Post, 17 Feb 1852; London Daily News, 17 Feb 1852; London Evening Standard, 17 Feb 1852; Belfast Mercury, 19 Feb 1852 Com App: Morning Advertiser, 2 Mar 1852 Rep: Morning Advertiser, 23 Mar 1852 3R: The Times, 26 Mar 1852; Globe, 26 Mar 1852; Morning Chronicle, 26 Mar 1852; Morning Post, 26 Mar 1852; Evening Mail, 26 Mar 1852; London Daily News, 26 Mar 1852; London Evening Standard, 26 Mar 1852; Leeds Intelligencer, 27 Mar 1852; Leeds Mercury, 27 Mar 1852; Reading Mercury, 27 Mar 1852; Bell's Weekly Messenger, 27 Mar 1852; Bell's New Weekly Messenger, 28 Mar 1852; Bell's Weekly Messenger, 29 Mar 1852 Royal Assent: The Times, 4 May 1852
Archives
House Bill: HL/PO/JO/10/9/132 Unopposed Bill C'tee Minutes: HC/CL/WM/UB/1/3 SOC Minutes: 30 Mar 1852 (p 8–9): HL/PO/CO/1/167 SOC Rep: HL/PO/JO/10/9/92 (No 315) Unopposed Bill C'tee Minutes: 6 Apr 1852 (p 3–5): HL/PO/CO/1/165
Notes
To re-incorporate and extend powers: Patent Solid Sewage Manure Company's Act 1854 (17 & 18 Vict. c. clxvi) (see s 8 and Sch 1)

North British Flax Company's Act 1852

PRVA71	1852
North British Flax Company's Act 1852 (15 & 16 Vict. c. cxxiv)	
An Act for the Incorporation, Establishment, and Regulation of the North British Flax Company, and to enable the said Company to purchase and work certain Letters Patent [Claussen's Patent]	

Table of contents (patent provisions only)
s 4 Company incorporated for the Purpose of working the Patents s 24 Patents may be assigned to Company without causing a Forfeiture s 25 Assignments to be valid, and not cause a Forfeiture s 26 Licences may be granted to the Company without causing a Forfeiture of the Patents s 27 This Act not to give Validity to Patents s 28 Confirmations and Prolongations may be granted to the Company s 29 Disclaimers may be made under the Seal of the Company [Letters Patent for Inventions Act 1835] 5 & 6 W 4 c. 83 s 30 The Company may grant Licences

Relevant patent	
12 Feb 1851 [Scots patent]	Improvements in Bleaching in the Preparation of Materials for spinning and felting, and in Yarns and Felts, and in the Machinery employed therein [Peter Claussen]

Journal					
House of Commons			**House of Lords**		
Pres: Joseph Brothernton Rep: Ralph Bernal (Ch W&M)			Rep: Lord Redesdale (Ld Ch)		
12 Feb 1852	107 CJ 38	Pet/Leave	21 May 1852	84 LJ 168	Brought HC/1R/Ref SOC
16 Feb 1852	107 CJ 47	1R	28 May 1852	84 LJ 199	**SOC Rep**
27 Feb 1852	107 CJ 79	2R/C'tted	5 Jun 1852	84 LJ 213	2R/C'tted
10 May 1852	107 CJ 202	Rep with Amds	11 Jun 1852	84 LJ 240	**Rep with Amds**
17 May 1852	107 CJ 218	Cons	18 Jun 1852	84 LJ 281	3R
21 May 1852	107 CJ 232	3R	24 Jun 1852	84 LJ 316	HC Ag Amds
18 Jun 1852	107 CJ 312	HL pass with Amds	30 Jun 1852	84 LJ 423	Royal Assent
23 Jun 1852	107 CJ 326	HL Amds Ag			
30 Jun 1852	107 CJ 366	Royal Assent			

Representation

Solicitor: Vardy and Delmar

Parliamentary debates

None

Parliamentary papers and cases

None

Gazette notices

London Gazette: 28 Nov 1851 (Iss: 21,268, p 3331)
Edinburgh Gazette: 28 Nov 1851 (Iss: 6129, p 1101)

Newspaper coverage of debates

House of Commons

SO cw: Morning Advertiser, 12 Feb 1852; Morning Chronicle, 12 Feb 1852; Morning Post, 12 Feb 1852; London Daily News, 12 Feb 1852; Dundee, Peth and Upar Advertiser, 17 Feb 1852; Edinburgh Evening Courant, 17 Feb 1852; Dundee Courier, 18 Feb 1852; Falkirk Herald, 19 Feb 1852; Fife Herald, 19 Feb 1852; Perthshire Advertiser, 19 Feb 1852; Durham Chronicle, 20 Feb 1852; Elgin Courant, 20 Feb 1852; Montrose, Arbroath and Brechin Review, 20 Feb 1852

1R: Edinburgh Evening Courant, 19 Feb 1852; The Scotsman, 21 Feb 1852

2R: Globe, 28 Feb 1852; Morning Advertiser, 28 Feb 1852; Morning Chronicle, 28 Feb 1852; Morning Post, 28 Feb 1852; London Daily News, 28 Feb 1852; London Evening Standard, 28 Feb 1852; Caledonian Mercury, 1 Mar 1852; Cork Constitution, 2 Mar 1852; Edinburgh Evening Courant, 2 Mar 1852; Southern Reporter and Cork Commercial Courier, 2 Mar 1852; Dundee Courier, 3 Mar 1852; Caledonian Mercury, 4 Mar 1852; Falkirk Herald, 4 Mar 1852; Stirling Observer, 4 Mar 1852; Elgin Courier, 5 Mar 1852; John O'Groat Journal, 5 Mar 1852; The Scotsman, 6 Mar 1852

Com App: Edinburgh Evening Courant, 6 Apr 1852

C'tee adj: Elgin Courant, and Morayshire Advertiser, 30 Apr 1852

Rep: Edinburgh Evening Courant, 13 May 1852; The Scotsman, 15 May 1852

Cons: Caledonian Mercury, 17 May 1852; Edinburgh Evening Courant, 18 May 1852

Cons: London Daily News, 18 May 1852; Caledonian Mercury, 20 May 1852; Edinburgh Evening Courant, 20 May 1852

3R: Globe, 21 May 1852; The Times, 22 May 1852; Morning Advertiser, 22 May 1852; Morning Chronicle, 22 May 1852; Morning Post, 21 May 1852; London Evening Standard, 22 May 1852; Edinburgh Evening Courant, 22 May 1852; Bell's New Weekly Messenger, 23 May 1852; Edinburgh Evening Courant, 25 May 1852; Southern Reporter and Cork Commercial Courier, 25 May 1852; The Scotsman, 26 May 1852; Newcastle Courant, 28 May 1852; Elgin Courant, 28 May 1852

HL pass: The Scotsman, 23 Jun 1852

HL Amds Ag: Globe, 23 Jun 1852; Morning Advertiser, 24 Jun 1853; London Daily News, 24 Jun 1852; Edinburgh Evening Courant, 24 Jun 1852; Reading Mercury, 26 Jun 1852; The Scotsman, 30 Jun 1852; Banbury Guardian, 1 Jul 1852; Falkirk Herald, 1 Jul 1852; Fife Herald, 1 Jul 1852

Royal Assent: The Times, 1 Jul 1852; Morning Chronicle, 1 Jul 1852; Morning Post, 1 Jul 1852; Belfast Mercury, 3 Jul 1852; Reading Mercury, 3 Jul 1852

Archives

House Bill: HL/PO/JO/10/9/132

SOC Rep: HL/PO/JO/10/9/100 (No 707)

Unopposed Bill C'tee Minutes: 3 May 1852 (p 43–44); 10 May 1852 (p 46): HC/CL/WM/UB/1/3

SOC Minutes: 28 May 1852 (p 185–186): HL/PO/CO/1/167

Unopposed Bill C'tee Minutes: 7 Jun 1852 (p 196) 11 Jun 1852 (p 242–246): HL/PO/CO/1/165

Claussen's Patent Flax Company's Act 1852

PRVA72	1852
Claussen's Patent Flax Company's Act 1852 (15 & 16 Vict. c. cxli)	
An Act for incorporating Claussen's Patent Flax Company, and to enable the said Company to purchase and work certain Letters Patent	

Table of contents (patent provisions only)
s 3 Company formed for the Purpose of working the Patent
s 25 Recited patent may be assigned to Company
s 26 Assignments to be valid, and not cause a Forfeiture
s 27 After Assignment the Patents &c, to vest in and be exercised by the Company, free from Conditions against Assignment, &c.
s 28 Licences may be granted to the Company without occasioning a Forfeiture
s 29 This Act not to give greater Validity to the Patents
s 30 Confirmation and Prolongations may be granted to the Company
s 31 Disclaimers may be made under the Seal of the Company
s 32 Power to Company to grant Licences

Relevant patent	
16 Aug 1850 (No 13,224)	Bleaching; preparation of materials for spinning and felting; yarns and felts [Peter Claussen] {extended to Channel Islands and colonies}

Journal

House of Commons			House of Lords		
Pres: Richard Spooner Rep: Ralph Bernal (Ch W&M)			Rep: Lord Redesdale (Ld Ch)		
16 Feb 1852	107 CJ 47	Pet /Leave	17 May 1852	84 LJ 157	Brought HC/1R/Ref SOC
19 Feb 1852	107 CJ 61	1R	25 May 1852	84 LJ 183	SOC Rep/Leave
27 Feb 1852	107 CJ 78	2R/C'tted	3 Jun 1852	84 LJ 205	2R/C'tted
3 May 1852	107 CJ 184	Rep with Amds	7 Jun 1852	84 LJ 222	Rep w/o Amds
10 May 1852	107 CJ 203	Cons	17 Jun 1852	84 LJ 271	**3R with Amds**
14 May 1852	107 CJ 212	3R	22 Jun 1852	84 LJ 307	Returned HC
18 Jun 1852	107 CJ 312	HL pass with Amds	30 Jun 1852	84 LJ 422	Royal Assent
22 Jun 1852	107 CJ 320	HL Amds Ag			
30 Jun 1852	107 CJ 366	Royal Assent			

Representation
Solicitor: Vardy and Delmar

Parliamentary debates
None

Parliamentary papers and cases
None

Gazette notices
London Gazette: 28 Nov 1851 (Iss: 21,268, p 3322)

Newspaper coverage of debates

House of Commons

SO cw: London Evening Standard, 12 Feb 1852; Morning Advertiser, 13 Feb 1852; Morning Chronicle, 13 Feb, 1852; Morning Post, 13 Feb 1852; Evening Mail, 13 Feb 1852; London Daily News, 13 Feb 1852; Liverpool Mercury, 13 Feb 1852; Cambridge Chronicle and Journal, 14 Feb 1852; Leeds Intelligencer, 14 Feb 1852; Oxford Journal, 14 Feb 1852; Staffordshire Advertiser, 14 Feb 1852; Belfast News-Letter, 16 Feb 1852; Hereford Journal, 18 Feb 1852; Newry Examiner and Louth Advertiser, 18 Feb 1852; Worcester Journal, 19 Feb 1852; Essex Standard, 20 Feb 1852; Hertford Mercury, 21 Feb 1852

2R: The Times, 28 Feb 1852; Morning Advertiser, 28 Feb 1852; Morning Chronicle, 28 Feb 1852; Morning Post, 28 Feb 1852; London Daily News, 28 Feb 1852; London Evening Standard, 28 Feb 1852; Cambridge Independent Press, 28 Feb 1852; Glasgow Herald, 1 Mar 1852; Cork Constitution, 2 Mar 1852; Limerick and Clare Examiner, 3 Mar 1852; Wexford Independent, 3 Mar 1852; Stirling Observer, 4 Mar 1852

3R: The Times, 15 May 1852; Globe, 15 May 1852; Morning Advertiser, 15 May 1852; Morning Chronicle, 15 May 1852; Morning Post, 15 May 1852; London Daily News, 15 May 1852; London Evening Standard, 15 May 1852; Belfast Mercury, 18 May 1852; Northern Whig, 18 May 1852; Cork Examiner, 19 May 1852; Essex Standard, 21 May 1852; Coleraine Chronicle, 22 May 1852

HL Am: London Evening Standard, 22 Jun 1852; Dublin Evening Mail, 23 Jun 1852; Belfast Mercury, 24 Jun 1852; Southern Reporter and Cork Commercial Courier, 24 Jun 1852; Coleraine Chronicle, 26 Jun 1852; Downpatrick Recorder, 26 Jun 1852

Royal Assent: The Times, 1 Jul 1852; Morning Chronicle, 1 Jul 1852; Morning Post, 1 Jul 1852; Belfast Mercury, 3 Jul 1852; Reading Mercury, 3 Jul 1852

Archives
House Bill: HL/PO/JO/10/9/126
Bill Amds: HL/PO/JO/10/9/102 (No 812)
SOC Rep: HL/PO/JO/10/9/99a (No 646)
Unopposed Bill C'tee Minutes: 6 Apr 1852 (p 35); 29 Apr 1852 (p 39); 3 May 1852 (p 44): HC/CL/WM/UB/1/3
SOC Minutes: 25 May 1852 (p 140–141): HL/PO/CO/1/167
Unopposed Bill C'tee Minutes: 7 Jun 1852 (p 188): HL/PO/CO/1/165

Electric Telegraph Company of Ireland Act 1853

PRVA73	1853
Electric Telegraph Company of Ireland Act 1853 (16 & 17 Vict. c cxxiii)	

An Act for Incorporating and regulating the Electric Telegraph Company of Ireland, and for better enabling the Company to establish and work Telegraphs in Scotland and Ireland and between those Countries, and for other Purposes

Table of contents (patent provisions only)

s 51 Patents may be assigned to the Company without causing a forfeiture
s 52 Disclaimers may be made under the Seal of the Company

Relevant patents

None particularised

Journal

House of Commons			House of Lords		
Pres: Joseph Brotherton Rep: Edward Pleydell-Bouverie (Ch W&M)			Rep: Lord Redesdale (Ld Ch)		
10 Feb 1853	180 CJ 217	Pet/Ord	17 Jun 1853	85 LJ 347	Brought HC/1R
11 Feb 1853	180 CJ 229	1R	27 Jun 1853	85 LJ 374	SOC Rep/Leave
16 Feb 1853	180 CJ 248	2R/C'tted	1 Jul 1853	85 LJ 397	2R/C'tted
2 Jun 1853	180 CJ 539	Rep wth Amds	4 Jul 1853	85 LJ 421	**Rep with Amds**
3 Jun 1853	180 CJ 544	Re-C'tted	7 Jul 1853	85 LJ 434	R consent
3 Jun 1853	180 CJ 546	Rep with Amds	7 Jul 1853	85 LJ 436	3R
13 Jun 1853	180 CJ 573	Cons	14 Jul 1853	85 LJ 478	HC Ag Amds
16 Jun 1853	180 CJ 586	R consent/3R with Amds	4 Aug 1853	85 LJ 566	Royal Assent
8 Jul 1853	180 CJ 661	HL pass with Amds			
12 Jul 1853	180 CJ 672	HL Amds day app			
13 Jul 1853	180 CJ 675	HL Amds Ag			
4 Aug 1854	180 CJ 762	Royal Assent			

Representation

Solicitor: Alfred Mayhew

Parliamentary debates

None

Parliamentary papers and cases

None

Gazette notices

London Gazette: 30 Nov 1852 (Iss: 21,368, p 3470)

Edinburgh Gazette: 30 Nov 1852 (Iss: 6234, p 1043)

Dublin Gazette: 30 Nov 1852 (Iss: 14,584, p 975)

(continued)

(continued)

Newspaper coverage of debates
House of Commons
2R: Morning Advertiser, 17 Feb 1853; Dublin Evening Post, 17 Feb 1853; Cork Examiner, 18 Feb 1853; Cork Constitution, 19 Feb 1863; Downpatrick, 19 Feb 1853; Glasgow Constitutional, 19 Feb 1853; Newry Examiner and Louth Advertiser, 19 Feb 1853; The Ulsterman, 19 Feb 1853; Kings County Chronicle, 23 Feb 1853
3R: The Times, 17 Jun 1853; Globe, 17 Jun 1853; Morning Advertiser, 17 Jun 1853; Morning Chronicle, 17 Jun 1853; Morning Post, 17 Jun 1853; Evening Mail, 17 Jun 1853; London Daily News, 17 Jun 1853; London Evening Standard, 17 Jun 1853; Dublin Evening Mail, 17 Jun 1853; Dublin Evening Post, 18 Jun 1853; Galway Mercury, 18 Jun 1853; Kerry Evening Post, 18 Jun 1853; Southern Reporter and Cork Commercial Courier, 18 Jun 1853; Saunders's News-Letter, 18 Jun 1853; Bell's New Weekly Messenger, 19 Jun 1853; Derry Journal, 22 Jun 1853; Newry Examiner and Louth Advertiser, 22 Jun 1853; Kilkenny Journal, 22 Jun 1853; Armagh Guardian, 24 Jun 1853
HL Amds day app: Globe, 12 Jul 1853; The Evening Freeman, 13 Jul 1853
HL Amds Ag: London Daily News, 14 Jul 1853; Belfast Mercury, 15 Jul 1853; Dublin Evening Mail, 15 Jul 1853; Catholic Telegraph, 16 Jul 1853; Dublin Weekly Nation, 16 Jul 1853; Galway Mercury, 16 Jul 1853; Ulster Gazette, 16 Jul 1853; Weekly Freeman's Journal, 16 Jul 1853; Banner of Ulster, 19 Jul 1853; Derry Journal, 20 Jul 1853; Dundalk Democrat and People's Journal, 23 Jul 1853
Royal Assent: The Times, 5 Aug 1853; Morning Chronicle, 5 Aug 1853; Morning Post, 6 Aug 1853; Illustrated London, 6 Aug 1853; Saunders's News-Letter, 6 Aug 1853; Freeman's Journal, 6 Aug 1853; Galway Mercury, and Connaught Weekly Advertiser, 6 Aug 1853; Belfast Commercial Chronicle, 8 Aug 1853; Banner of Ulster, 9 Aug 1853; Northern Whig, 9 Aug 1853; Dundalk Democrat and People's Journal, 13 Aug 1853

Archives
House Bill: HL/PO/JO/10/9/176
Unopposed Bill C'tee Minutes: 28 Apr 1853 (p 101); 5 May 1853 (p 118) (the following pages are indexed but no longer in the records, p 128, 135, 138 and 141): HC/CL/WM/UB/1/4
SOC Minutes: 27 Jun 1853 (p 193–194): HL/PO/CO/1/172
Unopposed Bill C'tee Minutes: 4 Jul 1853 (p 248–251): HL/PO/CO/1/170

Royal Conical Flour Mill Company's Act 1854

PRVA74	1854				
Royal Conical Flour Mill Company's Act 1854 (17 & 18 Vict. c. cxc)					
An Act for incorporating and regulating a Company to be called "The Royal Conical Flour Mill Company," and to enable the said Company to purchase, work, and use certain Letters Patent, and for other Purposes					
Table of contents (patent provisions only)					
s 3 Company incorporated for the purpose of working the Patents, but subject to the Provisions herein-after contained s 30 Licences may be granted to Company					
Relevant patent					
24 Jan 1850 (No 12,939)	Cleaning and grinding corn or grain, and dressing meal or flour [Walter Westrup]				
Journal					
House of Commons			**House of Lords**		
Pres: Joseph Brotherton Rep: Edward Pleydell-Bouverie (Ch W&M)			Rep: Lord Redesdale (Ld Ch)		
10 Mar 1854	109 CJ 125	Pet/Leave	30 Jun 1854	86 LJ 330	Brought HC/1R/Ref SOC
14 Mar 1854	109 CJ 130	1R	6 Jul 1854	86 LJ 353	SOC Rep/Leave
24 Mar 1854	109 CJ 152	2R	11 Jul 1854	86 LJ 370	2R/C'tted
27 Apr 1854	109 CJ 194	C'tted	13 Jul 1854	86 LJ 380	Rep w/o Amds
9 Jun 1854	109 CJ 295	Rep w/o Amds	17 Jul 1854	86 LJ 394	3R
21 Jun 1854	109 CJ 325	Cons day app	24 Jul 1854	86 LJ 422	Royal Assent
22 Jun 1854	109 CJ 327	Cons			
30 Jun 1854	109 CJ 349	3R			
18 Jul 1854	109 CJ 407	HL pass w/o Amds			
24 Jul 1854	109 CJ 431	Royal Assent			

Representation
Solicitor: Durnford & Co

Parliamentary debates
None

Parliamentary papers and cases
None

Gazette notices
London Gazette, 22 Nov 1853 (Iss: 21,496, p 3283)

Newspaper coverage of debates

House of Commons

2R: The Globe, 25 Mar 1854;

C'tted: London Evening Standard, 27 Apr 1854; Morning Advertiser, 28 Apr 1854; Morning Chronicle, 28 Apr 1854; Morning Post, 28 Apr 1854; London Evening Standard, 28 Apr 1854

Cons day app: Globe, 21 Jun 1854; London Evening Standard, 21 Jun 1854 (both misrep)

Cons: Morning Advertiser, 23 Jun 1854; Morning Post, 23 Jun 1854; London Daily News, 23 Jun 1854; Bell's Weekly Messenger, 24 Jun 1854; Carlisle Patriot, 24 Jun 1854; Leeds Intelligencer, 24 Jun 1854; Bell's Weekly Messenger, 26 Jun 1854

3R: The Times, 1 Jul 1854; Globe, 1 Jul 1854; Morning Advertiser, 1 Jul 1854; Morning Chronicle, 1 Jul 1854; Morning Post, 1 Jan 1854; London Daily News, 1 Jul 1854; London Evening Standard, 1 Jul 1854; Bell's Weekly Messenger, 1 Jul 1854; Bell's Weekly Messenger, 3 Jul 1854

Royal Assent: The Times, 25 Jul 1854; London Evening Standard, 25 Jul 1854; Dublin Evening Packet and Correspondent, 25 Jul 1854; Newcastle Journal, 29 Jul 1854

Archives

House Bill: HL/PO/JO/10/9/233

Unopposed Bill C'tee Minutes: 9 Jun 1854 (p 65): HC/CL/WM/UB/1/5

SOC Minutes: 6 Jul 1854 (p 306–307): HL/PO/CO/1/177

SOC Rep: HL/PO/JO/10/9/207 (No 955)

Unopposed Bill C'tee Minutes: 13 Jul 1854 (p 342): HL/PO/CO/1/175

Notes
Amended by Royal Conical Flour Mill Company's Amendment Act 1855 (18 & 19 Vict. c. cxcvii)

Webb and Craig's Patent Act 1862

PRVA75	1862
Webb and Craig's Patent Act 1862 (25 & 26 Vict. c. xvii)	
An Act for rendering valid certain Letters Patent granted to Thomas Webb, of Tutbury in the County of Derby, Cotton Spinner, and James Craig, of the same Place, Manager	

Table of contents

s 1 Power to Commissioners of Patents to stamp Letters Patent
s 2 Letters Patent confirmed
s 3 Saving of Rights
Schedule

Relevant patent	
30 July 1858 (1858 No 1725)	Spinning, doubling, winding, and warping yarns or threads [Thomas Webb and James Craig]

Journal	
House of Commons	**House of Lords**
Rep: William Massey (Ch W&M)	Pres: Lord Westbury LC Rep: Lord Redesdale (Ld Ch)

(continued)

(continued)

10 Feb 1862	117 CJ 21	Bill originate HL	13 Feb 1862	94 LJ 18	Ex Cert
14 Feb 1862	117 CJ 43	SO cw	14 Feb 1862	94 LJ 22	1R
18 Mar 1862	117 CJ 99	Brought HL	20 Feb 1862	94 LJ 26	Ex Cert
18 Mar 1862	117 CJ 100	Ref Ex	24 Feb 1862	94 LJ 32	2R
24 Mar 1862	117 CJ 109	SO cw	6 Mar 1862	94 LJ 60	C'tted
31 Mar 1862	117 CJ 123	2R/C'tted	10 Mar 1862	94 LJ 66	C'tee to meet
6 May 1862	117 CJ 179	Rep w/o Amds	11 Mar 1862	94 LJ 68	Rep w/o Amds
9 May 1862	117 CJ 189	3R	14 Mar 1862	94 LJ 76	3R
16 May 1862	117 CJ 205	Royal Assent	12 May 1862	94 LJ 196	HC pass w/o Amds
			16 May 1862	94 LJ 219	Royal Assent

Representation

Solicitor: Harrison Blair
Agent: Wyatt & Metcalf

Parliamentary debates

Royal Assent: HL Deb, 16 May 1862, Vol 166 (3rd), col 1785
Table of Acts: HC Deb, 7 Aug 1862, Vol 168 (3rd), col 1218

Parliamentary papers and cases

None

Gazette notices

London Gazette: 26 Nov 1861 (Iss: 22,569, p 4878)
Edinburgh Gazette: 26 Nov 1861 (Iss: 7174, p 1455)
Dublin Gazette: 26 Nov 1861 (Iss: 15,530, p 1353)

Newspaper coverage of debates

House of Commons

SO cw: London Daily News, 14 Feb 1862; London Evening Standard, 14 Feb 1862

3R: The Times, 10 May 1862; Morning Advertiser, 10 May 1862; Morning Post, 10 May 1862; London Evening Standard, 10 May 1862; Bell's Weekly Messenger, 10 May 1862; Bell's Weekly Messenger, 12 May 1862

Royal Assent: The Times, 17 May 1862; Morning Advertiser, 17 May 1862; Morning Post, 17 May 1862; London Daily News, 17 May 1862; London Evening Standard, 17 May 1862; Royal Cornwall Gazette, 23 May 1862

Archives

House Bill: HL/PO/JO/10/9/493 (2 copies)

Unopposed Bill C'tee Minutes: 6 May 1862 (p 36): HC/CL/WM/UB/1/13

Unopposed Bill C'tee Minutes: 11 Mar 1862 (p 4–5): HL/PO/CO/1/209

Rammell's Patent Act 1864

PRVA76	1864
Rammell's Patent Act 1864 (27 & 28 Vic, c. clxvii)	

An Act for rendering valid Letters Patent granted to Thomas Webster Rammell for Improvements in Pneumatic Railways and Tube [Pneumatic Despatch Company]

Table of contents

s 1 Power to stamp Letters Patent
s 2 Letters Patent confirmed
s 3 Saving Rights
s 4 Short Title
Schedule

Relevant patent

10 Feb 1860 (1860 No 356)	Pneumatic railways and tubes [Thomas Webster Rammell]

Journal

House of Commons	House of Lords
Rep: William Massey (Ch W&M)	Rep: Lord Redesdale (Ld Ch)

22 Apr 1864	119 CJ 187	Pet/Leave	22 Apr 1864	96 LJ 180	Ex Cert
25 Apr 1864	119 CJ 190	1R/Short title changed	31 May 1864	96 LJ 314	Brought HC/1R/Ref Ex
2 May 1864	119 CJ 208	2R/C'tted	6 Jun 1864	96 LJ 337	No further SO App
26 May 1864	119 CJ 258	Rep w/o Amds	10 Jun 1864	96 LJ 366	2R/C'tted
30 May 1864	119 CJ 268	3R	13 Jun 1864	96 LJ 373	Rep w/o Amds
6 Jul 1864	119 CJ 398	HL pass w/o Amds	5 Jul 1864	96 LJ 496	3R
14 Jul 1864	119 CJ 420	Royal Assent	14 Aug 1864	96 LJ 563	Royal Assent

Representation

Solicitor: Baxter, Rose, Norton & Co

Parliamentary debates

None

Parliamentary papers and cases

None

Gazette notices

London Gazette: 27 Nov 1863 (Iss: 22,792, p 6085) [general notice by Pneumatic Despatch Company]
No Edinburgh or Dublin Gazette

Newspaper coverage of debates

House of Commons

2R: London Evening Standard, 3 May 1864

3R: The Times, 31 May 1865; Morning Advertiser, 31 May 1864; Morning Post, 31 May 1864; London Daily News, 31 May 1864; Reading Mercury, 4 Jun 1864

House of Lords

2R: Globe, 11 Jun 1864

3R: Globe, 17 Jun 1864; Morning Advertiser, 17 Jun 1864

Royal Assent: Globe, 15 Jul 1864; Morning Advertiser, 15 Jul 1864; London Evening Standard, 15 Jul 1864; Bell's Weekly Messenger, 16 Jul 1864; Bell's Weekly Messenger, 18 Jul 1864

Archives

House Bill: HL/PO/JO/10/9/555

Unopposed Bill C'tee Minutes: 26 May 1864 (p 81): HC/CL/WM/UB/1/15

Unopposed Bill C'tee Minutes: 13 Jun 1864 (p 305–307): HL/PO/CO/1/215

Gardiner's Patent Act 1868

PRVA77	1868

Gardiner's Patent Act 1868 (31 & 32 Vict. c. lxiii)

An Act for Rendering Valid Certain Letters Patent Granted to Perry Gardiner of the City of New York in the United States of America

Table of contents

s 1 Power of Commissioners of Patents to stamp Letters Patent as in Schedule
s 2 Letters Patent confirmed
s 3 Saving Rights
Schedule

Relevant patent

1 Dec 1863 (1863 No 3007)	Railroad Car Springs [Perry Gardiner]

Journal

House of Commons			House of Lords		
Rep: John Dodson (Ch W&M)			Pres and Rep: Lord Redesdale (Ld Ch)		
14 Feb 1868	123 CJ 40	Bill originate HL	17 Feb 1868	100 LJ 31	Ex Cert
16 Mar 1868	123 CJ 84	SO cw	18 Feb 1868	100 LJ 34	1R
17 Mar 1868	123 CJ 86	Brought HL/1R	24 Feb 1868	100 LJ 39	2R

(continued)

(continued)

17 Mar 1868	123 CJ 86	Ref Ex	6 Mar 1868	100 LJ 51	C'tted
20 Mar 1868	123 CJ 95	SO cw	9 Mar 1868	100 LJ 52	C'tee to meet
25 Mar 1868	123 CJ 104	2R/C'tted	12 Mar 1868	100 LJ 57	**Rep with Amds**
23 Apr 1868	123 CJ 135	Rep w/o Amds	16 Mar 1868	100 LJ 62	3R
27 Apr 1868	123 CJ 140	3R	28 Apr 1868	100 LJ 131	HC pass w/o Amds
29 May 1868	123 CJ 214	Royal Assent	29 May 1868	100 LJ 243	Royal Assent

Representation

Agent: Wyatt & Metcalf

Parliamentary debates

None

Parliamentary papers and cases

None

Gazette notices

London Gazette: 19 Nov 1867 (Iss: 23,325, p 6165)
Edinburgh Gazette: 26 Nov 1867 (Iss: 7801, p 1399)
Dublin Gazette: 26 Nov 1867 (Iss: 16,170, p 1457)

Newspaper coverage of debates

House of Lords

SO cw: Globe, 14 Feb 1868; Morning Advertiser, 15 Feb 1868; London Daily News, 15 Feb 1868; Waterford Standard, 19 Feb 1868

2R: London Evening Standard, 25 Feb 1868

HL Com: Globe, 13 Mar 1868; London Daily News, 13 Mar 1868; London Evening Standard, 13 Mar 1858

3R: The Times, 17 Mar 1868; Morning Post, 17 Mar 1868; London Evening Standard, 17 Mar 1868

House of Commons

SO cw: Globe, 23 Apr 1868; Morning Advertiser, 24 Apr 1868; London Daily News, 24 Apr 1868

2R: London Evening Standard, 26 Mar 1868

3R: The Times, 28 Apr 1868; Morning Advertiser, 28 Apr 1868; Morning Post, 28 Apr 1868; London Daily News, 28 Apr 1868; London Evening Standard, 28 Apr 1868; Reading Mercury, 2 May 1868; Bell's Weekly Messenger, 2 May 1868; Bell's Weekly Messenger, 4 May 1868

Royal Assent: The Times, 30 May 1868; Morning Post, 30 May 1868; London Daily News, 30 May 1868; London Evening Standard, 30 May 1868

Archives

House Bill: HL/PO/JO/10/9/665

Unopposed Bill C'tee Minutes: 23 Apr 1868 (p 16): HC/CL/WM/UB/1/21

Unopposed Bill C'tee Minutes: 10 Mar 1868 (p 2–6): HL/PO/CO/1/230

Vellum: HL/PO/PB/1/1868/31&32V1n63 [not otherwise printed]

Mills' Patent Act 1873

PRVA78	1873

Mills' Patent Act 1873 (36 & 37 Vict. c. xxxiv)

An Act for rendering valid certain Letters Patent granted to Benjamin Joseph Barnard Mills for Improvements in the Manufacture of Boots and Shoes and in Machinery employed therein

Table of contents

s 1 Power to Commissioners of Patents to stamp letters patent
s 2 Letters patent confirmed
s 3 Restricting charge for royalty
s 4 Saving rights
Schedule

Relevant patent

13 Apr 1869 (1869 No 1131)	Manufacture of boots and shoes; machinery employed therein [Benjamin Joseph Barnard Mills]

Journal					
House of Commons			**House of Lords**		
Rep: John Bonham-Carter (Ch W&M)			Pres and Rep: Lord Redesdale (Ld Ch)		
10 Feb 1873	128 CJ 26	Bill originate HL	11 Feb 1873	105 LJ 18	Ex Cert
27 Mar 1873	128 CJ 116	SO cw	13 Feb 1873	105 LJ 22	1R
27 Mar 1873	128 CJ 117	Brought HL	20 Feb 1873	105 LJ 34	2R day app
28 Mar 1873	128 CJ 119	1R/Ref Ex	28 Feb 1873	105 LJ 68	2R
1 Apr 1873	128 CJ 128	SO cw	7 Mar 1873	105 LJ 81	C'tted
7 Apr 1873	128 CJ 143	2R day app	13 Mar 1873	105 LJ 101	C'tee to meet
21 Apr 1873	128 CJ 149	2R/C'tted	24 Mar 1873	105 LJ 127	**Rep with Amds**
1 May 1873	128 CJ 179	Rep with Amds	25 Mar 1873	105 LJ 158	3R
5 May 1873	128 CJ 184	Cons	13 May 1873	105 LJ 346	HC pass with Amds/Ag
12 May 1873	128 CJ 202	3R	15 May 1873	105 LJ 353	Royal Assent
15 May 1873	128 CJ 216	HL Agree Amds			
15 May 1873	128 CJ 217	Royal Assent			

Representation
Solicitor: Wilson, Bristow and Carpmaels
Agent: Wyatt, Hoskins and Hooker

Parliamentary debates
None

Parliamentary papers and cases
None

Gazette notices
London Gazette: 22 Nov 1872 (Iss: 23,922, p 5587)
Edinburgh Gazette: 26 Nov 1872 (Iss: 8323, p 838)
Dublin Gazette: 22 Nov 1872 (Iss: 16,794, p 801)

Newspaper coverage of debates

House of Lords

2R day app: The Times, 21 Feb 1873; Morning Post, 21 Feb 1873; London Evening Standard, 21 Feb 1873

2R: The Times, 1 Mar 1873; Morning Post, 1 Mar 1873; London Evening Standard, 1 Mar 1873

3R: The Times, 26 Mar 1873; Morning Post, 26 Mar 1873; London Daily News, 26 Mar 1873; London Evening Standard, 26 Mar 1873

House of Commons

2R day app: Morning Post, 8 Apr 1873; London Evening Standard, 8 Apr 1873

2R: The Times, 22 Apr 1873; Morning Post, 22 Apr 1873; London Evening Standard, 22 Apr 1873

3R: The Times, 13 May 1873; Morning Post, 13 May 1873; London Evening Standard, 13 May 1873

Royal Assent: The Times, 16 May 1873

Archives

House Bill: HL/PO/JO/10/9/819 (two copies)

Unopposed Bill C'tee Minutes: 1 May 1873 (p 52): HC/CL/WM/UB/1/26

Unopposed Bill C'tee Minutes: 14 Mar 1873 (p 43–45): HL/PO/CO/1/250

Barlow's Patent Act 1874

PRVA79	1874
Barlow's Patent Act 1874 (37 & 38 Vict. c. xci)	
An Act for rendering valid certain Letters Patent granted to Henry Bernoulli Barlow for Improvements in Embroidering Machines	
Table of contents	

s 1 Power to Commissioners of Patents to stamp letters patent
s 2 Letters patent confirmed
s 3 Saving rights
Schedule

(continued)

(continued)

Relevant patent	
3 Dec 1870 (1870 No 3177)	Embroidering machines [Henry Bernoulli Barlow]

Journal					
House of Commons			**House of Lords**		
SOC Rep: John Mowbray Rep: Henry Raikes (Ch W&M)			Rep: Lord Redesdale (Ld Ch)		
14 Apr 1874	129 CJ 78	SOC Rep	27 Apr 1874	106 LJ 86	Ex Cert
27 Apr 1874	129 CJ 105	SO ncw/Ref SOC	11 May 1874	106 LJ 134	Ref SOC
1 May 1874	129 CJ 119	Pet/Ref SOC	15 May 1874	106 LJ 174	SOC Rep/Disp
8 May 1874	129 CJ 135	SOC Rep/SO Disp /Leave	5 Jun 1874	106 LJ 217	Brought HC/1R/Ref Ex
11 May 1874	129 CJ 138	1R	12 Jun 1874	106 LJ 248	Ex Cert
18 May 1874	129 CJ 159	2R/C'tted	16 Jun 1874	106 LJ 260	2R/C'tted
2 Jun 1874	129 CJ 192	Rep w/o Amds	22 Jun 1874	106 LJ 285	Rep with Amds
5 Jun 1874	129 CJ 204	3R	25 Jun 1874	106 LJ 299	3R
27 Jun 1874	129 CJ 262	HL pass with Amds	2 Jul 1874	106 LJ 329	HC Ag Amds
30 Jun 1874	129 CJ 266	HL Amds Ag	16 Jul 1874	106 LJ 374	Royal Assent
16 Jul 1874	129 CJ 304	Royal Assent			

Representation
Agent: Wyatt, Hoskins and Hooker

Parliamentary debates
None

Parliamentary papers and cases
None

Gazette notices
London Gazette: 27 Feb 1874 (Iss: 24,069, p 894)
Edinburgh Gazette: 27 Feb 1874 (Iss: 8454, p 132)
Dublin Gazette: 27 Feb 1874 (Iss: 16,841, p 137)

Newspaper coverage of debates

House of Commons

2R: The Times, 19 May 1874; Morning Post, 19 May 1874; London Evening Standard, 19 May 1874

3R: The Times, 6 Jun 1874; Morning Post, 6 Jun 1874; London Evening Standard, 6 Jun 1874

House of Lords

2R: The Times, 17 Jun 1874; Morning Post, 17 Jun 1874; London Daily News, 17 Jun 1874; London Evening Standard, 17 Jun 1874

3R: The Times, 26 Jun 1874; Morning Post, 26 Jun 1874; London Evening Standard, 26 Jun 1874

Royal Assent: The Times 17 Jul 1874; Morning Post, 17 Jul 1874; London Daily News, 17 Jul 1874; London Evening Standard, 16 Jul 1874; London Evening Standard, 17 Jul 1874

Archives

House Bill: HL/PO/JO/10/9/839

Unopposed Bill C'tee Minutes: 2 Jun 1874 (p 60): HC/CL/WM/UB/1/27

SOC Minutes: 15 May 1874 (4 pages – no page numbers) [Ex Cert; Statement of Promoter]: HL/PO/CO/1/256

Unopposed Bill C'tee Minutes: 22 Jun 1874 (p 165): HL/PO/CO/1/254

Whitthread's Patent Act 1875

PRVA80	1875
Whitthread's Patent Act 1875 (38 & 39 Vict. c. cxv)	
An Act for rendering valid certain Letters Patent granted to Francis Gerard Prange and William Whitthread for Improvements in the Utilization of Sewage	

Table of contents
s 1 Power to Commissioners of Patents to stamp letters patent s 2 Letters patent confirmed s 3 Saving rights Schedule

Relevant patent	
6 Feb 1872 (1872 No 379)	Improvements in the Utilization of Sewage [Francis Gerard Prange and William Whitthread]

Journal

House of Commons			House of Lords		
SOC Rep: John Mowbray Rep: Henry Raikes (Ch W&M)			Rep: Lord Redesdale (Ld Ch)		
23 Mar 1875	130 CJ 113	SOC Rep	8 Apr 1875	107 LJ 87	Ex Cert
6 Apr 1875	130 CJ 121	SOC ncw/Ref SOC	16 Apr 1875	107 LJ 102	Ref SOC
7 Apr 1875	130 CJ 126	Pet/Ref SOC	20 Apr 1875	107 LJ 107	SOC Rep/Disp
13 Apr 1875	130 CJ 140	SOC Rep/Disp /Leave	13 May 1875	107 LJ 196	Brought HC/1R/Ref Ex
14 Apr 1875	130 CJ 142	1R	31 May 1875	107 LJ 211	Ex Cert
19 Apr 1875	130 CJ 151	2R/C'tted	3 Jun 1875	107 LJ 219	2R/C'tted
5 May 1875	130 CJ 193	Rep with Amds	7 Jun 1875	107 LJ 230	Rep w/o Amds
10 May 1875	130 CJ 200	Cons	15 Jun 1875	107 LJ 260	3R
13 May 1875	130 CJ 212	3R	29 Jun 1875	107 LJ 306	Royal Assent
17 Jun 1875	130 CJ 284	HL pass w/o Amds			
29 Jun 1875	130 CJ 316	Royal Assent			

Representation
Agent: Simson, Wakeford, and Simson

Parliamentary debates
None

Parliamentary papers and cases
None

Gazette notices
London Gazette: 19 Mar 1875 (Iss: 24,192, p 1724) Edinburgh Gazette: 19 Mar 1875 (Iss: 8564, p 191) Dublin Gazette: 19 Mar 1875 (Iss: 16,953, p 208)

Newspaper coverage of debates

House of Commons

2R: The Times, 20 Apr 1875; Morning Post, 20 Apr 1875; London Evening Standard, 20 Apr 1875

3R: The Times, 14 May 1875; Morning Post, 14 May 1875; London Evening Standard, 14 May 1875

House of Lords

2R: The Times, 4 Jun 1875; Morning Post, 4 Jun 1875; London Evening Standard, 4 Jun 1875

3R: The Tines, 16 Jun 1875; Morning Post, 16 Jun 1875; London Evening Standard, 16 Jun 1875

Royal Assent: London Daily News, 30 Jul 1875; London Evening Standard, 30 Jun 1875

Archives

House Bill: HL/PO/JO/10/9/888

Unopposed Bill C'tee Minutes: 5 May 1875 (p 57): HC/CL/WM/UB/1/28

SOC Minutes: 20 Apr 1875 (5 pages – no page numbers) [Ex Cert; Promoter's Statement]: HL/PO/CO/1/260

SOC Rep: HL/PO/JO/10/9/860 (No 316)

Unopposed Bill C'tee Minutes: 7 Jun 1875 (p 116–117): HL/PO/CO/1/258

Campbell's Sewage Patent Act 1875

PRVA81	1875

Campbell's Sewage Patent Act 1875 (38 & 39 Vict. c. cxcii)

An Act for rendering valid certain Letters Patent granted to Dugald Campbell for an improved process for the treatment of sewage and the production of manures therefrom

Table of contents
s 1 Power to Commissioners of Patents to stamp letters patent s 2 Letters patent confirmed s 3 Saving rights Schedule

Relevant patent	
30 Mar 1872 (1872 No 944)	Treatment of sewage and the production of manures therefrom [Dugald Campbell]

Journal					
House of Commons			**House of Lords**		
Rep: Henry Raikes (Ch W&M)			Pres and Rep: Lord Redesdale (Ld Ch)		
2 Jul 1875	130 CJ 324	Brought HL	3 Jun 1875	107 LJ 219	Pet/Ref Ex/1R
2 Jul 1875	130 CJ 324	1R/Ref Ex	7 Jun 1875	107 LJ 229	Ex Cert
6 Jul 1875	130 CJ 332	SO ncw/Ref SOC	7 Jun 1875	107 LJ 230	Ref SOC
8 Jul 1875	130 CJ 338	SOC Rep/Disp	11 Jun 1875	107 LJ 243	SOC Rep/Disp /1R
13 Jul 1875	130 CJ 352	2R/C'tted	15 Jun 1875	107 LJ 260	2R
27 Jul 1875	130 CJ 390	Rep w/o Amds	22 Jun 1875	107 LJ 283	C'tted
30 Jul 1875	130 CJ 400	3R	28 Jun 1875	107 LJ 298	Rep with Amds
2 Aug 1875	130 CJ 409	Royal Assent	1 Jul 1875	107 LJ 311	Cons/3R
			30 Jul 1875	107 LJ 384	HC pass w/o Amds
			2 Aug 1875	107 LJ 389	Royal Assent

Representation
Agent: Wyatt, Hoskins and Hooker

Parliamentary debates
None

Parliamentary papers and cases
None

Gazette notices
London Gazette: 7 May 1875 (Iss: 24,206, p 2465) Edinburgh Gazette: 7 May 1875 (Iss: 8578, p 303) Dublin Gazette: 7 May 1875 (Iss: 16,967, p 303)

Newspaper coverage of debates
House of Lord 2R: The Times, 16 Jun 1875; Morning Post, 16 Jun 1875; London Evening Standard, 16 Jun 1875 3R: The Times, 2 Jul 1875; Morning Post, 2 Jul 1875; London Evening Standard, 2 Jul 1875 *House of Commons* 2R: The Times, 14 Jul 1875; London Evening Standard, 14 Jul 1875 3R: The Times, 31 Jul 1875; London Evening Standard, 31 Jul 1875 Royal Assent: The Times, 3 Aug 1875; Morning Post, 3 Aug 1875; London Daily News, 3 Aug 1875; London Evening Standard, 3 August 1875

Archives
Pet: HL/PO/JO/10/9/863 (No 508) House Bill: HL/PO/JO/10/9/873 Unopposed Bill C'tee Minutes: 27 Jul 1877 (p 108): HC/CL/WM/UB/1/28 SOC Minutes: 11 Jun 1877 (5 pages – no page numbers) [Ex Cert; Statement of Promoter]: HL/PO/CO/1/260 SOC Rep: HL/PO/JO/10/9/864 (No 578) Unopposed Bill C'tee Minutes: 24 Jun 1877 (p 171–175): HL/PO/CO/1/258

Bousfield's Patent Act 1876

PRVA82	1876

Bousfield's Patent Act 1876 (39 & 40 Vict. c. xxi)

An Act for rendering valid certain Letters Patent granted to George Tomlinson Bousfield for Improvements in Lacing Devices and in the Mode of Lacing and Fastening Wearing Apparel and other Articles with the same

Table of contents
s 1 Power to Commissioners of Patents to stamp letters patent s 2 Letters patent confirmed s 3 Saving rights Schedule

Relevant patent	
12 Sep 1872 (1872 No 2707)	Improvements in lacing devices, and in the mode of lacing and fastening wearing apparel and other articles with the same [George Tomlinson Bousfield]

Journal					
House of Commons			**House of Lords**		
Rep: Henry Raikes (Ch W&M)			Pres: Lord Cairns LC Rep: Lords Redesdale (Ld Ch)		
11 Feb 1876	131 CJ 28	Bill originate HL	11 Feb 1876	108 LJ 19	Ex Cert
9 Mar 1876	131 CJ 85	SO cw	14 Feb 1876	108 LJ 23	1R
30 Mar 1876	131 CJ 129	Brought HL	18 Feb 1876	108 LJ 31	2R
31 Mar 1876	131 CJ 130	1R/Ref Ex	23 Mar 1876	108 LJ 85	C'tted
6 Apr 1876	131 CJ 141	SO cw	24 Mar 1876	108 LJ 91	Rep with Amds
11 Apr 1876	131 CJ 155	2R/C'tted	28 Mar 1876	108 LJ 98	3R
2 May 1876	131 CJ 173	Rep w/o Amds	8 May 1876	108 LJ 155	HC pass w/o Amds
5 May 1876	131 CJ 179	3R	1 Jun 1876	108 LJ 223	Royal Assent
1 Jun 1876	131 CJ 238	Royal Assent			

Representation
Solicitor: Wilson, Bristow and Carpmael Agent: Wyatt, Hoskins, and Hooker

Parliamentary debates
None

Parliamentary papers and cases
None

Gazette notices
London Gazette: 30 Nov 1875 (Iss: 24,271, p 6166) Edinburgh Gazette: 30 Nov 1875 (Iss: 8639, p 866) Dublin Gazette: 30 Nov 1875 (Iss: 17,026, p 767)

Newspaper coverage of debates

House of Lords

SO cw: Globe, 26 Jan 1876; Manchester Times, 29 Jan 1876

2R: The Times, 19 Feb 1876; Morning Post, 19 Feb 1876; London Evening Standard, 19 Feb 1876

3R: The Times, 29 Mar 1876; Morning Post, 29 Mar 1876; London Evening Standard, 29 Mar 1876

House of Commons

2R: The Times, 12 Apr 1876; Morning Post, 12 Apr 1876; London Evening Standard, 12 Apr 1876

3R: The Times, 6 May 1876; Morning Post, 6 May 1876; London Evening Standard, 6 May 1876

Royal Assent: The Times, 2 Jun 1876; Morning Post, 2 Jun 1876; London Daily News, 2 Jun 1876; London Evening Standard, 2 Jun 1876

Archives

House Bill: HL/PO/JO/10/9/901

Unopposed Bill C'tee Minutes: 2 May 1876 (p 26): HC/CL/WM/UB/1/29

Unopposed Bill C'tee Minutes: 24 Mar 1876 (p 17): HL/PO/CO/1/262

Hall's Patent Act 1876

PRVA83	1876

Hall's Patent Act 1876 (39 & 40 Vict. c. xxii)
An Act for rendering valid certain Letters Patent granted to Charles Henry Hall for Improvement in Steam Pumps or Apparatus for Elevating Fluids by Steam

Table of contents

s 1 Power to Commissioners of Patents to stamp letters patent
s 2 Letters patent confirmed
s 3 Saving rights
Schedule

Relevant patent

1 Oct 1872 (1872 No 2885)	Steam pumps or apparatus for elevating fluids by steam [Charles Henry Hall]

Journal

House of Commons			House of Lords		
Rep: Henry Raikes (Ch W&M)			Pres: Lord Cairns LC Rep: Lord Redesdale (Ld Ch)		
11 Feb 1876	131 CJ 28	Bill originate HL	11 Feb 1876	108 LJ 19	Ex Cert
9 Mar 1876	131 CJ 85	SO cw	14 Feb 1876	108 LJ 23	1R
30 Mar 1876	131 CJ 129	Brought HL	18 Feb 1876	108 LJ 31	2R
31 Mar 1876	131 CJ 130	1R/Ref Ex	23 Mar 1876	108 LJ 85	C'tted
6 Apr 1876	131 CJ 141	No further SO App	24 Mar 1876	108 LJ 91	Rep with Amds
11 Apr 1876	131 CJ 155	2R/C'tted	28 Mar 1876	108 LJ 98	3R
2 May 1876	131 CJ 173	Rep w/o Amds	8 May 1876	108 LJ 155	HC pass w/o Amds
5 May 1876	131 CJ 179	3R	1 Jun 1876	108 LJ 223	Royal Assent
1 Jun 1876	131 CJ 238	Royal Assent			

Representation

Solicitor: J Henry Johnson
Agent: Wyatt, Hoskins, and Hooker

Parliamentary debates

None

Parliamentary papers and cases

None

Gazette notices

London Gazette: 23 Nov 1875 (Iss: 24,269, p 5771)
Edinburgh Gazette: 23 Nov 1875 (Iss: 8637, p 824)
Dublin Gazette: 23 Nov 1875 (Iss: 17,024, p 720)

Newspaper coverage of debates

House of Lords

SO cw: London Evening Standard, 27 Jan 1876

2R: The Times, 19 Feb 1876; Morning Post, 19 Feb 1876; London Evening Standard, 19 Feb 1876

3R: The Times, 29 Mar 1876; Morning Post, 29 Mar 1876; London Evening Standard, 29 Mar 1876

House of Commons

2R: The Times, 12 Apr 1876; Morning Post, 12 Apr 1876; London Evening Standard, 12 Apr 1876

3R: The Times, 6 May 1876; Morning Post, 6 May 1876; London Evening Standard, 6 May 1876

Royal Assent: The Times, 2 Jun 1876; Morning Post, 2 Jun 1876; London Daily News, 2 Jun 1876; London Evening Standard, 2 Jun 1876

Archives

House Bill: HL/PO/JO/10/9/904

Unopposed Bill C'tee Minutes: 30 May 1876 (p 27): HC/CL/WM/UB/1/29

Unopposed Bill C'tee Minutes: 24 Mar 1876 (p 17–18): HL/PO/CO/1/262

Milner's Patent Act 1876

PRVA84	1876

Milner's Patent Act 1876 (39 & 40 Vict. c. xxiii)

An Act for rendering valid certain Letters Patent granted to Edward Milner for Improvement in the Method of producing White Pigments from Lead

Table of contents

s 1 Power to Commissioners of Patents to stamp letters patent
s 2 Letters patent confirmed
s 3 Saving rights
Schedule

Relevant patent

22 Jun 1872 (1872 No 1881)	Producing white pigments from lead [Edward Milner]

Journal

House of Commons			House of Lords		
Rep: Henry Raikes (Ch W&M)			Pres: Lord Cairns LC Rep: Lord Redesdale (Ld Ch)		
11 Feb 1876	131 CJ 28	Bill originate HL	11 Feb 1876	108 LJ 20	Ex Cert
9 Mar 1876	131 CJ 85	SO cw	14 Feb 1876	108 LJ 24	1R
30 Mar 1876	131 CJ 129	Brought HL	18 Feb 1876	108 LJ 32	2R
31 Mar 1876	131 CJ 130	1R/Ref Ex	23 Mar 1876	108 LJ 85	C'tted
6 Apr 1876	131 CJ 141	No SO app	24 Mar 1876	108 LJ 91	Rep with Amds
11 Apr 1876	131 CJ 155	2R/C'tted	28 Mar 1876	108 LJ 98	3R
2 May 1876	131 CJ 173	Rep w/o Amds	8 May 1876	108 LJ 155	HC pass w/o Amds
5 May 1876	131 CJ 179	3R	1 Jun 1876	108 LJ 223	Royal Assent
1 Jun 1876	131 CJ 238	Royal Assent			

Representation

Agent: Wyatt, Hoskins, and Hooker

Parliamentary debates

None

Parliamentary papers and cases

None

Gazette notices

London Gazette: 26 Nov 1875 (Iss: 24,270, p 5994)
Edinburgh Gazette: 26 Nov 1975 (Iss: 8638, p 854)
Dublin Gazette: 26 Nov 1875 (Iss: 17,025, p 750)

Newspaper coverage of debates

House of Lords

SO cw: Globe, 26 Jan 1876; Liverpool Mercury, 27 Jan 1876

2R: The Times 19 Feb 1976; Morning Post, 19 Feb 1876; London Evening Standard, 19 Feb 1876

3R: The Times, 29 Mar 1876; Morning Post, 29 Mar 1876; London Evening Standard, 29 Mar 1876

House of Commons

2R: The Times, 12 Apr 1876; Morning Post, 12 Apr 1876; London Evening Standard, 12 Apr 1876

3R: The Times, 6 May 1876; Morning Post, 6 May 1876; London Evening Standard, 6 May 1876

Royal Assent: The Times, 2 Jun 1876; Morning Post, 2 Jun 1876; London Daily News, 2 Jun 1876; London Evening Standard, 2 Jun 1876

Archives

House Bill: HL/PO/JO/10/9/906

Unopposed Bill C'tee Minutes: 30 May 1876 (p 27): HC/CL/WM/UB/1/29

Unopposed Bill C'tee Minutes: 24 Mar 1876 (p 19): HL/PO/CO/1/262

Sillar's and Wigner's Patent Act 1876

PRVA85	1876

Sillar's and Wigner's Patent Act 1876 (39 & 40 Vict. c. xxix)

An Act for rendering valid certain Letters Patent granted to William Cameron Sillar, Rother George Sillar, and George William Wigner, for Improvements in deodorising and purifying Sewage and making Manure therefrom

Table of contents

s 1 Power to Commissioners of Patents to stamp letters patent
s 2 Letters patent confirmed
s 3 Saving rights
Schedule

Relevant patent

15 Jun 1868 (1868 No 1954)	Deodorising and purifying sewage and making manure therefrom [William Cameron Sillar, Robert George Sillar and George William Wigner]

Journal

House of Commons			House of Lords		
Rep: Henry Raikes (Ch W&M)			Pres: Lord Cairns LC Rep: Lord Redesdale (Ld Ch)		
11 Feb 1876	131 CJ 28	Bill originate HL	11 Feb 1876	108 LJ 20	Ex Cert
9 Mar 1876	131 CJ 85	SO cw	14 Feb 1876	108 LJ 24	1R
28 Mar 1876	131 CJ 125	Brought HL	21 Feb 1876	108 LJ 35	2R
29 Mar 1876	131 CJ 126	1R/Ref Ex	20 Mar 1876	108 LJ 80	C'tted
3 Apr 1876	131 CJ 134	No further SO App	23 Mar 1876	108 LJ 85	Rep with Amds
10 Apr 1876	131 CJ 151	2R/C'tted	27 Mar 1876	108 LJ 96	3R
2 May 1876	131 CJ 173	Rep with Amds	12 May 1876	108 LJ 167	HC pass with Amds/Ag
8 May 1876	131 CJ 182	Cons	1 Jun 1876	108 LJ 223	Royal Assent
11 May 1876	131 CJ 190	3R			
16 May 1876	131 CJ 198	HL Ag Amds			
1 Jun 1876	131 CJ 238	Royal Assent			

Representation

Solicitor: Davidson & Co
Agent: Marriott and Jordan

Parliamentary debates

None

Parliamentary papers and cases

None

Gazette notices

London Gazette: 30 Nov 1875 (Iss: 24,271, p 6166)

Edinburgh Gazette: 30 Nov 1875 (Iss: 8639, p 868)

Dublin Gazette: 30 Nov 1875 (Iss: 17,026, p 767)

Defunct Notices (Solicitor of J Henry Johnson)

London Gazette: 30 Nov 1875 (Iss: 24,271, p 6166)

Edinburgh Gazette: 30 Nov 1875 (Iss: 8639, p 869)

Dublin Gazette: 30 Nov 1875 (Iss: 17,026, p 767)

Newspaper coverage of debates

House of Lords

SO cw: Globe, 2 Feb 1876; Morning Post, 2 Feb 1876; London Daily News, 2 Feb 1876; London Evening Standard, 2 Feb 1876

2R: The Times, 22 Feb 1876; Morning Post, 22 Feb 1876; London Evening Standard, 22 Feb 1876

3R: The Times, 12 May 1876

House of Commons

2R: The Times, 11 Apr 1876; Morning Post, 11 Apr 1876; London Evening Standard, 11 Apr 1876

3R: The Times, 12 May 1876; Morning Post, 12 May 1876

Royal Assent: The Times, 2 Jun 1876; Morning Post, 2 Jun 1876; London Daily News, 2 Jun 1976; London Evening Standard, 2 Jun 1876

Archives	
House Bill: HL/PO/JO/10/9/909	
Table Bill: HL/PO/JO/10/9/890 (No 87)	
Unopposed Bill C'tee Minutes: 30 May 1876 (p 28): HC/CL/WM/UB/1/29	
Unopposed Bill C'tee Minutes: 31 Mar 1876 (p 4–5): HL/PO/CO/1/262	

Notes
Related cases
Sillar's Patent (1882) (PC) 10 HPC 781; Goodeve's Abr 581

Goux's Patent Act 1876

PRVA86	1876

Goux's Patent Act 1876 (39 & 40 Vict. c. ccvi)
An Act for rendering valid certain Letters Patent granted to Pierre Nicolas Goux for Improvements in collecting and in disinfecting Human Excreta and converting the same into Manure; also in the Apparatus or Means employed therein

Table of contents
s 1 Power to Commissioners of Patents to stamp letters patent
s 2 Letters patent confirmed
s 3 Saving rights
Schedule

Relevant patent	
20 Feb 1868 (1868 No 566)	Collecting and disinfecting human excreta; converting the same into manure; also apparatus or means employed therein [Pierre Nicolas Goux]

Journal					
House of Commons			**House of Lords**		
SOC Rep: John Mowbray Rep: Henry Raikes (Ch W&M)			Rep: Lord Redesdale (Ld Ch)		
28 Apr 1876	131 CJ 166	SOC Rep	15 May 1876	108 LJ 170	Ex Cert
9 Apr 1876	131 CJ 186	Pet/Ref SOC	15 May 1876	108 LJ 170	Ref SOC
9 Apr 1876	131 CJ 186	Ex Rep SO ncw/Ref SOC	19 May 1876	108 LJ 181	SOC Rep/Disp
12 May 1876	131 CJ 192	SOC Rep/Disp	13 Jun 1876	108 LJ 231	Brought HC/1R/Ref Ex
15 May 1876	131 CJ 195	Rep read/Leave/1R	16 Jun 1876	108 LJ 242	Ex Cert
22 May 1876	131 CJ 208	2R/C'tted	19 Jun 1876	108 LJ 248	2R
30 May 1876	131 CJ 232	Rep with Amds	20 Jun 1876	108 LJ 255	C'tted
8 Jun 1876	131 CJ 243	Cons	11 Jul 1876	108 LJ 322	Rep with Amds
12 Jun 1876	131 CJ 251	3R	18 Jul 1876	108 LJ 350	3R
20 Jul 1876	131 CJ 351	HL pass with Amds	25 Jul 1876	108 LJ 367	HC Ag Amds
24 Jul 1876	131 CJ 358	HL Amds Ag	11 Aug 1876	108 LJ 403	Royal Assent
11 Aug 1876	131 CJ 413	Royal Assent			

Representation
Solicitor: J Henry Johnson
Agent: Wm T Manning

Parliamentary debates
None

Parliamentary papers and cases
None

Gazette notices
London Gazette: 14 Apr 1876 (Iss: 24,314, p 2483)
Edinburgh Gazette: 21 Apr 1876 (Iss: 8680, p 279)
Dublin Gazette: 21 Apr 1876 (Iss: 17,068, p 240)

(continued)

(continued)

Newspaper coverage of debates
House of Commons
Cons: Morning Post, 9 Jun 1876;
3R: The Times, 13 Jun 1876; Morning Post, 13 Jun 1876; London Evening Standard, 13 Jun 1876
HL Amds: Morning Post, 25 Jul 1876
House of Lords
2R: The Times, 20 Jun 1876; London Evening Standard, 20 Jun 1876
3R: The Times, 19 Jul 1876; Morning Post, 19 Jul 1876
Royal Assent: The Times, 12 Aug 1876; Morning Post, 12 Aug 1876; London Daily News, 12 Aug 1876; Liverpool Mercury, 12 Aug 1876; Manchester Times, 12 Aug 1876; Yorkshire Post and Leeds Intelligencer, 12 Aug 1876

Archives
House Bill: HL/PO/JO/10/9/904
SOC Minutes: 19 May 1875 (p 123–134): HL/PO/CO/1/264
SOC Rep: HL/PO/JO/10/9/894 (No 302)
Unopposed Bill C'tee Minutes: 11 Jun 1876 (p 162–163): HL/PO/CO/1/262
Unopposed Bill C'tee Minutes: 30 May 1876 (p 71–72): HC/CL/WM/UB/1/29

Harper's Patent Act 1877

PRVA87	1877		
Harper's Patent Act 1877 (40 & 41 Vict. c. xix)			
An Act for rendering valid certain Letters Patent granted to William Harper for Improvements in Machinery or Apparatus for suspending Fabrics in Drying Stoves			

Table of contents
s 1 Power to Commissioners of Patents to stamp letters patent
s 2 Letters patent confirmed
s 3 Saving rights
Schedule

Relevant patent	
25 Sep 1869 (1869 No 2787)	Machinery for suspending fabrics in drying stoves [William Harper]

Journal					
House of Commons			**House of Lords**		
SOC Rep: John Mowbray Rep: Henry Raikes (Ch W&M)			Pres and Rep: Earl Redesdale (Ld Ch)		
9 Feb 1877	132 CJ 9	Ex Rep SO ncw/Ref SOC	9 Feb 1877	109 LJ 21	Ex Cert
12 Feb 1877	132 CJ 18	Bill originate HL	12 Feb 1877	109 LJ 23	1R
13 Mar 1877	132 CJ 94	SOC Rep/Disp	22 Feb 1877	109 LJ 37	Ref SOC
24 Mar 1877	132 CJ 120	Brought HL	27 Feb 1877	109 LJ 44	SOC Rep/Disp
24 Mar 1877	132 CJ 120	1R/Ref Ex	2 Mar 1877	109 LJ 47	2R
5 Apr 1877	132 CJ 129	SO cw	9 Mar 1877	109 LJ 56	C'tted
10 Apr 1877	132 CJ 142	2R/C'tted	20 Mar 1877	109 LJ 75	Rep with Amds
12 Apr 1877	132 CJ 147	Ex Rep SO ncw	22 Mar 1877	109 LJ 79	3R
8 May 1877	132 CJ 207	Rep w/o Amds	14 May 1877	109 LJ 158	HC pass w/o Amds
11 May 1877	132 CJ 214	3R	17 May 1877	109 LJ 167	Royal Assent
17 May 1877	132 CJ 233	Royal Assent			

Representation
Agent: Wyatt, Hoskins and Hooker

Parliamentary debates
None

Parliamentary papers and cases
None

Gazette notices
London Gazette: 19 Dec 1876 (Iss: 24,395, p 7005) Edinburgh Gazette: 19 Dec 1876 (Iss: 8749, p 950) Dublin Gazette: 19 Dec 1876 (Iss: 17,137, p 882)

Newspaper coverage of debates

House of Lords

2R: The Times, 3 Mar 1877; London Evening Standard, 3 Mar 1877

3R: The Times, 23 Mar 1877; Morning Post, 23 Mar 1877

House of Commons

2R: The Times, 11 Apr 1877; Morning Post, 11 Apr 1877; London Evening Standard, 11 Apr 1877

3R: The Times, 12 May 1877; Morning Post, 12 May 1877

Royal Assent: The Times, 18 May 1877; Morning Post, 18 May 1877; London Evening Standard,18 May 1877; London Daily News, 18 Mar 1877

Archives
House Bill: HL/PO/JO/10/9/926
Unopposed Bill C'tee Minutes: 8 May 1877 (p 56): HC/CL/WM/UB/1/30
SOC Minutes: 27 Feb 1877 (p 1–6) [Ex Cert; Statement of Promoter]: HL/PO/CO/1/268
Unopposed Bill C'tee Minutes: 20 Mar 1877 (p 27–28): HL/PO/CO/1/266

Robey and Chantrell's Patent Act 1877

PRVA88	1877
	Robey and Chantrell's Patent Act 1877 (40 & 41 c. ccxlii)

An Act for rendering valid certain Letters Patent granted to James Robey and George Frederick Chantrell for A New or Improvement Filtering and deodorising Medium

Table of contents

s 1 Power to Commissioners of Patents to stamp letters patent
s 2 Letters patent confirmed
s 3 Saving rights
Schedule

Relevant patent

15 Mar 1873 (1873 No 957)	Filtering and deodorising medium [James Robey and George Fredrick Chantrell]

Journal					
House of Commons			**House of Lords**		
SOC Rep: John Mowbray Rep: Henry Raikes (Ch W&M)			Pres and Rep: Earl Redesdale (Ld Ch)		
15 Jun 1877	132 CJ 278	Brought HL	30 Apr 1877	109 LJ 134	1R/Ref Ex
15 Jun 1877	132 CJ 278	1R/Ref Ex	4 May 1877	109 LJ 142	Ex Cert
22 Jun 1877	132 CJ 292	SO ncw/Ref SOC	4 May 1877	109 LJ 142	Ref SOC
29 Jun 1877	132 CJ 308	SOC Rep/SO Disp	8 May 1877	109 LJ 147	SOC Rep/Disp
5 Jul 1877	132 CJ 319	2R day app	14 May 1877	109 LJ 158	2R
12 Jul 1877	132 CJ 337	2R/C'tted	4 Jun 1877	109 LJ 180	C'tted
25 Jul 1877	132 CJ 374	Rep w/o Amds	11 Jun 1877	109 LJ 204	Rep with Amds
30 Jul 1877	132 CJ 388	3R	14 Jun 1877	109 LJ 211	3R
2 Aug 1877	132 CJ 402	Royal Assent	3 Jul 1877	109 LJ 361	HC pass w/o Amds
			2 Aug 1877	109 LJ 368	Royal Assent

Representation
Agent: Wyatt, Hoskins and Hooker

Parliamentary debates
None

(continued)

(continued)

Parliamentary papers and cases
None

Gazette notices
London Gazette: 20 Apr 1877 (Iss: 24,445, p 2692) Edinburgh Gazette: 20 Apr 1877 (Iss: 8784, p 296) Dublin Gazette: 20 Apr 1877 (Iss: 17,173, p 282)

Newspaper coverage of debates
House of Lords
2R: The Times, 15 May 1877; Morning Post, 15 May 1877
3R: The Times, 15 Jun 1877; Morning Post, 15 Jun 1877; London Evening Standard, 15 Jun 1877
House of Commons
2R: The Times, 13 Jul 1877; Morning Post, 13 Jul 1877; London Evening Standard, 13 Jul 1877
3R: The Times, 31 Jul 1877; Morning Post, 31 Jul 1877; London Evening Standard, 31 Jul 1877
Royal Assent: The Times, 3 Aug 1877; Morning Post, 3 Aug 1877; London Daily News, 3 Aug 1877; London Evening Standard, 3 Aug 1877

Archives
House Bill: HL/PO/JO/10/9/932
Unopposed Bill C'tee Minutes: 25 Jul 1877 (p 106): HC/CL/WM/UB/1/30
SOC Minutes: 8 May 1877 (p 383–387) [Ex Cert; Statement of Promoters]: HL/PO/CO/1/268
Unopposed Bill C'tee Minutes: 5 Jun 1877 (p 121–122): HL/PO/CO/1/266
Vellum: HL/PO/PB/1/1877/40&41V1n242 [not otherwise printed]

Aspinwall's Patent Act 1878

PRVA89	1878
Aspinwall's Patent Act 1878 (41 & 42 Vict. c. iv)	
An Act for rendering valid certain Letters Patent granted to Lewis Augustus Aspinwall for a new or improved implement for planting Potatoes	

Table of contents
s 1 Power to Commissioners of Patents to stamp Letters Patent s 2 Letters patent confirmed s 3 Saving rights Schedule

Relevant patent	
27 Oct 1874 (1874 No 3703)	Implement for planting potatoes [Lewis Augustus Aspinwall]

Journal					
House of Commons			**House of Lords**		
Rep: Henry Raikes (Ch W&M)			Pres: Lord Cairns LC Rep: Earl Redesdale (Ld Ch)		
21 Jan 1878	133 CJ 17	Bill originate HL	26 Jan 1878	110 LJ 26	Ex Cert
25 Feb 1878	133 CJ 82	Brought HL	1 Feb 1878	110 LJ 27	1R
25 Feb 1878	133 CJ 82	1R/Ref Ex	8 Feb 1878	110 LJ 38	2R
1 Mar 1878	133 CJ 90	No further SO App	15 Feb 1878	110 LJ 47	C'tted
6 Mar 1878	133 CJ 97	2R/C'tted	19 Feb 1878	110 LJ 52	Rep w/o Amds
15 Mar 1878	133 CJ 112	Rep w/o Amds	22 Feb 1878	110 LJ 55	3R
19 Mar 1878	133 CJ 120	3R	21 Mar 1878	110 LJ 98	HC pass w/o Amds
28 Mar 1878	133 CJ 146	Royal Assent	28 Mar 1878	110 LJ 109	Royal Assent

Representation
Agent: Wyatt, Hoskins and Hooker

Parliamentary debates
None

Parliamentary papers and cases
None

Gazette notices
London Gazette: 13 Nov 1877 (Iss: 24,521, p 6201) Edinburgh Gazette: 16 Nov 1877 (Iss: 8844, p 848) Dublin Gazette: 16 Nov 1877 (Iss: 17,233, p 774)

Newspaper coverage of debates
House of Lords
2R: The Times, 9 Feb 1878; London Evening Standard, 9 Feb 1878
3R: The Times, 23 Feb 1878; London Evening Standard, 23 Feb 1878; Hertford Mercury and Reformer, 2 Mar 1878
House of Commons
2R: The Times, 7 Mar 1878; Morning Post, 7 Mar 1878; London Evening Standard, 7 Mar 1878
3R: The Times, 20 Mar 1878; London Evening Standard, 20 Mar 1878
Royal Assent: The Times, 29 Mar 1878; Morning Post, 29 Mar 1878; London Daily News, 29 Mar 1878; London Evening Standard, 29 Mar 1878

Archives
House Bill: HL/PO/JO/10/9/947
Unopposed Bill C'tee Minutes: 15 Mar 1878 (p 8): HC/CL/WM/UB/1/31
Unopposed Bill C'tee Minutes: 19 Feb 1878 (p 8–9): HL/PO/CO/1/270

Vicars and Smith's Patent Act 1879

PRVA90	1879

Vicars and Smith's Patent Act 1879 (42 & 43 Vict. c. xxxiv)
An Act for rendering valid certain Letters Patent granted to Thomas Vicars the elder and Thomas Vicars the younger, of Liverpool in the County of Lancaster, and James Smith, of the same place, for the Invention of Improvements in Self-stoking Furnaces

Table of contents
s 1 Power to Commissioners of Patents to stamp letters patent s 2 Letters patent confirmed s 3 Saving rights Schedule

Relevant patent	
22 Dec 1875 (1875 No 4443)	Self-stoking Furnaces [Thomas Vicars Eld, Thomas Vicars Yng and James Smith]

Journal					
House of Commons			**House of Lords**		
SOC Rep: John Mowbray Rep: Henry Raikes (Ch W&M)			Pres and Rep: Earl Redesdale (Ld Ch)		
28 Mar 1879	134 CJ 123	Brought HL	27 Feb 1879	111 LJ 37	Pet/1R/Ref Ex
31 Mar 1879	134 CJ 125	1R/Ref Ex	3 Mar 1879	111 LJ 42	SOC ncw
4 Apr 1879	134 CJ 135	SO ncw/Ref SOC	7 Mar 1879	111 LJ 48	Ref SOC
22 Apr 1879	134 CJ 154	SOC Rep/Disp	11 Mar 1879	111 LJ 52	SOC Rep/Disp
22 Apr 1879	134 CJ 154	SOC Rep read	14 Mar 1879	111 LJ 61	2R
28 Apr 1879	134 CJ 163	2R/C'tted	21 Mar 1879	111 LJ 97	C'tted
13 May 1879	134 CJ 201	Rep w/o Amds	4 Mar 1879	111 LJ 100	Rep w/o Amds
16 May 1879	134 CJ 214	3R	27 Mar 1879	111 LJ 108	3R
23 May 1879	134 CJ 239	Royal Assent	19 May 1879	111 LJ 198	HC pass w/o Amds
			23 May 1879	111 LJ 209	Royal Assent

Representation
Solicitor: Walter William Wynne
Agent: Sherwood and Company

(continued)

(continued)

Parliamentary debates
None

Parliamentary papers and cases
None

Gazette notices
London Gazette: 21 Feb 1879 (Iss: 24,681, p 873)
Edinburgh Gazette: 25 Feb 1879 (Iss: 8977, p 184)
Dublin Gazette: 25 Feb 1879 (Iss: 17,371, p 155)

Newspaper coverage of debates
House of Lords
2R: The Times, 15 Mar 1879; London Evening Standard, 15 Mar 1879
3R: The Times, 28 Mar 1879; Morning Post, 28 Mar 1879; London Evening Standard, 28 Mar 1879
House of Commons
2R: Morning Post, 29 Apr 1879
3R: The Times, 28 Mar 1879; Morning Post, 17 May 1879; London Evening Standard, 17 May 1879
Royal Assent: The Times, 24 May 1879; Morning Post, 24 May 1879; London Evening Standard, 24 May 1879

Archives
House Bill: HL/PO/JO/10/9/979
Unopposed Bill C'tee Minutes: 13 May 1879 (p 40): HC/CL/WM/UB/1/32
SOC Minutes: 11 Mar 1879 (p 177–181) [Ex Cert; Statement of Promoter]: HL/PO/CO/1/276
Unopposed Bill C'tee Minutes: 24 Mar 1879 (p 24–25): HL/PO/CO/1/274

Hunt's Patent Act 1880

PRVA91	1880
Hunt's Patent Act 1880 (43 & 44 Vict. c. cxi)	
An Act for rendering valid certain Letters Patent granted to Bristow Hunt for the Invention of improved Machinery or Apparatus for setting and distributing Types	

Table of contents
s 1 Short Title
s 2 Power to Commissioners of Patents to stamp letters patent
s 3 Letters patent confirmed
s 4 Saving rights
Schedule

Relevant patent	
24 Mar 1876 (1876 No 1255)	Machinery or apparatus for setting and distributing types [Bristow Hunt]

Journal					
House of Commons			House of Lords		
SOC Rep: Sir John Mowbray Rep: Lyon Playfair (Ch W&M)			Rep: Earl Redesdale (Ld Ch)		
28 May 1880	135 CJ 163	SOC Rep	10 Jun 1880	112 LJ 185	Ex Cert
7 Jun 1880	135 CJ 183	Pet/Ref SOC	11 Jun 1880	112 LJ 191	Ref SOC
7 Jun 1880	135 CJ 184	SO ncw/Ref SOC	15 Jun 1880	112 LJ 200	SOC Rep/SO Disp
11 Jun 1880	135 CJ 197	SOC Rep/SO Disp /Leave	6 Jul 1880	112 LJ 247	Brought HC/1R/Ref Ex
15 Jun 1880	135 CJ 209	1R	12 Jul 1880	112 LJ 262	No SO applicable
21 Jun 1880	135 CJ 226	2R/C'tted	15 Jul 1880	112 LJ 272	2R/C'tted
2 Jul 1880	135 CJ 268	Rep w/o Amds	16 Jul 1880	112 LJ 277	Rep with Amds
5 Jul 1880	135 CJ 274	3R	20 Jul 1880	112 LJ 289	3R
20 Jul 1880	135 CJ 319	HL pass with Amds	26 Jul 1880	112 LJ 307	HC Ag Amds
23 Jul 1880	135 CJ 327	HL Amds Ag	2 Aug 1880	112 LJ 326	Royal Assent
2 Aug 1880	135 CJ 346	Royal Assent			

Representation
Solicitor: Bower and Cotton
Agent: Dyson and Co

Parliamentary debates
List of Acts: HC Deb, 7 Sep 1880, Vol 256(3rd), col 1344

Parliamentary papers and cases
None

Gazette notices
London Gazette: 30 Apr 1880 (Iss: 24,840, p 2797)
Edinburgh Gazette: 30 Apr 1880 (Iss: 9100, p 425)
Dublin Gazette: 30 Apr 1880 (Iss: 17,496, p 426)

Newspaper coverage of debates

House of Commons

2R: The Times, 22 Jun 1880; Morning Post, 22 Jun 1880

Rep: London Daily News, 3 Jul 1880

3R: The Times, 6 Jul 1880; Morning Post, 6 Jul 1880; London Evening Standard, 6 Jul 1880

HL Amds: Morning Post, 24 Jul 1880

House of Lords

2R: The Times,16 Jul 1880; London Evening Standard, 16 Jul 1880

3R: The Times, 21 Jul 1880; London Evening Standard, 21 Jul 1880

Royal Assent: The Times, 3 Aug 1880; Morning Post, 3 Aug 1880; London Evening Standard, 3 Aug 1880

Archives
House Bill: HL/PO/JO/10/9/997
Unopposed Bill C'tee Minutes: 2 Jul 1880 (p 59): HC/CL/WM/UB/1/33
SOC Minutes: 15 Jun 1880 (p 361 and 379–385) [Ex Cert; Promoter's Statement; Pet for Bill]: HL/PO/CO/1/280
Unopposed Bill C'tee Minutes: 16 Jul 1880 (p 147–148): HL/PO/CO/1/278

Williamson's Patent Act 1880

PRVA92	1880

Williamson's Patent Act 1880 (43 & 44 Vict. c. cxxi)

An Act for rendering valid certain Letters Patent granted to William Shepherd Williamson, of Congleton in the County of Chester, for the Invention of Improvements in Blast Furnaces

Table of contents

s 1 Power to Commissioners of Patents to stamp letters patent
s 2 Letters patent confirmed
s 3 Saving rights
Schedule

Relevant patent

17 May 1877 (1877 No 1931)	Blast Furnaces [William Shepherd Williamson]

Journal					
House of Commons			**House of Lords**		
SOC Rep: Sir John Mowbray Rep: Lyon Playfair (Ch W&M)			Rep: Earl Redesdale (Ld Ch)		
28 Jun 1880	135 CJ 253	Brought HL	3 Jun 1880	112 LJ 172	Pet/1R/Ref Ex
28 Jun 1880	135 CJ 253	1R/Ref Ex	7 Jun 1880	112 LJ 180	SOC ncw/Ref SOC
2 Jul 1880	135 CJ 270	SO ncw/Ref SOC	11 Jun 1880	112 LJ 191	Rep SOC Disp
9 Jul 1880	135 CJ 289	SOC Rep/Disp	15 Jun 1880	112 LJ 200	2R
12 Jul 1880	135 CJ 293	SOC Rep read/1R	22 Jun 1880	112 LJ 216	C'tted

(continued)

14 Jul 1880	135 CJ 300	SO 235 Susp/2R day app		24 Jun 1880	112 LJ 218	Rep with Amds
15 Jul 1880	135 CJ 303	2R/C'tted		28 Jun 1880	112 LJ 226	3R
23 Jul 1880	135 CJ 327	Rep w/o Amds		29 Jul 1880	112 LJ 315	HC pass w/o Amds
27 Jul 1880	135 CJ 334	3R adj		2 Aug 1880	112 LJ 326	Royal Assent
28 Jul 1880	135 CJ 337	3R				
2 Aug 1880	135 CJ 346	Royal Assent				

Representation

Solicitor: A MacDonald Blair
Agent: Lewin and Gregory

Parliamentary debates

2R: HC Deb, 15 Jul 1880, Vol 254(3rd), col 467

List of Acts: HC Deb, 7 Sep 1880, Vol 256(3rd), col 1344

Parliamentary papers and cases

None

Gazette notices

London Gazette: 28 May 1880 (Iss: 24,848, p 3223)
Edinburgh Gazette: 1 Jun 1880 (Iss: 9109, p 526)
Dublin Gazette: 1 Jun 1880 (Iss: 17,505, p 557)

Newspaper coverage of debates

House of Lords

2R: The Times, 15 Jun 1880

3R: The Times, 29 Jun 1880; The Scotsman, 29 Jun 1880

House of Commons

SO cw: London Daily News, 3 Jul 1880

2R: The Times, 16 Jul 1880; Morning Post, 16 Jul 1880

3R: Glasgow Herald, 29 Jul 1880

Royal Assent: The Times, 3 Aug 1880; Morning Post, 3 Aug 1880; London Evening Standard, 3 Aug 1880

Archives

House Bill: HL/PO/JO/10/9/1004

Unopposed Bill C'tee Minutes: 23 Jul 1880 (p 79–80): HC/CL/WM/UB/1/33

SOC Minutes: 11 Jun 1880 (p 351 and 257–360) [Ex Cert; Statement of Promoter]: HL/PO/CO/1/280

Unopposed Bill C'tee Minutes: 24 Jun 1880 (p 106–107): HL/PO/CO/1/278

Muirhead's Patent Act 1880

PRVA93	1880

Muirhead's Patent Act 1880 (43 & 44 Vict. c. cxciii)

An Act for rendering valid certain Letters Patent granted to John Muirhead the younger and Alexander Muirhead, of Regency Street, in the City of Westminster, for the Invention of Improvements in Electric Telegraphs

Table of contents

s 1 Power to Commissioners of Patents to stamp letters patent
s 2 Letters patent confirmed
s 3 Saving rights
Schedule

Relevant patent

2 Jul 1877 (1877 No 2538)	Electric telegraphs [John Muirhead]

Journal					
House of Commons			**House of Lords**		
SOC Rep: Sir John Mowbray Rep: Lyon Playfair (Ch W&M)			Rep: Earl Redesdale (Ld Ch)		
21 Jul 1880	135 CJ 324	SOC Rep	23 Jul 1880	112 LJ 301	SO ncw
22 Jul 1880	135 CJ 324	SO 70 Susp/Ex to proc	29 Jul 1880	112 LJ 314	Ref SOC
23 Jul 1880	135 CJ 327	Pet/Ref SOC	2 Aug 1880	112 LJ 327	SOC Rep/Disp
23 Jul 1880	135 CJ 327	SOC ncw	6 Aug 1880	112 LJ 341	Brought HC /1R/Ref Ex
27 Jul 1880	135 CJ 334	SO Disp	10 Aug 1880	112 LJ 341	No further SO app
27 Jul 1880	135 CJ 335	SOC Rep/Leave	10 Aug 1880	112 LJ 346	2R/C'tted
28 Jul 1880	135 CJ 337	1R/SO 204/235 Susp	13 Aug 1880	112 LJ 353	Rep w/o Amds
29 Jul 1880	135 CJ 340	2R/C'tted	17 Aug 1880	112 LJ 360	3R
30 Jul 1880	135 CJ 344	SO 211 Susp/C'tee app	26 Aug 1880	112 LJ 375	Royal Assent
3 Aug 1880	135 CJ 349	Rep w/o Amds			
6 Aug 1880	135 CJ 361	3R			
20 Aug 1880	135 CJ 395	HL pass w/o Amds			
26 Aug 1880	135 CJ 406	Royal Assent			

Representation

Agent: JC Rees
Solicitor: Bircham and Co

Parliamentary debates

2R: HC Deb, 29 Jul 1880, Vol 254(3rd), col 1660
List of Acts: HC Deb, 7 Sep 1880, Vol 256(3rd), col 1344

Parliamentary papers and cases

None

Gazette notices

London Gazette: 20 Jul 1880 (Iss: 24,865, p 4045)

Edinburgh Gazette: 20 Jul 1880 (Iss: 9123, p 664)

Dublin Gazette: 20 Jul 1880 (Iss: 17,519, p 711)

Newspaper coverage of debates

House of Commons

2R: The Times, 30 Jul 1880; Morning Post, 30 Jul 1880

3R: London Evening Standard, 7 Aug 1880

House of Lords

2R: The Times, 11 Aug 1880

3R: The Times, 18 Aug 1880; London Evening Standard, 18 Aug 1880; Morning Post, 18 Aug 1880

Royal Assent: The Times, 27 Aug 1880; Morning Post, 27 Aug 1880; London Daily News, 27 Aug 1880; London Evening Standard, 27 Aug 1880

Archives

House Bill: HL/PO/JO/10/9/1000

Unopposed Bill C'tee Minutes: 3 Aug 1880 (p 84): HC/CL/WM/UB/1/33

SOC Minutes: 2 Aug 1880 (p 469 and 475–478) [Ex Cert; Statement of Promoter]: HL/PO/CO/1/280

Unopposed Bill C'tee Minutes: 13 Aug 1880 (p 212): HL/PO/CO/1/278

Hancock's Patent Act 1881

PRVA94	1881
Hancock's Patent Act 1881 (44 & 45 Vict. c. vi)	
An Act for rendering valid certain Letters Patent granted to James Hancock for Improvements in Bobbin Net or Twist Lace Machines	

(continued)

(continued)

Table of contents
s 1 Power to Commissioners of Patents to stamp letters patent
s 2 Letters patent confirmed
s 3 Saving rights
s 4 Short Title
Schedule

Relevant patent	
11 Aug 1873 (1873 No 2672)	Bobbin Net or Twist Lace Machines [James Hancock]

Journal					
House of Commons			**House of Lords**		
Rep: Lyon Playfair (Ch W&M)			Pres: Lord Selborne LC Rep: Earl Redesdale (Ld Ch)		
25 Jan 1881	136 CJ 31	Bill originate HL	27 Jan 1881	113 LJ 25	SO cw
2 Mar 1881	136 CJ 101	Brought HL	28 Jan 1881	113 LJ 27	1R
3 Mar 1881	136 CJ 103	1R/Ref Ex	1 Feb 1881	113 LJ 32	2R
7 Mar 1881	136 CJ 106	No further SO App	8 Feb 1881	113 LJ 44	C'tted
14 Mar 1881	136 CJ 123	2R/C'tted	21 Feb 1881	113 LJ 61	C'tee to meet
25 Mar 1881	136 CJ 155	Rep w/o Amds	24 \Feb 1881	113 LJ 66	Rep with Amds
25 Mar 1881	136 CJ 156	SO cw	28 Feb 1881	113 LJ 74	3R
29 Mar 1881	136 CJ 162	3R	31 Mar 1881	113 LJ 150	HC pass w/o Amds
8 Apr 1881	136 CJ 192	Royal Assent	8 Apr 1881	113 LJ 165	Royal Assent

Representation
Solicitor: A Braham Cann
Agent: Wyatt, Hoskins and Hooker

Parliamentary debates
None

Parliamentary papers and cases
None

Gazette notices
London Gazette: 26 Nov 1880 (Iss: 24,906, p 6126)
Edinburgh Gazette: 26 Nov 1880 (Iss: 9160, p 1117)
Dublin Gazette: 26 Nov 1880 (Iss: 17,556, p 1071)

Newspaper coverage of debates
House of Lords
SO cw: Leigh Chronicle and Weekly District Advertiser, 29 Jan 1881; Leeds Mercury, 31 Jan 1881
2R: The Times, 2 Feb 1881; Morning Post, 2 Feb 1881; Cornubian and Redruth Times, 4 Feb 1881; Diss Express, 4 Feb 1881
3R: The Times, 1 Mar 1881; Morning Post, 1 Mar 1881
House of Commons
2R: The Times, 15 Mar 1881; Morning Post, 15 Mar 1881; Manchester Courier and Lancashire General Advertiser, 15 Mar 1881; Yorkshire Post and Leeds Intelligencer, 15 Mar 1881
3R: The Times, 30 Mar 1881; Morning Post, 30 Mar 1881
Royal Assent: The Times, 9 Apr 1881; Morning Post, 9 Apr 1881; London Evening Standard, 9 Apr 1881; London Daily News, 9 Apr 1881

Archives
House Bill: HL/PO/JO/10/9/1021
Unopposed Bill C'tee Minutes: 22 Mar 1881 (p 24): HC/CL/WM/UB/1/34
Unopposed Bill C'tee Minutes: 24 Feb 1881 (p 3–5): HL/PO/CO/1/282

Notes
Related Case
Cropper v Smith (1883) (CA) 10 HPC 891; LR 24 Ch D 305

Greene's Patent Act 1881

PRVA95	1881	
	Greene's Patent Act 1881 (44 & 45 Vict. c. cxxvii)	
	An Act for rendering valid certain Letters Patent granted to John Greene for the invention of improvements in the manufacture of Types Logotypes and Phrasotypes and in Apparatus therefor	

Table of contents

s 1 Power to Commissioners of Patents to stamp letters patent
s 2 Letters patent confirmed
s 3 Saving rights
Schedule

Relevant patent

10 Apr 1872 (1872 No 1056)	Manufacture of types logotypes and phrasotypes [John Greene]

Journal

House of Commons			House of Lords		
Rep: Lyon Playfair (Ch W&M)			Pres: Lord Selborne LC		
			Rep: Earl Redesdale (Ld Ch)		
25 Jan 1881	136 CJ 31	Bill originate HL	15 Feb 1881	113 LJ 52	SO cw
25 Mar 1881	136 CJ 156	SO cw	17 Feb 1881	113 LJ 56	1R
5 Apr 1881	136 CJ 180	Brought HL	24 Feb 1881	113 LJ 66	2R
6 Apr 1881	136 CJ 180	1R/Ref Ex	3 Mar 1881	113 LJ 80	C'tted
16 May 1881	136 CJ 238	No further SO App	18 Mar 1881	113 LJ 129	C'tee to meet
23 May 1881	136 CJ 252	2R/C'tted	25 Mar 1881	113 LJ 141	Rep with Amds
17 Jun 1881	136 CJ 309	Rep w/o Amds	31 Mar 1881	113 LJ 150	3R
7 Jul 1881	136 CJ 355	3R	8 Jul 1881	113 LJ 312	HC pass w/o Amds
18 Jul 1881	136 CJ 380	Royal Assent	18 Jul 1881	113 LJ 334	Royal Assent

Representation

Agent: P Burrows Sharkey

Parliamentary debates

None

Parliamentary papers and cases

None

Gazette notices

London Gazette: 2 Mar 1880 (Iss: 24,819, p 1803); 26 Nov 1880 (Iss: 24,906, p 6126)
Edinburgh Gazette: 5 Mar 1880 (Iss: 9084, p 226); 26 Nov 1880 (Iss: 9160, p 1117)
Dublin Gazette: 26 Nov 1880 (Iss: 17,556, p 1067)

Newspaper coverage of debates

House of Lords

2R: The Times, 25 Feb 1881; Morning Post, 25 Feb 1881; London Evening Standard, 25 Feb 1881

3R: The Times, 1 Apr 1881; Morning Post, 1 Apr 1881; London Evening Standard, 1 Apr 1881

House of Commons

2R: The Times, 24 May 1881; Morning Post, 24 May 1881; London Evening Standard, 24 May 1881

3R: The Times, 8 Jul 1881

Royal Assent: The Times, 19 Jul 1881; Morning Post, 19 Jul 1881; Stamford Mercury, 22 Jul 1881

Archives

House Bill: HL/PO/JO/10/9/1020

Unopposed Bill C'tee Minutes: 17 Jun 1881 (p 80): HC/CL/WM/UB/1/34

Unopposed Bill C'tee Minutes: 25 Mar 1881 (p 38–39): HL/PO/CO/1/282

Copland's Patent Act 1881

PRVA96	1881
	Copland's Patent Act 1881 (44 & 45 Vict. c. clxxxvii)

An Act for rendering valid certain Letters Patent granted to Henry Syed Smart Copland for improvements in the formation of roads or ways with wood paving with or without rails and in apparatus for the purpose

Table of contents

s 1 Power to Commissioners of Patents to stamp letters patent
s 2 Letters patent confirmed
s 3 Saving rights
Schedule

Relevant patent

27 Dec 1872 (1872 No 3925)	Formation of roads or ways with wood paving with or without rails; apparatus for same [Henry Syed Smart Copland]

Journal

House of Commons			House of Lords		
Rep: Lyon Playfair (Ch W&M)			Pres: Lord Selbourne LC Rep: Earl Redesdale (Ld Ch)		
25 Jan 1881	136 CJ 31	Bill originate HL	15 Feb 1881	113 LJ 52	SO cw
14 Mar 1881	136 CJ 124	Brought HL/1R/Ref Ex	18 Feb 1881	113 LJ 58	1R
18 Mar 1881	136 CJ 140	No further SO App	25 Feb 1881	113 LJ 71	2R
23 Mar 1881	136 CJ 151	2R/C'tted	4 Mar 1881	113 LJ 82	C'tted
25 Mar 1881	136 CJ 156	SO cw	7 Mar 1881	113 LJ 87	Rep with Amds
31 May 1881	136 CJ 275	Rep w/o Amds	11 Mar 1881	113 LJ 95	3R
25 Jul 1881	136 CJ 399	3R	26 Jul 1881	113 LJ 350	HC pass w/o Amds
11 Aug 1881	136 CJ 451	Royal Assent	11 Aug 1881	113 LJ 404	Royal Assent

Representation

Agent: Holmes, Anton and Greig

Parliamentary debates

None

Parliamentary papers and cases

None

Gazette notices

London Gazette: 26 Nov 1880 (Iss: 24,906, p 6136)
Edinburgh Gazette: 26 Nov 1990 (Iss: 9160, p 1112)
Dublin Gazette: 26 Nov 1880 (Iss: 17,556, p 1071)

Newspaper coverage of debates

House of Lords

2R: The Times, 26 Feb 1881; Morning Post, 26 Feb 1881

3R: The Times, 12 Mar 1881; London Evening Standard, 12 Mar 1881

House of Commons

2R: The Times, 24 Mar 1881; Morning Post, 24 Mar 1881; London Evening Standard, 24 Mar 1881

3R: The Times, 26 Jul 1881; Morning Post, 26 Jul 1881

Royal Assent: The Times, 12 Aug 1881; Morning Post, 12 Aug 1881; Belfast Morning News, 12 Aug 1881

Archives

House Bill: HL/PO/JO/10/9/1018

Unopposed Bill C'tee Minutes: 31 May 1881 (p 70): HC/CL/WM/UB/1/34

Unopposed Bill C'tee Minutes: 7 Mar 1881 (p 16–18): HL/PO/CO/1/282

Lecky and Smyth's Patent Act 1882

PRVA97	1882
	Lecky and Smyth's Patent Act 1882 (45 & 46 Vict. c. lxxxiv)

An Act for reviving and rendering valid certain Letters Patent, granted to Francis Boyce Lecky and William Hugh Smyth, for improvements in the manufacture of soles, and in the machinery or apparatus employed therefor

Table of contents

Relevant patent	
14 Mar 1879 (1879 No 1010)	Manufacture of soles; Apparatus employed therefor [Francis Boyce Lecky and William Hugh Smyth]

Journal

House of Commons			House of Lords		
SOC Rep: Sir John Mowbray Rep: Lyon Playfair (Ch W&M)			Rep: Earl Redesdale (Ld Ch)		
21 Apr 1882	137 CJ 150	SOC Rep	1 May 1882	114 LJ 127	Ex Cert
1 May 1882	137 CJ 168	Pet/Ref SOC	8 May 1882	114 LJ 139	Ref SOC
1 May 1882	137 CJ 169	SO ncw/Ref SOC	12 May 1882	114 LJ 149	SOC Rep/Disp
5 May 1882	137 CJ 180	SO Rep/Disp	6 Jun 1882	114 LJ 187	Brought HC/1R/Ref Ex
5 May 1882	137 CJ 181	SOC Rep read/Leave	12 Jun 1882	114 LJ 203	No further SO App
8 May 1882	137 CJ 184	1R	15 Jun 1882	114 LJ 219	2R/C'tted
15 May 1882	137 CJ 198	2R/C'tted	22 Jun 1882	114 LJ 240	Rep w/o Amds
25 May 1882	137 CJ 231	Rep with Amds	26 Jun 1882	114 LJ 257	3R
1 Jun 1882	137 CJ 237	Cons	3 Jul 1882	114 LJ 279	Royal Assent
5 Jun 1882	137 CJ 245	3R			
27 Jun 1882	137 CJ 307	HL pass w/o Amds			
3 Jul 1882	137 CJ 326	Royal Assent			

Representation

Solicitor: Bannatyne, Kirkwood, McJannett and France
Agent: Grahams and Currey

Parliamentary debates

None

Parliamentary papers and cases

None

Gazette notices

London Gazette: 14 Apr 1882 (Iss: 25,095, p 1704)
Edinburgh Gazette: 14 Apr 1882 (Iss: 9304, p 295)
Dublin Gazette: 14 Apr 1882 (Iss: 17,709, p 438)

Newspaper coverage of debates

House of Commons
2R: The Times, 16 May 1882
3R: The Times, 6 Jun 1882; Morning Post, 6 Jun 1882
House of Lords
2R: The Times, 16 Jun 1882; Morning Post, 16 Jun 1882; London Evening Standard, 16 Jun 1882
3R: The Times, 27 Jun 1882; Morning Post, 27 Jun 1882; London Evening Standard, 27 Jun 1882
Royal Assent: The Times, 4 Jul 1882; Morning Post, 4 Jul 1882

Archives

House Bill: HL/PO/JO/10/9/1055
Minute Bill: HL/PO/JO/10/9/1041 (No 500)
Unopposed Bill C'tee Minutes: 25 May 1882 (p 61): HC/CL/WM/UB/1/35
SOC Minutes: 12 May 1882 (p 271–277) [Ex Cert; Statement of Promoters): HL/PO/CO/1/288
Unopposed Bill C'tee Minutes: 22 Jun 1882 (p 164–166): HL/PO/CO/1/286

Chetham's Patent Act 1883

PRVA98	1883
	Chetham's Patent Act 1883 (46 & 47 Vict. c. i)

An Act for rendering valid certain Letters Patent granted to William Chetham for Improvements in Self-acting Temples for Looms

Table of contents
s 1 Power to Commissioners of Patents to stamp letters patent s 2 Letters patent confirmed s 3 Saving rights s 4 Short Title Schedule

Relevant patent	
8 Aug 1879 (1879 No 3187)	Self-acting temples for looms [William Chetham]

Journal

House of Commons			House of Lords		
Rep: Sir Arthur Otway (Ch W&M)			Pres: Lord Selborne LC Rep: Earl Redesdale (Ld Ch)		
19 Feb 1883	138 CJ 19	Bill originate HL	20 Feb 1883	115 LJ 17	Ex Cert
5 Mar 1883	138 CJ 65	SO cw	22 Feb 1883	115 LJ 21	1R
12 Mar 1883	138 CJ 85	Brought HL	26 Feb 1883	115 LJ 27	2R
12 Mar 1883	138 CJ 85	1R/Ref Ex	5 Mar 1883	115 LJ 36	C'tted
16 Mar 1883	138 CJ 97	No further SO App	8 Mar 1883	115 LJ 45	Rep with Amds
29 Mar 1883	138 CJ 106	2R/C'tted	9 Mar 1883	115 LJ 49	3R
6 Apr 1883	138 CJ 122	Rep with Amds	17 Apr 1883	115 LJ 91	HC pass with Amds/Ag
11 Apr 1883	138 CJ 132	Cons	26 Apr 1883	115 LJ 113	Royal Assent
16 Apr 1883	138 CJ 139	3R			
20 Apr 1883	138 CJ 152	HL Ag Amds			
26 Apr 1883	138 CJ 163	Royal Assent			

Representation
Agent: Wyatt, Hoskins and Hooker

Parliamentary debates
None

Parliamentary papers and cases
None

Gazette notices
London Gazette: 24 Nov 1882 (Iss: 25,171, p 5333)
Edinburgh Gazette: 24 Nov 1882 (Iss: 9368, p 918)
Dublin Gazette: 24 Nov 1882 (Iss: 17,781, p 1256)

Newspaper coverage of debates
House of Lords
2R: The Times, 27 Feb 1883; Morning Post, 27 Feb 1883
3R: The Times, 10 Mar 1883; Morning Post, 10 Mar 1883; London Evening Standard, 10 Mar 1883
House of Commons
2R: The Times, 30 Mar 1883; Morning Post, 30 Mar 1883; London Evening Standard, 30 Mar 1883
3R: The Times, 17 Apr 1883; Morning Post, 17 Apr 1883; London Evening Standard, 17 Apr 1883
Royal Assent: The Times, 27 Apr 1883; Morning Post, 27 Apr 1883

Archives
House Bill: HL/PO/JO/10/9/1087
Minute Bill: HL/PO/JO/10/9/1066 (No 48)
Unopposed Bill C'tee Minutes: 6 Apr 1883 (p 4): HC/CL/WM/UB/1/36
Unopposed Bill C'tee Minutes: 8 Mar 1883 (p 3–4): HL/PO/CO/1/290

Mullings' Patent Act 1883

PRVA99	1883

Mullings' Patent Act 1883 (46 & 47 Vict c. v)

An Act for reviving and rendering valid certain Letters Patent granted to Thomas John Mullings for a new and improved process for extracting Oil and Fat and oil and fatty matters from Wool and other substances and the apparatus connected therewith and applicable thereto

Table of contents

s 1 Power to stamp Letters Patent
s 2 Letters patent revived and confirmed
s 3 Saving rights
s 4 Short Title
Schedule

Relevant patent

1879 No 4262 (21 Oct 1879)	Extracting oil and fat and oil and fatty matters from wool and other substances; apparatus connected therewith [Thomas John Mullings]

Journal

House of Commons			House of Lords		
Rep: Sir Arthur Otway (Ch W&M)			Pres: Lord Selbourne LC Rep: Earl Redesdale (Ld Ch)		
19 Feb 1883	138 CJ 19	Bill originate HL	20 Feb 1883	115 LJ 18	Ex Cert
5 Mar 1883	138 CJ 65	SO cw	22 Feb 1883	115 LJ 21	1R
12 Mar 1883	138 CJ 85	Brought HL	26 Feb 1883	115 LJ 28	2R
12 Mar 1883	138 CJ 85	1R/Ref Ex	5 Mar 1883	115 LJ 36	C'tted
16 Mar 1883	138 CJ 97	No further SO App	8 Mar 1883	115 LJ 45	Rep w/o Amds
29 Mar 1883	138 CJ 107	2R/C'tted	9 Mar 1883	115 LJ 49	3R
6 Apr 1883	138 CJ 122	Rep w/o Amds	24 Apr 1883	115 LJ 109	HC pass w/o Amds
23 Apr 1883	138 CJ 155	3R	26 Apr 1883	115 LJ 113	Royal Assent
26 Apr 1883	138 CJ 163	Royal Assent			

Representation

Agent: Durnford and Co

Parliamentary debates

None

Parliamentary papers and cases

None

Gazette notices

London Gazette: 21 Nov 1882 (Iss: 25,170, p 5206)

Edinburgh Gazette: 24 Nov 1882 (Iss: 9368, p 918)

Dublin Gazette: 24 Nov 1882 (Iss: 17,781, p 1240)

Newspaper coverage of debates

House of Lords

2R: The Times, 27 Feb 1883

3R: The Times, 10 Mar 1883; Morning Post, 10 Mar 1883; London Evening Standard, 10 Mar 1883

House of Commons

2R: The Times, 30 Mar 1883; Morning Post, 30 Mar 1883; London Evening Standard, 30 Mar 1883

3R: The Times, 24 Apr 1883; Morning Post, 24 Apr 1883; London Evening Standard, 24 Apr 1883

Royal Assent: The Times, 27 Apr 1883; Morning Post, 27 Apr 1883; London Evening Standard, 27 Apr 1883

Archives

House Bill: HL/PO/JO/10/9/1096

Minute Bill: HL/PO/JO/10/9/1066 (No 61)

Unopposed Bill C'tee Minutes: HC/CL/WM/UB/1/36

Unopposed Bill C'tee Minutes: 8 Mar 1883 (1–2): HL/PO/CO/1/290

Laws' Patent Act 1883

PRVA100	1883

Laws' Patent Act 1883 (46 & 47 Vict. c. liii)

An Act for rendering valid certain Letters Patent granted to Joseph Law and Henry Law for Improvements in appliances for heating hardening and tempering Wire used in the manufacture of Cards for Carding Fibres

Table of contents

s 1 Power to Commissioners of Patents to stamp letters patent
s 2 Letters patent confirmed
s 3 Saving rights
Schedule

Relevant patent

14 Jan 1880 (1880 No 162)	Appliances for heating hardening and tempering Wire used in the manufacture of cards for carding fibres [Joseph Law and Henry Law]

Journal

House of Commons			House of Lords		
SOC Rep: Sir John Mowbray Rep: Sir Arthur Otway (Ch W&M)			Rep: Lord Speaker		
13 Mar 1883	138 CJ 87	SO Pet	3 Apr 1883	115 LJ 68	Ex Cert
29 Mar 1883	138 CJ 107	Pet/Ref SOC	5 Apr 1883	115 LJ 70	Ref SOC
29 Mar 1883	138 CJ 107	SO ncw/Ref SOC	10 Apr 1883	115 LJ 80	SOC Rep/Disp
3 Apr 1883	138 CJ 114	SO Rep/Disp/Leave	24 May 1883	115 LJ 150	Brought HC/1R/Ref Ex
5 Apr 1883	138 CJ 119	1R	28 May 1883	115 LJ 154	No further SO App
11 Apr 1883	138 CJ 132	2R/C'tted	1 Jun 1883	115 LJ 168	2R/C'tted
9 May 1883	138 CJ 195	Rep w/o Amds	11 Jun 1883	115 LJ 190	C'tee to meet
21 May 1883	138 CJ 205	3R	15 Jun 1883	115 LJ 208	Rep w/o Amds
22 Jun 1883	138 CJ 295	HL pass w/o Amds	19 Jun 1883	115 LJ 223	3R
29 Jun 1883	138 CJ 310	Royal Assent	29 Jun 1883	115 LJ 260	Royal Assent

Representation

Solicitor: George Brierley
Agent: Torr & Co

Parliamentary debates

None

Parliamentary papers and cases

None

Gazette notices

London Gazette: 6 Mar 1883 (Iss: 25,209, p 1269)

Edinburgh Gazette: 6 Mar 1883 (Iss: 9397, p 163)

Dublin Gazette: 3 Mar 1883 (Iss: 17,812, p 249)

Newspaper coverage of debates

House of Commons

2R: The Times, 12 Apr 1883

House of Lords

2R: The Times, 2 Jun 1883; Morning Post, 2 Jun 1883

3R: The Times, 20 Jun 1883; Morning Post, 20 Jun 1883; London Evening Standard, 20 Jun 1883

Royal Assent: The Times, 30 Jun 1883; Morning Post, 30 Jun 1883

Archives

House Bill: HL/PO/JO/10/9/1094

Minute Bill: HL/PO/JO/10/9/1074 (No 386)

Unopposed Bill C'tee Minutes: 9 May 1883 (p 30): HC/CL/WM/UB/1/36

SOC Minutes: 10 Apr 1883 (p 443 and 453–455) [Ex Cert; Statement of Promoter]: HL/PO/CO/1/292

Unopposed Bill C'tee Minutes: 16 Jun 1883 (p 106–107): HL/PO/CO/1/290

Haddan's Patent Act 1883

PRVA101	1883	
Haddan's Patent Act 1883 (46 & 47 Vict. c. clxxxv)		
An Act for rendering valid certain Letters Patent granted to Herbert John Haddan for Improvements in Electric Lamps		

Table of contents

s 1 Power to Commissioners of Patents to stamp letters patent
s 2 Letters patent confirmed
s 3 Saving rights
s 4 Short Title
Schedule

Relevant patent

26 Apr 1880 (1880 No 1704)	Electric Lamps [Herbert John Haddan]

Journal

House of Commons			House of Lords		
Rep: Sir Arthur Otway (Ch W&M)			Rep: Earl Redesdale (Ld Ch)		
5 Jun 1883	138 CJ 277	SO Pet	16 Jul 1883	115 LJ 339	Brought HC/1R/Ref Ex
18 Jun 1883	138 CJ 279	SO Susp/Ex sat	17 Jul 1883	115 LJ 341	Ex Cert/Ref SOC
19 Jun 1883	138 CJ 285	Pet/SOC ncw/Ref SOC	23 Jul 1883	115 LJ 352	SOC Rep/Disp
22 Jun 1883	138 CJ 296	SOC Rep/Disp	24 Jul 1883	115 LJ 357	2R/C'tted
25 Jun 1883	138 CJ 296	Leave/1R	30 Jul 1883	115 LJ 366	Rep with Amds
2 Jul 1883	138 CJ 313	2R/C'tted	2 Aug 1883	115 LJ 373	3R
13 Jul 1883	138 CJ 350	Rep w/o Amds	20 Aug 1883	115 LJ 424	Royal Assent
16 Jul 1883	138 CJ 352	SO Susp/3R			
3 Aug 1883	138 CJ 414	HL pass with Amds/Ag			
20 Aug 1883	138 CJ 473	Royal Assent			

Representation

Solicitor: Johnson, Upton, Budd and Atkey

Parliamentary debates

None

Parliamentary papers and cases

None

Gazette notices

London Gazette: 15 Jun 1883 (Iss: 25,242, p 3103)

Edinburgh Gazette: 15 Jun 1883 (Iss: 9426, p 447)

Dublin Gazette: 15 Jun 1883 (Iss: 17,842, p 796)

Newspaper coverage of debates

House of Commons

2R: The Times, 3 Jul 1883; Morning Post, 3 Jul 1883

3R: Morning Post, 17 Jul 1883

House of Lords

2R: The Times, 25 Jul 1883; London Evening Standard, 25 Jul 1883

3R: Morning Post, 3 Aug 1883; The Times, 3 Aug 1883

Royal Assent: The Times, 21 Aug 1883; Morning Post, 21 Aug 1883

Archives

House Bill: HL/PO/JO/10/9/1093

Minute Bill: HL/PO/JO/10/9/1081 (No 601)

Unopposed Bill C'tee Minutes: 17 Jul 1883 (p 86): HC/CL/WM/UB/1/36

SOC Minutes: 23 Jul 1883 (p 675–679) [Ex Cert; Statement of Promoter]: HL/PO/CO/1/292

Unopposed Bill C'tee Minutes: 30 Jul 1883 (p 221–223): HL/PO/CO/1/290

Bradbury and Lomax's Patent Act 1884

PRVA102	1884
Bradbury and Lomax's Patent Act 1884 (47 & 48 Vict. c. ix)	
An Act for rendering valid certain Letters Patent granted to George Francis Bradbury and Henry Lomax for Improvements in Sewing Machines	

Table of contents
s 1 Power to Comptroller General of Patents to stamp Letters Patent [Confirmation and Saving] s 2 Short title Schedule

Relevant patent	
21 Oct 1875 (1875 No 3653)	Sewing Machines [George Francis Bradbury and Henry Lomax]

Journal					
House of Commons			**House of Lords**		
SOC Rep: Sir John Mowbray Rep: Sir Arthur Otway (Ch W&M)			Pres: Lord Selborne LC Rep: Earl Redesdale (Ld Ch)		
8 Feb 1884	139 CJ 30	Bill originate HL	11 Feb 1884	116 LJ 20	Ex Cert
11 Feb 1884	139 CJ 34	SO ncw/Ref SOC	12 Feb 1884	116 LJ 23	Pres/1R
27 Feb 1884	139 CJ 77	SOC Rep/Disp	15 Feb 1884	116 LJ 32	Ref SOC
3 Mar 1884	139 CJ 84	Cert SO ncw	19 Feb 1884	116 LJ 36	Rep SOC/Disp
18 Mar 1884	139 CJ 119	Brought HL	22 Feb 1884	116 LJ 42	2R
19 Mar 1884	139 CJ 120	1R/Ref Ex	29 Feb 1884	116 LJ 58	C'tted
24 Mar 1884	139 CJ 134	No further SO App	4 Mar 1884	116 LJ 65	C'tee to meet
31 Mar 1884	139 CJ 146	2R/C'tted	13 Mar 1884	116 LJ 79	Rep with Amds
7 Apr 1884	139 CJ 164	Rep w/o Amds	17 Mar 1884	116 LJ 85	3R
21 Apr 1884	139 CJ 170	3R	22 Apr 1884	116 LJ 136	HC pass w/o Amds
28 Apr 1884	139 CJ 186	Royal Assent	28 Apr 1884	116 LJ 144	Royal Assent

Representation
Solicitor: Charles Colchester Agent: Sherwood and Co

Parliamentary debates
List of Acts: HC Deb, 14 Aug 1884, Vol 292(3rd), col 656

Parliamentary papers and cases
None

Gazette notices
London Gazette: 18 Dec 1883 (Iss: 25,297, p 6523)
Edinburgh Gazette: 18 Dec 1883 (Iss: 9480, p 999)
Dublin Gazette: 18 Dec 1883 (Iss: 17,897, p 1819)

Newspaper coverage of debates
House of Lords
2R: The Times, 23 Feb 1844; Morning Post, 23 Feb 1884
3R: Morning Post, 18 Mar 1884
House of Commons
2R: Morning Post, 1 Apr 1884
3R: The Times, 22 Apr 1884; Morning Post, 22 Apr 1884
Royal Assent: The Times. 29 Apr 1884; Yorkshire Post, 29 Apr 1884; Manchester Courier and Lancashire General Advertiser, 29 Apr 1884

Archives
House Bill: HL/PO/JO/10/9/1125
Minute Bill: HL/PO/JO/10/9/1102 (No 53)
Unopposed Bill C'tee Minutes: 7 Apr 1884 (p 34): HC/CL/WM/UB/1/37
SOC Minutes: 19 Feb 1884 (p 3 and 9–13) [Ex Cert; Statement of Promoter]: HL/PO/CO/1/296
Unopposed Bill C'tee Minutes: 7 Mar 1884 (p 5–6): HL/PO/CO/1/294

Boult's Patent Act 1884

PRVA103	1884

Boult's Patent Act 1884 (47 & 48 Vict c. xi)

An Act for rendering valid certain Letters Patent granted to Alfred Julius Boult of 323 High Holborn in the County of Middlesex for Improvements in the method and means of removing Dust from Carpets

Table of contents

s 1 Powers to Comptroller-General and confirmation of Letters Patent
s 2 Saving rights
s 3 Short title
Schedule

Relevant patent

1 Dec 1880 (1880 No 5010)	Removing dust from carpets [Alfred Julius Boult]

Journal

House of Commons			House of Lords		
SOC Rep: Sir John Mowbray Rep: Sir Lyon Playfair			Pres: Lord Selborne LC Rep: Earl Redesdale (Ld Ch)		
8 Feb 1884	139 CJ 30	Bill originate HL	11 Feb 1884	116 LJ 20	Ex Cert
11 Feb 1884	139 CJ 34	SO ncw/Ref SOC	12 Feb 1884	116 LJ 23	1R
3 Mar 1884	139 CJ 84	Cert SO ncw/Ref SOC	15 Feb 1884	116 LJ 32	Ref SOC
4 Mar 1884	139 CJ 89	SOC Rep/Disp	19 Feb 1884	116 LJ 36	SOC Rep/Disp
14 Mar 1884	139 CJ 111	Brought HL	22 Feb 1884	116 LJ 42	2R
14 Mar 1884	139 CJ 111	1R/Ref Ex	29 Feb 1884	116 LJ 58	C'tted
18 Mar 1884	139 CJ 118	No further SO App	4 Mar 1884	116 LJ 69	C'tee to meet
24 Mar 1884	139 CJ 131	2R/C'tted	10 Mar 1884	116 LJ 75	Rep with Amds
2 Apr 1884	139 CJ 155	Rep with Amds	13 Mar 1884	116 LJ 80	3R
7 Apr 1884	139 CJ 163	Cons	22 Apr 1884	116 LJ 136	HC pass with Amds
21 Apr 1884	139 CJ 170	3R	24 Apr 1884	116 LJ 137	HC Amds Ag
25 Apr 1884	139 CJ 184	HL pass with Amds	28 Apr 1884	116 LJ 144	Royal Assent
28 Apr 1884	139 CJ 186	Royal Assent			

Representation

Agent: JC Rees

Parliamentary debates

List of Acts: HC Deb, 14 Aug 1884, Vol 292(3rd), col 656

Parliamentary papers and cases

None

Gazette notices

London Gazette: 18 Dec 1883 (Iss: 25,297, p 6523)

Edinburgh Gazette: 18 Dec 1883 (Iss: 9480, p 999)

Dublin Gazette: 18 Dec 1883 (Iss: 17,897, p 1819)

Newspaper coverage of debates

House of Lords

2R: The Times, 23 Feb 1884; Morning Post, 23 Feb 1884

3R: The Times, 14 Mar 1884; Morning Post, 14 Mar 1884

House of Commons

2R: Morning Post, 25 Mar 1884

3R: The Times, 22 Apr 1884; Morning Post, 22 Apr 1884

Royal Assent: The Times, 29 Apr 1884; Yorkshire Post, 29 Apr 1884; Manchester Courier and Lancashire General Advertiser, 29 Apr 1884

Archives

House Bill: HL/PO/JO/10/9/1125

Minute Bill: HL/PO/JO/10/9/1102 (No 52)

Unopposed Bill C'tee Minutes: 2 Apr 1884 (p 23–24): HC/CL/WM/UB/1/37

SOC Minutes: 19 Feb 1884 (p 3–8) [Ex Cert; Statement of Promoter]: HL/PO/CO/1/296

Unopposed Bill C'tee Minutes: 7 Mar 1884 (p 9–10): HL/PO/CO/1/294

Wright's Patent Act 1884

PRVA104	1884

Wright's Patent Act 1884 (47 & 48 Vict. c. cxciv)

An Act for reviving and rendering valid certain Letters Patent granted to Edward Wright for Improvements in Paint Brushes

Table of contents

s 1 Power to stamp Letters Patent; Letters Patent, &c., confirmed
s 2 Saving rights
s 3 Short title
Schedule

Relevant patent

22 Oct 1880 (1880 No 4319)	Paint brushes [Edward Wright]

Journal

House of Commons				House of Lords		
SOC Rep: Sir John Mowbray Rep: Sir Arthur Otway (Ch W&M)				Rep: Earl Redesdale (Ld Ch)		
13 May 1884	139 CJ 226	SOC Rep on Pet for Pet		26 May 1884	116 LJ 210	Ex Cert
26 May 1884	139 CJ 259	SO ncw/Ref SOC		13 Jun 1884	116 LJ 228	Ref SOC
27 May 1884	139 CJ 264	SOC Pet		17 Jun 1884	116 LJ 238	SOC Rep/Disp
10 Jun 1884	139 CJ 282	SOC Rep read/Disp		7 Jul 1884	116 LJ 307	Brought HC/1R/Ref Ex
10 Jun 1884	139 CJ 282	Bill Ord		8 Jul 1884	116 LJ 310	No further SO App
12 Jun 1884	139 CJ 285	1R		15 Jul 1884	116 LJ 334	2R/SO Disp
17 Jun 1884	139 CJ 296	2R/C'tted		18 Jul 1884	116 LJ 344	Rep w/o Amds
2 Jul 1884	139 CJ 333	Rep with Amds		22 Jul 1884	116 LJ 352	3R
7 Jul 1884	139 CJ 341	SO 243 Susp/3R		28 Jul 1884	116 LJ 371	Royal Assent
24 Jul 1884	139 CJ 391	HL pass w/o Amds				
28 Jul 1884	139 CJ 402	Royal Assent				

Representation

Solicitor: John Walford
Agent: Durnford and Co

Parliamentary debates

List of Acts: HC Deb, 14 Aug 1884, Vol 292(3rd), col 656

Parliamentary papers and cases

None

Gazette notices

London Gazette: 16 May 1884 (Iss: 25,354, p 2189)
Edinburgh Gazette: 16 May 1884 (Iss: 9523, p 384)
Dublin Gazette: 16 May 1884 (Iss: 17,942, p 570)

Newspaper coverage of debates

House of Commons

Com to Meet: London Evening Standard, 2 Jul 1884

2R: The Times, 18 Jun 1884

3R: Morning Post, 8 Jul 1884

House of Lords

2R: The Times, 17 Jul 1884; Morning Post, 16 Jul 1884; Birmingham Daily Post, 16 Jul 1884

3R: The Times, 23 Jul 1884; Morning Post, 23 Jul 1884; London Evening Standard, 23 Jul 1884

Archives

House Bill: HL/PO/JO/10/9/1138

Minute Bill: HL/PO/JO/10/9/1119 (No 557)

Unopposed Bill C'tee Minutes: 27 Jun 1884 (p 92): HC/CL/WM/UB/1/37

SOC Minutes: 17 Jun 1884 (p 467 and 473–476) [Ex Cert; Statement of Promoter]: HL/PO/CO/1/296

Unopposed Bill C'tee Minutes: 18 Jul 1884 (p 256–257): HL/PO/CO/1/294

Auld's Patent Act 1885

PRVA105	1885

Auld's Patent Act 1885 (48 & 49 Vict. c. xviii)

An Act for rendering valid certain Letters Patent granted to William Wallace Auld for Improvements in the Preparation and Combination of Animal Substances for Use as Food

Table of contents
s 1 Powers to Comptroller-General to give certificate of payment; Letters Patent confirmed; [Saving rights] s 2 Short title Schedule

Relevant patent	
11 Dec 1876 (1876 No 4782)	Preparation and combination of animal substances for use as food [William Wallace Auld]

Journal

House of Commons			House of Lords		
Rep: Sir John Mowbray			Pres: Lord Selborne LC Rep: Earl Redesdale (Ld Ch)		
20 Feb 1885	140 CJ 44	Bill originate HL	23 Feb 1885	117 LJ 61	Ex Cert
23 Mar 1885	140 CJ 115	Brought HL	24 Feb 1885	117 LJ 65	1R
23 Mar 1885	140 CJ 115	1R/Ref Ex	3 Mar 1885	117 LJ 80	2R
27 Mar 1885	140 CJ 125	SO cw	10 Mar 1885	117 LJ 93	C'tted
9 Apr 1885	140 CJ 136	2R/C'tted	13 Mar 1885	117 LJ 100	C'tee to meet
21 Apr 1885	140 CJ 160	Chair W&M replaced	17 Mar 1885	117 LJ 107	Rep with Amds
22 Apr 1885	140 CJ 164	Rep with Amds	20 Mar 1885	117 LJ 116	3R
29 Apr 1885	140 CJ 181	Cons	5 May 1885	117 LJ 193	HC pass with Amds/Ag
4 May 1885	140 CJ 197	3R with Amds	21 May 1885	117 LJ 244	Royal Assent
7 May 1885	140 CJ 209	HL pass with Amds/Ag			
21 May 1885	140 CJ 251	Royal Assent			

Representation
Agent: A. Beveridge

Parliamentary debates
None

Parliamentary papers and cases
None

Gazette notices
London Gazette: 28 Nov 1884 (Iss: 25,418, p 5511)
Edinburgh Gazette: 28 Nov 1884 (Iss: 9579, p 1004)
Dublin Gazette: 28 Nov 1884 (Iss: 17,999, p 1255)

Newspaper coverage of debates

House of Lords

2R: The Times, 4 Mar 1885; Morning Post, 4 Mar 1885; London Evening Standard, 4 Mar 1885; Lloyd's Weekly News, 8 Mar 1885

3R: The Times, 21 Mar 1885; Morning Post, 21 Mar 1885

House of Commons

2R: The Times, 10 Apr 1885; Morning Post, 10 Apr 1885; London Evening Standard, 10 Apr 1885

Com to Meet: London Evening Standard, 22 Apr 1885

Rep: Morning Post, 30 Apr 1885

3R: The Times, 5 May 1885; Morning Post, 5 Mar 1885

Royal Assent: Manchester Courier and Lancashire General Advertiser, 22 May 1885; Yorkshire Post and Leeds Intelligencer, 22 May 1885

Archives
House Bill: HL/PO/JO/10/9/1157 (two copies)
Minute Bill: HL/PO/JO/10/9/1140 (No 150)
Unopposed Bill C'tee Minutes: 22 Apr 1885 (p 18): HC/CL/WM/UB/1/38
Unopposed Bill C'tee Minutes: 17 Mar 1885 (p 3–4): HL/PO/CO/1/298

Potter's Patent Act 1887

PRVA106	1887

Potter's Patent Act 1887 (50 & 51 Vict. c. cxxi)

An Act for rendering valid certain Letters Patent granted to Richard Potter for Improvements in Furnaces for melting Glass

Table of contents

s 1 Letters Patent confirmed
s 2 Saving rights
s 3 Short title

Relevant patents

27 Jun 1882 (1882 No 2971)	Furnaces for melting glass [Richard Potter]

Journal

House of Commons			House of Lords		
Rep: Leonard Courtney (Ch W&M)			Pres: Lord Halsbury LC Rep: Duke of Buckingham and Chandos (Ld Ch)		
28 Jan 1887	142 CJ 10	Bill originate HL	31 Jan 1887	119 LJ 18	Ex Cert
8 Feb 1887	142 CJ 54	SO cw	3 Feb 1887	119 LJ 23	Pres/1R
23 Jun 1887	142 CJ 313	1R/Ref Ex	10 Feb 1887	119 LJ 36	2R day app
27 Jun 1887	142 CJ 318	No further SO App	17 Feb 1887	119 LJ 48	2R adj
4 Jul 1887	142 CJ 339	2R/C'tted	22 Feb 1887	119 LJ 64	2R adj
12 Jul 1887	142 CJ 363	Rep w/o Amds	24 Feb 1887	119 LJ 66	2R adj
15 Jul 1887	142 CJ 371	3R day app	25 Feb 1887	119 LJ 70	2R
18 Jul 1887	142 CJ 376	3R	4 Mar 1887	119 LJ 81	C'tted
19 Jul 1887	142 CJ 382	Royal Assent	2 May 1887	119 LJ 171	Ref SC
			16 May 1887	119 LJ 194	SC Rep
			20 May 1887	119 LJ 210	Com to Meet
			13 Jun 1887	119 LJ 234	Rep with Amds
			17 Jun 1887	119 LJ 246	**3R with Amds**
			18 Jul 1887	119 LJ 341	HC pass w/o Amds
			19 Jul 1887	119 LJ 347	Royal Assent

Representation

Solicitor: Learoyd, Piercy and Simpson
Agent: S. Learoyd and James

Parliamentary debates

3R: HC Deb, 18 Jul 1887, Vol 317(3rd), col 1145	2R: **HL Deb, 25 Feb 1887, Vol 311(3rd), col 557–559**

Parliamentary papers and cases

Report of Select Committee on Potter's Patent Bill, Skirvanow's Patent Bill and Gilbert and Sinclair's Patent Bill (1887 HL Papers 100), Vol 9, p 469 [witnesses: Wilton Brook; Thomas Johnson; Ambrose Myall; Ann Ryland; Dan Rylands]

Gazette notices

London Gazette: 26 Nov 1886 (Iss: 25,649, p 5803)

Edinburgh Gazette: 30 Nov 1886 (Iss: 9760, p 1126)

Dublin Gazette: 30 Nov 1886 (Iss: 18,213, p 1042)

Newspaper coverage of debates

House of Lords

2R: **Morning Post, 26 Feb 1887**; **London Evening Standard, 26 Feb 1887**; *The Times, 26 Feb 1887*; *Glasgow Herald, 26 Feb 1887*; *Leeds Mercury, 26 Feb 1887*; *Northern Daily Mail, 26 Feb 1887*; *Shields Daily Gazette and Shipping Telegraph, 26 Feb 1887*

Ref SC: *The Times, 3 May 1887*; *Morning Post, 3 May 1887*; *Glasgow Herald, 3 May 1887*; Chepstow Weekly Advertiser, 7 May 1887; Whitby Gazette, 7 May 1887

3R: The Times, 18 Jun 1887; Morning Post, 18 Jun 1887

House of Commons

2R: Morning Post, 5 Jul 1887; The Times, 5 Jul 1887

3R adj: The Times, 16 Jul 1887

3R: Morning Post, 19 Jul 1887

Royal Assent: The Times, 20 Jul 1887; Freeman's Journal 28 Jul 1887

Archives
House Bill: HL/PO/JO/10/9/1229
Minute Bill: HL/PO/JO/10/9/1206 (No 111)
Office Papers: HL/PO/PB/18/3/37
Unopposed Bill C'tee Minutes: 23 May 1887 (p 116–117): HL/PO/CO/1/306
Unopposed Bill C'tee Minutes: 12 Jul 1887 (p 60): HC/CL/WM/UB/1/40

Worms and Balé's Patent Act 1891

PRVA107	1891
	Worms and Balé's Patent Act 1891 (54 & 55 Vict. c. clxxxii)

An Act for rendering valid certain Letters Patent granted to Eugene Worms of Paris in the Republic of France and Jean Bale of the same place Engineers for Improved Process and Apparatus for Tanning by aid of Electricity

Table of contents
s 1 Short title
s 2 Power to Comptroller-General of Patents, &c to antedate Letters Patent
s 3 Letters Patent confirmed
s 4 For protection of persons who may have availed themselves of subject-matter of patent after it has been declared void
s 5 Costs of Act

Relevant patent	
5 Jul 1887 (1887 No 9515)	Tanning by aid of electricity [Eugene Worms and Jean Balé]

Journal					
House of Commons			House of Lords		
SOC Rep: Sir John Mowbray Rep: Leonard Courtney (Ch W&M)			Pres: Lord Halsbury LC Rep: Earl of Launderdale (no committee met) Rep: Earl of Morley (Ld Ch)		
19 Mar 1891	146 CJ 162	SO ncw/Ref SOC	12 Mar 1891	123 LJ 106	Pet/Ref Ex
11 Jun 1891	146 CJ 349	Brought HL	13 Mar 1891	123 LJ 109	Procs Vacated
11 Jun 1891	146 CJ 349	1R/Ref Ex	13 Mar 1891	123 LJ 109	Pet/Ref Ex
15 Jun 1891	146 CJ 358	No further SO App	19 Mar 1891	123 LJ 118	Ex Cert
30 Jun 1891	146 CJ 404	Rep SOC/SO Disp	13 Apr 1891	123 LJ 139	Ref SOC/Pet Ag
6 Jul 1891	146 CJ 417	2R/C'tted	20 Apr 1891	123 LJ 150	Rep/SO Disp
14 Jul 1891	146 CJ 439	Rep with Amds	21 Apr 1891	123 LJ 152	1R
20 Jul 1891	146 CJ 455	Cons	23 Apr 1891	123 LJ 156	Ref Ex
23 Jul 1891	146 CJ 467	3R	27 Apr 1891	123 LJ 164	Ex Cert no further SO App
27 Jul 1891	146 CJ 482	HL Ag Amds	30 Apr 1891	123 LJ 171	2R
28 Jul 1891	146 CJ 484	Royal Assent	8 May 1891	123 LJ 186	Pet Ag to be heard
			12 May 1891	123 LJ 198	C'tted
			29 May 1891	123 LJ 208	C'tee to meet
			2 Jun 1891	123 LJ 213	C'tee did not meet/Ord Disc
			2 Jun 1891	123 LJ 213	Rep with Amds
			9 Jun 1891	123 LJ 228	3R
			23 Jul 1891	123 LJ 383	HC pass with Amds/Ag
			28 Jul 1891	123 LJ 399	Royal Assent

Petition		
13 Apr 1891	123 LJ 139	Lorentz Albert Groth

Representation
Agent: Burchell and Co

Parliamentary debates
None

Parliamentary papers and cases
None

Gazette notices
London Gazette: 3 Mar 1891 (Iss: 26,140, p 1213)
Edinburgh Gazette: 3 Mar 1891 (Iss: 10,234, p 261)
Dublin Gazette: 3 Mar 1891 (Iss: 18,674, p 797)
Office Journal of the Patent Office: 4 Mar 1891 (No 113, p viii); 25 Feb 1891 (No 112, p viii)

(continued)

(continued)

Newspaper coverage of debates
House of Lords
2R: The Times, 1 May 1891; Morning Post, 1 May 1891
3R: The Times, 10 Jun 1891
House of Commons
2R: The Times, 7 Jul 1891
3R: The Times, 24 Jul 1891

Archives
House Bill: HO/PO/JO/10/9/1371
Opposed Bill (no evidence): Evidence 1891, Vol 17 (HL/PO/PB/5/57/17)
Minute Bill: HL/PO/JO/10/9/1346 (No 250)
Unopposed Bill C'tee Minutes: 14 Jul 1891 (p 60): HC/CL/WM/UB/1/44
SOC Minutes: 30 Apr 1891 (p 166–168): HL/PO/CO/1/324 [Ex Cert; Statement of the Promoter; Petition Against SO Being Dispensed With; Shorthand Writers Notes of Hearing (22 pages)]
Unopposed Bill C'tee Minutes: 2 Jun 1891 (p 114): HL/PO/CO/1/322
Opposed Bill Minutes: 29 May 1891 (p 141): HL/PO/CO/1/323

Notes
Related cases
British Tanning Company v Groth (1891) 8 RPC 113

Horsfall's Patent Act 1892

PRVA108	1892

Horsfall's Patent Act 1892 (55 & 56 Vict. c. cxiv)
An Act for rendering valid certain Letters Patent granted to William Horsfall for a new or improved Construction of Furnace for burning Towns' or other Refuse

Table of contents
s 1 Letters patent confirmed
s 2 Saving rights
s 3 Short title

Relevant patent	
24 Jun 1887 (1887 No 8999)	Construction of furnace for burning towns' or other refuse [William Horsfall]

Journal					
House of Commons			**House of Lords**		
Rep: Leonard Courtney (Ch W&M)			Pres: Lord Halsbury LC Rep: Earl of Morley (Ld Ch)		
25 Mar 1892	147 CJ 132	SO ncw	21 Mar 1892	124 LJ 84	Pet
19 May 1892	147 CJ 263	Brought HL/1R/Ref Ex	25 Mar 1892	124 LJ 92	Ex Cert
23 May 1892	147 CJ 271	No further SO App	25 Mar 1892	124 LJ 92	Ref SOC
27 Mat 1892	147 CJ 296	Rep SOC/SO Disp	1 Apr 1892	124 LJ 106	SOC Rep/SOC Disp
2 Jun 1892	147 CJ 312	2R/C'tted	4 Apr 1892	124 LJ 110	1R
10 Jun 1892	147 CJ 331	Rep w/o Amds	2 May 1892	124 LJ 127	2R
14 Jun 1892	147 CJ 347	3R	9 May 1892	124 LJ 142	C'tted
20 Jun 1892	147 CJ 386	Royal Assent	10 May 1892	124 LJ 146	Rep with Amds
			17 May 1892	124 LJ 162	3R
			16 Jun 1892	124 LJ 307	HC pass w/o Amds
			20 Jun 1892	124 LJ 337	Royal Assent

Representation
Solicitor: Risdale and sons
Agent: Sherwood and Co

Parliamentary debates
None

Parliamentary papers and cases
None

Gazette notices
London Gazette: 27 Nov 1891 (Iss: 26,227, p 6581)
Edinburgh Gazette: 27 Nov 1891 (Iss: 10,311, p 1339)
Dublin Gazette: 27 Nov 1891 (Iss: 18,753, p 1779)
Office Journal of the Patent Office: 2 Dec 1891 (No 152, p 1022); 31 Dec 1891 (No 156, p 1100); 13 Jan 1892 (No 158, p 20)

Newspaper coverage of debates
House of Lords
2R: Morning Post, 3 May 1892; London Evening Standard, 3 May 1892; The Times, 3 May 1892
3R: The Times, 18 May 1892
House of Commons
2R: The Times, 3 Jun 1892
3R: The Times, 15 Jun 1892

Archives
House Bill: HL/PO/JO/10/9/1394
Minute Bill: HL/PO/JO/10/9/1379 (No 254)
Examiner's Rep: HL/PO/PB/19/27 (No 41)
Unopposed Bill C'tee Minutes: 10 Jun 1892 (p 51): HC/CL/WM/UB/1/45
SOC Minutes: 1 Apr 1892 (p 251, 259 and 263) [Ex Cert; Statement of Promoter]: HL/PO/CO/1/328
Unopposed Bill C'tee Minutes: 10 May 1892 (p 83–84): HL/PO/CO/1/326

Notes
There was an earlier Bill in the same session: PRVB149

Nussey and Leachman's and Nussey's Patents Act 1892

PRVA109	1892

Nussey and Leachman's and Nussey's Patents Act 1892 (55 & 56 Vict. c. cxv)

An Act for rendering valid certain Letters Patent granted to George Henry Nussey and William Bradshaw Leachman (1) for Improvements in Machinery or Apparatus for pressing and tentering Woollen and other Woven or Felted Fabrics (2) for Improvements in Machinery or Apparatus for pressing Woollen and other Woven or Felted Fabrics and (3) to the said George Henry Nussey for an Improved Knitted Fabric

Table of contents
s 1 Letters patent confirmed
s 2 Saving rights
s 3 Short title
Schedule

Relevant patent	
17 Mar 1885 (1885 No 3450)	Machinery or apparatus for pressing and tentering woollen and other woven or felted fabrics [George Henry Nussey and William Leachman]
8 May 1886 (1886 No 6264)	Machinery or apparatus for pressing woollen and other woven or felted fabrics [George Henry Nussey and William Leachman]
9 Feb 1887 (1887 No 2052)	Knitted Fabric [George Henry Nussey]

Journal	
House of Commons	**House of Lords**
Rep: Leonard Courtney (Ch W&M)	Pres: Lord Halsbury LC Rep: Earl of Morley (Ld Ch)

(continued)

(continued)

25 Mar 1892	147 CJ 132	SO ncw	21 Mar 1892	124 LJ 84	Pet	
19 May 1892	147 CJ 263	Brought HL/1R/Ref Ex	25 Mar 1892	124 LJ 92	Ex Cert	
23 May 1892	147 CJ 271	No further SO App	25 Mar 1892	124 LJ 92	Ref SOC	
27 Mat 1892	147 CJ 296	Rep SOC/SO Disp	1 Apr 1892	124 LJ 106	SOC Rep/SOC Disp	
2 Jun 1892	147 CJ 312	2R/C'tted	4 Apr 1892	124 LJ 109	1R	
10 Jun 1892	147 CJ 331	Rep w/o Amds	2 May 1892	124 LJ 127	2R	
14 Jun 1892	147 CJ 347	3R	9 May 1892	124 LJ 142	C'tted	
20 Jun 1892	147 CJ 386	Royal Assent	10 May 1892	124 LJ 146	Rep with Amds	
			17 May 1892	124 LJ 162	3R	
			16 Jun 1892	124 LJ 307	HC pass w/o Amds	
			20 Jun 1892	124 LJ 337	Royal Assent	

Representation
Solicitor: Risdale and Sons
Agent: Sherwood and Co
Parliamentary debates
None
Parliamentary papers and cases
None
Gazette notices
London Gazette: 27 Nov 1891 (Iss: 26,227, p 6581)
Edinburgh Gazette: 27 Nov 1891 (Iss: 10,311, p 1339)
Dublin Gazette: 27 Nov 1891 (Iss: 18,753, p 1779)
Office Journal of the Patent Office: 2 Dec 1891 (No 152, p 1022); 31 Dec 1891 (No 156, p 1100); 13 Jan 1892 (No 158, p 20)

Newspaper coverage of debates
House of Lords
2R: The Times, 3 May 1892; Morning Post, 3 May 1892; London Evening Standard, 3 May 1892
3R: The Times, 18 May 1892
House of Commons
2R: The Times, 3 Jun 1892
3R: The Times, 15 Jun 1892

Archives
House Bill: HL/PO/JO/10/9/1397
Minute Bill: HL/PO/JO/10/9/1379 (No 255)
Examiner's Rep: HL/PO/PB/19/27 (No 42)
Unopposed Bill C'tee Minutes: 10 Jun 1892 (p 51): HC/CL/WM/UB/1/45
SOC Minutes: 1 Apr 1892 (p 251, 259 and 265) [Ex Cert; Statement of Promoter]: HL/PO/CO/1/328
Unopposed Bill C'tee Minutes: 10 May 1892 (p 84–85): HL/PO/CO/1/326

Notes
There was an earlier Bill in the same session: PRVB149.

Whitehead's and Pickles' Patents Act 1892

PRVA110	1892
	Whitehead's and Pickles' Patents Act 1892 (55 & 56 Vict. c. cxvi)

An Act for rendering valid certain Letters Patent granted to (1) John Henry Whitehead for Improvements in Feed Boxes of Combing Machines and (2) John Pickles and Henry Walton Whitehead for Improvements in Noble's Combing Machines

Table of contents
s 1 Letters patent confirmed
s 2 Saving rights
s 3 Short title
Schedule

Relevant patents	
2 Jun 1886 (1886 No 7398)	Feed boxes of combing machines [John Henry Whitehead]
10 May 1887 (1887 No 3665)	Improvements to Noble's combing machines [John Pickles and Henry Walton Whitehead]

Journal					
House of Commons			**House of Lords**		
Rep: Leonard Courtney (Ch W&M)			Pres: Lord Halsbury LC Rep: Earl of Morley (Ld Ch)		
25 Mar 1892	147 CJ 132	SO ncw	21 Mar 1892	124 LJ 84	Pet
19 May 1892	147 CJ 263	Brought HL/1R/Ref Ex	25 Mar 1892	124 LJ 92	Ex Cert
23 May 1892	147 CJ 271	No further SO app	25 Mar 1892	124 LJ 92	Ref SOC
27 Mat 1892	147 CJ 296	Rep SOC/SO Disp	1 Apr 1892	124 LJ 106	Rep/SO Disp
2 Jun 1892	147 CJ 312	2R/C'tted	4 Apr 1892	124 LJ 110	1R
10 Jun 1892	147 CJ 331	Rep w/o Amds	2 May 1892	124 LJ 127	2R
14 Jun 1892	147 CJ 347	3R	9 May 1892	124 LJ 142	C'tted
20 Jun 1892	147 CJ 386	Royal Assent	10 May 1892	124 LJ 146	Rep with Amds
			17 May 1892	124 LJ 162	3R
			16 Jun 1892	124 LJ 307	HC pass w/o Amds
			20 Jun 1892	124 LJ 337	Royal Assent

Representation
Solicitor: Risdale and Sons Agent: Sherwood and Co

Parliamentary debates
None

Parliamentary papers and cases
None

Gazette notices
London Gazette: 27 Nov 1891 (Iss: 26,227, p 6581)
Edinburgh Gazette: 27 Nov 1891 (Iss: 10,311, p 1339)
Dublin Gazette: 27 Nov 1891 (Iss: 18,753, p 1779)
Office Journal of the Patent Office: 2 Dec 1891 (No 152, p 1022); 31 Dec 1891 (No 156, p 1100); 13 Jan 1892 (No 158, p 20)

Newspaper coverage of debates
House of Lords 2R: The Times, 3 May 1892; Morning Post, 3 May 1892; London Evening Standard, 3 May 1892 3R: The Times, 18 May 1892 *House of Commons* 2R: The Times, 3 Jun 1892 3R: The Times, 15 Jun 1892

Archives
House Bill: HL/PO/JO/10/9/1404
Minute Bill: HL/PO/JO/10/9/1379 (No 256)
Examiner's Rep: HL/PO/PB/19/27 (No 40)
Unopposed Bill C'tee Minutes: 10 Jun 1892 (p 51): HC/CL/WM/UB/1/45
SOC Minutes: 1 Apr 1892 (p 251, 259 and 261) [Ex Cert; Statement of Promoter]: HL/PO/CO/1/328
Unopposed Bill C'tee Minutes: 10 May 1892 (p 86–87): HL/PO/CO/1/326

Notes
There was an earlier Bill in the same session: PRVB149.

Simpson's and Fawcett's Patent Act 1892

PRVA111	1892
Simpson's and Fawcett's Patent Act 1892 (55 & 56 Vict. c. ccxxix)	
An Act for rendering valid certain Letters Patent granted to James Simpson and Samuel Thomas Fawcett for Improvements in the Construction of Perambulators	

(continued)

(continued)

Table of contents
s 1 Letters Patent confirmed s 2 Saving rights s3 Short title

Relevant patent	
3 Jan 1887 (1887 No 56)	Construction of Perambulators [James Simpson and Samuel Thomas Fawcett]

Journal					
House of Commons			**House of Lords**		
Rep: Leonard Courtney (Ch W&M)			Pres: Lord Halsbury LC Rep: Earl of Morley (Ld Ch)		
10 May 1892	147 CJ 233	SO ncw/Ref SOC	6 May 1892	124 LJ 138	Pet
14 Jun 1892	147 CJ 351	Brought HL	10 May 1892	124 LJ 145	Ex Cert
14 Jun 1892	147 CJ 351	1R/Ref Ex	10 May 1892	124 LJ 145	Ref SOC
16 Jun 1892	147 CJ 364	SO 70 susp /Ex sits	16 May 1892	124 LJ 158	SOC Rep/SO Disp
16 Jun 1892	147 CJ 365	SO not app	19 May 1892	124 LJ 171	1R
20 Jun 1892	147 CJ 382	SO 235 susp/2R/C'tted	24 May 1892	124 LJ 190	2R
21 Jun 1892	147 CJ 389	Var SO susp /Com sits	13 Jun 1892	124 LJ 226	C'tted
27 Jun 1892	147 CJ 398	Rep w/o Amds	14 Jun 1892	124 LJ 297	Rep with Amds/3R
27 Jun 1892	147 CJ 402	SO 223 and 243 susp /3R	27 Jun 1892	124 LJ 384	HC pass w/o Amds
28 Jun 1892	147 CJ 406	Royal Assent	28 Jun 1892	124 LJ 389	Royal Assent

Representation
Solicitor: Ridsdale and Co Agent: Sherwood and Co

Parliamentary debates
None

Parliamentary papers and cases
None

Gazette notices
London Gazette: 6 May 1892 (Iss: 26,285, p 2647) Edinburgh Gazette: 6 May 1892 (Iss: 10,359, p 611) Dublin Gazette: 6 May 1892 (Iss: 18,800, p 504) Office Journal of the Patent Office: 25 May 1892 (No 177, p 461); 1 Jun 1892 (No 178, p 485)

Newspaper coverage of debates
House of Lords 2R: The Times, 25 May 1892 3R: The Times, 15 Jun 1892 *House of Commons* 2R: The Times, 21 Jun 1892 3R: The Times, 28 Jun 1892; Morning Post, 28 Jun 1892 Royal Assent: The Times, 29 Jun 1892

Archives
House Bill: HL/PO/HI/10/9/1402 Minute Bill: HL/PO/JO/10/9/1383 (No 349) Examiner's Rep: HL/PO/PB/19/27 (No 36) Unopposed Bill C'tee Minutes: 21 Jun 1892 (p 68): HC/CL/WM/UB/1/45 SOC Minutes: 16 May 1892 (p 307–311) [Ex Cert; Statement of Promoter]: HL/PO/CO/1/328 Unopposed Bill C'tee Minutes: 14 Jun 1892 (p 186–188): HL/PO/CO/1/326

Whiting's Patent Act 1897

PRVA112	1897

Whiting's Patent Act 1897 (60 & 61 Vict. c. xi)

An Act for rendering valid certain Letters Patent granted to William John Whiting for Improvements in Revolver Firearms

Table of contents

s 1 Letters patent confirmed
s 2 Saving rights
s 3 Short title
Schedule

Relevant patent

25 Feb 1891 (1891 No 3427)	Revolver Firearms [William John Whiting]

Journal

House of Commons			House of Lords		
Rep: James Lowther (Ch W&M)			Pres: Lord Halsbury LC Rep: Earl of Morley (Ch W&M)		
2 Feb 1897	152 CJ 34	Originate HL	18 Feb 1897	129 LJ 44	Ex Cert
18 Feb 1897	152 CJ 72	SO cw	22 Feb 1897	129 LJ 48	1R
18 Mar 1897	152 CJ 121	Brought HL/1R/Ref Ex	26 Feb 1897	129 LJ 59	2R
22 Mar 1897	152 CJ 125	No further SO app	11 Mar 1897	129 LJ 69	C'tted
29 Mar 1897	152 CJ 143	2R/C'tted	12 Mar 1897	129 LJ 84	Rep with Amds
5 Apr 1897	152 CJ 160	Rep w/o Amds	16 Mar 1897	129 LJ 89	3R
6 Apr 1897	152 CJ 162	SO 243 susp/3R	8 Apr 1897	129 LJ 135	HC pass w/o Amds
3 Jun 1897	152 CJ 281	Royal Assent	3 Jun 1897	129 LJ 240	Royal Assent

Representation

Solicitor: Michael Abrahams
Agent: Sherwood and Co

Parliamentary debates

Ord HL: HC Deb, 2 Feb 1897, Vol 45(4th), col 1033	Royal Assent: HL Deb, 3 Jun 1897, Vol 50(4th), col 150
Royal Assent: HC Deb, 3 Jun 1897, Vol 50(4th), col 153	
List of Acts: HC Deb, 6 Aug 1897, Vol 52(4th), col 532	

Parliamentary papers and cases

None

Gazette notices

London Gazette: 24 Nov 1896 (Iss: 26,797, p. 6536)
Edinburgh Gazette: 24 Nov 1896 (Iss: 10,834, p 1160)
Dublin Gazette: 24 Nov 1896 (Iss: 19,279, p 1203)
Office Journal of the Patent Office: 2 Dec 1896 (No 413, p 1495); 9 Dec 1896 (No 414, p 1533)

Newspaper coverage of debates

House of Lords

3R: The Times, 17 Mar 1897

House of Commons

2R: The Times, 30 Mar 1897

3R The Times, 7 Apr 1897

Royal Assent: The Times, 4 Jun 1897

Archives

Unopposed Bill C'tee Minutes: 5 Apr 1897 (p 16): HC/CL/WM/UB/1/50
Unopposed Bill C'tee Minutes: 12 Mar 1897 (p 9–11): HL/PO/CO/1/346

Holmes's Patent Act 1898

PRVA113	1898

Holmes's Patent Act 1898 (61 & 62 Vict. c. xliv)

An Act for rendering valid certain Letters Patent granted to Thomas Holmes for Improvements in Apparatus applicable to Twist Lace Machines

Table of contents
s 1 Letters patent confirmed s 2 Saving rights s 3 Short title Schedule

Relevant patent	
16 Jul 1892 (1892 No 11,786)	Apparatus applicable to twist lace machines [Thomas Holmes]

Journal

House of Commons			House of Lords		
Rep: James Lowther (Ch W&M)			Pres: Lord Halsbury LC Rep: Earl of Morley (Ld Ch)		
11 Feb 1898	153 CJ 17	Bill originate HL	28 Feb 1898	130 LJ 54	Ex Cert
28 Feb 1898	153 CJ 60	SO cw	1 Mar 1898	130 LJ 57	1R
22 Apr 1898	153 CJ 149	Brought HL/1R/Ref Ex	7 Mar 1898	130 LJ 66	2R
26 Apr 1898	153 CJ 154	No further SO app	14 Mar 1898	130 LJ 77	C'tted
2 May 1898	153 CJ 167	2R/C'tted	28 Mar 1898	130 LJ 97	C'tee to meet
12 May 1898	153 CJ 198	Rep with Amds	31 Mar 1898	130 LJ 106	Rep with Amds
17 May 1898	153 CJ 207	Cons	21 Apr 1898	130 LJ 117	3R
20 May 1898	153 CJ 214	3R	20 May 1898	130 LJ 162	HC pass with Amds
10 Jun 1898	153 CJ 250	HL Ag Amds	9 Jun 1898	130 LJ 177	HC Amds Ag
1 Jul 1898	153 CJ 305	Royal Assent	1 Jul 1898	130 LJ 243	Royal Assent

Representation
Solicitor: Wells and Hind Agent: Sherwood and Co

Parliamentary debates	
Bill in HL: HC Deb, 11 Feb 1898, Vol 53(4th), col 350 Rep: HC Deb, 17 May 1898, Vol 57(4th), col 1523 Royal Assent: HC Deb, 1 Jul 1898, Vol 60(4th), col 7776	Royal Assent: HL Deb, 1 Jul 1898, Vol 60(4th), col 753

Parliamentary papers and cases
None

Gazette notices
London Gazette: 26 Nov 1897 (Iss: 26,914, p 6903)
Edinburgh Gazette: 26 Nov 1897 (Iss: 10,939, p 1184)
Dublin Gazette: 26 Nov 1897 (Iss: 19,384, p 1367)
Office Journal of the Patent Office: 8 Dec 1897 (No 466, p 1626); 15 Dec 1897 (No 467, p 1666)

Newspaper coverage of debates
House of Lords 2R: Morning Post, 8 Mar 1898 3R: The Times, 22 Apr 1898; Morning Post, 22 Apr 1898; London Evening Standard, 22 Apr 1898 *House of Commons* 2R: The Times, 3 May 1898 3R: The Times, 21 May 1898

Archives
Unopposed Bill C'tee Minutes: 11 May 1898 (p 27): HC/CL/WM/UB/1/51
Unopposed Bill C'tee Minutes: 29 Mar 1898 (p 18–20): HL/PO/CO/1/350

Uralite Patent Act 1900

PRVA114	1900	
	Uralite Patent Act 1900 (63 & 64 Vict. c. xi)	
	An Act for rendering valid certain Letters Patent granted to Alexander Imschenetzky for an Invention for manufacture of fireproof and insulating compounds known as Uralite [Imschenetzky's Uralite Patent]	

Table of contents

s 1 Letters patent confirmed
s 2 Saving rights
s 3 Short title
Schedule

Relevant patent

12 May 1895 (1895 No 5254)	Manufacture of fireproof and insulating compounds known as uralite [Alexander Imschenetzky]

Journal

House of Commons			House of Lords		
Rep: James Lowther (Ch W&M)			Pres: Lord Speaker Rep: Earl of Morley (Ld Ch)		
6 Feb 1900	155 CJ 20	Orig HL	12 Feb 1900	132 LJ 26	Ex Cert
12 Feb 1900	155 CJ 36	SO cw	13 Feb 1900	132 LJ 33	Pres/1R/Ref Ex
5 Apr 1900	155 CJ 142	Brought HL/1R/Ref Ex	19 Feb 1900	132 LJ 41	Ex Cert
9 Apr 1900	155 CJ 148	Further SO cw	22 Feb 1900	132 LJ 49	2R
27 Apr 1900	155 CJ 157	2R/C'tted	1 Mar 1900	132 LJ 65	C'tted
10 May 1900	155 CJ 183	Rep w/o Amds	29 Mar 1900	132 LJ 105	C'tee to meet
14 May 1900	155 CJ 190	3R	30 Mar 1900	132 LJ 108	Rep with Amds
25 May 1900	155 CJ 221	Royal Assent	3 Apr 1900	132 LJ 114	3R
			15 May 1900	132 LJ 165	HC pass w/o Amds
			25 May 1900	132 LJ 185	Royal Assent

Representation

Solicitor: Golding and Hargrove
Agent: Sherwood and Co

Parliamentary debates

Orig HL: HC Deb, 6 Feb 1900, Vol 78(4th), col 692	SO cw: HL Deb, 12 Feb 1900, Vol 78(4th), col 1161
SO cw: HC Deb, 12 Feb 1900, Vol 78(4th), col 1195	1R: HL Deb, 13 Feb 1900, Vol 78(4th), col 1353
Br HL/1R: HC Deb, 5 Apr 1900, Vol 81(4th), col 1250–1251	Ex Cert: HL Deb, 19 Feb 1900, Vol 79(4th), col 341
SO cw: HC Deb, 9 Apr 1900, Vol 81(4th), col 1505	Rep: HL Deb, 30 Mar 1900, Vol 81(4th), col 781
2R: HC Deb, 27 Apr 1900, Vol 82(4th), col 111	3R: HL Deb, 3 Apr 1900, Vol 81(4th), col 1045
Rep: HC Deb, 10 May 1900, Vol 82(4th), col 1230	HC pass: HL Deb, 15 May 1900, Vol 83(4th), col 150
3R: HC Deb, 14 May 1900, Vol 83(4th) col 20	Royal Assent: HL Deb, 25 May 1900, Vol 83(4th), col 1221

Parliamentary papers and cases

None

Gazette notices

London Gazette: 24 Nov 1899 (Iss: 27,138, p 7422)

Edinburgh Gazette: 24 Nov 1899 (Iss: 11,148, p 1186)

No Dublin Gazette

Office Journal of the Patent Office: 29 Nov 1899 (No 569, p 1438); 6 Dec 1899 (No 570, p 1472)

Newspaper coverage of debates

House of Lords

3R: The Times, 4 Apr 1900

House of Commons

2R: The Times, 28 Apr 1900

3R: The Times, 15 May 1900

Archives

House Bill: HL/PO/JO/10/10/35 (No 174)

Minute Bill: HL/PO/JO/10/10/8 (No 162)

Unopposed Bill C'tee Minutes: 10 May 1900 (p 19): HC/CL/WM/UB/1/53

Unopposed Bill C'tee Minutes: 30 Mar 1900 (p 28–29): HL/PO/CO/1/358

Church's Patent Act 1900

PRVA115	1900

Church's Patent Act 1900 (63 & 64 Vict. c. xxiv)

An Act for rendering valid certain Letters Patent granted to Melvin Batchlor Church for the manufacture of an improved compound for coating and decorating walls and others surfaces and the production of casts or mouldings and for analogous purposes

Table of contents
s 1 Letter patent confirmed s 2 Date [of Letters patent confirmed] s 3 Saving rights s 4 Short title Schedule

Relevant patent	
2 Apr 1895 (1895 No 13,154)	Compound for coating and decorating walls and others surfaces and the production of casts or mouldings and for analogous purposes [Melvin Batchlor Church]

Journal

House of Commons			House of Lords		
Rep: Sir Henry Fletcher			Pres: Lord Halsbury LC Rep: Earl of Camperdown		
6 Feb 1900	155 CJ 20	Originate HL	9 Feb 1900	132 LJ 23	Ex Cert
9 Feb 1900	155 CJ 24	SO cw	12 Feb 1900	132 LJ 27	1R
30 Mar 1900	155 CJ 128	Brought HL	16 Feb 1900	132 LJ 38	Pet Ag
30 Mar 1900	155 CJ 129	1R/Ref Ex	16 Feb 1900	132 LJ 39	2R
5 Apr 1900	155 CJ 141	Further SO cw	23 Feb 1900	132 LJ 55	C'tted
26 Apr 1900	155 CJ 152	2R/C'tted	6 Mar 1900	132 LJ 73	C'tte named
15 May 1900	155 CJ 197	Wit to attend	8 Mar 1900	132 LJ 85	Peer sub/witness Sum
21 May 1900	155 CJ 210	Rep w/o Amds	22 Mar 1900	132 LJ 94	Rep with Amds
24 May 1900	155 CJ 218	3R day app	30 Mar 1900	132 LJ 108	3R
25 May 1900	155 CJ 221	3R	25 May 1900	132 LJ 188	HC pass w/o Amds
25 Jun 1900	155 CJ 264	Royal Assent	25 Jun 1900	132 LJ 238	Royal Assent

Representation
Solicitor: E Grover Watkins Agent: A & W Beveridge

Parliamentary debates

Orig HL: HC Deb, 6 Feb 1900, Vol 78(4th), col 691	Ex Cert: HL Deb, 9 Feb 1900, Vol 78(4th), col 1017
Ex Cert: HC Deb, 9 Feb 1900, Vol 78(4th), col 1024	1R: HL Deb, 12 Feb 1900, Vol 78(4th), col 1162
Br HL/1R: HC Deb, 30 Mar 1900, Vol 81(4th), col 786	2R: HL Deb, 16 Feb 1900, Vol 79(4th), col 194
SO cw: HC Deb, 5 Apr 1900, Vol 81(4th), col 1237	C'tted: HL Deb, 23 Feb 1900, Vol 79(4th), col 910
Wit: HC Deb, 15 May 1900, Vol 83(4th), col 227	3R: HL Deb, 30 Mar 1900, Vol 81(4th), col 782
Rep: HC Deb, 21 May 1900, Vol 83(4th), col 718	HC pass: HL Deb, 25 May 1900, Vol 83(4th), col 1224
3R: HC Deb, 25 May 1900, Vol 83(4th), col 1281	Royal Assent: HL Deb, 25 Jun 1900, Vol 84(4th), col 873

Parliamentary papers and cases
None

Gazette notices
London Gazette: 24 Nov 1899 (Iss: 27,138, p. 7421)
Edinburgh Gazette: 24 Nov 1899 (Iss: 11,148, p 1190)
Dublin Gazette: 24 Nov 1899 (Iss: 19,592, p 2038)
Office Journal of the Patent Office: 29 Nov 1899 (No 569, p 1437); 6 Dec 1899 (No 570, p 1471)

Newspaper coverage of debates
House of Lords 2R: The Times, 17 Feb 1900 3R: The Times, 31 Mar 1900 *House of Commons* 3R: The Times, 26 May 1900 Royal Assent: The Times, 26 Jun 1900

Archives
House Bill: HL/PO/JO/10/10/27 (No 46)
Minute Bill: HL/PO/JO/10/10/2 (No 71)
Minutes Opposed Bill C'tee: Divider H: 18 May 1900 (1 page – no page number); 21 May 1900 (1 page – no page number): HC/CL/PB/1/111
Opposed Bill Evidence (1900), Vol 3 [witnesses: Melvin Church and Cornelius Dalton]: HL/PO/PB/5/66/3
Opposed Bill C'tee Minutes: 13 Mar 1900 (p 23–25): HL/PO/CO/1/359

Roe's Patent Act 1900

PRVA116	1900
Roe's Patent Act 1900 (63 & 64 Vict. c. clxv)	
An Act for rendering valid certain Letters Patent granted to John Pearce Roe for an Invention for improvements in apparatus for shipping or transferring coal and other materials	

Table of contents
s 1 Letters Patent confirmed s 2 Saving rights s 3 Short title Schedule

Relevant patent	
3 Sep 1895 (1895 No 16,525)	Apparatus for shipping or transferring coal and other materials [John Pearce Roe]

Journal

House of Commons			House of Lords		
Rep: James Lowther (Ch W&M)			Pres: Lord Halsbury LC Rep: Earl of Morley (Ld Ch)		
18 Jun 1900	155 CJ 240	SO ncw/Ref SOC	14 May 1900	132 LJ 160	Pet
26 Jun 1900	155 CJ 272	SO Disp	18 Jun 1900	132 LJ 217	Ex Cet
10 Jul 1900	155 CJ 311	Brought HL/1R/Ref Ex	18 Jun 1900	132 LJ 217	Ref SOC
13 Jul 1900	155 CJ 319	Remaining SO cw	22 Jun 1900	132 LJ 232	SOC Rep/SO Disp
18 Jul 1900	155 CJ 330	2R/C'tted	22 Jun 1900	132 LJ 232	1R
23 Jul 1900	155 CJ 341	SO 211 and 236 susp	28 Jun 1900	132 LJ 256	2R
24 Jul 1900	155 CJ 345	Rep w/o Amds	5 Jul 1900	132 LJ 279	C'tted
27 Jul 1900	155 CJ 353	3R	6 Jul 1900	132 LJ 285	Rep with Amds
30 Jul 1900	155 CJ 357	Royal Assent	10 Jul 1900	132 LJ 299	3R
			27 Jul 1900	132 LJ 356	HC pass w/o Amds
			30 Jul 1900	132 LJ 366	Royal Assent

Representation
Agent: Sherwood and Co

Parliamentary debates

SO ncw: HC Deb, 18 Jun 1900, Vol 84(4th), col 267	Pet: HL Deb, 14 May 1900, Vol 83(4th), col 2–3
SO Disp: HC Deb, 26 Jun 1900, Vol 84(4th), col 1110	Ref SOC: HL Deb, 18 Jun 1900, Vol 84(4th), col 250
1R: HC Deb, 10 Jul 1900, Vol 85(4th), col 1105	1R: HL Deb, 22 Jun 1900, Vol 84(4th), col 737
SO cw: HC Deb, 13 Jul 1900, Vol 85(4th), col 1446–1447	SO Disp: HL Deb, 22 Jun 1900, Vol 84(4th), col 738
2R: HC Deb, 18 Jul 1900, Vol 86(4th), col 341	2R: HL Deb, 28 Jun 1900, Vol 84(4th), col 1266
SO Disp: HC Deb, 23 Jul 1900, Vol 86(4th), col 846	Rep: HL Deb, 6 Jul 1900, Vol 85(4th), col 725
Rep: HC Deb, 24 Jul 1900, Vol 86(4th), col 1038	3R: HL Deb, 10 Jul 1900, Vol 85(4th), col 1080
3R: HC Deb, 27 Jul 1900, Vol 86(4th), col 1496	HC pass: HL Deb, 27 Jul 1900, Vol 86(4th), col 1456
	Royal Assent: HL Deb, 30 Jul 1900, Vol 87(4th), col 4

Parliamentary papers and cases
None

(continued)

(continued)

Gazette notices
London Gazette: 15 May 1900 (Iss: 27,192, p 3084) Edinburgh Gazette: 15 May 1900 (Iss: 11,197, p 485) Dublin Gazette: 15 May 1900 (Iss: 19,642, p 710) Office Journal of the Patent Office: 24 May 1900 (No 594, p 581); 30 May 1900 (No 595, p 613)
Newspaper coverage of debates
House of Lords 2R: The Times, 29 Jun 1900 *House of Commons* 3R: The Times, 28 Jul 1900
Archives
House Bill: HL/PO/JO/10/10/43 (No 328) Minute Bill: HL/PO/JO/10/10/20 (No 449a) SOC Minutes: 22 Jun 1900 (p 261 and 273–277) [Ex Cert; Statement of Promoter]: HL/PO/CO/1/360 Unopposed Bill C'tee Minutes: 6 Jul 1900 (p 113): HL/PO/CO/1/358 Unopposed Bill C'tee Minutes: 24 Jul 1900 (p 63): HC/CL/WM/UB/1/53

Rodgers' Patent Act 1901

PRVA117	1901
Rodgers' Patent Act 1901 (1 Edw 7. c. lvi)	

An Act for rendering valid certain Letters Patent granted to James Godman Rodgers for an Invention for improvements in rubber tyres for vehicles
Table of contents
s 1 Letters Patent confirmed s 2 Saving rights s 3 Short title Schedule

Relevant patent	
3 Sep 1895 (1895 No 16,525)	Rubber tyres for vehicles [James Godman Rodgers]

Journal					
House of Commons			**House of Lords**		
Rep: James Lowther (Ch W&M)			Pres: Lord Halsbury LC Rep: Earl of Morley (Ld Ch)		
28 Mar 1901	156 CJ 105	SO ncw	12 Mar 1901	133 LJ 66	Pet
30 Apr 1901	156 CJ 150	SO Disp	28 Mar 1901	133 LJ 88	Ex Cert
21 May 1901	156 CJ 203	Brought HL	22 Apr 1901	133 LJ 100	Ref SOC
21 May 1901	156 CJ 204	1R/Ref Ex	26 Apr 1901	133 LJ 110	Rep/SO Disp
7 Jun 1901	156 CJ 217	SO cw	29 Apr 1901	133 LJ 115	1R
12 Jun 1901	156 CJ 228	2R/C'tted	3 May 1901	133 LJ 125	2R
18 Jun 1901	156 CJ 245	Rep w/o Amds	10 May 1901	133 LJ 138	C'tted
24 Jun 1901	156 CJ 257	3R	17 May 1901	133 LJ 148	Rep with Amds
2 Jul 1901	156 CJ 282	Royal Assent	21 May 1901	133 LJ 160	3R
			25 Jun 1901	133 LJ 219	HC pass w/o Amds
			2 Jul 1901	133 LJ 245	Royal Assent

Representation
Agent: Sherwood and Co

Parliamentary debates	
SO ncw: HC Deb, 28 Mar 1901, Vol 92(4th), col 37	SO ncw: HL Deb, 28 Mar 1901, Vol 92(4th), col 1rodg
Brought HL/1R: HC Deb, 21 May 1901, Vol 94(4th), col 848	SO Disp: HL Deb, 26 Apr 1901, Vol 92(4th), col 1414
SO cw: HC Deb, 7 Jun 1901, Vol 94(4th), col 1309	1R: HL Deb, 29 Apr 1901, Vol 93(4th), col 2
2R: HC Deb, 12 Jun 1901, Vol 95(4th), col 145	SO Disp: HL Deb, 30 Apr 1901, Vol 93(4th), col 179
3R: HC Deb, 24 Jun 1901, Vol 95(4th), col 1189	2R: HL Deb, 3 May 1901, Vol 93(4th), col 561
HL pass: HC Deb, 25 Jun 1901, Vol 95(4th), col 1335	C'tted: HL Deb, 10 May 1901, Vol 93|(4th), col 1277
	Rep: HL Deb, 17 May 1901, Vol 94(4th), col 398
	3R: HL Deb, 21 May 1901, Vol 94(4th), col 722
	HL Ag: HL Deb, 25 Jun 1901, Vol 95(4th), col 1336
	Royal Assent: HL Deb, 2 Jul 1901, Vol 96(4th), col 534

Parliamentary papers and cases
None

Gazette notices
London Gazette: 8 Mar 1901 (Iss: 27,292, p 1665)
Edinburgh Gazette: 8 Mar 1901 (Iss: 11,283, p 283)
Dublin Gazette: 8 Mar 1991 (Iss: 19,732, p 381)
Office Journal of the Patent Office: 13 Mar 1901 (No 636, p 282); 27 Mar 1901 (No 638, p 348)

Newspaper coverage of debates
House of Lords
2R: The Times, 4 May 1901
3R: The Times, 22 May 1901
House of Commons
2R: The Times, 13 Jun 1901
3R: The Times, 25 Jun 1901

Archives
House Bill: HL/PO/JO/10/10/91 (No 905)
Minute Bill (Proof and Amended): HL/PO/JO/10/10/62 (No 275)
SOC Minutes: 26 Apr 1901 (p 129 and 135–137) [Ex Cert; Statement of Promoter]: HL/PO/CO/1/364
Unopposed Bill C'tee Minutes: 17 May 1901 (p 46): HL/PO/CO/1/362
Unopposed Bill C'tee Minutes: 18 Jun 1901(p 40): HC/CL/WM/UB/1/54

Kip's Patents Act 1903

PRVA118	1903
Kip's Patents Act 1903 (3 Edw 7. c. cci)	
An Act for rendering valid certain letters patent granted to William Phillips Thompson in respect of inventions communicated to him from abroad by Frederic Ellsworth Kip (1) for improvements in stop-motions for looms warping machines and the like and (2) for improvements in electrical stop-motions for warps	

Table of contents
s 1 Letters patent confirmed
s 2 Saving rights
s 3 Short title
Schedule

Relevant patents	
28 Oct 1898 (1898 No 22,703)	Stop-motions for looms warping machines and the like [William Phillips Thompson]
17 Nov 1898 (1898 No 24,277)	Electrical stop-motions for warps [William Phillips Thompson]

(continued)

(continued)

Journal					
House of Commons			**House of Lords**		
Rep: Arthur Frederick Jeffreys (Dep Ch W&M)			Pres: Lord Halsbury LC Rep: Earl of Morley (Ld Ch)		
14 May 1903	158 CJ 171	Pet/SOC ncw	4 May 1903	135 LJ 97	Pet
16 Jun 1903	158 CJ 237	SO Disp	14 May 1903	135 LJ 116	Ex Cert
29 Jun 1903	158 CJ 269	Brought HL	14 May 1903	135 LJ 116	Ref SOC
29 Jun 1903	158 CJ 270	1R/Ref Ex	19 May 1903	135 LJ 124	SOC Rep/SO Disp
3 Jul 1903	158 CJ 285	SO cw	22 May 1903	135 LJ 128	1R/Ref Ex
8 Jul 1903	158 CJ 300	2R/C'tted	25 May 1903	135 LJ 138	Ex Cert
28 Jul 1903	158 CJ 359	Rep w/o Amds	26 May 1903	135 LJ 144	2R
31 Jul 1903	158 CJ 372	3R	11 Jun 1903	135 LJ 153	C'tted
11 Aug 1903	158 CJ 411	Royal Assent	23 Jun 1903	135 LJ 186	Rep with Amds
			29 Jun 1903	135 LJ 205	3R
			3 Aug 1903	135 LJ 296	HC pass w/o Amds
			11 Aug 1903	135 LJ 350	Royal Assent

Representation
Agent: James Mellor and Coleman

Parliamentary debates	
Ref SOC: HC Deb, 14 May 1903, Vol 122(4th) col 664	Pet: HL Deb, 4 May 1903, Vol 121(4th), col 1137
SO Disp: HC Deb, 16 Jun 1903, Vol 123(4th), col 1049	Ex Cert/Ref SOC: HL Deb, 14 May 1903, Vol 122(4th), col 653
Brought HL: HC Deb, 29 Jun 1903, Vol 124(4th), col 767	SOC Rep: HL Deb, 19 May 1903, Vol 122(4th), col 1045
1R: HC Deb, 29 Jun 1003, Vol 124(4th), col 768	1R: HL Deb, 22 May 1903, Vol 122(4th), col 1453
SO cw: HC Deb, 3 Jul 1903, Vol 124(4th), col 1254	Ex Cert: HL Deb, 25 May 1903, Vol 122(4th), col 1573
2R: HC Deb, 8 Jul 1903, Vol 125(4th), col 1	2R: HL Deb, 26 May 1903, Vol 122(4th), col 1750
Rep: HC Deb, 28 Jul 1903, Vol 126(4th), col 529	C'tted: HL Deb, 11 Jun 1903, Vol 123(4th), col 589
3R: HC Deb, 31 Jul 1903, Vol 126(4th), col 1067	Rep: HL Deb, 23 Jun 1903, Vol 124(4th), col 194
	3R: HL Deb, 29 Jun 1903, Vol 124(4th), col 721
	HC pass: HL Deb, 3 Aug 1903, Vol 126(4th), col 1153

Parliamentary papers and cases
None

Gazette notices
London Gazette: 21 Apr 1903 (Iss: 27,545, p 2540)
Edinburgh Gazette: 21 Apr 1903 (Iss: 11,506, p 420)
Dublin Gazette: 21 Apr 1903 (Iss: 19,959, p 492)
Office Journal of the Patent Office: 29 Apr 1903 (No 747, p 549); 6 May 1903 (No 748, p 585); 13 May 1903 (No 749, p 621)

Newspaper coverage of debates
House of Lords 2R: The Times, 27 May 1903 3R: The Times, 30 Jun 1903
House of Commons 2R: The Times, 9 Jul 1903 3R: The Times, 1 Aug 1903

Archives
Unopposed Bill C'tee Minutes: 28 Jul 1903 (p 63): HC/CL/WM/UB/1/56
SOC Minutes: 18 May 1903 (p 105–109) [Ex Cert; Statement of Promoter]: HL/PO/CO/1/372
Unopposed Bill C'tee Minutes: 24 Jul 1903 (p 70): HL/PO/CO/1/370

Richard Jaeger's Patent Act 1904

PRVA119	1904

Richard Jaeger's Patent Act 1904 (4 Edw 7. c. cii)

An Act for rendering valid certain letters patent granted to Richard Jaeger in respect of an invention for an improved process for the dry slaking of lime and apparatus therefor

Table of contents

s 1 Letters patent confirmed
s 2 Saving rights
s 3 Short title
Schedule

Relevant patent

20 Feb 1899 (1899 No 3760)	Process for the dry slaking of lime and apparatus therefor [Richard Jaeger]

Journal

House of Commons			House of Lords		
Rep: James Lowther (Ch W&M)			Pres: Lord Halsbury LC Rep: Lord Balfour of Burleigh		
21 Apr 1904	159 CJ 136	Pet/SOC ncw	24 Mar 1904	136 LJ 92	Pet
3 May 1904	159 CJ 160	SO Disp	21 Apr 1904	136 LJ 111	Ex Cert
9 Jun 1904	159 CJ 225	Brought HL/1R/Ref Ex	22 Apr 1904	136 LJ 114	Ref SOC
9 Jun 1904	159 CJ 225	SO cw	26 Apr 1904	136 LJ 119	SOC Rep/SO Disp
20 Jun 1904	159 CJ 246	2R/C'tted	28 Apr 1904	136 LJ 124	1R
1 Jul 1904	159 CJ 280	Rep with Amds	2 May 1904	136 LJ 130	2R
8 Jul 1904	159 CJ 302	Cons	9 May 1904	136 LJ 146	C'tted
12 Jul 1904	159 CJ 311	3R	13 May 1904	136 LJ 154	C'tee to meet
15 Jul 1904	159 CJ 325	HL Ag Amds	17 May 1904	136 LJ 163	Rep with Amds
22 Jul 1904	159 CJ 342	Royal Assent	7 Jun 1904	136 LJ 173	3R
			14 Jul 1904	136 LJ 261	HC pass with Amds
			22 Jul 1904	136 LJ 282	Royal Assent

Representation

Agent: Baker, Lees and Co

Parliamentary debates

SOC ncw: HC Deb, 21 Apr 1904, Vol 133(4th), col 832–833

SO Disp: HC Deb, 3 May 1904, Vol 134(4th), col 271

Brought HL: HC Deb, 9 Jun 1904, Vol 135(4th), col 1202

SO cw: HC Deb, 13 Jun 1904, Vol 135(4th), col 1460

2R: HC Deb, 20 Jun 1904, Vol 136(4th), col 459

Rep: HC Deb, 1 Jul 1904, Vol 137(4th), col 315

Cons: HC Deb, 8 Jul 1904, Vol 137(4th), col 1085

3R: HC Deb, 12 Jul 1904, Vol 137(4th), col 1346

HL Ag Amds: HC Deb, 15 Jul 1904, Vol 138(4th), col 153

Royal Assent: HC Deb, 22 Jul 1904, Vol 138(4th), col 939

Pet: HL Deb, 24 Mar 1904, Vol 132(4th), col 581

Ex Cert: HL Deb, 21 Apr 1904, Vol 133(4th), col 797

Ref SOC: HL Deb, 22 Apr 1904, Vol 133(4th), col 941

SO Disp: HL Deb, 26 Apr 1904, Vol 133(4th), col 1165

1R: HL Deb, 28 Apr 1904, Vol 133(4th), col 1405

2R: HL Deb, 2 May 1904, Vol 134(4th), col 74

C'tted: HL Deb, 9 May 1904, Vol 134(4th), col 701

Rep: HL Deb, 17 May 1904, Vol 135(4th), col 1

3R: HL Deb, 7 Jun 1904, Vol 135(4th), col 906

HL pass: HL Deb, 14 Jul 1904, Vol 138(4th), col 3

Royal Assent: HL Deb, 22 Jul 1904, Vol 138(4th), col 887

Parliamentary papers and cases

None

Gazette notices

London Gazette: 29 Jan 1904 (Iss: 27,640, p 619)

Edinburgh Gazette: 2 Feb 1904 (Iss: 11,590, p 118)

Dublin Gazette: 2 Feb 1904 (Iss: 20,046, p 130)

Office Journal of the Patent Office: 3 Feb 1904 (No 786, p 115); 10 Feb 1904 (No 787, p 151)

(continued)

(continued)

Newspaper coverage of debates
House of Lords
2R: The Times, 3 May 1904
3R: The Times, 8 Jun 1904
House of Commons
2R: The Times, 21 Jun 1904
3R: The Times, 13 Jul 1904

Archives
House Bill: HL/PO/JO/10/10/210 (No 812)
Minute Bill (Proof, HC Amds, C'tee Bill): HL/PO/JO/10/10/188 (No 321)
Unopposed Bill C'tee Minutes: 1 Jul 1904 (p 34): HC/CL/WM/UB/1/57
SOC Minutes: 26 Apr 1904 (p 39–42) [Ex Cert; Statement of Promoter]: HL/PO/CO/1/376
Unopposed Bill C'tee Minutes: 17 May 1904 (p 69): HL/PO/CO/1/374

Young and Bell's Patents Act 1904

PRVA120	1904

Young and Bell's Patents Act 1904 (4 Edw 7. c. iv)
An Act for rendering valid certain Letters Patent granted to William Young and Alexander Bell in respect of an invention for improvements in the decomposition of mineral oils for the production of illuminating gas and to William Young in respect of inventions (1) for improvements in the production of illuminating gas from mineral oils and in apparatus therefor and for producing water gas and (2) for improvements in the production of illuminating gas and bye-products from liquid hydrocarbons and in apparatus therefor [Passed in accordance with Private Legislation Procedure (Scotland) Act 1899]

Table of contents
s 1 Short title s 2 Letters patent confirmed s 3 Saving rights Schedule

Relevant patent	
5 Jul 1892 (1892 No 12,421)	Production of illuminating gas from mineral oils and in apparatus therefor and for producing water gas [William Young and Alexander Bell]
23 Jun 1893 (1893 No 12,355)	Production of illuminating gas and bye-products from liquid hydrocarbons and in apparatus therefor [William Young and Alexander Bell]

Journal					
House of Commons			**House of Lords**		
Rep: Arthur Jeffreys (Dep Ch W&M)			Pres: Lord Halsbury LC Rep: Lord Balfour of Burleigh		
10 Feb 1904	159 CJ 31	Bill originate HL	9 Feb 1904	136 LJ 26	Ord under 1899 Act
15 Feb 1904	159 CJ 34	SO cw	15 Feb 1904	136 LJ 35	Ex Cert/1R
15 Mar 1904	159 CJ 85	Brought HL	19 Feb 1904	136 LJ 48	Ex Cert
15 Mar 1904	159 CJ 86	1R/Ref Ex	23 Feb 1904	136 LJ 56	2R/C'tted
21 Mar 1904	159 CJ 96	SO cw	1 Mar 1904	136 LJ 64	C'tee to meet
28 Mar 1904	159 CJ 111	2R/C'tted	8 Mar 1904	136 LJ 71	Rep with Amds
14 Apr 1904	159 CJ 123	Rep w/o Amds	14 Mar 1904	136 LJ 79	3R
18 Apr 1904	159 CJ 127	3R	19 Apr 1904	136 LJ 107	HC pass w/o Amds
28 Apr 1904	159 CJ 152	Royal Assent	28 Apr 1904	136 LJ 123	Royal Assent

Representation
Agent: John Kennedy WS

Parliamentary debates	
Under 1899 Act: HC Deb, 9 Feb 1904, Vol 129(4th), col 713	Under 1899 Act: HL Deb, 9 Feb 1904, Vol 129(4th), col 709–710
SO cw: HC Deb, 10 Feb 1904, Vol 129(4th), col 1299	Ex Cert/1R: HL Deb, 15 Feb 1904, Vol 129(4th), col 1257
Originate HL: HC Deb, 10 Feb 1904, Vol 129(4th), col 841	Ex Cert: HL Deb, 19 Feb 1904, Vol 130(4th), col 345

Brought HL/1R: HC Deb, 15 Mar 1904, Vol 131(4th), col 1118–1119	2R: HL Deb, 23 Feb 1904, Vol 130(4th), col 673
2R: HC Deb, 28 Mar 1904, Vol 132(4th), col 808	Rep: HL Deb, 8 Mar 1904, Vol 131(4th), col 433
Rep: HC Deb, 14 Apr 1904, Vol 133(4th), col 182	3R: HL Deb, 14 Mar 1904, Vol 131(4th), col 917
3R: HC Deb, 18 Apr 1904, Vol 133(4th), col 349	HC pass: HL Deb, 19 Apr 1904, Vol 133(4th), col 477
Royal Assent: HC Deb, 28 Apr 1904, Vol 133(4th), col 1421	Royal Assent: HC Deb, 28 Apr 1904, Vol 133(4th), col 1405

Parliamentary papers and cases

None

Gazette notices

London Gazette, 13 Nov 1903 (Iss: 27,615, p 6950)

Edinburgh Gazette, 13 Nov 1903 (Iss: 11,567, p 1155)

Dublin Gazette: 13 Nov 1903 (Iss: 20,023, p 1367)

Office Journal of the Patent Office: 25 Nov 1903 (No 777, p 1575); 2 Dec 1903 (No 778, p 1613)

Newspaper coverage of debates

Should be dealt with by Bill not Provisional Order: The Scotsman, 11 Feb 1904

House of Lords

3R: The Times, 15 Mar 1904

House of Commons

2R: The Times, 29 Mar 1904

3R: The Times, 19 Apr 1904

Archives

House Bill: HL/PO/JO/10/10/213 (No 883)

Minute Bill (Proof and C'tee) Bill: HL/POJO/10/10/185 (No 174)

Unopposed Bill C'tee Minutes: 14 Apr 1904 (p 12): HC/CL/WM/UB/1/57

Unopposed Bill C'tee Minutes: 8 Mar 1904 (p 1): HL/PO/CO/1/374

Notes

The notices also included Patent No (1893 No 13,126) (Improvement in the Production of Illuminating Gas and Bye-Products from Liquid Hydrocarbons and in Apparatus thereof), which was not in the final Act

Leven Patent Act 1905

PRVA121	1905
	Leven Patent Act 1905 (5 Edw 7. c. lxi)
	An Act for rendering valid certain letters patent granted to Adolph Leven in respect of an invention for improvements in appliances for protection against projectiles

Table of contents

s 1 Letter patent confirmed
s 2 Saving rights
s 3 Short title
Schedule

Relevant patent

6 Apr 1900 (1900 No 6463)	Appliances for protection against projectiles [Adolph Leven]

Journal

House of Commons			House of Lords		
Rep: James Lowther (Ch W&M)			Pres: Lord Halsbury LC Rep: Earl of Onslow (Ld Ch)		
20 Mar 1905	160 CJ 73	SO ncw	16 Mar 1905	137 LJ 66	Pet
11 Apr 1905	160 CJ 128	SOC Disp	20 Mar 1905	137 LJ 70	Ex Cert
23 May 1905	160 CJ 203	Brought HL	30 Mar 1905	137 LJ 88	Ref SOC
23 May 1905	160 CJ 203	1R/Ref Ex	4 Apr 1905	137 LJ 98	SOC Rep/SO Disp

(continued)

(continued)

29 May 1905	160 CJ 218	SO cw	6 Apr 1905	137 LJ 100	1R
5 Jun 1905	160 CJ 236	2R/C'tted	13 Apr 1905	137 LJ 114	2R
21 Jun 1905	160 CJ 255	Rep w/o Amds	8 May 1905	137 LJ 126	C'tted
26 Jun 1905	160 CJ 263	3R	9 May 1905	137 LJ 133	C'tee to meet
30 Jun 1905	160 CJ 281	Royal Assent	16 May 1905	137 LJ 147	Rep with Amds
			22 May 1905	137 LJ 159	3R
			27 Jun 1906	137 LJ 213	HC pass w/o Amds
			30 Jun 1906	137 LJ 223	Royal Assent

Representation

Solicitor: JH and JY Johnson

Agent: Rees and Freres

Parliamentary debates

SO ncw: HC Deb, 20 Mar 1905, Vol 143(4th), col 421	Pet: HL Deb, 16 Mar 1905, Vol 143(4th), col 157
SO Disp: HC Deb, 11 Apr 1905, Vol 144(4th), col 1246	Ex Cert: HL Deb, 20 Mar 1905, Vol 143(4th), col 397
Brought HL/1R: HC Deb, 23 May 1905, Vol 146(4th), col 1109	Ref SOC: HL Deb, 30 Mar 1905, Vol 143(4th), col 1649
	SOC Disp: HL Deb, 4 Apr 1905, Vol 144(4th), col 261
SO cw: HC Deb, 29 May 1905, Vol 147(4th), col 55	1R: HL Deb, 6 Apr 1905, Vol 144(4th), col 589
2R: HC Deb, 5 Jun 1905, Vol 147(4th), col 668	2R: HL Deb, 13 Apr 1905, Vol 145(4th), col 2
Rep: HC Deb, 21 Jun 1905, Vol 147(4th), col 1206	C'tted: HL Deb, 8 Mar 1905, Vol 145(4th), col 1091
3R: HC Deb, 26 Jun 1905, Vol 148(4th), col 53	Rep: HL Deb, 16 May 1905, Vol 146(4th), col 405
	3R: HL Deb, 22 May 1905, Vol 146(4th), col 918
	HC pass: HL Deb, 27 Jun 1905, Vol 148(4th), col 226
	Royal Assent: HL Deb, 30 Jun 1905, Vol 148(4th), col 627

Parliamentary papers and cases

None

Notices

London Gazette: 17 Feb 1905 (Iss: 27,765, p 1211)

Edinburgh Gazette: 17 Feb 1905 (Iss: 11,699, p 173)

Dublin Gazette: 17 Feb 1905 (Iss: 20,158, p 278)

Office Journal of the Patent Office: 22 Feb 1905 (No 841, p 208); 1 Mar 1905 (No 842, p 246)

Newspaper coverage of debates

House of Lords

2R: The Times, 14 Apr 1905

House of Commons

2R: The Times, 6 Jun 1905

3R: The Times, 27 Jun 1905

Archives

House Bill: HL/PO/JO/10/10/241 (No 658)

Minute Bill (Corrected Amended, Proof): HL/PO/JO/10/10/225 (No 217a)

Unopposed Bill C'tee Minutes: 21 Jun 1905 (p 27): HC/CL/WM/UB/1/58

SOC Minutes: 4 Apr 1905 (at p 58 and 68–78) [Ex Cert; Statement of Promoters]: HL/PO/CO/1/380

Unopposed Bill C'tee Minutes: 16 May 1905 (p 30): HL/PO/CO/1/378

Vauclain's Patent Act 1906

PRVA122	1906
Vauclain's Patent Act 1906 (6 Edw 7. c. v)	
An Act for rendering valid certain letters patent granted to Samuel Mathews Vauclain for an invention for improvements in compound steam locomotives.	

Table of contents

s 1 Letter patent confirmed
s 2 Saving rights
s 3 Short title
Schedule

Relevant patent

3 Jun 1901 (1901 No 11,342)	Compound steam locomotives [Samuel Vauclain]

Journal

House of Commons				House of Lords		
Rep: Laurence Hardy (Dep Ch W&M)				Pres: Lord Loreburn LC Rep: Earl of Onslow (Ld Ch)		
20 Feb 1906	161 CJ 17	Bill originate HL		22 Feb 1906	138 LJ 59	Ex Cert
21 Feb 1906	161 CJ 20	SO cw		26 Feb 1906	138 LJ 62	1R
27 Mar 1906	161 CJ 91	Brought HL		5 Mar 1906	138 LJ 74	2R day app
27 Mar 1906	161 CJ 91	1R/Ref Ex		12 Mar 1906	138 LJ 83	2R/C'tted
2 Apr 1906	161 CJ 104	SO cw		13 Mar 1906	138 LJ 85	C'tee to meet
9 Apr 1906	161 CJ 126	2R/C'tted		20 Mar 1906	138 LJ 95	Rep with Amds
3 May 1906	161 CJ 160	Rep w/o Amds		26 Mar 1906	138 LJ 101	3R
7 May 1906	161 CJ 164	3R		8 May 1906	138 LJ 149	HC pass w/o Amds
29 May 1906	161 CJ 220	Royal Assent		29 May 1906	138 LJ 190	Royal Assent

Representation

Agent: Sherwood and Co

Parliamentary debates

Originate HL: HC Deb, 20 Feb 1906, Vol 152(4th), col 208

SO cw: HC Deb, 21 Feb 1906, Vol 152(4th), col 315

Brought HL/1R: HC Deb, 27 Mar 1906, Vol 154(4th), col 1039

SO cw: HC Deb, 2 Apr 1906, Vol 155(4th), col 124

2R: HC Deb, 9 Apr 1906, Vol 155(4th), col 953

Rep: HC Deb, 3 May 1906, Vol 156(4th), col 683

3R: HC Deb, 7 May 1906, Vol 156(4th), col 943–944

SO cw: HL Deb, 22 Feb 1906, Vol 152(4th), col 453

1R: HL Deb, 26 Feb 1906, Vol 152(4th), col 701

2R: HL Deb, 12 Mar 1906, Vol 153(4th), col 850

Rep: HL Deb, 20 Mar 1906, Vol 154(4th), col 177

3R: HL Deb, 26 Mar 1906, Vol 154(4th), col 805

HC pass: HL Deb, 8 May 1906, Vol 156(4th), col 1102

Royal Assent: HL Deb, 29 May 1906, Vol 158(4th), col 233

Parliamentary papers and cases

None

Gazette notices

London Gazette: 24 Nov 1905 (Iss: 27,857, p 8239)

Edinburgh Gazette: 24 Nov 1905 (Iss: 11,780, p 1206)

Dublin Gazette: 24 Nov 1905 (Iss: 20,239, p 1504)

Office Journal of the Patent Office: 29 Nov 1905 (No 881, p 1641); 6 Dec 1905 (No 882, p 1684)

Newspaper coverage of debates

House of Lords
2R: The Times, 13 Mar 1906

House of Commons
2R: The Times, 10 Apr 1906

3R: The Times, 8 May 1906

Archives

Pet: HC/CL/PB/104

House Bill: HL/PO/JO/10/10/283 (No 299)

Minute Bill (Proof and Corrected Amended): HL/PO/JO/10/10/255 (No 442)

Unopposed Bill C'tee Minutes: 3 May 1906 (p 11): HC/CL/WM/UB/1/59

Unopposed Bill C'tee Minutes: 20 Mar 1906 (p 8): HL/PO/CO/1/382

Crellin's Patents Act 1906

PRVA123	1906

Crellin's Patents Act 1906 (6 Edw 7. c. xlvii)
An Act for rendering valid certain letters patent granted to John Caesar Crellin for inventions for (1) an appliance for raising lowering supporting and transporting portions of machinery and the like (2) improvements relating to lifting-jacks and (3) improved apparatus for raising lowering supporting and transporting portions of machinery and like uses

Table of contents

s 1 Letter patent confirmed
s 2 Saving rights
s 3 Short title
Schedule

Relevant patents

20 Feb 1900 (1900 No 3318)	Appliance for raising lowering and supporting and transporting portions of machinery [John Crellin]
5 Jun 1900 (1900 No 10,254)	Lifting-jacks [John Crellin]
15 Jan 1901 (1901 No 942)	Apparatus for raising lowering, supporting and transporting portions of machinery and like uses [John Crellin]

Journal

House of Commons			House of Lords		
Rep: Sir John Lawson Walton (Ch W&M)			Pres: Lord Loreburn LC Rep: Earl of Onslow (Ld Ch)		
30 Apr 1906	161 CJ 147	SO ncw	5 Apr 1906	138 LJ 120	Pet/Ref Ex
15 May 1906	161 CJ 184	SOC Disp	30 Apr 1906	138 LJ 126	Ex Cert
29 May 1906	161 CJ 222	Brought HL	1 May 1906	138 LJ 134	Ref SOC
29 May 1906	161 CJ 223	1R/Ref Ex	7 May 1906	138 LJ 143	SOC Rep/SO Disp
8 Jun 1906	161 CJ 230	SO cw	8 May 1906	138 LJ 148	1R
13 Jun 1906	161 CJ 239	2R/C'tted	14 May 1906	138 LJ 159	2R
21 Jun 1906	161 CJ 266	Rep w/o Amds	21 May 1906	138 LJ 172	C'tted
25 Jun 1906	161 CJ 272	3R	22 May 1906	138 LJ 174	Rep w/o Amds
20 Jul 1906	161 CJ 356	Royal Assent	28 May 1906	138 LJ 184	3R
			26 Jun 1906	138 LJ 230	HC pass w/o Amds
			20 Jul 1906	138 LJ 287	Royal Assent

Representation

Agent: Recheck-Gazette

Parliamentary debates

SO ncw: HC Deb, 30 Apr 1906, Vol 156(4th), col 209

SO Disp: HC Deb, 15 May 1906, Vol 157(4th), col 335

Brought HL/1R: HC Deb, 29 May 1906, Vol 158(4th), col 251–252

SO cw: HC Deb, 8 Jun 1906, Vol 158(4th), col 613

2R: HC Deb, 13 Jun 1906, Vol 158(4th), col 933

Rep: HC Deb, 21 Jun 1906, Vol 159(4th), col 340

3R: HC Deb, 25 Jun 1906, Vol 159(4th), col 582

Pet: HL Deb, 5 Apr 1906, Vol 155(4th), col 617

SO ncw: HL Deb, 30 Apr 1906, Vol 156(4th), col 193

Ref SOC: HL Deb, 1 May 1906, Vol 156(4th), col 370

Rep SOC: HL Deb, 7 May 1906, Vol 156(4th), col 913

1R: HL Deb, 8 May 1906, Vol 156(4th), col 1101

2R: HL Deb, 14 May 1906, Vol 157(4th), col 97

Rep: HL Deb, 22 May 1906, Vol 157(4th), col 1073

3R: HL Deb, 28 May 1906, Vol 158(4th), col 3

HC pass: HL Deb, 26 Jun 1906, Vol 159(4th), col 746

Royal Assent: HL Deb, 20 Jul 1906, Vol 161(4th), col 534

Parliamentary papers and cases

None

Gazette notices

London Gazette: 30 Mar 1906 (Iss: 27,899, p 2257)

Edinburgh Gazette: 30 Mar 1906 (Iss: 11,816, p 376)

Dublin Gazette: 30 Mar 1806 (Iss: 20,276, p 420)

Office Journal of the Patent Office: 4 Apr 1906 (No 899, p 482); 11 Apr 1906 (No 900, p 523)

Newspaper coverage of debates	

House of Lords

2R: The Times, 15 May 1906

House of Commons

2R: The Times, 14 Jun 1906

3R: The Times, 26 Jun 1906

Archives

Minute Bill (1R Bill; Proofs Bill; C'tee Bill): HL/PO/JO/10/10/263

House Bill: HL/PO/JO/10/10/273 (No 46)

Unopposed Bill C'tee Minutes: 21 Jun 1906 (p 37): HC/CL/WM/UB/1/59

SOC Minutes: 7 May 1906 (p 136 and 144–147) [Ex Cert and Statement of Promoters]: HL/PO/CO/1/384

Unopposed Bill C'tee Minutes: 22 May 1906 (p 56–57): HL/PO/CO/1/382

Harrison's Patent Act 1907

PRVA124	1907
Harrison's Patent Act 1907 (7 Edw 7. c. xxxviii)	

An Act for rendering valid certain Letters Patent granted to Richard Harrison for an invention for improvements in or connected with elastic wheels applicable to motor and other vehicles

Table of contents

s 1 Letter patent confirmed
s 2 Saving rights
s 3 Short title
Schedule

Relevant patent

30 Jan 1902 (1902 No 2471)	Elastic wheels applicable to motor and other vehicles [Richard Harrison]

Journal

House of Commons			House of Lords		
Rep: Alfred Emmott (Ch W&M)			Pres: Lord Speaker / Rep: Earl of Onslow (Ld Ch)		
13 Feb 1907	162 CJ 7	Bill originate HL	14 Feb 1907	139 LJ 12	Ex Cert
14 Feb 1907	162 CJ 10	SO cw	18 Feb 1907	139 LJ 16	1R
29 May 1907	162 CJ 214	Brought HL	25 Feb 1907	139 LJ 31	2R/Ctted
29 May 1907	162 CJ 215	1R/Ref Ex	8 May 1907	139 LJ 120	C'tee to meet
3 Jun 1907	162 CJ 221	SO cw	14 May 1907	139 LJ 128	Rep with Amds
10 Jun 1907	162 CJ 238	2R day app	28 May 1907	139 LJ 137	3R
11 Jun 1907	162 CJ 243	2R/C'tted	25 Jun 1907	139 LJ 190	HC pass w/o Amds
20 Jun 1907	162 CJ 269	Rep w/o Amds	4 Jul 1907	139 LJ 211	Royal Assent
24 Jun 1907	162 CJ 274	3R			
4 Jul 1907	162 CJ 305	Royal Assent			

Representation

Agent: Blundell, Gordon and Co

Parliamentary debates

HL Originate: HC Deb, 13 Feb 1907, Vol 169(4th), col 153	SO cw: HL Deb, 14 Feb 1907, Vol 169(4th), col 273
SO cw: HC Deb, 14 Feb 1907, Vol 169(4th), col 277	1R: HL Deb, 18 Feb, 1907, Vol 169(4th), col 493
Brought HL/1R: HC Deb, 29 May 1907, Vol 174(4th), col 1609–1610	2R: HL Deb, 25 Feb 1907, Vol 169(4th), col 1218
SO cw: HC Deb, 3 Jun 1907, Vol 175(4th), col 250	Rep: HL Deb, 14 May 1907, Vol 174(4th), col 733
2R: HC Deb, 11 Jun 1907, Vol 175(4th), col 1196	3R: HL Deb, 28 May 1907, Vol 174(4th), col 1449
Rep: HC Deb, 20 Jun 1907, Vol 176(4th), col 584	HC pass: HL Deb, 25 Jun 1907, Vol 176(4th), col 1013
3R: HC Deb, 24 Jun 1907, Vol 176(4th), col 849	Royal Assent: HL Deb, 4 Jul 1907, Vol 177(4th), col 814

(continued)

(continued)

Parliamentary papers and cases
None
Gazette notices
London Gazette: 23 Nov 1906 (Iss: 27,970, p 7998)
Edinburgh Gazette: 23 Nov 1906 (Iss: 11,884, p 1256)
Dublin Gazette: 23 Nov 1906 (Iss: 20,344, p 1617)
Office Journal of the Patent Office: 8 Nov 1906 (No 933, p 1757); 5 Dec 1906 (No 934, p 1799)
Newspaper coverage of debates

House of Lords

2R: The Times, 26 Feb 1907

3R: The Times, 29 May 1907

House of Commons

2R: The Times, 12 Jun 1907

3R: The Times, 25 Jun 1907

Archives

Pet: HL/CL/PB/10/6

House Bill: HL/PO/JO/10/10/304 (No 93)

Minute Bill (Proof Bill, Letter from Comptroller and Amended Bill): HL/PO/JO/10/10/286

Unopposed Bill C'tee Minutes: 20 Jun 1907 (p 23): HC/CL/WM/UB/1/60

Unopposed Bill C'tee Minutes: 14 Mar 1907 (p 39): HL/PO/CO/1/386

Harrison's Patent Bill Renewal: National Archives (BT 15/54)

Private Bills and notices

Henry Heron's Bill 1621

PRVB1	1621
Henry Heron's Bill 1621 (18 Ja 1)	

Bill for Confirmation of a Judgement given for His Majesty in a Scire Facias in the Time of this Session of Parliament against H. Heron, and for a declaration of the Letters Patents, therein mentioned, to be void

Purpose
To confirm a judgment; the text was exactly the same as that enacted in 1624

Relevant patent	
5 Aug 1819	For salting, drying and packing of fish in Devon and Cornwall [Henry Heron] (1619) (STC 8609) [EEBO]

Journal

House of Commons			House of Lords		
29 Nov 1621	1 CJ 650	1R	9 May 1621	3 LJ 118	1R
			18 May 1621	3 LJ 128	2R
			30 May 1621	3 LJ 142	3R

Parliamentary debates
None

Parliamentary papers and cases
Wallace Notestein, Frances Relf and Hartley Simpson, *Commons Debates 1621* (Yale 1935), Vol 7 Text of Patent, p 359–360

Archives
Letters Patent (19 Aug 1619): Third Report of the Royal Commission on Historical Manuscripts (1872 C 673), Vol 33, p 337 at p 116 [HL/PO/JO/10/2/2A]
Ing (9 May 1621): House of Lords Manuscripts (New Series), Addenda, 1514–1714, Vol 11, p 147 (No 3351) [HL/PO/JO/10/2/2B]

Notes
The text of the Bill is exactly the same as that enacted in 1624: see PRVA2

Draft Ordnance Ordinance 1645

PRVB2	1645
Draft Ordnance Ordinance 1645	

Draft Ordinance that Peter Cannon shall have the Benefit of his Invention for the making of Ordnance and Guns, which will prove very advantageous for the Commonwealth

Contents (based on petition)
[Cl 1 Sole benefit of invention for loading iron and brass ordnance at the britche, not mouth; any other person making such ordnance to forfeit it]

Relevant patent
None

(continued)

(continued)

Journal							
House of Commons				**House of Lords**			
29 Sep 1645	4 CJ 293	Brought HL		29 Sep 1645	7 LJ 607	Passed	
8 Oct 1645	4 CJ 301	Message from HL		11 Feb 1646	8 LJ 156	Message to HC	
14 Oct 1645	4 CJ 306	Message from HL		24 Mar 1646	8 LJ 234	Message to HC	
22 Oct 1645	4 CJ 317	1R Ord		20 Apr 1646	8 LJ 279	Message to HC	
10 Nov 1645	4 CJ 337	Message from HL					
12 Feb 1645	4 CJ 438	1R adj					
16 Feb 1646	4 CJ 444	1R adj					
26 Mar 1646	4 CJ 491	1R adj					
20 Apr 1646	4 CJ 517	Message from HL					
Parliamentary debates							
None							
Parliamentary papers and cases							
None							
Archives							
Pet for Ordinance (26 Sep 1645): Sixth Report of the Royal Commission on Historical Manuscripts (1877 C 1745), Vol 47, p 1 at p 78 [HL/PO/JO/10/1/193]							

Chamberlen's Draft Ordinance 1648

PRVB3	1648
Chamberlen's Draft Ordinance 1648	
Draft Ordinance for granting to Doctor Peter Chamberlen the Benefit of his Invention of making Baths, &c. for Fourteen Years, according to the Statute	

Purpose	
No further details	

Relevant patent	
None	

Journal					
House of Commons			**House of Lords**		
4 Apr 1648	5 CJ 525	Brought HL	31 Mar 1648	10 LJ 165	Passed

Parliamentary debates					
None					

Parliamentary papers and cases					
To the Honourable House of Commons assembled in Parliament, the humble petition of Peter Chamberlen, doctor in physic (1649) C1908 (Wing 2nd) [This is the date provided, but queried, in the bibliographic details held, but it is more likely to be 1648 as this was when the Ordinance was before the House of Commons]					

Archives					
None					

Leather Trade Bill 1660

PRVB4	1660
Leather Trade Bill 1660 (12 Chas 2) [FL: 1.093]	
Bill for the more speedy and better Way for Tanning and Dressing, of all Sorts of Leather	

Table of contents
[Cl 1 Charles Howard, son of late Earl of Arundel, invention for tanning hides more quickly and without use of Oak bark shall have sole benefit of invention for 14 years; on payment of one fifth of profits and one forth of all penalties to His Majesty]

Relevant patent	
27 Oct 1660 (No 130)	Tanning, tawing, dressing, and preparing raw hides and skins, and making the same into leather [Charles Howard]

Journal					
House of Commons			**House of Lords**		
				Rep: Earl of Portland	
17 Dec 1660	8 CJ 213 – V	Unspecified	26 Nov 1660	11 LJ 192	1R
18 Dec 1660	8 CJ 215 – V	1R	27 Nov 1660	11 LJ 193	2R/C'tted
			30 Nov 1660	11 LJ 195	Rep w/o Amds
			1 Dec 1660	11 LJ 196	3R

Parliamentary debates
None

Parliamentary papers and cases
None

Archives
Bill (26 Nov 1660) (List of C'tee; Amds to Bill): Seventh Report of the Royal Commission on Historical Manuscripts (1879 C 2340), Vol 40, p 1 at p 135 [HL/PO/JO/10/1/300]

Notes
There was a similar Bill presented in the next session: PRVB5

Leather Trade Bill 1661

PRVB5	1661
	Leather Trade Bill 1661 (13 Chas 2) [FL: 2.015]
	Bill for the more speedy Way for Tanning, Currying, and Dressing, of all Sorts of Leather

Table of contents
All materials relating to this Bill are presumed lost, but it is probable that it was the same as the Bills considered in the previous session

Relevant patent (presumed)	
27 Oct 1660 (No 130)	Tanning, tawing, dressing, and preparing raw hides and skins, and making the same into leather [Charles Howard]

Journal			
House of Commons			**House of Lords**
			Pres: No Information
28 May 1661	8 CJ 260	Bill Ord	*Never considered by House of Lords*
30 May 1661	8 CJ 262	1R	
21 Jun 1661	8 CJ 277	2R	

Parliamentary debates
None

Parliamentary papers and cases
None

Archives
None

Colnett's Patent Bill 1662

PRVB6	1662
	Colnett's Patent Bill 1662 (14 Chas 2) [FL: 2.089]
	Bill for confirming Letters Patents, granted to John Colvett [sic], for making Glass Bottles, and for preventing frauds therein

(continued)

(continued)

Purpose
All materials relating to this Bill are presumed lost, but it is probable that it was the same as the Bills considered by the House of Lords

Relevant patent	
6 Sep 1661 (1661) PR 13, Cas II, Pt 25, No 8	Manufacturing of glass bottles and for preventing frauds and abuses in the making and public vending thereof [John Colnett]

Journal			
House of Commons			**House of Lords**
Pres: No information			
26 Feb 1662	8 CJ 373	Bill Ord	*Never considered by House of Lords*

Parliamentary debates
None

Parliamentary papers and cases
None

Archives
None

Notes
This Bill is presumed to be the same as PRVB7 and PRVB8

[Colnett's] Glass Bottle Bill 1662

PRVB7	1662
Glass Bottle Bill 1662 (14 Chas 2) [FL: 2.152]	
Bill for confirming the invention and manufacture of glass bottles, and for the prevention of fraud and abuses in the making and public vending thereof	

Proposed clauses (based on breviate)
[Cl 1 The invention shall be treated as new for the purposes of the Letters Patent granted 6 Sep 1661 despite it being used previously] [Cl 2 All bottles shall use the proper measures; 5l penalty for selling bottles without the proper measure; such bottles may be seized and broken]

Relevant patent	
6 Sep 1661 (1661) PR 13, Cas II, Pt 25, No 8	Manufacturing of glass bottles and for preventing frauds and abuses in the making and public vending thereof [John Colnett]

Journal			
House of Commons	**House of Lords**		
	Pres: No information		
Never considered by House of Commons	10 Apr 1662	11 LJ 426	1R
	11 Apr 1662	11 LJ 427	2R/C'tted
	24 Apr 1662	11 LJ 436	CWH day app

Parliamentary debates
None

Parliamentary papers and cases
None

Archives
Bill and Breviate (10 Apr 1662) (Annexed List of C'tee, Amd to Bill, Pets against, Rep of AG on Proc): *Seventh Report of the Royal Commission on Historical Manuscripts* (HMSO 1879) (C 2340), p 164 [HL/PO/JO/10/1/314]

Notes
This Bill is presumed to be the same as PRVB6 and PRVB8

[Colnett's] Glass Bottle Bill 1663

PRVB8	1663
Glass Bottle Bill 1663 (15 Ch. 3) [FL: 2.152]	
Bill for the better regulating the Manufacture of Glass Bottles, and for preventing of Abuses committed therein	

Table of contents (based on reference for Bill)

[Cl 1 The invention shall be treated as new for the purposes of the Letters Patent granted 6 Sep 1661 despite it being used previously]
[Cl 2 All bottles shall use the proper measures; 5l penalty for selling bottles without the proper measure; such bottles may be seized and broken]

Relevant patent

6 Sep 1661 (1661) PR 13, Cas II, Pt 25, No 8	Manufacturing of glass bottles and for preventing frauds and abuses in the making and public vending thereof [John Colnett]

Journal

House of Commons		House of Lords		
		Pres: No information		
Never considered by House of Commons		16 Mar 1663	11 LJ 493	1R

Parliamentary debates

None

Parliamentary papers and cases

None

Archives

Bill (16 Mar 1663): Seventh Report of the Royal Commission on Historical Manuscripts (1879 C 2340), Vol 40, p 1 at p 168 [HL/PO/JO/10/1/316]

Notes

This Bill is presumed to be the same as PRVB6 and PRVB7

Moreland's Pump Bill 1674

PRVB9	1674
Moreland's Pump Bill 1674 (24 Chas 2) [FL: 16.038]	
Bill to enable Sir Samuell Moreland to enjoy the sole Benefit of certain Pumps by him invented	

Purpose

No further details

Relevant patent

None

Journal

House of Commons			House of Lords
Pres: No information			
12 Feb 1674	9 CJ 308	1R	Never considered by House of Lords
13 Feb 1674	9 CJ 308	2R/C'tted	

Parliamentary debates

None

Parliamentary papers and cases

None

Archives

None

Notes

This might relate to the same invention as covered by PRVB10

Moreland's Pump Bill 1677

PRVB10	1677
Moreland's Pump Bill 1677 (29 Chas 2) [FL: 16.038]	
Bill for allowing Sir Samuel Moreland the Benefit of Pumps and Water Engines, by him invented	

Tables of contents (based on cases against)
[Cl 1 Sole property in the Engine and any improvements made to the engine]
[Cl 2 Within three months deliver a model of the invention, but in relation to any improvements delivery at any time after improvements made]
[Cl 3 Forfeiture to be approved by two justices of peace]

Relevant patent	
14 Mar 1674 (No 175)	Engine for raising great quantities of water [Samuel Moreland]

Journal			
House of Commons			**House of Lords**
Pres: No information			
20 Mar 1677	9 CJ 402	1R	*Never considered by House of Lords*
2 Apr 1677	9 CJ 412	2R/C'tted	

Parliamentary debates
None

Parliamentary papers and cases
Anon [James Ward], Reasons offered against passing Sir Samuel Morland's Bill (1677) Wing R576
Samual Morland, Sir Samuel Morland's answer to several papers of reasons against his mill for his new water-engines (1677) Wing M2776 [EEBO]

Archives
None

Notes
This might relate to the same invention as covered by PRVB9

[Walcot's] Salt-Water Patent Bill 1678

PRVB11	1678
Salt-Water Patent Bill 1678 (30 Chas 2) [FL: 16.141]	
Bill for making salt Water fresh and wholesome at Land and Sea	

Table of contents
[Cl 1 William Walcot &c shall exercise and enjoy the art of making salt water fresh for [Blank] Years]
[Cl 2 Any infringement punished by forfeiture of furnaces, vessels and fine; treble damages]
[Cl 3 Power of search and seizure to Walcot]

Relevant patent	
28 Oct 1675 (No 184)	Purifying corrupted water, and making sea water fresh, clear, and wholesome [William Walcot]

Journal			
House of Commons		**House of Lords**	
		Pres: No information	
Never considered by House of Commons	13 Mar 1678	13 LJ 181	1R

Parliamentary debates
None

Parliamentary papers and cases
None

Archives
Bill (13 Mar 1678) Ninth Report of Historical Manuscripts Commission, Part II, Appendix (1884 C-3773–I), Vol 37, p 1 at p 109 (No 521) [HL/PO/JO/10/1/375]
Notes
There were other Bills related to this invention: PRVB13, 15, 18 and 19; and the Act PRVA11

Hutchinson's Lamp Petition 1685

PRVB12	1685
Hutchinson's Lamp Bill 1685 (1 Ja 2) [FL: 22.016]	
Bill for granting to Samuel Hutchinson the Benefit of the Invention of Lights and Lamps	

Purpose
No further details
Relevant patent

27 Feb 1684 (No 232)	New experiment for the great and durable increase of light by means of extraordinary glasses and lamps, for the great improvement of ship lanterns, lighthouses, dispersing of lights in mines, and other uses where light and heat are required [Edward Wyndus, who was a proxy for Samuel Hutchinson]

Journal			
House of Commons			**House of Lords**
3 Jun 1685	9 CJ 726	Pet/Bill Ord	*Never considered by House of Lords*

Parliamentary debates
None
Parliamentary papers and cases
None
Archives
None
Notes
A later enactment related to the same patent: PRVA10

[Fitzgerald's] Salt-Water Patent Bill 1685

PRVB13	1685
Salt-Water Patent Bill 1685 (1 Ja 2) [FL: 22.026]	
Bill for making salt Water fresh and wholesome at Land and Sea	

Purpose
No further details
Relevant patent

9 Jun 1683 (No 226)	Engine for purifying salt and brackish water, making it sweet and fit for drinking and purposes of cooking [Robert Fitzgerald, Theophilus Oglethorp, William Bridgman, Patrick Trant and Thomas Maule]

Journal			
House of Commons			**House of Lords**
Pres: No information			
5 Jun 1685	9 CJ 729	Pet	*Never considered by House of Lords*
13 Jun 1685	9 CJ 736	Bill Ord	
15 Jun 1685	9 CJ 736	1R	

(continued)

(continued)

Parliamentary debates
None
Parliamentary papers and cases
None
Archives
None
Notes
There were other Bills related to this invention: PRVB11, 15, 18 and 19; and the Act PRVA11

White Paper Company Bill 1690

PRVB14	1690
White Paper Company Bill 1690 (2 Will & Mar) [FL: 24.055]	
Bill for the Encouraging and Better Establishing the Manufacture of White Paper	

Purpose
No details, but presumed the same as the subsequent Act

Relevant patent (presumed)	
21 Jan 1675 (No 178)	Making white paper for writing and printing [Inventor: Eustace Burneby] [Nathaniel Bladen – 1682] [Christopher Jackson – 1684] [John Briscoe – 1685] [Nicholas Dupin, Adam de Cardonell and Elias de Grunch – 1686]

Journal			
House of Commons			**House of Lords**
Pres: No information			
16 Jan 1690	10 CJ 333	Pet/Bill Ord	*Never considered by House of Lords*
22 Jan 1690	10 CJ 338	1R	
25 Jan 1690	10 CJ 343	2R	

Parliamentary debates
None
Parliamentary papers and cases
None
Archives
None
Notes
The Bill lapsed at the end of the session, and a new Bill was introduced in the next session: PRVA9

Walcott's Salt-Water Petition 1690

PRVB15	1690
Walcott's Salt-Water Petition 1690 (2 Will & Mar) [FL 25.054]	
Petition whereby William Walcott may be restored to his ancient right, and have his term renewed and enlarged	

Purpose
No further details

Relevant patent	
28 Oct 1675 (No 184)	Purifying corrupted water, and making sea water fresh, clear, and wholesome [William Walcott]

Journal			
House of Commons			**House of Lords**
15 May 1690	10 CJ 414	Pet/Bill Ord	*Never considered by House of Lords*
Parliamentary debates			
None			
Parliamentary papers and cases			
None			
Archives			
None			
Notes			
There were other Bills related to this invention: PRVB11, 13, 18 and 19; and the Act PRVA11			

Making Saltpetre Bill 1691

PRVB16	1691
Making Saltpetre Bill 1691 (3 Will & Mar) [FL: 27.026]	
Bill for the Encouragement of making Saltpetre here in England	
Purpose	
No further details	
Relevant patent	
7 Feb 1691 (No 266)	Making saltpetre [Richard Price, [Andrew Parry] and others]

Journal			
House of Commons			**House of Lords**
Pres: No information Rep: Sir Matthew Andrews			
25 Nov 1691	10 CJ 561	Com Intro Bill	*Never considered by House of Lords*
27 Nov 1691	10 CJ 562	**Pet**	
28 Nov 1691	10 CJ 564	Mem app	
2 Dec 1691	10 CJ 570	Mem app	
2 Dec 1691	10 CJ 571	Mem app	
5 Dec 1691	10 CJ 574	Mem app	
15 Dec 1691	10 CJ 587	Mem app	
16 Dec 1691	10 CJ 590	Mem app	
30 Dec 1691	10 CJ 603	Mem app	
7 Jan 1692	10 CJ 614	Rep/Bill Ord	
13 Jan 1692	10 CJ 621	1R	
21 Jan 1692	10 CJ 635	2R	
21 Jan 1692	10 CJ 636	**Pet Ag**	
23 Jan 1692	10 CJ 640	C'tted (All voices)	
1 Feb 1692	10 CJ 648	**Pet Ag**	
17 Feb 1692	10 CJ 678	Rep day app	
Petitions			
21 Jan 1692	10 CJ 636	Talbot Clerke and William. Terry [that they are first and true inventors]	
1 Feb 1692	10 CJ 648	William Tyndall [petitioners' invention not novel]	
Parliamentary debates			
None			
Archives			
None			
Parliamentary papers and cases			
None			

Convex Light Bill 1692

PRVB17	1692
	Convex Light Bill 1692 (4 Will & Mar) [FL: 28.012]
	Bill for the Granting a Further Term of Years to the Patentees of the Convex Lights

Purpose
No further details

Relevant patent	
27 Feb 1684 (No 232)	New experiment for the great and durable increase of light by means of extraordinary glasses and lamps, for the great improvement of ship lanterns, lighthouses, dispersing of lights in mines, and other uses where light and heat are required [Edward Wyndus]

Journal

House of Commons			House of Lords
Pres: Robert Waller			
Rep: Sir John Trenchard			
18 Nov 1692	10 CJ 706	Pet	*Never considered by House of Lords*
19 Nov 1692	10 CJ 707	1R	
22 Nov 1692	10 CJ 709	**2R/Pet Ag/C'tted**	
24 Nov 1692	10 CJ 710	**Pets Ag**	
24 Nov 1692	10 CJ 711	Mem add	
25 Nov 1692	10 CJ 714	Mem add	
6 Dec 1692	10 CJ 734	Rep/**Pet Ag**/Re-C'tted	
10 Dec 1692	10 CJ 740	Mem add	
19 Dec 1692	10 CJ 746	**Pet Ag**	
19 Dec 1962	10 CJ 747	**Pet Ag**/Rep	
30 Dec 1692	10 CJ 765 – V	3R	

Petitions

22 Nov 1692	10 CJ 709	Craven Howard [Bill establishes monopoly and against public good]
24 Nov 1692	10 CJ 710	Anthony Vernatty [prejudice patent owned by petitioner]
24 Nov 1692	10 CJ 710	Horner's Company London [Bill would reduce price of tallow to prejudice of makers]
6 Dec 1692	10 CJ 734	City of London Corp
19 Dec 1692	10 CJ 746	Company of Spectaclemaker [not read]
19 Dec 1692	10 CJ 747	City of London Corp

Parliamentary debates

None

Parliamentary papers and cases

Objections against passing the bill by the Proprietors of the Lights Now Generally Used (1692) Wing O85B

Archives

None

Notes

25 Mar 1695 – Books of the Company Ordered (11 CJ 281) (Listed as FL: 30.039) The Company got protection under a later Act: PRVA10

[Walcot's] Salt Water Bill 1692

PRVB18	1692
	Salt Water Bill 1692 (4 Will & Mar) [FL: 28.030]
	Bill for making sea water fresh, clear and wholesome

Table of contents

[s 1 William Walcot &c. to have to have exclusive rights over his invention and improvements in his Majesty's Dominions and Ireland and His Majestys Ships; and that no other person shall not do so without licence] [s 2 Any infringement under pain of forfeiture and treble value of the whole profit; one third part to His Majesty; one third part to informer and one third part to William Walcot] [s 3 Walcot can obtain a warrant for the better discovery of offences]

Relevant patent	
28 Oct 1675 (No 184)	Purifying corrupted water, and making sea water fresh, clear, and wholesome [William Walcott]

Journal					
House of Commons			**House of Lords**		
			Rep: Earl of Stamford		
14 Dec 1692	10 CJ 743	**Pet**/Bill Ord	28 Feb 1693	15LJ 252	Brought HC
9 Jan 1693	10 CJ 772	1R	2 Mar 1693	15 LJ 256	1R
4 Feb 1693	10 CJ 804	2R	4 Mar 1693	15 LJ 273	2R/C'tted
28 Feb 1693	10 CJ 837	3R	10 Mar 1693	15 LJ 284 – V	Rep w/o Amds/3R (negative)

Parliamentary debates
None

Parliamentary papers and cases
None

Archives
Committee Minutes: 6 Mar 1693 (p 174); 7 Mar 1693 (p 175–176) [HL/PO/CO/1/5] (these are summarised in Fourteenth Report of Historical Manuscripts Commission, Appendix, Part VI (1894 C7573), L Pt.I.479, p 378 (No 723))
Ing: 28 Feb 1692/3 – Engrossment of an Act for making sea-water fresh, clear and wholesome (Walcot's Patent) Fourteenth Report of Historical Manuscripts Commission, Appendix, Part VI (1894 C7573), L Pt.I.479, p 378(No 723) [HL/PO/JO/10/2/22]

Notes
There were other Bills related to this invention: PRVB11, 13, 15 and 19; and the Act PRVA11

[Walcot's] Salt Water, Making into Fresh Bill 1694

PRVB19	1694
Salt Water, Making into Fresh Bill 1694 (5 & 6 Will & Mar) [FL: 29.072]	
Bill for the making of salt Water fresh and useful	

Table of contents
[s 1 William Walcot &c. to have [blank] of exclusive rights over his invention and improvements in his Majesty's Dominions and Ireland and His Majestys Ships; and that no other person shall not do so without licence]
[s 2 Any infringement under pain of forfeiture and treble value of the whole profit; one third part to His Majesty; one third part to informer and one third part to William Walcot]
[s 3 Walcot can obtain a warrant for the better discovery of offences]

Relevant patent	
28 Oct 1675 (No 184)	Purifying corrupted water, and making sea water fresh, clear, and wholesome [William Walcot]

Journal			
House of Commons	**House of Lords**		
	Pres: No information		
Never considered by House of Commons	21 Mar 1694	15 LJ 399	1R

Parliamentary debates
None

Parliamentary papers and cases
None

Archives
Bill and Breviate: 21 Mar 1694 - House of Lords Manuscripts (New Series), Vol 1 (HMSO 1900), p 376 (No 825) [HL/PO/JO/10/1/465/825]

Notes
There were other Bills related to this invention: PRVB11, 13, 15 and 18; and the Act PRVA11

Robert Ledgingham's Invention for Ship Pumps Bill 1698

PRVB20	1698		
Robert Ledgingham's Invention for Ship Pumps Bill 1698 (10 Will 3) [FL: 33.063]			
Bill for the Encouragement of Robert Ledginham's New-Invented Pumps for Ships			
Purpose			
No further details			
Relevant patent			
12 Jul 1695 (No 340)	Making chain-pumps and hand-pumps for ships of war and merchant ships [Robert Ledingham]		
Journal			
House of Commons		**House of Lords**	
Rep: John Manley			
19 Feb 1698	12 CJ 120	**Pet**	*Never considered by House of Lords*
24 Feb 1698	12 CJ 127	Mem add	
6 May 1698	12 CJ 257	**Pet Rep**/Leave	
21 May 1698	12 CJ 280	Pres	
23 May 1698	12 CJ 283	1R	
28 May 1698	12 CJ 289	2R/C'tted	
1 Jun 1698	12 CJ 294	Mem add	
7 Jun 1698	12 CJ 302	**Pet Ag**	
9 Jun 1698	12 CJ 306	**Pet Ag**	
Petitions			
7 Jun 1698	12 CJ 302	Sir Robert Gordon [his invention better than Ledgingham's]	
9 Jun 1698	12 CJ 306	Pumpmakers of London [hand pump not novel]	
Parliamentary debates			
None			
Parliamentary papers and cases			
To the honourable the Commons of England, in Parliament assembled. The humble representation of Robert Ledgingham, merchant (1698) Wing L837A			
To the honourable the Commons of England in Parliament assembled. The humble recital of Robert Ledgingham, merchant (1699) No Bib Ref (JISC)			
Advert, The uses and conveniences of Mr. Ledgingham's new invented chain pumps (1700) Wing L837B			
Archives			
None			

Robert Ledgingham's Fire Engine Petition 1699

PRVB21	1699		
Robert Ledgingham's Fire Engine Petition 1699 (11 & 12 Will 3) [FL: 34.024]			
Purpose			
No further details			
Relevant patent			
None			
Journal			
House of Commons		**House of Lords**	
Rep: Lord Cornbury			
26 Jan 1699	12 CJ 450	**Pet**	*Never considered by House of Lords*
28 Jan 1699	12 CJ 463	Mem Add	
2 Feb 1699	12 CJ 469	Mem Add	
16 Feb 1699	12 CJ 513	Mem Add	
20 Feb 1699	12 CJ 518	**Rep to Conduct Exp**	
23 Mar 1699	12 CJ 610	Arrest of witness	

Parliamentary debates
None
Parliamentary papers and cases
None
Archives
None

Hildeyard's Navigation Instruments Petition 1702

PRVB22	1702
Hildeyard's Navigation Instruments Petition 1702 (1 Ann) [FL: 37.016]	
Petition for a Bill for Encouraging the invention [of Two Several Instruments, for the Improvement of Navigation]	

Purpose
No further details

Relevant patent
None, but the inventor was Edward Hildeyard

Journal

House of Commons			House of Lords
3 Feb 1702	13 CJ 714	Pet	*Never considered by House of Lords*

Parliamentary debates
None
Parliamentary papers and cases
None
Archives
None

Damasking Stuffs Bill 1702

PRVB23	1702
Damasking Stuffs Bill 1702 (1 Ann) [FL: 37.027]	
Bill for the Encouragement of an Invention of Damasking, Striking, and Fixing, Colours into all Sorts of Stuffs, and Clothes; and Raising and Embossing Flowers of Various Colours of the Same	

Purpose [from reasons against]
Bill to extend a patent

Relevant patent

14 Dec 1695 (No 346)	Damasking, striking, and fixing colours on both sides on leather, stuffs, cloths, velvets and hair; making tapestry with grogram yarn [Thomas Matthews and Thomas Ferrers]

Journal

House of Commons			House of Lords
Pres and Rep: Lord Fairfax			
23 Feb 1702	13 CJ 756	**Pet**/Leave	*Never considered by the House of Lords*
26 Feb 1702	13 CJ 766	Pres	
2 Mar 1702	13 CJ 770	1R	
6 Mar 1702	13 CJ 778	2R/C'tted	
7 Mar 1702	13 CJ 780	**Pet Ag**	
10 Mar 1702	13 CJ 785	**Pet Ag**	
13 Mar 1702	13 CJ 794	Mem Add	
23 Mar 1702	13 CJ 817	**Pet Ag**	
27 Mar 1702	13 CJ 821	**Pet Ag**	

(continued)

(continued)

31 Mar 1702	13 CJ 831	Mem Add	
11 Apr 1702	13 CJ 842	Mem Add	
13 Apr 1702	13 CJ 843	Mem Add	
15 Apr 1702	13 CJ 845	C'tee Ord Rep	
17 Apr 1702	13 CJ 848	**Interim Rep**	
20 Apr 1702	13 CJ 857	Inst to C'tee	

Petitions		
7 Mar 1702	13 CJ 780	Woollen-drapers [prejudicial to Woollen Manufacturers]
10 Mar 1702	13 CJ 785	Robert Parker [first inventor and Bill will prevent working]
23 Mar 1702	13 CJ 817	Thomas Freeman, John Rowland, John Mould [apprentices in invention could no longer work it]
27 Mar 1702	13 CJ 821	Levant Company [Bill great prejudice to manufacturers]

Parliamentary debates
None

Parliamentary papers and cases
Reasons humbly offered for the passing a bill for the encouraging an invention of damasking, striking and fixing colours into all sorts of cloths, stuffs, &c. And raising and embossing various flowers and shades on the same; in answer to several objections which have been made against it (ESTC T020637)

Archives
None

Watches, Inventions, Extension of Patent Bill 1704

PRVB24	1704

Watches, Inventions, Extension of Patent Bill 1704 (3 & 4 Ann) [FL: 40.017]

Bill for the further encouragement of the new art or invention of working and applying precious and more common stones, for the greater perfection of watches, clocks and other engines

Purpose
Term extension

Relevant patent	
1 May 1704 (No 371)	Working stones, crystals, or glass and other matters different from metal, for use in clocks or watch work, and in other engines [Nicholas Facio, Peter Debaufre and Jacob Debaufre]

Journal			
House of Commons			**House of Lords**
Pres: Marquis of Hartington			
6 Dec 1704	14 CJ 445	**Pet**/Leave	*Never considered by the House of Lords*
9 Dec 1704	14 CJ 451	1R	
14 Dec 1704	14 CJ 458	2R/C'tted	
15 Dec 1704	14 CJ 459	Mem Add	
18 Dec 1704	14 CJ 462	**Pet Ag**	
21 Dec 1704	14 CJ 467	**Pet Ag**	

Petitions		
18 Dec 1704	14 CJ 462	Clockmakers and Watchmakers [Bill on false basis]
21 Dec 1704	14 CJ 567	Jewellers, Diamond Cutters &c. [Bill will stop jewellers doing things already working]

Parliamentary debates
None

Parliamentary papers and cases
Reasons of the English watch and clockmakers against the bill to confirm the pretended new invention of using precious and common stones about watches, clocks, and other engines (1704) [ESTC T046472]
Reasons humbly offer'd by the jewellers, diamond-cutters, lapidaries, engravers in stone, &c. against the bill for jewel-watches (1704) (EEBO)

Archives
None

Hutchinson's Time Movement Bill 1712

PRVB25	1712		
	Hutchinson's Time Movement Bill 1712 (12 Ann) [FL: 48.022]		
	Bill for securing to Mr John Hutchinson the property of a Movement, Invented by Him, for the more exact measuring of time, both in motion, and at rest		
	**Purpose**		
	To give patent-like protection (for more than 14 years) to his invention		
	**Relevant patent**		
	None		
	**Journal**		

House of Commons			House of Lords
Pres: Sir William Windham			*Never considered by the House of Lords*
14 May 1712	17 CJ 223	**Pet**/Leave	
17 May 1712	17 CJ 229	Bill Pr	
19 May 1712	17 CJ 229	1R	
22 May 1712	17 CJ 233	2R/C'tted/**Pet Ag**	
23 May 1722	17 CJ 239	Mem Add	
28 May 1712	17 CJ 246	Mem Add	

Petitions		
22 May 1712	17 CJ 233	Company of Clockmakers [Bill would be prejudicial to them and a discouragement to others in the trade]

Parliamentary debates
None

Parliamentary papers and cases
None

Archives
Papers on Bill: London Metropolitan Archives (Guildhall Library): CLC/L/CD/E/004/MS03952 [(1) Petition of John Hutchinson; (2) Petition of Company of Clockworkers; (3) The Clockworker's Reasons Against Mr Hutchinsons Pretended Invention; (4) Reasons for the Bill offered in Answer to those offered by the Clockmakers; (5) The Clockmakers farther reasons Against the Bill; (6) Further reasons For the Bill in Response to the farther reasons offer; (7) Account of Report of Proceedings of Clockworker's Company in relation to Bill]

Le Blon's Petition 1734

PRVB26	1734
	Le Blon's Petition 1734 (8 Geo 2) [NFL]
	Petition to incorporate James Christopher Le Blon and his Copartners in a Patent for weaving Tapestry, in order to encourage the manufacturing Tapestry in the Loom
	**Purpose**
	No further details
	**Relevant patent**

1 May 1727 (No 492)	Weaving tapestry in the loom [James Christopher Le Blon]

Journal		

House of Commons		House of Lords
27 Feb 1734	22 CJ 259 – V	**Pet**
		Never considered by the House of Lords

Parliamentary debates
None

Parliamentary papers and cases
None

Archives
None

Tuite's Water Engine Bill 1742

PRVB27	1742

Tuite's Water Engine Bill 1742 (16 Geo 2) [FL: 80.018]
Bill for vesting, for a certain time, in John Tuite, his executors, administrators, and assigns, the sole property of a water engine by him invented

Table of contents (from Ingrossment)
[C1 1 From 24 Jun 1742 John Tuite &c to have the benefit and use of water engine invented by him for 21 years; for each infringement the article is forfeited and £400 paid to John Tuite &c]   [Cl 2 Does not extend to any water engine already invented]

Relevant patent	
30 Jul 1742 (No 585)	Engine for raising water [John Tuite]

Journal

House of Commons			House of Lords		
Pet Rep and Pres: Nicholas Fenwick Bill Rep: Thomas Gore					
15 Mar 1742	24 CJ 123	**Pet (before grant)/Ref** C'tee	14 Apr 1742	26 LJ 99	1R
29 Mar 1742	24 CJ 152	**Pet Rep**	27 Apr 1742	26 LJ 103	2R/C'tted
1 Apr 1742	24 CJ 161	1R			
5 Apr1742	24 CJ 165	2R/C'tted			
13 Apr 1742	24 CJ 177	Rep			
14 Apr 1742	24 CJ 181	3R			

Parliamentary debates
None

Parliamentary papers and cases
None

Archives
Ing: 14 April 1742 – Act for vesting for a certain term chosen mentioned in John Tuite, his executors, administrators and assigns the vote property of water engine by him invented [HL/PO/JO/10/2/41]   C'tee Minutes: 13 May 1742: [HL/PO/CO/1/12]

Tuite's Water Engine Petition 1743

PRVB28	1743

Tuite's Water Engine Petition 1743 (17 Geo 2) [FL: 81.010]
Petition for a Bill for Enlarging the Term Granted to John Tuite for his Patent [for supplying towns and cities with water, for draining mines, and saving ships by springing leaks at sea]

Purpose
No further details

Relevant patent	
30 Jul 1742 (No 585)	Engine for raising water [John Tuite]

Journal

House of Commons			House of Lords
11 Jan 1743	24 CJ 374	Pet/Ref C'tee	*Never considered by the House of Lords*

Parliamentary debates
None

Parliamentary papers and cases
None

Archives
None

Champion's Patent Petition 1751

PRVB29		1751	
Champion's Patent Petition 1751 (25 Geo 2) [FL: 89.008]			
Petition for a Bill for Enlarging the Term Granted by His Present Majesty's Letters Patent to William Champion, of the City of Bristol, Merchant, for the Making, Using, and Vending of Spelter			
Purpose			
The property in the invention in William Champion for such term of years as the House shall deem fit			
Relevant patent			
1 July 1738 (No 564)		Reducing sulphureous British minerals into a body of metallic sulphur [William Champion]	
Journal			
House of Commons			**House of Lords**
Rep: Edward Southwell			
21 Feb 1751	26 CJ 54	Pet/Ref C'tee	*Never considered by the House of Lords*
4 Mar 1751	26 CJ 81	**Pet Rep**	
26 Mar 1751	26 CJ 150	**Pet Ag**	
Petition			
26 Mar 1751	26 CJ 510	Merchants and Traders of Preston [against general interest]	
Parliamentary debates			
None			
Parliamentary papers and cases			
None			
Archives			
None			

Lyddell's Ballast Engine Petition 1755

PRVB30		1755	
Lyddell's Ballast Engine Petition 1755 (28 Geo 2) [FL: 94.007]			
Petition for a Bill for Extending the Term of Letters Patent for [a new sort of Machine, or Vessel, for the Removal of Earth, Ballast, sand, or any of kind of matter, from any Port, River, Harbour, Creak, or Inlett]			
Purpose			
The property in the invention to Richard Lyddell such term of years as the House shall deem fit			
Relevant patent			
12 Apr 1753 (No 682)		Machines or vessels for removing earth, ballast, sand, rubbish, or any other matter [Richard Liddell]	
Journal			
House of Commons			**House of Lords**
Rep: George Cooke			
8 Jan 1755	27 CJ 66	**Pet**	*Never considered by the House of Lords*
21 Jan 1755	27 CJ 111	**Pet Ag**	
21 Jan 1775	27 CJ 112	**3 × Pet Ag**	
28 Jan 1755	27 CJ 122	**2 × Pet Ag**	
3 Feb 1755	27 CJ 134	**Pet Ag**	
6 Feb 1755	27 CJ 143	**Pet Fav**	
7 Feb 1755	27 CJ 144	**Pet Fav**	
12 Feb 1755	27 CJ 154	**Pet Fav**	
12 Mar 1755	27 CJ 203	**Rep**	
13 Mar 1755	27 CJ 204	**Re-C'tted**	
14 Mar 1755	27 CJ 213	**Question for Com**	
17 Mar 1755	27 CJ 235	**Rep/not proc**	

(continued)

(continued)

Petitions			
21 Jan 1755	27 CJ 111		Mayor &c. Newcastle-Upon-Tyne [use of invention dangerous and may affect trade in Newcastle]
21 Jan 1755	27 CJ 112		JPs of Durham [ballast should only be thrown out onto dry land]
21 Jan 1755	27 CJ 112		JPs of Morpeth [invention should not be used to prejudice navigation of the Tyne]
21 Jan 1755	27 CJ 112		Masters and Pilots Trinity House in Newcastle [invention would be damaging to the port]
28 Jan 1755	27 CJ 122		Fishermen and Pilots Newcastle [use of invention damaged fishing waters]
28 Jan 1755	27 CJ 122		Fraternity of Hollmen of Newcastle [discharge of ballast will cause hazards]
3 Feb 1755	27 CJ 134		Commissioners of River Wear [damage to port and hard of Shields]
6 Feb 1755	27 CJ 143		Owners and Masters of Starbough [invention is cheaper]
7 Feb 1755	27 CJ 144		Owners and Masters Louden [is better than current method and cheaper]
12 Feb 1755	27 CJ 154		Owners and Masters Yarmouth [invention of great benefit]

Parliamentary debates
None

Parliamentary papers and cases
None

Archives
None

Cox's Unloading Machine Petition 1757

PRVB31	1757

Cox's Unloading Machine Petition 1757 (30 Geo 2) [FL: 96.012]

Petition for a Bill for the Securing to Edward Cox, his Heirs or Assigns, the Sole Use and Benefit of the [Engine for the more speedy unloading of Coal Ships]

Purpose (based on petition)
The property in the machine to vest in Edward Cox for such term of years as the House shall deem fit

Relevant patent	
23 Feb 1757 (No 712)	Machine for unloading coal-ships in the Pool of the river Thames [Edward Cox] [after House of Commons petition]

Journal			
House of Commons			**House of Lords**
Rep: William Hammond			
10 Feb 1757	27 CJ 693	**Pet**/Ref C'tee	*Never considered by the House of Lords*
28 Apr 1757	27 CJ 859	**Pet Rep**	

Parliamentary debates
None

Parliamentary papers and cases
None

Archives
None

Hunter Morris Petition 1759

PRVB32	1759

Hunter Morris Petition 1759 (33 Geo 2) [NFL]

Manufacture of salt in North America

Table of contents (based on petition)
[Cl 1 Profits arising from marine salt manufacture in British North American Colonies for a Term of Years] [Cl 2 No restriction on the current methods of salt production in the Colonies]

Relevant patent		
None		
Journal		
House of Commons		**House of Lords**
11 Feb 1758	28 CJ 85	**Pet**	*Never considered by the House of Lords*
2 Mar 1758	28 CJ 114	Pet read/Ref C'tee	
Parliamentary debates		
None		
Parliamentary papers and cases		
None		
Archives		
None		

Bindley's Verdigrease Manufacture Petition 1760

PRVB33	1760
Bindley's Verdigrease Manufacture Petition 1760 (1 Geo 3) [FL: 101.008]	
Petition for a Bill for vesting in [John Bindley] the sole Right and Property of using and exercising [the method of making either from British or Foreign Materials Verdigrease of equal Goodness with that of the French Manufacture]	

Table of contents (based on petition)		
[Cl 1 Sole right in method of making Verdigrease [a green dye pigment] discovered by John Bindley to be granted for a term of years]		
Relevant patent		
None		
Journal		
House of Commons		**House of Lords**
19 Dec 1760	28 CJ 1000	**Pet /Ref C'tee**	*Never considered by the House of Lords*
23 Jan 1761	28 CJ 1039	**Pet Rep/Ref CWH**	
26 Jan 1761	28 CJ 1044	CWH adj	
27 Jan 1761	28 CJ 1045	CWH adj	
28 Jan 1761	28 CJ 1047	CWH adj	
2 Feb 1761	28 CJ 1055	CWH adj	
4 Feb 1761	28 CJ 1055	CWH adj	
Parliamentary debates		
None		
Parliamentary papers and cases		
None		
Newspaper coverage of debates		
The Gentleman and London Magazine, 19 Dec, May 1762, p 258–259		
Archives		
None		

Dingley's Saw Mill Petition 1768

PRVB34	1768
Dingley's Saw Mill Petition 1768 (8 Geo 3) [FL: 109.003]	
Petition for Protection and Encouragement to Repair Immediately his Saw Mill, that the Public may not be sufferers, as well as the petitioners, by it not being re-established and repaired immediately	

Purpose
Protection to prevent competition with saw mill
Relevant patent
None

(continued)

(continued)

Journal			
House of Commons			**House of Lords**
19 May 1768	32 CJ 15	Pet	*Never considered by the House of Lords*
Parliamentary debates			
None			
Parliamentary papers and cases			
None			
Newspaper coverage of debates			
None			
Archives			
None			
Notes			
He was awarded a prize: PRZA12			

Swaine's Patent Petition 1775

PRVB35	1775
Swaine's Patent Petition 1775 (15 Geo 3) (NFL)	
Petition for a Bill for enlarging the Term granted by [the Letters Patent for the Application of Smelting Furnaces to a Fire Engine for draining Mines], for securing to [Sampson Swain] and his assigns the benefit of the said invention, for such further term as the house sees fit	
Purpose	
No further details	
Relevant patent	
21 May 1762 (No 774)	Furnace for smelting and refining metals, and for other purposes [Sampson Swain]

Journal			
House of Commons			**House of Lords**
27 Feb 1775	35 CJ 155	Pet/Ref C'tee	*Never considered by the House of Lords*
Parliamentary debates			
None			
Parliamentary papers and cases			
None			
Newspaper coverage of debates			
None			
Archives			
Notes			

Marine Acid Bill 1780

PRVB36	1780
Marine Acide Bill 1780 (20 Geo 3) [FL: 121.051]	
Bill to take off the Duties on Salt used in preparing Marine Acide, and a fixed Fossil or Mineral Alkai, for a Time to be limited	
Purpose	
No further details	
Relevant patent	
1 Aug 1781 (No 1303)	Process by which the alkalies contained in sea-salt, salt-water, rock-salt, salt-springs, and vitriolated tartar are separated from the marine and vitriolic acids [Alexander Fordyce]

Journal			
House of Commons			**House of Lords**
Rep Fordyce: Charles Brett Rep Keir et al: Richard Sutton Pres: George Dempster			*Never considered by the House of Lords*
22 May 1780	37 CJ 865	**Pet [Fordyce]**	
31 May 1780	37 CJ 891	**Pet [Keir]**	
31 May 1780	37 CJ 892	**Pets [De Bruges and Watt]**	
31 May 1780	37 CJ 893	**Pet Rep [Fordyce]/Ref CWH**	
1 Jun 1780	37 CJ 897	**Pet [Collison]**	
6 Jun 1780	37 CJ 903	CWH [Fordyce] adj	
19 Jun 1780	37 CJ 908	**Pet [Fry]**	
19 Jun 1780	37 CJ 909	CWH [Forydce] adj	
19 Jun 1780	37 CJ 909	Keir Com Ord given	
19 Jun 1780	37 CJ 909	**Pet Ag**	
21 Jun 1780	37 CJ 912	**Pet Ag**	
21 Jun 1780	37 CJ 913	**Pet Rep [All others]**	
21 Jun 1780	37 CJ 916	**Pet Ag**	
21 Jun 1780	37 CJ 917 – V	Cons/Bill Ord	
23 Jun 1780	37 CJ 921	1R	
28 Jun 1780	37 CJ 929	**Further Pet Rep [all others]**	
Petitions			
31 May 1780	37 CJ 891	James Keir [that all persons working in manufacture of marine acid given duties exemption]	
31 May 1780	37 CJ 892	Peter Theodore De Bruges [he allowed same exemption from duty or given to all manufacturers]	
31 May 1780	37 CJ 892	James Watt and Dr Joseph Black [same exemption of duty to all manufactures of marine alkali]	
1 Jun 1780	37 CJ 897	John Collison [same exemption to all manufactures of marine acid]	
19 Jun 1780	37 CJ 908	Joseph Fry [same exemption to all manufactures of marine acid]	
19 Jun 1780	37 CJ 909	Richard Shannon [can produce marine acid without being duty free/so reject all other petitions]	
21 Jun 1780	37 CJ 912	Samuel Garbett [granting reduction of duty to Fordyce will injure petitioner]	
21 Jun 1780	37 CJ 916	Isaac Cookson and Edward Wilson [same exemption to be granted to all manufacturers]	
Parliamentary debates			
None			
Parliamentary papers and cases			
None			
Newspaper coverage of debates			
None			
Archives			
None			

Arkwright's Cotton Machine Petition 1782

PRVB37	1782
Arkwright's Cotton Machine Petition 1782 (22 Geo 3) [NFL]	
Petition for a Bill to extend the Term granted by the Patent in the Year 1769, so as to make the same expire with the Term granted by the patent in the year 1775, as some Recompence or Satisfaction for what, he humbly conceives, he may call his Public Service and Suffering &c.	
Purpose	
No further details	
Relevant patents	
3 Jul 1769 (No 931)	Machinery for the making of weft or yarn from cotton, flax, and wool [Richard Arkwright]
16 Dec 1775 (No 1111)	Preparing silk, cotton, flax, and wool for spinning [Richard Arkwright]

(continued)

(continued)

Journal					
House of Commons			**House of Lords**		
6 Feb 1782	38 CJ 687	**Pet**	*Never considered by the House of Lords*		
4 Mar 1782	38 CJ 865	**Pet Ag × 4**			
11 Mar 1782	38 CJ 882	**Pet Ag**			
11 Mar 1782	38 CJ 883	**Pet Ag**			
18 Mar 1782	38 CJ 897	**Pet Ag**			
20 Apr 1782	38 CJ 938	**Pet Ag**			

Petitions		
4 Mar 1782	38 CJ 865	Cotton and Calico Mfg Blackburn [Arkwright allegations unsupported; detriment to industry]
4 Mar 1782	38 CJ 865	Cotton Mfg Manchester [Arkwright allegations unsupported; detriment to industry]
4 Mar 1782	38 CJ 865	Cotton Mfg Bolton [Arkwright allegations unsupported; detriment to industry]
4 Mar 1782	38 CJ 865	Cotton Mfg Stockport [Arkwright allegations unsupported; detriment to industry]
11 Mar 1782	38 CJ 882	Merchants of Liverpool [Arkwright already obtained all advantages]
18 Mar 1782	38 CJ 897	Merchants of Lancaster [Arkwright already obtained all advantages]
20 Apr 1782	38 CJ 938	Landowners Manchester [Bill would prejudice manufacturers and commerce]

Parliamentary debates
None

Parliamentary papers and cases
Case of Mr Richard Arkwright & Co, in relation to Mr Arkwright's invention of an engine for spinning yarn (1782) (ESTC T188828)
[There was a shortened version of the case in Report from the Select Committee on the Law Relative to Patents for Inventions (1829 HC Papers 332), Vol 3, p 415 at p. 184, with a note that it may never have been lodged before Parliament]

Newspaper coverage of debates
None

Archives
None

Notes
There was a further petition in a later session: PRVB39

Wharam's Patent Stirrup Bill 1782

PRVB38	1782
Wharam's Patent Stirrup Bill 1782 (22 Geo 3) [FL: 123.011]	
Bill for enlarging the Term of a Patent granted to Ann. Wharam, for making a certain Sort of Spring Stirrup	

Table of contents (from Ingrossment)
[Cl 1 Said invention vests in Anne Wharam &c in Great Britain and in plantations from passing of this Act for term of fourteen years; who shall get benefit of invention for that term; and no other shall use it without licence]
[Cl 2 Cannot be assigned to more than five persons]
[Cl 3 Public Act]

Relevant patent	
23 May 1769 (No 926)	Preventing the dangers arising to equestrians from their hanging by the foot in the stirrup, in case of falling or being thrown from their horses [Anne Stell]

Journal					
House of Commons			**House of Lords**		
Pres and Rep: Richard Hill					
31 Jan 1782	38 CJ 655	**Pet** /Ref C'tee	30 Apr 1782	36 LJ 451	Brought HC
6 Feb 1782	38 CJ 679	**Pet Rep**			
11 Feb 1782	38 CJ 700	1R			
19 Feb 1782	38 CJ 801	2R/C'tted			
28 Feb 1782	38 CJ 862	**Rep**/Ing			
5 Mar 1782	38 CJ 868	3R			

Parliamentary debates
None
Parliamentary papers and cases
None
Newspaper coverage of debates
None
Archives
Ing: 30 April 1782 – Bill to enlarge the term of the spinning stirrup patent, granted to Anne Wharam (includes Breviate) [HL/PO/JO/10/2/57]
Notes
There was a similar Bill in the next session: PRVB40

Arkwright's Cotton Machine Petition 1783

PRVB39	1783
Arkwright's Cotton Machine Petition 1783 (23 Geo 3) [NFL]	
Petition for a Bill to extend the Term granted by the First Patent in the Year 1769, so far as to make the same expire with the Term granted by the Patent in the Year 1775, as some Recompence or Satisfaction for what, he humbly conceives, he may call his public Services and Suffering &c.	

Purpose
No further details

Relevant patents	
3 Jul 1769 (No 931)	Piece of machinery for the making of weft or yarn from cotton, flax, and wool, much superior in quality to any heretofore manufactured or made [Richard Arkwright]
16 Dec 1775 (No 1111)	Machines for preparing silk, cotton, flax, and wool for spinning [Richard Arkwright]

Journal			
House of Commons			**House of Lords**
5 Feb 1783	39 CJ 147	**Pet/Ref** C'tee	*Never considered by the House of Lords*
4 Mar 1783	39 CJ 269	**Pet Ag**	
21 Mar 1783	39 CJ 313	**Pet Ag**	

Petitions		
4 Mar 1783	39 CJ 269	Mayor &c. Wigan [Bill would prejudice country]
21 Mar 1783	39 CJ 313	Cotton and Calico [Bill give stability to a dangerous monopoly]

Parliamentary debates
None
Parliamentary papers and cases
None
Newspaper coverage of debates
None
Archives
None
Notes
There was a petition in an earlier session: PRVB37

Wharam's Patent Stirrup Petition 1783

PRVB40	1783
Wharam's Patent Stirrup Petition 1783 (23 Geo 3) [FL: 124.027]	
Petition for a Bill for enlarging the Term granted to [Anne Wharam] by the said Letters Patent	

(continued)

(continued)

Purpose		
No information, but likely to be the same as the earlier Bill in the previous session		

Relevant patent		
23 May 1769 (No 926)	Preventing the dangers arising to equestrians from their hanging by the foot in the stirrup, in case of falling or being thrown from their horses [Anne Wharam]	

Journal		
House of Commons		**House of Lords**
5 Feb1783	39 CJ 151	**Pet**/Ref C'tee	*Never considered by the House of Lords*

Parliamentary debates
None

Parliamentary papers and cases
None

Newspaper coverage of debates
None

Archives
None

Notes
There was a similar Bill in the previous session: PRVB38

Legh Master's Petition 1788

PRVB41	1788
Legh Master's Petition 1788 (28 Geo 3) [NFL]	
Petition for a Bill to vest in and secure to the petitioner and his assigns, for some reasonable term of years, the sole right of erecting and vending machinery which shall be erected or used on board ships or vessels which shall be navigated or conducted upon the principle and method discovered by him	

Purpose		
No further details		

Relevant patent		
None		

Journal		
House of Commons		**House of Lords**
8 Feb 1788	43 CJ 199	**Pet**	*Never considered by the House of Lords*

Parliamentary debates
None

Parliamentary papers and cases
None

Newspaper coverage of debates
None

Archives
None

Anthony Bourboulon de Boneuil's Petition 1788

PRVB42	1788
Anthony Bourboulon de Boneuil's Petition 1788 (28 Geo 3) [NFL]	
Petition for a Bill to be secured in the full and exclusive possession of their Invention of a method of bleaching cloths made of flax, hemp and cotton, for a longer term of years than are granted by Royal Letters Patent	

Purpose			
No further details			

Relevant patent			
None			

Journal			
House of Commons			**House of Lords**
8 Feb 1788	43 CJ 202	**Pet**	*Never considered by the House of Lords*
19 May 1788	43 CJ 480	Motion ref C'tee	
26 May 1788	43 CJ 507	Adj for 6m	

Parliamentary debates
None

Parliamentary papers and cases
None

Newspaper coverage of debates
None

Archives
None

James Turner Dye Invention Bill 1791

PRVB43	1791

James Turner Dye Invention Bill 1791 (31 Geo 3) [FL: 133.035]

Bill for vesting in James Turner, his Executors, Administrators, and Assigns, the sole Use and Property of certain Yellow Colour of his Invention, throughout that Part of Great Britain, called England, the Dominion of Wales, and Town of Berwick upon Tweed, for a Time to be limited

Table of contents (from Ingrossment)

[Cl 1 Patent extended to last for 18 years from 24 Jun 1791 and James Turners &c may use invention during said term; no other to work the invention without the consent of James Turner &c]
[Cl 2 Dye not to be sold by James Turner for more than 5Guineas per cwt]
[Cl 3 Nothing to prevent the working of any invention previously worked]
[Cl 4 Any challenge to validity of the patent can be raised against the Act]
[Cl 5 Not to be assigned to more than five persons]
[Cl 6 Public Act]

Relevant patent

26 Feb 1781 (No 1281)	Producing a yellow colour for painting in oil or water; making white lead separating mineral-alkai from common salt, all in one single process [James Turner]

Journal

House of Commons			**House of Lords**		
Pres and Rep: Sir James Murray					
25 Feb 1791	46 CJ 224	**Pet**	12 May 1791	39 LJ 183	Brought HC/1R
10 Mar 1791	46 CJ 295	**Pet Rep**	13 May 1791	39 LJ 188	Pet Ag/Counsel Ord
21 Mar 1791	46 CJ 317	1R	23 May 1791	39 LJ 203	2R day app
25 Mar 1791	46 CJ 348	2R/C'tted	31 May 1791	39 LJ 226	2R adj
4 Apr 1791	46 CJ 377	All voices	3 Jun 1791	39 LJ 237	2R adj
7 Apr 1791	46 CJ 385	**Pet Ag**	7 Jun 1791	39 LJ 249	2R adj 3 wks
8 Apr 1791	46 CJ 395	**Pet Rep /**Counsel Ord			
18 Apr 1791	46 CJ 431	**Pet Ag**			
3 May 1791	46 CJ 451	**Pet Ag**			
4 May 1791	46 CJ 456	**Pet Ag**			
5 May 1791	46 CJ 460 – V	**Counsel heard**			
9 May 1791	46 CJ 468	Rep with Amds/Ing			
10 May 1791	46 CJ 478	**3R with Amds**			

(continued)

(continued)

Petitions		
7 Apr 1791	46 CJ 385	Colourmen, Druggists and Painters from London and Westminster
18 Apr 1791	46 CJ 431	Colourmen, Druggists and Painters from London, Westminster and Southwark
3 May 1791	46 CJ 451	Colourmen, Druggists and Painters from Kent and Sussex
4 May 1791	46 CJ 456	Colourmen, Druggists and Painters from Birmingham and elsewhere

Parliamentary debates	
1R: The Senator, 21 Mar 1791, Vol 2, p 154	
2R: The Senator, 25 Mar 1791, Vol 2, p 207	
Pet Ag: The Senator, 7 Apr 1791, Vol 2, p 546	
Pet Ag: The Senator, 18 Apr 1791, Vol 3, p 19	
Pet Ag: The Senator, 3 Mar 1791, Vol 3, p 26	
Counsel heard: The Senator, 5 May 1791, Vol 3, p 28	
Rep: The Senator, 9 May 1791, Vol 3, p 119	
3R: The Senator, 10 May 1791, Vol 3, p 126	

Parliamentary papers and cases
None

Newspaper coverage of debates

House of Commons

Rep: General Evening Post, 10–12 Mar 1791

2R: Diary or Woodfall's Register, 26 Mar 1791; Star, 26 Mar 1791

Pet Ag: *Diary or Woodfall's Register, 19 Apr 1791*; The Times, 19 Apr 1791; Diary or Woodfall's Register, 19 Apr 1791; Morning Post and Daily Advertiser, 19 Apr 1791

Counsel: **Evening Mail, 4–6 May 1791**; **Whitehall Evening Post, 5–7 May 1791**; **Morning Post and Daily Advertiser, 6 May 1791**; **Star, 6 May 1791**; *General Evening Post, 5–7 May 1791*; *London Chronicle, 5–7 May 1791*; *The Times, 6 May 1791*; Lloyd's Evening Post, 4–6 May 1791

Rep: London Chronicle, 7–10 May 1791; St. James's Chronicle or the British Evening Post, 7–10 May 1791; Whitehall Evening Post, 7–10 May 1791; Evening Mail, 9–11 May 1791; The Times, 10 May 1791; Diary or Woodfall's Register, 10 May 1791; Morning Post and Daily Advertiser, 10 May 1791

3R: General Evening Post, 10–12 May 1791; Public Advertiser, 11 May 1791

House of Lords

Brought HC: Star, 13 May 1791

2R adj: *The Times, 4 Jun 1791*; St. James's Chronicle or the British Evening Post, 2–4 Jun 1791; Evening Mail, 3–6 Jun 1791; Star, 4 Jun 1791

2R adj: London Chronicle, 7–9 Jun 1791; St. James's Chronicle or the British Evening Post, 7–9 Jun 1791; The Times, 8 Jun 1791; Public Advertiser, 8 Jun 1791

Archives

Ing: 12 May 1791 – Act for vesting in James Turner, his executors, etc, a certain yellow colour, his invention [HL/PO/JO/10/2/65A]

Pet Ag: 13 May 1791 – Turner's Patent Bill, petition against of Colourman (in Large Parchments). Druggists, painters etc. [HL/PO/JO/10/7/893 and HL/PO/JO/10/3/283/3]

Notes

He successfully obtained an Act in a later session: PRVA26

Hornblower's Patent Bill 1792

PRVB44	1792
Hornblower's Patent Bill 1792 (32 Geo 3) [FL: 134.007]	
Bill for vesting in Jonathan Hornblower, his Executors, Administrators, and Assigns, the Sole Use and Property of certain Machines or Engines for raising Water and other Liquids, commonly called Fire Engines, of his Invention, described therein, for a limited time	

Table of contents
[Cl 1] Sole Privilege &c of making these Engines, vested in Jonathan Hornblower for Years
[Cl 2] Not to hinder any Person from making or using any Engine not the Invention of Jonathan Hornblower
[Cl 3] Objections at Law, same as if this Act not passed
[Cl 4] Privileges by this Act given, not to be transferred to more than [space] Persons
[Cl 5] Public Act

Relevant patent	
13 Jul 1781 (No 1298)	Machine and engine for raising water and other liquids by means of fire and steam, and for other purposes [Jonathan Hornblower]

Journal

House of Commons			House of Lords
Rep and Pres: Sir William Lemon			
24 Feb 1792	47 CJ 416	**Pet**/Ref C'tee	*Never considered by the House of Lords*
5 Mar 1792	47 CJ 478	**Pet Rep**/Leave	
8 Mar 1792	47 CJ 514	1R	
13 Mar 1792	47 CJ 546	**Pet Ag**	
21 Mar 1792	47 CJ 580	2R adj	
30 Mar 1792	47 CJ 630	2R adj	
4 Apr 1792	47 CJ 689 – V	2R adj	
20 Apr 1792	47 CJ 717	2R adj	
24 Apr 1792	47 CJ 726	2R adj	
1 May 1792	47 CJ 756	**2R (Counsel Hrd/adj)**	
3 May 1792	47 CJ 762	2R Ord Disc	

Petition		
13 Mar 1792	47 CJ 546	James Watt [invention not better than his engine and not new]

Parliamentary debates
None

Parliamentary papers and cases
James Watt and the Steam Revolution: A Documentary History (Ed Eric Robinson and A.E Musson) (Adam & Dart 1969)
Mr Hornblower's Case Relative to a Petition to Parliament for the Extension of the Term of his Patent, p 158–160
Short Statement, on the Part of Messrs. Boulton and Watt, in Opposition to Mr Jonathan Hornblower's Application to Parliament for an Act to prolong the Term of his Patent, p 160–161

Newspaper coverage of debates
House of Commons
1R: Diary or Woodfall's Register, 9 Mar 1792
2R adj: Diary or Woodfall's Register, 30 Mar 1792; Star, 30 Mar 1792; Morning Herald, 31 Mar 1792; Diary or Woodfall's Register, 31 Mar 1792
2R adj: **Morning Chronicle, 5 Apr 1792**; **Public Advertiser, 5 Apr 1792**; **Star, 5 Apr 1792**; **Diary or Woodfalls' Register, 7 Apr 1792**
2R adj: *Diary or Woodfall's Register, 21 Apr 1792*; The Times, 21 Apr 1792; Star, 21 Apr 1792
2R adj: Lloyd's Evening Post, 23–25 April 1792; St. James's Chronicle or the British Evening Post, 24–26 April 1792; The Times, 25 Apr 1792; Diary or Woodfall's Register, 25 April 1792; Morning Herald, 25 April 1792
2R: *The Times, 2 May 1792*; St. James's Chronicle or the British Evening Post, 1–3 May 1792; London Chronicle, 1–3 May 1792; Morning Herald, 2 May 1792; Star, 2 May 1792
Gone off to other session: General Evening Post, 3–5 May 1792; Diary or Woodfall's Register, 4 May 1792

Archives
Pet: Hornblower's Petition 24 Feb 1792 [Birmingham Library: MS 3147/2/35/27]
Hornblower's Case: Mr. Hornblower's Case Relative to a Petition to Parliament for the Extension of the Term of his Patent [Birmingham Library: MS 3147/2/36/3]
Bill: A Bill for Vesting in Jonathan Hornblower, his Executors, Administrators and Assigns, the sole Use and Property of certain Machines or Engines for raising Water and other Liquids, commonly called Steam Engines, of his Invention, described therein, for a Limited Time [Birmingham Library: MS 3147/2/36/1]
Second Reading Minutes: 1 May 1792 Minutes on Second reading of Mr. Hornblower's Patent Bill [Birmingham Library: MS 3147/2/35/23]
Hornblower's Case: 2 Apr 1792 Copy of Hornblower's printed paper given at the House of Commons [Birmingham Library: MS 3147/2/35/28]
Boulton & Watt's Case Against: Apr 1792 Arguments in favour of Boulton & Watt. Apr. 1792 [Birmingham Library: MS 3147/2/35/29]; "Heads of arguments favour of B & W." [Birmingham Archives: MS 3147/2/35/31]; Observations on the Part of Messrs. Boulton and Watt concerning Mr. Hornblower's Steam-Engine Bill 17 Apr. 1792 [Birmingham Library: MS 3147/2/36/2]; "Short Statement, on the Part of Messrs. Boulton and Watt, in Opposition to Mr. Jonathan Hornblower's Application to Parliament for an Act to prolong the Term of his Patent." [Birmingham Library: MS 3147/2/36/4]

Cuthbert Gordon's Petition 1793

PRVB45	1793		
Cuthbert Gordon Petition (33 Geo 3) [FL: 135.061]			
Petition for a Bill for ascertaining and establishing [Cuthbert Gordon's Discoveries] on a proper advantageous Footing for the Benefit of the Community and of the Petitioner			
Purpose			
No further details			
Relevant patent			
12 Aug 1758 (No 727)	Dye called cudbear [Cuthbert Gordon]		
Journal			
House of Commons		**House of Lords**	
25 Feb 1793	48 CJ 266	**Pet/Ref C'tee**	*Never considered by the House of Lords*
Parliamentary debates			
None			
Parliamentary papers and cases			
None			
Newspaper coverage of debates			
None			
Archives			
None			
Notes			
He was also given two rewards: PRZA19 and PRZA21			

Kendrew and Porthouse's Bill 1794

PRVB46	1794
Kendrew and Porthouse's Bill 1794 (34 Geo 3) [FL: 136.018]	

Bill for vesting in John Kendrew and Thomas Porthouse, their Executors, Administrators, and Assigns, the sole Use and Property of a certain Mill or Machine, for Spinning Yarn from Flax and Hemp, of their Invention, for a limited Time

Table of contents (from Ingrossment)

[Cl 1 Invention vests in John Kendrew and Thomas Porthouse for 17 years from 19 Jun 1794; may enjoy sole benefit of invention; no other person to use invention without licence]
[Cl 2 Nothing in Act extends to Mills or Machines not invented by Kendrew or Porthouse which have been publicly used by another person before the date of the recited Letters Patent]
[Cl 3 Objections relating to the novelty of the patent may be made against the Act]
[Cl 4 May not be assigned to more than five persons]
[Cl 5 Public Act]

Relevant patent

19 Jun 1787 (No 1613)	Machine for spinning yarn from hemp, tow, flax or wood [John Kendrew and Thomas Porthouse]

Journal

House of Commons			House of Lords		
Rep and Pres: Rowland Burdon					
19 Feb 1794	49 CJ 199	**Pet**/Ref C'tte	9 Apr 1794	40 LJ 106	1R
21 Mar 1794	49 CJ 362	**Pet Rep**	28 Apr 1794	40 LJ 137	2R adj
24 Mar 1794	49 CJ 363	1R	5 May 1794	40 LJ 154	2R adj for 2m
28 Mar 1794	49 CJ 388	2R/C'tted	5 May 1794	40 LJ 156	Pet Ag
4 Apr 1794	49 CJ 419	Rep with Amds			
8 Apr 1794	49 CJ 430	3R			

Petition		
5 May 1794	40 LJ 156	Inhabitants of Knaresborough

Parliamentary debates	
3R: Senator, 8 Apr 1794, Vol 9, p 902 (Kendren's Patent)	

Parliamentary papers and cases
None

Newspaper coverage of debates

House of Commons

Pet: Whitehall Evening Post, 18–20 Feb 1794; Public Advertiser or Political Literary Diary, 20 Feb 1794

Pet Rep: Oracle and Public Advertiser, 22 Mar 1794

1R: Whitehall Evening Post, 22–25 Mar 1794; Oracle and Public Advertiser, 25 Mar 1794

2R: Lloyd's Evening Post, 28–31 Mar 1794; Sun, 29 Mar 1794; World, 29 Mar 1794

Rep: Whitehall Evening Post, 3–5 Apr 1794; World, 5 Apr 1794

3R: Lloyd's Evening Post, 7–9 Apr 1794; Oracle and Public Advertiser, 9 Apr 1794

Archives

Ing: Kendrew and Porthouse's Patent Bill: 9 April 1794 [HL/PO/JO/10/2/67]

Petition against, of spinners of yarn etc, in the counties of York, Lancaster and Westmoreland: 28 Apr 1794 [HL/PO/JO/10/3/286/22A];

Petition against, of manufacturers of sail cloth in the County of Lancaster: 18 April 1794 [HL/PO/JO/10/3/286/22B]

Petition against, of Mayor, Aldermen etc, of Borough of Leeds: 28 April 1794 [HL/PO/JO/10/3/286/22C]

Petition against, of mill owners of town of Knaresborough 5 May 1794[HL/PO/JO/10/3/286/22D]

[All petitions also held under HL/PO/JO/10/7/973]

Abraham Bosquet's Invention Petition 1794

PRVB47	1794

Abraham Bosquet's Invention Petition 1794 (34 Geo 3) [FL: 136.057]
Petition for right to use a vessel of 200 or 300 Tones Burdened, Duty Free, for Fourteen Years, which vessel shall have a perpetual Breach or Leak in her Bottom, which no Pump can relieve, and though even destitute of Pump, yet the Cargo shall not be injured [such grant a sufficient compensation, and would thereby be enabled to evince to the Maritime World, at his own Risque, the Practicability and Importance of this extensive Object, without any Expence to, or further Claim]

Purpose
No further details

Relevant patent

8 Jun 1798 (No 2242)	Method by the application of which ships are rendered durable sound, and free from bilge water [Abraham Bosquet] (this patent was subsequent to the petition, but it appears to be a related invention)

Journal

House of Commons		House of Lords
4 Mar 1794	49 CJ 278	**Pet**	*Never considered by the House of Lords*
30 Mar 1794	49 CJ 636	Pet ref C'tte	

Parliamentary debates
None

Parliamentary papers and cases
None

Newspaper coverage of debates
None

Archives
None

Edmund Cartwright Petition 1794 [Woolcombers Bill]

PRVB48	1794

Edmund Cartwright Petition 1794 (4 Geo 3) [FL: 136.072]

Petition to be heard regarding other petitions regarding a Petition and then Bill for the Purposes of protecting Woolcombers from being injured in their Manufacture by the Use of Certain Machines latterly introduced for the combing of Wool

Table of contents
[Cl 1] From [date to be set] it shall be unlawful for any person to use a machine to comb wool

Relevant patent
No particular patent particularised

Journal

House of Commons			House of Lords
Pres: (John) Bastard			*Never considered by the House of Lords*
24 Jan 1794	49 CJ 21	Woolcombers Pet	
27 Jan 1794	49 CJ 22	Woolcombers Pet	
4 Feb 1794	49 CJ 104	Woolcombers Pet	
6 Feb 1794	49 CJ 135	Woolcombers Pet	
7 Feb 1794	49 CJ 144	Woolcombers Pet	
10 Feb 1794	49 CJ 147	Woolcombers Pet	
11 Feb 1794	49 CJ 152	Woolcombers Pet	
12 Feb 1794	49 CJ 158	Woolcombers Pet	
17 Feb 1794	49 CJ 185	Woolcombers Pet	
19 Feb 1794	49 CJ 201	Woolcombers Pet	
27 Feb 1794	49 CJ 249	Woolcombers Pet	
4 Mar 1794	49 CJ 280	Woolcombers Pet	
4 Mar 1794	49 CJ 289	Various petitions ref C'tee	
7 Mar 1794	49 CJ 307	Woolcombers Pet	
12 Mar 1794	49 CJ 319	Woolcombers Pet	
13 Mar 1794	49 CJ 322	Rep of C'tee	
14 Mar 1794	49 CJ 331	Woolcombers Pet	
18 Mar 1794	49 CJ 347	**Pet of Cartwright**	
19 Mar 1794	49 CJ 352	Woolcombers Pet	
31 Mar 1794	49 CJ 395	**Pet of Toplis**	
4 Apr 1794	49 CJ 422	Rep and Pets Cons	
7 Apr 1794	49 CJ 430	Adj	
8 Apr 1794	49 CJ 439	Bill Ord	
10 Apr 1794	49 CJ 450	1R	
14 Apr 1794	49 CJ 463	2R adj	
28 Apr 1794	49 CJ 491	Woolcombers Pet	
29 Apr 1794	49 CJ 497	2R adj	
2 May 1794	49 CJ 545	2R/C'tted CWH/Pet	
5 May 1794	49 CJ 552	Woolcombers Pet	
6 May 1794	49 CJ 555	CWH adj	
8 May 1794	49 CJ 564	**2d Pet of Toplis**	
9 May 1794	49 CJ 571 – V	CWH adj 6m	

Parliamentary debates	
Pet: Senator, 27 Jan 1794, Vol 8, p 94; Woodfall, 27 Jan 1794, Vol 1, p 250	
Pets: Woodfall, 4 Mar 1794, Vol 2, p 172	
Bill Ord: Senator, 8 Apr 1794, Vol 9, p 902	
1R: Woodfall, 10 Apr 1794, Vol 3, p 163	
Put off: Senator, 8 May 1794, Vol 10, p 1162–1163; Woodfall, 8 May 1794, Vol 3, p 469	

Parliamentary papers and cases
Bill for the Purpose of protecting Woolcombers from being injured in their Manufacture, by the Use of certain Machines, latterly introduced, for the combing of Wool (1794), Vol 92
Catalogue of Papers printed by Order of the House of Commons, from the year 1731 to 180. In the Custody of the Clerk of the Journals (1807) (Reprint: HMSO 1954): Woolcomber's Petition, 1794, Vol 14, No 117; Woolcomber for protecting them from injury in their Manufactures by the use of certain Machines, 1794, Vol 24, No 719

Newspaper coverage of debates
House of Commons
Pet (27 Jan): Sun, 28 Jan 1794
Pet (4 Feb): General Evening Post, 4–6 Feb 1794
Pet (10 Feb): World, 11 Feb 1794
Pet (11 Feb): Lloyd's Evening Post, 10–12 Feb 1794
Pet (12 Feb): World, 13 Feb 1794
Pet (13 Feb): Public Advertiser or Political Literary Diary, 20 Feb 1794
Pet (18 Feb): The Times, 19 Feb 1794
Com App: The Times, 5 Mar 1794
Pet Com: The Times, 11 Apr 1794
2R/Pet Ag: London Chronicle, 1–3 May 1794; Morning Chronicle, 3 May 1794
2R adj: Morning Chronicle, 30 Apr 1794
CWH adj: *London Chronicle, 8–10 May 1794*

Archives
None

Sabatier's Petition 1795

PRVB49	1795

Sabatier's Petition 1795 (35 Geo 3) [FL: 137.019]
Petition for a Bill for subjecting all Cotton imported by Individuals from the East Indies, packed and retained by Means of the Machinery and Contrivances invented and discovered by William Sabatier, to the per Centage which the [East India] Company have engaged to pay him on Cotton imported by them

Purpose
No further details

Relevant patent	
4 Jul 1796 (No 2215)	Retaining cotton tobacco, hemp, flax, hops, hay and other articles in nearly the same compass into which they can be compressed by machinery, without being liable to any material expansion after they are removed from such machinery [William Sabatier] (this was subsequent to the petition, but appears related)

Journal			
House of Commons			**House of Lords**
3 Feb 1795	50 CJ 118	**Pet**/Ref C'tte	*Never considered by the House of Lords*

Parliamentary debates
None

Parliamentary papers and cases
None

Newspaper coverage of debates
None

Archives
None

Notes
An Act was subsequently enacted: PRVA30

Noble's Patent Water Engine Bill 1797

PRVB50	1797

Noble's Patent Water Engine Bill 1797 (37 Geo 3) [FL: 139.070]
Bill for vesting in Mark Noble, his Executors, Administrators, and Assigns, the sole Use and Property of a certain Pump or Engine, of his Invention, throughout that Part of Great Britain called England, for a further Time to be limited

(continued)

Purpose		
Presumed term extension		

Relevant patent		
29 Jan 1784 (No 1453)	Pump for raising water [Mark Noble]	

Journal		
House of Commons		**House of Lords**
Rep and Pres: Charles Dundas		
24 Feb 1797	52 CJ 331	**Pet**/Ref C'tte
6 May 1797	52 CJ 544	**Pet Rep**
10 May 1797	52 CJ 561	1R

(House of Lords column, spanning the three journal rows): *Never considered by the House of Lords*

Parliamentary debates		
None		

Parliamentary papers and cases		
None		

Newspaper coverage of debates		
None		

Archives		
None		

Bramah's Bill 1798

PRVB51	1798
(Joseph) Bramah's Bill 1798 (38 Geo 3) [FL: 140.033]	
Bill for vesting in him the sole use and property of his invention of a new kind of lock for doors, drawers, &c	

Purpose		
Term extension		

Relevant patent		
23 Apr 1784 (No 1430)	Lock for doors, cabinets, and other things on which locks are used (without wheels or ward) [Joseph Bramah]	

Journal		
House of Commons		**House of Lords**
Rep and Pres: Gabriel Tucker Steward		
22 Feb 1798	53 CJ 297	**Pet**
15 Mar 1798	53 CJ 371	**Pet Rep**
21 Mar 1798	53 CJ 392	Bill Ord
23 Mar 1798	53 CJ 400	1R
27 Mar 1798	53 CJ 425 – V	2R/C'tted
2 Apr 1798	53 CJ 438	**Pet Ag**

(House of Lords column, spanning the journal rows): *Never considered by the House of Lords*

Petitions		
2 Apr 1798	53 CJ 438	Manufactures and Vendors of Locks [interests will be affected]

Parliamentary debates		
2R: **Woodfall, 27 Mar 1798, Vol 2, p 170**		

Parliamentary papers and cases		
None		

Newspaper coverage of debates
House of Commons
2R: **Star, 28 Mar 1798**; *Lloyd's Evening Post, 26–28 Mar 1798*; *Express and Evening Chronicle, 27–29 Mar 1798*; *London Chronicle, 27–29 Mar 1798*; *St. James's Chronicle or the British Evening Post, 27–29 Mar 1798*; *The Times, 28 Mar 1798*; *The Sun, 28 Mar 1798*; *Johnson's British Gazette and Sunday Monitor, 1 April 1798*
Pet Ag: *Whitehall Evening Post, 31 Mar–3 Apr 1798*; *Star, 3 Apr 1798*; *Sun, 3 Apr 1798*

Archives		
None		

Tanning Leather Bill 1798

PRVB52	1798
	Tanning Leather Bill 1798 (38 Geo 3) [FL: 140.051]

Bill to amend an Act, made in the Second Year of the Reign of King James the First, intituled, "An Act concerning Tanners, Curriers, Shoemakers, and other Artificers occupying the Cutting of Leather" [Amendment for Sealy]

Table of contents (relevant clauses only) (1798 HL Papers)

[Cl 3 Nothing in the recited Act should prevent Edward Sealy from enjoying the benefit and advantage under his Letters Patent (assigned from George Hawkes)]
[This clause was omitted again by the House of Lords before it returned to the Commons]

Relevant patent

2 Jun 1795 (No 2054)	Manufacture for tanning [George Hawkes]

Journal

House of Commons			House of Lords		
Pet Rep Sealy: William Dickinson Pres: (Dudley) Ryder Bill Rep: Henry Hobart			Rep: Lord Walsingham (Ld Ch)		
19 Mar 1798	53 CJ 385	Bill Ord	31 May 1798	41 LJ 614	Brought HC/1R
20 Mar 1798	53 CJ 391	1R	1 Jun 1798	41 LJ 619	Bill Pr
21 Mar 1798	53 CJ 397	2R adj	5 Jun 1798	41 LJ 622	2R/C'tted CWH
28 Mar 1798	53 CJ 431	2R adj	8 Jun 1798	41 LJ 630	CWH adj
2 Apr 1798	53 CJ 441	2R/C'tted	11 Jun 1798	41 LJ 633	CWH (Seely clause omitted)
18 Apr 1798	53 CJ 466	C'tee adj	12 Jun 1798	41 LJ 634	Rep adj
23 Apr 1798	53 CJ 480	**Pet Sealy**	13 Jun 1798	41 LJ 637	**Rep with Amds**
25 Apr 1798	53 CJ 504	C'tee adj	14 Jun 1798	41 LJ 639	3R
1 May 1798	53 CJ 521	**Rep Sealy Pet**			
2 May 1798	53 CJ 531	CWH adj			
3 May 1798	53 CJ 532	Rep Re-C'tted			
7 May 1798	53 CJ 543	**Rep Sealy Pet Re-C'tted**			
9 May 1798	53 CJ 556	CWH day app			
10 May 1798	53 CJ 561	Sealy Rep ref CWH			
14 May1798	53 CJ 577	CWH adj			
17 May 1798	53 CJ 596	CWH adj			
18 May 1798	53 CJ 601	CWH			
21 May 1798	53 CJ 613	Rep adj			
22 May 1798	53 CJ 615	**Rep/Ing**			
25 May 1798	53 CJ 627	3R			
14 Jun 1798	53 CJ 672	HL pass with Amds			
15 Jun1798	53 CJ 678	HL Amds Cons day app			
19 Jun 1798	53 CJ 685	HL Amds Cons adj			
20 Jun1798	53 CJ 689	HL Amds Cons adj			
21 Jun 1798	53 CJ 693	HL Amds Cons adj 3m			

Parliamentary debates

1R: **Parliamentary Register, 20 Mar 1798, Vol 5, p 345** Rep **Parliamentary Register, 7 May 1798, Vol 6, p 187–193** CWH: **Parliamentary Register, 18 May 1798, Vol 6, p 176**	CWH: **Parliamentary Register, 18 May 1798, Vol 6, p 352–353**

Parliamentary papers and cases

Bill intitled An Act to amend an Act, made in the Second Year of the Reign of King James the First, An Act concerning Tanners, Curriers, Shoemakers, and other Artificers occupying the Cutting of Leather (1798 HL Papers), Vol 1

Catalogue of Papers printed by Order of the House of Commons, from the year 1731 to 1800. In the Custody of the Clerk of the Journals (1807) (Reprint: HMSO 1954): Sealy's Petition, Tanning with Elm Bark, 1797/8, Vol 21, No 145

Report from the Committee on Mr Sealy's Petition respecting his Patent for Tanning of Leather with Elm Bark (1798)

(continued)

(continued)

Newspaper coverage of debates
House of Commons
1R: **The Times, 20 Mar 1798**

Archives
None

Dr Bancroft's Patent Bill 1799

PRVB53	1799

Dr Bancroft's Patent Bill 1799 (39 Geo 3) [FL: 41.011]
Bill for enlarging for the term of seven years, from the fourteenth day of June, One thousand seven hundred and ninety-nine, the Term, and continuing the Powers of an Act, passed in the Twenty-fifth Year of the Reign of His present Majesty, Chapter Thirty-eight, on the Thirteenth Day of June, One thousand seven hundred and eight-five, intituled "An Act vesting in Edward Bancroft, Doctor in Physick, his Executors, Administrators, and Assigns, the sole property of his invention or discovery of the use and application of certain Vegetables for dying, staining, printing, and painting, certain valuable Colours, throughout that Part of His Majesty's Kingdom of Great Britain called England, the Dominion of Wales and Town of Berwick-upon-Tweed, for a limited time" and for extending the same to and throughout that Part of Great Britain called Scotland, for the Term of Seven Years, from the Fourth Day of June One thousand seven hundred and ninety-nine

Table of contents (based on Ingrossment)
[Cl 1 Bancroft's Patent Act 1785 extended for a further term of 14 years after its original expiry] [Cl 2 Bancroft not permitted to charge more than 33 s for each hundred pounds of Quercitron bark; not permitted to charge more than 45 s for ground mangrove bark] [Cl 3 Public Act] [Cl 4 Bancroft's Patent Act 1785 to stay in force for further term of 14 years]

Relevant patents	
23 Oct 1775 (No 1103)	Use of certain vegetables for dyeing, staining, printing, painting or otherwise colouring, wool, hair, fur, silk, hemp, cotton, linen, skins, leather, paper, and wool [Edward Bancroft]

Journal					
House of Commons			**House of Lords**		
Pres and Rep: Sir William Young					
10 Dec 1798	54 CJ 67	**Pet**/Ref C'tee	18 Feb 1799	42 LJ 59	Brought HC
14 Dec 1798	54 CJ 76	**Pet Rep**	20 Feb 1799	42 LJ 63	1R
27 Dec 1798	54 CJ 98	Must publish notices	22 Feb 1799	42 LJ 64	Pet Ag
31 Dec 1798	54 CJ 104	1R	19 Mar 1799	42 LJ 97	Pet Ag
7 Jan 1799	54 CJ 135	2R/C'tted	9 Apr 1799	42 LJ 113	Pet Ag
22 Jan 1799	54 CJ 142	Rep with Amds	10 May 1799	42 LJ 201	Adj
23 Jan 1799	54 CJ 146	3R	24 May 1799	42 LJ 220	2R adj 6m

Petitions		
22 Feb 1799	42 LJ 64	Manufacturers and Calico Printers and those concerned with dying from Manchester
19 Mar 1799	42 LJ 97	Manufacturers and Calico Printers and those concerned with dying from Glasgow
9 Apr 1799	42 LJ 113	Dyers and Calico Printers of Essex, Surrey and Kent

Parliamentary debates	
	Pet: Woodfall, 22 Feb 1799, Vol 2, p273
	Pet: Woodfall, 9 Apr 1799, Vol 2, p 429
	2R: Woodfall, 24 May 1799, Vol 3, p 77

Representation
None – posted notice personally

Parliamentary papers and cases
Edward Bancroft, *Facts and Observations, Briefly Stated in Support of an Intended Application to Parliament* (London 1798)

Gazette notices	

London Gazette: 15 Dec 1798 (Iss: 15,089, p 1206); 18 Dec 1798 (Iss: 15,090, p 1219); 22 Dec 1798 (Iss: 15,092, p 1241)

Newspaper coverage of debates

House of Lords

2R: **St. James's Chronicle, 23–25 May 1799**; **Whitehall Evening Post, 23–25 May 1799**; **Sun, 24–27 May 1799**; **True Briton, 25 May 1799**; **Morning Herald, 25 May 1799**; **Morning Post and Gazetteer, 25 May 1799**; **Oracle and Daily Advertiser, 25 May 1799**; **Kentish Weekly Post or Canterbury Journal, 28 May 1799**; **Kentish Gazette, 28 May 1799**; **Staffordshire Advertiser, 1 June 1799**; *Lloyd's Evening Post, 24–27 May 1799*; *London Packet or New Lloyd's Evening Post, 24–27 May 1799*; *The Times, 25 May 1799*; *Morning Chronicle, 25 May 1799*; *Observer, 26 May 1799*; *Salisbury and Winchester Journal, 27 May 1799*

Pet Ag: Star, 23 Feb 1799; Courier and Evening Gazette, 23 Feb 1799

Archives

Ing: 20 Feb 1799 – Dr Bancroft's Patent Bill [HL/PO/JO/10/2/70] and [HL/PO/JO/10/3/293/33]

Bill: 19 Mar 1799 Dr Bancroft's Patent Bill [HL/PO/JO/10/3/293/46]

Petition against, of manufacturers of London: 20 Feb 1799 [HL/PO/JO/10/3/293/33 and HL/PO/JO/10/7/1083]

Petition against, of manufacturers in Manchester: 22 Feb 1799: [HL/PO/JO/10/3/293/34 and HL/PO/JO/10/7/1083]

Petition against, of manufacturers etc. of Glasgow: 19 Mar 1799: [HL/PO/JO/10/3/293/46 and HL/PO/JO/10/7/1085]

Petition in support of, of Dyers and Calico Printers of Middlesex, Essex, Surrey and Kent: 9 Apr 1799: [HL/PO/JO/10/3/293/53 and HL/PO/JO/10/7/1087]

Notes

The Bill was to extend an earlier private act: PRVA24

Related case

Bancroft v Warden (1786) 11 HPC App

Koops Papermaking Patent Bill 1800

PRVB54	1800
Koops Papermaking Patent Bill 1800 (39 & 40 Geo 3)	

Bill to incorporate certain Persons and their Successors, with proper Powers for the Purpose of establishing a Manufactory for extracting Ink from printed and written paper, and making other Paper therefrom, for Writing, Printing and Other Purposes

Purpose (from report)

To allow transfer of patent to 60 people and also to keep specification secret

Relevant patent

17 Feb 1801 (No 2481)	Manufacturing paper from straw, hay, thistles, waste and refuse of hemp and flax, and different kinds of wood and bark [Matthias Koops]

Journal

House of Commons			House of Lords
Rep and Pres: William Adams			*Never considered by House of Lords*
11 Jun 1800	55 CJ 635	**First Pet/Ref C'tee**	
11 Jun 1800	55 CJ 636	**Second Pet/Ref C'tee**	
13 Jun 1800	55 CJ 647	**Pet Rep**	
16 Jun 1800	55 CJ 652	1R	

Representation

No information

Parliamentary debates

Rep: Woodfall, 13 Jun 1800, Vol 3, p. 199 1R: **Parliamentary Register, 16 Jun 1800, Vol 12 p 118**; Woodfall, 16 Jun 1800, Vol 3, p 202	

(continued)

(continued)

Parliamentary papers and cases
Report on Mr. Koops' Petition, Respecting his Invention for making Paper from various Refuse materials (1801 HL Papers), Vol 1
Report on Mr Koops' Petition, respect his invention for making paper from various refuse materials (1801) (HC Papers 55), Vol 3, p 127
Gazette notices
Not required by SO
Newspaper coverage of debates
Pet: General Evening Post, 10–12 Jun 1800; London Chronicle or Universal Evening Post, 10–12 Jun 1800; Whitehall Evening Post, 10–12 Jun 1800; Evening Mail, 11–13 Jun 1800; London Packet or New Lloyd's Evening Post, 11–13 Jun 1800; Lloyd's Evening Post, 11–13 Jun 1800; The Times, 12 Jun 1800; Morning Herald, 12 Jun 1800; Morning Post and Gazetteer, 12 Jun 1800; Sun, 12 Jun 1800; True Briton, 12 Jun 1800   Pet Rep: General Evening Post, 12–14 Jun 1800; Morning Chronicle, 14 Jun 1800; Morning Post and Gazetteer, 14 Jun 1800; Sun, 14 June 1800; Albion and Evening Advertiser, 14 June 1800
Archives
None

John Garnett's Notice 1801

PRVB55	1801
John Garnett's Notice 1801 (42 Geo 3)	
Purpose	
Bill to vest in John Garnett for a Term to be limited by such Act, the sole Right, Benefit, and Advantage of making, using, and vending certain Machinery for reducing Friction for which John Garnett received letters patent	
6 Jan 1787 (No 1580)	Method of reducing the friction of an axis or fulcrum; useful for wheels, beams, levers, pendulums blocks, pulleys, and other instruments that have a partial, total, or repeated revolution or oscillation [John Garnett]
Representation	
Solicitor: Thomas Jacques	
Gazette notices	
London Gazette: 1 Sep 1801 (Iss: 15,403, p 1077); 8 Sep 1801 (Iss: 15,405, p 1106); 29 Sep 1801 (Iss: 15,410, p 1183)	

Richard Willcox's Notice 1802

PRVB56	1802
Richard Willcox's Notice 1802 (43 Geo 3)	
Purpose	
Bill for vesting in Richard Willcox for a Term of Years to be limited by such Act, the sole right to use his invention on Steam Engines protected by Letters Patent granted to him	
23 Jan 1802 (No 2574)	Steam-engine or boiler and air-pump [lessening the consumption of fuel] [Richard Wilcox]
Representation	
No information	
Gazette notices	
London Gazette: 28 Aug 1802 (Iss: 15,510, p 920); 31 Aug 1802 (Iss: 15,511, p 932); 4 Sep 1802 (Iss: 15,512, p 946)	

Browell and Jack's Petition 1809

PRVB57	1809	
	Browell and Jack's Petition 1809 (49 Geo 3)	
	Petition for Bill for allowing delivery of the Specification to be Secretly Enrolled instead of being enrolled in the Court of Chancery	
	**Purpose**	
	No further details	
	**Relevant patent**	
11 Jul 1803 (No 3150)	Chemical preparation for preserving woollen and vegetable substances from mildew, rot, or fermentation, and also rendering cloths and other fabrics impervious to rain [James Browell, James Jacks and Thomas Lermitte]	
	**Journal**	
House of Commons		**House of Lords**
31 Jan 1809	64 CJ 15	Pet	*Never considered by House of Lords*
	**Representation**	
	No information	
	**Parliamentary debates**	
	None	
	**Parliamentary papers and cases**	
	None	
	**Gazette notices**	
	Not required by SO	
	**Newspaper coverage of debates**	
	None	
	**Archives**	
	None	

Parker's Cement Notice 1809

PRVB58	1809
Parker's Cement Notice 1809 (49 Geo 3)	
Purpose	
Bill for enlarging the Term granted to James Parker of His Majesty's Letter Patent for an Invention of certain Cement or Terras	
Relevant patent	
28 June 1796 (No 2120)	Cement or tarrass to be used in aquatic and other buildings and stucco-work [James Parker]
Representation	
Solicitor: Smith and Sons	
Gazette notices	
London Gazette: 13 Sep 1808 (Iss: 16,183, p 1265); 17 Sep 1808 (Iss: 16,184, p 1292); 20 Sep 1808 (Iss: 16,185, p 1309); 24 Sep 1808 (Iss: 16,186, p 1324)	

Parker's Cement Petition 1810

PRVB59	1810
Parker's Cement Petition 1810 (50 Geo 3)	
Petition for Prolonging the Term of Letters Patent for Invention of Cement or Terra granted to James Parker	

(continued)

(continued)

Purpose		
No further details		
Relevant patent		
28 June 1796 (No 2120)	Cement or tarrass to be used in aquatic and other buildings and stucco-work [James Parker]	
Journal		
House of Commons		**House of Lords**
7 Feb 1810	65 CJ 48	**Pet**	*Never considered by House of Lords*
Parliamentary debate		
None		
Representation		
None		
Parliamentary papers and cases		
None		
Gazette notices		
London Gazette: 29 Aug 1809 (Iss: 16,293, p 1387); 2 Sep 1809 (Iss: 16,294, p 1421); 15 Sep 1809 (Iss: 16,295, p 1440)		
Newspaper coverage of debates		
None		
Archives		
None		

Robert Barber's Notice 1810

PRVB60	1810
Robert Barber's Notice 1810 (50 Geo 3)	
Purpose	
Bill for prolonging the term of certain Letters Patent granted to Robert Barber, for the invention of manufacturing Double Looped Stocking Frame Work by machinery	
Relevant patent	

25 March 1797 (No 2175)	Gigger stocking frame [Robert Barber]

Representation
John Barber
Gazette notices
London Gazette: 8 Aug 1809 (Iss: 16,284 p 1260); 12 Aug 1809 (Iss: 16,286, p 1285); 15 Aug 1809 (Iss: 16,287, p 1301)
Notes
This notice was followed by another notice and Bill in the following sessions: see PRVB61

Robert Barber's Bill 1811

PRVB61	1811
Robert Barber's Bill 1811 (51 Geo 3)	
Bill for prolonging the term of certain Letters Patent granted to Robert Barber, for the invention of manufacturing Double Looped Stocking Frame Work by machinery	
Purpose	
No further details	
Relevant patent	

25 March 1797 (No 2175)	Gigger stocking frame [Robert Barber]

Journal			
House of Commons			**House of Lords**
Rep and Pres: Davies Giddy			*Never considered by the House of Lords*
23 Jan 1811	66 CJ 41	Pet	
31 Jan 1811	66 CJ 61	Pet Rep	
3 Feb 1811	66 CJ 77	Leave to publish notices	
5 Feb 1811	66 CJ 81	Leave for Bill	
7 Feb 1811	66 CJ 83	1R	
18 Feb 1811	66 CJ 97	Pet Ag	
20 Feb 1811	66 CJ 101	Pets Ag	
22 Feb 1811	66 CJ 109	Pets Ag	
27 Feb 1811	66 CJ 124	2R adj	
7 Mar 1811	66 CJ 153	2R adj	
8 Mar 1811	66 CJ 157 – V	2R rej	
1 Apr 1811	66 CJ 221	Pet Ag	
Petitions			
18 Feb 1811	66 CJ 97	Hosiers of Leicester	
20 Feb 1811	66 CJ 101	(1) Hosiers of Derby; (2) Hosiers of Nottingham	
22 Feb 1811	66 CJ 109	(1) Hosiers of Leicester; (2) Hosiers of Nottingham	
1 Apr 1811	66 CJ 221	Hosiers of Leicester	
Representation			
Solicitor: Barker and Bishop			
Parliamentary debates			
None			
Parliamentary papers and cases			
None			
Gazette notices			
London Gazette: 8 Aug 1810 (Iss: 16,397, p 1246); 21 Aug 1810 (Iss: 16,398, p 1264); 28 Aug 1810 (Iss: 16,400, p 1306); 2 Feb 1811 (Iss: 16,449, p 205); 5 Feb 1811 (Iss: 16,451, p 230); 12 Feb 1811 (Iss: 16,455, p 297)			
Newspaper coverage of debates			
House of Commons Leave: Salisbury and Winchester Journal, 11 Feb 1811; Perthshire Courier, 14 Feb 1811 Adj: *Globe, 2 Mar 1811* 2R: **Globe, 9 Mar 1811**; **Kentish Gazette, 12 Mar 1811**; *Morning Chronicle, 9 Mar 1811*; *Morning Post, 9 Mar 1811*; *Public Ledger and Daily Advertiser, 9 Mar 1811*; *London Courier and Evening Gazette, 9 Mar 1811*; *Leicester Journal, 15 Mar 1811*; *Cheltenham Chronicle, 14 Mar 1811*; *Hereford Journal, 13 Mar 1811*			
Archive			
None			

Patent Tessera Bill 1811

PRVB62	1811	
Patent Tessera Bill 1811 (51 Geo 3)		
Bill for enabling the Proprietors of an Invention, known by the name of John's Patent Tessera, to assign the same to a greater number of persons than is at present limited by the Letters Patent		
Purpose		
No further details		
Relevant patent		
22 Dec 1806 (No 2998)	Compositions; mode of making the same for covering and facing houses and for other purposes [Ambrose Bowden Johns]	
Journal		
House of Commons		**House of Lords**
Pres: No information		

(continued)

(continued)

1 Feb 1811	66 CJ 74	Pet	*Never considered by the House of Lords*
1 Mar 1811	66 CJ 133	Pet Rep/Leave	
4 Mar 1811	66 CJ 140	Pres	
12 Mar 1811	66 CJ 163	1R	
9 Apr 1811	66 CJ 250	2R adj	
10 Apr 1811	66 CJ 253	2R adj	
11 Apr 1811	66 CJ 255	2R adj	
24 Apr 1811	66 CJ 265	2R adj	
25 Apr 1811	66 CJ 271	2R adj	

Representation
No information
Parliamentary debates
None
Parliamentary papers and cases
None
Gazette notices
Not required by SO
Newspaper coverage of debates

House of Commons

2R adj: **The Times, 9 Mar 1811**

2R adj: Globe, 12 Apr 1811; Public Ledger and Daily Advertiser, 12 Apr 1811

Archives
None
Notes
There was a related Act passed in 1810: PRVA34

Frederick Albert Winsor's Petition 1812

PRVB63	1812
Frederick Albert Winsor's Petition 1812 (2 Geo 3)	
Petition for the extension of his patent for gas lights and for issuing shares	

Purpose
No further details

Relevant patent	
3 March 1808 (No 3113)	Oven, stove, or apparatus for carbonizing raw fuel and combustibles, and reducing them into superior fuel of coke and charcoal; extracting during the same process the oil, acids, and gas ; and extracting and refining all the inflammable air or gas, so as to deprive it of all disagreeable odour during combustion, and render it fit for human respiration when diluted with atmospheric air dated [Fredrick Albert Winsor]

Journal			
House of Commons			**House of Lords**
18 Dec 1812	68 CJ 97	Pet	*Never considered by the House of Lords*

Representation
No details
Parliamentary debates
None
Parliamentary papers and cases
None

Gazette notices
Not required by SO
Newspaper coverage of debates
None
Archives
None

John Vancouver's Bill 1814

PRVB64	1814
John Vancouver's Bill 1814 (54 Geo 3)	

Bill for securing to John Vancouver, and the Public, the benefit of his invention of a new method of preparing Paint free from Noxious qualities
Table of contents (from Ingrossment)
[Cl 1 Specification of Letters Patent shall be sealed delivered to Lord Chancellor within 15 months instead of inrolling it in the Chancery; to be lodged in office of the Master of the Chancery] [Cl 2 Seal on specification not to be removed unless ordered by the Lord Chancellor or Keepers of Great Seal where similar to earlier later specification or infringement; to be sealed again after inspection] [Cl 3 Specification to remain sealed for 14 years; after which shall be enrolled in Court of Chancery by John Vancouver] [Cl 4 The proviso in the Letters Patent to enrol a specification is deemed complied] [Cl 5 Docket of Patent (abstract) and date of Specification to be entered on patent roll within 4 months] [Cl 6 Public Act]

Relevant patent	
17 May 1814 (No 3808)	Method of painting walls of apartments and other surfaces, by the preparation, use and application of certain materials [John Vancouver]

Journal					
House of Commons			**House of Lords**		
Pet Rep and Pres: Charles Harvey Rep: Sir James Graham					
26 May 1814	69 CJ 308	**Pet**	29 Jun 1814	49 LJ 1023	Brought HC/1R
27 May 1814	69 CJ 312	New Pet			
3 Jun 1814	69 CJ 320	Pet Rep/Bill Ord			
6 Jun 1814	69 CJ 328	1R			
10 Jun 1814	69 CJ 340	2R/C'tted			
27 Jun 1814	69 CJ 385	Rep with Amds			
29 Jun 1814	69 CJ 405	3R			

Representation
No information
Parliamentary debates
None
Parliamentary papers and cases
None
Gazette notices
Not required by SO
Newspaper coverage of debates
None
Archives
Ing: 29 June 1814 – Act for securing to John Vancouver and the public benefit of his invention of a new method of preparing paint free from noxious qualities [HL/PO/JO/10/2/88C]

Lee's Patent Bill 1816

PRVB65	1816

Lee's Patent Bill 1816 (56 Geo 3)

Bill for extending the provisions of an Act of His present Majesty, for securing James Lee and the Public, the benefit of his invention of certain new methods of preparing Hemp and Flax, to certain improvements since made by him in the said invention; and for enabling the said James Lee to assign the benefit of the said invention and improvements to a great number of Persons than those limited by the Letters Patent granted to him

Table of contents (from Ingrossment)

[Cl 1 Specification of Letters Patent shall be sealed delivered to Lord Chancellor within 15 months instead of inrolling it in the Chancery; to be lodged in office of the Master of the Chancery; to be accompanied by affidavit stating it makes a complete disclosure of the invention]

[Cl 2 Seal on specification not to be removed unless ordered by the Lord Chancellor or Keepers of Great Seal where similar to earlier later specification or infringement; to be sealed again after inspection]

[Cl 3 Specification for Ireland may be delivered sealed to the Lord Chancellor of Ireland within 15 months; and to the Chief Baron in Scotland within 15 months]

[Cl 4 Seal on specification on Irish specification not to be removed unless ordered by the Lord Chancellor of Ireland; or in Scotland by Chief Baron]

[Cl 5 Specifications to remain sealed for 7 years; after which shall be enrolled in Court of Chancery]

[Cl 6 Enrolment in Chancery within 4 months of the expiry of that 7–year period deemed adequate to satisfy the proviso]

[Cl 7 Docket (abstract) of the invention should be filed and enrolled within 4 months of passing of the Act]

[Cl 8 Any improvements in the Letters Patent may be enrolled as aforesaid]

[Cl 9 It is lawful to transfer to Letters Patent to more than five persons]

[Cl 10 Provided it is not transferred to more than 60 persons; nothing in the Act to give greater validity to the Letters Patent than they had before]

[Cl 11 Public Act]

Relevant patent

5 Dec 1815 (No 3964)	Preparing flax and hemp for various uses, by which also other vegetable substances may be made applicable to many purposes for which hemp and flax are now used [James Lee]

Journal

House of Commons			House of Lords		
Pres and Rep: [Thomas] Courtney			Rep: Lord Redesdale		
16 Feb 1816	71 CJ 54	**Pet**	10 May 1816	50 LJ 601	Brought HC/1R
18 Mar 1816	71 CJ 213	Pet Rep/Leave	24 May 1816	50 LJ 642	Papers delivered
22 Mar 1816	71 CJ 234	1R	17 Jun 1816	50 LJ 719	2R
5 Apr 1816	71 CJ 274	2R Ord	18 Jun 1816	50 LJ 725	Adj
8 Apr 1816	71 CJ 275	2R/C'tted	19 Jun 1816	50 LJ 736	All voices
29 Apr 1816	71 CJ 318	All voices	24 Jun 1816	50 LJ 767	**Rep with Amds**
3 May 1816	71 CJ 327	Rep with Amds	28 Jun 1816	50 LJ 798 – V	3R negative
9 May 1816	71 CJ 349	3R			

Representation

No information

Parliamentary debates

None

Parliamentary papers and cases

Minutes of Evidence taken before Lords Committee to whom James Lee's Bill was referred (1816 HL Papers 110), Vol 81, p 21 [Hannah Brighton; Francis Dacre; Charles Grant; Patrick Milne; Lettia Thomas; George Tyer]

Papers circulated by the Trustees of the Linen and Hempen Manufacturers of Ireland on the Subject of Hemp and Flax prepared by the Mode of Mr Lee's Patent (1816 HL Papers 70), Vol 81, p 77

Report of the Trustees for Fisheries, Manufactures and Improvements in Scotland on Experiments made under their Direction to prepare Flax in the Manner practised under Mr Lees patent (1816 HL Papers 58), Vol 81, p 121

Report from Committee on Petitions Relating to Machinery for Manufacturing of Flax (1817 HC Papers 311), Vol 3, p 99 [allegation of infringement]

Gazette notices

Not required by SO

Newspaper coverage of debates

House of Lords

Certain papers ordered: *The Times, 1 May 1816; Morning Post, 1 May 1826; Evening Mail, 1 May 1816; London Courier and Evening Gazette, 1 May 1816*

1R: The Times, 11 May 1816; Morning Post, 11 May 1816

2R: **The Times, 18 Jun 1816**; Morning Chronicle, 18 Jun 1816; Public ledger and Daily Advertiser, 18 Jun 1816; London Courier and Evening Gazette, 18 Jun 1816; Hampshire Telegraph, 24 Jun 1816; Hereford Journal, 26 Jun 1816

Pet Ag: Public Ledger and Daily Advertiser, 14 May 1816

3R: **London Courier and Evening Gazette, 29 Jun 1816**; **Caledonian Mercury, 4 Jul 1816**; *The Times, 29 Jun 1816; Morning Chronicle, 29 Jun 1816; Public Ledger and Daily Advertiser, 29 Jun 1816; Bell's Weekly Messenger, 30 Jun 1816; The Examiner, 30 Jun 1816;* 1816; Hereford Journal, 3 Jul 1816; Norfolk Chronicle, 6 Jul 1816; Leicester Chronicle, 6 Jul 1816; Yorkshire Gazette, 2 May 1829

Archives

Ing: Act for extending the provision of an Act for securing to James Lee and the public the benefit of his invention of certain new methods of preparing hemp, etc. (includes amendments sheet): 10 May 1816 [HL/PO/JO/10/2/90B]

Motions for Papers Respecting: 30 Apr 1816: [HL/PO/JO/10/8/378]

C'tee Minutes: 20 Jun 1816 (p 335); 22 Jun 1816 (p 349–351): [HL/PO/CO/1/62]

Additional papers 13 May 1816 (revenues); 15 May 1816 (Minutes of Trustees and Letter from Lee to James Corry): [HL/PO/JO/10/8/379]

Good Hope Company Petition 1816

PRVB66	1816	
Good Hope Company Petition 1816 (56 Geo 3)		
Petition for Bill to establish a Company under the title of the Good Hope Company, for the purposes of bringing forwards and prosecuting the said plans and invention [of impelling Vessels or Ships of any burthen with great speed and safety, against the wind or tide] and other matters directly and indirectly connected therewith		
Purpose		
No further details		
Relevant patent		
There does not appear to be a patent, but an invention by Isaac Hadley Reddell		
Journal		
House of Commons		**House of Lords**
16 Feb 1816	71 CJ 53	**Pet**	*Never considered by the House of Lords*
Representation		
No information		
Parliamentary debates		
None		
Parliamentary papers and cases		
None		
Gazette notices		
Not required by SO		
Newspaper coverage of debates		
None		
Archives		
None		

Bradbury's Bill 1818

PRVB67	1818

Bradbury's Bill 1818 (58 Geo 3)

Bill for securing to John Leigh Bradbury and the Public, the benefit of a certain method of Engraving, by enabling him to lodge the specifications of any Patents he may obtain, under certain restrictions

Table of contents (1818 HL Papers 100)

[Cl 1 Mr Bradbury to apply for Letters Patent within a certain Time]
[Cl 2 Specification to be deposited under the Seal, instead of being enrolled]
[Cl 3 Regulations as to the Custody and Use of the Specification previous to Enrolment]
[Cl 4 Specification to be delivered in Scotland and Ireland]
[Cl 5 Specification to be produced in Scotland and Ireland when necessary]
[Cl 6 Where Specification to be deposited after expiration of 14 Years]
[Cl 7 The Delivery of the Specification, according to this Act, to be deemed a Compliance with the Proviso in the Letters Patent requiring Enrolment]
[Cl 8 Abstract to be deposited]
[Cl 9 Public Act]

Relevant patent

9 Jan 1821 (No 4525)	Engraving and etching metal rollers used for prining woollen, cotton, linen, paper, cloth, silk and other fibrous substances [John Leigh Bradbury] [Patent not yet applied for at the time Bill was prosecuted, it was for future Patent, but this appears the most likely invention]

Journal

House of Commons			House of Lords		
Pres and Rep: Peter Moore					
28 Apr 1818	73 CJ 292	Pet	3 Jun 1818	51 LJ 740	Brought HC/1R
4 May 1818	73 CJ 311	Pet Pres	5 Jun 1818	51 LJ 752	2R/rej
19 May 1818	73 CJ 356	Pet Rep			
22 May 1818	73 CJ 371	Pet/Bill Ord			
22 May 1818	73 CJ 372	1R			
26 May 1818	73 CJ 388	2R/C'tted			
27 May 1818	73 CJ 391	Ord Rep			
28 May 1818	73 CJ 398	Rep with Amds			
30 May 1818	73 CJ 404	3R			

Representation

No information

Parliamentary debates

None

Parliamentary papers and cases

Report from the committee on Mr. Bradbury's petition relative to machinery for engraving and etching (1818 HC Papers 328), Vol 3, p 361

Bill for securing to John Bradbury and the Public, the benefit of a certain method of Engraving, by enabling him to lodge the specification under certain restrictions (1818 HL Papers 100), Vol 88, p 485

Gazette notices

Not required by SO

Newspaper coverage of debates

House of Commons

Pet Rep: **Evening Mail, Monday 25 May 1818**; *Worcester Journal, 28 May 1818*; *Huntingdon, Bedford & Peterborough Gazette, 30 May 1818*

2R: *The Times, 27 May 1818*; *Stamford Mercury, 29 May 1818*; *Huntingdon, Bedford & Peterborough Gazette, 30 May 1818*; *Caledonian Mercury, 30 May 1818*; *The Suffolk Chronicle, 30 May 1818*; *Hereford Journal, 3 June 1818*; Royal Cornwall Gazette, 6 June 1818; Morning Post, 27 May 1818

3R: Morning Advertiser, 1 June 1818

House of Lords
1R: Morning Post, 4 June 1818
2R: *The Times, 6 Jun 1818; Evening Mail, 8 June 1818; Manchester Mercury, 9 June 1818; Kentish Weekly Post or Canterbury Journal, 9 June 1818; Lancaster Gazette, 13 June 1818; Royal Cornwall Gazette, 13 June 1818*
Archives
Ing: 3 June 1818 – Act to enable John L Bradbury to lodge specifications of patents for engraving [HL/PO/JO/10/2/93]

Arthur Woolf's Notice 1818

PRVB68	1818
Arthur Woolf's Notice 1818 (58 Geo 3)	
Purpose	
Bill for prolonging the term of fourteen years granted to him by Letters patent for his invention of certain improvements relating to steam engines	
7 Jun 1804 (No 2772)	Construction of steam-engines [Arthur Woolf]
Representation	
Solicitor: F Abbott	
Gazette notices	
London Gazette: 13 Sep 1817 (Iss: 17,285, p 1936); 16 Sep 1817 (Iss: 17,286, p 1958); 20 Sep 1817 (Iss: 17,287, p 1979)	
Notes	
A subsequent notice related to a similar invention was posted in the following session: PRVB69	

Arthur Woolf's Notice 1819

PRVB69	1819
Arthur Woolf's Notice 1819 (69 Geo 3)	
Purpose	
Bill for prolonging the term of fourteen years granted to him by Letters Patent for his invention in relation to steam engines	
2 Jul 1805 (No 2863)	Steam engines [Arthur Woolf] {Scottish patent: 23 Oct 1805}
Representation	
Solicitor: F Abbott	
Gazette notices	
London Gazette: 25 Aug 1818 (Iss: 17,391, p 1516); 29 Aug 1818 (Iss: 17,393, p 1546); 1 Sep 1818 (Iss: 17,394, p 1567)	
Notes	
A notice related to a similar invention was published in the previous session: PRVB68	

Antimephetic Company Bill 1819

PRVB70	1819
Antimephetic Company Bill 1819 (60 Geo 3)	
Bill for the establishment of a Company to be called the Antimephetic Company	
Purpose	
Presumed to be permitting the assignment of patents to a company	

(continued)

(continued)

Relevant patent	
18 Nov 1819 (No 4410)	Moveable and inodorous Conveniences [Louis Fauche Borel]

Journal	
House of Commons	**House of Lords**

			House of Lords
Rep and Pres: John Curwen			*Never considered by House of Lords*

House of Commons			House of Lords
6 Dec 1819	75 CJ 24	**Pet**	*Never considered by House of Lords*
2 May 1820	75 CJ 131	**Renewed Pet (Masse)**	
12 May 1820	75 CJ 201	**Renewed Pet (Borel)**	
30 May 1820	75 CJ 250	Pet Rep/Bill Ord	
31 May 1820	75 CJ 256	Pres/1R	
6 Jun 1820	75 CJ 279	Pet Ag	
26 Jun 1820	75 CJ 353	2R/C'tted	
28 Jun 1820	75 CJ 364	Time enlarged	
3 Jul 1820	75 CJ 385	Pet Ag/Counsel Ord	

Petitions		
6 Jun 1820	75 CJ 279	Joseph Clarke
3 Jul 1820	75 CJ 385	Scavengers and Nightmen in Cities of London and Westminster

Representation
No information

Parliamentary debates
None

Parliamentary papers and cases
None

Gazette notices
Not required by SO

Newspaper coverage of debates
House of Commons 2R: Globe, 27 Jun 1820

Archives
None

Edward Heard's Notice 1820

PRVB71	1820
Edward Heard's Notice 1820 (60 Geo 3)	
Purpose	
Bill for vesting in Edward Heard for a term of years to be limited thereby the sole privilege of using an invention of certain means of inflammable gas from pit coal	
Relevant patent	
12 Jun 1806 (No 2941)	Obtaining inflammable gas from pit-coals, to burn without producing offensive smell [Edward Heard]
Representation	
Solicitor: William P Bartlett	
Gazette notices	
London Gazette: 18 Sep 1819 (Iss: 17,517, p 1661); 21 Sep 1819 (Iss: 17,518, p 1683); 25 Sep 1819 (Iss: 17,519, p 1703)	

James Winter's Notice 1821

PRVB72	1821
	James Winter's Notice 1821 (2 Geo 4)

Purpose
Bill for prolonging the term of letters patent for the term of fourteen years for sewing and point leather gloves

Relevant patent	
20 Feb 1807 (No 3012)	Machine for sewing, &c, leather gloves [James Winter]

Representation
Solicitor: James W Lyon

Gazette notices
London Gazette: 19 Sep 1820 (Iss: 17,635, p 1784); 23 Sep 1820 (Iss: 17,636, p 1801); 30 Sep 1820 (Iss: 17,638, p 1850)

Antimephetic Company Bill 1821

PRVB73	1821
	Antimephetic Company Bill 1821 (2 Geo 4)
	Bill for the establishment of a Company to be called The Antimephetic Company

Purpose
Presumed to be permitting the assignment of patents to a company

Relevant patent	
18 Nov 1819 (No 4410)	Moveable and inodorous Conveniences [Louis Fauche Borel]

Journal			
House of Commons			**House of Lords**
Rep: John Curwen Pres: Sir Eliab Harvey			
8 Feb 1821	76 CJ 46	**Pet**	*Never considered by House of Lords*
6 Mar 1821	76 CJ 142	Pet Rep/Bill Ord	
9 Mar 1821	76 CJ 149	Pres/1R	
12 Mar 1821	76 CJ 156	Pet Ag	
20 Mar 1821	76 CJ 185 – V	2R adj 6m	

Petitions		
12 Mar 1821	76 CJ 156	Joseph Clarke, Manure Manufacturer

Parliamentary debates
None

Representation
None

Parliamentary papers and cases
None

Gazette notices
Not required by SO

Newspaper coverage of debates
2R adj 6m: **Public Ledger and Daily Advertiser, 21 Mar 1821**; *The Times, 21 Mar 1821*; *Globe, 21 Mar 1821*; *Morning Chronicle, 21 Mar 1821*; *Morning Post, 21 Mar 1821*; *Evening Mail, 21 Mar 1821*

Fourdrinier's Patent Petition 1822

PRVB74	1822
	Fourdrinier's Patent Petition 1822 (3 Geo 4)

Petition for Bill for further prolonging the Term of the Letters Patent assigned to Henry Fourdrinier and Sealy Fourdrinier

Purpose
No further details

Relevant patent	
20 Apr 1801 (No 2487)	Machine for making paper in single sheets without seam or joinings [John Gamble]
7 Jun 1803 (No 2708)	Machine for making paper in single sheets without seam or joinings [John Gamble]
14 Aug 1807 (No 3068*)	Machine for making paper in single sheets without seam or joinings, &c. (inrolled under s 5) [Henry Fourdrinier, Sealy Fourdrinier and John Gamble]

Journal			
House of Commons	**House of Lords**		
Never considered by House of Commons	14 Mar 1822	55 LJ 70	**Pet/Bill Ord**

Representation
No information

Parliamentary debates
None

Parliamentary papers and cases
None

Gazette notices
None

Newspaper coverage of debates
None

Notes
This was the end of the fifteen-year period granted by the 1807 Act (and it had been indicated that a further seven years might be available)
There was an earlier Act, PRVA33, and a later Bill, PRVB85, and eventually a reward: PRZA42

Thomas Bruton's Notice 1823

PRVB75	1823
	Thomas Bruton's Notice 1823 (4 Geo 4)

Purpose
Bill for confirming to Thomas Brunton &c. during the remainder of the term granted by certain letters patent, the sole and exclusive right of making, using, exercising and vending of certain improved chain cables or mooring invented by him, in such and the same manner as if such letters patent had been granted in relation to the chain cables and moorings only [amend the patent]

Relevant patent	
26 Mar 1813 (No 3671)	Manufacturing ship's anchors, windlasses, of chain-cables or moorings [Thomas Brunton]

Representation
Solicitor: R Abbott

Gazette notices
London Gazette: 7 Sep 1822 (Iss: 17,850, p 1464); 10 Sep 1822 (Iss: 17,851, p 1485); 14 Sep 1822 (Iss: 17,852, p 1504)

John Heathcoat's Notice 1823

PRVB76	1823
	John Heathcoat's Notice 1823 (4 Geo 4)

Purpose
Bill for vesting in John Heathcoat for a term of years to be limited by such Act the exclusive right to use his invention of making an manufacturing of bobbin lace

Relevant patent	
20 Mar 1809 (No 3216)	Machine for making bobbin-lace [John Heathcoat]
29 Mar 1813 (No 3673)	Machine for making bobbin-lace [John Heathcoat]

Representation
Solicitor: F Abbott

Gazette notices
London Gazette: 27 Aug 1822 (Iss: 17,847, p 1412); 21 Sep 1822 (Iss: 17,854, p 1543); 25 Sep 1822 (Iss: 17,856, p 1582)

Simeon Thompson's Petition 1823

PRVB77	1823
	Simeon Thompson's Petition 1823 (4 Geo 4)

Petition for Bill for the renewal of [his Patent for raising Weights applicable to the erection of Buildings for the discharge of Vessels] on the condition that the exclusive right of using it for the discharge of Colliers within the port London, and the for the benefit of the Coal whippers, shall be given to the Corporation of the city of London, with the power to form the Coal whippers into a society

Purpose
No further details

Relevant patent	
20 Mar 1809 (No 3218)	Machinery for raising, lowering, drawing, driving, forcing, impressing, or moving bodies, substances, materials, fluids, articles, or commodities [Simeon Thompson]

Journal			
House of Commons			**House of Lords**
21 Feb 1823	78 CJ 59	**Pet/Ref** C'tee	*Never considered by House of Lords*

Representation
No details

Parliamentary debates
None

Parliamentary papers and cases
None

Gazette notices
Not required by SO

Newspaper coverage of debates
None

Archives
None

John Badams' Notice 1826

PRVB78	1826
	John Badams' Notice 1826 (7 Geo 4)

Purpose
Bill for securing to John Badams the benefit of his invention of extracting metals by enabling him to lodge the specification under certain restriction

Relevant patent	
16 May 1825 (No 5174)	Extracting Certain Metals from Ores, and for purifying certain metals [John Badams]

Representation
Solicitor and Agent: William Seymour

Gazette notices
London Gazette: 6 Sep 1825 (Iss: 18,173, p 1635); 10 Sep 1825 (Iss: 18,174, p 1652); 13 Sep 1825 (Iss: 18,175, p 1673)

Joseph Tilt's Bill 1827

PRVB79	1827

Joseph Tilt's Bill 1827 (7 & 8 Geo 4)
Bill to enable him to grant a greater Number of Licences, under certain Letters Patent, relating to Salt Pans

Purpose
No further details

Relevant patent	
4 Apr 1827 (No 5483)	Salt-pans used for making salt [Joseph Tilt]

Journal			
House of Commons			**House of Lords**
Rep and Pres: Matthew Wood Bill Rep: David Barclay			Never considered by House of Lords
18 May 1827	82 CJ 471	Pet to Pet late	
22 May 1827	82 CJ 481	Pet Rep/Leave	
23 May 1827	82 CJ 486	Pet for Bill	
30 May 1827	82 CJ 504	Pet Rep/Bill Ord/1R	
8 Jun 1827	82 CJ 533	2R/C'tted	
20 Jun 1827	82 CJ 585	Rep/Not proved	

Representation
No information

Parliamentary debates
None

Parliamentary papers and cases
None

Gazette notices
Not required by SO

Newspaper coverage of debates
None

Archives
None

Crossley's Petition (Gas Lights) Bill 1829

PRVB80	1829
	Crossley's Petition (Gas Lights) Bill 1829 (10 Geo 4)

Bill for prolonging the terms of certain Letters Patent, for England and Scotland respectively, assigned to Samuel Crosley, for an improved Gas Apparatus, in so far as regards certain parts of such improved Gas Apparatus

Purpose

No further details

Relevant patent

9 Dec 1815 (No 3968)	Gas-apparatus [Samuel Clegg]

Journal

House of Commons			House of Lords
Rep and Pres: Matthew Wood			
13 Feb 1829	84 CJ 27	**Pet**	*Never considered by House of Lords*
27 Feb 1829	84 CJ 87	**Pet Rep/Ref SOC**	
6 Mar 1829	84 CJ 108	SOC Rep (publish notices)	
9 Mar 1829	84 CJ 111	Bill Ord	
12 Mar 1829	84 CJ 125	1R	
30 Mar 1829	84 CJ 180	2R/C'tted	
7 Apr 1829	84 CJ 206	Pet Ag	
8 Apr 1829	84 CJ 210	Pet Ag	
9 Apr 1829	84 CJ 211	Pet Ag	
10 Apr 1829	84 CJ 217	Pet Ag	
14 Apr 1829	84 CJ 226	Pet Ag	
28 Apr 1829	84 CJ 242	Pet Ag	
1 May 1829	84 CJ 248	Pet Ag	
8 May 1829	84 CJ 275	Pet Ag	
3 Jun 1829	84 CJ 366	Pet Ag	

Petitions

7 Apr 1829	84 CJ 206	Leeds Gas Company
8 Apr 1829	84 CJ 210	Burnley Gas Company
9 Apr 1829	84 CJ 211	Gainsbourg Gas Works
9 Apr 1829	84 CJ 211	Doncaster Gas Company
10 Apr 1829	84 CJ 217	Whitby Gas Company
10 Apr 1829	84 CJ 217	Wakefield Gas Company
14 Apr 1829	84 CJ 226	Ashton-under-Lyne Gas Lights and Water Works Company
28 Apr 1829	84 CJ 242	Liverpool Gas Light Company
1 May 1829	84 CJ 248	City of London Gas Light and Coke Company
8 May 1829	84 CJ 275	Carlisle Gas Light and Coke Company
8 May 1829	84 CJ 275	Commissioners for Lighting and Paving Keighley
3 Jun 1829	84 CJ 366	Leicester Gas Company

Representation

No information

Parliamentary debates

Pet: Mirror, 13 Feb 1829, Vol 1, p 124

Ref SOC: Mirror, 27 Feb 1829, Vol 1, p 307

Rep SOC: Mirror, 6 Mar 1829, Vol 1, p 439

Leave: Mirror, 9 Mar 1829, Vol 1, p 478

1R: Mirror, 12 Mar 1829, Vol 1, p 538

2R: Mirror, 30 Mar 1829, Vol 2, p 889

Pet Ag: **Mirror, 7 Apr 1829, Vol 2, p 1142 -43**

Pet Ag: Mirror, 8 Apr 1829, Vol 2, p 1177

Pet Ag: Mirror, 9 Apr 1829, Vol 2, p 1199

(continued)

(continued)

Pet Ag: Mirror, 10 Apr 1829, Vol 2, p 1240
Pet Ag: Mirror, 14 Apr 1829, Vol 2, p 1292
Pet Ag: **Mirror, 28 Apr 1829, Vol 2, p 1345**
Pet Ag: Mirror, 1 May 1829, Vol 2, p 1358
Pet Ag: **Mirror, 1 May 1829, Vol 2, p 1359–1360**
Pet Ag: Mirror, 8 May 1829, Vol 2, p 1504
Pet Ag: Mirror, 3 Jun 1829, Vol 3, p 1990

Parliamentary papers and cases

None

Gazette notices

London Gazette: 10 Mar 1829 (Iss 18,557, p 447); 13 Mar 1829 (Iss 18,558, p 471); 17 Mar 1829 (Iss 18,559, p 503); 20 Mar 1829 (Iss 18,560, p 528)

Newspaper coverage of debates

House of Commons

Pet: **Morning Chronicle, 29 Apr 1829; Evening Mail, 29 Apr 1829; London Courier and Evening Gazette, 29 Apr 1829; London Evening Standard, 29 Apr 1829**; *The Times, 29 Apr 1829; Morning Advertiser, 29 Apr 1829:* Public Ledger and Daily Advertiser, 29 Apr 1829

Pet: **Morning Advertiser, 2 May 1829; Morning Chronicle, 2 May 1829; London Courier and Evening Gazette, 2 May 1829; Leeds Patriot and Yorkshire Advertiser, 9 May 1829**; *The Times, 2 May 1829; Public Ledger and Daily Advertiser, 2 May 1829; Newcastle Courant, 9 May 1829;* London Evening Standard, 2 May 1829; Bath Chronicle and Weekly Gazette, 7 May 1829

Archives

None

Notes

Proposal to change Standing Orders following Bill: *The Times, 29 Apr 1829*

John Hague's Notice 1830

PRVB81	1830
John Hague's Notice 1830 (11 Geo 4 & 1 Will 4)	
Purpose	
Bill to prolong John Hague's Patent for expelling molasses from sugar	
Relevant patent	
27 Jul 1816 (No 4048)	Expelling molasses from sugars [John Hague]
Representation	
Solicitor: Freshfield & Co	
Gazette notices	
London Gazette: 22 Sep 1829 (Iss: 18,613, p 1749); 25 Sep 1829 (Iss: 18,614, p 1767); 2 Oct 1829 (Iss: 18,616, p 1807)	

Richard Williams' Notice 1831

PRVB82	1831
Richard Williams' Notice 1831 (1 & 2 Will 4)	
Purpose	
Bill to prolong Richard Williams's Patent for elastic and dense fluid	
Relevant patent	
15 Dec 1828 (No 5736)	Application of elastic and dense fluids to the propelling of machinery of various descriptions [Richard Williams]

Representation
Solicitor: Tooke & Parker
Gazette notices
London Gazette: 17 Sep 1830 (Iss: 18,727, p 1973); 21 Sep 1830 (Iss: 18,728, p 1997); 24 Sep 1830 (Iss: 18,729, p 2021)
Notes
In the notices, the patent is incorrectly stated to be dated 15 September 1828. This is probably because the notice was dated 15 September 1830.

Peter Young's Notice 1832

PRVB83	1832	
Peter Young's Notice 1832 (2 & 3 Will 4)		
Purpose		
Bill to confirm and render available Peter Young's patent for fourteen years from the date of the said letters patent.		
Relevant patent		
6 Oct 1831 (No 6176)	Manufacturing mangel-wurzel for producing various known articles of commerce [vinegar] [Peter Young]	
Representation		
In person		
Gazette notices		
London Gazette: 15 Nov 1831 (Iss 18,872, p 2357); 18 Nov 1831 (Iss 18,873, p 2426); 22 Nov 1831 (Iss 18,876, p 2384)		

Morton's Patent Slip Bill 1832

PRVB84	1832		
Morton's Patent Slip Bill 1832 (2 & 3 Will 4)			
Bill for prolonging the terms of certain Letters Patent granted to Thomas Morton, for a method of dragging Ships out of the Water on dry Land, commonly called "Morton's Patent Slip"			
Purpose			
No further details			
Relevant patent			
23 Mar 1819 (No 4352)	Method of dragging ships out of water on to dry land [by means of a railway] [Thomas Morton] {Scottish patent: 6 Jun 1818}		
Journal			
House of Commons			**House of Lords**
Rep and Pres: Sir Michael Shaw Stewart			
15 Dec 1831	87 CJ 25	Pet	*Never considered by House of Lords*
5 Mar 1832	87 CJ 163	Pet Rep/Bill Ord	
6 Mar 1832	87 CJ 166	1R	
28 Mar 1832	87 CJ 230	2R adj	
30 Mar 1832	87 CJ 234	2R adj	
6 Apr 1832	87 CJ 252	2R adj	
13 Apr 1832	87 CJ 271	SC Rep	
Representation			
Solicitor: Greig and Morton			

(continued)

(continued)

Parliamentary debates	
Pet: Mirror, 15 Dec 1831, Vol 1, p 97	
Rep: Mirror, 5 Mar 1832, Vol 2, p 1000	
1R: Mirror, 6 Mar 1832, Vol 2, p 1024	
2R adj: **Mirror, 28 Mar 1832, Vol 2, p 1491–1492**	
Appoint SC: **Mirror, 30 Mar 1832, Vol 2, p 1526**	
Send for papers: Mirror, 6 Apr 1832, Vol 2, p 1632	
SC Rep: Mirror, 13 Apr 1832, Vol 2, p 1817	

Parliamentary papers and cases
Select Committee on Expediency of extending Patent for Morton's Patent Slip (1831–32 HC Papers 380), Vol 5, p 295

Gazette notices
London Gazette: 13 Sep 1831 (Iss: 18,849, p 1879); 16 Sep 1831 (Iss: 18,851, p 1902); 20 Sep 1831 (Iss: 18,852, p 1926)

Newspaper coverage of debates
2R adj: Morning Advertiser, 29 Mar 1832; *Public Ledger and Daily Advertiser, 29 Mar 1832*

Archives
None

Fourdrinier's Patent Bill 1837

PRVB85	1837
	Fourdrinier's Patent Bill 1837 (7 Will 4 & 1 Vict)
	Bill for reviving and prolonging the Term of certain Letters Patent assigned to Henry Fourdrinier and Sealy Fourdrinier, for the invention of making Paper by means of Machinery

Purpose
No further details

Relevant patents	
20 Apr 1801 (No 2487)	Machine for making paper in single sheets without seam or joinings [John Gamble]
7 Jun 1803 (No 2708)	Machine for making paper in single sheets without seam or joinings [John Gamble]
14 Aug 1807 (No 3068)	Machine for making paper in single sheets without seam or joinings, &c. (inrolled under s 5) [Henry Fourdrinier, Sealy Fourdrinier and John Gamble]

Journal			
House of Commons			**House of Lords**
Pres and Second Rep: Sir Oswald Mosley SC Rep: William MacKinnon			
17 Feb 1837	92 CJ 60	Pet	*Never considered by House of Lords*
1 Mar 1837	92 CJ 100	Rep	
1 Mar 1837	92 CJ 101	Bill Ord	
15 Mar 1837	92 CJ 170	1R	
1 May 1837	92 CJ 309	Pet renewed/Ref SC	
1 Jun 1837	92 CJ 425	SC Rep	
15 Jun 1837	92 CJ 476	Pet for share of reward	
15 Jun 1837	92 CJ 478	Re-C'tted	
16 Jun 1837	92 CJ 482	Second Rep	
22 Jun 1837	92 CJ 494	Cons adj	
29 Jun 1837	92 CJ 552	Cons adj	
5 Jul 1837	92 CJ 596	Cons adj	
12 Jul 1837	92 CJ 619	Cons adj 3m	

Representation
No information

Parliamentary debates	
Pet: Mirror, 21 Apr 1836, Vol 2, p 1089	
Pet: Mirror, 17 Feb 1837, Vol 1, p 212	
Rep: Mirror, 27 Feb 1837, Vol 1, p 350	
Bill Ord: Mirror, 1 Mar 1837, Vol 1, p 395	
1R: Mirror, 15 Mar 1837, Vol 1, p 667	
Ref SC: Mirror, 1 May 1837, Vol 2, p 1266	
Power to SC: Mirror, 1 Jun 1837, Vol 3, p 1663	
Re-C'tted: **HC Deb, 15 Jun 1837, Vol 38 (3rd), col 1492–1494; Mirror, 15 Jun 1837, Vol 3, p 1888–1889**	
Pet for share: Mirror, 15 Jun 1837, Vol 3, p 1875	
Rep table: Mirror, 16 Jun 1837, Vol 3, p 1903	
Rep adj: Mirror, 29 Jun 1837, Vol 3, p 2055	
Rep adj: Mirror, 5 Jul 1837, Vol 3, p 2141	
Rep adj: **Mirror, 12 Jul 1837, Vol 3, p 2203**	

Parliamentary papers and cases
Report from the Select Committee on Fourdrinier's Patent; with the minutes of evidence, and appendix (1837 HC Papers 351), Vol 20, p 35
Report on Re-Committed Report from the Select Committee on Fourdriniers' Patent (1837 HC Papers 405), Vol 20, p 91

Gazette notices
London Gazette: 4 Nov 1836 (Iss: 19,434, p 1924); 8 Nov 1836 (Iss: 19,435, p 1958); 15 Nov 1836 (Iss: 19,437, p 2032)
Edinburgh Gazette: 11 Nov 1836 (Iss: 4537, p 294); 18 Nov 1836 (Iss: 4539, p 306); 25 Nov 1836 (Iss: 4541, p 319)

Newspaper coverage of debates

House of Commons

Pet: *Derby Mercury, 22 Feb 1837*; London Courier and Evening Gazette, 18 Feb 1837

1R: London Courier and Evening Gazette, 16 Mar 1837

2R: *The Times, 2 May 1837; London Evening Standard, 2 May 1837; Coventry Standard, 5 May 1837; Carlisle Journal, 6 May 1837; Staffordshire Advertiser, 6 May 1837*; Morning Advertiser, 2 May 1837; Pubic Ledger and Daily, 2 May 1837; Kendal Mercury, 6 May 1837

Rep: **The Times, 7 Jun 1837; London Courier and Evening Gazette, 8 Jun 1837; Staffordshire Advertiser, 10 Jun 1837**

Re-C'tted: **The Times, 16 Jun 1837; Morning Advertiser, 16 Jun 1837; Globe, 16 Jun 1837; Morning Chronicle, 16 Jun 1837; Evening Chronicle, 16 Jun 1837; Evening Mail, 16 Jun 1837; Public Ledger and Daily Advertiser, 16 Jun 1837; London Courier and Evening Gazette, 16 Jun 1837; London Evening Standard, 16 Jun 1837; Windsor and Eaton Express, 17 Jun 1837; Freeman Journal, 19 Jun 1837;** *Morning Post, 16 Jun 1837; Birmingham Journal, 17 Jun 1837; Dublin Morning Register, 19 Jun 1837; Oxford Journal, 17 Jun 1837; The Pilot, 19 Jun 1837; West Kent Guardian, 17 Jun 1837; Yorkshire Gazette, 17 Jun 1837; Devizes and Wiltshire Gazette, 22 Jun 1837; Bucks Herald, 24 Jun 1837; Carlisle Journal, 24 Jun 1837; Derbyshire Courier, 24 Jun 1837; Kendal Mercury, 24 Jun 1837; Leicestershire Mercury, 24 Jun 1837; Manchester Courier and Lancashire General Advertiser, 24 Jun 1837; Derby Mercury, 28 Jun 1837;* Bell's New Weekly Messenger, 18 Jun 1836; The Examiner, 18 Jun 1837; Kentish Gazette, 20 Jun 1837; Blackburn Standard, 21 Jun 1837; Hereford Journal, 21 Jun 1837; Perthshire Advertiser, 22 Jun 1837; Wiltshire Independent, 22 Jun 1837

Cons adj 3m: *Globe, 13 Jul 1837; Evening Chronicle, 13 Jul 1837; London Evening Standard, 13 Jul 1837; Saunders's News-Letter, 17 Jul 1837; Sherborne Mercury, 17 Jul 1837; Bradford Observer, 20 July 1837; Carlisle Journal, 22 Jul 1837; Kendal Mercury, 22 Jul 1837;* Morning Advertiser, 13 Jul 1837; Morning Chronicle, 13 Jul 1837; Morning Post, 13 Jul 1837; Public Ledger and Daily Advertiser, 13 Jul 1837; Royal Cornwall Gazette, 21 Jul 1837; Monmouthshire Merlin, 22 Jul 1837

Editorial comment: **The Times, 14 Jun 1837; Morning Chronicle, 15 Jun 1837; Morning Post, 14 Jun 1837; Evening Mail, 14 Jun 1837; London Evening Standard, 14 Jun 1837; Blackburn Standard, 19 Jul 1837; Sherborne Mercury, 19 Jun 1837; Hereford Journal, 21 Jun 1837; Monmouthshire Merlin, 24 Jun 1837; Preston Chronicle, 24 Jun 1837; London Dispatch, 25 Jun 1837**

(continued)

(continued)

Archives
None

Notes
There was an earlier Act, PRVA33, and an earlier Bill, PRVB74, and eventually a reward: PRZA42

Sievier's Petition 1837

PRVB86	1837
Sievier's Petition 1837 (7 Will 4 & 1 Vict)	
Petition for Bill to enable Robert William Sievier to assign certain Letters Patent to a Joint Stock Company his Patent and patent rights for certain improvements in the making and manufacture of cables, ropes, whale-fishing and other lines	

Purpose
No further details

Relevant patent	
1 Dec 1831 (No 6193)	Manufacture of cables, ropes, whale-fishing and other lines, lath and rigger-bands, bags, and purses [Robert William Sievier]

Journal			
House of Commons			House of Lords
Rep: Henry Aglionby			
17 Feb 1837	92 CJ 60	Pet	*Never considered by House of Lords*
13 Mar 1837	92 CJ 160	Pet Rep/Bill Ord	

Representation
No information

Parliamentary debates	
Pet: Mirror, 17 Feb 1837, Vol 1, p 212 Rep: Mirror, 13 Mar 1837, Vol 1, p 607	

Parliamentary papers and cases
None

Gazette notices
Not required by SO

Newspaper coverage of debates
None

Archives
None

Notes
This appears to have been replaced by the London Caoutchouc Company Act 1837 (PRVA41)

Westhead's Patent Petition 1837

PRVB87	1837
Westhead's Patent Petition 1837 (7 Will 4 & 1 Vict)	
Bill to enable Joshua Proctor Westhead to assign to a Company certain Letters Patent	

Purpose
No further details

Relevant patents	
23 May 1831 (No 6114)	Manufacture of smallwares [Joshua Proctor Westhead]
24 Sep 1835 (No 6896)	Manufacture of smallwares; arrangement of machinery for covering or forming a case around wire, cord, gut, thread, or other substances, to render the same applicable to various purposes [Joshua Proctor Westhead]
16 Feb 1836 (No 7004)	Cutting caoutchouc, india-rubber, leather, hides, and similar substances, to render them applicable to various purposes [Joshua Proctor Westhead]
	There is no evidence of which (if any) of these patents was to be subject of the Bill

Journal			
House of Commons			**House of Lords**
Rep: Henry Aglionby			
17 Feb 1837	92 CJ 60	Pet	*Never considered by House of Lords*
13 Mar 1837	92 CJ 159	Pet Rep/Bill Ord	

Representation
No information

Parliamentary debates	
Pet: Mirror, 17 Feb 1837, Vol 1, p 212	
Rep: Mirror, 13 Mar 1837, Vol 1, p 607	

Parliamentary papers and cases
None

Gazette notices
Not required by SO

Newspaper coverage of debates
None

Archives
None

Notes
This appears to have been replaced by the London Caoutchouc Company Act 1837 (PRVA41)

Birmingham Plate and Crown Glass Company Bill 1837

PRVB88	1837
Birmingham Plate and Crown Glass Company Bill 1837 (7 Will 4 & 1 Vict)	
Bill to enable Birmingham Plate and Glass Company to Sue and be Sued in Nature of Name of the Chairman or Manager for the time being of the said Company, and for other Purposes	

Relevant patent
No information

Journal			
House of Commons			**House of Lords**
Rep and Pres: William Dugdale Rep: Charles Villers			
13 Feb 1837	92 CJ 38	Pet	*Never considered by House of Lords*
24 Feb 1837	92 CJ 81	Pet Rep	
27 Feb 1837	92 CJ 88	Bill Ord	
1 Mar 1837	92 CJ 99	1R	
6 Mar 1837	92 CJ 121	2R/C'tted	
24 Apr 1837	92 CJ 287	Rep	
25 Apr 1837	92 CJ 295 – V	3R	

Representation
No information

(continued)

(continued)

Parliamentary debates	
Pet: Mirror, 13 Feb 1837, Vol 1, p 139	
Pet Rep: Mirror, 24 Feb 1837, Vol 1, p 323	
Bill Ord: Mirror, 27 Feb 1837, Vol 1, p 350	
1R: Mirror, 1 Mar 1837, Vol 1, p 395	
2R: Mirror, 6 Mar 1837, Vol 1, p 454	
Rep: Mirror, 24 Apr 1837, Vol 2, p 1180	
3R: **Mirror, 25 Apr 1837, Vol 2, p 1204–1205**	

Parliamentary papers and cases
None

Gazette notices
Not required by SO

Newspaper coverage of debates
House of Commons
Pet: Coventry Herald, 17 Feb 1837; Drogheda Argus and Leinster, 18 Feb 1837
Rep: Morning Advertiser, 25 Feb 1837; London Courier and Evening Gazette, 25 Feb 1837
1R: London Courier and Evening Gazette, 2 Mar 1837
2R: Morning Advertiser, 7 Mar 1837; Morning Post, 7 Mar 1837; London Evening Standard, 7 Mar 1837; London Courier and Evening Gazette, 7 Mar 1837; Bristol Mercury, 11 Mar 1837; Bell's Weekly Messenger, 12 Mar 1837; Sherborne Mercury, 13 Mar 1837; Wolverhampton Chronicle and Staffordshire Advertiser, 15 Mar 1837
Rep: The Times, 25 Apr 1837; Globe, 25 Apr 1837; Morning Advertiser, 25 Apr 1837; Coventry Herald, 28 Apr 1837
3R: **The Times, 26 Apr 1837**; **Globe, 26 Apr 1837**; **Morning Advertiser, 26 Apr 1837**; **Evening Chronicle, 26 Apr 1837**; **Public Ledger and Daily Advertiser, 26 Apr 1837**; **London Courier and Evening Gazette, 26 Apr 1837**; **London Evening Standard, 26 Apr 1837**; **Coventry Standard, 28 Apr, 1837**; **Manchester Courier and Lancashire General Advertiser, 29 Apr 1837**; **Leamington Spa Courier, 29 Apr 1837**; **The Jurist, Vol 1, 1837, p 268**; *The Pilot, 28 Apr 1837*; *Nottingham Review and General Advertiser for the Midland Counties, 28 Apr 1837*; *Carlisle Journal, 29 Apr 1837*; *Freeman's Journal, 29 Apr 1837*; *Saunders's News-Letter, 29 Apr 1837*; *Warder and Dublin Weekly Mail, 29 Apr 1837*; *Dublin Evening Packet and Correspondent, 29 Apr 1837*; *Yorkshire Gazette, 29 Apr 1837*

Archives
None

Anti-Dry Rot Company Bill 1837

PRVB89	1837
Anti-Dry Rot Company Bill 1837 (7 Will 4 & 1 Vict)	

Bill for vesting in and securing to The Anti-Dry Rot Company certain Profits and Emoluments for a limited time [Discharged Order: Bill for vesting in and securing to The Anti-Dry Rot Company certain Profits and Emoluments for a limited time, and for incorporating the said Company, and other purposes]	

Purpose	
No further details	

Relevant patents	
31 Mar 1832 (No 6253)	A New Mode of Preserving Certain Vegetable Substances from Decay [John Howard Kyan] {Scottish patent: 1 Aug 1832; Irish patent: 5 Nov 1832; Colonies: 11 Feb 1836}
22 Sep 1832 (No 6309)	An Improved Mode of preserving Paper, Canvass, Cloth, and Cordage for Ships, and other Uses, and the ray Materials of Hemp, Flax, or Cotton from which the same may wholly or in part be made [John Howard Kyan]

Journal	
House of Commons	**House of Lords**
Rep: Henry Aglionby	

17 Feb 1837	92 CJ 60	Pet	*Never considered by House of Lords*
13 Mar 1837	92 CJ 159	Pet Rep SO not app/Bill Ord	
18 Mar 1837	92 CJ 187	Ord Disc/New Ord	
18 Mar 1837	92 CJ 187	1R	
22 Mar 1837	92 CJ 205	2R/C'tted	
2 Jun 1837	92 CJ 427	C'tee adj	

Representation
No information

Parliamentary debates

Pet: Mirror, 17 Feb 1837, Vol 1, p 212	
Rep: Mirror, 13 Mar 1837, Vol 1, p 607	
1R: Mirror, 18 Mar 1837, Vol 1, p 756	
2R: Mirror, 22 Mar 1837, Vol 1, p 794	
Rep adj: Mirror, 2 Jun 1837, Vol 3, p 1676	

Parliamentary papers and cases
None

Gazette notices
Not required by SO

Newspaper coverage of debates

House of Commons

Pet: London Courier and Evening Gazette, 18 Feb 1837

Leave/Bill Ord: London Courier and Evening Gazette, 14 Mar 1837; Evening Chronicle, 15 Mar 1837; Bell's New Weekly Messenger, 19 Mar 1837

1R: Morning Post, 20 Mar 1837; Public Ledger and Daily Advertiser, 20 March 1837; County Chronicle, Surrey Herald and Weekly Advertiser for Kent, 21 Mar 1837; Cheltenham Chronicle, 23 Mar 1837; Liverpool Mercury, 24 Mar 1837; Hereford Journal, 29 Mar 1837

2R: London Courier and Evening Gazette, 22 Mar 1837; Globe, 23 Mar 1837; Morning Chronicle, 23 Mar 1837; London Courier and Evening Gazette, 23 Mar 1837; Dublin Evening Post, 25 Mar 1837; Oxford Chronicle and Reading Gazette, 25 Mar 1837; Saunder's News-Letter, 25 Mar 1837

C'tee adj: London Courier and Evening Gazette, 3 Jun 1837

Archives
None

Notes
Similar Bill introduced in following session: PRVB90. An Act was passed in the previous session: PRVA40

Anti-Dry Rot Company Bill 1838

PRVB90	1838
	Anti-Dry Rot Company Bill 1838 (1 & 2 Vict)
	Bill for regulating the sums to be taken for licences by the Anti-Dry Rot Company, and for vesting the Profits therefor in the Company for a limited time

Table of contents (based on notice)
[Cl 1 Assignment of Letters Patent of John Howard Kyan for Invention of preventing vegetable matter from decay] [Cl 2 Repealing, altering, amending, or enlarging the provisions of the Anti-Dry Rot Company (Letters Patent) Act 1836]

Relevant patents	
31 Mar 1832 (No 6253)	A New Mode of Preserving Certain Vegetable Substances from Decay [John Howard Kyan]
22 Sep 1832 (No 6309)	An Improved Mode of preserving Paper, Canvass, Cloth, and Cordage for Ships, and other Uses, and the ray Materials of Hemp, Flax, or Cotton from which the same may wholly or in part be made [John Howard Kyan]

(continued)

(continued)

Journal	
Rep: Charles Shaw Lefevre Pres: Sir Robert Price	
House of Commons	**House of Lords**
7 Dec 1837 93 CJ 186 Pet 7 Feb 1838 93 CJ 255 Pet Rep/Leave 23 Feb 1838 93 CJ 301 Bill Ord 26 Feb 1838 93 CJ 306 1R 16 Mar 1838 93 CJ 365 2R day app 20 Mar 1838 93 CJ 373 2R adj 26 Mar 1838 93 CJ 402 2R adj 6m	*Never considered by House of Lords*

Representation
Solicitor: Hall, Thompson, and Sewell

Parliamentary debates	
Pet: Mirror, 7 Dec 1837, Vol 1, p 493	
Rep Pet: Mirror, 7 Feb 1838, Vol 2, p 1624	
Bill Ord: Mirror, 23 Feb 1838, Vol 3, p 2108	
1R: Mirror, 26 Feb 1838, Vol 3, p 2152	
2R day app: Mirror, 16 Mar 1838, Vol 4, p 2766	
2R adj: Mirror, 19 Mar 1838, Vol 4 p 2806 and 2831 (no record in journal)	
2R adj 6m: Mirror, 26 Mar 1838, Vol 4, p 3041 and 3068	

Parliamentary papers and cases
None

Gazette notices
London Gazette: 19 Sep 1837 (Iss: 19,542, p 2447); 22 Sep 1837 (Iss: 19,543, p 2477); 26 Sep 1837 (Iss: 19,544, p 2497)
Edinburgh Gazette: 19 Sep 1837 (Iss: 4626, p 296); 22 Sep 1837 (Iss: 4628, p 299); 26 Sep 1837 (Iss: 4629, p 301)
Dublin Gazette: 22 Sep 1837 (Iss: 12,869, p 779); 26 Sep 1837 (Iss: 12,870, p 790); 29 Sep 1837 (Iss: 12,871, p 796)

Newspaper coverage of debates
House of Commons
Pet: London Courier and Evening Gazette, 8 Dec 1837
2R adj 6m: London Courier and Evening Gazette, 27 Mar 1838

Archives
None

Galvanization of Metals Petition 1838

PRVB91	1838
Galvanization of Metals Petition 1838 (1 & 2 Vict)	
Petition for Bill to enable certain Persons to assign to a Company their interests in Patents for preventing the Oxidation of Metals	
Table of contents (based on notice)	
[Cl 1 Assigning Letters Patent to a Company for the invention of converting metal to prevent oxidation] [Cl 2 To allow the said company to vend and licence the said invention] [Cl 3 To make regulation for the said company]	
Relevant patent	
29 Apr 1837 (No 7355)	Method of coating or covering iron and copper for the prevention of oxydation [Henry William Craufurd]

Journal				
House of Commons			**House of Lords**	
Rep: Thomas Greene			*Never considered by the House of Lords*	
16 May 1838	93 CJ 524	Pet to Pet Late		
23 May 1838	93 CJ 544	**Pet Rep/Leave/Pet**		

Representation
No information

Parliamentary debates	
Pet: Mirror, Vol 5, 16 May 1838, p 4079	
Rep: Mirror, Vol 6, 23 May 1838, p 4227	

Parliamentary papers and cases
None

Gazette notices
London Gazette: 25 May 1838 (Iss: 19,620, p 1195); 29 May 1838 (Iss: 19,621, p 1221); 5 Jun 1838 (Iss: 19,623, p 1270)

Newspaper coverage of debates
None

Archives
None

Notes
A further notice was issued with other patents in a later session: PRVB95

Burnett's Patent Bill 1839

PRVB92	1839
Burnett's Patent Bill 1839 (2 & 3 Vict)	
Bill for extending the number of Proprietors allowed by a Patent granted to him for improvements in preserving Wood	

Purpose
No further details

Relevant patent	
26 Jul 1838 (No 7747)	Preserving wood and other vegetable matter from decay [Sir William Burnett]

Journal				
House of Commons			**House of Lords**	
Rep: Charles Shaw Lefevre SOC Rep: George Estcourt			*Never considered by House of Lords*	
12 Jan 1839	94 CJ 52	Pet		
15 Mar 1839	94 CJ 116	Pet (Extending Time)		
27 Mar 1839	94 CJ 153	Pet Rep/Pet Ref SOC		
12 Apr 1839	94 CJ 176	SOC Rep SOC not Disp		

Representation
No information

Parliamentary debates	
Pet for Ex Tim: Mirror, 15 Mar 1839, Vol 2, p 1256	
Rep: Mirror, 27 Mar 1839, Vol 2, p 1593	
SOC Rep: **Mirror, 12 Apr 1839, Vol 2, p 1674**	

Parliamentary papers and cases
None

(continued)

(continued)

Gazette notices
None
Newspaper coverage of debates
None
Archives
None

Daniel Stafford's Patent Bill 1839

PRVB93	1839

Daniel Stafford's Patent Bill 1839 (2 & 3 Vict)

Table of contents (based on notice)
[Cl 1 To incorporate a company with proper and necessary powers] [Cl 2 To assign and put into effect the Letters Patent of Daniel Stafford in relation to his invention of improvement in carriages] [Cl 3 To grant certain other powers in relation to the Letters Patent]

Relevant patents	
24 Dec 1824 (No 5063)	Carriages [Daniel Stafford]
21 Dec 1838 (No 7919)	Carriages [Daniel Stafford] [extension of earlier patent for seven years]

Journal			
House of Commons			**House of Lords**
Rep: Charles Shaw Lefevre SOC Rep: Thomas Greene			
27 Feb 1839	94 CJ 63	Pet to be late	*Never considered by House of Lords*
5 Mar 1839	94 CJ 78	Pet Rep/Leave	
6 Mar 1839	94 CJ 83	Pet	
19 Mar 1839	94 CJ 127	Pet Rep/SO cw	

Representation
Solicitor: HM Vane

Parliamentary debates	
Pet: Mirror, 27 Feb 1839, Vol 1, p 560	
Leave: Mirror, 5 Mar 1839, Vol 1, p 766	
Pet: Mirror, 8 Mar 1839, Vol 1, p 803	
Rep: Mirror, 18 Mar 1839, Vol 2, p 1317	

Parliamentary papers and cases
None

Gazette notices
London Gazette: 14 Nov 1838 (Iss: 19,673, p 2531); 21 Nov 1838 (Iss: 19,676, p 2641); 27 Nov 1838 (Iss: 19,678, p 2723)
Edinburgh Gazette: 16 Nov 1838 (Iss: 4748, p 330); 23 Nov 1838 (Iss: 4750, p 339); 30 Nov 1838 (Iss: 4752, p 345)

Newspaper coverage of debates
None

Archives
None

Notes
A further petition was lodged in following session: PRVB97

National Steel and Iron Company Notice 1839

PRVB94	1839
National Steel and Iron Company Notice 1839 (2 & 3 Vict)	
Table of contents (based on notice)	
[Cl 1 To incorporate a company by the name of the National Steel Iron-Company or to enable the said company to sue and be sued in the name of any member or officer] [Cl 2 To grant other powers to the company] [Cl 3 To give them a power to purchase certain Letters Patent]	
Relevant patent	
No information	
Representation	
Solicitor: Few, Hamilton and Few	
Gazette notices	
London Gazette: 2 Nov 1838 (Iss: 19,669, p 2381); 9 Nov 1838 (Iss: 19,671, p 2450); 14 Nov 1838 (Iss: 19,673, p 2508)	

Crauford, Fontainemoreau and Berry's Notice 1839

PRVB95	1839
Crauford, Fontainemoreau and Berry's Notice 1839 (2 & 3 Vict)	
Table of contents (based on notice)	
[Cl 1 Assignment of Letters Patent of William Crauford, Pierre Armand de Fontainemoreau and Miles Berry for Invention of Improved Modes of preserving or preventing the oxidation of iron and copper, or other metals to a company] [Cl 2 To enable the company to make, use and licence the said invention] [Cl 3 To incorporate the said company]	
Relevant patents	
29 Apr 1837 (No 7355)	Coating iron and copper, to prevent or other metals [Henry William Craufurd]
3 May 1838 (No 7630)	Alloying metals by cementation; – applicable to the preservation of copper, iron, and other metals [Miles Berry]
5 May 1838 (No 7635)	Preventing the oxidation of metals [Pierre Fontaineoreau (Le Comte de Armand)]
Representation	
Solicitor: Swain, Stephens & Co	
Gazette notices	
London Gazette: 14 Nov 1838 (Iss: 19,673, p 2523); 20 Nov 1838 (Iss: 19,675, p 2609); 30 Nov 1838 (Iss: 19,680, p 2779) Edinburgh Gazette: 13 Nov 1838 (Iss: 4747, p 328); 20 Nov 1838 (Iss: 4749, p 335); 27 Nov 1838 (Iss: 4751, p 342) Dublin Gazette: 13 Nov 1838 (No 12,988, p 701); 20 Nov 1838 (No 12,990, p 725); 27 Nov 1838 (No 12,992, p 741)	
Notes	
A further notice was issued with other patents in an earlier session: PRVB91	

David Mushet's Notice 1840

PRVB96	1840
David Mushet's Notice 1840 (3 & 4 Vict)	
Table of contents (based on notice)	
[Cl 1 For transferring or authorising the assignment to a company of letters patent granted to David Musket] [Cl 2 To confer powers on such company to sue and be sued] [Cl 3 For incorporating such company, and granting all other necessary or usual powers]	

(continued)

(continued)

Relevant patents	
22 Oct 1835 (No 6908)	Manufacture of bar-iron or malleable iron [David Mushet]

Representation
Solicitor: MacDougall and Upton

Gazette notices
London Gazette: 18 Oct 1839 (Iss: 19,779, p 1947); 25 Oct 1839 (Iss: 19,782 p 1998); 1 Nov 1839 (Iss:19,785, p 2062)

Daniel Stafford's Petition 1840

PRVB97	1840

Daniel Stafford's Petition 1840 (3 & 4 Vict)

Petition for a Bill for enabling the Trustees of Daniel Stafford to assign certain Letters Patent granted to him, for certain inventions on carriages, and for incorporating them

Table of contents (based on notice)
[Cl 1 To incorporate a Company with all proper and necessary powers] [Cl 2 To enable Daniel Stafford to assign to the company the Letters Patent in his invention for Improvement in Carriages] [Cl 3 To grant certain other privileges in relation to the Letters Patent]

Relevant patent	
24 Dec 1824 (No 5063)	Carriages [Daniel Stafford]
21 Dec 1838 (No 7919)	Carriages [Daniel Stafford] [extension of earlier patent for seven years]

Journal			
House of Commons			**House of Lords**
Rep: Thomas Greene			
24 Feb 1840	95 CJ 107	Pet	*Never considered by House of Lords*
5 Mar 1840	95 CJ 145	Pet Rep	

Representation
Solicitor: H. A.T. Vane

Parliamentary debates	
Pet: Mirror, 24 Feb 1840, Vol 2, p 1200 Rep: Mirror, 5 Mar 1840, Vol 2, p 1525	

Parliamentary papers and cases
None

Gazette notices
London Gazette: 16 Nov 1839 (Iss: 19,790, p 2267); 23 Nov 1839 (Iss: 19,794, p 2403); 26 Nov 1839 (Iss: 19,796, p 2418) Edinburgh Gazette: 19 Nov 1839 (Iss: 4853, p 314); 26 Nov 1839 (Iss: 4855, p 325); 29 Nov 1839 (Iss: 4856, p 329)

Newspaper coverage of debates
None

Archives
None

Notes
A Bill had been lodged in an earlier session: PRVB93

United Wood Paving Company's Bill 1840

PRVB98	1840
United Wood Company's Bill 1840 (3 & 4 Vict)	
Petition for a Bill for Incorporating the Petitioner and Others, by the name The United Wood Paving Company, with power to sue and be sued in the name of any Member or Officer of the Company, and for enabling the said company to purchase and hold certain letters patent granted to David Stead and Stephen Geary	

Table of contents (based on notice)
[Cl 1 To incorporate the United Wood Paving Company or to enable the company to be sued in the name of any Member or Officer]   [Cl 2 To grant powers to the company including the power to purchase Letters Patent for paving with timber or wooden blocks]

Relevant patents	
19 May 1838 (No 7645)	Making or paving streets, ways, roads, courts, and bridges, with timber or wooden blocks [David Stead]
23 Apr 1839 (No 8041)	Making and paving streets, ways, roads, paths, courts, and bridges, with timber or wooden block [David Stead]
1 Jun 1839 (No 8085)	Paving or covering streets, roads, and other ways [Stephen Geary]

Journal			
House of Commons			**House of Lords**
31 Jan 1840	95 CJ 50	Pet	*Never considered by House of Lords*

Representation
Solicitor: White and Borrett

Parliamentary debates	
Pet: Mirror, 31 Jan 1840, Vol 1, p 555	

Parliamentary papers and cases
None

Gazette notices
London Gazette: 16 Nov 1839 (Iss: 19,790, p 2267); 23 Nov 1839 (Iss: 19,794, p 2403); 26 Nov 1839 (Iss: 19,796, p 2418)   Edinburgh Gazette: 15 Nov 1839 (Iss: 4852, p 307); 22 Nov 1839 (Iss: 4854, p 321); 29 Nov 1839 (Iss: 4856, p 330)

Newspaper coverage of debates
None

Archives
None

Notes
A successful Bill was enacted relating to some of these patents in the next session: PRVA53

Robert Carey's Patent Notice 1840

PRVB99	1840
Robert Carey's Patent Notice 1840 (3 & 4 Vict)	

Table of contents (based on notice)
[Cl 1 Authorise the assignment to a company of certain Letters Patent granted to Robert Carey for certain improvements in paving or covering streets, roads and other ways]   [Cl 2 To make, use and vend the said invention]   [Cl 3 To incorporate a company and to give them powers for said ends]

Relevant patent	
29 Jan 1839 (No 7957)	Paving or covering streets, roads, or other ways [Robert Carey]

(continued)

(continued)

Representation
None
Gazette notices
London Gazette: 16 Nov 1839 (Iss: 19,790, p 2247); 23 Nov 1839 (Iss: 19,794, p 2391); 27 Nov 1839 (Iss: 19,797, p 2453)

Ambrose Johns' Patent Notice 1840

PRVB100	1840
	Ambrose Johns' Patent Notice 1840 (3 & 4 Vict)

Table of contents (based on notice)	
[Cl 1 Authorise the assignment, or transfer, to a company of certain Letters Patent granted to Ambrose Bowden Johns for invention of improvements in colouring or painting walls] [Cl 2 To make, use, license and vend the said invention] [Cl 3 To incorporate a company and to give them powers for said ends]	
Relevant patents	
1 Dec 1839 (No 7885)	Colouring or painting walls or other surfaces [Ambrose Bowden Johns]
19 Jun 1839 (No 8115)	Colouring or painting walls and other surfaces; preparing materials used for that purpose [Ambrose Bowden Johns] [It is not clear whether one or both of these patents were proposed to be held by the company]
Representation	
Solicitor: Little and Woolcombe	
Gazette notices	
London Gazette: 16 Nov 1839 (Iss: 19,790, p 2267); 23 Nov 1839 (Iss: 19,794, p 2403); 26 Nov 1839 (Iss: 19,796, p 2418)	

Robert Logan's Patent Notice 1840

PRVB101	1840
	Robert Logan's Notice 1840 (3 & 4 Vict)

Table of contents (based on notice)	
[Cl 1 Authorise the assignment, or transfer, to a company of certain Letters Patent granted to Robert Logan for invention of a new cloth constructed from Coca Nut Fibre and for improvements in preparing such fibrous material] [Cl 2 To make, use, license and vend the said invention] [Cl 3 To incorporate a company and to give them powers for said ends]	
Relevant patent	
11 Jan 1839 (No 7934)	Preparing cocoa-nut fibre for manufacturing [Robert Logan]
Representation	
No information	
Gazette notices	
London Gazette: 22 Nov 1839 (Iss: 19,793, p 2355); 26 Nov 1839 (Iss: 19,796, p 2414); 29 Nov 1839 (Iss: 19,798, p 2491)	

Michael Joseph John Donlan's Petition 1840

PRVB102	1840	
	Michael Joseph John Donlan's Petition 1840 (3 & 4 Vict)	
Petition for a Bill for enabling him to convey to a trading Company his Discoveries, inventions and improvements, for preparing, preserving and manufacturing articles of Hemp and Flax for and other purposes, secured to him by Patents and for enabling such Company to sue and be sued in the name of their Public Officers or Secretary for the time being		
Purpose		
No further details		
Relevant patent		
No information		
Journal		
House of Commons		**House of Lords**
31 Jan 1840	95 CJ 49	Pet	*Never considered by House of Lords*
Representation		
No information		
Parliamentary debates		
Pet: Mirror, 31 Jan 1840, p 555		
Parliamentary papers and cases		
None		
Gazette notices		
None		
Newspaper coverage of debates		
None		
Archives		
None		

Electric Telegraph Company Notice 1841

PRVB103	1841
Electric Telegraph Company Notice (5 Vict)	
Table of contents (based on notice)	
[Cl 1 To assign to a company certain letters patent] [Cl 2 To enable a company to make use, exercise and practise the inventions certain letters patent] [Cl 3 To incorporate the company and to enable it to sue and be sued]	
Relevant patents	
12 Jun 1837 (No 7390)	Giving signals and sounding alarum in distant places, by means of electric-currents transmitted through metallic-circuits [Charles Wheatstone and William Fothergill Cooke] {Scottish patent: 12 Dec 1837}
18 Apr 1838 (No 7614)	Giving signals and sounding alarum in distant places, by means of electric-currents transmitted through metallic-circuits [William Fothergill Cooke]
21 Jan 1840 (No 8345)	Giving signals and sounding alarum in distant places, by means of electric-currents transmitted through metallic-circuits [Charles Wheatstone and William Fothergill Cooke] {extends to Crown dependencies and colonies} {Scottish patent: 21 Aug 1840}
Representation	
Solicitor: WH Ashurt Solicitor: Robert Wilson	

(continued)

(continued)

Gazette notices
London Gazette: 14 Nov 1840 (Iss: 19,914, p 2573); 20 Nov 1840 (Iss: 19,917, p 2689); 25 Nov 80 (Iss 19,921, p 2801)   Edinburgh Gazette: 10 Nov 1840 (Iss: 4955, p 343); 17 Nov 1840 (Iss: 4957, p 355); 24 Nov 1840 (Iss: 4959, p 372)
Notes
A successful Bill which assigned a number of other patents was passed a few years later: see PRVA55

General Salvage Company Notice 1841

PRVB104	1841
General Salvage Company Notice 1841 (5 Vict)	

Table of contents (based on notice)
[Cl 1 To authorise the assignment of John William Fraser's patents to the General Salvage Company for improvements in apparatus for descending under water and for improvements in diving or descending or working under water and for raising and floating stranded vessels; and any future letters patent granted]   [Cl 2 To enable the Company to make, use exercise, license and vend the same invention]

Relevant patents (presumed)	
22 Jun 1835 (No 6852)	Apparatus for descending under water [John William Fraser]
15 Oct 1835 (No 6905)	Raising weights from below water to the surface of the same [John William Fraser]
14 Nov 1835 (No 6929)	Apparatus for descending under water [John William Fraser]
22 Jun 1835 (No 7696)	Raising or floating sunken and stranded vessels and other bodies [John William Fraser]

Representation
Solicitor: Martineau, Malton and Trollope
Gazette notices
London Gazette: 17 Nov 1840 (Iss: 19,915, p 2621); 25 Nov 1840 (Iss: 19,921, p 2806); 30 Nov 1840 (Iss: 19,924, p 2894)

William Hannis Taylor's Bill 1841

PRVB105	1841
William Hannis Taylor's Bill 1841 (5 Vict)	
Bill to enable William Hannis Taylor to sell and assign certain Letters Patent to a Joint Stock Company [Taylor's Patent Wood-cutting Company]	

Purpose
No further details

Relevant patent	
20 May 1840 (No 8512)	Improvements in the mode of forming or manufacturing Stave, Shingles and the Laths [William Hannis Taylor] [The petition before Parliament suggests 20 Mar 1840, but it appears to have be that granted on 20 May 1840]

Journal			
House of Commons			**House of Lords**
Rep: Thomas Greene SOC Rep: George Estcourt			*Never considered by House of Lords*
9 Feb 1841	96 CJ 33	Pet	
1 Mar 1841	96 CJ 87	Pet Rep/Ref SOC	
3 Mar 1841	96 CJ 95	SOC Rep/Must pub notices	

Representation
Agent: Elderton and Hoare

Parliamentary debates	
Pet: Mirror, 9 Feb 1841, Vol 1, p 176	
Pet Rep: Mirror, 1 Mar 1841, Vol 1, p 467	
SOC Rep: **Mirror, 3 Mar 1841, Vol 1, p 527**	
Parliamentary papers and cases	
None	
Gazette notices	
London Gazette: 18 Nov 1840 (Iss: 19,916, p 2652); 25 Nov 1840 (Iss: 19,921, p 2794); 30 Nov 1840 (Iss: 19,924, p 2890)	
Newspaper coverage of debates	
None	
Archives	
None	
Notes	
There was a further notice (PRVB109) and a bill (PRVB111) in subsequent sessions.	

Safety Rotation Railway Company Notice 1842

PRVB106	1842
Safety Rotation Railway Company Notice 1842 (5 & 6 Vict)	
Table of contents (relevant provisions only) (based on notice)	
[Cl 1 To incorporate The Safety Rotation Railway Company] [Cl 2 Company to sue and be sued in the name of one or more of the trustees or directors &c] [Cl 3 to authorise the purchase and exercise improvements in the construction of railways]	
Relevant patent	
3 Mar 1840 (No 8410)	Construction of railways; means of applying power to propelling carriages and machinery [John Rangeley]
Representation	
Solicitor: CB Wilson Agent: A Cassels Howden	
Gazette notices	
London Gazette: 12 Oct 1841 (Iss: 20,027, p 2517); 19 Oct 1841 (Iss: 20,029, p 2568); 26 Oct 1841 (Iss: 20,031, p 2626)	

David Redmund Notice 1842

PRVB107	1842
David Redmund Notice 1842 (5 & 6 Vict)	
Table of contents (relevant provisions only) (based on notice)	
[Cl 1 To authorise assignment to a company of certain Letters Patent granted to David Redmund; and of any other letters patent which may be granted for such improvements, so far as the same are applicable for canals] [Cl 2 To enable such company to make use, exercise, and vend the said improvements, or any of them, and to grant licences for making, using, exercising, and vending the same] [Cl 3 To incorporate the said company, or to give them power to sue and be sued in the name of directors or officers] [Cl 4 To grant other powers for the general regulations of the said company]	
Relevant patents	
18 Oct 1832 (No 6322)	Steam-engines [David Redmund]
28 Oct 1833 (No 6494)	Steam-carriages, applicable to other purposes [David Redmund]
10 Apr 1838 (No 7612)	Construction and apparatus of steam-boats, or vessels used for war or commerce [David Redmund]

(continued)

(continued)

Representation
Solicitor: Carchile, Cardale, and Iliffe

Gazette notices
London Gazette: 5 Nov 1841 (Iss: 20,034, p 2727); 13 Nov 1841 (Iss: 20,038, p 2824); 17 Nov 1841 (Iss: 20,040, p 2888) Edinburgh Gazette: 9 Nov 1841 (Iss: 5059, p 382); 16 Nov 1841 (Iss: 5062, p 398); 23 Nov 1841 (Iss: 5064, p 418)

National Floating Breakwater Bill 1842

PRVB108	1842

National Floating Breakwater Bill 1842 (5 & 6 Vict)

Bill for forming Breakwater Company Bill and regulating the National Floating Breakwater and Refuge Harbour Company, and to enable the said Company to purchase certain Letters Patent

Table of contents (based on notice)
[Cl 1 To authorise the assignment to a company of Letters Patent granted to Joseph Needham for the Invention of reducing the shock force of waves of the ocean] [Cl 2 To make, use, exercise and vend the Invention] [Cl 3 To incorporate a company and to give the company the right to sue and be sued in its name or that of directors or officers] [Cl 4 To grant powers for the general regulation of the company]

Relevant patent	
4 July 1838 (No 7718)	Abating or lessening the mischief arising from the force of the waves, and reducing waves to broken water, thereby preventing injury to breakwaters, mole-heads, piers, fortifications, lighthouses, docks, wharfs, landing-places, embankments, bridges; also adding security and defence to harbours and other places exposed to the action of the water [Joseph Needham Tayler]

Journal					
House of Commons			**House of Lords**		
Rep and Pres: Edward Strutt Rep Bill: Robert Vernon Smith			Rep SC: Lord Colborne		
18 Feb 1842	97 CJ 41	Pet	7 Jul 1842	74 LJ 399	Brought HC/1R
2 Mar 1842	97 CJ 77	Pet Rep/Bill Ord	18 Jul 1842	74 LJ 438	Ref SOC
11 Mar 1842	97 CJ 107	1R	22 Jul 1842	74 LJ 448	SOC Rep/Leave
15 Mar 1842	97 CJ 117	2R/C'tted	26 Jul 1842	74 LJ 459	2R/C'tted SC
5 Apr 1842	97 CJ 161	Ord produce patent	28 Jul 1842	74 LJ 483	Peers named
6 Apr 1842	97 CJ 163	Pet Ag	29 Jul 1842	74 LJ 488	Papers Ref
25 Apr 1842	97 CJ 221	Pet Ag	1 Aug 1842	74 LJ 496	Rep/Preamble not proven
2 May 1842	97 CJ 242	C'tee adj			
6 May 1842	97 CJ 262	Rep with Amds			
6 Jul 1842	97 CJ 456 – V	3R			

Petitions		
6 Apr 1842	97 CJ 163	Dame Mary Sophia Bentham
25 Apr 1842	97 CJ 221	Dame Mary Sophia Bentham

Representation
Solicitor: A Clarke

Parliamentary debates	
Debate (patent not valid): HC Deb, 5 Apr 1842, Vol 61(3rd), col 295–297	

Parliamentary papers and cases
None

Gazette notices
London Gazette: 17 Nov 1841 (Iss: 20,040, p 2905); 25 Nov 1831 (Iss: 20,044, p 3041); 30 Nov 1841 (Iss: 20,047, p 3113)

Newspaper coverage of debates
House of Commons
2R: **The Times, 16 Mar 1842**; **Morning Advertiser, 16 Mar 1842**; **Morning Post, 16 Mar 1842**; **Evening Mail, 16 Mar 1842**; **London Evening Standard, 16 Mar 1842**; **Freeman's Journal, 17 Mar 1842**; **Newcastle Courant, 18 Mar 1842**; *North Devon Journal, 17 Mar 1842*; *Kendal Mercury, 19 Mar 1842*; *Norwich Mercury, 19 Mar 1842*; *The Scotsman, 19 Mar 1842*; *Warwick and Warwickshire Advertiser, 19 Mar 1842*; *Windsor and Eton Express, 19 Mar 1842*; *Caledonian Mercury, 24 Mar 1842*; Worcester Journal, 17 Mar 1842; Liverpool Mercury, 18 Mar 1842; Bell's Weekly Messenger, 19 Mar 1842; Sussex Advertiser, 21 Mar 1842; Northern Standard, 26 Mar 1842; Enniskillen Chronicle and Erne Packet, 24 Mar 1842
Produce patent: **The Times, 6 Apr 1842**; **Morning Advertiser, 6 Apr 1842**; **Morning Chronicle, 6 Apr 1842**; **Morning Post, 6 Apr 1842**; **Evening Chronicle, 6 Apr 1842**; **London Evening Standard, 6 Apr 1842**; **Sussex Advertiser, 12 Apr 1842**; *Hull Advertiser and Exchange Gazette, 8 Apr 1842*; *The Scotsman, 9 Apr 1842*; *Warwick and Warwickshire Advertiser*; *Manchester Time, 9 Apr 1842*; John O'Groats Journal, 15 Apr 1842 (also see **The Times, 19 Apr 1842**)
3R: **Morning Advertiser, 7 Jul 1842**; **Morning Chronicle, 7 Jul 1842**; **Morning Post, 7 Jul 1842**; **London Evening Standard, 7 Jul 1842**; **Newcastle Courant, 8 Jul 1842**; *The Times, 7 Jul 1842*; *Bucks Herald, 9 Jul 1842*; *Dublin Evening Packet and Correspondent, 9 Jul 1842*; *Oxford Journal, 9 Jul 1842*; *Reading Mercury, 9 Jul 1842*; *The Scotsman, 9 Jul 1842*; *Bell's Weekly Messenger, 9 Jul 1842*; *Aris's Birmingham Gazette, 11 Jul 1842*; *Bell's Weekly Messenger, 11 Jul 1842*; *Inverness Courier, 13 Jul 1842*; *Royal Cornwall Gazette, 15 Jul 1842*; Buck Gazette, 9 Jul 1842; Newcastle, 9 Jul 1842; Northern Whig, 9 Jul 1842; Illustrated London News, 9 Jul 1842; West Kent Guardian, 9 Jul 1842; Manchester Courier and Lancashire General Advertiser, 9 Jul 1842; Carlisle Patriot, 9 Jul 1842
Comment about failure: **Morning Chronicle, 5 Aug 1842**; **Morning Post, 5 Aug 1842**; **London Evening Standard, 5 Aug 1842**
Archives
SOC Minutes: 22 Jul 1842 (p 136–137): HL/PO/CO/1/118
Opposed Bill C'tee Minutes: 1 Aug 1842 (p 162–167): HL/PO/CO/1/117
Opposed Bill Evidence, 1842, Vol 2: HL/PO/PB/5/8/2 [Dame Mary Bentham; Bickerton (Parliamentary Agent); John Charretie (Company Secretary); Ambrose Clare (Company Solicitor); Samuel Kettlewell (Civil Engineer); John Milnes; James Nevill (Civil Engineer); Nicholson (Parliamentary Agent); Richard Saumarez (Captain Royal Navy); Sladen (Parliamentary Agent); Talbot (Parliamentary Agent); Toriano (Counsel); unnamed]

William Hannis Taylor's and Francis Roubiliac's Notice 1843

PRVB109	1843
William Hannis Taylor's and Francis Roubiliac's Notice 1843 (6 & 7 Vict)	
Table of contents (based on notice)	
[Cl 1 To enable a Company to make, use, exercise, and vend the said several inventions and improvements, and each of them, and to grant licences for making, using, exercising, and vending the same] [Cl 2 To give the said Company power to sue and be sued in the name of one or more of their directors or officers, and to grant other powers for the general regulation of the Company] [Cl 3 Provision to enable William Hannis Taylor and Francis Roubiliac Conder to assign over to the said Company patents or improvements, with reference to the said several methods and improvements]	
Relevant patents	
20 May 1840 (No 8512)	Certain improvements in the mode of forming or manufacturing staves, shingles, and laths, and in the machinery used for that purpose [William Hannis]
23 Feb 1843 (No 9644)	Cutting and shaping of wood; machinery for that purpose [Francis Roubiliac Conder]
Representation	
Agent: Elderton and Hoare	
Gazette notices	
London Gazette: 4 Nov 1842 (Iss: 20,157, p 3044); 12 Nov 1842 (Iss: 20,160, p 3130); 19 Nov 1842 (Iss: 20,164, p 3277)	
Notes	
There was an earlier bill (PRVB105) as well as a subsequent bill (PRVB111)	

Stephen Goldner's Petition 1843

PRVB110	1843

Stephen Goldner's Petition 1843 (6 & 7 Vict)
Petition for a Bill to authorize the transfer to more than twelve person of certain Patents relating to Improvements in preserving Animal and Vegetable Substances and Liquids

Table of contents (based on notice)
[Cl 1 To authorise the transfer to more than twelve people of the Letters Patent granted to John Wertheimer and Stephen Goldner for an invention in the improvements in the preservation of animal and vegetable substances and liquids]

Relevant patents	
20 Jun 1839 (No 8117)	Preserving animal and vegetable substances and liquids [John Wertheimer][unclear if included in petition]
8 Feb 1840 (No 8378)	Preserving animal and vegetable substances and liquids [John Wertheimer] [unclear if included in petition]
8 Mar 1841 (No 8873)	Preserving animal and vegetable substances and fluids [Stephen Golder and John Wertheimer]

Journal				
House of Commons				**House of Lords**
Rep: Edward Strutt Rep: George Estcourt				*Never considered by House of Lords*
25 Feb 1842	97 CJ 67	Pet		
9 Mar 1842	97 CJ 98	Pet Rep/Ref SOC		
15 Mar 1842	97 CJ 116	SOC Rep/SOC not Disp		

Representation
Solicitor: Swain, Stevens, and Co

Parliamentary debates
None

Parliamentary papers and cases
None

Gazette notices
London Gazette: 25 Feb 1482 (Iss: 20,075, p 538); 1 Mar 1842 (Iss: 20,77, p 602); 8 Mar 1842 (Iss: 20,079, p 667)

Newspaper coverage of debates
None

Archives
None

General Wood-Cutting Company Bill 1843

PRVB111	1843

General Wood-Cutting Company Bill 1843 (6 & 7 Vict)
Bill for forming and regulating the General Wood-cutting Company, and to enable the said Company to purchase certain Letters Patent

Table of contents (based on notice)
[Cl 1 To authorise the assignment to, and purchase by, a Company of certain letters patent, granted to William Hannis Taylor and Francis Roubiliac Conder] [Cl 2 To enable Company to make, use, exercise, and vend the said several inventions and improvements] [Cl 3 To enable company to grant licences for making, using, exercising, and vending the same] [Cl 4 To give the said Company power to sue and be sued in the name of one or more of their directors or officers] [Cl 5 To grant other powers for the general regulation of the Company]

Relevant patents	
20 May 1840 (No 8512)	Mode of forming or manufacturing staves, shingles, and laths; and machinery used for that purpose [William Hannis Taylor]
23 Feb 1843 (No 9644)	Cutting and shaping wood; machinery for the purpose [Francis Roubiliac Conder]

Journal			
House of Commons			**House of Lords**
Rep: Henry Aglionby Pres: John Bowring			
24 Feb 1843	98 CJ 52	Pet	*Never considered by House of Lords*
23 Mar 1843	98 CJ 143	Pet Rep/Bill Ord	
24 Mar 1843	98 CJ 148	1R	

Representation
Agent: Elderton and Hoare

Parliamentary debates
None

Parliamentary papers and cases
None

Gazette notices
London Gazette: 4 Nov 1842 (Iss: 20,157, p 3044); 12 Nov 1842 (Iss: 20,160, p 3130); 14 Nov 1842 (Iss: 20,164, p 3277)

Newspaper coverage of debates
None

Archives
None

Notes
There was an earlier bill (PRVB105) and notice (PRVB109).

Aerial Transit Company Bill 1843

PRVB112	1843

Aerial Transit Bill 1843 (6 & 7 Vict)
Bill to authorise the Transfer to more than twelve persons of a Patent granted to William Samuel Henson, relating to Locomotive Apparatus and Machinery, and for the establishment of a Company for carrying out the Objects of the said Patent

Table of contents (based on notice)
[Cl 1 To authorise the assignment to a company of Letters Patent granted to William Samuel Henson for improvements in locomotive apparatus; and of any other Letters patent which may be granted for improvements] [Cl 2 To make, use, exercise and vend and licence the Letters Patent] [Cl 3 To incorporate the Company and give it power to sue or be sued in the name of the company, its directors or officers] [Cl 4 To grant other powers for the general regulation of the company]

Relevant patent	
16 Feb 1841 (No 8849)	Steam Engines [William Samuel Henson]

Journal			
House of Commons			**House of Lords**
Rep: Edward Strutt Pres: John Roebuck			
24 Feb 1843	98 CJ 54	Pet	*Never considered by the House of Lords*
24 Mar 1843	98 CJ 148	Pet Rep/Leave	
24 Mar 1843	98 CJ 148	1R	

Representation
Solicitor: DE Columbine

Parliamentary debates
None

Parliamentary papers and cases
None

(continued)

(continued)

Gazette notices
London Gazette: 19 Nov 1842 (Iss: 20,164 p 3295); 26 Nov 1842 (Iss: 20,170, p 3481); 30 Nov 1842 (Iss: 20,172, p 3555)
Newspaper coverage of debates
None
Archives
None

James Anthony Emslie Notice 1843

PRVB113	1843
James Anthony Emslie Notice 1843 (6 & 7 Vict)	
Table of contents (based on notice)	

[Cl 1 To authorize the assignment to, and purchase by, a company of more than twelve persons, of certain Letters Patent, granted to James Anthony Emslie]
[Cl 2 To enable such company to make use, exercise, and vend the said Letters Patent, and to grant licences for making, using, exercising, and vending the same]
[Cl 3 To incorporate the said company, or to give them power to sue and be sued in the names of one or more of their directors or officers]
[Cl 4 To grant other powers for the general regulations of the said company]

Relevant patent	
9 Jun 1842 (No 9386)	Pumps [James Anthony Emslie]
Representation	
No information	
Gazette notices	
London Gazette: 19 Nov 1842 (Iss: 20,164 p 3295); 26 Nov 1842 (Iss: 20,170, p 3481); 30 Nov 1842 (Iss: 20,172, p 3555)	

William Henry Stuckey Notice 1843

PRVB114	1843
William Henry Stuckey Notice 1843 (6 & 7 Vict)	
Table of contents (based on notice)	

[Cl 1 To authorize the assignment to, and purchase by, a company of more than twelve persons, of certain Letters Patent, granted to William Henry Stuckey]
[Cl 2 To enable the company to make use, exercise, and vend the said inventions and engines, and to grant licences for making, using, exercising, and vending the same]
[Cl 3 to give the company power to sue and be sued in the name of one or more of their directors or officers, and to grant other powers and privileges to the said company]
[Cl 4 To be made to enable the William Henry Stuckey to assign over to the said company any other patent or patents, with reference to the said inventions]

Relevant patent	
12 Jul 1842 (No 9419)	Pneumatic-engines for producing motive power [William Henry Stuckey]
Representation	
Solicitor: DE Columbine	
Gazette notices	
London Gazette: 19 Nov 1842 (Iss: 20,164 p 3295); 26 Nov 1842 (Iss: 20,170, p 3481); 30 Nov 1842 (Iss: 20,172, p 3555)	

William Henry Stuckey's Notice (No 2) 1843

PRVB115	1843
	William Henry Stuckey Notice (No 2) 1843 (6 & 7 Vict)

Table of contents (based on notice)
[Cl 1 To authorize the assignment to, and purchase by, a company of more than twelve persons, of certain Letters Patent, granted to William Henry Stuckey] [Cl 2 To enable such company to make, use, exercise, and vend the said inventions and improvements, and to grant licences for making, using, exercising, and vending the same] [Cl 3 To give the company power to sue and be sued in the name of one or more of their directors or officers, and to grant other powers and privileges to the company] [Cl 4 To enable the said William Henry Stuckey to assign over to the company any other patent or patents with reference to the said inventions and improvements]

3 Dec 1842 (No 9539)	Filtering water and other fluids [William Henry Stuckey]

Representation
No information

Gazette notices
London Gazette: 19 Nov 1842 (Iss: 20,164, p 3295); 26 Nov 1842 (Iss: 20,170, p 3481); 30 Nov 1842 (Iss: 20,172, p 3555)

British Watch and Clockmakers Company Bill 1843

PRVB116	1843
	British Watch and Clockmakers Company Bill (6 & 7 Vict)

Table of contents (based on notice)
[Cl 1 To authorize the assignment to, and purchase by, a company of more than twelve persons, of certain Letters Patent granted to Pierre Frederick Ingold] [Cl 2 To enable such company to make, use, exercise, and vend the said inventions and improvements, and to grant licences for making, using, exercising, and vending the same] [Cl 3 To give the said company power to sue and be sued in the name of one or more of their directors or officers] [Cl 4 To grant other powers and privileges to the said company] [Cl 5 To be made in the said Bill to enable the said Pierre Frederick Ingold to assign over to the said company any other patent or patents with reference to the said methods, inventions, and improvements]

Relevant patent
8 Nov 1842 (No 9511)	Machinery for making parts of watches and other timekeepers [Pierre Frederick Ingold]

Journal

House of Commons			House of Lords
Rep: Sir William Heathcote Pres: John Masterman			*Never considered by House of Lords*
24 Feb 1843	98 CJ 50	Pet	
9 Mar 1843	98 CJ 92	Pet Rep	
21 Mar 1843	98 CJ 134	1R	
31 Mar 1843	98 CJ 164	Pet Ag × 2	
31 Mar 1843	98 CJ 164 – V	2R adj 6m	

Petitions		
31 Mar 1843	98 CJ 164	Person connected with the Watch and Clock Trade present at meeting [Against]
31 Mar 1843	98 CJ 164	Coventry Watchmakers [Against]

Representation
No information

(continued)

(continued)

Parliamentary debates
2R adj: **HC Deb, 31 Mar 1843, Vol 68(3rd), col 273–285**

Parliamentary papers and cases
None

Gazette notices
London Gazette: 19 Nov 1842 (Iss: 20,164 p 3295); 26 Nov 1842 (Iss: 20,170, p 3481); 30 Nov 1842 (Iss: 20,172, p 3555)

Newspaper coverage of debates
2R: **The Globe, 31 Mar 1843; The Times, 1 Apr 1843**

Archives
None

General Steam Carriage Company Bill 1844

PRVB117	1844
	General Steam Carriage Company Bill 1844 (7 & 8 Vict)
	Bill for establishing and regulating a Company to be called The General Steam Carriage Company, and to enable the said Company to purchase certain Letters Patent

Table of contents (based on notice)
[Cl 1 To incorporate a certain joint stock Company or co-partnership, called or known by the name of The General Steam Carriage Company]
[Cl 2 Formed for the purpose of conveying passengers and goods on public roads, in carriages propelled by steam]
[Cl 3 To enable the said Company to sue and be sued in the name of some one or more-of their Directors or Officers]
[Cl 4 To raise, levy, and collect rates, duties, or charges in respect of the business conducted by them]
[Cl 5 To grant other powers and privileges to the said Company]
[Cl 6 To obtain powers to purchase letters patent, granted to Frank Hills and John Squire]
[Cl 7 To obtain powers for authorizing equitable tolls to be levied in respect of such carriages passing through any toll-gate]

Relevant patents	
29 Jan 1839 (No 7958)	Construction of steam-boilers, and locomotive engines [Frank Hills]
5 May 1840 (No 8495)	Construction of steam-boilers and engines, and locomotive-carriages [Frank Hills]
30 Mar 1843 (No 9684)	Steam-boilers; locomotive-carriages [Frank Hills]
21 Dec 1842 (No 9564)	Steam-boilers or generators [John Squire]

Journal			
House of Commons			House of Lords
Rep: Thomas Bramston Pres: James Emerson Tennent			
22 Feb 1844	99 CJ 50	Pet/Ref SOC	*Never considered by House of Lords*
6 Mar 1844	99 CJ 89	SOC Rep/Bill Ord	
18 Mar 1844	99 CJ 143	1R	

Representation
Solicitor: Risley and Chappell Agent: William Brydon

Parliamentary debates
None

Parliamentary papers and cases
None

Gazette notices
London Gazette: 8 Nov 1843 (Iss: 20,277, p 3652); 18 Nov 1843 (Iss: 20,283, p 3876); 25 Nov 1843 (Iss: 20,288, p 4072)
Newspaper coverage of debates
None
Archives
None

Bude Light Company Notice 1844

PRVB118	1844
Bude Light Company Notice (7 & 8 Vict)	
Table of contents (based on notice)	
[Cl 1 To incorporate a certain company by the name of the Bude Light Company] [Cl 2 To give the said company powers to sue and be sued in the name or names of one or more of its directors or officers, and to grant other powers to the said company] [Cl 3 To grant a power to enable the said company to purchase certain letters patent]	
Relevant patent	
No information	
Representation	
John Bethell	
Gazette notices	
London Gazette: 18 Nov 1843 (Iss: 20,283, p 3889); 23 Nov 1843 (Iss: 20,286, p 3969); 30 Nov 1843 (Iss: 20,291, p 4173)	

Pierre Frederick Ingold Notice 1844

PRVB119	1844
Pierre Frederick Ingold Notice 1844 (7 & 8 Vict)	
Table of contents (based on notice)	
[Cl 1 To authorize the assignment to and purchase by a company of more than twelve persons, of certain letters patent granted to Pierre Frederick Ingold] [Cl 2 To enable such company to make, use, exercise, and vend the said inventions and improvements] [Cl 3 To grant licences for making, using, exercising, and vending the same] [Cl 4 To give the said company power to sue and be sued in the name of one or more of their directors or officers] [Cl 5 To grant other powers and privileges to the said company] [Cl 6 To enable the said Pierre Frederick Ingold to assign over to the said company any other patent or patents with reference to the said inventions]	
Relevant patent	
1 Jun 1843 (No 9752)	Machinery for making parts of watches and other timekeepers [Pierre Frederick Ingold]
Representation	
Solicitor: Mullins and Paddison	
Gazette notices	
London Gazette: 16 Nov 1843 (Iss: 20,281, p 3801); 25 Nov 1843 (Iss: 20,288, p 4061); 30 Nov 1843 (Iss: 20,291, p 4189)	
Notes	
This is the same inventor, but a different patent, as that behind the British Watch and Clock Makers Bill: PRVB116	

Scottish Patent Wood Carving Company Notice 1846

PRVB120	1846
Scottish Patent Wood Carving Company Notice 1846 (9 & 10 Vict)	

Table of contents (based on notice)

[Cl 1 To incorporate and establish a company called the Scottish Patent Wood Carving Company, or to enable such company to sue and be sued in the name of any director or officer of the company]
[Cl 2 To enable such company to purchase and acquire certain letters patent for Scotland granted to Matthew Allen now owned by Hamilton Wood]
[Cl 3 To enable the Company to use, exercise and vend the invention]
[Cl 5 To enable them to purchase letters patent with reference to said invention]

Relevant patent

16 Dec 1841	An improvement in producing uneven surfaces on Wood [Matthew Allen] {Scottish patent: 2 Mar 1842}

Representation

Solicitor: Dundas & Jamieson

Solicitor (London): Deans, Dunlop & Hope

Gazette notices

Edinburgh Gazette: 14 Nov 1845 (Iss: 5483, p 605)

No other notices posted

Universal Salvage Company Notice 1846

PRVB121	1846
Universal Salvage Company Notice 1846 (9 & 10 Vict)	

Table of contents (based on notice)

[Cl 1 To incorporate and establish a company called the Universal Salvage Company, or to enable such company to sue and be sued in the name of any director or officer of the company]
[Cl 2 To enable such company, or any trustee or trustees on their behalf, to purchase from the General Salvage Company, or the trustees thereof, certain letters patent to Edward Austin]
[Cl 3 To enable the directors or trustees of the General Salvage Company to make an assignment of the said letters patent to the Universal Salvage Company]
[Cl 4 To carry out and confirm certain articles of agreement]
[Cl 5 To enable them to purchase certain letters patent Ireland, and Scotland, granted to the Edward Austin]
[Cl 6 To enable Edward Austin any other letters patent for improvements in raising, floating, or buoying sunken, wrecked, or distressed vessels or other bodies, or for lifting vessels over bars or shallow places, or other improvements in salvage operations]
[Cl 7 To exempt the company from Merchant Seaman Act 1845, s 5 and 63]

Relevant patent

12 May 1837 (No 7372)	Raising sunken vessels and other bodies [Edward Austin]

Representation

Solicitor for company: John Watson

Solicitor for Bill: Thomas Eyre Wyche

Gazette notices

London Gazette: 15 Nov 1845 (Iss: 20,534, p 4312); 22 Nov 1845 (Iss: 20,540, p 5752); 29 Nov 1845 (Iss: 20,546, p 6808)

William Irving's Notice 1846

PRVB122	1846
	William Irving's Notice 1846 (9 & 10 Vict)

Table of contents (based on notice)
[Cl 1 To authorize the assignment to a company of certain letters patent granted to William Irving]
[Cl 2 And of any other letters patent which may be hereafter granted for such improvements]
[Cl 3 To enable such company to accept such transfer or assignment, and to use and exercise the said patents or inventions]
[Cl 4 To grant licenses for using and exercising the same]
[Cl 5 To incorporate the said either to incorporate the said company, or to give them powers to sue and be sued in the name of one or more of their directors or officers]

Relevant patents	
25 Nov 1843 (No 9962)	Machinery and apparatus, for cutting and carving substances to be applied for inlaying and other purposes [William Irving]
10 Feb 1845 (No 10,517)	Construction of apparatus for cutting ornamental forms, beads, recesses, and mouldings in wood, stone, and other materials [William Irving]

Representation
Solicitor: Baker and Co

Gazette notices
London Gazette: 8 Nov 1845 (Iss: 20,528, p 3523); 12 Nov 1845 (Iss: 20,531, p 3926); 17 Nov 1845 (Iss: 20,535, p 4976)

Alexander Bain's Petition 1846

PRVB123	1846
	Alexander Bain's Petition 1846 (9 & 10 Vict)

Petition for a Bill to authorize Alexander Bain to assign certain Letters Patent to, and for forming and regulating a Company, to enable to company to work such Letters Patents

Purpose
No further details

Relevant patent
No information

Journal			
House of Commons			**House of Lords**
Rep: George Estcourt			
8 Mar 1846	101 CJ 659	Pet for late Pet	*Never considered by House of Lords*
12 May 1846	101 CJ 682	Pet Rep/SO Disp	
15 May 1846	101 CJ 706	Pet for Bill	
20 May 1846	101 CJ 733	Pet Ag	
26 May 1846	101 CJ 774	Rep SO ncw	
29 May 1846	101 CJ 792	SO Disp	

Petitions		
20 May 1846	101 CJ 733	Pet Ag: William Fothergill Cook [SO ncw]

Representation
No information

Parliamentary debates
None

Parliamentary papers and cases
None

Gazette notices
None

Newspaper coverage of debates
None

Archives
None

John McIntosh's Notice 1847

PRVB124	1847
John McIntosh's Notice 1847 (10 & 11 Vict)	
Table of contents (based on notice)	
[Cl 1 To authorise the assignment to a company or more than twelve individuals of the Letters Patent granted to John McIntosh for rotary engines] [Cl 2 To authorise the purchase of any other Letters Patent for any similar invention] [Cl 3 To authorise the assignment to the company of other interest or interests] [Cl 4 To Licence the Letters Patent] [Cl 5 To enable such company or persons to make, use, exercise, and vend such inventions and improvements] [Cl 6 To enable such company or persons to grant licenses, to make, use, exercise, and vend such revolving engines, methods, inventions, and improvements] [Cl 7 To enable such company or persons to sell or otherwise dispose of the privileges granted by Letters Patent] [Cl 8 To incorporate the said company, or to grant to the said company power to sue and be sued in the name or names of the said company, or one or more of the directors or officers] [Cl 9 To make provision and grant powers for the constitution and regulation of the company]	
Relevant patent	
17 May 1844 (No 10,189)	Rotary engines; producing motive-power; propelling vessels [John McIntosh] {extended to Channel Islands}
Representation	
Solicitor: Macdougall and Co	
Gazette notices	
London Gazette: 14 Nov 1846 (Iss: 20,665, p 4432); 21 Nov 1846 (Iss: 20,671, p 4960); 28 Nov 1846 (Iss: 20,677, p 5538)	

British and Irish Peat Company Notice 1850

PRVB125	1850
British and Irish Peat Company Notice 1850 (14 & 15 Vict)	
Table of contents (based on notice)	
[Cl 1 To authorise the assignment to by a Company to be incorporated, of Letters Patent granted to Rees Reece (and any future related Letters Patent)] [Cl 2 To enable or permit the Company to make use, exercise, and vend, and to sell and grant licences to the inventions or improvements] [Cl 3 To enable the patentees or grantees named in the Letters Patent to sell, transfer, assign and to grant licences in the Letters Patent] [Cl 4 To vary or extinguish all rights and privileges which the patentees or grantees named in the Letters Patent]	
Relevant patent	
23 Jan 1849 (No 12,436)	Treating peat and obtaining products therefrom [Rees Reece] {extended to Channel Islands and colonies; Scottish patent: 5 Feb 1849; Irish patent: 29 Aug 1849}
Representation	
Solicitor: Mullins and Paddison	
Gazette notices	
London Gazette: 26 Nov 1850 (Iss: 21,157, p 3173)	
Edinburgh Gazette: 26 Nov 1850 (Iss: 6024, p 1007)	
Dublin Gazette: 26 Nov 1850 (Iss: 14,370, p 895)	

Submarine Telegraph Company's Bill 1851

PRVB126	1851
Submarine Telegraph Company's Bill 1851 (14 & 15 Vict)	
Bill for incorporating and regulating a Company to establish a system of Submarine Electric Telegraph Communication between the Kingdom of England and France	

Table of contents (based on notice)	

[Cl 1 To enable the Company to make, construct, and use all other inventions and improvements relating to the transmission of electronic telegraph]
[Cl 2 To enable the Company to take assignments of any letters patents for the invention and improvement in electric telegraphs]
[Cl 3 To work and use the powers and privileges granted by such letters patent]
[Cl 4 To Licence, any use, any present or future letters patent belonging to person relating to telegraphic communications]
[Cl 5 To enable the Company to licence the use of any such inventions as may become vested in them]

Relevant patent
No information

Journal			
House of Commons			**House of Lords**
Pres: Sir Charles Burrell			
17 Feb 1851	106 CJ 52	Pet	*Never considered by House of Lords*
18 Feb 1851	106 CJ 59	1R	
28 Feb 1851	106 CJ 80	2R/C'tted	
6 May 1851	106 CJ 204	**Pet [Disp SO]**	
9 May 1851	106 CJ 212	Pet Ag	

Petitions		
6 May 1851	106 CJ 204	Promoter Disp SO
9 May 1851	106 CJ 212	John Parson for Manchester, Sheffield and Lincolnshire Railway Company [not Disp SO]

Representation
Solicitor: Edwards and Radcliffe

Parliamentary debates
None

Parliamentary papers and cases
None

Gazette notices
London Gazette: 26 Nov 1850 (Iss: 21,157, p 3207)
(Two notices for Great Britain to Ireland and England to France)
Dublin Gazette: 19 Nov 1850 (Iss: 14,368, p 863)

Newspaper coverage of debates

House of Commons

SO cw: Globe, 13 Feb 1851; Morning Advertiser, 13 Feb 1851; Caledonian Mercury, 17 Feb 1851

Ref SC: Morning Advertiser, 22 Apr 1851; London Daily News, 22 Apr 1852; Caledonian Mercury, 24 Apr 1851; Leicestershire Mercury, 26 Apr 1851; Newry Telegraph, 1 May 1851

Com: Morning Advertiser, 30 May 1851; London Daily News, 30 May 1851

Bill w/d: Globe, 3 Jun 1851; Morning Advertiser, 3 Jun 1851; London Daily News, 3 Jun 1851; London Evening Standard, 3 Jun 1851; Cork Constitution, 5 Jun 1851; Dundee, Perth and Cupar Advertiser, 6 Jun 1851; Huddersfield Chronicle, 7 Jun 1851; Staffordshire Advertiser, 7 Jun 1851; Yorkshire Gazette, 7 Jun 1851; Belfast News-Letter, 9 Jun 1851; Brechin Advertiser, 10 Jun 1851; Aberdeen Press and Journal, 11 Jun 1851; Worcestershire Chronicle, 11 Jun 1851; Durham Chronicle, 13 Jun 1851; Dublin Evening Packet and Correspondent, 14 Jun 1851; Cumberland Pacquet, 17 Jun 1851

Severn Steam Tug Bill 1851

PRVB127	1851
Severn Steam Tug Bill 1851 (14 &15 Vict)	
Bill for forming and regulating [the Severn Steam Tug Company] and enabling it to work certain Letters Patent	

(continued)

(continued)

Table of contents (based on notice)
[Cl 1 To incorporate a Company, and to transfer Cornelius Bonell's Letters Patent]
[Cl 2 To enable the same Company to use the invention]
[Cl 3 To grant licences to others for the use of the invention]

Relevant patent	
12 Oct 1849 (No 12,810)	Rotatory engines; construction of carriages, vessels, or other vehicles, to be worked or propelled by the said improvements in rotatory engines, or other motive-power; machinery connected therewith [Cornelius Bonell]

Journal			
House of Commons			**House of Lords**
Pres: Joseph Brotherton			
11 Feb 1851	106 CJ 33	Pet	*Never considered by House of Lords*
12 Feb 1851	106 CJ 41	Pres/1R	
18 Feb 1851	106 CJ 60	2R adj 6m	

Representation
Solicitor: Wilkinson, Gurney, and Stevens

Parliamentary debates
None

Parliamentary papers and cases
None

Gazette notices
None

Newspaper coverage of debates
London Gazette: 12 Nov 1850 (Iss: 21,152, p 2947)

Archives
None

Patent Marble Company Notice 1851

PRVB128	1851
Patent Marble Company Notice 1850 (14 & 15 Vict)	

Table of contents (based on notice)
[Cl 1 To authorise assignment of Letter Patent of Charles Iles and future Letters Patent in the invention for moulding]
[Cl 2 To enable the Company to make, use, and exercise the inventions, rights and licence the Letters Patent]
[Cl 3 To vary or extinguish all rights and privileges which the Patentees named in such Letters Patent may have]
[Cl 4 To provide for incorporating the Company and to sue and be sued in the name of the Company or one of the directors or officers]
[Cl 5 To generally regulate the Company using such powers and provisions as are usually inserted into such a Bills]

Relevant patent	
26 Apr 1849 (No 12,587)	Manufacture of picture-frames, inkstands, and other articles in dies or moulds; producing ornamental surfaces [Charles Iles]

Representation
Solicitor: Scott and Edwards

Gazette notices
London Gazette: 29 Nov 1850 (Iss: 21,158, p 3271)
Edinburgh Gazette: 29 Nov 1850 (Iss: 6025, p 1019)
Dublin Gazette: 29 Nov 1850 (Iss: 14,371, p 903)

Patent Inventions Society Bill 1851

PRVB129	1851

Patent Inventions Society Bill 1851 (14 & 15 Vict)

Bill for incorporating The Patent Inventions Society for the encouragement of Inventions and the Protection of Inventors

Table of contents (based on notice)
[Cl 1 To incorporate a Society or Company for the purpose of enquiring into the merits of inventions] [Cl 2 To aid inventors or patentees with the advance of money to obtain Letters Patent whether British or foreign for approved inventions; and to protect against infringements] [Cl 3 To regulate the management of the Society; and to authorise the Society to hold Letters Patent in certain cases and to receive profits in those Letters Patent] [Cl 4 To grant limited liability to stock holders]

Journal			
House of Commons			**House of Lords**
Pres: Lord John Manners			*Never considered by House of Lords*
20 Feb 1851	106 CJ 68	Pet	
24 Feb 1851	106 CJ 75	Pres/1R	
7 Mar 1851	106 CJ 86	2R/C'tted	

Representation
Agent: Burchell and Parsons

Parliamentary debates
None

Parliamentary papers and cases
None

Gazette notices
London Gazette: 26 Nov 1850 (Iss: 21,157, p 3165)
Edinburgh Gazette: 26 Nov 1850 (Iss: 6024, p 1009)
Dublin Gazette: 26 Nov 1850 (Iss: 14,370, p 895)

Newspaper coverage of debates
None

Archives
None

Patent Inventions Society Notice 1852

PRVB130	1852

Patent Inventions Society Notice 1852 (15 & 16 Vict)

Table of contents (based on notice)
[Cl 1 To incorporate a Society or Company for the purpose of enquiring into the merits of inventions] [Cl 2 To aid inventors or patentees with the advance of money to obtain Letters Patent whether British or foreign for approved inventions; and to protect against infringements] [Cl 3 To regulate the management of the Society; and to authorise the Society to hold Letters Patent in certain cases and to receive profits in those Letters Patent] [Cl 4 To grant limited liability to stock holders]

Representation
Agent: George Henry Drew

Gazette notices
London Gazette: 28 Nov 1851 (Iss: 21,268, p 3335)
Edinburgh Gazette: 28 Nov 1851 (Iss: 6129, p 1102)
Dublin Gazette: 18 Nov 1851 (Iss: 14,478, p 966)

Use of Grant's Apparatus Bill 1852

PRVB131	1852
	Use of Grant's Apparatus Bill 1852 (15 & 16 Vict)

Bill for further amending the Act for regulating the Construction and the Use of Buildings in the Metropolis and its Neighbourhood [Authorizing the use of Grant's Apparatus/Metropolitan Building Act Further Amendment]

Table of contents
[Cl 1] Authorizing the Use of Apparatus for ventilating Buildings; notwithstanding [Metropolitan Buildings Act 1844]

Relevant patent	
18 Apr 1844 (No 10,146)	Ventilation of apartments in which gas and other combustible matters are consumed by ignition [Donald Grant]

Journal

House of Commons			House of Lords		
				Pres: Viscount Hutchinson Rep: Lord Redesdale (Ld Ch)	
21 Jul 1853	108 CJ 702	Brought HL	25 Nov 1852	85 LJ 35	Pres/1R
22 Jul 1853	108 CJ 708	1R	4 Jul 1853	85 LJ 425	2R day app
26 Jul 1853	108 CJ 723	2R adj 3m	12 Jul 1853	85 LJ 475	2R/C'tted CWH
			14 Jul 1853	85 LJ 486	CWH
			18 Jul 1853	85 LJ 498	Rep with Amds
			19 Jul 1853	85 LJ 504	3R
			19 Aug 1853	85 LJ 710	**Pet for relief**

Representation
No information

Parliamentary debates
None

Parliamentary papers and cases
Report on Petition of Donald Grant, respecting his patent for Ventilation (1846 HL Papers 261), Vol 26, p 1 [Reprinted (1852–53 HL Papers 17), Vol 31, p 693] (reprint order 25 Nov 1852, 85 LJ 35)
Further report on Petition of Donald Grant, respecting his patent for Ventilation (1847–48 HL Papers 66), Vol 24. p 633 [Reprinted (1852–53 HL Papers 17), Vol 31, p 713]
Bill for further amending the Act for regulating the Construction and the Use of Buildings in the Metropolis and its Neighbourhood [Authorizing the use of Grant's Apparatus] (1852–53 HL Papers 19), Vol 4, p 495
Bill for further amending the Act for regulating the Construction and the Use of Buildings in the Metropolis and its Neighbourhood [Authorizing the use of Grant's Apparatus] (as amended in Committee) (1852–53 HL Papers 304), Vol 4, p 495
Bill for further amending the Act for regulating the Construction and the Use of Buildings in the Metropolis and its Neighbourhood [Authorizing the use of Grant's Apparatus] (1852–53 HC Papers 808), Vol 5, p 37

Gazette notices
None

Newspaper coverage of debates
None

Archives
Proceedings at Select Committee (1846): 16 Jul 1846 (p 218–219); 23 Jul 1846 (p 219); 4 Aug 1846 (p 261–263) [includes printed report]: HL/PO/CO/1/136

Notes
Petition - PET223

Severn Steam Tug Bill 1852

PRVB132	1852
	Severn Steam Tug Bill 1852 (15 & 16 Vict)

Bill for forming and regulating [the Seven Steam Tug Company] and enabling it to work certain Letters Patent

Table of contents (based on notice)
[Cl 1 To authorise the laying down of flexible iron cable along a stated route]
[Cl 2 To incorporate a company for the purposes of that undertaking]
[Cl 3 To enable the company to enter agreements with Commissioners for navigation]
[Cl 4 To vest in the Company the Letters Patent granted to Conelius Bonell for certain improvements in rotary engines]
[Cl 5 To enable the Company to grant licenses to the use the invention]
[Cl 5 To enable the Company to charge rates or dues for the use of their steam tugs, works, and apparatus]
[Cl 6 To vary, repeal, or extinguish all rights or privileges which would in any manner impede or interfere with the works or objects, or any of them, and to confer other powers]

Relevant patent	
12 Oct 1849 (No 12,810)	Rotatory Engines; construction of carriages, vessels, or other vehicles to be worked or propelled by means of the said improvements in rotatory engines, by or other motive-power; machinery connected therewith [Cornelius Bonell]

Journal			
House of Commons			**House of Lords**
Rep: Joseph Brotherton			*Never considered by House of Lords*
15 Mar 1852	107 CJ 90	Pet/Bill Ord	
16 Mar 1852	107 CJ 93	Pet w/d	
16 Mar 1852	107 CJ 96	Pet for Bill/Ref SOC	
18 Mar 1852	107 CJ 99	Pet Ag	
22 Mar 1852	107 CJ 107	Pet Ag	
26 Mar 1852	107 CJ 124	SOC 151 Disp	
29 Mar 1852	107 CJ 129	SOC Rep/Bill Ord	
1 Apr 1852	107 CJ 137	Disc/Bill Ord/1R	
20 Apr 1852	107 CJ 158	2R Disc/Bill w/d	

Petitions		
18 Mar 1852	107 CJ 99	Dyson & Co against SO Disp
22 Mar 1852	107 CJ 107	Thomas Waters, Clerks to Navigation of Severn River, against SO Disp

Representation
Agent: H Brooks

Parliamentary debates
None

Parliamentary papers and cases
None

Gazette notices
London Gazette: 28 Nov 1851 (Iss: 21,268, p 3335)

Newspaper coverage of debates
House of Commons
2R: Globe, 21 Apr 1852; Morning Chronicle, 21 Apr 1852; Worcestershire Chronicle, 21 Apr 1852

Archives
None

Permanent Way Company Bill 1852

PRVB133	1846
Permanent Way Company Bill 1852 (15 & 16 Vict)	
Bill for Incorporating a company to work Letters Patent relating to the Permanent Way of Railways	

Table of contents (based on notice)
[Cl 1 To incorporate a Company with no limit or restriction in respect of numbers for the purpose of working Letters Patent granted to William Henry Barlow, Peter William Barlow, William Bridges Adams, Robert Richardson and James Samuel relating to the construction of the permanent way of railways]
[Cl 2 To transfer to or vest in the said Company several letters patent (and future letters patent)]
[Cl 3 To authorize the sale, purchase, and transfer to the Company of the benefit of all and every or any other Letters Patent granted, or which may hereafter be granted to any of the named persons]

(continued)

(continued)

Relevant patents	
23 Jan 1849 (No 12,438)	Construction of permanent ways of railway [William Henry Barlow]
14 Jun 1849 (No 12,659)	Permanent ways of railways [Peter William Barlow] {Scottish patent: 14 Nov 1849}
3 Jan 1850 (No 12,917)	Permanent ways of railways [William Henry Barlow and Peter William Barlow] {Scottish patent: 22 July 1850; Irish patent: 5 Oct 1850}
24 May 1847 (No 11,715)	Construction of railways; engines, and carriages used thereon; also transport and storage arrangements for the conveyance, management, and preservation of perishable articles [William Bridges Adams and Robert Richardson] {Scottish patent: 27 Jul 1848; Irish patent: 7 Aug 1848; both granted to William Bridges Adams only}
5 Apr 1850 (No 13,029)	Construction of railways and steam-engines; machinery for the same [James Samuel] {Scottish patent: 12 Nov 1850}

Journal			
House of Commons			**House of Lords**
Pres: Joseph Brotherton Rep: Lord Hotham			
13 Feb 1852	107 CJ 42	Bill Ord	*Never considered by House of Lords*
16 Feb 1852	107 CJ 47	1R	
23 Feb 1852	107 CJ 72	2R/C'tted	
20 May 1852	107 CJ 226	Rep/not proc	

Representation
Solicitor: Hodgson, Concanen, and Noyes Agent: Philetus Richardson

Parliamentary debates
None

Parliamentary papers and cases
None

Gazette notices
London Gazette: 28 Nov 1851 (Iss: 21,268, p 3321)
Edinburgh Gazette: 28 Nov 1851 (Iss: 6129, p 1100)
Dublin Gazette: 28 Nov 1851 (Iss: 14,478, p 960)

Newspaper coverage of debates
House of Commons
2R: Globe, 24 Feb 1852; Morning Advertiser, 24 Feb 1852; Morning Chronicle, 24 Feb 1852; Morning Post, 24 Feb 1852; London Daily News, 24 Feb 1852; London Evening Standard, 24 Feb 1852

Archives
None

Imperial Parafine and Peat Bill 1852

PRVB134	1852
Imperial Parafine and Peat Bill 1852 (15 & 16 Vict)	
Bill to incorporate the Company, and to enable them to work certain Letters Patent	
Table of contents (based on notice)	

[Cl 1 To authorize the assignment of Rees Reeces's Letter Patent and any future letters patent relating to the invention]
[Cl 2 To permit the Company to make, use, exercise, and vend, and to sell and grant licenses in relation to the Inventions or improvements]
[Cl 3 To enable the patentees and grantees named in the Letters Patent and every person in whom such letters patent vested to sell, transfer and grant licenses for the Invention]
[Cl 4 To confirm all agreements already entered into by the Irish Peat Company for the purchase and use of the Letters Patent]
[CL 5 To vary or extinguish all rights and privileges of the patentees or grantees of the Letters Patent]
[Cl 6 If need be, to reincorporate the Irish Peat Company, a company with a Royal Charter of Incorporation, as a Company under the Act]

Relevant patent	
23 Jan 1849 (No 12,436)	Treating peat and obtaining products therefrom [Rees Reece] {extended to Channel Islands and colonies; Scottish patent: 5 Feb 1849}

Journal	
House of Commons	**House of Lords**

House of Commons			House of Lords
Pres: Joseph Brotherton Rep: Ralph Bernal (Ch W&M)			
11 Feb 1852	107 CJ 33	Pet/Bill Ord	*Never considered by House of Lords*
12 Feb 1852	107 CJ 38	1R	
17 Feb 1852	107 CJ 53	2R/C'tted	
24 Feb 1852	107 CJ 236	Rep with Amds	

Representation
Solicitor: Mullins and Paddisons

Parliamentary debates
None

Parliamentary papers and cases
None

Gazette notices
London Gazette: 18 Nov 1851 (Iss: 21,264, p 3048)
Edinburgh Gazette: 21 Nov 1851 (Iss: 6127, p 1070)
Dublin Gazette: 25 Nov 1851 (Iss: 14,477, p 937)

Newspaper coverage of debates
House of Commons 2R: Morning Advertiser, 18 Feb 1852; Morning Chronicle, 18 Feb 1852; Morning Post, 18 Feb 1852; London Daily News, 18 Feb 1852; London Evening Standard, 18 Feb 1852;

Archives
Unopposed C'tee Minutes: 1 Apr 1852 (p 21); 29 Apr 1852 (p 41); 10 May 1852 (p 46); 24 May 1852 (p 49): HC/CL/WM/UB/1/3

English and Australian Copper Company's Bill 1853

PRVB135	1853
English and Australian Copper Company's Bill 1853 (16 & 17 Vict)	
Bill for incorporating the English and Australian Copper Company; for enabling such Company to raise additional Capital, and to take an Assignment of certain Letters Patent	

Table of contents (based on notice)
[Cl 1 To enable the English and Australian Copper Company to purchase Letters Patent belonging to James Napier, Alfred Trueman and John Cameron; and any future Letters Patent granted to those persons] [Cl 2 To vary or extinguish the rights and privileges which the patentees or grantees might have in the Letters Patent and confer the same rights on the Company] [Cl 3 To enable the company to raise more by share or loan than it is currently authorised to do] [Cl 4 To enable the company to purchase and hold lands] [Cl 5 To insert such clauses as are usually included in Bills of this sort]

Relevant patents	
20 Jul 1846 (No 11,301)	Smelting copper-ores [James Napier] {extends to Crown dependencies and colonies}
2 Mar 1847 (No 11,600)	Smelting copper and other ores [James Napier] {extends to Crown dependencies and colonies}
4 Mar 1852 (No 13,996)	Obtaining copper from ore [Alfred Trueman and John Cameron] {extends to Crown dependencies and colonies}

(continued)

(continued)

Journal	
House of Commons	**House of Lords**
Pres: Benjamin Oliveira	
22 Feb 1853 · 108 CJ 268 · Pet/Bill Ord 25 Feb 1853 · 108 CJ 286 · 1R 4 Mar 1853 · 108 CJ 308 · 2R day app 7 Mar 1853 · 108 CJ 313 · 2R adj 18 Mar 1853 · 108 CJ 351 · 2R disc	*Never considered by House of Lords*
Representation	
Solicitor: CS Gilman	
Parliamentary debates	
None	
Parliamentary papers and cases	
None	
Gazette notices	
London Gazette: 12 Nov 1852 (Iss: 21,379, p 2982)	
Newspaper coverage of debates	
None	
Archives	
None	

Pownall's Patent Flax Company Notice 1853

PRVB136	1853
	Pownall's Patent Flax Company Notice 1853 (16 & 17 Vict)
Table of Contents (based on notice)	

[Cl 1 To authorize the assignment of Letters Patent granted to Charles James Pownall for treating fibrous materials (and any other existing or any future letters patent relating to the invention)]
[Cl 2 To authorize the assignment to the Company of any interest or license under the said letters patent]
[Cl 3 To permit the Company to sell, lease, and grant licenses for the use and exercise of improvements]
[Cl 4 To permit the Company to make, use, and exercise the inventions, rights, and privileges granted by, or incident to such letters patent]
[Cl 5 To incorporate the Company and limit the responsibility of shareholders]
[Cl 6 To enable persons to sue and be sued in the name of the Company or one or more of the directors or officers]
[Cl 7 To vary or extinguish all rights and privileges which the patentee or grantee named in such letters patent]

Relevant patent	
15 Jul 1852 (No 14,224)	Treatment and preparation of flax and other fibrous vegetable substances [Charles James Pownall]
Representation	
Agent: RH Wyatt	
Gazette notices	
London Gazette: 30 Nov 1852 (Iss: 21,386, p 3485)	

Patent Office Bill 1864

PRVB137	1864
	Patent Office Bill 1864 (27 & 28 Vict)
Bill to enable the Inventors Association (Limited) to acquire a Site in the Parish of Saint Andrew, Holborn, in the County of Middlesex, for a Patent Office, and for other Purposes	

Table of contents (based on House Bill)
Cl 1 Short Title Cl 2 Incorporation of Lands Clauses Consolidation Acts, 1845 and 1860 Cl 3 Same meaning to words in this and incorporated Acts Cl 4 Power to take lands Cl 5 Period within which lands are to be purchased by compulsion Cl 6 Power to stop up streets, &c Cl 7 Costs of Act

Journal				
House of Commons		**House of Lords**		
		Pres: Lord Redesdale (Ld Ch)		
Never considered by House of Commons		22 Feb 1864	96 LJ 39	Ex Cert/SO cw
		26 Feb 1864	96 LJ 47	1R

Representation
No information

Parliamentary debates
None

Parliamentary papers and cases
None

Gazette notices
None

Newspaper coverage of debates
None

Archives
House Bill: HL/PO/JO/10/9/555

Shepard's Patent Bill 1865

PRVB138	1865
	Shepard's Patent Bill 1865 (28 & 29 Vict)
Bill for rendering valid certain Letters Patent granted to William Albert Shepard of Pall Mall in the County of Middlesex	

Table of contents (from House Bill)
Cl 1 Power of Commissioners to stamp Letters Patent Cl 2 Letters Patent confirmed Cl 3 Saving of rights Schedule

Relevant patent	
7 Nov 1861 (No 2800)	Preparing and Treating Gutta Percba and India Rubber [William Albert Shepard]

Journal					
House of Commons			**House of Lords**		
			Pres: Lord Westbury LC		
13 Feb 1865	120 CJ 48	Bill originate HL	13 Feb 1865	97 LJ 17	Ex Cert/SO cw
24 Feb 1865	120 CJ 92	Ex Cert	14 Feb 1865	97 LJ 21	1R

Representation
Solicitor: H. Wellington Vallance
Agent: Wyatt and Metcalf

Parliamentary debates	
	2R adj: HL Deb, 24 Feb 1865, Vol 177(3rd), col 635
	2R not moved: HL Deb, 27 Feb 1865, Vol 177(3rd), col 736

(continued)

(continued)

Parliamentary papers and cases
None

Gazette notices
London Gazette: 22 Nov 1864 (Iss: 22,914, p 5763)
Edinburgh Gazette: 25 Nov 1864 (Iss: 7487, p 1605)
Dublin Gazette: 25 Nov 1864 (Iss: 15,845, p 1311)

Newspaper coverage of debates
House of Lords
2R adj: **The Times, 25 Feb 1865; Morning Post, 25 Feb 1865; London Daily News, 25 Feb 1865; London Evening Standard, 25 Feb 1865**; *Morning Advertiser, 25 Feb 1865*
2R not moved: **The Times, 28 Feb 1865; Morning Advertiser, 28 Feb 1865; Morning Post, 28 Feb 1865; London Daily News, 28 Feb 1865; London Evening Standard, 28 Feb 1865; Birmingham Daily Gazette, 28 Feb 1865; Caledonian Mercury, 28 Feb 1865; Dublin Evening Mail, 28 Feb 1865; Evening Freeman, 28 Feb 1865; Glasgow Herald, 28 Feb 1865; Glasgow Morning Journal 28 Feb 1865; Leeds Mercury, 28 Feb 1865; Liverpool Mercury, 28 Feb 1865; Northern Whig, 28 Feb 1865; Saunders's News-Letter, 28 Feb 1865; Sheffield Daily Telegraph, 28 Feb 1865; Sheffield Independent, 28 Feb 1865; Southern Reporter and Cork Commercial Courier, 28 Feb 1865; Western Daily Press, 28 Feb 1865; Western Morning News, 28 Feb 1865; Belfast Morning News, 1 Mar 1865; Armagh Guardian, 3 Mar 1865; Cardiff and Merthyr Guardian, 3 Mar 1865; Elgin Courier, 3 Mar 1865; Royal Cornwall Gazette, 3 Mar 1865**

Archives
House Bill: HL/PO/JO/10/9/585

Wright's Patent Bill 1865

PRVB139	1865
Wright's Patent Bill 1865 (28 & 29 Vict)	
Bill for rendering valid Letters Patent granted to John Wright for Improvements in preparing or treating Strips of Steel for hardening and tempering	

Table of contents (from House Bill)
Cl 1 Power to stamp Letters Patent Cl 2 Letters Patent confirmed Cl 3 Saving Rights Cl 4 Name of Act Schedule

Relevant patent	
16 Oct 1857 (1857 No 2649)	Improvements in preparing or treating Strips of Steel for hardening and tempering [John Wright]

Journal					
House of Commons			**House of Lords**		
				Pres: Lord Westbury LC	
13 Feb 1865	120 CJ 48	Bill originate HL	13 Feb 1865	97 LJ 17	Ex Cert/SO cw
24 Feb 1865	120 CJ 92	Ex Cert	14 Feb 1865	97 LJ 22	1R

Representation
Solicitor: Smith & Burdekin

Parliamentary debates
2R adj: HL Deb, 24 Feb 1865, Vol 177(3rd), col 635
2R not moved: HL Deb, 27 Feb 1865, Vol 177(3rd), col 736

Parliamentary papers and cases
None

Gazette notices
London Gazette: 29 Nov 1864 (Iss: 22,916, p 6219)
Edinburgh Gazette: 29 Nov 1864 (Iss: 7488, p 1637)
Dublin Gazette: 29 Nov 1864 (Iss: 15,846, p 1368)

Newspaper coverage of debates
House of Lords
2R adj: **The Times, 25 Feb 1865**; **Morning Post, 25 Feb 1865**; **London Daily News, 25 Feb 1865**; **London Evening Standard, 25 Feb 1865**; *Morning Advertiser, 25 Feb 1865*
2R not moved: **The Times, 28 Feb 1865**; **Morning Advertiser, 28 Feb 1865**; **Morning Post, 28 Feb 1865**; **London Daily News, 28 Feb 1865**; **London Evening Standard, 28 Feb 1865**; **Birmingham Daily Gazette, 28 Feb 1865**; **Caledonian Mercury, 28 Feb 1865**; **Dublin Evening Mail, 28 Feb 1865**; **Evening Freeman, 28 Feb 1865**; **Glasgow Herald, 28 Feb 1865**; **Glasgow Morning Journal 28 Feb 1865**; **Leeds Mercury, 28 Feb 1865**; **Liverpool Mercury, 28 Feb 1865**; **Northern Whig, 28 Feb 1865**; **Saunders's News-Letter, 28 Feb 1865**; **Sheffield Daily Telegraph, 28 Feb 1865**; **Sheffield Independent, 28 Feb 1865**; **Southern Reporter and Cork Commercial Courier, 28 Feb 1865**; **Western Daily Press, 28 Feb 1865**; **Western Morning News, 28 Feb 1865**; **Belfast Morning News, 1 Mar 1865**; **Armagh Guardian, 3 Mar 1865**; **Cardiff and Merthyr Guardian, 3 Mar 1865**; **Elgin Courier, 3 Mar 1865**; **Royal Cornwall Gazette, 3 Mar 1865**

Archives
House Bill: HL/PO/JO/10/9/587

Spencer's Patent Bill 1865

PRVB140	1865
	Spencer's Patent Bill 1865 (28 & 29 Vict)

Bill for rendering valid certain Letters Patent granted to John Fredrick Spencer, late of Brighton in the County of Sussex, but now of Saint Nicholas Buildings, Newcastle-on-Tyne, in the County of Northumberland, Marine Engineer

Table of contents (from House Bill)
Cl 1 Power of Commissioners to stamp Letters Patent Cl 2 Letters Patent confirmed Cl 3 Saving of rights Schedule

Relevant patent	
16 Nov 1857 (1857 No 2874)	Invention of obtain improvements in steam engines and in the apparatus connected therewith [John Fredrick Spencer]

Journal					
House of Commons			**House of Lords**		
			Pres: Lord Redesdale (Ld Ch)		
13 Feb 1865	120 CJ 48	Bill originate HL	14 Feb 1865	97 LJ 22	Ex Cert
24 Feb 1865	120 CJ 92	Ex Cert	17 Feb 1865	97 LJ 27	1R

Representation
Solicitor: Elliot and Pierce
Agent: Henry Moon

Parliamentary debates
2R adj: HL Deb, 24 Feb 1865, Vol 177(3rd), col 635
2R not moved: HL Deb, 27 Feb 1865, Vol 177(3rd), col 736

Parliamentary papers and cases
None

Gazette notices
London Gazette: 29 Nov 1864 (Iss: 22,916, p 6271)
Edinburgh Gazette: 29 Nov 1864 (Iss: 7488, p 1637)
Dublin Gazette: 29 Nov 1864 (Iss: 15,846, p 1368)

(continued)

(continued)

Newspaper coverage of debates
House of Lords
2R adj: **The Times, 25 Feb 1865; Morning Post, 25 Feb 1865; London Daily News, 25 Feb 1865; London Evening Standard, 25 Feb 1865;** *Morning Advertiser, 25 Feb 1865*
2R not moved: **The Times, 28 Feb 1865; Morning Advertiser, 28 Feb 1865; Morning Post, 28 Feb 1865; London Daily News, 28 Feb 1865; London Evening Standard, 28 Feb 1865; Birmingham Daily Gazette, 28 Feb 1865; Caledonian Mercury, 28 Feb 1865; Dublin Evening Mail, 28 Feb 1865; Evening Freeman, 28 Feb 1865; Glasgow Herald, 28 Feb 1865; Glasgow Morning Journal 28 Feb 1865; Leeds Mercury, 28 Feb 1865; Liverpool Mercury, 28 Feb 1865; Northern Whig, 28 Feb 1865; Saunders's News-Letter, 28 Feb 1865; Sheffield Daily Telegraph, 28 Feb 1865; Sheffield Independent, 28 Feb 1865; Southern Reporter and Cork Commercial Courier, 28 Feb 1865; Western Daily Press, 28 Feb 1865; Western Morning News, 28 Feb 1865; Belfast Morning News, 1 Mar 1865; Armagh Guardian, 3 Mar 1865; Cardiff and Merthyr Guardian, 3 Mar 1865; Elgin Courier, 3 Mar 1865; Royal Cornwall Gazette, 3 Mar 1865**

Archives
House Bill: HL/PO/JO/10/9/585

Henry William Putnam's Notice 1871

PRVB141	1871
Henry William Putnam's Notice 1871 (34 & 35 Vict)	
Table of contents (based on notice)	
[Cl 1 To continue and confirm certain Letters-paten granted to Henry William Putnam (and transferred to James Miller)] [Cl 2 To enable the said James Miller to pay the Stamp-duty on the said Letters-patent]	
Relevant patent	
6 Nov 1863 (1863 No 2132)	An improved machine for wringing clothes [Henry Putnam]
Representation	
Solicitor: Connell & Hope	
Gazette notices	
London Gazette: 29 Nov 1870 (Iss: 23,683, p 5585)	
Edinburgh Gazette: 29 Nov 1870 (Iss: 8115, p 1474)	
Dublin Gazette: 29 Nov 1870 (Iss: 16,490, p 1579)	

Shaw's Patent (Lining Lead Pipes) Bill 1871

PRVB142	1871
Shaw's Patent (Lining Lead Pipes) Bill 1871 (34 & 35 Vict)	
Bill to continue and confirm certain Letters Patent granted to William Anthony Shaw of the City and State of New York in the United States of America	
Table of contents (from House Bill)	
Cl 1 Power to Commissioners of Patents to stamp Letters Patent Cl 2 Letters Patent confirmed Cl 3 Saving Rights Schedule	
Relevant patent	
24 Apr 1863 (No 1025)	Mode of lining lead pipes with tin or its alloys [William Anthony Shaw]

Journal	
House of Commons	**House of Lords**
	Pres: Lord Hatherley LC Rep: Lord Greville

Never considered by House of Commons	21 Feb 1871	103 LJ 30	SO cw
	27 Feb 1871	103 LJ 39	1R
	6 Mar 1871	103 LJ 51	2R
	13 Mar 1871	103 LJ 60	Pet Ag
	13 Mar 1871	103 LJ 61	C'tted
	16 Mar 1871	103 LJ 71	SC nom
	30 Mar 1871	103 LJ 163	Wit to attend
	31 Mar 1871	103 LJ 165	Rep/Not to proc

Petitions		
13 Mar 1871	103 LJ 60	M Rogers Jr and another
13 Mar 1871	103 LJ 60	James J Harrop

Representation

Solicitor: Laces, Banner, Newton, Bushby, and Richardson

Agent: Wyatt and Hoskins

Parliamentary debates

None

Parliamentary papers and cases

None

Gazette notices

London Gazette: 11 Nov 1870 (Iss: 23,677, p 4831)

Edinburgh Gazette: 15 Nov 1870 (Iss: 8111, p 1336)

Dublin Gazette: 15 Nov 1870 (Iss: 16,486, p 1473)

Newspaper coverage of debates

House of Lords

2R: Morning Advertiser, 7 Mar 1871; Morning Post, 7 Mar 1871; London Evening Standard, 7 Mar 1871

Rep: London Daily News, 1 Apr 1871; London Evening Standard, 1 Apr 1871

Archives

House Bill: HL/PO/JO/10/9/760

Opposed Bill C'tee Minutes: 30 Mar 1871 (p 91); 31 Mar 1871 (p 91–92); HL/PO/CO/1/243

SC Rep: 31 Mar 1871: HL/PO/JO/10/9/733

Opposed Private Bill C'tee Evidence, 1871, Vol 6 [witnesses: George Campbell; Alexander Gordon; James Harrop; M Rogers; Norman Walker; Rev Richard Workman]: HL/PO/PB/5/37/6

Smith's Patent Bill 1876

PRVB143	1876

Smith's Patent Bill 1876 (39 & 40 Vict)

Table of contents (based on notice)

[Cl 1 To pay the £50 stamp duty on the patent]
[Cl 2 To enable the Commissioners to stamp the said paid]

Relevant patent

15 Jun 1872 (1872 No 1802)	Improvements in the Extraction of Indigo and other similar Substances from Plants containing such Substances [Christopher Webb Smith]

Journal

House of Commons			House of Lords
11 Feb 1876	131 CJ 28	Bill originate HL	*Never considered by House of Lords*

Representation

Solicitor: Carr, Bannister, Davidson, and Morris

Agent: JC Rees

Parliamentary debates

None

(continued)

(continued)

Parliamentary papers and cases
None
Gazette notices
London Gazette: 7 Dec 1875 (Iss 24,273, p 6317)
Edinburgh Gazette: 15 Nov 1870 (Iss: 8111, p 1336)
Dublin Gazette: 10 Dec 1875 (Iss: 17,029, p 794)
Newspaper coverage of debates
SO adj: Globe, 2 Feb 1876
Archives
None

Leigh's Patent Bill 1877

PRVB144	1877				
Leigh's Patent Bill 1877 (40 & 41 Vict)					
Bill for rendering valid certain Letters Patent granted to Evan Arthur Leigh for certain Improvements in carding and spinning Cotton, Wool, and other Fibrous Substances, and Machinery and Apparatus therefor					

Table of contents (based on notice)

[Cl 1 To continue and confirm certain Letters patent]
[Cl 2 To enable Evan Leigh &c. to pay the stamp duty of £50; and the Commissioner of Patents to issue a certificate]

Relevant patent

31 Jan 1874 (1874 No 398)	Carding and Spinning Cottonwool, and other fibrous substances and machinery and apparatus therefore [Evan Leigh]

Journal

House of Commons			House of Lords		
SOC Rep: John Mowbrey Rep: Henry Raikes (Ch W&M)			SOC Rep: Lord Redesdale (Ld Ch)		
27 Feb 1877	132 CJ 66	Pet SO Disp	12 Mar 1877	109 LJ 60	SO ncw
9 Mar 1877	132 CJ 89	SOC Rep	19 Mar 1877	109 LJ 71	Ref SOC
16 Mar 1877	132 CJ 91	Pet/Ref SOC	23 Mar 1877	109 LJ 90	SOC Rep/Disp
16 Mar 1877	132 CJ 102	Rep SOC/Disp			
19 Mar 1877	132 CJ 106	1R			
26 Mar 1877	132 CJ 121	2R/C'tted			
5 Jun 1877	132 CJ 251	Rep w/o Amds			
13 Jun 1877	132 CJ 271	3R day app			
14 Jun 1877	132 CJ 273	3R adj			
15 Jun 1877	132 CJ 277	3R dis/Bill w/d			

Representation

Agent: Simson, Wakeford, and Simson

Parliamentary debates

None

Parliamentary papers and cases

None

Gazette notices

London Gazette: 23 Feb 1877 (Iss 24,424, p 928); 2 Mar 1877 (Iss 24,428, p 1848); 6 Mar 1877 (Iss: 24,429, p 1919)
Edinburgh Gazette: 23 Feb 1877 (Iss: 8768, p 148); 2 Mar 1877 (Iss: 8770, p 167); 6 Mar 1877 (Iss: 8771, p 176)
Dublin Gazette: 2 Mar 1877 (Iss: 17,159, p 165)

Newspaper coverage of debates

House of Commons

2R: The Times, 27 Mar 1877; Morning Post, 27 Mar 1877; London Evening Standard, 27 Mar 1877; Manchester Courier and Lancashire General Advertiser, 27 Mar 1877

Archives	
Unopposed Bill C'tee: 5 Jun 1877 (p 79): HC/CL/WM/UB/1/30	
SOC Minutes: 28 Mar 1877 (p 265–272) [Ex Cert; Statement from Promoter]: HL/PO/CO/1/268	
SOC Rep: HL/PO/JO/10/9/914 (No 189)	

Taylor's Notice 1882

PRVB145	1882
Taylor's Notice 1882 (45 & 46 Vict)	

Table of contents (based on notice)

[Cl 1 To continue and confirm certain Letters Patent granted to William Taylor]
[Cl 2 To enable the said William Taylor to pay the Stamp Duty of £50 on the said Letters Patent]
[Cl 3 To enable the Commissioners of Patents or their clerk to stamp the said Letters Patent or a duplicate thereof]

Relevant patent

3 Aug 1878 (1878 No 3072)	Construction of Receptacles for the Carriage of Oil [William Taylor]

Representation

Agent: JC Rees

Gazette notices

London Gazette: 29 Nov 1881 (Iss: 25,042, p 6425)
Edinburgh Gazette: 29 Nov 1881 (Iss: 9265, p 1010)
Dublin Gazette: 29 Nov 1881 (Iss: 17,668, p 1261)

Gilbert and Sinclair's Patent Bill 1887

PRVB146	1887
Gilbert and Sinclair's Patent Bill 1887 (50 & 51 Vict)	

Bill for rendering valid certain Letters Patent granted to Edward Gilbert and Daniel Sinclair for an Invention for a New or Improved Fastener for securing the Coverings of Railways and other Waggons or Vehicles

Table of contents (from House Bill)

Cl 1 Renewal Fee to be paid to Comptroller-General and there-upon Letters patent to become valid
Cl 2 Short title
Schedule

Relevant patent

11 Oct 1881 (1881 No 4424)	New or Improved fastener for securing the coverings of railway and other waggons or vehicles [Edward Gilbert and Daniel Sinclair]

Journal

House of Commons	House of Lords		
	Pres and Rep: Duke of Buckingham and Chandos (Ld Ch)		
Never considered by House of Commons	15 Mar 1887	119 LJ 98	1R/Ref Ex
	21 Mar 1887	119 LJ 109	Ex Cert/SOC ncw
	25 Mar 1887	119 LJ 121	Rep/SOC Disp
	29 Mar 1887	119 LJ 129	2R
	21 Apr 1887	119 LJ 149	C'tted
	2 May 1887	119 LJ 171	Ref SC
	16 May 1887	119 LJ 194	**SC Rep**/not proc

Representation

Agent: Sherwood & Co

Parliamentary debates

None

(continued)

(continued)

Parliamentary papers and cases
Report of Select Committee on Potter's Patent Bill, Skirvanow's Patent Bill and Gilbert and Sinclair's Patent Bill (1887 HL Papers 100), Vol 9, p 469

Gazette notices
London Gazette: 15 Mar 1887 (Iss: 25,683, p 1563)
Edinburgh Gazette: 15 Mar 1887 (Iss: 9820, p 232)
Dublin Gazette: 15 Mar 1887 (Iss: 18,244, p 289)

Newspaper coverage of debates
House of Lords
2R: Morning Post, 30 Mar 1887; The Times, 30 Mar 1887
Ref SC: *Morning Post, 3 May* 1887; *The Times, 3 May 1887; Glasgow Herald, 3 May 1887*; Chepstow Weekly Advertiser, 7 May 1887; Whitby Gazette, 7 May 1887

Archives
House Bill: HL/PO/JO/10/9/1224
House Bill and correspondence: HL/PO/PB/18/3/37
SOC Minutes: 25 Mar 1887 (p 175 and 183–188) [Ex Cert; Statement of the Promoters]: HL/PO/CO/1/308

Skrivanow's Patent Bill 1887

PRVB147	1887
Skrivanow's Patent Bill 1887 (50 & 51 Vict)	
Bill for rendering valid Letters Patent granted to Gregory George Skrivanow for Improvements in and connected wth Batteries for generating electricity	

Table of contents (from House Bill)
Cl 1 Renewal Fee to be paid to Comptroller-General and there-upon Letters patent to become valid; Saving Rights Cl 2 Short title Schedule

Relevant patent	
19 Sep 1882 (1882 No 4460)	Improvements in and connected with batteries for generating electricity [Gregory George Skrivanow]

Journal			
House of Commons	**House of Lords**		
	Pres and SC Rep: Duke of Buckingham and Chandos (Ld Ch)		
Never considered by House of Commons	15 Mar 1887	119 LJ 98	1R/Ref Ex
	21 Mar 1887	119 LJ 109	Ex Cert
	25 Mar 1887	119 LJ 121	Rep/SO Disp
	29 Mar 1887	119 LJ 129	2R
	21 Apr 1887	119 LJ 149	C'tted to SC
	2 May 1887	119 LJ 171	Ref SC
	16 May 1887	119 LJ 194	**SC Rep**/not proc

Representation
Agent: Sherwood and Co

Parliamentary debates
None

Parliamentary papers and cases
Report of Select Committee on Potter's Patent Bill, Skirvanow's Patent Bill and Gilbert and Sinclair's Patent Bill (1887 HL Papers 100), Vol 9, p 469

Gazette notices
London Gazette: 15 Mar 1887 (Iss: 25,683, p 1562)
Edinburgh Gazette: 15 Mar 1887 (Iss: 9820, p 232)
Dublin Gazette: 15 Mar 1887 (Iss: 18,244, p 289)

Newspaper coverage of debates
House of Lords
2R: The Times, 30 Mar 1887; Morning Post, 30 Mar 1887
Ref SC: *The Times, 3 May 1887; Morning Post, 3 May 1887; Glasgow Herald, 3 May 1887*; Chepstow Weekly Advertiser, 7 May 1887; Whitby Gazette, 7 May 1887

Archives
House Bill: HL/PO/JO/10/9/1229
House Bill and correspondence: HL/PO/PB/18/3/37
SOC Minutes: 25 Mar 1887 (p 175–182) [Ex Cert; Statement if the Promoters]: HL/PO/CO/1/308

Clark's Patent Bill 1887

PRVB148	1887

Clark's Patent Bill 1887 (50 & 51 Vict)

Bill for rendering valid certain Letters Patent granted to Alexander Melville Clark, of 53, Chancery Lane, in the County of Middlesex, for an improved Method of, and Apparatus for, Transmitting Motion

Table of contents (from House Bill)
Cl 1 Power to Comptroller-General and confirmation of Letters Patent Cl 2 Saving rights Cl 3 Short title Schedule

Relevant patents

18 Apr 1882 (1882 No 1864)	Transmitting motion [Alexander Melville Clark]

Journal

House of Commons			House of Lords		
SOC Rep: Sir John Mowbrey Rep: Leonard Courtney (Ch W&M)			SOC Rep: Duke of Buckingham and Chandos (Ld Ch)		
22 May 1887	142 CJ 130	Pet Disp SO	18 Apr 1887	119 LJ 142	Ex Cert
4 Apr 1887	142 CJ 157	Pet/Ref SOC	21 Apr 1887	119 LJ 150	Ref SOC
19 Apr 1887	142 CJ 177	SOC Rep/SO Disp	26 Apr 1887	119 LJ 158	SOC Rep/SO Disp
19 Apr 1887	142 CJ 177	Rep/Bill Ord	28 Jun 1887	119 LJ 272	Brought HC/1R/Ref Ex
20 Apr 1887	142 CJ 178	1R	30 Jun 1887	119 LJ 275	Ex Cert
25 Apr 1887	142 CJ 187	2R/C'tted			
23 Jun 1887	142 CJ 312	Rep with Amds			
27 Jun 1887	142 CJ 319	SO Disp (SO 243)			
28 Jun 1887	142 CJ 324	3R			

Representation
Agent: Wyatt, Hoskins, Hooker, and Williams

Parliamentary debates
3R: HC Deb, 28 Jun 1887, Vol 316(3rd), col 1142

Parliamentary papers and cases
None

Gazette notices
London Gazette: 25 Mar 1887 (Iss: 25,686, p 1774)
Edinburgh Gazette: 25 Mar 1887 (Iss: 9823, p 273)
Dublin Gazette: 25 Mar 1887 (Iss: 18,247, p 338)

Newspaper coverage of debates
House of Commons
2R: Morning Post, 26 Apr 1887
3R: Morning Post, 29 Jun 1887
House of Lords
2R: The Times, 15 Jul 1887

(continued)

(continued)

Archives
House Bill: HL/PO/JO/10/9/1222
SOC Minutes: 26 Apr 1887 (p 207–208 and 215–218) [Ex Cert; Statement of Promoters]: HL/PO/CO/1/308

Nussey and Leachman's and Other Patents Bill 1892

PRVB149	1892 (55 & 56 Vict)
	Nussey and Leachman's and Other Patents Bill 1892

Bill for rendering valid certain Letters Patent granted to (1) George Henry Nussey and William Bradshaw Leachman for improvements in machinery or apparatus for pressing and terntering woollen and other woven or felted fabrics; (2) John Midgley for improvement in wool combing machines; (3) Benjamin Preston for improvements in and connected with stocks employed in the manufacture of leather yarns and woollen or other woven or felted fabrics; (4) the said George Henry Nussey and William Bradshaw Leachman for improvements in machinery and apparatus for pressing woollen and other woven or felted fabrics; (5) John Henry Whitehead for improvements in feed boxes in combing machines; (6) the said George Henry Nussey for an improved knitted fabric; (7) John Pickles and Henry Walton Whitehead for improvements in Noble's combing machines; (8) William Horsfall for a new or improved construction of furnace for burning towns' or other refuse

Table of contents (from House Bill)
s 1 Letters patent confirmed s 2 Saving rights s 3 Short title Schedule

Relevant patents	
17 Mar 1885 (1885 No 3450)	Machinery or apparatus for pressing and tentering woollen and other woven or felted fabrics [George Henry Nussey and William Leachman]
8 May 1886 (1886 No 6264)	Machinery or apparatus for pressing woollen and other woven or felted fabrics [George Henry Nussey and William Leachman]
9 Feb 1887 (1887 No 2052)	Knitted Fabric [George Henry Nussey]
1 May 1885 (1885 No 53,780	Improvement in Wool Combing Machines [John Midgley]
6 May 1885 (1885 No 5613)	Stocks employed in the manufacture of leather, yarns and woollen, or other woven or felted fabrics [Benjamin Preston]
24 Jun 1887 (1887 No 8999)	Construction of furnace for burning towns' or other refuse [William Horsfall]
2 Jun 1886 (1886 No 7398)	Feed boxes of combing machine [John Henry Whitehead]
10 May 1887 (1887 No 3665)	Improvements to Noble's combing machines [John Pickles and Henry Walton Whitehead]

Journal					
House of Commons			**House of Lords**		
			Pres: Lord Halsbury LC		
12 Feb 1892	147 CJ 30	Bill originate HL	15 Feb 1892	124 LJ 19	Ex Cert
18 Feb 1892	147 CJ 50	SO cw	18 Feb 1892	124 LJ 28	1R
			25 Feb 1892	124 LJ 39	2R day app
			7 Mar 1892	124 LJ 60	2R adj
			21 Mar 1892	124 LJ 85	Not proc

Representation
Solicitor: Ridsdale & Sons Agent: Sherwood & Co

Parliamentary debates
None

Parliamentary papers and cases
None

Gazette notices
London Gazette: 27 Nov 1891 (Iss: 26,227. p 6581)
Edinburgh Gazette: 27 Nov 1891 (Iss: 10,311, p 1339)
Dublin Gazette: 27 Nov 1891 (Iss: 18,753, p 1779)
Office Journal of the Patent Office: 2 Dec 1891 (No 152, p 1022); 31 Dec 1891 (No 156, p 1100); 13 Jan 1892 (No 158, p 20)

Newspaper coverage of debates
House of Lords 2R day app: The Times, 26 Feb 1892

Archives
House Bill: HL/PO/JO/10/9/1397

Notes
The Bill was withdrawn and was replaced by the following Acts: PRVA108 to PRVA110 It should be noted that there were no Acts or Bills for Benjamin Preston or John Midgely's Patent

Holmes' Patent Petition 1895

PRVB150	1895

Holmes' Patent Petition 1895 (58 & 59 Vict)

Petition for a Bill to continue and confirm certain Letters Patent granted to John Henry Holmes for Improvements in or applicable to switches or circuit-closers for electrical conducting apparatus

Table of contents (based on notice)
Cl 1 [Continue and confirm Letters Patent] Cl 2 [Patentee or assigns able to pay renewal fee notwithstanding the time limit as expired] Cl 3 [Enable the Comptroller-General to grant certificates that fees paid] Cl 4 [Letters patent shall be deemed valid as if payment made]

Relevant patent	
14 Feb 1884 (1884 No 3256)	Switches or circuit-closers for electrical conducting apparatus [John Henry Holmes]

Journal					
House of Commons			**House of Lords**		
7 Feb 1895	150 CJ 12	Originate HL	8 Feb 1895	127 LJ 17	Ex Cert/SO cw
8 Feb 1895	150 CJ 13	SO cw			

Representation
Agent: Faithfull and Owen

Parliamentary debates
None

Parliamentary papers and cases
None

Gazette notices
London Gazette: 23 Nov 1894 (Iss: 26,573, p 6644)
No Dublin or Edinburgh Gazette notice
Office Journal of the Patent Office: 28 Nov 1894 (No 308, p 1230); 5 Dec 1894 (No 309, p 1261); 19 Dec 1894 (No 311, p 1321)

Newspaper coverage of debates
None

Archives
None

Livet's Patent Petition 1895

PRVB151	1895

Livet's Patent Petition 1895 (58 & 59 Vict)
Petition for a Bill to continue and confirm certain Letters Patent of Fountain Livet notwithstanding that the periodical payment last due and payable to the Patent Office has not been made

Table of contents (based on notice)
Cl 1 [Continue and confirm Letters Patent] Cl 2 [To authorize the Comptroller-General to receive payment of the late fee and make the necessary endorsements]

Relevant patent	
1890 No 11,472 (22 Jul 1890)	Construction and disposition of the parts of steam generators [Fountain Livet]

Journal					
House of Commons			**House of Lords**		
7 Feb 1895	150 CJ 12	Bill originate HL	8 Feb 1895	127 LJ 17	Ex Cert/SO cw
8 Feb 1895	150 CJ 13	SO cw			

Parliamentary debates
None

Representation
Agent: W and WM Bell

Parliamentary papers and cases
None

Gazette notices
London Gazette: 30 Nov 1894 (Iss 26,575, p 7062)
Edinburgh Gazette: 30 Nov 1894 (Iss: 10,627, p 1366)
Dublin Gazette: 30 Nov1894 (Iss: 19,071, p 1405)
Office Journal of the Patent Office: 5 Dec 1894 (No 309, p 1261); 12 Dec 1894 (No 310, p 1292)

Newspaper coverage of debates
None

Archives
None

Salomon's Patent Petition 1895

PRVB152	1895

Salomon's Patent Petition 1895 (58 & 59 Vict)
Petition for Bill to empower the Comptroller General of Patents, Designs and Trade Marks ... [to re-date] the provisional specification which accompanied the application to the Patent Office Authorities for a British patent by George Downing on behalf of Joseph Salomon, of Hanover

Table of contents (based on notice)
Cl 1 [Re-dating the Provisional Specification] Cl 2 [Deeming that new date to be the date of the Provisional Specification for all purposes] Cl 3 [Saving]

Relevant patent	
9 Oct 1894 (1894 No 19,201)	Machines for distributing type for printing [Joseph Salomon]

Journal					
House of Commons			**House of Lords**		
7 Feb 1895	150 CJ 12	Bill originate HL	8 Feb 1895	127 LJ 17	Ex Cert/SO cw
8 Feb 1895	150 CJ 13	SO cw			

Representation
Agent: W and WM Bell
Parliamentary debates
None
Parliamentary papers and cases
None
Gazette notices
London Gazette: 27 Nov 1894 (Iss: 26,574, p 6912)
Edinburgh Gazette: 27 Nov 1894 (Iss: 10,626, p 1353)
Dublin Gazette: 27 Nov1894 (Iss: 19,070, p 1385)
Office Journal of the Patent Office: 5 Dec 1894 (No 309, p 1260); 12 Dec 1894 (No 310, p 1292)
Newspaper coverage of debates
None
Archives
None

Willson's Patent Bill 1896

PRVB153	1896
Willson's Patent Bill 1896 (59 & 60 Vict)	

Bill antedating rendering valid and confirming certain Letters Patent granted or to be granted to Thomas Leopold Willson for Improved Metallic Carbides applicable for use in the production of Acetylene and means for producing the same and certain other Letters Patent granted or to be granted to George Beloe Ellis (as a communication from Thomas Leopold Willson) for improvements in the production of Metallic Carbides and of illuminating gas derived therefrom

Table of contents (from House Bill)
Cl 1 Short title Cl 2 Power to Comptroller-General of Patents &c, to antedate Letters Patent Cl 3 Letters Patent confirmed Schedule

Relevant patents	
1894 No 16,705 (Not yet sealed)	Metallic Carbides for the use in the production of Acetylene and means for producing the same [Thomas Leopold Willson]
1894 No 16,342 (Not yet sealed)	Metallic Carbides and of Illuminating Gas derived therefrom [Thomas Leopold Willson]

Journal					
House of Commons			**House of Lords**		
			Pres: Lord Halsbury LC Rep: Viscount Bangor		
13 Feb 1896	151 CJ 14	Bill originate HL	14/Feb 1896	128 LJ 29	Ex Rep/SO cw
14 Feb 1896	151 CJ 18	SO cw	17 Feb 1896	128 LJ 34	1R
			21 Feb 1896	128 LJ 42	2R
			28 Feb 1896	128 LJ 55	Pets Ag
			28 Feb 1896	128 LJ 56	C'tted
			6 Mar 1896	128 LJ 69	Com named/Pet ref
			9 Mar 1896	128 LJ 71	Mem Sub
			16 Mar 1896	128 LJ 83	Wit Sum
			23 Mar 1896	128 LJ 95	Rep/not proc

Petitions		
28 Feb 1896	128 LJ 55	1. Messrs Read, Holliday, and Sons, Limited 2. Louis Michel Bullier 3. Messrs Exley and Holliday

(continued)

(continued)

Representation
Agent: Sherwood and Co
Parliamentary debates
None
Parliamentary papers and cases
None
Gazette notices
London Gazette: 26 Nov 1895 (Iss: 26,683, p 6691)
Edinburgh Gazette: 26 Nov 1895 (Iss: 10,730, p 1572)
Dublin Gazette: 26 Nov 1895 (Iss: 19,174, p 1312)
Office Journal of the Patent Office: 26 Dec 1895 (No 364, p 1392); 31 Dec 1895 (No 365, p 1421)
Newspaper coverage of debates

House of Lords

2R: The Times, 22 Feb 1886

C'tee: **Huddersfield Daily Chronicle, 25 Mar 1896**; **Huddersfield Daily Chronicle, 28 Mar 1896**; **Sheffield Daily Telegraph, 24 Mar 1896**

Archives

House Bill: HL/PO/JO/10/9/1566

Opposed Private Bill C'tee Evidence, 1896, Vol 29 [Holliday of Exley & Holliday; John Mewburn; Read of Read, Holliday & Sons; Henry Cameron; George Ellis]: HL/PO/PB/5/62/29

Opposed C'tee Book: 20 Mar 1896 (p 29–30) [HL/PO/CO/1/343]

Rawson's Notice 1898

PRVB154	1898
Rawson's Notice 1898 (61 & 62 Vict)	
Table of contents (based on notice)	

[Cl 1 To enable the assignee of the Letters Patent to pay the renewal fee]
[Cl 2 To enable the Comptroller General to grant a certificate that the renewal fee has been paid]
[Cl 3 To provide that upon payment the Letters Patent shall be deemed to be valid as if all payments had been made]

Relevant patent	
16 Jul 1892 (1886 No 11,161)	Production of Light by Incandence of Refractory Material [Frederick Lawrence Rawson and William Stepney Rawson]
Representation	
Agent: Sherwood and Co	
Gazette notices	
London Gazette: 26 Nov 1897 (Iss: 26,914, p 6903)	
Edinburgh Gazette: 26 Nov 1897 (Iss: 10,939, p 1185)	
Dublin Gazette: 26 Nov 1897 (Iss: 19,384, p 1368)	
Office Journal of the Patent Office: 1 Dec 1897 (No 465, p 1587); 8 Dec 1897 (No 466, p 1626)	

3 Standing Orders for private Bills

House of Commons

Standing Order 1690 [letters patent annexed]

PSO1	1690
Original version: 13 May 1690 (10 CJ 412)	
That when any Bill shall be brought into this House for confirming of Letters Patents, there be a true Copy of such Letters Patents annexed to the Bill	
1891: 30 Jul 1891 (146 CJ 404)	
When any Bill shall be brought into The House for restoring any Letter Patent, there shall be a true Copy of such Letters Patent annexed to the Bill, and the total amount of fees (including the prescribed fee for the enlargement under Section 17 of "The Patents, Designs and Trade Marks Act, 1883"), due and to become due on the patent, shall be deposited with the Comptroller General of Patents, Designs and Trade Marks, before the meeting of the Committee on the Bill, and such deposit proved before the Committee	
1909: 6 Aug 1909 (164 CJ 362)	
When any Bill shall be brought into The House for restoring any Letter Patent, there shall be a true Copy of such Letters Patent annexed to the Bill, and the total amount of fees (including the prescribed fee for the enlargement under Section 17 of "The Patents and Designs Act, 1907"), due and to become due on the patent, shall be deposited with the Comptroller General of Patents, Designs and Trade Marks, before the meeting of the Committee on the Bill, and such deposit proved before the Committee	
Numbering	
1801	Restated (30 Jun 1801: 56 CJ 660)
1810–13	Part XV Ord 2
1813–	Part XVI, Ord 4
1837	Part XVI, Ord 4
1840	SO 80 (opposed Bills) and 108 (unopposed Bills)
1842	SO 86
1843–45	SO 89
1846	SO 100
1847	SO 131
1847–48	SO 137
1849–52	SO 138
1852–53	SO 150
1854–55	SO 148
1856	SO 147
1857–60	SO 143
1861–62	SO 144
1862	SO 156
1863	SO 158
1864	SO 164
1865–66	SO 169
1867	SO 170
1867–68	SO 166

(continued)

(continued)

1868–69	SO 167
1870	SO 169
1871	SO 166
1872–73	SO 173
1874–75	SO 176
1876–1930	SO 175
1931	Omitted

Parliamentary debates
1909: **HC Deb, 5 Aug 1909, Vol 8(5th), col 1966; HC Deb, 6 Aug 1909, Vol 8(5th), col 2104**

Newspaper coverage of debates
None

Notes
See O Cyprian Williams, *The Historical Development of Private Bill Procedure and Standing Orders in the House of Commons* (HMSO 1949), Vol 2, p 202

Standing Order 1798 [notices in *Gazette*]

PSO2	1798

Original version: 1 May 1798 (53 CJ 524)
That, before any Petition be presented to this House for confirming or prolonging the Term of Letters Patent, granted by His Majesty to any Person or Persons, on account of any Invention, Notice of such intended Application shall be inserted Three Times in The London Gazette (and also Three Times in One of the Edinburgh Papers where the Letters Patent extend to Scotland) in the Months of August and September, or either of them, immediately preceding the Session of Parliament in which such Application is intended to be made; and that Such Notice shall have prefixed to it, in Capital Letters, the Name by which the Invention is usually distinguished, and shall contain a distinct Description of the Invention for which such Letters Patent have been obtained, and also an Account of the Term of their Duration: and that Such Notice shall have prefixed to it, in Capital Letters, the Name by which the Invention is usually distinguished, and shall contain a distinct Description of the Invention for which such Letters Patent have been obtained, and also an Account of the Term of their Duration; and that the Chairman of the Committee to whom the Petition for confirming or prolonging the Term of such Letters Patent, is referred, do report to the House how far the Order contained in the said Resolution has been complied with

1801: 30 Jun 1801 (56 CJ 660)
That, before any Petition be presented to this House, for confirming or prolonging the Term of Letters Patent granted by His Majesty to any Person or Persons on Account of any Invention, Notice of such intended Application shall be inserted Three Times in The London Gazette (and also Three Times in one of the Edinburgh Papers, where the Letters Patent extend to Scotland, and also Three Times in the Dublin Gazette, where the Letters Patent extend to Ireland) in the Months of August and September, or either of them, immediately preceding the Session of Parliament in which such Application is intended to be made; and that such Notice shall have prefixed to it in Capital Letters the Name by which the Invention is usually distinguished, and shall contain a distinct Description of the Invention for which such Letters Patent have been obtained, and also an Account of the Term of their Duration; and that the Chairman of the Committee, to whom the Petition for confirming or prolonging the Term of such Letters Patent is referred, do report to the House how far the Order contained in the said Resolution has been complied with

1810 (1810 HC Papers 355), Vol 2, p 211–20 Jun 1810 (65 CJ 509)
1. That when any Application is intended to be made to the House, for leave to bring in a Bill for confirming or prolonging the Term of Letters Patent, granted by His Majesty to any Person or Persons, on account of any Invention, Notice of such intended application shall be inserted Three Times in The London Gazette (and also Three Times in One of the Edinburgh Papers where the Letters Patent extend to Scotland, and also Three Times in the Dublin Gazette, where the Letters Patent extend to Ireland) in the months of August and September, or either of them, immediately preceding the Session of Parliament in which such Application is intended to be made; and that Such Notice shall have prefixed to it in Capital Letters, the Name by which the Invention is usually distinguished, and shall contain a distinct Description of the Invention for which such Letters Patent have been obtained, and also an account of the Term of their duration

   . . .

3. That the Committee to whom the Petition shall be referred, do examine, in the first place, how far the Orders contained in these Resolutions have been complied with; and do report the same to the House, on the Report of such Petition |

1811 (1810–11 HC Papers 248), Vol 11, p 477–21 Jun 1811 (66 CJ 444 and 66 CJ 681 – App)

That when any Application is intended to be made to the House, for leave to bring in a Bill for confirming or prolonging the Term of Letters Patent, granted by His Majesty to any Person or Persons, on account of any Invention, Notice of such intended Application be given

That such Notices be inserted Three Times in The London Gazette (and also Three Times in One of the Edinburgh Papers where the Letters Patent extend to Scotland, and also Three Times in the Dublin Gazette, where the Letters Patent extend to Ireland) in the months of August and September, or either of them, immediately preceding the Session of Parliament in which such Application is intended to be made: And each such Notice shall have prefixed to it in Capital Letters, the name by which the Invention is usually distinguished, and shall contain a distinct description of the Invention for which such Letters Patent have been obtained, and also an account of the Term of their duration

That the Committee, to whom such Petitions shall be referred do examine, in the first place, how far the proceeding Orders contained in these Resolutions have been complied with; and do report the same to the House, on the Report of such Petition

1837: 13 Jul 1837 (92 CJ 643)

[The requirement to give notices was added to a general order]
That each Notice shall have prefixed to it in Capital Letters, the name by which the Invention is usually distinguished, and shall contain a distinct description of the Invention for which such Letters Patent have been obtained, and also an account of the Term of their Duration

1840: 15 Aug 1840 (95 CJ 651)

That in cases of Bills for confirming or prolonging the terms of Letters Patent, each Notice shall have prefixed to it in Capital Letters the name by which the Invention is usually distinguished, and shall contain a distinct description of the Invention for which such Letters Patent have been obtained, and also an account of the Term of their Duration

Numbering

1801–10	Restated (30 Jun 1801: 56 CJ 660)
1810–11	Part XV, Ord 1 and 3
1811–40	Part XVI, Ord 1, 2 and 3
1840	SO 45
1842	SO 44
1843–45	SO 45
1846	SO 56
1847–52	SO 14
1852–53	SO 19
1854–62	SO 18
1862–66	SO 17
1867–75	SO 18
1876–1930	SO 8
1945	Omitted

Parliamentary debates

1798: Parliamentary Register, 1 May 1798, Vol 6, p 84; Woodfall, 1 May 1798, Vol 2, p 433
1945: HC Deb, 9 Mar 1945, Vol 408(5th), col 2382–2383

Newspaper coverage of debates

1798: Evening Mail, 30 Apr – 2 May 1798; London Chronicle, May 1-3 May 1798; Whitehall Evening Post, 1-3 May 1798; The Times, 2 May 1798; Sun, 2 May 1798; True Briton, 2 May 1798; Craftsman or Say's Weekly Journal, 5 May 1798

Notes

Report from Select Committee on Private Bill Standing Orders with the proceedings of the Committee and an Appendix (1944–45 HC Papers 30), Vol 3, p 485 at p 19

O Cyprian Williams, *The Historical Development of Private Bill Procedure and Standing Orders in the House of Commons* (HMSO 1949), Vol 2, p 24–25 (includes fuller explanation than HC Papers 30)

Standing Order 1884 [deposit of Bills]

PSO3	1884
Added to existing SO 33: 1 Aug 1884 (139 CJ 420)	
On or before the 21st December ... a printed Copy of every Bill relating to Railways, Tramways, Subways, Canals, Gas, Water, Patents, or Electric Lighting, or for incorporating or giving powers to any Company, shall be deposited at the Office of the Board of Trade ...	
1899: 4 Aug 1899 (154 CJ 409)	
On or before the 21st day of December, a printed Copy shall be deposited: . . . (1) Of every Bill relating to Railways, Tramways, Subways, Canals, Gas, Water, Patents, or Electric Lighting, or for incorporating or giving powers to any Company, shall be deposited at the Office of the Board of Trade; . . .	
1911: 1 Aug 1911 (166 CJ 370)	
On or before the 21st day of December, a printed Copy shall be deposited: . . . Of every Bill relating to railways, tramways, trolley vehicles, subways, canals, gas, water, patents, or Electric lighting, or for incorporating or giving powers to any Company, shall be deposited at the Office of the Board of Trade; . . .	
1920: 23 Nov 1920 (175 CJ 438)	
On or before the 21st day of December, a printed Copy shall be deposited: ... Of every Bill relating to gas, patents, or for incorporating or giving powers to any Company, shall be deposited at the Office of the Board of Trade ...	
1922: 11 Jul 1922 (177 CJ 259)	
On or before the 21st day of December, a printed Copy shall be deposited: ... Of every Bill relating to gas, patents, designs, trade marks or copyrights, or for incorporating or giving powers to any Company, shall be deposited at the Office of the Board of Trade ...	
Numbering and minor amendments	
1903	Date changed to 18 Dec
1908	SO 33(4)
1925	SO 33(5)
1930–31	SO 39(4) and date changed to 4 Dec
1935–36	SO 39(3)
1944–45	SO 39(2)
1950–51	Omitted so as to fall with a general provision to deposit all Bills at the Board of Trade
Parliamentary debates	
1920: HC Deb, 23 Nov 1920, Vol 135(5th), col 188 1922: HC Deb, 11 July 1922, Vol 156(5th), col 1013	
Newspaper coverage of debates	
None	
Notes	
O Cyprian Williams, *The Historical Development of Private Bill Procedure and Standing Orders in the House of Commons* (HMSO 1949), Vol 2, p 25	

Standing Order 1889 [publication in Patent Office Journal]

PSO4	1889
1889: 15 Aug 1889 (144 CJ 428)	
In addition to the ordinary Notices, Notice of the intention to apply to Parliament for a Bill relating to Letters Patent shall be published twice in the Official Journal of the Patent Office, before the introduction of the Bill in this House; and the total amount of fees including the prescribed fee for enlargement under Section 17 of the "The Patents, Designs, and Trade Marks Act, 1883," due and to become due on the Patent shall be deposited with the Comptroller before the meeting of the Committee on the Bill, and such deposit proved before the Committee	
1891: 30 Jul 1891 (146 CJ 494)	
In addition to the ordinary Notices, Notice of the intention to apply to Parliament for a Bill relating to Letters Patent shall be published twice in the Official Journal of the Patent Office, before the introduction of the Bill in this House	
Numbering	
1889–1930	SO 8A
1931	SO 9
1945	Omitted
Parliamentary debates	
1945: HC Deb, 9 Mar 1945, Vol 408(5th), col 2382–2383	
Newspaper coverage of debates	
1889: The Times, 16 Aug 1889	
Notes	
O Cyprian Williams, *The Historical Development of Private Bill Procedure and Standing Orders in the House of Commons* (HMSO 1949), Vol 2, p 25	

House of Lords

Standing Order 1808 [notices]

PSO5	1808
Original version: 28 Mar 1808 (46 LJ 516) **[based on Motions: 25 Mar 1808 (46 LJ 512)]**	
That no Bill for extending the Term of any Letters Patent, granted by His Majesty under the Great Seal of England, Scotland, or Ireland, shall be read a Third Time in this House unless Notices shall have been inserted Three Times in the London Gazette (and also Three Times in the Edinburgh Gazette, if the Letters Patent be under the Great Seal of Scotland; and Three Times in the Dublin Gazette, if under the Great Seal of Ireland), in the Months of August and September, or either of them, immediately preceding the Session in which Application for such Bill shall be made to Parliament, that an Application was intended to be made to Parliament to obtain such Bill	
1825: 8 Feb 1825 (57 LJ 25)	
That no Bill for extending the Term of any Letters Patent for any Invention or Discovery, granted by His Majesty under the Great Seal of England, Scotland, or Ireland, shall be read a Third Time in this House unless Notices shall have been inserted Three Times in the London Gazette (and also Three Times in the Edinburgh Gazette, if the Letters Patent be under the Great Seal of Scotland; and Three Times in the Dublin Gazette, if under the Great Seal of Ireland), in the Months of August and September, or either of them, immediately preceding the Session in which Application for such Bill shall be made to Parliament, that an Application was intended to be made to Parliament to obtain such Bill	
Numbering	
1838	Omitted: 70 LJ 751 (16 Aug 1838)
Parliamentary debates	
1808: HL Deb, 25 Mar 1808, Vol 10(1st), col 1254	
Newspaper coverage of debates	
1808: The Times, 25 Mar 1808; Morning Advertiser, 26 Mar 1808; Public Ledger and Daily Advertiser, 26 Mar 1808; Morning Chronicle, 26 Mar 1808; Kentish Gazette, 29 Mar 1808; Hereford Journal, 30 Mar 1808; Royal Cornwall Gazette, 2 Apr 1808	

Standing Order 1808 (No 2) [expiry of patent: time limit]

PSO6	1808

Original version: 28 Mar 1808 (46 LJ 516) **[based on Motions: 25 Mar 1808 (46 LJ 512)]**	
That no Bill for the Purpose aforesaid shall be read a Third Time in this House, unless it shall appear that the Letters Patent, the Term of which is intended by such Bill to extend, will expire within Two Years from the Commencement of the Session of Parliament in which the Application for such Bill shall be made	
1838: 16 Aug 1838 (70 LJ 751)	
That no Bill for extending the Term of any Letters Patent for any Invention or Discovery granted under the Great Seal of England, Scotland, or Ireland, shall be read a Third Time in this House, unless it shall appear that the Letters Patent, the Term of which is intended by such Bill to extend, will expire within Two Years from the Commencement of the Session of Parliament in which the Application for such Bill shall be made	
1875: 10 Aug 1875 (107 LJ 420)	
The term of any letters patent for any invention or discovery granted under the Great Seal of England, Scotland, or Ireland, shall not be extended unless such letters patent will expire within two years from the commencement of the Session of Parliament in which the application for the Bill shall be made unless it shall appear that the application to Parliament for extending the term of the letters patent is made by the person, or by the representatives of the person, who himself originally made the invention or discovery for which such letters patent were granted; and that the knowledge of such invention or discovery was not acquired by such person by purchase or otherwise, or by information that such invention or discovery was known and pursued in any foreign country	

Numbering	
1807	SO No 173
1838	SO No 229.1
Before 1845	SO No 230.1
After 1845	SO No 225.1
1849	SO No 187.1 (CLXXXVII.1)
1875	SO No 136 (and merged with SO below) – 107 LJ 420 (10 Aug 1875)
1876	SO No 137
1889	Omitted (replaced with different patents provisions: see below)
Parliamentary debates	
1808: HL Deb, 25 Mar 1808, Vol 10(1st), col 1254	
Newspapers Coverage of Debates	
1808: The Times, 25 Mar 1808; Morning Advertiser, 26 Mar 1808; Public Ledger and Daily Advertiser, 26 Mar 1808; Morning Chronicle, 26 Mar 1808; Kentish Gazette, 29 Mar 1808; Hereford Journal, 30 Mar 1808; Royal Cornwall Gazette, 2 Apr 1808	

Standing Order 1808 (No 3) [application by inventor]

PSO7	1807

Original version: 28 Mar 1808 (46 LJ 516) **[based on Motions: 25 Mar 1808 (46 LJ 512)]**	
That no Bill for the Purpose aforesaid shall be read a Third Time in this House, unless it shall appear that the Application to Parliament for extending the Term of the Letters Patent is made by the Person, or by the Representatives of the Person, who himself originally discovered the Invention for which such Letters Patent were granted by His Majesty; and that the Knowledge of such Invention was not acquired by such Person as aforesaid, by Purchase or otherwise, from the Invention or Owner of the same, or by Information that such Invention was known and pursued in any Foreign Country	

Numbering	
1807	SO No 174
1838	SO No 229.2
Before 1845	SO No 230.2
After 1845	SO No 225.2
1849	SO No 187.2 (CLXXXVII, No 2)
1875	Merged with SO (above) and renumbered SO No 136: 107 LJ 420 (10 Aug 1875)

Parliamentary debates
1808: HL Deb, 25 Mar 1808, Vol 10(1st), col 1254
Newspaper coverage of debates
1808: The Times, 25 Mar 1808; Morning Advertiser, 26 Mar 1808; Public Ledger and Daily Advertiser, 26 Mar 1808; Morning Chronicle, 26 Mar 1808; Kentish Gazette, 29 Mar 1808; Hereford Journal, 30 Mar 1808; Royal Cornwall Gazette, 2 Apr 1808

Standing Order 1819 [trade report required]

PSO8	1819
Original version: 7 Jul 1819 (52 LJ 879)	

That for the future no Bill, regulating the Conduct of any Trade; altering the Law of Apprenticeship in relation to any particular Business; affixing Marks to designate the Quality of any Manufacture; prohibiting the Manufacture of any Species of Commodity, or extending the Term of any Patent; shall be read a first Time in this House, until a Select Committee shall have inquired into the Expediency or Inexpediency of the proposed Regulations, and shall have reported to the House the result of such Inquires
Amended: 30 Jun 1823 (55 LJ 826)
That for the future no Bill, regulating the Conduct of any Trade; altering the Law of Apprenticeship in relation to any particular Business; affixing Marks to designate the Quality of any Manufacture; prohibiting the Manufacture of any Species of Commodity, or extending the Term of any Patent; shall be read a Second Time in this House, until a Select Committee shall have inquired into the Expediency or Inexpediency of the proposed Regulations, and shall have reported upon the Expediency or Inexpediency of this House proceeding to take the Bill into further Consideration
Numbering

1819	SO No 198
1849	SO No 175 (CLXXV)
1875	Omitted

Parliamentary debates
None
Parliamentary papers and cases
1819: The Times, 7 Jul 1819; The Times, 8 Jul 1819
Newspaper coverage of debates
None
Notes
A similar Standing Order was proposed for the House of Commons, but never adopted: see The Times, 5 Jul 1820

Standing Order 1875 [notices]

PSO9	1875
SO No 8: 107 LJ 420 (10 Aug 1875)	

In cases of Bills for confirming or prolonging or other relating to letters patent, each notice shall have prefixed to it in capital letters the name by which the invention is usually distinguished, and shall contain a distinct description of the invention for which such letters patent have been obtained, and also an account of the term of their duration
Numbering

1931	Omitted

Parliamentary debates
1931: HL Deb, 27 Jul 1931, Vol 81(5th), col 1164 and 1166–1167
Newspaper coverage of debates
None

Standing Order 1875 (No 2) [letters patent annexed]

PSO10	1875
SO No 135: 10 Aug 1875 (107 LJ 420)	

Every Bill for confirming any letters patent shall have a true copy of such letters patent annexed thereto

(continued)

(continued)

1889: 6 Aug 1889 (121 LJ 341)
Every Bill for restoring any letters patent shall have a true copy of such letters patent annexed thereto

1891: 28 Jul 1891 (123 LJ 401)
Every Bill for restoring any letters patent shall have a true copy of such letters patent annexed thereto; and the total amount of fees (including the prescribed fee for enlargement under Section 17 of the Patents, Designs, and Trade Marks Act, 1883) due and to become due on the patent shall be deposited with the Comptroller General of Patents, Designs and Trade Marks before the meeting of the Committee on the Bill, and such deposit proved before the Committee

Numbering	
1876	SO No 136
1931	Omitted: 163 LJ 340 (27 Jul 1931)

Parliamentary debates
1931: HL Deb, 27 Jul 1931, Vol 81(5th), col 1166–1167

Newspaper coverage of debates
None

Notes
See Report of Select Committee on Potter's Patent Bill, Skirvanow's Patent Bill and Gilbert and Sinclair's Patent Bill (1887 HL Papers 100), Vol 9, p 469

Standing Order 1884 [deposit of Bills]

PSO11	1884

SO No 33: 29 Jul 1884 (116 LJ 377)
On or before the twenty-first day of December a printed copy of every Local Bill shall be deposited at the Office of Her Majesty's Treasury and the General Post Office: A printed copy of every Local Bill relating to railways, tramways, subways, canals, gas, water, patents, or electric lighting or for incorporating or giving power to any company, shall be deposited at the Office of the Board of Trade; . . . .

1911: 1 Aug 1911 (143 LJ 360)
On or before the twenty-first day of December a printed copy shall be deposited . . . (4) Of every Local Bill relating to railways, tramways, trolley vehicles, subways, canals, gas, water, patents, or electric lighting or for incorporating or giving power to any company, at the Office of the Board of Trade

1919: 30 Oct 1919 (151 LJ 417)
On or before the twenty-first day of December a printed copy shall be deposited . . . (4a) Of every Bill relating to gas, water, patents, or to the generation and supply of electricity, or for incorporating or giving power to any company, at the Office of the Board of Trade

1920: 10 Aug 1920 (152 LJ 392)
On or before the twenty-first day of December a printed copy shall be deposited . . . (4a) Of every Bill relating to gas, or patents, or for incorporating or giving power to any company, at the Office of the Board of Trade

1922: 1 Aug 1922 (154 LJ 355)
On or before the twenty-first day of December a printed copy shall be deposited . . . (4a) Of every Bill relating to gas, water power, or patents, designs, trade marks, or copy rights, or for incorporating or giving power to any company, at the Office of the Board of Trade

Numbering	
1930	SO No 33(4)
1931	References to patents and other intellectual property rights omitted: 163 LJ 340 (27 Jul 1931)

Parliamentary debates
1911: HL Deb, 1 Aug 1911, Vol 9(5th), col 703 1919: HL Deb, 30 Oct 1919, Vol 37(5th), col 119–120 1922: HL Deb, 1 Aug 1922, Vol 51(5th), col 1002–1004 1931: HL Deb, 27 Jul 1931, Vol 81(5th), col 1166–1167

Newspaper coverage of debates
None

Standing Order 1889 [publication in Patent Office Journal]

PSO12	1889
SO No 8a: 6 Aug 1889 (121 LJ 340)	
In addition to the ordinary notices, notice of the intention to apply to Parliament for a Bill relating to letters patent shall be published twice in the Official Journal of the Patent Office, before the introduction of the Bill in this House; and the total amount of fees (including the prescribed fee for enlargement under Section 17 of the Patents, Designs, and Trade Marks Act, 1883) due and to become due on the patent shall be deposited with the Comptroller before the meeting of the Committee on the Bill, and such deposit proved before the Committee	
1891: 28 Jul 1891 (123 LJ 401)	
In addition to the ordinary notices, notice of the intention to apply to Parliament for a Bill relating to letters patent shall be published twice in the Official Journal of the Patent Office, before the introduction of the Bill in this House	
Numbering	
1931	Omitted: 163 LJ 340 (27 Jul 1931)
Parliamentary debates	
HL Deb, 27 Jul 1931, Vol 81(5th), col 1166–1167	
Newspaper coverage of debates	
None	
Notes	
See Report of Select Committee on Potter's Patent Bill, Skirvanow's Patent Bill and Gilbert and Sinclair's Patent Bill (1887 HL Papers 100), Vol 9, p 469	

Standing Order 1889 (No 2) [require inclusion of clause]

PSO13	1889
SO No 137 (121 LJ 341 – 6 Aug 1889)	

In any case in which a Bill to restore a patent is entertained, the following clauses shall be inserted for the protection of persons who may have availed themselves of the subject-matter of the patent after it has been announced as void in the Official Journal of the Patent Office, with such alterations as the circumstances of each case may require:
"No action or other proceedings shall be commenced or prosecuted nor any damage recovered:–

(1) In respect of any infringement of the said patent which shall have taken place after the day of (the day on which the patent was announced to be void in the Official Journal), and before the passing of this Act

(2) In respect of the use or employment at any time hereafter of any machine, machinery, process or operation actually made or carried on within the British Islands, or of the use or sale of any article manufactured or made in infringement of the said Paid, after the said day of and before the passing of this Act. Provided that such use, sale, or employment is by the person or corporation by or for whom such machine or machinery or article was bona fide manufactured or made, or such process or operation was bona fide carried on, his or their executors, administrators, successors, or vendees, or his or their assigns

(3) In respect of the use, employment, or sale at any time hereafter by any person or corporation entitled for the time being under the proceeding sub-section to use or employ any machine, machinery, process or operation or any improved or additional machine or machinery, or any improved, extended or developed process or operation, or of any article manufactured or made by any of the means aforesaid, in infringement of the said patent. Provided that the use or employment of any such improved or additional machine or machinery, or of any such improved, extended or developed process or operation, shall be limited to the buildings, works, or premises of the person or corporation by or for whom such machine or machinery was manufactured or such process or operation was carried on within the meaning of the preceding sub-section, his or their executors, administrators, successors, or assigns

If any person shall, within one year after the passing of this act, make an application to the Board of Trade for compensation in respect of money, time or labour expended by the applicant upon the subject-matter of the said patent, in the bona fide belief that such patent had become and continued to be void, it shall be lawful for the said Board, after hearing the parties concerned, or their agents, to assess the amount of such compensation, if in their opinion the application ought to be granted, and to specify the party by whom and the day on which such compensation shall be paid, and if default shall be made in payment of the sum awarded, then the said patent shall, by virtue of this Act, become void, but the sum awarded shall not in that case be recoverable as a debt or damages.

(continued)

(continued)

Numbering	
1931	Omitted: 163 LJ 340 (27 Jul 1931)
Parliamentary debates	
1931: HL Deb, 27 Jul 1931, Vol 81(5th), col 1166–1167	
Newspaper coverage of debates	
None	
Notes	
See Report of Select Committee on Potter's Patent Bill, Skirvanow's Patent Bill and Gilbert and Sinclair's Patent Bill (1887 HL Papers 100), Vol 9, p 469	

Part 3 Acts and legislation of the Old Scottish and Irish Parliaments

Part 3 contents

Chapter 1: Scottish Acts granting exclusive rights

There is no table of contents for Chapters 2 and 3.

Chapter 4: Irish Bills

Acts of the Old Scottish Parliament

The Old Scottish Parliament evolved from the King's Council and Parliament, and it first became identifiable as a Parliament in the early thirteenth century. It continued to exist until the Act of Union in 1707. The procedure of the Parliament of Scotland changed radically over its life, from being a body which did little more than ratify the decisions of the Lords of the Articles (a committee delegated from the Parliament which carried out most of its functions) to becoming a legislative body similar to the Westminster model.[1]

The records of the old Parliament of Scotland have been extensively catalogued and now digitised. At the beginning of the nineteenth century, antiquarian interest developed and William Robertson published *The Parliamentary Records of Scotland in the General Register House 1240–1571*. This edition was criticised, and between 1814 and 1817 Thomas Thomson and Cosmo Innes published a complete edition of the *Acts of the Parliaments of Scotland* (APS) over twelve volumes. It included any known paper judged to be in any way Parliamentary between 1125 and 1707.

This series was used as the starting point for what is now the premier collection of Parliamentary records for Scotland: the *Records of the Parliaments of Scotland to 1707* (RPS) compiled by St Andrews University and hosted digitally.[2] The collection has assembled all the official records of the Parliament and Conventions of the Estates both in the original version and a modern English translation; although there is some other material available which is not included in this collection (some of which was included in APS), none of it relates to patents and inventions.

In Chapter 1 of this part, all the Acts (and petitions, supplications and so forth) which would grant exclusive rights in or in relation to inventions are given an individual record. In each case, a short title is assigned, a coding reference (SCOT) and the "long" title[3] of the enactment. In respect of each Act, the year[4] and chapter number is as assigned by the APS.[5] However, the numbering of statutes is erratic as some private Acts are given chapter numbers, others are not, and some Acts are not included at all. The reference number assigned in the RPS is included in square brackets.

The record continues with a synthesised table of contents of the Act, so all entries are in square brackets. These tables are based on the English-language version of the material in the RPS. Where there are related papers included in the RPS collection, these are included under the heading "Parliamentary papers". From the middle of the seventeenth century, as decisions moved from the Lords of the Article to Parliament, the Parliamentary records increased. Accordingly, where there were Parliamentary or committee minutes, these are included, and where the event is recorded twice in different documents, both entries are included. In each case, the date of the event, a brief summary of the document and in square brackets the RPS (and in curvy brackets the APS) reference are included. Those seeking archival references to the original documents can obtain these through the RPS.

The Scottish Parliament adopted an extraordinarily pro-active industrial policy from the middle of the seventeenth century. The policy began with textile manufacturers being given exclusion from taxes and duties and other privileges under a series of manufactory Acts. Chapter 2 of this part includes a list of the many manufactory Acts passed. In relation to the key Acts for Manufactories 1641, 1661 and 1681, a table of contents is provided. In the later period, when the Parliamentary material for a particular Act increases, references have been provided to that material using the RPS reference number.

There were various other papers included in the Acts of the Parliament of Scotland which related to patents and inventions. These papers have been included in Chapter 3 with their title and the relevant references.

Irish Parliamentary legislation

While enactments of the old Irish Parliament have been printed and are widely available, there were no patent enactments, either public or private, passed by the Irish Parliament. There were, however, some Bills which were heard (and even passed by the Parliament). Tragically, the records of the Irish Parliament were entirely lost when the Public Records of Ireland was destroyed in 1922 during the Irish civil war. While there are some documents in other archives or libraries, there is no record of the text of any patent Bill.

The journals of the Irish Parliament (both House of Commons and House of Lords) were printed, so it is possible to know the legislation that was considered by the Parliament. Working from these journals, the Irish Legislation Project[6] at Queen's University, Belfast has provided a database of all the material that is available. This includes a Bill (ILD) number for each entry. This database was used to identify three private patent/invention-related Bills which were considered by the Irish Parliament (coded as IRE). Once the Bills

---

1 For a history, see Charles Terry, *The Scottish Parliament: Its Constitution and Procedure 1603–1707* (James Mac Lehose 1905).

2 www.rps.ac.uk.

3 It is the only title, in fact, as short titles were never given officially.

4 In Scotland, the calendar year began in January from 1600.

5 Another set of statutes published by Sir Thomas Murray of Glendook, *Laws and Acts of Parliament made by James the First and his royal successors, kings and queens of Scotland* (2 Vols, 1682), has different chapter numbers. Comparison charts are available on the RPS website.

6 www.qub.ac.uk/ild/.

were identified, the Irish House of Commons Journal (ICJ) was consulted and the entries from that journal included in the same way as for the Westminster Parliament (i.e. a bold entry means that there was detail beyond procedural). In each case, the journal includes a summary of the petition for the private Bill, so it is possible to work out its scope, if not its contents. Some limited reporting of Parliamentary debates can be found in the *Parliamentary Register of the House of Commons of Ireland*, and reference is made where it is available. One Bill, the Silk Crapes Bill 1725, passed the Irish House of Commons and the Irish Privy Council[7] and then went for approval by the English Privy Council. The references in the Privy Council register in the State Papers are therefore included although there is no substantive detail in that register.

---

7 All records of this Irish Privy Council were also lost in 1922.

1 Scottish Acts granting exclusive rights

Salt Act 1563

SCOT1	1563
	Salt Act 1563 (1563 c. 7) {ii APS 538} [1581/10/83]
	Act granting monopoly for making salt
	**Table of contents**
	[s 1 Grant for 50 years to make or cause to be made any salt of the new fashion and manner invented or used by the said strangers different from the fashion now and of before used within this realm] [s 2 Use without special licence under the pain of death and confiscation of the lands, grounds and houses where the said salt shall happen to be made] [s 3 After 50 years, any person using the invention must pay 7.5 bolls to Her Majesty and one to the Salt Conservator of every hundred]
	**Parliamentary minutes**
	None
	**Parliamentary papers**
	None

Robert Dickson's Ratification 1581

SCOT2	1581
	Robert Dickson's Ratification 1581 (1581 c. 64) {iii APS 240} [1581/10/83]
	Ratification of the privilege of silk-making to Robert Dickson
	**Table of contents**
	[s 1 Ratification of the privilege and liberty granted to Robert Dickson, upon his offer to bring in and to learn within this realm the art of the making and working of silks from France or Flanders] [s 2 Privilege to last thirty years to come; all others to not to exercise art without his leave] [s 3 Raw and unwrought silks to be brought home by him shall be custom free] [s 4 Grant subject to working a year and a day after the date hereof, with 100 servants, and continue in the said work thereafter, certifying that if he does in the contrary, he shall lose his privilege]
	**Parliamentary minutes**
	None
	**Parliamentary papers**
	None

Fleming Craftsmen Act 1587

SCOT3	1587
	Fleming Craftsmen Act 1587 (1587 c. 119) {iii APS 507} [1587/7/142]
	Act in favour of the craftsmen Flemings (John Garden, Philip Fermant and John Banko)
	**Table of contents**

(continued)

(continued)

[s 1 Craftsmen shall remain within this realm for at least 5 years, and shall bring 30 weavers, fullers &c. with them and work the craft as worked in Flanders, Holland or England]
[s 2 No obligation to take Scots apprentices; but Edinburgh bairns to be preferred if any taken on certain conditions (5-year apprenticeship)]
[s 3 Duties paid same as those in Flanders]
[s 4 Shall sell wares in Edinburgh on ordinary market days]
[s 5 Exemption from all but certain taxes]
[s 6 Strangers may only buy on open market]
[s 7 Religious Minister may be appointed when certain numbers]
[s 8 Loom wright may be engaged]
[s 9 1000 merks advances]
[s 10 Payment to King for each unit sold]
[s 11 Oaths and obligations on craftsmen]
Parliamentary minutes
None
Parliamentary papers
None

Margaret Balfour's Act 1587

SCOT4	1587
Margaret Balfour's Act 1587 (1587 c. 101) {iii APS 494} [1587/7/123]	
Act in favour of [Margaret Balfour], Lady Burleigh, touching the privilege of refined salt	
Table of contents	
[s 1 Granted and full liberty and privilege to the said Dame Margaret, her heirs, assignees, servants and factors having commission and power, to her to make and cause be made the said refined salt, otherwise called salt upon salt, in any other manner than the same was made in this realm before]	
[s 2 To sell and convey the same in small or great during the space of seven years coming after the date hereof; not be lawful any other person to make said salt]	
[s 3 Full power to make searchers; committers of deforcement shall be rigorously punished as if they had deforced our sovereign lord's officers in execution of his office]	
Parliamentary minutes	
None	
Parliamentary papers	
None	

Smith and Acheson's Act 1598

SCOT5	1598
Smith and Acheson's Act 1598 {iv APS 176} [1598/10/7]	
Act regarding the sole making of pumps	
Table of contents	
[s 1 Grant and commit to the said Gavin Smith and James Acheson and their deputes the gift, use and only privilege to make, use, erect and exercise knowledge of an artificial engine in making of pumps and devices during the space of 21 years next after the day and date hereof]	
[s 2 With power to them and their deputes to uptake and receive such profits and commodities as they may have thereof to their own benefit and utility]	
[s 3 Persons prohibited to make, erect, use or exercise the invention without licence]	
[s 5 Any person, owner of the ground, to pay £2,000 yearly so long as any metals, coals or stones shall be extracted in their mines; one half to be paid to his Majesty and the other half to the said Gavin and James equally]	
Parliamentary minutes	
None	
Parliamentary papers	
None	

Eustatius Rough [Eustachius Roghe] (Great Salt) Act 1597–99

SCOT6	1599
Eustatius Rough [Eustachius Roghe] (Great Salt) Act 1597–99	
Act in favour of Eustatius Rough (1599 c. 69) {iv APS 156} [1597/11/76] Act regarding great Salt {iv APS 182} [1599/7/5]	
Table of contents	
[s 1 Annual Rent on any Salt Pan 10 in every 100] [s 2 Eustatius Rough to receive 10s for each boll of salt] [s 3 First two pans to be used to build two further pans; no assignment or conveyance of same] [s 4 Eustatius Rough to receive 30s for each of the said pans; thereafter only contractual right with His Majesty for tenth part of just profit] [s 5 Annual accounts to be given in July each year] [s 6 William, Commendator of Pittenweem, Comptroller of Salt Pans shall be given allowance of 40s for each chalder of salt which is given to him as part of his office; Comptroller to present himself in July when accounts made] [s 7 No profits from any pans to be used except to build further salt pans, until there are four] [s 8 Once four pans built, third of free profit to Comptroller of Salt Pans until £25,000 reached; whereafter only allowance as Comptroller to remain]	
Parliamentary minutes	
None	
Parliamentary papers	
None	

Salt Pans Act 1599

SCOT7	1599
Salt Pans Act 1599 {iv APS 187} [1599/7/13]	
Act regarding salt pans	
Table of contents	
[s 1 Eustatius Rough devised some more inventions: a form of stove; method for venting of chimneys; new form of kiln] [s 2 Privy Council to produce letter to perpetually confirm licences granted to Rough] [s 3 Grant to Eustatius Rough to build, reform and renew any kiln or stove, venting chimney, furnace or vat] [s 4 Possessors of said stoves &c. to pay a reasonable fee to Eustatius Rough built to design] [s 5 Any person who imitates the invention to pay 500 merks, one half to His Majesty other half to Eustatius Rough; also the stove &c. forfeited]	
Parliamentary minutes	
None	
Parliamentary papers	
None	

Armour Act 1599

SCOT8	1599
Armour Act 1599 {iv APS 190} [1599/7/17]	
Act regarding armour	
Table of contents	
[s 1 Sir Michael Balfour of Burleigh shall purchase sufficient armour to arm 10,000 men from overseas] [s 2 Obligation on subjects to buy armour] [s 3 Exclusive right to sell armour for three years]	
Parliamentary minutes	
None	
Parliamentary papers	
None	

Sir George Hay's Act 1612

SCOT9	1612
Sir George Hay's Act 1612 (1612 c. 59) {iv APS 515} [1612/10/66]	
Ratification to Sir George Hay [of Nether Liff] of his gift and privilege of making of iron and glassworks	
Table of contents	
[s 1 Parliament, ratifies, approves and confirms the licence to Sir George Hay of Nether Liff to make iron and glass within the said kingdom of Scotland for 31 years]	
Parliamentary minutes	
None	
Parliamentary papers	
Licences to sell iron notwithstanding privileges of burghs: (1) Ratification to Archibald Primrose of his licence of making of iron within the sheriffdom of Perth (permission to make iron) (1612 c. 60) {iv APS 515} [1612/10/67] (2) Licence to Sir George Hay [of Kinfauns] regarding selling of his iron (1621 c. 100) {iv APS 686} [1621/6/119]	

Act of Monopolies 1641

SCOT10	1641
Act of Monopolies 1641 (1641 c. 98) {v APS 411} [1641/8/192]	
Act discharging monopolies	
Table of contents	
[s 1 Patent selling tobacco to Sir Samuel Leslie and Thomas Dalmahoy; patent of selling leather to [James Erskine] Earl of Mar; patent of pearling to [James] Bannatyne; patent of pearl to Robert Buchan; patent of armory to Henry William Mauld all discharged] [s 2 All patents of that nature purchased for a particular person in prejudice of the public, to cease and be ineffectual in all times coming]	
Parliamentary minutes	
16 Nov 1641 – Parliamentary Minutes [M1641/8/75]	
Parliamentary papers	
Supplication . . . business regarding patent for tanning of leather remitted to commission for manufactories; article against monopolies continued [C1639/8/30]	
Notes	
Burghs desire a general Act against monopolies (1639) {v APS 602} [C1639/8/30] Act rescinded by: Rescissory Act 1661 (1661 c. 15) {vii APS 86, c.126} [1661/1/158] Also included in Webster's Patent Cases (1 WPC 33)	

Sir Robert Bruce's Act 1646

SCOT11	1646
Sir Robert Bruce's Act (1647 c. 472) {vi(i) APS 820} [1646/11/547]	
Act [Sir Robert Bruce], Laird of Clackmannan	
Table of contents	
[s 1 Grant invention for drying out all mine shafts filled with water to Sir Robert Bruce and his assignees for 19 years from the date hereof] [s 2 All persons who work his invention without licence to pay Sir Robert Bruce has 1000 merks]	
Note	
Act rescinded by: Rescissory Act 1661 (1661 c. 15) {vii APS 86, c.126} [1661/1/158]	

Colonel James Wemyss' Act 1648

SCOT12	1648
Colonel James Wemyss' Act (1648 c. 40) {vi(ii) APS 18} [1648/3/48]	
Act in favour of Colonel James Wemyss	

[s 1 Colonel James Wemyss and assigns have for three terms of 19 years successively after each other from the date hereof to put invention into practice light ordnance (otherwise called leather ordnance), shooting ordnance from a pound bullet to a demi-cannon, with various others engines of war such as mortar pieces, petards and the like of leather]
[s 2 All persons who made such articles to have them forfeited to Wemyss]
[s 3 Right to administer oath to those to whom the invention is shown to prohibit the secret being disclosed to keep secrets within the Realm]
[s 4 Right to sell ordnance to any person who are at amity with this Realm]

Parliamentary minutes

21 March 1648 – Unofficial Minute of Parliament [A1648/3/7]

Parliamentary papers

None

Notes

Act rescinded by: Rescissory Act 1661 (1661 c. 15) {vii APS 86, c.126} [1661/1/158]

Colonel James Wemyss' Act 1649

SCOT13	1649
Colonel James Wemyss' Act 1649 (1649 c. 226) {vi(i) APS 482} [1649/5/233]	
Act in favour of Colonel James Wemyss anent the making of leather ordnances and several other engines of war	
Table of contents	

[s 1 Colonel James Wemyss and assigns to put invention into effect for three terms of 19 years successively; all persons prohibited for those periods to make the leather ordnances]
[s 2 All persons who made articles to have them forfeited to Wemyss]
[s 3 Right to administer oath to those to whom the invention is shown to prohibit the secret being disclosed to keep secrets within the Realm]
[s 4 Right to sell ordnance to any person who are at amity with this Realm]

Parliamentary minutes

None

Parliamentary papers

None

Notes

Act rescinded by: Rescissory Act 1661 (1661 c. 15) {vii APS 86, c.126} [1661/1/158]

Soap Act 1649

SCOT14	1649
Soap Act 1649 (1649 c. 275) {vi (ii) APS 300} [1649/1/310]	
Act anent the soap-works	
Table of contents	

[s 3 All former private monopolies over soap discharged]

Parliamentary minutes

16 November 1641 – Parliamentary Minutes [M1641/8/75]

Parliamentary papers

(continued)

(continued)

None
Notes
Act rescinded by: Rescissory Act 1661 (c. 15) {APS vii 86, c.126} [1661/1/158]

Colonel James Wemyss' Act 1661

SCOT15	1661
Colonel James Wemyss' Act 1661 (1661 c. 65) {vii APS 46} [1661/1/91]	
Act in favour of Colonel James Wemyss	
Table of contents	
[s 1 Act of 1648 was lost at Sea, new grant of three terms of 19 years from date hereof to put in practice invention of light ordnance] [s 2 His Heirs and successors may administer an oath to those who see invention to keep it secret] [s 3 All persons who make or sell the light ordnance to forfeit the same and pay under penalty of 500 merks]	
Parliamentary minutes	
21 March 1648 – Unofficial Minute of Parliament [A1648/3/7]	
Parliamentary papers	
Report by the Commissioners for Bills and Trade Concerning James Wemyss, General of the Artillery, 1 March 1661 [A1661/1/29]	

Major Lun's Act 1661

SCOT16	1661
Major Lun's Act 1661 (1661 c. 274) {vii APS 274} [1661/1/367]	
Act for Major Lun anent the making of needles	
Table of contents	
[s 1 Major Edward Lun permitted to set up a manufactory for the making of needles] [s 2 All materials imported by him in this country to be free of custom or any other imposition for the space of nineteen years] [s 3 All persons prohibited from making needles for 19 years, except such native apprentices as they shall teach and instruct in the said trade] [s 4 Must set up trade within six months after the date hereof]	
Parliamentary minutes	
None	
Parliamentary papers	
None	

Leslie and Scott's Act 1661

SCOT17	1661
Leslie and Scott's Act 1661 (1661 c. 66) {vii APS 47} [1661/1/92]	
Act in favour of colonels Ludovic Leslie and James Scott	
Table of contents	
[s 1 Grant for 19 years after date of Act to make in more easy and profitable way the following commodities: saltpetre, salt upon salt, potashes, tanning of skins and hides without bark, pitch, tar, white iron, iron-thread, making of iron with coal, castlesoap, raising of water and weights out of pits, improving of ground, making of ploughs and salt pans, and for making of anything in crystal as well for ornament as use] [s 2 Any person who uses any such invention, without consent, to pay 500 merks for first contravention and prohibited for rest of 19-year term] [s 3 Leslie and Scott to make experiment for the commodities within three years of Act; otherwise persons free to make said commodities in any way they see fit]	

Parliamentary minutes
None
Parliamentary papers
None

Wemyss, Leslie and Scott's Act 1661

SCOT18	1661
Wemyss, Leslie and Scott's Act 1661 (1661 c. 163) {vii APS 127} [1661/1/200]	
Act in favour of James Wemyss, general of artillery, and colonels Leslie and Scott	
Table of contents	
[s 1 Grant to Wemyss and assigns of 19 years after erection of Mill works to make works to invention of draining mines; without prejudice to those making known mills] [s 2 Any person making Mill invention a penalty of 500 merks for first fault and 500 for each subsequent contravention] [s 3 Invention to be compared to that of Ludovic Leslie and James Scott; if invention the same Wemyss may not use invention for Mines and Coalpits; if different, subjects free to choose between inventions] [s 4 Ludovic Leslie and James Scott to disclose secret to His Majesty or representative within three months; James Wemyss to do likewise; if the same invention then Wemyss' grant be void to the extent the same; if invention not disclosed by Leslie and Scott then rights to Wemyss]	
Parliamentary minutes	
None	
Parliamentary papers	
1 Mar 1661 – Report by the Commissioners for Bills and Trade Concerning James Wemyss, General of the Artillery [A1661/1/29]	

James Lockhart's Petition 1672

SCOT19	1672
James Lockhart's Petition 1672 {viii APS App 23} [A1672/6/37]	
Petition of James Lockhart for making alum	
Table of contents	
[Cl 1 James Lockhart be granted the rights of a manufactory] [Cl 2 James Lockhart to have the sole right to make alum for the space of [ ] years] [Cl 3 Manufactory to be erected within three years]	
Parliamentary minutes	
None	
Parliamentary papers	
10 Sep 1672 – Warrant to James Lockhart of Cleghorn [M1672/6/19]	

Gordon's Gunpower Manufactory Bill 1690

SCOT20	1690
Gordon's Gunpower Manufactory Bill 1690 {ix APS App 42} [A1690/4/7]	
Gunpower Manufactory Bill	
Table of contents	
[C 1 Prohibit all persons from importing any gunpowder under the penalty and forfeiture of the powder] [Cl 2 All gunpowder made in Scotland shall be sealed by a particular seal to be made by the said Mr James Gordon; and any unsealed powder shall be forfeited] [Cl 3 James Gordon to bring any contravener before any judge for seizure and forfeiting]	

(continued)

(continued)

[Cl 4 It is a crime to counterfeit the said seal or to put foreign powder into any of these sealed barrels]
[Cl 5 James Gordon declared to be the only maker of gunpowder and saltpetre within this kingdom during his lifetime, and his successors for [ ] years after his death]
[Cl 6 Free of all public taxes and impositions whatsoever during the said space]
[Cl 7 Power of search for gunpowder]
[Cl 8 All raw material imported free of duty]
[Cl 9 James Gordon can require magistrates to furnish work horses on certain fee]
[Cl 10 Privy Council may give any other such encouragement]

Parliamentary minutes
14 May 1690 – Parliamentary Minutes – Proposal for Making Gunpowder [M1690/4/11]
30 Jun 1690 – Parliamentary Register – Proposal Remitted to C'tee [1690/4/73]
30 Jun 1690 – Proceedings concerning a gunpowder manufactory (including draft of Bill) [1690/4/7]
30 Jun 1690 – Parliamentary Minutes – Rep of C'tee read [M1690/4/29]
Parliamentary papers
None

Hudson and Hog's Act 1693

SCOT21	1693
Hudson and Hog's Act 1693 (1693 c. 49) {ix APS 313} [A1693/1/19]	
Act to Marmaduke Hudson and William Hog	
Table of contents	

[s 1 Prohibit the using of the invention [baize] by any other person without the consent of Hudson and Hog or assignees for 19 years from the date hereof]
[s 2 Grant the privilege of manufacturing it during the said period]
[s 3 Provided that the work is set up within a year and a day of this date]

Parliamentary minutes
5 Jun 1693 – Parliamentary Minutes – Pet read [M1693/4/22]
6 Jun 1693 – C'tee Minutes – Pet read [C1693/4/40]
14 Jun 1693 – Parliamentary Minutes – Pet granted [M1693/4/28]
Parliamentary papers
14 Jun 1693 – Supplication of Marmaduke Hudson and William Hogg {ix APS App 91} [A1693/4/19]

Hamilton's Act 1693

SCOT22	1693
Hamilton's Act 1693 (1693 c. 88) {ix APS 340}[1693/4/149]	
Ratification in favour of James Hamilton of Little Earnock	
Table of contents	

[s 1 Ratification of agreement with James Hamilton of Little Earnock dated 26 August 1690]
[s 2 James Hamilton to have privilege of making, vending and selling playing cards within this kingdom]
[s 3 Granting the liberties and privileges granted to manufactories of a paper mill given to Peter Bruce]
[s 4 Penalty of £100 Scots money on each occasion and confiscation of any foreign playing cards]

Parliamentary minutes
None
Parliamentary papers
None

James Lyall's Oil Act 1695

SCOT23	1695
James Lyall's Oil Act 1695 (1695 c. 33) {ix APS 419} [1695/5/153]	
Act in favour of James Lyall of Garden anent an oil manufactory and rabbit and hare skin manufactory	

Table of contents
[s 1 James Lyall of Garden to set up manufactory for making of lint, hemp and rape seed oils, as also a manufactory for rabbit and hare skins] [s 2 The said manufactories shall have all the liberties, privileges and immunities granted by the act of 1661] [s 3 In place of 2s Scots as the duty of export for each hogshead of old lint seed there be 24s Scots exacted] [s 4 In place of 30s money for each hundred of rabbit and hare skins there be £3 Scots exacted] [s 5 Discharging all farmers and collectors of his majesty's customs and excise or others to quit anything of the said 24s per hogshead of old lint seed or of the £3 for the hundred of hare and rabbit skins] [s 6 Any intimation requires the payment to of his Majesty's treasury of £100 Scots money for each breach of this present act; one half to be paid to his majesty and the other half to the informer] [s 7 The liberties, privileges and immunities hereby granted shall continue for the space of nineteen years after the date hereof for the said oil, hare and rabbit skin manufactories] [s 8 James Lyall shall have the sole power and privilege for making lint, hemp and rape seed oil for the space foresaid, and that it shall not be rightful during that space for any other person or persons to make lint, hemp or rape seed oils within this kingdom, providing the said James Lyall do set up the said manufactory between now and Martinmas [11 November] 1696] [s 9 This act shall be without prejudice to the importation of the said oils and hats from foreign parts by merchants as they have been in use to do before the making hereof]

Parliamentary minutes
None

Parliamentary papers
None

Alexander Hope's Act 1695

SCOT24	1695
Alexander Hope's Act 1695 (1695 c. 34) {ix APS 420} [1695/5/154]	
Act in favour of [Alexander] Hope of Kerse and co-partnery for erecting a manufactory for making of gunpowder and alum	

Table of contents
[s 1 Sir Alexander Hope of Kerse, Sir Robert Dickson of Sornbeg, George Clark and James Balfour's two works for making of gunpowder and for making of alum are manufactories and enjoy benefits under 1661 Act] [s 2 They shall have the sole power and privilege of making of the same for the space of 19 years from and after the setting up of their works] [s 3 Said undertakers do set up the said alum work between now and Martinmas [11 November] 1698] [s 4 Without prejudice to the importation of alum and gunpowder from foreign parts by merchants as they have been in use before the making hereof]

Parliamentary minutes
4 Jul 1695 – Parliamentary Minutes – Approval [M1695/5/27]
5 Jul 1695 – Parliamentary Minutes – Royal Assent [M1695/5/28]

Parliamentary papers
None

John Hamilton's Act 1696

SCOT25	1696
John Hamilton's Act (1696 c. 42) {xi APS 78} [1696/9/153]	
Act in favour of John Hamilton for shelling and preparing barley	

(continued)

(continued)

Table of contents
[Cl 1 John Hamilton shall have privileges of a manufactory in relation to making so called "French barley"; but must not import the same]
[Cl 2 All other persons prevents from making or preparing "French barley" under penalty of 500 merks; confiscation of mills & engines]
[Cl 3 Nothing prevents any person preparing barley in any way or manner which is different from John Hamilton]
[Cl 4 John Hamilton to work invention within two years or Act becomes null and void]
[Cl 5 Nothing in Act prevents a private person from making French barley for their own use]
Parliamentary minutes
12 Sep 1696 – Parliamentary Minutes – Remitted to C'tee for Trade [1696M/9/3]
24 Sep 1696 – Parliamentary Register – Overture for Act [1696/9/48]
24 Sep 1696 – Parliamentary Minutes – Rep laid on table [1696M/9/9]
Parliamentary papers
None

James Melville's Ratification 1696

SCOT26	1696
James Melville's Ratification 1696 (1696 c. 60) {x APS 103} [1696/9/202]	
Ratification in favour of Mr James Melville of Halhill	

[s 1 The prorogation and ratification of a letter patent for making sailcloth granted to James Melville, Robert Burleigh and James Melville

(a) Confirms patent of 1 January 1694 to Melville, Burleigh and Melville granting a monopoly in the making and selling of sailcloth for seven years.
(b) To set up the Sailcloth Society
(c) Time for setting up a society prolonged to 19 years a start to made within seven years, with same privilege as before]

Parliamentary minutes
None
Parliamentary papers
None

Wemyss Manufactory Act 1698

SCOT27	1698
Wemyss Manufactory Act 1698 (1698 c. 45) {x APS 179} [A1693/1/19]	
Act and ratification in favour of the glass manufactory at the Wemyss	
Table of contents	

[s 1 Ratify Privy Council Act so that David, lord Elcho, enjoys the privileges, liberties and immunities granted by former Acts of Parliament to such glass manufactory]
[s 2 All persons prohibited for nine years from making any new species of glasses, namely, mirror or looking-glass plates, coach glasses, moulded glasses and window glasses]
[s 3 Does not apply where said person sets up and make the said species of glasses within two years from today]
[s 4 Does not apply to anything imported within the next nine months]
[s 5 Where infringed one half to be applied for the use of the said manufactory and the other half to the discoverer]
[s 5 David Wemyss must furnish to the kingdom as good and as cheap as the foresaid species of glass as has been sold at London, and if he fails the privilege and benefit is let go]
[s 7 This Act shall not prejudge the privileges granted to the glass manufactory at Leith]
[s 8 It is declared that this present Act shall be in no way prejudicial to the Act granted in favour of the glass manufactory at Atcheson's Haven]

Parliamentary minutes
18 Aug 1698 – Parliamentary Register – First Reading [1698/7/86]
18 Aug 1698 – Parliamentary Minutes – First Reading [M1698/7/8]
29 Aug 1698 – Parliamentary Register – Second Reading [1698/7/104]

| 29 Aug 1698 – Parliamentary Minutes – Second Reading [M1698/7/18] |
| 1 Sep 1698 – Parliamentary Register – Touched with Sceptre [1698/7/157] |
| 1 Sep 1698 – Parliamentary Minutes – Touched with Sceptre [M1698/7/21] |
| **Parliamentary papers** |
| None |

Morison's Haven Glass Manufactory Act 1698

SCOT28	1698
Morison's Haven Glass Manufactory Act 1698 (1698 c. 46) {x APS 180} [A1698/7/171]	
Act and ratification in favour of the glass manufactory at Morison's Haven	
Table of contents	
[s 1 Ratifying Act of Privy Council allowing manufactory at Atcheson's Haven (Morison's Haven) date 27 April 1697] [s 2 All persons prohibited for nine years from making any new species of glasses, namely, mirror or looking-glass plates, coach glasses, moulded glasses and window glasses] [s 3 Does not apply where said person sets up and make the said species of glasses within two years from today] [s 4 Does not apply to anything imported within the next nine months] [s 5 William Morrison must furnish to the kingdom as good and as cheap as the foresaid species of glass has been sold at London, and if he fails the privilege and benefit is let go] [s 7 This Act shall not prejudge the privileges granted to the glass manufactory at Leith] [s 8 It is declared that this present Act shall be in no way prejudicial to the Act granted in favour of the glass manufactory set up by David Wemyss, Lord Elcho] [s 9 William Morrison to give bond to the Privy Council to the said effect under the penalty of £100 sterling]	
Parliamentary minutes	
3 Aug 1698 – Parliamentary Register – Pet read [1698/7/47] 3 Aug 1698 – Parliamentary Minutes – Pet read [M1698/7/7] 4 Aug 1698 – C'tee Minutes [C1698/7/20] 5 Aug 1698– Parliamentary Register – First Reading [1698/7/54] 5 Aug 1698 – Parliamentary Minutes – First Reading [M1698/7/8] 18 Aug 1698 – Parliamentary Register – Second Reading (but put off) [1698/7/86] 18 Aug 1698 – Parliamentary Minutes – Second Reading (but put off) [M1698/7/13] 29 Aug 1698 – Parliamentary Register – Second Reading [1698/7/104] 29 Aug 1698 – Parliamentary Minutes – Second Reading [M1698/7/18] 1 Sep 1698 – Parliamentary Register – Touched with Sceptre [1698/7/157] 1 Sep 1698 – Parliamentary Minutes – Touched with Sceptre [M1698/7/21]	
Parliamentary papers	
None	

Thomas Rome's Bill 1701

SCOT29	1701
Thomas Rome's Bill 1701	
Draft Act in favour of Mr Thomas Rome and partners {x APS App 101} [A1700/10/56]	
Table of contents	
[s 1 Grant to John Rome, Matthew Colson, Thomas Rome and assignees to erect smelting manufactory; and to exercise their trade for 21 years] [s 2 Prohibition on any party setting up the same art of smelting, extracting and manufacturing during the period of 21 years; those who do contrary forfeit the minerals smelted and the tools for doing so] [s 3 Persons are free to smelt using any other method as used before] [s 4 Not permissible to hire any servants or artists employed by Mr Rome or his partners without their consent; any challenge of the hiring of the servant may be done within a year and a day and if so challenged must return them within 24 hours, pay damages for loss of the servant and a fine of £100 to Mr Rome and partners] [s 5 Mr Rome and partners may use any engine formerly made use of them in England, notwithstanding any particular Act made in the Realm]	

(continued)

(continued)

Parliamentary minutes
31 Jan 1701 – Parliamentary Minutes – First Reading [M1700/10/56]

Parliamentary papers
None

James Gregory's Petition 1701

SCOT30	1701
James Gregory's Petition {x APS 240} [A1700/10/153]	
Petition for the sole right to use a Machine invented by him for raising water	

Table of contents
No further details

Parliamentary minutes
3 Jan 1701 - Parliamentary Register [1700/10/153]
3 Jan 1701 – Parliamentary Minutes [M1700/10/34]
25 Jan 1701 – Parliamentary Register – Pets read {x APS 267} [1700/10/217]
25 Jan 1701 – Parliamentary Minutes [M1700/10/51]

Parliamentary papers
None

James Smith's Act 1701

SCOT31	1701
James Smith's Act 1701	
Act in favour of Mr James Smith {x APS 267} [A1700/10/218]	

Table of contents
[s 1 No person may make use of the invention without James Smith's permission for the remaining space of 34 years yet to run on Thomas Savory's extended patent]

Parliamentary minutes
None

Parliamentary papers
25 Jan 1701 – Parliamentary Register Pet [1700/10/217]
25 Jan 1701 – Parliamentary Minutes – Pet [M1700/10/51]

Montgomery and Linn's Act 1703

SCOT32	1703
Montgomery and Linn's Act 1703 {xi APS 112} [1703/5/199]	
Act in favour of William Montgomery and George Linn for a manufactory of lame, purslane and earthen ware	

Table of contents
[s 1 William Montgomery and George Linn, their heirs and assignees and such other persons as they shall assume in company and society with themselves, to enjoy all privileges of manufactory for making lame, purslane and earthen ware] [s 2 Grant to William Montgomery and George Linn, their heirs and assignees and such other persons as they shall assume, is, the sole power of making the said lame or earthen ware within this kingdom for the space of fifteen years; prohibits all other persons to make the same, without special licence of the Montgomery and Linn under the penalty of two thousand pounds] [s 3 Act shall not stop or impede any person from bringing into this kingdom from abroad any of the said lame, purslane and earthen ware or to sell the same as they could have done of before, nor to make it where it is in use at this present time] [s 4 Any Act or gift by Her Majesty for lame, purslane or earthenware which has not taken effect shall be thereafter be of no force or effect]

Parliamentary minutes
31 Aug 1703 – Parliamentary Register – First Reading [1703/5/152]
31 Aug 1703 – Parliamentary Minutes – First Reading [M1703/5/52]
7 Sep 1703 – Parliamentary Register – Second Reading [1703/5/171]
7 Sep 1703 – Parliamentary Minutes – Second Reading [M1703/5/57]
16 Sep 1703 – Parliamentary Register – Royal Assent [1703/5/188]
16 Sep 1703 – Parliamentary Minutes – Royal Assent [M1703/5/63]
Parliamentary papers
None

George Campbell's Act 1705

SCOT33	1705
George Campbell's Act 1705 {xi APS 220–221} [A1705/6/48]	
Act in favour of Mr George Campbell	
Table of contents	
[s 1 Grant of the exclusive right to use the invention for making salt for twenty five years from date of Act] [s 2 It is lawful to accept the contracts already made and must be accepted on the same terms] [s 3 Manufactories retain immunities under the Acts of 1661 and 1681] [s 4 None should present themselves as the inventor of the technology] [s 5 Court may order the ceasing of the salt pans upon summary complaint &c.; and answerable to George Campbell]	
Parliamentary minutes	
3 Aug 1705 – Parliamentary Register – Pet be read [1705/6/41]	
3 Aug 1705 – Parliamentary Minutes – Pet be read [M1705/6/14]	
8 Aug 1705 – Parliamentary Register – Pet read again [1705/6/46]	
8 Aug 1705 – Parliamentary Minutes – Pet read again [M1705/6/16]	
9 Aug 1705 – Parliamentary Register – Pet read [1705/6/47]	
Parliamentary papers	
None	

2 Manufactory Acts

Manufactories Acts 1641

SCOT34	Commission for manufactories (1641 c. 100) {v APS 412, 659} [1641/8/194]

[s 1 Persons establishing manufactories within this kingdom granted all liberties, privileges and immunities to the erectors thereof]

[s 2 Persons nominated by the lords of secret council full power to consult, advise and determine upon the best rules, overtures and propositions and ways for erecting and maintaining the said manufactories of all sorts]

[s 3 Secret council appoint correction houses for the good of the said manufactories and restraint of idle and masterless beggars]

[s 4 Secret council has power to prescribe rules for those who have already or shall during the time of this commission erect and maintain any of the said manufactories; secret council to direct letters against masterless people and their receivers, as well to burgh as landward, commanding them to work at such reasonable rates as the said Commissioners or quorum thereof shall appoint]

[s 5 Secret council has power to make corporations and to grant them privileges according to the laws of the kingdom]

[s 6 Said manufactories granted following privileges and immunities following:

(a) all Spanish and foreign fine wool for making of fine cloth shall be custom free;
(b) all dyed wares, oil and other necessaries for the use of the said works only shall be free of all custom;
(c) all parcels of cloth, serge and others made by any who have erected or shall erect any of the said works shall be custom and impost free for the space of 15 years after the erecting thereof;
(d) the workers of the said works erected or to be erected shall be free of any taxation or imposition to be imposed on the kingdom for any occasion bygone or to come;
(e) it shall not be lawful to any in the kingdom to hire, reserve or maintain any of the servants of the said works without consent of the masters thereof]

8 Sep 1641 – Overtures on Manufactories	[M1641/8/19]/[A1641/8/31]	
10 Sep 1641 – Commission Appointed	[M1641/8/21]	
16 Nov 1641 – Minutes	[M1641/8/75]	
17 Nov 1641 – Ratification in favour of the weavers of Edinburgh	[1641/8/290]	
SCOT35	Act in favour of manufactories, masters, workers therein, servants and apprentices [no requirement to quarter soldiers or apprentices to serve] (3 Mar 1645)	(1645 c. 154) {vi (i) APS 367}	[1645/1/163]
SCOT36	Ratification of the Acts and articles concerning the advancement of manufactories within this kingdom [Ratification of Commission decision] (4 Feb 1646)	(1646 c. 290) {vi(i) APS 608}	[1646/11/307]
SCOT37	Act in favour of the silver and gold lace weavers (John and Anne Hunter) (26 Mar 1647)	(1647 c. 408) {vi(i) APS 794}	[1646/11/479]
SCOT38	Act anent the soap-works (15 Mar 1649) [Also included as SCOT14]	(1649 c. 275) {vi (ii) APS 300}	[1649/1/310]

Manufactories Acts 1661

SCOT39	Act for erecting of manufactories (1661 c. 280) {vii APS 261} [1661/1/344]

[s 1 Persons as have or shall set up any manufactories granted the following privileges]

[s 2 Any foreigner who comes to kingdom to work and teach making cloth stuffs, stockings, soap or any other kind of manufactory, to enjoy the benefit and privileges that a native enjoys, with power to erect manufactories, either in burgh or landward as they shall think fit, and there to dwell and exercise their trade without any stop or trouble]

[s 3 All oil, dying stuffs, foreign wool, potashes, or other materials used manufactories that are imported, to be free of custom dues]

[s 4 All cloth stuffs, stockings, or any other commodities to be made and exported by manufactory to be free of custom and excise for nineteen years after January 1662]

[s 5 Any stock employed for the manufactories is to be free of all public and private taxes; all customers, collectors, and others are discharged to demand any such customs]

[s 6 Every person prohibited from exporting any wool or skins with wool upon them or any materials useful for manufactories, until they be made in work or put to the best price for the good of the kingdom; penalty forfeit half to King half to informer and further penalty as should be imposed]

[s 7 All regraters and forestallers of markets of wool prohibited; no merchant or person whatsoever to buy and keep up wool, but must sell it on the open market]

[s 8 Any wool undersold by weight shall be confiscated; one half to his majesty's use and the other half to the discoverer]

[s 9 Manufactories are exempt from quarterings or levying of soldiers upon manufactories or the masters]

[s 10 No person shall take the servants or apprentices of the manufactories without consent of their master]

[s 11 Masters of manufactories to meet by themselves for making of ordinances for the good and advancement of their trade, for ordering servants, appointing inspector, to affix a mark to show sufficient]

[s 12 Privy council or exchequer to consider overtures for the good of manufactories, and to make such orders and grant such further liberties and privileges to them as they shall think just]

[s 13 Exchequer may grant licence for exporting of wool and skins]

SCOT40	Act establishing companies and societies for making linen cloth, stuffs etc. (12 Jun 1661)	(1661 c. 275) {vii APS 255}	[1661/1/339]
SCOT41	Act discharging the exportation of woollen yarn, worsted, broken copper and pewter (28 Jun 1661)	(1661 c. 23) {vii APS 465}	[1661/1/385]
SCOT42	Act concerning beggars and vagabonds (manufactories can seize beggars to work) (25 Sep 1663)	(1663 c. 52) {vii APS 485}	[1663/6/75]
SCOT43	Act in favour of silk weavers, printers etc. (21 Aug 1663)	(1663 c. 25) {vii APS 466}	[1663/6/42]
SCOT44	Act concerning the making of cards (John Aikman, James Riddell, James Currie and James Auchterlony) (29 Sep 1663)	(1663 c. 59) {vii APS 488}	[1663/6/83]
SCOT45	Act anent linseed, hemp seed and steel (exempting these industries from duties) (2 Oct 1663)	(1663 c. 63) {vii APS 491}	[1663/6/87]
SCOT46	Act concerning the excise and customs (limited immunities to those conforming to 1661 Act) (15 Dec 1669)	(1669 c. 18) {vii APS 563}	[1669/10/31]
SCOT47	Act in favour of printers and stationers [exempting duties for paper] (23 Dec 1669)	(1669 c. 115) {vii APS 655}	[1669/10/132]
SCOT48	Act concerning the privileges of royal burghs (allowing exemptions from duties for manufactories) (10 Jul 1672)	(1672 c. 5) {viii APS 63}	[1672/6/13]
SCOT49	Act for establishing correction-houses for idle beggars and vagabonds (coalmasters can seize vagabonds to work) (4 Sep 1672)	(1672 c. 41) {viii APS 91}	[1672/6/52]

Manufactories Acts 1881

| SCOT50 | Act for encouraging trade and manufactories (1681 c. 78) {viii APS 348} [1681/7/36] |

[s 1 All persons prohibited from importing gold or silver thread, gold or silver lace &c.; all patterned or embroidered silk stuff; all such imported without certification to be destroyed and importer fined]

[s 2 The wearing of any said prohibited goods after 1 April 1682 fined 500 merks Scots money; clothes confiscated (extended period for King's army)]

[s 3 All persons prohibited from importing linen, cotton, wool or lint &c.; gloves, slippers &c. all such imported without certification to be destroyed and importer fined]

[s 4 Any collector of customs who does not stop the entry of these goods lose their office, banned from public office and fined value of goods; the fine to go to the informer]

[s 5 All Acts already made for the encouragement of the manufactories ratified; strangers coming to Kingdom to set up manufactories given privileges and freedoms of native]

(continued)

(continued)

[s 6 All materials useful for manufactories which are imported are free of custom duties in all time coming]

[s 7 All cloths, stuffs, stockings or any other commodities to be made and exported by manufactories free of all custom and for the space of nineteen years]

[s 8 All material for erecting and entertaining any manufactories free of taxes]

[s 9 All quartering and levying of soldiers, and that all servants of the said manufactories shall be free of watching, warding, militia or levies during their actual service for the space of seven years]

[s 10 Masters of manufactories to make ordinances for the right ordering of their servants, sufficiency of their stuffs, cloths and others, and appointing inspectors]

[s 11 Ratifying 43rd Act of the first session of his majesty's first Parliament, and the 46th Act of the same session of Parliament]

[s 12 All linen brought to market must be certain specified sizes or confiscated]

[s 13 Privy council to declare these manufactories already set up, or that hereafter shall be set up, to be such to the effect they may enjoy the privileges, liberties and immunities granted by the said Acts of Parliament]

[s 14 Collectors must under oath give details of those infringing Act failure to do so lose office and banned in future; halve of penalties collected to customs collector and the other half to King; where a different informer that informer gets share]

[s 15 Any proceedings must be brought within three months]

[s 16 This Act is in place of any former sumptuary law in relation to apparel]

5 Sep 1681 – C'tee Minutes – Petition related to Manufactories (Edinburgh Merchants)		[C1681/7/24]	
9 Sep 1681 – C'tee Minutes – Draft approved		[C1681/7/30]	
9 Sep 1681 – Parliamentary Minutes – Twice Read [some comments of prices]		[M1681/7/17] also see [A1681/7/17]	
12 Sep 1681 – C'tee Minutes – Act approved		[C1681/7/32]	
13 Sep 1681 – Parliamentary Minutes – Act approved		[M1681/7/18]	
SCOT51	Act declaring the woollen work of serge, called serge de Nime and other stuff erected by James Armour, to be a manufactory (17 Sep 1681)	(1681 c. 104) {viii APS 361}	[1681/7/65]
	15 Sep 1681 – C'tee Minutes (Pet granted)		[C1681/7/36]
SCOT52	Act declaring the sugar-work at Glasgow to be a manufactory (Frederick Hamilton and John Corse) (17 Sep 1681)	(1681 c. 103) {viii APS 360}	[1681/7/641]
	5 Sep 1681 – C'tee Minutes (Pet Pres)		[C1681/7/25]
	15 Sep 1681 – C'tee Minutes (Pet approved)		[C1681/7/36]
SCOT53	Act anent the prices of French and Spanish salt (17 Sep 1681)	(1681 c. 93) {viii ASP 356}	[1681/7/51]
SCOT54	Act declaring the Greenland fishing to be a manufactory (16 Jun 1685)	(1685 c. 51) {viii APS 490}	[1685/4/75]
SCOT55	Act Concerning Trade and Manufactures 1685 [confirming Act of 1681] (30 May 1685)	(1685 c. 28) {viii APS 478}	[1685/4/51]
	30 May 1685 - Parliamentary Minutes (Read and approved)		[M1685/4/14]
SCOT56	Act of reference to the council ament allowing importation of prohibited goods (14 Jun 1686)	(1686 c. 32) {viii APS 600}	[1686/4/48]
SCOT57	Act in favour of John Meikle (15 Jun 1686)	(1686. c. 43) {viii APS 608}	[1686/4/60]
SCOT58	Act in favour of Robert Gibb (27 Apr 1689)	(1689 c. 76) {ix APS 76}	[1689/3/191]
SCOT59	Proposal for Gunpowder Manufactory (30 Jun 1690)		
	30 Jun 1690 – Parliamentary Minutes (Rep)		[M1690/4/29]
	30 Jun 1690 – Rep		[A1690/4/7]
SCOT60	Draft Act anent the manufactory of cards (17 Jul 1690)		
	17 Jul 1690 – Parliamentary Minutes (Remitted to C'tee)		[M1899/4/41]
SCOT61	Manufactory at Leith (17 Jul 1690)		[C1681/7/36]
SCOT62	Draft Act for Robert Douglas in Leith Manufactory of Starch (24 May 1693)		
	24 May 1693 – C'tee Minutes		[C1693/4/35]
SCOT63	Act for erecting a manufactory for making Colchester baize (14 Jun 1693)	(1693 c. 49) {ix APS 313}	[1693/4/106]
	3 Jun1693 – C'tee Minutes (Act Pres)		[C1693/4/38]

	6 Jun 1693 – C'tee Minutes (Day appointed)		[C1693/4/40]
	13 Jun 1693 – Parliamentary Minutes (Act approved)		[M1693/4/27]
SCOT64	Act in favour of William Scott, cabinet maker, for the making of coaches (14 Jun 1693)	(1693 c. 55) {ix APS 319}	[1693/4/112]
	Pet – 14 Jun 1693		[M1693/4/28]
SCOT65	Act in favour of the linen manufactory erecting them in a free incorporation (Leith) (14 Jun 1693)	(1693 c. 52) {ix APS 316}	[1693/4/109]
	8 May 1693 – C'tee Minutes		[C1693/4/26]
	16 May 1693 – C'tee Minutes (Witness summons)		[C1693/4/32]
	22 May 1693 – C'tee Minutes (Date to hear witnesses)		[C1693/4/34]
	13 Jun 1693 – Parliamentary Minutes (Act approved)		[M1693/4/27]
	14 Jun 1693 – Parliamentary Minutes (Royal Assent)		[M1693/4/28]
SCOT66	Act for the woollen manufactory at Newmills (14 Jun 1693)	(1693 c. 53) {ix APS 317}	[1693/4/110]
	1 Jun 1693 – C'tee Minutes (Act read)		[C1693/4/36]
	2 Jun 1693 – C'tee Minutes (Rep read –Favourable)		[C1693/4/37]
	3 Jun 1693 – C'tee Minutes (Amds made)		[C1693/4/38]
	6 Jun 1693 – C'tee Minutes (Approve Bill)		[C1693/4/39]
	13 Jun 1693 – Parliamentary Minutes (Act approved)		[M1693/4/27]
	14 Jun 1693 – Parliamentary Minutes (Royal Assent)		[M1693/4/28]
SCOT67	Act anent the right making and measuring of linen cloth (14 Jun 1693)	(1693 c. 48) {ix APS 311}	[1693/4/105]
	Overture (6 May 1693)		[C1693/4/25]
SCOT68	Act in favour of the manufactory of linen cloth, woollen and baize (14 Jun 1693)	(1693 c. 49) {ix APS 313}	[1693/4/109]
	8 May 1693 – C'tee Minutes (Act suggested)		[C1693/4/26]
	3 Jun 1693 – C'tee Minutes (Approved)		[C1693/4/38]
	6 Jun 1693 – C'tee Minutes (Cons)		[C1693/4/40]
	13 Jun 1693 – Parliamentary Minutes (Approved)		[M1693/4/27]
	14 Jun 1693 – Parliamentary Minutes (Royal Assent)		[M1693/4/28]
SCOT69	William Scott (14 Jun 1693)	(1693 c. 55) {ix APS 321}	[1693/4/112]
	14 Jun 1693 – Minutes (Act passed)		[M1693/4/28]
SCOT70	Ratification in favour of James Hamilton of Little Earnock (making playing card) (15 Jun 1693)	(1693 c. 83) {ix APS 341}	[1693/4/149]
SCOT71	Draft Act in favour of Robert Douglas for establishing a manufactory in Leith of soap work, sugar, porcelain, lime works and starch (7 Jun 1695)	(1695 c. 84) {ix APS 491}	[M1695/5/14]
SCOT72	Act for a manufactory of white paper (10 Jul 1695)	(1695 c. 41) {ix APS 429}	[1695/5/169]
	5 Jul 1695 – Parliamentary Minutes (Act approved)		[M1695/5/28]
	10 Jul 1695 – Parliamentary Minutes (Royal Assent)		[M1695/5/31]
SCOT73	Act in favour of the linen manufactory (11 Jul 1695)	(1695 c. 43) {ix APS 430}	[1695/5/173]
SCOT74	Act in favour of Whitfield Heyter and others (denied right of manufactory) (17 Jul 1695)	(1695 c. 86) {ix APS 492}	[1695/5/237]
SCOT75	Act in favour of Robert Douglas (17 Jul 1695)	(1695 c. 100) {ix APS 88}	[1695/5/235]
	7 Jun 1695 – Parliamentary Register (Act remitted to C'tee)		[1695/5/56]

(continued)

(continued)

	7 Jun 1695 – C'tee Minutes (C'tee Cons)		[C1695/5/22]
	12 Jun 1695 – C'tee Minutes (C'tee approve)		[C1695/5/23]
	4 Jul 1695 – Parliamentary Minutes (Brought from C'tee)		[M1695/5/27]
	16 Jul 1695 – Parliamentary Minutes (Act approved)		[M1695/5/36]
SCOT76	Act in favour of Alexander Fearn for engraving (17 Jul 1695)	(1695 c. 82) {ix APS 490}	[1695/5/233]
	17 Jul 1695 – Parliamentary Minutes (Act approved)		[M1695/5/37]
SCOT77	Act in favour of comb-makers (John Holmes, Thomas Leishman and William Park) (17 Jul 1695)	(1695 c. 81) {ix APS 490}	[1695/5/232]
	17 Jul 1695 – Parliamentary Minutes (Act approved)		[M1695/5/37]
SCOT78	Act anent the skinners (17 Jul 1695)	(1695 c. 67) {ix APS 461}	[1695/5/202]
SCOT79	Act for discharging the vending of rum (17 Jul 1695)	(1695 c. 70) {ix APS 462}	[1695/5/205]
	25 Sep 1696 – Repealed by Act		[1696/9/59]
SCOT80	Draft of an Act for encouraging woollen manufactory of Newmills (9 Oct 1696)		[1696/9/121]
	8 Oct 1696 – Parliamentary Register (Pet)		[1696/9/156]
	9 Oct 1696 – Parliamentary Minutes (1R)		[M1696/9/18]
SCOT81	Act for erecting a new sugar manufactory at Glasgow (9 Oct 1696)	(1696 c. 33) {x APS 66}	[1696/9/152]
	5 Oct 1696 – Parliamentary Register (1R)		[1696/9/94]
	5 Oct 1696 – Parliamentary Minutes (Read)		[M1696/9/15]
	8 Oct 1696 – Parliamentary Minutes (Act approved)		[M1696/9/17]
	8 Oct 1696 – Parliamentary Register (Act approved)		[1696/9/120]
	9 Oct 1696 – Parliamentary Minutes (Royal Assent)		[M1696/9/18]
	9 Oct 1696 – Parliamentary Register (Royal Assent)		[1696/9/128]
SCOT82	Act in favour of William Erskine for making salt (12 Oct 1696)	(1696 c. 49) {x APS 80}	[1696/9/179]
SCOT83	Act Making Salt (12 Oct 1696)	(1696 c. 49) {x APS 80}	[1669/9/177]
SCOT84	Act in favour of Sir John Shaw of Greenock and others for making salt after a new manner (12 Oct 1696)	(1696 c. 48) {x APS 80}	[1696/9/178]
SCOT85	Act in favour of John Hamilton for shelling and preparing barley (12 Oct 1696)		[1696/9/153]
SCOT86	Petition of Joseph Ormiston and William Elliot [to set up a silk manufactory] (10 Aug 1698)		[A1698/7/7]
	4 Aug 1698 – C'tee Minutes (Adj)		[C1698/7/19]
	9 Aug 1698 – C'tee Minutes (Overture adj)		[C1698/7/21]
	10 Aug 1698 – Overture for Act		[A1698/7/9]
SCOT87	Petition for Woollen Manufactory in Aberdeen (22 Aug 1698)		[1698/7/96]
	22 Aug 1698 – Pet		
SCOT88	Overture for prohibiting the exportation of wool (24 Aug 1698)		[1698/7/101]
	24 Aug 1698 – Parliamentary Minutes (Noted)		[M1698/7/16]
SCOT89	Overture for encouraging the woollen manufactory (24 Aug 1698)		[1698/7/101]
	24 Aug 1698 – Parliamentary Minutes (Noted)		[M1698/7/16]
SCOT90	Act in favour of the manufactory for ropes and cordage at Glasgow (30 Aug 1698)	(1698 c. 13) {x APS 154}	[1698/7/120]
	22 Aug 1698 – Parliamentary Register (1R)		[1698/7/96]

	22 Aug 1698 – Parliamentary Minutes (1R)		[M1698/7/15]
	29 Aug 1698 – Parliamentary Register (2R)		[1698/7/104]
	30 Aug 1698 – Parliamentary Register (Royal Assent)		[1698/7/108]
	30 Aug 1698 – Parliamentary Minutes (Royal Assent)		[M1698/7/19]
SCOT91	Act for Glass Manufactory at Morison's Haven (1 Sep 1698)	(1698 c. 46) {x APS 180}	[1698/7/171]
	3 Aug 1698 – Parliamentary Register (Pet)		[1698/7/47]
	3 Aug 1698 – Parliamentary Minutes (Pet)		[M1698/7/7]
	5 Aug 1698 – Parliamentary Register (1R)		[1698/7/54]
	5 Aug 1698 – Parliamentary Minutes (1R)		[M1698/7/8]
	18 Aug 1698 – Parliamentary Register (2R adj)		[1698/7/86]
	18 Aug 1698 – Parliamentary Minutes (2R adj)		[M1698/7/13]
	29 Aug 1698 – Parliamentary Register (2R)		[1698/7/104]
	29 Aug 1698 – Parliamentary Minutes (2R)		[M1698/7/18]
	1 Sep 1698 – Parliamentary Register (Royal Assent)		[1698/7/157]
	1 Sep 1698 – Parliamentary Minutes (Royal Assent)		[M1698/7/21]
SCOT92	Act in favour of the manufactory of white paper (30 Aug 1698)		[1698/7/123]
	30 Aug 1698 – Parliamentary Register (Pres)		
	30 Aug 1698 – Parliamentary Minutes (Pres)		[M1698/7/19]
SCOT93	Act in favour of the glass manufactory at the Wemyss (1 Sep 1698)	1698 c. 45 {x APS 179}	[1698/7/170]
	18 Aug 1698 – Parliamentary Register (Debated and adj)		[1698/7/86]
	18 Aug 1698 – Parliamentary Minutes (Debated and adj)		[M1698/7/13]
	29 Aug 1698 – Parliamentary Register (2R)		[1698/7/104]
	29 Aug 1698 – Parliamentary Minutes (2R)		[M1698/7/18]
	1 Sep 1698 – Parliamentary Register (Royal Assent)		[1698/7/157]
	1 Sep 1698 – Parliamentary Minutes (Royal Assent)		[M1698/7/21]
SCOT94	Overture for glass manufactory in favour of William Morrison of Prestongrange (4 Sep 1698)		
	4 Aug 1698 – C'tee Minutes		[C1698/7/19]
SCOT95	Petitions for encouraging manufactories East Lothian (27 May 1700)		
	27 May 1700 – Parliamentary Register		[1700/5/41]
	27 May 1700 – Parliamentary Minutes		[M1700/5/3]
SCOT96	Petitions to restrict imports to support local manufactories (27 May 1700)		
	27 May 1700 – Lanark		[A1700/5/5]
	27 May 1700 – Stirlingshire		[A1700/5/6]
	27 May 1700 – Haddington		[A1700/5/8]
	27 May 1700 – Cupar		[A/1700/5/9]
	27 May 1700 – East Lothian (Parliamentary Register)		[1700/5/41]
SCOT97	Petition of James Montgomery manufactory of glass and soap works Glasgow (12 Nov 1700)		[A1700/10/4]
	Reasons for granting Petition (12 Nov 1700)		[A1700/10/5]
	12 Nov 1700 – Parliamentary Register (Pet)		[1700/10/34]
	12 Nov 1700 – Parliamentary Minutes (Pet)		[M1700/10/6]
SCOT98	Petition of William Barclay making ale-aigre or vinegar a manufactory [and discharge, i.e. exclusive right] (14 Nov 1700)	{x APS 210, 212}	[1700/10/43]
	14 Nov 1700 – Parliamentary Minutes (Pet)		[M1700/10/7]

(continued)

(continued)

SCOT99	Petition of David Maxwell woollen manufactory at Newmills fleece wool manufactory (14 Nov 1700)		
	14 Nov 1700 – Parliamentary Register (Pet)		[1700/10/41]
	14 Nov 1700 – Parliamentary Minutes (Pet)		[M1700/10/7]
SCOT100	Petition of Matthew and Daniel Campbell sugar works as manufactory (18 Nov 1700)	{x APS 212} {x APS App 52}	[A1700/10/6]
	18 Nov 1700 – Parliamentary Register (Pet)		[1700/10/58]
SCOT101	Petition of James Cowan vinegar manufactory (18 Nov 1700)		
	18 Nov 1700 – Parliamentary Register (Pet)		[1700/10/58]
	18 Nov 1700 – Parliamentary Minutes (Pet)		[M1700/10/10]
SCOT102	Petition of Matthew and Daniel Campbell sugar manufactory and a manufactory for distilling of brandy and strong waters (18 Nov 1700)		[A1700/10/6]
	18 Nov 1700 – Parliamentary Minutes (Pet ref to C'tee)		[M1700/10/10]
SCOT103	Draft Act Woollen Manufactory at Musselburg (21 Nov 1700)		
	21 Nov 1700 – Parliamentary Register (Read and C'tted)		[1700/10/62]
	21 Nov 1700 – Parliamentary Minutes (Read and C'tted)		[M1700/10/12]
SCOT104	Draft of an Act for prohibiting the importing, using and wearing of all foreign woollen manufactories (26 Nov 1700)		
	8 Nov 1700 – Parliamentary Minutes (Overture)		[M1700/10/5]
	26 Nov 1700 – Parliamentary Minutes (1R)		[M1700/10/15]
SCOT105	Petition of John Sochon (21 Nov 1700)	{x APS 220} {x APS App 56}	[A1700/10/10]
SCOT106	Petition of John Corse that his works for making shearing hooks etc. be erected in a manufactory (21 Nov 1700)		
	27 Nov 1700 – Parliamentary Register (Pet)		[1700/10/81]
	27 Nov 1700 – Parliamentary Minutes (Pet)		[M1700/10/16]
SCOT107	Petition of Alexander Monteith for the art discovered by him to draw spirits from malt equal in goodness to true French brandy be declared a manufactory (27 Nov 1700)	{x APS 220}	
	27 Nov 1700 – Parliamentary Register (Pet/C'tted)		[1700/10/81]
	27 Nov 1700 – Parliamentary Minutes (Pet)		[M1700/10/16]
SCOT108	Petition of the undertakers of the manufactory of worsted and other stuffs at Paul's Work and Bonnington be declared a manufactory (27 Nov 1700)		[A1700/10/11]
	27 Nov 1700 – Parliamentary Register (Pet)		[1700/10/81]
	27 Nov 1700 – Parliamentary Minutes (Pet)		[M1700/10/16]
SCOT109	Petition for John Schochan for grant for making hangings and factory declared a manufactory (27 Nov 1700)		[A1700/10/10]
	27 Nov 1700 – Parliamentary Register (Pet)		[1700/10/80]
	27 Nov 1700 – Parliamentary Minutes (Pet)		[M1700/10/16]
SCOT110	Draft of an Act to anent the woollen manufactories (13 Dec 1700)		
	2 Dec 1700 – Parliamentary Register (Brought Com for Trade)		[1700/10/91]
	2 Dec 1700 – Parliamentary Minutes (Brought Com for Trade)		[M1700/10/18]

	5 Dec 1700 – Parliamentary Register (Read and debated)		[1700/10/93]
	5 Dec 1700 – Parliamentary Minutes (Read and debated)		[M1700/10/19]
	6 Dec 1700 – Parliamentary Register (Read and debated)		[1700/10/96]
	6 Dec 1700 – Parliamentary Minutes (Read and debated)		[M1700/10/20]
	11 Dec 1700 – Parliamentary Register (Read and debated)		[1700/10/103]
	11 Dec 1700 – Parliamentary Minutes (Read and debated)		[M1700/10/22]
	13 Dec 1700 – Parliamentary Register (Read and clause added)		[1700/10/104]
	13 Dec 1700 – Parliamentary Minutes (Read and clause added)		[M1700/10/23]
SCOT111	Petition of James Dunlop trade of working stockings upon frames into a manufactory (23 Dec 1700)		
	23 Dec 1700 – Parliamentary Register (Pet)		[1700/10/126]
	23 Dec 1700 – Parliamentary Minutes (Pet)		[M1700/10/27]
SCOT112	Petition of William Park, comb-maker for rights of manufactory (23 Dec 1700)		
	23 Dec 1700 – Parliamentary Register (Pet)		[1700/10/128]
	23 Dec 1700 – Parliamentary Minutes (Pet)		[M1700/10/27]
SCOT113	Petition of William Corse a new sugar manufactory at Glasgow (23 Dec 1700)		
	23 Dec 1700 – Parliamentary Register (Pet)		[1700/10/126]
	23 Dec 1700 – Parliamentary Minutes (Pet)		[M1700/10/27]
SCOT114	Petition of James Turner, cabinet maker in Edinburgh (23 Dec 1700)	{x APS App 67)	[A1700/10/20]
	23 Dec 1700 – Parliamentary Register (Pet)		[1700/10/127]
	23 Dec 1700 – Parliamentary Minutes (Pet)		[M1700/10/27]
SCOT115	Petition of James and William Walkinshaw for a manufactory of cordage, canvas	{x APS 231}	
	23 Dec 1700 – Parliamentary Register (Pet)		[1700/10/126]
	23 Dec 1700 – Parliamentary Minutes (Pet)		[M1700/10/27]
SCOT116	Petitions to restrain the import of anything that can be imported into Scotland (9 Jan 1701)		
	9 Jan 1701 – Mid Lothian		[A1700/10/25]
	9 Jan 1701 – Wigtown		[A1700/10/26]
	9 Jan 1701 – Ayr		[A1700/10/25]
	9 Jan 1701 – Dunbarton		[A1700/10/28]
	9 Jan 1701 – Renfrew		[A1700/10/29]
	9 Jan 1701 – Inverness		[A1700/10/30]
	9 Jan 1701 – Nairn		[A1700/10/31]
	9 Jan 1701 – Fife		[A1700/10/32]
	9 Jan 1701 – Banff		[A1700/10/33]
	9 Jan 1701 – Elgin and Forres		[A1700/10/34]
	9 Jan 1701 – Orkney		[A1700/10/35]
	9 Jan 1701 – Perth		[A1700/10/36]
	9 Jan 1701 – Dysart		[A1700/10/37]
	9 Jan 1701 – Kirkcaldy		[A1700/10/38]
	9 Jan 1701 – Anstruther Easter		[A1700/10/39]
	9 Jan 1701 – Inverness		[A1700/10/40]
	9 Jan 1701 – Crail		[A1700/10/41]

(continued)

(continued)

SCOT117	Draft of Act for encouraging manufactories (17 Jan 1701)	{x APS 251}	
	17 Jan 1701 – Parliamentary Register (1R)		[1700/10/187]
	17 Jan 1701 – Parliamentary Minutes (1R)		[M1700/10/44]
SCOT118	Act in favour of Mr Thomas Rome and partners [for improving extraction of minerals] declared manufactory (31 Jan 1701)	{x APS App 101}	[A1700/10/56]
	[Also included as SCOT29]		
SCOT119	Overture by James Moir for improving woollen manufactories (22 Jun 1703)	{xi APS 63}	
	22 Jun 1703 – Parliamentary Register (Adj)		[1703/5/86]
	22 Jun 1703 – Parliamentary Minutes (Adj)		[M1703/5/18]
SCOT120	Act in favour of Mr William Black (1 Sep 1703)	{xi APS 81}	[1703/5/155]
	1 Sep 1703 – Parliamentary Register (Pet)		[1703/5/154]
	1 Sep 1703 – Parliamentary Minutes (Pet)		[M1703/5/53]
SCOT121	Act in favour of William Hogg of Harcarse (2 Sep 1703)	{xi APS 82}	
	14 Jun 1703 – Parliamentary Register (Pet)		[1703/5/67]
	14 Jun 1703 – Parliamentary Minutes (Pet)		[M1703/5/15]
	2 Sep 1703 – Parliamentary Register (Pet/Act annexed)		[1703/5/158]
	2 Sep 1703 – Parliamentary Minutes (Pet)		[M1703/5/54]
SCOT122	Act in favour of the woollen manufactory of Musselburg (2 Sep 1703)	{xi APS 82}	
	2 Sep 1703 – Parliamentary Register (Pet/Act annexed)		[1703/5/157]
	2 Sep 1703 – Parliamentary Minutes (Pet)		[M1703/5/54]
SCOT123	Act in favour of William Montgomery and George Lind for a manufactory of china, porcelain and earthenware (16 Sep 1703)	(1703 c. 12) {xi APS 111}	[1703/5/199]
	31 Aug 1703 – Parliamentary Register (Overture)		[1703/5/12]
	31 Aug 1703 – Parliamentary Minutes (Overture)		[M1703/5/52]
	7 Sep 1703 – Parliamentary Register (Read and approved)		[1703/5/171]
	7 Sep 1703 – Parliamentary Minutes (Read and approved)		[M1703/5/57]
	16 Sep 1703 – Parliamentary Register (Royal Assent)		[1703/5/188]
	16 Sep 1703 – Parliamentary Minutes (Royal Assent)		[M1703/5/63]
SCOT124	Representations of Merchants of Edinburgh to ban wearing silk to support local woollen production (3 Aug 1704)	{xi APS App 53, 54}	
	3 Aug 1704 – Representations		[A1704/7/24]
	3 Aug 1704 – Answer to representations from silk makers		[A1704/7/25]
	3 Aug 1704 – Parliamentary Register (Representations)		[1704/7/57]
	3 Aug 1704 – Parliamentary Minutes (Representations)		[M1704/7/8]
SCOT125	Petition of Lyle of Garden for a cloth manufactory (9 Aug 1704)	{xi APS 152]	
	9 Aug 1704 – Parliamentary Register (Pet)		[1704/7/75]
	9 Aug 1704 – Parliamentary Minutes (Pet)		[M1704/7/12]

SCOT126	Petition against Act discharging of all woollen manufacturing and allowing the exporting of wool (22 Aug 1704) 22 Aug 1704 – Parliamentary Register (Pet against)		[A1704/7/49] [1704/7/113]
SCOT127	Act declaring linen and woollen manufactory free of duty (21 Sep 1705) 5 Sep 1705 – Parliamentary Register (Overture/1R) 5 Sep 1705 – Parliamentary Minutes (Overture/1R) 7 Sep 1705 – Parliamentary Register (Read and approved) 7 Sep 1705 – Parliamentary Minutes (Read and approved) 21 Sep 1705 – Parliamentary Register (Royal Assent) 21 Sep 1705 – Parliamentary Minutes (Royal Assent)	(1705 c. 52) {xi APS 296}	[1705/6/196] [1705/6/96] [M1705/6/32] [1705/6/107] [M1705/6.34] [1705/6/190] [M1705/6/40]
SCOT128	Petition for Sarah for privilege of a japanning manufactory (14 Sep 1705)		[M1705/6/38]
SCOT129	Petition for Sarah Dalrymple craving the privilege of a japanning manufactory (14 Sep 1705) 14 Sep 1705 – Parliamentary Register (Pet) 14 Sep 1705 – Parliamentary Minutes (Pet)	{xi APS 249}	 [1705/6/125] [M1705/6/38]
SCOT130	Act appointing a council of trade (21 Sep 1705)	(1705 c. 49) {xi APS 294}	[1705/6/193]
SCOT131	Petition of Alexander Black for a starch manufactory (24 Mar 1707) 24 Mar 1707 – Parliamentary Register (Pet/ Recommend) 24 Mar 1707 – Parliamentary Minutes (Pet/ Recommend)	{xi APS 474} {xi APS App 137}	[A1706/10/55] [1706/10/410] [M1706/10/122]

3 Other Scottish Parliamentary material

SCOT132	Ratification of the Grant of the gold, silver and other metals for 43 years to Joachim Hoeckscatter (17 Nov 1526)	{ii APS 310} [1526/11/18]
SCOT133	Grant to Eustance Rough of tin and other mines for 21 years (22 Aug 1584)	(1584 c. 32) {iii APS 368} [1584/5/108]
SCOT134	Recommendation that societies and manufactories be established in principal burghs (1 Nov 1625)	{v APS 178} [A1625/10/24]
SCOT135	Grievance of the barkers regarding tannage inquired into (2 Nov 1625)	{v APS 185}[A1625/10/52]
SCOT136	Lord Erskine's Patent for tanning leather remitted to Committee; Act regarding the matter of the process of tanning (4 Aug 1630)	{v APS 225} {v APS 228} [A1630/7/48] [A1630/7/60]
SCOT137	Request to consider Thorton's patent and whether it is prejudicial (29 Jul 1630)	{v APS 219} [A1630/7/20]
SCOT138	Request that gunpowder patent be exercised or recalled (29 Jul 1630) Act in favour of Lord Spynie (4 Aug 1630) Remitted to Privy Council (4 Aug 1630)	{v APS 219} [A1630/7/20] {v APS 224} [A1630/7/50] {v APS 225} [A1630/7/47]
SCOT139	Complaint against Buchan's fish pearl patent (2 Aug 1630) Remitted to Privy Council (28 Jun 1633) Agent heard in support (26 Sep 1639)	{v APS 224}[A1630/7/39] {v APS 490}[1633/6/49] {v APS 597}[C1639/8/31]
SCOT140	Article desiring steps taking for bringing in manufactory (28 Jun 1633)	{v APS 49}[1633/6/49]
SCOT141	Earl of Mar & others to heard in relation to tanning patent (12 Sep 1639) Lord Burley to state prejudices relating to patent (16 Sep 1639) Rep to be produced (24 Sep 1639) Rep of C'tee (25 Sep 1639)	{v APS 597} [C1639/8/11] {v APS 598} [C1639/8/17] [C1639/8/28] {v APS 601} [C1639/8/30]
SCOT142	Petition from manufactories for discharge of customs (21 Oct 1639)	{v APS 614} [C1639/8/73]
SCOT143	Act in favour of John Erskine, Earl of Mar and Alexander Livingstone, earl of Linlithgow (consider expenses incurred seeking patent) (16 Nov 1641)	{v APS 411} [1641/8/193]
SCOT144	Letter from Magistrates in Aberdeen relating to patent granted to Captain William King (28 Mar 1651)	{vi(ii) APS 654} [M1651/3/17]
SCOT145	Instructions to Protector to Scottish Council to encourage manufactories; renewed (1658)	{vi(ii) APS 827, 876}
SCOT146	Proposal to include clause in Act of Union to preserve manufactures (30 Dec 1706)	{xi APS 338, 355} [M1706/10/64] and [1706/10/178]

4 Irish Bills

Silk Crapes Bill 1725

IRE1		1725			
Silk Crapes Bill 1725 [ILD: 1790]					
Bill to encourage the making of silk crapes, commonly called by the names of Vallee-Cypress, or Bologna crapes in this kingdom [Petition of Richard Brennan]					
Purpose					
A grant for further encouragement as the House sees fit					
Journal					
House of Commons			**Privy Council**		
Pres: Henry Maxwell					
11 Nov 1725	3 ICJ 418	**Pet**	21 Jan 1726	5 Geo 1 PCR	Law Officers' approval
25 Nov 1725	3 ICJ 426	Rep/Leave			Approved Irish PC
2 Dec 1725	3 ICJ 430	Read C'tted CWH			Rejected English PC
8 Dec 1725	3 ICJ 434	Rep			
8 Dec 1725	3 ICJ 434	Sent to Governor			
Parliamentary debates					
None					
Privy Council					
Pet Ag: 21 Jan, Register of Privy Council, Vol 89, f 143–144 (State Papers PC2/89)					
Lords Report read and approved, 12 Feb, Vol 89, f 189 (State Papers PC2/89)					

Turner Camac's Bill 1793

IRE2		1793	
Turner Camac's Bill 1793 [ILD: 1796]			
Bill for vesting in Turner Camac, esquire, his executors, administrators and assigns the sole use and property of making oil of vitriol or vitriolic acid from materials the produce of this kingdom, of his invention, to be hereafter described, for a limited time			
Purpose			
A term of years granted for the sole use of his invention of making vitriolic acid			
Journal			
House of Commons			**House of Lords**
Pres: Barry Maxwell			
22 Jun 1793	15 ICJ 211	**Pet**	*Never reached Irish House of Lords*
27 Jun 1793	15 ICJ 219	Rep/Leave	
5 Jul 1793	15 ICJ 236	1R	
8 Jul 1793	15 ICJ 241	**Pet Ag**	
8 Jul 1793	15 ICJ 242	**Pet Ag**	
8 Jul 1793	15 ICJ 242	2R set to 30 Sep 1793	
Parliamentary debates			
1R: Parliamentary Register of the House of Commons of Ireland, Vol 13, 5 Jul 1793, p 515			
Pet Ag: **Parliamentary Register of the House of Commons of Ireland, Vol 13, 8 Jul 1793, p 517–519**			

Thomas and William Blair's Bill 1795

IRE3	1795
Thomas and William Blair's Bill 1795 [ILD: 2240]	
Bill for vesting in Thomas Blair and William Blair of the city of Dublin, merchants, their executors, administrators and assigns the sole use and property of manufactures of tinplates and rolled iron, for a limited time	
Purpose	
Patent term extension	
Journal	
House of Commons	**House of Lords**

Pres: Barry Maxwell			
13 May 1795	16 ICJ 143	**Pet**	*Never reached Irish House of Lords*
14 May 1795	16 ICJ 145	Pet ref to C'tee/Rep/1R	

Parliamentary debates
1R: **Parliamentary Register of the House of Commons of Ireland, Vol 15, 14 May 1795, p 387**

Part 4 | Statutory instruments

Part 4 contents

Statutory instruments

The first rules concerning patents regulated the procedure before the Privy Council in relation to the extension of patents under the Letters Patent for Inventions Act 1835. Since that time there have been a plethora of different rules. Orders in Council were published in the *London Gazette*, but otherwise there was no regular publication of statutory instruments until 1890. Accordingly, any rules made before that date were published in different places. Before the Office of the Commissioners of Patents was set up under the Patent Law Amendment Act 1852, the most reliable source of patent information was the *Reparatory of Arts and Manufactures, the Reparatory of Patent Inventions* and *The Mechanics Magazine*, and early rules are found there. In 1854 and every year thereafter, the Commissioners, and then the Comptroller, of Patents provided an annual report to Parliament. In this report, the text of new rules made to regulate the office were included. Occasionally, however, rules were published in the Patent Office Journal (and not elsewhere).

The central publication of statutory instruments began in 1890 with the annual publication of Statutory Rules & Orders (SR & O). This included (almost) every statutory instrument made, arranged in thematic order. In 1890, a consolidated volume of statutory instruments then in force was provided, again arranged thematically.[1] This publication was given statutory force, and the instruments numbered from 1894.[2] A new series of statutory instruments, which included the statutory instruments in numerical order, began in 1949, and the Statutory Rules & Orders slowly declined and ceased publication in the 1950s.

The tables in this part include the short title of the instrument, the date it was made and the date it was laid before Parliament (if laying was required), and the references in the House of Commons Journal and

---

1 There were subsequent consolidated editions, but these are not referred to in this Guide.
2 See Rules Publication Act 1893 and the Regulations, dated 9 Aug 1894, in pursuance of the Rules Publication Act (1894 No 734).

House of Lords Journal recording it being laid. The tables record the primary publication of the instrument, so from 1890 this was usually the Statutory Rules and Orders, and then, from 1949, the Statutory Instrument Series. Where there is any reference or debate in *Hansard*, this could be a note of the motion or a substantive debate.

Early rules

Rules of Practice before the Attorney and Solicitor-General for Petitions to leave to enter Disclaimers and Memorandums of Alteration pursuant to the statute 5 & 6 Will IV c. 83 Undated (circa 1835)	London Journal and Repertory of Patent Inventions (Conjoined Series) (1835), Vol 7 (No 47), p 373	
Law Officer's Rule Requiring Outline Descriptions Made: 2 Nov 1850	The Mechanics Magazine, Vol 53, 9 Nov 1850, (No 1422), p 371	
Law Officer's Rules on Deposit of Outline Descriptions Made: 15 Jan 1851	The Mechanics Magazine, Vol 54, 25 Jan 1851 (No 1433), p 73	
Order of Lord Chancellor on the form to be taken by Specifications	Repertory of Patent Inventions, Oct 1852, Vol 20 (No 4), p 262	
Rules and Instructions to be observe in applications respecting Patents for Inventions, and by Persons petitioning for Letters Patent for Inventions, and for Liberty to enter Disclaimers and Alterations according to the Statutes	Repertory of Patent Inventions, Oct 1852, Vol 20 (No 4), p 263	
Rule in respect of oppositions to patents at the Great Seal Made: 15 Oct 1852 Not laid	(1854 HL Papers 321), Vol 36, p 1 at p 9	

Commencement orders

Order made by Board of Trade in pursuance of Section 1 Sub-section 2 of the Patents Act 1902 fixing date for coming into operation of section Made: 12 Aug 1904 Laid: 13 Aug 1904 (159 CJ 420; 136 LJ 350)	Patent Office Journal, 31 Aug 1904, No 816, p 1155	HC Deb, 13 Aug 1904, Vol 140(4th), col 515 HL Deb, 13 Aug 1904, Vol 140(4th), col 497
Order of the Board of Trade Bringing Section 8 of the Patents and Designs Act 1907 into Operation on 1 January 1909 Laid: 18 Nov 1908 (163 CJ 449; 140 LJ 405)	(No number) 1914, SR & O, Vol III, p 355	HC Deb, 18 Nov 1908, Vol 196(4th), col 1198 HL Deb, 19 Nov 1908, Vol 196(4th), col 1353
Date of Operation of Section 29(3) of Patents and Designs Act, as Amended by Section 8 of the Patents and Designs Act 1919 Made: 21 Jan 1920 Not laid	(1920 No 59) 1919, SR & O, Vol II, p 104	
Date of Operation of Sections 24 and 27 of Patents and Designs Act, as Respectively Amended by Sections 2 and 1 of the Patents and Designs Act 1919 Made: 15 Mar 1920 Not laid	(1920 No 413) 1919, SR & O, Vol II, p 104	
Date of Operation of Section 29(1)(2) and (4) of Patents and Designs Act, as Amended by Section 8 of the Patents and Designs Act 1919 Made: 23 Apr 1920 Not laid	(1920 No 658) 1919, SR & O, Vol II, p 105	
Order in Council Appointing 1 August 1938 as the Date of Operation of the Patents &c. (International Conventions) Act 1938 Made: 28 Jul 1938 Not laid	(1938 No 742) 1938, SR & O, Vol II, p 2766	

Patents rules

First Set of Rules and Regulations under the Act 15 & 16 Vict. c. 83 for the passing of Letters Patent for Invention Made: 1 Oct 1852 Laid: 24 Nov 1852; 22 Nov 1852 (108 CJ 88; 85 LJ 32)	(1854 HL Papers 321), Vol 36, p 1 at p 7	
Second Set of Rules and Regulations under the Act 15 & 16 Vict. c. 83 for the passing of Letters Patent for Invention Made: 15 Oct 1852 Laid: 24 Nov 1852 (108 CJ 88; 85 LJ 32)	(1854 HL Papers 321), Vol 36, p 1 at p 8	
Third Set of Rules and Regulations under the Act 15 & 16 Vict. c. 83 for the passing of Letters Patent for Invention Made: 12 Dec 1853 Laid: 24 Nov 1852 (108 CJ 88; 85 LJ 32)	(1854 HL Papers 321), Vol 36, p 1 at p 19	
Order in respect of Applications to the Lord Chancellor to extend the time for Sealing Patents Made: 17 Jul 1854 Not laid	Commissioners of Patents Journal (1854), 5 Sep 1954, No 70, p 309	
Order of Law Officers as to Forms of Declarations for Patents Communications from Abroad Made: 23 Feb 1859 Not laid	Commissioners of Patents Journal (1859), 18 Mar 1859, No 543, p 309	
Additional Rule requiring the filing of an abridgement of the provisional or complete specification Made: 17 Dec 1866 Not laid	(1867 HL Papers 310), Vol 32, p 437 at p 9	
Additional Rule on timing of payment of stamp duties Made: 14 May 1867 Not laid	(1867–68 HL Papers 299), Vol 36, p 507 at p 9	
Rule amending rule 2 of the First Set of Rules and Regulations Made: 1 Jul 1871 Laid: 13 Jul 1871 (126 CJ 338; 103 LJ 529)	(1872 HC Papers 385), Vol 24 p 221 at p 12	
Rule or Regulation made by Commission Made: 17 May 1876 Laid: 8 Jun 1876; 13 Jun 1876 (131 CJ 243; 108 LJ 230)	(1877 HC Papers 459), Vol 33, p 959 at p 5	
Rules by the Commissioner under the Patent Law Amendment Act Made: 14 May 1878 Laid: 16 May 1878 (133 CJ 224; 110 LJ 172)	(1878–79 HC Papers 355), Vol 26, p 809 at p 2	
Three Sets of Rules and Regulations under the Patent Law Amendment Act (called "Order repealing Rules III, IV and V of the First Set of Rules and Regulations") Made: 30 Nov 1878 Laid: 6 Dec 1878; 5 Dec 1878 (134 CJ 7; 111 LJ 8)	(1878–79 HC Papers 355), Vol 26, p 809 at p 2	
Rules under the Patent Law Amendment Act Made: 9 Feb 1880 Laid: 13 Feb 1880; 12 Feb 1880 (135 CJ 40; 112 LJ 19)	HL/PO/JO/10/9/985	
Rules and Regulations & Passing of Letters Patent Made: 8 Nov 1882 Laid: 22 Nov 1882 (137 CJ 513; 114 LJ 442)	Not printed	
Patents Rules 1883 Made: 21 Dec 1883 Laid: 5 Feb 1883 (139 CJ 7; 116 LJ 10)	(1884 C 4040), Vol 28, p 45 at p 11	
Patents Rules 1885 Made: 15 Aug 1885 Laid: 22 Jan 1886; 25 Jan 1886 (141 CJ 24; 118 LJ 24)	(1886 C 4756), Vol 29, p 697 at p 9	

(continued)

(continued)

Rules in lieu of and substitution for Rules 28, 29, 30 and 31 of Patents Rules 1883 Made: 16 Sep 1886 Laid: 16 May 1886 (141 CJ 372; 118 LJ 374)	(1887 C 5066), Vol 35, p 585 at p 14	
Patents (International and Colonial Arrangements) Rules 1888 Made: 15 May 1888 Laid: 16 May 1888 (143 CJ 231; 120 LJ 186)	(1889 C 5728), Vol 34, p 649 at p 14	
Patents Rules 1890 Made: 31 Mar 1890 Laid: 14 Apr 1890; 17 Apr 1890 (145 CJ 234; 122 LJ 223)	(No number) 1890, SR & O, p 889	
Patents Rules 1892 (First Set) Made: 19 Feb 1892 Laid: 25 Feb 1892 (147 CJ 63; 124 LJ 39)	(No number) 1892, SR & O, p 981	
Patents Rules 1892 (Second Set) Made: 4 Jul 1892 Laid: 11 Aug 1892; 15 Aug 1892 (147 CJ 418; 124 LJ 410)	(No number) 1892, SR & O, p 983	
Patent Rules 1898 Made: 15 Sep 1898 Laid: 7 Feb 1899 (153 CJ 18; 131 LJ 17)	(1898 No 675) 1898, SR & O, p 763	HC Deb, 7 Feb 1899, Vol 66(4th), col 55 HL Deb, 7 Feb 1899, Vol 66(4th), col 42
Patents Rules 1901 Made: 18 Dec 1901 Laid: 17 Jan 1902 (157 CJ 11; 134 LJ 11)	(1902 HC Papers 178), Vol 34, p 521 at p 25	HC Deb, 16 Jan 1902, Vol 101(4th), col 56 HL Deb, 17 Jan 1902, Vol 101(4th), col 168
Patents Rules 1902 Made: 4 Jun 1902 Laid: 6 Jun 1902 (157 CJ 267; 134 LJ 207)	(1902 No 477) 1902, SR & O, p 313	HC Deb, 6 Jun 1902, Vol 109(4th), col 10 HL Deb, 6 Jun 1902, Vol 109(4th), col 5
Patents Rules 1903 Made: 12 Jan 1903 Laid: 17 Feb 1903 (158 CJ 6; 135 LJ 8)	(1903 No 231) 1903, SR & O, p 1173	HC Deb, 17 Feb 1903, Vol 118(4th), col 54 HL Deb, 17 Feb 1903, Vol 118(4th), col 42
Patents Rules 1905 Made: 20 Oct 1904 Laid: 15 Feb 1905; 16 Feb 1905 (160 CJ 13; 137 LJ 20)	(1904 No 1652) 1904, SR & O, p 576	HC Deb, 15 Feb 1905, Vol 141(4th), col 172 HL Deb, 16 Feb 1905, Vol 141(4th), col 284
Patents Rules 1908 Made: 17 Dec 1907 Laid: 29 Jan 1908 (163 CJ 10; 140 LJ 14)	(1907 No 949) 1907, SR & O, p 779	HC Deb, 29 Jan 1908, Vol 183(4th), col 107 HL Deb, 29 Jan 1908, Vol 183(4th), col 71
Patents Rules 1920 Made: 25 Feb 1920 Laid: 8 Mar 1920; 9 Mar 1920 (175 CJ 48; 152 LJ 67)	(1920 No 338) 1919, SR & O, Vol II, p 109	
Patents Rules 1932 Made: 25 Oct 1932 Laid: 31 Oct 1932; 1 Nov 1932 (187 CJ 324; 164 LJ 328) Re-laid: 16 Mar 1933 (188 CJ 100; 165 LJ 107)	(1932 No 873) 1932, SR & O, p 1321	
Patents (Amendment) Rules 1938 Made: 20 Jul 1938 Laid: 5 Oct 1938 (193 CJ 407; 170 LJ 377) Re-laid: 8 Nov 1938 (194 CJ 6; 171 LJ 7)	(1938 No 718) 1938, SR & O, Vol II, p 2772	
Patents Rules 1939 Made: 24 Jul 1939 Laid: 24 Aug 1939 (194 CJ 401; 171 LJ 373)	(1939 No 858) 1939, SR & O, Vol II, p 2453	
Patents (Amendment) Rules 1942 Made: 11 Feb 1942 Laid: 3 Mar 1942 (197 CJ 58; 174 LJ 68)	(1942 No 273) 1942, SR & O, Vol I, p 705	

Patents (Amendment) Rules 1946 Made: 28 May 1946 Laid: 3 Jun 1946; 4 Jun 1946 (201 CJ 279; 178 LJ 296)	(1946 No 756) 1946, SR & O, Vol I, p 1236	
Patents Rules 1947 Made: 17 Mar 1947 Laid: 20 Mar 1947 (202 CJ 145; 179 LJ 145)	(1947 No 484) 1947, SR & O, Vol I, p 1531	
Patents (No 2) (Nauchatel Agreement) Rules 1947 Made: 24 Jul 1947 Laid: 30 July 1947 (202 CJ 336; 179 LJ 454)	(1947 No 1588) 1947, SR & O, Vol I, p 1534	
Patents (Canada) Rules 1947 Made: 7 Nov 1947 Laid: 13 Nov 1947 (203 CJ 47; 180 LJ 27)	(1947 No 2392) 1947, SR & O, Vol I, p 1537	
Patents (No 3) (Amendment) Rules 1947 Made: 7 Nov 1947 Laid: 13 Nov 1947 (203 CJ 47; 180 LJ 27)	(1947 No 2393) 1947, SR & O, Vol I, p 1536	
Patents Rules 1949 Laid: 6 Mar 1950 (205 CJ 16; 182 LJ 110)	(1949 No 2385) 1949, SR & O, p 2933	
Patents (Amendment) Rules 1955 Made: 24 Jan 1955 Laid: 31 Jan 1955; 1 Feb 1955 (210 CJ 42; 187 LJ 43)	SI 1955/117	
Patents (Amendment) Rules 1957 Made: 8 Apr 1957 Laid: 16 Apr 1957 (212 CJ 169; 189 LJ 151)	SI 1957/618	
Patents Rules 1958 Made: 16 Jan 1958 Laid: 23 Jan 1958 (190 LJ 65; 213 CJ 68)	SI 1958/73	
Patents (Amendment) Rules 1959 Made: 23 Mar 1959 Laid: 26 Mar 1959; 7 Apr 1959 (214 CJ 162; 191 LJ 164)	SI 1959/524	
Patents (Amendment) Rules 1961 Made: 23 Jun 1961 Laid: 29 Jun 1961 (216 CJ 276; 193 LJ 322)	SI 1961/1185	
Patents (Amendment No 2) Rules 1961 Made: 16 Aug 1961 Laid: 29 Aug 1961; noted 17 Oct 1961 (216 CJ 335; 193 LJ 425)	SI 1961/1619	
Patents (Amendment) Rules 1962 Made: 13 Dec 1962 Laid: 19 Dec 1962 (218 CJ 66; 195 LJ 82)	SI 1962/2730	
Patents (Amendment) Rules 1963 Made: 5 Dec 1963 Laid: 11 Dec 1963 (219 CJ 48; 196 LJ 51)	SI 1963/1982	
Patents (Amendment) Rules 1964 Made: 18 Feb 1964 Laid: 25 Feb 1964 (219 CJ 123; 196 LJ 146)	SI 1964/228	
Patents (Amendment No 2) Rules 1964 Made: 24 Aug 1964 Laid: 31 Aug 1964 Laid and noted: 3 Nov 1964 (220 CJ 18; 197 LJ 30)	SI 1964/1337	
Patents (Amendment) Rules 1966 Made: 28 Nov 1966 Laid: 5 Dec 1966 (222 CJ 273; 199 LJ 283)	SI 1966/1482	
Patents (Amendment) Rules 1967 Made: 14 Mar 1967 Laid: 21 Mar 1967 (222 CJ 403; 199 LJ 463)	SI 1967/392	
Patents (Amendment No 2) Rules 1967 Made: 29 Jul 1967 Laid: 4 Aug 1967, noted 23 Oct 1967 (222 CJ 602; 199 LJ 759)	SI 1967/1171	Motion to approve: HC Deb, 30 Nov 1967, Vol 755(5th), col 783–797 [223 CJ 42]

(continued)

(continued)

Patents Rules 1968 Made: 27 Aug 1968 Laid: 12 Sep 1968, noted 14 Oct 1968; 7 Oct 1968 (223 CJ 375; 200 LJ 613)	SI 1968/1389	
Patents (Amendment) Rules 1968 Made: 25 Oct 1968 Laid: 31 Oct 1968 (224 CJ 7; 201 LJ 11)	SI 1968/1702	Motion to annul: HC Deb, 17 Dec 1968, Vol 775(5th), col 1332–1338 [224 CJ 72]
Patents (Amendment) Rules 1969 Made: 27 Mar 1969 Laid: 14 Apr 1969; 15 Apr 1969 (224 CJ 190; 201 LJ 185)	SI 1969/482	
Patents (Amendment No 2) Rules 1969 Made: 1 Dec 1969 Laid: 8 Dec 1969 (225 CJ 74; 202 LJ 67)	SI 1969/1706	Motion to annul: HC Deb, 10 Feb 1970, Vol 795(5th), col 1202–1216 [225 CJ 151]
Patents (Amendment) Rules 1970 Made: 26 Jun 1970 Laid: 7 Jul 1970 (226 CJ 29; 203 LJ 26)	SI 1970/955	
Patents (Amendment) Rules 1971 Made: 17 Feb 1971 Laid: 26 Feb 1971; 2 Mar 1971 (226 CJ 294; 203 LJ 290)	SI 1971/263	
Patents (Amendment No 2) Rules 1971 Made: 24 Nov 1971 Laid: 2 Dec 1971 (227 CJ 61; 204 LJ 54)	SI 1971/1917	
Patents (Amendment) Rules 1973 Made: 18 Jan 1973 Laid: 25 Jan 1973 (228 CJ 110; 205 LJ 110)	SI 1973/66	
Patents (Amendment) Rules 1974 Made: 21 Jan 1974 Laid: 28 Jan 1974 (229 CJ 138; 206 LJ 155)	SI 1974/87	
Patents (Amendment) Rules 1975 Made: 13 Mar 1975 Laid: 21 Mar 1975; 24 Mar 1975 (231 CJ 315; 208 LJ 409)	SI 1975/371	Standing Committee on Statutory Instruments Minutes of proceedings on the Patents (Amendment) Rules 1975: (1974–75 HC Paper 385), Vol 36, p 435
Patents (Amendment No 2) Rules 1975 Made: 21 May 1975 Laid: 30 May 1975 (as printed) Laid: 9 Jun 1975 (231 CJ 465; 208 LJ 608)	SI 1975/891	
Patents (Amendment No 3) Rules 1975 Made: 23 Jun 1975 Laid: 23 Jun 1975 (231 CJ 501; 208 LJ 688)	SI 1975/1021	
Patents (Amendment No 4) Rules 1975 Made: 28 Jul 1975 Laid: 31 Jul 1975 (231 CJ 608; 208 LJ 882)	SI 1975/1262	

English and Welsh Supreme Court rules

Rules of the Supreme Court (Patents and Designs) 1908 Made: 3 Jun 1908 Laid: 4 Jun 1908; 16 Jun 1908 (163 CJ 241; 140 LJ 203)	(1908 No 445) 1908, SR & O, p 934	HC Deb, 4 Jun 1908, Vol 190(4th), col 163 HC Deb, 16 Jun 1908, Vol 190(4th), col 682
Rules of the Supreme Court (No 2) 1920 Made: 10 May 1920 Laid: 12 May 1920; 11 May 1920 (175 CJ 158; 152 LJ 162)	(1920 No 713) 1920, SR & O, Vol II, p 703	

Rules of the Supreme Court (Patents and Designs) 1925 Made: 22 Jun 1925 Laid: 2 Jul 1925 (180 CJ 293; 157 LJ 258)	(1925 No 1467) 1925, SR & O, p 1467	
Rules of the Supreme Court (No 1) 1931 Made: 2 Feb 1931 Laid: 13 Feb 1931; 17 Feb 1931 (186 CJ 122; 163 LJ 115)	(1931 No 54) 1931, SR & O, p 1236	
Rules of the Supreme Court (No 3) 1936 Made: 26 Jun 1936 Laid: 6 Jul 1936; 7 Jul 1936 (191 CJ 312; 168 LJ 284)	(1936 No 680) (L 19) 1936, SR & O, Vol II, p 2543	
Rules of Supreme Court (No 2) 1938 Made: 23 Dec 1938 Laid: 6 Feb 1939; 7 Feb 1939 (194 CJ 73; 171 LJ 66)	(1938 No 1575) (L 28) 1938, SR & O, Vol II, p 3150 (at p 3151)	
Rules of the Supreme Court (Patents) 1944 Made: 2 Aug 1944 Laid: 26 Sep 1944 (199 CJ 178) Re-laid: 5 Dec 1944 (200 CJ 11; 177 LJ 10)	(1944 No 906) (L 36) 1944, SR & O, Vol I, p 930	
Rules of the Supreme Court (Patents) 1945 Made: 16 Nov 1945 Laid: 22 Nov 1945; 21 Nov 1945 (201 CJ 91; 178 LJ 102)	(1945 No 1450) (L 21) 1945, SR & O, Vol I, p 1124	
Rules of the Supreme Court (No 1) 1950 Made: 3 Apr 1950 Laid: 6 Apr 1950 (205 CJ 69; 182 LJ 33)	SI 1950/572 (L 13)	
Rules of the Supreme Court (No 3) 1954 Made: 21 Dec 1954 Laid: 25 Jan 1955 (187 LJ 38)	SI 1954/1726(L 23)	
Rules of the Supreme Court (Appeals) 1955 Made: 13 Dec 1955 Laid: 19 Dec 1955 (211 CJ 159; 188 LJ 162)	SI 1955/1885 (L 18)	
Rules of the Supreme Court (No 3) 1959 Made: 17 Nov 1959 Laid: 27 Nov 1959; 24 Nov 1959 (215 CJ 54; 192 LJ 58)	SI 1959/1958 (L 13)	
Rules of the Supreme Court (Revision) 1965 Made: 30 Sep 1965 Laid: 2 Nov 1965 (220 CJ 428; 197 LJ 28)	SI 1965/1776 (L 23)	
Rules of the Supreme Court (Amendment No 2) 1975 Made: 27 May 1975 Laid: 7 Jun 1975; 9 Jun 1975 (231 CJ 214; 208 LJ 609)	SI 1975/911 (L 10)	

Acts of Sederunt (Scottish Court rules)

Act of Sederunt providing for the Manner of Advertising Petitions for Extension of Terms of Patent Made: 11 Jan 1908	(1908 No 41) 1908, SR & O, p 886	
Act of Sederunt further to regulate Procedure under the Patents and Designs Act 1907 Made: 16 Jul 1910	(1910 No 767) (S 24) 1910, SR & O, p 672	
Act of Sederunt to Consolidate and Amend the Acts of Sederunt Made: 4 Jun 1913	(1913 No 638) (S 44) 1913, SR & O, p 2013 (at p 2065)	
Act of Sederunt to Regulate Proceedings by a Patentee for Leave to Amend His Specification Made: 7 Jul 1921	(1921 No 1228) (S 60) 1921, SR & O, p 843	
Act of Sederunt Consolidating Rules of Court (Section 9) Made: 19 Jul 1934	(1936 No 88) (S 4) 1936, SR & O, Vol II, p 2231 (at p 2365)	
Act of Sederunt (Rules of Court, Consolidation and Amendment) 1965 Made: 10 Nov 1964	SI 1965/321 (S 16)	

Irish Supreme Court rules

Rules of the Supreme Court (Ireland) 1919 (Procedure under s 18 of Patents and Designs Act 1907) Made: 22 Dec 1919 Laid: 17 Feb 1919; 18 Feb 1919 (174 CJ 29; 151 LJ 46)	(1919 No 1956) 1920, SR & O, Vol II, p 489	
Rules of Supreme Court (No 1) (Application for Patent Extension) amending Rules of the Irish Supreme Court Made: 22 Mar 1921 Laid: 4 Apr 1921 (176 CJ 77; 153 LJ 96)	(1921 No 839) 1921, SR & O, p 1313	
Rules of the Supreme Court (Northern Ireland) 1936, Order LXXX Made: 22 Oct 1936 Laid: 20 Mar 1936; 24 Mar 1936 (191 CJ 140; 168 LJ 139)	(1936 No 1173) 1936, SR & O, Vol II, p 2551 (at p 2923)	

Privy Council rules

Rules of Practice to be observed in Proceedings before the Judicial Committee of the Privy Council under the Act of 5 & 6 Will IV. c. 83 Made: 18 Nov 1835	1890 Cons, SR & O, Vol 5, p 139 Repertory of Patent Inventions, (1835) (NS), No 26, Vol 4, p. 369 Macpherson's Privy Council Practice, pp 24–26 The Times, 24 Nov 1835	
Additional Rules to be observed in Proceedings before the Judicial Committee of the Privy Council under the Act of 5 & 6 Will IV. c. 83 Made: 21 Dec 1835	1890 Cons, SR & O, Vol 5, p 139 Repertory of Patent Inventions (1835) (NS), No 32, Vol 6, p. 117	
Order in Council making Regulations as to the Extension of the Term of Patents on Petition Made: 26 Nov 1897	(No number) 1899, SR & O, p 1837 Official Journal of the Patent Office, 15 Dec 1897, Issue 467, p 1633	
Order in Council making Rules regulating Proceedings before the Judicial Committee on Petitions for Grant of Compulsory Licences Made: 16 Feb 1903	(1903 No 124) 1903, SR & O, p 1167	

Patent Appeal Tribunal rules

Patent Appeal Tribunal Fees Order 1932 Made: 26 Oct 1932	(1932 No 874) 1932, SR & O, p 1428	
Patents Appeal Tribunal Rules 1932 Made: 31 Oct 1932	(1932 No 887) 1932, SR & O, p 1423	
Patents Appeal Tribunal Rules 1950 Made: 24 Mar 1950	SI 1950/392 (L 8)	
Patents and Registered Designs Appeal Tribunal Fees Order 1950 Made: 24 Mar 1950	SI 1950/458 (L 10)	
Patents Appeal Tribunal (Amendment) Rules 1956 Made: 27 Mar 1956	SI 1956/470 (L 2)	
Patents Appeal Tribunal Rules 1959 Made: 17 Feb 1959	SI 1959/278	
Patents Appeal Tribunal (Amendment) Rules 1961 Made: 17 May 1961	SI 1961/1016	
Patents Appeal Tribunal (Amendment) Rules 1969 Made: 20 Mar 1969	SI 1969/500	
Patents and Registered Designs Appeal Tribunal Fees Order 1970 Made: 26 Mar 1970	SI 1970/529 (L 13)	

Patents Appeal Tribunal (Amendment) Rules 1970 Made: 16 Jul 1970	SI 1970/1074 (L 22)	
Patents Appeal Tribunal (Amendment) Rules 1971 Made 5 Mar 1971	SI 1971/394 (L 9)	
Patents Appeal Tribunal Rules 1972 Made: 8 Dec 1972	SI 1972/1940 (L 28)	
Patents Appeal Tribunal (Fees) Order 1973 Made: 1 Feb 1973	SI 1973/164 (L 1)	

Statutory instruments relating to fees

Fees to be paid to laws officers and Clerks Made: 1 Oct 1852	(1854 HL Papers 321), Vol 36, p 1 at p 12	
Treasury Order directing that certain fees payable in the Patent Office shall be collected in cash instead of by stamps Made: 13 May 1890 Not laid	(No number) 1890, SR & O, p 922	
Treasury Order as to the taking by stamps of the fees and percentages under the Patents Act Made: 14 Dec 1892 Not laid	(No number) 1892, SR & O, p 651	
Treasury Notice under the Public Office Fees Act 1879 and the Patents, Designs and Trade Marks Act 1883 Made: 26 Nov 1898 Not laid	(1898 No 796) 1898, SR & O, p 764	
Public Offices Fees (Patents, Designs and Trade Marks) Order 1940 Made: 23 May 1940 Not laid	(1940 No 911) 1940, SR & O, Vol I, p 899	
Public Offices Fees (Patents, Designs and Trade Marks) Order 1964 Made: 16 Jan 1964 Not laid	SI 1964/45	
Patents (Fees Amendment) Order 1961 Draft laid: 29 Jun 1961 (216 CJ 276; 193 LJ 322) Rep: 12 Jul 1961 (193 LJ 345) Approved: 21 Jul 1961; 24 Jul 1961 (216 CJ 307; 193 LJ 380) Made: 2 Aug 1961	SI 1961/1499	Motion: HC Deb, 21 Jul 1961, Vol 644(5th), col 1684–1685 HL Deb, 24 Jul 1961, Vol 233 (5th), col 833–836 and 850–851
Patents (Fees Amendment) Order 1970 Draft laid: 29 Oct 1970 (226 CJ 93; 203 LJ 100) Rep: 4 Nov 1970 (203 LJ 112) Approved: 20 Nov 1970; 19 Nov 1970 (226 CJ 128; 203 LJ 139) Made: 17 Dec 1970	SI 1970/1953	Motion: HC Deb, 20 Nov 1970, Vol 806(5th), col 1667–1670 HL Deb, 19 Nov 1970, Vol 312(5th), col 1244–1245
Patents (Fees Amendment) Order 1974 Draft laid: 26 Nov 1974 (231 CJ 93; 208 LJ 106) JCSI Rep: 3 Dec 1974 (208 LJ 123) Approved: 12 Dec 1974; 16 Dec 1974 (231 CJ 136; 208 LJ 162) Made: 18 Dec 1974	SI 1974/2145	Ref to SC: HC Deb, 2 Dec 1974, Vol 882(5th), col 1131 Motion: HC Deb,12 Dec 1974, Vol 883(5th), col 969 HL Deb, 16 Dec 1974, Vol 355 (5th), col 1001–1003 Standing Committee on Statutory Instruments Minutes of proceedings on the Patents (Fees Amendment) Rules 1974: (1974–75 HC Paper 385), Vol 36, p 435

Patent agents rules

Register of Patent Agents Rules 1889 Made: 18 Jun 1889 Laid: 17 Jun 1889; 18 Jun 1889 (144 CJ 241; 121 LJ 201)	1890 Cons, SR & O, Vol 5, p 147 Official Patent Office Journal, 19 Jun 1889, Issue 24, p 530 London Gazette, 14 Jun 1889, p 3228 (1889 C 5747), Vol 60, p 941	
Register of Patent Agents Rules 1891 Made: 18 Nov 1891 Laid: 9 Feb 1892 (147 CJ 9; 124 LJ 8)	(No Number) 1891, SR & O, p 572	
Rule amending rule 7 of Register of Patents Agents Rules 1889 Made: 29 Oct 1902 Laid: 5 Nov 1902 (157 CJ 464; 134 LJ 384)	(1902 HC Papers 366), Vol 94, p 261	HC Deb, 5 Nov 1902, Vol 114(4th), col 129 HL Deb, 17 Nov 1902, Vol 114(4th), col 1098
Register of Patent Agents Rules 1908 Made: 17 Dec 1907 Laid: 21 Jan 1908; 29 Jan 1908 (163 CJ 10; 140 LJ 14)	(1907 No 951) 1907, SR & O, p 856	
Register of Patent Agent Rules 1919 Made: 26 Feb 1919 Laid: 4 Mar 1919 (174 CJ 51; 151 LJ 66)	(1919 No 228) (1920 HC Papers 106), Vol 22, p 353 p 9	
Order of the Board of Trade altering Fees Prescribed in Appendix B to the Register of Patent Agents Rules Made: 30 Aug 1919 Not laid	(1919 No 1177) (1920 HC Papers 106), Vol 22, p 11	
Register of Patent Agents Rules 1920 Made: 30 Jan 1920 Laid: 8 Feb 1920; 10 Feb 1920 (175 CJ 7; 152 LJ 21)	(1920 No 145) 1919, SR & O, Vol II, p 191	
Register of Patent Agents Rules 1926 Made: 19 Jan 1926 Laid: 4 Feb 1926; 10 Feb 1926 (181 CJ 11; 158 LJ 25)	(1926 No 58) 1926, SR & O, p 1100	
Register of Patent Agents Rules 1932 Made: 4 Oct 1932 Laid: 18 Oct 1932 (187 CJ 303) Re-laid: 16 Mar 1933 (164 LJ 318; 188 CJ 100)	(1932 No 820) 1932, SR & O, p 1417	
Register of Patent Agent Rules 1950 Made: 18 May 1950 Laid: 22 May 1950; 23 May 1950 (205 CJ 117; 182 LJ 110)	SI 1950/804	
Register of Patent Agent (Amendment) Rules 1957 Made: 19 Sep 1957 Laid: 26 Sep 1957; noted 29 Oct 1957 (212 CJ 295; 189 LJ 304)	SI 1957/1657	
Register of Patent Agent (Amendment) Rules 1959 Made: 7 Sep 1959 Laid: 18 Nov 1959; 18 Sep 1959 (214 CJ 323; 191 LJ 386)	SI 1959/1569	
Register of Patent Agent (Amendment) Rules 1964 Made: 21 Dec 1964 Laid: 31 Dec 1964 (as printed) Laid: 19 Jan 1965 (220 CJ 97; 197 LJ 114)	SI 1964/2029	
Register of Patent Agent (Amendment) Rules 1968 Made: 31 Oct 1968 Laid: 7 Nov 1968 (224 CJ 15; 201 LJ 19)	SI 1968/1741	
Register of Patent Agent (Amendment) Rules 1975 Made: 8 Sep 1975 Laid: 16 Sep 1975 (noted 13 Oct 1975); 22 Sep 1975 (231 CJ 640; 208 LJ 919)	SI 1975/1467	

Early war legislation

Memorandum for Inventors from the Secretary of State for the War Department as to Patents for Improvements in Instruments and Munitions of War [Signed B Hawes] Made: 13 Oct 1859	Repertory of Patent Inventions, Vol 35 (Jan–Jun 1860), p 166	

World War I laws

Patents, Designs and Trade Marks (Temporary) Rules 1914 Made: 21 Aug 1914 Laid: 31 Aug 1914 (169 CJ 453; 146 LJ 409)	(1914 No 1255) 1914, SR & O, Vol III, p 40	
Patents, Designs and Trade Marks (Temporary) Rules 1914 Made: 21 Aug 1914 Laid: 31 Aug 1914 (169 CJ 453; 146 LJ 409)	(1914 No 1256) 1914, SR & O, Vol III, p 43	
Patents, Designs and Trade Marks (Temporary) Rules 1914 Made: 5 Sep 1914 Laid: 10 Sep 1914 (169 CJ 457; 146 LJ 412)	(1914 No 1327) 1914, SR & O, Vol III, p 45	HC Deb, 31 Aug 1914, Vol 66(5th), col 354
Patents, Designs and Trade Marks (Temporary) Rules 1914 Made: 7 Sep 1914 Laid: 10 Sep 1914 (169 CJ 457; 146 LJ 412)	(1914 No 1328) 1914, SR & O, Vol III, p 48	HC Deb, 10 Sep 1914, Vol 66(5th), col 617
Order in Council under the Isle of Man (War Legislation) Act 1914 extending the Patents, Designs and Trade Marks (Temporary Rules) Act 1914 and the Rules thereunder Made: 7 Jan 1915	(1915 No 6) 1915, SR & O, Vol 1, p 341	
Patents, Designs and Trade Marks (Temporary) Rules 1915 Made: 17 Jun 1915 Laid: 28 Jun 1915; 29 Jun 1915 (170 CJ 167; 147 LJ 204)	(1915 No 591) 1915, SR & O, Vol III, p 45	HC Deb, 28 Jun 1915, Vol 72(5th), col 1444 HL Deb, 29 Jun 1915, Vol 19(5th), col 151
Order in Council further amending the Defence of the Realm (Consolidation) Regulations Made: 14 Oct 1915 Not laid	(1915 No 998) 1915, SR & O, Vol I, 172	
Patents, Designs and Trade Marks (Temporary) Rules 1915 (Second Set) Made: 19 Oct 1915 Laid: 2 Nov 1915 (170 CJ 273; 147 LJ 311)	(1915 No 1011) 1915, SR & O, Vol III, p 46	HC Deb, 2 Nov 1915, Vol 75(5th), col 435 HL Deb, 2 Nov 1915, Vol 20(5th), col 77
Order in Council further amending the Defence of the Realm (Consolidation) Regulations 1914 Made: 2 Dec 1915 Not laid	(1915 No 1220) 1915, SR & O, Vol I, p 177	
Order in Council extending Section 30 of the Patents and Designs Act 1907 to Air Force Made: 7 May 1916 Not laid	(1916 No 548) 1916, SR & O, Vol I, p 50	
General Licence of the Board of Trade as to payment of Fees for Patents in Enemy Countries Made: 4 Jul 1919 Not laid	(1919 No 840) 1919, SR & O, Vol II, p 834	
Order as to "Vested Patents", "Vested Applications" and "Restored Patents" of German Nationals Made: 19 Jul 1920 Not laid	(1920 No 1336) 1920, SR & O, Vol II, p 354	
Patents (Treaty of Paris) Rules 1920 Made: 24 Jul 1920 Not laid	(1920 No 1371) 1920, SR & O, Vol II, p 354	

(continued)

(continued)

Order as to "Vested Patents", "Vested Applications" and "Restored Patents" of Austrian and Bulgarian Nationals Made: 9 Nov 1920 Not laid	(1920 No 2118) 1920, SR & O, Vol II, p 369	
Patents (Treaties of Peace – Austria and Bulgaria) Rules 1920 Made: 29 Nov 1920 Not laid	(1920 No 2247) 1920, SR & O, Vol II, p 374	
Order in Council extending the Patents, Designs and Trade Marks (Temporary Rules) Act 1914 to the Isle of Man Made: 14 Feb 1921 Not laid	(1921 No 266) 1921, SR & O, p 439	
Orders of the Board of Trade under s 5(1) of the Trading with the Enemy Amendment Act 1914 further defining "Restored Application" – German Nationals Made: 12 Mar 1921 Not laid	(1921 No 331) 1921, SR & O, p 857	
Orders of the Board of Trade under s 5(1) of the Trading with the Enemy Amendment Act 1914 further defining "Restored Application" – Austrian Nationals Made: 12 Mar 1921 Not laid	(1921 No 332) 1921, SR & O, p 858	
Orders of the Board of Trade under s 5(1) of the Trading with the Enemy Amendment Act 1914 further defining "Restored Application" – Hungarian Nationals Made: 16 Aug 1921 Not laid	(1921 No 1315) 1921, SR & O, p 859	
Trading with the Enemy (Custodian Direction) Order Made: 10 Aug 1921 Not laid	(1921 No 1405) 1921, SR & O, p 1381	
Patents (Treaty of Peace – Hungary) Rules 1920 Made: 5 Sep 1921 Not laid	(1921 No 1453) 1921, SR & O, p 864	
Orders of the Board of Trade under s 5(1) of the Trading with the Enemy Amendment Act 1914 for the restoration of Vested Patents Made: 26 Oct 1923 Not laid	(1923 No 1386) 1923, SR & O, p 738	
Patents (Treaty of Peace) Rules 1920 Revocation Rules 1930 Made: 17 May 1930 Not laid	(1930 No 342) 1930, SR & O, p 1379	
Order of Board of Trade revoking orders of 1920 and 1921 as to German nationals Made: 17 May 1930 Not laid	(1930 No 343) 1930, SR & O, p 1379	
Order of Board of Trade revoking orders of 1920 and 1921 as to Austrian nationals Made: 29 Oct 1930 Not laid	(1930 No 853) 1930, SR & O, p 1381	
Patents (Treaty of Peace – Hungary) Rules 1921 Revocation Rules 1931 Made: 9 Apr 1931 Not laid	(1931 No 312) 1931, SR & O, p 1029	
Order of Board of Trade revoking order of 1920 as to Hungarian nationals Made: 18 May 1931 Not laid	(1931 No 313) 1931, SR & O, p 1029	

Patents (Treaty of Peace – Austria and Bulgaria) Rules 1920 Revocation Rules 1931 Made: 18 May 1931 Not laid	(1931 No 397) 1931, SR & O, p 1027	
Order of Board of Trade revoking order of 1920 as to Bulgarian nationals Made: 18 May 1931 Not laid	(1931 No 398) 1931, SR & O, p 1027	

World War II laws

Defence (General) Regulations 1939 Made: 25 Aug 1939 Not laid	(1939 No 927) 1939, SR & O, Vol I, p 715 (at p 813)	
Patents, Designs, Copyright and Trade Marks (Emergency) Rules 1939 Made: 26 Sep 1939 Not laid	(1939 No 1375) 1939, SR & O, Vol II, p 2547	
Order in Council amending the Defence (General) Regulations 1939 Made: 23 Nov 1939 Not laid	(1939 No 1682) 1939, SR & O, Vol I, p 840	
General Licence Issued by Board of Trade Made: 7 Jan 1940 Not laid	(1940 No 181) 1940, SR & O, Vol I, p 1056	
Aircraft Production (Transfer of Functions) Order 1940 Made: 20 May 1940 Not laid	(1940 No 762) 1940, SR & O, Vol I, p 30 (at p 31)	
Patents, Designs, Copyright and Trade Marks (Emergency) (Amendment) Rules 1940 Made: 7 May 1940 Not laid	(1940 No 693) 1940, SR & O, Vol I, p 740	
Order in Council amending the Defence Regulations (Isle of Man) 1939 Made: 19 Jun 1940 Not laid	(1940 No 1067) 1940, SR & O, Vol II, p 1474 (at p 1475)	
Order in Council amending the Defence (General) Regulations 1939 Made: 24 Jun 1940 Not laid	(1940 No 1328) 1940, SR & O, Vol II, p 91	
General Licence Authorised by Board of Trade as to Fees in Respect of Patents, Designs and Trade Marks Made: 5 Jun 1941 Not laid	(1941 No 794) 1941, SR & O, Vol I, p 1142	
Defence (Patents, Trade Marks, etc) Regulations 1941 Made: 11 Nov 1941 Not laid	(1941 No 1780) 1941, SR & O, Vol II, p 189	
Defence (Patents, Trade Marks, etc) Rules 1942 Made: 15 Jan 1942 Not laid	(1942 No 72) 1942, SR & O, Vol II, p 1860	
Order in Council amending the Defence (Armed Forces) Regulations 1939, the Defence (Companies) Regulations 1940, the Defence (Evacuated Areas) Regulations 1940, the Defence (Home Guard) Regulations 1940 and the Defence (Patents, Trade Marks, etc) Regulations 1941 Made: 17 Sep 1942 Not laid	(1942 No 1882) 1942, SR & O, Vol II, p 116 (at p 117)	

(continued)

(continued)

General Licence Authorised by Board of Trade as to Fees in Respect of Patents, Designs and Trade Marks Made: 10 Oct 1942 Not laid	(1942 No 2104) 1942, SR & O, Vol I, p 820	
Ordering in Council amending the Defence (Evacuated Areas) Regulations 1940 and the Defence (Patents, Trade Marks, etc) Regulations 1941 Made: 16 Dec 1942 Not laid	(1942 No 2563) 1942, SR & O, Vol II, p 136 (at p 137)	
Use of Inventions, &c., in USA (Exemption) (No 1) Order 1943 Made: 19 Jan 1943 Not laid	(1943 No 124) 1943, SR & O, Vol II, p 1742	
Order in Council adding regulation 5A to the Defence (Patents, Trade Marks, etc) Regulations 1941 Made: 11 Mar 1943 Not laid	(1943 No 376) 1943, SR & O, Vol II, p 67	
Order in Council adding amending regulation 7 of the Defence (Patents, Trade Marks, etc) Regulations 1941 Made: 20 May 1943 Not laid	(1943 No 746) 1943, SR & O, Vol II, p 68	
Order in Council Revoking and Amending Certain Defence Regulations Made: 9 May 1945 Not laid	(1945 No 504) 1945, SR & O, Vol II, p 13 (at p 23)	
Patents (Extension of Period of Emergency) Order 1950 Delivered: 17 Oct 1950 (205 CJ 228; 182 LJ 224) Rep: 20 Oct 1950 (182 LJ 231) Res: 23 Oct 1950; 25 Oct 1950 (205 CJ 238; 182 LJ 240) HM answer: 26 Oct 1950 (205 CJ 244; 182 LJ 241) Made: 2 Nov 1950	SI 1950/1778	Res: HC Deb, 23 Oct 1950, Vol 478(5th), col 2641 Motion: HL Deb, 25 Oct 1950, Vol 168(5th), col 1367 HM message: HC Deb, 26 Oct 1950, Vol 478(5th), col 2940; HL Deb, 26 Oct 1950, Vol 168(5th), col 1416
Emergency Laws (Continuance) Order 1950 Motion: 23 Oct 1950; 25 Oct 1950 (205 CJ 236; 182 LJ 240) HM answer: 26 Oct 1950 (205 CJ 244; 182 LJ 241) Made: 2 Nov 1950	SI 1950/1770	Motion: HC Deb, 23 Oct 1950, Vol 478(5th), col 2589–2637; HL Deb, 25 Oct 1950, Vol 168(5th), col 1364–1367 HM answer: HC Deb, 26 Oct 1950, Vol 478(5th), col 2939–2940; HL Deb, 26 Oct 1950, Vol 168(5th), col 1416
Patents (Extension of Period of Emergency) Order 1951 Delivered: 6 Nov 1951 (207 CJ 17; 184 LJ 20) SpOC day app: 13 Nov 1951 (184 LJ 24) Rep: 14 Nov 1951 (184 LJ 27) Res: 14 Nov 1951; 20 Nov 1951 (207 CJ 37) HM answer: 19 Nov 1951; 21 Nov 1951 (207 CJ 42; 194 LJ 34) Made: 4 Dec 1951	SI 1951/2123	Motion: HC Deb, 14 Nov 1951, Vol 493(5th), col 1125–1126; HL Deb, 20 Nov 1951, Vol 174(5th), col 380 HM answer: HC Deb, 19 Nov 1951, Vol 494(5th), col 1; HL Deb, 21 Nov 1951, Vol 174(5th), col 403
Emergency Laws (Continuance) Order 1951 Motion: 14 Nov 1951; 20 Nov 1951 (207 CJ 35; 184 LJ 32) HM answer: 19 Nov 1951; 21 Nov 1951 (207 CJ 42; 184 LJ 34) Made: 4 Dec 1951	SI 1951/2117	Motion: HC Deb, 14 Nov 1951, Vol 493(5th), col 986–1124; HL Deb, 20 Nov 1951, Vol 174(5th), col 378–380 HM answer: HC Deb, 19 Nov 1951, Vol 494(5th), col 1; HL Deb, 21 Nov 1951, Vol 174(5th), col 403

Patents (Extension of Period of Emergency) Order 1952 Delivered: 4 Nov 1952 (208 CJ 4; 185 LJ 4) Rep: 12 Nov 1952 (185 LJ 12) Res: 27 Nov 1952; 20 Nov 1952 (208 CJ 41; 185 LJ 16) HM answer: 4 Dec 1952 (208 CJ 49; 185 LJ 29) Made: 4 Dec 1952	SI 1952/2101	Motion: HC Deb, 27 Nov 1952, Vol 508(5th), col 941; HL Deb, 20 Nov 1952, Vol 179(5th), col 511 HM answer: HC Deb, 4 Dec 1952, Vol 508(5th), col 1727; HL Deb, 4 Dec 1952, Vol 179(5th), col 749
Emergency Laws (Continuance) Order 1952 Motion: 20 Nov 1952; 2 Dec 1952 (208 CJ 27; 185 LJ 24) Resumed: 27 Nov 1952 (208 CJ 38) HM answer: 4 Dec 1952 (208 CJ 49; 185 LJ 29) Made: 4 Dec 1952	SI 1952/2095	Motion: HC Deb, 20 Nov 1952, Vol 507(5th), col 2183–2212; HC Deb, 27 Nov 1952, Vol 508(5th), col 761–940; HL Deb, 20 Nov 1952, Vol 179(5th), col 511 HM answer: HC Deb, 4 Dec 1952, Vol 508(5th), col 1727; HL Deb, 4 Dec 1952, Vol 179(5th), col 749
Patents (Extension of Period of Emergency) Order 1953 Delivered: 3 Nov 1953 (209 CJ 4; 186 LJ 5) Ref SpOC: 10 Nov 1953, (186 LJ 12) Rep: 18 Nov 1953 (186 LJ 18) Res: 24 Nov 1953; 26 Nov 1953 (209 CJ 32; 186 LJ 30) HM answer: 27 Nov 1953; 2 Dec 1953 (209 CJ 40; 186 LJ 35) Made: 4 Dec 1953	SI 1953/1775	Motion: HC Deb, 24 Nov 1953, Vol 521(5th), col 305–306; HL Deb, 26 Nov 1953, Vol 184(5th), col 757 HM answer: HC Deb,18 Nov 1953, Vol 521(5th), col 1127; HL Deb, 2 Dec 1953, Vol 184(5th), col 864
Emergency Laws (Continuance) Order 1953 Motion: 24 Nov 1953; 26 Nov 1953 (209 CJ 32; 186 LJ 29) HM answer: 2 Dec 1953 (209 CJ 40; 186 LJ 35) Made: 4 Dec 1953	SI 1953/1768	Motion: HC Deb, 24 Nov 1953, Vol 521(5th), col 271; HL Deb, 26 Nov 1953, Vol 184(5th), col 755–757 HM answer: HC Deb, 2 Dec 1953, Vol 521(5th), col 1127; HL Deb, 2 Dec 1953, Vol 184(5th), col 863–864
Patents (Extension of Period of Emergency) Order 1954 Delivered: 3 Nov 1954 (209 CJ 333; 186 LJ 370) Rep: 10 Nov 1954 (186 LJ 376) Res: 15 Nov 1954; 17 Nov 1954 (209 CJ 348; 186 LJ 400) HM answer: 18 Nov 1954 (209 CJ 350; 186 LJ 401) Made: 24 Nov 1954	SI 1954/1563	Motion: HC Deb, 15 Nov 1954, Vol 533(5th), col 157–158; HL Deb,17 Nov 1954, Vol 189(5th), col 1595–1599 HM answer: HC Deb, 18 Nov 1954, Vol 533(5th), col 535; HL Deb, 18 Nov 1954, Vol 189(5th), col 1637
Emergency Laws (Continuance) Order 1954 Motion: 15 Nov 1954; 17 Nov 1954 (209 CJ 347; 186 LJ 399) HM answer: 18 Nov 1954 (209 CJ 350; 186 LJ 401) Made: 24 Nov 1954	SI 1954/1560	Motion: HC Deb, 15 Nov 1954, Vol 533(5th), col 156–157; HL Deb, 17 Nov 1954, Vol 189(5th), col 1594–1595 HM answer: HC Deb, 18 Nov 1954, Vol 533(5th), col 535; HL Deb, 18 Nov 1954, Vol 189(5th), col 1637
Patents (Extension of Period of Emergency) Order 1955 Delivered: 25 Oct 1955 (211 CJ 96; 188 LJ 100) Rep: 2 Nov 1955 (188 LJ 110) Res: 14 Nov 1955; 24 Nov 1955 (211 CJ 123; 188 LJ 132) HM answer: 1 Dec 1955 (211 CJ 142; 188 LJ 139) Made: 1 Dec 1955	SI 1955/1812	Motion: HC Deb, 14 Nov 1955, Vol 546(5th), col 31–45; HL Deb, 24 Nov 1955, Vol 194(5th), col 851–852 HM answer: HC Deb, 1 Dec 1955 Vol 546(5th), col 2479; HL Deb, 1 Dec 1955, Vol 194(5th), col 1009

(continued)

(continued)

Emergency Laws (Continuance) Order 1955 Motion: 14 Nov 1955; 24 Nov 1955 (211 CJ 123; 188 LJ 132) HM answer: 1 Dec 1955 (211 CJ 142; 188 LJ 139) Made: 1 Dec 1955	SI 1955/1813	Motion: HC Deb, 14 Nov 1955, Vol 546(5th), col 31–44; HL Deb, 24 Nov 1955, Vol 194(5th), col 850–851 HM answer: HC Deb, 1 Dec 1955 Vol 546(5th), col 2479; HL Deb, 1 Dec 1955, Vol 194(5th), col 1009
Patents (Extension of Period of Emergency) Order 1956 Delivered: 6 Nov 1956; 25 Oct 1956 (212 CJ 4; 188 LJ 100) Rep: 2 Nov 1956 (188 LJ 110) Res: 20 Nov 1956; 24 Nov 1956 (212 CJ 21; 188 LJ 132) HM answer: 21 Nov 1956; 1 Dec 1956 (212 CJ 22; 188 LJ 139)	SI 1956/1889	Motion: HC Deb, 20 Nov 1956, Vol 560(5th), col 1610; HL Deb, 20 Nov 1956, Vol 200(5th), col 389–390 HM answer: HC Deb, 21 Nov 1956, Vol 560(5th), col 1715; HL Deb, 27 Nov 1956, Vol 200(5th), col 549
Emergency Laws (Continuance) Order 1956 Motion: 20 Nov 1956 (212 CJ 21; 189 LJ 18) HM answer: 21 Nov 1956; 27 Nov 1956 (212 CJ 22; 189 LJ 22) Made: 29 Nov 1956	SI 1956/1883	Motion: HC Deb, 20 Nov 1956, Vol 560(5th), col 1563–1610; HL Deb, 20 Nov 1956, Vol 200(5th), col 388–389 HM answer: HC Deb, 21 Nov 1956, Vol 560(5th), col 1715; HL Deb, 27 Nov 1956, Vol 200(5th), col 549
Patents (Extension of Period of Emergency) Order 1957 Delivered: 5 Nov 1957; 6 Nov 1957 (213 CJ 4; 189 LJ 6) Ref to SpOC: 13 Nov 1957 (189 LJ 11) Rep: 14 Nov 1957 (189 LJ 14) Res: 21 Nov 1957; 20 Nov 1957 (213 CJ 17; 189 LJ 19) HM answer: 21 Nov 1957; 27 Nov (213 CJ 29; 189 LJ 22) Made: 27 Nov 1957	SI 1957/2062	Motion: HC Deb, 14 Nov 1957, Vol 577(5th), col 1195; HL Deb,19 Nov 1957, Vol 206(5th), col 393 HM answer: HC Deb, 21 Nov 1957, Vol 578(5th), col 533; HL Deb, 26 Nov 1957, Vol 206(5th), col 477
Emergency Laws (Continuance) Order 1957 Motion: 14 Nov 1957; 19 Nov 1957 (213 CJ 17; 190 LJ 19) HM answer: 21 Nov 1957; 26 Nov 1957 (213 CJ 29; 190 LJ 24) Made: 27 Nov 1957	SI 1957/2057	Motion: HC Deb, 14 Nov 1957, Vol 577(5th), col 1173–1194; HL Deb,19 Nov 1957, Vol 206(5th), col 392–393 HM answer: HC Deb, 21 Nov 1957, Vol 578(5th), col 533; HL Deb, 26 Nov 1957, Vol 206(5th), col 477

Foreign Jurisdiction Acts 1843 to 1913

Africa Order in Council 1889 (art 55) Made: 15 Oct 1889	London Gazette, 22 Oct 1889 (Iss: 25,986, p 5557)	
Morocco Order in Council 1889 (art 112) Made: 28 Nov 1889	1890 Con, SR & O, Vol 3, p 524 London Gazette, 13 Dec 1889 (Iss: 26,001, p. 7163)	
Persia Order in Council 1889 (art 292) Made: 13 Dec 1889	1890 Con, SR & O, Vol 3, p 698 London Gazette, 24 Dec 1889 (Iss: 26,005,p. 7417)	
Persian Coast and Islands Order in Council 1889 (art 50) Made: 13 Dec 1889	1890 Con, SR & O, Vol 3, p 796 London Gazette, 24 Dec 1889 (Iss: 26,005, p. 7459)	

Africa Order in Council 1889 (art 55) Made: 15 Oct 1889	London Gazette, 22 Oct 1889 (Iss: 25,986, p 5557)	
Somali Coast Order in Council 1889 (art 4) Made: 13 Dec 1889	London Gazette, 24 Dec 1889 (Iss: 26,005, p. 7467)	
Brunei Order in Council 1890 (art 40) Made: 22 Nov 1890	(No number) 1890 SR & O, p 664	
China, Japan and Corea (Patents & C) Order in Council 1899 Made: 2 Feb 1899	(1899 No 82) 1899 SR & O, Vol 1, p 639	HC Deb, 7 Feb 1899, Vol 66(4th), col 71 HL Deb, 7 Feb 1899, Vol 66(4th), col 38
Ottoman Order in Council 1899 (art 57) Made: 8 Aug 1899	(1899 No 595) 1899, SR & O, p 643	
Siam Order in Council 1903 (art 59) Made: 16 Feb 1903	(1903 No 123) 1903, SR & O, p 793	
China Order in Council 1925 (art 73) Made: 17 Mar 1925	(1925 No 603) 1925, SR & O, p 379	
Egypt Order in Council 1930 (arts 69 and 117) Made: 28 Jul 1930	(1930 No 744) 1930, SR & O, p 539	
India and Burman (Transitory Provisions) Order 1937 Made: 18 Mar 1937	(1937 No 266) 1937, SR & O, p 1262	

Convention Country orders

Order in Council applying the provisions of Patents, Designs and Trade Marks Act 1883 to Members of the Paris Convention Made: 26 Jun 1884	1890 Cons, SR & O, Vol 5, p 142 London Gazette, 1 Jul 1884 (Iss: 25,372, p 2993)	
Order in Council applying the provisions of Patents, Designs and Trade Marks Act 1883 to Sweden and Norway Made: 9 Jul 1885	1890 Cons, SR & O, Vol 5, p 143 London Gazette, 10 Jul 1885 (Iss: 25,489, p 3173)	
Order in Council applying the provisions of Patents, Designs and Trade Marks Act 1883 to Paraguay and Uruguay Made: 24 Sep 1886	1890 Cons, SR & O, Vol 5, p 144 London Gazette, 24 Sep 1886 (Iss: 25,629, p 4725)	
Order in Council applying the provisions of Patents, Designs and Trade Marks Act 1883 to the United States Made: 12 Jul 1887	1890 Cons, SR & O, Vol 5, p 145 London Gazette, 15 Jul 1887 (Iss: 25,721, p 3827)	
Order in Council applying the provisions of Patents, Designs and Trade Marks Act 1883 to the Netherlands, East India Colonies Made: 17 Nov 1888	1890 Cons, SR & O, Vol 5, p 145 London Gazette, 23 Nov 1888 (Iss: 25,877, p 6412)	
Order in Council applying the provisions of Patents, Designs and Trade Marks Act 1883 to Mexico Made: 26 Jun 1884	1890 Cons, SR & O, Vol 5, p 146 London Gazette, 31 May 1889 (Iss: 25,941, p 2955)	
Order in Council applying the provisions of the Patents, Designs and Trade Marks Act 1883 to the Netherlands East Indian Colonies (Curacao and Surinam) Made: 17 May 1890	(No number) 1890, SR & O p 886	
Order in Council applying the provisions of the Patents, Designs and Trade Marks Act 1883 to Santo Domingo 1890 Made: 21 Oct 1890	(No number) 1890, SR & O, p 887	
Order in Council applying the provisions of the Patents, Designs and Trade Marks Act 1883 to Roumania Made: 5 Aug 1892	(No number) 1892, SR & O, p 650	
Order in Council Applying the Patents &c. Acts to Greece Made: 15 Oct 1894	(1894 No 234) 1894, SR & O, p 57	

(continued)

(continued)

Order in Council applying the provisions of the Patents, Designs and Trade Marks Act 1883 to Denmark and the Faroe Islands Made: 20 Nov 1894	(1894 No 542) 1894, SR & O, p 56	
Order in Council applying the provisions of the Patents, Designs and Trade Marks Act 1883 to Guatemala Made: 2 Feb 1895	(1895 No 62) 1895, SR & O, p 585	
Order in Council applying the provisions of the Patents, Designs and Trade Marks Act 1883 to Japan Made: 7 Oct 1899	(1899 No 759) 1899, SR & O, p 964	
Order in Council applying The Provisions of the Patents, Designs and Trade Marks 1883 to the Republic of Honduras Made: 26 Sep 1901	(1901 No 799) 1901, SR & O, p 320	
Order in Council applying The Provisions of the Patents, Designs and Trade Marks 1883 to Germany Made: 9 Oct 1903	(1903 No 867) 1903, SR & O, p 1170	
Order in Council applying s 91 of the Patents and Designs Act 1907 to French Morocco Protectorate Made: 12 Feb 1918	(1918 No 250) 1918, SR & O, Vol II, p 628	
Order in Council applying s 91 of the Patents and Designs Act 1907 to Poland Made: 25 Nov 1919	(1919 No 816) 1919, SR & O, Vol II, p 106	
Order in Council applying s 91 of the Patents and Designs Act 1907 to Austria-Hungary Made: 17 May 1909	(1909 No 585) 1909, SR & O, p 614	
Order in Council applying s 91 of the Patents and Designs Act 1907 to Czecho-Slovakia Made: 11 Mar 1920	(1920 No 575) 1920, SR & O, Vol II, p 347	
Order in Council applying s 91 of the Patents and Designs Act 1907 to Roumania Made: 13 Oct 1920	(1920 No 1992) 1920, SR & O, Vol II, p 350	
Order in Council applying s 91 of the Patents and Designs Act 1907 to Serb-Croat-Slovene State Made: 14 Feb 1921	(1921 No 267) 1921, SR & O, p 845	
Order in Council applying s 91 of the Patents and Designs Act 1907 to Bulgaria Made: 14 Jul 1921	(1921 No 1213) 1921, SR & O, p 848	
Order in Council applying s 91 of the Patents and Designs Act 1907 to Free City of Danzig Made: 21 Nov 1921	(1921 No 1808) 1921, SR & O, p 854	
Order in Council applying s 91 of the Patents and Designs Act 1907 to Finland Made: 11 Oct 1921	(1921 No 1643) 1921, SR & O, p 851	
Industrial Property Convention (Accession of Luxembourg) Order 1922 Made: 14 Jul 1922	(1922 No 814) 1922, SR & O, p 799	
Industrial Property Convention (Accession of Estonia) Order 1924 Made: 20 Oct 1924	(1924 No 251) 1924, SR & O, p 1423	
Industrial Property Convention (Accession of Syria and Lebanon) Order 1924 Made: 9 Oct 1924	(1924 No 1224) 1924, SR & O, p 1428	
Industrial Property Convention (Accession of Greece) Order 1924 Made: 9 Oct 1924	(1924 No 1225) 1924, SR & O, p 1426	
Industrial Property Convention (Accession of Syria Latvia) Order 1925 Made: 12 Oct 1925	(1925 No 1014) 1925, SR & O, p 1314	

Industrial Property Convention (Accession of Turkey) Order 1925 Made: 12 Oct 1925	(1925 No 1015) 1925, SR & O, p 1315	
Hague Industrial Property Convention Order 1928 Made: 14 Aug 1928	(1928 No 637) 1928, SR & O, p 1041	
Industrial Property Convention (Serb-Croat-Slovene) Order 1928 Made: 1 Nov 1928	(1928 No 909) 1928, SR & O, p 1042	
Industrial Property Convention (Portugal) Order 1928 Made: 21 Dec 1928	(1928 No 1048) 1928, SR & O, p 1044	
Industrial Property Convention (Hungary) Order 1929 Made: 8 Jun 1929	(1929 No 480) 1929, SR & O, p 1135	
Industrial Property Convention (Switzerland) Order 1929 Made: 5 Jul 1929	(1929 No 549) 1929, SR & O, p 1137	
Industrial Property Convention (Belgium) Order 1929 Made: 15 Aug 1929	(1929 No 652) 1929, SR & O, p 1132	
Industrial Property Convention (Brazil) Order 1929 Made: 17 Dec 1929	(1929 No 1162) 1929, SR & O, p 1134	
Industrial Property Convention (Mexico) Order 1930 Made: 27 Feb 1930	(1930 No 124) 1930, SR & O, p 1375	
Industrial Property Convention (France, Morocco (French Zone) and Tunis) Order 1930 Made: 27 Oct 1930	(1930 No 926) 1930, SR & O, p 1373	
Industrial Property Convention (Turkey) Order 1930 Made: 27 Oct 1930	(1930 No 927) 1930, SR & O, p 1377	
Industrial Property Convention (United States) Order 1931 Made: 29 Jun 1931	(1931 No 547) 1931, SR & O, p 1025	
Industrial Property Convention (Poland) Order 1931 Made: 17 Dec 1931	(1931 No 1096) 1931, SR & O, p 1024	
Industrial Property Convention (Libya, Eritrea and Italian Aegean Islands) Order 1932 Made: 11 Feb 1932	(1932 No 63) 1932, SR & O, p 1429	
Industrial Property Convention (Syria and Lebanon) Order 1932 Made: 15 Dec 1932	(1932 No 1060) 1932, SR & O, p 1430	
Industrial Property Convention (Czecho-Slovakoa) Order 1933 Made: 16 Mar 1933	(1933 No 232) 1933, SR & O, p 1520	
Industrial Property Convention (Netherlands East Indies, Surinam and Curacao) Order 1933 Made: 16 Mar 1933	(1933 No 258) 1933, SR & O, p 1522	
Industrial Property Convention (Liechtenstein) Order 1933 Made: 24 Jul 1933	(1933 No 738) 1933, SR & O, p 1524	
Industrial Property Convention (French Possessions Overseas) Order 1934 Made: 26 Feb 1934	(1934 No 219) 1934, SR & O, Vol II, p 34	
Industrial Property Convention (Sweden) Order 1934 Made: 14 Aug 1934	(1934 No 927) 1934, SR & O, Vol II, p 35	
Industrial Property Convention (Japan) Order 1935 Made: 21 Feb 1935	(1935 No 136) 1935, SR & O, p 1307	
Industrial Property Convention (Morocco (Tangier Zone)) Order 1936 Made: 24 Mar 1936	(1936 No 303) 1936, SR & O, Vol II, p 2027	
Industrial Property Convention (Denmark) Order 1937 Made: 22 Oct 1937	(1937 No 956) 1937, SR & O, p 1910	
Patents &c. (Convention Countries) (No 1) Order 1938 Made: 28 Jul 1938	(1938 No 767) 1938, SR & O, Vol II, p 2766	

(continued)

(continued)

Patents &c. (Convention Countries) (No 2) Order 1938 Made: 28 Jul 1938	(1938 No 768) 1938, SR & O, Vol II, p 2770	
Patents &c. (Luxemburg) Order 1946 Made: 19 Feb 1946	(1946 No 170) 1946, SR & O, Vol I, p 1239	
Patents &c. (Union of South Africa) (Convention) Order 1948 Made: 26 Jan 1948	(1948 No 104) 1948, SR & O, Vol I, p 3186	
Patents &c. (Austria) (Convention) Order 1948 Made: 27 Apr 1948	(1948 No 872) 1948, SR & O, Vol I, p 872	
Patents &c. (Spanish Colonies) (Convention) Order 1948 Made: 12 May 1948	(1948 No 1006) 1948, SR & O, Vol I, p 1006	
Patents etc. (Singapore) Order 1949 Made: 15 Dec 1949	SI 1949/2338	
Patents etc. (Israel) (Convention) Order 1950 Made: 31 Mar 1950	SI 1950/522	
Patents etc. (Dominican Republic) (Convention) Order 1950 Made: 9 Oct 1950	SI 1950/1653	
Patents etc. (Egypt) (Convention) Order 1951 Made: 1 Aug 1951	SI 1951/1389	
Patents etc. (Indonesia) (Convention) Order 1952 Made: 4 Dec 1952	SI 1952/2107	
Patents etc. (Ceylon) (Convention) Order 1953 Made: 11 Nov 1953	SI 1953/394	
Patents etc. (Finland) (Convention) Order 1953 Made: 19 Jun 1953	SI 1953/971	
Patents etc. (Greece) (Convention) Order 1953 Made: 22 Dec 1953	SI 1953/1899	
Patents etc. (Monaco) (Convention) Order 1956 Made: 29 Jun 1956	SI 1956/1003	
Patents etc. (Vietnam) (Convention) Order 1957 Made: 5 Apr 1956	SI 1957/600	
Patents etc. (Federation of Rhodesia and Nyasaland) (Convention) Order 1958 Made: 19 Feb 1958	SI 1958/263	
Patents etc. (Republic of Haiti) (Convention) Order 1958 Made: 25 Jun 1958	SI 1958/1053	
Patents etc. (Republic of Ireland) (Convention) Order 1958 Made: 25 Jun 1958	SI 1958/1054	
Patents etc. (Iran) (Convention) Order 1960 Made: 8 Feb 1960	SI 1960/201	
Patents etc. (The Republic of San Marino) (Convention) Order 1960 Made: 16 Mar 1960	SI 1960/437	
Patents etc. (United Arab Republic) (Convention) Order 1960 Made: 12 Sep 1960	SI 1960/1651	
Patents etc. (Vatican City) (Convention) Order 1960 Made: 26 Oct 1960	SI 1960/1958	
Patents etc. (Iceland) (Convention) Order 1962 Made: 23 May 1962	SI 1962/1083	
Patents etc. (Cuba) (Convention) Order 1963 Made: 27 Feb 1963	SI 1963/366	
Patents etc. (U.S. Dependencies and Tanganyika) (Convention) Order 1963 Made: 29 Jul 1963	SI 1963/1326	

Patents etc. (Nigeria and Congo (Brazzaville) (Convention) Order 1963 Made: 29 Aug 1963	SI 1963/1487	
Patents etc. (Ivory Coast) (Convention) Order 1963 Made: 23 Oct 1963	SI 1963/1757	
Patents etc. (Central African Republic, Chad, Laos, Upper Volta and Roumania) (Convention) Order 1963 Made: 27 Nov 1963	SI 1963/1919	
Patents etc. (Malagasy and Senegal) (Convention) Order 1963 Made: 20 Dec 1963	SI 1963/2082	
Patents etc. (Gabon) (Convention) Order 1964 Made: 26 Feb 1964	SI 1964/265	
Patents etc. (Cameroon) (Convention) Order 1964 Made: 12 May 1964	SI 1964/692	
Patents etc. (Niger) (Convention) Order 1964 Made: 3 Jul 1964	SI 1964/998	
Patents etc. (Trinidad and Tobago) (Convention) Order 1964 Made: 27 Jul 1964	SI 1964/1196	
Patents etc. (Mauritania) (Convention) Order 1965 Made: 14 Apr 1965	SI 1965/977	
Patents etc. (Union of Soviet Socialist Republics) (Convention) Order 1965 Made: 14 May 1965	SI 1965/1123	
Patents etc. (Uganda and Kenya) (Convention) Order 1965 Made: 24 Jun 1965	SI 1965/1304	
Patents etc. (Philippines) (Convention) Order 1965 Made: 18 Sep 1965	SI 1965/1711	
Patents etc. (Malawi) (Convention) Order 1965 Made: 29 Nov 1965	SI 1965/2013	
Patents etc. (Algeria) (Convention) Order 1966 Made: 31 Jan 1966	SI 1966/80	
Patents etc. (Cyprus) (Convention) Order 1966 Made: 31 Jan 1966	SI 1966/81	
Patents etc. (Bulgaria) (Convention) Order 1966 Made: 6 Apr 1966	SI 1966/396	
Patents etc. (Dahomey) (Convention) Order 1967 Made: 10 Feb 1967	SI 1967/158	
Patents etc. (Argentina and Uruguay) (Convention) Order 1967 Made: 23 Mar 1967	SI 1967/481	
Patents etc. (Togo) (Convention) Order 1967 Made: 10 Oct 1967	SI 1967/1492	
Patents etc. (Bahamas) (Convention) Order 1967 Made: 13 Nov 1967	SI 1967/1681	
Patents etc. (Malta)(Convention) Order 1967 Made: 13 Nov 1967	SI 1967/1682	
Patents etc. (Laos) (Convention) Order 1969 Made: 25 Jun 1969	SI 1969/865	
Patents etc. (Jordan) (Convention) Order 1972 Made: 28 Jun 1972	SI 1972/972	
Patents etc. (Federal Republic of Germany and German Democratic Republic) (Convention) Order 1973 Made: 18 Apr 1973	SI 1973/773	

(continued)

(continued)

Patents etc. (Zaire) (Convention) Order 1974 Made: 18 Dec 1974	SI 1974/2146	
Patents etc. (Iraq) (Convention) Order 1975 Made: 19 Dec 1975	SI 1975/2195	
Patents etc. (Ghana, Libya and Mauritius) (Convention) Order 1976 Made: 27 Oct 1976	SI 1976/1785	

Extension of time rules

Patents (Extension of Time) (Israel) Rules 1950 Made: 14 Dec 1950 Laid: 15 Dec 1950; 23 Jan 1951 (206 CJ 58; 183 LJ 55)	SI 1950/2024	
Patents (Extension of Time) (Federal Republic of Germany) Rules 1951 Made: 16 Mar 1951 Laid: 19 Mar 1951 (206 CJ 143; 183 LJ 105)	SI 1951/457	
Patents (Extension of Time) (Federal Republic of Germany) (Amendment) Rules 1951 Made: 5 Sep 1951 Laid: 4 Oct 1951 (206 CJ 325; 183 LJ 1416)	SI 1951/1632	

Application of Acts to dominions and colonies

Order in Council applying the provisions of the Patents, Designs and Trade Marks Act 1883 to Queensland 1885 Made: 17 Sep 1885	1890 Cons, SR & O, Vol 5, p 141 London Gazette, 22 Sep 1885 (Iss: 25,513, p 4429)	
Order in Council applying the provisions of the Patents, Designs and Trade Marks Act 1883 to New Zealand 1890 Made: 8 Feb 1890	(No Number) 1890, SR & O, p 887	
Order in Council applying the provisions of the Patents, Designs and Trade Marks Act 1883 to Tasmania Made: 30 Apr 1894	(1894 No 123) 1894, SR & O, p 54	
Order in Council applying the provisions of the Patents, Designs and Trade Marks Act 1883 to Western Australia Made: 11 May 1895	(1895 No 245) 1895, SR & O, p 587	
Order in Council applying The Provisions of the Patents, Designs and Trade Marks 1883 to Cuba Made: 12 Jan 1905	(1905 No 10) 1905, SR & O, p 270	
Order in Council applying The Provisions of the Patents, Designs and Trade Marks 1883 to Ceylon Made: 7 Aug 1905	(1905 No 933) 1905, SR & O, p 268	
Order in Council applying The Provisions of the Patents, Designs and Trade Marks 1883 to Commonwealth of Australia Made: 12 Aug 1907	(1907 No 651) 1907, SR & O, p 776	
Order in Council applying The Provisions of the Patents, Designs and Trade Marks 1883 to Trinidad and Tobago Made: 12 Aug 1907	(1907 No 652) 1907, SR & O, p 777	
Order in Council applying The Provisions of the Patents, Designs and Trade Marks 1883 to Commonwealth of Australia Made: 26 Mar 1907	(1907 No 263) 1907, SR & O, p 773	

Order in Council applying s 91 of the Patents and Designs Act 1907 to Union of South Africa Made: 25 Jun 1918	(1918 No 816) 1918, SR & O, Vol II, p 627	
Order in Council applying s 91 of the Patents and Designs Act 1907 and 1919 to British India Made: 13 Oct 1920	(1920 No 2034) 1920, SR & O, Vol II, p 346	
Patents, Designs and Trade Marks (Canada) Order 1923 Made: 11 Oct 1923	(1923 No 1226) 1923, SR & O, p 737	
Patents, Designs and Trade Marks (Irish Free State) Order 1927 Made: 3 Nov 1927	(1927 No 1062) 1927, SR & O, p 944	
Patents, Designs and Trade Marks (Canada) Order 1928 Made: 14 Aug 1928	(1928 No 636) 1928, SR & O, p 1039	
Patents, Designs and Trade Marks (Trinidad and Tobago) Order 1929 Made: 17 Dec 1929	(1929 No 1204) 1929, SR & O, p 1131	
Patents, Designs and Trade Marks (New Zealand) Order 1931 Made: 1 Oct 1931	(1931 No 850) 1931, SR & O, p 1022	
Patents, Designs and Trade Marks (Commonwealth of Australia) Order 1933 Made: 16 Mar 1933	(1933 No 256) 1933, SR & O, p 1517	
Patents, Designs and Trade Marks (Palestine) Order 1933 Made: 9 Oct 1933	(1933 No 978) 1933, SR & O, p 1519	
Patents, Designs and Trade Marks (Tanganyika Territory) Order 1937 Made: 23 Nov 1937	(1937 No 1067) 1937, SR & O, p 1912	

Exhibition orders

Order in Council applying certain provisions of the Patents, Designs and Trade Marks Act 1883 to the Paris Universal Exhibition in 1889 Made: 17 Nov 1888	London Gazette, 23 Nov 1888 (Iss: 25,877, p 6412)	
Order in Council applying certain provisions of the Patents, Designs and Trade Marks Act 1883 to the International Exhibition to be held at Chicago in 1893 Made: 24 Nov 1891	(No number) 1891, SR & O, p 276	
Order in Council applying certain provisions of the Patents, Designs and Trade Marks Act 1883 to the International Exhibition to be held at Vienna in 1894 Made: 29 Jan 1894	(1894 No 75) 1894, SR & O, p 75	
Order in Council applying certain provisions of the Patents, Designs and Trade Marks Act 1883 to the International Exhibition to be held at Paris in 1900 Made: 2 Feb 1899	(1899 No 80) 1899, SR & O, p 601	
Order in Council applying certain provisions of the Patents, Designs and Trade Marks Act 1883 to the International Exhibition to be held at St Louis in 1904 Made: 10 Aug 1899	(1903 No 670) 1903, SR & O, p 741	
Application of the Patents, Designs and Trade Marks Act 1883 to the Milan 1906 Exhibition Made: 16 Feb 1906	(1906 No 148) 1906, SR & O, p 169	
Order in Council applying certain provisions of the Patents and Designs Act 1907 to the International Exhibition to be held at Brussels in 1910 Made: 2 Apr 1909	(1909 No 395) 1909, SR & O, p 294	

(continued)

(continued)

Order in Council applying certain provisions of the Patents and Designs Act 1907 to the International Exhibition to be held at Turin in 1911 Made: 17 May 1909	(1909 No 581) 1909, SR & O, p 296	
Order in Council applying certain provisions of the Patents and Designs Act 1907 to the International Exhibition to be held at Rome in 1911 Made: 17 May 1909	(1909 No 582) 1909, SR & O, p 297	
Order in Council applying certain provisions of the Patents and Designs Act 1907 to the International Exhibition to be held at Buenos Aires (Agriculture) in 1910 Made: 10 Jan 1910	(1910 No 65) 1910, SR & O, p 95	
Order in Council applying certain provisions of the Patents and Designs Act 1907 to the International Exhibition to be held at Buenos Aires (Hygiene) in 1910 Made: 10 Jan 1910	(1910 No 66) 1910, SR & O, p 97	
Order in Council applying certain provisions of the Patents and Designs Act 1907 to the International Exhibition to be held at Vienna (Shooting and Field Sports) in 1910 Made: 10 Jan 1910	(1910 No 63) 1910, SR & O, p 100	
Order in Council applying certain provisions of the Patents and Designs Act 1907 to the International Exhibition to be held at Buenos Aires (Railways and Land Transport) in 1910 Made: 10 Jan 1910	(1910 No 64) 1910, SR & O, p 98	
Order in Council applying certain provisions of the Patents and Designs Act 1907 to the Ghent International Exhibition Made: 19 Jul 1912	(1912 No 1135) 1911, SR & O, p 141	
Order in Council applying certain provisions of the Patents and Designs Act 1907 to Leipzig (Book Industry and Graphic Arts) Exhibition in 1914 Made: 9 Mar 1914	(1914 No 405) 1914, SR & O, Vol I, p 563	
Order in Council applying certain provisions of the Patents and Designs Act 1907 to Paris (British Arts and Crafts) Exhibition in 1914 Made: 9 Mar 1914	(1914 No 406) 1914, SR & O, Vol I, p 564	
Defence of the Realm Regulations as to prohibiting on exhibition prejudicing production of war material, revoked Made: 25 Nov 1918	(1918 No 1550) 1918, SR & O, Vol I, p 376	
Inventions and Designs (Gothenburg Exhibition) Order 1923 Made: 26 Jun 1923	(1923 No 766) 1923, SR & O, p 319	
Inventions and Designs (Paris Exhibition) Order 1925 Made: 17 Mar 1925	(1925 No 255) 1925, SR & O, p 334	

Aircraft orders

Aircraft (Exemption from Seizure on Patent Claims) Order 1957 Made: 8 Oct 1957 Laid: 29 Oct 1957 (212 CJ 295; 189 LJ 304)	SI 1957/1740	
Aircraft (Exemption from Seizure on Patent Claims) Order 1961 Made: 27 Feb 1961 Laid: 3 Mar 1961; 7 Mar 1961 (216 CJ 127; 193 LJ 161)	SI 1961/332	

Aircraft (Exemption from Seizure on Patent Claims) Order 1964 Made: 20 Jan 1964 Laid: 24 Jan 1964; 28 Jan 1964 (219 CJ 82; 196 LJ 103)	SI 1964/56	
Aircraft (Exemption from Seizure on Patent Claims) Order 1966 Made: 24 Feb 1966 Laid: 1 Mar 1966; 2 Mar 1966 (221 CJ 114; 198 LJ 134)	SI 1966/188	
Aircraft (Exemption from Seizure on Patent Claims) Order 1969 Made: 10 Feb 1969 Laid: 14 Feb 1969; 18 Feb 1969 (224 CJ 117; 201 LJ 120)	SI 1969/150	
Aircraft (Exemption from Seizure on Patent Claims) Order 1972 Made: 28 Jun 1972 Laid: 4 Jul 1972 (227 CJ 419; 204 LJ 397)	SI 1972/969	

Miscellaneous

Rules Regulating the Practice and Procedure on Appeals to the Law Officers Laid: 5 Feb 1884 (139 CJ 7)	(1884 C 4040), Vol 28, p 45 at p 15 (Appendix to Patents Rules 1883)	
World Intellectual Property Organisation (Immunities and Privileges) Order 1968 Made: 7 Jun 1968 Not laid	SI 1968/890	HC Deb, 16 May 1968, Vol 764(5th), col 1522–1526 HL Deb, 21 May 1968, Vol 292(5th), col 639–646

Part 5 Parliamentary rewards

Part 5 Contents

Chapter 1: Parliamentary rewards granted

Chapter 2: Parliamentary rewards sought but not granted

Introduction

The role of Parliament in giving rewards (i.e. payments) to individual inventors is often mentioned in the biographic literature of particular inventors or as part of broader scheme of encouraging innovation.[1] The difficulty for researchers has long been that the key list relied upon is Patrick Colquhoun's 1815 compendium of rewards,[2] because it was included as an Appendix to the Report of the 1829 Select Committee.[3] This list is defective in three ways. First, it rolled up certain rewards (it has an entry for "miscellaneous rewards at various times"), secondly it included some typographical errors (so it referred to Dr Irvine when it was Charles Irving) and thirdly it ended in 1815. There was a slightly updated list produced in the *Mechanics Magazine* in 1832,[4] and additions (not in list form) have been made by Burrell and Kelly.[5] However, the errors in earlier lists have confounded later researchers (Burrell and Kelly, for instance, could not, for obvious reasons, find Irvine in the Parliamentary record[6]).

The purpose of this part is to provide a full list of rewards made by Parliament and the supporting records and, hopefully, to correct the errors made in earlier lists. Importantly, the list is confined to rewards made as a result of a specific resolution of the Committee of Supply of the House of Commons. It does not include rewards made by government departments or the War Office from their supply, and neither does it include the numerous rewards made by non-governmental bodies. It also does not include payments for work done[7] or for purchasing patents or resolving infringement disputes,[8] except where the reward is included in Colquhoun's list.[9]

---

1 E.g. Robert Burrell and Catherine Kelly, "Public Rewards and Innovation Policy: Lessons from the Eighteenth and Nineteenth Century" (2014) 77 *MLR* 858.

2 Patrick Colquhoun, *A Treatise on the Wealth, Power and Resources of the British Empire* (Joseph Mawman 1814) at p 231–232.

3 *Report of the Select Committee on the Law Relative to Patents for Inventions* (1829 HC Papers 332), Vol 3, p 415 (at p 181).

4 "List of Parliament Rewards Granted for Useful Discoveries, Inventions and Improvements" (1832) 13 *Mechanics Magazine: Museum, Register, Journal and Gazette*, p 61–62.

5 Robert Burrell and Catherine Kelly, "Public Rewards and Innovation Policy: Lessons from the Eighteenth and Nineteenth Century" (2014) 77 *MLR* 858.

6 Robert Burrell and Catherine Kelly, "Public Rewards and Innovation Policy: Lessons from the Eighteenth and Nineteenth Century" (2014) 77 *MLR* 858 at 862, fn 25.

7 E.g. the dispute between Sir Marc Isambard Brunel and the government over the block tackle: see Richard Beamish, *Memoir of the Life of Sir Marc Isambard Brunel* (Longman 1862), Ch 4–6.

8 E.g. the use of the screw propeller and the payments made to resolve potential infringement claims between the various patentees (one being Francis Pettit Smith); see HC Deb, 15 May 1855, Vol 138(3rd), col 639–660.

9 John Palmer, who was being compensated under a contract for setting up a postal service, and Charles Dingle and Edmund Cartwright, who were really being given money following riots and destruction rather than for their inventions.

The requests for rewards were started by either a petition (usually from the inventor) or a motion. It was necessary for Crown consent[10] to be indicated before any resolution could be passed to make a payment out of public funds. It was common, although not universal, that the petition would be accompanied by a statement from Chancellor of the Exchequer (or other relevant minister) indicating that the government was content to make the reward. Once read, the petition would usually be referred to a Select Committee to consider the merits of the award and what, if any, payment should be made. The report from this Select Committee (if favourable) would be referred to the Committee of Supply (COS). A COS resolution would follow, and it would be referred to the Committee of Ways and Means, and then eventually it would be incorporated in the general Supply or Appropriation Act or, exceptionally, a special enactment would be proposed to make the payment. Importantly, there can be no payment made without statutory authority, so each resolution would eventually have to be part of an Act of Parliament (and so be approved by the House of Lords[11] and given Royal Assent).

Rewards to inventors have also been made in a slightly different fashion. This involved a COS resolution being passed and then an Address being made by the Commons to the Crown asking for payment to be made. The Crown would then make the payment and, in the subsequent session, present an account to Parliament of payments made pursuant to Addresses of the House of Commons. The Appropriation Act would then authorise the payment of the sum to reimburse the money.

Structure of record

In respect of each record, there is a year and a coding for rewards granted (PRZA) and for those claimed (PRZC). This is followed by the name of the recipient and the sum of money awarded. Immediately beneath this is the statutory authority for granting the award. This will usually be the section of a Supply or Appropriation Act, and this is followed by an extract of the relevant part of that section authorising the supply.[12] As the payment was usually one of hundreds made under the same section, the approach taken has been to include the opening words of the section and then just the words relating to the particular reward. Where the statutory authority was to reimburse the Crown for payments made following Address of the House of Commons, the relevant extract is included as well as an extract from the Commons Journal particularising the Crown payment. The next section of the record includes the entry from the Commons Journal[13] from the original petition to the final COS resolution. This is followed by the journal entries for passage of the Appropriation Act, or other enactment, making the supply in the same way as is done for enactments in Part 1.

Where there are Parliamentary reports (e.g. in *Hansard*), these are listed in the next section. This only includes debates relating to the supply of the particular reward, and not the passage of the Supply Acts more generally. This is followed by any Parliamentary papers relating to the reward (which often included a report from the relevant Select Committee[14]), after which are detailed any newspaper reports relating to stages before the COS resolution (as for *Hansard*). The newspaper reports are coded and dealt with in the same way as for public Bills. As before, there is a notes section at the end which records archival material and related matters.

In relation to claims for rewards which were not actually made, it went as far as the Act being rejected by the House of Lords after passing through the Commons.[15] In some cases, where there were repeated requests which failed at early stages, entries have been grouped (in particular those of William Mallison 1811–20). There are also some entries where a Parliamentary reward was sought, but a payment made other than following a resolution of the COS.[16] Throughout the rest of the nineteenth century a number of inventors petitioned Parliament for a reward or an inquiry into their inventions. All these petitions are included in Part 7. Only those petitions which got beyond being presented have an entry in Chapter 2.

10 15 CJ 211 (11 Dec 1706).

11 However, during the relevant time, the House of Lords did not interfere with the Supply, so it was common for Appropriation Acts to have a very short passage through the Lords.

12 It should be noted for most years, the Statutes at Large series only includes a summary of the Supplies in Appropriation Acts rather than their entire text. Accordingly, the text has usually been taken from the Public Acts Series.

13 There would never be an entry in the House of Lords Journal at this stage, as the Supply was the Commons' exclusive domain.

14 For the earlier rewards, this is included in the Commons Journal itself.

15 Henry Phillips 1781. The basis for the Lords rejecting it is unclear, but it is probably because it was not part of the general Supply, rather by way of his own private Bill.

16 E.g. Thomas Chapman 1819.

Thomas Lombe 1732

PRZA1	1732

Thomas Lombe for engine for winding silk

£14,000

Lombe's Silk Engines Act 1731 (5 Geo 2. c. viii), s 1
"that it may be enacted, and be it enacted by the King's most excellent Majesty, by and with the Advice and Consent of the Lords Spiritual and Temporal, and Commons, in this present Parliament assembled, and by the Authority of the same, That out of all or any of the Aids or Supplies granted to His Majesty for the Service of the Year One thousand seven hundred and thirty two, there shall and may be applied and paid to the said Sir Thomas Lombe, his Executors, Administrators, or Assigns, the Sum of Fourteen thousand Pounds, as a Reward and Recompence to him, for the eminent service he has done this Nation, in discovering, introducing, and bring to full Perfection, at his own great Expence as aforesaid, a Work so useful and beneficial to this Kingdom; and the Lords Commissioners of his Majesty's Treasury, or the Lord High Treasurer for the time being, are hereby authorized and impowered to direct the Payment of, and issue the said sum of fourteen thousand Pounds to the said Sir Thomas Lombe, his Executors, Administrators, or Assigns accordingly"
[Provided model supplied]

Journal

House of Commons			House of Lords		
Pres and Rep: Micajah Perry			Rep: Lord De La Warr		
1 Feb 1731	21 CJ 782	Pet (term extension)	23 Mar 1731	24 LJ 63	Brought HC
11 Feb 1731	21 CJ 795	Pet Rep	24 Mar 1731	24 LJ 65	1R
14 Feb 1731	21 CJ 798	Cons/Bill Ord	27 Mar 1732	24 LJ 67	2R/C'tted
15 Feb 1731	21 CJ 801	Ord patent	30 Mar 1732	24 LJ 73	Rep w/o Amds
18 Feb 1731	21 CJ 804	Patent Pres	31 Mar 1732	24 LJ 77	3R
21 Feb 1731	21 CJ 806	Lombe appears at Bar	3 Apr 1732	24 LJ 79	Royal Assent
6 Mar 1731	21 CJ 832	1R			
7 Mar 1731	21 CJ 836	Pet Ag			
9 Mar 1731	21 CJ 840	Pet Ag			
10 Mar 1731	21 CJ 842	Pet Ag			
14 Mar 1731	21 CJ 846	2R/C'tted CWH/Money Res			
20 Mar 1731	21 CJ 855	CWH			
21 Mar 1731	21 CJ 856	Rep with Amds			
22 Mar 1731	21 CJ 858	Cons			
23 Mar 1731	21 CJ 859	3R			
27 Mar 1732	21 CJ 865	Deliver patent back			
3 Apr 1732	21 CJ 876	Royal Assent			

Parliamentary debates

Pet: Chandler, The History and Proceedings of the House of Commons, Vol 7, p 140; Torbuck, A Collection of Parliamentary Debates in England from the Year MDCLXVIII to the present time (1741), Vol 10, p 101–108; Corbett's Parliamentary History, Vol 8, p 924–929

Parliamentary papers and cases etc.

The following papers are included in Harper's Collection of Private Bill, Vol 9, No 31

(1) The Case of the Silk Throwers Company
(2) The Case of the Manufacturers of Wollen, Linnen, Mohair and Cotton in the Towns of Manchester &c.
(3) A Brief State of the Case relating to the Machine erected at Derby for making Italian Organizine Silk
(4) Original Bill for Term Extension (2 versions), read 1732

Notes

This entry is also included in the private Act section (it was originally an attempt to extend Patent No 422): see PRVA14
Repealed by: Statute Law Revision Act 1948

Joanna Stephens 1738

PRZA2	1738

Joanna Stephens for her cure for stone

£5000

Joanna Stephens' Reward (Cure for Stone) Act 1738 (12 Geo 2. c. xxiii), s 1
"now for encouraging the said Joanna Stephens to make a Discovery thereof, and for providing a Recompence, in case the said Medicines shall be submitted to the Examination of proper Judges, and by them be found worthy of the Reward hereby provided; may it please Your Majesty that it may be enacted, and be it enacted by the King's most excellent Majesty, by and with the Advice and Consent of the Lords Spiritual and Temporal, and Commons, in this present Parliament assembled, and by the Authority of the same, That out of all or any the Aids or Supplies granted to His Majesty for the Service of the year One thousand seven hundred and thirty nine, there may, and shall be applied and paid to the said Joanna Stephens, or her Executors, Administrators or Assigns, the Sum of five thousand pounds"
[Provided discovery made public]

Journal					
House of Commons			**House of Lords**		
Pres: Thomas Townshend Rep: Francis Fane			Rep: Earl of Warwick		
26 Mar 1739	23 CJ 302 – V	Pet (Royal Consent)	17 May 1739	25 LJ 388	Brought HC/1R
10 Apr 1739	23 CJ 325	Money Res £5000	22 May 1739	25 LJ 394	2R/C'tted CWH
11 Apr 1739	23 CJ 326	Bill Ord	25 May 1739	25 LJ 398	CWH/Rep w/o Amds
26 Apr 1739	23 CJ 340	1R	28 May 1739	25 LJ 399	3R
2 May 1739	23 CJ 346 – V	**2R**	14 Jun 1739	23 LJ 419	Royal Assent
8 May 1739	23 CJ 353	CWH			
9 May 1739	23 CJ 354	Rep with Amds			
16 May 1739	23 CJ 365	**3R with Amds**			
30 May 1739	23 CJ 376	HL pass w/o Amds			
14 Jun 1739	23 CJ 380	Royal Assent			

Parliamentary debates
26 Mar 1739 (Pet): History and Proceedings (Minutes) (5th Sess [1737–39], Vol 10, p viii) 2 May 1739 (2R): History and Proceedings (Minutes) (5th Sess [1737–39], Vol 10, p x) 14 Jun 1739 (Royal Assent): History and Proceedings (Minutes) (5th Sess [1737–39], Vol 10, p xiii)

Parliamentary papers and cases etc.
None

Notes
The recipe for the "cure" was published in the London Gazette, 16 Jun 1739 (Iss: 7815, p 1) Repealed by: Statute Law Revision Act 1948

John Harrison 1753

PRZA3	1753

John Harrison for his work relating to discovering longitude using timepieces

£1250

Discovery of Longitude at Sea Act 1753 (26 Geo 2. c. 25), s 1
"And whereas a competent Number of the said Commissioners for the Discovery of the said Longitude … heard and received several Proposals made to them at different Times for discovering the said Longitude, and were so far satisfied of the Probabilities of such Discoveries, that they thought it proper to make Experiments thereof, and accordingly certified the same from Time to Time to the Commissioners of the Navy for the Time being, together with the Name of Master John Harrison, who was Author of the said Proposals whereupon Bills were made out for several Sums of Money, amounting in the Whole to one thousand two hundred and fifty Pounds, all which respective Sums were paid to the said John Harrison by the Treasurer of the Navy … the said Commissioners for discovering the said Longitude have at present, by virtue of the said Acts of Parliament, Power only to apply the Sum of two hundred and fifty Pounds, and no more (being the Remainder of the said two thousand Pounds) towards making any further Experiments which they may think proper and necessary to be made, in order to discover the said Longitude … Be it enacted … the said Commissioners of the Navy are hereby authorized and required to make out a Bill or Bills for any such Sum or Sums of Money not exceeding two thousand Pounds, over and above the aforesaid Sum of two hundred and fifty Pounds …"

Journal					
House of Commons			**House of Lords**		
Pres: John Clevland (Sec to Adm) Rep: Coulson Fellowes			Rep: Earl Warwick		
26 Mar 1753	26 CJ 717	Longitude Board a/c Req	21 May 1753	28 LJ 135	Brought HC/1R
29 Mar 1753	26 CJ 729	Longitude Board a/c Pre	22 May 1753	28 LJ 136	2R/C'tted CWH
13 Apr 1753	26 CJ 763	Considering Longitude Act	23 May 1753	28 LJ 137	CWH adj
16 Apr 1753	26 CJ 772	Considering Longitude Act	28 May 1753	28 LJ 142	CWH/Rep w/o Amds
19 Apr 1753	26 CJ 795	Considering Longitude Act	30 May 1753	28 LJ 144	3R
1 May 1753	26 CJ 799	Considering Longitude Act	6 Jun 1753	28 LJ 154	Royal Assent
2 May 1753	26 CJ 801	Money Res £2000/Bill Ord			
7 May 1753	26 CJ 808	Unrelated clause			
9 May 1753	26 CJ 811	1R			
11 May 1753	26 CJ 817	2R/C'tted			
15 May 1753	26 CJ 823	CWH			
16 May 1753	26 CJ 824	Rep with Amds			
18 May 1753	26 CJ 826	3R			
30 May 1753	26 CJ 833	HL pass w/o Amds			
6 Jun 1753	26 CJ 838	Royal Assent			

Parliamentary debates
None

Parliamentary papers and cases etc.
None

Notes
This was to reimburse the Board of Longitude for monies already paid out to Harrison There was also a reward to Whiston: see PRZA4

William Whiston 1753

RPZA4	1753
William Whiston for a survey of Great Britain headlands to assist in finding longitude	
£500	

Discovery of Longitude at Sea Act 1753 (c. 25), s 1
"did . . . appoint Master William Whiston to survey and determine the Longitude and Latitude of the chief Ports and Head Lands on the Coasts of Great Britain and Ireland, and the Islands and Plantations thereto belonging; and did also apply the further Sum or five hundred Pounds ..which they thought necessary for the making such Survey, and determining the said last-mentioned Longitude and Latitude, and which said Sum of five hundred Pounds was paid to the said William Whiston accordingly by the Treasurer of the Navy ... the said Commissioners for discovering the said Longitude have at present, by virtue of the said Acts of Parliament, Power only to apply the Sum of two hundred and fifty Pounds, and no more (being the Remainder of the said two thousand Pounds) towards making any further Experiments which they may think proper and necessary to be made, in order to discover the said Longitude ... Be it enacted ... the said Commissioners of the Navy are hereby authorized and required to make out a Bill or Bills for any such Sum or Sums of Money not exceeding two thousand Pounds, over and above the aforesaid Sum of two hundred and fifty Pounds ..."

Journal					
House of Commons			**House of Lords**		
Pres: John Clevland (Sec to Adm) Rep: Coulson Fellowes			Rep: Earl Warwick		
26 Mar 1753	26 CJ 717	Longitude Board a/c Req	21 May 1753	28 LJ 135	Brought HC/1R
29 Mar 1753	26 CJ 729	Longitude Board A/C Pres	22 May 1753	28 LJ 136	2R/C'tted CWH
13 Apr 1753	26 CJ 763	Considering Longitude Act	23 May 1753	28 LJ 137	Com adj
16 Apr 1753	26 CJ 772	Considering Longitude Act	28 May 1753	28 LJ 142	C'tee/Rep w/o Amds
19 Apr 1753	26 CJ 795	Considering Longitude Act	30 May 1753	28 LJ 144	3R
1 May 1753	26 CJ 799	Considering Longitude Act	6 Jun 1753	28 LJ 154	Royal Assent
2 May 1753	26 CJ 801	Money Res £2000/Bill Ord			
7 May 1753	26 CJ 808	Unrelated clause			

(continued)

(continued)

9 May 1753	26 CJ 811	1R			
11 May 1753	26 CJ 817	2R/C'tted			
15 May 1753	26 CJ 823	CWH			
16 May 1753	26 CJ 824	Rep with Amds			
18 May 1753	26 CJ 826	3R			
30 May 1753	26 CJ 833	HL pass w/o Amds			
6 Jun 1753	26 CJ 838	Royal Assent			

Parliamentary debates
None

Parliamentary papers and cases etc.
None

Notes
This was to reimburse the Board of Longitude for monies already paid out to Whiston There was also a reward to Harrison: see PRZA3

Thomas Stephens 1755

PRZA5	1755
Thomas Stephens for a method of making potash	
£3000	

Supply, etc. Act 1755 (28 Geo 2. c. 22), s 19
"And it is hereby also enacted, That out of all or any the Aids or Supplies provided as aforesaid, there shall and may be issued and applied … any Sum or Sums of Money, not exceeding three thousand Pounds, to be paid to Thomas Stephens, as a Reward for discovering his Method of making Pot Ash, and introducing that Manufacture into the British Plantations in America"

Journal
Resolution of Committee of Supply

28 Feb 1755	27 CJ 181	**Pet/Ref C'tee/**Request for papers
28 Feb 1755	27 CJ 182	Ord document to be produced
3 Mar 1755	27 CJ 185	Person added to C'tee
17 Mar 1755	27 CJ 233	**Rep of C'tee by John Thornhagh**
24 Mar 1755	27 CJ 253	Ord document to be produced
25 Mar 1755	27 CJ 264	Stephens examined at Bar
26 Mar 1755	27 CJ 267	**Pet Against by patentees**
2 Apr 1755	27 CJ 271	Patentees Pres/Re-C'tted
2Apr 1755	27 CJ 272	C'tee met
11 Apr 1755	27 CJ 280	Ref COS
12 Apr 1755	27 CJ 281	COS Res £3000

Supply, etc Act 1755					
House of Commons			**House of Lords**		
15 Apr 1755	27 CJ 284	Bill Ord	21 Apr 1755	28 LJ 406	Brought HC/1R
16 Apr 1755	27 CJ 285	1R	22 Apr 1755	28 LJ 408	2R/Com CWH
17 Apr 1755	27 CJ 287	2R/C'tted CWH	23 Apr 1755	28 LJ 409	CWH/Rep w/o Amds
18 Apr 1755	27 CJ 288	**CWH**	24 Apr 1755	28 LJ 411	3R
19 Apr 1755	27 CJ 289	Rep with Amds/Ing	25 Apr 1855	28 LJ 412	Royal Assent
21 Apr 1755	27 CJ 290	3R			
25 Apr 1755	27 CJ 294	HL pass w/o Amds			
25 Apr 1755	27 CJ 294	Royal Assent			

Parliamentary debates
None

Parliamentary papers and cases etc.
None

Thomas Lowndes 1759

PRZA6	1759		
Thomas Lowndes (to his executor Roger Long) for a method of improving salt brine			
£1280			

Supply, etc. Act 1758 (32 Geo 2. c. 36), s 15
"And it is hereby also further enacted by the Authority aforesaid, That out of all or any the Aids or Supplies provided as aforesaid, there shall and may be issued and applied … and any Sum or Sums of Money, not exceeding one thousand two hundred and eighty Pounds, to be paid to Roger Long Doctor in Divinity, Lowndes Astronomical and Geometrical Professor in the University of Cambridge, without Account, to enable him to discharge, in pursuance of the Will of Thomas Lowndes Esquire, (the Inventor of a Method for meliorating the Brine Salt of this Kingdom) a Mortgage upon an Estate devised for the Endowment of the said Professorship by the said Thomas Lowndes, and to reimburse to the said Roger Long the Interest Monies he hath paid, and that are growing due, and the Expences he hath incurred in Respect of the said Mortgage, and that the same be paid without Fee or Reward …"

Journal		
Resolution of Committee of Supply		
26 May 1746	25 CJ 157	**Pet** (Royal consent)/**Ref C'tee**
3 Jun 1746	25 CJ 163	**Rep of Charles Cotes/Res for Royal Address**
3 Feb 1759	28 CJ 399	**Pet of executor (Roger Long)** (Royal consent)/Ref C'tee
20 Feb 1759	28 CJ 435	**Rep of C'tee by Edward Finch**
19 Mar 1759	28 CJ 492	Res £1280

Supply, etc. Act 1758					
House of Commons			**House of Lords**		
23 May 1759	28 CJ 594	1R	28 May 1759	29 LJ 522	Brought HC/1R
24 May 1759	28 CJ 595	2R/C'tted CWH	29 May 1759	29 LJ 523	2R/C'tted CWH
25 May 1759	28 CJ 596	CWH	30 May 1759	29 LJ 524	CWH/Rep w/o Amds
26 May 1759	28 CJ 597	Rep/Ing	31 May 1759	29 LJ 525	3R
28 May 1759	28 CJ 598	3R	2 Jun 1759	29 LJ 531	Royal Assent
31 May 1759	28 CJ 601	HL pass w/o Amds			
2 Jun 1759	28 CJ 623	Royal Assent			

Parliamentary debates
None

Parliamentary papers and cases etc.
None

John Harrison 1762

PRZA7	1762
John Harrison for the disclosure of how to make his timekeeper	
£5000	

Discovery of Longitude at Sea Act 1762 (3 Geo 3. c 14), s 1
"That so soon as the said John Harrison, his Executors or Administrators, shall make or cause to be made a full and clear Discovery of the Principles of his said Instrument or Watch for Discovery of the Longitude, and of the true Manner and Method in which the same is and may be constructed, unto the Right Honourable Lord Charles Cavendish, the Right Honourable the Earl of Morton, the Right Honourable Lord Willoughby of Parham, George Lewis Scott Esquire Fellow of the Royal Society, Master James Short Fellow of the Royal Society, the Reverend Master John Mitchell Woodwardian Professor at Cambridge, Master Alexander Cumming, Master Mudge of Fleet Street, Master William Frodsham, Master Andrew Dickie, and Master James Green of Fenchurch Street, who, as well as the said John Harrison, are hereby required to publish and make the same known, so that other Workmen may be enabled to make other such Instruments or Watches for the same Purpose; and so soon as the said Lord Charles Cavendish, the Earl of Morton, Lord Willoughby of Parham, George Lewis Scott, James Short, John Mitchell, Alexander Cumming, Master, Mudge, William Frodsham, Andrew Dickie, and James Green, or the major Part of them shall certify in Writing under their Hands

(continued)

(continued)

and Seals, to the Commissioners of his Majesty's Navy for the Time being, that the said John Harrison hath fully and clearly made the said Discovery for the Purposes aforesaid, then, upon producing such Certificate, the said Commissioners of the Navy are hereby authorized and required to make out a Bill or Bills for the Sum of five thousand Pounds payable to the said John Harrison, his Executors or Administrators, by the Treasurer of the Navy; which Sum the Treasurer of the Navy for the Time being, is hereby required to pay immediately to him the said John Harrison, his Executors or Administrators, out of any Money that shall be in the said Treasurer's Hands unapplied for the Use of the Navy"

Journal						
House of Commons			**House of Lords**			
Pres: John Clevland (Sec to Adm) Rep: George Hay (Ld Adm)			Rep: Earl Macclesfield			
1 Mar 1762	29 CJ 201	Ref a/c	1 Apr 1762	30 LJ 217	Brought HC/1R	
3 Mar 1762	29 CJ 206	Cons a/c	5 Apr 1762	30 LJ 222	2R/C'tted CWH	
4 Mar 1762	29 CJ 209	Bill Ord/Money Res	6 Apr 1762	30 LJ 227	C'tee/Rep w/o Amds	
15 Mar 1762	29 CJ 233	1R	7 Apr 1762	30 LJ 229	3R	
23 Mar 1762	29 CJ 254	2R/C'tted CWH	8 Apr 1762	30 LJ 232	Royal Assent	
25 Mar 1762	29 CJ 266	CWH				
26 Mar 1762	29 CJ 272	Rep with Amds/Ing				
30 Mar 1762	29 CJ 277	3R				
7 Apr 1762	29 CJ 296	HL pass w/o Amds				
8 Apr 1762	29 CJ 298	Royal Assent				

Parliamentary debates
None

Parliamentary papers and cases etc.
None

Notes
Harrison never made the disclosure, so the reward was never given.

John Blake 1764

PRZA8	1764
John Blake for his scheme for transporting fish	
£2500	

Supply, etc. Act 1763 (4 Geo 3. c. 23), s 22
"And it is hereby also enacted by the Authority aforesaid, That out of all or any the Aids or Supplies aforesaid, there shall and may be issued and applied … any Sum or Sums of Money, not exceeding two thousand five hundred Pounds, to be applied towards encouraging and enabling John Blake Esquire, further to carry into execution the Plan concerted by him for the better supplying the Cities of London and Westminster with Fish at moderate Rates …"

Journal		
Resolution of Committee of Supply		
22 Feb 1762	29 CJ 187	**Fish Committee Reps on supply**
18 Mar 1763	29 CJ 575	**Fish Committee Res for reward**
24 Feb 1764	29 CJ 879	**Pet from Blake Ref C'tee**
1 Mar 1764	29 CJ 892	COS Res

Passage of Supply, etc. Act 1763						
House of Commons			**House of Lords**			
7 Apr 1764	29 CJ 1040	Bill Ord	13 Apr 1764	30 LJ 573	Brought HC/1R	
9 Apr 1764	29 CJ 1042	Bill Pres/1R	16 Apr 1764	30 LJ 580	2R/C'tted CWH	
10 Apr 1764	29 CJ 1044	2R/C'tted CWH	17 Apr 1764	30 LJ 581	CWH/Rep w/o Amds	
11 Apr 1764	29 CJ 1048	CWH	17 Apr 1764	30 LJ 582	3R	
12 Apr 1764	29 CJ 1049	Rep/Ing	19 Apr 1764	30 LJ 583	Royal Assent	
13 Apr 1764	29 CJ 1050	3R				
18 Apr 1764	29 CJ 1053	HL pass w/o Amds				
19 Apr 1764	29 CJ 1056	Royal Assent				

Parliamentary debates
None
Parliamentary papers and cases etc.
None

John Harrison 1765

PRZA9	1765

John Harrison for his timekeeper used to find longitude
£10,000 (less £2500 already paid)

Discovery of Longitude at Sea Act 1765 (5 Geo 3. c. 20)

s 1 "… That one Moiety of the greatest Reward which is directed in and by the said Act, made in the twelfth Year of the Reign of Queen Anne, to be paid to the first Author or Authors, Discoverer or Discoverers, of a proper Method for finding the said Longitude at Sea, shall be paid to the said John Harrison, his Executors, Administrators, or Assigns, when and so soon as the Principles upon which his said Watch or Time Keeper is constructed are fully discovered, and explained to the Satisfaction of the said Commissioners for the Discovery of the Longitude, or the major Part of them; and when and so soon as the said John Harrison hath assigned to the said Commissioners, for the Use of the Publick, the Property of the three several Time Keepers which, in and by the said Articles he agreed to deliver up, and also the Property of the said last mentioned Watch or Time Keeper, deducting from and out of the said Moiety, so to be paid to the said John Harrison, his Executors, Administrators, or Assigns, the Sum of two thousand five hundred Pounds already advanced and paid to him; and that the other Moiety of the said greatest Reward mentioned in the said Act shall, when and so soon as other Time Keepers of the same Kind shall be made, and shall, upon Trial, be found to be of a sufficient Correctness to determine the said Longitude within half a Degree of a Great Circle, or thirty Geographical Miles, to the Satisfaction of the said Commissioners, or the major Part of them, be paid to the said John Harrison, his Executors, Administrators, or Assigns."

s 2 "Provided always, and be it enacted by the Authority aforesaid, That the said Master John Harrison shall not be intitled, by virtue of any thing contained in this Act, to the said Reward, or any Part thereof, unless the Discovery and Explanation of the Principles upon which his said Time Keeper is constructed, shall be made within six Months after the passing of this Act"

Journal					
House of Commons			**House of Lords**		
Pres: Philip Stephens (Sec Adm) Rep: Sir George Pocock			Rep: Lord Delamer		
8 Feb 1765	30 CJ 105	Com app to consider Acts	29 Apr 1765	31 LJ 163	Brought HC
11 Feb 1765	30 CJ 116	Longitude C'tee	30 Apr 1765	31 LJ 167	1R
12 Feb 1765	30 CJ 123	Longitude C'tee First Rep	1 May 1765	31 LJ 171	2R/C'tted CWH
18 Feb 1765	30 CJ 157	Longitude C'tee	3 May 1765	31 LJ 177	C'tee/Rep w/o Amds
19 Feb 1765	30 CJ 160	Papers Pres	6 May 1765	31 LJ 178	3R
22 Feb 1765	30 CJ 176	Sum Wit	10 May 1765	31 LJ 194	Royal Assent
25 Feb 1765	30 CJ 180	**Pet (John Harrison)**			
25 Feb 1765	30 CJ 181	Earl of Morton Sum			
25 Feb 1765	30 CJ 181	Longitude C'tee adj			
26 Feb 1765	30 CJ 184	HL Leave for Morton			
26 Feb 1765	30 CJ 186	Wit Sum			
5 Mar 1765	30 CJ 225	Papers ref Longitude C'tee			
5 Mar 1765	30 CJ 225	Longitude C'tee			
6 Mar 1765	30 CJ 228	Longitude C'tee			
8 Mar 1765	30 CJ 234	Longitude C'tee			
8 Mar 1765	30 CJ 235	Longitude C'tee			
19 Mar 1765	30 CJ 261	Rep Harrison's trial			
19 Mar 1765	30 CJ 275	Longitude C'tee			
20 Mar 1765	30 CJ 280	Longitude C'tee Rep/Res			
20 Mar 1765	30 CJ 281	Bill Ord			
1 Apr 1765	30 CJ 326	1R			
2 Apr 1765	30 CJ 334	2R/C'tted CWH			
4 Apr 1765	30 CJ 344	CWH adj			
22 Apr 1765	30 CJ 355	CWH			
23 Apr 1765	30 CJ 372	Rep with Amds/Ing			

(continued)

(continued)

29 Apr 1765	30 CJ 386	3R			
6 May 1765	30 CJ 403	HL pass w/o Amds			
10 May 1765	30 CJ 415	Royal Assent			
21 May 1765	30 CJ 432	Papers returned to Board			

Parliamentary debates
None

Parliamentary papers and cases etc.
None

Leonhard Euler 1765

PRZA10	1765

Prof Leonhard Euler for his mathematical work

£300

Discovery of Longitude at Sea Act 1765 (5 Geo 3. c. 20), s 3 "And be it further enacted by the Authority aforesaid, That a Reward or Sum of Money, not exceeding three hundred Pounds in the Whole, shall be paid to the said Professor Euler"

Journal					
House of Commons			**House of Lords**		
Pres: Philip Stephens (Sec Adm) Rep: Sir George Pocock			Rep: Lord Delamer		
8 Feb 1765	30 CJ 105	Com app to Cons Acts	29 Apr 1765	31 LJ 163	Brought HC
11 Feb 1765	30 CJ 116	Longitude C'tee	30Apr 1765	31 LJ 167	1R
12 Feb 1765	30 CJ 123	Longitude C'tee First Rep	1 May 1765	31 LJ 171	2R/C'tted CWH
18 Feb 1765	30 CJ 157	Longitude C'tee	3 May 1765	31 LJ 177	C'tee/Rep w/o Amds
19 Feb 1765	30 CJ 160	Papers Pres	6 May 1765	31 LJ 178	3R
22 Feb 1765	30 CJ 176	Sum Wit	10 May 1765	31 LJ 194	Royal Assent
25 Feb 1765	30 CJ 180	**Pet (John Harrison)**			
25 Feb 1765	30 CJ 181	Earl of Morton Sum			
25 Feb 1765	30 CJ 181	Longitude C'tee adj			
26 Feb 1765	30 CJ 184	HL Leave for Morton			
26 Feb 1765	30 CJ 186	Wit Sum			
5 Mar 1765	30 CJ 225	Papers ref Longitude C'tee			
5 Mar 1765	30 CJ 225	Longitude C'tee			
6 Mar 1765	30 CJ 228	Longitude C'tee			
8 Mar 1765	30 CJ 234	Longitude C'tee			
8 Mar 1765	30 CJ 235	Longitude C'tee			
19 Mar 1765	30 CJ 261	Rep Harrison's trial			
19 Mar 1765	30 CJ 275	Longitude C'tee			
20 Mar 1765	30 CJ 280	Longitude C'tee Rep/Res			
20 Mar 1765	30 CJ 281	Bill Ord			
1 Apr 1765	30 CJ 326	1R			
2 Apr 1765	30 CJ 334	2R/C'tted CWH			
4 Apr 1765	30 CJ 344	CWH adj			
22 Apr 1765	30 CJ 355	CWH			
23 Apr 1765	30 CJ 372	Rep with Amds/Ing			
29 Apr 1765	30 CJ 386	3R			
6 May 1765	30 CJ 403	HL pass w/o Amds			
10 May 1765	30 CJ 415	Royal Assent			
21 May 1765	30 CJ 432	Papers returned to Board			

Parliamentary debates
None

Parliamentary papers and cases etc.
None

Tobais Mayer (his heirs) 1765

PRZA11	1765

Tobais Mayer (his heirs) for his lunar tables

£3000

Discovery of Longitude at Sea Act 1765 (5 Geo 3. c. 20), s 4

"And be it further enacted by the Authority aforesaid, That a Reward or Sum of Money, not exceeding three thousand Pounds in the Whole, shall be paid to the Widow or other Representatives of the said Professor Mayer, upon her or their assigning the Property of the Set of the latest Manuscript Lunar Tables, constructed by the said Tobias Mayer, to the said Commissioners, to and for the Use of the Publick"

Journal					
House of Commons			**House of Lords**		
Pres: Philip Stephens (Sec Adm) Rep: Sir George Pocock			Rep: Lord Delamer		
8 Feb 1765	30 CJ 105	Com app to consider Acts	29 Apr 1765	31 LJ 163	Brought HC
11 Feb 1765	30 CJ 116	Longitude C'tee	30Apr 1765	31 LJ 167	1R
12 Feb 1765	30 CJ 123	Longitude C'tee First Rep	1 May 1765	31 LJ 171	2R/C'tted CWH
18 Feb 1765	30 CJ 157	Longitude C'tee	3 May 1765	31 LJ 177	C'tee/Rep w/o Amds
19 Feb 1765	30 CJ 160	Papers Pres	6 May 1765	31 LJ 178	3R
22 Feb 1765	30 CJ 176	Sum Wit	10 May 1765	31 LJ 194	Royal Assent
25 Feb 1765	30 CJ 180	**Pet (John Harrison)**			
25 Feb 1765	30 CJ 181	Earl of Morton Sum			
25 Feb 1765	30 CJ 181	Longitude C'tee adj			
26 Feb 1765	30 CJ 184	HL Leave for Morton			
26 Feb 1765	30 CJ 186	Witness Sum			
5 Mar 1765	30 CJ 225	Papers ref Longitude C'tee			
5 Mar 1765	30 CJ 225	Longitude C'tee			
6 Mar 1765	30 CJ 228	Longitude C'tee			
8 Mar 1765	30 CJ 234	Longitude C'tee			
8 Mar 1765	30 CJ 235	Longitude C'tee			
19 Mar 1765	30 CJ 261	Rep Harrison's trial			
19 Mar 1765	30 CJ 275	Longitude C'tee			
20 Mar 1765	30 CJ 280	Longitude C'tee Rep/Res			
20 Mar 1765	30 CJ 281	Bill Ord			
1 Apr 1765	30 CJ 326	1R			
2 Apr 1765	30 CJ 334	2R/C'tted CWH			
4 Apr 1765	30 CJ 344	CWH adj			
22 Apr 1765	30 CJ 355	CWH			
23 Apr 1765	30 CJ 372	Rep with Amds/Ing			
29 Apr 1765	30 CJ 386	3R			
6 May 1765	30 CJ 403	HL pass w/o Amds			
10 May 1765	30 CJ 415	Royal Assent			
21 May 1765	30 CJ 432	Papers returned to Board			
Parliamentary debates					
None					
Parliamentary papers and cases etc.					
None					

Charles Dingley 1769

PRZA12	1769

Charles Dingley for the repair of his destroyed windsaw

£2000

Supply Act 1769 (9 Geo 3. c. 34), s 24

"And it is hereby also enacted by the Authority aforesaid, That, out of all or any the Aids or Supplies aforesaid, there shall and may be issued and applied … any Sum or Sums of Money not exceeding Two thousand pounds, to be applied and

(continued)

(continued)

paid to Charles Dingley of London, Merchant, as a Reward to him for having erected and brought to Perfection, for the Benefit of the Public, a Wind Saw Mill, at Limehouse in the County of Middlesex, for the Purpose of manufacturing Timber into Wainscot and Deals, and as Recompence for the Loss he sustained in the wilful Destruction of the said Wind Saw, by a number of riotous and disorderly persons in the month of May last"

Journal		
Resolution of Committee of Supply		
19 Dec 1768	32 CJ 15	**Pet**
28 Jan 1769	32 CJ 160	**Renewed Pet** (Royal consent)/Ref C'tee
9 Feb 1769	32 CJ 194	**Rep of C'tee by Sir Charles Whitworth**
22 Feb1769	32 CJ 237	Ref COS
23 Feb1769	32 CJ 240	COS Res

Supply Act 1769					
House of Commons			**House of Lords**		
23 Feb 1769	32 CJ 240	Bill Ord	15 Mar 1769	32 LJ 293	Brought HC/1R
28 Feb 1769	32 CJ 255	1R	16 Mar 1769	32 LJ 296	2R/Com CWH
3 Mar 1769	32 CJ 267	2R/C'tted CWH	20 Mar 1769	32 LJ 298	C'tee/Rep w/o Amds/3R
6 Mar 1769	32 CJ 289	CWH adj	21 Mar 1769	32 LJ 304	Royal Assent
7 Mar 1769	32 CJ 293	CWH			
8 Mar 1769	32 CJ 296	Rep/Ing			
9 Mar 1769	32 CJ 297	3R			
20 Mar 1769	32 CJ 327	HL pass w/o Amds			
21 Mar 1769	32 CJ 334	Royal Assent			

Parliamentary debates
None
Parliamentary papers and cases etc.
None
Newspaper coverage of debates
Comment: *Gazetteer and New Daily Advertiser, 25 Feb 1769*
Notes
Listed in Failed Legislation: [FL: 110.035] (never requested a Bill)

Charles Irving 1772

PRZA13	1772
Charles Irving for making sea water fresh	
£5000	

Supply, etc. Act 1772 (12 Geo 3. c. 70), s 24
"And it is hereby also enacted by the Authority aforesaid, That out of all or any the Aids or Supplies aforesaid, there shall and may be issued and applied … any Sum or Sums of Money not exceeding Five thousand Pounds; to be paid to Charles Irving, for the Discovery of an easy and practicable Method of making Sea Water fresh and wholesome"

Journal		
Committee of Supply resolution		
28 Feb1772	33 CJ 534	**Pet**(Royal Consent)/Ref SC/All voices
20 Mar 1772	33 CJ 600	**Pet Against by Daniel Scott**
24 Mar 1772	33 CJ 609	**Pet Against by Bartholomew Dominiccii**
6 Apr 1772	33 CJ 661	**Rep of C'tee by Sir George Colebrooke**/Ref COS
30 Apr1772	33 CJ 714	Letters laid before House
1 May 1772	33 CJ 717	Reps laid before House
8 May 1772	33 CJ 740	Papers ref COS
11 May 1772	33 CJ 745	COS Res

Supply, etc. Act 1772	
House of Commons	**House of Lords**

11 May 1772	33 CJ 745	Bill Ord	26 May 1772	33 LJ 434	Brought HC/1R
18 May 1772	33 CJ 767	1R	27 May 1772	33 LJ 436	2R/Com CWH
19 May 1772	33 CJ 772	2R/C'tted CWH	28 May 1772	33 LJ 439	CWH/Rep w/o Amds
22 May 1772	33 CJ 783	CWH	3 Jun 1772	33 LJ 454	3R
25 May 1772	33 CJ 786	Rep/Ing	9 Jun 1772	33 LJ 456	Royal Assent
26 May 1772	33 CJ 790	3R			
3 Jun 1772	33 CJ 953	HL pass w/o Amds			
9 Jun 1772	33 CJ 957	Royal Assent			

Parliamentary debates
None

Parliamentary papers and cases etc.
None

Newspaper coverage of debates
Pet: **Caledonian Mercury, 7 March 1772 (extracted in letter)**; Oxford Journal, 9 May 1772 Res: Kentish Gazette, 12 May 1772; Gazetteer and New Daily Advertiser, 13 May 1772; Reading Mercury, 18 May 1772

Notes
In both Colquhoun and the *Mechanics Magazine*, the recipient is misnamed as "Irvine": see Introduction to this Part.

Richard Williams 1773

PRZA14	1773		
Richard Williams for inventing yellow dye			
£2000			
Supply, etc. Act 1773 (13 Geo 3. c. 77), s 24 "And it is hereby also enacted by the Authority aforesaid, That, out of all or any the Aids or Supplies aforesaid, there shall and may be issued and applied … any Sum or Sums of Money, not exceeding Two thousand Pounds, to be advanced to Doctor Richard Williams, of Saint Margaret's Westminster, as a Reward for his inventing a fast Greet Yellow Dye on Cotton Yarns and Thread, and for discovering the Secret thereof"			

Journal

Committee of Supply resolution

2 Feb 1773	34 CJ 104	**Pet** (Royal consent)/Ref C'tee
14 Jun 1773	34 CJ 371	**Rep of C'tee by Charles Whitworth**
18 Jun 1773	34 CJ 381	Rep ref COS
19 Jun 1773	34 CJ 382	COS Res

Supply, etc. Act 1773					
House of Commons			**House of Lords**		
15 Jun 1773	34 CJ 373	Bill Ord	28 Jun 1773	33 LJ 691	Brought HC/1R
17 Jun 1773	34 CJ 378	1R	29 Jun 1773	33 LJ 693	2R/C'tted CWH
18 Jun 1773	34 CJ 380	2R/C'tted CWH	30 Jun 1773	33 LJ 695	CWH/Rep/3R
19 Jun 1773	34 CJ 382	CWH	1 Jul 1773	33 LJ 697	Royal Assent
21 Jun 1773	34 CJ 383	Rep/Ing			
28 Jun 1773	34 CJ 385	3R			
30 Jun 1773	34 CJ 387	HL pass w/o Amds			
1 Jul 1773	34 CJ 389	Royal Assent			

Parliamentary debates
None

Parliamentary papers and cases etc.
None

Newspaper coverage of debates

(continued)

(continued)

Rep ref COS: Lloyd's Evening Post, 14–16 Jun 1773; General Evening Post, 15–17 Jun 1773; London Chronicle, 15–17 Jun 1773; Middlesex Journal or Universal Evening Post, 15–17 Jun 1773; Morning Chronicle and London Advertiser, 16 Jun 1773; Hibernian Journal; or, Chronicle of Liberty, 18 Jun 1773
COS Rep: London Chronicle 17–19 Jun 1773; Middlesex Journal or Universal Evening Post, 19–22 Jun 1773; Daily Advertiser, 21 Jun 1773; Caledonian Mercury, 23 Jun 1773; Craftsman or Say's Weekly Journal, 26 Jun 1773
COS Res: General Evening Post, 17–19 Jun 1773; Lloyd's Evening Post, 18–21 Jun 1773; Morning Chronicle and London Advertiser, 19 Jun 1773; London Chronicle, 19–22 Jun 1773; London Evening Post, 19–22 Jun 1773; St. James's Chronicle or the British Evening Post, 19–22 Jun 1773; Middlesex Journal or Universal Evening Post, 19–22 Jun 1773; Daily Advertiser, 21 Jun 1773; Kentish Gazette, 23 Jun 1773; Kentish Gazette, 23 Jun 1773; Ipswich Journal, 26 Jun 1773; Newcastle Chronicle, 26 Jun 1773
Notes
The Supply, etc. Act 1773 is sometimes dated 1772

John Harrison 1773

PRZA15	1773
John Harrison for inventions relating to his timekeepers for finding longitude	
£8750	

Supply, etc Act 1773 (13 Geo 3. c. 77), s 29
"And whereas John Harrison of Red Lion Square, having, under the Encouragement of an Act, made in the Twelfth Year of Her Majesty Queen Anne, intituled, An Act for granting a Reward for the Discovery of the Longitude at Sea, applied himself, with unremitting Industry for the Space of Forty-eight Years, to the making an Instrument for ascertaining the Longitude at Sea; and having constructed a Time-keeper for that Purpose, and discovered the Principles of constructing the same, by which other Time-keepers have been already made, and found to answer with great Exactness; from which Discovery, it is apprehended that great Benefit will arise to the Trade and Navigation of these Kingdoms, is highly deserving of publick Encouragement and Reward; be it therefore enacted by the Authority aforesaid, That it shall and may be lawful to and for the Treasurer of His Majesty's Navy, and he is hereby directed, out of any Sums of Money now in His Hands, to pay, or cause to be paid to the said John Harrison , a Sum not exceeding Eight thousand seven hundred and fifty Pounds, as a further Reward and Encouragement over and above the Sums already received by him for his said Invention of a Time-keeper, and his Discovery of the Principles upon which the same was constructed"

Journal
Committee of Supply resolution

2 Apr 1773	34 CJ 244	**Pet** (no Royal consent)
27 Apr 1773	34 CJ 285	Pet read
30 Apr 1773	34 CJ 293	Longitude papers laid on table
4 May 1773	34 CJ 298	Papers from Longitude Board read
6 May 1773	34 CJ 302	Pet withdrawn
6 May 1773	34 CJ 302	**Fresh Pet** (Royal consent)
11 Jun 1773	34 CJ 367	Ref COS
14 Jun 1773	34 CJ 369	COS Res
19 Jun 1773	34 CJ 383	COS Res re-read

Supply, etc. Act 1773					
House of Commons			**House of Lords**		
15 Jun 1773	34 CJ 373	Bill Ord	15 Jun 1774	34 LJ 253	Brought HC/1R
17 Jun 1773	34 CJ 378	1R	16 Jun 1774	34 LJ 254	2R/C'tted CWH
18 Jun 1773	34 CJ 380	2R/C'tted CWH	17 Jun 1774	34 LJ 255	CWH/rep w/o Amds
19 Jun 1773	34 CJ 382	CWH	20 Jun 1774	34 LJ 257	3R
21 Jun 1773	34 CJ 383	Rep/Ing	22 Jun 1774	34 LJ 259	Royal Assent
28 Jun 1773	34 CJ 385	3R			
30 Jun 1773	34 CJ 387	HL pass w/o Amds			
1 Jul 1773	34 CJ 389	Royal Assent			

Parliamentary debates
None
Parliamentary papers and cases etc.
None
Newspaper coverage of debates

Pet: General Evening Post, 27–29 Apr 1773; London Chronicle, 27–29 Apr 1773; London Evening Post, 27–29 Apr 1773

Proceedings laid before Parliament: Lloyd's Evening Post, 26–28 Apr 1773; Daily Advertiser, 27 Apr 1773; Middlesex Journal or Universal Evening Post, 27–29 Apr 1773; Morning Chronicle and London Advertiser, 28 Apr 1773

Longitude reps read: St. James's Chronicle or the British Evening Post, 29 Apr–1 May 1773; Daily Advertiser, 1 May 1773; Morning Chronicle and London Advertiser, 1 May 1773; Morning Post and Daily Advertiser, 1 May 1773; Craftsman or Say's Weekly Journal, 1 May 1773; Shrewsbury Chronicle, 8 May 1773

Pet: **Caledonian Mercury, 5 May 1773**; *Stamford Mercury, 6 May 1773*; General Evening Post, 4–6 May 1773; London Chronicle, 4–6 May 1773; St. James's Chronicle or the British Evening Post, 4–6 May 1773; Middlesex Journal or Universal Evening Post, 4–6 May 1773; Daily Advertiser, 6 May 1773

Pet w/d/new Pet: *Middlesex Journal or Universal Evening Post, 6–8 May 1773*; Morning Chronicle and London Advertiser, 7 May 1773

Pet follow-on comment: Kentish Gazette, 5 May 1773; Hibernian Journal, or Chronicle of Liberty, 12 May 1773

Notes
The Supply, etc. Act 1773 is sometimes dated 1772

David Hartley 1774

PRZA16	1774	
	David Hartley for invention to protect buildings and shops from fire	
	£2500	

Supply, etc. Act 1774 (14 Geo 3. c. 85), s 24
"And it is hereby also enacted by the Authority aforesaid, That out of all or any of the Aids or Supplies aforesaid, there shall and may be issued and applied … any Sum or Sums of Money, not exceeding two thousand five hundred Pounds, to be paid to David Hartley Esquire, towards enabling him to defray the Charge of Experiments, in order to ascertain the Practicability and Utility of his Discovery of a Method to secure Buildings and Ships from Fire, and that the same be paid without Fee or Reward"

Journal

Committee of Supply resolution

11 May 1774	34 CJ 740	**Pet** (Royal consent)/Ref C'tee
13 May 1774	34 CJ 746	**C'tee Rep by Thomas Townshend**/Ref COS
16 May 1774	34 CJ 756	COS Res

Supply, etc Act 1774

House of Commons			House of Lords		
31 May 1774	34 CJ 792	Bill Ord	15 Jun 1774	34 LJ 253	Brought HC/1R
8 Jun 1774	34 CJ 807	1R	16 Jun 1774	34 LJ 254	2R/C'tted
10 Jun 1774	34 CJ 808	2R/C'tted CWH	17 Jun 1774	34 LJ 255	CWH/Rep w/o Amds
13 Jun 1774	34 CJ 813	CWH	20 Jun 1774	34 LJ 257	3R
14 Jun 1774	34 CJ 817	Rep/Ing	22 Jun 1774	34 LJ 259	Royal Assent
15 Jun 1774	34 CJ 817	3R			
21 Jun 1774	34 CJ 819	HL pass w/o Amds			
22 Jun 1774	34 CJ 820	Royal Assent			

Parliamentary debates

None

Parliamentary papers and cases etc.

None

Newspaper coverage of debates

Pet: *London Evening Post, 10–12 May 1774; Daily Advertiser, 13 May 1774; Derby Mercury, 13 May 1774, Craftsman or Say's Weekly Journal, 14 May 1774; Oxford Journal, 14 May 1774; Hibernian Journal, 18 May 1774*; St. James's Chronicle or the British Evening Post, 10–12 May 1774; Gazetteer and New Daily Advertiser, 12 May 1774; Kentish Gazette, 18 May 1774

COS Res: General Evening Post, 14–17 May 1774; Daily Advertiser, 16 May 1774; Public Advertiser, 17 May 1774; Bath Chronicle and Weekly Gazette, 19 May 1774; Kentish Gazette, 21 May 1774; Newcastle Chronicle, 21 May 1774; Newcastle Courant, 21 May 1774; Leeds Intelligencer, 24 May 1774

Notes
Hartley also had a separate private Act to extend his patent in relation to shipping (see PRVA23)

James Berkenhout and Thomas Clark 1779

PRZA17	1779

James Berkenhout and Thomas Clark for crimson dye

£5000

Appropriation Act 1779 (19 Geo 3. c. 71), s 20 "Any it is hereby also enacted by the Authority aforesaid, that out of all or any of the Aids or Supplies aforesaid, there shall and may be issued and applied … any Sum or Sums of Money not exceeding five thousand pounds, to be paid to James Berkenhout Esquire, and Thomas Clark, of the Town of Leeds, Dyer, upon a proper Discovery to be made by them for the use of the Publick of their Method of dying Scarlet and Crimson, as well as other Colours, on Linen and Cotton"

Journal

Committee of Supply resolution

4 May 1779	37 CJ 367	**Pet** (Royal consent)/Ref C'tee
12 May 1779	37 CJ 392	**C'tee Rep by Sir Herbert Mackworth**
26 May 1779	37 CJ 420	Ref COS
27 May 1779	37 CJ 422	COS Res

Appropriation Act 1779					
House of Commons			**House of Lords**		
27 May 1779	37 CJ 423	Bill Ord	10 Jun 1779	35 LJ 785	Brought HC/1R
5 Jun 1779	37 CJ 437	1R	11 Jun 1779	35 LJ 789	2R/C'tted CWH
7 Jun 1779	37 CJ 438	2R/C'tted CWH	12 Jun 1779	35 LJ 792	CWH/Rep w/o Amds
8 Jun 1779	37 CJ 440	CWH	17 Jun 1779	35 LJ 801	3R
9 Jun 1779	37 CJ 442	Rep/Ing	30 Jun 1779	35 LJ 810	Royal Assent
10 Jun 1779	37 CJ 443	3R			
18 Jun 1779	37 CJ 455	HL pass w/o Amds			
30 Jun 1779	37 CJ 457	Royal Assent			

Parliamentary debates
None

Parliamentary papers and cases etc.
None

Newspaper coverage of debates
Pet: *Morning Chronicle and London Advertiser, 5 May 1779*
Res: Morning Chronicle and London Advertiser, 27 May 1779; Derby Mercury, 28 May 1779; Ipswich Journal, 29 May 1779; Oxford Journal, 29 May 1779; Hampshire Chronicle, 31 May 1779; Northampton Mercury, 31 May 1779

Louis Borell 1786

PRZA18	1786

Louis Borel for Turkey Red dye

£2500

Appropriation Act 1786 (26 Geo 3. c 61), s 27 "And it is hereby also enacted by the Authority aforesaid, That out of all or any of the Aids or Supplies aforesaid, there shall and may be issued and applied … any Sum or Sums of Money, not exceeding Two thousand five hundred Pounds, to be paid to Louis Borel, and Abraham Henry Borel, Dyers, upon a proper Discovery to be made by them for the Use of the Public, and their Method of dying the Colour called Turkey Red, upon Cotton in Banks, and in the Piece"

Journal

Committee of Supply resolution

3 Mar 1786	41 CJ 289	**Pet** (Royal consent)/Ref C'tee
3 Apr1786	41 CJ 467	**C'tee Rep by John Blackburne**
2 Jun 1786	41 CJ 878	Rep ref COS
7 Jun 1786	41 CJ 882	COS Res

Appropriation Act 1786	
House of Commons	**House of Lords**

20 Ju 1786	41 CJ 920	Bill Ord		29 Jun 1786	37 LJ 544	Brought HC/1R
21 Jun 1786	41 CJ 923	1R		30 Jun 1786	37 LJ 548	2R/Com neg
22 Jun 1786	41 CJ 925	2R/C'tted CWH		3 Jul 1786	37 LJ 551	3R
26 Jun 1786	41 CJ 936	CWH		4 Jul 1786	37 LJ 557	Royal Assent
27 Jun 1786	41 CJ 940	Rep/Ing				
28 Jun 1786	41 CJ 948	3R				
3 Jul 1786	41 CJ 955	HL pass w/o Amds				
4 Jul 1786	41 CJ 957	Royal Assent				

Parliamentary debates
None

Parliamentary papers and cases etc.
None

Newspaper coverage of debates
Pet: General Advertiser, 4 Mar 1786
CWH: Morning Chronicle and London Advertiser, 22 May 1786
Rep: Whitehall Evening Post, 3–6 Jun 1786; Caledonian Mercury, 7 Jun 1786; Bath Chronicle and Weekly Gazette, 8 Jun 1786; Norfolk Chronicle, 10 Jun 1786

Cuthbert Gordon 1789

PRZA19	1789
Cuthbert Gordon for substances useful in dying	
£200	

Appropriation Act 1789 (29 Geo 3. c. 61), s 22
"And it is hereby also enacted by the Authority aforesaid, That, out of all or any the Aids or Supplies aforesaid, there shall and may be issued and applied any Sum or Sums of Money, not exceeding Thirty-four thousand three hundred and seventy pounds One Shilling and four-pence, to make good the like Sum which has been issued by His Majesty's Orders, in pursuance of the Addresses of the House of Commons"
Address A/C: "Doctor Cuthbert Gordon, as a further Reward for his Merit in discovering Substances useful in Dyeing, and as an Encouragement to him to proceed in the said Discoveries [£200 – –]" (44 CJ 411)

Journal

Committee of Supply resolution

7 Mar 1786	41 CJ 305	**Pet** (Royal consent)
4 Jul 1786	41 CJ 963	Res Address to King
10 Jul 1786	41 CJ 977	King ref matter to Privy Council
25 May 1789	44 CJ 411	A/C unpaid Royal Addresses
27 May 1789	44 CJ 428	A/C ref COS
28 May 1789	44 CJ 432	COS Res

Appropriation Act						
House of Commons			**House of Lords**			
11 Jun 1789	44 CJ 453	Bill Ord	24 Jul 1789	38 LJ 508	Brought HC
20 Jul 1789	44 CJ 543	1R	28 Jul 1789	38 LJ 509	1R
21 Jul 1789	44 CJ 547	2R/C'tted	29 Jul 1789	38 LJ 510	2R/C'tted CWH
22 Jul 1789	44 CJ 550	CWH	30 Jul 1789	38 LJ 511	CWH
23 Jul 1789	44 CJ 551	Rep/Ing	3 Aug 1789	38 LJ 516	CWH/Rep w/o Amds
24 Jul 1789	44 CJ 640	3R	4 Aug 1789	38 LJ 517	3R
6 Aug 1789	44 CJ 645	HL pass w/o Amds	11 Aug 1789	38 LJ 524	Royal Assent
11 Aug 1789	44 CJ 647	Royal Assent			

Parliamentary debates
None

Parliamentary papers and cases etc.
None

(continued)

(continued)

Newspaper coverage of debates
Res: The Times, 5 Jul 1786; Morning Chronicle and London Advertiser, 5 Jul 1786; Morning Herald, 5 Jul 1786; Morning Post and Daily Advertiser, 5 Jul 1786; The Ipswich Journal, 8 Jul 1786; Newcastle Courant, 15 Jul 1786

Notes
Gordon had already had a patent over the dye (No 727); see Bill PRVB45 and later prize PRZA21

William Forsyth 1791

PRZA20	1791

William Forsyth for curing defects in trees

£1500

Appropriation Act 1791 (31 Geo 3. c. 41), s 25
"And it is hereby also enacted by the Authority aforesaid, That out of all or any the Aids or Supplies aforesaid, there shall and may be issued and applied, any Sum or Sums of Money, not Sixty-seven thousand nine hundred and forty-eight Pounds Twelve Shillings and Ten-pence, to make good the like Sum which has been issued by His Majesty's Orders, in pursuance of the Addresses of the House of Commons"

Address A/C: "To William Forsyth, for the discovery of a Composition to cure Defects in Trees, arising from Injuries in the Bark [1500 – –]" (46 CJ 585)

Journal

Committee of Supply resolution		
24 Jul 1789	44 CJ 640	**Letter from Lords Commissioners**
24 Jul 1789	44 CJ 641	Res for Royal Address
30 Jul 1789	44 CJ 643	Royal Address/reward for disclosure
17 May 1791	46 CJ 585	A/C unpaid Royal Address
19 May 1791	46 CJ 615	COS Res

Appropriation Act 1791					
House of Commons			**House of Lords**		
19 May 1791	46 CJ 616	Bill Ord	30 May 1791	39 LJ 221	Brought HC/1R
20 May 1791	46 CJ 622	1R	31 May 1791	39 LJ 223	2R/C'tted CWH
21 May 1791	46 CJ 625	2R/C'tted CWH	1 Jun 1791	39 LJ 229	CWH
24 May 1791	46 CJ 633	CWH	2 Jun 1791	39 LJ 230	3R
25 May 1791	46 CJ 638	Rep/Ing	6 Jun 1791	39 LJ 242	Royal Assent
30 May 1791	46 CJ 661	3R			
2 Jun 1791	46 CJ 668	HL pass w/o Amds			
6 Jun 1791	46 CJ 685	Royal Assent			

Parliamentary debates
None

Parliamentary papers and cases etc.
None

Newspaper coverage of debates
Rep (24 Jul): *Public Advertiser, 25 Jul 1789*; World, 25 Jul 1789

Notes
The method was disclosed: (1791) 33 *Annual Register* 351 (Reprint 1824)

Cuthbert Gordon 1793

PRZA21	1793

Cuthbert Gordon for cultivating Galium Vecum

£100 (+ fees £18 12s)

	**Appropriation Act 1793 (33 Geo 3. c. 72), s 24**

"And it is hereby also enacted by the Authority aforesaid, That, out of all or any the Aids or Supplies aforesaid, there shall and may be issued and applied any Sum or Sums of Money, not exceeding Thirty-seven thousand six hundred fifty-seven Pounds Seventeen Shillings and Three-pence, to make good the like Sum, which has been issued by His Majesty's Orders, in pursuance of the Addresses of the House of Commons"

Address A/C: "To Doctor Cuthbert Gordon, as a Remuneration for his Trouble and Attention to Cultivation and Management of the said Plant [Galium Vecum, or Luteum] [£100 – –]" (48 CJ 292)

Journal

Committee of Supply resolution

28 Feb 1791	46 CJ 241	**Pet** for reward (Royal consent)
25 Feb 1793	48 CJ 266	Pet renewed
27 Feb 1793	48 CJ 292	A/C unpaid Royal Addresses
5 Mar 1793	48 CJ 342	COS Res

Appropriation Act 1793

House of Commons			**House of Lords**		
28 May 1793	48 CJ 811	1R	10 Jun 1793	39 LJ 737	Brought HC/1R
30 May 1793	48 CJ 821	2R/C'tted CWH	11 Jun 1793	39 LJ 744	2R/C'tted CWH
3 Jun 1793	48 CJ 832	CWH	12 Jun 1793	39 LJ 748	CWH/Rep w/o Amds
5 Jun 1793	48 CJ 844	Rep/Ing	17 Jun 1793	39 LJ 764	3R
10 Jun 1793	48 CJ 866	3R	21 Jun 1793	39 LJ 768	Royal Assent
17 Jun 1793	48 CJ 945	HL pass w/o Amds			
21 Jun 1793	48 CJ 996	Royal Assent			

Parliamentary debates

Pet: The Senator, 28 Feb 1793, Vol 1, p 412
Res: The Senator, 5 Mar 1793, Vol 1, p 430

Parliamentary papers and cases etc.

None

Newspaper coverage of debates

None

Notes

Archive

Brief Statement of the Importance of Dr. Cuthbert Gordon's "Discoveries in the Art of Dying", with copies of the answers of the woollen manufacturers and dyers to the Queries of the select committee (Gloucestershire Archives D421/X5/7)

Also see Cuthbert Gordon Petition 1793 (PRVB45) and earlier prize: PRZA19

Thomas Mudge 1795

PRZA22	1795
	Thomas Mudge for a timekeeper
	£2500

	**Appropriation Act 1795 (35 Geo 3. c. 120), s 24**

"And it is hereby also enacted by the Authority aforesaid, That, out of all or any the Aids or Supplies aforesaid, there shall and may be issued and applied any Sum or Sums of Money, not exceeding Forty-seven thousand six hundred and forty-nine Pounds One Shilling and Five-pence, to make good the like Sum, which has been issued by His Majesty's Orders, in pursuance of the Addresses of the House of Commons"

Address A/C: "To Thomas Mudge, Gentleman, as a Reward for his Pains and Labour in an Invention for the better Construction of Time Keepers [£2500 – –]" (50 CJ 240)

Journal

Committee of Supply resolution

21 Feb 1793	48 CJ 246	**Pet** for reward (Royal consent)
8 Mar 1793	48 CJ 367	Pet ref SC
29 Apr 1793	48 CJ 700 – V	**Rep by William Windham**/Ref SC
8 May 1793	48 CJ 750	Quorum of C'ttee

(continued)

(continued)

17 May 1793	48 CJ 793	C'tee to sit outside session
11 Jun 1793	48 CJ 877	**SC Rep by William Windham**
17 Jun 1793	48 CJ 946	Res for Royal Address (£2500)
19 Jun 1793	48 CJ 993	Royal Address Answered
19 Feb 1795	50 CJ 240	A/C unpaid Royal Addresses
20 Feb 1795	50 CJ 259	Ref COS
23 Feb 1795	50 CJ 265	COS Res

Appropriation Act 1795					
House of Commons			**House of Lords**		
24 Apr 1795	50 CJ 468	1R	18 Jun 1795	40 LJ 487	Brought HC/1R
12 Jun 1795	50 CJ 596	2R/C'tted CWH	19 Jun 1795	40 LJ 490	2R/C'tted CWH
15 Jun 1795	50 CJ 601	CWH adj	20 Jun 1795	40 LJ 492	CWH/Rep w/o Amds
16 Jun 1795	50 CJ 603	CWH	22 Jun 1795	40 LJ 499	3R
17 Jun 1795	50 CJ 606	Rep/Ing	26 Jun 1795	40 LJ 508	Royal Assent
18 Jun 1795	50 CJ 612	3R			
22 Jun 1795	50 CJ 620	HL pass w/o Amds			
26 Jun 1795	50 CJ 637	Royal Assent			

Parliamentary debates
Rep: **The Senator, 20 Apr 1793, Vol 7, p 697–698** Res: **Parliamentary Register, 17 Jun 1793, Vol 35, p 651–652**; The Senator, 17 Jun 1793, Vol 7, p 947

Parliamentary papers and cases etc.
Catalogue of Papers printed by Order of the House of Commons, from the year 1731 to 1800. In the Custody of the Clerk of the Journals (1807) (Reprint: HMSO 1954): Mudge's Timekeeper Report, 1793, Vol 11, No 106

Newspaper coverage of debates
Pet: Lloyd's Evening Post, 8–11 Mar 1793
Pet Rep: *The Times, 30 Apr 1793*; *Courier, 30 Apr 1793*
Rep: E. Johnson's British Gazette and Sunday Monitor, 16 Jun 1793
Pet: *The Times, 12 Jun 1793*
Comment: *The Times, 13 Jun 1793*
Minutes of proceedings: Gazetteer and New Daily Advertiser, 17 Jun 1793
Res: *Lloyd's Evening Post, 17–19 Jun 1793*; *The Times, 18 Jun 1794*; *Public Advertiser*, 19 Jun 1793; St. James's Chronicle or the British Evening Post, 15–18 Jun 1793

Joseph Elkington 1799

PRZA23	1799
Joseph Elkington for a system of draining	

£1000

Appropriation Act 1799 (39 Geo 3. c. 114), s 21
"And it is hereby also enacted, That, out of all or any the Aids or Supplies aforesaid, there shall and may be issued and applied any Sum or Sums of Money, not exceeding Nine thousand three hundred and thirty-seven Pounds Five Shillings and Sixpence, to make good the like Sum which has been issued by His Majesty's Orders, pursuant to Addresses of the House of Commons, and which has not been made good by Parliament"
Address A/C: "Jos^{ph} Elkington, for the Discovery of his System of Draining [1000]" (54 CJ 507)

Journal		
Committee of Supply resolution		
18 Jun 1795	50 CJ 612	Rep of Agriculture Board
19 Jun 1795	50 CJ 616 – V	Res for Royal Address (£1000)
25 Jun 1795	50 CJ 622	Royal Address Answered
3 May 1799	54 CJ 507	A/C unpaid Royal Addresses
8 May 1799	54 CJ 526	Ref COS
9 May 1799	54 CJ 528	COS Res

Appropriation Act 1799					
House of Commons			**House of Lords**		
24 Jun 1799	54 CJ 684	1R	5 Jul 1799	42 LJ 317	Brought HC/1R
25 Jun 1799	54 CJ 693	2R/C'tted CWH	8 Jul 1799	42 LJ 320	2R/C'tted
28 Jun 1799	54 CJ 709	CWH	9 Jul 1799	42 LJ 324	Com/Rep w/o Amds
1 Jul 1799	54 CJ 717	CWH	12 Jul 1799	42 LJ 335	3R
2 Jul 1799	54 CJ 720	Rep/Ing	12 Jul 1799	42 LJ 333	Royal Assent
3 Jul 1799	54 CJ 723	3R			
12 Jul 1799	54 CJ 739	HL pass w/o Amds			
12 Jul 1799	54 CJ 743	Royal Assent			

Parliamentary debates

Board Rep: Parliamentary Register, 18 Jun 1795, Vol 41, p 613; Senator, 18 Jun 1795, Vol 12, p 1360; Woodfall, 18 Jun 1795, Vol 4, p 85

Parliamentary papers and cases etc.

None

Newspaper coverage of debates

Board Rep: The Times, 19 Jun 1795

Res: *St. James's Chronicle or the British Evening Post, 18–20 Jun 1795; Whitehall Evening Post, 18–20 Jun 1795; The Times, 20 Jun 1795*

Joke on Res: *Morning Chronicle, 23 Jun 1795*

Notes

This is misreported in Colquhoun as Elkinston.

John Davis 1800

PRZA24	1800

John Davis for cleaning smutty wheat
£1000
Exchequer Bills Act 1800 (39 & 40 Geo 3. c. 109), s 28
"And it is hereby also enacted That out of all or any of the Aids or Supplies aforesaid, there shall and may be issued and applied … any Sum or Sums of Money, not exceeding One thousand Pounds, to be paid to Master John Davis, upon his making a proper Discovery for the Use of the Publick of his Method of cleaning and purifying Wheat damaged by Smut, and rendering it fit for the Food of Man"

Journal

Committee of Supply resolution

14 May 1800	55 CJ 529	**Pet reward** (Royal consent)
15 May 1800	55 CJ 532	Pet ref C'tee
17 Jul 1800	55 CJ 660	**Rep from C'tee by Sir Henry St. John Mildmay**
18 Jul 1800	55 CJ 767	Rep ref COS
19 Jul 1800	55 CJ 768	COS Res (£1000)

Exchequer Bills Act 1800					
House of Commons			**House of Lords**		
20 Jul 1800	55 CJ 769	Bill Ord	25 Jul 1800	42 LJ 641	Brought HC/1R
21 Jul 1800	55 CJ 770	1R	26 Jul 1800	42 LJ 642 – V	2R/Com neg/3R
22 Jul 1800	55 CJ 773	2R/C'tted CWH	28 Jul 1800	42 LJ 644	Royal Assent
23 Jul 1800	55 CJ 775	CWH			
24 Jul 1800	55 CJ 779	Rep/Ing			
25 Jul 1800	55 CJ 781	3R			
28 Jul 1800	55 CJ 784	HL pass w/o Amds			
28 Jul 1800	55 CJ 783	Royal Assent			

Parliamentary debates

Res: Parliamentary Register, 19 Jul 1800, Vol 12, p 424; Woodfall, 19 Jul 1800, Vol 3, p 462

(continued)

(continued)

Parliamentary papers and cases etc.
None

Newspaper coverage of debates
Res: General Evening Post, 17–19 Jul 1800; St. James's Chronicle or the British Evening Post, 17–19 Jul 1800; Whitehall Evening Post, 17–19 Jul 1800; Lloyd's Evening Post, 18–20 Jul 1800; London Packet or New Lloyd's Evening Post, 18–21 Jul 1800; Morning Herald, 19 Jul 1800; Sun, 19 Jul 1800; True Briton, 19 Jul 1800; E. Johnson's British Gazette and Sunday Monitor, 20 Jul 1800; Bell's Weekly Messenger, 20 Jul 1800; Bath Chronicle and Weekly Gazette, 24 Jul 1800; Chester Chronicle, 25 Jul 1800; Newcastle Courant, 26 Jul 1800

Thomas Foden 1801

PRZA25	1801

Thomas Foden for a wheat flour substitute

£500

Appropriation Act 1801 (41 Geo 3. c. 84), s 35
"And it is hereby also enacted, That out of all or any the Aids or Supplies aforesaid, there shall and may be issued and applied any Sum or Sums of Money not exceeding twenty-one thousand eight hundred and eight Pounds six Shillings and Threepence, to make good the like Sum which has been issued by his Majesty's Orders, pursuant to Addresses of the House of Commons, and which has not been made good by Parliament"

Address A/C: "To Thomas Foden, towards enabling him to prosecute a Discovery made by him of a Chrystalline Paste, as a substitute of Wheat Flour in all Purposes of Manufacture where Wheat Flour is used [£500]" |

Journal		
Committee of Supply resolution		
5 May 1800	55 CJ 474	**Pet reward** (Royal consent)
7 May 1800	55 CJ 481	Pet ref C'tee
2 Jun 1800	55 CJ 564	**Rep of C'tee by Robert Peel**
13 Jun 1800	55 CJ 649	Cons by CWH
16 June 1800	55 CJ 657	Rep/Res for Royal Address (no sum)
18 June 1800	55 CJ 669	Answer to Royal Address (no sum)
3 Mar 1801	56 CJ 104	A/Cs withdrawn Re-Ord
9 Mar1801	56 CJ 122	A/Cs (No 18) laid on table
24 Apr 1801	56 CJ 311	A/C ref COS
27 Apr 1801	56 CJ 319	COS Rep Res
27 Apr 1801	56 CJ 320	COS Res Agreed
App No 18	56 CJ 774	A/C unpaid Royal Address

Appropriation Act 1801					
House of Commons			**House of Lords**		
17 Jun 1801	56 CJ 577	1R	23 Jun 1801	43 LJ 334	Brought HC
18 Jun 1801	56 CJ 587	2R/C'tted CWH	23 Jun 1801	43 LJ 335	1R
19 Jun 1801	56 CJ 596	CWH	24 Jun 1801	43 LJ 339	2R/C'tted CWH
20 Jun 1801	56 CJ 606	Rep/Ing	25 Jun 1801	43 LJ 347	CWH/Rep w/o Amds
22 Jun 1801	56 CJ 618	3R	26 Jun 1801	43 LJ 355	3R
26 Jun 1801	56 CJ 638	HL pass w/o Amds	27 Jun 1801	43 LJ 367	Royal Assent
27 Jun 1801	56 CJ 640	Royal Assent			

Parliamentary debates
CWH: Parliamentary Register, 13 Jun 1800, Vol 12, p 112; Senator, 13 Jun 1800, Vol 26, p 1690; Woodfall, 13 Jun 1800, Vol 3, p 199
Rep: Parliamentary Register, 16 Jun 1800, Vol 12, p 117; Senator, 16 Jun 1800, Vol 26, p 1613; Woodfall, 16 Jun 1800, Vol 3, p 203
Answer: Woodfall, 18 Jun 1800 Vol 3, p 212
Accounts: Parliamentary Register, Appendix, Vol 12, p 764

Parliamentary papers and cases etc.
Report on Mr. Foden's Petition respecting his Chrystalline Size, &c. (23 May 1800), Eighteenth Century Parliamentary Papers, Vol 130
Catalogue of Papers printed by Order of the House of Commons, from the year 1731 to 1800. In the Custody of the Clerk of the Journals (1807) (Reprint: HMSO 1954): Foden's Cristalline Size, 1799/1800, Vol 26, No 162

Newspaper coverage of debates
CWH: **Morning Chronicle, 14 Jun 1800**; **Albion and Evening Advertiser, 14 Jun 1800**; **Sun, 14 Jun 1800**; **True Briton, 14 Jun 1800**; *General Evening Post, 12–14 Jun 1800*; *London Chronicle or Universal Evening Post, 12–14 Jun 1800*; *St. James's Chronicle or the British Evening Post, 12–14 Jun 1800*; *English Chronicle or Universal Evening Post, 12–14 Jun 1800*; *Whitehall Evening Post, 12–14 Jun 1800*; *Evening Mail, 13–16 Jun 1800*; *Morning Herald, 14 Jun 1800*; *Wheeler's Manchester Chronicle, 21 Jun 1800*; London Packet or New Lloyd's Evening Post, 13–16 Jun 1800; Star, 14 Jun 1800; Bell's Weekly Messenger, 15 Jun 1800
Res: Whitehall Evening Post, 14–17 Jun 1800; Evening Mail, 15–14 Jun 1800; Lloyd's Evening Post, 16–18 Jun 1800; Morning Herald, 17 Jun 1800; Star, 17 Jun 1800; True Briton, 17 Jun 1800
Address: General Evening Post, 17–20 Jun 1800

Arthur Young 1801

PRZA26	1801
	Arthur Young for essays for breaking up grass lands
	£800

Appropriation, etc. Act 1801 (41 Geo 3. c. 84), s 38
"And it is hereby also enacted, That out of all or any the Aids or Supplies aforesaid, there shall and may be issued and applied … any Sum or Sums of Money not exceeding eight hundred Pounds, to make good the like Sum has been issued to Arthur Young Esquire, Secretary to the Board of Agriculture, at the Receipt of the Exchequer, out of his Majesty's Civil List Revenues, for Premiums to be paid for Essays for breaking up of Grass Lands"

Journal
Committee of Supply resolution

3 June 1801	56 CJ 505	A/C laid on table
11 June 1801	56 CJ 541	COS res
App (No 50)	56 CJ 882	A/C of Civil List unpaid

Appropriation, etc. Act 1801

House of Commons			House of Lords		
17 Jun 1801	56 CJ 577	1R	23 Jun 1801	43 LJ 334	Brought HC
18 Jun 1801	56 CJ 587	2R/C'tted	23 Jun 1801	43 LJ 335	1R
19 Jun 1801	56 CJ 596	CWH	24 Jun 1801	43 LJ 339	2R/C'tted CWH
20 Jun 1801	56 CJ 606	Rep/Ing	25 Jun 1801	43 LJ 347	CWH/Rep w/o Amds
22 Jun 1801	56 CJ 618	3R	26 Jun 1801	43 LJ 355	3R
26 Jun 1801	56 CJ 638	HL pass w/o Amds	27 Jun 1801	43 LJ 367	Royal Assent
27 Jun 1801	56 CJ 640	Royal Assent			

Parliamentary debates
COS Res: Parliamentary Register, 10 Jun 1801, Vol 17, p 523

Parliamentary papers and cases etc.
None

Newspaper coverage of debates
COS Res: The Times, 11 Jun 1801; E. Johnson's British Gazette and Sunday Monitor, 14 Jun 1801; Bell's Weekly Messenger, 14 Jun 1801; Oxford Journal, 13 Jun 1801; Caledonian Mercury, 15 Jun 1801; Derby Mercury, 18 Jun 1801

Henry Greathead 1802

PRZA27	1802
	Henry Greathead for life boats
	£1200

Appropriation Act 1802 (42 Geo 3. c. 120), s 18
"And it is hereby also enacted, That, out of all or any the Aids or Supplies aforesaid, there shall and may be issued and applied … any Sum or Sums of Money not exceeding One thousand two hundred Pounds, to be paid to Henry Greathead of South Shields in the Country of Durham, Boat Builder, as a Reward for his Invention of the Life Boat, whereby many Lives have already been saved, and great Security is afforded to Seamen and Property in Cases of Shipwreck"

(continued)

(continued)

Journal		
Committee of Supply resolution		
25 Feb 1802	57 CJ 173	**Pet** (Royal consent)/Ref C'tee
31 Mar 1802	57 CJ 281	Rep of C'tee by Rowland Burden (laid on table)
26 May 1802	57 CJ 506	Ref COS
3 June 1802	57 CJ 544	COS Res
9 June 1802	57 CJ 554	CWH adopt COS Res

Appropriation Act 1802					
House of Commons			**House of Lords**		
14 Jun 1802	57 CJ 585	Bill Ord	22 Jun 1802	43 LJ 720	Brought HC/1R
16 Jun 1802	57 CJ 615	1R	23 Jun 1802	43 LJ 725	2R/C'tted CWH
17 Jun 1802	57 CJ 623	2R/C'tted CWH	24 Jun 1802	43 LJ 728	CWH/Rep w/o Amds
18 Jun 1802	57 CJ 632	CWH	26 Jun 1802	43 LJ 736	3R
19 Jun 1802	57 CJ 635	Rep/lng	28 Jun 1802	43 LJ 737	Royal Assent
21 Jun 1802	57 CJ 637	3R			
26 Jun 1802	57 CJ 661	HL pass w/o Amds			
28 Jun 1802	57 CJ 662	Royal Assent			

Parliamentary debates
Pet: **Senator (2d), 24 Feb 1802, Vol 3, p 617–618**; Parliamentary Register, 24 Feb 1802, Vol 17, p 66; Woodfall, 24 Feb 1802, Vol 1, p 513
Rep on table: Senator (2d), 31 Mar 1802, Vol 4, p 931
COS: **Parliamentary Register, 2 Jun 1802, Vol 18, p 600–602**
CWH adopt Res: Parliamentary Register, 9 Jun 1802, Vol 18, p 660; Woodfall, 9 Jun 1802, Vol 3, p 482

Parliamentary papers and cases etc.
Report from the committee on Mr. Greathead's petition, respecting his new invention of a life-boat (1801–1802 HC Papers 37), Vol 2, p 169 (First Series, Vol 10, p 730)

Newspaper coverage of debates
Pet: **The Times, 26 Feb 1802; Morning Chronicle, 26 Feb 1802; Morning Post, 26 Feb 1802; London Courier and Evening Gazette, 26 Feb 1802; Corbett's Weekly Political Register, 27 Feb 1802; Bell's Weekly Messenger, 28 Feb 1802**
Rep: Morning Chronicle, 1 Apr 1802; Morning Post, 1 Apr 1802
Ref COS: *The Times, 27 May 1802*; Morning Chronicle, 27 May 1802; Morning Post, 27 May 1802; London Courier and Evening Gazette, 27 May 1802; Bell's Weekly Messenger, 30 May 1802
COS Res: **The Times, 3 Jun 1802; Morning Chronicle, 3 Jun 1802; Morning Post, 3 Jun 1802; Evening Mail, 4 Jun 1802; Bell's Weekly Messenger, 6 Jun 1802;** *London Courier and Evening Gazette, 3 Jun 1802;* Corbett's Weekly Political Register, 5 Jun 1802
Res app: Morning Chronicle, 10 Jun 1802

Notes
There was another reward given in 1812: PRZA33

Edward Jenner 1802

PRZA28	1802
Dr Edward Jenner for vaccine innoculation	
£10,000 + £725 10s expenses	

Appropriation Act 1802 (42 Geo 3. c. 120), s 18
"And it is hereby also enacted, That, out of all or any the Aids or Supplies aforesaid, there shall and may be issued and applied … any Sum or Sums of Money not exceeding Ten thousand Pounds, to be paid to Doctor Edward Jenner, as a Reward for promulgating his Discoveries of Vaccine Inoculation, by which a mild and efficacious Mode of superseding that dreadful Malady the Small Pox, is established"
Appropriation Act 1803 (43 Geo 3. c. 162), s 18
"And it is hereby also enacted, That, out of all or any the Aids or Supplies aforesaid, there shall and may be issued and applied … any Sum or Sums of Money not exceeding Seven hundred twenty-five Pounds Ten Shillings and Sixpence, to reimburse to Doctor Jenner the Amount of the Fees and Charges on the Receipt of the Sum granted by an Act of the last Session of Parliament, as a Reward to him for promulgating his Discoveries of the Vaccine Innoculation"

Journal		
Committee of Supply resolution for £10,000 reward		
17 Mar 1802	57 CJ 240	**Pet** (Royal consent)/Ref C'tee
6 May 1802	57 CJ 413	Rep of C'tee by Henry Bankes
20 May 1802	57 CJ 481	Day app to Rep
25 May 1802	57 CJ 502	Rep read, ref COS
3 Jun 1802	57 CJ 544	COS Res (£10,000)
9 Jun 1802	57 CJ 554	CWH adopt COS Res
Committee of Supply resolution for £725 10s 6d expenses		
27 Jul 1803	58 CJ 641	A/C Pres (App 83)
29 Jul 1803	58 CJ 649	A/C ref COS
30 Jul 1803	58 CJ 658	COS Res (£725 10s 6d)
App (25)	58 CJ 818	A/C Pres from last year (detailing reward)
App (83)	58 CJ 1223	A/C setting out the costs from obtaining the reward (£725 10s 6d)

Appropriation Act 1802

House of Commons			House of Lords		
14 Jun 1802	57 CJ 585	Bill Ord	22 Jun 1802	43 LJ 720	Brought HC/1R
16 Jun 1802	57 CJ 615	1R	23 Jun 1802	43 LJ 725	2R/C'tted CWH
17 Jun 1802	57 CJ 623	2R/C'tted CWH	24 Jun 1802	43 LJ 728	CWH/Rep w/o Amds
18 Jun 1802	57 CJ 632	CWH	26 Jun 1802	43 LJ 736	3R
19 Jun 1802	57 CJ 635	Rep/Ing	28 Jun 1802	43 LJ 737	Royal Assent
21 Jun 1802	57 CJ 637	3R			
26 Jun 1802	57 CJ 661	HL pass w/o Amds			
28 Jun 1802	57 CJ 662	Royal Assent			

Appropriation Act 1803

House of Commons			House of Lords		
1 Aug 1803	58 CJ 664	1R	6 Aug 1803	44 LJ 383	Brought HC/1R
2 Aug 1803	58 CJ 671	2R/C'tted CWH	8 Aug 1803	44 LJ 385	2R/C'tted CWH
3 Aug 1803	58 CJ 675	CWH	9 Aug 1803	44 LJ 387	CWH/Rep w/o Amds
4 Aug 1803	58 CJ 679	Rep/Ing	11 Aug 1803	44 LJ 398	3R
5 Aug 1803	58 CJ 683	3R	12 Aug 1803	44 LJ 400	Royal Assent
11 Aug 1803	58 CJ 692	HL pass w/o Amds			
12 Aug 1803	58 CJ 693	Royal Assent			

Parliamentary debates

Prop: **Parliamentary Register, 15 Mar 1802, Vol 17, p 203**

Pet: **Parliamentary Register, 17 Mar 1802, Vol 17, p 239–241**; **Senator (2d), 17 Mar 1802, Vol 4, p 813–814**

Res: **Parliamentary Register, 2 Jun 1802, Vol 18, p 592–600**; **Woodfall, 1802, 2 Jun 1802, Vol 3, p 451**

CWH adopt Res: Parliamentary Register, 9 Jun 1802, Vol 18, p 660; Woodfall, 9 Jun 1802, Vol 3, p 482

Civil List expenses Pres: Parliamentary Register, 29 Jul 1802, Vol 4, p 745

Parliamentary papers and cases etc.

Vaccine Inoculation, Inquiry into its Efficacy, and into Dr Jenner's Claim to the merit of the Discovery (1802 HC Papers 85), Vol 2, p 267 (First Series, Vol 14, p 172)

Newspaper coverage of debates

Pet: **The Times, 16 Mar 1802**; **Morning Post, 16 Mar 1802**; *Morning Chronicle, 16 Mar 1802*; *London Courier and Evening Gazette, 16 Mar 1802*; *Cobett's Weekly Political Register, 13 Mar 1802*

Rep: Morning Chronicle, 7 May 1802

Ref COS: The Times, 26 May 1802; Morning Chronicle, 26 May 1802; Morning Post, 26 May 1802; London Courier and Evening Gazette, 26 May 1802; Evening Mail, 26 May 1802

COS: **The Times, 3 Jun 1802**; **Morning Chronicle, 3 Jun 1802**; **Morning Post, 3 Jun 1802**; **London Courier and Evening Gazette, 3 Jun 1802**; **Evening Mail, 4 Jun 1802**; *Bell's Weekly Messenger, 6 Jun 1802*

Req to exempt from fees: *The Times, 4 Jun 1802*; *Morning Chronicle, 4 Jun 1802*; *Morning Post, 4 Jun 1802*; *London Courier and Evening Gazette, 4 Jun 1892*; *Evening Mail, 4 Jun 1802*; *Cobett's Weekly Political Register, 5 Jun 1802*

Res app: *Times, 10 Jun 1802 (vote for fees prop)*; Morning Chronicle, 10 Jun 1802; Morning Post, 10 Jun 1802; London Courier and Evening Gazette, 10 Jun 1802

Notes

The second reward was to cover the exchequer and other fees Jenner faced in relation to the £10,000 reward. He received a further reward in 1807 (PRZA30)

James Carmichael Smyth 1803

PRZA29	1803

James Carmichael Smyth for nitrous fumigation to prevent contagion

£5000 (plus expenses of £258 17s)

Appropriation Act 1803 (43 Geo 3. c 162), s 15

"And it is hereby also enacted, That, out of all or any the Aids of Supplies aforesaid, there shall and may be issued and applied any Sum or Sums of Money not exceeding Fifteen thousand one hundred sixty Pounds and Sixpence, to make good the like Sum, which has been issued by His Majesty's Orders, pursuant to Addresses of the House of Commons, and which has not been made good by Parliament"

Address A/C: "Doctor James Carmichael Smyth, in consideration of the merit of his Discovery of Nitric Fumigation, to prevent the Communication of Contagion" (58 CJ 733)

Journal

Committee of Supply resolution

25 Feb 1802	57 CJ 173	**Pet** (Royal consent)/Ref C'tee
31 Mar 1802	57 CJ 282	All voices in C'tee
10 Jun 1802	57 CJ 565	Rep of C'tee by Henry Bankes
11 Jun 1802	57 CJ 575	Rep Prt
24 Jun 1802	57 CJ 650	Res for £5000 to Royal Address
26 Jun 1802	57 CJ 662	Answer to Royal Address
14 Dec 1802	58 CJ 91	A/Cs Pres (App 12)
15 Dec 1802	58 CJ 96	Ref COS
16 Dec 1802	58 CJ 100	COS Res
App (No 12)	58 CJ 733	**A/C of Addresses**

Appropriation Act 1803

House of Commons			House of Lords		
1 Aug 1803	58 CJ 664	1R	6 Aug 1803	44 LJ 383	Brought HC/1R
2 Aug 1803	58 CJ 671	2R/C'tted CWH	8 Aug 1803	44 LJ 385	2R/C'tted CWH
3 Aug 1803	58 CJ 675	CWH	9 Aug 1803	44 LJ 387	CWH/Rep w/o Amds
4 Aug 1803	58 CJ 679	Rep/Ing	11 Aug 1803	44 LJ 398	3R
5 Aug 1803	58 CJ 683	3R	12 Aug 1803	44 LJ 400	Royal Assent
11 Aug 1803	58 CJ 692	HL pass w/o Amds			
12 Aug 1803	58 CJ 693	Royal Assent			

Parliamentary debates

Pet: **Parliamentary Register, 25 Feb 1802, Vol 17, p 64–65**; **Senator (2d), 25 Feb 1802, Vol 3, p 616–617**

Res: **Parliamentary Register, 24 Jun 1802, Vol 18, p 790–792**; **Senator (2d), 24 Jun 1802, Vol 5, 1869–72**

Answer: Parliamentary Register, 26 Jun 1802, Vol 18, p 306; Senator (2d), 26 Jun 1802, Vol 5, p 1884

Appendix K, HC Deb (no date), Vol 1, col 1132

Parliamentary papers and cases etc.

Nitrous Fumigation, its efficacy in destroying Contagion and Claim of Dr James Carmichael Smith (1801–1802 HC Papers 114), Vol 2, p 381 (First Series, Vol 14, p 189)

Also see On the Health of the Prisoners of War confined to the King's House at Winchester (Appendix in HC Papers) (First Series, Vol 10, p 766) (which showed the efficacy of Nitrous Fumigation)

Newspaper coverage of debates

Pet: **The Times, 26 Feb 1802**; **Morning Chronicle, 26 Feb 1802**; **Morning Post, 26 Feb 1802**; *London Courier and Evening Gazette, 26 Feb 1802*; *Cobett's Weekly Political Register, 27 Feb 1802*; *Bell's Weekly Messenger, 28 Feb 1802*

Res: **The Times, 25 Jun 1802**; **Morning Chronicle, 25 Jun 1802**; **Morning Post, 25 Jun 1802**; **London Courier and Evening Gazette, 25 Jun 1802**; Cobett's Weekly Political Register, 26 Jun 1802; Bell's Weekly Messenger, 27 Jun 1802;

Address: The Times, 28 Jun 1802; Morning Chronicle, 28 Jun 1802; Morning Post, 28 Jun 1802; Evening Mail, 28 Jun 1802; London Courier and Evening Gazette, 28 Jun 1802

Notes

This reward was misdated as 1813 in both Colquhoun and the *Mechanics Magazine*

Edward Jenner 1807

PRZA30	1807
Dr Edward Jenner for vaccine Innoculation	
£20,000	

Appropriation Act 1807 (47 Geo 3. Sess 2. c. 76), s 20
"And it is hereby also enacted, That out of all or any the Aids or Supplies aforesaid, there shall and may be issued and applied … any Sum or Sums of Money, not exceeding Twenty thousand Pounds, as a further Reward to Doctor Edward Jenner, for promulgating his Discovery of the Vaccine Inoculation, by which a mild, efficacious, and not contagious Mode of superseding that Malady the Small Pox is established, and that the said Sum be issued and paid without any Fee or other Deduction whatsoever"

Journal

Committee of Supply resolution		
8 Jul 1807	62 CJ 660	Rep of Royal College of Surgeons Pres
29 Jul 1807	62 CJ 795	Royal College Rep ref COS
30 Jul 1807	62 CJ 798	COS Res
App	62 CJ 870	Appendix 51 (Rep)

Appropriation Act 1807					
House of Commons			**House of Lords**		
1 Aug 1807	62 CJ 807	Bill Ord	10 Aug 1807	46 LJ 376	Brought HC/1R
3 Aug 1807	62 CJ 811	1R	11 Aug 1807	46 LJ 380	2R/C'tted
4 Aug 1807	62 CJ 816	2R/C'tted CWH	12 Aug 1807	46 LJ 382	CWH/Rep w/o Amds
5 Aug 1807	62 CJ 821	Clause added	13 Aug 1807	46 LJ 393	3R
6 Aug 1807	62 CJ 823	Rep/Ing	14 Aug 1807	46 LJ 398	Royal Assent
7 Aug 1807	62 CJ 828	3R			
13 Aug 1807	62 CJ 840	HL pass w/o Amds			
14 Aug 1807	62 CJ 847	Royal Assent			

Parliamentary debates
Rep: HC Deb, 29 Jul 1907, Vol 9(1st), col 1007–1015

Parliamentary papers and cases etc.
None

Newspaper coverage of debates
Rep RCS: Morning Chronicle, 9 Jul 1807; Morning Post, 9 Jul 1807
Rep COS: **The Times, 30 Jul 1807**; **Morning Chronicle, 30 Jul 1807**; *Morning Post, 30 July 1807*; *Public Ledger and Daily Ledger, 30 July 1807*; Morning Advertiser, 30 July 1807
COS Res: The Times, 31 Jul 1807; Morning Advertiser, 31 Jul 1807; Morning Chronicle, 31 Jul 1807; Public Ledger and Daily Advertiser, 31 Jul 1807

Location of Acts
This was to supplement an earlier reward said to be inadequate (see PRZA28)

Edmund Cartwright 1809

PRZA31	1809
Edmund Cartwright for various woolcombing inventions	
£10,000	

Appropriation Act 1809 (49 Geo 3. c. 128), s 21
"And it is hereby also enacted, That out of all or any the Aids or Supplies aforesaid, there shall and may be issued and applied … any Sum or Sums of Money not exceeding Ten thousand Pounds, to be paid to Edmund Cartwright Clerk, Doctor in Divinity, in Compensation for the great Expence he has incurred in the Discovery and Application of various mechanical Inventions to the Process of Wearing, by which he has rendered essential Services to the Manufacturers of this Country, and that the said Sum be issued and paid without any Fee or other Deduction whatsoever"

(continued)

(continued)

Journal		
Committee of Supply resolution		
24 Mar 1808	63 CJ 206	**Pet**
13 Apr 1808	63 CJ 263	Rep by Issac Hawkins Brown
24 Feb 1809	64 CJ 96	**Pet** (Royal consent)
7 Jun 1809	64 CJ 391	13 Apr 1909 Rep ref COS
8 Jun 1809	64 CJ 393	COS Res

House of Commons			House of Lords		
Appropriation Act 1809					
2 Jun 1809	64 CJ 380	Bill Ord	13 Jun 1809	47 LJ 375	Brought HC/1R
6 Jun 1809	64 CJ 386	1R	14 Jun 1809	47 LJ 380	2R/C'tted CWH
8 Jun 1809	64 CJ 392	2R/C'tted CWH	15 Jun 1809	47 LJ 386	CWH/Rep w/o Amds
9 Jun 1809	64 CJ 395	CWH	19 Jun 1809	47 LJ 392	3R
10 Jun 1809	64 CJ 399	Rep/Ing	20 Jun 1809	47 LJ 397	Royal Assent
12 Jun 1809	64 CJ 400	3R			
19 Jun 1809	64 CJ 409	HL pass w/o Amds			
20 Jun 1809	64 CJ 415	Royal Assent			

Parliamentary debates
Rep ref to COS: **HC Deb, 7 Jun 1809, Vol 14(1st), col 922–923**

Parliamentary papers and cases etc.
Report from the committee on Dr. Cartwright's petition respecting his weaving machine (1808 HC Papers 179), Vol 2, p 135

Newspaper coverage of debates
Ref COS: *The Times, 8 Jun 1809*; Morning Chronicle, 8 Jun 1809; Morning Post, 8 Jun 1809; London Courier and Evening Gazette, 8 Jun 1809
COS Res: **Morning Advertiser, 9 Jun 1809**; *The Times, 9 Jun 1809*; *Morning Chronicle, 9 Jun 1809*; *Morning Post, 9 Jun 1809*

Notes
Cartwright also had a private Act to extend various patents: PRVA32; also see PRVB48

George Manby 1810

PRZA32	1810
Captain George Manby for communicating with stranded ships	
£2000	

Appropriation Act 1810 (50 Geo 3. c. 115), s 23
"And it is hereby also enacted, That out of all or any the Aids or Supplies aforesaid, there shall and may be issued and applied … any Sum or Sums of Money not exceeding Two thousand Pounds, to be paid to Captain George Manby, as a Reward for his Invention for effecting a Communication with Ships stranded, and that the said Sum be issued and paid without any Fee or other Deduction whatsoever"

Journal		
Committee of Supply resolution		
7 Jun 1809	64 CJ 389	Board/Ordinance Reps Pres
23 Mar 1810	65 CJ 212	**Pet** (Royal Consent)
26 Mar 1810	65 CJ 219	Pet Rep by John Curwen
13 Apr 1810	65 CJ 285	**Rep ref COS**
16 Apr 1810	65 CJ 289	COS Res
App No 8	66 CJ 610	A/C showing money paid

House of Commons			House of Lords		
Appropriation Act 1810					
1 Jun 1810	65 CJ 441	Bill Ord	15 Jun 1810	47 LJ 787	Brought HC/1R
2 Jun 1810	65 CJ 447	1R	16 Jun 1810	47 LJ 795	2R/C'tted CWH
2 Jun 1810	65 CJ 452	2R/C'tted CWH	18 Jun 1810	47 LJ 797	CWH/Rep w/o Amds
5 Jun 1810	65 CJ 458	CWH adj	19 Jun 1810	47 LJ 801	3R

8 Jun 1810	65 CJ 473	CWH		20 Jun 1810	47 LJ 805	Royal Assent
9 Jun 1810	65 CJ 481	Rep/Ing				
14 Jun 1810	65 CJ 494	3R day app				
15 Jun 1810	65 CJ 498	3R				
20 Jun 1810	65 CJ 506	HL pass w/o Amds				
20 Jun 1810	65 CJ 505	Royal Assent				

Parliamentary debates
None

Parliamentary papers and cases etc.
Papers relating to Capt. Manby's experiments for effecting a communication with ships stranded (1809 HC Papers 255), Vol 10, p 373
Report from the committee on Capt. Manby's petition (1810 HC Papers 163), Vol 4, p 5
Copy of report from the Committee of Field Officers of Artillery; containing, an account of the experiments made at Woolwich on the 18th and 20th May last; on Captain Manby's invention for saving the lives of shipwrecked mariners (1810–11 HC Papers 215), Vol 11, p 111

Newspaper coverage of debates
Rep: *Morning Post, 27 Mar 1810*; *London Courier and Evening Gazette, 27 Mar 1810*; Morning Advertiser, 27 Mar 1810
Ref COS: *Morning Post, 14 Apr 1810*; The Times, 14 Apr 1810; Morning Chronicle, 14 Apr 1810; Public Ledger and Daily Advertiser, 14 Apr 1810; London Courier and Evening Gazette, 14 Apr 1810;
COS Res: The Times, 17 Apr 1810; Morning Advertiser, 17 Apr 1810; Public Ledger and Daily Advertiser, 14 Apr 1810

Notes
Manby received three further rewards: PRZA35, PRZA37 and PRZA39

Henry Greathead 1812

PRZA33	1812
Henry Greathead for his Life Boat	
£650	

Appropriation Act 1812 (52 Geo 3. c. 154), s 24
"And it is hereby also enacted, That out of all or any the Aids or Supplies aforesaid, there shall and may be issued and applied … any Sum or Sums of Money not exceeding Six hundred and fifty Pounds, to enable His Majesty to make further Remuneration to Mr. Greathead for his useful Invention of the Life Board, and that the said Sum be issued and paid without any Fee or other Deduction whatsoever"

Journal

Committee of Supply resolution

10 Jun 1811	66 CJ 412	**Pet** (Royal Consent)
11 Jun 1811	66 CJ 416	Pet ref C'tee
13 Jun 1811	66 CJ 425	Rep from C'tee by Robert Ward
14 Jun 1811	66 CJ 431	Further consideration of Rep
27 Apr 1812	67 CJ 327	13 Jun 1811 Rep ref COS
28 Apr 1812	67 CJ 333	COS Res

Appropriation Act 1812						
House of Commons				**House of Lords**		
2 Jul 1812	67 CJ 502	Bill Ord		15 Jun 1810	47 LJ 787	Brought HC/1R
9 Jul 1812	67 CJ 520	1R		16 Jun 1810	47 LJ 795	2R/C'tted CWH
10 Jul 1812	67 CJ 521	2R/C'tted CWH		18 Jun 1810	47 LJ 797	CWH/Rep w/o Amds
13 Jul 1812	67 CJ 525	CWH		19 Jun 1810	47 LJ 801	3R
14 Jul 1812	67 CJ 526	Rep/Ing		20 Jun 1810	47 LJ 805	Royal Assent
16 Jul 1812	67 CJ 532	3R				
23 Jul 1812	67 CJ 550	HL pass w/o Amds				
28 Jul 1812	67 CJ 599	Royal Assent				

Parliamentary debates
Pet: **HC Deb, 10 Jun 1811, Vol 20(1st), col 558–559**

(continued)

(continued)

Parliamentary papers and cases etc.
Report on Mr. Greathead's petition (1810–11 HC Papers 230), Vol 2, p 387
Newspaper coverage of debates
Rep ref COS: **Public Ledger and Daily Advertiser, 28 Apr 1812**; Morning Chronicle, 28 Apr 1812; Globe, 28 Apr 1812
Note
This supplemented an earlier reward to Greathead: PRZA27

Samuel Crompton 1812

PRZA34	1812

Samuel Crompton for the spinning mule

£5000

Appropriation Act 1812 (52 Geo 3. c. 154), s 24
"And it is hereby also enacted, That out of all or any the Aids or Supplies aforesaid, there shall and may be issued and applied … any Sum, or Sums of Money not exceeding Five thousand Pounds, to enable His Majesty to advance the like Sum to Master Crompton, for his Invention of the Machine called The Mule, and that the said Sum be issued and paid without any Fee or other Deduction whatsoever"

Journal
Resolution of Committee of Supply

5 Mar 1812	67 CJ 175	Pet (Royal Consent)/ref C'tee
24 Mar 1812	67 CJ 225	Rep on Pet by John Blackburne
24 Jun 1812	67 CJ 468	Rep ref COS
25 Jun 1812	67 CJ 476	COS Res
App (No 13)	67 CJ 838	Rep on Mr Crompton's Pet

Journal					
House of Commons			**House of Lords**		
2 Jul 1812	67 CJ 502	Bill Ord	15 Jun 1810	47 LJ 787	Brought HC/1R
9 Jul 1812	67 CJ 520	1R	16 Jun 1810	47 LJ 795	2R/C'tted CWH
10 Jul 1812	67 CJ 521	2R/C'tted CWH	18 Jun 1810	47 LJ 797	CWH/Rep w/o Amds
13 Jul 1812	67 CJ 525	CWH	19 Jun 1810	47 LJ 801	3R
14 Jul 1812	67 CJ 526	Rep/Ing	20 Jun 1810	47 LJ 805	Royal Assent
16 Jul 1812	67 CJ 532	3R			
23 Jul 1812	67 CJ 550	HL pass w/o Amds			
28 Jul 1812	67 CJ 599	Royal Assent			

Parliamentary debates
Pet: HC Deb, 5 Mar 1812, Vol 21(1st), col 1173–1174
Parliamentary papers and cases etc.
Report on Mr Crompton's Petition (1812 HC Papers 126), Vol 2, p 89
Newspaper coverage of debates
Rep ref COS: **Morning Chronicle, 25 Jun 1812**; **London Courier and Evening Gazette, 25 Jun 1812**; *Globe, 25 Jun 1812*

George Manby 1812

PRZA35	1812

Captain George Manby for communicating with stranded ships to save mariners lives

£1250 (+ expenses)

Appropriation Act 1812 (52 Geo 3. c. 154), s 24
"And it is hereby also enacted, That out of all or any the Aids or Supplies aforesaid, there shall and may be issued and applied … any Sum or Sums of Money not exceeding One thousand two hundred and fifty Pounds, for defraying Captain Manby's Allowance and travelling Expences in carrying in Execution on suitable Parts of the Coasts of Great Britain his Plans for saving the Lives of shipwrecked Mariners for the Year One thousand eight hundred and twelve"

Journal		
Resolution of Committee of Supply		
30 May 1811	66 CJ 386	A/C of Captain Manby's experiments
14 Jun 1811	66 CJ 430	Address to HRH Prince Regent
18 Jun 1811	66 CJ 437	Reply from HRH Prince Regent
22 Jan 1812	67 CJ 57	Estimate in accordance with Address
27 Jan1812	67 CJ 81	COS Res
App (No 3)	67 CJ 641	Estimate of cost to defray Captain Manby's expenses

Journal					
House of Commons			**House of Lords**		
2 Jul 1812	67 CJ 502	Bill Ord	18 Jul 1812	48 LJ 996	Brought HC/1R
9 Jul 1812	67 CJ 520	1R	20 Jul 1812	48 LJ 1003	2R/C'tted CWH
10 Jul 1812	67 CJ 521	2R/C'tted CWH	21 Jul 1812	48 LJ 1007	CWH adj
13 Jul 1812	67 CJ 525	CWH	22 Jul 1812	48 LJ 1012	CWH/Rep w/o Amds
14 Jul 1812	67 CJ 526	Rep/Ing	23 Jul 1812	48 LJ 1016	3R
16 Jul 1812	67 CJ 532	3R	28 Jul 1812	48 LJ 1028	Royal Assent
23 Jul 1812	67 CJ 550	HL pass w/o Amds			
28 Jul 1812	67 CJ 599	Royal Assent			

Parliamentary debates
HM address: HC Deb, 14 Jun 1811, Vol 20(1st), col 625–626

Parliamentary papers and cases etc.
Select Committee on Reports and Papers respecting Captain Manby's Experiments for saving lives of Shipwrecked Mariners (1813–14 HC Papers 227), Vol 3, p 343
Papers relating to Captain Manby's Plan for saving Lives of Shipwrecked Mariners (1813–14 HC Papers 48), Vol 11, p 415

Newspaper coverage of debates
HM address: **Morning Chronicle, 15 Jun 1811**; **Morning Post, 15 Jun 1811**; **Globe, 15 Jun 1811**; *Public Ledger and Daily Advertiser, 15 Jun 1811*; *London Courier and Evening Gazette, 15 Jun 1811*
Est Add: Globe, 25 Jan 1812; Public Ledger and Daily Advertiser, 25 Jan 1812; London Courier and Evening Gazette, 25 Jan 1812

Notes
The was the second of four rewards paid to Manby (Manby also received three further rewards: PRZA32, PRZA37 and PRZA39)

John Palmer 1813

PRZA36	1813
John Palmer for the postal service (pursuant to an earlier contract)	
£50,000	

Grant of John Palmer, Esquire (Post Office Services) Act 1813 (53 Geo 3. c. 158), s 1
"That the Sum of Fifty thousand Pounds shall be issued and paid, out of the said Consolidated Fund of Great Britain, to the said John Palmer Esquire, without any Fee or other Deduction whatsoever, in full Satisfaction and Discharge for the Services performed by the said John Palmer, in the Accommodation so afforded to the Public, and the Benefit derived to the Post Office Revenue as aforesaid; and which said Sum of Fifty thousand Pounds the said John Palmer accepts in full Satisfaction of such Services: Provided always, that nothing herein contained shall affect the Payment of a certain Pension or annual Allowance of Three thousand Pounds heretofore made to the said John Palmer out of the Revenues of the Post Office, by virtue of an Order of the Lords Commissioners of His Majesty's Treasury, bearing Date the Twenty eighth Day of June One thousand seven hundred and ninety three"

Journal	
1st Bill Pr: Charles Nicholas Palmer 2nd Bill Pr: Nicholas Vansittart (Ch Ex) 1st Bill Rep: Charles Moore 2nd Bill Rep: John Croker C'tee on LJ: Stephen Rumbold Lushington	1st Bill Rep: Earl of Harrowby (Ld Pr) 2nd Bill Rep: Lord Douglas of Lochleven

(continued)

(continued)

House of Commons			House of Lords		
20 May 1813	68 CJ 504	**Res ref CWH**	22 Jun 1813	49 LJ 524	Brought HC/1R
21 May 1813	68 CJ 510	**CWH**/Bill Ord	22 Jun 1813	49 LJ 525	A/Cs Ord
24 May 1813	68 CJ 514	1R	23 Jun 1813	49 LJ 529	A/Cs Ord
24 May 1813	68 CJ 517	Re-prt Rep of 9 Jun 1808	24 Jun 1813	49 LJ 533	Lords App
25 May 1813	68 CJ 519	Bill Prt	24 Jun 1813	49 LJ 534	Wit Sum
31 May 1813	68 CJ 531	2R/C'tted CWH	23 Jun 1813	49 LJ 535	Wit Sum
31 May 1813	68 CJ 531	Rep 13 Jul 1797 ref	24 Jun 1813	49 LJ 536	A/Cs Rec
11 Jun 1813	68 CJ 555	CWH adj	25 Jun 1813	49 LJ 537	A/Cs ref C'tee
14 Jun 1813	68 CJ 563	**R't Supply** (award £84,920)	25 Jun 1813	49 LJ 538	A/C and Wit Sum
15 Jun 1813	68 CJ 568 – V	CWH	28 Jun 1813	49 LJ 542	Wit Sum
21 Jun 1813	68 CJ 585	**Rep with Amds**/Ing	28 Jun 1813	49 LJ 544	A/C Ord
22 Jun 1813	68 CJ 591	3R	29 Jun 1813	49 LJ 547	Wits Sum
5 Jul 1813	68 CJ 642	C'tee to inspect LJ	29 Jun 1813	49 LJ 548	A/C Ord
6 Jul 1813	68 CJ 643	**Com Rep**	5 Jul 1813	49 LJ 568	Rep on Dispute
8 Jul 1813	68 CJ 651	Rep C'tee on Services	5 Jul 1813	49 LJ 572	2R, adj 3m
		Second Bill			*Second Bill*
10 Jul 1813	68 CJ 656	1R	14 Jul 1813	49 LJ 615	Brought HC/1R
12 Jul 1813	68 CJ 658	2R/C'tted	15 Jul 1813	49 LJ 618	2R/C'tted CWH
13 Jul 1813	68 CJ 661	CWH/**Rep with Amds**/Ing	16 Jul 1813	49 LJ 619	CWH/Rep w/o Amds
14 Jul 1813	68 CJ 666	3R	20 Jul 1813	49 LJ 653	3R
20 Jul 1813	68 CJ 670	HL pass w/o amend	21 Jul 1813	49 LJ 659	Royal Assent
21 Jul 1813	68 CJ 673	Royal Assent			

Parliamentary debates
COS Resolution: **HC Deb, 20 May 1813 Vol 26(1st), col 253**

Parliamentary papers and cases etc.

Bill to secure to J. Palmer Future Percentage on Revenue of Post Office: (as amended by Committee on Report) (1812–13 HC Papers 230), Vol 2, p 863

Minutes of evidence taken before the committee appointed to consider of the agreement made with Mr. Palmer, for the reform and improvement of the Post-Office and its revenue (1812–13 HC Papers 260), Vol 4, p 735

Report from the Select Committee of the House of Lords, in 1813, on the Agreement made with Mr Palmer, for the Reform and Improvement of the Post Office; with Minutes of Evidence (1812–13 HL Papers 123), Vol 63, p 1

Account of the net revenue of the Post Office, from 5th April 1798 to 5th January 1813 (1812–13 HC Papers 217), Vol 13, p 163

Reports and Accounts relating to J. Palmer's Agreement with Post Office, and its Revenue (1812–13 HC Papers 222), Vol 4, p 761

Account of the Per-centage, including the Salary, paid to Mr Palmer, from the Date of his Appointment to 5th Apr 1793 (1812–13 HL Papers 103), Vol 63, p 133

Account of all Sums paid to Mr Palmer over and above his Allowance for Salary, and the Sum of 2½ per Cent on the increased Revenue (1812–13 HL Papers 111), Vol 63, p 123

Account of the Per-centage, including the Salary, paid to Mr Palmer, from 5th Apr 1793 to 5th Jan 1813 (1812–13 HL Papers 113), Vol 63, p 132

Account of the net Revenue of the Post Office, from 6th April 1793 to 5th January 1813 (1812–13 HL Papers 104, Vol 63, p 127

Newspaper coverage of debates

First Bill: House of Commons

Res: **The Times, 21 May 1813; Morning Chronicle, 21 May 1813; Morning Post, 21 May 1813; London Courier and Evening Gazette, 21 May 1813**; *Public Ledger and Daily Advertiser, 21 May 1813*

Bill Ord: *Morning Chronicle, 22 May 1813*; Morning Post, 22 May 1813; Public Ledger and Daily Advertiser, 22 May 1813; London Courier and Evening Gazette, 22 May 1813

2R: **The Times, 1 Jun 1813; Morning Chronicle, 1 Jun 1813; Morning Post, 1 Jun 1813**; *Public Ledger and Daily Advertiser, 1 Jun 1813*; London Courier and Evening Gazette, 1 Jun 1813

Wit Att: **The Times, 2 Jun 1813**

COS Rep: **Morning Chronicle, 15 Jun 1813**; Public Ledger and Daily Advertiser, 15 Jun 1813;

COS: **The Times, 16 Jun 1813; Morning Chronicle, 16 Jun 1813; Morning Post, 16 Jun 1813**; *Public Ledger and Daily Advertiser, 16 Jun 1813: London Courier and Evening Gazette, 16 Jun 1813*

Rep: **Morning Chronicle, 16 Jun 1813; Morning Post, 16 Jun 1813; Public Ledger and Daily Advertiser, 16 Jun 1813: London Courier and Evening Gazette, 16 Jun 1813**

3R: Public Ledger and Daily Advertiser, 23 Jun 1813

First Bill: House of Lords

1R: Morning Chronicle, 23 Jun 1813; Morning Post, 23 Jun 1813; Public Ledger and Daily Advertiser, 23 Jun 1813; London Courier and Evening Gazette, 23 Jun 1813

Add info: **The Times, 24 Jun 1813; Morning Post, 24 Jun 1813**; *London Courier and Evening Gazette, 24 Jun 1813*; Morning Chronicle, 24 Jun 1813

Papers Del: Morning Chronicle, 29 Jun 1813; Morning Post, 29 Jun 1813; Public Ledger and Daily Advertiser, 29 Jun 1813

2R adj: **The Times, 6 Jul 1813; Morning Chronicle, 6 Jul 1813; Morning Post, 6 Jul 1813; London Courier and Evening Gazette, 6 Jul 1813**; Public Ledger and Daily Advertiser, 6 Jul 1813

Second Bill: House of Commons

2R: Morning Chronicle, 13 Jul 1813; Morning Post, 13 Jul 1813; London Courier and Evening Gazette, 13 Jul 1813

Rep: Morning Chronicle, 14 Jul 1813; Morning Post, 14 Jul 1813; London Courier and Evening Gazette, 14 Jul 1813

3R: **The Times, 15 Jul 1813; Morning Chronicle, 15 Jul 1813; Morning Post, 15 Jul 1813; London Courier and Evening Gazette, 15 Jul 1813**

Second Bill: House of Lords

2R: **The Times, 16 Jul 1813; Morning Post, 16 Jul 1813; London Courier and Evening Gazette, 16 Jul 1813**; *Morning Chronicle, 16 Jul 1813*

CWH: **The Times, 17 Jul 1813; Morning Chronicle, 17 Jul 1813; Morning Post, 17 Jul 1813**

3R: Public Ledger and Daily Advertiser, 21 Jul 1813

Royal Assent: Morning Post, 22 Jul 1813; London Courier and Evening Gazette, 22 Jul 1813

Notes
There were two earlier Bills: one in 1808 (PRZC10) and one in 1812 (PRZC14). This Act was the outcome of a long fight with the government by Palmer trying to obtain money under a contract he had with them. It was not a reward as such

George Manby 1814

PRZA37	1814

George Manby for communicating with stranded ships

£2000

Appropriation Act 1814 (54 Geo 3. c. 167), s 26
"And it is hereby also enacted, That out of all or any of the Aids or Supplies aforesaid, there shall and may be issued and applied … any Sum or Sums of Money not exceeding Two thousand Pounds, to be issued to Captain Manby as a further Reward for his Invention for effecting a Communication with Ships stranded, and that the said Sum be issued and paid without any Fee or other Deduction whatsoever"

Journal		
Resolution of Committee of Supply		
7 Dec1813	69 CJ 105	Reps relating to Manby experiments laid before Parliament
6 May 1814	69 CJ 244	Reps ref SC
19 May 1814	69 CJ 285	Whitfield Pet
3 Jun 1814	69 CJ 323	Papers ref COS
10 Jun 1814	69 CJ 341	Rep from C'tee by George Rose
20 Jun 1814	69 CJ 367	Rept ref COS
23 Jun 1814	69 CJ 375	COS Res
23 Jul 1814	69 CJ 497	Rep sent to Prince Regent
27 Jul 1814	69 CJ 513	Prince Regent to give directions

Appropriation Act 1814					
House of Commons			**House of Lords**		
18 Jul 1814	69 CJ 475	1R	26 Jul 1814	49 LJ 1133	Brought HC/1R
20 Jul 1814	69 CJ 481	2R/C'tted CWH	27 Jul 1814	49 LJ 1146	2R (misrep) (not C'tted)
20 Jul 1814	69 CJ 501	CWH adj	28 Jul 1814	49 LJ 1152	3R
21 Jul 1814	69 CJ 491	CWH	29 Jul 1814	49 LJ 1159	Royal Assent
22 Jul 1814	69 CJ 494	Rep/Ing			
23 Jul 1814	69 CJ 499	3R day app			
25 Jul 1814	69 CJ 501	3R			
28 Jul 1814	69 CJ 516	HL pass w/o Amds			
29 Jul 1814	69 CJ 516	Royal Assent			

(continued)

(continued)

Parliamentary debates
HC Deb, 14 Jun 1811, Vol 20(1st), col 625–626
Ref SC: **HC Deb, 6 May 1814, Vol 27(1st), col 728–739**
Pet Rep: **HC Deb, 10 Jun 1814, Vol 28(1st), col 44–50**
COS: HC Deb, 20 Jun 1814, Vol 28(1st), col 104
Res: **HC Deb, 22 Jun 1814, Vol 28(1st), col 121–122**

Parliamentary papers and cases etc.
Papers relating to Captain Manby's plan for saving the lives of ship-wrecked mariners (1813–14 HC Papers 48), Vol 11, p 415
Report from committee on reports and other papers respecting Captain Manby's experiments for saving the lives of shipwrecked mariners (1813–14 HC Papers 227), Vol 3, p 343

Newspaper coverage of debates
Res ref SC: **The Times, 7 May 1814**; **Morning Chronicle, 7 May 1814**; **Morning Post, 7 May 1814**; **Public Ledger and Daily Advertiser, 7 May 1814**; **London Courier and Evening Gazette, 7 May 1814**
Pet Rep: Morning Chronicle, 11 Jun 1814; Morning Post, 11 Jun 1814; London Courier and Evening Gazette, 11 Jun 1814; Public Ledger and Daily Advertiser, 11 Jun 1814
COS: **Morning Post, 21 Jun 1814**; **London Courier and Evening Gazette, 21 Jun 1814**; Morning Chronicle, 21 Jun 1814

Notes
The was the third of four rewards paid to Manby (Manby also received three further rewards: PRZA32, PRZA35 and PRZA39)

John Bell (by daughter Elizabeth Whitfield) 1815

PRZA38	1815
Lt John Bell (by daughter Elizabeth Whitfield) for invention of preserving lives of shipwrecked mariners	
£500	

Appropriation Act 1815 (55 Geo 3. c. 187), s 25
"And it is hereby also enacted, That out of all or any Aids or Supplies aforesaid there shall and may be issued and applied . . . any Sum or Sums of Money not exceeding Five hundred Pounds, to be paid to Elizabeth Whitfield, only surviving Daughter of the late Lieutenant Bell of the Royal Invalid Artillery, in Consideration of the Merit and Exertions of the said Lieutenant Bell, towards the Attainment of the Object of preserving Lives of shipwrecked Seamen and others, and that the said Sum be issued and paid without any Fee or other Deduction whatsoever"

Journal		
Resolution of Committee of Supply		
19 May 1814	69 CJ 285	**Pet** (Royal consent)
1 Jul 1814	69 CJ 417	Pet ref C'tee
11 Jul 1814	69 CJ 448	C'tee Rep by Charles Moore
23 Jun 1815	70 CJ 423	Rep ref COS
26 Jun 1815	70 CJ 428	COS Res £500

Appropriation Act 1815					
House of Commons			**House of Lords**		
27 Jun 1815	70 CJ 434	1R	5 Jul 1815	50 LJ 380	Brought HC/1R
28 Jun 1815	70 CJ 440	2R/C'tted CWH	6 Jul 1815	50 LJ 389	2R/C'tted CWH
29 Jun 1815	70 CJ 444	CWH adj	7 Jul 1815	50 LJ 398	CWH/Rep
30 Jun 1815	70 CJ 450	CWH	8 Jul 1815	50 LJ 399	3R
3 Jul 1815	70 CJ 455	Rep/Ing	11 Jul 1815	50 LJ 406	Royal Assent
5 Jul 1815	70 CJ 462	3R			
11 Jul 1815	70 CJ 469	HL pass w/o Amds			
11 Jul 1815	70 CJ 468	Royal Assent			

Parliamentary debates
None

Parliamentary papers and cases etc.
Report on Mrs. Whitfield's petition (1813–14 HC Papers 309), Vol 3, p 347
Newspaper coverage of debates
Ref COS: *Morning Post, 24 Jun 1815*; *Public Ledger and Daily Advertiser, 24 Jun 1815*; Morning Chronicle, 24 Jun 1815; London Courier and Evening Gazette, 24 Jun 1815
Notes
This follows on from a petition lodged in relation to Manby's Invention: PRZA37

George Manby 1823

PRZA39	1823

George Manby for communicating with stranding ships
£2000
Appropriation Act 1823 (4 Geo 4, c. 100), s 26 "And it is hereby also enacted, That out of all or any of the Aids or Supplies aforesaid, there shall and may be issued and applied . . . any Sum or Sums of Money not exceeding Two thousand Pounds, to be issued to Captain Manby, as a further Reward for his Invention for effecting a Communication with Ships stranded, whereby One hundred and twenty-nine Lives have been saved, and that the said Sum be issued and paid without any Fee or other Deduction whatsoever"
Journal
Resolution of Committee of Supply

28 Apr 1823	78 CJ 261	**Pet** (Royal Consent)
5 May 1823	78 CJ 285	Pet ref SC
16 May 1823	78 CJ 370	Leave to rep evidence
9 Jun 1823	78 CJ 379 – V	C'tee Rep by James Brogden/Ref COS
25 Jun 1823	78 CJ 422	COS Res

Appropriation Act 1823					
House of Commons			**House of Lords**		
25 Jun 1823	78 CJ 425	1R	7 Jul 1823	55 LJ 845	Brought HC/1R
26 Jun 1823	78 CJ 430	2R/C'tted CWH	14 Jul 1823	55 LJ 875	2R/C'tted CWH
28 Jun 1823	78 CJ 438	CWH adj	15 Jul 1823	55 LJ 878	CWH/Rep w/o Amds
2 Jul 1823	78 CJ 448	CWH	18 Jul 1823	55 LJ 888	3R
4 Jul 1823	78 CJ 452	Rep/Ing	19 Jul 1823	55 LJ 892	Royal Assent
4 Jul 1823	78 CJ 454	3R			
18 Jul 1823	78 CJ 482	HL pass w/o Amds			
19 Jul 1823	78 CJ 485	Royal Assent			

Parliamentary debates
None
Parliamentary papers and cases etc.
Report from the Select Committee on Captain Manby's Apparatus for Saving the Lives of Shipwrecked Seamen; &c. (1823 HC Papers 351), Vol 4, p 155
Also see: Papers relating to Captain Manby's plan for affording relief in cases of shipwreck (1816 HC Papers 409), Vol 19, p 193
Newspaper coverage of debates
Pet: **Morning Chronicle, 29 Apr 1823**; **Morning Post, 29 Apr 1823**; **Public Ledger and Daily Advertiser, 29 Apr 1823**; *Morning Advertiser, 29 Apr 1823*
COS Rep: *Morning Chronicle, 10 Jun 1823*; *Morning Post, 10 Jun 1823*; *The Times, 21 Jun 1823*
Notes
The was the last of four rewards paid to Manby (Manby received three further rewards: PRZA32, PRZA35 and PRZA37)

John McAdam 1826

PRZA40	1826
	John McAdam for improvement in constructing roads
	£2000

Appropriation Act 1825 (6 Geo 4. c. 134), s 9

"And it is hereby also enacted, That out of all or any of the Aids or Supplies aforesaid, there may be issued and applied … any Sum or Sums of Money not exceeding Two thousand Pounds, to enable His Majesty to remunerate John Louden McAdam, for the Service which he has rendered by the Introduction of a valuable Improvement in the Method of constructing the public Roads of this Country, and that the said Sum be issued and paid without any Fee or other Deduction whatsoever"

Journal

Resolution of Committee of Supply

19 May 1820	75 CJ 229	**Pet/Ref SC**
26 May 1820	75 CJ 246	SC member added
31 May 1820	75 CJ 261	SC member added
16 Jun 1820	75 CJ 321	SC member added
18 Jul 1820	75 CJ 465	Rep of SC by Davies Gilbert
27 Mar 1821	76 CJ 204	A/C MacAdam
5 Apr 1821	76 CJ 233	MacAdam A/C Pres
14 May 1823	78 CJ 309	**Pet** (Royal Consent)
23 May 1823	78 CJ 333	Pet ref SC
26 May 1823	78 CJ 341	Leave for HL to be Wit
5 Jun 1823	78 CJ 368	SC sit out of session
20 Jun 1823	78 CJ 412	SC Rep
19 May 1824	79 CJ 386	Royal Address for information about McAdam's salaries
14 Apr 1825	80 CJ 304	Pet Against reward
22 Apr 1825	80 CJ 334	McAdam Ord salaries
29 Apr 1825	80 CJ 352	Return for McAdam salaries
3 May 1825	80 CJ 369	Pet Against reward
13 May 1825	80 CJ 414	COS
1 Jun 1825	80 CJ 476	COS Rep
2 Jun 1825	80 CJ 482	Pet Against reward
2 Jun 1825	80 CJ 484	COS Res £2000

Appropriation Act 1825

7 Jun 1825	80 CJ 501	Bill Ord	30 Jun 1825	57 LJ 1200	Brought HC/1R
8 Jun 1825	80 CJ 509	1R	1 Jul 1825	57 LJ 1207	2R/C'tted CWH
8 Jun 1825	80 CJ 511	2R/C'tted	2 Jul 1825	57 LJ 1256	CWH/Rep w/o Amds
14 Jun 1825	80 CJ 538	CWH adj	5 Jul 1825	57 LJ 1285	3R
17 Jun 1825	80 CJ 551	Receive Clause/CWH	6 Jul 1825	57 LJ 1294	Royal Assent
20 Jun 1825	80 CJ 575	Rep adj			
23 Jun 1825	80 CJ 593	Rep/lng			
24 Jun 1825	80 CJ 601	3R			
5 Jul 1825	80 CJ 629	HL pass w/o Amds			
6 Jul 1825	80 CJ 642	Royal Assent			

Parliamentary debates

Pet Ag Rew: **HC Deb, 15 Apr 1825, Vol 12(2nd), col 1352–1354**

COS Res: **HC Deb, 13 May 1825, Vol 13(2nd), col 593–599**

Parliamentary papers and cases etc.

Report from Select Committee on Mr. McAdam's Petition, relating to his improved system of constructing and repairing the public roads of the kingdom (1823 HC Papers 476), Vol 5, p 53

Mr. McAdam. Return of salaries, gratuities, or remunerations, due and to be received by Messieurs McAdam; 1818–1825 (1825 HC Papers 248), Vol 20, p 149

Newspaper coverage of debates

Speech for a grant: **The Times, 16 Apr 1825; Morning Chronicle, 16 Apr 1825; Morning Post, 16 Apr 1825**; *Morning Advertiser, 16 Apr 1825*; Public Ledger and Daily Advertiser, 16 Apr 1825; London Courier and Evening Gazette, 16 Apr 1825

COS Debate: **The Times, 14 May 1825; Morning Advertiser, 14 May 1825; Morning Chronicle, 14 May 1825; Morning Post, 14 May 1825; Public Ledger and Daily Advertiser, 14 May 1825; London Courier and Evening Gazette, 14 May 1825**

Thomas Morton 1833

PRZA41	1833

Thomas Morton for patent slip

£2500

Appropriation Act 1833 (3 & 4 Will 4. c. 96), s 17
"And it is hereby also enacted, That out of all or any the Aids or Supplies aforesaid there shall and may be issued and applied … any Sum or Sums of Money not exceeding Two thousand five hundred Pounds, to defray, to the Thirty-first Day of March One thousand eight hundred and thirty-four, the Charge of a Grant to Mr Morton on account of his Invention of a Patent Slip, and that the said Sum be issued and paid without any Fee or other Deduction whatsoever"

Journal

Resolution of Committee of Supply		
15 Dec 1831	87 CJ 25	Pet for Bill
5 Mar 1832	87 CJ 163	Pet Rep/Bill Ord
5 Mar 1832	87 CJ 166	1R
28 Mar 1832	87 CJ 230	2R adj
16 Aug 1833	88 CJ 684	COS Res
17 Aug 1833	88 CJ 689	COS Res (£2500)

Journal					
House of Commons			**House of Lords**		
20 Aug 1833	88 CJ 700	1R	24 Aug 1833	65 LJ 621	Brought HC/1R
21 Aug 1833	88 CJ 703	2R/C'tted CWH	26 Aug 1833	65 LJ 627	2R/C'tted CWH
22 Aug 1833	88 CJ 711	CWH	27 Aug 1833	65 LJ 630	CWH/Rep w/o Amds
23 Aug 1833	88 CJ 716	Rep/Ing	28 Aug 1833	65 LJ 636	3R
24 Aug 1833	88CJ 721	3R	29 Aug 1833	65 LJ 642	Royal Assent
28 Aug 1833	88 CJ 727	HL pass w/o Amds			
29 Aug 1833	88 CJ 734	Royal Assent			

Parliamentary debates
COS Res: Mirror of Parliament, 16 Aug 1833, Vol 4, p 3879

Parliamentary papers and cases etc.
Report from the Select Committee appointed to consider how far it is expedient to extend the patent granted for Morton's slip (1831–32 HC Papers 380), Vol 5, p 295
Estimates, &c. Miscellaneous services: for four quarters of 1833–34 (1833 HC Papers 168), Vol 14, p 451 (at p 6) [Estimate for payment of reward]

Newspaper coverage of debates
2R adj: *Public Ledger and Daily Advertiser, 29 Mar 1832*; Morning Advertiser, 29 Mar 1832
COS Res Supply: The Times, 17 Aug 1833; Morning Advertiser, 17 Aug 1833; Morning Chronicle, 17 Aug 1833; London Courier and Evening Gazette, 17 Aug 1833

Notes
This prize began as attempt to extend a patent: see PRVB84

Henry Fourdrinier and Sealy Fourdrinier 1840

PRZA42	1840

Henry and Sealy Fourdrinier for improvements in the manufacture of paper

£7000

Appropriation Act 1840 (3 & 4 Vict. c. 112), s 16
"And it is hereby also enacted, That out of all or any the Aids or Supplies aforesaid there shall and may be issued and applied … any Sum or Sums of Money not exceeding Seven thousand Pounds, to enable Her Majesty to make a Grant to Messieurs Fourdrinier, in consideration of the great Benefits conferred on the Public by the Introduction of their Machinery for the Improvement of the Manufacture of Paper"

(continued)

(continued)

Journal		
Resolution of Committee of Supply		
31 Mar 1840	95 CJ 239	Estimate of grant Pres
4 Mar 1840	95 CJ 303	Ref COS
16 May 1840	95 CJ 341	COS Res

Appropriation Act 1840					
House of Commons			**House of Lords**		
30 Jul 1840	95 CJ 584	1R	4 Aug 1840	72 LJ 603	Brought HC/1R
31 Jul 1840	95 CJ 591	2R/C'tted CWH	5 Aug 1840	72 LJ 609	2R/C'tted CWH
1 Aug 1840	95 CJ 595	CWH	6 Aug 1840	72 LJ 620	CWH/Rep w/o Amds
3 Aug 1840	95 CJ 598	Rep/Ing	10 Aug 1840	72 LJ 659	3R
4 Aug 1840	95 CJ 605	3R	11 Aug 1840	72 LJ 681	Royal Assent
10 Aug 1840	95 CJ 650	HL pass w/o Amds			
11 Aug 1840	95 CJ 670	Royal Assent			

Parliamentary debates
Motion: **HC Deb, 25 Apr 1839, Vol 47 (3rd), col 512–522**
Supply: **HC Deb, 8 May 1840, Vol 54 (3rd), col 1328–1330**
Pets: Mirror, 4 Jul 1838, Vol 7, p 5251
Pet: Mirror, 10 Jul 1838, Vol 7, p 5400
Pet: Mirror, 16 Jul 1838, Vol 7, p 5535
Pet: Mirror, 17 Jul 1838, Vol 7, p 5574
Pet: Mirror, 18 Jul 1838, Vol 7, p 5603
Rep Cons: **Mirror, 25 Feb 1839, p 2066–2071**

Parliamentary papers and cases etc.
Estimate of the Amount required to make a Grant to Messrs Fourdrinier for the Introduction of their Machinery for the Improvement of Manufacture of Paper (1840 HC Papers 179, IV), Vol 30, p 843, p 11

Newspaper coverage of debates
Rep (Re-C'tted): **The Times, 26 Apr 1839**; **Morning Chronicle, 26 Apr 1839**; **Morning Post, 26 Apr 1839**; **Evening Chronicle, 26 Apr 1839**; **Evening Mail, 26 Apr 1839**; **London Evening Standard, 26 Apr 1839**; *Morning Advertiser, 26 Apr 1839*; *London Courier and Evening Gazette, 26 April 1839*
Supply Debate: The Times, 9 May 1840; Morning Post, 9 May 1840; London Evening Standard, 9 May 1840

Notes
The Fourdrinier brothers obtained a private Act to extend their patent (PRVA33), but the patent was revoked. They then unsuccessfully sought two further private acts to revive and extend the patent (PRVB74 and PRVB85)
There were a number of petitions from those in the industry: see PET55; PET77 to PET83; PET86 to PET104

William Snow Harris 1853

PRZA43	1853
Sir William Snow Harris for lightning conductors	
£5000	
Appropriation Act 1853 (16 & 17 Vict. c. 110), s 26	
"Out of all or any the Aids or Supplies aforesaid there shall and may be issued and applied … any Sum or Sums of Money not exceeding Five thousand Pounds, to enable Her Majesty to make Compensation to Sir William Snow Harris for his Expenditure of Time and Money in perfecting a Mode of applying Electrical Conductors on board Ships"	
Journal	
Resolution of Committee of Supply	

5 Aug 1853	108 CJ 794	COS Res
8 Aug 1853	108 CJ 804	COS Res Agreed

Appropriation Act 1853

House of Commons			House of Lords		
10 Aug 1853	108 CJ 812	Pres/1R	15 Aug 1853	85 LJ 648	Brought HC/1R
10 Aug 1853	108 CJ 813	2R/C'tted CWH	15 Aug 1853	85 LJ 650	2R day app
11 Aug 1853	108 CJ 817	CWH	16 Aug 1853	85 LJ 671	2R/Com neg
12 Aug 1853	108 CJ 821	Rep	18 Aug 1853	85 LJ 701	3R
13 Aug 1853	108 CJ 822	3R	20 Aug 1853	85 LJ 717	Royal Assent
19 Aug 1853	108 CJ 840	HL pass w/o Amds			
20 Aug 1853	108 CJ 846	Royal Assent			

Parliamentary debates

Res: **HC Deb, 5th Aug 1853, Vol 129 (3rd), col 1412**

Parliamentary papers and cases etc.

Estimates for Civil services, 1853–54 (VIII) (1852–53 HC Papers 824), Vol 58, p 547 at p 7

Newspaper coverage of debates

COS Res: **Morning Advertiser, 6 Aug 1853**; **Morning Chronicle, 6 Aug 1853**; **Morning Post, 6 Aug 1853**; **London Daily News, 6 Aug 1853**; **London Evening Standard, 6 Aug 1853**

Notes

Report and evidence from the commission appointed to inquire into the plan of Sir William Snow Harris, Esq. FRS relating to the protection of ships from the effects of lightning. (1840 HC Papers 64), Vol 45, p 127

There were a number of mentions of the invention:

HC Deb, 23 April 1839, Vol 47(3rd), col 474–477

HL Deb, 18 Feb 1841, Vol 56(3rd), col 707–722

HL Deb, 25 Feb 1841, Vol 56(3rd), col 1019–1020

HL Deb, 11 May 1849, Vol 105(3rd), col 257–258

HC Deb, 25 July 1851, Vol 118(3rd), col 1554–1555 (mentioned during passage of Patent Law Amendment Bill)

See earlier petition: PET84

Peter Andreas Hansen 1860

PRZA44	1860

(Professor) Peter Andreas Hansen for lunar tables

£1000

Appropriation Act 1860 (23 & 24 Vict. c 131), s 27   "Out of all or any the Aids or Supplies aforesaid there shall and may be issued and applied … any Sum or Sums of Money not exceeding One thousand Pounds, as a Grant to Professor Hansen of Gotha in acknowledgement of the practical Value of his Lunar Tables to Her Majesty's Navy and the British Mercantile Marine"

Journal

Resolution of Committee of Supply

20 Aug 1860	115 CJ 488	COS Res

Appropriation Act 1860

House of Commons			House of Lords		
20 Aug 1860	115 CJ 488	Bill Ord	23 Aug 1860	92 LJ 712	Brought HC
20 Aug 1860	115 CJ 488	1R	23 Aug 1860	92 LJ 720	1R
21 Aug 1860	115 CJ 491	2R/C'tted CWH	24 Aug 1860	92 LJ 722	2R/Com neg
22 Aug 1860	115 CJ 496	CWH/Rep	25 Aug 1860	92 LJ 725	3R
23 Aug 1860	115 CJ 500	3R	28 Aug 1860	92 LJ 732	Royal Assent
28 Aug 1860	115 CJ 501	HL pass w/o Amds			
28 Aug 1860	115 CJ 508	Royal Assent			

Parliamentary debates

COS Res: HC Deb, 18 August 1860, 3rd Series, Vol 160, col 1546

Parliamentary papers and cases etc.

(continued)

(continued)

Civil services estimates, 1860–61 (VII) (1860 HC Papers 203), Vol 43, p 319 at p 38
Newspaper coverage of debates
None
Notes
Professor Hansen was also paid £100 in two instalments by the Navy to produce the tables:
Navy estimates for the year 1856–57 (1856 HC Papers 16), Vol 29, p 149 at p 24
Navy estimates for the year 1857–58 (1857 Sess 1 HC Papers 20), Vol 8, p 20 at p 25

Percy Scott 1872

PRZA45	1872

£2000 + £6000
(Captain) Percy Scott for gunnery inventions

Appropriation Act 1872 (35 & 36 Vict. c 87), s 3 and Sch B-Part 2, Navy

s 3 "All sums granted by this Act and the other Acts mentioned in Schedule (A.) annexed to this Act out of the said Consolidated Fund towards making good the supply granted to Her Majesty, amounting, as appears by the said Schedule, in the aggregate to the sum of forty-three million six hundred and fifteen thousand five hundred and sixty-seven pounds three shillings and threepence, are appropriated and shall be deemed to have been appropriated as from the date of the passing of the first of the Acts mentioned in the said Schedule (A.) for the purposes and services expressed in Schedule (B.) annexed hereto.

The abstract of schedules and schedules annexed hereto, with the notes (if any) to such schedules, shall be deemed to be part of this Act, in the same manner as if they had been contained in the body thereof."

"Schedule (B) – Part 2 Supplementary – Navy, viz– Miscellaneous grant to Captain Scott, RN [£2000]"

Appropriation Act 1873 (36 & 37 Vict. c. 79), s 3 and Sch B

s 3 "All sums granted by this Act and the other Acts mentioned in Schedule (A.) annexed to this Act out of the said Consolidated Fund towards making good the supply granted to Her Majesty, amounting, as appears by the said Schedule, in the aggregate to the sum of forty-seven million seven hundred and eighty-eight thousand and sixty-two pounds nineteen shillings and ninepence, are appropriated and shall be deemed to have been appropriated as from the date of the passing of the first of the Acts mentioned in the said Schedule (A.) for the purposes and services expressed in Schedule (B.) annexed hereto.

The abstract of schedules and schedules annexed hereto, with the notes (if any) to such schedules, shall be deemed to be part of this Act in the same manner as if they had been contained in the body thereof."

"Schedule (B) – Part 2 Supplementary – Navy, viz– Miscellaneous – reward to Captain Scott, RN, for his gunnery inventions [£6000]"

Journal		
Resolution of Committee of Supply		
12 Mar 1872	127 CJ 87	COS Res (£2000)
10 Aug 1872	128 CJ 56	COS Res (£6000)

Appropriation Act 1872					
House of Commons			**House of Lords**		
7 May 1872	127 CJ 181	Bill Ord	10 May 1872	104 LJ 286	Brought HC
7 May1872	127 CJ 184	1R	11 May 1872	104 LJ 288	1R
8 May1872	127 CJ 187	2R/C'tted CWH	11 May 1872	104 LJ 294	2R/Com neg/3R
10 May1872	127 CJ 192	CWH/Rep	13 May 1872	104 LJ 298	Royal Assent
10 May1872	127 CJ 195	3R			
13 May1872	127 CJ 199	HL pass w/o Amds			
13 May1872	127 CJ 196	Royal Assent			

Appropriation Act 1873					
House of Commons			**House of Lords**		
17 May 1873	128 CJ 224	Bill Ord	23 May 1872	105 LJ 386	Brought HC
17 May 1873	128 CJ 225	1R	23 May 1872	105 LJ 387	1R
20 May 1873	128 CJ 229	2R/C'tted CWH	26 May 1872	105 LJ 399	2R/C'tted CWH
21 May 1873	128 CJ 234	CWH/Rep	27 May 1872	105 LJ 408	CWH/Rep w/o Amds
22 May 1873	128 CJ 238	3R	9 Jun 1872	105 LJ 413	3R
10 Jun 1873	128 CJ 269	HL pass w/o Amds	16 Jun 1872	105 LJ 437	Royal Assent
16 Jun 1873	128 CJ 279	Royal Assent			
Parliamentary debates					
None					
Parliamentary papers and cases etc.					
Navy Estimates: 1873–74 (HC Papers 60), Vol 42, p 60 at p 115					
Newspaper coverage of debates					
None					

2 Parliamentary rewards sought but not granted

John Wadsworth 1747

PRZC1		1747	
Proposed reward: No estimate			
John Wadsworth for paper cartridges for artillery			
Journal			
House of Commons			
6 Feb 1747	25 CJ 276	**Pet/Motion to ref C'tee neg**	
Parliamentary debates			
None			
Parliamentary papers and cases etc.			
None			
Notes			
The petition is included in Failed Legislation [FL: 85.010]			

Henry Delamaine 1754

PRZC2		1754	
Proposed reward: No estimate			
Henry Delamaine's Kilns for burning earthenware			
Journal			
House of Commons			
21 Jan 1754	26 CJ 913	**Pet (Royal consent)/Ref C'tee**	
Parliamentary debates			
None			
Parliamentary papers and cases etc.			
None			
Newspaper coverage of debates			
Pet: Gentleman's Magazine (21 Jan 1754) September 1754, Vol 23, p 437			
Notes			
The petition is included in failed legislation [FL: 92.010]			

Charles Dingley 1768

PRZC3	1768
Proposed reward: No estimate	
Charles Dingley for his saw mill	
Journal	
House of Commons	

19 May 1768	32 CJ 15	**Pet/Lie on the table**
Parliamentary debates		
None		
Parliamentary papers and cases etc.		
None		
Newspaper coverage of debates		
None		
Notes		
The petition was included in failed legislation [FL 109.003]. He received an award in the following session: see PRZA12		

William Storer 1780

PRZC4	1780
Proposed reward: No estimate	
William Storer for optical instruments	
Journal	
House of Commons	

8 Feb 1780	37 CJ 579	**Pet** (Royal consent)**/Ref C'tee**
Parliamentary debates		
None		
Parliamentary papers and cases etc.		
None		
Newspaper coverage of debates		
None		

Henry Phillips 1781

PRZC5	1781
Proposed reward: £500 and £3000	
Henry Phillip Composition for destroying insects [FL: 122.047]	

Bill for providing a reward to Henry Phillips, on his revealing for the public use the composition of his powder for the destruction of insects

"And be it enacted by the King's most Excellent Majesty by and with the advice and consent of the Lords Spiritual and temporal and Commons in this present Parliament assembled and by the authority of the same that out of all or any the aids or supplies granted to his Majesty for the service of the year one thousand seven hundred and eighty one there shall and may be applied and paid to the said Henry Phillips his executors and administrators the sum of five hundred pounds immediately after the passing of this Act and that the further sum of three thousand pounds shall be paid to the said Henry Phillips his executors or assigns upon his or their making a proper discovery for the use of the public of the composition of the said powder for the destruction of insects and also upon the said Henry Phillips his executors administrators and assigns presenting to the Commissioners of his Majesty's Treasury or any three or more of them or the Lord High Treasurer for the time being a certificate signed by any three or more of the Commissioners of the Navy of the efficacy of the said powder in the preservation of dry provisions on board of his Majesty's Ships of War and also of his having made a full discovery of the materials of the said powder and the method of preparing and using the same and the commissioners of his Majesty's Treasury or any three or more of them or the Lord High Treasurer or any three or more of the commissioners of the treasury for the time being are thereby authorised and required to direct the payment of an issue the said sum of six hundred pounds and three thousand pounds respectively to the said Henry Phillips his executors administrators or assigns and that the said sum shall be issued and paid without any fees or deductions whatsoever"

Journal	
House of Commons	**House of Lords**
Pres: Sir Gilbert Elliot Rep: Edmund Burke	

(continued)

(continued)

21 Mar 1781	38 CJ 311	**Pet**	26 Jun 1781	36 LJ 330	Brought HC/1R	
16 May 1781	38 CJ 467	**Pet ref**	27 Jun 1781	36 LJ 331	2R day app/A/Cs Ord	
6 Jun 1781	38 CJ 504	Ref COS	28 Jun 1781	36 LJ 331	A/C Pres	
7 Jun 1781	38 CJ 506 – V	COS Res	28 Jun 1781	36 LJ 332 – V	2R/C'tted CWH	
8 Jun 1781	38 CJ 508	Ord/1R	29 Jun 1781	36 LJ 334	CWH	
13 Jun 1781	38 CJ 514	2R/C'tted CWH	2 Jul 1781	36 LJ 335	Papers Ord	
21 Jun 1781	38 CJ 533	CWH	3 Jul 1781	36 LJ 341	Wit/CWH	
22 Jun 1781	38 CJ 535	Rep with Amds/Ing	5 Jul 1781	36 LJ 345	Wit Sum	
26 Jun 1781	38 CJ 538	3R	10 Jul 1781	36 LJ 354	Experiments/CWH adj	
			21 Jun 1782	36 LJ 543	Letter from Admiralty	

Parliamentary debates
None

Parliamentary papers and cases etc.
None

Newspaper coverage of debates

House of Commons

Ref COS: *St. James's Chronicle or the British Evening Post, 5–7 Jun 1781*; *Lloyd's Evening Post, 6–8 Jun 1781*; *London Courant and Westminster Chronicle, 7 Jun 1781*; *Stamford Mercury, 14 Jun 1781*; *Newcastle Chronicle, 16 Jun 1781*

COS Res: **Morning Chronicle and London Advertiser, 7 Jun 1781**; **London Courant and Westminster Chronicle, 8 Jun 1781**; *Lloyd's Evening Post, 6–8 Jun 1781*; *Morning Herald and Daily Advertiser, 7 Jun 1781*; *St. James's Chronicle or the British Evening Post, 7–9 Jun 1781*; *St. James's Chronicle or the British Evening Post, 7–9 Jun 1781*; *Leeds Intelligencer, 12 Jun 1781*; *Public Advertiser, 6 Jun 1781*

2R: *St. James's Chronicle or the British Evening Post, 12–14 Jun 1781*; *Public Advertiser, 14 Jun 1781*; *London Courant and Westminster Chronicle, 14 Jun 1781*; *Stamford Mercury, 21 Jun 1781*; *Stamford Mercury, 14 Jun 1781*; *Hampshire Chronicle, 18 Jun 1781*

CWH: Morning Chronicle and London Advertiser, 22 Jun 1781

Rep: Morning Chronicle and London Advertiser, 23 Jun 1781

House of Lords

1R: Morning Chronicle and London Advertiser, 27 Jun 1781

2R: *London Chronicle, 28–30 Jun 1781*; *London Courant and Westminster Chronicle, 29 Jun 1781*; *Morning Chronicle and London Advertiser, 29 Jun 1781*; Morning Herald and Daily Advertiser, 30 Jun 1781; Hampshire Chronicle, 2 Jul 1781; Saunders's News-Letter, 6 Jul 1781; Hibernian Journal or, Chronicle of Liberty, 6 Jul 1781

CWH: *Morning Chronicle and London Advertiser, 30 Jun 1781*; Public Advertiser, 30 Jun 1781

Papers Ord: Morning Chronicle and London Advertiser, 3 Jul 1781

CWH: **St. James's Chronicle or the British Evening Post, 3–5 Jul 1781**; **Morning Chronicle and London Advertiser, 4 July 1781**; **Morning Herald and Daily Advertiser, 4 Jul 1781**; **Stamford Mercury, 12 Jul 1781**; Public Advertiser, 4 July 1781; Hampshire Chronicle, 9 Jul 1781

Wit Sum: Morning Chronicle and London Advertiser, 6 Jul 1781

CWH adj: **Ipswich Journal, 14 Jul 1781**; **Dublin Evening Post, 17 Jul 1781**; **Newcastle Chronicle, 21 Jul 1781 (Lord Abingdon's Speech)**; *Caledonian Mercury, 16 Jul 1781*; *Hampshire Chronicle, 16 Jul 1781*; *Stamford Mercury, 19 Jul 1781*; *Newcastle Chronicle, 21 Jul 1781*

Abstract of Bill: Morning Chronicle and London Advertiser, 29 Jun 1781

Notes

Archive

2 Jul 1781: Letter from Grenada Merchants: HL/PO/JO/10/7/629

2 Jul 1781: Letter from Commissioner of Victualling: HL/PO/JO/10/7/629

2 Jul 1781: Further evidence: HL/PO/JO/10/7/629

5 Jul 1781: Witness Summons (John Dudgeon): HL/PO/JO/10/7/629

10 Jul 1781: Address for Account of Experiments: HL/PO/JO/10/7/631

21 Jun 1782: Letter from Commissioner for Victualling: HL/PO/JO/10/7/650

28 May 1783: Experiments ordered: HL/PO/JO/10/7/658

17 Jun 1783: Papers Respecting Powder: HL/PO/JO/10/7/660

26 June 1781 – Ing: Bill for providing a reward to Henry Phillips, on his revealing for the public use the composition of his powder for the destruction of insects: HL/PO/JO/10/2/56

This was the first of four failed attempts for rewards: see PRZC6, PRZC7 and PRZC8

Henry Phillips 1783

PRZC6	1783				
Proposed reward: No estimate					
Henry Phillip Composition for destroying insects					
Journal					
House of Commons			**House of Lords**		
Rep: John Luttrell					
17 June 1783	39 CJ 488	**Pet**/Ref C'tee neg	28 May 1783	36 LJ 686	Address/Rep read
10 Dec 1783	39 CJ 832	**Pet** (Royal consent)/Ref C'tee	17 June 1783	36 LJ 694	A/C provided
16 Mar 1784	39 CJ 1031	**Pet Rep**/Lie on table			
Parliamentary debates					
None					
Parliamentary papers and cases etc.					
None					
Newspaper coverage of debates					
None					
Notes					
This was the second of four failed attempts for rewards: see PRZC5, PRZC7 and PRZC8					

Henry Phillips 1784

PRZC7	1784	
Proposed reward: No estimate		
Henry Phillip Composition for destroying insects		
Journal		
House of Commons		
27 May 1784	40 CJ 31	**Pet** (Royal consent)/Ref C'tee
15 Jun 1784	40 CJ 206	**Pet rep by John Luttrell**
18 Jun 1784	40 CJ 222	Admiralty Papers Pres
23 Jun 1784	40 CJ 249	Rep read/Ref COS
Parliamentary debates		
None		
Parliamentary papers and cases etc.		
None		
Newspaper coverage of debates		
None		
Notes		
It was included in failed legislation [FL: 122.047]. This was the third of four failed attempts for rewards: see PRZC5, PRZC6 and PRZC8		

Henry Phillips 1785

PRZC8	1785
Proposed reward: £1000	
Phillips' Insect Destroying Power [FL: 127.055]	
Bill for providing a Reward to Henry Phillips on his making a proper Discovery for the Use of the Public of the Composition of his Powder for the Destruction of Insects "shall and may be issued applied and paid to the said Henry Phillips his executors administrators or assigns the sum of one thousand pounds upon his or their making a proper discovery for the use of the powder for the destruction of	

(continued)

(continued)

insects and also upon the said Henry Phillips his executors administrators or assigns producing to the commissioners of his Majesty's Treasury or any three or more of them or the Lord High Treasurer for the time being a certificate signed by any three of the commissioners of the navy of the efficacy of the said powder in the preservation of dry provisions on board of his Majesty's Shops of war and also of his having made a full discovery of the materials of the said powder and the method of preparing and using the same and the commissioners of his Majesty's Treasury or any three of more of them now being or the Lord High Treasurer or any three or more of the Commissioners of the Treasury for the time being one hereby authorized and required to divert the payment of and issued the said sum of one thousand pounds to the said Henry Phillips his executors administrators or assigns that out of all or any the aids or supplies granted to his Majesty for the service of the year one thousand seven hundred and eight five there"

Journal					
House of Commons			**House of Lords**		
Pres: Sir James Johnstone Pet Rep: Henry Pye Bill Rep: Thomas Gilbert					
7 Mar 1785	40 CJ 596	**Pet**/Ref C'tee	11 Jul 1785	37 LJ 351	Brought HC/1R
14 Mar1785	40 CJ 631	Papers ref C'tee	20 Jul 1785	37LJ 368 – V	2R/C'tted
11 Apr1785	40 CJ 832	**Pet Rep**	20 Jul 1785	37LJ 368	Address relating to use
20 Jun 1785	40 CJ 1090	Rep ref COS	25 Jul 1785	37 CJ 373	Bill adj sine dine
21 Jun 1785	40 CJ 1092	COS Res			
1 Jul 1785	40 CJ 1119	Bill Ord			
4 Jul 1785	40 CJ 1120	1R			
6 Jul 1785	40 CJ 1128	2R/C'tted CWH			
7 Jul 1785	40 CJ 1132	CWH			
8 Jul 1785	40 CJ 1132	Rep with Amds/Ing			
11 Jul 1785	40 CJ 1135	3R			

Parliamentary debates
None

Parliamentary papers and cases etc.
None

Newspaper coverage of debates

House of Commons

Rep ref SOC: *The Times, 21 Jun 1785*; St. James's Chronicle or the British Evening Post, 18–21 Jun 1785; General Advertiser, 21 Jun 1785; Chelmsford Chronicle, 24 Jun 1785; Kentish Gazette, 24 Jun 1785; Stamford Mercury, 24 Jun 1785; Caledonian Mercury, 25 Jun 1785; Ipswich Journal, 25 Jun 1785; Newcastle Courant, 25 Jun 1785; Saunders's News-Letter, 27 Jun 1785; Sussex Advertiser, 27 Jun 1785

CWH: Kentish Gazette, 12 Jul 1785

2R: Hampshire Chronicle, 11 Jul 1785

3R: Morning Chronicle and London Advertiser, 12 Jul 1785

House of Lords

1R: *The Times, 13 Jul 1785*; General Evening Post, 12–14 Jul 1785

2R: *Whitehall Evening Post, 19–21 July 1785*; *Public Advertiser, 21 Jul 1785*; *Oxford Journal, 23 Jul 1785*; Whitehall Evening Post, 18–21 Jun 1785; Morning Herald and Daily Advertiser, 21 Jun 1785; Public Advertiser, 21 Jul 1785; Stamford Mercury, 29 Jul 1785

Adj sin die: **Saunder's News-Letter, 27 Jul 1785**; *General Evening Post, 23–26 Jul 1785*; *Morning Herald and Daily Advertiser, 26 Jul 1785*; *Morning Post and Daily Advertiser, 26 Jul 1785*; *Kentish Gazette, 29 Jul 1785*; Leeds Intelligencer, 2 Aug 1785

Notes

Archive

20 Jul 1785: Address for papers relating to Powder: HL/PO/JO/10/7/712

Ing: 11 July 1785 – Act for providing a reward to Henry Phillips on his revealing for public use the composition of his powder for the destruction of insects: HL/PO/JO/10/2/59B

This was the final of four failed attempts for rewards: see PRZC5, PRZC6 and PRZC7

Thomas Chapman 1807

PRZC9	1807
	Proposed reward: No estimate
	Thomas Chapman for separating seal hair for use in the manufacture of hats
	**Journal**
	**House of Commons**

20 Jul 1807	62 CJ 747	**Pet** (Royal consent)
28 Jul 1807	62 CJ 790	Ref C'tee

Parliamentary debates

None

Parliamentary papers and cases etc.

None

Newspaper coverage of debates

None

Notes

Some years later Chapman was paid money out of the Civil Contingency fund for the invention, but this was not the result of Parliamentary resolution: Appendix No 3, 76 CJ 574 (76 CJ 80: 16 Feb 1621).

There were two other failed petitions for a reward: PRZC12 and PRZC15

John Palmer 1808

PRZC10	1808

Proposed reward: £54,702 0s 7d

John Palmer for setting up the postal service
(under a contract)

Journal

House of Commons			House of Lords		
Pet and Pres: Thomas Lethbridge			Rep: Lord Eliot		
24 Mar 1807	62 CJ 285	Pet	13 Jun 1808	46 LJ 711	Com App
27 Jun 1807	62 CJ 572	Sec Pet/Royal consent	14 Jun 1808	46 LJ 713	Papers Ord
27 Jun 1807	62 CJ 575	Rep 17 Jul 1797 Re-prt	14 Jun 1808	46 LJ 715	Papers Req
30 Jun 1807	62 CJ 596	Ref SC	15 Jun 1808	46 LJ 716	Wit Ord
13 Jul 1807	62 CJ 697	SC Rep/Prt	15 Jun 1808	46 LJ 718	Papers Del
20 Jul 1807	62 CJ 748	Ref CWH	16 Jun 1808	46 LJ 720	Brought HC/1R
23 Jul 1807	62 CJ 766	CWH Disc	16 Jun 1808	46 LJ 720	Rep ref C'tee
1 Apr 1808	63 CJ 256	Motion/Ref CWH	17 Jun 1808	46 LJ 726	**C'tee Rep**
12 May 1808	63 CJ 319-V	Rep Rec/Neg	17 Jun 1808	46 LJ 728	Prt Bill
17 May 1808	63 CJ 337-V	Rep Rec/Neg	18 Jun 1808	46 LJ 728	Mins Pres
18 May 1808	63 CJ 340	A/Cs and Mins Pres	20 Jun 1808	46 LJ 737	2R day app
20 May 1808	63 CJ 353	Bill Ord	21 Jun 1808	46 LJ 745	2R rejected
23 May 1808	63 CJ 360	1R			
25 May 1808	63 CJ 366	A/C Pres/2R adj			
26 May 1808	63 CJ 371	A/C ref SC			
30 May 1808	63 CJ 383	2R/C'tted CWH			
3 Jun 1808	63 CJ 406	CWH adj			
8 Jun 1808	63 CJ 411	CWH			
9 Jun 1808	63 CJ 412	Rep/Ing			
10 Jun 1808	63 CJ 422	3R adj			
13 Jun 1808	63 CJ 429	SC Rep ref COS			

(continued)

(continued)

13 Jun 1808	63 CJ 431	3R adj			
14 Jun 1808	63 CJ 434	COS Rep			
14 Jun 1808	63 CJ 435	HL Req Rep			
15 Jun 1808	63 CJ 436	3R adj			
15 Jun 1808	63 CJ 439	Rep sent HL			
15 Jun 1808	63 CJ 441	3R			
		Second Bill			
23 Jun 1808	63 CJ 468	1R/COS Res			
24 Jun 1808	63 CJ 469	2R/Rep COS			

Parliamentary debates

Earlier debates

Consider Agreement: **Parliamentary Register, 31 May 1799, Vol 8, p 611–635**

Pet: **HC Deb, 25 Mar 1807, Vol 9(1st), col 220–229**

Com Res: HC Deb, 12 May 1808, Vol 11(1st), col 161–252	Rep Req: HL Deb, 13 Jun 1808, Vol 11(1st), col 870
CWH: HC Deb, 16 May 1808, Vol 11(1st), col 289–300	2R: HL Deb, 21 Jun 1808, Vol 11(1st), col 959–973
Motion for papers: **HC Deb, 18 May 1808, Vol 11(1st), col 394–395**	
Leave: HC Deb, 20 May 1808, Vol 11(1st), col 473–475	
COS: HC Deb, 13 Jun 1808, Vol 11(1st), col 865	
Separate Bill/Not Appropriation Act: HC Deb, 20 Jun 1808, Vol 11(1st), col 956	
New Bill: HC Deb, 23 Jun 1808, Vol 11(1st), col 1010–1042	

Parliamentary papers and cases etc.

Bill to secure to John Palmer, Esquire, his future per centage on the net increased revenue of the Post-Office, according to the provisions of his appointment of one thousand seven hundred and eighty-nine (1808 HC Papers 253), Vol 1, p 493

Bill to secure to John Palmer, esquire his future Per-centage on the net increased Revenue to the Post Office, according to the Provisions of his Appointment, dated 11th September 1789 (1808 HL Papers 105), Vol 15, p 765

Report from the Committee of Mr Palmer's Petition (1807 HC Papers 31), Vol 2, p 101

Minutes of Evidence before Select Committee on Petition of J. Palmer, relating to his Agreement with Post Office (1808 HC Papers 241), Vol 6, p 215

Catalogue of Papers printed by Order of the House of Commons, from the year 1731 to 1800. In the Custody of the Clerk of the Journals (1807) (Reprint: HMSO 1954): Palmer, Report Respecting Palmer's Agreement with Post Office, 1796?/7, Vol 19, No 136 (also House of Commons Papers of Eighteenth Century (1715–1800), Vol 105)

Report of the Select Committee of the House of Commons, in 1797, on the Agreement made with John Palmer, Esquire, for the Improvement of the Post Office and its Revenue (1808 HL Papers 95), Vol 18, p 1

Report from the Committee who were appointed to consider the agreement made with Mr Palmer for the reform and improvement of the Post Office (1797 Reprint) (1807 HC Papers 1), Vol 2, p 105

Account of Net Revenue of Post Office, and J Palmer's Percentage, 1793–1807 (1808 HC Papers 259), Vol 6, p 221

Warrant of the Treasury to the Postmaster Genera to make out the Commission for Mr Palmer to Surveyor and Report from the Committee on Mr Palmer's Account (1808 HC Papers 294), Vol 3, p 155

Report from the Lords Committee, in 1808, on the Agreement with Mr Palmer for this Reform and Improvement of the Post Office, and to inquire into the Causes of his Suspension from the Office of Comptroller General (1808 HL Papers 111), Vol 18, p 169

Return from the Treasure and Postmaster General's Minute; dated 7th March 1792, respecting the Suspension and Dismissal of John Palmer, Esquire, from the Office of Comptroller General of the Post Office (1808 HL Papers 112), Vol 18, p 177

Newspaper coverage of debates

Earlier proceedings

Cons Ag: **The Times, 1 Jun 1799**

Pet: *Morning Post, 25 Mar 1807*

Cons Pet: **The Times, 1 Jul 1807; Morning Post, 1 Jul 1807**

Rep: *Morning Post, 14 Jul 1807*

Pet: **The Times, 13 May 1808; Morning Advertiser, 13 May 1808; Morning Chronicle, 13 May 1808; Morning Post, 13 May 1808; Public Ledger and Daily Advertiser, 13 May 1808**

Rep Pet: **The Times, 17 May 1808**; **Morning Chronicle, 17 May 1808**; **Morning Post, 17 May 1808**; **Public Ledger and Daily Advertiser, 17 May 1808**

Ref: **The Times, 21 May 1808**; **Morning Advertiser, 21 May 1808**; **Morning Chronicle, 21 May 1808**; **Morning Post, 21 May 1808**; **Cobett's Weekly Political Register, 21 May 1808**; **Public Ledger and Daily Advertiser, 21 May 1808**

First Bill

1R: **Morning Advertiser, 24 May 1808**; **Morning Post, 24 May 1808**; The Times, 24 May 1808

2R adj: **The Times, 26 May 1808**; **Morning Post, 26 May 1808**; **Public Ledger and Daily Advertiser, 26 May 1808**

A/C Ord: **The Times, 27 May 1808**

2R: **Morning Advertiser, 31 May 1808**; **Morning Chronicle, 31 May 1808**; **Public Ledger and Daily Advertiser, 31 May 1808**

Rep: *Morning Advertiser, 10 Jun 1808*; *Morning Chronicle, 10 Jun 1808*; *Morning Post, 10 Jun 1808*; *Public Ledger and Daily Advertiser, 10 Jun 1808*

Separate Bill: Morning Chronicle 21 Jun 1808; Morning Post, 21 Jun 1808

Second Bill- House of Commons

Obs: The Times, 13 Jun 1808

COS: The Times, 14 Jun 1808; Morning Advertiser, 14 Jun 1808

Papers: The Times, 15 Jun 1808

Leave: **Morning Chronicle, 24 Jun 1808**; **Morning Post, 24 Jun 1808**

1R: **Morning Chronicle, 25 Jun 1808**; **Morning Post, 25 Jun 1808**; *Public Edger and Daily Advertiser, 25 Jun 1808*

2R rej: *Morning Chronicle, 27 Jun 1808*; *Morning Post, 27 Jun 1808*

House of Lords

Comment: Morning Chronicle, 14 Jun 1808; Morning Post, 14 Jun 1808

Papers laid before House: Morning Advertiser, 15 Jun 1808

Rep brought HL: Morning Advertiser, 16 Jun 1808; Morning Chronicle, 16 Jun 1808

Obs: The Times, 21 Jun 1808;

2R: **The Times, 22 Jun 1808**; **Morning Chronicle, 22 Jun 1808**; **Morning Post, 22 Jun 1808**; *Morning Advertiser, 22 Jun 1808*; *Public Ledger and Daily Advertiser, 22 Jun 1808*

Comment: **The Times, 24 Jun 1808**

Comment: *The Times, 25 Jun 1808*

Notes
There was a second Bill in 1812 (PRZC14), and finally an award was made: see PRZA36

Thomas Earnshaw 1809

PRZC11		1809
Proposed reward: No estimate		
Thomas Earnshaw for invention of Timekeepers for ascertaining the Longitude at Sea		
Journal		
House of Commons		
24 Feb 1808	63 CJ 101	**Pet** (Royal consent)/Ref C'tee
2 Feb 1809	64 CJ 22	**Pet**/Ref C'tee
25 May 1809	64 CJ 344	C'tee Ord to rep
31 May 1809	64 CJ 363	C'tee to be revived
31 May 1809	64 CJ 367	**Rep by Davies Giddy against reward as could not decide who was first**
Parliamentary debates		
None		
Parliamentary papers and cases etc.		
Report from the committee on Mr. Earnshaw's petition (1809 HC Papers 245), Vol 3, p 379		
Newspaper coverage of debates		
None		

Thomas Chapman 1809

PRZC12	1809

PRZC12	1809
Proposed reward: No estimate	
Thomas Chapman for discovery of mode of separating fur of South Sea Seal Skin from long hair (in 1795) to be used in manufacture of hats	
Journal	
House of Commons	
24 Feb 1809 64 CJ 95 **Pet ref C'tee** (Royal consent)	
Parliamentary debates	
None	
Parliamentary papers and cases etc.	
None	
Newspaper coverage of debates	
None	
Notes	
Some years later Chapman was paid money out of the Civil Contingency fund for the invention, but this was not the result of Parliamentary resolution: Appendix No 3, 76 CJ 574 (76 CJ 80: 16 February 1621)	
There were two other failed petitions for a reward: PRZC9 and PRZC15	

Henry Cort (by Coningsby Cort) 1812

PRZC13	1812
Proposed reward: £250	
Henry Cort (by Coningsby Cort his son) for his iron furnace invention	
Journal	
House of Commons	
24 Jan 1812 67 CJ 77 **Pet** (Royal consent)	
27 Jan 1812 67 CJ 82 Ref C'tee	
4 Mar 1812 67 CJ 170 Power to Rep	
20 Mar 1812 67 CJ 217 Rep laid on the table	
10 Apr 1812 67 CJ 256 Estimate (App 3)	
3 July 1812 67 CJ 506 Estimate withdrawn	
8 July 1812 67 CJ 516 COS met to consider resolution, but no resolution as no quorum	
App (No 3) 67 CJ 653 Estimate £250	
Parliamentary debates	
Pet: HC Deb, 24 Jan 1812, Vol 21, col 329–331	
Parliamentary papers and cases etc.	
Report on Mr. Cort's petition (1812 HC Papers 118), Vol 2, p 85	
Newspaper coverage of debates	
Pet: *Globe, 25 Jan 1812; Morning Chronicle, 25 Jan 1812 (misrep)*; London Courier and Evening Gazette, 25 Jan 1812 COS: *Morning Chronicle, 9 Jul 1912; London Courier and Evening Gazette, 9 Jul 1812*; Globe, 9 Jul 1812 (res withdrawn quorum)	
Notes	
The claim was based on two patents (No 1351; 17 Jan 1783) and (No 1420; 14 Feb 1784) which were claimed never to have given any benefit to Henry Cort	

John Palmer 1812

PRZC14	1812

Proposed reward: £78, 344 12s 9d

John Palmer for the postal service (pursuant to an earlier contract)

Bill to secure to John Palmer, Esquire, his future per-centage on the net increased revenue of the Post Office; according to the provisions of his appointment of one thousand seven hundred and eighty-nine

"That the sum of Seventy-eight thousand three hundred and forty-four Pounds Twelve Shillings and Ninepence, of lawful Money of Greta Britain, shall be paid, out of any of the Aids or Supplies granted for the Service of the year one thousand eight hundred and twelve, to John Palmer, Esquire, being the Balance of the Per-Centage due to him on the net Revenue of the Post Office, from the fifth day of April one thousand seven hundred and ninety-three, to the fifth day of January one thousand eight hundred and twelve"

Journal

Pres: Charles Palmer
Rep: Stephen Rumbold Lushington

House of Commons			House of Lords		
17 Jun 1812	67 CJ 432	**Motion/1808 Res read**	29 Jun 1812	48 LJ 935	Brought HC
19 Jun 1812	67 CJ 435	Bill Ord	30 Jun 1812	48 LJ 938	1R
20 Jun 1812	67 CJ 447	1R	1 Jul 1812	48 LJ 941	Papers Ord
22 Jun 1812	67 CJ 459	2R/C'tted CWH	2 Jul 1812	48 LJ 942	Papers Ord
23 Jun 1812	67 CJ 464	CWH adj	2 Jul 1812	48 LJ 945	Papers delivered
26 Jun 1812	67 CJ 484	**Instructions to CWH**	3 Jul 1812	48 LJ 950	2R
27 Jun 1812	67 CJ 487	Rep/lng	6 Jul 1812	48 LJ 953	**Papers Ord**
29 Jun 1812	67 CJ 492	3R	6 Jul 1812	48 LJ 954	**Papers delivered**
			7 Jul 1812	48 LJ 956	Committed CWH
			20 Jul 1812	48 LJ 977	CWH/Rep w/o Amds
			14 Jul 1812	48 LJ 984	3R adj 3m

Parliamentary debates

Earlier debates

Motion for payment: **HC Deb, 25 May 1809, Vol 14(1st), col 696–711**

Motion for payment: **HC Deb, 21 May 1811, Vol 20(1st), col 255–268**

Ans to Royal Address: **HC Deb, 24 May 1811, Vol 20(1st), col 305**

Ans to Royal Address: **HC Deb, 30 May 1811, Vol 20(1st), col 343–365**

COS Res: **HC Deb, 25 Jun 1812, Vol 23(1st), col 768–771**

Parliamentary papers and cases etc.

Bill (as amended by the committee, and on the report) to secure to John Palmer, Esquire, his future per-centage on the net increased revenue of the Post Office; according to the provisions of his appointment of one thousand seven hundred and eighty-nine (1812 HC Papers 296), Vol 1, p 1171

Bill to provide for the Payment of the Arrears due to John Palmer, Esquire, from the net increased Revenue of the Post Office, and to secure his future Per-centage on the same according to the Provisions of his Appointment (1812 HL Papers 136), Vol 48, p 1127

Report of the Select Committee of the House of Commons, in 1797, on the Agreement made with John Palmer, Esquire, for the Improvement of the Post Office and its Revenue (1812 HL Papers 138), Vol 53, p 265

Report from the Lords Committee, in 1808, on the Agreement with Mr Palmer for this Reform and Improvement of the Post Office, and to inquire into the Causes of his Suspension from the Office of Comptroller General (1812 HL Papers 137), Vol 53, p 257

Account of the per-centage due to Mr. Palmer, on the net revenue of the Post-Office; from 5th April 1793 to 5th January 1812 (1812 HC Papers 284), Vol 284, p 231

Account of the Per-centage, including the Salary, paid to Mr Palmer, from 5th Apr 1793 to 5th Jan 1812 (1812 HL Papers 141), Vol 53, p 133

Account of the net Revenue of the Post Office, from 6th April 1793 to 5th January 1812 (1812 HL Papers 151), Vol 53, p 443

Account of the net Revenue of the Post Office, for Ten Years ending 5th April 1789 (1812 HL Papers 156), Vol 53, p 445

Commission dated 11 October 1786 to John Palmer, Esquire, as Comptroller and Surveyor General of the Post Office (1812 HL Papers 140), Vol 53, p 437

Comptroller General of the Post Office, dated 5th Aug 1786 (1812 HL Papers 150), Vol 53, p 433

(continued)

(continued)

Newspaper coverage of debates of Debates
Earlier proceedings since 1808 Act
Motion: **The Times, 22 May 1811; The Globe, 22 May 1811;** Morning Chronicle, 22 May 1811; **Morning Post, 22 May 1811; Public Ledger and Daily Advertiser, 22 May 1811;** Evening Mail, 22 May 1811; **London Courier and Evening Gazette, 22 May 1811;**
HM Answer: **The Times, 25 May 1811; The Globe, 25 May 1811; Morning Chronicle, 25 May 1811; London Courier and Evening Gazette, 25 May 1811**
House of Commons
Rep: *The Times, 20 Jun 1812; Globe, 20 Jun 1812: Morning Chronicle, 20 Jun 1812; London Courier and Evening Gazette, 20 Jun 1812*
2R: *The Times, 23 Jun 1812; Globe, 23 Jun 1812; Morning Chronicle, 23 Jun 1812; Morning Post, 23 Jun 1812; Public Ledger and Daily Advertiser, 23 Jun 1812*
Rep: **The Times, 26 Jun 1812; Public Ledger and Daily Advertiser, 26 Jun 1812; London Courier and Evening Gazette, 26 Jun 1812;** Morning Chronicle, 26 Jun 1812; Globe, 26 Jun 1812
Rep: Morning Chronicle, 29 Jun 1812
3R: **Morning Chronicle, 30 Jun 1812;** *Public Ledger and Daily Advertiser, 30 Jun 1812*
Motion: **Globe, 23 June 1812; Morning Chronicle, 23 Jun 1812; London Courier and Evening Gazette, 23 Jun 1812; Morning Post, 23 Jun 1812; Public Ledger and Daily Advertiser, 23 Jun 1812**
COS Res: Morning Chronicle, 25 Jun 1812
Rep C'ttee on Res for £70,000: **The Times, 26 Jun 1812; Globe, 26 Jun 1812; Morning Chronicle, 26 Jun 1812; Public Ledger and Daily Advertiser, 26 Jun 1812; London Courier and Evening Gazette, 26 Jun 1812**
Obs: **The Times, 30 Jun 1812; Morning Chronicle, 30 Jun 1812; Public Ledger and Daily Advertiser, 30 Jun 1812; London Courier and Evening Gazette, 30 Jun 1812**
Comment: **The Times 14 Jul 1812; Globe, 14 Jul 1814; Morning Chronicle, 14 Jul 1812; Public Ledger and Daily Advertiser, 14 Jul 1812; London Courier and Evening Gazette, 14 Jul 1812**
House of Lords
1R: Morning Chronicle, 1 Jul 1812; London Courier and Evening Gazette, 1 Jul 1812; Globe, 1 Jul 1812
2R day app: **The Times, 2 Jul 1812; Globe, 2 Jul 1812; Morning Chronicle, 2 Jul 1812**
Papers Ord: Morning Chronicle, 3 Jul 1812
Whether motion for claim brought forward: **The Times, 4 Jul 1812;** *Globe, 4 Jul 1812; Morning Chronicle, 4 Jul 1812; London Courier and Evening Gazette, 4 Jul 1812*
2R: **The Times, 7 Jul 1812; Globe, 7 Jul 1812; Morning Chronicle, 7 Jul 1812; Public Ledger and Daily Advertiser, 7 Jul 1812; London Courier and Evening Gazette, 7 Jul 1812**
C'tted/CWH: **The Times, 11 Jul 1812; Morning Chronicle, 11 Jul 1812; Public Ledger and Daily Advertiser, 11 Jul 1812**
CWH adj: Globe, 8 Jul 1812; Morning Chronicle, 8 Jul 1812
3R: **The Times, 15 Jul 1812; Morning Chronicle, 15 Jul 1812; Public Ledger and Daily Advertiser, 15 Jul 1812; London Courier and Evening Gazette, 15 Jul 1812**
Notes
There were an earlier Bill in 1808 (PRZC10) and a successful Act (PRZA36)

Thomas Chapman 1819

PRZC15	1819
Proposed reward: No estimate	
Thomas Chapman for discovery of mode of separating fur of South Sea Seal Skin from long hair (in 1795) to be used in manufacture of hats	
Journal	
House of Commons	
4 Feb 1819	74 CJ 94	**Pet**/Lie on table
Parliamentary debates	

None
Parliamentary papers and cases etc.
None
Newspaper coverage of debates
Pet: Morning Chronicle, 5 Feb 1819; Evening Mail, 5 Feb 1819
Notes
A reward of £218 2s 6d paid from Civil List: see 76 CJ 574 (App 3); HC Papers 1821 (43), p 5 There were two other failed petitions for a reward: PRZC9 and PRZC12

William Mallison 1811–21

PRZC16	1811–21

Proposed reward: No estimate
William Mallison for preservation of life at sea (cork life jacket)
Journal
House of Commons

21 May 1811	66 CJ 357	**Pet for investigation into merits (reward)**
22 May 1811	66 CJ 360	Pet read
24 May 1811	66 CJ 370	Sit during adj
5 Jun 1811	66 CJ 394	**Rep by Samuel Whitbread**
13 May 1814	69 CJ 264	**Pet generally**
28 Jun 1815	70 CJ 441 – V	Motion to form C'tee
19 Jun 1816	71 CJ 485	**Pet generally**
18 May 1819	74 CJ 456	**Pet for SC**
6 Jul 1819	74 CJ 622	Motion to act on rep
7 Dec 1819	75 CJ 30	**Pet generally**
13 Jul 1820	75 CJ 446	**Pet for SC**
4 Jun 1821	76 CJ 412	**Pet for SC**

Parliamentary debates
Pet: HC Deb, 21 May 1811, Vol 20(1st), col 255–268
Pet read: HC Deb, 22 May 1811, Vol 20(1st), col 272–274
Rep: HC Deb, 5 Jun 1811, Vol 20(1st), col 430–431
Pet Pres: HC Deb, 13 May 1814, Vol 27(1st), col 867
Question: HC Deb, 27 Jul 1814, Vol 28(1st), col 861
Motion: HC Deb, 28 Jul 1814, Vol 28(1st), col 864–868
Motion: HC Deb, 28 Jun 1815, Vol 31(1st), col 1018–1021
Pet: HL Deb, 4 Jul 1815, Vol 31(1st), col 1087–1088
Parliamentary papers and cases etc.
Report of the committee on Mr. Mallison's petition (Preservation from drowning) (1810–11 HC Papers 206), Vol 2, p 375
Correspondence of Ordnance and Admiralty Boards with Mr. Mallison on Apparatus for preventing Loss of Life from Shipwrecks (1818 HC Papers 272), Vol 13, p 341
Newspaper coverage of debates
Pet Pres: **The Times, 22 May 1811**; **Globe, 22 May 1811**; **Morning Chronicle, 22 May 1811**; **Morning Post, 22 May 1811**; **Evening Mail, 22 May 1811**; **London Courier and Evening Gazette, 22 May 1811**
Pet read: **The Times, 23 May 1811**; **Globe, 23 May 1811**; **Morning Chronicle, 23 May 1811**; **Morning Post, 23 May 1811**; **London Courier and Evening Gazette, 23 May 1811**
Pet: *Morning Post, 14 May 1814*; Morning Chronicle, 14 May 1814; Public Ledger and Daily Advertiser, 14 May 1814; London Courier and Evening Gazette, 14 May 1814
Motion: **The Times, 20 Jul 1814**; **Morning Chronicle, 29 Jul 1814**; **Morning Post, 29 Jul 1814**; **London Courier and Evening Gazette, 29 Jul 1814**; **Evening Mail, 29 Jul 1814**; **Public Ledger and Daily Advertiser, 29 Jul 1814**

(continued)

(continued)

Ref C'tee: **The Times, 29 Jun 1815**; **Globe, 29 Jun 1815**; **Morning Chronicle, 29 Jun 1815**; **Morning Post, 29 Jun 1815**; **London Courier and Evening Gazette, 29 Jun 1815**; **Public Ledger and Daily Advertiser, 29 Jun 1815**
Pet: **Globe, 19 May 1819**; **Public Ledger and Daily Advertiser, 19 May 1819**; Morning Advertiser, 9 May 1819; Morning Chronicle, 19 May 1819; Morning Post, 19 May 1819;
Motion: **The Times, 7 Jul 1819**; **Globe, 7 Jul 1819**; **Morning Chronicle, 7 Jul 1819**; **Morning Post, 7 Jul 1819**; **Public Ledger and Daily Advertiser, 7 Jul 1819**; *Morning Advertiser, 7 Jul 1819*
Pet: *Globe, 8 Dec 1819*; *Morning Chronicle, 8 Dec 1819*; *Morning Post, 8 Dec 1819*; Morning Advertiser, 8 Dec 1819; Public Ledger and Daily Advertiser, 8 Dec 1819
Pet: Globe, 14 Jul 1820; Evening Mail, 14 Jul 1820; Public Ledger and Daily Advertiser, 14 Jul 1820
Pet: The Times, 5 Jun 1821

John Couch 1822

PRZC17		1822	
Proposed reward: No estimate			
John Couch for the dobephone (direction bearer) which simplifies navigation			
Journal			
House of Commons			
25 Feb 1822	77 CJ 59	**Pet**	
27 Feb 1822	77 CJ 67	Pet Prt	
Parliamentary debates			
None			
Parliamentary papers and cases etc.			
None			
Newspaper coverage of debates			
Pet: *Morning Advertiser, 26 Feb 1822*; *Morning Chronicle, 26 Feb 1822*; *Morning Post, 26 Feb 1822*; *Public Ledger and Daily Advertiser, 26 Feb 1822*			

Henry Trengrouse 1822

PRZC18		1822	
Proposed reward: No estimate			
Henry Trengrouse for preservation of life at sea			
Journal			
House of Commons			
9 July 1822	77 CJ 413	**Pet**	
3 Jun 1825	80 CJ 488	**Pet**	
3 Jun 1825	80 CJ 489	Papers Ord	
7 Jun 1825	80 CJ 505	Papers Pres	
Parliamentary debates			
None			
Parliamentary papers and cases etc.			
Letters relating to Mr. Trengrouse's invention (1825 HC Papers 415), Vol 21, p 361			
Report of a committee of elder brethren of the Trinity House, to whom Mr. Henry Trengrouse's invention, for saving seamen from shipwreck, was referred (1825 HC Papers 489), Vol 21, p 363			
Newspaper coverage of debates			
Pet: Morning Advertiser, 10 Jul 1822; Public Ledger and Daily Advertiser, 10 Jul 1822;			
Pet: **Morning Chronicle, 4 Jun 1825**; **Morning Post, 4 Jun 1825**; **Public Ledger and Daily Advertiser, 4 Jun 1825**; **London Courier and Evening Gazette, 4 Jun 1825**; Morning Advertiser, 4 Jun 1825			

John Grant 1862

PRZC19	1862
Proposed reward: No estimate	
(Captain) John Grant for improvement in field and permanent cooking in the army	
Journal	
House of Commons	
22 Jul 1862 | 117 CJ 358 – V | Motion to recognise grant	
Parliamentary debates	

Debate: **HC Deb, 11 May 1860, Vol 158(3rd), col 1087–1090**

Motion for reward: **HC Deb, 22 Jul 1862, Vol 168(3rd), col 664–669**

Debate on refusal to reward: **HC Deb, 25 Jul 1862, Vol 168(3rd), col 851–876**

Motion for reward: **HC Deb, 20 May 1864, Vol 175(3rd), col 523–526**

Parliamentary papers and cases etc.

Reports respecting Working of Captain Grant's Kitchens, at Aldershot and Woolwich Barracks (1857–58 HC Papers 301 and 301-I), Vol 37, p 327 and p 349

Return of Cost of Alteration of Captain Grant's Model Kitchen at Aldershot by Introduction of Mr. Warriner's Apparatus (1861 HC Papers 303), Vol 36, p 407

Correspondence between Under Secretary of State for War and Captain Grant, respecting Claims for Remuneration; Reports on Captain Grant's System of Cooking (1862 HC Papers 402), Vol 32, p 327

Report on Captain Grant's Cooking Apparatus (1863 C 3116), Vol 32, p 463

Committee to consider Claims of Captain Grant to Remuneration for Services to Public by Introduction of System of Cookery, Report, Minutes of Evidence, Appendix (1864 C 3279), Vol 35, p 507

Newspaper coverage of debates

Debate: **The Times, 12 May 1860; Globe, 12 May 1860; Morning Advertiser, 12 May 1860; Morning Chronicle, 12 May 1860; Morning Post, 12 May 1860; London Daily News, 12 May 1860; London Evening Standard, 12 May 1860**

Motion for reward: **The Times, 23 Jul 1862; Morning Advertiser, 23 Jul 1862; Morning Post, 23 Jul 1862; London Daily News, 23 Jul 1862; London Evening Standard, 23 Jul 1862**

Debate on refusal: **The Times, 26 Jul 1862; Morning Advertiser, 26 Jul 1862; Morning Post, 26 Jul 1862; London Daily News, 26 Jul 1862; London Evening Standard, 26 Jul 1862;**

Motion for reward: **The Times, 21 May 1864; Morning Advertiser, 21 May 1864; Morning Post, 21 May 1864; London Daily 21 May 1864; London Evening Standard, 21 May 1864;** *Globe, 21 May 1864*

Part 6 — Parliamentary and Command Papers

Introduction

This part provides details of Parliamentary and Command Papers which have not been included in another Part. While there were Parliamentary papers (including Command Papers) printed during the eighteenth century,[1] there were no papers on the patent system.[2] However, during the nineteenth century there were a substantial number of papers ordered and published relating to patents, individual inventions and similar. This part of the Guide provides a list of all those papers, with journal references for the date the paper was ordered, when it was presented and, if appropriate, when it was ordered to be printed. Each record also includes the location in the published Parliamentary papers (where it was published) and references to debates published by *Hansard*, the *Mirror of Parliament* or *The Times*. The starting point for this part was Peter Chadwick's index of House of Commons papers",[3] but Chadwick did not include all orders for papers, and obviously those for the House of Lords, so the Journals of each House were searched to identify any further papers.

Chapter 1 details the papers and reports relating to reviews of the patent system from the first in 1829 to the last during the relevant period in 1971. Most of these reports have been published as Parliamentary or Command Papers, but a handful were published by Her Majesty's Stationery Office in the usual way, and two were originally unpublished but have now been made available. Chapter 2 provides a list of Parliamentary papers where the paper is not otherwise recorded in this Guide.

Commissioners' and Comptrollers' reports

The Patent Law Amendment Act 1852[4] required a report to be laid before Parliament every year by the Commissioners of Patents, and this continued when the Comptroller took over responsibility under the Patents, Designs and Trade Marks Act 1883.[5] A list of these reports is set out in Chapter 3. Each report includes a vast amount of statistical information regarding the number of applications made and granted, details about renewal fees, the number of appeals, private Acts of Parliament, as well as setting out any new patent rules.

The early reports of the Commissioners were published as House of Lords papers, but later they became House of Commons papers before being printed as Command Papers and returning once more to being House of Commons papers. The report was provided, but not printed, from 1940 to 1947. However, a type-script version of those reports is available at the British Library. There is a record of every report from the first in 1852–53 to that in 1976.

Reports on exhibitions

The Commissioners of the Great Exhibition of 1851 made various reports on the success of the exhibition. These reports include some significant information about technologies exhibited and the occasional reference to patent matters. The reports continued for many years after 1851, but eventually such reports related to the fund created by the Great Exhibition.[6] Therefore, references are not included after the point when the exhibition itself was no longer the subject of the Commissioner's reports. Where other exhibitions were held

---

1 Shelia Lambert, "House of Commons Papers of the Eighteenth Century" (1976) 3 *Government Publications Review* 195.
2 There were reports on individual patents or inventions, and these are recorded under the relevant private enactment or reward.
3 Peter Chadwick, *House of Commons Parliamentary Papers, 1801–1900: Guide to the Chadwyck-Healey Microfiche Edition* (Chadwyck-Healey 1991).
4 Patent Law Amendment Act 1852, s 3.
5 Patents, Designs and Trade Marks Act 1883, s 102; Patents and Designs Act 1907, s 76; Patents Act 1949, s 100.
6 Which still pays scholarships to this day.

elsewhere in the world, such as those in Paris, Philadelphia and New York, it was usual practice for reports to be obtained from experts and these reports to be published as Command Papers. Chapter 4 provides an entry for each such international exhibition.

Awards to inventions

After both World War I and World War II, Royal Commissions were set up to reward inventors whose inventions had been used for the war effort. These awards were usually meant to represent the compensation an inventor might have received had the invention been purchased or licensed in the normal way (or under Crown use[7]). Chapter 5 records the journal entries and Command Paper numbers of the six reports of the Royal Commission which considered the awards relating to the World War I and the four reports of the Commissioners following World War II.

Command Papers relating to international treaties

Chapter 6 similarly lists the Command Papers which have been laid before Parliament in relation to international treaties. It includes the Command Paper number as well as its number in the Treaty Series or other series. In the later period, the practice developed that a treaty when signed would be laid as a Command Paper in the Miscellaneous Series, and when ratified re-laid in the Treaty Series. Both versions are included in the list, provided the paper was presented before 1977.

British Empire patent

In the first two decades of the twentieth century, the idea of a British Empire patent gained traction.[8] It was debated at the Colonial, later Imperial, conferences which were held between 1902 and 1924. The papers for these conferences were usually printed as Command Papers, so Chapter 7 provides a list of the conference papers, with page references, which dealt with the proposal for a British Empire patent. There is also a section at the end detailing all the archival references to the British Empire patent.

---

7 See HC Deb, 22 May 1919, Vol 116(5th), col 586–588W.

8 For a history of the proposal, see Christopher Wadlow, "The British Empire Patent 1901–1923: The 'Global' Patent that Never Was" [2006] *IPQ* 311.

1 Parliamentary reports on the patent system

1829 Select Committee Report

Select Committee Report 1829 [REP1]		
House of Commons Select Committee		
Report from the Select Committee on the Law Relative to Patents for Inventions (1829 HC Papers 332), Vol 3, p 415 [Also published: British Parliamentary Papers, Inventions (Irish Academic Press 1972), Vol 1]		
Terms of reference		
To inquire into the present state of the Law and practice relative to Letters Patent for Inventions		
Appointment and members nominated	84 CJ 214 (9 Apr 1829)	Motion postponed: Mirror, 12 Mar 1829, Vol 1, p 546 Motion for SC: HC Deb, 9 Apr 1829, Vol 21(2nd), col 599–608; Mirror 9 Apr 1829, Vol 2, p 1205 to 1208; The Times, 10 Apr 1829
Member added	84 CJ 278 (9 May 1829)	
Member added	84 CJ 301 (14 May 1829)	
Leave to sit in adj	84 CJ 369 (3 Jun 1829)	
Rep Pres	84 CJ 395 (12 Jun 1829)	Mirror, 12 Jun 1829, Vol 3, p 2104
Witnesses		
Francis Abbott; Arthur Aikin; Thomas Aspinwall (Consul of US); Mark Brunel (Engineer); Samuel Clegg; Davies Gilbert MP; John Farey (Engineer, Patent Agent); Charles Few (Patentee); John Isaac Hawkins; Arthur How Holdsworth MP; John Macarthy; Joseph Merry (Ribbon Manufacturer); John Millington (Civil Engineer); Samuel Morton (Inventor); William Newton (Patent Agent); Moses Poole (Clerk to Attorney-General); Benjamin Rotch; John Taylor (Manufacturer); Walter Wyatt (Editor of Repertory of Arts and Manufactures)		

1835 Select Committee Report

1835 Select Committee Report [REP2]		
House of Lords Select Committee on Letters Patent for Inventions Bill		
Unpublished		
Terms of reference		
The Select Committee considered the ten clauses which were the subject of the Bill at the time		
Reference	67 LJ 227 (19 Jun 1835)	
Rep Pres	67 LJ 290 (10 Jul 1835)	
Witnesses		
John Heatcoat MP; Archibald Rosser (Solicitor, Patents); John Farey (Patent Agent)		
Notes		
The unpublished evidence has now been published: Phillip Johnson "Minutes of Evidence of the Select Committee on the Letters Patent for Inventions Act 1835" (2017) 7(1) *Queen Mary Journal of Intellectual Property* 99		

1835–36 Select Committee Report

1835–36 Select Committee Report [REP3]		
House of Commons Select Committee		
Report of the Select Committee on Arts and their Connexion with Manufactures (1836 HC Papers 568), Vol 9, p 18 (Also see Report of the Select Committee on Arts and their Connexion with Manufactures (1835 HC Papers 598), Vol 5, p 375)		
Terms of reference		
Inquire into: The State of Art in this country and in other countries, as manifested in their different Manufactures; The best means of extending among the People, especially the Manufacturing Classes, a knowledge of and a taste for Art; The state of the higher branches of Art, and the best mode of advancing them;		
Appointment	90 CJ 451 (14 Jul 1835)	
Member added	90 CJ 480 (23 Jul 1835)	
Member added	90 CJ 525 (8 Aug 1835)	
Rep presented	90 CJ 645 (4 Sep 1835)	
Appointment	91 CJ 17 (9 Feb 1836)	
Nominated	91 CJ 21 (10 Feb 1836)	
Papers Ref	91 CJ 69 (22 Feb 1836)	Paper: Returns of Communications made to and received from His Majesty's Ministers abroad respecting encouragement given to the cultivation of the Arts in Foreign Countries Pres: 91 CJ 38 (16 Feb 1836)
Papers Ref	91 CJ 94 (29 Feb 1836)	Paper: Returns of Communications made to and received from His Majesty's Ministers abroad respecting encouragement given to the cultivation of the Arts in Foreign Countries Pres: 91 CJ 87 (27 Feb 1836)
Pet/Ref	91 CJ 223 (29 Mar 1836)	Petition from Artists
Papers Ref	91 CJ 524 (20 Jun 1836)	Paper: Returns of Communications made to and received from His Majesty's Ministers abroad respecting encouragement given to the cultivation of the Arts in Foreign Countries Pres: 91 CJ 502 (18 Jun 1836)
Pet/Ref	91 CJ 566 (27 Jun 1836)	Petition from Engravers
Papers Ref	91 CJ 617 (4 Jul 1836)	Paper: Returns of Communications made to and received from His Majesty's Ministers abroad respecting encouragement given to the cultivation of the Arts in Foreign Countries Pres: 91 CJ 613 (2 Jul 1836)
Leave to sit	91 CJ 668 (15 Jul 1836)	
Rep/Prt	91 CJ 818 (16 Aug 1836)	
Witnesses		

1835: Philip Barnes (Architect); Robert Barnes; Professor Felix Bogaerts (History, Antwerp); Robert Butt (Retailer); Charles Cockerell (Architect); James Crabb (Designer); George Eld (Corn Trader); George Foggo (Designer); Thomas Gibson (Silk Manufacturer); Claude Guillotte (Loom Maker); Robert Harrison (Silk Manufacturer); John Henning (Sculptor); John Howell (Retailer); Thomas James (Silk Buyer); John Martin (Painter); James Morrison MP (Merchant); John Papworth (Architect); George Rennie (Traveller); Joseph Robertson (Editor of Mechanics Magazine); James Skene (Royal Institution for Encouragement of Fine Arts) ; Charles Smith (Sculptor Architectural Ornaments); John Smith (Iron Manufacturer); Samuel Smith (Merchant); Benjamin Spalding (Merchant); Charles Toplis (Director of Museum of Manufactures); Professor Gustave Waagen (Director Royal Gallery, Berlin); Samuel Wiley (Japanning); William Wyon (Chief Engraver Mint)

1836: John Bowring MP; John Burnet (Painter); George Clint (painter); Charles Cockerell (Member Royal Academy); Edward Cowper (Steam Printing Machine Patentee); Mr Cheverton (Ivory Worker); George Foggo (Art Historian); D Hay (House Painter); Thomas Donaldson (Architect); Benjamin Haydon (Painter); William Hilton (Keeper Royal Academy); T Hofland (Secretary to Society of British Artists); Henry Howard (Secretary Royal Academy); Thomas Howell (factory inspector); Frederick Hurlstone (President Royal Society of Artists); John Landseer (Royal Academy Member); James Leigh (Artist); John Martin (Painter); John Millward (Lace Manufacturer); George Morant (House Decorator); James Nasmyth (Engineer); Sir John Paul (Royal Academy); John Peel (Art Restorer); John Pye (Engraver); Henry Sass (Design Teacher); William Seguier (Keeper National Gallery); Sir Martin Shee (President Royal Academy); Edward Solly (Art Collector); George Stanley (Art Dealer); Noel St Leon (Paper Manufacturer); Robert Stothard (Draftsman and Artist); Ramsay Reinagle (Royal Academician); George Rennie (Sculptor); Baron Von Klenze (Architect); William Wilkins (Architect); Samuel Woodburn (Art Dealer)

1844 Judicial Committee Report

1844 Judicial Committee Report [REP4]		
House of Lords Select Committee		
Report of Select Committee of House of Lords appointed to consider of the Bill intitled An Act for amending an Act passed in the Fourth Year of the Reign of His late Majesty, intituled An Act for the better Administration of Justice in His Majesty's Privy Council; and to extend its Jurisdiction and Powers with Minutes of Evidence (1844 HL Papers 34), Vol 19, p 323		
Terms of reference		
To consider the [Judicial Committee Bill] [PUBA44]		
Appointment	76 LJ 58 (8 Mar 1844)	
Prt	76 LJ 71 (14 Mar 1844)	
Rep	76 LJ 421 (25 Jun 1844)	
Witnesses		
There were numerous witnesses, but only three dealt with patents: Lord Brougham, p 82–83 (Q916); Earl Dundonald (Inventor), p 70–74, p 91–93 (Q791-Q853; Q923-934); Henry Reeve (Privy Council, Appeal Clerk), p 54 (Q624)		

1849 Privy Seal Office Report

1849 Privy Seal Office Report [REP5]		
Treasury Committee		
Report of the Committee on the Signet and Privy Seal Offices: with minutes of evidence and appendix (1849 C 1099), Vol 22, p 453		
Terms of reference		
To inquire into the circumstances connected with the offices of the Clerks of the Signet and of the Lord Privy Seal		
Appointment		Minute of Treasury, dated 23 June 1848
Rep Pres	104 CJ 530; 81 LJ 462 (21 Jul 1849; 20 Jul 1849)	
Witnesses		
Charles Barlow (Patent Agent); Frederick Campin (Patent Agent); William Carpmael (Patent Agent); Leonard Edmunds (Clerk of the Patents); William Goodwin (Junior Clerk at Privy Seal Office); David Johnstone (Clerk to Attorney-General); William Newton (Patent Agent); Moses Poole (Clerk of Inventions to Attorney-General); Thomas Ruscoe (Chief Clerk in Great Seal Patent Office); Joseph Robertson (Patent Agent); Henry Sanders (Record Keeper at Signet Office); William Spence (Patent Agent); Thomas Webster (Special Pleader, Patents); Bennet Woodcroft (Inventor with experience of patents – later Superintendent at Patent Office)		

1851 Protection of Inventions Report

1851 Protections of Invention Report [REP6]		
Select Committee of House of Lords		
Select Committee of House of Lords to consider Bill, intituled, Act to extend provisions of Designs Act, 1850, and to give Protection from Piracy to Persons exhibiting new Inventions in Exhibition of Works of Industry of all Nations in 1851 (1851 HC Papers 145), Vol 18, p 671		
Terms of reference		
To Consider the Protection of Inventions Bill 1851		
Appointment	83 LJ 60 (6 Mar 1851)	
Rep Pres	83 LJ 63 (10 Mar 1851)	
Witnesses		
William Carpmael (Patent Agent); Charles May (Civil Engineer); Alfred Newton (Patent Agent); Thomas Webster (Barrister, Patents); Bennett Woodcroft (Professor of Machinery, UCL)		

1851 Select Committee Report

1851 Select Committee Report [REP7]
House of Lords Select Committee
Report and minutes of evidence taken before the Select Committee of the House of Lords appointed to consider of the bills amending the Law touching Letters Patent for Invention (1851 HC Papers 486), Vol 18, p 233 [Also published: British Parliamentary Papers, Inventions (Irish Academic Press 1972), Vol 1]

Terms of reference

To consider the Patent Law Amendment Bill 1851; Patent Law Amendment (No 2) Bill 1851		
Appointment	83 LJ 130 (11 Apr 1851)	
Rep presented	83 LJ 304 (1 Jul 1851)	

Witnesses

Sir David Brewster (Principal of United College); Isambard Kingdom Brunel (Engineer); William Carpmael (Patent Agent); Frederick Campin (Patent Agent); Henry Cole (Member Society of Arts); William Cubutt (President Institute of Civil Engineers); John Duncan (Patent Solicitor); William Fairbarn (Civil Engineer); John Fairrie (Sugar Refiner); Benjamin Fothergill (Mechanical Engineer); Warren Hale (Manufacturer); Matthew Hill QC (Non-practising Barrister); Paul Hodge; John Lloyd (Barrister); Charles May; Robert Macfie (Sugar Refiner); John Mercer (Calico Printer); Alfred Newton (Patent Agent); John Prevost (Consul-General Switzerland); Richard Prosser (Civil Engineer); William Reid (former Governor of Bermuda); James Rendel (Civil Engineer); Richard Roberts (Civil Engineer); Lord Romilly (Master of the Rolls); William Spence (Patent Agent); Thomas Webster (Barrister, Patents); William Weddinge (Prussian Patent Commission); Joshua Westhead MP (Chair Inventors' Association); Louis Wolowski (National Assembly France); Sir William Wood (SG); Bennet Woodcroft (Professor Machinery, UCL); Richard Wyatt (Patent Solicitor)

1864 Royal Commission Report

1864 Royal Commission Report [REP8]
Royal Commission
Report of the commissioners appointed to inquire into the working of the law relating to letters patent for inventions (1864 C 3419), Vol 29, p 321 [Also published: British Parliamentary Papers, Inventions (Irish Academic Press 1972), Vol 2, p 9]

Terms of reference

To inquire into the working of the law relating to letters patent		
Appointment	117 CJ 232 (27 May 1864) 117 CJ 243 (2 Jun 1864)	Motion: HC Deb, 27 May 1862, Vol 167(3rd), col 31–52; The Times, 28 May 1862 Answer: HC Deb, 2 Jun 1862, Vol 167(3rd), col 237; The Times, 3 Jun 1862
Rep presented	119 CJ 481; 96 LJ 681 (29 Jul 1864)	

Witnesses

Frederick Abel (Chemical Department, War Office); Sir William Armstrong (Inventor); William Carpmael (Patent Agent); Sir Francis Crossley MP; Matthew Curtis (Manufacturer); Leonard Edmunds (Patent Office); W Grove; John Lefroy (War Office); Robert Macfie (Manufacturer); Alfred Newton (Patent Agent); Sir Roundell Palmer (Attorney-General); Henry Reeve (Registrar Privy Council); Richard Roberts (Engineer); Robert Robinson (Admiralty); M Smith; Duke of Somerset (Admiralty); William Spence (Patent Agent); Thomas Webster (Barrister, Patents); Bennet Woodcroft (Superintendent of Specifications)

1864 Patent Library Report

1864 Patent Library Report [REP9]
House of Commons Select Committee
Report of Select Committee into Patent Library (1864 HC Papers 504), Vol 12, p 1

Terms of reference

To inquire as to the most suitable Arrangements respecting the Patent Office Library and Museum

Appointment	119 CJ 231 – V (10 May 1864)	HC Deb, 9 May 1864, Vol 175(3rd), col 245; The Times, 10 May 1864
Nominated	119 CJ 257 (23 May 1864)	
Member discussed/added	119 CJ 267 (28 May 1864)	
C'tee Rep	119 CJ 439 (19 Jul 1864)	HC Deb, 23 May 1864, Vol 175(3rd), col 587; The Times, 24 May 1864 HC Deb, 27 May 1864, Vol 175(3rd), col 718

Witnesses
Joseph Bazalgette (Civil Engineer); Sir David Brewster (Principal Edinburgh University); William Carpmael (Patent Agent); Frederick Chifferial (Law Stationer); Henry Cole (Secretary South Kensington Museum); Edward Cowper (Mechanical Engineer); William Fairbairn (former Royal Commissioner); Captain Fishbourne (Chairman Services Museum); Sir Charles Fox (Civil Engineer); William Lefeuvre (Civil Engineer); John Johnson (Patent Agent); Leonard Edmunds (Clerk Commissioner Patents); Robert Richardson (Civil Engineer); James Pennethorne (Government Surveyor); Francis Petitt Smith (Curator Patent Museum); Rigby Wason; Thomas Webster (Barrister, Patents); Bennett Woodcroft (Superintendent of Patent Library)

1865 Patent Office Accounts Report

1864 Patent Office Accounts [REP10]
House of Commons Select Committee
Report to Commissioners of Patents in reference to Patent Office Accounts and Evidence (1865 HC Papers 173), Vol 43, p 495
Terms of reference
To institute Inquiries in reference to the Patent Office Accounts, and of any Evidence on which such Reports were founded, and of any Answers that may have been made thereto

Appointment		Letter from Lord Chancellor and Commissioners of Patents dated 3 May 1864
C'tee Rep	120 CJ 168 (Prt: 176) (28 Mar 1865; 30 Mar 1865)	The Times, 23 Mar 1865

Witnesses
None

1865 Edmunds Committee Report

1865 Edmunds Committee Report [REP11]
House of Lords Select Committee
Report from the Select Committee of the House of Lords appointed to inquire into the Circumstances connected with the Resignation by Mr Edmunds of the Officers of the Patents and Clerk (1865 HC Papers 294), Vol 9, p 1; (1865 HL Papers 30), Vol 22, p 1
Terms of reference
To inquire into all the Circumstances connected with the resignation of Mr Edmunds of the Offices of Clerk of the Patents and Clerk to the Commissioners of Patents, and with his Resignation of the Office of Reading Clerk and Clerk of Out-Door Committees in this House; and also into all the Circumstances connected with the Grant of a retiring pension to him by this House; and to report to the House

Pet from Edmunds	97 LJ 22 (14 Feb 1865)	
Rep from SC of Office of Clerk	97 LJ 27 (17 Feb 1865)	
Rep agreed	97 LJ 38 (24 Feb 1865)	

(continued)

(continued)

Appointment	97 LJ 55 (7 Mar 1865)	HL Deb, 7 Mar 1865, Vol 177(3rd), col 1203–1221
Member appointed	97 LJ 58 (9 Mar 1865)	
Documents Ord	97 LJ 61 (10 Mar 1865)	
Witness on oath Evidence Pres	97 LJ 67 (14 Mar 1865)	
Chancellor of Exchequer summoned	97 LJ 95 (24 Mar 1865)	
Chancellor of Exchequer leave	97 LJ 100; 120 CJ 160 (27 Mar 1865; 25 Mar 1865)	
Attorney-General summoned	97 LJ 140 (6 Apr 1865)	
Attorney-General leave	97 LJ 161; 120 CJ 199 (7 Apr 1865; 6 Apr 1865)	
Rep	97 LJ 179 (2 May 1865)	
HC request Rep	97 LJ 230; 120 CJ 252 (9 May 1865)	
Rep received	120 CJ 258 (11 May 1865)	
HC printed	120 CJ 275 (17 May 1865)	

Witnesses

George Arbuthnot; William Brougham; Leonard Edmunds; Pemberton Gipps (Secretary to Patents Museum); William Gladstone (Chancellor of Exchequer); John Greenwood QC (Solicitor to the Treasury); George Hamilton; William Hindmarch QC; Charles Hooper (Public Accountant); James Leman (Solicitor to Leonard Edmunds); John Miller (Chief Registrar Court of Bankruptcy); Alfred Montgomery (friend of Lord Brougham); Sir Roundell Palmer (Attorney-General); Lord Redesdale (Lord Chairman of Committee); Sir John Romilly (Master of the Rolls); Thomas Ruscoe (Clerk to Leonard Edmunds); Sir John Shaw (Clerk of the Parliaments)

Notes

Motion for Rep: The Times, 22 Mar 1865

Motion of Lord Chancellor Censure: HC Deb, 3 Jul 1865, Vol 180(3rd), col 1045–1138

Motion for Evidence: HC Deb, 29 Jul 1868, Vol 193(3rd), col 1929–1933

Motion for a Select Committee: HL Deb, 4 Jul 1879, Vol 247(3rd), col 1407–1414 (111 LJ 294; 4 Jul 1879)

Motion for Address: HL Deb, 9 Aug 1872, Vol 213(3rd), col 831–834 (104 LJ 749; 9 Aug 1872)

Related papers to Leonard Edmunds and fallout

Copy of the reports made to the Commissioners of Patents by Mr. Hindmarch, Q. C., and Mr. Greenwood, Q. C., the commissioners appointed to institute inquiries in reference to the Patent Office accounts (1865 HC Papers 173), Vol 43, p 495; Ord: 120 CJ 148 (21 Mar 1865); Pres: 120 CJ 168 (28 Mar 1865); Prt: 120 CJ 176 (30 Mar 1865)

Warrant or order of court for the commitment to prison of Leonard Edmunds at the suit of the Crown (1870 HC Papers 380), Vol 57, p 97; Ord: 125 CJ 344 (19 Jul 1870); Pres: 125 CJ 349 (21 Jul 1870); Prt: 125 CJ 354 (22 Jul 1870)

Treasury Minute, December 1869, recorded as State Paper and signed by First Lord of Treasury, relating to Leonard Edmunds (1872 HC Papers 299), Vol 50, p 195; Ord: 127 CJ 328 (8 Jul 1870); Pres: 127 CJ 335 (10 Jul 1870); Prt: 127 CJ 342 (12 Jul 1870)

Copy of Correspondence between the Earl of Redesdale and the Chancellor of the Exchequer, relative to the Accounts of Leonard Edmunds (1878–79 HL Papers 13), Vol 12, p 1; Ord: 111 LJ 27 (17 Feb 1879); Pres and Prt: 111 LJ 32 (20 Feb 1879)

Copy of the "Document", dated the 2nd of May instant (deposited in the Treasury on the 7th instant), and entitled "In the matter of the claims of Leonard Edmunds, formerly 'Reading and Outdoor Committee Clerk in the House of Lords, and Clerk of the Patents, for the Statutory audit of his accounts with the Crown; for payment of his statutory pensions and arrears of pensions; and for payment of the several sums of money due to him by the Crown in relation to his said accounts" (1878–79 HL Papers 81), Vol 12, p 1; Pres and Prt: 111 LJ 183 (13 May 1879)

First Report from the Select Committee on the Office of the Clerk of the Parliaments and Office of the Gentleman Usher of the Black Rod (1884–85 HL Papers 22), Vol 7, p 1; also see 117 LJ 68 (24 Feb 1885); Agreed: 117 LJ 74 (27 Feb 1885)

Petitions – PET283; PET288; PET301; PET308; PET309; PET312 to PET314; PET570

Samuelson Committee 1871

1871 Select Committee Report [REP12]		
House of Commons Select Committee		
Report from the Select Committee on Letters Patent; together with the proceedings of the committee, minutes of evidence, appendix and index (1871 HC Papers 368), Vol 10, p 603 [Also published: British Parliamentary Papers, Inventions (Irish Academic Press 1972), Vol 2, p 265]		
Terms of reference		
To inquire into the Law and Practice and the effects of Grants of Letters Patent for Inventions		
Appointment	126 CJ 76 (7 Mar 1871)	HC Deb, 7 Mar 1871, Vol 204(3rd), col 1512–1534; The Times, 8 Mar 1871; Morning Advertiser, 8 Mar 1871; Morning Post, 8 Mar 1871; London Daily News, 8 Mar 1871; London Evening Standard, 8 Mar 1871
Nominated	126 CJ 90 (17 Mar 1871)	
Member added	126 CJ 92 (18 Mar 1871)	
1864 Royal Commission Rep referred	126 CJ 103 (23 Mar 1871)	
Witness Ord (Lord Romilly)	126 CJ 168; 103 LJ 231 (2 Mar 1871)	
Leave to sit out of session	126 CJ 202 (18 May 1871)	
Rep	126 CJ 354 (20 Jul 1871)	HC Deb, 20 Jul 1871, Vol 208(3rd), col 12
Witnesses		
Theo Aston (Barrister, Patents); Sir William Armstrong (Inventor and Manufacturer); Henry Bessemer (Inventor); Lucius Chittenden (former Registrar of the US Treasury); William Groove QC (Commissioner 1964 Royal Commission); Peter Hall Henson (Clerk to Attorney-General); Isaac Holden (Woollen Manufacturer); Robert Macfie MP; William Michell (First Class Clerk Patent Office); James Nasmyth (Inventor); Eugene Schneider (Managing Partner of Creuzot Works); Lord Romilly (Master of the Rolls); Thomas Webster QC (Barrister, Patents)		
Notes		
Notice of Motion: The Times, 10 Feb 1871		

Second Samuelson Committee 1872

Second Samuelson Committee 1872 [REP13]		
House of Commons Select Committee		
Report from the Select Committee on Letters Patent; together with the proceedings of the committee, minutes of evidence, appendix, and index (1872 HC Papers 193), Vol 11, p 395 [Also published: British Parliamentary Papers, Inventions (Irish Academic Press 1972), Vol 2, p 519]		
Terms of reference		
To inquire into the Law and Practice and the effects of Grants of Letters Patent for Inventions		
Appointment	127 CJ 22 (8 Feb 1872)	HC Deb, 8 Feb 1872, Vol 209(3rd), col 179
Nominated	127 CJ 43 (15 Feb 1872)	HC Deb, 15 Feb 1872, Vol 209(3rd), col 462; The Times, 16 Feb 1872
Evidence of 1871 Committee Ref	127 CJ 60 (22 Feb 1872)	
Rep	127 CJ 188 (8 May 1872)	HC Deb, 8 May 1872, Vol 211(3rd), col 447

(continued)

(continued)

Witnesses
Christian Allhusen (President Newcastle Chamber of Commerce); Frederick Beaumont MP (also Patentee); Arthur Bower (Solicitor, Patents); Frederick Campin (Barrister and former Patent Agent); William Carpmael (Patent Agent); George Haseltine (experience of US patent law); James Howard MP (also Agricultural Manufacturer); John Johnson (Patent Agent); Anthony Mundella MP; Edmund Muspratt (President Liverpool Chamber of Commerce); Alfred Newton (Patent Agent); Bernhard Samuelson MP; C William Siemens (President of Institute of Mechanical Engineers); Thomas Webster QC (Barrister, Patents); William Wise (Patent Agent); Bennet Woodcraft (Chief Clerk Patent Office); John Wright (Manufacturer)

Herschell Report 1887–88

Herschell Report 1887–88 [REP14]		
Board of Trade Committee		
(First) Report of the committee appointed by the Board of Trade to inquire into the duties, organisation, and arrangements of the Patent Office under the Patents, Designs, and Trade Marks Act, so far as it relates to patents 1883 (1887 C 4968), Vol 66, p 495		
(Second) Report of the committee appointed by the Board of Trade to inquire into Duties, Organisation and Arrangements of Patent Office, as relates to Trade Marks and Designs, Report, Minutes of Evidence, Appendices (1888 C 5350), Vol 81, p 37 [this report related to trade marks and designs; witnesses and terms of reference not included]		
Terms of reference		
To Inquire into the Duties, Organisation, and Arrangements of the Patent Office under the Patents, Designs, and Trade Marks Act, 1883 (46 & 47 Vict cap 57), having especial regard to the system of examination of Specifications which accompany applications for Patents now in force under that Act		
Appointment		Letter from Board of Trade dated 30 Dec 1885
C'tee Rep	142 CJ 64; 119 LJ 43 (14 Feb 1887) 142 CJ 130; 120 LJ 104 (5 Apr 1888; 13 Apr 1888)	
Witnesses		
Alfred Boult (Patent Agent); John Hall (Deputy Comptroller of the Patent Office); Henry Hatfield (Patent Office Examiner); John Imray (CIPA President); Henry Reader Lack (Comptroller General of Patents); SJ Mackie (Inventors Institute); Richard Prosser (Superintendent of Examiners); J Selwyn (President of Inventors Institute); Sir William Thomson (Professor of Natural Philosophy, Glasgow University); W Phillips Thompson (Patent Agent); Andrew Walke (Patent Officer Examiner); Henry Wood (Secretary Society of Arts)		

Patent Agent Committee Report 1894

Patent Agent Committee Report 1894 [REP15]		
Select Committee on Patent Agents Bills		
Select Committee on Patent Agents Bill, Special Report, Proceedings, Evidence, Appendix, Index (1894 HC Papers 235), Vol 14, p 247		
Terms of reference		
To consider Patent Agents Bill and the Patent Agents Registration Bill		
Appointment	149 CJ 55 (4 Apr 1894)	
Pres	149 CJ 319 (25 Jul 1894)	
Witnesses		
Sir Courtney Boyle (Permanent Secretary Board of Trade); Ebenezer Bristow (Solicitor, Patents); Edward Carpmael (Patent Agent); John Fairfax (Patent Agent); William Gadd (Patent Agent); Herbert Haddan (Patent Agent); Francis Hopwood (Assistant Secretary to Board of Trade); Henry Howgrave Graham (CIPA Secretary); John Imray (CIPA Past President); Sir Henry Reader Lack (Comptroller); Joseph Lockwood (Patent Agent); John Mewburn (Fellow CIPA, Patent Agent); James Wann (Patent Agent); Thomas Wilkins (Patent Agent); Lloyd Wise (CIPA President)		

Hopwood Committee 1900

Hopwood Committee 1900 [REP16]		
Departmental Committee		
Report of the committee appointed by the Board of Trade to consider various suggestions which have been made for developing the benefits afforded by the Patent Office to inventors (1900 Cd 210), Vol 26, p 821		
Terms of reference		
To consider various suggestions which have been made for developing the benefits afforded by the Patent Office to Inventors		
Appointment		Minute from Board of Trade dated 29 Nov 1899
C'tee Rep	155 CJ 235; 132 LJ 220 (7 May 1900; 18 Jun 1900)	HC Deb, 14 Jun 1900, Vol 84(4th), col 8; HL Deb, 18 Jun 1900, Vol 84(4th), col 255–256
Witnesses		
None		

Fry Committee 1901

Fry Committee 1901 [REP17]		
Departmental Committee		
Report of the Committee appointed by the Board of Trade to inquire into the Works of the Patents Acts on certain specified Questions (1901 Cd 506), Vol 23, p 506 Appendices: (1901 Cd 530), Vol 23, p 599 Solicitor-General's Report (1902 Cd 1030), Vol 83, p 729		
Terms of reference		

"While Here Majesty's Government do not think it desirable and do not propose to establish any general system of examination as to the novelty of inventions in respect of which applications for Letters Patent are made, and do not require any inquiry in any such system of examination; the Committee hereinbefore appointed is to inquire into the working of the Patents Acts with reference to the following question:
 	
(1) Whether any, and, if so, what additional powers should be given to the Patent Office to-
 	
   (a) control;
   (b) impose conditions on, or
   (c) otherwise limit
 	
   the issue of Letters Patent in respect of inventions which are obviously old, or which the information recorded in the Office shows to have been previously protected by Letters Patent in this country.
 	
(2) Whether any, and, if so, what amendments are necessary in the provisions of Section 22 of the Patents, &c., Act, 1883, and
(3) Whether the period of seven months priority allowed by Section 103 of that Act to applications for Letters Patent under the International Convention may properly be extended, and, if so, on what conditions"		

Appointment		Minute of Board of Trade dated 24 May 1900
Rep	156 CJ 70; 133 LJ 64 (11 Mar 1901)	HL Deb, 11 Mar 1901, Vol 90(4th), col 1139; HC Deb, 11 Mar 1901, Vol 90(4th), col 1147
Appendix	156 CJ 92; 133 LJ 83 (22 Mar 1901)	HC Deb, 22 Mar 1901, Vol 91(4th), col 833 and 846 and 854
Solicitor-General report	157 CJ 112; 134 LJ 106 (14 Mar 1902)	
Witnesses		
Moses Adams (Inventor); W Bousfield QC MP (Barrister, Patents); Griffith Brewer (Patent Agent); Robert Cunliffe (Board of Trade Solicitor); T Croker (Sanitary Appliance manufacturer); Cornelius Dalton (Comptroller); George Ellis (Solicitor and CIPA Member); John Fairfax (Patent Agent); Samuel Flood-Page (London Chamber of Commerce); J Gordon (Barrister, Patents); G Hardingham (Patent Agent); John Imray (CIPA Council) ; Lennox Lee (Calico Printers Association); Ivan Levinstein (Manchester Chamber of Commerce); Philip Justice (CIPA Fellow); Henry Hatfield (Chief Examiner Patent Office); Roger Wallace (Barrister, Patents) ; Dr Weinberg (Dyeing Company Representative); E Wethered (Inventor); W Wise (Patent Agent, CIPA past President)		

Parker Committee 1916

Parker Committee 1916 [REP18]
Departmental Committee
Unpublished
Terms of reference (informal)
"To enquire whether any and what amendments are required in the Patents Act or other Statutes with the object (1) of preventing the exploitation of the Patent Laws by foreigners to the detriment of British trade, (2) of affecting the better encouragement of invention and securing more adequate and certain remuneration to inventors, (3) of securing that in the public interest all useful inventions should be brought into use at the earliest possible moment"
Witnesses
None
Notes
There were no formal terms of reference, but that set out above is mentioned in a letter to Sir Hubert Llewellyn Smith (Permanent Secretary, Board of Trade) from Temple Franks dated 24 May 1916: National Archive BT 209/485 The unpublished report, and certain accompanying memorandums, have now been published as: Phillip Johnson, "The Report of the Parker Committee 1916" (2017) 7(1) Queen Mary Journal of Intellectual Property 156 This committee has also been called the Franks Committee after the Comptroller-General of Patents

Inventions by Public Funds Committee 1922

Inventions by Public Funds Committee 1922 [REP19]
Departmental Committee
Report of the Inter-Departmental Committee appointed to consider the Methods of dealing with Inventions made by Workers aided or maintained from Public Funds (HMSO 1922)
Terms of reference
"1. To consider the methods of dealing with inventions made by the workers aided or maintained from public funds, whether such workers be engaged (a) as research workers, or (b) in some other technical capacity, so as to give a fair reward to the inventor and thus encourage further effort, to secure the utilisation in industry of suitable inventions and to protect the national interest, and 2 To outline a course of procedure in respect of inventions arising out of State-aided or supported work, which shall further these aims and be suitable for adoption by all Government Departments concerned"
Witnesses
There was no live evidence

Dating of Patents Committee 1927

Dating of Patents Committee 1927 [REP20]
Departmental Committee
Report of the Dating of Patents Committee (HMSO 1927)
Terms of reference
"To enquire into and report whether any, and if so, what change is desirable in the practice of the United Kingdom of: (a) Dating and sealing patents applied for under Section 91 of the Patents Act, 1907 and 1919, as of the date of the application in the foreign State; (b) Dating and sealing other patents as of the date of application in the United Kingdom as provided by Section 13 of the Acts"
Witnesses
There were no live witnesses, but evidence was provided by the persons listed in the appendix.

Sargant Committee 1931

Sargant Committee 1931 [REP21]		
Departmental Committee		
Report of the Departmental Committee on the Patents and Designs Act and the practice of the Patent Office (Sargant Committee) (1931 Cmd 3829), Vol 16, p 709		
Terms of reference		
"To be a Committee to consider and report whether any, and if so what, amendments in the Patents and Designs Acts, or changes in the practice of the Patent Office are desirable"		
Appointment		Minute of Board of Trade dated 18 May 1929
Pres	186 CJ 191; 163 LJ 166 (26 Mar 1931)	
Witnesses		
No minutes of evidence are included in the report, but there is a list of witnesses on p 100		

Swann Committee 1945–47

Swann Committee 1945–47 [REP22]		
Departmental Committee		
First Interim Report of the Departmental Committee on Patents and Designs Act (First Interim Report) (1944–45 Cmd 6618), Vol 5, p 421 Second Interim Report of the Departmental Committee on Patents and Designs Act (Second Interim Report) (1945–46 Cmd 6789), Vol 14, p 155 Final Report of the Departmental Committee on Patents and Designs Act (1946–47 Cmd 7206), Vol 13, p 457		
Terms of reference		
"Report on: (a) The initiation, conduct and determination of legal proceedings arising under or out of the Patents and Designs Acts, including the constitution of the appropriate tribunal; and (b) The provisions of these Acts for the prevention of the abuse of monopoly rights"		
Appointment		President of Board of Trade, Apr 1944
First	200 CJ 89; 177 LJ 93 (10 Apr 1945)	
Second	201 CJ 223; 178 LJ 245 (10 Apr 1946)	
Final	202 CJ 381; 179 LJ 500 (20 Oct 1947)	
Witnesses		
There are no minutes of evidence, but there is a list of witnesses: Second Interim Report, p 37, and Final Report, p 84		
Notes		
National Archive Swann Committee: BT306/1 to BT306/66		

Howitt Committee 1956

Howitt Committee 1956 [REP23]
Departmental Committee
Report of the Committee of Enquiry on the powers of the Crown to authorise the use of unpatented inventions and unregistered designs in connection with defence contracts (1955–56 Cmd 9788), Vol 14, p 187

(continued)

(continued)

Terms of reference
"To Consider and report:
(i)   Whether the Crown should have permanent powers to authorise the use, in connection with defence contracts, of unpatented inventions and unregistered designs (and models, documents, and information relating thereto), and thereby to override contractual obligations as to such use; and
(ii)   if so, the conditions under which any such powers should be exercised"

Appointment		President of Board of Trade, November 1955
Pres	211 CJ 338; 188 LJ 334 (20 Jun 1956)	

Witnesses
There was inter-departmental evidence, but no live evidence

Notes
National Archive
Committee of Enquiry to Investigate and Report: BT258/574 to BT258-590

Banks Committee 1971

Banks Committee 1971 [REP24]
Departmental Committee
Report of the Committee to Examine the Patent System and Patent Law (1970–71 Cmnd 4407), Vol 43, p 1
Terms of reference
Original: "To examine and report with recommendations upon the British patent system and patent law, in light of the increasing need for international collaboration in patent matters and, in particular, of the United Kingdom Government's intention to ratify the recent Council of Europe Convention on patent laws"
Further clarified to include:
"Its effectiveness and suitability as an instrument for strengthening the national economy by encouraging invention, the making known of new inventions and the bringing of new inventions into commercial operation.
The changes which might, or should, be made in the present system of granting patents, having regard to:
(1)   the conclusions reached about its effectiveness and suitability;
(2)   the continual increase in the number of applications for British patents and the difficulty of maintaining a staff of suitability qualified Examiners to deal with them;
(3)   the preponderance of applications from countries other than the United Kingdom.
The relationship of the United Kingdom system to international and foreign patent systems, with particular regard to:
(i)   simplifying the procedure to be followed by British applicants in obtaining patent protection in other countries;
(ii)   the desirability of harmonising national patent laws and the degree of protection obtained by the same invention in different countries;
(iii)   the possibility of lightening the load on the British Patent Office.
Legislative changes aimed at giving effective protection without detriment to the public interest and facilitating the settlement speedily and cheaply of all matters concerning patents, whether before the Patent Office or the Courts.
The desirability, or practicability, of complementing the patent system by legislation for the protection of 'know-how'"

Appointment		HC Deb, 10 May 1967, Vol 746(5th), col c241W
Pres	226 CJ 43; 203 LJ 39 (14 Jul 1970)	

Witnesses
There are no minutes of evidence, but there is a list of witnesses on p 188

Notes
National Archive
Committee on the Patent System and Patent Law (Banks Committee): BT136/1 to BT 136/15

2 Parliamentary papers

PPP1	Correspondence between Treasury and Royal Society relative to Invention of Charles Babbage [on his Application of Machinery for calculating Mathematical Tables] Pres: 22 May 1823 (78 CJ 330)	(1823 HC Papers 370), Vol 15, p 9	
PPP2	Return of Expenses in taking out Patent in Scotland Ord: 23 Mar 1826 (81 CJ 206) Pres/Prt: 14 Apr 1826 (81 CJ 242)	(1826 HC Papers 270), Vol 23, p 251	
PPP3	Return of Expenses in taking out Patent in England Ord: 23 Mar 1826 (81 CJ 206) Pres: 5 Apr 1826 (81 CJ 211) Prt: 6 Apr 1826 (81 CJ 216)	(1826 HC Papers 216), Vol 21, p 139	
PPP4	Return of Expenses in taking out Patent at the Attorney General's and the Attorney and Solicitor General's Officers for England Ord: 23 Mar 1826 (81 CJ 206) Pres/Prt: 10 Apr 1826 (81 CJ 221)	(1826 HC Papers 242), Vol 21, p 143	The Times, 11 Apr 1826
PPP5	Return of Expenses in taking out Patent in England (The Great Seal) Ord: 23 Mar 1826 (81 CJ 206) Pres: 18 Apr 1826 (81 CJ 252)	(1826 HC Papers 282), Vol 21, p 145	
PPP6	Return of Expenses in taking out Patent in England and Ireland (Signet Office) Ord: 23 Mar 1826 (81 CJ 206) Pres/Prt: 20 Apr 1826 (81 CJ 264)	(1826 HC Papers 294), Vol 21, p 147	
PPP7	Return of the Expenses incurred in taking out a Patent in Ireland, independent of the Specification; distinguishing the items or heads of that expense Ord: 23 Mar 1826 (81 CJ 206) Pres: 13 Apr 1826 (81 CJ 233)	Not published	
PPP8	Return of Expenses in taking out Patent, independent of the Specification; distinguishing the Items or Heads of that Expense; also the Lowest and Highest Expense of the Specification-so far as relates to the Office of Secretary of State for the Home Department Ord: 23 Mar 1826 (81 CJ 206) Pres/Prt: 7 Apr 1826 (81 CJ 218)	(1826 HC Papers 239), Vol 21, p 141	
PPP9	Minute of the Lords of the Committee of Privy Council for Trade dated 4 November 1834 on granting Letters Patent Address: 24 May 1837 (92 CJ 403) Pres: 25 May 1837 (92 CJ 406) Prt: 27 May 1837 (92 CJ 413)	(1837 HC Papers 337), Vol 39, p 287	

(continued)

(continued)

PPP10	Return of Fees and Expenses on taking out Patent of Invention in United Kingdom Address: 19 Apr 1838 (83 CJ 724) Answer: 24 Jul 1838 (83 CJ 744) Pres: 15 Aug 1838 (83 CJ 882) Prt: 16 Aug 1838 (83 CJ 885)	(1837–38 HC Papers 729), Vol 36, p 421	Mirror, 7 Mar 1838, Vol 3, p 2530
PPP11	Return of Fees and Expenses on taking out Patent of Invention in England, Scotland and Ireland Ord: 18 Jul 1838 (93 CJ 341) Pres: 8 Apr 1838 (94 CJ 167) Prt: 9 April 1838 (94 CJ 170)	(1839 HC Papers 172), Vol 30, p 573	Mirror, 15 Aug 1838, Vol 8, p 6311
PPP12	Report from Select Committee on Arts and Manufactures: together with the minutes of evidence, and appendix [also included as REP3] Rep/Prt: 4 Sep 1835 (90 CJ 645)	(1835 HC Papers 598), Vol 5, p 375	
PPP13	Report from the Select Committee on Arts and their Connexion with Manufactures; with the minutes of evidence, appendix and index [also included as REP3] Rep/Prt: 16 Aug 1836 (91 CJ 818)	(1836 HC Papers 568), Vol 9, p 1	
PPP14	Return of Expenditure of Sums voted in 1838 for Rewards, Experiments and Expenses for Scientific Purposes Ord: 26 Mar 1839 (94 CJ 150) Pres: 9 Apr 1839 94 CJ 169 Prt: 13 Apr 1839 (94 CJ 179)	(1839 HC Papers 181), Vol 30, p 659	
PPP15	Minute of Committee of Privy Council for Trade (Nov 1834) on granting Letters Patent Ord Re-Prt: 7 Jul 1840 (95 CJ 491)	(1840 HC Papers 449), Vol 29, p 557	Mirror, 7 Jul 1840, Vol 5, p 4369
PPP16	Return of Cases in which Judicial Committee of Privy Council have reported on Persons having Letters Patent; Applications for Prolongation of Patents Ord: 27 Feb 1840 (95 CJ 122) Pres: 20 Mar 1840 (95 CJ 192) Prt: 24 Mar 1840 (95 CJ 208)	(1840 HC Papers 155), Vol 29, p 559	Mirror, 27 Feb 1840, Vol 2, p 1317; *The Times*, 28 Feb 1840 Mirror, 20 Mar 1840, Vol 2, p 1824 Mirror, 24 Mar 1840, Vol 2, p 1927
PPP17	Account of Number of Days on which Judicial Committee of Privy Council has during nine years ending 19th Feb 1842 Ord: 18 Feb 1842 (74 LJ 36) Pres/Prt: 21 Feb 1842 (74 LJ 40) Amended: 28 Feb 1842 (74 LJ 53) Updated Ord: 5 Aug 1842 (74 LJ 520) Pres: 9 Aug 1842 (74 LJ 537)	(1842 HL Papers 31), Vol 18, p 39 Amended (1842 HL Papers 38), Vol 18, p 39 Not Prt HL/PO/JO/10/8/1416	
PPP18	Letters Patent for England on Breakwater at Plymouth to J Needham Taylor Ord: 5 Apr 1842 (97 CJ 161) Pres: 8 Apr 1842 (97 CJ 170) Prt: 12 Apr 1842 (97 CJ 178)	(1842 HC Papers 157), Vol 39, p 503	
PPP19	Fees and Expenses payable on taking out a Patent of Invention Ord: 14 Feb 1845 (100 CJ 34)	Never presented	

PPP20	Correspondence between HMG and Mr Warner relative to Experiments	(1844 HC Papers 620), Vol 33, p 419	
	Ord: 31 Jul 1844 (99 CJ 565) Pres: 7 Aug 1844 (99 CJ 628) Prt: 8 Aug 1844 (99 CJ 636)		
	Correspondence since Aug 1944	(1846 HC Papers 351), Vol 26, p 499	
	Address: 13 May 1846 (101 CJ 687) Answer: 18 May 1846 (101 CJ 719) Pres/Prt: 29 May 1846 (101 CJ 794)		
PPP21	Fees on Patents for Invention: Return of all Fees charged on passing a Patent for Invention through the different Public Offices in Scotland	(1845 HL Papers 4), Vol 16, p 133	
	Ord: 6 Aug 1844 (76 LJ 668) Pres/Prt: 10 Feb 1845 (77 LJ 12)		
PPP22	Fees on Patents for Invention: Return of all Fees charged on passing a Patent for Invention through the different Public Offices in Ireland	(1845 HL Papers 13), Vol 16, p 135	
	Ord: 6 Aug 1844 (76 LJ 668) Pres/Prt: 14 Feb 1845 (77 LJ 21)		
PPP23	Major-General Pasley's Report on Powell's Patent Sectional Transferable Railway Carriage for carrying Goods on Broad or Narrow Gauge	(1846 HC Papers 415), Vol 38, p 377	
	Pres on command: 18 Jun 1846 (101 CJ 900); Prt: 20 Jun 1846 (101 CJ 908)		
PPP24	Reports to Admiralty of Trials of Rettie's Signals for Prevention of Collision of Vessels at Sea	(1846 HC Papers 568), Vol 26, p 471	
	Ord: 13 May 1846 (101 CJ 687) Pres: 29 May 1846 (101 CJ 797) Prt: 4 Aug 1846 (101 CJ 1156)		
PPP25	Report on Trial of Warner's "Long Range"	(1847 HC Papers 165), Vol 36, p 473	
	Ord: 25 Feb 1847 (102 CJ 163) Pres: 9 Mar 1847 (102 CJ 221) Prt: 10 Mar 1847 (102 CJ 228)		
	Instructions of Board of Ordnance to Officers to conduct Experiments of Warner's Long Range	(1847 HC Papers 250), Vol 36, p 475	
	Ord: 25 Mar 1847 (102 CJ 282) Pres/Prt: 12 Apr 1847 (102 CJ 318)		
	Account of money spent on trials	(1847 HC Papers 302), Vol 36, p 485	
	Ord: 26 Mar 1847 (102 CJ 289) Pres: 20 Apr 1847 (102 CJ 383) Prt: 21 Apr 1847 (102 CJ 388)		
PPP26	Abstract Return of Number of Letters Patent for Invention in England, Ireland and Scotland 1845–47	(1847–48 HC Papers 457), Vol 39, p 421	
	Address: 13 Mar 1848 (103 CJ 317) Answer: 21 Mar 1848 (103 CJ 350) Pres: 29 Jun 1848 (103 CJ 665) Prt (abstract only): 3 Jul 1848 (103 CJ 676)		
PPP27	Correspondence and Reports relative to Water Bulkheads invented by AH Holdsworth	(1847–48 HC Papers 554 and 554-II), Vol 41, p 283 and 289	
	Ord: 5 Jul 1848 (103 CJ 685) Pres: 25 Jul 1848 (103 CJ 784) Prt: 28 Jul 1848 (103 CJ 799)		

(continued)

(continued)

PPP28	Return of Number of Letters Patent for Inventions sealed at Westminster and in Scotland and Ireland and Colonies 1838–47 Address: 14 Aug 1848 (103 CJ 921) Answer: 18 Aug 1848 (103 CJ 947) Pres: 9 Feb 1849 (104 CJ 44) Prt: 12 Feb 1849 (104 CJ 51)	(1849 HC Papers 23), Vol 45, p 381	
PPP29	Report by Professors of Chemistry to Board of Inland Revenue and Correspondence, to Dr J Scoffern's Patent for refining sugar Ord/Pres/Prt: 14 Aug 1850 (105 CJ 664)	(1850 HC Papers 708), Vol 52, p 477	
PPP30	Copies of all Memorials and Petitions address to the Board of Trade on Patent Law Ord: 1 Apr 1851 (83 LJ 108) Pres/Prt: 10 Apr 1851 (83 LJ 126)	(1851 HL Papers 72), Vol 16, p 455	
PPP31	Correspondence relative to Construction of Machine by Mr Archer for perforating Sheets of Postage Label Stamps Ord: 21 Jun 1851 (106 CJ 301) Pres: 22 Jul 1851 (106 CJ 384) Prt: 24 Jul 1851 (106 CJ 393)	(1851 HC Papers 582), Vol 51, p 51	
PPP32	Report by Board of General Officers on Fitness of Dowie's Patent Boots for Use of Army Ord: 16 Mar 1852 (107 CJ 95) Pres: 18 Mar 1852 (107 CJ 101) Prt: 19 Mar 1852 (107 CJ 104)	(1852 HC Papers 170), Vol 30, p 141	
PPP33	Letter to Chancellor of Exchequer by Patentee of Plan for perforating Postage Labels Ord: 9 Feb 1852 (107 CJ 26) Pres/Prt: 27 Feb 1852 (107 CJ 82)	(1852 HC Papers 129), Vol 49, p 363	
PPP34	Agreement of August 1851 between Inland Revenue and Messer Bacon & Petch for Engraving, Printing and gumming Postage Labels Ord: 12 Feb 1852 (107 CJ 41) Pres: 12 Mar 1852 (107 CJ 88) Prt: 15 Mar 1852 (107 CJ 91)	(1852 HC Papers 145), Vol 49, p 359	
PPP35	Mr Gurney's Memorial to Treasury Jun 1849 respecting Claim to Remuneration for Use of his Patent Light in lighting House of Commons Libraries Ord: 15 May 1852 (107 CJ 216) Pres (No 481): 15 Jun 1852 (107 CJ 296) Prt (No 481): 15 Jun 1852 (107 CJ 298) Pres/Prt (No 511): 30 Jun 1852 (107 CJ 370)	(1852 HC Papers 481), Vol 42, p 163 (1852 HC Papers 511), Vol 42, p 155	
PPP36	Return of the Amount of Fees and Stamps Duties in lieu of Fees received under the Patent Law Amendment Act 1852 between 1 October 1852 and 31 July 1853 Ord: 1 Aug 1853 (85 LJ 553) Pres: 5 Aug 1853 (85 LJ 585)	Not printed HL/PO/JO/10/9/162	
PPP37	Return of the Amount of Fees and Stamps Duties in lieu of Fees received under the Patent Law Amendment Act 1852 between 1 October 1852 and 31 December 1853; and also Salaries, Fees, Allowances, Sums and Compensation under that Act Ord: 23 Jun 1854 (86 LJ 278)	Not returned	

PPP38	Letters to Mr Rettie, Inventor of Coloured Light System of Signals for Saving Collisions at Sea Ord: 27 May 1852 (107 CJ 245) Pres: 1 Jul 1852 (107 CJ 370) Prt: 7 Dec 1852 (108 CJ 176)	(1852–53 HC Papers 59), Vol 60, p 269	
PPP39	Correspondence relating to the Trials of Rettie's Invention Ord: 2 Jun 1853 (108 CJ 538)	Never presented	
PPP40	Correspondence on Dowie's Patent Boots Ord: 11 Apr 1853 (108 CJ 384) Pres: 9 May 1853 (108 CJ 473) Prt: 10 May 1853 (108 CJ 477)	(1852–53 HC Papers 469), Vol 59, p 423	The Times, 16 Mar 1852
PPP41	Correspondence between Admiralty and Mr Richardson and Mr Bentinck, on Richardson's Tubular Life-Boat Ord: 10 Jun 1853 (108 CJ 568) Pres: 20 Jun 1853 (108 CJ 598) Prt: 21 Jun 1853 (108 CJ 603)	(1852–53 HC Papers 640), Vol 60, p 503	
PPP42	Papers and Correspondence between Admiralty and Mr Bovill, on his Patent Machinery for grinding Corn at Deptford Ord: 23 Nov 1852 (108 CJ 67) Pres: 5 Apr 1853 (108 CJ 365) Prt: 6 Apr 1853 (108 CJ 369)	(1852–53 HC Papers 301), Vol 60, p 293	
PPP43	Statement of Compensation under Patent Law Amendment Act Pres: 4 Apr 1854 (109 CJ 176)	Not printed HC/CL/JO/10/25/116	
PPP44	A Return of the Amount of Fees and Stamp Duties in lieu of Fees received under the Patent Law Amendment Act 1852, between 1st October 1852 and 31st December 1853; and also, of all Salaries, Fees, Allowances, Sums, and Compensation appointed, allowed, or granted under the aforesaid Act Ord: 23 Jun 1854 (86 LJ 278)	Not returned	
PPP45	Correspondence and Reports relating to Mr Redl's Cone Telegraph Ord: 23 Mar 1854 (109 CJ 150) Pres: 5 May 1854 (109 CJ 213) Prt: 16 May 1854 (109 CJ 245)	(1854 HC Papers 249), Vol 42, p 361	
PPP46	Major Wynne's Report on the Practical Working of Professor Gluckman's Apparatus for effecting a Means of Communication between Guards and Engine Drivers of Railway Trains, dated 27th June 1854 Pres/Prt: 1 May 1854 (86 LJ 112)	(1854 HL Papers 320), Vol 34, p 1	Also see: HL Deb, 25 Jul 1854, Vol 135(3rd), col 696–9
PPP47	Report of Master Shipwrights of Portsmouth on Berthon's Collapsing Life-Boat Ord: 19 Jun 1854 (109 CJ 318) Pres: 29 Jun 1954 (109 CJ 342) Prt: 29 Jun 1854 (109 CJ 345)	(1854 HC Papers 336), Vol 42, p 437	
PPP48	Report of Captain Wynne to Committee of Privy Council for Trade on Prof Gluckman's Invention of Communication between Guards and Drivers of Trains Pres: 11 Aug 1854; 7 Aug 1854 (109 CJ 492; 86 LJ 471)	(1854 C 1769), Vol 62, p 555	
PPP49	Letter from General Board of Health with Digest of Information for Consumption of Smoke Pres: 28 Jul 1854 (109 CJ 447; 28 LJ 440)	(1854 C 1854), Vol 61, p 533	

(continued)

(continued)

PPP50	Correspondence on Dowie's Patent Boots Ord: 17 Mar 1854 (109 CJ 138) Forthwith: 8 May 1854 (109 CJ 223) Pres/Prt: 16 May 1854 (109 CJ 245)	(1854 HC Papers 252), Vol 41, p 49	
PPP51	Report by Sir B Walker on Patent Tubular Life-Raft invented by Mr Parratt Ord: 19 Jun 1854 (109 CJ 318) Pres: 23 Jun 1854 (109 CJ 331) Prt: 27 Jun 1854 (109 CJ 339)	(1854 HC Papers 332), Vol 42, p 441	
PPP52	Return of Names who have petitioned Lord Chancellor to extend Time for Sealing Letters Patent or filing Specifications Ord: 26 Apr 1855 (110 CJ 182) Pres: 7 May 1855 (110 CJ 207) Prt: 18 Jun 1855 (110 CJ 300)	(1854–55 HC Papers 323), Vol 50, p 499	
PPP53	Returned of Names and Addresses who have petitioned Lord Chancellor for extending the time limit for proceeding with their patent Ord: 10 May 1855 (110 CJ 218) Pres: 18 May 1855 (110 CJ 241)	Never printed	
PPP54	Monies paid to Law Officers and their Clerks in Cases of Hearings and Oppositions in any Matter of Patents for Inventions Address: 13 Jul 1855 (110 CJ 374)	Never answered	
PPP55	Names of HM Ships fitted with Grant's Apparatus for obtaining Fresh-Water distilled from Sea Ord: 24 Jul 1857 (112 CJ 344) Pres: 6 Aug 1857 (112 CJ 380) Prt: 10 Aug 1857 (112 CJ 390)	(1857 Sess 2 HC Papers 254), Vol 27, p 271	
PPP56	Rep by Captain Denman Jan 1855 on Trials in HM Steam – yacht Tender Elfin of [Thomas] Prideaux's Self-closing Furnace-Valve door Ord: 23 Apr 1858 (113 CJ 131) Pres: 28 Apr 1858 (113 CJ 141) Prt: 29 Apr 1858 (113 CJ 143) Report of Mr Murray on Same Ord: 4 May 1858 (113 CJ 149) Pres: 13 May 1858 (113 CJ 173) Prt: 14 May 1858 (113 CJ 175)	(1857–58 HC Papers 243), Vol 39, p 285 (1857–58 HC Papers 277 and 277-I), Vol 39, p 287 and 293	
PPP57	Report on the Capabilities of Boydell's Traction Engine (Sir F Abbott to East India Company) Ord: 22 Apr 1858 (113 CJ 129) Pres: 29 Apr 1858 (113 CJ 143) Prt: 30 Apr 1858 (113 CJ 145)	(1857–58 HC Papers 249), Vol 42, p 513	
PPP58	Report by Chief Engineer of Trinity Steamship Argus relative to results from Use of Stevens' Patent Regulating Air Doors Ord: 2 July 1858 (113 CJ 275) Pres: 13 Jul 1858 (113 CJ 304) Prt: 14 Jul 1858 (113 CJ 310)	(1857–58 HC Papers 432), Vol 52, p 463	

PPP59	Report of Trials of Jeffries Smoke-Consuming Apparatus on Board *Vivid* between Dover and Ostend Apr 1857 Ord: 10 Jun 1858 (113 CJ 219) Pres: 15 Jun 1858 (113 CJ 230) Prt: 16 Jul 1858 (113 CJ 318)	(1857–58 HC Papers 435), Vol 39, p 281	
PPP60	Report to War Department on Applicability of Bray's Improved Traction Engine Address: 14 Jul 1858 (113 CJ 309) Pres: 20 Jul 1858 (113 CJ 329) Prt: 21 Jul 1858 (113 CJ 332)	(1857–58 HC Papers 451), Vol 37, p 175	
PPP61	Names of Officers employed by the Commissioners of Patents, Fees, Salaries, and Duties; Publications issued by Commissioners Ord: 5 Aug 1859 (114 CJ 344)	Never presented	
PPP62	Sums paid for Patents annually, from 1855 to 1860 and how disposed of Address: 23 Mar 1860 (115 CJ 153) Pres: 19 Apr 1860 (115 CJ 190)	Not printed	
PPP63	Report of Anchor Committee (including invention of tumbling fluke anchor) Rep/Prt: 27 Mar 1860 (115 CJ 162)	(1860 HC Papers 71), Vol 41, p 145	
PPP64	Amount of Public Money advanced by Private Persons for Experiments for improving Weapons of War Address: 28 Feb 1869 (115 CJ 93) Pres: 14 Jun 1869 (115 CJ 302) Prt: 15 Jun 1869 (115 CJ 306)	(1860 HC Papers 386), Vol 41, p 657	
PPP65	Correspondence between J Clare, Admiralty and Surveyor of Navy on Clare's Patent and Plans for building Iron Vessels for Royal Navy 1853 and 1854 Ord: 22 Feb 1861 (116 CJ 74) Pres: 8 Mar 1861 (116 CJ 97) Prt: 11 Mar 1861 (116 CJ 99)	(1861 HC Papers 94), Vol 37, p 129	HC Deb, 22 Feb 1861, Vol 161 (3rd), col 860–861
PPP66	Return of Amount of Fees realized by Patents of Inventions, and Amount paid into the Exchequer Address: 11 Mar 1863 (118 CJ 105) Pres: 27 Mar 1863 (118 CJ 147); 27 Jul 1863 (118 CJ 342) Prt: 8 Jul 1863 (118 CJ 343)	Not printed But included in (1863 HC Papers 423), Vol 37, p 525	
PPP67	Return showing Particulars relative to the Civil Service Estimates, No 7, respecting Patent Law Expenses 1862–63 Ord: 19 Jun 1863 (118 CJ 294) Pres: 7 Jul 1863 (118 CJ 342) Prt: 8 Jul 1863 (118 CJ 343)	(1863 HC Papers 423), Vol 37, p 525	
PPP68	Letters and Detailed Accounts of Costs incurred in Trial of Clare v Queen Ord: 17 Feb 1863 (118 CJ 60) Pres: 19 Mar 1863 (118 CJ 122) Prt: 24 Mar 1863 (118 CJ 132)	(1863 HC Papers 123), Vol 35, p 119	

(continued)

(continued)

PPP69	Correspondence between J Clare and Admiralty, 1854–56 Ord: 3 Mar 1863 (118 CJ 92) Pres: 20 Mar 1863 (118 CJ 125) Prt: 24 Mar 1863 (118 CJ 132)	(1863 HC Papers 124), Vol 36, p 123	
PPP70	Correspondence between War Office and Mr Metford on his Explosive Percussion Bullets Address: 3 Jun 1864 (119 CJ 285) Pres: 25 Jul 1864 (119 CJ 462) Prt: 26 Jul 1864 (119 CJ 467)	(1864 HC Papers 543), Vol 35, p 539	
PPP71	Return of Number of Patents for Inventions granted for England, Scotland, Ireland and Colonies 1650, 1750 &c. Address: 2 Mar 1869 (124 CJ 60) Pres: 5 Apr 1869 (124 CJ 111) Prt: 9 Apr 1869 (124 CJ 122)	(1868–69 HC Papers 138), Vol 50, p 601	
PPP72	Annual and Total Receipts of the Patent Office under the Patent Law Amendment Act of 1852 Ord: 11 May 1869 (124 CJ 193) Pres: 1 Jun 1869 (124 CJ 218) Prt: 3 Jun 1869 (124 CJ 222)	(1868–69 HC Papers 242), Vol 34, p 351	
PPP73	Public Official Documents received at the Foreign Office, showing why the Government of Prussia, and Dutch Government and others have recommend the Abolition of Patents for Inventions Ord: 2 Aug 1869 (124 CJ 387) Pres: 11 Feb 1870 (125 CJ 29) Prt: 17 Feb 1870 (125 CJ 41)	(1870 HC Papers 41), Vol 61, p 527	
PPP74	Correspondence between War Office and Colonel Boxer relating to his Patent for Fuses Address: 18 Mar 1870 (125 CJ 91) Pres: 5 Apr 1870 (125 CJ 128) Prt: 8 Apr 1870 (125 CJ 135)	(1870 HC Papers 161), Vol 42, p 501	
PPP75	Reports explaining Item (Reward to Inventors) in Army Estimates Address: 31 May 1871 (125 CJ 239) Pres/Prt: 31 May 1871 (125 CJ 240)	(1870 HC Papers 266), Vol 42, p 375	
PPP76	Reports to War Department on Mr Thomson's Road Steamer and its advantages for military purposes Address: 30 May 1870 (125 CJ 234) Pres: 16 Jun 1870 (125 CJ 256) Prt: 2 Aug 1870 (125 CJ 389)	(1870 HC Papers 408), Vol 42, p 653	
PPP77	Memorial by HPD Cunningham to Admiralty on Claims for Inventions Ord/Pres/Prt: 1 Aug 1871 (126 CJ 385)	(1871 HC Papers 400), Vol 40, p 613	
PPP78	Supplementary Army Estimate (Rewards to Inventors 1871–72) Pres/Prt: 7 Aug 1871 (126 CJ 401) (No 426) Pres/Prt: 11 Aug 1871 (126 CJ 415) (No 451)	(1871 HC Papers 426 and 451), Vol 38, p 365 and 367	
PPP79	Correspondence on Letters Patent for Inventions, since Report of Select Committee on Law, Practice and Effect of Letters Patent Address: 9 Aug 1872 (127 CJ 435) Pres: 6 Feb 1873 (128 CJ 4) Prt: 13 Feb 1873 (128 CJ 42)	(1873 HC Papers 23), Vol 53, p 505	

PPP80	Report by Her Majesty's Secretaries of Embassy and Legation respecting the Law and Practice in Foreign Countries regarding to inventions Delivered: 5 Jun 1873; 22 May 1873 (128 CJ 256; 106 LJ 196)	(1873 C 741), Vol 41, p 519	
PPP81	Report to Board of Trade on Results of Experiments with Dillon's and Roger's Mortar Apparatus and Rocket Apparatus for saving Life from Shipwreck on Coasts Ord: 26 May 1873 (128 CJ 246) Pres: 6 Jun 1873 (128 CJ 261) Prt: 9 Jun 1873 (128 CJ 266)	(1873 HC Papers 238), Vol 40, p 309	
PPP82	Correspondence respecting International Arrangements for Assimilation in Law and Practice in regard to Letters Patent of Invention Pres: 22 May 1874 (129 CJ 180; 106 LJ 196)	(1874 C 999), Vol 54, p 211	
PPP83	Correspondence between Admiralty and Rev CM Ramus on certain experiments [Hull Designs] Ord: 31 March 1873 (129 CJ 124) Pres: 16 May 1873 (129 CJ 222) Prt: 21 Jul 1874 (129 CJ 319)	(1874 HC Papers 313), Vol 38, p 585	
PPP84	Mr Froude Report to Admiralty on Rev Ramus Proposal June 1873 Ord: 10 Jul 1874 (129 CJ 292) Pres: 4 Aug 1874 (129 CJ 365) Prt: 6 Aug 1874 (129 CJ 372)	(1874 HC Papers, 388), Vol 38, p 653	
PPP85	Statement of Results on Trials of Griffith's Screw-Casting in Bruiser Gun-Boat and Steam Pinnace Ord: 17 Mar 1876 (131 CJ 103) Pres: 30 Mar 1876 (131 CJ 128) Prt: 4 Apr 1876 (131 CJ 138)	(1876 HC Papers 147), Vol 45, p 639	
PPP86	Correspondence between Board of Trade and Gas Referees, in reference to Mr Patterson taking out Patent for Gas Purification Ord/Pres: 29 May 1877 (131 CJ 229) Prt: 1 Jun 1877 (131 CJ 236)	(1876 HC Papers 260), Vol 68, p 109	
PPP87	Return of Fees received in Crown Office for Great Seal, Petty Bag Office and Patent Office of Attorney and Solicitor General, 1874, 1875 and 1876 Address: 19 Apr 1877 (132 CJ 164) Pres: 15 May 1877 (132 CJ 225) Prt: 31 May 1877 (132 CJ 239)	(1877 HC Papers 224), Vol 69, p 315	
PPP88	Patent Act of First Session of 1877 of German Parliament Pres/Prt: 15 Jun 1877 (132 CJ 278)	(1877 HC Papers 270), Vol 68, p 511	
PPP89	Report of Committee of Board of Trade to carry out Experiments in connection with Construction of Ships-of-War, Guns, Torpedoes, Rifles and Small Arms 1854–78 Address: 18 Jul 1877 (132 CJ 352) Pres: 13 Jun 1878 (133 CJ 284) Prt: 14 Jun 1878 (133 CJ 288)	(1878 HC Papers 233), Vol 47, p 495	
PPP90	Statement showing, from 1870 to 1878 inclusive, the Number of Patents then in the Fourteenth Year; and those being prolonged Ord/Prt: 24 May 1879 (134 CJ 243)	(1878–79 HC Papers 205), Vol 58, p 551	

(continued)

(continued)

PPP91	Report by TE Harrison to NE Railway Co on Westinghouse Automatic Brake Ord: 21 Jul 1879 (134 CJ 360) Pres: 25 Jul 1879 (134 CJ 373) Prt: 28 Jul 1879 (134 CJ 377)	(1878–79 HC Papers 317), Vol 63, p 399	
PPP92	Return of Annual and Total Receipts of Patent Office under Patent Law Amendment Act 1852 Ord: 21 Jun 1880 (135 CJ 228) Pres: 4 Sep 1880 (135 CJ 432) Prt: 7 Sep 1880 (135 CJ 434)	(1880 HC Papers 412), Vol 40, p 395	
PPP93	Return of Receipts from Patent Office 1880–81 Ord: 20 Jun 1881 (136 CJ 312) Pres: 6 Jul 1881 (136 CJ 351) Prt: 12 Jul 1881 (136 CJ 366)	(1881 HC Papers 325), Vol 57, p 317	
PPP94	Return of Receipts from Patent Office, 1881–82 Ord: 20 Apr 1882 (137 CJ 148) Pres: 25 Apr 1882 (137 CJ 157) Prt: 27 Apr 1882 (137 CJ 162)	(1882 HC Papers 163), Vol 37, p 317	
PPP95	Correspondence between Admiralty and Rev CM Ramus on certain experiments [Hull Designs] Ord: 22 May 1887 (137 CJ 218) Pres: 2 Jun 1887 (137 CJ 242) Prt: 8 May 1888 (138 CJ 191)	(1883 HC Papers 159), Vol 41, p 499	
PPP96	Report of Board of Trade on Experimental Testing of Copper Pipe Ord/Pres/Prt: 12 Jun 1888 (143 CJ 278)	(1888 HC Papers 219), Vol 90, p 111	
PPP97	Treasury Minute relating to Award to Major Watkin on Adoption and Use of his Artillery Position-Finder Pres: 27 Mar 1888 (143 CJ 127) Prt: 22 Jun 1888 (143 CJ 310)	(1888 HC Papers 235), Vol 45, p 417	
PPP98	Return of Comparative Statement of Number of Parts of Martini-Henry and new Magazine Rifles, Number of Workmen and Hours required to turn out Rifles, and Patents taken out by Mr Speed Address: 23 Jan 1891 (146 CJ 39) Pres/Prt: 29 Jan 1891 (146 CJ 49)	(1890–91 HC Papers 63), Vol 50, p 251	
PPP99	Treasury Minute under the Superannuation Act 1859 dated 15 June 1898 declaring that the office of Law Clerk in the Patent Office under the Board of Trade professional or other peculiar qualifications not ordinarily to be acquired in public service Pres: 22 Jun 1898 (153 CJ 278)	Not printed HC/CL/JO/10/192/151	HC Deb, 22 Jun 1898, Vol 59(4th), col 1080
PPP100	Report from the Select Committee on Patent Medicines together with the proceedings of the committee [Note: While called patent medicines, most such medicines were not patented, so patent law was only a small part of the inquiry] Appointed: 25 Apr 1922 (167 CJ 124) Member appointed: 21 May 1912 (167 CJ 178) Member appointed: 10 Oct 1912 (167 CJ 359) Rep/Pres: 6 Feb 1913 (167 CJ 529): stated inquiry not complete	1912–13 HC Papers 508), Vol 9, p 99	HC Deb, 25 Apr 1912, Vol 37(5th), col 1371–1373 HC Deb, 21 May 1912, Vol 38(5th), col 1757 HC Deb, 10 Oct 1912, Vol 42(5th), col 662 HC Deb, 6 Feb 1913, Vol 48(5th), col 3

PPP101	Report from the Select Committee on Patent Medicines Appointed: 14 Mar 1913 (168 CJ 18) Evidence Ord: 28 Mar 1913 (168 CJ 41) Member appointed: 22 Apr 1913 (168 CJ 89) Rep/Pres: 6 Aug 1913 (168 CJ 338): stated inquiry not complete	(1913 HC Papers 258), Vol 10, p 51	HC Deb, 14 Mar 1913, Vol 50(5th), col 670 HC Deb 28 Mar 1913, Vol 50(5th), col 1977 HC Deb, 22 Apr 1913, Vol 52(5th), col 322 HC Deb, 6 Aug 1913, Vol 56(5th), col 1455
PPP102	Report from the Select Committee on Patent Medicines, together with the proceedings of the committee, minutes of evidence, and appendices. [Evidence from all 1912–13, 1913 and 1914 committees] Appointed: 10 Jun 1914 (169 CJ 252) Evidence ref: 2 Jul 1914 (169 CJ 311) Rep/Pres: 4 Aug 1914 (169 CJ 411)	(1914 HC Papers 414), Vol 9, p 1	HC Deb, 10 Jun 1914, Vol 63(5th), col 451–452 HC Deb, 2 July 1914, Vol 64(5th), col 569
PPP103	Report of the Royal Commission on Income Tax Pres: 15 Mar 1920; 16 Mar 1920 (175 CJ 62; 152 LJ 78) [See par 197]	(1920 Cmd 618), Vol 18, p 97	
PPP104	United Kingdom Law: the Effects of the Strasbourg Convention of 1963: Report on Legislative Changes which would be involved in ratification Pres: 7 Dec 1965 (221 CJ 43; 198 LJ 40)	(1965–66 Cmnd 2835), Vol 6, p 763	
PPP105	Report of the Committee of Enquiry into the relationship of the pharmaceutical industry with the National Health Service 1965–67 (The Sainsbury Committee) Pres: 23 Oct 1967 (222 CJ 601; 199 LJ 757)	(1967 Cmnd 3410, Vol 45), p 687	

3 Reports of the Commissioner and Comptroller under the Patents Act

Report of the Commissioner of Patents 1852–53	(1854 HL Papers 321), Vol 36, p 1	109 CJ 462; 86 LJ 456 (Prt: 471) (1 Aug 1854) (Prt: 7 Aug 1854)	
Report 1854	(1854–45 C. 1972), Vol 15, p 717	110 CJ 414; 87 LJ 369 (26 Jul 1854)	
Report 1855	(1856 HL Papers 300), Vol 39, p 1	111 CJ 372; 88 LJ 458 (22 Jul 1856)	
Report 1856	(1857 Sess 2 HL Papers 156), Vol 28, p 1	112 CJ 380; 89 LJ 329 (6 Aug 1857)	
Report 1857	(1857–58 HL Papers 249), Vol 32, p 93	113 CJ 319; 90 LJ 412 (Prt: 438) (16 Jul 1858) (Prt: 22 Jul 1858)	
Report 1858	(1859 Sess 2 HC Papers 120), Vol 14, p 679	114 CJ 304 (Prt: 306); 91 LJ 395 (26 Jul 1859; 25 Jul 1859) (Prt: 27 Jul 1859; 25 Jul 1859)	
Report 1859	(1860 HL Papers 317), Vol 33, p 1	115 CJ 425; 92 LJ 625 (27 Jul 1860)	
Report 1860	(1861 HL Papers 200), Vol 32, p 39	116 CJ 376; 93 LJ 527 (19 Jul 1861; 16 Jul 1861)	
Report 1861	(1862 HL Papers 254), Vol 32, p 135	117 CJ 373; 94 LJ 531 (Prt: 568) (28 Jul 1862) (Prt: 7 Aug 1862)	
Report 1862	(1863 HL Papers 255), Vol 41, p 217	118 CJ 401; 95 LJ 596 (24 Jul 1863)	
Report 1863	(1864 HL Papers 257), Vol 35, p 307	119 CJ 482; 96 LJ 681 (29 Jul 1864)	
Report 1864	(1866 HL Papers 9), Vol 34, p 441	122 CJ 58; 97 LJ 639 (Prt: 98 LJ 33) (18 Feb 1867; 6 Jul 1865) (Prt: 13 Feb 1866)	
Report 1865	(1866 HL Papers 209), Vol 34, p 451	122 CJ 252; 98 LJ 610 (9 Jul 1967; 23 Jul 1866)	
Report 1866	(1867 HL Papers 310), Vol 32, p 437	122 CJ 438; 99 LJ 556 (8 Aug 1867)	
Report 1867	(1867–68 HL Papers 299), Vol 36, p 507	123 CJ 346; 100 LJ 437 (Prt: 487) (18 Jul 1868; 20 Jul 1868) (Prt: 29 Jul 1868)	
Report 1868	(1868–69 HL Papers 284), Vol 30, p 497	124 CJ 394; 101 LJ 562 (Prt: 574) (4 Aug 1869) (Prt: 6 Aug 1869)	
Report 1869	(1870 HL Papers 312), Vol 13, p 365	125 CJ 406; 102 LJ 555 (8 Aug 1870)	
Report 1870	(1871 HL Papers 327), Vol 14, p 393	126 CJ 435; 103 LJ 664 (17 Aug 1871)	
Report 1871	(1872 HC Papers 385), Vol 24, p 221	127 CJ 421 (Prt: 425); 104 LJ 722 (6 Aug 1872) (Prt: 7 Aug 1872)	
Report 1872	(1873 HC Papers 391), Vol 26, p 473	128 CJ 414 (Prt: 417); 105 LJ 706 (1 Aug 1873; 31 Jul 1873) (Prt: 2 Aug 1873)	
Report 1873	(1874 HC Papers 390), Vol 21, p 83	129 CJ 369 (Prt: 372); 106 LJ 432 (5 Aug 1874) (Prt: 6 Aug 1874)	
Report 1874	(1875 HC Papers 392), Vol 27, p 101	130 CJ 415 (Prt: 418); 107 LJ 398 (3 Aug 1875; 5 Aug 1875) (Prt: 4 Aug 1875)	

Report 1875	(1876 HC Papers 451), Vol 26, p 79	131 CJ 421 (Prt: 423); 108 LJ 414 (14 Aug 1876) (Prt: 15 Aug 1876)	
Report 1876	(1877 HC Papers 459), Vol 33, p 959	132 CJ 439; 109 LJ 404 (14 Aug 1877; 13 Aug 1877)	
Report 1877	(1878 HC Papers 400), Vol 36, p 585	133 CJ 437 (Prt: 438); 110 LJ 386 (15 Aug 1878) (Prt: 16 Aug 1878)	
Report 1878	(1878–79 HC Papers 355), Vol 26, p 809	134 CJ 416 (Prt: 419); 111 LJ 366 (8 Aug 1879) (Prt: 9 Aug 1879)	
Report 1879	(1880 HC Papers 369), Vol 25, p 785	135 CJ 370 (Prt: 401); 112 LJ 345 (10 Aug 1880) (Prt: 24 Aug 1880)	
Report 1880	(1881 HC Papers 397), Vol 37, p 821	136 CJ 451 (Prt: 457); 113 LJ 414 (11 Aug 1881; 12 Aug 1881)	
Report 1881	(1882 HC Papers 374), Vol 27, p 381	137 CJ 484 (Prt: 485); 114 LJ 423 (16 Aug 1882) (Prt: 17 Aug 1882)	
Report 1882	(1883 C 3780), Vol 27, p 835	138 CJ 477; 115 LJ 403 (21 Aug 1883; 13 Aug 1883)	
Report 1883	(1884 C 4164), Vol 28, p 785	139 CJ 442; 116 LJ 381 (8 Aug 1884; 31 Jul 1884)	
Comptroller General of Patents, Designs and Trade Marks First Report 1884	(1884 C 4040), Vol 28, p 805	139 CJ 259; 116 LJ 205 (26 May 1884; 23 May 1884)	
Second Report 1884	(1884–85 C 4428), Vol 28, p 627	140 CJ 245; 117 LJ 231 (19 May 1885)	
Third Report, 1885	(1886 C 4756), Vol 29, p 697	141 CJ 230; 118 LJ 225 (27 May 1886)	
Fourth Report 1886	(1887 C 5066), Vol 35, p 585	142 CJ 262; 119 LJ 217 (23 May 1887)	
Fifth Report 1887	(1888 C 5396), Vol 44, p 615	143 CJ 221; 120 LJ 175 (14 May 1888)	
Sixth Report 1888	(1889 C 5728), Vol 34, p 649	144 CJ 197; 121 LJ 155 (22 May 1889; 21 May 1889)	
Seventh Report 1889	(1890 C 6033), Vol 32, p 865	145 CJ 322; 122 LJ 304 (16 May 1890)	
Eighth Report 1890	(1890–91 C 6359), Vol 32, p 993	146 CJ 281; 123 LJ 199 (12 May 1891)	
Ninth Report 1891	(1892 C 6696), Vol 33, p 735	147 CJ 283; 124 LJ 191 (25 May 1892; 24 May 1892)	The Times, 30 May 1892
Tenth Report 1892	(1893–94 C 7020), Vol 30, p 921	148 CJ 297; 124 LJ 205 (19 May 1893; 30 May 1893)	
Eleventh Report 1893	(1894 C 7386), Vol 33, p 403	149 CJ 146; 126 LJ 99 (23 May 1894; 28 May 1894)	
Twelfth Report 1894	(1895 C 7750), Vol 34, p 527	150 CJ 217; 127 LJ 163 (20 May 1895)	HC Deb, 20 May 1895, Vol 33(4th), col 1573
Thirteenth Report 1895	(1896 C 8090), Vol 32, p 567	151 CJ 216; 128 LJ 184 (13 May 1896; 15 May 1896)	
Fourteenth Report 1896	(1897 C 8411), Vol 33, p 879	152 CJ 159; 129 LJ 124 (5 Apr 1897)	
Fifteenth Report 1897	(1898 C 214), Vol 32, p 811	153 CJ 222; 130 LJ 170 (23 May 1898)	HC Deb, 23 May 1898, Vol 58(4th), col 319 HL Deb, 23 May 1898, Vol 58(4th), col 264

(continued)

(continued)

Sixteenth Report 1898	(1899 HC Papers 202), Vol 29, p 447	154 CJ 208 (Prt: 214); 131 LJ 175 16 May 1899; 18 May 1899 (Prt: 17 May 1899)	HC Deb, 16 May 1899, Vol 71(4th), col 727 HC Deb, 17 May 1899, Vol 71(4th), col 889 HC Deb, 18 May 1899, Vol 71 (4th), col 910
Seventeenth Report 1899	(1900 HC Papers 165), Vol 26, p 837	155 CJ 175 (Prt: 178); 13 LJ 146 (16 May 1900; 7 May 1900) (Prt: 17 May 1900)	HC Deb, 7 May 1900, Vol 82(4th), col 867 HL Deb, 8 May 1900, Vol 82(4th), col 871
Eighteenth Report 1900	(1901 HC Papers 163), Vol 23, p 781	156 CJ 174; 133 LJ 139 (10 May 1901; 10 May 1901)	HC Deb, 10 May 1901, Vol 93(4th), col 1304 HL Deb, 10 May 1901, Vol 93(4th), col 1279
Nineteenth Report 1901	(1902 HC Papers 178), Vol 34, p 521	157 CJ 228; 134 LJ 183 (14 May 1902; 15 May 1902)	HC Deb, 14 May 1902, Vol 108(4th), col 172 HL Deb, 15 May 1902, Vol 108(4th), col 345
Twentieth Report 1902	(1903 HC Papers 177), Vol 23, p 523	158 CJ 192; 135 LJ 132 (22 May 1903)	HC Deb, 22 May 1903, Vol 122(4th), col 1507 HL Deb, 22 May 1903, Vol 122(4th), col 1457
Twenty-First Report 1903	(1904 HC Papers 178), Vol 22, p 519	159 CJ 188; 136 LJ 155 (16 May 1904; 13 May 1904)	HC Deb, 16 May 1904, Vol 134(4th), col 1363 HL Deb, 16 May 1904, Vol 134(4th), col 1273
Twenty-Second Report 1904	(1905 HC Papers 175), Vol 30, p 459	160 CJ 216; 137 LJ 170 (26 May 1905)	HC Deb, 26 May 1905, Vol 146(4th), col 1531 HL Deb, 26 May 1905, Vol 146(4th), col 1516
Twenty-Third Report 1905	(1906 HC Papers 167), Vol 31, p 1083	161 CJ 179; 138 LJ 166 (14 May 1906; 17 May 1906)	HC Deb, 14 May 1906, Vol 157(4th), col 142 HL Deb, 17 May 1906, Vol 157(4th), col 587
Twenty-Fourth Report 1906	(1907 HC Papers 164), Vol 24, p 541	162 CJ 206; 139 LJ 139 (27 May 1907; 28 May 1907)	HC Deb, 27 May 1907, Vol 174(4th), col 1295 HL Deb, 28 May 1907, Vol 174 (4th), col 1455
Twenty-Fifth Report 1907	(1908 HC Papers 156), Vol 25, p 1	163 CJ 221; 140 LJ 197 (28 May 1908; 1 Jun 1908)	HC Deb, 28 May 1908, Vol 189(4th), col 1231 HL Deb, 1 Jun 1908, Vol 189(4th), col 1489
Twenty-Sixth Report 1908	(1909 HC Papers 98), Vol 35, p 783	164 CJ 106; 141 LJ 89 (7 Apr 1909)	
Twenty-Seventh Report 1909	(1910 HC Papers 94), Vol 44, p 505	165 CJ 86; 142 LJ 93 (12 Apr 1910)	
Twenty-Eighth Report 1910	(1911 HC Papers 95), Vol 38, p 1	166 CJ 90; 143 LJ 87 (20 Mar 1911)	
Twenty-Ninth Report 1911	(1912–13 HC Papers 66), Vol 42, p 697	167 CJ 62; 144 LJ 62 (18 Mar 1912)	HC Deb, 18 Mar 1912, Vol 35(5th), col 1504
Thirtieth Report 1912	(1913 HC Papers 48), Vol 38, p 61	168 CJ 45; 145 LJ 39 (1 Apr 1913)	
Thirty-First Report 1913	(1914 HC Papers 161), Vol 44, p 49	169 CJ 95; 146 LJ 115 (24 Apr 1914; 25 Apr 1914)	HC Deb, 24 Apr 1914, Vol 60(5th), col 166
Thirty-Second Report 1914	(1914–16 HC Papers 160), Vol 32, p 1	170 CJ 87; 147 LJ 102 (16 Mar 1915)	HC Deb, 16 Mar 1915, Vol 70(5th), col 1895

Thirty-Third Report 1915	(1916 HC Papers 58), Vol 14, p 463	171 CJ 59; 148 LJ 80 (17 Apr 1916)	HC Deb, 17 Apr 1916, Vol 81(5th), col 2046 HL Deb,17 Apr 1916, Vol 21 (5th), col 745
Thirty-Fourth Report 1916	(1917–18 HC Papers 79), Vol 17, p 823	172 CJ 93; 149 LJ 106 (9 May 1917)	
Thirty-Fifth Report 1917	(1918 HC Papers 87), Vol 12, p 537	173 CJ 159; 150 LJ 181 (15 Jul 1918; 16 Jul 1918)	
Thirty-Sixth Report 1918	(1919 HC Papers 172), Vol 27, p 31	174 CJ 296; 151 LJ 365 (11 Aug 1919)	
Thirty-Seventh Report 1919	(1920 HC Papers 106), Vol 22, p 353	175 CJ 186; 152 LJ 199 (2 Jun 1920; 8 Jun 1920)	
Thirty-Eighth Report 1920	(1921 HC Papers 74), Vol 16, p 1	176 CJ 88; 153 LJ 105 (12 Apr 1921)	
Thirty-Ninth Report 1921	(1922 HC Papers 90), Vol 10, p 285	177 CJ 164; 154 LJ 192 (22 May 1922; 23 May 1922)	
Fortieth Report 1922	(1923 HC Papers 71), Vol 12, Pt 2, p 247	178 CJ 152; 155 LJ 134 (14 May 1923; 15 May 1923)	
Forty-First Report 1923	(1924 HC Papers 65), Vol 12, p 1	179 CJ 157; 156 LJ 151 (30 Apr 1924; 6 May 1924)	
Forty-Second Report 1924	(1924–25 HC Papers 113), Vol 15, p 157	180 CJ 238; 157 LJ 215 (27 May 1925; 27 May 1925)	
Forty-Third Report 1925	(1926 HC Papers 87), Vol 15, p 147	181 CJ 193; 158 LJ 144 (7 Jun 1926)	
Forty-Fourth Report 1926	(1927 HC Papers 65), Vol 11, p 915	182 CJ 148; 159 LJ 105 (9 May 1927; 10 May 1927)	
Forty-Fifth Report 1927	(1928 HC Papers 69), Vol 11, p 849	183 CJ 128; 160 LJ 109 (30 Apr 1928; 1 May 1928)	
Forty-Sixth Report 1928	(1928–29 HC Papers 111), Vol 9, p 1	184 CJ 252; 161 LJ 281 (7 May 1929)	
Forty-Seventh Report 1929	(1929–30 HC Papers 123), Vol 16, p 899	185 CJ 338; 162 LJ 336 (12 May 1930; 13 May 1930)	
Forty-Eighth Report 1930	(1930–31 HC Papers 101), Vol 16, p 685	186 CJ 259; 163 LJ 241 (18 May 1931; 19 May 1931)	
Forty-Ninth Report 1931	(1931–32 HC Papers 80), Vol 12, p 515	187 CJ 212; 164 LJ 198 (27 May 1932; 31 May 1932)	
Fiftieth Report 1932	(1932–33 HC Papers 116), Vol 15, p 235	188 CJ 197; 165 LJ 180 (18 May 1933)	
Fifty-First Report 1933	(1933–34 HC Papers 60), Vol 14, p 677	189 CJ 135; 166 LJ 119 (27 Mar 1934)	
Fifty-Second Report 1934	(1934–35 HC Papers 77), Vol 10, p 853	190 CJ 176; 167 LJ 152 (17 Apr 1935; 30 Apr 1935)	
Fifty-Third Report 1935	(1935–36 HC Papers 79), Vol 14, p 243	191 CJ 174; 168 LJ 168 (21 Apr 1936; 28 Apr 1936)	
Fifty-Fourth Report 1936	(1936–37 HC Papers 104), Vol 14, p 669	192 CJ 220; 169 LJ 192 (21 Apr 1937)	
Fifty-Fifth Report 1937	(1937–38 HC Papers 107), Vol 14, p 453	193 CJ 223; 170 LJ 168 (28 Apr 1938; 2 May 1938)	
Fifty-Sixth Report 1938	(1938–39 HC Papers 115), Vol 14, p 135	194 CJ 213; 171 LJ 197 (4 May 1939)	
Fifty-Seventh Report 1939	(1939–40 HC Papers 125), Vol 5, p 99	195 CJ 134; 172 LJ 129 (13 May 1940)	

(continued)

(continued)

Fifty-Eighth Report 1940	Not printed – typescript in British Library	196 CJ 130; 173 LJ 123 (27 May 1941)	
Fifty-Ninth Report 1941	Not printed – typescript in British Library	197 CJ 99; 174 LJ 111 (12 May 1942)	
Sixtieth Report 1942	Not printed – typescript in British Library	198 CJ 105; 175 LJ 118 (11 May 1943)	
Sixty-First Report 1943	Not printed – typescript in British Library	199 CJ 98; 176 LJ 92 (25 Apr 1944)	
Sixty-Second Report 1944	Not printed – typescript in British Library	200 CJ 137; 177 LJ 122 (29 May 1945)	
Sixty-Third Report 1945	Not printed – typescript in British Library	201 CJ 264; 178 LJ 283 (21 May 1946)	
Sixty-Fourth Report 1946	Not printed – typescript in British Library	202 CJ 236; 179 LJ 234 (21 May 1947)	
Sixty-Fifth Report 1947	Not printed – typescript in British Library	203 CJ 285; 180 LJ 271 (28 May 1948)	
Sixty-Sixth Report 1948	(1948–49 HC Papers 175), Vol 19, p 171	204 CJ 252; 181 LJ 239 (25 May 1949)	
Sixty-Seventh Report 1949	(1950 HC Papers 72), Vol 13, p 227	205 CJ 122; 182 LJ 114 (24 May 1959)	
Sixty-Eighth Report 1950	(1950–51 HC Papers 193), Vol 18, p 93	206 CJ 217; 183 LJ 172 (29 May 1951)	
Sixty-Ninth Report 1951	(1951–52 HC Papers 197), Vol 17, p 785	207 CJ 241; 184 LJ 195 (21 May 1952)	
Seventieth Report 1952	(1952–53 HC Papers 166), Vol 16, p 237	208 CJ 207; 185 LJ 173 (5 May 1953)	
Seventy-First Report 1953	(1953–54 HC Papers 185), Vol 18, p 219	209 CJ 220; 186 LJ 207 (27 May 1954)	
Seventy-Second Report 1954	(1955–56 HC Papers 6), Vol 26, p 205	211 CJ 17; 188 LJ 20 (9 Jun 1955)	
Seventy-Third Report 1955	(1955–56 HC Papers 293), Vol 26, p 235	211 CJ 313; 188 LJ 312 (30 May 1956)	
Seventy-Fourth Report 1956	(1956–57 HC Papers 179), Vol 18, p 1	212 CJ 200; 189 LJ 194 (21 May 1957)	
Seventy-Fifth Report 1957	(1957–58 HC Papers 202), Vol 17, p 1	213 CJ 207; 190 LJ 179 (15 May 1958)	
Seventy-Sixth Report 1958	(1958–59 HC Papers 190), Vol 18, p 727	214 CJ 212; 191 LJ 225 (8 May 1959; 12 May 1958)	
Seventy-Seventh Report 1959	(1959–60 HC Papers 207), Vol 20, p 1	215 CJ 225; 192 LJ 244 (18 May 1960)	
Seventy-Eighth Report 1960	(1960–61 HC Papers 197), Vol 20, p 1	216 CJ 209; 193 LJ 220 (1 May 1961)	
Seventy-Ninth Report 1961	(1961–62 HC Papers 182), Vol 20, p 1	217 CJ 207; 184 LJ 210 (18 Apr 1962)	
Eightieth Report 1962	(1962–63 HC Papers 222), Vol 23, p 1	218 CJ 210; 195 LJ 257 (8 May 1963)	
Eighty-First Report 1963	(1963–64 HC Papers 217), Vol 18, p 1	219 CJ 233; 196 LJ 263 (12 May 1964)	
Eighty-Second Report 1964	(1964–65 HC Papers 197), Vol 21, p 1	220 CJ 262; 197 LJ 281 (12 May 1965)	
83rd Report 1965	(1966–67 HC Papers 45), Vol 45, p 445	222 CJ 82; 199 LJ 73 (26 May 1966)	

84th Report 1966	(1966–67 HC Papers 469), Vol 45, p 477	222 CJ 464; 199 LJ 514 (1 May 1967)	
85th Report 1967	(1967–68 HC Papers 238), Vol 30, p 181	223 CJ 255; 200 LJ 337 (22 May 1968; 23 May 1968)	
86th Report 1968	(1968–69 HC Papers 277), Vol 44, p 379	224 CJ 276; 201 LJ 256 (9 Jun 1969; 22 May 1969)	
87th Report 1969	(1969–70 HC Papers 262), Vol 24, p 327	225 CJ 322; 202 LJ 297 (11 May 1970)	
88th Report 1970	(1970–71 HC Papers 393), Vol 43, p 263	226 CJ 464; 203 LJ 546 (26 May 1971)	
89th Report 1971	(1971–72 HC Papers 247), Vol 33, p 749	227 CJ 341; 204 LJ 282 (19 May 1971; 5 Jun 1971)	
90th Report 1972	(1972–73 HC Papers 271), Vol 28, p 773	228 CJ 339; 205 LJ 388 (23 May 1973)	
91st Report 1973	(1974 HC Papers 135), Vol 14, p 379	230 CJ 149; 207 LJ 169 (23 May 1974)	
92nd Report 1974	(1974–75 HC Papers 376), Vol 30, p 129	231 CJ 456; 208 LJ 594 (21 May 1975)	
93rd Report 1975	(1975–76 HC Papers 333), Vol 39, p 433	232 CJ 292; 209 LJ 594 (28 Apr 1976)	

4 Reports on international exhibitions

EXB1	First Report of the Commissioners for the Exhibition of 1851	107 CJ 220; 84 LJ 158 (17 May 1852)	(1852 C 1485), Vol 32, p 1
	Second Report of the Commissioners for the Exhibition of 1851	108 CJ 64; 85 LJ 36 (22 Nov 1852; 26 Nov 1852)	(1852–53 C 1566), Vol 54, p 407
	Third Report of the Commissioners for the Exhibition of 1851	111 CJ 146; 88 LJ 98 (18 Apr 1856; 17 Apr 1856)	(1856 C 2065), Vol 24, p 501
	Fourth Report of the Commissioners for the Exhibition of 1851	116 CJ 199; 93 LJ 273 (9 May 1861; 10 May 1861)	(1861 C 2819), Vol 32, p 245
	Fifth Report of the Commissioners for the Exhibition of 1851	122 CJ 464; 99 LJ 599 (16 Aug 1867)	(1867 C 3933), Vol 23, p 319
	Further reports not included as they relate to the fund		
EXB2	General Report of the British Commissioners to attend the Industrial Exhibition at New York	109 CJ 98; 84 LJ 36 (24 Feb 1854; 27 Feb 1854)	(1854 C 1716), Vol 26, p 1
	Special Report: George Wallis	109 CJ 98; 84 LJ 36 (24 Feb 1854; 27 Feb 1854)	(1854 C 1717), Vol 26, p 9
	Special Report: Joseph Whitworth	109 CJ 98; 84 LJ 36 (24 Feb 1854; 27 Feb 1854)	(1854 C 1718), Vol 26, p 103
	Special Report: Sir Charles Lyell	109 CJ 349; 84 LJ 326 (30 Jun 1854; 29 Jun 1854)	(1854 C 1793), Vol 26, p151
	Special Report: Mr Dilke	109 CJ 385; 84 LJ 370 (11 Jul 1854)	(1854 C 1801), Vol 26, p 203
	Special Report: Professor Wilson	109 CJ 491; 84 LJ 495 (10 Aug 1854)	(1854 C 1830), Vol 26, p 321
EXB3	Report on the Paris Universal Exhibition Part I	111 CJ 49; 88 LJ 28 (15 Feb 1856)	(1856 C 2049-I), Vol 50, p 1
	Part II	111 CJ 333; 88 LJ 388 (9 Jul 1856; 8 Jul 1856)	(1856 C 2049-II), Vol 36, p 1
	Part III	111 CJ 333; 88 LJ 388 (9 Jul 1856; 8 Jul 1856)	(1856 C 2049-III), Vol 36, p 413
	Report of the Commissioners for the Exhibition of 1862	118 CJ 170; 95 LJ 152 (20 Apr 1863)	(1863 C), Vol 14, p 565
EXB4	Report on the Paris Exhibition of 1867 Vol I	123 CJ 21; 100 LJ 16 (3 Dec 1867)	(1867–68 C 3968-I), Vol 30, Pt 1, p 1
	Vol II		(1867–68 C 3968-II), Vol 30, Pt 1, p 323,
	Vol III		(1867–68 C 3968-III), Vol 30, Pt 2, p 1
	Vol IV		(1867–68 C 3968-IV), Pt 3, Vol 30, p 1
	Vol V		(1867–68 C 3968-V), Vol 30, Pt 3, p 801
	Report of Her Majesty's Commissioners for the Universal Exhibition of Wares of Industry, Agriculture, and Fine Art held in Paris in 1867	124 CJ 387; 101 LJ 554 (2 Aug 1869)	(1868-9 C 4195), Vol 23, p 15

EXB5	Report on the Vienna Exhibition of 1873 Vol I	129 CJ 324; 106 LJ 393 (23 Jul 1874)	(1874 C 1072), Vol 73, p 1
	Vol II		(1874 C 1072-I), Vol 74, p 1
	Vol III		(1874 C 1072-II), Vol 75, p 1
	Vol IV		(1874 C 1072-III), Vol 76, p 1
	Appendix		(1874 C 1072-IV), Vol 77, p 1
EXB6	Report of the Education Department on the Philadelphia International Exhibition of 1876 Vol I	132 CJ 233; 109 LJ 172 (17 May 1877)	(1877 C 1774 and C 1774-I), Vol 34, p 1 and 435
	Vol II	132 CJ 417; 109 LJ 384 (6 Aug 1877; 7 Aug 1877)	(1877 C 1848), Vol 35, p 1
	Vol III	132 CJ 417; 109 LJ 384 (6 Aug 1877; 7 Aug 1877)	(1877 C 1890), Vol 36, p 505
EXB7	Report for the Paris Universal Exhibition of 1878 Vol I	135 CJ 179; 112 LJ 173 (3 Jun 1880)	(1880 C 2588), Vol 32, p 1
	Vol II		(1880 C2588-I), Vol 33, p 1
EXB8	Report for the Australian International Exhibition with Speeches &c.	137 CJ 20; 114 LJ 19 (10 Feb 1882)	(1882 C 3099), Vol 46, p 1
EXB9	Report of the Royal Commission for the Paris International Exhibition 1900, Vol I	156 CJ 222; 133 LJ 168 (10 Jun 1901)	(1901 Cd 629), Vol 31, p 1
	Vol II		(1901 Cd 630), Vol 31, p 1
EXB10	Report of His Majesty's Commissioners for the International Exhibition, St Louis 1904	161 CJ 7; 138 LJ 39 (19 Feb 1906)	(1906 Cd 2800), Vol 54, p 297
EXB11	Report on the Argentine Centennial Exhibition, Buenos Aires 1910	166 CJ 220; 143 LJ 197 (16 May 1911)	(1911 Cd 5677), Vol 21, p 813
EXB12	Report of the Royal Commission for International Exhibitions at Brussels, Rome and Turin in 1910 and 1911	167 CJ 520; 144 LJ 377 (31 Jan 1913; 4 Feb 1913)	(1912–13 Cd 6609), Vol 12, p 1
EXB13	British Empire Exhibition – Report from Chair of Executive Council of the British Empire Exhibition	178 CJ 4; 155 LJ 17 (13 Feb 1923)	(1923 Cmd 1799), Vol 19, p 1
EXB14	Report of the Committee to examine the present situation as regards the British Industries Fair	186 CJ 45; 163 LJ 48 (27 Nov 1930)	(1930–31 Cmd 3726), Vol 10, p 311

5 Reports of Royal Commissions on Awards to Inventors

After World War I			
ATI1	Commission on Awards to Inventors, First Report of The Commissioners	176 CJ 5; 153 LJ 19 (15 Feb 1921)	(1921 Cmd 1112), Vol 8, p 507
ATI2	Commission on Awards to Inventors, Second Report of The Commissioners	177 CJ 371; 154 LJ 446 (8 Dec 1922; 12 Dec 1922)	(1922 Sess II Cmd 1782), Vol 2, p 17
ATI3	Commission on Awards to Inventors, Third Report of The Commissioners	180 CJ 18; 157 LJ 18 (9 Dec 1924)	(1924–25 Cmd 2275), Vol 9, p 225
ATI4	Commission on Awards to Inventors, Fourth Report of The Commissioners	181 CJ 176; 158 LJ 133 (17 May 1926)	(1926 Cmd 2656), Vol 8, p 319
ATI5	Commission on Awards to Inventors, Fifth Report of The Commissioners	183 CJ 34; 160 LJ 38 (22 Feb 1928)	(1928 Cmd 3044), Vol 7, p111
ATI6	Commission on Awards to Inventors, Sixth Report of The Commissioners	186 CJ 445; 163 LJ 377 (7 Oct 1931)	(1930–31 Cmd 3957), Vol 10, p 283
ATI7	Commission on Awards to Inventors, Final Report of The Commissioners	193 CJ 32; 170 LJ 24 (17 Nov 1937)	(1937–38 Cmd 5594), Vol 12, p 649
After World War II			
ATI8	First Report of Royal Commission on Awards to Inventors	204 CJ 66; 181 LJ 52 (15 Dec 1948)	(1948–49 Cmd 7832), Vol 17, p 377
ATI9	Second Report of Royal Commission on Awards to Inventors	204 CJ 415; 181 LJ 473 (29 Nov 1949)	(1948–49 Cmd 7586), Vol 17, p 345
ATI10	Third Report of Royal Commission on Awards to Inventors	208 CJ 87; 185 LJ 58 (29 Jan 1953; 29 Mar 1853)	(1952–53 Cmd 8743), Vol 7, p 505
ATI11	Royal Commission on Awards to Inventors fourth and final report	211 CJ 286; 188 LJ 291 (2 May 1956)	(1955–56 Cmd 9744), Vol 11, p 353
Archives			
Royal Commission 1919–37: National Archive: T173/1 to T173/830 (except 35–71, 132 and 322) Royal Commission 1946–55: National Archive: T166/1 to T166/138 (index T166/100 to 104)			

6 Command Papers relating to international treaties

TRE1	International Convention for Protection of Industrial Property, Paris, March 1883; acceded to by H.M. Government, March 1884	(1884 C 4043), Vol 87, p 225 (1884 Commercial Series 28)	139 CJ 307; 116 LJ 252 (20 Jun 1884)
TRE2	Papers relative to Conference at Rome on Industrial Property; Correspondence relating to Fraudulent Use of Trade Marks	(1886 C 4837), Vol 60, p 413	141 CJ 206; 118 LJ 290 (21 Jun 1886)
TRE3	Correspondence relative to Accession of United States to International Union for Protection of Industrial Property	(1887 C 5044 (C 5046)), Vol 81, p 411 & 415 (1887 Commercial Series 10)	142 CJ 220; 119 LJ 172 (9 May 1887)
TRE4	Extracts from Treaties and Declarations between Great Britain and Foreign Powers relating to Trade Marks, Designs and Industrial Property, August 1888	(1888 C 5554), Vol 98, p 745 (1888 Commercial Series 12)	143 CJ 456; 120 LJ 416 (13 Aug 1888; 6 Nov 1888)
TRE5	Accession of Dutch E. Indies to International Union for Protection of Industrial Property	(1888 C 5517), Vol 109, p 393 (1888 Switzerland 2)	143 CJ 455; 120 LJ 404 (11 Aug 1888; 10 Aug 1888)
TRE6	Correspondence relative to Protection of Industrial Property	(1888 C 5521), Vol 98, p 385 (1888 Miscellaneous Series 3)	143 CJ 455; 120 LJ 410 (11 Aug 1888)
TRE7	Papers and Correspondence relative to Conference at Madrid on Industrial Property and Merchandise Marks	(1890 C 6023), Vol 67, p 725	145 CJ 297; 122 LJ 288 (8 May 1890)
TRE8	Accession of Dutch Colonies of Curaçao and Surinam to International Union for Protection of Industrial Property	(1890 C 5971), Vol 81, p 971 (1890 Switzerland 1)	145 CJ 220; 122 LJ 215 (28 Mar 1890)
TRE9	Papers and Correspondence relative to Conference at Madrid on Industrial Property and Merchandise Marks	(1890–91 C 6417), Vol 77, p 507	146 CJ 409; 123 LJ 307 (2 Jul 1891; 3 Jul 1891)
TRE10	Protocol between Great Britain, Spain, United States of America, France, Sweden, Norway, Switzerland and Tunis respecting Expenses of International Office (Industrial Property), Madrid, April 1891	(1892 C 6819), Vol 95, p 143 (1892 Treaty Series 14)	147 CJ 418; 124 LJ 411 (11 Aug 1892; 15 Aug 1892)
TRE11	Ratification by Portugal of Protocols 1, 2 and 3 of Madrid Conference for Protection of Industrial Property, November 1893	(1893 C 7206), Vol 109, p 303 (1893 Treaty Series 16)	148 CJ 612; 125 LJ 472 (5 Dec 1893)
TRE12	Accession of Denmark to Industrial Property Convention of March 1883, October 1894	(1894 C 7590), Vol 109, p 7 (1894 Treaty Series 25)	150 CJ 6; 127 LJ 10 (5 Feb 1892)
TRE13	Withdrawal of Guatemala from Industrial Property Convention of March 1883	(1894 C 7591), Vol 109, p 87 (1894 Treaty Series 26)	150 CJ 6; 127 LJ 10 (5 Feb 1892)
TRE14	Accession of Serbia and Dominican Republic to Protocol 111 of Madrid Conference respecting Endowment of International Office (Industrial Property), October 1897	(1897 C 8682), Vol 105, p 413 (1897 Treaty Series 15)	153 CJ 5; 130 LJ 14 (5 Feb 1898; 8 Feb 1898)
TRE15	Papers and Correspondence relative to Conference at Brussels on Industrial Property and Merchandise Marks	(1898 C 9014), Vol 92, p 155 [Cont. C. 6417] [TRE9]	153 CJ 419; 130 LJ 365 (8 Aug 1898)
TRE16	Protocol between Great Britain and Japan respecting Patents, Trade Marks and Designs, October 1897	(1898 C 8679), Vol 105, p 367 (1898 Treaty Series 12)	153 CJ 5; 130 LJ 14 (5 Feb 1898; 27 Oct 1897 noted 8 Feb 1898)

(continued)

(continued)

TRE17	Accession of Japan to Industrial Property Convention of March 1883, May 1899	(1899 C 9327), Vol 110, p 63 (1899 Treaty Series 12)	154 CJ 230; 131 LJ 186 (2 Jun 1899)
TRE18	Industrial property and merchandise marks. Papers and correspondence relative to the recent meeting at Brussels of the adjourned conference of the Union for the Protection of Industrial Property	(1901 Cd 603), Vol 80, p 443	156 CJ 179; 133 LJ 144 (13 May 1901; 14 May 1901)
TRE19	Additional Act modifying the Industrial Property Convention of March 20, 1883	(1902 Cd 1084), Vol 130, p 15 (1902 Treaty Series 15)	157 CJ 502; 134 LJ 400 (2 Dec 1902)
TRE20	Accession of Mexico to the Industrial Property Convention, 1883, and additional Act of 1900	(1903 Cd 1773), Vol 110, p 373 (1903 Treaty Series 13)	159 CJ 8; 136 LJ 9 (2 Feb 1904)
TRE21	Accession of Germany to the Industrial Property Convention of March 20, 1883, &c.	(1903 Cd 1774), Vol 110, p 359 (1903 Treaty Series 14)	159 CJ 8; 136 LJ 9 (2 Feb 1904)
TRE22	Accession of Cuba to the Industrial Property Convention, 1883, &c.	(1904 Cd 2314), Vol 103, p 215 (1904 Treaty Series 12)	160 CJ 7; 137 LJ 8 (14 Feb 1905)
TRE23	Industrial Property Convention. Accession of New Zealand to the additional Act of December 14, 1900; and accession of Ceylon to the convention of 1883, as modified by the additional Act of December 14, 1900	(1905 Cd 2533), Vol 103, p 349 (1905 Treaty Series 17)	160 CJ 261; 137 LJ 208 (23 Jun 1905; 26 Jun 1905)
TRE24	Accession of the Commonwealth of Australia to the industrial property convention of 1883, as modified by the Additional Act of 1900	(1907 Cd 3609), Vol 99, p 99 (1907 Treaty Series 21)	162 CJ 351; 139 LJ 262 (23 Jul 1907)
TRE25	Accession of the colony of Trinidad and Tobago to the Industrial Property Convention of 1883, as modified by the Additional Act of 1900	(1908 Cd 3967), Vol 125, p 579 (1908 Treaty Series 11)	163 CJ 164; 140 LJ 138 (5 May 1908)
TRE26	Agreement between the United Kingdom and the United States respecting protection of patents in Morocco	(1908 Cd 3752), Vol 125, p 4 (1908 Treaty Series 33)	163 CJ 4; 140 LJ 8 (29 Jan 1908) HL Deb, 29 Jan 1908, Vol 183(4th), col 51
TRE27	Accession of Servia to the Industrial Property Convention of 1883, as modified by the additional Act of 1900	(1908 Cd 4872), Vol 105, p 897 (1909 Treaty Series 24)	164 CJ 479; 141 LJ 334 (7 Oct 1909)
TRE28	Accession of Austria and Hungary to the industrial property convention, 1883, &c.	(1909 Cd 4649), Vol 105, p 273 (1909 Treaty Series 15)	164 CJ 222; 141 LJ 160 (14 Jun 1909; 23 Jun 1909)
TRE29	Notes exchanged between the United Kingdom and Russia respecting protection of trade-marks and patents in Morocco	(1909 Cd 4902), Vol 105, p 6 (1909 Treaty Series 29)	164 CJ 530; 141 LJ 419 (23 Nov 1909; 19 Nov 1909)
TRE30	Notes exchanged between the United Kingdom and Belgium, Italy, Portugal and Spain respecting protection of patents in Morocco	(1909 Cd 4951), Vol 105, p 12 (1909 Treaty Series 30)	164 CJ 530; 141 LJ 419 (23 Nov 1909; 19 Nov 1909)
TRE31	Colonial Reports: A List of Colonial Laws dealing with patents, designs, trade marks, and the marking of merchandise	(1910 Cd 4996), Vol 65, p 549 (1910 Miscellaneous Series 70)	165 CJ 8; 142 LJ 19 (21 Feb 1910)
TRE32	Industrial property and merchandise marks. Papers and correspondence relative to the recent conference at Washington, for the revision of the International Convention for the Protection of Industrial Property and the arrangement for the prevention of false indications of origin on goods	(1911 Cd 5842), Vol 87, p 189	166 CJ 404; 143 LJ 397 (14 Aug 1911; 15 Aug 1911)
TRE33	International Convention for the Protection of Industrial Property	(1913 Cd 6805), Vol 81, p 51 (1913 Treaty Series 8)	168 CJ 155; 145 LJ 122 (6 Jun 1913; 9 Jun 1913)

TRE34	Agreement respecting the preservation or the restoration of the rights of industrial property affected by the world war	(1920 Cmd 1040), Vol 51, p 465 (1920 Treaty Series 18)	175 CJ 446; 152 LJ 481 (26 Nov 1920; 29 Nov 1920)
TRE35	International convention for the protection of industrial property signed at the Hague, November 6, 1925	(1928 Cmd 3167), Vol 26, p 321 (1928 Treaty Series 16)	183 CJ 326; 160 LJ 275 (2 Aug 1928)
TRE36	Exchange of Notes between Union of South Africa and German Government respecting registration of patents, models and designs	(1931–32 Cmd 4082), Vol 27, p 4 (1932 Treaty Series 14)	187 CJ 202; 164 LJ 189 (23 May 1932; 25 May 1932)
TRE37	International convention for the protection of industrial property	(1937–38 Cmd 5833), Vol 31, p 21 (1938 Treaty Series 55)	193 CJ 403; 170 LJ 372 (28 Sep 1938)
TRE38	Agreement between United Kingdom and United States regarding exchange of patent rights information	(1941–42 Cmd 6392), Vol 9, p 681 (1942 Treaty Series 8)	197 CJ 168; 174 LJ 191 (29 Sep 1942)
TRE39	Agreement between His Majesty's Government in the United Kingdom and the provisional government of the French Republic relating to certain rights in respect of industrial, literary and artistic property which have been affected by the war	(1945–46 Cmd 6674), Vol 25, p 261 (1945 Treaty Series 5)	201 CJ 34; 178 LJ 49 (9 Oct 1945)
TRE40	Agreement between His Majesty's Government in the United Kingdom and the government of Mexico regarding compensation in respect of expropriated petroleum industrial properties	(1945–46 Cmd 6768), Vol 25, p 483 (1946 Treaty Series 5)	201 CJ 199; 178 LJ 225 (25 Mar 1946; 26 Mar 1946)
TRE41	Exchange of notes between the government of the United Kingdom of Great Britain and Northern Ireland and the government of the French Republic extending the time-limit in article 1 of the Anglo-French agreement of the 29th August, 1945, concerning industrial, literary and artistic property	(1945–46 Cmd 6917), Vol 25, p 267 (1946 Treaty Series 33)	201 CJ 369; 178 LJ 402 (8 Oct 1946)
TRE42	Agreement between United Kingdom and United States regarding exchange of patent rights information	(1945–46 Cmd 6795), Vol 25, p 875 (1946 Treaty Series 10)	201 CJ 229; 178 LJ 256 (16 Apr 1946)
TRE43	Agreement between the government of the United Kingdom and the government of Denmark relating to certain rights in respect of industrial property which have been affected by the war	(1946–47 Cmd 7208), Vol 26, p 327 (1947 Treaty Series 69)	202 CJ 380; 179 LJ 500 (20 Oct 1947)
TRE44	Correspondence incorporating the texts of the agreement between the government of Mexico and the Mexican Eagle Oil Company regarding compensation to be paid in respect of expropriated petroleum industrial properties	(1947–48 Cmd 7275), Vol 31, p 5 (1947 Mexico 1)	203 CJ 78; 180 LJ 46 (4 Dec 1947)
TRE45	Treaty of German owned patents. Final Act of Conference 15–27 July 1946 and Protocol 17 July 1947	(1947–48 Cmd 7359), Vol 27, p 311 (1948 Treaty Series 15)	203 CJ 184; 180 LJ 190 (22 Mar 1948; 17 Dec 1948)
TRE46	Agreement for the preservation or restoration of industrial property rights affected by the Second World War [with final protocol and additional final protocol]	(1946–47 Cmd 7111), Vol 24, p 161 (1947 Miscellaneous Papers 10) (1948–49 Cmd 7784), Vol 34, p 309 (1949 Treaty Series 54)	202 CJ 186; 179 LJ 198 (23 Apr 1947) 204 CJ 362; 181 LJ 377 (18 Oct 1949)

(continued)

(continued)

TRE47	Exchanges of notes between the government of the United Kingdom of Great Britain and Northern Ireland and the government of Israel for the reciprocal extension of the periods of priority stipulated in article 4 of the industrial property convention of 2nd June, 1934	(1950–51 Cmd 8216), Vol 33, p 285 (1951 Treaty Series 29)	206 CJ 193; 183 LJ 141 (26 Apr 1951)
TRE48	Agreement between United Kingdom, French Republic and the United States and Italy on German Owned Patents	(1950–51 Cmd 8156), Vol 23, p 323 (1951 Treaty Series 14)	206 CJ 96; 183 LJ 78 (15 Feb 1951)
TRE49	Agreement between the United Kingdom and Italian Republic on the prolongation of patents for inventions	(1950–51 Cmd 8305), Vol 23, 329 (1951 Italy 1)	206 CJ 292; 183 LJ 246 (19 Jul 1951)
TRE50	Agreement between the United Kingdom and the United States to facilitate the interchange of patents and technical information for defence purposes	(1952–53 Cmd 8757), Vol 30, p 1171 (1953 Treaty Series 9)	208 CJ 93; 185 LJ 60 (3 Feb 1953)
TRE51	Agreement between the United Kingdom and Italian Republic on the prolongation of patents for inventions	(1952–53 Cmd 8831), Vol 30, p 697 (1953 Treaty Series 33)	208 CJ 215; 185 LJ 180 (12 May 1953)
TRE52	European Convention relating to the formalities required for patent applications	(1953–54 Cmd 9095), Vol 31, p 1025 (1954 Miscellaneous 6) (1955–56 Cmd 9526), Vol 41, p 573 (1955 Treaty Series 43)	209 CJ 126; 186 LJ 123 (16 Mar 1954) 211 CJ 76; 188 LJ 67 (19 Jul 1955)
TRE53	European Convention on the international classification of patents for inventions	(1954–55 Cmd 9427), Vol 18, p 153 (1955 Miscellaneous 4) (1955–56 Cmd 9862). Vol 41, p 593 (1956 Treaty Series 42)	210 CJ 122; 187 LJ 124 (5 Apr 1955) 211 CJ 413; 188 LJ 448 (23 Oct 1955)
TRE54	International convention for the protection of industrial property	(1959–60 Cmnd 875), Vol 34, p 825 (1959 Miscellaneous Papers 15) (1961–62 Cmnd 1715), Vol 37, p 613 (1962 Treaty Series 38)	215 CJ 45; 192 LJ 56 (19 Nov 1959) 217 CJ 234; 194 LJ 240 (17 May 1962; 31 Oct 1962)
TRE55	Agreement for the mutual safeguarding of secrecy of inventions relating to defence and for which applications for patents have been made	(1960–61 Cmnd 1220), Vol 32, 373 (1960 Miscellaneous 18) (1961–62 Cmnd 1595), Vol 37, p 915 (1962 Treaty Series 9)	216 CJ 27; 193 LJ 29 (22 Nov 1960) 217 CJ 73; 194 LJ 78 (23 Jan 1962)
TRE56	European Convention on the international classification of patents for inventions with amended form of Annex	(1962–63 Cmnd 1956), Vol 37, p 289 (1963 Treaty Series 12)	218 CJ 136; 195 LJ 176 (12 Mar 1963)
TRE57	Procedures implementing the agreement for the mutual safeguarding of secrecy of inventions relating to defence for which applications for patents have been made	(1963–64 Cmnd 2167), Vol 32, p 67 (1963 Miscellaneous 17)	219 CJ 4; 196 LJ 11 (12 Nov 1963)
TRE59	Convention on the unification of certain points of substantive law on patents for invention [See PPP104]	(1963–64 Cmnd 2362), Vol 32, p 77 (1964 Miscellaneous 15)	219 CJ 242; 196 LJ 276 (2 Jun 1964)
TRE60	Exchange of Notes between United Kingdom and Netherlands concerning the mutual safeguarding of secrecy of inventions relating to defence for which applications for patents have been made	(1963–64 Cmnd 2252), Vol 33, p 407 (1964 Treaty Series 7)	219 CJ 89; 196 LJ 109 (30 Jan 1964)

TRE61	Agreement concerning the establishment of an International Patent Bureau	(1964–65 Cmnd 2672), Vol 33, p 17 (1965 Miscellaneous 15)	220 CJ 320; 197 LJ 348 (22 Jun 1965)
		(1964–65 Cmnd 2789), Vol 33, p 31 (1965 Treaty Series 84)	220 CJ 417; 197 LJ 467 (26 Oct 1965)
TRE62	Agreement revising the agreement concerning the establishment of the International Patent Bureau	1964–65 Cmnd 2673, Vol 33, p 45 (1965 Miscellaneous 16)	220 CJ 320; 197 LJ 348 (22 Jun 1965)
TRE63	International convention for the protection of industrial property	(1967 Cmnd 3474), Vol 40, p 3474 (1967 Miscellaneous 21)	223 CJ 49; 200 LJ 69 (7 Dec 1967)
		(1970 Cmnd 4431), Vol 43, p 335 (1970 Treaty Series 61)	226 CJ 76; 203 LJ 83 (27 Oct 1970)
TRE64	Patent Co-operation Treaty with Regulations	(1970–71 Cmnd 4530), Vol 43, p 395 (Miscellaneous 24)	226 CJ 159; 203 LJ 166 (8 Dec 1970)
TRE65	Strasbourg Agreement Concerning the International Patent Classification	(1971–72 Cmnd 4878), Vol 33, p 781 (Miscellaneous 9)	227 CJ 168; 204 LJ 153 (22 Feb 1972)
		(1974–75 Cmnd 6238), Vol 30, p 349 (Treaty Series 113)	231 CJ 635; 208 LJ 951 (13 Oct 1975)
TRE66	Convention on the grant of European Patents	(1975–76 Cmnd 5656), Vol 30, p 197 (1976 Miscellaneous 24)	231 CJ 46; 208 LJ 59 (5 Nov 1975)
TRE67	Convention for the European patent for the Common market including implement regulations and Final Act	(1975–76 Cmnd 6553), Vol 39, p 477 (1976 European Communities 18)	232 CJ 530; 209 LJ 692 (11 Oct 1976; 27 Sep 1976)

7 Command Papers relating to the British Empire patent proposal

EMP1	Colonial Conference, 1902. Papers relating to a conference between the Secretary of State for the Colonies and the prime ministers of self-governing colonies; June to August, 1902	(1902 Cd 1299), Vol 66, p 451 (see p 39 and App X, p 131–144)	157 CJ 451; 134 LJ 377 (27 Oct 1902; 3 Nov 1902)
EMP2	Despatch from the Secretary of State for the Colonies, with enclosures, respecting the agenda of the Colonial Conference, 1907	(1907 Cd 3337), Vol 54, p 727 (see p 4, 5, 8, 10 and 12)	162 CJ 25; 139 LJ 29 (21 Feb 1907)
EMP3	Colonial Conference, 1907: Correspondence relating to the Colonial Conference	(1907 Cd 3340), Vol 54, p 739 (see p 31)	162 CJ 51; 139 LJ 49 (7 Mar 1907)
EMP4	Published proceedings and précis of the Colonial Conference, 30th April to 14th May, 1907	(1907 Cd 3406), Vol 55, p 29 (see p 25)	162 CJ 197; 139 LJ 133 (16 May 1907)
EMP5	Colonial Conference, 1907. Minutes of proceedings of the Colonial Conference, 1907	(1907 Cd 3523), Vol 55, p 61 (see p ix, 221, 366, 484–489 and 513)	162 CJ 291; 139 LJ 139 (27 Jun 1911; 28 May 1911)
EMP6	Colonial Conference, 1907. Papers laid and before the Colonial Conference, 1907	(1907 Cd 3524), Vol 55, p 691 (see p 6–7, 31, 37 and 501–520)	162 CJ 291; 139 LJ 139 (27 Jun 1911; 28 May 1911)
EMP7	Further correspondence relating to the Imperial Conference	(1910 Cd 5273), Vol 65, p 87 (see p xiii–xiv, 67–85)	165 CJ 276; 1422 LJ 245 (27 Jul 1910)
EMP8	Imperial Conference. Correspondence relating to the Imperial Conference, 1911	(1911 Cd 5513), Vol 54, p 1 (see p 7, 9 and 11)	166 CJ 25; 143 LJ 39 (13 Feb 1911; 15 Feb 1911)
EMP9	Imperial Conference, 1911. Précis of the proceedings	(1911 Cd 5741), Vol 54, p 17 (see p 35)	166 CJ 291; 143 LJ 253 (27 Jun 1911; 28 Jun 1911)
EMP10	Imperial Conference, 1911. Dominions No 7. Minutes of proceedings of the Imperial Conference, 1911	(1911 Cd 5745), Vol 54, p 103 (see p 15, 162–165, 175, 179–180 and 185)	166 CJ 360; 143 LJ 300 (27 Jul 1911; 12 Jul 1911)
EMP11	Imperial Conference, 1911. Dominions No 8. Papers laid before the conference	(1911 Cd 5746-I), Vol 54, p 547 (see p 137–163 and 208)	166 CJ 360; 143 LJ 310 (27 Jul 1911; 17 Jul 1911)
EMP12	Imperial War Conference, 1917. Extracts from minutes of proceedings and papers laid before the conference	(1917–18 Cd 8566), Vol 23, p 319 (see p 4)	172 CJ 102; 149 LJ 124 (17 May 1917; 21 May 1917)
EMP13	Conference of prime ministers and representatives of the United Kingdom, the dominions, and India, held in June, July, and August, 1921. Summary of proceedings and documents	(1921 Cmd 1474), Vol 14, p 1 (see p 9 and 63–64)	166 CJ 356; 153 LJ 360 (16 Aug 1921)
EMP14	British Empire Patent Conference. Report of the Conference held at the Patent Office, London, 1922 (HMSO 1923)	Not published as Parliamentary paper	
EMP15	Imperial Economic Conference, 1923. Summary of conclusions	(1923 Cmd 1990), Vol 20, Pt 1, p 17 (see p 10–11)	178 CJ 329; 155 LJ 292 (13 Nov 1923)

EMP16	Imperial Economic Conference of Representatives of Great Britain, the Dominions, India, and the Colonies and Protectorates, held in October and November, 1923. Record of proceedings and documents	(1924 Cmd 2009), Vol 10, p 313 (see p 18, 32, 84 and 430–437)	179 CJ 17; 156 LJ 14 (15 Jan 1924)

Archive

National Archive

Patents, designs and trade marks: Patent Office provisional scheme for legislation in colonies and protectorates in response to resolution of Imperial Economic Conference, 1923; includes printed copies of draft ordinance and "Report of Conference Patent Office, 12–23 June 1922": CO 323/951/28

Imperial Economic Conference 1923: printed conclusions on Patents, Designs and Trade Marks: CO323/923/34

Patents Committee: CAB 32/34

British Empire Patent Conference: forwards copy of report considering patents applied for in UK and those applied for in the Bahamas; await views of other Colonial Governments: CO 23/291/51

Empire Patent Conference: forwarded copy of Conference of Prime Ministers and Representatives of the United Kingdom (Cmd 1474): CO 323/875/33

Colonial patents: draft colonial ordinance in respect to the Provisional Scheme recommended by the British Empire Patent Conference, 1922; memorandum on patent legislation in colonies and protectorates: CO 323/903/46

Empire Patent Conference: Report by Mr G Seth: CO 323/900/40

Empire Patent Conference 1922: complete typed copy of report and appendices: National Archive: BT 209/656

Imperial Economic Conference 1923: report of Patents Committee: National Archive: BT 209/657

Part 7   Public petitions

Introduction

The petitioning of Parliament has occurred since the earliest times, and in 1669 the House of Commons resolved that it was the right of every commoner to prepare and present petitions to the House. In the seventeenth and eighteenth centuries, petitions to the Commons were still recorded, often at length, in the Votes and Proceedings (and then the journal). As the nineteenth century progressed and political activity of the general population increased, so did the number of petitions presented to Parliament. To avoid the Votes and Proceedings becoming too extensive, in 1819 Parliament began printing an Appendix to the Votes and Proceedings. The Appendix included a printed version of many (but not all) the petitions lodged. This version was usually longer than that which had been printed in the Votes and Proceedings, and it remained the case that the petition was noted in the Votes (and the journal), but usually only briefly.

As the number of petitions further increased, it became necessary for the House of Commons to appoint a Select Committee on Public Petitions in 1833.[1] The committee issued reports periodically throughout a Parliamentary session setting out the general subject of the petition, the origin of the petitioners, and the number of signatures. Sometimes it might include a short summary of what the petition was about, other times it might simply indicate the general subject matter. Indeed, where there were co-ordinated campaigns with very similar petitions lodged by different groups, this was noted (and these are cross-referenced in this Guide). The number of reports varied between sessions; sometimes a single report of the committee would cover the petitions lodged on a single day, other times it was weekly or even over longer periods. It depended on Parliamentary activity. The number of petitions lodged sometimes exceeded 20,000 a session, but there were often far fewer. Nevertheless, each individual petition was noted in the Select Committee Reports. In addition to the reports of the committee, an Appendix was also provided.[2] This sets out the full text (although between 1834 and 1839 they were summaries) of selected petitions. The petitioning of Parliament waned as the nineteenth century progressed, and it became an unusual form of Parliamentary lobbying after World War I. The last public petition related to patent law in the period documented in the Guide was in 1906.

In comparison to the House of Commons, the Lords was petitioned infrequently. Any such petition was always recorded in the House of Lords journal, but in summary form only. In only one session did the House of Lords form a Select Committee to deal with public petitions,[3] and no petitions relating to patents were recorded by that committee. Where a petition was presented to both Houses one entry includes both petitions.

The petitions in both the House of Commons and Lords usually included requests for reform of the patent law in general, for specific provision being made, or simply opposing a particular change. There were also petitions to encourage the government to adopt a particular invention or to reward a particular inventor.[4] In other words, they provide an invaluable source of information about the public mood in respect of patent law at any particular time and the reception and concerns the public had about particular measures or proposed reforms. They also demonstrate where the greatest political activity was taking place and which groups were most active.

The table of public petitions in this part provides the date of the petition, the reference in the House of Commons or Lords journal (where there is one[5]), the number of the Public Petitions Report where it is found, the number of that petition, and the page number in the report and the number of signatures appended. Where the petition is included in the Appendix of Public Petitions, its number and page number are also provided.

---

1   See Maurice Bond, *Guide to the Records of Parliament* (HMSO 1971), p 222–223

2   A handful of petitions were published in the *Supplement to Votes and Proceedings* rather than the Appendix where they were of more general interest, so references are made to the Supplement in such cases; as to the Supplement, see Introduction to Part 1.

3   House of Lords Public Petitions Committee (1867–68 House of Lords Paper 91), Vol 30, p 1.

4   In particular, there were a number of petitions in 1839 to reward the Fourdriner brothers.

5   The Commons ceased documenting individual petitions in the journal in 1849.

The entry also includes the organisation (or individual) who petitioned. The final column sets out in square brackets a note of any concerns or facts relied upon by the petitioner and, where it exists, the prayer is set out in "full". The number of signatures is also noted, but as the seal of association counted as one signature, this can be misleading since the association may have had hundreds of members.

It should be noted that many newspapers recorded the petitions that were lodged before Parliament. This would usually include the name of the person presenting the report, the name of the petition and the broad subject matter (e.g. reform of patent law). Unfortunately, there are many false positives in the newspapers – that is, petitions which are said to have been lodged which do not appear on the official record.

In handful of cases, there were debates in *Hansard* or the *Mirror of Parliament*, and in such cases this has been recorded (but no reference to *The Times* has been included). Where there was other Parliamentary activity connected to a petition, this is also recorded, but such activity is rare.

Public petitions

PET1	10 Mar 1819 74 CJ 209	Not printed	Edwin Thrackson	[Expenses incurred in developing lifeboat] Favourable consideration
PET2	14 Jun 1820 75 CJ 310	V&P App, p 182–184 (No 179)	Patentees of the Metropolis for the alteration of the Law of Patents	"that such alterations or amendments may be made in the law of Patents, and such new regulations established as Parliament thinks proper"
PET3	16 Jun 1820 75 CJ 316	V&P App, p 186 (No 183)	Several Manufacturers and Tradesmen of the Metropolis	"That the law relating to patents be amended"
PET4	7 Jul 1820 75 CJ 418 13 Jul 1820 53 LJ 297	V&P App, p 312–313 (No 237)	Alexander Tilloch	[Developed an anti-forgery plan, which was rejected by Bank of England] Against Bank Notes Bill
PET5	19 Jul 1820 53 LJ 328	Not printed	John Leigh Bradbury	[Artist whose plan had been adopted by bank without recognition] Against Bank Notes Bill
PET6	31 Jan 1821 76 CJ 16	Not printed	Several Gentlemen, Merchants, Manufacturers, Artists, Engineers, Mechanics and others	"that regulations . . . for affording to inventor's protection from piracy during the progress of experiment, and for more effectively securing to the public a full and just specification of inventions" [i.e. less than 6 months]
PET7	20 Jun 1822 77 CJ 359	V&P, p 487–488 (No 705)	Thomas Walker	[Patents are very expensive] "to cause such a reduction of the expense upon obtaining a Patent as will put it in his power to procure one, by which means the House will prevent in future both the Country at large and indigent individuals from being further injured"
PET8	23 May 1823 78 CJ 337	Not printed	William Lester	[Developed inventions for improving roads; McAdam had petitioned for further reward, requesting certain witnesses attend a Select Committee]
PET9	22 Mar 1826 81 CJ 201	V&P, p 331–332 (No 534)	Charles Broderip	"To pass such law or laws as will give him, in common with other authors and inventors and discoverer, the same rights and security as are now enjoyed by literary authors and artists, or such other relief" HC Deb, 22 Mar 1826, Vol 15(2nd), col 71–76

PET10	1 May 1826 81 CJ 309 26 May 1826 58 LJ 375	V&P, p 498–499 (No 761)	Thomas Morton	"To pass such law or laws as will give to him, in common with authors of inventions and discoveries, the protection of statute law to their rights and privileges in clear and positive terms, as may extend the period of property to twenty-eight years, and for life, as may limit the obligation touching the publicity of specifications, and also the expense of obtaining Patents, within just and proper bounds, and as may confer on any number of individuals the power of holding patent rights"
PET11	10 Mar 1829 84 CJ 122	V&P, p 663–664 (No 1586)	Several Manufacturers, Engineers, Inventors and Artists	"That the existing laws, by which Letters Patent are allowed to be granted to the inventors of improvements in the processes of arts and manufactures, may undergo a Revision; and that such alterations and amendments may be made therein as found advisable" Mirror, 10 Mar 1829, Vol 1, p 513
PET12	12 Mar 1829 84 CJ 128	V&P, p 748–749 (No 1802 and 1803)	Thomas Flannagan	"That application is about to be made to appoint a Select Committee …[in Ireland] the Attorney General's and other fees amount to an insuperable barrier … that it would be desirable to inquire into the state of patent law in Ireland … that granting patents free of expense, would be most beneficially felt with a certain portion of taxation upon machinery in general" Mirror, 12 Mar 1829, Vol 1, p 546
PET13	31 Mar 1829 84 CJ 187	V&P, p 1213–1214 (No 2839)	John Birkinshaw	"to pass such a law as may be best adapted to secure to the Petitioner, and every other author of useful inventions, the protection of their just Rights and Privileges, for such an extended period of time as in their wisdom they shall think fit, and to adopt such other measures as shall reduce within a narrow limit the obligation of publishing the nature and details of their inventions, and diminish the expenses of obtaining patents, or grant to the Petitioners such other relief as they shall think fit" Mirror, 31 Mar 1829, Vol 2, p 936
PET14	25 May 1829 84 CJ 339	V&P, p 1393–1398 (No 3084)	Joseph Astley	"To adopt steps for abolishing the system of Patents, as inconsistent with the maxims of sound political economy, and as exercising an injurious influence upon the rights and interests of the public, the welfare of science, and even the interests of the Patentees themselves; or at all events, for restoring the provision of the system to the state in which they were fixed by the terms of the fifth Clause in the Statute of Monopolies" Mirror, 25 Mar 1829, Vol 3, p 1848
PET15	28 Feb 1833 88 CJ 132	2nd Rep, p 48 (No number)	Thomas Richard Yare	"House speedily revise the laws relating to the obtaining and securing of Patents for inventions" [1 petition – 1 signature] Mirror, 28 Feb 1833, Vol 1, p 456
PET16	18 Mar 1833 88 CJ 179	7th Rep, p 176 (No number)	Richard Roberts	[Provision of blank forms which would reduce costs] "House to adopt such means as may cause Letters Patent for Inventions to be granted in such a cheap, expeditious and secure manner as shall give encouragement to inventors" [2 petitions – 2 signatures] Mirror, 18 Mar 1833, Vol 1, p 805

(continued)

(continued)

PET17	28 Mar 1833 88 CJ 231	10th Rep, p 294 (No 2140)	John Kitchen	[Prevented by expense in obtaining Letters Patent] "to pass the present Bill [PUBB10] to amend the Laws relating to Patents for Inventions, or otherwise give the Petitioner relief" [1 signature] Mirror, 28 Mar 1833, Vol 1, p 1047
PET18	20 Jun 1833 88 CJ 505	13th Rep, p 1150 (No 9382) App, p 1192 (App No 1090)	Joseph Holiday	[Inventors to be placed on the same footing as authors; there should be one patent for the whole of the UK] "House to make modifications in the law relative to Patents for Inventions" [3 petitions – 4 signatures] Mirror, 20 Jun 1833, Vol 2, p 2446
PET19	1 Jul 1833 80 CJ 535	33rd Rep, p 1268 (No 9559)	Julius Ludolphus Schroder	"Taking notice of the Report of the Select Committee of 1829 [REP1] and also on the Present Bill [PUBB10], which he deems totally inadequate in its principle; and provisions for the security and protection of inventors and an inquiry into the fees paid under the present system" [1 signature] Mirror, 1 Jul 1833, Vol 3, p 2645
PET20	13 Mar 1834 89 CJ 117 17 Mar 1834 66 LJ 74	8th Rep, p 91 (No 1292) App, p 289 (App No 410)	Edward Moxhay	[High cost of obtaining a patent] "House will take this Law into consideration, and have it altered, which appears to him to be a tax on the ingenuity of man" [1 signature] Mirror, 13 Mar 1834, Vol 1, p 698 Mirror, 17 Mar 1834, Vol 1, p 759
PET21	29 Apr 1834 89 CJ 229	16th Rep, p 197 (No 3176) App, p 643–644 (App No 926)	Goldsworthy (George) Gurney	[Patented invention in 1825 for propelling engines along turnpike roads; carried out lots of experiments and incurred cost; but law changed to make working invention unlawful; committee considered matter and recommended repeal of restriction] "to repeal the Legislative restrictions as recommended by your Committee" [1 signature] HC Deb, 29 Apr 1834, Vol 23(3rd), col 203–207 Mirror, 29 Apr 1834, Vol 2, p 1356–1358
PET22	28 Apr 1834 89 CJ 227	16th Rep, p 198 (No 3186) App, p 648–649 (App No 932)	William Ivory	[Inventor lost capital, so the invention could not be exploited; invented instrument showing strength of spirits used in conjunction with Revenue] "take Petition into its favourable consideration" [2 petitions – 2 signatures] Mirror, 28 Apr 1834, Vol 1, p 1351
PET23	4 Jul 1834 89 CJ 460 89 CJ 464 (Ref to Com)	36th Rep, p 499 (No 7974) App, p 1470–1471 (App No 2146)	Goldsworthy (George) Gurney	[Patent almost expired; seeking remedy to repeal the legislation] "for the sympathy of your Honourable House, and for such measure as you in your wisdom may consider just to himself, and beneficial to the public" [1 signature] HC Deb, 4 Jul 1834, Vol 24(3rd), col 134 Mirror, 4 Jul 1834, Vol 3, p 2616 Mirror, 10 Jul 1834, Vol 3, p 2721 Select Committee on Mr. G. Gurney's Case (Steam Carriages): Report, Minutes of Evidence (1834 HC Papers 483), Vol 11, p 223

PET24	28 Jul 1834 89 CJ 531	43rd Rep, p 572 (No 8961) App, p 1680 (App No 2475)	John Howard Kyan	[Navy has tested his anti-dry rot invention; it has been widely taken up] "to take the premises into consideration, and that an immediate inquiry may be may be instituted as to the experiments which have already been made, and their results, with a view to the adoption of your Petitioner's process for the Timber used in the Navy" [1 signature] HC Deb, 28 Jul 1834, Vol 25(3rd), col 617–620 Mirror, 28 Jul 1834, Vol 4, p 3033
PET25	28 Jul 1835 90 CJ 492	33rd Rep, p 253 (No 3249) App, p 1138–1141 (App No 1522)	Michael Joseph John Donlan	"to investigate the merits of his improved method of manufacturing Flax and Hemp" [1 signature] Mirror, 28 Jul 1835, Vol 3, p 2129
PET26	21 Aug 1835 90 CJ 578	39th Rep, p 292 (No 3718) App, p 1331–1332 (App No 1733)	James Marsh	[For inserting a clause in the Letters Patent for Inventions Bill [PUBA2] to replace upfront fees with annual licence; not forfeit his Patent right where he describes in specification something that has been done before, but should retain the rest of it] [1 signature] Mirror, 21 Aug 1835, Vol 3, p 2665
PET27	24 Aug 1835 90 CJ 584	40th Rep, p 300 (No 3806) App, p 1372–1373 (App No 1785)	Patentees, Merchants and Others of Birmingham	[Reduce expense and create a UK patent; simplification of the law and removing the bar on trifling matter previously known invalidating a patent; extension of patent term; protection should start from depositing petition; jury of scientific persons to hear patent cases] "not to sanction any measure for the amendment of the Laws touching Letters Patent for Inventions [PUBA2] that does not embody the above principles, and afford such practical relief to the great body of manufacturers and artizens in Great Britain" [81 signatures] HC Deb, 24 Aug 1835, Vol 30(3rd), col 936 Mirror, 24 Aug 1835, Vol 3, p 2713
PET28	2 Sep 1835 90 CJ 628	41st Rep, p 308 (No 3898) App, p 1442–1444 (App No 1837)	Edward Edwards	[Invented a new form of chain pump used at a capstan; would be more efficient; plan rejected by the Admiralty] [1 signature] "inquiry into his improved method of working Chain Pumps on board His Majesty's ships"
PET29	23 Mar 1836 91 CJ 196	8th Rep, p 55 (No 780) App, p 172 (App No 347)	Friends and Promoters of the Arts and Sciences	[High expense in obtaining patents and bringing infringement proceedings] [81 signatures] HC Deb, 23 Mar 1836, Vol 32(3rd), col 501 Mirror, 23 Mar 1836, Vol 1, p 746
PET30	11 May 1836 91 CJ 347	15th Rep, p 166 (No 2845) App, p 472 (App No 1041)	Matthew Phillips	[His son invented a new design of ship which was much faster; the King suggested that the matter be laid before the Admiralty] [1 signature] "inquiry into his son's improvements in Naval Architecture, with a view to the prevention of the loss of life and property by shipwreck" Mirror, 11 May 1836, Vol 2, p 1425

(continued)

(continued)

PET31	17 May 1836 91 CJ 376	16th Rep, p 182 (No 3122)	William Pickman	"For an alteration of the Law of Patents for Inventions" [1 signature] Mirror, 17 May 1836, Vol 2, p 1506
PET32	17 May 1836 91 CJ 376	16th Rep, p 182 (No 3123) App, p 513 (App No 1113)	Manufacturers and Iron-founders in Middlesex	"That the Honourable House will be pleased to adopt such Laws [WA Mackinnon's Bill, PUBB12] that will secure to the manufacturers and iron founders some security against the impositions which are so frequently committed on them" [15 signatures] Mirror, 17 May 1836, Vol 2, p 1506
PET33	1 Jun 1836 91 CJ 416	17th Rep, p 204 (No 3606)	Hugh Bidwell	[Petitioner cannot afford to patent his invention and prays that the House reduces the fees payable] [1 signature] Mirror, 1 Jun 1836, Vol 2, p 1626
PET34	13 Jun 1836 91 CJ 471	19th Rep, p 246 (No 4412) App, p 681 (App No 1469)	Patentees, Inventors and Projectors in the City of London and Westminster	[Section 2 of the Patents for Inventions Act 1835 [PUBA2] is injurious to poor man (that which allows disclaimers); inventors not seeking patents should be able to deposit inventions at a newly established Patent Office] [11 signatures] HC Deb, 13 Jun 1836, Vol 34(3rd), col 486 Mirror, 13 Jun 1836, Vol 2, p 1873
PET35	1 Jul 1836 91 CJ 607	21st Rep, p 274 (No 4865) App, p 775 (App No 1649)	Hely Dutton	[Plan for draining soil; requesting a bounty for teaching method to the public] "for an inquiry into his system of for the Drainage of Land" [1 signature] Mirror, 1 Jul 1836, Vol 3, p 2183
PET36	4 Jul 1836 91 CJ 616	22nd Rep, p 292 (No 5,40) App, p 826–830 (App No 1757)	Michael Joseph and John Donlan	[Made three discoveries in relation to fibrous substances; description of inventions; letters supporting use set out; requesting a Select Committee] "that a Select Committee … may be appointed to investigate and examine … the discoveries he has made will assist in saving a large portion of life and Property annual lost in the maritime service of Great Britain" [1 signature] Mirror, 13 Jul 1836, Vol 3, p 2205
PET37	12 Jul 1836 91 CJ 652	23rd Rep, p 306 (No 5328) App, p 871 (App No 1845)	Patentees and Manufacturers of Artificial Skins and Japanned Silk Wares	[Owners of a patent to make a product; Petitioners were informed by the government that the product was not considered to be paper and so not liable to paper duty; Paper Duty Bill will change this] "that the same exception is granted to the manufactures of patent artificial skins as is specially granted to the manufacturers of scale board" [2 signatures] Mirror, 12 Jul 1836, Vol 3, p 2335
PET38	13 Jul 1836 91 CJ 658	23rd Rep, p 307 (No 5340) App, p 875–876 (App No 1836)	John Pond Drake	[Made certain developments in Naval Architecture; another person took out a patent; he therefore made a loss of £4000; consideration of the issue] "improvements in Naval Architecture introduced by him, and praying the consideration of the House to the merits of his service" [1 signature] Mirror, 13 Jul 1836, Vol 3, p 2355

PET39	21 Jul 1836 91 CJ 684	24th Rep, p 320 (No 5503) App, p 919 (App No 1939)	James Marsh	[The cost of obtaining a patent should be reduced so that any inventor should be able to obtain a patent free followed by yearly instalments] [1 signature] Mirror, 19 Jul 1836, Vol 4, p 2453
PET40	21 Jul 1836 91 CJ 684	24th Rep, p 320 (No 5504)	Manufacturers and Others	"that the Letters Patent Bill [PUBB12] may pass into law" [11 signatures] Mirror, 21 Jul 1836, Vol 3, p 2480
PET41	28 Jul 1836 91 CJ 709	25th Rep, p 329 (No 5596)	Patentees, Inventors and Manufacturers	Letters Patent Bill [PUBB12] pass into law [That the House change its plan and sit on the day that the Bill is scheduled to be read so it may pass into Law this Session] [4 signatures] Mirror, 28 Jul 1836, Vol 3, p 2586
PET42	4 Aug 1836 91 CJ 750 5 Aug 1836 68 LJ 796	25th Rep, p 329 (No 5597) App, p 956–957 (App No 1992)	William James	"That their Lordships will take into their Consideration the present inadequate Protection to scientific Discoveries, Plans, Models, and Labours, and by extending the Law of Copyrights to the Laws of Patent or by amending Compensation and Remuneration to the original Inventors of all Engines, Plans, Models, &c., where they are successfully appropriated by other Persons to the same or other Purposes, afford that Encouragement to Science and Invention which the great Railroads and other Works now contemplated (from the Success of the Petitioner's Project, the Liverpool and Manchester Railroad) imperatively call for" [1 signature] Mirror, 5 Aug 1836, Vol 4, p 2737
PET43	10 Aug 1836 91 CJ 775 (Misdated 13 Aug 1836 in SC Rep)	26th Rep, p 341 (No 5769)	Manufacturers and Others Interested in Patent Amendment Bill	Letters Patent Bill [PUBB12] – In Favour [73 signatures] HC Deb, 10 Aug 1836, Vol 35(2nd), col 1057 Mirror, 10 Aug 1836, Vol 4, p 2818
PET44	16 Aug 1836 91 CJ 818	26th Rep, p 341 (No 5770) App, p 1000 (App No 2080)	Dennis McCarthy	"Patent to grant protection over all three kingdoms of the United Kingdom or even the whole Empire" [1 signature] Mirror, 16 Aug 1836, Vol 4, p 2922
PET45	17 Aug 1836 91 CJ 823	26th Rep, p 341 (No 5771)	Manufacturers, Patentees and Inventors at Exeter Hall	Letters Patent Bill [PUBB12] – In Favour [11 signatures] Mirror, 17 Aug 1836, Vol 3, p 2938
PET46	8 Mar 1837 92 CJ 139	8th Rep, p 120 (No 2764)	James Marsh	Patents for Inventions Bill [PUBB13] pass into law [1 signature] Mirror, 8 Mar 1837, Vol 1, p 512
PET47	10 Mar 1837 92 CJ 152	8th Rep, p 120 (No 2765)	Timothy and Thomas Burstall	Patents for Inventions Bill [PUBB13] pass into Law [1 signature] Mirror, 10 Mar 1837, Vol 1, p 570
PET48	11 Mar 1837 92 CJ 158	9th Rep, p 167 (No 3963)	John Walsh	[Petitioner invented a Theory of Reasoning; asks the House to take the subject into consideration] [1 signature] Mirror, 11 Mar 1837, Vol 1, p 598

(continued)

(continued)

PET49	4 Apr 1837 92 CJ 222	10th Rep, p 180 (No 4187)	William Roberts	[Petitioner invented method of preserving bodies for anatomy instruction] "to make this means attainable by enabling him to grant to all anatomical schools in United Kingdom free use of his invention" [1 signature] Mirror, 4 Apr 1837, Vol 2, p 818
PET50	19 Apr 1837 92 CJ 277	13th Rep, p 244 (No 5557) App, p 224 (App No 444)	Henry Harrison	[Petitioner aquatinted with navigation; developed a new way of determining longitude at sea; seeking a trial to prove his method] "inquiry into the merits of his discovery of a method of determining longitude" [1 signature] Mirror, 19 Apr 1837, Vol 2, p 1096
PET51	18 May 1837 92 CJ 384	16th Rep, p 337 (No 7378)	William Robert	Similar to earlier petition, No 4187 [PET49] [1 signature] Mirror, 18 May 1837, Vol 2, p 1502
PET52	5 Jun 1837 92 CJ 435	18th Rep, p 400 (No 8644)	James Davis	"that the House will not remove from Ireland the right hitherto enjoyed of preparing, sealing and enrolling Patents for Inventions and Specifications at Dublin" [See PUBB13] [1 signature] Mirror, 5 Jun 1837, Vol 3, p 1702
PET53	5 Jun 1837 92 CJ 435	18th Rep, p 400 (No 8645)	Hugh Bidwell	Patents for Inventions Bill [PUBB13] pass into law [1 signature] Mirror, 5 Jun 1837, Vol 3, p 1702
PET54	5 Jun 1837 92 CJ 435	18th Rep, p 400 (No 8646)	Julius Ludolphus Schroder	Patents for Inventions Bill [PUBB13] pass into law [1 signature] Mirror, 5 Jun 1837, Vol 3, p 1702
PET55	15 Jun 1837 92 CJ 476	19th Rep, p 421 (No 9030) App, p 413 (App No 846)	Henry Towgood	[Fourdrinier lost £50,000 of Matthew Towgood's money in developing invention and so family of the same entitled to a share of any compensation paid to Fourdrinier] [1 signature] Mirror, 15 Jun 1837, Vol 3, p 1875
PET56	7 Dec 1837 93 CJ 186	1st Rep, p 9 (No 104) Supp V&P *All known copies lost*	Michael Donovan	"an inquiry into a mode discovered by the Petitioner for illumining Lighthouses" [1 signature] Mirror, 7 Dec 1837, Vol 1, p 494
PET57	26 Jan 1838 93 CJ 237	5th Rep, p 36 (No 346)	Hugh Bidwell	Patterns and Inventions Bill [PUBB16] pass into law [10 signatures] HC Deb, 26 Jan 1838, Vol 40(3rd), col 453 Mirror, 26 Jan 1838, Vol 2, p 1416
PET58	29 Jan 1838 93 CJ 239	6th Rep, p 46 (No 451)	John Collier and George Harvey	Patterns and Inventions Bill [PUBB16] pass into law [2 signatures] Mirror, 29 Jan 1838, Vol 2, p 1464
PET59	29 Jan 1838 93 CJ 239	6th Rep, p 46 (No 452)	Orsmond Stickwood &c.	Patterns and Inventions Bill [PUBB16] pass into law [7 signatures] Mirror, 29 Jan 1838, Vol 2, p 1464

PET60	2 Feb 1838 93 CJ 242	6th Rep, p 46 (No 453)	Robert Shorter &c.	Patterns and Inventions Bill [PUBB16] pass into law [4 signatures] HC Deb, 2 Feb 1838, Vol 40(3rd), col 715 Mirror, 2 Feb 1838, Vol 2, p 1526
PET61	5 Feb 1838 93 CJ 247	7th Rep, p 60 (No 633)	Thomas Parkin	[Petitioner complaining about infringement of his patent by London and Croydon Railway] "to pass a Law prohibiting, for the protection of inventors such temporary use" [1 signature] Mirror, 5 Feb 1838, Vol 2, p 1573
PET62	7 Feb 1838 93 CJ 253	7th Rep, p 60 (No 634)	Merchants and Wholesale and Retail Details in Silks, Calicoes, Cottons in London	Patterns and Inventions Bill [PUBB16] pass into law [8 signatures] Mirror, 7 Feb 1838, Vol 2, p 1625
PET63	7 Feb 1838 93 CJ 253	7th Rep, p 60 (No 635)	Merchants and Wholesale and Retail in Westminster	Patterns and Inventions Bill [PUBB16] pass into law [28 signatures] HC Deb, 7 Feb 1838, Vol 24(3rd), col 832 Mirror, 7 Feb 1838, Vol 2, p 1625
PET64	21 Feb 1838 93 CJ 296	11th Rep, p 121 (No 1561)	Merchants, Tradesmen and Mechanics in Marylebone	Patterns and Inventions Bill [PUBB16] pass into law [35 signatures] Mirror, 21 Feb 1838, Vol 3, p 2062
PET65	21 Feb 1838 93 CJ 296	11th Rep, p 121 (No 1562)	Carpet and Rug Manufacturers in Middlesex	Patterns and Inventions Bill [PUBB16] pass into law [3 signatures] Mirror, 21 Feb 1838, Vol 3, p 2062
PET66	21 Feb 1838 93 CJ 296	11th Rep, p 121 (No 1563)	Manufacturers and Dealers in Paper Hangings and Fancy and Ornamental Paper in Middlesex	Patterns and Inventions Bill [PUBB16] pass into law [13 signatures] Mirror, 21 Feb 1838, Vol 3, p 2062
PET67	21 Feb 1838 93 CJ 296	11th Rep, p 121 (No 1564)	Manufacturers and Dealers in Floor and Oil Cloth in Middlesex	Patterns and Inventions Bill [PUBB16] pass into law [11 signatures] Mirror, 21 Feb 1838, Vol 3, p 2062
PET68	23 Feb 1838 93 CJ 303	11th Rep, p 124 (No 1594)	Samuel Hall	"for a full investigation of the advantages of his improved steam engine" [1 signature] Mirror, 23 Feb 1838, Vol 3, p 2110
PET69	28 Feb 1838 93 CJ 316	12th Rep, p 138 (No 1755) App, p 83–84 (App No 164)	Calico Printers, Engravers to Calico Printers and Engravers in Lancaster [Manchester]	"That your Petitioners contend, that any interference by Parliament on the subject of printing is uncalled for, and will be positively mischievous … most respectfully protest against the present Bill [PUBB16]" [182 signatures] Mirror, 28 Feb 1838, Vol 3, p 2262
PET70	26 Mar 1838 93 CJ 400	19th Rep, p 238 (No 3990)	James Burns	For reducing the price of patents for inventions [1 signature] Mirror, 26 Mar 1838, Vol 4, p 3041
PET71	9 Apr 1838 93 CJ 442	24th Rep, p 326 (No 4657)	George and Son	For an inquiry into the Merits of their Invention of a Steam War Chariot [2 signatures] Mirror, 9 Apr 1838, Vol 5, p 3449

(continued)

(continued)

PET72	9 Apr 1838 93 CJ 442	24th Rep, p 328 (No 4670)	Hosiery and Lace Artizans and Mechanics of Nottingham	Patterns and Inventions Bill [PUBB16] pass into law [19 signatures] Mirror, 9 Apr 1838, Vol 5, p 3449
PET73	30 Apr 1838 93 CJ 474	26th Rep, p 358 (No 5167) App, p 231 (App No 420)	William Roberts	[Amend the Anatomy Act to enable his discovery to be worked to preserve bodies for anatomical examination] [1 signature] Mirror, 30 Apr 1838, Vol 5, p 3601
PET74	12 Jun 1838 93 CJ 601	31st Rep, p 523 (No 8261)	James Jones &c.	Patterns and Inventions Bill [PUBB16] pass into law [11 signatures] Mirror, 12 Jun 1838, Vol 6, p 4709
PET75	12 Jun 1838 93 CJ 601	31st Rep, p 523 (No 8262)	John Bidwell &c.	Patterns and Inventions Bill [PUBB16] pass into law [3 signatures] Mirror, 12 Jun 1838, Vol 6, p 4709
PET76	15 Jun 1838 93 CJ 612	31st Rep, p 524 (No 8263)	James Welsford	Patterns and Inventions Bill [PUBB16] pass into law [1 signatures] Mirror, 15 Jun 1838, Vol 6, p 4806
PET77	4 Jul 1838 93 CJ 670	35th Rep, p 570 (No 8623) App, p 397 (App No 699)	Merchants, Bankers, Solicitors, Booksellers and other consumers of paper in London	[The greater diffusion of knowledge by reason of the machine invented by Fourdrinier greatly outweighing displacement of labour; it caused Messrs Fourdrinier to be ruined] "To take into favourable consideration the case of Messrs Fourdrinier relative to their Patent for manufacture of Paper" [286 signatures] Mirror, 4 Jul 1838, Vol 7, p 5251
PET78	4 Jul 1838 93 CJ 670	35th Rep, p 570 (No 8624) App, p 397–398 (App No 700)	Paper makers working in Scotland	[Advantages of Fourdrinier invention and public benefit annually of £586,240] "To take into favourable consideration the case of Messrs Fourdrinier relative to their Patent for manufacture of Paper" [30 signatures] Mirror, 4 Jul 1838, Vol 7, p 5251
PET79	6 Jul 1838 93 CJ 683	35th Rep, p 570 (No 8625)	Earthenware, Manufacturers in York, Durham, Northumberland and Scotland	"To take into favourable consideration the case of Messrs Fourdrinier relative to their Patent for manufacture of Paper" [26 signatures]
PET80	10 Jul 1838 93 CJ 691	36th Rep, p 583 (No 8732) App, p 409 (App No 726)	Bankers, Printers, Booksellers &c. of Oxford	[Great benefit of invention; increase in revenue for others by Messrs Fourdrinier spending a vast sum of money] "To take into favourable consideration the case of Messrs Fourdrinier relative to their Patent for manufacture of Paper" [59 signatures] Mirror, 10 Jul 1838, Vol 7, p 5400
PET81	16 Jul 1838 93 CJ 708	37th Rep, p 603 (No 8960)	Merchants, Booksellers, Printers, Stationers and Consumers in Nottingham	"To take into favourable consideration the case of Messrs Fourdrinier relative to their Patent for manufacture of Paper" [57 signatures] Mirror, 16 Jul 1838, Vol 7, p 5535

PET82	17 Jul 1838 93 CJ 713	37th Rep, p 603 (No 8961)	Printers, Booksellers, Grocers &c. of Sheffield	"To take into favourable consideration the case of Messrs Fourdrinier relative to their Patent for manufacture of Paper" [58 signatures] Mirror, 17 Jul 1838, Vol 7, p 5574
PET83	18 Jul 1838 93 CJ 724	37th Rep, p 603 (No 8962)	Merchants, Bankers, Solicitors, Booksellers and other consumers of paper in Edinburgh	"To take into favourable consideration the case of Messrs Fourdrinier relative to their Patent for manufacture of Paper" [55 signatures] Mirror, 18 Jul 1838, Vol 7, p 5603
PET84	21 Feb 1839 94 CJ 47	5th Rep, p 85 (No 1878) Supp V&P, p 27–28 (21 Feb 1839)	William Snow Harris	[Petitioner requests an inquiry into the cause of damage to Ships by Lightning; the Petitioner discovered a complete method of avoiding lightening] "institute an inquiry into the subject, so that the facts and evidence relating to this question" [1 signature] Mirror, 21 Feb 1839, Vol 1, p 431 HC Deb, 23 Apr 1839, Vol 47(3rd), col 474–477
PET85	14 Mar 1839 94 CJ 111	11th Rep, p 199 (No 4032)	James Couch	[Petitioner complaining of the infringement of his patent, under Admiralty Order, for his invention of the Ship's Solid Safety Channel for the Preservation of Life and Property at Sea] [1 signature] Mirror, 14 Mar 1839, Vol 2 p 1197
PET86	24 Apr 1839 94 CJ 217	20th Rep, p 350 (No 6495)	Printers, Booksellers and Stationers &c. in Derby	To take into consideration of the Case of Messrs Fourdrinier relative to their Patent for the Manufacture of Paper [52 signatures] Mirror, 24 Apr 1839, Vol 3, p 2045
PET87	25 Apr 1839 94 CJ 221	20th Rep, p 350 (No 6496)	Merchants, Bankers and Traders of Manchester	To take into consideration of the Case of Messrs Fourdrinier relative to their Patent for the Manufacture of Paper [67 signatures]
PET88	25 Apr 1839 94 CJ 221	20th Rep, p 350 (No 6497)	Merchants, Bankers, Booksellers, Printers, Stationers &c. in Newcastle-upon-Tyne	To take into consideration of the Case of Messrs Fourdrinier relative to their Patent for the Manufacture of Paper [28 signatures]
PET89	25 Apr 1839 94 CJ 221	20th Rep, p 351 (No 6498)	Bankers, Merchants and Consumers in Staffordshire Potteries	To take into consideration of the Case of Messrs Fourdrinier relative to their Patent for the Manufacture of Paper [132 signatures]
PET90	25 Apr 1839 94 CJ 221	20th Rep, p 351 (No 6499)	Earthenware and China Manufacturers in Staffordshire Potteries	To take into consideration of the Case of Messrs Fourdrinier relative to their Patent for the Manufacture of Paper [69 signatures]
PET91	25 Apr 1839 94 CJ 221	20th Rep, p 351 (No 6500)	Manufacturers of Paper in Dublin	To take into consideration of the Case of Messrs Fourdrinier relative to their Patent for the Manufacture of Paper [9 signatures]

(continued)

(continued)

PET92	25 Apr 1839 94 CJ 221	20th Rep, p 351 (No 6501)	Merchants, Bankers, Booksellers, Printers, Stationers, and Consumers in Glasgow	To take into consideration of the Case of Messrs Fourdrinier relative to their Patent for the Manufacture of Paper [46 signatures]
PET93	25 Apr 1839 94 CJ 221	20th Rep, p 351 (No 6502)	Booksellers Printers, Bankers, Merchants, &c. in Wolverhampton	To take into consideration of the Case of Messrs Fourdrinier relative to their Patent for the Manufacture of Paper [52 signatures]
PET94	25 Apr 1839 94 CJ 221	20th Rep, p 351 (No 6503)	Bankers, Merchants and Consumers in Newcastle-under-Lyme	To take into consideration of the Case of Messrs Fourdrinier relative to their Patent for the Manufacture of Paper [86 signatures]
PET95	25 Apr 1839 94 CJ 221	20th Rep, p 351 (No 6504)	Bankers, Merchants and Consumers of Paper in Birmingham	To take into consideration of the Case of Messrs Fourdrinier relative to their Patent for the Manufacture of Paper [68 signatures]
PET96	25 Apr 1839 94 CJ 221	20th Rep, p 351 (No 6505)	Gentlemen, Bankers, Merchants, Manufacturers, Printers, Stationers in Kendal	To take into consideration of the Case of Messrs Fourdrinier relative to their Patent for the Manufacture of Paper [91 signatures]
PET97	25 Apr 1839 94 CJ 221	20th Rep, p 351 (No 6506)	Advocates, Merchants, Bankers, Booksellers, Stationers and Consumers in Aberdeen	To take into consideration of the Case of Messrs Fourdrinier relative to their Patent for the Manufacture of Paper [79 signatures]
PET98	25 Apr 1839 94 CJ 221	20th Rep, p 351 (No 6507)	Wholesale and Retail Stationers in London &c.	To take into consideration of the Case of Messrs Fourdrinier relative to their Patent for the Manufacture of Paper [77 signatures]
PET99	25 Apr 1839 94 CJ 221	20th Rep, p 351 (No 6508)	Bankers, Merchants, Booksellers, Printers and Consumers in Stone	To take into consideration of the Case of Messrs Fourdrinier relative to their Patent for the Manufacture of Paper [51 signatures]
PET100	25 Apr 1839 94 CJ 221	20th Rep, p 351 (No 6509)	Bankers, Printers, Booksellers and Consumers of Paper in Cambridge	To take into consideration of the Case of Messrs Fourdrinier relative to their Patent for the Manufacture of Paper [85 signatures]
PET101	25 Apr 1839 94 CJ 221	20th Rep, p 351 (No 6510)	Papermakers in Manchester	To take into consideration of the Case of Messrs Fourdrinier relative to their Patent for the Manufacture of Paper [12 signatures]
PET102	1 May 1839 94 CJ 238	22nd Rep, p 386 (No 6987)	Wholesale Stationers, Booksellers, Printers and Publishers in Dublin	To take into consideration of the Case of Messrs Fourdrinier relative to their Patent for the Manufacture of Paper [38 signatures] Mirror, 1 May 1839, Vol 3, p 2195
PET103	1 May 1839 94 CJ 238	22nd Rep, p 386 (No 6988)	Booksellers, Printers and Manufacturers, Banker, Merchants, Warehousemen in Leeds	To take into consideration of the Case of Messrs Fourdrinier relative to their Patent for the Manufacture of Paper [6 signatures] Mirror, 1 May 1839, Vol 3, p 2195

PET104	3 May 1839 94 CJ 247	22nd Rep, p 386 (No 6989)	Merchants, Bankers and Traders of Liverpool	To take into consideration of the Case of Messrs Fourdrinier relative to their Patent for the Manufacture of Paper [71 signatures] Mirror, 3 May 1839, Vol 3, p 2266
PET105	13 May 1839 94 CJ 261	24th Rep, p 432 (No 7692)	Samuel Hall	"inquiry into his improvements to the Steam Engine" [1 signature] Mirror, 13 May 1839, Vol 3, p 2400
PET106	8 Aug 1839 94 CJ 527	40th Rep, p 792 (No 13,607)	Anthony Mackenrot	[Petitioner invented a certain Shipwreck Preventive device, which is called Orthodromic Navigation, enabling Vessels to proceed against the wind; requesting permission to give evidence before the Select Committee of the Mathematical Proofs] [1 signature] Mirror, 8 Aug 1839, Vol 6, p 4867
PET107	20 Aug 1839 71 LJ 626	HL Pet	William Roberts	[Petitioner invented method for preserving bodies for anatomical purposes; he did not take out a patent as requested not to do so but was put to great expense perfecting invention] "to immediately [redress] the injury set forth" [1 signature] Mirror, 20 Aug 1839, Vol 6, p 5120–5121
PET108	6 Mar 1840 95 CJ 152	13th Rep, p 153 (No 2775)	William Joseph Curtis	"invented various contrivances calculated to reduce the risk and promote the convenience of travelling by Railway … and the same be taken into consideration" [1 signature] Mirror, 6 Mar 1840, Vol 2, p 1579
PET109	3 Apr 1840 95 CJ 252	21st Rep, p 433 (No 9916) Supp V&P, p 135–136 (3 Apr 1840)	William Roberts	[Merits of Petitioner's invention for keeping subjects intended for anatomical purposes free from decomposition should be investigated] [1 signature] Mirror, 3 Apr 1840, Vol 3, p 2269 Also see: HC Deb, 21 May 1840, Vol 34(3rd), col 488–493 (95 CJ 360)
PET110	8 Jul 1840 95 CJ 500	42nd Rep, p 936 (No 17,932)	Samuel Hill	"discovered a method for the more economical manufacture of Bread … inquiry into the merits of the same" [1 signature] Mirror, 8 Jul 1840, Vol 5, p 4398
PET111	14 Jul 1840 72 LJ 506	HL Pet	William Roberts	"appoint a committee to investigate … a matured Invention by which Subjects intended for Dissection can be kept in nature Condition by antiseptic means" [1 signature] Mirror, 14 Jul 1840, Vol 5, p 4556–4557
PET112	15 Feb 1841 96 CJ 52	4th Rep, p 28 (No 289) App, p 35–36 (App No 63)	Master Machine-makers of Manchester and Salford	[Export of machinery is prohibited; originated to secure inventions for the advantage of this country exclusively; machinery made aboard already; artisans can go abroad; superiority of the country sufficient; unfair to put restrictions on the trade not known in other fields] "that such Laws may be revised or repealed" [40 signatures] Mirror, 15 Feb 1841, Vol 1, p 241

(continued)

(continued)

PET113	16 Feb 1841 96 CJ 57	4th Rep, p 28 (No 290) App, p 36 (App No 64)	Operative Machine-makers of Manchester and Salford	[Restriction on exporting machinery leads to a depression in the trade; artisans can leave to take the knowledge with them] "that the law which prohibits the exportation of machinery may be repealed" [1964 signatures] HC Deb, 16 Feb 1841, Vol 56(3rd), col 670–692 Mirror, 16 Feb 1841, Vol 1, p 261–268
PET114	16 Feb 1841 96 CJ 57	4th Rep, p 28 (No 291) App, p 36 (App No 65)	Operative Machine-makers of Leeds	[Wool and flax machines allowed only to be sent abroad if of a preparatory kind; considerable number sent abroad in defiance of the law; no restriction on steam engines or skilled artisans leaving; created a premium on machine manufacture on the continent] "that such Laws may be revised or repealed" [1660 signatures] HC Deb, 16 Feb 1841, Vol 56(3rd), col 670–692 Mirror, 16 Feb 1841, Vol 1, p 261–268
PET115	16 Feb 1841 96 CJ 57	4th Rep, p 28 (No 292) App, p 37 (App No 66)	Master Machine-makers of Leeds	[That despite the ban on exporting machinery, licences have been granted to do so; the raw materials can be freely exported; machines smuggled out and used as models; artisans emigrate] "that such Laws may be revised or repealed" [14 signatures] HC Deb, 16 Feb 1841, Vol 56(3rd), col 670–692 Mirror, 16 Feb 1841, Vol 1, p 261–268
PET116	16 Feb 1841 96 CJ 57	4th Rep, p 28 (No 293)	Master Machine-makers of Blackburn	"for the Repeal of the Laws restricting the export of Machinery" [6 signatures] HC Deb, 16 Feb 1841, Vol 56(3rd), col 670–692 Mirror, 16 Feb 1841, Vol 1, p 261–268
PET117	16 Feb 1841 96 CJ 57	4th Rep, p 28 (No 294)	Master Machine-makers of Ashton-Under-Lyme	"for the Repeal of the Laws restricting the export of Machinery" [6 signatures] HC Deb, 16 Feb 1841, Vol 56(3rd), col 670–692 Mirror, 16 Feb 1841, Vol 1, p 261–268
PET118	16 Feb 1841 96 CJ 57	4th Rep, p 28 (No 295)	Master Machine-makers of Bolton	"for the Repeal of the Laws restricting the export of Machinery" [4 signatures] HC Deb, 16 Feb 1841, Vol 56(3rd), col 670–692 Mirror, 16 Feb 1841, Vol 1, p 261–268
PET119	16 Feb 1841 96 CJ 57	4th Rep, p 28 (No 296)	Master Machine-makers of Preston	"for the Repeal of the Laws restricting the export of Machinery" [5 signatures] HC Deb, 16 Feb 1841, Vol 56(3rd), col 670–692 Mirror, 16 Feb 1841, Vol 1, p 261–268
PET120	16 Feb 1841 96 CJ 57	4th Rep, p 28 (No 297)	Master Machine-makers of Stockport	"for the Repeal of the Laws restricting the export of Machinery" [7 signatures] HC Deb, 16 Feb 1841, Vol 56(3rd), col 670–692 Mirror, 16 Feb 1841, Vol 1, p 261–268

PET121	16 Feb 1841 96 CJ 57	4th Rep, p 28 (No 298)	Master Machine-makers of Rochdale	"for the Repeal of the Laws restricting the export of Machinery" [15 signatures] HC Deb, 16 Feb 1841, Vol 56(3rd), col 670–692 Mirror, 16 Feb 1841, Vol 1, p 261–268
PET122	16 Feb 1841 96 CJ 57	4th Rep, p 28 (No 299)	Master Machine-makers of Bury	"for the Repeal of the Laws restricting the export of Machinery" [6 signatures] HC Deb, 16 Feb 1841, Vol 56(3rd), col 670–692 Mirror, 16 Feb 1841, Vol 1, p 261–268
PET123	16 Feb 1841 96 CJ 57	4th Rep, p 28 (No 300) App, p 37 (App No 67)	Master Machine-makers of Bradford	"for the Repeal of the Laws restricting the export of Machinery" [37 signatures] HC Deb, 16 Feb 1841, Vol 56(3rd), col 670–692 Mirror, 16 Feb 1841, Vol 1, p 261–268
PET124	22 Mar 1841 96 CJ 155	14th Rep, p 177 (No 2714)	William Henry Lassalle	"Claims to be the original inventor of the Electric Telegraph, and for inquiry into the circumstances connected with such claims" [1 signature] Mirror, 22 Mar 1841, Vol 2, p 925
PET125	18 May 1841 96 CJ 317	27th Rep, p 545 (No 9736)	Richard Joseph Smith	For the House to institute an inquiry into the state of the Law relating to Patents for Inventions [1 signature] Mirror, 18 May 1841, Vol 3, p 1787
PET126	7 Feb 1842 97 CJ 12	1st Rep, p 387 (No 1056)	John Snooke	"to investigate his plans for lighting Ships at sea, with the view of preventing collisions" [1 Signature]
PET127	26 May 1842 97 CJ 309	27th Rep, p 475 (No 8189) Supp V&P, p 83 (27 May 1842)	George Manby	[Perfecting Plan for Ship wrecks using his inventions] [1 signature] Prt: 28 May 1842 (97 CJ 318) Ref to SC, adj: 1 Jun 1842 (97 CJ 326) Adj: 3 Jun 1842 (97 CJ 335) Adj: 7 Jun 1842 (97 CJ 343) Adj: 8 Jun 1842 (97 CJ 351) Adj: 9 Jun 1842 (97 CJ 355)
PET128	25 Jul 1842 97 CJ 525 29 Jul 1842 74 LJ 487	43rd Rep, p 678 (No 9347)	William Henry Stuckey	"to cause an inquiry to be made into his plan of the filtration of Water by machinery, for the benefit of the Metropolis" [1 signature] HC Deb, 25 Jul 1842, Vol 65(3rd), col 588 HL Deb, 29 Jul 1842, Vol 65(3rd), col 834
PET129	11 May 1843 75 LJ 274	HL Pet	William Henry Stuckey	"accept on Behalf of the Nation at large, his Plan of effectually filtering Water" HL Deb, 11 May 1843, Vol 69(3rd), col 174
PET130	11 May 274 75 LJ 274	HL Pet	John Fell Christy, John Harvey, George Rhan and Charles Speare Tosswill	[Proprietors of Fire Preventive Cement] "Offer of sufficient of the Cement … to make the new House of Parliament Fire-proof"

(continued)

(continued)

PET131	20 Feb 1844 99 CJ 44 16 Feb 1844 76 LJ 32	3rd Rep, p 19 (No 147) App, p 18 (App No 32)	Earl of Dundonald	[Reciting various problems faced by his father in relation to his patents not being profitable due to prejudices; trials of his steam engine] "An Act giving to the Privy Council ... Power in his Case to grant such further Extension of Patent Right as may afford a Chance of recovering his heavy Expenses and suitable Recompense" [i.e. longer than that granted under the Letters Patent for Invention Act 1835] [1 signature] HL Deb, 16 Feb 1844, Vol 72(3rd), col 996–998 HL Deb, 16 Feb 1844, Vol 72(3rd), col 993 HC Deb, 20 Feb 1844, Vol 72(3rd), col 1208
PET132	16 Feb 1844 76 LJ 32	HL Pet	Earl of Dundonald	[To allow him to extend his patent further] HL Deb, 16 Feb 1844, Vol 72(3rd), col 993
PET133	1 Apr 1844 99 CJ 184	15th Rep, p 163 (No 2271)	Adderley Willcocks Sleigh	[Invented a floating sea and wind barrier and breakwater] "a temporary loan may be granted" [1 signature] HC Deb, 1 Apr 1844, Vol 73(3rd), col 1691
PET134	1 Apr 1844 99 CJ 184	15th Rep, p 163 (No 2273)	William Pringle Green	"consider ... certain discoveries he has made in naval matters" [1 signature] HC Deb, 1 Apr 1844, Vol 73(3rd), col 1691
PET135	2 Aug 1844 99 CJ 580	44th Rep, p 891 (No 12,161)	William Bridges	"Use of Payne's Patent Process for the preservation of Wood to be used in the construction of Railways in Ireland; and petition referred to Committee now sitting on Irish Railways" [1 signature] HC Deb, 2 Aug 1844, Vol 76(3rd), col 1706
PET136	8 Aug 1844 99 CJ 630	45th Rep, p 914 (No 12,443) App, p 472 (App No 771)	Earl of Dundonald	[Invention of method of destroying batteries and ships [method not mentioned, but it was poison gas] which will bring war to an end and request for consideration of money] [1 signature]
PET137	3 Mar 1845 100 CJ 84	7th Rep, p 55 (No 402) App, p 58–60 (App No 104) Supp V&P, p 19 (4 Mar 1845)	Joseph D'Aguilar Samuda and Samuel Clegg	[Use of Atmospheric System of Railway] "that a Committee be appointed by your honourable House to inquire into the merits of the Atmospheric System of Railway, and to hear the evidence of engineers and other persons upon the subject and that your Petitioners be allowed to attend before such Committee, and be heard by counsel, or otherwise, as your honourable House shall direct" [2 signatures] HC Deb, 3 Mar 1845, Vol 78(3rd), col 234
PET138	30 Jun 1845 100 CJ 659	38th Rep, p 395 (No 15,656)	James Hantler	"inventor of mechanical improvement ... he is unable to avail himself of that protection which it is the intention of the Law to afford, as a reward for scientific improvements, in consequence of the expense attending the same and prays the House find a remedy" [1 signature]

PET139	10 Feb 1846 101 CJ 99	4th Rep, p 78 (No 2228)	Thomas Parkin	[Petitioner invented a system of locomotion which dispenses with tunnels, earthwork, viaducts etc.] "permit him to exhibit the said model in one of the Committee Rooms of the House, and to appoint a Committee" [1 signature] HC Deb, 10 Feb 1846, Vol 83(3rd), col 638
PET140	24 Jul 1846 101 CJ 1097	44th Rep, p 593 (No 7950) App, p 447–448 (App No 845)	Earl of Dundonald	"To adopt such measures as shall afford him the means of proving that Enterprises [of war] may be achieved by his secret plan for infallibly dismantling or destroying Forts or Fleets" [1 signature]
PET141	7 Aug 1846 101 CJ 1178	47th Rep, p 640 (No 8092) App, 470–471 (App No 882)	Frederick Maberley	[Invented new method of steam vessels whereby they are divided into compartments; plan submitted to the Admiralty; never acknowledged for his invention] "his improvements regarding the construction and working of Steam Vessels, have been used by the Board of Admiralty with acknowledgement" [1 signature]
PET142	18 Aug 1846 101 CJ 1224	50th Rep, p 679 (No 8384)	George Walter	"to inspect and report upon the efficiency of his Life Boat" [1 signature] HC Deb, 18 Aug 1846, Vol 88(3rd), col 845
PET143	19 Aug 1846 101 CJ 1235	50th Rep, p 681 (No 8450)	Robert Scott Burn and John Howden	"That they will be pleased to take into Consideration the present Patent Laws of Great Britain, with a view to their Alteration or Amendment, or their Assimilation to the Patent Laws of Continental Kingdoms, or to the Law of Copyright at present existing in this Kingdom" [2 signatures] HC Deb, 19 Aug 1846, Vol 88(3rd), col 875
PET144	15 Mar 1847 79 LJ 86	HL Pet	Robert Scott Burn and John Howden	[For alteration of the Patent Law] "That they will be pleased to take into Consideration the present Patent Laws of Great Britain, with a view to their Alteration or Amendment, or their Assimilation to the Patent Laws of Continental Kingdoms, or to the Law of Copyright at present existing in this Kingdom, by such Means as to this House may seem proper"
PET145	7 May 1847 102 CJ 492	27th Rep, p 572 (No 7977)	Henry Needham Scrope Shrapnel	[Great success of his father's shell invention; various claims against East India Company; insufficient pension] "take … case into consideration" Also see Return of Number of Shrapnel Shells ordered for British and East India Company (1847 HC Papers 596 and 755), Vol 36, p 596 and Vol 41, p 425 Ord: 10 Jun 1847 (102 CJ 651) Pres: 25 Jun 1847 (102 CJ 742) Prt: 1 Jul 1847 (102 CJ 776) Pres: 15 Jul 1847 (102 CJ 875) Prt: 23 Jul 1847 (102 CJ 959) [1 signature] HC Deb, 7 Deb 1847, Vol 92(3rd), col 523

(continued)

(continued)

PET146	14 May 1847 102 CJ 526	29th Rep, p 631 (No 8787) App, p 353–956 (App No 717)	Henry Needham Scrope Shrapnel	[Provides details of father's invention of Shrapnel; the expenses and debts he incurred and so forth] "take his case into consideration" [1 signature]
PET147	22 Jun 1847 102 CJ 719	38th Rep, p 792 (No 10,251) App, p 440 (App No 852)	Inhabitants of Bradford	In supporting petitions of Henry Needham Scrope Shrapnel [PET145] [36 signatures] HC Deb, 22 Jun 1847, Vol 93(3rd), col 798
PET148	1 Jul 1847 102 CJ 775 Prt: 6 Jul 1847 102 CJ 807	41st Rep, p 828 (No 10,356)	Samuel Porter	"Electric Telegraph originated with him … cause the merit of the discovery to fall upon the right country and the right individual" [1 signature] HC Deb, 1 Jul 1847, Vol 93(3rd), col 1089
PET149	9 Jul 1847 102 CJ 841	43rd Rep, p 854 (No 10,437) App, p 470 (App No 888)	Inhabitants of Southampton &c.	In supporting petitions of Henry Needham Scrope Shrapnel [PET145] [117 signatures] HC Deb, Jul 1847, Vol 94(3rd), col 102
PET150	3 Mar 1848 103 CJ 289	17th Rep, p 267 (No 3567)	Robert Young	"Consideration of the effective mode given by [his invention] for an instantaneous communication between the Passengers, Guards and Engine Drivers of all Trains" [1 signature]
PET151	9 Mar 1848 103 CJ 305	20th Rep, p 313 (No 3885) App, p 258–260 (App No 488)	Henry Archer	[Details of cost of taking out patents in England, Scotland and Ireland; comparison of costs with other countries; to reduce expense of patents; to create one patent for whole of United Kingdom] "A Select Committee of your Honourable House be appointed to resume the said inquiry [i.e. the 1829 Inquiry] this Session" [1 signature]
PET152	31 Mar 1848 103 CJ 402	29th Rep, p 446 (No 4663) App, p 350 (App No 658)	Captain Henry Needham Scrope Shrapnel	[Enormous expense in taking out a patent; "intellectual property"; reduce cost of patent to £5 for England, £5 Scotland and £5 Ireland; adopt Crown prosecutions for patent infringement] "to consider the great importance of such reductions and alterations in the law of patents" [22 signatures]
PET153	2 Aug 1848 103 CJ 843	74th Rep, p 1323 (No 18,037)	Robert Rettie	[System of Marine Light Signals; and other naval inventions; consideration of time and outlay on inventions] Praying for inquiry into merits of his invention [1 signature] HC Deb, 2 Aug 1848, Vol 100(3rd), col 1094
PET154	16 Aug 1848 103 CJ 931	80th Rep, p 1425 (No 18,254) App, p 812–813 (App No 1514)	Fredrick William Campin	[System of patents and designs flawed: 1. High level of fees up to £400; 2. Practice of allowing patents to pass with vague titles and the problem of applicants coming between patent and specification problems; 3. High Cost of litigation and need for presumption of validity and specially qualified tribunal; 4. Non-suiting where a registered design conflicts with a patent; 5. Lack of coherence in patent records (being stored in three places) and need for a patent register; Proposals: (a) lower cost patents; (b) patents bear the date of application; (c) titles need to be precise or a provisional specification should be filed;

				(e) presumption of validity; (f) specialist patent tribunal set up; (g) caveats allowed against designs; (h) that a patent office be formed where all records collated] [158 signatures] HC Deb, 16 Aug 1848, Vol 101(3rd), col 145
PET155	29 Aug 1848 103 CJ 988	85th Rep, p 1506 (No 18,451)	John Snooke	[Invented a more efficient Life Boat than has yet has been produced; inquiry into the merits of an invention which would prevent a repetition as occurred on the destruction of the Ocean Monarch Emigrant Ship] [1 signature] HC Deb, 29 Aug 1848, Vol 101(3rd), col 615
PET156	22 Feb 1849 104 CJ 85	9th Rep, p 50 (No 226)	Henry Archer	"That either a Commission or Select Committee may be appointed this Session to inquire into the present State of the Patent Laws, or that a Law may be passed to give Effect, not only to the Recommendations of the Commissioners appointed to inquire into the Nature of the Duties of the Signet and Privy Seal Offices, but to provide that such Persons as may be compelled to exhibited unpatented, their Inventions, at the proposed National Exhibition of Arts and Manufactures, shall not be disqualified from subsequently taking out Patents by reason of such Publications" [Extract from Lords, Select Committee noted it was the same as the petition in the previous session] [1 signature] HC Deb, 22 Feb 1849, Vol 102(3rd), col 1098
PET157	8 Mar 1849 104 CJ 120	15th Rep, p 102 (No 483)	James Dowie	[In May 1838, petitioner submitted his boots for inspection at Horse Guards eventually reported unfavourably by Clothing Board; reason to believe that reports of Clothing Board and Horse Guards were different] "House to call for said Reports together with all correspondence on the matter" [1 signature] HC Deb, 12 Mar 1849, Vol 103(3rd), col 538
PET158	10 Jul 1849 104 CJ 474	62nd Rep, p 975 (No 9489)	William Henry Lassalle	[Invented an improved Life Boat; and plan for converting ordinary boats to the improve version] "for an inquiry" into invention [1 signature] HC Deb, 10 Jul 1849, Vol 107(3rd), col 101
PET159	16 Jul 1849 104 CJ 498 9 Jul 1849 81 LJ 414	64th Rep, p 1008 (No 9585)	James Godfrey Wilson and William Pidding	"For inquiry into invention for abolition of smoke nuisance" [2 signatures]
PET160	28 Jul 1849 104 CJ 607	69th Rep, p 1098 (No 9875)	Donald Grant	[Petitioner spent a large sum of money in developing improvements in ventilation] "from want of funds unable to carry out his views … praying for an inquiry" [1 signature] HC Deb, 28 Jul 1849, Vol 107(3rd), col 1074

(continued)

(continued)

PET161	13 Feb 1850 105 CJ 66	5th Rep, p 41 (No 484)	John Jones	[Heavy amount of Stamp and Office charges under Patent Law; disparity for securing an English Patent compared with an American patent for the same invention (80:1 difference)] "Immediate revision of those laws" [1 signature]
PET162	15 Mar 1850 82 LJ 62	HL Pet	Henry Archer	[Expense of obtaining a patent] "That either a Commission or Select Committee may be appointed this Session to inquire into the present State of the Patents Laws, or that a Law may be passed to give Effect, not only to the Recommendations of the Commissioners appointed to inquire into the Nature of the Duties of the Select and Privy Seal Office, but to provide, that such Persons as may be compelled to exhibit unpatented their Inventions, at the proposed National Exhibition of Arts and Manufactures, shall not be disqualified from subsequently taking out Patent by reason of such Publications"
PET163	15 Apr 1850 105 CJ 222	27th Rep, p 442 (No 5725)	Henry Olding	[Discovered method for consuming coal smoke in a furnace, but unable to take out a patent due to expense] "Alter the Laws relating to the Registration of Mechanical Inventions by diminishing the cost of such Registration to one or two pounds" [1 signature]
PET164	23 May 1850 105 CJ 632	42nd Rep, p 844 (No 10,226) App, p 496–497 (App No 1091)	Fredrick William Campin	[Inconvenience of patent law; recommendations of Report of Committee into Privy Seal and Signet Office dated 30 Jan 1849 put into effect [REP5]; (a) that patent takes date of application not sealing; (b) a memorandum or specification is filed at the time of making the application; (c) properly classified index produced; (d) a reduction of fees and patent for whole of United Kingdom; (e) a method for transferring surreptitiously obtained patents] For alteration of the Law of Patents [75 signatures]
PET165	27 Jun 1850 105 CJ 469	55th Rep, p 1159 (No 12,922)	Henry Needham Scrope Shrapnel	[Father never received any public reward or acknowledgement; various complaints against East India Company] "take his case into consideration" [1 signature]
PET166	22 Jul 1850 105 CJ 548	66th Rep, 1429 (No 15,690)	Fredrick Herbert Maberley	[Petitioner the inventor of certain improvements in steam and sailing vessels by the division of vessels into watertight compartments; invention used by Lords of Admiralty with no payment to the petitioner; this use prevents him from getting a patent] "For consideration of his case" [1 signature]
PET167	29 Jul 1850 105 CJ 578	69th Rep, p 1485 (No 15,837) App, p 774–776 (App No 1652)	Donald Grant	Complaining of Official Referees under the Metropolitan Building Act precluding him from working his invention [1 signature]

PET168	17 Feb 1851 14 Feb 1851 83 LJ 24	6th Rep, p 73 (No 1916) App, p 81 (App No 175)	Members of the Huddersfield Local Committee to Promote the Exhibition of the Works of Industry of all Nations in 1851	"to alter the Patent Law, and abolish the heavy Fees, so that new Manufactures and Inventions may be freely exhibited without entailing Penalties on the Exhibitor of them for doing so, and to pass a Measure of Relief similar to that which was passed by the House of Lords in the last Session of Parliament, but which was altered by the Commons" [See PUBA4] [28 signatures]
PET169	17 Mar 1851 13 Mar 1851 83 LJ 65	16th Rep, p 218 (No 4245) App, p 178 (App No 383)	Inhabitants of the borough of Bradford	[That the method of getting letters patent not suited to present time; no means of ascertaining what has been patented already; no real guarantee as to validity; much more expensive than other countries] "That these Grievances may be redressed; and there may be an Office established for the Registration of Inventions, and that the Procedure may be as simple as possible; that the Cost of Registration should not exceed Five Pounds in the first instance and that the Right secured thereby should extend throughout the United Kingdom and Ireland; that complete Indices of all past and existing Specifications be forthwith made, printed and published and that all future Specifications may be printed and periodically published" [148 signatures]
PET170	18 Mar 1851	17th Rep, p 237 (No 4522) App, p 193 (App No 426)	National Patent Law Amendment Association	[The current patent law prevents many things being exhibited at the Great Exhibition; proposes that: (a) the legal protection of inventors should be provisionally available at nominal cost; (b) full patents available in a straightforward manner; (c) judicial proceedings for patent matters be made inexpensive; (d) scientific assessors used; (e) a power to compel fraudulent patentee to assignee it to inventor] [See PUBA4] [1 signature]
PET171	20 Mar 1851 4 Apr 1851 83 LJ 114	18th Rep, p 274 (No 5462) App, p 210–211 (App No 472)	Inhabitants of Kirkcaldy	[Law relating to letters patent unsuitable to present age and very expensive; means of determining what has been patented very difficult; no real guarantee provided to patentee; United Kingdom is far behind France, Belgium, Austria, the United States and Spain; there should be one patent office] "That these Grievances may be redressed; and there may be an Office established for the Registration of Inventions, and that the Procedure may be as simple as possible; that the Cost of Registration should not exceed Five Pounds in the first instance and that the Right secured thereby should extend throughout the United Kingdom and Ireland; that complete Indices of all past and existing Specifications be forthwith made, printed and published and that all future Specifications may be printed and periodically published" [158 signatures]

(continued)

(continued)

PET172	24 Mar 1851 25 Mar 1851 83 LJ 82	19th Rep, p 300 (No 5965) App, p 226 (App No 504)	Mayor, Alderman and Burgesses of the Borough of Bridport	"That these Grievances may be redressed; and there may be an Office established for the Registration of Inventions, and that the Procedure may be as simple as possible; that the Cost of Registration should not exceed Five Pounds in the first instance and that the Right secured thereby should extend throughout the United Kingdom and Ireland; that complete Indices of all past and existing Specifications be forthwith made, printed and published and that all future Specifications may be printed and periodically published" [1 signature]
PET173	25 Mar 1851	20th Rep, p 319 (No 6294) App, p 234–235 (App No 521)	Belfast Chamber of Commerce	[Delays and cost of getting a patent too high; method of discovering what is patented too difficult] "that there may be one patent office for the United Kingdom; that the present useless, dilatory, and expensive forms may be dispensed with and some, simple, cheap, and expeditious forms introduced instead thereof; that the novelty of inventions may be ascertained by the registrar before registration of the specification; that models of all inventions may be required to be lodged in a museum to be provided for that purpose; that the expense of a patent may not exceed £70, and for the convenience and encouragement of poor inventors only £10 pounds of that sum to be paid a time of registry, and the remainder by instalments; and that the public and inventors should have early and accurate information of all patented inventions by the periodical publication, at cost price, of a printed catalogue therefore, with drawings and specifications of all patents existing at the time of publication" [3 signatures]
PET174	25 Mar 1851 28 Mar 1851 83 LJ 89	20th Rep, p 319 (No 6295)	Inhabitants of Reading	"That these Grievances may be redressed; and there may be an Office established for the Registration of Inventions, and that the Procedure may be as simple as possible; that the Cost of Registration should not exceed Five Pounds in the first instance and that the Right secured thereby should extend throughout the United Kingdom and Ireland; that complete Indices of all past and existing Specifications be forthwith made, printed and published and that all future Specifications may be printed and periodically published" [58 signatures]
PET175	4 Apr 1851 83 LJ 114	HL Pet	Patentees and others interested in the Laws affecting Patents	"Patent Law Amendment Bill [PUBB20] may be referred to a Select Committee of their Lordships"
PET176	4 Apr 1851 83 LJ 114	HL Pet	Inhabitants of Kirby	[Great expense in taking out a patent; an Office should be established for the registration of inventions; and a simplified procedure adopted; the cost of registration should not exceed £5; and the right should extend through the United Kingdom and Ireland; and there should be a complete index of specifications]

PET177	14 Apr 1851 14 Apr 1851 83 LJ 137	28th Rep, p 439 (No 7471) App, p 319 (App No 709)	Inhabitants of Manchester	[Patents very expensive with no real service rendered] "That these Grievances may be redressed; and there may be one Office established for the Registration of Inventions, and that the Procedure may be as simple as possible; that the Cost of Registration should not exceed Five Pounds in the first instance and that the Right secured thereby should extend throughout the United Kingdom and Ireland; that complete Indices of all past and existing Specifications be forthwith made, printed and published and that all future Specifications may be printed and periodically published" [1 signature]
PET178	30 May 1851 83 LJ 223	HL Pet	Local Committee at Newbury appointed to assist with the Exhibition of all Nations 1851	[Great expense taking out a patent] "That these Grievances may be redressed, and that there may be One Office established for granting Patents for Inventions for the United Kingdom, and that the Procedure may be as simple as possible; that the Cost of obtaining Patents may not be more than is absolutely necessary for the Maintenance of the One Office in a State of Efficiency; that complete Indies of all past and existing Specifications be forthwith made, printed, and published and that all future Specifications be printed and periodically published" [See PUBB20 and PUBB21]
PET179	16 Jun 1851 83 LJ 253	HL Pet	Belfast Chamber of Commerce	"That the Patent Office for the United Kingdom may be presided over by a Single Commissioner; that the Mode of obtaining Letters Patent be as simple and expeditious as possible; that Models and Drawings of Inventions be required to be lodged in a Museum provided for the Purpose; that the Expense of a Patent may not exceed £70, and, for the Convenience and Encouragement of poor Inventors, only £10 of that Amount be paid at the Time of Registry, and the Remainder by periodic Instalments; that the Public and Inventors shall have early and accurate Information of all patented Inventions, by the periodical Publication, at Cost Price, of a printed Catalogue, with Drawings and Specifications of all Patents existing at the Time of Publication" [See PUBB20 and PUBB21]
PET180	23 Jun 1851 1 Jul 1851 83 LJ 307	53rd Rep, p 854 (No 10,327) App, p 578–580 (App No 1222)	Sugar Refiners of the Port of Liverpool	[Better to abolish the patent system than pass the Bill [PUBB22] as currently proposed; the petitioners propose: (a) no patent granted where used or published in Europe, America or a British Dominion; (b) no patent granted for a trivial invention; (c) every patentee bound to grant a licence on a reasonable fee; (d) such licence should be subject to modification where unjust; (e) all patents should cover the whole of the British Empire; (f) the government should be able to withdraw a patent on fair payment; (g) the duration of the patent should be determined on a case by case basis] "to make some new and effectual Provision for securing the Commerce and Manufacturers of the United Kingdom from the evil Consequences of which may follow a Reduction of the Cost of

(continued)

(continued)

				patenting Inventions, and to put the whole British Dominions on the same Footing, so that no Exemption may be shown the Colonies, to the Disadvantage of the British Producers and Manufacturers, but on the contrary, that both may be favoured alike in any intended Change of Practice" [92 signatures]
PET181	24 Jun 1851 83 LJ 281	HL Pet	Edinburgh Chamber of Commerce	That the Patent Law Amendment Bill [PUBB22] be passed
PET182	30 Jun 1851	56th Rep, p 902 (No 10,471)	James Dowie	[In July 1849, his invention received formal approval of Horse Guards, but only partially received into service and has been unable to bring his invention into full use] "for investigation and the production of all correspondence upon the subject" [1 signature]
PET183	30 Jun 1851	56th Rep, p 903 (No 10,483) App, p 602 (App No 1264)	Sugar Refiners of Greenock, Port Glasgow, Glasgow and Leith	[(a) patent law should grant a right of compensation and not an exclusive right; (b) inventors should be rewarded by the state rather than patents; (c) court should be set up to referee between patentee and public; (d) sugar refiners will have to pay patent fees in United Kingdom but not in colonies so will not be able to compete] "to reform the patent laws, and reform them in accordance with the foregoing representations" [14 signatures]
PET184	4 Jul 1851 106 CJ 335	58th Rep, p 947 (No 11,007) App, p 623 (App No 1294)	Henry Needham Scrope Shrapnel	[Eldest son and heir of Lt-Gen Shrapnel developer of the Shrapnel shell; father received a pension; huge loss sustained due to shells supplied to East India Company being taken out of hands of the inventor; give the late General's family the reward he was entitled to] [1 signature]
PET185	14 Jul 1851 15 Jul 1851 83 LJ 378	62nd Rep, p 1020 (No 11,364) App, p 682 (App No 1398)	Greenock Chamber of Commerce	[That the Patent Law Amendment Bill [PUBB22] means colonies will not be subject to patent laws] "That in passing any Law on the Subject of Patents they will provide that all Parts of Her Majesty's Dominions shall be subject to the same Rules on that Behalf" [1 signature]
PET186	15 Jul 1851	63rd Rep, p 1037 (No 11,453) App, p 692 (App No 1418)	National Patent Law Amendment Association	[Proposed Bill [PUBB22] lacks certain important provisions: (a) the rule that foreign publications destroying novelty should be omitted; (b) no provision for scientific advisers in court; (c) new system will be too expensive; (d) patent cases should be heard in county courts] [1 signature]
PET187	15 Jul 1851	63rd Rep, p 1037 (No 11,444)	John Fordham Stanford	For certain alteration of the Patent Law Amendment Bill [PUBB22] [1 signature]
PET188	17 Jul 1851	63rd Rep 1038 (No 11,445) App, p 692–693 (App No 1419)	Incorporated Society for the Encouragement of Arts, Manufactures and Commerce	[While Bill [PUBB22] is great improvement it still includes much cumbersome and useless machinery] "to pass the proposed [Patent Law Amendment] Bill in the present Session of Parliament" [1 signature]

PET189	17 Jul 1851	63rd Rep, p 1038 (No 11,446) App, p 693 (App No 1420)	Manchester Patent Law Reform Association	[Cl 14 which makes publication abroad the same as local publication is an injustice to British inventors as it is necessary to ascertain whether an invention is novel in many other countries; but advantages greatly outweigh disadvantages] "to pass the proposed Bill [PUBB22] into a law in the present Session of Parliament, leaving further amendments to be introduced hereafter if found to be necessary" [1 signature]
PET190	17 Jul 1851	63rd Rep, p 1038 (No 11,447)	Borough of Bradford	To pass the Patent Law Amendment Bill [PUBB22] [42 signatures]
PET191	18 Jul 1851	64th Rep, p 1054 (No 11,516) App, p 698 (App No 1433)	Association of Patentees for the Protection and Regulation of Patent Property	[Novelty examination is unnecessary and would make it difficult for inventor to substantiate their claims and so increase the cost further; excepting the ability to extend it to the colonies; publication in any foreign country would stop the importance of bringing inventions from abroad and make it too easy to evade patents] "to take the premises into your consideration, and either reject the said Bill [PUBB22] altogether or to make such alterations as the interests of the country and rights of inventors may in your wisdom seem to require" [11 signatures]
PET192	22 Jul 1851	66th Rep, p 1095 (No 11,717)	Charles Barlow (Ed Patent Journal)	"to refer Patent Law Amendment Bill [PUBB22] to a Select Committee to consider the same, and take Evidence thereon" [1 signature]
PET193	28 Jul 1851	68th Rep, p 1131 (No 11,836) App, p 735 (App No 1506)	Members of the Wortley Improvement Society, the Armly Youth Guardian Society and the Churwell Mechanics Institute	[The Patent Amendment Bill [PUBB22] will reduce the incentives that currently exist; that preliminary examination is unnecessary and will increase the cost of a patent; there should be an increase in the cost of getting a patent in the colonies] "to reject the said Bill entirely or to make such alterations, therein as may preserve inviolate the statute" [90 signatures]
PET194	30 Jul 1851	69th Rep, p 1149 (No 11,904)	Bleachers, Dyers and Printers of the County of Lancaster	"to induce the House to reject the Patent Law Amendment Bill [PUBB22]" [16 signatures]
PET195	30 Jul 1851	69th Rep, p 1149 (No 11,905)	Members of the Mechanics' Institute at Leck in Stafford	"to induce the House to reject the Patent Law Amendment Bill [PUBB22]" [127 signatures]
PET196	4 Aug 1851	71st Rep, p 1188 (No 12,010) App, p 764 (App No 1553)	Council of the Board of Irish Manufacturers and Industry	[Cost and delay of getting patent protection in Ireland; provide in the Bill that patents may be obtained from an office in Dublin as well as London] Pray for amendment of Patent Amendment Bill [PUBB22] [15 signatures]

(continued)

(continued)

PET197	11 Feb 1852 12 Feb 1852 84 LJ 20	3rd Rep, p 15 (No 92) App, p 25 (App No 48)	Inhabitants of Blackburn	[Provisional protection under the Protection of Inventors Act 1851 [PUBA4] due to expire; pass law to make obtaining letters patent cheaper; an index of patents; ensure for protection of inventors] "Measure may be passed so that the Cost of obtaining Letters patent may be reduced to such a moderate Sum as will enable the Artizan to secure to himself the Rights of his intellectual labour" [See PUBA5] [1 signature]
PET198	12 Feb 1852 19 Feb 1852 84 LJ 28	3rd Rep, p 15 (No 93) App, p 25–26 (App No 49)	National Patent Law Amendment Association and Inhabitants of Manchester	[Inventors need a fair chance of remuneration only possible by granting an exclusive right; proposed: (a) provisional protection of inventions for little or no cost; (b) complete letters patent at moderate cost; (c) simple method of obtaining a patent; (d) a classified index of patents; (e) the introduction of scientific assessors for patent cases; (f) a declaratory statute setting out law of patents] "That an Act may be passed by which the ... Cost of obtaining Letters patent may be reduced to such a moderate Sum as will enable the Artizan to secure to himself the Rights of his intellectual labour" [1 signature] HL Deb, 19 Feb 1852, Vol 119(3rd), col 762–763
PET199	12 Mar 1852	9th Rep, p 62 (No 467)	Julius Jeffreys	[Found a means of removing all causes of accidents in deembarking ships by using mechanical principles] "inquiry into his plan" [1 signature]
PET200	19 Mar 1852 22 Mar 1852 84 LJ 64	13th Rep, p 107 (No 1010)	Inhabitants of Bradford	"That an Act may be passed for the Revision of the Patent Laws, by which the Cost of obtaining Letters Patent shall be reduced to such a moderate Sum as will enable the humble Artizan to secure to himself the Rights of his intellectual Labour, that the Processes or Forms may be simplified as much as possible, that perfect authenticated Indices of all Patents granted may be published at as short Intervals as may be found convenient, and that such further Provisions may be made for the Protection of Inventors and the Public as will secure to this Nation a Continuation of the proud Pre-eminence and Engineering Skill she has so long occupied" [1 signature]
PET201	23 Mar 1852 22 Mar 1852 84 LJ 64	14th Rep, p 135 (No 1309)	Inhabitants of Halifax	Similar to Blackburn, App 48 [PET197] [1 signature]
PET202	7 May 1852	28th Rep, p 383 (No 4346) App, p 329 (App No 659)	Sugar Refiners of Liverpool	[The exclusion of patents from the colonies should be struck out in PUBA6; inquiry into patent law] "to legislate with regard to patents in such as manner as not to put the home manufacturers and producers on a more unfavourable footing than colonial, and to modify the patent laws in such a manner as not to subject the Petitioners to unlimited charges for the use of patents" [6 signatures]

PET203	12 May 1852	30th Rep, p 417 (No 4671) App, p 348–349 (App No 701)	Inventors' Society	[While the Patent Law Amendment Bill [PUBA6] could be improved, the savings brought in would be worth it] "to pass the said Bill into a law with as little delay as the forms of your honourable House will admit" [12 signatures]
PET204	14 May 1852	31st Rep, p 430 (No 4755) App, p 356 (App No 714)	Liverpool Soap Manufacturers	[Bill ought not to pass without more than ordinary consideration and especially not without its being adapted to the interests of British producers] "to remit the Patent Law Amendment Bill [PUBA6] to a Select Committee to be amended" [11 signatures]
PET205	17 May 1852	32nd Rep, p 443 (No 4822) App, p 361–362 (App No 725)	Edinburgh Chamber of Commerce	[A general satisfaction with the proposed Patent Law Amendment Bill but some changes: (a) make provision for actions to be heard in Scotland; (b) a branch of Patent Office could be situated in Edinburgh; (c) all specifications should be open to inspection in Edinburgh if no office; (d) should not excluded Colonies from letters patent] "to adopt the same, and to make provision for carrying them into effect by the insertion of such words or clauses as may in your wisdom seem best adapted for the purpose and, with these amendments to pass the Patent Law Amendment Bill [PUBA6] now before your Honourable House" [1 signature]
PET206	20 May 1852	33rd Rep, p 457 (No 4922) App, p 366 (App No 737)	Inventors' Society	[Cl 25 foreign publication and use anticipating is objectionable; does not provide for extension to the colonies; unnecessary to refer to a Select Committee] "the progress of this Bill [PUBA6] may not be interrupted in any way, but that being duly amended it may be forthwith passed by your honourable House at present assembled" [83 signatures]
PET207	21 May 1852	34th Rep, p 471 (No 5026) App, p 373 (App No 750)	London Mechanics' Institution	[General approval of the Bill albeit some modification useful] "that the said Bill [PUBA6] may be passed during the present Session with as little delay as possible" [66 signatures]
PET208	24 May 1852	35th Rep, p 488 (No 5215) App, p 381 (App No 770)	Greenock Chamber of Commerce	[Patent Law has not yet properly been considered] "not to pass the said Bill [PUBA6] into a law, or otherwise to alter the laws affecting patents at present but to allow further time for mature consideration" [1 signature]
PET209	27 May 1852	35th Rep, p 488 (No 5216) App, p 381–382 (App No 771)	Council Members of National Patent Law Amendment Association	[Cl 25 foreign publication and use anticipating is objectionable; as is clause excluding colonies; do not refer to a Select Committee] "the said Bill [PUBA6] may be amended without being referred to a Select Committee, and then passed without delay" [30 signatures]

(continued)

(continued)

PET210	27 May 1852	35th Rep, p 488 (No 5217) App, p 382 (App No 772)	National Meeting of Patent Law Amendment Society, Pentonville	[Patent law very defective; Patent Law Amendment Bill inflict new injuries; Bill needs amendment] "the said Bill [PUBA6] may be thoroughly and effectively amended, and that it be referred to a Select Committee for that end, provided that this will not endanger the passing of the measure of patent law amendment this Session" [72 signatures]
PET211	7 Jun 1852	38th Rep, p 528 (No 5397) App, p 405–406 (App No 809)	Society of Solicitors, Supreme Court of Scotland	[(a) That actions should be possible before the Scottish Courts; (b) it should be possible to lodge specifications in Edinburgh as well as London; (c) duplicates of the register should be available in Edinburgh] "to adopt the alterations [to PUBA6] suggested by them; or to afford such other relief as to your honourable House may seem proper" [2 signatures]
PET212	15 Jun 1852	41st Rep, p 566 (No 5494) App, p 420–421 (App No 836)	Engineers, Machinists and Residents of Rochdale	[Omit Cl 25 in Patent Law Amendment Bill; to ensure that the work of Select Committee will not delay passage of Bill] "pass the Bill [PUBA6] without delay and thus afford substantial relief to a numerous and deserving class of persons many of whom have been benefactors to the public and an ornament to their country" [13 signatures]
PET213	18 Jun 1852	43rd Rep, p 592 (No 5556) App, p 435 (App No 857)	Merchants, Manufacturers, Traders in London	[Cl 14 for novelty examination should be restricted so it only takes a reasonable time; Cl 25 on foreign publication anticipating should be omitted; Cl 31 changed to make publication of the specifications optional; and fees reduced and no stamp duty imposed; Registrar of Designs be employed with putting Act into effect] "will adopt such measure as may be effectual for the passing of the said Bill [PUBA6] during the present Session of Parliament in an amended form, and thereby afford the relief" [54 signatures]
PET214	23 Jun 1852	45th Rep, p 620 (No 5611) App, p 443–444 (App No 868)	Sugar Refiners of Greenock	[Cl 19 of PUBA6 prohibiting extension to the colonies should be omitted] "not to put the home refiners on a more unfavourable footing than the colonial in regard to patents" [7 signatures]
PET215	29 Jun 1852	46th Rep, p 635 (No 5638)	William Burness Brixton	[Possesses several very important inventions but unable to bring them to use because of current patent law] "for the insertion of clauses in the Patent Law Amendment Bill [PUBA6] now before Parliament for the removal of obstacles to Patentees" [1 signature]
PET216	10 Mar 1853	29th Rep, p 296 (No 2378)	Robert Rettie	[Claims he is the inventor of the Red, White and Green signals used on the railways; and signals for showing distress at sea; his patent has been infringed; request Committee of Inquiry] [1 signature]

PET217	26 May 1853	52nd Rep, p 790 (No 6335)	Patrick Mac Enna	[Petitioner discovered method of remedy to reduce suffering; requests to be examined at bar of the house] [1 signature]
PET218	3 Jun 1853 9 May 1853 85 LJ 245	56th Rep, p 882 (No 6890) App, p 654 (App No 1312)	Convention of the Royal Burgh of Scotland	[Specifications should be filed at the Chancery Office in Edinburgh; proposed change of law is a violation of the rights of Scotland and Ireland] "that the Copies of Specifications Repeal Bill [PUBA8] may not pass into a Law" [1 signature]
PET219	26 May 1853 85 LJ 284	HL Pet	Leith Chamber of Commerce	"that the Copies of Specifications Repeal Bill [PUBA8] may not pass into a Law"
PET220	9 Jun 1853	58th Rep, p 925 (No 7085) App, p 678–679 (App No 1354)	Edinburgh Chamber of Commerce	[Specifications covering Scotland have always been deposited in Edinburgh; the new Bill will end this] "reject the aforesaid Copies of Specifications Repeal Bill [PUBA8]" [1 signature]
PET221	15 Jun 1853	61st Rep, p 1000 (No 7667) App, p 705 (App No 1406)	Company of Merchants of Edinburgh	[Ending the filing of specifications in Scotland will be injurious to its residents] "refuse your sanction to the Bill [PUBA8] in dependence being into a law" [1 signature]
PET222	16 Jun 1853	61st Rep, p 1000 (No 7668) App, p 705–706 (App No 1407)	Council of Inventors Rights	[Provision should be added to the Copies of Specifications Bill [PUBA8] to extend patents to the colonies; and the provisional specification should not be published] [1 signature]
PET223	19 Aug 1853 85 LJ 710	HL Pet	Donald Grant	Petition for relief following unsuccessful Private Bill [PRVB131]
PET224	17 Mar 1854	18th Rep, p 179 (No 1503) App, p 168 (App No 378)	National Patent Law Amendment Association	[The 1852 Act [PUBA6] has taken away the power to grant patents in respect of colonies and there is no longer a system for obtaining them; the period of protection granted by a provisional specification is too short] "to take the contents of this Petition into your favourable consideration, and revise and amend the said Patent Amendment Act as speedily as may be" [1 signature]
PET225	8 Jun 1854	41st Rep, p 702 (No 7620)	William Beard	[Petitioner's patent was opposed and once resolved, the time for sealing patent had expired; so no order for sealing could be made unless time had run out before passing of Patent Law Act 1853 [PUBA7] otherwise only a one month extension allowed] "that the [Patent Law Act 1853; PUBA7] be amended as to have retrospective action given to it whereby the Lord Chancellor may be authorised to seal his Patent; and that the Lord Chancellor may in future be unrestricted to any particular time for sealing the Patent in the cases provided for in the said Act" [1 signature]
PET226	12 Aug 1854	65th Rep, p 1142 (No. 10,374)	Fredrick Herbert Maberley	[Perfected certain inventions with respect to water-tight compartments in Steam Vessels; used by Admiralty but no recognition] [1 signature]

(continued)

(continued)

PET227	23 Dec 1854	2nd Rep, p 10 (No 49)	Fredrick Herbert Maberley	[Submitted various suggestions to the Admiralty with respect to water-tight compartments; suggestions returned unapproved, but since adopted by Admiralty without payment to the petitioner] [1 signature]
PET228	9 Mar 1855	15th Rep, p 108 (No 690) App, p 117–118 (App No 210)	Earl of Dundonald	[Discovered invention which would overcome ordinary weapons of war and overcome fortifications; provided to Prince Regent in 1812; the invention has yet to be taken up] "inquiry to ascertain whether the aforesaid secret plans are capable speedily, certainly, and cheaply to surmount obstacles which our gallant, preserving, and costly armies and fleets have failed to accomplish" [1 signature]
PET229	23 Apr 1855	26th Rep, p 307 (No 2558)	Thomas Bromley	[Petitioner owns patent for soap; it is well fitted for use in the Navy; House inquire into the matter] [1 signature]
PET230	26 Apr 1855	28th Rep, p 384 (No 3778)	Janet Adam	[As early as 1831, her husband James Adam had been propelling ships by means of the Screw; submitted plans to the Admiralty; no means to obtain a patent; request for an inquiry] [1 signature]
PET231	15 May 1855	36th Rep, p 618–619 (No 6778)	William Farquhar	[Alleges he is the inventor of the screen propeller; a working model produced in 1834; showed this invention for five years; inquiry requested] [1 signature]
PET232	10 Mar 1856	18th Rep, p 333–334 (No 6126)	George Shepherd	[Suggested to the Admiralty the use gunpowder for blasting passages through the ice; and using balloons for communicating message; seeking compensation for the work he has done] [1 signature]
PET233	31 Mar 1856	18th Rep, p 382 (No 6716)	Thomas Rose	[Use of his father's invention using Cream of Tartar to treat Small Pox; no fee paid; the method should be adopted] [1 signature]
PET234	18 Apr 1856 17 Apr 1856 88 LJ 99	26th Rep, p 581 (No 9380) App p 275–276 (App No 572)	Citizens of Manchester	[Large surplus developed; stamp duties should be reduced by one half; reserve used to reduce stamp duty further; Commissioners should be persons skilled in mechanical and chemical science and should be paid salary] "That Measures may be adopted for applying the Monies paid Inventors for Letters Patent exclusively to Objects and Purposes from which they may derive some Benefit, for reducing the Fees or Stamp Duties to such Amounts as may be sufficient for the Administration of the Patent Office, and that an Inquiry may be made into the present Expenditure and Application of Monies paid by Inventors, and for ascertaining what Charges may be necessary for the efficient Administration of the Patent System" [1 signature]
PET235	21 Apr 1856 29 Apr 1856 88 LJ 119	27th Rep, p 603 (No 9557) App, p 299 (App No 618)	George Scott	[Developed a furnace which saves a third on the consumption of coal; petitioner gave up business to become engineer to perfect invention; person appointed over petitioner's head] [1 signature] HL Deb, 29 April 1856, Vol 141(3rd), col 1690–1691

PET236	2 May 1856 6 May 1856 88 LJ 127	31st Rep, p 686 (No 10,215)	Inhabitants of the Borough of Halifax	Similar to Manchester, App 572 [PET234] [1 signature]
PET237	19 Jun 1856 25 Jul 1856 88 LJ 473	46th Rep, p 1054–1055 (No 12,771)	John Daines	[Invented and patented method for preserving Stone, Plaster and Cement and neutralising alkaline efflorescence; request an inquiry to make use of his invention] [1 signature] HL Deb, 25 July 1856, Vol 143(3rd), col 1419–1421
PET238	4 Jul 1856	51st Rep, p 1174 (No 13,485)	Richard Cort	[Petitioner's father was the inventor of a process for making wrought iron; Patents granted in 1783 and 1784; invention has be useful to the Navy, railways etc.; request relief from destitution] [1 signature]
PET239	4 Jul 1856	51st Rep, p 1174 (No 13,486) App, p 583–584 (App No 1230)	Manufacturers of ships using wrought iron	[Henry Cort was responsible for major improvements in the iron industry; take into consideration the claim of Richard Cort who has made improvements to the inventions at his own expense] [57 signatures]
PET240	17 Jul 1856	54th Rep, p 1241 (No 13,740)	Fredrick Herbert Maberley	[Various suggestions made to the Admiralty with respect to water-tight compartments; such inventions sent to Admiralty returned and then used without compensation] [1 signature]
PET241	15 Jun 1857	13th Rep, p 356 (No 1737)	Edward John Carpenter	[Claims he invented the screen propeller that has been adopted by the Royal Navy; applied for share of £20,000 but application refused; application to extend patent granted by Privy Council; take petition into consideration] [1 signature]
PET242	4 Dec 1857	1st Rep, p 5 (No 12)	Bartolommeo Predaville	[Presented to Royal Society discovery relating to projectiles; give favourable consideration to the invention] [1 signature]
PET243	12 Apr 1858	18th Rep, p 215 (No 1771)	Joseph Jopling	[Invited the Navy Board to use his discoveries in Naval Architecture; request inquiry into his inventions] [1 signature]
PET244	13 Apr 1858	19th Rep, p 231 (No 1904)	Fredrick Herbert Maberley	[Various suggestions made to the Admiralty with respect to water-tight compartments; such inventions sent to Admiralty returned and then used without compensation] [1 signature]
PET245	23 Jul 1858	51st Rep, p 885 (No 6982)	Fredrick Herbert Maberley	[Recognition of water-tight compartment invention] [1 signature]
PET246	30 Jul 1858	53rd Rep, p 920 (No 7063)	Adderley Willcocks Sleigh	[Petitioner invented new system of breakwater for shelter of shipping; requesting attendance at Royal Commission] [1 signature]
PET247	7 Feb 1859	1st Rep, p 10 (No 99) App, p 13–14 (App No 29)	Citizens of Manchester	[That the Patent Office is running a surplus; that the stamp duty on patents should be reduced; the surplus of the Patent Office should be dedicated to promoting invention and science; special Commissioners should be appointed under s 1 of the Patent Law Amendment Act 1852 [PUBA6] the

(continued)

(continued)

				Commissioners should investigate the working of patent law; there should be a special court appointed to try patent cases; there should be a penalty on people marking as patented when this is not the case; there should be a simple means to get a patent in colonies] "to take these suggestions into consideration" [1 signature]
PET248	22 Feb 1859	5th Rep, p 64 (No 717)	Fredrick Herbert Maberley	[Consideration of his inventions for loss of life at sea] [1 signature]
PET249	24 Feb 1859	6th Rep, p 80 (No 914) App p 57–58 (App No 137)	John Macintosh	[Developed method for destroying fortifications from the sea; favourable reports into invention; invention now universally known yet no reward received] "Committee may be appointed to fully investigate into the subject ... with a view of having your Petitioner's new system of warfare adopted" [1 signature]
PET250	4 Apr 1859	17th Rep, p 332 (No 3744)	Joseph Jopling	[Petitioner requests earlier petition referred to committee] [1 signature]
PET251	14 Apr 1859	Extra Rep, p 385 (No 4121)	Fredrick Herbert Maberley	[Consideration of his invention with respect to vessels of war; prays for adoption] [1 signature]
PET252	5 Jul 1859 91 LJ 313	HL Pet	Citizens of Manchester	"For a Revision of Law of Patents, and for the Appointment of a Special Court to hear Patent Cases"
PET253	29 Jul 1859	9th Rep, p 523 (No 1407) App, p 286–287 (App No 169)	John Benjamin Daines	[Method of treating stone; trial successful on the Palace of Westminster; patent solution has now had five years trial] "to cause an inquiry to be made into the matter of this Petition" [1 signature]
PET254	9 Mar 1860	12th Rep, p 406 (No 7661)	John Benjamin Daines	[Patented solution has been used on Houses of Parliament; inquiry into the matter] [1 signature] Also see: HC Deb, 1 Jun 1863, Vol 171(3rd), col 229–233
PET255	16 Apr 1860	20th Rep, p 885–886 (No 16,557)	Thomas Meriton	[Erroneous decision of the Law Officers should be appealable, particularly in case of oppositions] [1 signature]
PET256	8 Jun 1860 12 Jun 1860 92 LJ 391	34th Rep p 1301 (No 20,284)	John Clare	[Vessels used by the Royal Navy infringe his Letters Patent; full investigation into his claim] [1 signature]
PET257	2 Aug 1860	48th Rep, p 1737 (No 24,006)	Adderley Willcocks Sleigh	[Petitioner has patent on floating batteries; requests trial of his plan] [1 signature] Also see HL Deb, 26 Mar 1860, Vol 157(3rd), col 1234
PET258	24 Jul 1860	53rd Rep, p 1811 (No 24,261) App, p 562–563 (App No 1185)	Nicholas D Maillard	[Improved method of discovering longitude based on new charts] [1 signature]

PET259	8 Mar 1861	7th Rep, p 267 (No 6206)	John Clare	[Vessels used by the Royal Navy infringe his Letters Patent; he had supplied invention to the Navy four years earlier] [1 signature]
PET260	10 Mar 1862	9th Rep, p 91 (No 994) App, p 68–69 (App No 152)	Leeds Chamber of Commerce	[Means for investigating patent infringement are unsatisfactory and need expert judge and jury] "to take into consideration the system of trying patent cases, and make such alterations therein as will ensure the speedy and economical administration of justice" [1 signature]
PET261	19 Mar 1862	11th Rep, p 144 (No 1841)	Samuel Goddard	[Certain patented inventions belonging to him and William Church have been incorporated into the Armstrong gun; no compensation for their use] [1 signature]
PET262	20 Mar 1862	12th Rep, p 177 (No 2360) App, p 113 (App No 249)	Liverpool Chamber of Commerce	"that your honourable House will appoint a Select Committee to inquire into the policy and operation of [patent] laws" [1 signature]
PET263	27 Mar 1862	14th Rep, p 261 (No 3804)	Henry Reverley	[In 1854, published new mode of making ordnance; considered but dropped by Board of Ordnance; 1858 Sir William Armstrong's took out a patent for the gun which was bought by the Board of Ordnance; as specification impounded cannot prove it was copied] [1 signature]
PET264	31 Mar 1862	15th Rep, p 280 (No 3962) App, p 170 (App No 375)	Citizens of Manchester	[Inconvenience of trying cases without expert jury; Proposed: 1. A Court of Commissioners with eminent scientists; 2. The Court examined and grant provisions protection or indicate they have doubts about the novelty; 3. One month after consideration to file specification; 4. Period of opposition; 5 Reasonable fees for re-examination; 6. Infringement tried before specialist jury; 7. Special routes of appeal; 8. Ability to disclaim invalid parts; 9. Lower renewal fees] [1 signature]
PET265	4 Apr 1862	16th Rep, p 300 (No 4140) App, p 184 (App No 393)	Halifax Chamber of Commerce	Similar to Leeds, App 152 [PET260]; save additional paragraph relates to designs [1 signature]
PET266	11 Apr 1862	18th Rep, p 348 (No 4656) App, p 212 (App No 457)	William Bush	[Petitioner devised shield and cupola ship; plans submitted to admiralty; invention now claimed by Captain Cole RN] "your honourable House, that prior to the recognition of the claims of … Captain Cole … your petitioner may be heard" [1 signature]
PET267	11 Apr 1862	18th Rep, p 352 (No 4724)	Batley Chamber of Commerce	Similar to Leeds, App 152 [PET260] [1 signature]
PET268	26 Mar 1863	14th Rep, p 220 (No 2751) App, p 159 (App No 330)	William Bush	[Petitioner invented method of protecting ships by shield or cupola; Captain Coles been paid £5000 by the Admiralty; inquiry into his claim] [1 signature]

(continued)

(continued)

PET269	5 May 1863	20th Rep, p 467 (No 6631) App, p 242 (App 531)	John Clare	[Infringements by the Royal Navy for infringement of Letters Patent related to his invention; which Clare had supplied to the Navy four years earlier] [1 signature]
PET270	5 May 1863	20th Rep, p 471 (No 6688)	Charles Rose	[Claims late father discovered Cream of Tartar cures small pox; requests publication of the said virtue] [1 signature]
PET271	18 May 1863	24th Rep, p 596 (No 8154) App, p 293 (App No 643)	Edward Deane	[Petitioner developed cooking apparatus; costly experiments have been undertaking; inquiry for committee into the merits of the apparatus] [1 signature]
PET272	28 May 1863	25th Rep, p 636 (No 8799) App, p 304–305 (App No 656)	John Clare	[Complaints of infringement of patent by Royal Navy; describing correspondence] [1 signature]
PET273	2 Jun 1863	26th Rep, p 717 (No 10,417) App, p 317–318 (App No 688)	John Clare	[Complaints of infringement of patent by Royal Navy; describing correspondence] [1 signature] Also see: HC Deb, 30 Apr 1877, Vol 234(3rd), col 103–104
PET274	17 Feb 1864	2nd Rep, p 17 (No 170) App, p 17–18 (App No 31)	James Chalmers	[Admiralty has funds for experimenting with armour; petitioner's invention tested in April 1863; invention adopted on various warships; no compensation paid; requests a remedy] [1 signature] HL Deb, 14 April 1864, Vol 174(3rd), col 962–965
PET275	14 Mar 1864 8 Mar 1864 118 LJ 66	10th Rep, p 164 (No 2368) App, p 82–83 (App No 180)	William Joseph Curtis	[Screw propeller was presented to Admiralty; trials carried out; argues invention works] "to take cognizance of his petition that the country may not be deprived of the advantages of this important and successful invention" [1 signature] HL Deb, 8 Mar 1864, Vol 173(3rd), col 1622–1626
PET276	12 May 1864	23rd Rep, p 518 (No 7015) App, p 212–213 (App No 435)	John Clare	[Patentee of Warrior Steamship; Admiralty used his invention and compelled to sue the Crown; lost trial unfairly] [1 signature]
PET277	20 Jun 1864	32nd Rep, p 769 (No 9703)	John Clare	[Patentee of Warrior Steamship; Admiralty used his invention and compelled to sue the Crown; lost trial unfairly] [1 signature]
PET278	22 Jul 1864	41st Rep, p 873 (No 10,221)	George Bell Galloway	[Wrote to Admiralty with a plan to use his screw propeller; petitioner's invention used by navy since that time; but no payment received] "correspondence be laid before the House" [1 signature]
PET279	10 Feb 1865	1st Rep, p 9 (No 87)	James Henry Bennett	[Invention for manufacture of artillery guns; complained of patent infringement; others adopted his plan and received compensation] "consideration of his case" [1 signature]

PET280	14 Feb 1865	1st Rep, p 9 (No 89)	James Chalmers	[Petitioner designed submitted plan to armour plate committee; principle used on some warships] Appointment of a Select Committee to inquire into his case [1 signature]
PET281	24 Feb 1865	4th Rep, p 39 (No 349) App, p 31 (App No 57)	John Clare	[Investigate statement made about standing in *Clare v The Queen*] "to grant a Select Committee so that those erroneous charges and misrepresentations published in the Report of the Commissioners relating to Letters Patent [REP8] may be inquired into and eradicated" [1 signature]
PET282	6 Apr 1865	16th Rep, p 313 (No 4646) App, p 174 (App No 362)	John Clare	[Investigate the plans of John Clare into his iron shop invention] "to grant a Select Committee to investigate the facts connected with your Petitioner's plans and invention" [1 signature]
PET283	29 Apr 1865	18th Rep, p 385 (No 5547)	Holker Meggison	[Method of shelling cast iron ship; sent invention to war office; trial successful; inquiry into adopting plan] [1 signature]
PET284	1 Mar 1866	7th Rep, p 69 (No 576) App, p 56 (App No 123)	John Clare	[Claim against Admiralty relating to making of Iron Ships; correspondence with Edward Cardwell; history of dispute] "to place before the honourable Commons the original plans and models your Petitioner has recorded at the Admiralty since 1853, of which the Warrior is an exact copy" [1 signature]
PET285	9 Mar 1865 97 LJ 232	HL Pet	Leonard Edmunds	[Praying for a delay to the motion to rescind his pension relating to his role at the Patent Office] HL Deb, 9 May 1865, Vol 179(3rd), col 39–45
PET286	31 May 1866 4 Jun 1866 98 LJ 365	25th Rep, p 659 (No 8328) App, p 292–293 (App No 720)	Inventors' Institute	[Complaints as to: (a) exorbitant cost of patent; (b) imperfect security to patentee; (c) expense of litigation; (d) so, cost should be reduced to administrative cost; (e) novelty examination introduced; (f) law of copyright and patents should be assimilated] "take these matters into your consideration, and enact such amendments of the law as will remedy the evil complained of" [42 signatures]
PET287	11 Jun 1866 98 LJ 408	HL Pet	Manchester Patent Law Reform Association	"for certain alterations in the Law respecting Patents"
PET288	19 Feb 1867	3rd Rep, p 39 (No 599)	John Langford and Joseph Wilder	[Inventors of certain Signal Lights; experiments conducted by the War Office and the Admiralty; system universally allowed; no compensation received] [2 signatures]
PET289	22 Nov1867 100 LJ 10	HL Pet	Leonard Edmunds	"That the proper Officer of this House may be ordered to attend the … Court of Chancery"

(continued)

(continued)

PET290	6 Mar 1868 100 LJ 51	HL Pet	Henry Needham Scrope Shrapnel	[Request for national reward conferred on the family of the late Lt-Gen Henry Scrapnel for services during campaign of Duke of Wellington] HL Deb, 6 March 1868, Vol 190(3rd), col 1147–1149
PET291	8 Jul 1868	30th Rep, p 998 (No 17, 610)	John Vaughan Snider	[Take care of the family of the inventor of the Snider Rifle who are insolvent] [1 signature]
PET292	9 Jul 1868 24 Jul 1868 100 LJ 461	31st Rep, p 1016 (No 17,650) App, p 368 (App No 795)	Scientific Men, Inventors, Journalists at meeting in Westminster	[Building provided for the museum and machines at South Kensington and in Southampton Buildings are inadequate; that a new Patent Museum is needed in a central location and the surplus generated should be used to fund it] [1 signature] "for the Concentration of the Patent Office Museum and Public Library, and for their Removal to a more central Situation"
PET293	9 Jul 1868 24 Jul 1868 100 LJ 461	31st Rep, p 1016 (No 17,651)	Workmen's Technical Education Committee	Similar to Westminster, App 795[PET292] [1 signature] "for the Concertation of the Patent Office Museum and Public Library, and for their Removal to a more central Situation"
PET294	9 Jul 1868 24 Jul 1868 100 LJ 461	31st Rep, p 1016 (No 17,652)	St James & Soho Working Men's Club	Similar to Westminster, App 795 [PET292] [1 signature] "for the concentration of the Patent Office Museum and Public Library, and for their Removal to a more central Situation"
PET295	27 Jul 1868	32nd Rep p 1052 (No 17,792)	George Forster Jobson	[Complaint about treatment by War Office regarding Time Fuse] [1 signature]
PET296	29 Jul 1868 24 Jul 1868 100 LJ 461	32nd Rep, p 1053 (No 17,795)	Council of Public Museums and Free Libraries	Similar to Westminster, App 795 [PET292] [4 signatures] "for the concentration of the Patent Office Museum and Public Library, and for their Removal to a more central Situation"
PET297	26 Feb 1869	3rd Rep, p 28 (No 322)	George Forster Jobson	[In 1859 plan submitted for time fuses to War Office; and adopted without his knowledge; unable to obtain redress] [1 signature]
PET298	27 May 1869	22nd Rep, p 698 (No 12,655) App, p 265 (App No 662)	Newcastle and Gateshead Chamber of Commerce	[That the petitioners believe the proposed abolition of the patent system will be of great benefit to the country and the resolution for its abolition should be adopted] "to take measure for placing the Patent Office and the museum and library belonging to it in a manner befitting a national institution for the assistance, information, and instruction of inventors, manufacturers, and industrial classes of the community" [1 signature]
PET299	9 Jul 1869	29th Rep, 998 (No 17,468) App, p 370 (App No 918)	Liverpool Chamber of Commerce	[Despite the Departmental Committees appointed, there should be a Royal Commission to inquire into patent law] [1 signature]

PET300	13 Jul 1869	29th Rep, p 1000 (No 17,490) App, p 571–574 (App No 924)	Henry Needham Scrope Shrapnel	[Detailing the work of General Shrapnel and the benefits received from the pension; Will of Lt-General Henry Shrapnel: "Her Majesty's Government may be graciously pleased to confer some national reward on my family, inconsideration of the valuable service rendered to my country by my shells during the late wars, and the numerous victories which were gain by use of them"] [1 signature]
PET301	13 Jul 1869	29th Rep, p 1000 (No 17,491) App, p 574 (App No 925)	Edward Meade	[Support application of Henry Needham Scrope Shrapnel for an appropriate reward] [60 signatures]
PET302	23 Jul 1869 101 LJ 523	HL Pet	Attorney-General	Request for a Shorthand writer in relation to Leonard Edmunds case to be provided by House of Lords to attend the Court of Arbitration.
PET303	14 Feb 1870	2nd Rep, p 15 (No 123) App, p 19 (App No 50)	Edinburgh Chamber of Commerce	"to appoint a Select Committee for the purpose indicated [investigate patent laws], or otherwise as to your wisdom may seem proper" [2 signatures]
PET304	8 Mar 1870	6th Rep, p 69 (No 848) App, p 66 (App No 177)	Liverpool Chamber of Commerce	[Innocent dealers can be caught as infringers; that granting patents is injurious as it is a lottery] "before any legislation in connexion with inventions or with patents for inventions is undertaken by your honourable House, a Committee may be appointed to inquire into the policy of granting such patents" [1 signature]
PET305	8 Mar 1870	6th Rep, p 69 (No 849) App, p 66–67 (App No 178)	Newcastle and Gateshead Chamber of Commerce	"that your honourable House will be pleased to appoint the said Select Committee of inquiry" [1 signature]
PET306	28 Apr 1870	16th Rep, p 459 (No 8363) App, p 202–203 (App No 552)	Inventors, Patentees, Manufacturers of Westminster	[Details value of patent system to United Kingdom; chief defects are: 1. Inadequate assessment of whether something patented or not; 2. Conflict between owner and improver of invention; 3. costly adjudication of patent disputes; proposal: (a) indexing of patents; (b) a system of compulsory licences; (c) patent infringement trials should have a preliminary examination before being tried] "not to entertain the question of Committee to consider the policy of a patent law, but rather to appoint a Select Committee, if an inquiry be deemed desirable, to consider what amendments are required to render the law relating to letters patent for inventions thoroughly effective" [12 signatures]
PET307	10 May 1870	19th Rep p 562 (No 9829) App, p 240 (App No 662)	Mechanics, Engineers and Artizans of Sheffield	[Engineers and makers of things which will be shown at Workmen's International Exhibition held in London 1870; similar Act to the Industrial Exhibitions Act 1865 [PUBA11] (and earlier)] "that your honourable House will take these matters into your favourable consideration, and at once provide by legislative enactment the same or

(continued)

(continued)

				equal protection with regard to new inventions, improvements, and designs of utility exhibition at industrial exhibitions, as was by law provided in reference to the Great Exhibition of 1851, and that such protection shall entail no large payment or more complicated procedure than is required by the Arts Copyright Act, 1862 ..." [See PUBA13] [1 signature]
PET308	19 May 1870	22nd Rep, p 658 (No 10,941)	Charles Griffin	For an inquiry into his system of Telegraphy [1 signature]
PET309	16 Mar 1871	9th Rep, p 171 (No 3042)	Leonard Edmunds	[Grievances suffered by the Crown relating to his role at the Patent Office; refer petition to Comptroller and Auditor-General] [1 signature]
PET310	19 Jun 1871 16 Jun 1871 103 LJ 377	28th Rep, p 927 (No 15,748) App, p 339–341 (App No 925)	Leonard Edmunds	[Grievances suffered by the Crown relating to his role at the Patent Office; appoint a Select Committee] [1 signature]
PET311	9 Aug 1871	31st Rep, p 1118 (No 17,491)	Liverpool Chamber of Commerce	Patents for Inventions Bill – For Postponement [1 signature]
PET312	13 May 1872	23rd Rep, p 1103 (No 23,120) App, p 256–259 (App No 684)	William Rowcett	[Electric telegraph patent (No 782); application made to the Privy Council to extend the patent failed; so, asking Parliament to extend it] "extension of patent subsequent to the expiration of the patent – the application being made ten days prior to its expiration" [1 signature]
PET313	26 May 1873 105 LJ 398	HL Pet	Leonard Edmunds	[Accounts prepared by Petitioner referred to Comptroller and Auditor General] [1 signature] Request refused: 105 LJ 446 (16 Jun 1873) HL Deb, 16 Jun 1873, Vol 216(3rd), col 963–979
PET314	22 Jun 1874 106 LJ 287	HL Pet	Leonard Edmunds	[Complaining of certain grievances; asking for reference to Select Committee] Ref to C'ttee vacated: 106 LJ 312 (29 Jun 1874)
PET315	2 Jul 1874 106 LJ 329	HL Pet	Leonard Edmunds	[Complaining of certain grievances; asking for reference to Select Committee] Request refused: 106 LJ 356 (13 Jul 1874) HL Deb, 13 Jul 1874, Vol 220(3rd), col 1500–1516
PET316	11 Mar 1875 107 LJ 63	HL Pet	Council of the Society for Encouragement of Arts &c.	"for amendment of Patents for Inventions Bill [PUBB29]"
PET317	13 Apr 1875	14th Rep, p 308 (No 6344)	Associated Engineers, Sheffield	Patents for Invention – Against Proposed Bill [PUBB29] [2 signatures]
PET318	16 Apr 1875	15th Rep, p 335 (No 6730) App, p 116 (App No 253)	Sheffield Trades Council	[If the Bill passes into law it will materially lessen the encouragement of invention] "that the said Bill [PUBB29] may not pass into law" [2 signatures]
PET319	16 Apr 1875	15th Rep, p 335 (No 6731)	United Shopping Trades Council of Liverpool	Similar to Sheffield, App 253 [PET318] [2 signatures] [Related to PUBB29]

PET320	20 Apr 1875	16th Rep, p 359 (No 7055) App, p 126 (App No 276)	Bury Trade Council	[If the Bill [PUBB29] passes into law it will materially lessen the encouragement of invention] "that the said Bill may not pass into law" [2 signatures]
PET321	21 Apr 1875	17th Rep, p 390 (No 7608)	John Clare	[Claim against the Admiralty regarding iron ships] Inquiry into his case [1 signature]
PET322	23 Apr 1875	17th Rep, p 396 (No 7728)	Philosophical Society of Glasgow	Similar to Bury, App 276 [PET320] [2 signatures] [Related to PUBB29]
PET323	26 Apr 1875	18th Rep, p 436 (No 8403)	Walsall District Trade Council	Similar to Sheffield, App 253 [PET318] [2 signatures] [Related to PUBB29]
PET324	26 Apr 1875	18th Rep, p 436 (No 8404)	Oldham Trade Council	Similar to Sheffield, App 253 [PET318] [2 signatures] [Related to PUBB29]
PET325	26 Apr 1875	18th Rep, p 436 (No 8405)	Dundee United Trades Council	Similar to Sheffield, App 253 [PET318] [2 signatures] [Related to PUBB29]
PET326	27 Apr 1875	18th Rep, p 436 (No 8406)	James Napier and other inventors	Similar to Sheffield, App 253 [PET318] [180 signatures] [Related to PUBB29]
PET327	27 Apr 1875	18th Rep, p 436 (No 8407)	Glasgow Trades Council	Similar to Sheffield, App 253 [PET318] [2 signatures] [Related to PUBB29]
PET328	26 Apr 1875	18th Rep, p 436 (No 8408) App, p 139–140 (App No 296)	Birmingham Chamber of Commerce	[Cl 11(1), (4) and (6) are unnecessary as no need for official examination only novelty and sufficiency need examination; Cl 6 should be amended to leave out the number of examiners; a non-working clause for compulsory licence; fees too high] "that the measure [PUBB29] now before your honourable House (subject to the modifications and alterations now suggested) may be speedily passed into law" [1 signature]
PET329	30 Apr 1875	19th Rep, p 459 (No 8706) App, p 145 (App No 306)	Leeds Chamber of Commerce	[Examiners should only consider priority of inventions and not utility and only to offer advice not to reject; 7 years too short for a patent and should remain at 14 years] "that the said Bill [PUBB29] may be amended so as to limit the power of examiners of patents … and so that the duration of patents may be fourteen years as heretofore" [1 signature]
PET330	4 May 1875	20th Rep, p 488 (No 9119)	Inventors of Dundee	Similar to Sheffield, App 253 [PET318] [14 signatures] [Related to PUBB29]
PET331	7 May 1875	21st Rep, p 546 (No 10,210)	Manchester and Salford Trades Council	Similar to Sheffield, App 253 [PET318] [3 signatures] [Related to PUBB29]
PET332	10 May 1875	21st Rep, p 546 (No 10,211)	Wigan Trades Council	Similar to Sheffield, App 253 [PET318] [2 signatures] [Related to PUBB29]

(continued)

(continued)

PET333	25 May 1875	21st Rep, p 546 (No 10,212)	Hull Trades Council	Similar to Sheffield, App 253 [PET318] [2 signatures] [Related to PUBB29]
PET334	10 May 1875	21st Rep, p 546 (No 10,213) App, p 173–174 (App No 361)	Liverpool Polytechnic Society	[Paid Commissioner are absolutely necessary; provisional specifications should be retained; examinations as to utility or merit likely to be pointless; 7 years is insufficient duration; it should be possible to apply through agents; should not be a compulsory licence for improved working; prolongation should be before Commissioner; Museum under Minister and surplus should maintain the Patent Museum] "to take the premises into your favourable consideration and take such steps for amending the said Bill [PUBB29] and procuring the extension of the said Patent Museum as to your honourable House may seem meet and right" [1 signature]
PET335	12 May 1875	21st Rep, p 546 (No 10,214) App, p 174 (App No 362)	Society for the Encouragement of Arts, Manufactures and Commerce	[Paid Commissioners necessary; no adverse examiners report should preclude the grant of a patent at his own risk; compulsory licences in the Bill are unduly complicated; prolongation before Commissioners; Museum placed under Minister of Crown and surplus fund it] "to take the premises into your favourable consideration and take such steps for amending the said Bill [PUBB29] and procuring the extension of the said Patent Museum as to your honourable House may seem meet and right" [1 signature]
PET336	20 May 1875	21st Rep, p 546 (No 10,215) App, p 174–175 (App No 363)	Malleable Ironworkers' Association	[Provisional specifications should continue; novelty examination only; patent term should remain 14 years; no power to revoke for non-use; compulsory licences only where improvements to existing processes and such licence fixed by public authority; Crown use not fixed by Treasury but by authority; Stamp duties should not exceed £10; no models should be required] "to amend the Bill [PUBB29] so as to afford them the relief that they desire" [15 signatures]
PET337	24 May 1875	21st Rep, p 546 (No 10,216) App, p 175 (App No 364)	Liverpool Chamber of Commerce	[Doubts over honorary Commissioners of Patents; examiner appointed must be of highest calibre] "that the necessary provisions will be introduced into the aforesaid Bill [PUBB29] by your honourable House for securing the services of duly qualified persons as examiners under the Bill" [2 signatures]
PET338	2 Jun 1875	23rd Rep, p 681 (No 12,752)	Inventors, Aberdare	Similar to Sheffield, App 253 [PET318] [4 signatures] [Related to PUBB29]
PET339	2 Jun 1875	23rd Rep, p 681 (No 12,753)	Liverpool Trade Union Council	Similar to Sheffield, App 253 [PET318] [12 signatures] [Related to PUBB29]
PET340	7 Jun 1875	24th Rep, p 754 (No 14,194)	Inventors, Patentees and others interested in inventions	Similar to Leeds, App 443 [PET345] [171 signatures] [Related to PUBB29]

PET341	10 Jun 1875	24th Rep, p 754 (No 14,195)	Society of Arts	For alteration of Patents for Inventions Bill [PUBB29] [2 signatures]
PET342	11 Jun 1875	24th Rep, p 754 (No 14,196)	Artizans and Inventors Patent Bill Committee	For alteration of Patents for Inventions Bill [PUBB29] [4 signatures]
PET343	11 Jun 1875	24th Rep, p 754 (No 14,197)	Civil Gas and Electric Engineers	Similar to Leeds, App 443 [PET345] [37 signatures] [Related to PUBB29]
PET344	11 Jun 1875	24th Rep, p 754 (No 14,198)	Inhabitants of Stockport	Similar to Leeds, App 443 [PET345] [23 signatures] [Related to PUBB29]
PET345	11 Jun 1875	24th Rep, p 754 (No 14,199) App, p 210 (App No 443)	Inhabitants of Leeds	[1875 Bill [PUBB29] includes many good provisions; do not discontinue provisional specifications; duration should be extended to 21 years; novelty examination should be restricted; no link to validity of foreign patents; compulsory licence and Crown use terms fixed by Commissioners] "that your honourable House will be pleased to afford them the relief they desire" [73 signatures]
PET346	14 Jun 1875	25th Rep, p 826 (No 15,516)	Leicester Trades Council	Similar to Sheffield, App 253 [PET318] [3 signatures] [Related to PUBB29]
PET347	14 Jun 1875	25th Rep, p 826 (No 15,517)	Textile Trades	Similar to Leeds, App 443 [PET345] [50 signatures] [Related to PUBB29]
PET348	15 Jun 1875	25th Rep, p 826 (No 15,518)	Inhabitants of Bury and Bolton	Similar to Leeds, App 443 [PET345] [39 signatures] [Related to PUBB29]
PET349	15 Jun 1875	25th Rep, p 826 (No 15,519)	Cabinet Makers and others, North London	Similar to Leeds, App 443 [PET345] [77 signatures] [Related to PUBB29]
PET350	15 Jun 1875	25th Rep, p 826 (No 15,520)	Inhabitants of Crewe	Similar to Leeds, App 443 [PET345] [32 signatures] [Related to PUBB29]
PET351	18 Jun 1875	26th Rep, p 926 (No 17,835)	Inventors' Institute	Similar to Leeds, App 443 [PET345] [52 signatures] [Related to PUBB29]
PET352	18 Jun 1875	26th Rep, p 926 (No 17,836)	Inventors, patentees and others interested	Similar to Leeds, App 443 [PET345] [121 signatures] [Related to PUBB29]
PET353	18 Jun 1875	26th Rep, p 926 (No 17,837)	Inhabitants of Oldham	Similar to Leeds, App 443 [PET345] [24 signatures] [Related to PUBB29]
PET354	22 Jun 1875 24 Jun 1875 107 LJ 290	26th Rep, p 926 (No 17,838)	London Patent Agents	For alteration of Patents for Inventions Bill [PUBB29] [2 signatures]
PET355	22 Jun 1875	26th Rep, p 926 (No 17,839)	Inhabitants of Westminster	Similar to Leeds, App 443 [PET345] [105 signatures] [Related to PUBB29]

(continued)

(continued)

PET356	18 Jun 1875	26th Rep, p 926 (No 17,840) App, p 228 (App No 481)	Inventors, Patentees and others interested in inventions	[Provisional protection should continue; patents should last 21 years; no further examination necessary; stamp duty should be reduced; annual renewal fees should be introduced; more copies of printed specifications should be made available] "in the event of your honourable House being in doubt as to the policy or proprietary of complying with the prayer of our humble Petition in its entirety, a Select Committee of your honourable House may be appointed immediately to take the evidence of inventors and patentees" [179 signatures]
PET357	24 Jun 1875	27th Rep, p 996 (No 19,266)	Bradford Chamber of Commerce	"to reject the Patents for Inventions Bill [PUBB29]" [2 signatures]
PET358	24 Jun 1875	27th Rep, p 996 (No 19,267)	Bradford District Trades Council	Similar to Sheffield, App 253 [PET318] [2 signatures] [Related to PUBB29]
PET359	25 Jun 1875	27th Rep, p 996 (No 19,268)	Southampton Trades Council	"to reject the Patents for Inventions Bill [PUBB29]" [2 signatures]
PET360	23 Jun 1875	27th Rep, p 996 (No 19,269)	Inhabitants of Liverpool (Bootmakers)	Similar to Malleable Ironworker, App 363 [PET336] [36 signatures] [Related to PUBB29]
PET361	23 Jun 1875	27th Rep, p 996 (No 19,270)	Inhabitants of Bedford	Similar to Malleable Ironworker, App 363 [PET336] [38 signatures] [Related to PUBB29]
PET362	24 Jun 1875	27th Rep, p 996 (No 19,271) App, p 242–243 (App No 503)	Patent Law Committee	[Against removal of provisional specification; examination beyond capacity of examiner; reduction of term to 7 years is destructive; compulsory licence clause modified so only to apply to improvements; unpaid Commissioners inconsistent with objects] "it takes the premises under your favourable consideration and to take steps for amending the said Bill [PUBB29] as to your honourable House may seem meet and right" [1 signature]
PET363	24 Jun 1875	27th Rep, p 996 (No 19,272)	Working Men of Rochdale	Similar to Malleable Ironworker, App 363 [PET336] [21 signatures] [Related to PUBB29]
PET364	29 Jun 1875	27th Rep, p 996 (No 19,273) App, p 243 (App No 504)	CE Parker Rhodes	[Abolition of stamp duties; term fifty years; registration pure and simple; certain certificate size; penalty £100 fixed; annual licence from Patent Office; various fee arrangements; good indexing] "a Royal Commission be appointed to consider the foregoing project in the matter of patents for inventions" [1 signature]
PET365	2 Jul 1875 107 LJ 318	HL Pet	Meeting in London	"Praying for the Amendment of the Patent for Inventions Bill [PUBB29]"
PET366	6 Jul 1875	28th Rep, p 1023 (No 19,594) App, p 250 (App No 517)	Fredrick Bramwell, President of Institute of Engineers	[Patents for Inventions Bill [PUBB29] much worse than current law; examination should be limited to novelty and should not affect grant; Bill differs from recommendations of 1864 Committee [REP8]]

				"not pass the Bill in which … such grave defects exist, but that your honourable House will reject the Bill altogether, or will refer it to a Select Committee, in order that it may be amended so as to be an improvement upon the existing patent laws of this realm, for the promotion and protection of invention, instead of being, as I show, a Bill for … the commencement of the abolition of patents" [1 signature]
PET367	8 Jul 1875	29th Rep, p 1056 (No 20,010) App, p 259 (App No 536)	London Seamen's Mutual Protection Society	[That the invention of John Banting Rogers be adopted; that the failure to adopt the system shows a disregard of the lives of seamen] [1 signature]
PET368	16 Jul 1875	30th Rep, p 1073 (No 20,145)	Manufacturing, Engineers and Founders of Salford	Similar to Leeds, App 443 [PET345] [12 signatures] [Related to PUBB29]
PET369	19 Jul 1875	30th Rep, p 1073 (No 20,146)	Inhabitants of Warrington	Similar to Leeds, App 443 [PET345] [40 signatures] [Related to PUBB29]
PET370	20 Jul 1875	30th Rep, p 1074 (No 20,147)	Inhabitants of Norwich	Similar to Leeds, App 443 [PET345] [38 signatures] [Related to PUBB29]
PET371	27 Jul 1875	31st Rep, p 1103 (No 20,455)	Inhabitants of Luton	Similar to Leeds, App 443 [PET345] [38 signatures] [Related to PUBB29]
PET372	27 Jul 1875	31st Rep, p 1103 (No 20,456)	Committee of Inventors and Patentees, Dublin	"to make certain alterations in the Patents for Inventions Bill [PUBB29]" [2 signatures]
PET373	27 Jul 1875	31st Rep, p 1103 (No 20,457)	Marshall M Harris and others	Similar to Leeds, App 443 [PET345] [39 signatures] [Related to PUBB29]
PET374	5 Aug 1875	31st Rep, p 1124 (No 20,575)	Charles Henwood	[Naval designs for Admiralty to turn into turret designs; Confidential reports made to the Admiralty; inquiry into the report] [1 signature]
PET375	14 Feb 1876	1st Rep, p 12 (No 216) App, p 10 (App No 24)	National Trade Congress, Glasgow	[Patent laws need reform; patent should cost no more than £10; patent should last 21 years; novelty examination; no compulsory licensing; sufficient staff; notice to proceed abolished] [2 signatures]
PET376	16 Feb 1876	2nd Rep, p 26 (No 505)	Charles Henwood	[Naval designs for Admiralty to turn into turret designs; Confidential reports made to the Admiralty; inquiry into the report] Inquiry into case [1 signature; withdrawn: 10th Rep, p 227] HC Deb, 3 Mar 1876, Vol 227(3rd) col 1404–1405 HC Deb, 20 Mar 1876, Vol 228(3rd), col 342–345
PET377	2 Mar 1876	5th Rep, p 122 (No 2926)	John Clare	For printing his Petition on the Construction of Ships [1 signature]

(continued)

(continued)

PET378	14 Mar 1876 108 LJ 74	HL Pet	Inhabitants of London	"For Amendment of Patents for Inventions Bill" [PUBB30]
PET379	20 Mar 1876	10th Rep, p 226 (No 4410)	John Clare	[Claim against Admiralty regarding iron-ships] Inquiry into case [1 signature]
PET380	27 Mar 1876	12th Rep, p 287 (No 5295) App, p 96–97 (App No 261)	Charles Henwood	[Naval designs for Admiralty to turn into turret designs; Confidential reports made to the Admiralty; inquiry into the report] Inquiry into case [1 signature]
PET381	28 Mar 1876	12th Rep, p 283 (No 5233)	John Clare	[Claim against Admiralty regarding iron-ships] Inquiry into case [1 signature]
PET382	11 Apr 1876	15th Rep, p 405 (No 7142) App, p 144 (App No 377)	Faculty of Procurators of Glasgow	[Cl 38, 40 and 41 very valuable but confined to England should extend to Scotland] "to take the premises into consideration and to pass the said Bill [PUBB30] into a law, with such amendments as will give the courts of Scotland the benefit of the provisions of section thirty-eight, section forty, and section forty-one thereof" [1 signature]
PET383	24 Apr 1876	15th Rep, p 405 (No 7143) App, p 144–145 (App No 378)	Philosophical Society of Glasgow	[Proposed amendments to Cl 6, 7, 9, 10, 11 14, 15, 16, 18 and 18] "that these amendments be embodied in the Bill [PUBB30]" [2 signatures]
PET384	24 Apr 1876	15th Rep, p 405 (No 7144)	Engineers of Sheffield	Patents for Inventions Bill [PUBB30] – For Alteration [2 signatures]
PET385	24 Apr 1876	15th Rep, p 405 (No 7145)	Sheffield Trades Council	Patents for Inventions Bill [PUBB30] – For Alteration [2 signatures]
PET386	1 May 1876	17th Rep, p 488 (No 8443)	Glasgow Inventors	Patents for Inventions Bill [PUBB30] – For Alteration [40 signatures]
PET387	1 May 1876	17th Rep, p 488 (No 8444) App, p 165 (App No 423)	Mansfield Trade Council	[Provisional Specifications should continue; complete specification filed after six months; and examined; where no complete specification filed, the provisional specification should be returned to applicant; right to take patent notwithstanding adverse report; Cl 14 omitted; patents to last 21 years; total stamp duty £10; Cl 18 and 26 omitted] "to amend the Bill [PUBB30] so as to afford the relief desired" [2 signatures]
PET388	2 May 1876	17th Rep, p 488 (No 8445)	Bury Trades Council	Similar to Mansfield, App 423 [PET387] [2 signatures] [Related to PUBB30]
PET389	2 May 1876	17th Rep, p 489 (No 8446)	Oldham Trades Council	Similar to Mansfield, App 423 [PET387] [2 signatures] [Related to PUBB30]
PET390	3 May 1876	18th Rep, p 535 (No 9289)	Graduate Section of Institute of Engineers, Scotland	Similar to Mansfield, App 423 [PET387] [2 signatures] [Related to PUBB30]
PET391	3 May 1876	18th Rep, p 535 (No 9290)	Stalybridge Trades Council	Similar to Mansfield, App 423 [PET387] [2 signatures] [Related to PUBB30]

PET392	4 May 1876	18th Rep, p 535 (No 9291)	Manchester and Salford Trades Council	Similar to Mansfield, App 423 [PET387] [2 signatures] [Related to PUBB30]
PET393	8 May 1876	19th Rep, p 585 (No 10,193)	Leeds Trades Council	Similar to Mansfield, App 423 [PET387] [2 signatures] [Related to PUBB30]
PET394	8 May 1876	19th Rep, p 585 (No 10,194)	Birkenhead Trades Council	Similar to Mansfield, App 423 [PET387] [2 signatures] [Related to PUBB30]
PET395	9 May 1876	19th Rep, p 585 (No 10,195)	Wigan Trades Council	Similar to Mansfield, App 423 [PET387] [2 signatures] [Related to PUBB30]
PET396	10 May 1876	20th Rep, p 638 (No 11,131)	Leicester Trades Council	Similar to Mansfield, App 423 [PET387] [3 signatures] [Related to PUBB30]
PET397	12 May 1876	20th Rep, p 638 (No 11,132)	Wolverhampton Trades Council	Similar to Mansfield, App 423 [PET387] [2 signatures] [Related to PUBB30]
PET398	15 May 1876	21st Rep, p 686 (No 12,103)	Huddersfield Trades Council	Similar to Mansfield, App 423 [PET387] [2 signatures] [Related to PUBB30]
PET399	18 May 1876	22nd Rep, p 737 (No 12,942) App, p 206 (App No 508)	Society of Arts, Manufactures and Commerce	[Paid Commissioners should be appointed; no purpose for examination; adverse report should not stop person having patent at risk; prolongation on application to Commissioners; Patent Museum under Minister of Crown and new site found] "to take the premise into your favourable consideration, and take such steps for amending the Bill [PUBB30] and procuring the extension of the said patent museum as to your honourable House may seem meet and right" [1 signature]
PET400	18 May 1876	22nd Rep, p 737 (No 12,943)	Liverpool Trades Council	Similar to Mansfield, App 423 [PET387] [2 signatures] [Related to PUBB30]
PET401	18 May 1876	22nd Rep, p 737 (No 12,944)	W Smith and others	Patents for Inventions [PUBB30] – For Alteration [22 signatures]
PET402	22 May 1876	22nd Rep, p 737 (No 12,945)	Paisley Trades Council	Similar to Mansfield, App 423 [PET387] [2 signatures] [Related to PUBB30]
PET403	22 May 1876	22nd Rep, p 737 (No 12,946) App, p 206–207 (App No 509)	Council of Huddersfield	"that your honourable House will be pleased to pass the said Bill [PUBB30]" [1 signature]
PET404	18 May 1876	22nd Rep, p 738 (No 12,947)	William Smith and Others	Patents for Inventions – In Favour of Certain Returns [1 signature]
PET405	25 May 1876	23rd Rep, p 770 (No 13,335)	Inventors' Institute	Patents for Inventions Bill [PUBB30] – For Alteration [2 signatures]

(continued)

(continued)

PET406	25 May 1876	23rd Rep, p 770 (No 13,336)	Hull Trades Council	Similar to Mansfield, App 423 [PET387] [1 signatures] [Related to PUBB30]
PET407	26 May 1876	23rd Rep, p 770 (No 13,337)	Bradford Trades Council	Similar to Mansfield, App 423 [PET387] [2 signatures] [Related to PUBB30]
PET408	26 May 1876	23rd Rep, p 770 (No 13,338) App, p 210–211 (App No 521)	Inventors, Patentee and Manufacturers of Sheffield	[Provisional protection continued; patents last 21 years; no examination; stamp duties lowered; annual fees introduced (say £5); information dissemination around the country] "that your honourable House will be pleased to amend the Bill [PUBB30] so as to afford them the relief that they desire" [30 signatures]
PET409	25 May 1876	23rd Rep, p 770 (No 13,339)	Mayor of Hull	Patents for Inventions Bill [PUBB30] – For Alteration [53 signatures]
PET410	25 May 1876	23rd Rep, p 770 (No 13,340) App, p 211–212 (App No 522)	Institute of Mechanical Engineers	[Bill does not follow departmental or Royal Commission recommendations; and Bill detrimental] "that the said Bill [PUBB30] may be referred to a Select Committee of your honourable House, and that your Petitioners may have leave to be heard before the same, by themselves, their agents, and witnesses, against such of the clauses and provisions of the said Bill to which they object, and that they may have such other relief in the premises as to your honourable House may seem meet" [1 signature]
PET411	1 Jun 1876	24th Rep, p 816 (No 14,039) App, p 219 (App No 542)	Association of Employers, Foremen and Draughtsmen of Manchester	[Abolition of provisional specifications will be detrimental to inventors; staffing of examiners is inadequate and examination too comprehensive] "that the Bill [PUBB30] does not pass into law" [1 signature]
PET412	30 May 1876	24th Rep, p 816 (No 14,040)	Glasgow Trades Council	Similar to Mansfield, App 423 [PET387] [189 signatures] [Related to PUBB30]
PET413	30 May 1876	24th Rep, p 816 (No 14,041)	Maidstone Trades Council	Similar to Mansfield, App 423 [PET387] [2 signatures] [Related to PUBB30]
PET414	9 Jun 1876	24th Rep, p 816 (No 14,042)	Artizans and Inventors Patent Law Committee	Patents for Inventions Bill [PUBB30] – For Alteration [3 signatures]
PET415	15 Jun 1876	25th Rep, p 899 (No 15,297)	Birmingham Trades Council	Similar to Mansfield, App 423 [PET387] [2 signatures] [Related to PUBB30]
PET416	16 Jun 1876	25th Rep, p 899 (No 15,298)	Leith Trades Council	Similar to Mansfield, App 423 [PET387] [2 signatures] [Related to PUBB30]
PET417	16 Jun 1876	25th Rep, p 899 (No 15,299)	London Trades Council	Similar to Mansfield, App 423 [PET410] [2 signatures] [Related to PUBB30]
PET418	19 Jun 1876	25th Rep, p 900 (No 15,300)	Royal Scottish Society of Arts	Patents for Inventions Bill [PUBB30] – For Alteration [1 signature]

PET419	30 Jun 1876	28th Rep, p 982 (No 16,479)	Leeds Foremen, Engineers and Draftsmen	Similar to Mechanical Engineers, App 522 [PET410] [1 signature] [Related to PUBB30]
PET420	10 Jul 1876	29th Rep, p 1031 (No 17,284) App, p 268 (App No 636)	Charles Meade Ramus	[Developed instruments of war for destroying an enemy from a distance; submitted to the Admiralty; report from Admiralty was misleading; further trials undertaken; request further investigation of rocket floats] [1 signature]
PET421	18 Jul 1876	30th Rep, p 1092 (No 18,523)	Liverpool Chamber of Commerce	Patents for Inventions Bill [PUBB30] – In Favour [2 signatures]
PET422	14 Aug 1876	31st Rep, p 1147 (No 18,886)	Owners, Lessees and Occupiers of Houses in the vicinity of the Tower	"to appoint a Committee to inquire into the merits of Barnett's Patent for the erection of a bridge across the Thames" [236 signatures]
PET423	8 Feb 1877	1st Rep, p 13 (No 237) App, p 5–6 (App No 12)	Philosophical Society of Glasgow	[Reduce stamp duty; provision for extending patents to 21 years; novelty examinations but no power to reject; abolish notice to proceed; provision allowing for periods of grace for paying renewal fees] [2 signatures]
PET424	1 Mar 1877	5th Rep, p 80 (No 1325)	Inventors, Patentees and others Glasgow	"to make certain alterations in the Patents for Inventions Bill [PUBB31]" [60 signatures]
PET425	1 Mar 1877	5th Rep, p 80 (No 1326) App, p 25–28 (App No 48)	Philosophical Society of Glasgow	[Abolish all charges except the necessary payment of administrative costs; object to requiring printing costs to be paid; examination for sufficiency not necessary; change provisions so no disclosure before patent is granted; single examination but no further consideration; opportunity on payment of fee to extend to 21 years; non-working clause is unfair; object to compulsory licensing so cl 22 struck out; repeal of printing dissemination clauses of 1852 Act [PUBA6] should not happen] "that the Bill [PUBB31] be altered and amended in conformity with the suggestions of this Petition" [2 signatures]
PET426	5 Mar 1877	5th Rep, p 80 (No 1327)	Glasgow United Trades Council	"to make certain alterations in the Patents for Inventions Bill [PUBB31]" [2 signatures]
PET427	8 Mar 1877	6th Rep, p 112 (No 1798)	Birmingham Trades Council	"to make certain alterations in the Patents for Inventions Bill [PUBB31]" [2 signatures]
PET428	8 Mar 1877	6th Rep, p 112 (No 1799)	Walsall General Meeting	"to make certain alterations in the Patents for Inventions Bill [PUBB31]" [2 signatures]
PET429	8 Mar 1877	6th Rep, p 112 (No 1780)	Employers, Foremen and Draughtsmen and Engineers, Manchester	"to make certain alterations in the Patents for Inventions Bill [PUBB31]" [1 signature]
PET430	13 Mar 1877	6th Rep, p 112 (No 1781)	Inventors, Patentees, and Manufacturers, Camberwell	"to make certain alterations in the Patents for Inventions Bill [PUBB31]" [25 signatures]

(continued)

(continued)

PET431	13 Mar 1877	6th Rep, p 112 (No 1782) App, p 38–39 (App No 74)	Wolverhampton Trades Council	[Bill should encourage invention; examination solely for informing applicant of results and not refusing patent; no opposition should be allowed so as to prevent vexatious litigation; renewal period should change; non-use over three years (Cl 22) should be omitted; rules should be approved by Parliament (Cl 53, p 14, l 5 to 18 should be struck out); stamp duty should be reduced] "that the said amendments be made on the Bill [PUBB31]" [2 signatures]
PET432	14 Mar 1877	7th Rep, p 148 (No 2303)	Framework Knitters Trade Council	Similar to Wolverhampton, App 74 [PET431] [2 signatures] [Related to PUBB31]
PET433	19 Mar 1877	7th Rep, p 148 (No 2304)	Bury Trades Council	Similar to Wolverhampton, App 74 [PET431] [2 signatures] [Related to PUBB31]
PET434	20 Mar 1877	7th Rep, p 148 (No 2305)	Paisley Trades Council	Similar to Wolverhampton, App 74 [PET431] [3 signatures] [Related to PUBB31]
PET435	20 Mar 1877	7th Rep, p 148 (No 2306)	Leeds Trades Council	Similar to Wolverhampton, App 74 [PET431] [3 signatures] [Related to PUBB31]
PET436	23 Mar 1877	8th Rep, p 171 (No 2556)	Provost, Magistrates and Town Council of Paisley	"that the Bill [PUBB31] throws additional impediments in the way of Inventors, and they pray the House to reject it" [1 signature]
PET437	23 Mar 1877	8th Rep, p 172 (No 2557)	Aberdeen Chamber of Commerce	"to make certain alterations in the Patents for Inventions Bill [PUBB31]" [1 signature]
PET438	23 Mar 1877	8th Rep, p 172 (No 2558) App, p 62 (App No 126)	Inventors' Institute	[Additional fees of £100 excessive; examination should be advisory only; full participation of the colonies; object to references to Law Officers or Lord Chancellor as overburdened; compulsory licences interfere with law of supply and demand; Stamp duty should be lowered] "that your honourable House will take the above into your favourable consideration, and that the said Bill [PUBB31] many be so amended as to be in accordance therewith" [2 signatures]
PET439	26 Mar 1877	9th Rep, p 199 (No 2928)	Huddersfield Trades Council	Similar to Wolverhampton, App 74 [PET431] [2 signatures] [Related to PUBB31]
PET440	5 Apr 1877	9th Rep, p 199 (No 2929)	Wednesbury Trades Council	Similar to Wolverhampton, App 74 [PET431] [2 signatures] [Related to PUBB31]
PET441	11 Apr 1877	10th Rep, p 231 (No 3308)	London Trades Council	Similar to Wolverhampton, App 74 [PET431] [2 signatures] [Related to PUBB31]
PET442	11 Apr 1877	10th Rep, p 231 (No 3309)	Sheffield Trades Council	Similar to Wolverhampton, App 74 [PET431] [2 signatures] [Related to PUBB31]

PET443	12 Apr 1877	10th Rep, p 231 (No 3310)	Liverpool Chamber of Commerce	"to make certain alterations in the Patents for Inventions Bill [PUBB31]" [2 signatures]
PET444	16 Apr 1877	11th Rep, p 259 (No 3604)	Polytechnic Society of Liverpool	"to make certain alterations in the Patents for Inventions Bill [PUBB31]" [2 signatures]
PET445	17 Apr 1877	11th Rep, p 259 (No 3605)	Stalybridge Trades Council	Similar to Wolverhampton, App 74 [PET431] [2 signatures] [Related to PUBB31]
PET446	23 Apr 1877	12th Rep, p 283 (No 3873)	Maidstone Trades Council	Similar to Wolverhampton, App 74 [PET431] [2 signatures] [Related to PUBB31]
PET447	23 April 1877	13th Rep, p 311 (No 4190) App, p 96 (App No 199)	Edinburgh Chamber of Commerce	[Rivals should have opportunity to buy patent after three years (so dedicated to public); register of inventions which cannot be patented; every patentee must have address for service in the United Kingdom] "that your honourable House may pass the Patents for Inventions Bill [PUBB31] into law; that the stated term for which patents are granted should be continued as at present at fourteen years; and that the recommendations made above should be adopted by your honourable House" [2 signatures]
PET448	30 Apr 1877	15th Rep, p 364 (No 4775)	Oldham Trades Council	Similar to Wolverhampton, App 74 [PET431] [2 signatures] [Related to PUBB31]
PET449	1 May 1877	15th Rep, p 364 (No 4776)	Artizans and Inventors Patent Law Amendment Committee	"to make certain alterations in the Patents for Inventions Bill [PUBB31]" [2 signatures]
PET450	1 May 1877	15th Rep, p 364 (No 4777)	Leeds Chamber of Commerce	"to make certain alterations in the Patents for Inventions Bill [PUBB31]" [1 signature]
PET451	4 May 1877	16th Rep, p 394 (No 5187)	Cleveland Institute of Engineers	"to make certain alterations in the Patents for Inventions Bill [PUBB31]" [2 signatures]
PET452	9 May 1877	18th Rep, p 459 (No 6101)	Manchester Trades Council	Similar to Wolverhampton, App 74 [PET431] [2 signatures] [Related to PUBB31]
PET453	15 May 1877	19th Rep, p 483 (No 6333)	Inventors, Patentees and others, Dublin	"to appoint a Select Committee to take the evidence of inventors on the subject of Patents" [43 signatures]
PET454	11 Jun 1877	21st Rep, p 594 (No 8535)	South of Scotland Chamber of Commerce	"to make certain alterations in the Patents for Inventions Bill [PUBB31]" [1 signature]
PET455	13 Jun 1877	22nd Rep, p 629 (No 9026)	Philip Brannan	Patent Laws – For Alteration [1 signature] [Related to PUBB31]
PET456	27 Jun 1877	24th Rep, p 693 (No 9770)	Inventors, Patentees and others of Leeds	"to reject the Patents for Inventions Bill [PUBB31]" [115 signatures]
PET457	4 Apr 1878	14th Rep, p 515 (No 9242)	Glasgow United Trades Council	"to pass the Patent Law Amendment Bill [PUBB32]" [3 signatures]

(continued)

(continued)

PET458	9 Apr 1878	14th Rep, p 515 (No 9243)	Liverpool Trades Council	"to pass the Patent Law Amendment Bill [PUBB32]" [2 signatures]
PET459	15 Apr 1878	15th Rep, p 563 (No 10,159)	Glasgow Branch Society of Engineers	"to pass the Patent Law Amendment Bill [PUBB32]" [25 signatures]
PET460	15 Apr 1878	15th Rep, p 563 (No 10,160)	Glasgow District Committee of Society of Engineers	"to pass the Patent Law Amendment Bill [PUBB32]" [13 signatures]
PET461	16 Apr 1878	15th Rep, p 563 (No 10,161) App, p 116 (App No 254)	Inventors' Institute	[Patents obtainable for small sum of money; fourteen years too short a term and twenty-one as in proposed Bill is appropriate] "that your honourable House will take the above into your favourable consideration, and pass the said Bill [PUBB32] during the present Session." [2 signatures]
PET462	7 May 1878	15th Rep, p 563 (No 10,162)	Dyers of Paisley	"to pass the Patent Law Amendment Bill [PUBB32]" [2 signatures]
PET463	7 May 1878	15th Rep, p 563 (No 10,163)	Sheffield Trades Council	"to pass the Patent Law Amendment Bill [PUBB32]" [19 signatures]
PET464	8 May 1878	16th Rep, p 599 (No 10,668) App, p 121–122 (App No 267)	Greenock Chamber of Commerce	"that your honourable House will be pleased to defer legislation on this subject, and to refuse to pass the said Bill [PUBB32] into a law" [1 signature]
PET465	8 May 1878	16th Rep 599 (No 10,669)	Leeds Trades Council	Similar to French Polishers, App 268 [PET467] [2 signatures] [Related to PUBB32]
PET466	8 May 1878	16th Rep 599 (No 10,670)	Flint Glass Cutters, Glasgow	Similar to French Polishers, App 268 [PET467] [25 signatures] [Related to PUBB32]
PET467	8 May 1878	16th Rep 599 (No 10,671) App, p 122 (App No 268)	French Polishers' Trade and Friendly Society, Glasgow	[Reducing stamp duty and deferring payment will give inducement to discover] "that the Bill [PUBB32] may be passed into law this session" [1 signature]
PET468	8 May 1878	16th Rep 599 (No 10,672)	Coopers' Association, Glasgow	Similar to French Polishers, App 268 [PET467] [69 signatures] [Related to PUBB32]
PET469	8 May 1878	16th Rep 599 (No 10,673)	Society of Engineers, Dumbarton	Similar to French Polishers, App 268 [PET467] [2 signatures] [Related to PUBB32]
PET470	8 May 1878	16th Rep 599 (No 10,674)	Aberdeen Trades Council	Similar to French Polishers, App 268 [PET467] [2 signatures] [Related to PUBB32]
PET471	8 May 1878	16th Rep 599 (No 10,675)	Glasgow Associated Joiners	Similar to French Polishers, App 268 [PET467] [21 signatures] [Related to PUBB32]
PET472	9 May 1878	16th Rep 599 (No 10,676)	General Union of Saddlers, Glasgow	Similar to French Polishers, App 268 [PET467] [2 signatures] [Related to PUBB32]

PET473	9 May 1878	16th Rep 599 (No 10,677)	Artizans and Inventors Patent Law Amendment Committee	"to pass the Patent Law Amendment Bill [PUBB32]" [19 signatures]
PET474	10 May 1878	16th Rep 599 (No 10,678)	Blacksmiths of Glasgow	Similar to French Polishers, App 268 [PET467] [2 signatures] [Related to PUBB32]
PET475	14 May 1878	17th Rep, p 653 (No 11,704) App, p 131 (App No 289)	Patent Agents of London	[Inventors would approve of the Bill [PUBB32]; amendment should be made so that the Lord Chancellor in case of accidental omission of paying fees should be able to grant an extension of time] [20 signatures]
PET476	13 May 1878	17th Rep, p 653 (No 11,705)	Inventors, Patentees and others, Glasgow	"to pass the Patent Law Amendment Bill [PUBB32]" [28 signatures]
PET477	13 May 1878	17th Rep, p 653 (No 11,706)	Society of Associated Blacksmiths, Glasgow	Similar to French Polishers, App 268 [PET467] [43 signatures] [Related to PUBB32]
PET478	13 May 1878	17th Rep, p 653 (No 11,707)	Inventors, Patentees and others, Edinburgh	Similar to French Polishers, App 268 [PET467] [28 signatures] [Related to PUBB32]
PET479	13 May 1878	17th Rep, p 653 (No 11,708)	Society of Engineers, Paisley	Similar to French Polishers, App 268 [PET467] [12 signatures] [Related to PUBB32]
PET480	13 May 1878	17th Rep, p 653 (No 11,709)	Operative Plumbers of Paisley	Similar to French Polishers, App 268 [PET467] [3 signatures] [Related to PUBB32]
PET481	13 May 1878	17th Rep, p 653 (No 11,710)	Bury Trades Council	Similar to French Polishers, App 268 [PET467] [2 signatures] [Related to PUBB32]
PET482	13 May 1878	17th Rep, p 653 (No 11,711)	Amalgamated Engineers, Greenock Branch	Similar to French Polishers, App 268 [PET467] [1 signature] [Related to PUBB32]
PET483	14 May 1878	17th Rep, p 653 (No 11,712)	Society of Engineers, Aberdeen	Similar to French Polishers, App 268 [PET467] [2 signatures] [Related to PUBB32]
PET484	14 May 1878	17th Rep, p 653 (No 11,713)	Operative Printers, Greenock	Similar to French Polishers, App 268 [PET467] [2 signatures] [Related to PUBB32]
PET485	15 May 1878	17th Rep, p 653 (No 11,714)	Philosophical Society of Glasgow	"to pass the Patent Law Amendment Bill [PUBB32]" [2 signatures]
PET486	15 May 1878	17th Rep, p 653 (No 11,715)	Birmingham Trades Council	"to pass the Patent Law Amendment Bill [PUBB32]" [2 signatures]
PET487	15 May 1878	17th Rep, p 653 (No 11,716)	Aberdeen Chamber of Commerce	"to pass the Patent Law Amendment Bill [PUBB32]" [1 signature]
PET488	15 May 1878	17th Rep, p 653 (No 11,717)	Edinburgh Trades Council	Similar to French Polishers, App 268 [PET467] [3 signatures] [Related to PUBB32]

(continued)

(continued)

PET489	20 May 1878	18th Rep, p 701 (No 12,484)	Glasgow Calendermen's Funeral Protection Association	Similar to French Polishers, App 268 [PET467] [15 signatures] [Related to PUBB32]
PET490	21 May 1878	18th Rep, p 701 (No 12,485)	Scottish Operative Brass Founders' Association	Similar to French Polishers, App 268 [PET467] [2 signatures] [Related to PUBB32]
PET491	22 May 1878	19th Rep, p 758 (No 13,626)	London Trades Council	"to pass the Patent Law Amendment Bill [PUBB32]" [1 signature]
PET492	23 May 1878	19th Rep, p 758 (No 13,627)	Society of Engineers, Glasgow	"to pass the Patent Law Amendment Bill [PUBB32]" [23 signatures]
PET493	27 May 1878	19th Rep, p 758 (No 13,628)	Operative Bricklayers' Association, Scotland	Similar to French Polishers, App 268 [PET467] [11 signatures] [Related to PUBB32]
PET494	28 May 1878	19th Rep, p 758 (No 13,629)	Operative Bakers of Paisley	"to pass the Patent Law Amendment Bill [PUBB32]" [2 signatures]
PET495	14 Jun 1878	20th Rep, p 806 (No 14,474)	Edinburgh Chamber of Commerce	"to reject the Patent Law Amendment Bill [PUBB32]" [2 signatures]
PET496	31 May 1878	20th Rep, p 807 (No 14,475) App, p 165 (App No 351)	Patent Law Committee, Association for the Reform and Codification of the Law of Nations	[Term of patents should be extended to 21 years; and the fees should cover only the expenses] "to pass [Mr Anderson's Bill: PUBB32] into law" [19 signatures]
PET497	31 May 1878	20th Rep, p 807 (No 14,476)	Faculty of Procurators in Glasgow	"to pass the Patent Law Amendment Bill [PUBB32]" [2 signatures]
PET498	14 Mar 1879	6th Rep, p 166 (No 2953) App, p 40 (App No 85)	Greenock Chamber of Commerce	[Should be novelty examination; terms should not be extended beyond 14 years] "to pass the said Bill [PUBB33 or PUBB34] into law with a provision therein that the Commissioners should cause applications for patents to be examined by officers to be appointed by them before granting the same, and that, although no person should appear to oppose the grant, and father than the duration of the patents should not be prolonged beyond 14 years, subject to the power of condition extension, as at present, and if extend to 21 years that the law should not be retrospective" [1 signature]
PET499	17 Mar 1879	6th Rep, p 166 (No 2954) App, p 40 (App No 86)	Inventors, Patentees of Glasgow	[Making complete specification public and inviting comments before grant is damaging; procedural change; requiring compulsory licences is not necessary; no need for models and stamp duties too high] "that the Bill [PUBB33 or PUBB34] should be altered or amended accordingly, and in the direction of the Patents for Inventions (No 1) Bill, as to the extension of existing patents and applications pending at the passing of the Bill, from the 14th to the 21st year, and the remission or deferring and reduction of the stamp duties contained in Schedule 2" [2 signatures]

PET500	24 Mar 1879	7th Rep, p 210 (No 3670)	Philosophical Society of Glasgow	For alteration of Patents for Inventions Bill [PUBB33 or PUBB34] [3 signatures]
PET501	21 Mar 1879	7th Rep, p 210 (No 3671)	United Trades Council of Glasgow	In favour of Patents for Inventions Bill [PUBB33 or PUBB34] [1 signature]
PET502	17 Apr 1879	9th Rep, p 297 (No 5010)	Inventors, Patentees and others of Edinburgh and Leith	For alteration of Patents for Inventions Bill [PUBB33 or PUBB34] [2 signatures]
PET503	18 Apr 1879	9th Rep, p 297 (No 5011)	Inventors, Patentees and others of Edinburgh and Leith	For alteration of Patents for Inventions Bill [PUBB33 or PUBB34] [2 signatures]
PET504	21 Apr 1879	9th Rep, p 298 (No 5012) App, p 70 (App No 151)	Society of Engineers of Glasgow	[Approval of extension of patents to 21 years and reduction of stamp duty] "that the Patents for Inventions (No 1) Bill [PUBB33] may be passed into law, as its provisions are much to be preferred to the proposed contained in the Patents for Inventions (No 2) Bill" [12 signatures]
PET505	6 May 1879	11th Rep, p 396 (No 6479)	Commissioners of Supply for Elgin	In favour of Patents for Inventions Bill [PUBB33 or PUBB34] [1 signature]
PET506	15 May 1879	13th Rep, p 465 (No 7254)	Commissioners of Supply for Aberdeen	In favour of Patents for Inventions Bill [PUBB33 or PUBB34] [1 signature]
PET507	19 May 1879	13th Rep, p 465 (No 7255) App, p 130–131 (App No 253)	Liverpool Chamber of Commerce	[Approval of 1875 Bill [PUBB29] which did not get 2R in HC; Commissioners should be salaried; should appoint examiners; Commissioners should be familiar with commerce; 21-year term not necessary; amendment to Cl 19; possible for rivals to buy out the patent] "take the several points put forward in this their Petition, into your most favourable consideration, with a view to the Bill [PUBB33 or PUBB34] before your honourable House being amended in accordance with them, such as granting suitable salaries to commissioners, a fair proportion of whom to be acquainted with commerce and manufactures (IV and VII); the appoint of examiners of patents, with adequate salaries (V and VI); the amendments of clauses 6, 16 and 19 (VIII, IX and X); the stamping with the number of article patented (XI) and the introduction of a clause to enable traders or manufactures to purchase patent rights with consent of patentees (XII)" [2 signatures]
PET508	26 May 1879	14th Rep, p 515 (No 7921)	Sheffield Trade Council	Patents for Inventions Bill [PUBB33 or PUBB34] – In Favour [2 signatures]
PET509	17 Jun 1879	14th Rep, p 515 (No 7922) App, p 155	Huddersfield Chamber of Commerce	[Patent Law Amendment Bill [PUBA34], Cl 16 should be changed to limit patents to 14 years not 21 years; Cl 33 should be made final so no re-examination; fees too high]

(continued)

(continued)

		(App No 294)		"to amend the said Bill [PUBB33 or PUBB34] in accordance with the suggestions herein contained" [1 signature]
PET510	8 Aug 1879	20th Rep, p 786 (No 12,383)	Henry Wimshurst	[Designing ships; no recognition of his service while others have adopted his plans and been compensated] [1 signature]
PET511	19 Feb 1880	3rd Rep, p 31 (No 483)	John Clare	[Claim against Admiralty for his invention of iron-ships] Inquiry into his case [1 signature]
PET512	17 Jun 1880	6th Rep, p 317 (No 4193)	Alexander Louden	Patents for Inventions Bill [PUBB36]– In Favour [1 signature]
PET513	21 Jun 1880	7th Rep, p 353 (No 4950) App, p 79–80 (App No 109)	Inventors, Patentees in Glasgow	"the present Bill [PUBB36] contains all the most urgently-needed reforms, and if passed into law would practically settle legislation on the subject for many years to come" [1 signature]
PET514	23 Jun 1880	8th Rep, p 428 (No 6936)	Philosophical Society of Glasgow	Patents for Inventions Bill [PUBB36] – In Favour [1 signature]
PET515	23 Jun 1880	8th Rep, p 428 (No 6937)	Union Trade Council of Glasgow	Similar to Glasgow, App 109 [PET513] [3 signatures] [Related to PUBB36]
PET516	25 Jun 1880	8th Rep, p 428 (No 6938)	Inventors Meeting in Edinburgh	Patents for Inventions Bill [PUBB36]– In Favour [2 signatures]
PET517	30 Jun 1880	9th Rep, p 458 (No 7531) App, p 98–99 (App No 151)	Typographical Association	"that the Bill [PUBB36] may be passed into law this Session" [3 signatures]
PET518	30 Jun 1880	9th Rep, p 458 (No 7532)	Iron Moulders of Scotland	Similar to Typographical Association, App 151 [PET517] [2 signatures] [Related to PUBB36]
PET519	1 Jul 1880	9th Rep, p 458 (No 7533)	Amalgamated Engineers of Glasgow	Similar to Typographical Association, App 151 [PET517] [2 signatures] [Related to PUBB36]
PET520	1 Jul 1880	9th Rep, p 459 (No 7534)	Brass Founders Society of Glasgow	Similar to Typographical Association, App 151 [PET517] [2 signatures] [Related to PUBB36]
PET521	2 Jul 1880	9th Rep, p 459 (No 7535)	Glasgow Shipwrights Society	Similar to Typographical Association, App 151 [PET517] [2 signatures] [Related to PUBB36]
PET522	3 Jul 1880	10th Rep, p 481 (No 7796)	Council of Amalgamated Society of Engineers	Similar to Typographical Association, App 151 [PET517] [2 signatures] [Related to PUBB36]
PET523	3 Jul 1880	10th Rep, p 481 (No 7797)	Glasgow Operative Glaziers' Society	Similar to Typographical Association, App 151 [PET517] [2 signatures] [Related to PUBB36]

PET524	3 Jul 1880	10th Rep, p 481 (No 7798)	Glasgow Throwers' Protective Society	Similar to Typographical Association, App 151 [PET517] [4 signatures] [Related to PUBB36]
PET525	3 Jul 1880	10th Rep, p 481 (No 7799)	United Kingdom Pattern Makers Society	Similar to Typographical Association, App 151 [PET517] [2 signatures] [Related to PUBB36]
PET526	3 Jul 1880	10th Rep, p 481 (No 7800)	Scottish Operative Tailors' Trade Protection, Glasgow Branch	Similar to Typographical Association, App 151 [PET517] [2 signatures] [Related to PUBB36]
PET527	3 Jul 1880	10th Rep, p 481 (No 7801)	Glasgow Branch of Society of Tailors	Similar to Typographical Association, App 151 [PET517] [2 signatures] [Related to PUBB36]
PET528	5 Jul 1880	10th Rep, p 481 (No 7802)	Boiler Makers and Iron Shipbuilders Association	Similar to Typographical Association, App 151 [PET517] [2 signatures] [Related to PUBB36]
PET529	5 Jul 1880	10th Rep, p 481 (No 7803)	Union of Operative Masons Association of Scotland, Glasgow Branch	Similar to Typographical Association, App 151 [PET517] [2 signatures] [Related to PUBB36]
PET530	5 Jul 1880	10th Rep, p 481 (No 7804)	Glasgow Flint Glass Cutters' Society	Similar to Typographical Association, App 151 [PET517] [2 signatures] [Related to PUBB36]
PET531	5 Jul 1880	10th Rep, p 481 (No 7805)	Aberdeen Chamber of Commerce	Patents for Inventions Bill [PUBB36] – In Favour [1 signature]
PET532	6 Jul 1880	10th Rep, p 481 (No 7806)	Glasgow Typographical Society	Similar to Typographical Association, App 151 [PET517] [2 signatures] [Related to PUBB36]
PET533	6 Jul 1880	10th Rep, p 481 (No 7807)	No 2 Branch of Blacksmiths of Scotland Society	Similar to Typographical Association, App 151 [PET517] [2 signatures] [Related to PUBB36]
PET534	6 Jul 1880	10th Rep, p 481 (No 7808)	Inventors of Renfrewshire	Similar to Typographical Association, App 151 [PET517] [142 signatures] [Related to PUBB36]
PET535	6 Jul 1880	10th Rep, p 481 (No 7809)	Glasgow Central Lodge of United Operative Masons of Scotland	Similar to Typographical Association, App 151 [PET517] [2 signatures] [Related to PUBB36]
PET536	9 Jul 1880	11th Rep, p 505 (No 8092)	Glasgow Bakers' Society	Similar to Typographical Association, App 151 [PET517] [2 signatures] [Related to PUBB36]

(continued)

(continued)

PET537	9 Jul 1880	11th Rep, p 505 (No 8093)	Glasgow Carters' Society	Similar to Typographical Association, App 151 [PET517] [3 signatures] [Related to PUBB36]
PET538	9 Jul 1880	11th Rep, p 505 (No 8094)	Bakers' Association of Scotland	Similar to Typographical Association, App 151 [PET517] [2 signatures] [Related to PUBB36]
PET539	9 Jul 1880	11th Rep, p 505 (No 8095)	Glasgow Coachmakers' Society	Similar to Typographical Association, App 151 [PET517] [2 signatures] [Related to PUBB36]
PET540	9 Jul 1880	11th Rep, p 505 (No 8096)	Glasgow Iron Dressers' Society	Similar to Typographical Association, App 151 [PET517] [2 signatures] [Related to PUBB36]
PET541	9 Jul 1880	11th Rep, p 505 (No 8097)	Glasgow Coopers' Society	Similar to Typographical Association, App 151 [PET517] [2 signatures] [Related to PUBB36]
PET542	9 Jul 1880	11th Rep, p 505 (No 8098)	Glasgow Calendermen's Protection and Funeral Association	Similar to Typographical Association, App 151 [PET517] [5 signatures] [Related to PUBB36]
PET543	9 Jul 1880	11th Rep, p 505 (No 8099)	Bricklayers' Friendly and Protection Association of Scotland	Similar to Typographical Association, App 151 [PET517] [2 signatures] [Related to PUBB36]
PET544	9 Jul 1880	11th Rep, p 505 (No 8100)	Inhabitants of Dumbarton	"the Patent for Inventions Bill [PUBB36] contains all the most urgently-needed reforms; and if passed into law, would practically settle legislation on the subject for many years to come" [65 signatures]
PET545	12 Jul 1880	12th Rep, p 535 (No 8497)	United Flint Glass Cutters' Society	Similar to Typographical Association, App 151 [PET517] [2 signatures] [Related to PUBB36]
PET546	12 Jul 1880	12th Rep, p 535 (No 8498)	Inventors Interested in Industrial Progress and Patent Law Reform	"the Patent for Inventions Bill [PUBB36] contains all the most urgently-needed reforms; and if passed into law, would practically settle legislation on the subject for many years to come" [342 signatures]
PET547	13 Jul 1880	12th Rep, p 535 (No 8499)	Glasgow Branch of Association of Carpenters and Joiners of Scotland	Similar to Typographical Association, App 151 [PET517] [3 signatures] [Related to PUBB36]
PET548	13 Jul 1880	12th Rep, p 535 (No 8500)	Gilders' Society of Glasgow	Similar to Typographical Association, App 151 [PET517] [2 signatures] [Related to PUBB36]
PET549	13 Jul 1880	12th Rep, p 535 (No 8501)	Handloom Weavers' Society, Glasgow	Similar to Typographical Association, App 151 [PET517] [2 signatures] [Related to PUBB36]

PET550	14 Jul 1880	12th Rep, p 535 (No 8502)	Scottish Operative Tailors' Society	Similar to Typographical Association, App 151 [PET517] [2 signatures] [Related to PUBB36]
PET551	19 Jul 1880	13th Rep, p 570 (No 8958)	Glasgow Cabinetmakers' Society	Similar to Typographical Association, App 151 [PET517] [2 signatures] [Related to PUBB36]
PET552	19 Jul 1880	13th Rep, p 570 (No 8959)	Glasgow Lathsplitters' Society	Similar to Typographical Association, App 151 [PET517] [3 signatures] [Related to PUBB36]
PET553	19 Jul 1880	13th Rep, p 570 (No 8960)	Patternmakers' Society of Scotland	Similar to Typographical Association, App 151 [PET517] [2 signatures] [Related to PUBB36]
PET554	28 Jul 1880	14th Rep, p 596 (No 9238)	Workmen of Paisley	Similar to Typographical Association, App 151 [PET517] [187 signatures] [Related to PUBB36]
PET555	28 Jul 1880	14th Rep, p 596 (No 9239)	Glasgow Flint Glass Makers' Society	Similar to Typographical Association, App 151 [PET517] [2 signatures] [Related to PUBB36]
PET556	16 Aug 1880	16th Rep, p 650 (No 9821)	Carpenters and Joiners of Scotland	Similar to Typographical Association, App 151 [PET517] [2 signatures] [Related to PUBB36]
PET557	22 Feb 1881	4th Rep, p 57 (No 985)	Lord Provost, Magistrates and Council of Edinburgh	"to pass the Patents for Inventions Bill [PUBB37]" [No indication]
PET558	25 Feb 1881	5th Rep, p 79 (No 1389) App, p 42 (App No 70)	Glasgow United Trade Council	"that the Bill [PUBB37] just brought before your House contains all the more urgently needed reforms, and, if passed into law, will practically settle all legislation on the subject for many years to come" [4 signatures]
PET559	3 Mar 1881	6th Rep, p 96 (No 1585)	Inventors and Patentees of Glasgow	Similar to Glasgow, App 70 [PET558] [1 signature] [Related to PUBB37]
PET560	19 Mar 1881	7th Rep, p 125 (No 2079)	Alexander Londen	Patents for Inventions Bill [PUBB37]– In Favour [1 signature]
PET561	30 Mar 1881	8th Rep, p 161 (No 2877)	Inventors, Patentees of Edinburgh	Patents for Inventions Bill [PUBB37]– In Favour [2 signatures]
PET562	27 Apr 1881	10th Rep, p 239 (No 4246) App, p 97 (App No 203)	Philosophical Society of Glasgow	"that the Bill [PUBB37] may be passed into law this Session" [2 signatures]
PET563	5 May 1881	11th Rep, p 275 (No 4684) App, p 111 (App No 248)	Liverpool Chamber of Commerce	[Present Bill contains no provisions appointing examiners; Cl 5 extends patent term to 21 years should be 14 years; there should be a right for rivals to buy out the patent]

(continued)

(continued)

				"take the several points put forward in this their Petition into your most favourable consideration with a view to the Bill [PUBB37] now before the House being amended in accordance with them, such as a fair proportion of the Commissioners appointed to be acquainted with commerce and manufactures, the appointment of examiners of patents with adequate salaries, the limitation of patents to fourteen years, and the introduction of a clause to enable traders or manufacturers to purchase patent rights with the consent of the patentee" [2 signatures]
PET564	6 May 1881	11th Rep, p 275 (No 4685)	Royal and Parliamentary Burghs of Scotland	"to remove from the Bill [PUBB37] the provisions in regard to Paid Commissioners" [1 signature]
PET565	24 May 1881	13th Rep, p 343 (No 5671) App, p 136 (App No 301)	Society of Arts, Manufactures and Commerce for alteration of law	[all matter associated with patents should be administered by persons having knowledge of arts, manufactures, and commerce, and not be legal functionaries; the Patent Museum is unsafe and suitable accommodation should be found] "to cause the present patent law to be amended, and it administration be entrusted to the Lords of the Privy Council for Trade" [1 signature] [Related to PUBB37]
PET566	26 May 1881	14th Rep, p 376 (No 6121) App, p 143–144 (App No 316)	Inventors' Institute, London	Petitions in favour of Patents for Inventions Bill [PUBB37] [2 signatures]
PET567	14 Jun 1881	15th Rep, p 418 (No 6815)	Inventors, Patentees and Manufacturers of Edinburgh	Similar to Glasgow, App 203[PET562] [81 signatures] [Related to PUBB37]
PET568	15 Jun 1881	16th Rep, p 460 (No 7538)	Inhabitants of Lambeth and Southwark	Similar to Glasgow, App 203[PET562] [329 signatures] [Related to PUBB37]
PET569	16 Jun 1881	16th Rep, p 460 (No 7539)	Inventors of Kirkcaldy	Similar to Glasgow, App 203[PET562] [27 signatures] [Related to PUBB37]
PET570	28 Jun 1881	17th Rep, p 532 (No 9125) App, p 143 (App No 373)	Bristol Chamber of Commerce	[Need to improve patents laws and provide greater protection to patentees] "to take these matters into your consideration, and to pass the said Bill [PUBB37] into a law, and so give great relief to your Petitioners" [1 signature]
PET571	20 Jul 1881	20th Rep, p 686 (No 12,722)	Leonard Edmunds	[Claims relating to his time at Patent Office] Inquiry into his case [1 signature]
PET572	19 Apr 1882	7th Rep, p 179 (No 4052)	Manchester Chamber of Commerce	Patents for Inventions Bill [PUBB39]– In Favour [2 signatures]
PET573	18 Apr 1882	7th Rep, p 179 (No 4053) App, p 56 (App No 127)	Members of the Dewsbury Chamber of Commerce	"The Patents for Inventions (No 2) Bill [PUBB39] now before your honourable House, with such amendments as your honourable House may deem necessary, may be enacted and become law during the present Session of Parliament" [2 signatures]

PET574	8 Jun 1882	13th Rep, p 437 (No 8318) App, p 110 (App No 264)	Paisley Town Council	"That your Petitioners consider that every facility should be afforded to inventors in securing the results of their inventions, and that the provisions of the Bill [PUBB39] seem calculated to minimise the trouble and expense of obtaining patents, and they approve of it accordingly" [2 petitions – 3 signatures]
PET575	15 Jun 1882	14th Rep, p 471 (No 8824)	Convocation of the Royal and Parliamentary Burghs of Scotland	Patents for Inventions Bill [PUBB39] – In favour [3 petitions – 4 signatures]
PET576	16 Jun 1882	15th Rep, p 503 (No 9326)	Alexander Louden	Patents for Inventions Bill [PUBB39] – In favour [4 petitions – 5 signatures]
PET577	19 Jul 1882	22nd Rep, p 898 (No 18,065)	Halifax Chamber of Commerce	Patents for Inventions Bill [PUBB39]– In favour [5 petitions – 6 signatures]
PET578	18 Apr 1883	8th Rep, p 476 (No 13,478) App, p 71–73 (App No 170)	Croydon Public Affairs Committee	Patents for Inventions Bill [PUBA14]– For Alteration [1. Require the examiners appointed by the Act to examine whether the inventions proposed to be patented are new, useful, and real improvement; 2. Prevent a cotemporaneous or second applicant receiving letters patent; 3. Allow certificates of addition; 4. reduce patent fees; 5. Repeal Protection of Inventions Act 1870 [PUBA13] and have registration of specification of exhibits] [2 signatures]
PET579	16 Apr 1883	8th Rep, p 476 (No 13,479)	Montrose Town Council	Patents for Inventions Bill [PUBA14] – In Favour [1 signature]
PET580	19 Apr 1883	8th Rep, p 476 (No 13,480)	Glasgow United Trades Council	Patents for Inventions (No 3) Bill [PUBA14] – In Favour [3 signatures]
PET581	25 Apr 1883	9th Rep, p 556 (No 15,592) App, p 85 (App No 197)	Edinburgh Chamber of Commerce	Patents for Inventions Bill [PUBA14] – In Alteration [Include "adequate examination" in Cl 6; automatic compulsory licence in Cl 22; specifications lodged but not patented in Cl 23; that no exemption for foreign vessels in Cl 40] "to pass this Bill into law, after introducing such amendments as will secure the several objects herein proposed" [2 petitions – 2 signatures]
PET582	24 Apr 1883	9th Rep, p 557 (No 15,593) App, p 85 (App No 198)	Exhibitors of Electrical Light Exhibitions at the Royal Aquarium	Patents for Inventions Bill [PUBA14] – In Favour [Fees for 4th and 7th year are disproportionate and prejudicial to trade and commerce] "to pass the said Bill into a law, and so give great relief to your Petitioners" [2 petitions – 27 signatures]
PET583	30 Apr 1883	10th Rep, p 629 (No 17,197)	Glasgow Chamber of Commerce	Patents for Inventions Bill [PUBA14] – For Alteration [2 petitions – 4 signatures]
PET584	30 Apr 1883	10th Rep, p 629 (No 17,198)	Inventors, Patentees, Manufacturers at Glasgow	Patents for Inventions Bill [PUBA14] – For Alteration [2 petitions – 3 signatures]
PET585	3 May 1883	10th Rep, p 629 (No 17,199)	Inventors, Patentees, Manufacturers at Glasgow	Patents for Inventions (No 3) Bill [PUBA14] – For Alteration [2 petitions – 5 signatures]
PET586	4 Jun 1883	12th Rep, p 741 (No 18,886)	Paisley Town Council	Patents for Inventions Bill [PUBA14] – In Favour [3 petitions – 28 signatures]

(continued)

(continued)

PET587	9 Jul 1883	17th Rep, p 945 (No 21,735) App, p 153–154 (App No 338)	Sheffield Chamber of Commerce and Manufactures	Patents for Inventions Bill [PUBA14] – For Alteration [Reduction of patent fees in 4th and 7th year; various changes regarding TMs] "will pass the said Bill into law during the present Session of Parliament" [5 petitions – 8 signatures]
PET588	20 Jul 1883	18th Rep, p 991 (No 22,409)	Wakefield Chamber of Commerce	Patents for Inventions Bill [PUBA14] may be passed with further amendments [1 signature]
PET589	31 Jul 1888	18th Rep, p 765 (No 10,740) App, p 112 (App No 221)	Manchester Chamber of Commerce	Patents, Designs and Trade Marks Bill [PUBA17] – For Alteration (relating to trade marks) [1 petition – 41 signatures]
PET590	10 Aug 1888	19th Rep, 810 (No 11,489)	Manchester Manufacturers, Shippers and Merchants	No amendment to Clause 10 of the Patents, Designs, and Trade Marks Bill [PUBA17] [1 petition – 48 signatures]
PET591	5 Jun 1894	7th Rep, p 143 (No 1461)	Birmingham Law Society	Patent Agents Bill [PUBB42 and PUBB43]– For Alteration (to Save Rights of Solicitors) [1 petition – 3 signatures]
PET592	5 Jun 1894	7th Rep, p 143 (No 1462) App, p 59 (App No 83)	Birmingham Law Society	Patent Agents Registration Bill PUBB42 and PUBB43] – For Alteration [Clause 3 amended to exempt solicitors; Cl 6 amended to place solicitors on same footing as Patent Agents; NC to provide that nothing prevents solicitors acting for clients in patent matters; Sch 3 amended to add Law Society Member] "that the pending Bill may be amended accordingly with the suggestions above contained" [1 petition – 3 signatures]
PET593	7 May 1895	9th Rep, p 244 (No 5469)	Huddersfield Chamber of Commerce	To pass the Patents, Designs and Trade Marks (1883 to 1888) Amendment Bill [PUBB44] [1 petition – 1 signature]
PET594	6 May 1902	6th Rep, p 216 (No 3027) App, p 70 (App No 151)	Walsall and District Chamber of Commerce	[Omit clause 2 of the Patent Law Amendment Bill [PUBA20]; replacing compulsory licences with revocation] [2 signatures]
PET595	6 May 1902	6th Rep, p 216 (No 3028) App, p 71 (App No 152)	Edinburgh Chamber of Commerce	[That the Board of Trade rather than court decide on compulsory licences for non-working; requirement of local working should be added] [Related to PUBA20] [2 signatures]
PET596	12 Nov 1902	11th Rep, p 403 (No 5548) App, p 119 (App No 259)	Scottish Trade Protection Society	[Substituting the High Court of Justice in England and Ireland and Court of Session with the Judicial Committee of the Privy Council] "To amend the Bill [PUBA20] as suggested, and when so amended that it do pass into law" [2 signatures]
PET597	25 Jun 1903	7th Rep, p 220 (No 3122)	Prudential Assurance Company Ltd	Against Patent Office Extension Bill [PUBA21] [3 signatures]

PET598	18 Jul 1905 137 LJ 261	HL Pet	Patent Agents	Patents, Designs and Trade Marks (Registration of Agents) Bill [PUBB45] be referred to a Select Committee Archive: HL/PO/6/15/3
PET599	25 Apr 1907	2nd Rep, p 92 (No 1425)	Glasgow Chamber of Commerce	To pass the Patents and Designs Bill [PUBA22] [1 signature]
PET600	6 Jun 1907	3rd Rep, p 117 (No 1767)	Scottish Trade Protection Society	To pass the Patents and Designs Bill [PUBA22] [2 signatures]
PET601	11 Jun 1907	4th Rep, p 140 (No 2007)	Edinburgh Chamber of Commerce	To pass the Patents and Designs Bill [PUBA22] [2 signatures]

Part 8 Parliamentary questions and debates

Introduction

One of the central functions of Parliament is to hold the government to account. Asking the minister questions was, and is, a central way of doing so. Part 8 includes a summary of every question asked (rather than the answer), the person asking the question and the minister answering it (both their name and their office), and the reference in *Hansard*[1] or *The Times*. Chapter 1 includes every significant question relating to patents or inventions included in *Hansard* until the beginning of the 1976–77 Parliamentary session. Chapter 2 includes references to patents in other debates – those which are not related to anything included in any other part of the Guide. It does not indicate office holders as the references are more dynamic. It also marks where something is recorded in *Hansard* but there is no debate. This part includes any significant references to patents, rewards or inventions by any member of either House which was recorded in *Hansard*, the *Mirror of Parliament* or *The Times*.[2] In earlier periods, the reporting in *Hansard* was restricted,[3] and this meant that many questions asked were not recorded. Accordingly, the Parliamentary reports in *The Times* have also been searched up until the contemporaneous reporting in 1909.[4] The date in brackets for *The Times* is the date of the sitting. Where additional information about a person or patent has been identified this is included in square brackets.

---

1 Written answers have a column reference with a "W".
2 Or, for the first few entries: Simon D'Ewes, *Journals of All the Parliaments during the Reign of Queen Elizabeth* (John Starkey 1682).
3 See Introduction to Part 1.
4 In some instances, only the answer is recorded in *The Times*, so the question is synthesised from that answer.

1 Parliamentary questions

Q1	Whether it is the current intention of the government to introduce a Patent Law Bill?	Q: Sir Samuel Whalley A: Viscount Althorp (Ch Ex)	Mirror, 28 Feb 1834, Vol 1, p 409 The Times, 1 Mar 1834
Q2	Whether it is the government's intention to bring in a Bill for the improvement of the law relating to letters patent?	Q: Benjamin Hall A: Charles Thomson (Pr BoT)	Mirror, 11 Jun 1838, Vol 6, p 4662 The Times, 12 Jun 1838
Q3	Whether the government will grant a loan to the National Floating Breakwater Company pending the Bill [PRVB108] being passed?	Q: George Pechell A: Sir Robert Peel (PM)	The Times, 5 Aug 1842 (4 Aug)
Q4	Could further letters from Captain Warner regarding his long range be produced?	Q: Lord Ingestre Q: Sir Charles Napier A: Sir Robert Peel (PM)	The Times, 20 Mar 1845 (19 Mar)
Q5	Whether the government is going to adopt [William] Needham's patent self-priming guns?	Q: Frederick Polhill A: Sir Robert Peel (PM)	The Times, 6 Jun 1846 (5 Jun)
Q6	Will patent fees for the Attorney-General stand in the way of patent reform?	Q: Thomas Gibson A: Lord John Russell (PM)	The Times, 20 Jul 1850 (19 Jul)
Q7	Whether it is the government's intention to bring in any bill on the subject of patent law?	Q: Edward Cardwell A: Lord John Russell (PM)	The Times, 7 Feb 1851 (6 Feb)
Q8	Will there be patent reform this session?	Q: Sir George De Lacy Evans A: Sir George Grey (Hom Sec)	The Times, 11 Feb 1851 (10 Feb)
Q9	Whether Lord Brougham would delay the introduction of his Patent Bill [PUBB20] as the government is now introducing one?	Q: Earl Granville A: Lord Brougham	The Times, 18 Mar 1851 (18 Mar)
Q10	Will the government be introducing any patent legislation this session?	Q: Edward Cardwell A: Henry Labouchère (Pr BoT)	The Times, 12 Apr 1851 (11 Apr)
Q11	Would the second reading of the Patent Law Bill [PUBB22] be delayed to enable members to consider it?	Q: John Ricardo A: Sir Alexander Cockburn (A-G)	The Times, 12 Jul 1851 (11 Jul)
Q12	Will the Patent Act [PUBA6] come into effect before the partial suspension under the Protection of Inventions Act 1851 [PUBA4] expires?	Q: Sir George De Lacy Evans A: Joseph Henley (Pr BoT)	London Evening Standard, 26 Mar 1852 (25 Mar)

(continued)

(continued)

Q13	Would the government object to the Patents Bill [PUBA6] being referred to a Select Committee?	Q: John Ricardo A: Joseph Henely (Pr BoT) Comment: Henry Labouchere	The Times, 8 May 1852 (7 May)
Q14	Whether the extension of the Patents Bill [PUBA6] to the (sugar growing) colonies would be delayed until their wishes could be known?	Q: William Forbes Mackenzie A: Joseph Henley (Pr BoT)	The Times, 19 Jun 1852 (18 Jun)
Q15	Will the Patents Bill [PUBA6] pass this session?	Q: Sir Thomas Cochrane A: Benjamin Disraeli (Ch Ex)	The Times, 22 Jun 1852 (21 Jun)
Q16	Whether all patent specifications are open for inspection in Dublin and Edinburgh?	Q: Charles Cowan A: Sir Frederic Thesiger (A-G)	The Times, 19 Mar 1853 (18 Mar)
Q17	Will a measure be introduced to extend the new patent law to the colonies?	Q: Sir John Shelly A: Sir Alexaner Cockburn (A-G)	The Times, 20 May 1854 (19 May)
Q18	Whether the Commissioners of Patents had laid a report as required by the Act?	Q: Apsley Pellatt A: James Wilson (Fin Sec Tr)	The Times, 28 Jul 1854 (27 Jul)
Q19	Will the War Department acquire the breech-loading rifle?	Q: John Maguire A: Sir Frederick Peel (US War)	The Times, 3 Mar 1855 (2 Mar)
Q20	Whether the Admiralty is adopting the [George Bovill] patent for making iron [No 11,097]?	Q: Marquess Stafford A: Sir Charles Wood (Bd Control)	The Times, 27 Apr 1855 (26 Apr)
Q21	Whether patent law will be extended to India?	Q: Edward Ball A: Robert Smith (Bd Control)	The Times, 14 Jul 1855 (13 Jul)
Q22	Whether it is true that [Thomas] Prideaux's patent provides a saving of 8% in fuel? [1853 No 3000]	Q: Josceline Percy A: Sir Charles Wood (Bd Control)	The Times, 10 Mar 1856 (9 Mar)
Q23	Incomprehensible question on Pridhaux's Patent Valve [1853 No 3000]	Q: Edward Hutchins A: Sir Charles Wood (Fir Ld Adm)	The Times, 14 Mar 1856 (13 Mar)
Q24	Is it the intention of the government to reform patent law?	Q: Lord Lyndhurst A: Lord Cranworth LC	HC Deb, 25 Jul 1856, Vol 143(3rd), col 1419–1421 The Times, 26 Jul 1856
Q25	Whether the report of the trials by the Carriage Department at Woolwich into the Traction Engine for carrying siege artillery will be laid on the table?	Q: Sir George De Lacy Evans A: Jonathan Peel (Sec War)	HC Deb, 12 Jul 1858, Vol 151(3rd), col 1285 The Times, 13 July 1858
Q26	Is there any intention to reform patent law or reduce stamp duties?	Q: Thomas Duncombe A: Sir Stafford Northcoat (Fin Sec Tr)	HC Deb, 11 Feb 1859, Vol 152(3rd), col 248 The Times. 12 Feb 1859
Q27	What steps have been taken to secure the rights to Joseph Whitworth's gun?	Q: Earl of Camperdown A: Earl De Grey and Ripon (US War)	HL Deb, 30 Mar 1860, Vol 157(3rd), col 1611–1616 The Times, 31 Mar 1860
Q28	Who advised on the selection of guns for the navy; was the report from Sir William Armstrong on the device he was contracted to make?	Q: Earl of Camperdown A: Earl de Grey and Ripon (US War)	HC Deb, 15 Jun 1860, Vol 159(3rd), col 492–496 The Times, 16 Jun 1860

Q29	Are there any reports on Sir William Armstrong's patent gun?	Q: Henry Baillie A: Sidney Herbert (Sec War)	The Times, 20 Jun 1860 (19 Jun)
Q30	What progress, if any, has been made in erecting offices for the Commissioners of Patents?	Q: William Tite A William Cowper-Temple (VP BoT)	HC Deb, 26 Jun 1860, Vol 159(3rd), col 998 The Times, 27 Jun 1860
Q31	Has the government purchased the patent for the Whitworth gun?	Q: John Dodson A: Sidney Herbert (Sec War)	HC Deb, 10 Jul 1860, Vol 159(3rd), col 1667 The Times, 11 Jul 1860
Q32	What steps have been taken by the Admiralty relating to George Gill's patent (improvement of ships) [1860 No 2810]?	Q: Somerset Beaumont A: Lord Clarence Paget (Sec Adm)	HC Deb, 10 May 1861, Vol 162(3rd), col 1857 The Times, 11 May 1861
Q33	Whether the Admiralty has considered any of the smoke consuming patents?	Q: William Sykes A: Lord Clarence Paget (Sec Adm)	HC Deb, 27 Feb 1862, Vol 165(3rd), col 835 The Times, 28 Feb 1862
Q34	Whether experiments on the Cupola Shield prejudice the patent of Captain [CP] Coles?	Q: John Edward Walcott A: Lord Clarence Paget (Sec Adm)	HC Deb, 12 May 1862, Vol 166(3rd), col 1560–1561 The Times, 13 May 1862
Q35	Whether any money has been paid to Captain [CP] Coles for his invention of the Cupola iron tower for ships?	Q: William Williams A: Lord Clarence Paget (Sec Adm)	HC Deb, 26 May 1862, Vol 166(3rd), col 2193 The Times, 27 May 1862
Q36	Whether the experiment with "Chalmers' Target" was based on Clare's patent?	Q: John Maguire A: Lord Clarence Paget (Sec Adm)	HC Deb, 7 May 1863, Vol 170(3rd), col 1299 The Times, 8 May 1863
Q37	Whether the principles behind "Chalmers' Target" were based on Clare's patent?	Q: James Aspinall Turner A: Lord Clarence Paget (Sec Adm)	HC Deb, 15 May 1863, Vol 170(3rd), col 1768–1769 The Times, 16 May 1863
Q38	Whether the government will settle claim with John Clare over the Warrior vessel following the evidence in *R v Clare* (The Times 3, 4, 5, 6 and 7 Feb 1863)?	Q: William Coningham A: Lord Clarence Paget (Sec Adm)	HC Deb, 13 Jul 1863, Vol 172(3rd), col 656–657 The Times, 14 Jul 1863
Q39	What use would be made of the National Exhibition ground; could the Patent Office not be put there?	Q: Francis Charteris, Lord Elcho A: Viscount Palmerston (PM)	HC Deb, 24 Jul 1863, Vol 172(3rd), col 1419–1420
Q40	What steps are being taken for providing a proper [Patent] Museum and Library?	Q: Earl of Powis A: Earl Granville (Ld Pr)	HL Deb, 18 Feb 1864, Vol 173(3rd), col 706 The Times, 19 Feb 1864
Q41	Whether contracts, without competition, were awarded for making gunboats?	Q: William Ferrand A: Lord Clarence Paget (Sec Adm)	HC Deb, 3 Mar 1864, Vol 173(3rd), col 1366–1367 The Times, 4 Mar 1864
Q42	Whether the recommendation to properly house the Patent Office [REP9] could be satisfied by occupying Fife House, Whitehall?	Q: Lord Alfred Spencer-Churchill A: William Cowper-Temple (Ch Com W&B)	HC Deb, 17 Mar 1864, Vol 174(3rd), col 182 The Times, 18 Mar 1864
Q43	Whether plans for new museums in South Kensington have been made yet (including Patent Museum)?	Q: Sir Stafford Northcote Q: Lewis Dillwyn A: William Cowper-Temple (Ch Com W&B)	HC Deb, 15 Apr 1864, Vol 174(3rd), col 1078 The Times, 16 Apr 1864
Q44	When will the Patent Law Commission make its report [REP8]?	Q: Lewis Dillwyn A: Lord (Edward) Stanley (PM Gen)	HC Deb, 28 Apr 1864, Vol 174(3rd), col 1773 The Times, 29 Apr 1864

(continued)

(continued)

Q45	When will the Patent Committee report [REP8]?	Q: John Hibbert A: Lord (Edward) Stanley (PM Gen)	The Times, 3 Jun 1864 (2 Jun)
Q46	When will the Patent Law Committee Report [REP8]?	Q: Sir Samuel Morton Peto A: Lord (Edward) Stanley (PM Gen)	The Times, 20 Jul 1864 (19 Jul)
Q47	Whether the government will introduce a Bill to protect international exhibitions?	Q: Francis Henry Berkeley A: Thomas Gibson (Pr BoT)	London Evening Standard, 18 Feb 1865 (17 Feb)
Q48	Whether the Secretary to the Admiralty will lay the report on the patent of William Carpmael [No 6955] and John Clare [1853 No 2043] which is alleged to be used in iron ships for the Royal Navy before the House?	Q: John Maguire A: Lord Clarence Paget (Sec Adm)	HC Deb, 20 Feb 1865, Vol 177(3rd), col 449 The Times, 21 Feb 1865
Q49	Will any further trial be given to Captain [George] Sayer's lifeboat invention?	Q: Sir John Hay A: Lord Clarence Paget (Sec Adm)	HC Deb, 24 Feb 1865, Vol 177(3rd), col 659 The Times, 25 Feb 1865
Q50	Whether the government is aware that a manufacturer is making Armstrong guns for foreign governments (the patent being owned by the government)?	Q: John Laird A: Marquess of Hartington (US Adm)	HC Deb, 2 Mar 1865, Vol 177(3rd), col 960–961 The Times, 3 Mar 1865
Q51	Whether the inquiry into irregularities at the Patent Office [REP10] has been concluded, and whether the report will be laid on the table?	Q: Lord Edward Stanley Q: Sir James Elphinstone Q: James Whiteside A: Roundell Palmer (A-G)	HC Deb, 6 Mar 1865, Vol 177(3rd), col 1120–1123 The Times, 7 Mar 1865
Q52	Whether the government intends to introduce a Bill in this session to implement the recommendation of the commission into the working of letters patent [REP8]?	Q: John Hibbert A: Roundell Palmer (A-G)	HC Deb, 10 Mar 1865, Vol 177(3rd), col 1475 The Times, 11 Mar 1865
Q53	Whether a copy of the report into [Leonard] Edmunds' case will laid on the table of the House [REP10]?	Q: Grosvenor Hogkinson A: Sir George Grey (Sec Tr)	HC Deb, 20 Mar 1865, Vol 177(3rd), col 1920–1921 The Times, 21 Mar 1865
Q54	Is it the case that the Clerk of the Patents and Clerk of the Commissioners may hold in their hands as much public money as they think fit [Leonard] Edmunds' case)?	Q: Earl of Wicklow A: Earl Granville (Ld Pr)	HL Deb, 15 May 1865, Vol 179(3rd), col 260 The Times, 16 May 1865
Q55	Whether it is the government's intention to introduce a Bill to amend the patent law this session?	Q: William Cox A: Roundell Palmer (A-G)	HC Deb, 16 May 1865, Vol 179(3rd), col 392–393 The Times, 17 May 1875
Q56	Is it the case that the Clerk of the Patents and Clerk of the Commissioners may hold in their hands as much public money as they think fit [Leonard] Edmunds' case); does this apply to other offices as well?	Q: Edward Douglas-Pennant A William Gladstone (Ch Ex)	HC Deb, 22 May 1865, Vol 179(3rd), col 637 The Times, 23 May 1865
Q57	What role did Lord St Leonards play in appointing Leonard Edmunds?	Q: Lord Chelmsford A: Lord St Leonards	HL Deb, 23 May 1865, Vol 179(3rd), col 717–718 The Times, 24 May 1865

Q58	What steps are being taken with regard to the report of the commission into the working of letters patent [REP8]?	Q: Robert Lowe A: Lord (Edward) Stanley (PM Gen)	HC Deb, 19 Jun 1865, Vol 180(3rd), col 448 The Times, 20 Jun 1865
Q59	What is the intended purpose for the vacant ground at South Kensington (Patent Museum)?	Q: George Bentinck A: William Gladstone (Ch Ex)	HC Deb, 20 Feb 1866, Vol 181(3rd), col 814–815 The Times, 21 Feb 1866
Q60	Whether officers connected with the War Department (in relation to smalls arms) have taken out patents?	Q: Viscount Lifford A: Lord Dufferin Q: Earl of Harwicke A: Earl of Longford (US War)	HL Deb, 19 Apr 1866, Vol 182(3rd), col 1638–1640 The Times, 20 Apr 1866
Q61	What steps have been taken to recover funds from Leonard Edmunds said to be deficient?	Q: Sir James Fergusson A: Roundell Palmer (A-G)	HC Deb, 10 May 1866, Vol 183(3rd), col 767
Q62	Why have the proceedings against Leonard Edmunds started on 6 Mar 1865 not been proceeded with?	Q: Sir James Fergusson A: Roundell Palmer (A-G)	HC Deb, 11 May 1866, Vol 183(3rd), col 767–768 The Times, 12 May 1866
Q63	Whether the government is aware that the printing of patent specifications is months in arrears; and whether they should be printed as soon as possible?	Q: Christopher Darby Griffith A: Roundell Palmer (A-G)	HC Deb, 15 May 1866, Vol 183(3rd), col 961 The Times, 16 May 1866
Q64	Whether it is true that a sum will be awarded to Major [William] Palliser, the inventor of chilled iron projectiles?	Q: Henry Baille A: Jonathan Peel (Sec War)	HC Deb, 14 Feb 1867, Vol 185(3rd), col 340–341 The Times, 15 Feb 1867
Q65	Would the Admiralty consider utilising Captain [George] Sayer's lifeboat invention?	Q: Edward Knatchbull-Hugessen A: Sir John Pakington (Sec War)	HC Deb, 18 Feb 1867, Vol 185(3rd), col 476–478 The Times, 19 Feb 1867
Q66	Whether departmental officers, who saw certain trials, have taken out patents on small arms?	Q: Viscount Lifford A: Earl of Longford (US War)	HL Deb, 22 Feb 1867, Vol 185(3rd), col 807–808 The Times, 23 Feb 1867
Q67	How is the sum of £22,800 [in the supply] to be paid to inventors?	Q: Sir George Stucley A: Sir John Pakington (Sec War)	HC Deb, 21 Mar 1867, Vol 186(3rd), col 283 The Times, 22 Mar 1867
Q68	Whether the government will present the papers relating to John Clare's case?	Q: Sir Thomas Bazley A: Henry Lowry-Corry (Sec Adm)	HC Deb, 26 Mar 1867, Vol 186(3rd), col 563 The Times, 27 Mar 1867
Q69	Whether the government will enquire into the invention of rifled ordnance and a share of the £22,8000 as a reward for its inventors?	Q: Sir George Stucley A: Sir John Pakington (Sec War)	HC Deb, 4 Apr 1867, Vol 186(3rd), col 1103 The Times, 5 Apr 1867
Q70	Whether it was true that shot cast in sand at Woolwich, without chill, were as effective as Major [William] Palliser projectiles?	Q: Henry Baillie A: Sir John Pakington (Sec War)	HC Deb, 11 Apr 1867, Vol 186(3rd), col 1480–1481 The Times, 12 Apr 1867
Q71	What are the recommendations of the Ordnance Select Committee regarding the award to Major Palliser for his projectiles?	Q: Augustus Anson A: Sir John Pakington (Sec War)	HC Deb, 12 Apr 1867, Vol 186(3rd), col 1582–1583 The Times, 13 Apr 1867

(continued)

(continued)

Q72	Whether Captain Warren RN's patent cooking apparatus has been adopted by the army; and whether he will be referred to the Standing Committee for Rewards to Inventors?	Q: William Sykes Q: Thomson Hankey A: Sir John Pakington (Sec War)	HC Deb, 26 Mar 1868 Vol 191(3rd), col 257–258 The Times, 27 Mar 1868
Q73	Whether the government intends to carry out the recommendations of the Select Committee of 1864 [REP9] and find proper accommodation for the Patent Office Library?	Q: Austen Layard A: Lord John Manners (Ch Com W&B)	HC Deb, 14 May 1868, Vol 192(3rd), col 244 The Times, 15 May 1868
Q74	Whether Colonel [Edward] Boxer has a patent over his cartridges and whether he has received any royalty on it?	Q: Francis Dunne A: Sir John Pakington (Sec War)	HC Deb, 23 Jul 1868, Vol 193(3rd), col 1667–1668 The Times, 24 Jul 1868
Q75	Whether the government proposes to introduce a Bill to amend patent law to implement the recommendations of the 1864 Report [REP8]?	Q: James Howard A: Robert Collier (A-G)	HC Deb, 26 Feb 1869, Vol 194(3rd), col 356 The Times, 27 Feb 1869
Q76	Whether the paper entitled "The History of the Edmunds Scandal" by Leonard Edmunds is now in the Treasury?	Q: George Bentinck A: Acton Ayrton (Ch Com W&B)	HC Deb, 10 May 1869, Vol 196(3rd), col 469–470 The Times, 11 May 1869
Q77	Whether it is true a patent Bill will be introduced in the next session?	Q: Robert Macfie A: John Bright (Pr BoT)	The Times, 29 Jul 1869 (28 Jul 1689)
Q78	Whether there is likely to be reform of the patent law in the next session; and, if so, will it be preceded by an inquiry?	Q: Robert Macfie A: John Bright (Pr BoT)	HC Deb, 2 Aug 1869, Vol 198(3rd) col 1089–1090 The Times, 3 Aug 1869
Q79	Whether the government is aware that the new Canadian patent law only benefits those resident in Canada; whether Imperial consent should be withheld?	Q: Edward Bentall A: William Monsell (US Col)	HC Deb, 5 Aug 1869, Vol 198(3rd), col 1292–1293 The Times, 6 Aug 1869
Q80	Whether the government will read the minute relating to Colonel [Edward] Boxer's invention?	Q: Augustus Anson A: Sir John Pakington (Sec War)	HC Deb, 5 May 1870, Vol 201(3rd), col 277–279 The Times, 6 May 1870
Q81	Whether an order for the arrest of Leonard Edmunds has been issued (and if so, is it to be withdrawn)?	Q: Sir James Elphistone A: Robert Lowe (Ch Ex)	HC Deb, 19 May 1870, Vol 201(3rd), col 970 The Times, 20 May 1870
Q82	Whether unpatented inventions of workmen at the forthcoming Workman's International Exhibition might be protected?	Q: Thomas Hughes A: Sir Robert Collier (A-G)	HC Deb, 30 May 1870, Vol 201(3rd), col 1596–1597 The Times, 31 May 1870
Q83	On what authority has Leonard Edmunds been arrested and confined to prison?	Q: Sir James Elphinstone A: William Gladstone (PM)	HC Deb, 16 Jun 1870, Vol 202(3rd), col 264 The Times, 17 Jun 1870
Q84	Whether the government will lay on the table the reports into the trials of the Martini Henry rifle; and the sums paid to its inventors?	Q: Walter Barttelot A: Edward Cardwell (Sec War)	HC Deb, 7 Jul 1870 Vol 202(3rd), col 1616 The Times, 8 Jul 1870

Q85	Whether the government is proposing to set up a Royal Commission into the patent system?	Q: Robert Macfie A: William Gladstone (PM)	HC Deb, 29 Jul 1870, Vol 203(3rd), col 1230–1232 The Times, 30 Jul 1870
Q86	What steps have been taken for providing a Patent Museum and Office in pursuance of the 1864 Report [REP9]?	Q: John Hinde Palmer A: Acton Ayrton (Ch Com W&B)	HC Deb, 13 Feb 1871, Vol 204(3rd), col 168 The Times, 14 Feb 1871
Q87	To whom are disputed aspects of patent law referred to at the War Office?	Q: John Candlish A: Edward Caldwell (Sec War)	HC Deb, 30 Mar 1871, Vol 205(3rd), col 888 The Times, 31 Mar 1871
Q88	Why has no remuneration been paid to Henry PD Cunningham in relation to the use of his invention for working heavy guns [Same invention as Scott?]	Q: Henry Scott A: George Goschen (Fir Ld Adm)	HC Deb, 13 Jul 1871, Vol 207(3rd), col 1626–1627 The Times, 14 Jul 1871
Q89	Whether [George] Jobson has received any reward for his time fuse submitted to the War Office in 1869?	Q: Thomas Lea A: Sir Henry Storks (SG Ord)	HC Deb, 17 Jul 1871, Vol 207(3rd), col 1879–1880 The Times, 18 Jul 1871
Q90	What criteria are used to assess the compensation paid when a patent is infringed by the Government Manufacturing Department?	Q: Myles O'Reilly A: Edward Cardwell (Sec War)	HC Deb, 18 Jul 1871, Vol 207(3rd), col 1935 The Times, 19 Jul 1871
Q91	Whether any reports have been made to the War Department on the Stowmark gun cotton explosion; and whether the recent Treasury minute on patents for invention is meant to be retrospective?	Q: Francis Charteris, Lord Elcho A: Edward Caldwell (Sec War)	HC Deb, 26 Mar 1872, Vol 210(3rd), col 690–691 The Times, 27 Mar 1872
Q92	Whether the government will grant a sum of money to enable manufacturers to exhibition at the Vienna International Exhibition?	Q: Edgar Bowring A: Robert Lowe (Ch Ex)	HC Deb, 6 Jun 1872, Vol 211(3rd), col 1269–1270 The Times, 7 Jun 1872
Q93	Whether the government is intending an early implementation of the recommendations of the Select Committee on Letters Patent [REP12]; and are new Patent Commissioners going to be appointed?	Q: Edgar Bowring A: William Gladstone (PM)	HC Deb, 27 Jun 1872, Vol 212(3rd), col 283 The Times, 28 Jun 1872
Q94	Whether Leonard Edmunds' request to have the accounts of the Commissioners audited can be granted as part of the case against him?	Q: Lord Redesdale A: Earl Granville (For Sec)	HL Deb, 30 Jul 1872, Vol 213(3rd), col 107–108
Q95	Whether the Admiralty is aware of [Thomas] Prideaux's patent for preventing smoke on ships [1867 No 2154]?	Q: John Maguire A: George Shaw Lefevre (Par Sec Adm)	The Times, 5 Aug 1872 (3 Aug 1872)
Q96	Whether the government intends to bring in legislation to give effect to the recommendations of the Select Committee Inquiry [REP12 and REP13]?	Q: James Howard A: Sir John Coleridge (A-G)	HC Deb, 3 Mar 1873, Vol 214(3rd), col 1182 The Times, 4 Mar 1873
Q97	Whether the government will attend the International Conference in Vienna relating to patent rights?	Q: Robert Macfie A: Viscount Enfield (Par Sec FO)	HC Deb, 7 Apr 1873, Vol 215(3rd), col 636 The Times, 8 Apr 1873

(continued)

(continued)

Q98	Whether the government claims it can use patents without the payment of royalties (pre-Crown use)?	Q: Lord Claud Hamilton A: Edward Cardwell (Sec War)	HC Deb, 6 Jun 1873, Vol 216(3rd), col 552
Q99	Whether the principle of patents will be assumed to be acquiesced in by those attending the Vienna International Conference on Patents for Inventions?	Q: Robert Macfie A: George Byng (US FO)	HC Deb, 14 Jul 1873, Vol 217(3rd), col 310–311 The Times, 15 Jul 1873
Q100	Whether the government intends to make use of James Duffey's invention for protection of gunpowder, and which patent he has not extended?	Q: Henry Raikes A: Sir Henry Storks (SG Ord)	HC Deb, 24 Jul 1872, Vol 217(3rd), col 906–907 The Times, 25 Jul 1873
Q101	Whether Mr Thomas Webster QC has authority to represent the government in the Vienna Conference on Patent Rights?	Q: Robert Macfie A: William Baxter (Fin Sec Tre)	HC Deb, 31 Jul 1873, Vol 217(3rd), col 1328 The Times, 1 Aug 1873
Q102	A dispatch suggests that Thomas Webster QC represents the government; will the government correct any misapprehension?	Q: Robert Macfie A: Viscount Enfield (Par Sec FO)	HC Deb, 5 Aug 1873, Vol 217(3rd), col 1564 The Times, 6 Aug 1873
Q103	Whether the £80,000 surplus on patent fees can be applied to the Patent Office Museum premises?	Q: Frederick Beaumont A: William H Smith (Fin Sec to Tres)	HC Deb, 17 Apr 1874, Vol 218(3rd), col 715 The Times, 18 Apr 1874
Q104	Whether the government is prepared to take action to accommodate the Patent Office Museum?	Q: Anthony Mundella A: Benjamin Disraeli (PM)	HC Deb, 20 Jul 1874, Vol 221(3rd), col 296 The Times, 21 Jul 1874
Q105	Whether the proposal to move the Patent Museum next to the International Exhibition site has been considered?	Q: Edward Reed A: Lord Henry Lennox (Ch Com W&B)	HC Deb, 20 Jul 1874, Vol 221(3rd), col 301 The Times, 21 Jul 1874
Q106	Whether non-legislative proposals of the 1872 Report [REP13] will be implemented?	Q: Charles Cawley A: Richard Cross (Hom Sec)	HC Deb, 21 Jul 1874, Vol 221(3rd), coll 391 The Times, 22 July 1874
Q107	Is there any progress on the Patent Museum?	Q: Anthony Mundella A: Lord Henry Lennox (Ch Com W&B)	HC Deb, 12 Feb 1875, Vol 222(3rd), col 269 The Times, 13 Feb 1875
Q108	Will the Patent Bill [PUBB29] progress before Whitsun?	Q: Anthony Mundella A: Benjamin Disraeli (PM)	The Times, 27 Apr 1875 (26 Apr)
Q109	What steps have been taken for the Patent Museum to occupy the South Block of the International Exhibition Centre?	Q: Sir Harcourt Johnstone A: Alexander Beresford Hope	HC Deb, 15 Jul 1875, Vol 225(3rd), col 1478–1479 The Times, 16 Jul 1875
Q110	Will the Patent Bill [PUBB29] proceed this session?	Q: Lewis Dillwyn A: Sir Richard Baggallay (A-G)	The Times, 16 Jul 1875 (15 Jul)
Q111	Will any progress be made with the Patents Bill [PUBB29] this session?	Q: Lewis Dillwyn A: Sir Richard Baggallay (A-G)	HC Deb, 22 Jul 1875, Vol 225(3rd), col 1818 The Times, 23 Jul 1875

Q112	Whether the intention of government is to re-introduce the Bill from last session [PUBB29]?	Q: Anthony Mundella A: Sir John Holker (A-G)	HC Deb, 18 Feb 1876, Vol 227(3rd), col 484 The Times, 19 Feb 1876
Q113	Whether the government will make a statement on Patterson's patent on purification of coal gas [1872 No 930]?	Q: Sir William Makins A: Sir Charles Adderley (Pr BoT)	HC Deb, 23 May 1876, Vol 229(3rd), col 1110–1112 The Times, 24 May 1876
Q114	Will the Treasury report on the Patents Museum be laid before the House?	Q: Henry Samuelson A: William Smith (Fin Sec Tr)	HC Deb, 30 May 1876, Vol 229(3rd), col 1421–1422 The Times, 31 May 1876
Q115	Whether the publication of "confidential documents" was the conduct of the Admiralty and not Charles Henwood relating to his invention?	Q: (Francis) Marcus Beresford A: George Hunt (Fir Ld Adm)	HC Deb, 13 Jun 1876, Vol 229(3rd), col 1763–1764 The Times, 14 Jul 1876
Q116	Will the Patents Bill [PUBB30] progress this session?	Q: Lewis Dillwyn A: Sir John Holker (A-G)	The Times, 11 Jul 1876 (10 Jul)
Q117	Whether the German and Belgium delegations at the Philadelphia International Exhibition [EXB6] are refusing to describe British or colonial inventions?	Q: McCarthy Downing A: Viscount Sandon (VP Council)	HC Deb, 17 Jul 1876, Vol 230(3rd), col 1479 The Times, 18 Jul 1876
Q118	Will the decision in *Dixon v London Small Arms* (1876) 1 App Cas 632 limit the supply of small arms needed to defend the country?	Q: Sir Walter Barttelot A: Lord Eustace Cecil (Sur Ord)	HC Deb, 17 Jul 1876, Vol 230(3rd), col 1479–1480 The Times, 18 Jul 1876
Q119	Would the government object to the Patents Bill [PUBB31] having a Second Reading?	Q: Anthony Mundella A: Sir John Holker (A-G)	The Times, 21 Feb 1877 (20 Feb)
Q120	Whether the specifications of expired patents are destroyed by the Patent Office (only five saved)?	Q: Edward Reed A: Sir John Holker (A-G)	HC Deb, 26 Feb 1877, Vol 232(3rd), col 1014–1015 The Times, 27 Feb 1877
Q121	Will the Second Reading of the Patents Bill [PUBB31] be before Easter?	Q: Alexander Brown A: Sir Stafford Northcot (Ch Ex)	The Times, 6 Mar 1877 (5 Mar)
Q122	Why has the memorial dated 12 Feb 1873 regarding John Clare's claim against the Admiralty not been acted upon?	Q: Joseph Biggar A: George Hunt (Fir Ld Adm)	HC Deb, 16 Apr 1877, Vol 233(3rd), col 1212–1213 The Times, 17 Apr 1877
Q123	Will the government object to the memorials of John Clare relating to his claim against the government being laid on the table?	Q: Joseph Biggar A: Richard Assheton Cross (Hom Sec)	HC Deb, 19 Apr 1877, Vol 233(3rd), col 1440–1442 The Times, 20 Apr 1877
Q124	Will the government provide a translation of the new German patent law?	Q: John Nolan A: Sir John Holker (A-G)	The Times, 5 May 1877 (4 May)
Q125	Why John Clare's petition of 1866 [PET287] and the memorial have not been acted upon?	Q: Joseph Biggar A: Algernon Egerton (Par Sec Adm) A: Richard Assheton Cross (Hom Sec)	HC Deb, 8 May 1877, Vol 234(3rd), col 494–495 The Times, 9 May 1877

(continued)

(continued)

Q126	Does the government intend to pass the Patents Bill [PUBB31]?	Q: Henry Jackson A: Sir John Holker (A-G)	HC Deb, 4 Jun 1877, Vol 234(3rd), col 1237 The Times, 5 Jun 1877
Q127	Whether the intention of the government is to introduce a patent law Bill during this session?	Q: Anthony Mundella A: Sir John Holker (A-G)	HC Deb, 18 Feb 1878, Vol 237(3rd), col 1850 The Times, 19 Feb 1878
Q128	Whether the government is intending to introduce a patent law Bill during this session?	Q: Earl Granville A: Lord Cairns (LC)	HL Deb, 19 Mar 1878, Vol 238(3rd), col 1580 The Times, 20 Mar 1878
Q129	Whether the government is prepared to refer the claims of John Clare to a committee?	Q: Frank O'Donnell A: William H. Smith (Fir Ld Adm)	HC Deb, 21 Mar 1878, Vol 238(3rd), col 1757–1758 The Times, 22 Mar 1878
Q130	Whether a patent Bill will be introduced this session?	Q: Johan Nolan A: Henry Selwin-Ibbetson (Fin Sec Tr)	HC Deb, 13 May 1878, Vol 239(3rd), col 1773–1776 The Times, 14 May 1878 (13 May)
Q131	Whether it is true that £7,000,000 has been paid on rifled ordnance, but nothing given to its inventors?	Q: Francis O'Beirne A: Lord Eustace Cecil (SG Ord)	HC Deb, 24 May 1878, Vol 240(3rd), col 626 The Times, 25 May 1878
Q132	Whether the system of rifled ordnance now used is the same as that which was rejected twice in 1855 and the offer of £100 for the inventor was rejected?	Q: Francis O'Beirne A: Lord Eustance Cecil (SG Ord)	HC Deb, 3 Jun 1878, Vol 240(3rd), col 1075 The Times, 4 Jun 1878
Q133	Whether [Hugh Childers] has read the petition of Charles Henwood complaining of statements and whether something stated about the plan was accurate?	Q: Bedford Pim A: Hugh Childers (not a minister)	HC Deb, 1 Aug 1878, Vol 242(3rd), col 866–867 The Times, 2 Aug 1878
Q134	Will the minister make a statement about the number of patents prolonged during the period 1870–78?	Q: Bernhard Samuelson A: Sir John Holker (A-G)	HC Deb, 18 Mar 1879, Vol 244(3rd), col 1150 The Times, 19 Mar 1879
Q135	Will the statement promised on the number of patents prolonged be laid on the table? [PPP90]	Q: Bernhard Samuelson A: Sir John Holker (A-G)	HC Deb, 22 May 1879, Vol 246(3rd), col 1006 The Times, 23 May 1879
Q136	Whether any person other than WP Padwick has claimed to be the inventor of a system of elongated projectiles with studs of soft metal?	Q: William Beresford A: Lord Eustace Cecil (Sur Ord)	HC Deb, 21 Jul 1879, Vol 248(3rd), col 843–844 The Times, 22 Jul 1879
Q137	Why there is not a weekly gazette issued of new patents, similar to that in the USA?	Q: James Howard A: Sir Henry James (A-G)	HC Deb, 31 May 1880, Vol 252(3rd), col 772
Q138	What has happened regarding the Patent Museum?	Q: John Hinde Palmer A: Lord Fredrick Cavendish (Fin Sec Tr)	HC Deb, 9 Aug 1880, Vol 255(3rd), col 663–664 The Times, 10 Aug 1880
Q139	Whether a portion of the Natural History Museum or other buildings in South Kensington could be used to house the Patent Office Museum?	Q: John Hinde Palmer A: William Adam (Ch Com W&B)	HC Deb, 12 Aug 1880, Vol 255(3rd), col 976–977 The Times, 13 Aug 1880

Q140	Whether the government proposes to introduce any measure to reform patent law?	Q: Charles Monk A: Joseph Chamberlain (Pr BoT)	HC Deb, 10 Mar 1881, Vol 259(3rd), col 719 The Times, 11 Mar 1881
Q141	What has happened to the collective illustrations of mining, metallurgy and mineralogy at the 1862 Exhibition?	Q: Sir Edward Watkins A: Anthony Mundella (VP BoEd)	HC Deb, 22 Mar 1881, Vol 259(3rd), col 1662 The Times, 23 Mar 1881
Q142	Whether a patented item can be imported into France; or does it have to be manufactured there?	Q: Sir Henry Holland A: Sir Charles Dilke (US FO)	HC Deb, 24 Jun 1881, Vol 262(3rd), col 1224 The Times, 25 Jun 1881
Q143	Whether the Patent Museum has to refuse gifts of inventions offered to it?	Q: John Hinde Palmer A: Joseph Chamberlain (Pr BoT)	HC Deb, 11 Aug 1881, Vol 264(3rd), col 1531 The Times, 12 Aug 1881
Q144	Whether the Naval Armoured Train uses a patented process – John Liardet's patent [1872 No 2611]?	Q: Charles Warton A: Sir Thomas Brassey (Ld Adm)	HC Deb, 17 Aug 1882, Vol 273(3rd), col 2044–2045 The Times, 18 Aug 1882
Q145	When the government Bill for consolidation of patent law [PUBA14] will be made available to members; and will there be a memorandum?	Q: Charles Stuart-Wortley and William H Smith A: Joseph Chamberlin (Pr BoT)	HC Deb, 1 Mar 1883, Vol 276(3rd), col 1163 The Times, 2 Mar 1883
Q146	Whether manufacture of twine in dockyards relates to George Good's patent [1881 No 2028]?	Q: Thomas Paget A: Henry Campbell-Bannerman (Sec Adm)	HC Deb, 16 Mar 1883, Vol 277(3rd), col 698 The Times, 17 Mar 1883
Q147	Whether use of John Clare's patent should lead to a Crown use payment?	Q: Joseph Biggar A: Henry Campbell-Bannerman (Fin Sec War)	HC Deb, 16 Jul 1883, Vol 281(3rd), col 1644–1645 The Times, 17 Jul 1883
Q148	Whether the Patents Bill can be discussed in the House of Lords during its passage through the Commons?	Q: Earl of Redesdale A: Earl Granville (For Sec)	HC Deb, 17 Jul 1883, Vol 281(3rd), col 1659–1660 The Times, 18 Jul 1883
Q149	When will the revised Index of Patents be completed?	Q: Sir John Eardley Wimot A: Joseph Chamberlain (Pr BoT)	HC Deb, 13 Aug 1883, Vol 283(3rd), col 281 The Times, 14 Aug 1883
Q150	What are the new arrangements for the Patent Museum?	Q: Charles Stuart-Wortley A: Anthony Mundella (VP Ed)	HC Deb, 13 Aug 1883, Vol 283(3rd), col 396–397 The Times, 14 Aug 1883
Q151	Whether Lynal Thomas, who would have a claim against the government under the Patents Bill [PUBA14], has an equitable claim against the government?	Q: Donald Macfarlane A: Henry Brand (SG Ord)	HC Deb, 20 Aug 1883, Vol 283(3rd), vol 1372–1373
Q152	Whether General Newgate reported favourably on the [Richard] Morris patent system (gun loading system)?	Q: Viscount Lewisham A: Marquis of Hartington (SoS India)	HC Deb, 8 Feb 1884, Vol 284(3rd), col 300 The Times, 9 Feb 1884
Q153	When the terms for accession to the International Convention of Patents [TRE1] will be laid on the table, along with correspondence relating to it?	Q: Bernhard Samuleson A: Lord Edmond Fitzmaurice (Par Sec FO)	HC Deb, 4 Apr 1884, Vol 286(3rd), col 1649 The Times, 5 Apr 1884

(continued)

(continued)

Q154	Whether the International Patents Convention [TRE1] has been ratified; and whether the Order in Council will be published?	Q: Bernhard Samuleson A: Joseph Chamberlain (Pr BoT)	HC Deb, 23 Jun 1884, Vol 289(3rd), col 1089 The Times, 24 Jun 1884
Q155	When the Paris Convention [TRE1] will come into operation?	Q: Bernard Sameulson A: Joseph Chamberlain (Pr BoT)	HC Deb, 23 Jun 1884, Vol 289(3rd), col 1089 The Times, 24 Jun 1884
Q156	Will the government publish the law officer's opinion on telephone not infringing United Telephone Company's patent?	Q: Matthew Kenny A: Henry Fawcett (PM Gen)	HC Deb, 30 Oct 1884, Vol 293(3rd), col 530–531 The Times, 31 Oct 1884
Q157	How can the commercial interests of inventors be protected at an international exhibition?	Q: Coleridge Kennard A: Joseph Chamberlain (Pr BoT)	HC Deb, 31 Oct 1884, Vol 293(3rd), col 660 The Times, 1 Nov 1884
Q158	Whether there are any plans to improve the Patent Library due to higher demand?	Q: James Howard A: Joseph Chamberlain (Pr BoT)	HC Deb, 10 Nov 1884, Vol 293(3rd), col 1385 The Times, 11 Nov 1884
Q159	Which department is responsible for the failure to deliver the index of specifications to the Public Record Office, Four Courts Dublin; and whether it has now been supplied?	Q: Thomas Sexton A: Sir Charles Dilke (Pr B Loc Gov)	HC Deb, 14 Nov 1884, Vol 293(3rd), col 1711
Q160	Whether an index of patent specifications can be supplied to the National Library of Ireland?	Q: Joseph Biggar A: Josephy Chamberlain (Pr BoT)	HC Deb, 4 Dec 1884, Vol 294(3rd), col 642–643 The Times, 5 Dec 1884
Q161	Whether Sir James Douglas' burner had restricted licensing his patent to three firms despite giving his invention for free use?	Q: Edward King-Harman A: Joseph Chamberlain (Pr BoT)	HC Deb, 5 May 1885, Vol 297(3rd), col 1634–1635
Q162	What are the receipts from patents at the previous year end?	Q: Bernard Molloy A: Baron Henry De Worms (Par Sec BoT)	HC Deb, 6 Jul 1885, Vol 298(3rd), col 1732 The Times, 7 Jul 1885
Q163	Whether a particular patent for ensilage extends to wire-rope or flexible cord [1883 No 1970]?	Q: William Beach A: Charles Acland (Par Sec BoT)	HC Deb, 3 Jun 1886, Vol 306(3rd), col 831–832 The Times, 4 Jun 1886
Q164	Whether the government intends to take up the inquiry set up under the former government into the working of the Patent Office?	Q: William Tomlinson A: Baron Henry De Worms (Par Sec BoT)	HC Deb, 2 Sep 1886, Vol 308(3rd), col 1064 The Times, 3 Sep 1886
Q165	Whether the government will explain the cartridge contract and Lorenz's patent?	Q: Robert Hanbury A: Sir Stafford Northcote (Fin Sec to SG Ord)	HC Deb, 11 Feb 1887, Vol 310(3rd), col 1231–1233 The Times, 12 Feb 1887
Q166	Whether visitors to the Patent Museum have been curtailed since it was transferred to the Science and Art Department?	Q: Joseph Chamberlain A: Sir William Hart Dyke (VP Ed)	HC Deb, 10 Mar 1887, Vol 311(3rd), col 1722 The Times, 11 Mar 1887

Q167	Whether the published evidence accompanying the Patent Office inquiry [REP14] represents all the evidence heard?	Q: Sir John Lubbock A: Baron Henry De Worms (Par Sec BoT)	HC Deb, 5 Apr 1887, col 313(3rd), col 476 The Times, 6 Apr 1887
Q168	How many instances are there where the law officers asked for advice in non-contentious matters (which includes patent matters)?	Q: Sydney Buxton A: William Jackson (Sec Tr)	HC Deb, 5 May 1887, Vol 314(3rd), col 949
Q169	Whether the telegraph insulator now being used is the subject of a patent?	Q: Francis John Hughes-Hallett Hughes-Hallett A: Henry Raikes (PM Gen)	HC Deb, 12 May 1887, Vol 314(3rd), col 1679 The Times, 13 May 1887
Q170	Whether the Institute of Patent Agents will get a charter?	Q: Bernard Molloy A: Baron Henry De Worms (Par Sec BoT)	The Times, 13 May 1887 (12 May)
Q171	Whether the Patent Office Inquiry Committee [REP14] recommendation into simplifying specifications has been carried out? Also why has no successor to the superintendent of the indexes has been appointed?	Q: Arthur O'Connor and Robert Hanbury A: Baron Henry De Worms (Par Sec BoT)	HC Deb, 25 Aug 1887, Vol 319(3rd), col 1808–1809 The Times, 26 Aug 1887
Q172	Will patent law be reformed so as to protect innocent infringers?	Q: Sir Henry Roscoe A: Sir Michael Hicks Beach (Pr BoT)	HC Deb, 13 Apr 1888, Vol 324(3rd), col 1187–1188 The Times, 14 Apr 1888
Q173	What is the stamp duty on equitable and legal assignments of patents?	Q: No identification A: Edward Stanhope (Sec War)	The Times, 14 Apr 1888 (13 Apr)
Q174	Whether the government is aware the Inland Revenue has instructed officials to refuse registration of agreements bearing the 6d stamp and is requiring the higher stamp to be paid?	Q: Philip Stanhope A: George Goschen (Ch Ex)	HC Deb, 16 Apr 1888, Vol 324(3rd), col 1326–1327 The Times, 17 Apr 1888
Q175	Why is the Patent Office notoriously mismanaged?	Q: Arthur O'Connor A: William Smith (Ld House)	HC Deb, 17 May 1888, Vol 326(3rd), col 581
Q176	Why are Colonial Patent Specifications not sent to the United Kingdom?	Q: Sir Bernard Samelson A: Sir Michael Hicks Beach (Pr BoT)	HC Deb, 18 Jun 1888, Vol 327(3rd), col 423
Q177	Whether the Patent Bill [PUBA17] will be proceeding in this session?	Q: Anthony Mundella A: William Smith (Ld House)	HC Deb, 3 Aug 1888, Vol 329(3rd), col 1424 The Times, 4 Aug 1888
Q178	Whether there is any rule against officials taking out patents [regarding Sir Fredrick Abel]?	Q: David Thomas A: Edward Stanhope (Sec War)	HC Deb, 6 Aug 1888, Vol 329(3rd), col 1693–1694 The Times, 7 Aug 1888
Q179	Whether the Patents Bill [PUBA17] will be deferred until the next session?	Q: Cornelius Warmington A: William Smith (Ld House)	HC Deb, 8 Aug 1888, Vol 330(3rd), col 118–119
Q180	What rules relate to officials taking out patents [regarding Sir Fredrick Abel]?	Q: David Thomas A: Edward Stanhope (Sec War)	HC Deb, 10 Aug 1888, Vol 330(3rd), col 332–333 The Times, 11 Aug 1888
Q181	Whether the Patents Bill [PUBA17] will be proceeding in this session?	Q: Francis Channing A: William Smith (Ld House)	HC Deb, 15 Nov 1888. Vol 330(3rd), col 1254

(continued)

(continued)

Q182	Whether the Patents Bill [PUBA17] will be proceeding in this session?	Q: Anthony Mundella A: William Smith (Ld House)	HC Deb, 23 Nov 1888, Vol 331(3rd), col 29 The Times, 24 Nov 1888
Q183	Whether the retirement of officials from the Patent Office was in accordance with recommendation?	Q: Sir George Campbell A: William Jackson (Fin Sec Tr)	HC Deb, 7 Dec 1888, Vol 331(3rd), col 1418–1419 The Times, 8 Dec 1888
Q184	How many patents stand in the name of government officials in the new magazine rifle; and whether there is any assessment of the validity of these patents; and what has been paid to the patentees?	Q: Robert Hanbury A: Edward Stanhope (Sec War)	HC Deb, 26 Feb 1889, Vol 333(3rd), col 372 The Times, 27 Feb 1889
Q185	What rules exist to restrict members of War Office committees having an interest in inventions?	Q: Robert Hanbury A: Edward Stanhope (Sec War)	HC Deb, 6 May 1889, Vol 335(3rd), col 1237–1238 The Times, 7 May 1889
Q186	Whether the payments for the patents to improvements of the magazine rifle have been settled yet?	Q: Robert Hanbury A: Henry Campbell-Bannerman (Sec War)	HC Deb, 18 Jun 1889, Vol 337(3rd), col 192–193 The Times, 19 Jun 1889
Q187	Whether the fuses made at Woolwich and Elswick are made from Mr GF Jobson's plan?	Q: Robert Graham A: Edward Standhope (Sec War)	HC Deb, 21 Jun 1889, Vol 337(3rd), col 412–413 The Times, 22 Jun 1889
Q188	Whether railway companies can compel servants to transfer their patents to them?	Q: Henry Broadhurst A: Sir Michael Hicks Beach (Pr BoT)	HC Deb, 24 Jun 1889, Vol 337(3rd), col 531–532 The Times, 25 Jun 1889
Q189	Whether the Commissioners have reported favourably on [George] Jobson for compensation for his time fuse?	Q: Robert Graham A: Edward Standhope (Sec War)	HC Deb, 28 Jun 1889, Vol 337(3rd), col 1010 The Times, 29 Jun 1889
Q190	Whether the government will examine the claim of [George] Jobson in relation to his time fuse?	Q: Robert Graham A: Edward Standhope (Sec War)	HC Deb, 8 Jul 1889, Vol 337(3rd), col 1683
Q191	When Mayne's equipment was submitted to the equipment committee; and the date of Colonel Slade's patent [1888 No 6801]; and when Slade ceased to be a member of the committee?	Q: Robert Hanbury A: William Brodrick (Fin Sec War)	HC Deb, 19 Jul 1889, Vol 338(3rd), col 843–845 The Times, 20 Jul 1889
Q192	Who invented the new magazine rifle; and what reward has he received?	Q: Sir William Crossman A: Edward Stanhope (Sec War)	HC Deb, 28 Feb 1890, Vol 341(3rd), col 1489 The Times, 1 Mar 1890
Q193	Whether an invitation has been received for the Industrial Conference at Madrid; and who will represent the United Kingdom?	Q: Howard Vincent A: Sir Michael Hicks Beach (Pr BoT)	HC Deb, 13 Mar 1890, Vol 342(3rd), col 717 The Times, 14 Mar 1890
Q194	Whether the government will set up a Select Committee to investigate telephones, as the patents are expiring at the end of the year?	Q: Duke of Marlborough A: Lord Balfour of Burleigh (Par Sec BoT)	HL Deb, 14 Mar 1890, Vol 342(3rd), col 840–850 The Times, 15 Mar 1890

Q195	Whether payment has been made to [George] Jobson for time fuses made at Elswick Works?	Q: Robert Graham A: Edward Standhope (Sec War)	HC Deb, 28 Apr 1890, Vol 343(3rd), col 1518 The Times, 29 Apr 1890
Q196	Why certain firms cannot tender for War Office contracts (Crown use not available)?	Q: Robert Hanbury A: William Brodrick (Fin Sec War)	HC Deb, 8 May 1890, Vol 344(3rd), col 453–454 The Times, 9 May 1890
Q197	What patents are involved in the new rifles; how many are being made; and how many patents related to it are owned by government employees?	Q: Robert Hanbury A: Edward Stanhope (Sec War)	HC Deb, 16 May 1890, Vol 344(3rd), col 1115–1116
Q198	Whether it is true that the Treasury has agreed to pay Admiral [Philip] Colomb £2000?	Q: Edward Field A: Lord George Hamilton (Fir Ld Adm)	HC Deb, 4 Jul 1890, Vol 346(3rd), col 802–803 The Times, 5 Jul 1890
Q199	Whether Admiral [Philip] Colomb is obtaining any pecuniary benefit from the use of his signals system?	Q: Edward Field A: Lord Hamilton (Fir Ld Adm) A: Edward Stanhope (Sec War)	HC Deb, 11 Jul 1890, Vol 346(3rd), col 1465–1466 The Times, 12 Jul 1890
Q200	Whether consideration had been made relating to [George] Jobson's claim for his time fuse?	Q: Charles Conybeare A: Edward Stanhope (Sec War)	HC Deb, 12 Aug 1890, Vol 348(3rd), col 716
Q201	Whether the government will give operator licences to other telephone companies now the patents have expired?	Q: Charles Cameron A: Henry Raikes (PM Gen)	HC Deb, 8 Dec 1890, Vol 349(3rd), col 695 The Times, 9 Dec 1890
Q202	Can the Patent Office surplus be applied to reduce fees? [See comment: Political Notes, The Times, 9 Feb 1891 and 10 Mar 1891]	Q: John Leng A: George Goschen (Ch Ex)	HC Deb, 9 Feb 1891, Vol 350(3rd), col 199–200 The Times, 10 Feb 1891
Q203	What royalty will be paid to [Joseph] Speed in relation to the magazine rifle being adopted in India?	Q: Edward Marjoribanks A: Edward Stanhope (Sec War)	HC Deb, 10 Feb 1891, Vol 350(3rd), col 301–302 The Times, 11 Feb 1891
Q204	Why has the Patent Office failed to publish the abridgements of specifications?	Q: John Leng A: Sir Michael Hicks Beach (Pr BoT)	HC Deb, 12 Feb 1891, Vol 350(3rd), col 470 The Times, 13 Feb 1891
Q205	Why United States Patent Specifications are not sent to the United Kingdom when published?	Q: John Leng A: Archibald Stuart Wortley (US Hom Off)	HC Deb, 10 Mar 1891, Vol 351(3rd), col 588–589 The Times, 11 Mar 1891
Q206	Why is there a fee difference between the United Kingdom and the United States?	Q: Alpheus Morton and Hugh Watt A: Sir Michael Hicks Beach (Pr BoT)	HC Deb, 9 Apr 1891, Vol 352(3rd), col 124–125 The Times, 10 Apr 1891
Q207	How many appeals have there been against decisions of the Comptroller in 1890?	Q: Howard Vincent A: Sir Michael Hicks Beach (Pr BoT)	HC Deb, 28 May 1891, Vol 353(3rd), col 1179–1180 The Times, 29 May 1891
Q208	Whether the more important patents in the telephone will expire next July?	Q: Charles Cameron A: Henry Raikes (PM Gen)	HC Deb, 19 Jun 1891, Vol 354(3rd), col 895 The Times, 20 Jun 1891 (19 Jun)
Q209	Whether the Patents Department in Dublin can be made more accessible?	Q: Henry Campbell A: Dodgson Madden (A-G Ir)	HC Deb, 19 Jun 1891, Vol 354(3rd), Vol 904–905

(continued)

(continued)

Q210	Whether, considering the surplus of the Patent Office, the fees should be reduced, in particular the renewal fees for between four and eight years?	Q: John Leng A Sir Michael Hicks Beach (Pr BoT)	HC Deb, 16 Feb 1892, Vol 1(4th), col 559–560
Q211	Whether there has been a decision yet on the patents in connection with the new magazine rifle?	Q: Robert Hanbury A: Edward Stanhope (Sec War)	The Times, 2 Mar 1892 (1 Mar)
Q212	Whether the government is aware that residents of British India are at a disadvantage to other countries when applying for a British patent?	Q: John Leng A: Richard Curzon-Howe (Par Sec India)	HC Deb, 8 Mar 1892, Vol 2(4th), col 312–313 The Times, 8 Mar 1892
Q213	Whether the Chancellor has assented to the President of the Board of Trade's suggestion that renewal fees should be reduced after the eighth year?	Q: John Leng A George Goschen (Ch Ex)	HC Deb, 14 Mar 1892, Vol 2(4th), col 754–755 The Times, 15 Mar 1892
Q214	Whether the government will consider reducing the renewal fees?	Q: John Leng A George Goschen (Ch Ex)	HC Deb, 18 Mar 1892, Vol 2(4th), col 1231–1235 The Times, 19 Mar 1892
Q215	Supply: Whether the powder used is that made by Sir Frederick Abel, namely Cordite [1889 No 11,664]?	Q: Arthur Baumann A: Edward Standhope (Sec War)	HC Deb, 25 Mar 1892, Vol 2(4th), col 1864
Q216	When will the rules on the reduction of fees come into effect?	Q: John Brunner A: George Goschen (Ch Ex)	HC Deb, 11 Apr 1892, Vol 3(4th), col 1175 (Q) and 1177 (A)
Q217	Whether Cordite has been patented [1889 No 11,664] in any foreign country; and by whom?	Q: Arthur Baumann A: William Brodrick (Fin Sec War)	HC Deb, 12 Apr 1892, Vol 3(4th), col 1234 The Times, 13 Aug 1892
Q218	When was the patent on Cordite granted [1889 No 11,664]; should it be kept secret; and in what other countries has it been patented?	Q: Arthur Baumann A: William Brodrick (Fin Sec War)	HC Deb, 26 Apr 1892, Vol 3(4th), col 1388 The Times, 27 Apr 1892
Q219	How many patents have been secured by Englishmen in the United States in the last five years; and how many of those are subsequently taken out in the UK?	Q: William Summers A: Sir Michael Hicks Beach (Pr BoT)	HC Deb, 5 May 1892, Vol 4(4th), col 183 The Times, 6 May 1892
Q220	Have other smokeless powder patents been assigned to the Secretary of State other than Cordite [1889 No 11,664]?	Q: Arthur Baumann A: William Brodrick (US of War)	HC Deb, 12 May 1892, Vol 4(4th), col 710–711 The Times, 13 May 1892
Q221	How many copies of the Patent Office Journal were sold in 1891?	Q: James Elllis A: Sir Michael Hicks Beach (Pr BoT)	HC Deb, 19 May 1892, Vol 4(4th), col 1294–1295 The Times, 20 May 1892
Q222	Will the government further reduce patent fees to give same advantages as in the United States?	Debate on BoT supply Q: Alpheus Morton	HC Deb, 9 Jun 1892, Vol 5(4th) col 654 The Times, 10 Jun 1892

Q223	Whether consideration has been given to reducing the fees of persons who have already applied for a patent?	Q: Thomas Sexton A: George Goschen (Ch Ex)	HC Deb, 13 Jun 1892, Vol 5(4th), col 899 The Times, 14 Jun 1892
Q224	Whether the government will get more American specifications delivered to match the number of British specifications delivered to United States?	Q: Thomas Snape A: Anthony Mundella (Pr BoT)	HC Deb, 3 Feb 1893, Vol 8(4th), col 383 The Times, 4 Feb 1893
Q225	What rewards have been paid to inventors connected to the new magazine rifle?	Q: Robert Hanbury A: Henry Campbell-Bannerman (Sec War)	HC Deb, 7 Feb 1893, Vol 8(4th), col 666–667 The Times, 8 Feb 1893
Q226	Whether the government intends to introduce a Bill to assimilate the laws of the UK with those in the United States?	Q: Charles Schwann A: Anthony Mundella (Pr BoT)	HC Deb, 10 Feb 1893, Vol 8(4th), col 1047 The Times, 11 Feb 1893
Q227	Whether any licences granted for Cordite under the patent assigned to the War Office [1889 No 11,664]; and who assigned the patent to the government?	Q: Robert Handbury A: Henry Campbell-Bannerman (Sec War)	HC Deb, 27 Feb 1893, Vol 9(4th), col 428–429 The Times, 28 Feb 1892
Q228	What is the number of Second Division Clerks in the Civil Service (including the Patent Office)?	Q: Sir Frederick Dixon-Hartland A: Sir John Hibbert (Sec Tr)	HC Deb, 28 Feb 1893, Vol 9(4th), col 556–557 The Times, 1 Mar 1893
Q229	What patents were used in the new magazine rifle; and what rewards were paid to particular patentees?	Q: Robert Handbury A: William Woodall (Fin Sec War)	HC Deb, 28 Feb 1893, Vol 9(4th), col 560–561 The Times, 1 Mar 1893
Q230	The Court of Session declared the Patent Agent Rules 1889 invalid in *Lockwood v CIPA* (1893) 10 RPC 167; will new rules be introduced?	Q: James Parker Smith A: Anthony Mundella (Pr BoT)	HC Deb, 2 Mar 1893, Vol 9(4th), col 837–838
Q231	Whether a statement of voided patents (and agents' fees) can be included in future Comptroller-General reports?	Q: Henry Labouchère A: Anthony Mundella (Pr BoT)	HC Deb, 6 Mar 1893, Vol 9(4th), col 1084 The Times, 7 Mar 1893
Q232	Whether the War Office was given notice of the alleged infringement of Nobel's patent for Cordite? [1889 No 11,664]	Q: Thomas Cochrane A: Henry Campbell-Bannerman (Sec War)	HC Deb, 7 Mar 1893, Vol 9(4th), col 1239–1240 The Times, 8 Mar 1893
Q233	Why experimentation on Cordite has continued notwithstanding the government was aware of the patent being in dispute?	Q: Thomas Cochrane A: Henry Campbell-Bannerman (Sec War)	HC Deb, 9 Mar 1893, Vol 9(4th), col 1442
Q234	Whether any fresh volumes of the abridged specifications will be available; and will they be accurate enough for novelty examination?	Q: Charles Schwann A: Thomas Burt (Pr BoT)	HC Deb, 12 May 1893, Vol 12(4th), col 769–770
Q235	Whether the Lee Enfield is fitted with the Penn-Deeley patent [1892 No 12,324]?	Q: James Weir A: Henry Campbell-Bannerman (Sec War)	HC Deb, 19 May 1893, Vol 12(4th), col 1369 The Times, 20 May 1893

(continued)

(continued)

Q236	Whether the Stationery Office is using an American filing invention over a British one?	Q: Sir Frederick Milner A: Sir John Hibbert (Fin Sec)	HC Deb, 8 Jun 1893, Vol 13(4th), col 523–524
Q237	Why does the Comptroller-General's report not include an account of the fees paid in relation to the Patent Agents Register?	Q: James Parker Smith A: Anthony Mundella (Pr BoT)	HC Deb, 22 Jun 1893, Vol 13(4th), col 1647
Q238	What royalties have been paid on the magazine rifle?	Q: Robert Hanbury A: Henry Campbell-Bannerman (Sec War)	HC Deb, 11 Jul 1893, Vol 14(4th), col 1275–1276 The Times, 12 Jul 1883
Q239	Whether the Treasury issued a minute in 1872 relating to civil or military employees of the Crown holding patents?	Q: Robert Hanbury A: Sir John Hibbert (Tr Sec)	HC Deb, 14 Jul 1893, Vol 14(4th), col 1565 The Times, 15 Jul 1893
Q240	Whether complaints about defective illustrations in the abridgements have reached the Patent Office?	Q: Sir Bernhard Samuelson A: Anthony Mundella (Pr BoT)	HC Deb, 21 Jul 1893, Vol 15(4th), col 200 The Times, 22 Jul 1893
Q241	Whether Abel's patent [1889 No 11,664] has been assigned abroad; and other questions relating to Cordite?	Q: Robert Hanbury A: Henry Campbell-Bannerman (Sec War)	HC Deb, 17 Aug 1893, Vol 16(4th), col 429–432 The Times, 18 Aug 1893
Q242	Whether General [William Henry] Noble's widow should get an increased pension due to his EXE powder patent?	Q: Joseph Nolan A: Henry Campbell-Bannerman (Sec War)	HC Deb, 18 Aug 1893, Vol 16(4th), col 524
Q243	What inventions were sent to the Explosives Committee 1888–91; and secrecy of the Cordite patent?	Q: Robert Hanbury A: Henry Campbell-Bannerman (Sec War)	HC Deb, 21 Aug 1893, Vol 16(4th), col 633–636 The Times, 22 Aug 1893
Q244	Who were members of the Explosive Committee; and in which countries have [Frederick] Abel and [James] Dewar taken out Cordite patents?	Q: Robert Hanbury A: Henry Campbell-Bannerman (Sec War)	HC Deb, 24 Aug 1893, Vol 16(4th), col 976–978 The Times, 25 Aug 1893
Q245	Whether the Treasury in 1872 issued a Circular into Invention for the Public Service; and whether it allows officers to make decisions on products in which they have an interest?	Q: Robert Hanbury A: Henry Campbell-Bannerman (Sec War)	HC Deb, 25 Aug 1893, Vol 16(4th), col 1090–1091 The Times, 26 Aug 1893
Q246	Whether there will be a vote on the Cordite patent [1889 No 11,664]?	Q: Robert Hanbury A: Henry Campbell-Bannerman (Sec War)	HC Deb, 29 Aug 1893, Vol 16(4th), col 1361–1362 The Times, 30 Aug 1893
Q247	Whether the government recognises Davidson as the inventor of the coupling; and whether he will receive a reward?	Q: John Nolan A: William Woodall (Fin Sec War)	HC Deb, 14 Sep 1893, Vol 17(4th) col 1147 The Times, 15 Sep 1893
Q248	Whether the boilers purchased by the Royal Navy are patented?	Q: Robert Hanbury A: Sir Ughtred Kay-Shuttleworth (Fin Sec Adm)	HC Deb, 12 Dec 1893, Vol 19(4th), col 1176–1177 The Times, 13 Dec 1893
Q249	Whether drain pipes used by W Tyndale are being used by the War Office; and whether Tyndale is supervising the work?	Q: Edward Bayley A: Henry Campbell-Bannerman (Sec War)	HC Deb, 29 Dec 1893, Vol 20(4th), col 437 The Times, 30 Dec 1893

Q250	Whether it is possible to serve process in Scotland in English patent case?	Q: Robert Reid A: Sir John Rigby (S-G)	HC Deb, 2 Jan 1894, Vol 20(4th), col 646 The Times, 3 Jan 1894
Q251	What is the total value of fees forfeited between 1852 and 1893 arising from the refusal of applications and voiding of patents for non-payment of renewal fees; what was the number of applications refused; and the total reaching full term?	Q: Alpheus Morton A: Anthony Mundella (Pr BoT)	HC Deb, 12 Apr 1894, Vol 23(4th), col 195–196 The Times, 13 Apr 1894
Q252	What was the total amount of fees on patents which were voided for non-payment of renewal fees between 1852 and 1893; what are the aggregate surplus income and balance of account?	Q Alpheus Morton A: Anthony Mundella (Pr BoT)	HC Deb, 19 Apr 1894, Vol 23(4th), col 832 The Times, 20 Apr 1894
Q253	What fees would have accrued to the Patent Office in respect of the patents voided from 1852 to 1893 if renewal fees had been paid to the end of the term?	Q: Alpheus Morton A: Thomas Burt (Par Sec BoT)	HC Deb, 26 Apr 1894, Vol 23(4th), col 1426–1427
Q254	Whether the government is aware that British patents on potassium cyanide in Transvaal will be undermined by a government monopoly on the same?	Q: George Bartley A: Sydney Buxton (US Col)	HC Deb, 25 Jun 1894, Vol 26(4th), col 125
Q255	How many newspapers, within the statutory definition, does the government publish (including Patents Journal)?	Q: Thomas Gibson Bowles A: Sir John Hibbert (Fin Sec Tr)	HC Deb, 24 Jul 1894, Vol 27(4th), col 795–796 The Times, 25 Jul 1894
Q256	Whether new rules will be made regarding patent agents and fees following the recommendation of the Select Committee [REP15]?	Q: Howard Vincent A: James Bryce (Pr BoT)	HC Deb, 23 Aug 1894, Vol 29(4th), col 382
Q257	What does the government intend to do with the report of the Select Committee of the last session into the Patent Agents Bill [REP15]?	Q: Thomas Bolton A: James Bryce (Pr BoT)	HC Deb, 22 Feb 1895, Vol 30(4th), col 1421–1422
Q258	Whether the government is aware that the specification for an antitoxin was accepted from Germany; and whether it would affect the production of a serum here?	Q: Robert Farquhasrson A: James Bryce (Pr BoT)	HC Deb, 4 Mar 1895, Vol 31(4th), col 285–286 The Times, 5 Mar 1895
Q259	Whether there are abstract indexes of patents to consult in London, Manchester, Leeds, Glasgow or Dublin; and whether the government is aware the average life time of a patent is about four years?	Q: Alpheus Morton Q: John Burns A: James Bryce (Pr BoT)	HC Deb, 25 Apr 1895, Vol 32(4th), c 1618–1619 The Times, 26 Apr 1895
Q260	When is the name of the patent agent substituted for that of the inventor; when is the patent published in the journal; and has this affected oppositions?	Q: Sir John Leng A: Charles Ritchie (Pr BoT)	HC Deb, 20 Apr 1896, Vol 39(4th), col 1239–1240 The Times, 21 Apr 1896

(continued)

(continued)

Q261	Whether there should be novelty examination (following comment of Kay LJ) in *Savage v Harris* (1896) 13 RPC 354 at 371?	Q: Sir John Leng A: Charles Ritchie (Pr BoT)	HC Deb, 7 May 1896, Vol 40(4th), col 730–731 The Times, 8 May 1896
Q262	What payments have been made in relation to Belleville boilers (Royal Navy), including patent fees?	Q: William Allan A: William Macartney (Fin Sec Adm)	HC Deb, 26 Jan 1897, Vol 45(4th), col 513 The Times, 27 Jan 1897
Q263	Whether this country is the only country not to require home manufacturing of patented articles?	Q: William O'Malley A: Charles Ritchie (Pr BoT)	HC Deb, 1 Feb 1897, Vol 45(4th), col 914 The Times, 2 Feb 1897
Q264	Whether the Patent Office accounts can be published to determine the surplus under each type of right?	Q: Sir John Leng A: Charles Ritchie (Pr BoT)	HC Deb, 8 Feb 1897, Vol 46(4th), col 6
Q265	What remedies are there for non-working of patents in the United Kingdom; are they any moves towards harmonising patent laws?	Q: Arthur Phillpotts A: Charles Ritchie (Pr BoT)	HC Deb, 11 Feb 1897, Vol 46(4th), col 163–164 The Times, 12 Feb 1897
Q266	Whether a Select Committee should be appointed to consider reforming s 22 of the 1883 Act [PUBA14]?	Q: Charles Schwann A: Charles Ritchie (Pr BoT)	HC Deb, 26 Feb 1897, Vol 46(4th), col 1262–1263
Q267	What is the basis on which the Admiralty orders goods; and does it give preference to domestic manufacturers?	Q: Howard Vincent A: William Macartney (Par Sec Adm)	HC Deb, 1 Mar 1897, Vol 46(4th), col 1324–1325 The Times, 2 Mar 1897
Q268	Will the government withdraw the Patent Office Extension Act [PUBA18] until after the financial relations between Ireland and the Great Britain Commission are reported?	Q: Patrick O'Brien A: Arthur Balfour (PM)	HC Deb, 2 Apr 1897, Vol 48(4th), col 412
Q269	Whether royalties are still being paid on the Maxim machine gun?	Q: Edward Cardwell A: Joseph Powell-Williams (Fin Sec War)	HC Deb, 1 Jul 1897, Vol 50(4th), col 860–861 The Times, 2 Jul 1897
Q270	Whether the government is aware that people are deterred from applying under s 22 of the 1883 Act [PUBA14] due to its vagueness?	Q: Frederick Cawley A: Robert Hanbury (for Charles Ritchie (Pr BoT))	HC Deb, 2 Jul 1897, Vol 50(4th), col 954–955 The Times, 3 July 1897
Q271	Whether the Post Office has ever paid to use patents?	Q: Andrew Provand A: Robert Hanbury (Fin Sec Tr)	The Times, 10 Jul 1897 (9 Jul)
Q272	Whether Boulton's patent wood-block wheels are being used (said to be gratuitous advertisement of the invention)?	Q: Arthur Griffith-Boscawen A: Henry Chaplin (Pr Loc Gov B) Comment: Walter Hazell	HC Deb, 26 Jul 1897, Vol 51(4th), col 1065–1066
Q273	Whether the recommendations of the Select Committee on the 1894 Patent Agents Bill [REP15] have been carried out yet; in particular the transfer of functions from the Institute to the Board of Trade?	Q: William Smith A: Charles Ritchie (Pr BoT)	HC Deb, 4 Mar 1898, Vol 54(4th), col 601

Q274	Whether the Register of Patent Agents Rules 1889 has been repealed since 1890?	Q: Frederick Platt-Higgins A: Charles Ritchie (Pr BoT)	HC Deb, 10 Mar 1898, Vol 54(4th) col 1216
Q275	Whether the government will publish further accounts of the Chartered Institute of Patent Attorneys?	Q: Alban Gibbs A: Charles Ritchie (Pr BoT)	HC Deb, 14 Mar 1898, Vol 54(4th), col 1531
Q276	Whether consideration has been given to removing patent agents from the register when they do not pay the fees?	Q: Sir Howard Vincent A: Charles Ritchie (Pr BoT)	HC Deb, 17 Mar 1898, Vol 55(4th) col 92–93
Q277	Whether the referee in *Levinstein v Earbeverke* has given his decision yet under s 22 of the Patents Act 1883 [PUBA14]?	Q: Frederick Cawley A: Charles Ritchie (Pr BoT)	HC Deb, 29 Mar 1898, Vol 55(4th), col 1226
Q278	If the referee in *Levinstein v Earbeverke* finds for the petitioners, will the defendant be able to appeal to a higher court before the compulsory licence can be granted?	Q: Fredrick Cawley A: Charles Ritchie (Pr BoT)	HC Deb, 29 Mar 1898, Vol 55(4th), col 1649
Q279	Whether the decision of the referee in *Levinstein v Meister, Lucias and Bruing* (1898) 15 RPC 732 can be appealed twice before the compulsory licence is granted?	Q: Frederick Cawley A: Charles Ritchie (Pr BoT)	HC Deb, 1 Apr 1898, Vol 55(4th), col 1649
Q280	How much money had been paid under the Register of Patents Agents Rules; and who has control of the fund?	Q: Llewellyn Atherley-Jones A: Charles Ritchie (Pr BoT)	HC Deb, 5 Apr 1898, Vol 56(4th), col 221
Q281	What authority has the President of the Board of Trade to revive repealed patent rules?	Q: Frederick Platt-Higgins A: Charles Ritchie (Pr BoT)	HC Deb, 2 May 1898, Vol 57(4th), col 13–14 The Times, 3 May 1898
Q282	Why the decision of the referee in *Levinstein v Earbeverke* has not been given when promised on 29 Mar 1898?	Q: Fredrick Cawley A: Charles Ritchie (Pr BoT)	HC Deb, 3 May 1898, Vol 57(4th), col 173
Q283	What proportion of specifications have drawings compared to those without for the year 1896?	Q: Alfred Billsom A: Charles Ritchie (Pr BoT)	HC Deb, 10 May 1898, Vol 57(4th), col 838
Q284	Whether the government will use the Patent Office surplus to introduce a novelty examination?	Q: Sir John Leng A: Charles Ritchie (Pr BoT)	HC Deb, 13 Jun 1898, Vol 59(4th), col 33–34 The Times, 14 Jun 1898
Q285	Whether the government has considered the report of the referee into the matter of *Levinstein v Earbeverke* and others regarding foreigners obtaining patents in England and not working them?	Q: Arthur Phillpotts A: Charles Ritchie (Pr BoT)	HC Deb, 14 Jun 1898, Vol 59(4th), col 213–214
Q286	Whether the government has reached a conclusion on the report in *Levinstein v Earbeverke*; whether the government will pay the petitioners' expenses as a test case; and whether the law will be amended?	Q: Fredrick Cawley A: Charles Ritchie (Pr BoT)	HC Deb, 8 Jul 1898, Vol 61(4th), col 325

(continued)

(continued)

Q287	Whether a patent expiring in the USA, France or Germany automatically expires in the other two countries (but not the UK)?	Q: Fredrick Cawley A: Charles Ritchie (Pr BoT)	HC Deb, 14 Feb 1899, Vol 66(4th), col 854;
Q288	Whether patents, designs and trade marks rules can be included in the Parliamentary papers?	Q: Sir John Leng A: Charles Ritchie (Pr BoT)	HC Deb, 16 Feb 1899, Vol 66(4th), col 1080
Q289	Whether the government will introduce a Bill framed on the Patent Agents Registration Bill 1894 as amended in Select Committee [PUBB43]?	Q: Alban Gibbs A: Charles Ritchie (Pr BoT)	HC Deb, 27 Feb 1899, Vol 67(4th), col 598–599
Q290	Whether Belleville boilers are protected in England by a patent; and whether any payments are being made to France for use of these boilers?	Q: William Field A: George Goschen (Fir Ld Adm)	HC Deb, 2 Mar 1899, Vol 67(4th), col 1044
Q291	What are the terms of patents of addition in Germany and the differences from the approach in the United Kingdom; and what happens about the termination of a patent when the original expires in France and Germany?	Q: Fredrick Cawley A: Charles Ritchie (Pr BoT)	HC Deb, 7 Mar 1899, Vol 68(4th), col 17–18 The Times, 8 Mar 1899
Q292	Whether government buildings, including the Patent Office, will be fireproofed?	Q: Sir John Leng A: Aretas Akers-Douglass (Fir Com Works)	HC Deb, 13 Apr 1899, Vol 69(4th), col 968 The Times, 14 Apr 1899
Q293	Whether the government is aware that the British Commission has refused space to British manufacturers at the Paris Exhibition?	Q: Robert Ashcroft A: Charles Ritchie (Pr BoT)	HC Deb, 16 May 1899, Vol 71(4th), col 737 The Times, 17 May 1899
Q294	Whether the surplus of £95,000 is being spent on new buildings; and what is the status of the surplus now fees are reduced?	Q: Sir John Leng A: Walter Long (Pr BoAgric)	HC Deb, 26 Jun 1899, Vol 73(4th), col 590 The Times, 27 Jun 1899 Vote: HC Deb, 12 May 1899, Vol 71(4th), col 546
Q295	Whether patents granted to British subjects, in relation to carbide of calcium, in the Transvaal are being used by others without permission?	Q: Timothy Healy A: Joseph Chamberlain (SoS Colonial Office)	HC Deb, 27 Jul 1899, Vol 75(4th), col 495–496 The Times, 28 Jul 1899
Q296	Whether the committee will consider novelty examination; whether any amendment is contemplated; and when will the report be presented?	Q: Sir John Leng A: Charles Ritchie (Pr BoT)	HC Deb, 20 Feb 1900, Vol 79(4th), col 579
Q297	Whether inventions submitted to the War Office go before a departmental committee; and what steps are taken to stop piracy of inventions?	Q: James Weir A: George Wyndham (Par Sec War)	HC Deb, 23 Feb 1900, Vol 79(4th), col 925–926 The Times, 24 Feb 1900
Q298	Whether a departmental committee has been appointed to inquire into the facilities granted to inventors under patent laws; and its terms of reference and whether it will inquire into compulsory licences?	Q: Fredrick Cawley A: Charles Ritchie (Pr BoT)	HC Deb, 27 Feb 1900, Vol 79(4th), col 1216–1217

Q299	Whether the government is aware that the Armstrong gun patent used principles from the earlier patent of Captain [Theophilus] Blakely; so place Mrs Blakely on civil list?	Q: James Weir A: Arthur Balfour (Fir Ld Tr)	HC Deb, 6 Mar 1900, Vol 80(4th), col 204 The Times, 7 Mar 1900
Q300	Whether Dr [Arthur] Conan Doyle's invention of a high angle rifle would be investigated by the War Office?	Q: Radcliffe Cooke A: Joseph Powell Williams (US War)	HC Deb, 9 Mar 1900, Vol 80(4th), col 483 The Times, 10 Mar 1900
Q301	Whether the Patents Act 1859 [PUBA9] should be repealed because of Captain [Theophilus] Blakely and the failure to get a reward?	Q: James Weir A: Arthur Balfour (Fir Ld Tr)	HC Deb, 2 Apr 1900, Vol 81(4th), col 941 The Times, 3 Apr 1900
Q302	Whether the widow of Captain [Theophilus] Blakely can have the patent back after it was declared secret under the Patents Act 1859 [PUBA9]?	Q: James Weir A: George Wyndham (Par Sec War)	HC Deb, 11 May 1900, Vol 82(4th), col 1366–1367
Q303	Whether British patent rights extend to the Transvaal and the Orange River Colony?	Q: Sir John Brunner A Joseph Chamberlain (SoS Col)	HC Deb, 26 Feb 1901, Vol 89(4th), col 1179 The Times, 27 Feb 1901
Q304	Whether mines are recognising the validity of [Hutton] Hepplewaite's pit prop patent?	Q: Arthur Markham A: Charles Ritchie (Hom Sec)	HC Deb, 26 Feb 1901, Vol 89(4th), col 1195–1196
Q305	Whether and where the patent rules can be purchased in Ireland?	Q: John Mooney A: Gerald Balfour (Pr BoT)	HC Deb, 11 Mar 1901, Vol 90(4th), col 1176
Q306	When will the Committee of Patent Law's report be published [REP17]?	Q: Fredrick Cawley A: Gerald Balfour (Pr BoT)	HC Deb, 12 Mar 1901, Vol 90(4th), col 1346
Q307	What steps have been taken to give effect to the recommendation of the Departmental Committee on the Patents Act [REP17]?	Q: Sir John Leng A: Gerald Balfour (Pr BoT)	HC Deb, 22 Mar 1901, Vol 91(4th), col 853–854 The Times, 23 Mar 1901
Q308	Whether the papers relating to the International Union for the Protection of Industrial Property held in Brussels in 1900 will be printed [TRE18]?	Q: Charles Stuart-Wortley A: Gerald Balfour (Pr BoT)	HC Deb, 22 Mar 1901, Vol 91(4th), col 854
Q309	Whether the government is aware that a gift of United States patent specifications had to be declined?	Q: John Boland A: George Wyndham (Ch Sec Ir)	HC Deb, 26 Mar 1901, Vol 91(4th), col 1373–1374
Q310	Whether examination as to novelty of patent applications should be introduced?	Q: Herbert Lewis A: Gerald Balfour (Pr BoT)	HC Deb, 28 Mar 1901, Vol 92(4th), col 65 The Times, 29 Mar 1901
Q311	Why trustees of the library are unable to find space for a free gift of United States patent specifications?	Q: John Boland A: George Wyndham (Ch Sec Ir)	HC Deb, 2 Apr 1901, Vol 92(4th), col 484–485
Q312	Whether members of the Rayleigh Committee have taken out patents related to explosives?	Q: William Redmond A: William Brodrick (Sec War)	HC Deb, 22 Apr 1901, Vol 92(4th), col 905–906 The Times, 23 Aug 1901

(continued)

(continued)

Q313	Whether the government will introduce legislation to give effect to the Departmental Committee Report on Patent Law [REP17]?	Q: Herbert Lewis A: Arthur Balfour (PM)	HC Deb, 14 May 1901, Vol 94(4th), col 63 The Times, 15 May 1901
Q314	Whether the National Library of Ireland could have more space for a gift of United States patent specifications?	Q: John Boland A: George Wyndham (Ch Sec Ir)	HC Deb, 13 Jun 1901, Vol 95(4th), col 287–288
Q315	Whether the government is aware that patents and inventions will be placed under one administration in Australia; and whether the law and regulations could be co-ordinated to create an Empire patent?	Q: Sir John Leng A: Gerald Balfour (Pr BoT)	HC Deb, 5 July 1901, Vol 96(4th), col 987–988 The Times, 6 Jul 1901
Q316	Whether the governments is aware of [Charles] Mackintosh's Patent (1895 No 524,622), which is to prevent injuries to stokers; will experiments be made of this invention?	Q: James Majendie A: Hugh Arnold-Forster (Sec Adm)	HC Deb, 6 Aug 1901, Vol 98(4th), col 1413
Q317	Whether the government will amend patent law to assimilate British law to that in France and Germany?	Q: Joseph Lawrence A: Gerald Balfour (Pr BoT)	HC Deb, 15 Aug 1901, Vol 99(4th), col 914–915 The Times, 16 Aug 1901
Q318	What steps are being taken to give effect to recommendations of the Fry Committee [REP17]?	Q: Sir John Leng A: Gerald Balfour (Pr BoT)	HC Deb, 21 Jan 1902, Vol 101(4th), col 461 The Times, 22 Jan 1902
Q319	Whether the Solicitor-Genera's minority report to the Fry Committee will be printed [REP17]?	Q: Joseph Lawrence A: Gerald Balfour (Pr BoT)	HC Deb, 11 Mar 1902, Vol 104(4th), col 1015 The Times, 13 Mar 1901
Q320	Whether the government will take steps to compel local working of patents, to follow Continental countries?	Q: Jospeh Lawrence A: Gerald Balfour (Pr BoT)	HC Deb, 13 Mar 1902, Vol 104(4th), col 1271–1272
Q321	How many writs have been issued by the Welsbach Incandescent Light Company relating to allegations of its patent [1893 No 124] being infringed?	Q: James Weir A: Sir Robert Finlay (A-G)	HC Deb, 13 Mar 1902, Vol 104(4th), col 1277
Q322	How many persons have been committed to prison in connection with sale or use of Welsbach Incandescent Light Company's patent [1893 No 124]?	Q: James Weir A: Charles Ritchie (Hom Sec)	HC Deb, 21 Mar 1902, Vol 105(4th), col 718
Q323	Has the Post Office considered whether it has been subsidising the Marconi patent if it turns out that the Lodge patent is the master patent?	Q: Thomas Gibson Bowles A: Austen Chamberlain (PM Gen)	HC Deb, 18 Apr 1902, Vol 106(4th), col 701–702 The Times, 19 Apr 1902 (18 Apr)
Q324	As there is a surplus of £107,000, can patent fees be reduced?	Q: Sir John Leng A: Gerald Balfour (Pr BoT)	HC Deb, 9 Jun 1902, Vol 109(4th), col 95–96 The Times, 10 Jun 1902

Q325	Whether there will be any progress on the Patents Bill this session?	Q: John Denny A: Not identified	HC Deb, 17 Jun 1902, Vol 109(4th), col 832
Q326	How do the fees payable by an inventor taking out a patent in Great Britain and Ireland compare with the United States?	Q: Lord Charles Beresford A: Gerald Balfour (Pr BoT)	HC Deb, 31 Jul 1902, Vol 112(4th), col 274
Q327	Whether a return will be provided showing official fees paid for patents in the colonies and dependencies?	Q: Richard Rigg A: Gerald Balfour (Pr BoT)	HC Deb, 11 Nov 1902, Vol 114(4th), col 586–587
Q328	When does the government propose to bring the provisions of the 1902 Act [PUBA20] into force?	Q: Sir Alfred Hickman A: Gerald Balfour (Pr BoT)	HC Deb, 7 May 1903, Vol 122(4th), col 18–19 The Times, 8 May 1903
Q329	What was the average surplus of the Patent Office over the previous ten years?	Q: William Field A: Victor Cavendish (Fin Sec Tr)	HC Deb, 24 Feb 1904, Vol 130(4th), col 835–836
Q330	How many petitions have been presented under s 3(1) and (5) of the Patents Act 1902 [PUBA20]?	Q: John Denny A: Gerald Balfour (Pr BoT)	HC Deb, 25 Feb 1904, Vol 130(4th), col 968
Q331	What is the number of Civil Service clerks, including at the Patent Office?	Q: James Yoxall A: Victor Cavendish (Fin Sec Tr)	HC Deb, 15 Mar 1904, Vol 131(4th), col 1124–1125
Q332	What arrangements are being made for wireless telegraphic apparatus to be installed in lightships?	Q: John Heaton A: Gerald Balfour (Pr BoT)	HC Deb, 17 Mar 1904, Vol 131(4th), col 1383 The Times, 18 Mar 1904
Q333	How many patents currently in force have been granted to foreigners?	Q: Sir John Leng A: Gerald Balfour (Pr BoT)	HC Deb, 18 Apr 1904, Vol 133(4th), col 377–378
Q334	Whether the government is willing to consider the formation of a branch of the Patent Office in Ireland?	Q: William Field A: Gerald Balfour (Pr BoT)	HC Deb, 26 Apr 1904, Vol 133(4th), col 1178
Q335	Whether the subjects to be referred to the Committee on the Income-tax will include the collection of the tax in Scotland [inquiry included patent taxation]?	Q: John Ainsworth A: Austen Chamberlain (Ch Ex)	HC Deb, 28 Apr 1904, Vol 133(4th), col 1443–1444 The Times, 29 Apr 1904
Q336	How many compulsory licences have been obtained under the Patents Act?	Q: Sir John Leng A: Gerald Balfour (Pr BoT)	HC Deb, 3 May 1904, Vol 134(4th), col 241
Q337	Whether the use of the Bryant and May patent to make matches avoids phosphorus poisoning?	Q: William Crooks A: Aretas Akers-Douglas (Hom Sec)	HC Deb, 8 Jun 1904, Vol 135(4th), col 1065–1066
Q338	Why are the railway companies precluding the use of patented carriages for carrying cattle?	Q: William Field A: Gerald Balfour (Pr BoT)	HC Deb, 14 Jun 1904, Vol 136(4th), col 19–20
Q339	What is the value of the contracts given to British and foreign firms in relation to the London telephone service?	Q: Sir Thomas Dewar A: Lord Stanley (Fin Sec Tr)	HC Deb, 30 Jul 1904, Vol 139(4th), col 81–82 The Times, 1 Aug 1904
Q340	Whether there will be an opportunity to discuss the Patent Rules before the expiry of the 40–day period of annulment?	Q: Sir Howard Vincent A: Mr Bonar Law (Sec BoT)	HC Deb, 27 Mar 1905, Vol 143(4th), col 1175

(continued)

(continued)

Q341	Has permission been given for private companies to use government patents for the rifle?	Q: Sir Edgar Vincent A: Hugh Arnold-Forster (Sec War)	HC Deb, 3 Apr 1905, Vol 144(4th), col 117
Q342	Whether nitrogen bacteria will be freely distributed in the UK as they have been in the USA by the patentee (the United States government)?	Q: Sir Walter Palmer A: Ailwys Fellowes (Pr BoAgric)	HC Deb, 5 Apr 1905, Vol 144(4th), col 461–462 The Times, 6 Apr 1905
Q343	Why the Post Office, having experimented on electrical condensers, has only obtained seven patents, and why have there have been payments to foreign patentees?	Q: William Steadman A: Sydney Buxton (PM Gen)	HC Deb, 30 Apr 1906, Vol 156(4th), col 215
Q344	Whether the government is aware of the practice of inventors designating their agent's place of business as their own and how it might be misleading?	Q: James White A: Hudson Kearley (Sec BoT)	HC Deb, 24 May 1906, Vol 157(4th), col 1420
Q345	Whether the government will qualify the statement in the annual report of the Patent Office regarding the availability of abridgements and the effect on invalidating patents?	Q: James White A: David Lloyd-George (Pr BoT)	HC Deb, 21 Jun 1906, Vol 159(4th), col 368
Q346	How many patent agents have been registered; and how many struck off the register?	Q: James White A: Sir Rudolph Hudson Kearley (Sec BoT)	HC Deb, 11 Jul 1906, Vol 160(4th), col 860
Q347	How many British patents prolonged beyond 14 years are still in force; and the details thereof?	Q: Dymoke White A: Sir Rudolph Hudson Kearley (Par Sec BoT)	HC Deb, 28 Feb 1907, Vol 170(4th), col 221
Q348	What are the legal provisions in Germany as to revoking patents which are not worked in Germany?	Q: Dymoke White A: Sir Rudolph Hudson Kearley (Par Sec BoT)	HC Deb, 28 Feb 1907, Vol 170(4th), col 221–222
Q349	Whether the government is aware of a patent for non-poisonous matches; and whether the law will be changed to outlaw yellow phosphorus? [See PUBA49]	Q: Arthur Henderson A: Herbert Gladstone (Hom Sec)	HC Deb, 4 Mar 1907, Vol 170(4th), col 474–475
Q350	Whether there has been a test of C Beatt's patent trenching tool; and what was the result?	Q: Alexander Wilkie A: Richard Haldane (SoS War)	HC Deb, 11 Mar 1907, Vol 170(4th), col 1211–1121
Q351	Will the Patent Law Amendment Bill be introduced before Easter; will it protect British industry from foreign industry?	Q: Edward Carlile and William Mitchell-Thomson A: Hudson Kearley (Par Sec BoT)	HC Deb, 14 Mar 1907, Vol 171(4th), col 237 The Times, 15 Mar 1907
Q352	Whether the government will publish a memorandum on the Patents Bill showing its effect on existing legislation [PUBA22]?	Q: Lord Robert Cecil A: David Lloyd-Geroge (Pr BoT)	HC Deb, 15 Apr 1907, Vol 172(4th), col 602–603
Q353	What is the effect of Cl 10 of the 1907 Bill [PUBA22], and is it at variance with any treaty?	Q: Sir Alfred Mond A: David Lloyd-Geroge (Pr BoT)	HC Deb, 18 Apr 1907, Vol 172(4th), col 1154–1155

Q354	Whether the Patents and Designs (Consolidation) Bill [PUBA23] will affect the Patents and Designs (Amendment) Bill [PUBA22]?	Q: Samuel Roberts A: David Lloyd Geroge (Pr BoT)	HC Deb, 4 Jun 1907, Vol 175(4th), col 474
Q355	How many patents are in force; and how many have been prolonged?	Q: James White A: David Lloyd-George (Pr BoT)	HC Deb, 18 Jun 1907, Vol 176(4th), col 300–301
Q356	Whether a stamp office can be included in the new Patent Office building to allow for revenue stamping on site?	Q: George Croydon Marks A: David Lloyd-George (Pr BoT)	HC Deb, 1 Jul 1907, Vol 177(4th), col 333–334
Q357	Whether a contract has been awarded for the Reports of Patent Cases and Illustrated Journal?	Q: Edward Pickersgill A: Hudson Kearley (Par Sec BoT)	HC Deb, 8 Jul 1907, Vol 177(4th), col 1162
Q358	Whether a contract has been entered in relation to the printing of the Journal and the Reports of Patent Cases?	Q: Edward Pickersgill A: Hudson Kearley (Par Sec BoT)	HC Deb, 18 Jul 1907, Vol 177(4th), col 1162
Q359	How many patent appeals are presently waiting to be heard; what is the longest pending appeal; and what is the reason for delay?	Q: Harry Liddell A: Sir John Walter (A-G)	HC Deb, 31 Jul 1907, Vol 179(4th), col 961–962 The Times, 1 Aug 1907; Correction: The Times, 2 Aug 1907
Q360	Whether the government is aware that the Patent Office runs at a profit of 100% over the cost of maintenance; and whether the cost of the 17–year term in other countries is less than that for 14 years in the United Kingdom?	Q: George Barnes A: David Lloyd-George (Ch Ex)	HC Deb, 15 Aug 1907, Vol 180(4th), col 1603–1604
Q361	Whether the government is aware that the Patent Office runs at a profit of 100% over the cost of maintenance; and whether the 17–year term in other countries is less than that for 14 years in the United Kingdom; and whether the fees can be reduced?	Q: George Barnes A: David Lloyd-George (Ch Ex)	HC Deb, 16 Aug 1907, Vol 180(4th), col 1818–1819
Q362	What effect has the Patents and Designs Act 1907 [PUBA23] had on the manufacture of patented articles in the United Kingdom (which were formerly made abroad)?	Q: Sir Horatio Parker A: David Lloyd-George (Ch Ex)	HC Deb, 10 Feb 1908, Vol 183(4th), col 1417–1418
Q363	Whether employees transferred from the London Patent Office to the Manchester Branch will get compensation for losses from the transfer?	Q: Richard Essex A: David Lloyd-George (Ch Ex)	HC Deb, 17 Feb 1908, Vol 184(4th), col 411
Q364	Have any representations be made by Germany or any other foreign country regarding the new Patents and Designs Act 1907 [PUBA23]?	Q: George Haddock A Hudson Kearley (Par Sec BoT)	HC Deb, 31 Mar 1908, Vol 187(4th), col 318 The Times, 1 Aug 1908

(continued)

(continued)

Q365	Why is the cost of the Patent Office extension so great; and why has there been a reduction in its budget?	Q: Frederick Banbury A: Lewis Harcourt (Com Works)	HC Deb, 2 Apr 1908, Vol 187(4th), col 753, 754
Q366	Whether British inventors will be liable to have patents revoked where they are only worked outside the United Kingdom if British producers have only offered unreasonable licences?	Q: John Rees A: Winston Churchill (Pr BoT)	HC Deb, 20 May 1908, Vol 189(4th), col 269
Q367	Whether the government is aware of a new process of making salt; and should the government acquire such a patent when it will lead to unemployment in the industry?	Q: Fredrick Jowett A: Winston Churchill (Pr BoT)	HC Deb, 16 Jun 1908, Vol 190(4th), col 716–717 The Times, 17 Aug 1908
Q368	Whether representations have been received from the United States regarding the effect of the Patents and Designs Act 1907 [PUBA23] on American manufacturers?	Q: Edward Goulding A: Winston Churchill (Pr BoT)	HC Deb, 18 Jun 1908, Vol 190(4th), col 1007–1008
Q369	What reply has been made to the government as to the effect of the Patents and Designs Act 1907 [PUBA23] on German manufacturers?	Q: William Mitchell-Thomson A: Winston Churchill (Pr BoT)	HC Deb, 18 Jun 1908, Vol 190(4th), col 1038–1039
Q370	Whether there can be reciprocal protection for Canadian patents?	Q: William Joynson-Hicks A: Winston Churchill (Pr BoT)	HC Deb, 18 Jun 1908, Vol 190(4th), col 1042–1043
Q371	Whether the government has had representations to extend the one-year period in which foreign patentees have to work the invention in the United Kingdom under s 27 of the Patents and Designs Act 1907 [PUBA23]?	Q: Timothy Davies A: Winston Churchill (Pr BoT)	HC Deb, 1 Jul 1908, Vol 191(4th), col 763–764
Q372	Whether the government has had representations to extend the one-year period in which foreign patentees have to work the invention in the United Kingdom under s 27 of the Patents and Designs Act 1907 [PUBA23]?	Q: John Rees A: Winston Churchill (Pr BoT)	HC Deb, 2 Jul 1908, Vol 191(4th), col 965 The Times, 3 Jul 1908
Q373	Whether a paper will be issued regarding the representations to the government regarding the working of the Patents and Designs Act 1907 [PUBA23]?	Q: Sir Berkely Sheffield A: Winston Churchill (Pr BoT)	HC Deb, 13 Jul 1908, Vol 192(4th), col 406–407
Q374	What declaration has been made by the government to foreign governments regarding the working of s 27 of the Patents and Designs Act 1907 [PUBA23]?	Q: John Lonsdale A: Joseph Pease (Ch Whip)	HC Deb, 20 Jul 1908, Vol 192(4th), col 1483
Q375	Will the Foreign Office instruct British consuls and agents abroad to bring to notice of foreign patent holders the advantages of working in Ireland?	Q: Joseph Devlin A: Sir Edward Grey (For Sec)	HC Deb, 23 Jul 1908, Vol 193(4th), col 303

Q376	Whether the government is intending to waive compulsory working requirements where there is a good reason for the delay in working locally?	Q: George Croydon Marks A: Winston Churchill (Pr BoT)	HC Deb, 30 Jul 1908, Vol 193(4th), col 1695
Q377	What is the number of foreign patentees registered in England who are likely to work the invention in Britain by reason of the Patents and Designs Act 1907 [PUBA23]?	Q: Thomas Sloan A: Winston Chuchill (Pr BoT)	HC Deb, 26 Oct 1908, Vol 194(4th), col 1587
Q378	How many towns in the United Kingdom have had new industries established by reason of the recent Patents Act [PUBA23]?	Q: Thomas Sloan A: Winston Churchill (Pr BoT)	HC Deb, 28 Oct 1908, Vol 195(4th), col 247
Q379	Whether enquiries had been made into the merits of Dr [James] Churchward's steel and armour process?	Q: George Bowles A: Reginald McKenna (Pr BoEd)	HC Deb, 2 Nov 1908, Vol 195(4th), col 749–750
Q380	What measures will be taken to encourage foreign manufacturers to work their inventions in the British Isles and in Ireland?	Q: Laurence Ginnell A: Sir Thomas Russell (Dept Ag Ir)	HC Deb, 3 Nov 1908, Vol 195(4th), col 951–952
Q381	Whether the invention of Julius Bielefeld of nosebags [1898 No 18,593] has been used by the government without compensation?	Q: Sir William Bull A: Richard Haldane (Sec War)	HC Deb, 16 Nov 1908, Vol 196(4th), col 849–850
Q382	What is the treatment of patent royalties under the Finance Act 1907 [PUBA48]?	Q: Sir Henry Kimber A: David Lloyd-George (Ch Ex)	HC Deb, 25 Nov 1908, Vol 197(4th), col 392 The Times, 26 Nov 1908
Q383	Whether the War Office has tested Martin Hale's rifle-propelled shrapnel grenade [1906 No 14,605]?	Q: George Courthope A: Richard Haldane (Sec War)	HC Deb, 10 Dec 1908, Vol 198(4th), col 725
Q384	Whether the Comptroller should introduce scaled costs (as costs too high)?	Q: Thomas Arnold Herbert A: Winston Churchill (Pr BoT)	HC Deb, 23 Feb 1909, Vol 1(5th), col 575
Q385	Whether the government is aware that Captain [John Duncan] Fulton's sight finder [1906 No 14,903] is being supplied to the artillery of a foreign government?	Q: George Faber A: Richard Haldane (Sec War)	HC Deb, 24 Feb 1909, Vol 1(5th), col 854
Q386	How many factories have been attracted to Ireland by reason of the Patents and Designs Act 1907 [PUBA23]?	Q: Joseph Devlin A: Thomas Russell (VP Agric)	HC Deb, 1 Mar 1909, Vol 1(5th), col 1243W
Q387	How many patents have been revoked for non-working in the United Kingdom (under the Patents and Designs Act 1907 [PUBA23], s 27)?	Q: Sir William Bull A: Winston Churchill (Pr BoT)	HC Deb, 1 Mar 1909, Vol 1(5th), col 1254W
Q388	How many United States, German and French applications were made during the three months ending 31 Mar 1908 and 1909?	Q: George Croydon Marks A: Harold Tennant (Par Sec BoT)	HC Deb, 7 Apr 1909, Vol 3(5th), col 1252W

(continued)

(continued)

Q389	What are the details of the German-American Treaty; and what are its provisions as to non-working in one country?	Q: Leo Money A: Winston Churchill (Pr BoT)	HC Deb, 10 Jun 1909, Vol 6(5th), col 606–607W
Q390	How many United States, German, Austrian, Hungarian, Canadian and French applications where there during the seven months ending 31 Jul 1906 to 1909?	Q: George Croydon Marks A: Harold Tennant (Par Sec BoT)	HC Deb, 23 Aug 1909, Vol 9(5th), col 1912W
Q391	Whether junior clerks at the Patent Office are paid a living wage?	Q: William Field A: Charles Hobhouse (Fin Sec Tr)	HC Deb, 6 Oct 1909, Vol 11(5th), c 2173–2174W
Q392	What is the number of foreign firms opening factories in Great Britain since the coming into force of the Patents and Designs Act 1907 [PUBA23]?	Q: Arthur Fell A: Sydney Buxton (Pr BoT)	HC Deb, 28 Apr 1910, Vol 17(5th), col 772W
Q393	Whether the unification of patent and trade mark law will be debated at the next Colonial Conference?	Q: Basil Peto A: John Seely (US Col)	HC Deb, 28 Jul 1910, Vol 19(5th), col 2336
Q394	How many specifications were deposited from 1 Feb 1910 to 1 Feb 1911; and how many of the those remaining are still to be dealt with on 1 Feb 1911?	Q: William Mitchell-Thomson A: Sydney Buxton (Pr BoT)	HC Deb, 20 Feb 1911, Vol 21(5th), col 1527
Q395	Will the government provide statistics on the number of vacancies for Patent Examiners in 1910–11, the number of appointments made, the number of candidates examined and the fees charged?	Q: Sir Laming Worthington-Evans A: Charles Hobhouse (Fin Sec Tr)	HC Deb, 8 Mar 1911, Vol 22(5th), col 1348W
Q396	What is the cost of the army rifle; what royalties are paid to government factory employees?	Q: Christopher Addison A: Richard Haldane (Sec War)	HC Deb, 21 Mar 1911, Vol 23(5th), col 216–217
Q397	Why is a foreign tile being used on the Drill Hall in Tunbridge Wells; should not they use British ones because of the Patents Act [PUBA23]?	Q: Herbert Spender Clay A: John Seely (US War)	HC Deb, 4 Apr 1911, Vol 23(5th), col 1985
Q398	How many factories have been established in the United Kingdom as a consequence of the Patents and Designs Act 1907 [PUBA23]?	Q: Almeric Paget A: Sydney Buxton (Pr BoT)	HC Deb, 11 Apr 1911, Vol 24(5th), col 235–236
Q399	How many appeals were brought from the Comptroller to the law officers in 1911?	Q: Sir George Croydon Marks A: Sir Rufus Issacs (A-G)	HC Deb, 16 Aug 1911, Vol 29(5th), col 2074W
Q400	Whether the government is aware of the patent vacuum lock for railway coaches; and Board of Trade examination of the same?	Q: William Thorne A: Sydney Buxton (Pr BoT)	HC Deb, 20 Nov 1911, Vol 31(5th), col 818
Q401	Whether the Select Committee into patent matters will be appointed early in the next session?	Q: Arthur Lynch A: Reginald McKenna (Hom Sec)	HC Deb, 23 Nov 1911, Vol 31(5th), col 1379–1380

Q402	What was the net revenue from Patent Office fees in the last year?	Q: Horatio Bottomley A: Sydney Buxton (Pr BoT)	HC Deb, 25 Apr 1912, Vol 37(5th), col 1377W
Q403	Will the government consider setting up a department for aiding poor inventors in the development of patents which are of public utility?	Q: Horatio Bottomley A: Sydney Buxton (Pr BoT)	HC Deb, 25 Apr 1912, Vol 37(5th), col 1387W
Q404	How many factories have been erected in the UK by foreign manufacturers; what royalties have been paid and received resulting from the Patents and Designs Act 1907 [PUBA23]?	Q: Leo Amery A: Sydney Buxton (Pr BoT)	HC Deb, 6 May 1912, Vol 38(5th), col 176W–177W
Q405	How many applications for revocation on the grounds of non-working have been made from the commencement of the Patents and Designs Act 1907 [PUBA23] up to Jun 1912; and how many compulsory licences were granted over the same period?	Q: Sir George Croydon Marks A: Sydney Buxton (Pr BoT)	HC Deb, 2 Jul 1912, Vol 40(5th), col 1100–1101W
Q406	Under what conditions may the government acquire and use patent articles and inventions?	Q: Sir Henry Norman A: Sydney Buxton (Pr BoT)	HC Deb, 16 Jul 1912, Vol 41(5th), col 246W
Q407	What are the terms for extending the agreement with Marconi to use wireless technology outside the United Kingdom?	Q: Frederick Hall A: Herbert Samuel (PM Gen)	HC Deb, 9 Oct 1912, Vol 42(5th), col 354–355
Q408	Whether the government is aware that Colonel [Rookes EB] Crompton, who is consulting to the Road Board, is inviting local councils to investigate his patented method of road crusts?	Q: Timothy Healy A: David Lloyd-George (Ch Ex)	HC Deb, 17 Oct 1912, Vol 42(5th), col 1428–1430W
Q409	Whether it is consistent with Colonel [Rookes EB] Crompton's duty as a consultant to advise on methods of road surfacing when he has links to Taroads Ltd and Praed Construction?	Q: Timothy Healy A: David Lloyd-George (Ch Ex)	HC Deb, 24 Oct 1912, Vol 42(5th), col 2379–2380W
Q410	Whether the Income Tax Commissioners now refuse deductions for patent fees and expenses?	Q: George Terrell A: David Lloyd-George (Ch Ex)	HC Deb, 30 Oct 1912, Vol 43(5th), col 433–434
Q411	On what grounds was Bellini's patent [1911 No 11,339] revoked?	Q: Frederick Hall A: Sydney Buxton (Pr BoT)	HC Deb, 14 Nov 1912, Vol 43(5th), col 2073
Q412	Whether the masts to be erected by Marconi will use "Marconi patents" within the meaning of the agreement?	Q: Martin Archer-Shee A: Herbert Samuel (PM Gen)	HC Deb, 27 Nov 1912, Vol 44(5th), col 1303–1304W
Q413	Whether the Bill introduced in the Gold Coast legislature for granting a monopoly over palm oil extraction can be discussed?	Q: James Dundas White A: Herbert Asquith (PM)	HC Deb, 18 Dec 1912, Vol 45(5th), col 1500–1501
Q414	Under the Government of Ireland Bill, is the Parliament excluded from legislating on patents and the government from administering them?	Q: Godfrey Locker-Lampson A: Augustine Birrell (Ch Sec Ir)	HC Deb, 20 Dec 1912, Vol 45(5th), col 1869W

(continued)

(continued)

Q415	Whether the law officers' opinion has been taken on whether patents were secured by Marconi by payments from the Post Office?	Q: Sir Henry Norman A: Herbert Samuel (PM Gen)	HC Deb, 18 Jul 1913, Vol 55(5th), col 1593–1594W
Q416	Whether Marconi has patents in British East Africa?	Q: Martin Archer-Shee and Herbert Pike Pease and Lord Robert Cecil A: Herbert Samuel (PM Gen)	HC Deb, 31 Jul 1913, Vol 56(4th), col 732–734
Q417	Whether patent experts have considered the validity of the Marconi patents; and the paying of royalties?	Q: John Gretton A: Herbert Samuel (PM Gen) Q: Arnold Ward Q: George Faber	HC Deb, 4 Aug 1913, Vol 56(5th), col 1031–1032
Q418	Whether the government knew Marconi's patents were not protected in British East Africa?	Q: George Faber A: Herbert Samuel (PM Gen)	HC Deb, 4 Aug 1913, Vol 56(5th), col 1046–1047W
Q419	Whether a clause is included in the Marconi agreement because of concerns about the validity of the patents; and whether secret inventions are covered by patent?	Q: Herbert Pike Pease A: Herbert Samuel (PM Gen)	HC Deb, 6 Aug 1913, Vol 56(5th), col 1492–1493W
Q420	Whether Lieutenant [John] Dunne's patent for aeroplanes has been secured by a French company?	Q: Rowland Hunt A: Harold Baker (Fin Sec War)	HC Deb, 14 Aug 1913, Vol 56(5th), col 2676–2677W
Q421	Why does patent law not require Marconi to licence the Crown its wireless technology?	Q: Herbert Pike Pease A: Herbert Samuel (PM Gen)	HC Deb, 15 Aug 1913, Vol 56(5th), col 2830W
Q422	Whether the government intends to amend s 27 of the Patents and Designs Act 1907 [PUBA23] to put the burden back on the patentee?	Q: Sir Basil Peto A: John Burns (Pr BoT)	HC Deb, 16 Feb 1914, Vol 58(5th), col 583
Q423	Have Marconi acquired the rights to use Golschmidt's high-frequency alternator?	Q: Walter Guinness A: Cecil Norton (Ass PM Gen)	HC Deb, 26 Feb 1914, Vol 58(5th), col 1936
Q424	Whether the "Phillips Entry" for aircraft is being used by the British Navy?	Q: Lord Edmund Talbot A: Winston Churchill (Fir Ld Adm)	HC Deb, 2 Mar 1914, Vol 59(5th), col 56W
Q425	What are the number and description of promotions and special increments awarded since 1907 to each grade at the Patent Office?	Q: Charles Duncan A: John Robertson (Par Sec BoT)	HC Deb, 18 Mar 1914, Vol 59(5th), col 2075W
Q426	Whether the Admiralty has adopted [Thomas] Truss' patent [1905 No 15,033] air lock for submarines?	Q: Sir Godfrey Dalrymple White A: Thomas Macnamara (Par Sec Adm)	HC Deb, 30 Mar 1914, Vol 60(5th), col 821
Q427	Whether the government is aware that Admiralty inspectors have taken out a patent?	Q: James Remnant A: Thomas Macnamara (Par Sec Adm)	HC Deb, 27 Apr 1914, Vol 61(5th), col 1315–1316
Q428	Whether the government is aware of 12–month priority periods and the problems with revocation resulting from making mistakes on priority?	Q: Robert Harcourt A: John Burns (Pr BoT)	HC Deb, 15 Jul 1914, Vol 64(5th), col 1936–1937W
Q429	Whether, due to the inability to obtain raw materials from Germany, licences will be granted to allow British businesses to work patents?	Q: Sir Fredrick Cawley A: Walter Runciman (Pr BoT)	HC Deb, 10 Aug 1914, Vol 65(5th), col 2249

Q430	Whether German patents in England will be suspended or annulled, allowing domestic manufacture?	Q: John Rees A: Walter Runciman (Pr BoT)	HC Deb, 27 Aug 1914, Vol 66(5th), col 133–134
Q431	To whom are patent royalties on Krupp's patent paid?	Q: Lord Charles Beresford A: Harold Tennant (US War)	HC Deb, 28 Apr 1915, Vol 71(5th), col 714–715
Q432	To whom are patent royalties on Krupp's patent paid?	Q: Lord Charles Beresford A: Harold Baker (Fin Sec War)	HC Deb, 4 May 1915, Vol 71(5th), col 956
Q433	What royalty is paid by the government for fuses?	Q: Sir Arthur Markham A: Harold Baker (Fin Sec War)	HC Deb, 6 May 1915, Vol 71(5th), col 1285W
Q434	Whether there should be a special taxation on German patent royalties?	Q: Philip Snowden A: David Lloyd George (Min Mun)	HC Deb, 12 May 1915, Vol 71(5th), col 1632–1633
Q435	Why, if the patent has expired, are British firms paying a royalty to Krupp's?	Q: Sir Arthur Markham A: Harold Baker (Fin Sec War)	HC Deb, 13 May 1915, Vol 71(5th), col 1818
Q436	Whether the inquiry into royalty paid on Krupp patent has concluded?	Q: Carlyon Bellairs A: Henry Forster (Fin Sec War) Q: Sir Alfred Markham	HC Deb, 1 Jul 1915, Vol 72(5th), col 1938–1939
Q437	Whether the government is aware of the difficulties faced by certain patentees in relation to taxes when the country is disorganised or cutting expenditure?	Q: Joseph King A: Ernest Pretyman (Par Sec BoT)	HC Deb, 6 Jul 1915, Vol 73(5th), col 187–198
Q438	Whether certain patents applied for by German companies will be granted during the war?	Q: Sir Arthur Markham A: Walter Runciman (Pr BoT)	HC Deb, 26 Jul 1915, Vol 73(5th), col 1967–1969
Q439	Whether the law officers have considered the government paying royalties on expired patents?	Q: Sir Alfred Markham A: Henry Forster (Fin Sec War)	HC Deb, 26 Jul 1915, Vol 73(5th), col 1980–1981W
Q440	What price is the government paying for the Krupp patents?	Q: Sir Alfred Markham A: Henry Forster (Fin Sec War)	HC Deb, 20 Oct 1915, Vol 74(5th), col 1806–1807W
Q441	Whether legislation will be introduced to suspend the duration of patents where a patentee is not able to work the invention due to the war?	Q: Sir Basil Peto A: Ernest Pretyman (Par Sec BoT)	HC Deb, 2 Dec 1915, Vol 76(5th), col 851–852
Q442	Whether, following *Diamond Coal Cutter Company v Mining Appliances* (1915) 32 RPC 569, legislation will be introduced that licensees of enemy patents are not exempt from the Patents and Designs Act 1907, s 36 [PUBA23]?	Q: Sir Basil Peto A: Walter Runciman (Pr BoT)	HC Deb, 26 Jan 1916, Vol 78(5th), col 1256
Q443	Whether the government is aware that the Patent Office is refusing to recognise the successor of a Scottish deceased inventor as the patent is a purely English estate?	Q: George Currie A: Ernest Pretyman (Par Sec BoT)	HC Deb, 29 Feb 1916, Vol 80(5th), col 898
Q444	Whether the practice of requiring the resealing of the Scottish confirmation of the patent will be discontinued?	Q: George Currie A: Walter Runciman (Pr BoT)	HC Deb, 9 Mar 1916, Vol 80(5th), col 1724

(continued)

(continued)

Q445	Whether the government can make a statement as to the recent letter from the Probate Court regarding Scottish deceased inventors and the extractions made?	Q: George Currie A: Walter Runciman (Pr BoT)	HC Deb, 12 Apr 1916, Vol 81(5th), col 1766
Q446	What instructions have been given to the Patent Office to stop treating patents as a purely English estate?	Q: George Currie A: Walter Runciman (Pr BoT)	HC Deb, 10 May 1916, Vol 82(5th), col 688–689W
Q447	Will the government introduce legislation to extend the term of patents which could not be worked due to the war?	Q: Sir Basil Peto A: Lewis Harcourt (Ch Com W&B)	HC Deb, 26 Jun 1916, Vol 83(5th), col 554W
Q448	When will legislation be introduced which will deal with keeping British patents alive that are applied for during the war?	Q: Sir Basil Peto A: Lewis Harcourt (Ch Com W&B)	HC Deb, 20 Jul 1916, Vol 84(5th), col 1174–1175
Q449	How many patents have been applied for under Trading with the Enemy Act 1916 in the name of enemy aliens?	Q: Sir John Lonsdale A: Lewis Harcourt (Ch Com W&B)	HC Deb, 24 Jul 1916, Vol 84(5th), col 1298–1299
Q450	Whether legislation to extend patents affected by the war will be introduced before adjournment?	Q: Sir Basil Peto A: Lewis Harcourt (Ch Com W&B)	HC Deb, 10 Aug 1916, Vol 85(5th), col 1230–1231
Q451	What were the duties of the Board of Trade in 1906, 1914 and 1916?	Q: Sir Edwin Cornwall A: Walter Runciman (Pr BoT)	HC Deb, 10 Oct 1916, Vol 86(5th), col 26–28W
Q452	Whether legislation to extend patents affected by the war will be considered by the government?	Q: Athelstan Rendall A: Ernest Pretyman (Par Sec BoT)	HC Deb, 26 Oct 1916, Vol 86(5th), col 1300–1301
Q453	Whether a patent had been granted to an interned enemy alien (Dr Mensching); and how many patents have been granted to non-naturalised Germans?	Q: Gershom Stewart A: Ernest Pretyman (Par Sec BoT)	HC Deb, 23 Nov 1916, Vol 87(5th), col 1582
Q454	Whether the renewal fees for devices made of metal, now commandeered for munitions, should be waived during the term of the war?	Q: James O'Grady A: George Roberts (Par Sec BoT)	HC Deb, 22 Feb 1917, Vol 90(5th), col 1460
Q455	Whether the government will consider creating an Inventions Committee to assist poor people to place their inventions on the market?	Q: Charles Stanton A: George Roberts (Par Sec BoT)	HC Deb, 22 Feb 1917, Vol 90(5th), col 1461
Q456	Whether patents relating to munitions are open to public inspection?	Q: Alexander MacCallum Scott A: George Roberts (Par Sec BoT)	HC Deb, 7 Mar 1917, Vol 91(5th), col 395
Q457	Whether inventors in the armed services have to assign their inventions to the Crown; and what rules are there to dealing with their inventions?	Q: Sir William Bull A: Christopher Addison (Min Mun)	HC Deb, 20 Mar 1917, Vol 92(5th), col 48–49W
Q458	How many foreign applications were filed by enemies during 1915–16?	Q: Sir George Croydon Marks A: George Roberts (Par Sec BoT)	HC Deb, 5 Apr 1917, Vol 92(5th), col 1488–1489W

Q459	Has the government considered the question of extending the period for which patents are granted; and modifying fees for the later years of the patent?	Q: Sir James Flannery A: George Roberts (Par Sec BoT)	HC Deb, 9 May 1917, Vol 93(5th), col 1082W
Q460	Whether patents are granted to Alien Enemies under r 2 and 3 of the 1914 Rules; what about the patent of Badische Aniline and Soda Fabrik; and what is likely to be the position after the end of hostilities?	Q: Sir Basil Peto A: Sir Albert Stanley (Pr BoT)	HC Deb, 18 Jul 1917, Vol 96(5th), col 357–358
Q461	Whether the orders for aircraft engines have been subdivided due to patent rights?	Sir Basil Peto Q: Noel Billing A: Sir Laming Worthington-Evans (Min Blockade)	HC Deb, 19 Jul 1917, Vol 96(5th), col 579–580
Q462	What progress has there been made to amend patent law; and is a Bill proposed?	Q: Sir Basil Peto A: George Roberts (Par Sec BoT)	HC Deb, 23 Jul 1917, Vol 96(5th), col 854
Q463	Whether patentees whose patents relate to working metal are able to get the raw materials?	Q: James Rowlands A: Geroge Roberts (Par Sec BoT)	HC Deb, 27 Jul 1917, Vol 96(5th), col 1591–1592
Q464	Whether the government has been promoted to take action to protect patent owners who have to pay renewal fees for patents which cannot be worked due to the war?	Q: Athelstan Rendall A: George Wardle (Par Sec BoT)	HC Deb, 18 Oct 1917, Vol 98(5th), col 280–281W
Q465	Whether the government is aware that many persons who have taken out patents cannot work them due to shortage of materials; whether anything has been done to remit patent fees; or to extend the period of the patent?	Q: Thomas Wilson A: George Wardle (Par Sec BoT)	HC Deb, 22 Oct 1917, Vol 98(5th), col 519W
Q466	Whether any British patents (or shares) belong to Krupp's of Essen? And what is happening to any dividends?	Q: Rowland Hunt Q: George Faber Q: Sir John Butcher A: George Wardle (Par Sec BoT)	HC Deb, 8 Nov 1917, Vol 98(5th), col 2307–2308
Q467	What are the names of formerly patented chemicals being protected as trade marks?	Q: Sir Richard Cooper A: Sir Albert Stanley (Pr BoT)	HC Deb, 12 Nov 1917, Vol 99(5th), col 4–5
Q468	Whether chemicals known by their former patent name are registered to enemy aliens?	Q: Sir Richard Cooper A: Sir Albert Stanley (Pr BoT)	HC Deb, 12 Nov 1917, Vol 99(5th), col 4–5
Q469	Whether the government will take steps to allow the use of chemical names protected by trade marks owned by enemies?	Q: Sir Richard Cooper A: Christopher Addison (Min of Reconstruction)	HC Deb, 12 Nov 1917, Vol 99(5th), col 58–59W
Q470	Whether steps will be taken to obtain the names of chemicals known by their former patent name?	Q: Sir Richard Cooper A: Christopher Addison (Min Reconstruction)	HC Deb, 12 Nov 1917, Vol 99(5th), col 58–59W
Q471	What remuneration is available to an officer who is required to take out a secret patent?	Q: Sir Henry Norman A: Sir Laming Worthington-Evans (Min Par Sec Mun)	HC Deb, 15 Nov 1917, Vol 99(5th), col 600W

(continued)

(continued)

Q472	Whether trade marks for articles upon which the patent has expired should be expunged?	Q: Sir Richard Cooper A: Christopher Addison (Min Reconstruction)	HC Deb, 26 Nov 1917, Vol 99(5th), col 1665–1667W
Q473	Will the Patents Bill [PUBB49] have an explanatory memorandum; will the Bill extend the life of the patent by one year?	Q: James Dundas White and Sir John Harmood-Banner A: Sir Albert Stanley (Pr BoT)	HC Deb, 20 Dec 1917, Vol 100(5th), col 2173
Q474	Whether a committee has been set up to deal with the submarine menace; and whether monetary rewards have been considered?	Q: George Terrell A: Thomas Macnamara (Par Sec For Off)	HC Deb, 29 Apr 1918, Vol 105(5th), col 1277–1278
Q475	Whether a prize might be offered to encourage inventors to solve problems of identifying planes at night?	Q: George Terrell A: John Baird (US Air)	HC Deb, 29 Apr 1918, Vol 105(5th), col 1280
Q476	Whether the Haber process is protected by British patents?	Q: Sir William Beale A: Fredrick Kellaway (Par Sec Min Mun)	HC Deb, 2 May 1918, Vol 105(5th), col 1688–1692
Q477	Whether the government intends to reintroduce the Patents and Designs Bill [PUBB49] this session?	Q: Walter Perkins A: Sir Albert Stanley (Pr BoT)	HC Deb, 2 May 1918, Vol 105(5th), col 1727–1728W
Q478	Before the Patents Bill is read a second time, could the government publish the report and evidence of the Engineering Industrial Committee on shoe machinery?	Q: Charles McCurdy A: Sir Albert Stanley (Pr BoT)	HC Deb, 6 May 1918, Vol 105(5th), col 1893
Q479	Now that government has given a reward regarding oil fuel, could a reward be offered for overcoming the submarine menace?	Q: George Terrell A: Thomas Macnamara (Par Sec	HC Deb, 15 May 1918, Vol 106(5th), col 325–327
Q480	Now that government has given a reward regarding oil fuel, could a reward be offered for overcoming the submarine menace?	Q: George Terrell A: John Baird (US Air)	HC Deb, 15 May 1918, Vol 106(5th), col 362
Q481	Whether patents have been granted to enemy aliens during 1917; and have any patents been issued to British subjects in Germany?	Q: Henry Croft A: Sir Albert Stanley (Pr BoT)	HC Deb, 3 Jun 1918, Vol 106(5th), col 1200–1201
Q482	Whether British policy should follow United States policy of not allowing any payments for patents in enemy countries?	Q: John Higham Q: James Rowlands A: Sir Albert Stanley (Pr BoT)	HC Deb, 5 Jun 1918, Vol 106(5th), col 1569–1570
Q483	Whether patents have been granted to enemy aliens during the war?	Q: Henry Croft A: George Wardle (Par Sec BoT)	HC Deb, 13 Jun 1918, Vol 106(5th), col 2355
Q484	Whether an enlisted man can submit an invention to the Board without his officer's support?	Q: Bertram Falle A: Thomas Macnamara (Par Sec For Off)	HC Deb, 26 Jun 1918, Vol 107(5th), col 1028–1029
Q485	How was a patent was granted to Max Burg, an enemy alien in Berlin; and what is the procedure in Germany and Britain as to enemies?	Q: Sir Edward Carson A: Sir Albert Stanley (Pr BoT)	HC Deb, 1 Jul 1918, Vol 107(5th), col 1371–1373

Q486	Whether patent agents are allowed to correspond with inventors in Germany; and whether this is under any special licence?	Q: Sir Edward Carson A: Sir Albert Stanley (Pr BoT)	HC Deb, 3 Jul 1918, Vol 107(5th), col 1725–1726
Q487	Whether the patent granted to Siemens-Schuckertwerke for artificial limbs can be worked without infringing the patent?	Q: William Chapple A: Sir Albert Stanley (Pr BoT)	HC Deb, 4 Jul 1918, Vol 107(5th), col 1828
Q488	Why was the contract for Knight's patent shell slings [Patent No 102236] was given to a company other than the inventor?	Q: Henry Croft A: Sir Laming Worthington-Evans (Fin Sec Min Mun)	HC Deb, 4 Jul 1918, Vol 107(5th), col 1847–1848
Q489	How many applications have been received from enemy aliens since the outbreak of war; and how many accepted?	Q: Sir Edward Carson A: Sir Albert Stanley (Pr BoT)	HC Deb, 8 Jul 1918, Vol 108(5th), col 5
Q490	Whether there can be a statement on allowing enemy subjects to file specifications at the Patent Office?	Q: Sir Edward Carson (postponed)	HC Deb, 10 Jul 1918, Vol 108(5th), col 320
Q491	Whether inventors who want to submit their invention to the Inventions Department have to submit additional information?	Q: Henry Wright A: Frederick Kellaway (PM Gen)	HC Deb, 17 Jul 1918, Vol 108(5th), col 1038–1039
Q492	When can government official inventors apply for a patent; and what permissions do they need?	Q: Henry Wright A: Frederick Kellaway (PM Gen)	HC Deb, 22 Jul 1918, Vol 108(5th), col 1448–1449
Q493	What are the minimum payments under the Salvarsan [anti-syphilis drug] substitutes?	Q: Philip Snowden A: George Wardle (Par Sec War)	HC Deb, 23 Jul 1918, Vol 108(5th), col 1662W
Q494	Whether the order refusing payments for German patent applications will have the effect of revoking the German patents filed and accepted since commencement of the war?	Q: Lord Armaghdale A: Lord Somerleyton	HL Deb, 25 Jul 1918, Vol 30(5th), col 1194–1197
Q495	Whether steps are taken regarding the Comptroller demanding renewal fees for patents which could not be worked during the war?	Q: Henry Croft A: Sir Albert Stanley (Pr BoT)	HC Deb, 26 Jul 1918, Vol 108(5th), col 2165
Q496	Where an official (Arnold Bradley) are allowed to patent an invention [No 119,911]; can they use government time and materials to do so (and [Laurence] Richard's retort [Patent 278,298])?	Q: Henry Wright A: Frederick Kellaway (PM Gen)	HC Deb, 29 Jul 1928, Vol 109(5th), col 32–33
Q497	How many British patents have been taken out in Germany since the start of the war; and the approach of the German government to the same?	Q: Sir Fredrick Hall A: Sir Albert Stanley (Pr BoT)	HC Deb, 31 Jul 1918, Vol 109(5th), col 433–434
Q498	Whether RW Bates was given permission to apply for a patent; and whether, in his official duties, he had access to the Tozer retort?	Q: Henry Wright A: Frederick Kellaway (PM Gen)	HC Deb, 1 Aug 1918, Vol 109(5th), col 646W
Q499	Why a company was forced to accept a lower royalty than promised to the inventor in relation to Knight's patent shell sling [Patent No 102236]?	Q: Henry Croft A: Frederick Kellaway (PM Gen)	HC Deb, 5 Aug 1918, Vol 109(5th), col 935–936W

(continued)

(continued)

Q500	Whether it has been considered extending patents where their working has been interrupted by the war?	Q: Sir Harold Elverston A: Sir Albert Stanley (Pr BoT)	HC Deb, 5 Aug 1918, Vol 109(5th), col 941W
Q501	Whether the term of protection for patents can be extended for servicemen to cover their period of service?	Q: Fredrick Jowett A: Sir Albert Stanley (Pr BoT)	HC Deb, 24 Oct 1918, Vol 110(5th), col 958W
Q502	What is the government policy on enemy-owned patents etc.?	Q: Sir Richard Cooper A: George Wardle (Par Sec War)	HC Deb, 7 Nov 1918, Vol 110(5th), col 2295–2296
Q503	When can the Patent Library return to opening during its pre-war hours?	Q: Sir James Remnant A: William Bridgeman (Par Sec BoT)	HC Deb, 24 Feb 1919, Vol 112(5th), col 1440W
Q504	Whether renewal fees can be suspended for patents applied for and granted from Jun 1914 till the date when metal can be freely used?	Q: George Tryon A: William Bridgeman (Par Sec BoT)	HC Deb, 7 Mar 1919, Vol 113(5th), col 796W
Q505	Whether inventors who have been unable to work their inventions during the war should have their patents extended?	Q: Walter Preston A: William Bridgeman (Par Sec BoT)	HC Deb, 8 May 1919, Vol 115(5th), col 1108
Q506	Whether the government intends to grant relief to patentees who could not work their patents during the war?	Q: James Rowlands A: Sir Auckland Geddes (Pr BoT)	HC Deb, 14 May 1919, Vol 115(5th), col 1579
Q507	Whether renewal fees can be suspended and the patent extended where war conditions have prevented the inventor from working the invention?	Q: Sir Herbert Nield A: William Bridgeman (Par Sec BoT)	HC Deb, 15 May 1919, Vol 115(5th), col 1811–1812W
Q508	What are the powers and functions of the Royal Commission on Awards to Inventors?	Q: Sir Clement Kinloch-Cooke A: Stanley Baldwin (Fin Sec Tr)	HC Deb, 22 May 1919, Vol 116(5th), col 586–588W
Q509	Whether patented apparatus and methods which could not be used during the war will be extended by the Comptroller under legislation?	Q: Sir James Flannery A: William Bridgeman (Par Sec BoT)	HC Deb, 4 Jun 1919, Vol 116(5th), col 2050W
Q510	Whether the government is aware of the hardship inflicted on patentees by reason of the war; and whether patents can be extended accordingly?	Q: Sir William Seager and Cyril Entwistle A: William Bridgeman (Par Sec BoT)	HC Deb, 5 Jun 1919, Vol 116(5th), col 2208–2209
Q511	Whether an indication can be given when the Patents Bill will be introduced?	Q: Sir Herbet Nield A: Sir Auckland Geddes (Pr BoT)	HC Deb, 2 Jul 1919, Vol 117(5th), col 1000W
Q512	What arrangements have been made to safeguard British patentees in countries which are to be sub-divided under the peace terms?	Q: Thomas Griffiths A: William Bridgeman (Par Sec for BoT)	HC Deb, 10 Jul 1919, Vol 117(5th), col 2053–2054W
Q513	When will the Patents Bill be introduced?	Q: James Rowlands A: William Bridgeman (Par Sec for BoT)	HC Deb, 14 Jul 1919, Vol 118(5th), col 23

Q514	Whether the government is aware Mr Constantinescu, the inventor, cannot get reasonable royalties from the government, so is leaving the country?	Q: James Hodge A: Thomas Macnamara (Par Sec Adm)	HC Deb, 18 Aug 1919, Vol 119(5th), col 1873–1874
Q515	Whether Issac Gibson's invention for raising submarines was rejected by the Admiralty so he did not get an Award?	Q: Samuel McGuffin A: Thomas Macnamara (Par Sec Adm)	HC Deb, 29 Oct 1919, Vol 120(5th), col 647–648
Q516	Whether patents can be extended where war conditions have prevented the inventor from working the invention?	Q: Josiah Wedgwood A: Sir Auckland Geddes (Pr BoT)	HC Deb, 3 Nov 1919, Vol 120(5th), col 1158W
Q517	Whether the government will bring in a law to cheapen taking out patents and to prevent patentees from selling more than 50% of their interest to employers?	Q: Nicholas Gratton-Doyle A: William Bridgeman (Par Sec BoT)	HC Deb, 27 Nov 1919, Vol 121(5th), col 1937–1938W
Q518	Whether the government is aware that closing the Patent Office Library early is causing great inconvenience; whether it will be kept open until 10pm?	Q: Martin Conway A: William Bridgeman (Par Sec BoT)	HC Deb, 27 Nov 1919, Vol 121(5th), col 1938–1939W
Q519	When can the Patent Library return to opening during its pre-war hours?	Q: John Rawlinson A: Sir Auckland Geddes (Pr BoT)	HC Deb, 8 Dec 1919, Vol 122(5th), col 935–936W
Q520	Why the government is refusing permission to use the Graham patent single davit?	Q: Vivian Henderson A: Sir Auckland Geddes (Pr BoT)	HC Deb, 15 Dec 1919, Vol 123(5th), col 75W
Q521	Why a particular former serviceman was not selected for a job as assistant examiner following the selection examination?	Q: George Hirst A: Stanley Baldwin (Fin Sec to Tr)	HC Deb, 28 Dec 1919, Vol 123(5th), col 1284W
Q522	What is the result of the government's decision into W Glendinning's invention on airships?	Q: John Cairns A: George Tryon (US Air)	HC Deb, 11 Mar 1920, Vol 126(5th), col 1547W
Q523	Whether the government is aware of a gun with a range of 100–150 miles; and that the patent is owned by the French government?	Q: Richard Curzon-Howe A: David Lloyd George (PM)	HC Deb, 25 Mar 1920, Vol 127(5th), col 590–591
Q524	Whether the government is aware an inventor submitted his patent (No 101,646) for rear lights to the government asking whether it infringed lighting laws, but has as yet received no reply?	Q: George Bowyer A: Bonar Law (L Priv Seal)	HC Deb, 3 May 1920. Vol 128(5th), col 1716–1717W
Q525	Why George Littleproud's torpedo invention was rejected by the Royal Commission on Awards to Inventors?	Q: William Coote A: Sir James Craig	HC Deb, 14 Jun 1920, Vol 130(5th), col 898–599W
Q526	Whether an application for the renewal of a licence for a patent cancelled under the Treaty of Peace has been referred to a tribunal?	Q: Edward Manville A: Sir Robert Horne (Pr BoT)	HC Deb, 21 Jun 1920, Vol 130(5th), col 1711

(continued)

(continued)

Q527	Whether the Patent Library can revert to its pre-war opening hours so that it opens until 10pm?	Q: John Newman A: William Bridgeman (Par Sec BoT)	HC Deb, 24 Jun 1920, Vol 130(5th), col 2408W
Q528	Which judges are engaged on extra-judicial duties (include the Royal Commission on Awards to Inventors)?	Q: William Wedgewood Benn A: Sir Gordon Hewart	HC Deb, 24 Jun 1920, Vol 130(5th), col 2423–2424W
Q529	Why is there an inconsistency in the approach to offers to those who develop inventions during the war?	Q: Sir Henry Norman A: Bonar Law (L Priv Seal)	HC Deb, 5 Jul 1920, Vol 131(5th), col 1016–1017
Q530	Whether higher-placed civil servants are allowed to take out patents?	Q: Charles Edwards A: Bonar Law (L Priv Seal)	HC Deb, 6 Jul 1920, Vol 131(5th), col 1243W
Q531	Whether the government will allow payments to be made to German patent agents?	Q: Joseph Hood A: William Bridgeman (Par Sec BoT)	HC Deb, 14 Jul 1920, Vol 131(5th), col 2408–2409W
Q532	Whether the government will ask the Patent Office to be especially careful when examining motor fuel applications?	Q: Edward Manville A: Sir Robert Horne(Pr BoT)	HC Deb, 9 Aug 1920, Vol 133(5th), col 68W
Q533	Whether the Air Council committee investigating the misuse of technical information will be open to the press, and whether witnesses should be able to call Counsel?	Q: William Joynson-Hicks A: Winston Churchill (Sec War)	HC Deb, 30 Nov 1920, Vol 135(5th), col 100–101
Q534	Whether the government will make a statement regarding Commodore [Charles] Burney's claim before the Royal Commission on Awards to Inventors?	Q: Sir William Joynson-Hicks A: Sir James Craig (Par Sec Adm)	HC Deb, 2 Dec 1920, Vol 135(5th), col 1461W
Q535	Whether the terms of reference for the Royal Commission on Awards to Inventors have recently been altered?	Q: William Coote A: Stanley Baldwin (Fin Sec Tr)	HC Deb, 9 Dec 1920, Vol 135(5th), col 2460–2461W
Q536	When will the claim of Walton Motors Ltd be heard by the Royal Commission on Awards to Inventors?	Q: William Coote A: Winston Churchill (Sec War)	HC Deb, 9 Dec 1920, Vol 135(5th), col 2461–2462W
Q537	Whether patented unpullable screw plugs patents (No 28,789) were used exclusively during the war?	Q: William Murray A: Winston Churchill (Sec War)	HC Deb, 21 Dec 1920, Vol 136(5th), col 1536W
Q538	Why were outside solicitors instructed in *Denning v Secretary of State for India* (1920) 37 TLR 138?	Q: Thomas Griffiths A: Edwin Montagu (SoS India)	HC Deb, 6 Apr 1921, Vol 140(5th), col 280–281W
Q539	Whether the government is aware of the long delay in granting awards to inventors whose inventions were used during the war?	Q: Sir William Davison A: Hilton Young (Fin Sec Tr)	HC Deb, 2 May 1921, Vol 141(5th), col 644–645
Q540	What are Sundry Loans and Misc receipts in the Financial Statement?	Q: Godfrey Collins A: Hilton Young (Fin Sec Tr)	HC Deb, 1 Jun 1921, Vol 142(5th), col 1067W

Q541	Whether the Prime Minister is aware of the serious delays before the Royal Commission on Awards to Inventors?	Q: John Thorpe A: Hilton Young (Fin Sec Tr)	HC Deb, 13 Jun 1921, Vol 143(5th), col 50W
Q542	Whether the government is aware of a patent which might have prevented the mining accident at Tinsley Park Colliery?	Q: James Sexton A: Sir William Mitchell Thomson (Par Sec BoT)	HC Deb, 20 Jul 1921, Vol 144(5th), col 2204–2205
Q543	Whether there is an inquiry into charges against Major Wylie and Captain Thurston, who used confidential information to take out patents?	Q: Murdoch Wood A: James Parker (for SoS Air)	HC Deb, 11 Aug 1921, Vol 146(5th), col 620–621
Q544	Why Mr B Davies is still retained (who works on Awards to Inventors Commission) and the job not given to an ex-serviceman?	Q: Alfred Raper A: Frederick Guest (Par Sec Tr)	HC Deb, 16 Feb 1922, Vol 150(5th), col 1238–1239W
Q545	Whether the regulation made under Finance (No 2) Act 1915 relates to patent rights?	Q: Stanley Holmes A: Hilton Young (Fin Sec Tr)	HC Deb, 20 Feb 1922, Vol 150(5th), col 1528–1529W
Q546	Whether the government is aware that Lieutenant Colonel Guy Liddell had to pay Income Tax on his award from the Royal Commission?	Q: Sir William Davidson A: Hilton Young (Fin Sec Tr)	HC Deb, 1 May 1922, Vol 153(5th), col 982–983
Q547	What are the miscellaneous receipts received in the year to 31 Mar 1923 (patent stamps and fees)?	Q: Rhys Davies A: Sir Robert Horne (Ch Ex)	HC Deb, 11 May 1922, Vol 153(5th), col 2375–2376
Q548	How many promotions have there been at the Patent Office; how many ex-servicemen were promoted compared to non-servicemen?	Q: William Graham A: Sir William Mitchell-Thomson (Par Sec BoT)	HC Deb, 11 May 1922, Vol 153(5th), col 2382–2383
Q549	Will a public inquiry be held into the refusal to grant an award to Mr Hearne for inventing a method of firing through a propeller?	Q: Viscount Wolmer A: Hilton Young (Fin Sec Tr)	HC Deb, 17 May 1922, Vol 154(5th), col 389W
Q550	Has the Post Office ever considered a reward for creating an automatic recorder?	Q: Sir Harry Brittain A: Herbet Pease (Ass PM Gen)	HC Deb, 30 May 1922, Vol 154(5th), col 1908
Q551	Whether the government is aware of the delays at the Patent Office and the steps being taken to address them?	Q: William Wedgwood Benn A: Sir William Mitchell-Thomson (Par Sec BoT)	HC Deb, 14 Jul 1922, Vol 156(5th), col 1609–1610W
Q552	Whether the government has considered the monopoly it intends to confer on Marconi?	Q: John Newman A: Herbert Pease (Ass PM Gen)	HC Deb, 24 Jul 1922, Vol 157(5th), col 27–28
Q553	Why there are delays in a claim of [William] Prideaux regarding his machine gun before the Royal Commission on Awards to Inventors?	Q: Philip Colfox A: Hilton Young (Fin Sec Tr)	HC Deb, 27 Jul 1922, Vol 157(5th), col 680–682

(continued)

(continued)

Q554	Is the government aware of the complaints being made about the delays at the Patent Office?	Q: Joseph Kenworthy A: William Mitchell-Thomson (Par Sec BoT)	HC Deb, 31 Jul 1922, Vol 157(5th), col 965–966
Q555	Whether Marconi has any claims outstanding against the government?	Q: George Middleton A: Stanley Baldwin (PM)	HC Deb, 13 Dec 1922, Vol 159(5th), col 2952W
Q556	Whether the Admiralty was ever given the submarine indicating nets?	Q: Arthur Harbord A: Bolton Eyres-Monsell (Fin Sec Adm)	HC Deb, 7 Mar 1923, Vol 161(5th), col 463
Q557	Is the reward for helicopters still available?	Q: Joseph Kenworthy A: Sir Samuel Hoare (SoS Air)	HC Deb, 22 Mar 1923, Vol 161(5th), col 2752
Q558	What payment has been made to Campbell regarding his invention for protecting ships from torpedoes?	Q: Sir George Hamilton A: Bolton Eyres-Monsell (Fin Sec Adm)	HC Deb, 28 Mar 1923, Vol 162(5th), col 470–471
Q559	Whether the United States will be paying the British government back in relation to the patent licence fees it paid for United States aircraft?	Q: Sir George Hamilton A: Archibald Boyd-Carpenter (Fin Sec Tr)	HC Deb, 17 Apr 1923, Vol 162(5th), col 1868–1869
Q560	Why the war invention claim of T Bathgate for an anti-Zeppelin bullet was not given an award; and was an award for this bullet by the Royal Commission heard in secret?	Q: Sir Archibald Sinclair A: Walter Guinness (Fin Sec Tr)	HC Deb, 26 Apr 1923, Vol 163(5th), col 689–690W
Q561	How many patent applications have been submitted but not examined; and what steps have been taken to address the delay?	Q: James Ede A: Viscount Wolmer (Par Sec BoT)	HC Deb, 8 May 1923, Vol 163(5th), col 2133–2134
Q562	Whether British patents are current in the Irish Free State; any reduction in fees for losing the Free State; whether fees will follow American fees models; whether delays can be addressed?	Q: Patrick Hannon and James Ede A: Sir Philip Lloyd-Greame (Pr BoT)	HC Deb, 5 Jun 1923, Vol 164(5th), col 1939–1941
Q563	What steps are being taken to remedy the delay in settling applications for patents?	Q: Sir Edwin Stockton A: Sir Philip Lloyd-Greame (Pr BoT)	HC Deb, 5 Jun 1923, Vol 164(5th), col 1989W
Q564	Whether the weapons used against the Zeppelins during the war were identical to those forwarded to the War Office by Mr Bathgate?	Q: Sir Archibald Sinclair A: Walter Guinness (Fin Sec Tr)	HC Deb, 26 Jun 1923, Vol 165(5th), col 2150W
Q565	What is the number of patents now under consideration at the Patent Office which have been received within the past three months; three to six months; three to nine months; over 12 months?	Q: James Ede A: Sir Philip Lloyd-Greame (Pr BoT)	HC Deb, 19 Jun 1923, Vol 165(5th), col 1161W
Q566	Whether there has been communication with the Irish Free State regarding licences which covered the whole of the United Kingdom?	Q: John Newman A: Albert Buckley (Jr Ld Tr)	HC Deb, 5 Jul 1923, Vol 166(5th), col 650W

Q567	What number of civil service officers' pay in 1914 exceeded £1200, and what number now?	Q: John Gretton A: Philip Lloyd-Greame (Pr BoT)	HC Deb, 17 Jul 1923, Vol 166(5th), col 2067–2069W
Q568	How are certain sums in the Civil Service Estimate connected with, amongst others, the Patents, Designs and Trade Marks Acts?	Q: Patrick Hannon A: Viscount Wolmer (Par Sec BoT)	HC Deb, 2 Aug 1923, Vol 167(5th), col 1696
Q569	Whether a monopoly has been granted to the Automatic Telephone Manufacturing Company for two or three years?	Q: James Hogge A: Vernon Hartshorn (PM Gen)	HC Deb, 14 Feb 1924, Vol 169(5th), col 1047–1048W
Q570	Whether all expired patents should become the property of the nation?	Q: George Oliver A: Albert Alexander (Par Sec BoT)	HC Deb, 21 Feb 1924, Vol 169(5th), col 2034W
Q571	What Treaties were in force between Russia and Great Britain before the revolution?	Q: Edward Lessing A: Ramsay MacDonald (PM)	HC Deb, 25 Feb 1924, Vol 170(5th), col 15–21
Q572	What is the average fee received per patent application, and how many are kept in force for the full term (and Irish Free State patents)?	Q: Smedley Crooke A: Sidney Webb (Pr BoT)	HC Deb, 26 Feb 1924, Vol 170(5th), col 220–221
Q573	Whether the government is aware of the League of Nations Report on Scientific Property?	Q: Sir George Croydon Marks A: Arthur Ponsonby (US FO)	HC Deb, 26 Feb 1924, Vol 170(5th), col 280–281W
Q574	Whether the government is aware of dissatisfaction with the Patent Office; and that fees are being charged for the extra two years granted under the Patents and Designs Act 1919 [PUBA31]?	Q: Sir William Bull A: Albert Alexander (Par Sec BoT)	HC Deb, 10 Mar 1924, Vol 170(5th), col 1957W
Q575	Whether, considering the surplus of the Patent Office, the fees might be reduced?	Q: Smedley Crooke A: Sidney Webb (Pr BoT)	HC Deb, 11 Mar 1824, Vol 170(5th), col 2098
Q576	Whether the government is aware that the French government has taken out patents for the Haber-Bosch process to produce nitrates?	Q: Hugh Moulton A: Stephen Walsh (Sec War)	HC Deb, 11 Mar 1924, Vol 170(5th), col 2111
Q577	Whether the government is aware of the delays facing claims before the Royal Commission on Awards to Inventors?	Q: John Remer A: William Graham (Fin Sec Tr)	HC Deb, 12 Mar 1924, Vol 170(5th), col 2318–2319
Q578	Whether the government is aware of the lack of uniformity in patent and trade mark law; and whether the government will push for more uniformity at the Industrial Property Convention conference?	Q: Patrick Hannon A: Sidney Webb (Pr BoT)	HC Deb, 3 Apr 1924, Vol 171(5th), col 2451W
Q579	Whether the government will consider amending the law so that where there are good reasons for not working the invention, a sole licence can be given rights despite the patent expiring?	Q: Sir Gervase Beckett A: Albert Alexander (Par Sec BoT)	HC Deb, 10 Apr 1924, Vol 172(5th), col 628
Q580	What was the revenue excess over expenditure of the Patent Office in 1922–23 and 1923–24?	Q: John Black A: Sidney Webb (Pr BoT)	HC Deb, 15 Apr 1924, Vol 172(5th), col 1102

(continued)

(continued)

Q581	Whether there will be a re-hearing of Albert Close's case regarding his anti-submarine net?	Q: Sir Fredric Wise A: William Graham (Fin Sec Tr)	HC Deb, 6 May 1924, Vol 173(5th), col 263W
Q582	Whether the government is aware that [Harry] Grindell-Matthews' death ray may pass out of British hands?	Q: John Emlyn-Jones Q: Joseph Kenworthy Q: William Greene A: William Leach (US Air)	HC Deb, 22 May 1924, Vol 173(5th), col 2392–2393
Q583	Why is the Royal Commission on Awards to Inventors now only meeting one day a week?	Q: John Remer A: William Graham (Fin Sec Tr)	HC Deb, 29 May 1924, Vol 174(5th), col 629–630W
Q584	What powers does the government have to acquire wireless patents?	Q: Walter Baker A: Vernon Hartshorn (PM Gen)	HC Deb, 4 Jun 1924, Vol 174(5th), col 1272–1273W
Q585	Could a second division of the Royal Commission on Awards to Inventors be established to clear arrears?	Q: John Remer A: William Graham (Fin Sec Tr)	HC Deb, 5 Jun 1924, Vol 174(5th), col 1489W
Q586	Why did A Hearne not get his out of pocket expenses for his invention for a synchronised firing gear?	Q: Arthur Samuel A: William Leach (US Air)	HC Deb, 19 Jun 1924, Vol 174(5th), col 2354W
Q587	Why did Albert Close not get his out of pocket expenses for his claim before the Royal Commission on Awards to Inventors?	Q: Sir Fredric Wise A: Charles Ammon (Fin Sec Adm)	HC Deb, 14 Jul 1924, Vol 176(5th), col 48W
Q588	Whether there has been any consideration of the replacement for the Comptroller of Patents; and whether the memorandum by eminent persons will be considered?	Q: Sir Frederick Hall A: Sir Philip Cunliffe-Lister (Pr BoT)	HC Deb, 23 Jul 1925, Vol 186(5th), col 2396
Q589	Whether those tendering to make parachutes need to take liability in respect of patent rights?	Q: Sir Frederick Sykes A: Sir Samuel Hoare (SoS Air)	HC Deb, 24 Nov 1925, Vol 188(5th), col 1179W
Q590	Whether the government is aware the American [Leslie] Irvine type parachute infringes British patents?	Q: Sir Frederick Sykes A: Sir Samuel Hoare (SoS Air)	HC Deb, 25 Nov 1925, Vol 188(5th), col 1381–1383W
Q591	On what basis did the British patent vest in the American company making [Leslie] Irving type parachutes?	Q: Sir Frederick Sykes A: Sir Samuel Hoare (SoS Air)	HC Deb, 3 Dec 1925, Vol 188(5th), col 2539–2534W
Q592	Whether the government is aware that dyers are not able to get licences for naphthalol?	Q: William Kelly A: Sir Robert Chadwick (Par Sec BoT)	HC Deb, 16 Dec 1925, Vol 189(5th), col 1418–1419
Q593	What was the cost of the Patent Office in 1914 and 1925; and the number of staff employed?	Q: Sir Frank Nelson A: Sir Philip Cunliffe-Lister (Pr BoT)	HC Deb, 4 Feb 1926, Vol 191(5th), col 349W
Q594	Why did the government decline an inventor's offer to solve the traffic problem?	Q: Sir Cooper Rawson A: Wilfred Ashley (Min Trans)	HC Deb, 11 Feb 1926, Vol 191(5th), col 1268–1269W

Q595	Whether typewriters made according to British patents are imported entire or in parts?	Q: Sir Harry Brittain A: Arthur Samuel (Fin Sec Tr)	HC Deb, 22 Feb 1926, Vol 192(5th), col 26–28
Q596	Whether the government will introduce legislation to make anti-splash devices compulsory (a British patent)?	Q: Harry Day A: Wilfred Ashley (Min Trans)	HC Deb, 30 Mar 1926, Vol 193(5th), col 1867–1868W
Q597	Whether Brennan has received money beyond £7000 for his helicopter?	Q: Sir Walter de Frec A: Sir Samuel Hoare (SoS Air)	HC Deb, 21 Apr 1926, Vol 194(5th), col 1203–1204
Q598	How many dominion inventors have won claims before the Royal Commission on Awards to Inventors; and how many payments have been made which are not in the reports?	Q: Sir Fredric Wise A: Ronald McNeill (Fin Sec Tr)	HC Deb, 14 Jul 1926, Vol 198(5th), col 423–424W
Q599	What has been done in the colonies to implement the British Empire Patent Conference; and the status of British patents in Irish courts?	Q: Robert Boothby A: Leo Amery (SoS Col)	HC Deb, 19 Jul 1926, Vol 198(5th), col 872–873
Q600	Whether the government is aware of the decision of the Irish High Court (*British Thomson-Houston v Litton & Co* (unreported, 16 Jul 1926) that British patents are no longer valid?	Q: Sir William Davison A: William Ormsby-Gore (PM Gen)	HC Deb, 21 Jul 1926, Vol 198(5th), col 1220
Q601	Whether Scottish Dyes has sold its patent for jade green to Interessen Gemeinschaft?	Q: John Sandeman Allen A: Sir Robert Chadwick (Par Sec BoT)	HC Deb, 26 Jul 1926, Vol 198(5th), col 1678
Q602	Whether post-marking machines are protected by British patents?	Q: Herbert Williams A: Sir Philip Cunliffe-Lister (Pr BoT)	HC Deb, 23 Nov 1926, Vol 200(5th), col 192
Q603	Whether the Beam radio system is a monopoly?	Q: Carlyon Bellairs A: Viscount Wolmer (Par Sec BoT)	HC Deb, 29 Nov 1926, Vol 200(5th), col 845W
Q604	Whether Marten Hale should have paid Income Tax on his award from the Royal Commission?	Q: Cuthbert James A: Ronald McNeill (Fin Sec Tr)	HC Deb, 7 Apr 1927, Vol 204(5th), col 2258–2259
Q605	Whether the government will issue a memorandum about miscellaneous revenue during the present financial year?	Q: Herbert Williams A: Winston Churchill (Ch Ex)	HC Deb, 26 Apr 1927, Vol 205(5th), col 655–657
Q606	How many claimants before the Royal Commission on Awards to Inventors have had to take proceedings to establish their patent is valid?	Q: Cuthbert James A: Ronald McNeill (Fin Sec Tr)	HC Deb, 4 May 1927, Vol 205(5th), col 1636–1638W
Q607	When was Income Tax first deducted from awards made to inventors?	Q: Cuthbert James A: Ronald McNeill (Fin Sec Tr)	HC Deb, 11 May 1927, Vol 206(5th), col 389–390W
Q608	Whether an inquiry will be set up to consider inventors who submit inventions to government departments where the patent is subject to the Official Secrets Act?	Q: Arnold Townend A: Sir Philip Cunliffe-Lister (Pr BoT)	HC Deb, 23 Jun 1927, Vol 207(5th), col 2073W
Q609	Whether the government is aware of the hardship arising from a patent application received on 3–7 Jun?	Q: Sir William Bull A: Sir Philip Cunliffe-Lister (Pr BoT)	HC Deb, 21 Jul 1927, Vol 209(5th), col 595–596W

(continued)

(continued)

Q610	Which judges have been withdrawn from judicial duties (Royal Commission on Awards to Inventors)?	Q: Sir Herbert Nield A: Sir Thomas Inskip (S-G)	HC Deb, 5 Dec 1927, Vol 211(5th), col 970–971
Q611	Whether it is the government's intention to carry out the recommendations of the committee on the dating and sealing of patents [REP20]?	Q: Sir Wilfred Sugden A: Herbert Williams (Par Sec BoT)	HC Deb, 13 Feb 1928, Vol 213(5th), col 542W
Q612	What is the number of patents registered in 1928, and how many lapsed due to failure to pay renewal fees?	Q: Herbert Woodcock A: Sir Philip Cunliffe-Lister (Pr BoT)	HC Deb, 21 Feb 1928, Vol 213(5th), col 1387
Q613	What is the relative position of the government and Marconi in ownership of the Beam?	Q: Charles Ammon A: Sir William Mitchell-Thomson (PM Gen)	HC Deb, 7 Mar 1928, Vol 214(5th), col 1139–1140
Q614	Whether the prolonging of a patent could be changed to avoid the expense of High Court proceedings?	Q: Smedley Crooke A: Douglas Hacking (US FO)	HC Deb, 26 Apr 1928, Vol 216(5th), 1076–1077
Q615	Whether instructions were given to make Income Tax deductions from awards to inventors?	Q: Cuthbert James Q: George Hardie A: Arthur Samuel (Fin Sec Tr)	HC Deb, 17 May 1928, Vol 217(5th), col 1200–1201
Q616	Whether the government is aware that Marten Hale had Income Tax deducted from his award from the Royal Commission?	Q: Cuthbert James A: Arthur Samuel (Fin Sec Tr)	HC Deb, 17 May 1928, Vol 217(5th), col 1200–1201
Q617	Whether any patents owned by the Airship Guarantee Company will be embodied in the R100?	Q: Frank Rose A: Sir Samuel Hoare (SoS Air)	HC Deb, 23 May 1928, Vol 217(5th), col 1908–1909W
Q618	What are the miscellaneous receipts listed in the 1927–28 Financial Statement?	Q: Arabella Lawrence A: Arthur Samuel (Fin Sec Tr)	HC Deb, 24 May 1928, Vol 217(5th), col 2086W
Q619	Whether the government is aware that Marten Hale had Income Tax deducted from his award from the Royal Commission?	Q: Cuthbert James A: Arthur Samuel (Fin Sec Tr)	HC Deb, 26 Jun 1928, Vol 219(5th), col 230
Q620	What allowance was made to Martin Hale regarding his prosecution costs before the Royal Commission on Awards to Inventors?	Q: Cuthbert James Q: Harry Crookshank Q: Edward Campbell A: Arthur Samuel (Fin Sec Tr)	HC Deb, 28 Jun 1928, Vol 219(5th), col 697–699
Q621	What steps are being taken to change the practice for dating and sealing patents; and the implementation of the International Convention?	Q: Sir Wilfred Sugden A: Herbert Williams (Parly Sec BoT)	HC Deb, 4 Jul 1928, Vol 219(5th), col 1388–1389W
Q622	What was the total sum awarded by the Royal Commission on Awards to Inventors, and how much was deducted as Income Tax?	Q: Harry Crookshank A: Arthur Samuel (Fin Sec Tr)	HC Deb, 9 Jul 1928, Vol 219(5th), col 1855–1856
Q623	Whether the government is aware that the "slotted wing" invention is being sold to the French government?	Q: Percy Harris A: Sir Samuel Hoare (Sec War)	HC Deb, 18 Jul 1928, Vol 220(5th), col 406

Q624	What was the Patent Office revenue and surplus over the past ten years; how many applications are awaiting office action; what are the arrears of work; what is the strength of the examining stage during these periods; whether more staff will be engaged?	Q: Patrick Malone A: Herbert Williams (Par Sec BoT)	HC Deb, 18 Jul 1928, Vol 220(5th), col 428W
Q625	Whether the government has received the resolutions from the Association of Special Libraries relating to searches of patent specifications?	Q: Stuart Bevan A: Sir Philip Cunliffe-Lister (Pr BoT)	HC Deb, 2 Aug 1928, Vol 220(5th), col 2405W
Q626	What is the time allowed to work a patent in different countries before revocation on grounds of failure to work?	Q: Carlyon Bellairs A: Herbert Williams (Par Sec BoT)	HC Deb, 9 Nov 1928, Vol 222(5th), col 374W
Q627	Whether the government is aware of the report of the British Science Guild into reform of the patent system; and what is the government's response?	Q: Walter Forrest and Abraham England A: Herbert Williams (Par Sec BoT)	HC Deb, 13 Nov 1928, Vol 222(5th), col 711–712W
Q628	Whether the government is aware of the report of the British Science Guild into patent reform; and whether the surplus generated by the Patent Office is right?	Q: Walter Forrest and Sir Nicholas Grattan-Doyle A: Herbert Williams (Par Sec BoT)	HC Deb, 15 Nov 1928, Vol 222(5th), col 1101–1102W
Q629	What the surplus of revenue over expenditure at the Patent Office in each year from 1922?	Q: Sir Nicholas Grattan-Doyle A: Herbert Williams (Par Sec BoT)	HC Deb, 20 Nov 1928, Vol 222(5th), col 1526
Q630	Whether there is any prospect of an inquiry into reforming patent law?	Q: Sir George Butler A: Herbert Williams (Par Sec BoT)	HC Deb, 20 Nov 1928, Vol 222(5th), col 1565W
Q631	Whether the government is proposing to amend the patent law to reduce the cost of prosecution?	Q: Sir Robert Thomas A: Herbert Williams (Parly Sec BoT)	HC Deb, 12 Dec 1928, Vol 223(5th), col 2120
Q632	What is the total capital expenditure on the Beam wireless system?	Q: Wilfred Wellock A: Sir William Mitchell-Thomson (PM Gen)	HC Deb, 19 Dec 1928, Vol 223(5th), col 3013
Q633	What were the numbers of men and women of higher clerical and executive officer grade assigned to the Patent Office?	Q: William Kelly A: Arthur Samuel (Fin Sec Tr)	HC Deb, 20 Dec 1928, Vol 223(5th), col 3252–3259W
Q634	Whether inventions and improvements relating to cable and wireless discovered by research workers will be owned by the Communication Company?	Q: Albert Alexander A: Sir William Mitchell-Thomson (PM Gen)	HC Deb, 20 Dec 1928, Vol 223(5th), col 3267W
Q635	How many complete specifications are currently awaiting examination; and how quickly arrears are developing; and setting up a committee to inquiry into the patent system?	Q: Fredrick Pethick-Lawrence A: Herbert Williams (Par Sec BoT)	HC Deb, 26 Feb 1929, Vol 225(5th), col 1747–1748
Q636	What is the increase in staff since 31 Dec 1928; how many applications does a member of staff deal with each year; how many months before examination begins?	Q: Fredrick Pethick-Lawrence A: Sir Philip Cunliffe-Lister (Pr BoT)	HC Deb, 5 Mar 1929, Vol 226(5th), col 172–175

(continued)

(continued)

Q637	What was the number of complete specifications filed during the past 25 years; what was the total number of examining staff on 1 Jan each year; and the number of complete specifications examined on 1 Jan each year?	Q: Fredrick Pethick-Lawrence A: Herbert Williams (Par Sec BoT)	HC Deb, 22 Mar 1929, Vol 226(5th), col 1978–1979W
Q638	Whether an inquiry will be set up to explore the amendment of patent law?	Q: George Spero A: William Graham (Pr BoT)	HC Deb, 9 Jul 1929, Vol 229(5th), col 669
Q639	How many complete specifications have been awaiting adjudication for more than three months?	Q: James Ede A: William Graham (Pr BoT)	HC Deb, 23 Jul 1929, Vol 230(5th), col 1057
Q640	Whether royalties have been paid to Squadron Leader [George] Scott and Lieutenant Colonel [Vincent] Richmond for their Airship patents?	Q: Cecil Malone A: Frederick Montague (US FO)	HC Deb, 13 Nov 1929, Vol 231(5th), col 2036
Q641	What was the total amount awarded by the Royal Commission, and how many cases are left to be decided?	Q: Alexander West Russell A: Frederick Pethick-Lawrence (Fin Sec Tr)	HC Deb, 12 Dec 1929, Vol 233(5th), col 691–692W
Q642	What is the maximum term of protection afforded to inventors in the United States and Great Britain; and what is the maximum fee for protection over that period; how many last the full period?	Q: Edward Wise A: William Graham (Pr BoT)	HC Deb, 28 Jan 1930, Vol 234(5th), col 863–864W
Q643	What were the administrative expenses of the Industrial Property Department and receipts and revenue for 1928?	Q: Edward Wise A: William Graham (Pr BoT)	HC Deb, 28 Jan 1930, Vol 234(5th), col 868–869W
Q644	Whether there has yet been a re-organisation of the Patent Office to increase examining staff to enable examination with less delay?	Q: Arthur Samuel A: William Graham (Pr BoT)	HC Deb, 4 Feb 1930, Vol 234(5th), col 1706W
Q645	Whether Patent Office staff can be rearranged to accelerate work?	Q: Douglas Clifton-Brown and Charles Williams A: Walter Smith (Par Sec BoT)	HC Deb, 18 Feb 1930, Vol 235(5th), col 1119–1120
Q646	How much money has been paid by the Royal Commission on Awards to Inventors; can the Commission now be discharged?	Q: Ralph Glyn A: Frederick Pethick-Lawrence (Fin Sec Tr)	HC Deb, 27 Feb 1930, Vol 235(5th), col 2452W
Q647	Whether the validity of British patents is part of the negotiations with Soviet Russia?	Q: Carlyon Bellairs A: Arthur Henderson (For Sec)	HC Deb, 10 Mar 1930, Vol 236(5th), col 900
Q648	Whether adverts are accepted in the pamphlet entitled "Instructions to Applicants for Patents"?	Q: Cecil Malone A: Frederick Pethick-Lawrence (Fin Sec Tr)	HC Deb, 13 Mar 1930, Vol 236(5th), col1530W
Q649	How much was awarded to those involved in inventing the tank; and are there any claims outstanding?	Q: William Kelly A: Frederick Pethick-Lawrence (Fin Sec Tr)	HC Deb, 1 Apr 1930, Vol 237(5th), col 1111–1112W

Q650	What were the net receipts of the Patent Office for the last 12 months; and what is the average time it takes for an applicant to get examination results?	Q: Harry Day A: William Graham (Pr BoT)	HC Deb, 15 Apr 1930, Vol 237(5th), col 2694–2695
Q651	Whether the Committee of Inquiry (Sargeant Committee) [REP21] has finished its inquiry; and when will the report be published?	Q: Patrick Hannon A: William Graham (Pr BoT)	HC Deb, 15 Apr 1930, Vol 237(5th), col 2760W
Q652	What is the surplus of revenue over expenditure over the last 12 months; and whether this has increased over the last 12 months?	Q: Harry Day A: William Graham (Pr BoT)	HC Deb, 13 May 1930, Vol 238(5th), col 1622
Q653	Whether the government intends to introduce laws to amend patents within the present session?	Q: Harry Crookshank A: William Graham (Pr BoT)	HC Deb, 6 Jun 1930, Vol 239(5th), col 2559W
Q654	When will a bill amending patent law be introduced; whether action has been taken to accelerate procedures and reduce cost?	Q: Harry Day A: William Graham (Pr BoT)	HC Deb, 17 Jun 1930, Vol 240(5th), col 6
Q655	As Italian patent law has not been amended to give effect to Hague Conference, must patented articles be manufactured in Italy?	Q: John Wardlaw-Milne A: William Graham (Pr BoT)	HC Deb, 8 Jul 1930, Vol 241(5th), col 214–215
Q656	Are the problems Victor A Terry (patentee) faced due to Italy not modifying its patent law in accordance with the Hague Conference?	Q: John Wardlaw-Milne A: William Graham (Pr BoT)	HC Deb, 8 Jul 1930, Vol 241(5th), col 248–249W
Q657	When will the next report of the Royal Commission on Awards to Inventors be published?	Q: Sir George Hamilton A: Frederick Pethick-Lawrence (Fin Sec Tr)	HC Deb, 17 Jul 1930, Vol 241(5th), col 1496–1497W
Q658	What representations have been made to Italy regarding its failure to implement the Hague Conference; and the difficulty caused for British patentees?	Q: John Wardlaw-Milne A: William Graham (Pr BoT)	HC Deb, 22 Jul 1930, Vol 241(5th), col 1915
Q659	What is being done to cope with the arrears of work at the Patent Office?	Q: Sir Nicholas Grattan-Doyle Q: Arthur Samuel Q: Harry Crookshank A: William Graham (Pr BoT)	HC Deb, 22 Jul 1930, Vol 241(5th), col 1918–1919
Q660	Whether the government is aware that a hearing was not allowed on the U-boat net invention?	Q: Sir George Hamilton A: Frederick Pethick-Lawrence (Fin Sec Tr)	HC Deb, 30 Jul 1930, Vol 242(5th), col 524–525W
Q661	Whether the government is aware that Rochdale Library was asked to send a copy of the patent specifications to the USSR?	Q: Sir Nicholas Grattan-Doyle A: William Graham (Pr BoT)	HC Deb, 25 Nov 1930, Vol 245(5th), col 1068–1069
Q662	When will the report of the Committee of Inquiry be received [REP21]?	Q: Douglas Hacking A: William Graham (Pr BoT)	HC Deb, 24 Feb 1931, Vol 248(5th), col 1932
Q663	Whether the government has received from the committee the report [REP21] into the law of patents; and whether the report will be published?	Q: Douglas Hacking A: Walter Smith (Par Sec BoT)	HC Deb, 25 Mar 1931, Vol 250(5th), col 337

(continued)

(continued)

Q664	Whether the Committee of Inquiry Report [REP21] has been considered yet; and what measures will be taken to reduce the delay in examination?	Q: John Remer A: William Graham (Pr BoT)	HC Deb, 5 May 1931, Vol 252(5th), col 210–211
Q665	What steps will be taken to implement the recommendations of the British Science Guild in response to the Committee of Inquiry Report [REP21]?	Q: Archibald Church A: Walter Smith (Par Sec BoT)	HC Deb, 6 Jul 1931, Vol 254(5th), col 1709
Q666	What preparations have been made for the International Congress on Patent Law and Practice?	Q: Archibald Church A: Walter Smith (Par Sec BoT)	HC Deb, 6 Jul 1931, Vol 254(5th), col 1709
Q667	Whether the surplus in the 48th Report is funded or taken by the Treasury as income; whether pension liability is funded?	Q: Robert Aske A: Walter Smith (Par Sec BoT)	HC Deb, 14 Jul 1931, Vol 255(5th), col 243–244W
Q668	Whether the government will accept the offer of Dr Watson for the patent rights for his dentistry device?	Q: George Buchanan A: Arthur Greenwood (Min He)	HC Deb, 30 Jul 1931, Vol 255(5th), col 2482–2483W
Q669	Whether the British government will give assistance to claimants before the United States Commission on Awards to Inventors?	Q: Sir William Davison A: Sir John Simon (For Sec)	HC Deb, 24 Oct 1932, Vol 269(5th), col 606–607
Q670	What was the statutory authority for patent renewal fees in respect of the fifteenth and sixteenth years?	Q: Henry Procter A: Edward Burgin (Par Sec BoT)	HC Deb, 6 Dec 1932, Vol 272(5th), col 1405–1406
Q671	Whether it is possible to estimate the payments in royalties to rights controlled abroad?	Q: George Mitcheson A: Edward Burgin (Par Sec BoT)	HC Deb, 13 Dec 1932, Vol 273(5th), col 177
Q672	Whether the Admiralty has had a report on Beechey's device for saving the crew of sunken submarines?	Q: Herbert Williams A: Sir Bolton Eyres-Monsell (Ch Whip)	HC Deb, 22 Feb 1933, Vol 274(5th), col 1716
Q673	What authority is used for prescribing fees for the fifteenth and sixteenth years of a patent; whether Patents Rules 1932 have been laid before the House?	Q: Lord Askwith A: Lord Templemore (L in Waiting)	HL Deb, 23 Mar 1933, Vol 87(5th), col 83–89
Q674	Whether the government will speak to the Chinese government about protecting foreign patents?	Q: William Nunn A: Walter Runciman (Pr BoT)	HC Deb, 30 May 1933, Vol 278(5th), col 1672
Q675	Whether the government will accept responsibility for the infringement of Clive Liddell's (Nissen) Hut patent [1917 No 113,376] by the United States government?	Q: Andrew Gault A: Walter Womersley (Jr Ld Tr)	HC Deb, 18 Jul 1933, Vol 280(5th), col 1659–1660
Q676	How many specifications have been post-dated under s 6(3)(b) of the Patents and Designs Act 1932 [PUBA33]?	Q: Henry Procter A: Edward Burgin (Par Sec BoT)	HC Deb, 27 Jul 1933, Vol 280(5th), col 2777–2778

Q677	How many examiners are there at the Patent Office, and what is the total pay?	Q: Gilbert Gledhill A: Walter Runciman (Pr BoT)	HC Deb, 6 Dec 1933, Vol 283(5th), col 1470–1471
Q678	What were the grounds that Mrs Cloete Capron was refused permission to appear before the Tank Inquiry Commission?	Q: Edward Doran A: Duff Cooper (Fin Sec War)	HC Deb, 6 Dec 1933, Vol 283(5th), col 1477
Q679	What sum would be due in royalties under the hydrogenation of coal scheme?	Q: Gordon Hall-Caine A: Ernest Brown (SoS Mines)	HC Deb, 13 Feb 1934, Vol 285(5th), col 1766W
Q680	Was not Sir Charles Craven right to tell his business friends that the Electric Boat Company had a financial interest in the building of the Clyde?	Q: Arthur Marseden A: Lord (Edward) Stanley (Par Sec Adm)	HC Deb, 14 Nov 1934, Vol 293(5th), col 1939–1940
Q681	Whether the government will ascertain how much of the cost of traffic signals is patent royalties?	Q: Charles Summersby A: Leslie Hore-Belisha (Min Trans)	HC Deb, 26 Jun 1935, Vol 303 (5th), col 1115W
Q682	Is the government aware that manufacturers have been developing their patent rights abroad due to the handicap on industry in this country?	Q: Louis Smith A: Ernest Brown (Min Lab)	HC Deb, 27 Jun 1935, Vol 303(5th), col 1245–1246
Q683	Whether women examiners are required to have the same qualifications and duties as male examiners?	Q: Valentine McEntee A: Duff Cooper (Fin Sec Tr)	HC Deb, 2 Aug 1935, Vol 304(5th), col 3005–3007W
Q684	Will a committee be set up to consider whether want of subject matter should be a ground for objection to the grant of a patent?	Q: Sir Arnold Wilson A: George Davies (Whip)	HC Deb, 13 Feb 1936, Vol 308(5th), col 1144–1145
Q685	Whether renewal fees may be waived for an unemployed person who is not able to exploit their patent?	Q: Alfred Holland A: Walter Runciman (Pr BoT)	HC Deb, 12 Mar 1936, Vol 309(5th), col 2324–2325W
Q686	When the Fuel Research Board carries out experiments, are the patentees given the results?	Q: Thomas Magnay A: Ramsay MacDonald (Ld Pr)	HC Deb, 24 Jul 1936, Vol 315(5th), col 963–964W
Q687	Whether the Royal Commission on Awards to Inventors is still sitting, and when its final report will be published?	Q: Sir Arnold Wilson A: Neville Chamberlain (Ch Ex)	HC Deb, 12 Nov 1936, Vol 317(5th), col 1063W
Q688	What steps will be taken to accelerate patent procedure and to simplify it; and negotiations with the speeding up the registration of patents?	Q: Harry Day A: Edward Burgin (Par Sec BoT)	HC Deb, 8 Dec 1936, Vol 318(5th), col 1803–1804
Q689	Why alterations have been made to the [Frederich] Bergius system of hydrogenation at Billingham, and do the patentees hold rights over the alterations?	Q: George Hardie A: Harry Crookshank (SoS Mines)	HC Deb, 19 Jan 1937, Vol 319(5th), col 3–5
Q690	What is the approximate time it takes to get a patent through the Patent Office?	Q: Harry Day A: Walter Runciman (Pr BoT)	HC Deb, 9 Feb 1937, Vol 320(5th), col 192

(continued)

(continued)

Q691	How many women civil servants have applied to be retained in the Civil Service after marriage?	Q: William Astor A: John Colville (Fin Sec Tr)	HC Deb, 3 Mar 1937, Vol 321(5th), col 375–376W
Q692	Whether the extension of the search for novelty under the Patents and Designs Act 1932 [PUBA33] has given satisfactory results; and whether the search can be extended further?	Q: Ralph Assheton A: Walter Runciman (Pr BoT)	HC Deb, 9 Mar 1937, Vol 321(5th), col 985–986W
Q693	When will the final report of the Royal Commission on Awards to Inventors be published?	Q: Sir Arnold Wilson A: John Colville (Fin Sec Tr)	HC Deb, 22 Apr 1937, Vol 322(5th), col 1930W
Q694	How many inventions made by officials in the Postmaster-General's department in the course of their duties have been commercially exploited in the last five years?	Q: Sir Robert Young A: George Tryon (PM Gen)	HC Deb, 19 Jul 1937, Vol 326(5th), col 1769
Q695	How many foreign firms have been given patent rights to extract oil from coal; what objections have there been from British firms?	Q: Edward Dunn A: Oliver Stanley (Pr BoT)	HC Deb, 20 Jul 1937, Vol 326(5th), col 1948
Q696	How many useful inventions have been made by government servants; what rewards have been paid to them?	Q: Sir Robert Young A: John Coville (Fin Sec Tr)	HC Deb, 29 Jul 1937, Vol 326(5th), col 3326–3327W
Q697	Are any British patents being used by the Nippon Steel Company; if so, what are the financial arrangements?	Q: Ellis Smith A: Oliver Stanley (Pr BoT)	HC Deb, 8 Feb 1938, Vol 331(5th), col 817–818
Q698	What steps are being taken to reform the patent system to enable dedication of scientific discoveries and to prevent drug patenting?	Q: David Adams A: Euan Wallace (Par Sec BoT)	HC Deb, 16 May 1938, Vol 336(5th), col 58W
Q699	Whether a licence or royalty is payable to any foreign government for the Bren gun?	Q: Reginald Fletcher A: Sir Victor Warrender (Fin Sec PM Gen)	HC Deb, 19 Jul 1938, Vol 338(5th), col 1974–1975
Q700	Whether the high price of anti-malaria drugs is why they are not provided to natives; could they be produced here under licence?	Q: David Adams A: Oliver Stanley (Pr BoT)	HC Deb, 26 Jul 1938, Vol 338(5th), col 2917–2918W
Q701	What claims are being made on the government in respect of the [Archibald] Frazer-Nash (gun turret) patents?	Q: Ellis Smith Q: Sir Derrick Gunston A: Sir Thomas Inskip (Min Co-ordination Def)	HC Deb, 14 Dec 1938, Vol 342(5th), col 1985–1986
Q702	Why is there an increase in sales from the Patent Office publications department?	Q: Harry Nathan A: Euan Wallace (Par Sec BoT)	HC Deb, 6 Mar 1939, Vol 344(5th), col 1869–1870
Q703	What is the total sum to be paid in royalties to the owners of the patents in the Bren gun?	Q: Thomas Sexton A: Leslie Hore-Belisha (Sec War)	HC Deb, 2 May 1939. Vol 346(5th), col 1663
Q704	Whether the government is aware that the German government is blocking transfer of royalties from Germany?	Q: Thomas Sexton A: Oliver Stanley (Pr BoT)	HC Deb, 9 May 1939, Vol 347(5th), col 271

Q705	Finance Bill (Apportionment of Income) Whether it applies to patent holding companies?	Q: Edward Keeling A: Donald Somervell (A-G)	HC Deb, 28 Jun 1939, Vol 349(5th), col 467–468
Q706	Whether the government has considered the use of the patented lifebelt light?	Q: Valentine McEntee A: Geoffrey Shakespeare (Par Sec Tr)	HC Deb, 26 Oct 1939, Vol 352(5th), col 1579W
Q707	Where does the Patent Office now have its headquarter?	Q: Sir Stanley Reed A: Oliver Stanley (Pr BoT)	HC Deb, 7 Nov 1939, Vol 353(5th), col 55–56W
Q708	What salary is paid to officials, including those transferred from the Board of Trade?	Q: Abraham Lyons A: Sir Arthur Salter (Par Sec Min Ship)	HC Deb, 23 Jan 1940, Vol 356(5th), col 387–396
Q709	Whether patents are still be granted to German subjects; and if so, upon what grounds?	Q: Gilbert Gledhill A: Sir Andrew Duncan (Pr BoT)	HC Deb, 28 May 1940, Vol 361(5th), col 425W
Q710	Whether patent agents, due to technical expertise, should be a reserved occupation?	Q: Eleanor Rathbone A: Ralph Assheton (Par Sec Tr)	HC Deb, 30 May 1940, Vol 361(5th), col 633
Q711	Whether enemy-owned patents are being worked by the government; and if so, what happens to the royalties?	Q: Thomas Sexton A: Sir Andrew Duncan (Pr BoT)	HC Deb, 25 Jun 1940, Vol 362(5th), col 315W
Q712	What steps are being taken to pool patent rights in the national interest?	Q: Ellis Smith A: Arthur Greenwood (Min w/o Port)	HC Deb, 25 Jul 1940, Vol 363(5th), col 950–951
Q713	Whether the high demand for patented Vitamin B1 should lead to it no longer being exported?	Q: Sir Ernest Graham-Little A: Robert Boothby (Par Sec Food)	HC Deb, 8 Aug 1940, Vol 364(5th), col 462W
Q714	Whether the government is aware the Army and Air Force have entered contracts for providing patented Vitamin A and B?	Q: Sir Ernest Graham-Little A: Richard Law (Fin Sec War)	HC Deb, 20 Nov 1940, Vol 365(5th), col 2025W
Q715	What is the annual cost of supplying the Air Force with patented products to restore vitamin A?	Q: Sir Ernest Graham-Little A: Sir Archibald Sinclair (SoS Air)	HC Deb, 21 Jan 1941, Vol 368(5th), col 54W
Q716	What licence is the government relying on to use German IG patents to make Vitamin B1?	Q: Sir Ernest Graham-Little A: Harcourt Johnstone (Sec Overseas Tr)	HC Deb, 22 Jan 1941, Vol 368(5th), col 195–196W
Q717	Whether patents whose working has ceased by reason of the war will have their term extended?	Q: Walter Higgs A: Oliver Lyttelton (Pr BoT)	HC Deb, 4 Feb 1941, Vol 368(5th), col 775
Q718	Whether the government is going to take over all the patents connected with aircraft production?	Q: Pierse Loftus Q: Arthur Woodburn A: John Dillwyn-Llewellin (Par Sec War Trans)	HC Deb, 5 Feb 1941, Vol 368(5th), col 917–918
Q719	Whether the government is paying patent royalties to non-British firms now or will do so in the future?	Q: Ellis Smith A: Harry Crookshank (Fin Sec Tr)	HC Deb, 30 Apr 1941, Vol 371(5th), col 439–440
Q720	Whether any royalties are being paid to enemy subjects?	Q: John Parker A: Charles Waterhouse (Par Sec BoT)	HC Deb, 1 May 1941, Vol 371(5th), col 569

(continued)

(continued)

Q721	Whether the government is considering suspending fees which are temporarily rendered of little value due to the war?	Q: Sir Herbert Williams A: Oliver Lyttelton (Pr BoT)	HC Deb, 20 May 1941, Vol 371(5th), col 1367–1368
Q722	Whether the government is aware that the cost of applying to suspend patent fees is greater than the cost of the fees themselves?	Q: Sir Herbert Williams A: Oliver Lyttelton (Pr BoT)	HC Deb, 27 May 1941, Vol 371(5th), col 1681–1682
Q723	Whether the procedure for suspending patent fees has been simplified where patents cannot be worked during the war?	Q: Sir John Wardlaw-Milne A: Sir Andrew Duncan (Pr BoT)	HC Deb, 14 Oct 1941, Vol 374(5th), col 1219–1220
Q724	What part did the government play in the decision to install only one United States rubber plant in the United Kingdom, and what were the difficulties with patent rights?	Q: John Parker Q: Emanuel Shinwell A: George Garro-Jones (Par Sec Prod)	HC Deb, 30 Sep 1942, Vol 383(5th), col 772
Q725	What steps are being take to make officials address questions on patents?	Q: John Parker A: Sir Andrew Duncan (Min Supp)	HC Deb, 30 Sep 1942, Vol 383(5th), col 777–778W
Q726	Whether steps can be taken for firms to comply with requests from officials relating to information regarding turnover?	Q: John Parker A: Hugh Dalton (Pr BoT)	HC Deb, 17 Nov 1942, Vol 385(5th), col 209W
Q727	How many requests have been made by the United States government for patent rights under the Anglo-American Agreement [TRE38]?	Q: John Parker A: Anthony Eden (Ld House)	HC Deb, 18 Nov 1942, Vol 385(5th), col 383W
Q728	Whether the government has adequate information regarding patents etc. in synthetic rubber?	Q: John Parker A: George Garro-Jones (Par Sec Prod)	HC Deb, 25 Nov 1942, Vol 385(5th), col 715
Q729	Have powers under the Defence (Patents, Trade Marks, etc.) Regulations 1941 been used to obtain the watercraft invented by George Constantinescu?	Q: Robert Bower A: Albert Alexander (Fir Ld Adm) Comment: Richard Stokes	HC Deb, 12 May 1943, Vol 389(5th), col 619–620
Q730	Why Albert Products, a German firm, was taken over by the Public Custodian and sold to Imperial Chemical Industries, and not offered to the whole market?	Q: Wilfred Burke Q: Emanuel Shinwell Q: Aneurin Bevan A: Hugh Dalton (Pr BoT)	HC Deb, 27 Jul 1943, Vol 391(5th), col 1366–1367
Q731	Whether a departmental committee could be set up to consider the restrictive practices of patent holders?	Q: John Parker A: Charles Waterhouse (Par Sec BoT)	HC Deb, 22 Sep 1943, Vol 392(5th), col 222W
Q732	Is the government aware of "Germany's Master Plan" and enemy patents?	Q: Emanuel Shinwell A: Hugh Dalton (Pr BoT)	HC Deb, 2 Nov 1943, Vol 393(5th), col 501
Q733	Whether the government will give tax relief to industrial research?	Q: Ralph Etherton A: Sir John Anderson (Ch Ex)	HC Deb, 2 Nov 1943, Vol 393(5th), col 523–524
Q734	Will the government confirm no further payments will be made to IG, the German company, in relation to its patents?	Q: Ellis Smith A: Hugh Dalton (Pr BoT)	HC Deb, 9 Nov 1943, Vol 393(5th), col 1063–1064

Q735	Will the law be amended to prohibit refusals to work and to require a more precise specification of manufacturing?	Q: Sir William Davison A: Hugh Dalton (Pr BoT)	HC Deb, 14 Mar 1944, Vol 398(5th), col 18–19
Q736	Whether a paper is being published on payments and loans made regarding German patents used before the war?	Q: Ellis Smith A: Hugh Dalton (Pr BoT)	HC Deb, 21 Mar 1944, Vol 398(5th), col 663
Q737	Whether the government will consider setting up a committee to consider the taxation of royalties and its retardation of inventive activities?	Q: Abraham Lyons A: Sir John Anderson (Ch Ex)	HC Deb, 21 Mar 1944, Vol 398(5th), col 668
Q738	Whether the government will make a statement about patent law reform?	Q: Alfred Edwards A: Hugh Dalton (Pr BoT)	HC Deb, 25 Apr 1944, Vol 399(5th), col 600–601
Q739	Whether the costs of developing an invention should be tax-deductible (as the patent is not adequate)?	Q: William Wavell Wakefield A: Sir John Anderson (Ch Ex)	HC Deb, 16 May 1944, Vol 400(5th), col 29–30
Q740	Whether the government is aware inventors have no right to remuneration where their invention is used by the nation?	Q: William Wavell Wakefield A: Sir John Anderson (Ch Ex)	HC Deb, 16 May 1944, Vol 400(5th), col39W
Q741	Whether private companies who take advantage of research by Power Jets Ltd (government company) are able to take out a patent?	Q: Lord Faringdon A: Lord Sherwood	HL Deb, 14 Jun 1944, Vol 132(5th), col 232–233
Q742	What are the composition and terms of reference of the committee appointed to consider patent laws [REP22]?	Q: Edward Salt A: Hugh Dalton (Pr BoT)	HC Deb, 20 Jun 1944, Vol 401(5th), col 33W
Q743	How many claims for inventions, processes and designs have been admitted and rejected since the start of the war?	Q: Alfred Edwards A: Charles Waterhouse (Par Sec BoT)	HC Deb, 21 Jun 1944, Vol 401(5th), col 204W
Q744	How many actions by inventors against the government have been brought since the start of the war?	Q: Alfred Edwards A: Sir John Anderson (Ch Ex)	HC Deb, 28 Jun 1944, Vol 401(5th), col 728–729W
Q745	Whether the Inquiry Committee [REP22] will be empowered to investigate patentees' records to see if the use has been contrary to the public interest?	Q: John Parker A: Hugh Dalton (Pr BoT)	HC Deb, 4 Jul 1944, Vol 401(5th), col 982
Q746	Will a Royal Commission be set up to give rewards to inventors?	Q: Francis Bowles A: Sir John Anderson (Ch Ex)	HC Deb, 10 Oct 1944, Vol 403(5th), col 1570
Q747	Whether a term will be included in a peace treaty to prevent payments or royalties being made under pre-war industrial agreements?	Q: Ellis Smith A: Richard Law (Min War)	HC Deb, 1 Nov 1944, Vol 404(5th), col 774–775
Q748	Whether the government will take steps to protect specifications sent to Russia to prevent them being copied (as no copyright)?	Q: Sir Waldron Smithers A: Hugh Dalton (Pr BoT)	HC Deb, 5 Dec 1944, Vol 406(5th), col 341–342

(continued)

(continued)

Q749	Whether the government of the USSR grants patent protection to firms who advertise in Russian trade journals?	Q: Sir Waldron Smithers A: Charles Waterhouse (Par Sec BoT)	HC Deb, 6 Dec 1944, Vol 406(5th), col 545–546W
Q750	Are there any restrictions on exploiting or advertising an invention in the USA/GB agreement where that invention is used to further the war?	Q: Sir Alfred Beit A: Oliver Lyttelton (Min Prod)	HC Deb, 13 Dec 1944, Vol 406(5th), col 1225–1226
Q751	Whether steps will be taken to enable patentees who have suffered by the war to have the patent term extended?	Q: Sir William Davison A: Hugh Dalton (Pr BoT)	HC Deb, 10 Apr 1945, Vol 409(5th), col 1653
Q752	Is it the government's intention to set up a Royal Commission on Awards to Inventors again?	Q: Ellis Smith A: Sir John Anderson (Ch Ex)	HC Deb, 6 Jun 1945, Vol 411(5th), col 907–908W
Q753	Where patents have laid idle during the war, will the government allow for extensions of the patent term?	Q: John Parker A: Charles Waterhouse (Par Sec BoT)	HC Deb, 7 Jun 1945, Vol 411(5th), col 1095–1096W
Q754	Is it the government's intention to set up a Royal Commission on Awards to Inventors again?	Q: Neil Cooper-Key A: George Hall (SoS Col)	HC Deb, 15 Oct 1945, Vol 414(5th), col 745W
Q755	Whether the government will make a statement on Buchanan Reith (and patent rights in hatch fittings)?	Q: John MacKie A: Albert Alexander (Fir Ld Adm)	HC Deb, 17 Oct 1945, Vol 414(5th), col 1183–1184W
Q756	Whether the government will implement the Swann Committee [REP22] recommendation for the extension of the patent term?	Q: Sir Arnold Gridley A: Sir Stafford Cripps (Pr BoT)	HC Deb, 22 Oct 1945, Vol 414(5th), col 1829W
Q757	Whether the government intends to introduce any amendments to patent law in the near future?	Q: John Boyd-Carpenter A: Sir Stafford Cripps (Pr BoT)	HC Deb, 12 Nov 1945, Vol 415(5th), col 1722
Q758	Will the government make available technical information and patents discovered in enemy territory?	Q: Walter Fletcher A: Ellis Smith (Par Sec BoT)	HC Deb, 14 Nov 1945, Vol 415(5th), col 2262W
Q759	What is the average time between a patent application being received and issuing the first examiner's report?	Q: Emrys Roberts A Sir Stafford Cripps (Pr BoT)	HC Deb, 28 Jan 1946, Vol 418(5th), col 118W
Q760	Is the government now in a position to make a statement about Buchanan Reith's patent rights?	Q: John MacKie A: Albert Alexander (Fir Ld Adm)	HC Deb, 27 Feb 1946, Vol 419(5th), col 1895–1896
Q761	Whether patent applications are dealt with in date order; and the extent of delays caused to examination?	Q: Joseph Binns A: Sir Stafford Cripps (Pr BoT)	HC Deb, 6 Mar 1946, Vol 420(5th), col 78–80W
Q762	Whether a Royal Commission will be set up for inventions used during the war?	Q: Michael Clark Hutchinson A: Hugh Dalton (Pr BoT)	HC Deb, 19 Mar 1946, Vol 420(5th), col 1690

Q763	Whether the patents of German and Italian car manufacturers have been made available to British manufacturers?	Q: Hartley Shawcross A: John Wilmot (Min Supp)	HC Deb, 15 Apr 1946, Vol 421(5th), col 374–375W
Q764	Whether a statement will be made regarding Buchanan Reith's patent rights claim?	Q: John MacKie A: William Whiteley (Par Sec Tr)	HC Deb, 16 Apr 1946, Vol 421(5th), col 2524
Q765	What arrangements have been made to make known German trade processes discovered by the British Intelligence Objectives Sub-Committee?	Q: Sir John Maitland A: John Belcher (Par Sec BoT)	HC Deb, 3 Jun 1946, Vol 423(5th), col 1589–1590
Q766	Whether the delays related to the Capital Issues Committee can be resolved to acquire foreign patent rights?	Q: Earl Fortescue A: Lord Pakenham	HL Deb, 24 Jul 1946, Vol 142(5th), col 944–945
Q767	Whether a government office can be set up for people to submit inventions for public use?	Q: Somerville Hasting A: Clement Attlee (PM)	HC Deb, 9 Jun 1947, Vol 438(5th), col 700
Q768	Whether the Afga colour process patents are available to British filmmakers?	Q: Hector Hughes A: John Belcher (Par Sec BoT)	HC Deb, 17 Jun 1947, Vol 438(5th), col 202–203W
Q769	Whether the government is aware that a Patent Office official was disciplined for writing a society's objections to clauses in the Agriculture Bill?	Q: Sir Ernest Graham-Little A: Thomas Williams (Min Agric)	HC Deb, 23 Jun 1947, Vol 439(5th), col 6–7W
Q770	Whether the government will give help to patentees who have to pay patent fees, but have not been able to work the invention?	Q: David Jones A: Sir Stafford Cripps (Pr BoT)	HC Deb, 31 Jul 1947, Vol 441(5th), col 85–86W
Q771	Whether state-owned patents and designs should be treated as a public asset and vesting in a single body?	Q: John Williams A: Harold Wilson (Pr BoT)	HC Deb, 13 Nov 1947, Vol 444(5th), col 93–94W
Q772	Whether it is the government's intention to introduce legislation to implement the Departmental Committee recommendations [REP22]?	Q: Arnold Palmer A: Harold Wilson (Pr BoT)	HC Deb, 20 Nov 1947, Vol 444(5th), col 200W
Q773	Whether the government has studied the Gibbon-Cellan-Jones patent system for upgrading gas?	Q: Robin Turton A: Hugh Gaitskell (Min Fuel)	HC Deb, 27 Nov 1947, Vol 444(5th), col 2095–2096
Q774	What is the value of the patents and technical know-how taken from the Germans?	Q: Richard Stokes A: Christopher Mayhew (US FO)	HC Deb, 3 Dec 1947, Vol 445(5th), col 375–376
Q775	Will the government explain the delay in dealing with patent correspondence?	Q: Sir Waldron Smithers A: Wilfred Paling (PM Gen)	HC Deb, 17 Dec 1947, Vol 445(5th), col 348–349W
Q776	Whether the government is investigating the German government's use of IG Farbenindustrie Gesch's patent to cripple the war capacity?	Q: Sir Ernest Graham-Little A: Christopher Mayhew (US FO)	HC Deb, 18 Dec 1947, Vol 445(5th), col 420–421W

(continued)

(continued)

Q777	Whether the government is aware of Patent Office delays; and steps taken to remedy it?	Q: Peter Freeman A: John Belcher (Par Sec BoT)	HC Deb, 20 Jan 1948, Vol 446(5th), col 36
Q778	Whether, to encourage invention, the government will consider abolishing Income Tax on the sale of patents?	Q: Vernon Barlett A: Sir Stafford Cripps (Ch Ex)	HC Deb, 9 Mar 1948, Vol 448(5th), col 132W
Q779	What are the total patent royalties paid to the USA for penicillin?	Q: Woodrow Wyatt A: Sir Stafford Cripps (Ch Ex)	HC Deb, 20 Apr 1948, Vol 449(5th), col 121–122W
Q780	Whether the government will introduce legislation to reduce the cost of patents?	Q: Mervyn Wheatley A: Harold Wilson (Pr BoT)	HC Deb, 29 Apr 1948, Vol 450(5th), col 581
Q781	When the staff of the Patent Office Library will be informed about the results of the negotiations on the reorganisation which were concluded in Jun 1947?	Q: Albert Blackburn A: Harold Wilson (Pr BoT)	HC Deb, 27 May 1948, Vol 451(5th), col 28–29W
Q782	Whether German patents are still protected outside Germany, and whether their value is being taken into account for reparations?	Q: Richard Stokes A: Christopher Mayhew (US FO)	HC Deb, 7 Jul 1948, Vol 453(5th), col 352–353
Q783	Why the 65th Comptroller's Annual Report is not being printed?	Q: Frederick Erroll A: John Belcher (Par Sec BoT)	HC Deb, 13 Jul 1948, Vol 453(5th), col 86W
Q784	What taxation is paid in France on patent royalties of British nationals?	Q: Ian Mikardo A: Sir Stafford Cripps (Ch Ex)	HC Deb, 2 Nov 1948, Vol 457(5th). Col 681–682
Q785	Whether the government is satisfied with the arrangements for patent registration in Germany?	Q: Hugh Fraser A: Hector McNeil (Min FO)	HC Deb, 15 Nov 1948, Vol 458(5th), col 29
Q786	Whether steps are being taken to prevent unfair Japanese competition (opening of Japanese Patent Office)?	Q: Barlett Stross A: Harold Wilson (Pr BoT)	HC Deb, 15 Feb 1949, Vol 461(5th), col 148–149W
Q787	To what extent are British exports obstructed by Canadian patent law?	Q: Frederick Cobb A: Harold Wilson (Pr BoT)	HC Deb, 10 Mar 1949, Vol 462(5th), col 1374–1375
Q788	How many engineers and inventors served on the Swann Committee [REP22]?	Q: William Snadden A: John Edwards (Par Sec BoT)	HC Deb, 26 Apr 1949, Vol 464(5th), col 22
Q789	How many payment agreements now in force have a provision requiring prompt payment of patent royalties?	Q: Oliver Crosthwaite-Eyre A: Sir Stafford Cripps (Ch Ex)	HC Deb, 2 Jun 1949, Vol 465(5th), col 170–171W
Q790	What is the function of the Patents Division in the Ministry of Supply?	Q: Frederick Erroll A: George Strauss (Par Sec Trans)	HC Deb, 11 Jul 1949, Vol 467(5th), col 20–21
Q791	How many patent agents are currently practising in London?	Q: Fredrick Erroll A: John Edwards (Par Sec BoT)	HC Deb, 12 Jul 1949, Vol 467(5th), col 15–16W
Q792	Has the government considered organising the National Research and Development Corporation to promote British inventions and patents in North America?	Q: Sir William Wavell Wakefield A: Harold Wilson (Pr BoT)	HC Deb, 14 Jul 1949, Vol 467(5th), col 434–435

Q793	How much of the £2,000,000 saved by the Patents Department in the Ministry of Supply has been from resisting awards to inventors?	Q: Frederick Erroll A: John Jones (Par Sec Min Supp)	HC Deb, 28 Jul 1949, Vol 467(5th), col 166W
Q794	Whether special security regulations will be laid down for patents and inventions brought before the National Research Development Corporation?	Q: John Baker White A: John Edwards (Par Sec BoT)	HC Deb, 18 Oct 1949, Vol 468(5th), col 9W
Q795	Whether advertising in the Patent Office Journal will resume?	Q: Fredrick Erroll A: William Hall (Fin Sec)	HC Deb, 29 Nov 1949, Vol 470(5th), col 79W
Q796	Whether, in view of the disclosure of Professor Fuchs' invention by the National Research Development Corporation, the government thinks the current security arrangements are adequate?	Q: John Baker White A: Harold Wilson (Pr BoT)	HC Deb, 9 Mar 1950, Vol 472(5th), col 442–443
Q797	What sums has the USA paid to Power Jets Research for use of its patents from Sep 1945?	Q: Thomas Edmund Harvey A: John Freeman (US War)	HC Deb, 24 Apr 1950, Vol 474(5th), col 586
Q798	How much has been received from the USA for the use of radar patents?	Q: Charles Ian Orr-Ewing A: George Strauss (Min Supp)	HC Deb, 1 May 1950, Vol 474(5th), col 1384
Q799	Whether the government is aware of the delay in examination of applications and specifications; and what steps are being taken to remedy the situation?	Q: Derick Heathcoat-Amory A: Harold Wilson (Pr BoT)	HC Deb, 13 Feb 1951, Vol 484(5th), col 40W
Q800	When is it intended to extend the Patent Office Library opening hours?	Q: Sir Hugh Munro-Lucas-Tooth A: Hartley Shawcross (Pr BoT)	HC Deb, 11 May 1951, Vol 487(5th), col 277W
Q801	Why does the publication of patent specifications and abridgements continue to be in arrears; what representations have been received from Imperial Chemical Industries and the Federation of British Industry; how many patent applications were awaiting examination at the end of 1938, 1949, 1950 and 1951?	Q: Wilfred Vernon A: Arthur Bottomley (SoS Commonwealth)	HC Deb, 10 Jul 1951, Vol 490(5th), col 19–20W
Q802	Why does the front wall of the Patent Office remain unrepaired so that 28 rooms remain unserviceable; and the cost of relocating those staff displaced from the room?	Q: John Morrison A: George Brown (Min of Works)	HC Deb, 10 Jul 1951, Vol 490(5th), col 196–197
Q803	What international trade and intellectual property treaties will Japan have to join under the Peace Treaty?	Q: Arthur Colegate Q: Walter Fletcher A: Ernest Davies (US FO)	HC Deb, 25 Jul 1951, Vol 491(5th), col 435–437
Q804	How many cases has the National Research Development Corporation taken, which would otherwise be unprovided for?	Q: Arthur Pearson A: Peter Thorneycroft (Pr BoT)	HC Deb, 31 Jul 1952, Vol 504(5th), col 167W

(continued)

(continued)

Q805	What information is available on foreign currency earnings of British patented products?	Q: Barnett Janner A: Rab Butler (Ch Ex)	HC Deb, 21 Oct 1952, Vol 505(5th), col 845
Q806	Why has the number of the Patent Office examiners increased in 1951–52 and 1952–53, but staff overall decreased?	Q: William Wavell Wakefield A: Henry Strauss (Par Sec BoT)	HC Deb, 2 Dec 1952, Vol 508(5th), col 1275
Q807	What assets were purchased from the £251,000 advanced by the government?	Q: Sir Herbert Williams A: Henry Strauss (Par Sec BoT)	HC Deb, 10 Feb 1953, Vol 511(5th), col 20W
Q808	What is the average time between receipt of a complete specification and the sealing of a patent; and how does this compare with 1938?	Q: Sir David Campbell A: Peter Thorneycroft (Pr BoT)	HC Deb, 21 Jul 1953, Vol 518(5th), col 184–185
Q809	Whether the discovery of Dr Arthur Charlsby in relation to polythene is patentable?	Q: Ian Winterbottom A: Duncan Sandys (Min Supp)	HC Deb, 9 Nov 1953, Vol 520(5th), col 590
Q810	What is the maximum extension of time in proceedings before the Comptroller; what remedies are there against delay?	Q: Sir David Campbell A: Peter Thorneycraft (Par BoT)	HC Deb, 23 Nov 1953, Vol 521(5th), col 10–11W
Q811	What remittances were made to the USA in 1953 in relation to patents, dividends etc.?	Q: Arthur Blenkinsop A: Rab Butler (Ch Ex)	HC Deb, 9 Feb 1954, Vol 523(5th), col 101–102W
Q812	What is the average delay between a hearing being requested and the matter heard, and the decision being issued?	Q: Sir David Campbell A: Peter Thorneycraft (Pr BoT)	HC Deb, 2 Mar 1954, Vol 524(5th), col 991–992
Q813	What is the average time between the hearing of the opposition to the grant and the date when decisions of the Comptroller are issued?	Q: Sir David Campbell A: Henry Strauss (Par Sec BoT)	HC Deb, 16 Mar 1954, Vol 525(5th), col 19W
Q814	What steps are being taken to make sure British aircraft are made under patent licences while there is uncertainty over Comet?	Q: Eirene White A: Duncan Sandys (Min Supp)	HC Deb, 28 Jun 1954, Vol 529(5th), col 898–899
Q815	When will the Royal Commission on Awards to Inventors finish its work?	Q: Ian Orr-Ewing A: Winston Churchill (PM)	HC Deb, 17 Mar 1955, Vol 538(5th), col 137–138W
Q816	What progress has been made at the National Institute of Dairy Research on frozen milk?	Q: Norman Dodds A: Julian Amery (Min Agric)	HC Deb, 31 Oct 1955, Vol 545(5th), col 77–78W
Q817	What progress has been taken to set up a National Reference Library of Science and Inventions?	Q: Frederick Willey Q: Barlett Janner Q: Donald Wade A: Reginald Bevins (Par Sec Min Works)	HC Deb, 1 Nov 1955, Vol 545(5th), col 91–92W
Q818	What would be the capital expenditure be for a National Reference Library of Science and Inventions?	Q: Frederick Willey A: Reginald Bevins (Par Sec Min Works)	HC Deb, 8 Nov 1955, Vol 545(5th), col 170W

Q819	How many patent applications, in order for acceptance, are now awaiting their numbers and formal acceptance; considering the number, should it not be speeded up?	Q: Peter Remnant A: Peter Thorneycroft (Pr BoT)	HC Deb, 8 Mar 1956, Vol 549(5th), col 2307
Q820	What developments have there been in relation to patent rights in frozen milk by the National Research Development Corporation?	Q: Norman Dodds A: Julian Amery (Min Agric)	HC Deb, 23 Apr 1956, Vol 551(5th), col 1424
Q821	What funds have been made available in relation to a National Reference Library of Science?	Q: James Callaghan A: Harold Macmillan (Ch Ex)	HC Deb, 24 Apr 1956, Vol 551(5th), col 1595–1596
Q822	Why has no reply been sent to Melvin Picknell to his offer of his artificial arm appliance?	Q: Charles Simmons A: Robin Turton (Min He)	HC Deb, 7 May 1956, Vol 552(5th), col 807–807
Q823	What steps have been taken in relation to the proposal for a National Library of Science Innovation?	Q: Frederick Willey A: Reginald Bevins (Par Sec Min Works)	HC Deb, 8 May 1956, Vol 552(5th), col 91W
Q824	What was the value in 1955 of the drugs prescribed which were manufactured in the UK under United States patent licences?	Q: Julian Snow A: Robin Turton (Min He)	HC Deb, 14 May 1956, Vol 552(5th), col 140–141W
Q825	What are the government's plans for a National Science Centre?	Q: Frederick Willey A: Reginald Bevins (Par Sec Min Works)	HC Deb, 15 May 1956, Vol 552(5th), col 157W
Q826	When will the departmental discussions about a new Patent Office and Science Reference Library be completed?	Q: Frederick Willey A: Reginald Bevins (Par Sec Min Works)	HC Deb, 5 Jun 1956, Vol 553(5th), col 45–46W
Q827	What did the Committee of Inquiry [REP23] on the use of unpatented inventions for defence purposes report; and what action is the government proposing to take?	Q: Peter Kirk A: Peter Thorneycroft (Pr BoT)	HC Deb, 20 Jun 1956, Vol 554(5th), col 111–112W
Q828	How much foreign currency is earned and spent on patent royalties?	Q: Arthur Bottomley A: Harold Macmillan (Ch Ex)	HC Deb, 13 Nov 1956, Vol 560(5th), col 734–735
Q829	What steps are being taken to increase the speed at which patent applications are examined?	Q: Ronald Bell A: Sir David Eccles (Pr BoT)	HC Deb, 24 Jan 1957, Vol 563(5th), col 389–890
Q830	What progress has been made regarding the National Scientific Reference and Lending Library project?	Q: Frederick Willey A: Harmar Nicholls (Min Agric)	HC Deb, 2 Apr 1957, Vol 568(5th), col 213
Q831	What happens to the patentable research outcomes undertaken with the Organisation for European Economic Cooperation?	Q: Geoffrey Wilson A: Harmar Nicholls (Min Agric)	HC Deb, 14 May 1957, Vol 570(5th), col 205–206
Q832	Whether the government believes the present Income Tax rules are framed so as to encourage inventors to develop their work in this country?	Q: William Fletcher-Vane A: Peter Thorneycroft (Pr BoT)	HC Deb, 12 Nov 1957, Vol 577(5th), col 769

(continued)

(continued)

Q833	What representations have been made to the Japanese government on the subject of patent law?	Q: John Peyton A: Sir David Eccles (Pr BoT)	HC Deb, 12 Dec 1957, Vol 579(5th), col 407–408
Q834	Whether the government is aware of the taxation advantages open to inventors in other countries?	Q: William Fletcher-Vane A: Enoch Powell (Fin Sec Tr)	HC Deb, 19 Dec 1957, Vol 580(5th), col 595
Q835	What are the legal and scientific qualifications of the present Comptroller-General?	Q: Roger Cresham Cooke A: Sir David Eccles (Pr BoT)	HC Deb, 11 Mar 1958, Vol 584(5th), col 28W
Q836	What qualifications are held by the person appointed to be Comptroller-General of Patents?	Q: Frederick Willey A: Sir David Eccles (Pr BoT)	HC Deb, 18 Mar 1958, Vol 584(5th), col 1075–1076
Q837	What are the reasons for appointing an administrative officer without professional qualifications be Comptroller-General of Patents?	Q: Paul Williams A: Sir David Eccles (Pr BoT)	HC Deb, 18 Mar 1958, Vol 584(5th), col 114–115W
Q838	When was the last occasion when a man without scientific qualification or practical experience was appointed to be Comptroller of the Patent Office?	Q: Edward Mallalieu A: Sir David Eccles (Pr BoT)	HC Deb, 27 Mar 1958, Vol 585(5th), col 65W
Q839	Whether, because of the concerns regarding the appointment of the Comptroller, an inquiry will be appointed into the working of the office since 1926?	Q: Edward Mallalieu A: Sir David Eccles (Pr BoT)	HC Deb, 3 Apr 1958, Vol 585(5th), col 179W
Q840	Will the agreement with the United States lead to the surrendering of patent rights in the Calder Hall type of reactor?	Q: George Brown Q: Roy Mason A: Rab Butler (Hom Sec)	HC Deb, 17 Jul 1958, Vol 591(5th), col 113–114W
Q841	Whether the government will make a statement on the Science Centre and reconstructing the Patent Office?	Q: Viscount Bridgeman A: Viscount Hailsham (SoS Ed & Sc)	HL Deb, 30 Jul 1958 Vol 211(5th), col 566–567WA
Q842	Whether the government will investigate the cost of making drugs rather than buying them from where patents apply?	Q: Maurice Edelman A: Derek Walker-Smith (Min He)	HC Deb, 16 Feb 1959, Vol 600(5th), col 3–4W
Q843	How many applications have been received under s 41 of the Patents Act 1949 [PUBA40]?	Q: Jesse Dickson Mabon A: John Vaughan-Morgan (Par Sec BoT)	HC Deb, 17 Feb 1959, Vol 600(5th), col 183–184
Q844	What advice is given to hospitals on purchasing patent aspirin?	Q: Jon Rankin Q: Edith Summerskill A: Derek Walker-Smith (Min He)	HC Deb, 23 Mar 1959, Vol 602(5th), col 910–911
Q845	What representations have been made to the United States authorities relating to United States patent owners allowing British firms to offer plant to Russia?	Q: Frank Allaun A: David Ormsby-Gore (Min FO)	HC Deb, 24 Jun 1959, Vol 607(5th), col 1168–1169
Q846	Has the Post Office taken out patents for the new channel equipment?	Q: Ness Edwards A: Kenneth Thompson (Par Sec Ed)	HC Deb, 22 Jul 1959, Vol 609(5th), col 1251

Q847	Whether a statement will be made about the Industrial Property Conference in Lisbon?	Q: Sir John Barlow A: John Rodgers (Par Sec BoT)	HC Deb, 28 Jul 1959, Vol 610(5th), col 309–310
Q848	What is the delay between the ascertainment that a patent application is in order and its acceptance?	Q: Dudley Smith A: Reginald Maudling (Pr BoT)	HC Deb, 7 Dec 1959, Vol 615(5th), col 15W
Q849	What steps are being taken to record when copies or specifications are being made available for inspection?	Q: Dudley Smith A: Reginald Maudling (Pr BoT)	HC Deb, 27 Jan 1960, Vol 616(5th), col 47–48W
Q850	What inventions are now being developed and exploited by the National Research Development Corporation?	Q: Albert Evans A: Reginald Maudling (Pr BoT)	HC Deb, 24 Feb 1960, Vol 618(5th), col 65–66W
Q851	Whether the government will take steps to encourage agricultural seed research and development?	Q: John Wells A: Joseph Godber (Par Sec Agric)	HC Deb, 7 Apr 1960, Vol 621(5th), col 536
Q852	What progress has been made in relation to the proposed National Reference Library of Science and Invention?	Q: Viscount De L'Isle A: Viscount Hailsham (Min Sc)	HL Deb, 31 May 1960, Vol 224(5th), col 108–109
Q853	Who are the patentees of penicillin; and what royalties have they received?	Q: John Biggs-Davison A: John Rodgers (Par Sec BoT)	HC Deb, 5 Jul 1960, Vol 626(5th), col 19W
Q854	Whether the new telephone designs made by the Post Office will be made available?	Q: Kenneth Lewis A: Reginald Bevins (PM Gen)	HC Deb, 18 Jul 1960, Vol 627(5th), col 16W
Q855	Will the cut in capital expenditure delay the building of the Patent Office and the National Scientific Library?	Q: Arthur Skeffingron A: Lord John Hope (Min Works)	HC Deb, 19 Jul 1960, Vol 627(5th), col 35W
Q856	Whether patent and trade mark fees will be raised?	Q: Martin McLaren A: Reginald Maudling (Pr BoT)	HC Deb, 7 Nov 1960, Vol 629(5th), col 23–24W
Q857	What rules relating to statutory tribunals have been made under the Tribunals and Inquiries Act 1958?	Q: Frederick Corfield A: Reginald Manningham-Buller (A-G)	HC Deb, 21 Nov 1960, Vol 630(5th), col 82–83W
Q858	Whether the government will consult others about an international patent office; and whether European patent law will be harmonised?	Q: Trevor Skeet A: Frederick Erroll (Min Tr)	HC Deb, 2 Dec 1960, Vol 631(5th), col 106W
Q859	What were the Patent Office's receipts and its outgoings in each year from 1939 to 1959?	Q: Austen Albu A: Niall Macpherson (Par Sec BoT)	HC Deb, 12 Dec 1960, Vol 632(5th), col 21–22W
Q860	Will the government make a statement on the renewal of the voluntary scheme for drugs prices?	Q: Lord Balniel A: Enoch Powell (SoS He)	HC Deb, 15 Dec 1960, Vol 632(5th), col 84–85W
Q861	To what extent do hospitals buy drugs from the Continent, rather than Britain or America, and what savings are made?	Q: Marcus Lipton A: Enoch Powell (SoS He)	HC Deb, 19 Dec 1960, Vol 632(5th), col 861

(continued)

(continued)

Q862	What steps are being taken to avoid the NHS using expensive branded drugs; will s 46 of the Patents Act 1949 be used?	Q: Cyril Osborne Q: Julian Snow A: Enoch Powell (SoS He)	HC Deb, 30 Jan 1961, Vol 633(5th), col 84W
Q863	What steps are being taken to ensure the application of existing scientific knowledge?	Q: William Owen A: Sir David Eccles (Pr BoT)	HC Deb, 31 Jan 1961, Vol 633(5th), col 113–114W
Q864	What provision has been made to delegate the authority under the Patents Act 1949, s 46 to regional hospital boards?	Q: Laurie Pavitt A: Enoch Powell (SoS He)	HC Deb, 8 Mar 1961, Vol 636(5th), col 50W
Q865	What arrangements are there for research by the Atomic Energy Authority to be passed to British industry?	Q: Kenneth Lewis Q: Thomas Peart A: Denzil Freeth (Par Sec Sc)	HC Deb, 14 Mar 1961, Vol 636(5th), col 1166–1167
Q866	How are inventions derived from publicly funded research developed in Scotland commercially exploited?	Q: Cyril Bence A: Denzil Freeth (Par Sec Sc)	HC Deb, 14 Mar 1961, Vol 636(5th), col 95W
Q867	Which hospitals are buying chlorothiazide, tetracycline and chloramphenicol from the Continent?	Q: John Arbuthnot A: Enoch Powell (SoS He)	HC Deb, 9 May 1961, Vol 640(5th), col 33W
Q868	Will you make a further statement about the purchase of drugs from unlicensed sources?	Q: John Arbuthnot A: Enoch Powell (SoS He)	HC Deb, 18 May 1961, Vol 640, (5th), col 170–171W
Q869	Why has the government instructed hospitals to stop buying drugs from unlicensed sources?	Q: Kenneth Robinson Q: Barnett Stross A: Enoch Powell (SoS He)	HC Deb, 12 Jun 1961, Vol 642(5th), col 11–12
Q870	Who were the successful tenderers for the drugs, and how have royalty payments been fixed?	Q: Kenneth Robinson A: Enoch Powell (SoS He)	HC Deb, 28 Jul 1961, Vol 645(5th), col 98W
Q871	How have negotiations with drug manufacturers progressed over payment of royalties?	Q: Jesse Dickson Mabon Q: George Chetwynd A: Geoffrey Rippon (Par Sec He)	HC Deb, 31 Jul 1961, Vol 645(5th), col 903
Q872	What steps has the government taken to obtain cheaper drugs from abroad?	Q: Marcus Lipton Q: Lord Balniel A: Enoch Powell (SoS He)	HC Deb, 23 Oct 1961, Vol 646(5th), col 539–540
Q873	What changes would be necessary to patent law under the Treaty of Rome?	Q: Sir Derek Walker-Smith A: Niall Macpherson (Par Sec BoT)	HC Deb, 28 Nov 1961, Vol 650(5th), col 228–229
Q874	Which Civil Service offices have received a pay increase?	Q: Dame Irene Ward A: Henry Brooke (Ch Sec Tr)	HC Deb, 6 Feb 1962, Vol 653(5th), col 27–32W
Q875	What conditions are imposed by the Atomic Energy Authority when private industry uses its patents?	Q: Fenner Brockway A: Denzil Freeth (Par Sec Sc)	HC Deb, 20 Feb 1962, Vol 654(5th), col 28W
Q876	Whether the government has reconsidered the National Reference Library of Science and Invention?	Q: Austen Albu A: Denzil Freeth (Par Sec Sc)	HC Deb, 27 Feb 1962, Vol 654(5th), col 1118
Q877	How many applications have been made under s 41 of the Patents Act 1949 [PUBA40] in the last five years; and how far did they progress?	Q: Kenneth Robinson A: Fredrick Erroll (Pr BoT)	HC Deb, 12 Mar 1962, Vol 655(5th), col 132W

Q878	Whether the rules relating to applications under s 41 of the Patents Act 1949 [PUBA40] will be amended to prevent patentees delaying proceedings?	Q: Kenneth Robinson A: Fredrick Erroll (Pr BoT)	HC Deb, 15 Mar 1962, Vol 655(5th), col 173–174W
Q879	Whether the government is going to introduce legislation to cover patent rights on agriculture products?	Q: John Maginnis A: William Vane (Par Sec Agric)	HC Deb, 19 Apr 1962, Vol 658(5th), col 100W
Q880	How are the negotiations going with the drug companies over voluntary price regulation?	Q: Gilbert Longden A: Enoch Powell (SoS He)	HC Deb, 14 May 1962, Vol 659(5th), col 906
Q881	Whether the government is aware of the confusion following letters being sent to hospitals over purchasing patented drugs?	Q: Laurie Pavitt A: Enoch Powell (SoS He)	HC Deb, 26 Jun 1962, Vol 661(5th), col 131–132W
Q882	What obligations does the government have regarding disclosure of information under the Euratom Treaty?	Q: Lord Crathorne Q: Viscount Alexander A: Viscount Hailsham (Pr Council)	HL Deb, 11 Jul 1962, Vol 242(5th), col 243–244
Q883	Whether, following *Geigy v Biorex* (1963) 80 RPC 263; (1964) 81 RPC 391 hospitals will be allowed to buy from manufacturers with licences under s 41 of the Patents Act 1949 [PUBA40]?	Q: Kenneth Robinson A: Enoch Powell (SoS He)	HC Deb, 16 Jul 1962, Vol 663(5th), col 10W
Q884	What steps have been taken under Euratom to hand over British nuclear information?	Q: William Blyton A: Edward Heath (Lord Privy Seal)	HC Deb, 18 Jul 1962, Vol 663(5th), col 426–428
Q885	Who has the Atomic Energy Authority licensed to build irradiation plants?	Q: Roy Mason A: Denzil Freeth (Par Sec Sc)	HC Deb, 24 Jul 1962, Vol 663(5th), col 138W
Q886	Will hospitals be advised to buy drugs from firms who have licenses under s 41 of the Patents Act 1949 [PUBA40]?	Q: Laurie Pavitt A: Enoch Powell (SoS He)	HC Deb, 30 Jul 1962, Vol 664(5th), col 5
Q887	On what terms does the Atomic Energy Authority provide information to private firms?	Q: Fenner Brockway A: Denzil Freeth (Par Sec Sc)	HC Deb, 27 Nov 1962, Vol 668(5th), col 28–29W
Q888	Whether an inquiry into the patent system will be set up?	Q: Richard Marsh A: David Price (Par Sec BoT)	HC Deb, 4 Dec 1962, Vol 668(5th), col 164W
Q889	What steps is the government taking following Lloyd-Jacob J's judgment in *Pfizer v Ministry of Health* (1963) 80 RPC 173 and s 46 of the Patents Act 1949 [PUBA40]?	Q: Kenneth Robinson A: Enoch Powell (SoS He)	HC Deb, 22 Jan 1963, Vol 670(5th), col 15W
Q890	Will the government now apply for compulsory licences under s 41 of the Patents Act 1949 [PUBA40]?	Q: Laurie Pavitt A: Enoch Powell (SoS He)	HC Deb, 28 Jan 1963, Vol 670(5th), col 123W
Q891	What steps will be taken to expedite matters for considering compulsory licences under the Patents Act 1949, s 41 [PUBA40]; how many such applications have been made in the last ten years?	Q: Kenneth Robinson and Jeremy Thorpe A: David Price (Par Sec BoT) and Frederick Erroll (Pr BoT)	HC Deb, 5 Feb 1963, Vol 671(5th), col 37W

(continued)

(continued)

Q892	Whether the Attorney-General will make a statement regarding *Geigy v Biorex* (1963) 80 RPC 263; (1964) 81 RPC 391 and s 41 of the Patents Act 1949 [PUBA40]?	Q: Kenneth Robinson A: Sir John Hobson (A-G)	HC Deb, 25 Feb 1963, Vol 672(5th), col 895–896
Q893	Is the government satisfied with the extent to which the current world output of scientific literature is available in London?	Q: Richard Crossman A: Denzil Freeth (Par Sec Sc)	HC Deb, 23 Apr 1963, Vol 676(5th), col 19W
Q894	When does government expect to legislate for patent rights on agricultural produce?	Q: John Maginnis A: James Scott-Hopkins (Par Sec Agric)	HC Deb, 6 May 1963, Vol 677(5th), col 14
Q895	What money has been recovered as royalties by the Atomic Energy Authority for Magnox reactors?	Q: Roy Mason A: Denzil Freeth (Par Sec Sc)	HC Deb, 6 May 1963, Vol 677(5th), col 4–5W
Q896	Will the Atomic Energy Authority publish its expenditure on advanced gas-cooled reactors?	Q: Roy Mason A: Denzil Freeth (Par Sec Sc)	HC Deb, 6 May 1963, Vol 677(5th), col 5–6W
Q897	What led the Ministry of Aviation to recognise Westinghouse's claim to patent rights for transistors?	Q: Joseph Mallalieu A: Neil Marten (Par Sec Av)	HC Deb, 8 May 1963, Vol 677(5th), col 69W
Q898	What plans are there for moving the Patent Office out of Central London?	Q: Walter Elliot A: John Boyd-Carpenter (Paymaster-General)	HC Deb, 16 Jul 1963, Vol 681(5th), col 48W
Q899	Has the government received the advice of the Tookey Committee on patents (the European Patent Convention)	Q: Leonard Cleaver A: Frederick Erroll (Pr BoT)	HC Deb, 25 Jul 1963, Vol 681(5th), col 1760
Q900	Who are to parties to the 1963 Bulk Supply, and what are the terms?	Q: Roy Mason A: Reginald Bevins (PM Gen)	HC Deb, 18 Nov 1963, Vol 684(5th), col 51–52W
Q901	What inquiries have been made about patent for the drug Tetralysal (an antibiotic)?	Q: Sir Barnet Stross A: Anthony Barber (Min He)	HC Deb, 12 Feb 1964, Vol 689(5th), col 88W
Q902	What steps are being taken to patent magnetoplasmdynamic processes by the British government?	Q: William Warbey A: Frederick Erroll (Pr BoT)	HC Deb, 16 Apr 1964, vol 693(5th), col 86–87W
Q903	On how many occasions has s 46 of the Patents Act 1949 [PUBA40] been invoked to obtain cheap drugs?	Q: Maurice Edelman A: Anthony Barber (Min He)	HC Deb, 27 Apr 1964, Vol 694(5th), col 25–26
Q904	What explanation has there been for the huge difference in price between imported unlicensed Tetracycline (an antibiotic) and the domestic product?	Q: Maurice Edelman A: Anthony Barber (Min He)	HC Deb, 4 May 1964, Vol 694(5th), col 884–885
Q905	In relation to each of the patented drugs being imported under new hospital contracts, which stages are carried out abroad?	Q: Sir John Arbuthnot A: Bernard Braine (Par Sec He)	HC Deb, 8 May 1964, Vol 694(5th), col 190W
Q906	Has a scheme been agreed with the British pharmaceutical industry over drug price regulation?	Q: Michael Clark Hutchinson A: Anthony Barber (Min He)	HC Deb, 17 Jul 1964, Vol 698(5th), col 290–291W

Q907	What steps will be taken to stimulate the industrial and commercial applications of new technology?	Q: Viscount Hanworth A: Lord Drumalybyn	HL Deb, 28 Jul 1964, Vol 260(5th), col 1081–1083W
Q908	What steps will be taken to stimulate the industrial and commercial applications of new technology?	Q: Denzil Freeth A: Edward Heath (Pr BoT)	HC Deb, 28 Jul 1964, Vol 699(5th), col 260–262W
Q909	Whether legislation will be introduced to allow the Monopolies Commission to inquire into excessive prices charged by patentees?	Q: William Shepherd A: George Darling (Min BoT)	HC Deb, 17 Dec 1964, Vol 704(5th), col 539–540
Q910	What is the present position regarding the draft EEC Patent Convention?	Q: Alan Williams A: Douglas Jay (Pr BoT)	HC Deb, 2 Feb 1965, Vol 705(5th), col 271–272W
Q911	What savings will result from buying unpatented drugs under s 46 of the Patents Act 1949 [PUBA40]?	Q: Sir Barnett Janner A: Kenneth Robinson (Min He)	HC Deb, 8 Feb 1965, Vol 706(5th), col 15W
Q912	Will the government give details of statutory provisions for complaints to be heard by independent tribunals?	Q: Dame Patricia Hornsby-Smith A: Harold Wilson (PM)	HC Deb, 11 Feb 1965, Vol 706(5th), col 123–127W
Q913	What is the estimated annual payment from British firms to foreign firms by way of royalties?	Q: Allan Beany A: Edward Redhead (Min BoT)	HC Deb, 12 Feb 1965, Vol 706(5th), col 141–142W
Q914	What savings have been made by using powers under s 46 of the Patents Act 1949 [PUBA40] to buy drugs?	Q: Laurie Pavitt A: Kenneth Robinson (Min He)	HC Deb, 15 Feb 1965, Vol 706(5th), col 167W
Q915	Whether the government will set up an enquiry into the pharmaceutical industry (including patents)?	Q: Laurie Pavitt A: Kenneth Robinson (Min He)	HC Deb, 8 Mar 1965, Vol 708(5th), col 30–33
Q916	What reduction in royalties paid to Western Electric resulted from the refusal to extend the patent?	Q: Anthony Fell A: Roy Jenkins (Min Av)	HC Deb, 17 Mar 1965, Vol 708(5th), col 267–268W
Q917	What steps are being taken to try to bring the Patent Office under one roof (and ending dispersal of departments)?	Q: Lord Cawley A: Lord Rhodes (Par Sec BoT)	HL Deb, 24 Mar 1965, Vol 264(5th), col 619–620
Q918	Will the terms of reference of the Committee of Inquiry into the Pharmaceutical Industry allow consideration of patents [PPP105]?	Q: Derek Page A: Kenneth Robinson (Min He)	HC Deb, 9 Apr 1965, Vol 710(5th), col 112W
Q919	What steps are being taken to secure adequate quality of drugs imported under s 41 of the Patents Act 1949 [PUBA40]?	Q: Alasdair Mackenzie Q: Brian Walden Q: Geoffrey Lloyd Q: Leo Abse A: Kenneth Robinson (Min He)	HC Deb, 15 Apr 1965, Vol 710(5th), col 240–241W
Q920	Will the government make representations to the EEC Commission in relation to the proposed European Patent Convention?	Q: Michael Alison A: George Thomson (Min FO)	HC Deb, 3 May 1965, Vol 711(5th), col 895

(continued)

(continued)

Q921	What steps are being taken to supervise small firms trying to take advantage of the Patents Act 1949, s 41 and 46 [PUBA40]?	Q: Wyndham Davies A: Kenneth Robinson (Min He)	HC Deb, 31 May 1965, Vol 713(5th), col 1168–1169
Q922	Is the government aware that drugs made under s 46 of the Patents Act 1949 [PUBA40] have had a failure of quality?	Q: Wyndham Davies A: Kenneth Robinson (Min He)	HC Deb, 14 Jun 1965, Vol 714(5th), col 16W
Q923	Will the government take steps to standardise tribunal procedure?	Q: Geoffrey Howe A: Sir Elwyn Jones (A-G)	HC Deb, 16 Jun 1965, Vol 714(5th), col 85–86W
Q924	Will the government make a statement on its future intentions to purchase under s 41 of the Patents Act 1949 [PUBA40]?	Q: Lord Balniel A: Kenneth Robinson (Min He)	HC Deb, 21 Jun 1965, Vol 714(5th), col 147W
Q925	Does the minister intend to keep purchasing drugs from abroad for services of the Crown?	Q: Laurie Pavitt A: Kenneth Robinson (Min He)	HC Deb, 5 Jul 1965, Vol 715(5th), col 157W
Q926	Will the government make a statement on the future location of the Patent Office?	Q: Sydney Allen A: Douglas Jay (Pr BoT)	HC Deb, 13 Jul 1965, Vol 716(5th), col 58W
Q927	What representations have been received from the Chartered Institute of Patent Attorneys on the location of the Patent Office?	Q: Eric Lubbock A: Douglas Jay (Pr BoT)	HC Deb, 15 Jul 1965, Vol 716(5th), col 98W
Q928	What amount has been spent on purchasing drugs from Birex; DDSA; Inter-Continental; and what about the companies set up to sell drugs more cheaply?	Q: Wyndham Davies Q: Jeremy Thorpe A: Kenneth Robinson (Min He)	HC Deb, 19 Jul 1965, Vol 716(5th), col 1095–1098
Q929	What plans are there for training of recruits as patent examiners; how many will be recruited over the next three years?	Q: Ronald Bell A: Douglas Jay (Pr BoT)	HC Deb, 19 Jul 1965, Vol 716(5th), col 175–176W
Q930	Whether any steps are being adopted to adopt the Compact Prosecution procedure from the United States (by introducing interviews)?	Q: Arthur Irvine A: Douglas Jay (Pr BoT)	HC Deb, 20 Jul 1965, Vol 716(5th), col 203–204W
Q931	What proposals are they for the use of the present site or buildings of the Patent Office if it is moved?	Q: Sir Anthony Meyer A: Charles Pannell (Min Public Buildings)	HC Deb, 26 Jul 1965, Vol 717(5th), col 14W
Q932	With the increasing technological development and effective working of the Patent Office, what has been done about moving the office outside London?	Q: Dudley Smith A: Frank Cousins (Min Tech)	HC Deb, 26 Jul 1965, Vol 717(5th), col 42–43W
Q933	Whether the Patent Appeal Tribunal needs to be relocated with the Patent Office; and what steps have be taken to appoint an additional judge?	Q: Henry Brewis A: Sir Elwyn Jones (A-G)	HC Deb, 28 Jul 1965, Vol 717(5th), col 126–127W

Q934	Whether assurances will be given that any patent examiner and applicant who think an interview will help will not be hindered?	Q: Arthur Irvine A: Douglas Jay (Pr BoT)	HC Deb, 29 Jul 1965, Vol 717(5th), col 159W
Q935	What proportion of patent examiners have indicated their willingness to move outside London; similarly users?	Q: Charles Longbottom Q: Patrick Jenkin A: George Darling (Min BoT)	HC Deb, 5 Aug 1965, Vol 717(5th), col 399–400W
Q936	What proposals are there for the use of the present site or buildings of the Patent Office if it is moved?	Q: Patrick Jenkin A: Charles Pannell (Min Public Buildings)	HC Deb, 5 Aug 1965, Vol 717(5th), col 422W
Q937	When will a decision be announced about moving the Patent Office out of London?	Q: Patrick Jenkin A: Douglas Jay (Pr BoT)	HC Deb, 27 Oct 1965, Vol 718(5th), col 70W
Q938	Will the government make a statement on the development of the hovercraft?	Q: Sir Barnett Janner A: Frank Cousins (Min Tech)	HC Deb, 11 Nov 1965, Vol 720(5th), col 6–8W
Q939	Has a cost benefit analysis been carried out on moving the Patent Office out of London?	Q: Terence Higgins Q: Patrick Jenkin A: Douglas Jay (Pr BoT)	HC Deb, 2 Dec 1965, Vol 721(5th), col 1606–1607
Q940	What representations have been received from the Association of Chartered Patent Agents and others regarding moving the Patent Office out of London?	Q: John Biggs-Davison A: George Darling (Min BoT)	HC Deb, 16 Dec 1965, Vol 722(5th), col 330W
Q941	How many representations have been received in favour of and against the relocation of the Patent Office; whether the move could be to Croydon with the Library remaining in Central London?	Q: Raymond Mawby and Patrick Jenkin A: George Darling (Min BoT)	HC Deb, 10 Feb 1966, Vol 724(5th), col 121–122W
Q942	What is the expenditure over the three years ending 31 Dec 1965 on purchasing Tetracycline from patentees and other sources?	Q: John Parker A: Kenneth Robinson (Min He)	HC Deb, 14 Feb 1966, Vol 724(5th), col 903–904
Q943	Whether the memorandum submitted by the minority of the Patents Liaison Group on ratification of the Strasbourg Convention will be published?	Q: Patrick Jenkin Q: Sir John Hobson A: George Darling (Min BoT)	HC Deb, 17 Feb 1966, Vol 724(5th), col 1512–1513
Q944	What proposals have been made for the future use of the Patent Office site?	Q: Sir Anthony Meyer A: James Boyden (Par Sec Public Buildings)	HC Deb, 7 Mar 1966, Vol 725(5th), col 443W
Q945	What money is expected for the sale of hovercraft patents abroad?	Q: Reginald Bennett A: Peter Shore (Par Sec Econ Aff)	HC Deb, 3 May 1966, Vol 727(5th), col 1408–1409
Q946	Whether the Atomic Energy Authority will agree to sell patents and know-how for Dragon type reactor?	Q: David Crouch A: Peter Shore (Par Sec Econ Aff)	HC Deb, 10 May 1966, Vol 728(5th), col 201–202
Q947	Whether the Patent Office will be moved to Swindon?	Q: Arnold Shaw A: George Darling (Min BoT)	HC Deb, 26 May 1966, Vol 729(5th), col 137W
Q948	What steps have been taken for the National Reference Library of Science and Invention to be the centre of scientific information?	Q: John Osborn A: Goronwy Roberts (Min Ed & Sc)	HC Deb, 16 Jun 1966, Vol 729(5th), col 301W

(continued)

(continued)

Q949	Whether locating the Patent Office in Croydon is practicable?	Q: Arnold Shaw A: George Darling (Min BoT)	HC Deb, 28 Jun 1966, Vol 730(5th), col 261W
Q950	How can the National Reference Library of Science be moved to the South Bank?	Q: Lord Ironside A: Lord Hilton (Ld-in-Wait)	HL Deb, 28 Jul 1966, Vol 276(5th), col 898–900
Q951	What factors have caused an increase in staff at the Board of Trade?	Q: Evelyn King A: Douglas Jay (Pr BoT)	HC Deb, 7 Nov 1966, Vol 735(5th), col 239W
Q952	What requests have there been for the patented protein-producing plant from Pakistan?	Q: John Tilney A: Albert Oram (Par Sec Ov Dev)	HC Deb, 24 Nov 1966, Vol 736(5th), col 1569–1570
Q953	Will the government take steps to bring the drug industry into public ownership?	Q: Gwilym Roberts Q: Nigel Fisher Q: Bernard Braine A: Kenneth Robinson	HC Deb, 5 Dec 1966, Vol 737(5th), col 915–916
Q954	What steps are being taken for hearings in London when the Patent Office moves to Croydon?	Q: Parrick Jenkin Q: Frederick Corfield A: George Darling (Min BoT) Comment: David Winnick	HC Deb, 8 Dec 1966, Vol 737(5th), col 1545–1546
Q955	What is intended in relation to amending the law to prevent prior claiming so that multiple patents can be granted for the same invention?	Q: Lord Cawley A: Lord Rhodes (Par Sec BoT)	HL Deb, 21 Dec 1966, Vol 278(5th), col 2204W
Q956	Whether a final decision has been reached on moving the Patent Office?	Q: Sir John Rodgers A: George Darling (Min BoT)	HC Deb, 18 Jan 1967, Vol 739(5th), col 76–77W
Q957	Whether steps will be taken to stop British hovercraft patents going to the United States as part of the brain drain?	Q: John Osborn A: Edmund Dell (Par Sec Econ Aff)	HC Deb, 24 Jan 1967, Vol 739(5th), col 1250–1251
Q958	What consultations have been held with overseas users of the Patent Office about the relocation to Croydon?	Q: Patrick Jenkin A: George Darling (Min BoT)	HC Deb, 1 Feb 1967, Vol 740(5th), col 500
Q959	What sites, other than Croydon, have been considered for the Patent Office?	Q: Sir Ronald Russell A: George Darling (Min BoT)	HC Deb, 8 Feb 1967, Vol 740(5th), col 301W
Q960	Would the government list the UN, Council of Europe etc. conventions not yet ratified by the United Kingdom?	Q: Benjamin Whitaker A: George Thomson (Par Sec FO)	HC Deb, 8 Mar 1967, Vol 742(5th), col 313–317W
Q961	When will the government announce the review of where to move the Patent Office?	Q: Patrick Jenkin Q: Frederic Harris Q: John Rankin Q: Sir John Eden A: George Darling (Min BoT)	HC Deb, 15 Mar 1967, Vol 743(5th), col 481–483
Q962	Whether the Patent Rules will be consolidated?	Q: Patrick Jenkin A: Douglas Jay (Pr BoT)	HC Deb, 23 Mar 1967, Vol 743(5th), col 312W
Q963	Will the government reconsider a Central London location for the Patent Office?	Q: John Hunt Q: Frederick Corfield A: George Darling (Min BoT)	HC Deb, 26 Apr 1967, Vol 745(5th), col 1602–1603
Q964	With the Patent Office being moved out of London, why is the National Steel Corporation being moved to London, so far from mills?	Q: Roger Cooke A: Richard Marsh (Min Power)	HC Deb, 9 May 1967, Vol 746(5th), col 1256

Q965	Whether a review of the patent system will be undertaken; and whether a statement will be made?	Q: Benjamin Whitaker A: Douglas Jay (Pr BoT)	HC Deb, 10 May 1967, Vol 746(5th), col 241W
Q966	Whether the government can show the balance of trade in royalties etc.?	Q: Sir Henry Legge-Bourke A: Douglas Jay (Pr BoT)	HC Deb, 9 Jun 1967, Vol 747(5th), col 269W
Q967	What is the increase in cost of running the Patent Office caused by Selective Employment Tax?	Q: Patrick Jenkin A: George Darling (Min BoT)	HC Deb, 21 Jun 1967, Vol 748(5th), col 292W
Q968	Whether talks will be started in the Council of Europe to adopt the draft EEC Patent Convention?	Q: Patrick Jenkin A: George Darling (Min BoT)	HC Deb, 21 Jun 1967, Vol 748(5th), col 293W
Q969	How many bulk purchases have been made under s 41 and 46 of the Patents Act 1949 [PUBA40]?	Q: Laurie Pavitt Q: Bernard Braine A: Kenneth Robinson (Min He)	HC Deb, 3 Jul 1967, Vol 749(5th), col 1251–1252
Q970	Will the Ministry of Health present evidence on the working of the Patents Act to the Departmental Committee [REP24]?	Q: Laurie Pavitt A: Kenneth Robinson (Min He)	HC Deb, 3 Jul 1967, Vol 749(5th), col 164W
Q971	Will the government make a statement about the future location of the Patent Office?	Q: John Robertson A: Douglas Jay (Pr BoT)	HC Deb, 4 Jul 1967, Vol 749(5th), col 241W
Q972	What is the membership of the Departmental Committee looking into the Patent System and Law [REP24]?	Q: Alexander Lyon A: Douglas Jay (Pr BoT)	HC Deb, 28 Jul 1967, Vol 751(5th), col 317W
Q973	Will the government consider the suggestions from the Sainsbury Committee [PPP105] relating to patent law?	Q: John Dunwoody A: Kenneth Robinson (Min He)	HC Deb, 23 Oct 1967, Vol 751(5th), col 1326
Q974	Is it government policy to press for formation of an International Patents Office?	Q: Marquess of Hamilton A: George Darling (Min BoT)	HC Deb, 8 Nov 1967, Vol 753(5th), col 122W
Q975	What is the number of unexamined patent applications?	Q: Marquess of Hamilton A: George Darling (Min BoT)	HC Deb, 8 Nov 1967, Vol 753(5th), col 122–123W
Q976	What is the cost to the Patent Office for processing an extension of time for filing complete specification?	Q: Peter Emery A: George Darling (Min BoT)	HC Deb, 10 Nov 1966, Vol 753(5th), col 198–199W
Q977	What steps are being taken to stop patent infringement in relation to animal medicines?	Q: Peter Mills A: George Darling (Min BoT)	HC Deb, 15 Nov 1967, Vol 754(5th), col 123–124W
Q978	How much has been spent by Royal Armaments Research and Development on the plasma arc cutter; what steps have been taken to patent it?	Q: Eric Lubbock A: Roy Mason (Min Def Eq)	HC Deb, 13 Dec 1967, Vol 756(5th), col 138W
Q979	How many meetings have there been of the departmental committee looking at patent law [REP24]; and when will it report?	Q: Laurie Pavitt A: George Darling (Min BoT)	HC Deb, 24 Jan 1968, Vol 757(5th), col 119–120W
Q980	What is the policy about rehousing the Patent Office under one roof?	Q: Patrick Jenkin A: Anthony Crosland (Pr BoT)	HC Deb, 24 Jan 1968, Vol 757(5th), col 122W

(continued)

(continued)

Q981	How many patents were taken out by the National Research Development Council between 1965 and 1967?	Q: David Price A: Tony Benn (Min Tech)	HC Deb, 26 Jan 1968, Vol 757(5th), col 196–197W
Q982	Why did the department take two months to clear an export order to Holland?	Q: Jock Bruce-Gardyne A: Gerald Fowler (Par Sec Min Tech)	HC Deb, 5 Feb 1968, Vol 758(5th), col 27–28
Q983	What investigations have been made into a Scottish hydrofoil and hovercraft industry?	Q: Winifred Ewing A: Tony Benn (Min Tech)	HC Deb, 7 Feb 1968, Vol 758(5th), col 168W
Q984	How many staff are concerned with the formation of the European Technological Community?	Q: Eric Moonman A: George Darling (Min BoT)	HC Deb, 9 Feb 1968, Vol 758(5th), col 246W
Q985	When is the Banks Committee [REP24] report expected?	Q: Austen Albu A: George Darling (Min BoT)	HC Deb, 22 Feb 1968, Vol 759(5th), col 173W
Q986	What are the terms of the licence upon which CS gas is sold in the United States?	Q: Tam Dalyell A: Roy Mason (Min Def Eq)	HC Deb, 26 Feb 1968, Vol 759(5th), col 264W
Q987	What patent licences exist for CS?	Q: Tam Dalyell A: Roy Mason (Min Def Eq)	HC Deb, 29 Feb 1968, Vol 759(5th), col 407–408W
Q988	What is the proportion of profit of drugs prices when sold to the NHS?	Q: Benjamin Whitaker A: Kenneth Robinson (Min He)	HC Deb, 18 Mar 1968, Vol 761(5th), col 32–33W
Q989	How many times has the Minister of Health issued an authorisation under s 46(1) of the Patents Act 1949 [PUBA40]?	Q: Ronald Bell A: Kenneth Robinson (Min He)	HC Deb, 10 Apr 1968, Vol 762(5th), col 277–278W
Q990	How many meetings have there been of the Banks Committee [REP24]?	Q: Laurie Pavitt A: Edmund Dell (Min BoT)	HC Deb, 24 May 1968, Vol 765(5th), col 137W
Q991	Is the government aware that nerve gas manufactured under British licences is being made in foreign countries?	Q: David Kerr A: John Morris (Min Def Eq)	HC Deb, 12 Jun 1968, Vol 766(5th), col 221
Q992	What patent rights does the government have in the CS gas packed by Schermuly Ltd?	Q: Tam Dalyell A: John Morris (Min Def Eq)	HC Deb, 21 Jun 1968, Vol 766(5th), col 181–182W
Q993	Whether the Banks Committee [REP24] will produce an interim report?	Q: Maurice Macmillan A: Edmund Dell (Min BoT)	HC Deb, 27 Jun 1968, Vol 767(5th), col 117W
Q994	What payments are made into public funds by private funds for using techniques and devices by government research teams?	Q: Rory Roebuck A: John Stonehouse (PM Gen)	HC Deb, 26 Jul 1968, Vol 769(5th), col 256–257W
Q995	Which government offices close on New Year's Day?	Q: Michael Jopling A: Edmund Dell (Min BoT)	HC Deb, 27 Jan 1969, Vol 776(5th), col 268–269W
Q996	What is the British obligation to the United States for patent etc. royalties?	Q: Brandon Rhys Williams A: Edmund Dell (Min BoT)	HC Deb, 12 Feb 1968, Vol 777(5th), col 1312
Q997	Whether the present taxation system adequately compensates inventors?	Q: Lord Trefgarne Q: Lord Inglewood A: Lord Beswick	HL Deb, 19 Feb 1969, Vol 299(5th), col 817–819

Q998	Whether the government will discuss with the National Research Development Council alternative methods of rewarding inventors?	Q: Peter Horden Q: Sir Henry Legge-Bourke A: Jeremy Bray (Par Sec Power)	HC Deb, 5 Mar 1969, Vol 779(5th), col 410–412
Q999	Whether the government will identify the expenditure on non-defence research?	Q: Tam Dalyell A: John Morris (Min Def Eq)	HC Deb, 3 Apr 1969, Vol 781(5th), col 178W
Q1000	Whether patent rights in carbon fibre remain in British hands?	Q: John Rankin A: Gerald Fowler (Par Sec Tech)	HC Deb, 16 Apr 1969, Vol 781(5th), col 1142
Q1001	Whether a statement will be made on the licensing agreements for hovercraft?	Q: Sir Henry Legge-Bourke A: Tony Benn (Min Tech)	HC Deb, 17 Apr 1969, Vol 781(5th), col 292–293W
Q1002	What reply has the government made to the invitation from the Common Market ministers to negotiate a new European Patents Convention?	Q: Patrick Jenkin A: Fred Mulley (Min Disarmament)	HC Deb, 30 Apr 1969, Vol 782(5th), col 253W
Q1003	Will the government make a statement on the Ministerial Council Meeting of the European Free Trade Association?	Q: Bertie Hazell A: Anthony Crosland (Pr BoT)	HC Deb, 13 May 1969, Vol 783(5th), col 196–198W
Q1004	What is the percentage of drugs supplied by foreign companies; and how many are subject to fixed prices under foreign patent law?	Q: Henry Kerby A: Julian Snow (US DHSS)	HC Deb, 23 May 1969, Vol 784(5th), col 166W
Q1005	Whether the policy of prohibiting hospitals from buying patented drugs will be reversed?	Q: Laurie Pavitt A: Richard Crossman (SoS Soc Ser)	HC Deb, 16 Jun 1969, Vol 785(5th), col 8W
Q1006	Will the government consider a compulsory licence under s 41 of the Patents Act 1949 [PUBA40] for ampicillin?	Q: Laurie Pavitt A: Julian Snow (US DHSS)	HC Deb, 30 Jun 1969, Vol 786(5th), col 26
Q1007	Whether the government intends to make bulk purchase of drugs for the NHS under s 46 of the Patents Act 1949 [PUBA40]?	Q: Laurie Pavitt A: Julian Snow (US DHSS)	HC Deb, 30 Jun 1969, Vol 786(5th), col 6W
Q1008	Whether the government is considering using the patent device to protect tower blocks?	Q: Arthur Lewis A: James MacColl (Par Sec Min Housing)	HC Deb, 8 Jul 1969, Vol 786(5th), col 240–241W
Q1009	Whether the anti-explosion device will be fitted in government buildings?	Q: Arthur Lewis A: John Silkin (Min Pub Build)	HC Deb, 8 Jul 1969, Vol 786(5th), col 243W
Q1010	What plans does the government have to reduce the cost of patenting?	Q: Christopher Chataway A: Edmund Dell (Min BoT)	HC Deb, 9 Jul 1969, Vol 786(5th), col 262W
Q1011	What changes have been made to the contracts division since the Inquiry into Bristol Siddeley Ltd?	Q: Ernest Marples A: Tony Benn (Min Tech)	HC Deb, 15 Jul 1969, Vol 787(5th), col 83W
Q1012	What is the number of employees, investment etc. for the National Research Development Corporation?	Q: Frank Hooley A: Jeremy Bray (Par Sec Power)	HC Deb, 17 Jul 1969, Vol 787(5th), col 177–178W
Q1013	What inventions have there been for oil slicks patented by Shell or ICI in the last year?	Q: Hector Hughes A: Ernest Davies (Par Sec BoT)	HC Deb, 3 Nov 1969, Vol 790(5th), col 23W

(continued)

(continued)

Q1014	What was the outcome of the European Free Trade Association meeting?	Q: Bertie Hazell A: Roy Mason (Pr BoT)	HC Deb, 12 Nov 1969, Vol 791(5th), col 98W
Q1015	Who has received ex gratia payments for inventions in the last 50 years?	Q: Sir Ronald Russell A: Tony Benn (Min Tech)	HC Deb, 27 Nov 1969, Vol 792(5th), col 127W
Q1016	Whether Mr Hargreaves will get an ex gratia payment for his invention of the moving map?	Q: John Ellis Q: Michael McNair-Wilson A: Tony Benn (Min Tech)	HC Deb, 8 Dec 1969, Vol 793(5th), col 22–23W
Q1017	What advisory committees etc. are responsible to the President of the Board of Trade?	Q: Nicholas Ridley A: Roy Mason (Pr BoT)	HC Deb, 19 Dec 1969, Vol 793(5th), col 489–490W
Q1018	What increases in Patent Office expenses have there been which were not foreseen at the 1969 increase in fees; what is the effect of the Selective Employment Tax on the Patent Office; when fees were introduced and whether this covered fee-earning branches of Patent Office?	Q: Nicholas Ridley A: Gwyneth Dunwoody (Par Sec BoT)	HC Deb, 19 Dec 1969, Vol 793(5th), col 490–491W
Q1019	Whether the government will make a statement on the Anglo-Japanese Agreement on Carbon Fibre?	Q: Tam Dalyell A: Ernest Davies (Par Sec BoT)	HC Deb, 16 Feb 1970, Vol 796(5th), col 9W
Q1020	When will the Banks Committee report [REP24] be received by the minister?	Q: Dudley Smith A: Gwyneth Dunwoody (Par Sec BoT)	HC Deb, 17 Feb 1970, Vol 796(5th), col 108W
Q1021	What steps are being taken to make it easier for British inventors?	Q: Arnold Gregory A: Gwyneth Dunwoody (Par Sec BoT)	HC Deb, 25 Feb 1970, Vol 796(5th), col 1192–1193
Q1022	How many meetings of the Banks Committee [REP24] were held; and when is the report expected?	Q: Laurie Pavitt A: Gwyneth Dunwoody (Par Sec BoT)	HC Deb, 13 Mar 1970, Vol 797(5th), col 494W
Q1023	What bodies etc. does the President of the Board of Trade appoint people to?	Q: Henry Kerby A: Gwyneth Dunwoody (Par Sec BoT)	HC Deb, 20 Mar 1970, Vol 798(5th), col 244–246W
Q1024	Whether cosmetic arms are made under licence from foreign patent owners?	Q: Fred Silvester A: Richard Crossman (SoS Soc Ser)	HC Deb, 15 May 1970, Vol 801(5th), col 424W
Q1025	Whether the government has received the Banks Committee Report [REP24]?	Q: Edwin Brooks A: Gwyneth Dunwoody (Par Sec BoT)	HC Deb, 15 May 1970, Vol 801(5th), col 432W
Q1026	Will the government make a statement on the EFTA Ministerial Council meeting?	Q: Bertie Hazell A: Roy Mason (Pr BoT)	HC Deb, 28 May 1970, Vol 801(5th), col 575–578W
Q1027	When the Banks Committee Report will be published [REP24]?	Q: Michael Shaw A: Michael Noble (Min BoT)	HC Deb, 14 Jul 1970, Vol 803(5th), col 200W
Q1028	What is proposed on computer programs following the Banks Report publication [REP24]?	Q: Leslie Huckfield A: Nicholas Ridley (Par Sec T&I)	HC Deb, 27 Oct 1970, Vol 805(5th), col 85–86W
Q1029	Whether the government will amend the law relating to employee inventions?	Q: Henry Kerby A: Nicholas Ridley (Par Sec T&I)	HC Deb, 2 Nov 1970, Vol 805(5th), col 251–252W

Q1030	Whether the government contemplates amending the law to protect computer programs?	Q: Lord Cawley A: Lord Drumalbyn (Min w/o Port)	HL Deb, 24 Nov 1970, Vol 313(5th), col 114–116W
Q1031	When does the government intend to rehouse the Patent Office?	Q: Albert Roberts A: John Davies (Pr T&I)	HC Deb, 10 Dec 1970, Vol 808(5th), col 182–183W
Q1032	Whether the government will apply for a compulsory licence for ampicillin?	Q: Laurie Pavitt A: Michael Alison (Par Sec T&I)	HC Deb, 12 Jan 1971, Vol 809(5th), col 36W
Q1033	Whether drafts of the European Patent Agreement and EEC Agreement can be put in the library?	Q: Trevor Skeet A: Anthony Grant (Min T&I)	HC Deb, 18 Jan 1971, Vol 809(5th), col 489–490
Q1034	What progress has been made on the sale of the Rolls-Royce patents?	Q: John Gilbert A: Frederick Corfield (Min T&I)	HC Deb, 24 Mar 1971, Vol 814(5th), col 516–517
Q1035	What is the current position in respect of the Rolls-Royce patents?	Q: James Scott-Hopkins A: Frederick Corfield (Min T&I)	HC Deb, 21 Apr 1971, Vol 815(5th), col 388W
Q1036	Whether steps will be taken to avoid applications becoming invalid due to the postal strike?	Q: Geoffrey Finsberg A: Nicholas Ridley (Par Sec T&I)	HC Deb, 14 May 1971, Vol 817(5th), col 183W
Q1037	Whether the government will consider adopting the Australian law to allow for protection during a postal strike by extending time limits?	Q: Norman Tebbit A: Nicholas Ridley (Par Sec T&I)	HC Deb, 17 May 1971, Vol 817(5th), col 214W
Q1038	What plans does the government have to rehouse the Patent Office?	Q: David Mather A: Julian Amery (Min Environment)	HC Deb, 25 May 1971, Vol 818(5th), col 126W
Q1039	Whether millions of pounds would be lost in royalties due to the acquisition method of the Rolls-Royce patents?	Q: Edward Bishop A: David Price (US T&I)	HC Deb, 18 Oct 1971, Vol 823(5th), col 357–358
Q1040	Will the government list the amounts provided in connection with the Rolls-Royce purchase?	Q: Cranley Onslow A: John Davies (SoS T&I)	HC Deb, 22 Oct 1971, Vol 823(5th), col 214–215W
Q1041	Will the government make a statement on discussions with the United States government regarding Rolls-Royce engine patents?	Q: Tam Dalyell A: Frederick Corfield (Min T&I)	HC Deb, 25 Oct 1971, Vol 823(5th), col 237–238W
Q1042	Whether the government is ready to give its view of the Banks Committee Report [REP24]?	Q: David Crouch A: Nicholas Ridley (Par Sec T&I)	HC Deb, 22 Nov 1971, Vol 826(5th), col 265W
Q1043	What are the present prospects for a European patent?	Q: Trevor Skeet A: Nicholas Ridley (Par Sec T&I)	HC Deb, 9 Dec 1971, Vol 827(5th), col 391–392W
Q1044	What arrangements have been made for the government exploiting the Rolls-Royce patents?	Q: Bruce Millan A: Frederick Corfield (Min T&I)	HC Deb, 17 Feb 1972, Vol 831(5th), col 153–154W
Q1045	Whether the government will confirm that the licensing of the Rolls-Royce patents will be at full economic price?	Q: Bruce Millan A: Frederick Corfield (Min T&I)	HC Deb, 23 Feb 1972, Vol 831(5th), col 317–318W
Q1046	Whether the government will publish the agreement between the receiver of Rolls-Royce and the government where patents were assigned?	Q: Bruce Millan A: Frederick Corfield (Min T&I)	HC Deb, 28 Feb 1972, Vol 832(5th), col 15–16W

(continued)

(continued)

Q1047	Whether the government will offer to house the European Patent Office?	Q: Tom Boardman A: John Davies (SoS T&I)	HC Deb, 20 Mar 1972, Vol 833(5th), col 229–230W
Q1048	What use is made of the patent system by the ball bearing industry?	Q: Jack Ashley Q: Frank Tomney A: Nicholas Ridley (Par Sec T&I)	HC Deb, 29 Mar 1972, Vol 834(5th), col 93W
Q1049	Will the government make a statement as to how the British Patent Office will be effected by the European Patent Office?	Q: Robert Woof A: Michael Noble (Min T&I)	HC Deb, 24 Apr 1972, Vol 835(5th), col 183–184W
Q1050	Whether the discussions on the location of the European Patent Office have concluded?	Q: Sir John Rodgers Q: George Darling A: John Davies (SoS T&I)	HC Deb, 19 Jun 1972, Vol 839(5th), col 8–9W
Q1051	Whether the government can state where the European Patent Office will be situated?	Q: Walter Elliot A: John Davies (Pr T&I)	HC Deb, 29 Jun 1972, Vol 839(5th), col 406W
Q1052	What is Great Britain's balance of patent payments for pharmaceutical drugs?	Q: Laurence Reed A: Michael Noble (Min T&I)	HC Deb, 26 Jul 1972, Vol 841(5th), col 331W
Q1053	Whether the government will refuse to extend the patent term of any drugs used extensively by the NHS?	Q: Laurie Pavitt A: Michael Noble (Min T&I)	HC Deb, 31 Jul 1972, Vol 842(5th), col 10W
Q1054	Whether the minister will consider moving the Patent Office to Coventry as part of government decentralisation?	Q: Maurice Edelman No answer	HC Deb, 31 Jul 1972, Vol 842(5th), col 15–16W
Q1055	Whether the payments for patent royalties on pharmaceutical products can be included in the balance of payments in the future?	Q: Laurance Reed A: Michael Noble (Min T&I)	HC Deb, 31 Jul 1972, Vol 842(5th), col 17W
Q1056	How many patent specifications were received by the Patent Office in the last year?	Q: Trevor Skeet A: Michael Noble (Min T&I)	HC Deb, 2 Aug 1972, Vol 842(5th), col 143W
Q1057	When does the government expect to announce amendments to enable the United Kingdom to join the European Patent Convention?	Q: Henry Brewis A: Sir Geoffrey Howe (Pr T&I)	HC Deb, 20 Nov 1972, Vol 846(5th), col 274W
Q1058	Whether the co-ordination of government departments has been sufficient to harmonise the laws of patents as they relate to pharmaceuticals?	Q: Tam Dalyell A: Edward Heath (PM)	HC Deb, 5 Dec 1972, Vol 847(5th), col 387–388W
Q1059	What is the effect on patents, trade marks and copyright from joining the Common Market?	Q: Trevor Skeet A: Sir Geoffrey Howe (Pr T&I)	HC Deb, 29 Jan 1973, Vol 849(5th), col 287–288W
Q1060	What study has been made on the payback by patents of new drug discoveries?	Q: Tam Dalyell A: Michael Alison (US DHSS)	HC Deb, 31 Jan 1973, Vol 849(5th), col 417–418W
Q1061	Whether s 41 of the Patents Act 1949 [PUBA40] will be repealed; and whether research is damaged by patent law?	Q: Tam Dalyell A: Sir Geoffrey Howe (Pr T&I)	HC Deb, 5 Feb 1973, Vol 850(5th), col 50W

Q1062	When will legislation be introduced to implement the Banks Committee Report [REP24]?	Q: Trevor Skeet A: Sir Geoffrey Howe (Pr T&I)	HC Deb, 15 Feb 1973, Vol 850(5th), col 399W
Q1063	What impediments are there on intellectual property rights by reason of Article 85 of the EEC Treaty?	Q: Trevor Skeet A: Sir Geoffrey Howe (Pr T&I)	HC Deb, 12 Apr 1973, Vol 854(5th), col 366–368W
Q1064	What steps are being taken to secure the British patent system within the EEC and European patent system?	Q: Lord Ironside A: Lord Drumalbyn (Min w/o Port)	HL Deb, 14 May 1973, Vol 342(5th), col 604–605
Q1065	Will the government implement the Banks Committee Report [REP24] and implement the European Patent Treaties?	Q: Peter Trew A: Sir Geoffrey Howe (Min Tr Com Aff)	HC Deb, 18 May 1973, Vol 856(5th), col 409W
Q1066	What modifications of the draft European Patent Convention are the government proposing to seek?	Q: Enoch Powell A: Sir Geoffrey Howe (Min Tr Com Aff)	HC Deb, 25 Jun 1973, Vol 858(5th), col 1120–1121
Q1067	Whether a statement will be made regarding the European Patent Office?	Q: Neil Marten A: Sir Geoffrey Howe (Min Tr Com Aff)	HC Deb, 2 Jul 1973, Vol 859(5th), col 20–21
Q1068	What steps are being taken to ensure the British Patent Office handles English-language applications?	Q: Ronald Bell A: Sir Geoffrey Howe (Min Tr Com Aff)	HC Deb, 9 Jul 1973, Vol 859(5th), col 238W
Q1069	When does the government propose to implement the Banks Committee Report [REP24]?	Q: Nigel Fisher A: Sir Geoffrey Howe (Min Tr Com Aff)	HC Deb, 16 Oct 1973, Vol 861(5th), col 48W
Q1070	What representations by the government have been made regarding the European Patent Office?	Q: Edward Bishop Q: Kenneth Warren A: Geoffrey Howe (Min Tr Com Aff)	HC Deb, 17 Oct 1973, Vol 861(5th), col 203–204W
Q1071	Will the government make a statement about the outcome of the Diplomatic Conference on the European Patent Convention?	Q: Charles Fletcher-Cooke A: Sir Geoffrey Howe (Min Tr Com Aff)	HC Deb, 24 Oct 1973, Vol 861(5th), col 549–550W
Q1072	What is government policy regarding the future of the patent system and the EEC patent?	Q: Edward Bishop A: Sir Geoffrey Howe (Min Tr Com Aff)	HC Deb, 14 Nov 1973, Vol 864(5th), col 168W
Q1073	What royalties are payable to the Atomic Energy Authority?	Q: Edmund Dell A: Peter Emery (US Trade)	HC Deb, 19 Nov 1973, Vol 864(5th), col 307–308W
Q1074	When the White Paper on patents will be published?	Q: Trevor Skeet A: Sir Geoffrey Howe (Min Tr Com Aff)	HC Deb, 6 Dec 1973, Vol 865(5th), col 461–462W
Q1075	How many High Court judges have carried out inquiries etc. in the last 20 years (Patent Procedure Committee)?	Q: John Morris A: Sir Michael Havers (S-G)	HC Deb, 7 Dec 1973, Vol 865(5th), col 478–482W
Q1076	What provisions in patent law require industries using patent processes to indicate the pollutants they discharge?	Q: John Cordle A: Sir Geoffrey Howe (Min Tr Com Aff)	HC Deb, 11 Dec 1973, Vol 866(5th), col 112–113W
Q1077	When will the negotiations over the European patent and EEC patent be concluded?	Q: Edward Bishop A: Sir Geoffrey Howe (Min Tr Com Aff)	HC Deb, 21 Jan 1974, Vol 867(5th), col 215–217W

(continued)

(continued)

Q1078	What are the Secretary of State for Trade's responsibilities?	Q: Trevor Skeet Q: Kenneth Baker A: Peter Shore (SoS Tr)	HC Deb, 22 Mar 1974, Vol 870(5th), col 215–216W
Q1079	What is the government's attitude to the proposal to establish the European Patent Office in Munich?	Q: Trevor Skeet A: Peter Shore (SoS Tr)	HC Deb, 1 Apr 1974, Vol 871(5th), col 255W
Q1080	When will the proposals for a European patent system be completed; when will the EEC patent be agreed?	Q: Edward Bishop A: Peter Shore (SoS Tr)	HC Deb, 6 May 1974, Vol 873(5th), col 7–8W
Q1081	Will the government make a statement on the site of the European Patent Office?	Q: Kenneth Warren A: Stanley Clinton Davis (US Co Av Ship)	HC Deb, 18 Dec 1974, Vol 883(5th), col 493W
Q1082	Whether legal aid will be extended?	Q: John Watkinson A: Samuel Silkin (AG)	HC Deb, 19 Dec 1974, Vol 883(5th), col 515W
Q1083	Whether classification was given for the VX gas patent, and has it changed?	Q: Michael Shersby A: William Rodgers (Min Def)	HC Deb, 13 Jan 1975, Vol 884(5th), col 20W
Q1084	Will a statement be made on declassification of VX gas?	Q: Bruce George Q: Bruce Douglas-Mann A: William Rodgers (Min Def)	HC Deb, 14 Jan 1975, Vol 884(5th), col 61W
Q1085	How many patents are registered in the name of the department, and how many are classified as secret; and considerations for declassifying?	Q: Bruce Douglas-Mann A: William Rodgers (Min Def)	HC Deb, 14 Jan 1975, Vol 884(5th), col 63W
Q1086	What action will be taken in light of the answer of the European Commission to Written Question 135/74 in the Community Parliament [timing of EPC and EEC Patent Conventions]?	Q: Peter Emery A: Eric Deakins (US Tr)	HC Deb, 22 Jan 1975, Vol 884(5th), col 385–386W
Q1087	Which bodies is the Secretary of State responsible for?	Q: John Garrett A: Peter Shore (SoS Tr)	HC Deb, 23 Jan 1975, Vol 884(5th), col 479–480W
Q1088	What is the opportunity cost of the Patent Office accommodation; and the basis of calculation?	Q: Kenneth Warren A: Stanley Clinton Davis (US Co Av Ship)	HC Deb, 11 Feb 1975, Vol 886(5th), col 127–128W
Q1089	When fees are increased, will the government ensure that those filing new complete specifications do not have to subsidise the Patent Office?	Q: Keith Stainton A: Stanley Clinton Davis (US Co Av Ship)	HC Deb, 24 Feb 1975, Vol 887(5th), col 34W
Q1090	What steps are being taken to reduce the delays in patent prosecution?	Q: Kenneth Warren A: Stanley Clinton Davis (US Co Av Ship)	HC Deb, 26 Feb 1975, Vol 887(5th), col 195W
Q1091	What functions does the Secretary of State for Trade have in Scotland?	Q: Tam Dalyell A: Eric Deakins (Min Tr)	HC Deb, 3 Mar 1975, Vol 887(5th), col 297W
Q1092	Whether patents are taken out by the Post Office Research Unit?	Q: Lord Wallace A: Lord Beswick	HL Deb, 13 Mar 1975, Vol 358(5th), col 488WA
Q1093	Whether the Secretary of State will make a statement as to the future of the patents system?	Q: Peter Snape A: Stanley Clinton Davis (US Co Av Ship)	HC Deb, 25 Mar 1975, Vol 889(5th), col 136W

Q1094	What is the statutory authority for requiring Patent Office fees to operate under the price codes?	Q: Keith Stainton A: Stanley Clinton Davis (US Co Av Ship)	HC Deb, 29 Apr 1975, Vol 891(5th), col 109–110W
Q1095	How will public expenditure entrenchment affect the Trade Department?	Q: Robert Woof A: Stanley Clinton Davis (US Co Av Ship)	HC Deb, 2 May 1975, Vol 891(5th), col 282–283W
Q1096	What action is the government taking to give effect to the European patent?	Q: Tom Normanton A: Stanley Clinton Davis (US Co Av Ship)	HC Deb, 9 Jun 1975, Vol 893(5th), col 96–97W
Q1097	What steps are being taken to implement the Sainsbury Report [PPP105]?	Q: George Rodgers A: David Owen (Min He)	HC Deb, 13 Jun 1975, Vol 893(5th), col 257–258W
Q1098	What steps will be taken to reduce the backlog of 50,000 unexamined patent applications?	Q: Andrew Faulds A: Stanley Clinton Davis (US Co Av Ship)	HC Deb, 27 Jun 1975, Vol 894(5th), col 266–267W
Q1099	Who in the Department of Trade have salaries around £4500, how have they increased since 1972?	Q: Arthur Lewis A: Eric Deakins (Min Tr)	HC Deb, 21 Jul 1975, Vol 896(5th), col 24–25W
Q1100	What steps are being taken to regulate the fees charged by the Patent Office in light of incomes and prices policy?	Q: Tom Normanton A: Eric Deakins (Min Tr)	HC Deb, 14 Oct 1975, Vol 897(5th), col 699–700W
Q1101	How many orders have been made over the last five years under s 56(2) of the Patents Act 1949 [PUBA40]?	Q: Jeff Rooker A: Stanley Clinton Davis (US Co Av Ship)	HC Deb, 28 Oct 1975, Vol 898(5th), col 451W
Q1102	What increase has there been in patent fees over the last ten years (and what percentage increase)?	Q: Kenneth Clarke A: Stanley Clinton Davis (US Co Av Ship)	HC Deb, 29 Oct 1975, Vol 898(5th), col 546–548W
Q1103	Whether the government will ensure that British interests are protected in the proposed Community patent?	Q: Ronald Bell A: Peter Shore (SoS Tr)	HC Deb, 3 Nov 1975, Vol 899(5th), col 64W
Q1104	What is the policy on granting patent licences to South Africa?	Q: David Steel A: Roy Mason (SoS Def)	HC Deb, 3 Dec 1975, Vol 901(5th), col 601W
Q1105	Whether a conclusion has been reached as to discussions between the pharmaceutical industry on the White Paper on Patent Law Reform?	Q: Peter Hordern A: David Owen (Min He)	HC Deb, 9 Dec 1975, Vol 902(5th), col 144W
Q1106	What steps will be taken to enable the European Patent Conventions to be ratified during 1976?	Q: Peter Emery A: Stanley Clinton Davis (US Co Av Ship)	HC Deb, 10 Dec 1975, Vol 902(5th), col 265W
Q1107	Whether steps will be taken to implement the Banks Report [REP24] during the current session?	Q: Michael English A: Stanley Clinton Davis (US Co Av Ship)	HC Deb, 15 Dec 1975, Vol 902(5th), col 944–946
Q1108	What steps will be taken to enable the European Patent Conventions to be ratified during this session of Parliament?	Q: Peter Emery A: Stanley Clinton Davis (US Co Av Ship)	HC Deb, 18 Dec 1975, Vol 902(5th), col 782W

(continued)

(continued)

Q1109	What steps will be used for pattern approval for new inventions to follow Weights and Measures standards?	Q: Peter Hordern A: Alan Williams (Min Prices and Consum Prot)	HC Deb, 11 Feb 1976, Vol 905(5th), col 268–269W
Q1110	When will the government introduce legislation to ratify the European Patent Convention?	Q: Barney Hayhoe A: Stanley Clinton Davis (US Co Av Ship)	HC Deb, 27 Apr 1976, Vol 910(5th), col 69W
Q1111	What steps have been taken to redecorate and develop the Patent Office?	Q: Lena Jeger A: Peter Shore (SoS Tr)	HC Deb, 2 Aug 1976, Vol 916(5th), col 645W
Q1112	How many UK patent applications, complete specifications and sealed patents have been made for pharmaceutical patents; and what percentage is this of the whole?	Q: Patrick Jenkin A: Stanley Clinton Davis (US Co Av Ship)	HC Deb, 6 Aug 1976, Vol 916(5th), col 1095–1096W

2 Parliamentary debates and comments

DEB1	Abuse of monopolies and privileges	Debate: Robert Wingfield	D'Ewes, 8 Nov 1597, p 554
DEB2	Committee formed to consider monopolies and patents of privilege	Debate: Sir John Fortescue; William Cecil	D'Ewes, 16 Nov 1597, p 558
DEB3	Petition presented to Elizabeth I relating to monopolies	Speaker presented report of committee	D'Ewes, 9 Feb 1598, p 547
DEB4	Elizabeth I's "Golden Speech" on patents and Monopolies	Elizabeth I	D'Ewes, 30 Nov 1601, p 659–660 1 Parliamentary History, col 933–939
DEB5	Petition that Irish do not want patent regulation [No record in LJ]	No indication	The Times, 14 Jun 1785 (13 Jun 1785)
DEB6	Vote for £4000 for William Adams for Ophthalmic Hospital (never claimed merit of invention)	Motion: Lord Palmerston Debate: Henry Bennet; William Peel; George Dawson; Christopher Hely-Hutchinson; Joseph Hume	The Times, 25 Jul 1822 (24 Jul 1822)
DEB7	Silk Trade Inventors discovered inventions abroad and brought them to this country and obtained patents	Comment: Edward Ellice	HC Deb, 23 Feb 1826, Vol 13(2nd), col 746 The Times, 24 Mar 1826
DEB8	Supply: Objection to government payment to Charles Babbage for his counting machine; machine stated to be of great public utility	Joseph Hume; Thomas Spring-Rice; Henry Warburton	HC Deb, 28 Mar 1831, Vol 3(3rd), col 1122 and 1125 The Times, 29 Mar 1831
DEB9	Supply: Payment to Charles Babbage said to be waste; payment was not for invention, but for machine itself	Robert Gordon; Thomas Spring-Rice; Sir Charles Wetherall	HC Deb, 13 Feb 1832, Vol 10(3rd), 302, 303 and 306 The Times, 14 Feb 1832
DEB10	Charles Babbage calculating machine has collateral advantage, with some improvements in Glasgow	Comment: Lord Ashley	HC Deb, 13 Apr 1832, Vol 12(3rd), col 468–469 The Times, 14 Apr 1832
DEB11	Mention of £12,000 payment to Charles Babbage	Joseph Hume; Thomas Spring- Rice	The Times, 8 Aug 1833 (7 Aug)
DEB12	Query why so much money paid to people like Charles Babbage; money did not go to him, but to pay for him to make his machine	William Corbett; John Spencer	HC Deb, 15 May 1835, Vol 27(3rd), col 1154
DEB13	Motion for a Select Committee to be appointed to enquire into the law surrounding letters patent	Comment: William MacKinnon	Mirror, 28 Apr 1836, Vol 2, p 1245
DEB14	No need for legal knowledge when Privy Council considers a patent	Comment: Lord Cottenham LC	The Times, 29 Apr 1836 (28 Apr)
DEB15	Comparison between copyright and patents	Debate: Thomas Spring-Rice	Mirror, 25 Apr 1838, Vol 5, p 3532

(continued)

(continued)

DEB16	Comment on the perceived success of the Privy Council in dealing with prolonging patents	Debate: Lord Brougham and Vaux	HL Deb, 27 Jul 1838, Vol 44(3rd), col 702
DEB17	Motion on Kyan's patent to take note of its use by Dutch Navy	Motion: Sir Richard Price Debate: Joseph Brotherton; Charles Wood; Daniel O'Connell	Mirror, 6 Aug 1838, Vol 8, p 6117 The Times, 7 Aug 1838
DEB18	[William] Snow Harris' invention to protect ships from lightning; appointment of a Select Committee	Debate: Lord Eliot; Sir Edward Codrington; Charles Wood; Henry Warburton; Sir Charles Adam; Sir Robert Peel	The Times, 24 Apr 1839 (23 Apr 1839)
DEB19	Copyright Bill If the patents for the steam engine or printing press still existed, the legislature might extend them, but once it has expired, not right to extend it	Comment: Edward Rice	The Times, 2 May 1839 (1 May 1839)
DEB20	The combination of two or more patents in one construction not permitted by English law	Comment: Charles Tennent	The Times, 17 Feb 1841 (16 Feb 1841)
DEB21	Debate on [William] Snow Harris' invention to protect ships from lightning	Motion: Lord Eliot Debate: Richard More-O'Ferrall; Viscount Ingestre; Henry Warburton; Sir Robert Peel; Sir Thomas Cochrane; Sir Robert Inglis; Sir Charles Lemon; Charles A'Court Repington; Sir Charles Adam; John Collier; Viscount Sandon	HC Deb, 18 Feb 1841, Vol 56(3rd), col 707–722 The Times, 19 Feb 1841
DEB22	Patents frequently cost more than they are worth and can be circumvented by minor improvement; patents are too expensive to litigate	Comment: Robert Greg; Henry Warburton	HC Deb, 3 Mar 1841, Vol 56(3rd), col 1285–1286 and 1289–1290 The Times, 4 Mar 1841
DEB23	Captain [Samuel] Warner has complained about the Board of Ordnance and the interference with his patent; the new Board of Ordnance will not do the same	Comment: Thomas Wakley	HC Deb, 24 Sep 1841, Vol 59(3rd), col 812 The Times, 25 Sep 1841
DEB24	Corn laws impede progress – patents taken out cannot be worked	Comment: Sir Robert Peel	HC Deb, 11 Jul 1842, Vol 64(3rd), col 1338 The Times, 12 Jul 1842
DEB25	Motion for Select Committee to investigate Captain [Samuel] Warner's long range	Proposed: Sir Francis Burdett Debate: Sir Howard Douglas; Joseph Brotherton; Sir Robert Peel; James Plumridge; George Brooke-Pechell; Sir George Cockburn	HC Deb, 4 Aug 1842, Vol 65(3rd), col 1033–1051 The Times, 5 Aug 1842
DEB26	Coalwhippers Bill Patents being impeded by the Bill is regrettable	Debate: Marquess of Clanricarde; Earl of Dalhousie	HL Deb, 17 Aug 1843(3rd), Vol 71(3rd), col 907–908
DEB27	Government should investigate the utility of Captain [Samuel] Warner's invention of the long range and the contempt with which it was received	Proposed: Viscount Ingestre Debate: Sir Robert Peel; William Cowper-Temple; Sir Howard Douglas; Sir Charles Napier; Henry Aglionby; Joseph Brotherton; Thomas Wakley; Sir George Cockburn	HC Deb, 31 July 1844 Vol 76(3rd), col 1577–1623 The Times, 1 Aug 1844

DEB28	When he had been Attorney-General, Lord Campbell had granted patents for smoke consumption devices which would save money	Comment: Lord Campbell	HC Deb, 19 Mar 1846, Vol 84(3rd), col 1220 The Times, 20 Mar 1846
DEB29	The government should investigate Captain [Samuel] Warner's invention of the long range	Proposed: Viscount Ingestre Debate: George Brooke-Pechell; Sir Howard Douglas; Charles Wood; Joseph Brotherton; Thomas Wakley	HC Deb, 13 July 1846, Vol 87(3rd), col 1071–1097 The Times, 14 Jul 1846
DEB30	The government should appoint a Select Committee to investigate Captain [Samuel] Warner's invention of the long range	Proposed: Viscount Ingestre Debate: Robert Holland; Joseph Brotherton; Lord John Russell; Henry Aglionby; Sir Howard Douglas; Maurice Berkeley	HC Deb, 25 Jun 1847, Vol 93(3rd), col 921–946 The Times, 26 Jun 1847
DEB31	Patents for smoke consumption are not effective	Comment: William Copeland	The Times, 26 Jul 1849 (25 Jul 1849)
DEB32	Call for papers relating to the cost of obtaining a patent	Motion: Charles Sibthorp Debate: Sir George Lewis Lewis; Thomas Barrett-Lennard; Henry Aglionby; Thomas Sidney; William Crawford; William Carew; Sir George Grey; Benjamin Disraeli	HC Deb, 1 Apr 1851, Vol 115(3rd), col 890–895 The Times, 2 Apr 1851
DEB33	Bovill patent [No 11342 or 12636] discussed as solution to issues with milling flour	James Wilson; Lord Naas	HC Deb, 15 Jul 1851, Vol 118(3rd), col 808 and 832 The Times, 16 Jul 1851
DEB34	The need for the Patents Bill to be revived	Debate: Lord Lyndhurst; Earl of Ellenbourgh	HL Deb, 9 Feb 1852, Vol 119(3rd), col 318 The Times, 10 Feb 1852
DEB35	The need for patent reform as the current system is ineffectual	Comment: Lord Lyndhurst	HL Deb, 12 Mar 1852, Vol 119(3rd), col 942 The Times, 13 Mar 1852
DEB36	Motion: A Select Committee to investigate the agreement between the Inland Revenue and Henry Archer regarding his machine for perforating the sheets	Proposed: George Muntz Debate: Edward Grogan; George Hamilton; Francis Mowatt; Charles Geach; Richard Spooner; Henry Drummond	HC Deb, 16 Mar 1852, Vol 119(3rd), col 1156–1159 The Times, 17 Mar 1852
DEB37	Motion: A Select Committee should be formed to investigate Captain [Samuel] Warner's inventions	Debate: Earl Talbot; Earl of Hardwicke; Lord de Ros; Earl of Albemarle; Earl of Minto; Duke of Argyll; Earl of Malmesbury; Earl of Wicklow; Earl of Ellesmere; Lord Vivian; Earl Granville	HL Deb, 14 May 1852, Vol 121(3rd), col 620–628 The Times, 15 May 1852
DEB38	Patents Bill [PUBA6] has been referred to a Select Committee only for expedition	Debate: Earl of Minto; Earl of Derby	The Times, 19 May 1852 (18 May 1852)
DEB39	Motion: Report into Captain [Samuel] Warner's invention of long range to be laid before House	Debate: Duke of Wellington; Earl of Derby; Earl of Hardwicke; Lord Monteagle; Earl Talbot; Earl of Wicklow; Earl of Winchelsa; Earl of Albemarle; Earl of Rosse; Marquess of Lansdowne	HL Deb, 21 May 1852 vol 121(3rd), col 855–873 The Times, 22 May 1852
DEB40	Glass patent has increased production substantially	Comment: Apsley Pellatt	HC Deb, 3 Mar 1853, Vol 125(3rd), col 1027 The Times, 4 Mar 1853 (3 Mar 1853)

(continued)

(continued)

DEB41	[William] Hale took out the patent for rockets and offered it to the government, but taken by foreign governments	Comment: Thomas Duncombe	HC Deb, 16 Apr 1853, Vol 125(3rd), col 1211 The Times, 16 Apr 1853
DEB42	Whether the government intends to prosecute [William] Hale, the inventor of the war rocket	Comment: Thomas Duncombe	HC Deb, 6 May 1853, Vol 126(3rd), col 114206 The Times, 6 May 1853
DEB43	Supply: Fees paid to law officers in relation to patents	Debate: Apsley Pellatt; James Wilson; John Bright; Sir Alexander Cockburn	HC Deb, 4 Aug 1853, Vol 129(3rd), col 1311–1313 The Times, 5 Aug 1853
DEB44	Supply: Vote to buy Archer patent	Debate: Vivian Smith; William Gladstone	HC Deb, 5 Aug 1853, Vol 129(3rd), col 1412 The Times, 6 Aug 1853
DEB45	Supply – Naval Estimates: Payment to Captain [Edward] Carpenter for his invention of the screw propeller, rather than [James] Lowe	Debate: George Scobell; Sir Francis Baring	HC Deb, 27 Feb 1854, Vol 130(3rd), col 1387–1389 The Times, 28 Feb 1854
DEB46	Whether loss of Europa would have been mitigated by use of [Robert] Parratt's tubular lifeboat	Debate: Arthur Otway; Sir James Graham	The Times, 20 Jun 1854 (19 Jun 1854)
DEB47	Supply: Patent Act £23,700 Compensation paid to officers under the Patent Law Amendment Act 1852 [PUBA6]; pay to law officers in relation to patents	Debate: Apsley Pellat; Sir Alexander Cockburn; William Williams; James Wilson; James Heywood; Sir Henry Willoughby; Lord John Russell	HC Deb, 7 Jul 1854, Vol 134(3rd), col 1390–1394 The Times, 8 Jul 1854
DEB48	Screw Propeller Misapplication of money in relation to "rewards" given to the inventor	Debate: Lord Lyndhurst; Earl of Aberdeen; Earl of Hardwicke	HL Deb, 10 Jul 1854, Vol 134(3rd), col 1420–1429 The Times, 11 Jul 1854
DEB49	Objecting to proposition that patents for inventions not fit subject matter for a Select Committee	Comment: Lord Naas	The Times, 19 Jul 1854 (18 Jul 1854)
DEB50	Supply: £60,000 for printing of patents	Comment: James Wilson	HC Deb, 9 Feb 1855, Vol 136(3rd), col 1394–1395 The Times, 10 Feb 1855
DEB51	Arbitration would be particularly suitable to settle patent disputes	Comment: William Mackinnon	HC Deb, 6 Mar 1855, Vol 137(3rd), col 204–205 The Times, 7 Mar 1855
DEB52	The rule restricting the number of people to whom a patent can be assigned should be restricted	Comment: Lord Redesdale	HC Deb, 22 Mar 1855, Vol 137(3rd), col 947 The Times, 23 Mar 1855
DEB53	Motion for Select Committee into £20,000 voted in relation to the screw propeller	Motion: George Scobell Debate: Sir Francis Baring; Henry Keating; John Walcot; Sir Fredric Thesiger; Sir George Pechell; John Phillimore; Sir Charles Wood; Edward Rice; Montague Chambers; Henry Drummond	HC Deb, 15 May 1855, Vol 138(3rd), col 639–660 The Times, 16 May 1855
DEB54	Supply: Patent Law £22,572	No debate	HC Deb, 31 Jul 1855, Vol 139(3rd), col 1567 The Times, 1 Aug 1855

DEB55	Supply – Stationery and Printing: Printing costs of specifications	Comment: James Wilson	HC Deb, 31 Mar 1856, Vol 141(3rd), col 265 and 268
DEB56	Supply: Patent Act £21,842 Complaints about the amount paid to the law officers relating to patents	Debate: William Williams; James Wilson; John Cheetham	HC Deb, 2 Jun 1856, Vol 142(3rd), col 881 The Times, 3 Jun 1856
DEB57	Advancement of Science Urge a reduction in patent fees (pay officers out of consolidated fund)	Debate: James Heywood	HC Deb, 10 Jun 1856, Vol 142(3rd), col 1265 and 1273 The Times, 11 Jun 1856
DEB58	Supply – Stationery Office: Printing of patent specifications transferred to Stationery Office costs £40,000 per year	Comment: James Wilson; and Anthony Wilson	HC Deb, 12 Jun 1857, Vol 145(3rd), col 1695 The Times, 13 Jun 1857
DEB59	Supply: Stationery Office payment increases because it includes, amongst other things, printing patent specification	Comment: James Wilson	HC Deb, 22 Jun 1857, Vol 146(3rd), col 188 The Times, 23 Jun 1857
DEB60	Supply: Patent Act £20,988 Vote for an additional building; cost is more than the surplus generated by the office; comments about fees paid to law officers; review of patent law required	Debate: John Mowbray; James Wilson; William Williams; Sir John Trollope; Henry Pease; William Sykes; Joseph Henley; Sir Henry Willoughby; Richard Spooner; Sir Edward Watkin; Sir Denham Norreys	HC Deb, 23 Jul 1857, Vol 147(3rd), col 323–327
DEB61	Supply: Patent Act £26,198 Fees paid to law officers; profits from Patent Office; Patent Museum	Debate: William Williams; Spencer Walpole; Charles Gilpin; Sir George Lewis; Sir Hugh Cairns; William Cox; Sir Fitzroy Kelly: Benjamin Disraeli; Augustus Smith; Lewis Dillwyn	HC Deb, 13 Jul 1858, Vol 151(3rd), col 1412–1416 The Times, 14 Jul 1858
DEB62	Discussion of Armstrong's rifle and the use of his invention	Debate: Jonathan Peel; William Williams; Sir Henry Willoughby; Sir George De Lacy Evans	HC Deb, 4 Mar 1859, Vol 152(3rd), col 1318–1322 The Times, 5 Mar 1859
DEB63	Discussion of the advantages of the Armstrong gun and its role in fortification	Debate: Jonathan Peel; Sir Charles Napier; Robert Philips; William Codrington; William Williams; William Monsell; Sir Frederick Smith; Lord Palmerston	HC Deb, 7 Mar 1859, Vol 152(3rd), col 1409–1412 The Times, 8 Mar 1859
DEB64	Attorney-General present in all patent extension hearings	Comment: Lord Brougham and Vaux	HC Deb. 4 Jul 1859, Vol 154(3rd), col 562 The Times, 5 Jul 1859
DEB65	Divorce Court Bill Role of Attorney-General in patent proceedings	Comment: Lord Chelmsford	HL Deb, 21 Jul 1859. Vol 155(3rd), col 145
DEB66	Supply: Patent Act £20,095 Costs of getting a patent; fees paid to various officials	Debate: John Brady; Samuel Laing; William Williams; Sir Edward Grogan; John Wise; William Sykes; Edwin James	HC Deb, 1 Aug 1859, Vol 155(3rd), col 761–763 The Times, 2 Aug 1859
DEB67	Army camp at Aldershot has been used to test over 200 inventions	Comment: Sidney Herbert	HC Deb, 17 Feb 1860, Vol 156(3rd), col 1287–1288 The Times, 18 Feb 1860
DEB68	Paper Duty Repeal Bill Problem of a patent being precluded from being worked	Comment: William Gladstone	HC Deb, 12 Mar 1860, Vol 157(3rd), col 425

(continued)

(continued)

DEB69	Patenting of floating breakwater and trial of the same	Comment: Marquess of Clanricarde	HL Deb, 26 Mar 1860, Vol 157(3rd), col 1234 The Times, 27 Mar 1860
DEB70	If the government does not purchase Joseph Whitworth's invention, then some foreign government will do so	Comment: Sir Joseph Paxton	HC Deb, 18 Jun 1860, Vol 159(3rd), col 599 The Times, 19 Jun 1860
DEB71	Weights and Measures Bill Requirement to use a patented invention	Debate: Lord Chelmsford and Lord Teynham	HL Deb, 3 Jul 1860, Vol 159(3rd), col 1313–1314 The Times, 4 Jul 1860
DEB72	Supply: Patent Act £28,229	No debate	HC Deb, 17 Aug 1860, Vol 160(3rd), col 1508
DEB73	Motion for correspondence between John Clare and Admiralty relating to his patent to build iron ships [PPP65]	Motion: John Hennessy Debate: Lord Clarence Paget; George Bentinck; William Jackson; Sir John Pakington	HC Deb, 22 Feb 1861, Vol 161(3rd), col 860–861 The Times, 23 Feb 1861
DEB74	Paper Duty Comment on rules relating to paper duty precluding the working of a patent	Debate: William Gladstone	HC Deb, 2 May 1861, Vol 162(3rd), col 1408
DEB75	Government of the Navy Bill The adoption, or otherwise of new inventions in the navy	Debate: Earl of Carnarvon; Duke of Somerset; Earl Grey of Ripon	HL Deb, 11 Jun 1861, Vol 163(3rd), col 904, 909 and 914 The Times, 12 Jun 1861
DEB76	Supply: Cost of printing	Debate: Augustus Smith; Sir Henry Willougby	HC Deb, 9 Jul 1861, Vol 164(3rd), col 640 and 642 The Times, 10 Jul 1861
DEB77	Supply: Patent Act £29,005 Concerns about fees paid to law officers	Debate: William Williams; Henry Jervis-White-Jervis; Robert Peel; William Coningham	HC Deb, 23 Jul 1861, Vol 164(3rd), col 1415–1416 The Times, 24 Jul 1861
DEB78	Court of Chancery Bill Patent injunctions in Court of Chancery	Debate: Peter Rolt	HC Deb, 25 Feb 1862, Vol 165(3rd), col 723 The Times, 26 Feb 1862
DEB79	The development of new inventions in armaments	Comments: Sir George Lewis; Philip Martin	HC Deb, 6 Mar 1862, Vol 165(3rd), col 1079, 1082 and 1104 The Times, 7 Mar 1863
DEB80	Building of Patent Museum must wait until after Select Committee reports [See REP9]	Comment: William Gladstone	HC Deb, 29 Apr 1862, Vol 166(3rd), col 1064 The Times, 30 Apr 1862
DEB81	Improvements and developments in the weapons of war; the need to obtain weapons from foreign powers	Debate: Sir Stafford Northcote; Benjamin Disraeli	HC Deb, 8 May 1862, Vol 166(3rd), col 1368, 1376, 1379 and 1425 The Times, 9 May 1862
DEB82	Preparations for the Cupola trial; complaints that the Admiralty does not properly investigate inventions	Lord Robert Montagu; Lord Clarence Paget	HC Deb, 19 May 1862, Vol 166(3rd), col 1945 The Times, 20 May 1862
DEB83	Captain [CP] Coles' letter in *The Times* (12 May 1862) on his cupola; and the testing of it	Debate: John Walcott	HC Deb, 23 May 1862, Vol 166(3rd), col 2110–2111 The Times, 24 May 1862

DEB84	Captain [CP] Coles and the payment from the Admiralty for his invention of the Cupola Shield	Motion: William Monsell Debate: Lord Clarence Paget; Henry Lygon; Ralph Bernal; Viscount Palmerston	HC Deb, 18 Jul 1862, Vol 168(3rd), col 505–510 The Times, 19 Jul 1862
DEB85	Supply: Concerns about the fees paid to the law officers in relation to patents	Debate: William Williams; William Fitzgerald; Robert Peel; Christopher Darby Griffiths; Sir David Dundas	HC Deb, 21 Jul 1862, Vol 168(3rd), col 597 The Times, 22 Jul 1862
DEB86	Supply – Stationery Office: Printing costs; £19,000 repaid fees by Patent Office	Debate: Robert Peel	HC Deb, 26 Mar 1863, Vol 169(3rd), col 1962 The Times, 27 Mar 1863
DEB87	Supply: Purchase of land for Patent Museum	Debate: Viscount Palmerston; William Gregory; William Gladstone; Bernal Osborne	HC Deb, 15 Jun 1863, Vol 171(3rd), col 906–911, 913–917, 924, 926–927, 932, 933, 936 The Times, 16 Jun 1863
DEB88	Supply: Purchase of exhibition buildings, including for Patent Museum	Debate: William Gladstone; Lord Elcho; William Coningham; William Tite; George Bentinck; Sir John Shelly; Frederick Dalton; Henry Lennox; William Gregory; Sir Stafford Northcote; Joseph Henley	HC Deb, 2 Jul 1863, Vol 172(3rd), col 74–135 The Times, 3 Jul 1863
DEB89	Supply: Patent Act £17,015	No debate	HC Deb, 10 Jul 1863, Vol 172(3rd), col 540 The Times, 11 Jul 1863
DEB90	Discussion of the Armstrong gun and the Whitworth gun and their relative merits	Earl of Hardwicke; Duke of Somerset; Earl De Grey and Ripon	HL Deb, 9 Feb 1864, Vol 173(3rd), col 311–320 The Times, 10 Feb 1864
DEB91	Pamphlet by [John] Chalmers relating to his target	Observation: Sir Frederic Smith	HC Deb, 22 Feb 1864, Vol 173(3rd), col 89–90 The Times, 23 Feb 1864
DEB92	Use of Chalmers' target; the failure of the Admiralty to remunerate him	Debate: Sir John Hay; Sir John Pakington	HC Deb, 25 Feb 1864, Vol 173(3rd), col 112–113 The Times, 26 Feb 1864
DEB93	Supply: Estimates ought to be reduced; Patent Office should pay for itself	Motion: Matthew Marsh Reply: Robert Peel	HC Deb, 1 Mar 1864, Vol 173(3rd), col 1342 and 1354 The Times, 2 Mar 1864
DEB94	[John] Chalmers' invention (targeting device); inventors providing inventions to Admiralty; process for generally	Debate: Sir Frederic Smith; Sir James Elphinstone; Charles Seely; William Ferrand; William Sykes; Sir Samuel Morton Peto; Sir Henry Willoughby; John Laird; Lord Clarence Paget; Sir John Pakington	HC Deb, 14 Mar 1864, Vol 173(3rd), col 1963–1984 The Times, 15 Mar 1864
DEB95	Supply: Patent Act £4000	No debate	HC Deb, 17 Mar 1864, Vol 174(3rd), col 291
DEB96	Comment on the insufficiency of the accommodation provided for the Patent Museum at South Kensington	Debate: Lewis Dillwyn	HC Deb, 12 Apr 1864, Vol 174(3rd), col 915 The Times, 13 Apr 1864

(continued)

(continued)

DEB97	Motion: Select Committee into claims of John Clare against Admiralty (notwithstanding jury found against him); also mentioned John Chalmers	Debate: Thomas Dickson; Lord Clarence Paget; Sir Robert Collier; George Denman; John Hennessy; Sir John Pakington	HC Deb, 21 Apr 1864, Vol 174(3rd), col 1460–1469 The Times, 22 Apr 1864
DEB98	Observations on the need for a proper Patent Office Library in the same location as the Office of the Commissioners of Patents	Debate: Lewis Dillwyn; William Gregory; William Cowper-Temple; Sir Walter Barttelot; Augustus Smith; Acton Ayrton	HC Deb, 29 Apr 1864, Vol 174(3rd), col 1950–1957 The Times, 30 Apr 1864
DEB99	Unfairness of payments made by the government under the Lancaster rifle patents	Comment: Lord Elcho; Marquis of Hartington	HC Deb, 5 May 1864, Vol 175(3rd), col 58, 61–62 The Times, 6 May 1864
DEB100	Building of Patent Museum	Debate: Francis Powell; Michael Hassard; William Cowper-Temple	HC Deb, 30 May 1864, Vol 175(3rd), col 867 and 868 The Times, 31 Mar 1864
DEB101	Stamp Duties paid: Patents and misc £240,000	No debate	HC Deb, 14 Jun 1864, Vol 175(3rd), col 1733
DEB102	Supply: Patent Act £22,689	No debate	HC Deb, 1 Jul 1864, Vol 176(3rd), col 57 The Times, 2 Jul 1864
DEB103	Discussion of manufacturing Armstrong and Whitford guns	Debate: Richard Cobden; Jonathan Peel	HC Deb, 22 Jul 1864, Vol 176(3rd), col 1911–1912 and 1967 The Times, 23 Jul 1864
DEB104	Comment on Clare's patent claim against the Admiralty: "ridiculous claim and demands"	Debate: Sir Roundell Palmer	HC Deb, 26 Jul 1864, Vol 176(3rd), col 2123–2124 The Times, 27 Jul 1864
DEB105	Discussion of the criticisms of Captain [CP] Coles' Cupola ship	Lord Clarence Paget; Sir Frederic Smith; Sir John Pakington	HC Deb, 9 Mar 1865, Vol 177(3rd), col 1412 to 1428, 1452 The Times, 10 Mar 1865
DEB106	Discussion of Lancaster rifle patent and its renewal	Debate: Lord Elcho; Maquess of Hartington; Arthur Kinnaird	HC Deb, 20 Mar 1865, Vol 177(3rd), col 1993–1994, 1996, 1998 and 1999 The Times, 21 Mar 1865
DEB107	Supply: Patent Law Expenses £6000	No debate	HC Deb, 6 Apr 1865, Vol 178(3rd), col 851
DEB108	Purchase of land for museums, including Patent Museum	Comment: William Gladstone	HC Deb, 5 May 1865, Vol 178(3rd), col 1558 The Times, 6 May 1865
DEB109	Debate on Edmunds' case and the Lords Committee Report [REP11]	Debate: Lord Redesdale; Earl Hardwicke; Viscount Eversley; Earl of Wicklow; Lord Lyveden; Earl of Derby; Earl Russell; Earl of Harrowby; Duke of Somerset; Lord Russell; Lord Chelmsford; Lord Wynford; Earl of Donoughmore; Lord Tauton; Earl Granville; Lord Cranworth	HL Deb, 9 May 1865, Vol 179(3rd), col 6–45 The Times, 10 May 1865
DEB110	Supply: Debate relating to the building of the Patent Library	Debate: Lewis Dillwyn; Francis Powell; Henry Cowper	HC Deb, 12 May 1865, Vol 179(3rd), col 255–256 The Times, 13 May 1865

DEB111	Supply: Patent Law Expenses £25,003	No debate	HC Deb, 8 Jun 1865, Vol 179(3rd), col 1305 The Times, 9 Jun 1865
DEB112	Motion of Censure of Lord Chancellor, including allegations relating to Leonard Edmunds	Motion: George Hunt; James Moncreiff; John Hennessy; George Denman; Benjamin Disraeli; Sir George Grey	HC Deb, 3 Jul 1865, Vol 180(3rd), col 1045–1138 The Times, 4 Jul 1865
DEB113	Supply: Patent Office £5000; Patent Law Expenses £8000	No debate	HC Deb, 8 Mar 1866, Vol 181(3rd), col 1780–1782
DEB114	Discussion of Captain [CP] Coles' Cupola invention	Debate: Lord Dunsany; Duke of Somerset; Earl of Hardwicke; Earl of Ellenborough	HL Deb, 12 Mar 1866, Vol 182(3rd), col 1–14 The Times, 13 Mar 1866
DEB115	Supply: Poor condition of Patent Roll and Patent Office, in particular the furniture	Debate: William Bovill; Henry Cowper; George Bentinck	HC Deb, 9 Apr 1866, Vol 182(3rd), col 903, 910 and 931–957 The Times, 10 Apr 1866
DEB116	Supply: Patent Law Expenses £21,292 Discussion of fees	Debate: Christopher Sykes; Hugh Childers	HC Deb, 11 May 1866, Vol 183(3rd), col 834 The Times, 13 May 1866
DEB117	Everyone who thinks they have invented a better rifle than a Snider should be able to demonstrate it.	Comment: Jonathan Peel	HC Deb, 16 Jul 1866, Vol 184(3rd), col 839 The Times, 17 Jul 1866
DEB118	Motion: Select Committee on Sewage and Pollution of Rivers If the committee reports on the merits of Dover's sewage patent, then it should also report on that of any other inventor	Debate: Earl of Shrewsbury; Earl of Derby; Lord Denman; Lord Redesdale	HL Deb, 19 Jul 1866, Vol 184(3rd), col 1061–1063 The Times, 20 Jul 1866
DEB119	Increase in supply for rewards to inventors; mention of Major William Palliser and Mr Frazer	Comment: Jonathan Peel	HC Deb, 7 Mar 1867, Vol 185(3rd), col 1458 The Times, 8 Mar 1867
DEB120	Supply: Patent Law Expenses £8000	No debate	HC Deb, 15 Mar 1867, Vol 185(3rd), col 1995
DEB121	Whether officers in public departments in the War Office should be able to patent inventions?	Debate: Sir John Pakington; Jonathan Peel; Marquess of Hartington; Lord Elcho; Henry Liddell; Joseph Samuda	HC Deb, 6 Jun 1867, Vol 187(3rd), col 1707–1711 The Times, 7 Jun 1867
DEB122	Ordnance Department and call for Select Committee Criticisms of how it works, including claims that inventions submitted to the committee misappropriated	Motion: Henry Baillie; Sir John Hay; Lord Elcho; Jonathan Peel; Charles Shaw Lefevre; Sir John Pakington; Charles Newdegate	HC Deb, 13 Jun 1867, Vol 187(3rd), col 1785–1813 The Times, 14 Jun 1867
DEB123	Supply: Patent Law Expenses: £23,410 (to complete sum of £31,410)	No debate	HC Deb, 22 Jul 1867, Vol 188(3rd), col 1903 The Times, 23 Jul 1867
DEB124	Motion for an address in relation to the Museum in South Kensington, including Patent Museum	Debate: Henry Cowper; Alexander Beresford Hope; Lord John Manners	HC Deb, 1 Aug 1867, Vol 189(3rd), col 634–644
DEB125	Supply: Patent Office £4000	No debate	HC Deb, 2 Apr 1868, Vol 191(3rd), col 800

(continued)

(continued)

DEB126	Discussion of Major [William] Palliser's invention of compound ordnance	Augustus Anson; Lord Elcho; Sir John Pakington; Joseph Samuda	HC Deb, 13 Aug 1867, Vol 189(3rd), col 1500–1509 The Times, 14 Aug 1867
DEB127	War Office gave a reward to [William] Hale for rockets and then made them worthless	Comment: Arthur Otway	HC Deb, 6 Jul 1868, Vol 193(3rd), col 777–778 The Times, 7 Jul 1868
DEB128	Supply includes £14,800 for rewards for inventors	Comment: Sir John Pakington; Francis Dunne; Marquess of Hartington	HC Deb, 9 Jul 1868, Vol 193(3rd), col 957 and 966
DEB129	Supply: Patent Office £19,071	No debate	HC Deb, 14 Jul 1868, Vol 193(3rd), col 1210 The Times, 15 Jul 1868
DEB130	Leonard Edmunds' case and government's suggestions on the same	Debate: George Bentinck; Sir John Karslake	HC Deb, 29 Jul 1868, Vol 193(3rd), col 1929 The Times, 30 Jul 1868
DEB131	Supply: No patent rights against the Crown, but all sorts of claims from inventors	Comment: Edward Cardwell	HC Deb, 11 Mar 1869, Vol 194(3rd), col 1131–1132 The Times, 12 Mar 1869
DEB132	Notice of motion to abolish patents	Notice: Robert Macfie	The Times, 14 May 1869 (13 May)
DEB133	Motion to abolish patent laws	Proposed: Robert Macfie Debate: Sir Roundell Palmer; Lord Stanley; James Howard; Anthony Mundella; John Stapleton; Lord Elcho; Joseph Samuda; Sir Robert Collier; George Denman	HC Deb, 28 May 1869, Vol 196(3rd), col 888–923 The Times, 29 May 1869
DEB134	Supply: Patent Office £23,669; and debate on Patent Office buildings and museum	Debate: Lewis Dillwyn; Edgar Bowring; Acton Ayrton	HC Deb, 12 Jul 1869, Vol 197(3rd), col 1685–1686
DEB135	Supply: Whether officers in public departments should take patents; whether the patent system should continue	Debate: Walter Barttelot; Robert Macfie; Edward Cardwell; Charles Newdegate	HC Deb, 22 Jul 1869, Vol 198(3rd), col 493–498 The Times, 23 Jul 1869
DEB136	War Office Bill Will a return be laid on the table setting out expenses, including awards to inventors?	Comment: Walter Barttelot	HC Deb, 24 Feb 1870, Vol 199(3rd) col 784 The Times, 25 Feb 1870
DEB137	Notice of motion to abolish patents	Notice: Robert Macfie	The Times, 16 Mar 1870 (15 Mar)
DEB138	Inappropriate for juries to hear patent cases	Comment: Lord Penzance	HL Deb, 18 Mar 1870, Vol 200(3rd), col 184 The Times, 19 Mar 1870
DEB139	Supply: Patent Office £8000	No debate	HC Deb, 8 Apr 1870, Vol 200(3rd), col 586
DEB140	Motion for Select Committee to report upon patents for inventions	Proposed: Robert Macfie	HC Deb, 12 Apr 1870, Vol 200(3rd), col 1726 The Times, 13 Apr 1870
DEB141	Motion for Select Committee into resignation of Colonel [Edward] Boxer; and whether officers should be able to take out patents	Proposed: Myles O'Reilly Seconded: William Gregory Debate: Sir John Pakington; Edward Cardwell; Augustus Anson	HC Deb, 29 Apr 1870, Vol 200(3rd), col 2062–2089 The Times, 30 Apr 1870

DEB142	Supply: Patent Office £26,265 Whether Patent Museum has progressed; and fees paid to law officers in patent cases	Debate: Edgar Bowring; Andrew Lusk; Acton Ayrton; Ralph Neville-Grenville; Lewis Dillwyn; Sir John Coleridge; John Hinde Palmer; John Walter	HC Deb, 15 Jul 1870, Vol 203(3rd), col 376–377 The Times, 16 Jul 1870
DEB143	Arrest of Leonard Edmunds and the request for the government to produce papers	Debate: Russell Gurney; Sir John Hay; Henry West; George Schlater-Booth; Sir Robert Collier; George Denman; Sir James Elphinstone; John Ball; David Sherlock; Sir Roundell Palmer; Edward Horsman; Sir John Coleridge	HC Deb, 19 Jul 1870, Vol 203(3rd), col 509–535 The Times, 20 Jul 1880
DEB144	Supply: The fees paid to law officers for patent work made up for the work done in other areas	Debate: Sir Roundell Palmer; David Chadwick	HC Deb, 26 Jul 1870, Vol 203(3rd), col 991–992 The Times, 27 Jul 1870
DEB145	Suggestion that Patent Museum can put in South Kensington site	Debate: Robert Lowe	HC Deb, 2 Aug 1870, Vol 203(3rd), col 1476 The Times, 3 Aug 1870
DEB146	Supply: £24,539 Debate on patent fees	Debate: Andrew Lusk; William Baxter; Gabriel Goldney; George Leeman; George Gregory; Peter Rylands; Montague Chambers; Edward Herman; Acton Ayrton; George Sclater-Booth; Duncan McLaren; Robert Macfie	HC Deb, 1 Jun 1871, Vol 206(3rd), col 1414–1417
DEB147	Request for papers setting out the claims paid to inventors by the War Office, particularly Major William Pallister	Debate: Earl of Denbigh; Lord Northbrook; Duke of Somerset; Viscount Melville; Viscount Gough; Earl of Camperdown	HL Deb, 10 Jul 1871, Vol 207(3rd), col 1321–1331 The Times, 11 Jul 1871
DEB148	Comment: Suggestion of using patent fee surplus to give rewards to inventors	Debate: William Fowler; Robert Macfie	HC Deb, 25 Mar 1872, Vol 210(3rd), col 641 and 651 The Times, 26 Mar 1872
DEB149	Supply: Patent Office £4500	No debate	HC Deb, 4 Apr 1872, Vol 210(3rd), col 809
DEB150	Obnoxious nature of patent fees going to law officers	Comment: Henry Fawcett	HC Deb, 3 May 1872, Vol 211(3rd), col 252
DEB151	Supply – Patents Act: £20,428 fees being paid to Scottish law officers	Debate: John Hinde Palmer; Francis Powell; William Baxter; Robert MacFie; Andrew Lusk	HC Deb, 10 Jun 1872, Vol 211(3rd), col 1536–1537 The Times, 11 Jun 1872
DEB152	Paying of law officers by patent fees; and patent fees	Comment: John Hinde Palmer	HC Deb, 21 Jun 1872, Vol 212(3rd), col 69
DEB153	Comment: Enforceability of patent law in Egypt	Debate: Viscount Enfield	HC Deb, 5 Jul 1872, Vol 212(3rd), col 733 The Times, 6 Jul 1872
DEB154	Supply: Comment that Patent Museum is in a "shocking state"	Debate: John Hinde Palmer; Robert Macfie	HC Deb, 3 Aug 1872, Vol 213(3rd), col 401
DEB155	Address to audit accounts between Crown and Leonard Edmunds	Proposed: Lord Redesdale Debate: Lord Hatherley	HC Deb, 9 Aug 1872, Vol 213(3rd), col 831–834 The Times, 10 Aug 1872

(continued)

(continued)

DEB156	Supply: Patent Office £5000	No debate	HC Deb, 21 Mar 1873, Vol 214(3rd), col 2061
DEB157	[Robert] Whitehead torpedo patent purchased in 1870; asked for money last year; where did it go?	Comment: Lord Henry Lennox	HC Deb, 24 Mar 1873, Vol 215(3rd), col 58–60 The Times, 25 Mar 1873
DEB158	Supply: Suggestion that grounds for National History Museum in South Kensington ought to be used for a Patent Museum	Debate: John Hinde Palmer; Robert Macfie Debate: Lewis Dillwyn; Acton Ayrton	HC Deb, 21 Apr 1873, Vol 215(3rd), col 789–790 The Times, 22 Apr 1873
DEB159	Supply: Patent Office £23,456	No debate	HC Deb, 25 Apr 1873, Vol 215(3rd), col 1021 The Times, 26 Apr 1873
DEB160	Nitro-glycerine, Professor [Sir Frederick] Abel and his patent	Debate: Alexander Staveley Hill; Henry Bruce; George Elliot; John Hinde Palmer; Mitchell Henry; Sir George Stokes	HC Deb, 16 May 1873, Vol 216(3rd), col 54–59 The Times, 17 May 1873
DEB161	Motion to refer Leonard Edmunds to Comptroller and Auditor-General	Debate: Lord Redesdale; Lord Selborne; Lord Denman	HC Deb, 16 Jun 1873, Vol 216(3rd), col 963–969 The Times, 17 Jun 1873
DEB162	Supply: Discussion of invention of the gun by Bashley Britten	Debate: George Gregory; John Hick; Sir Henry Storks; Frederick Beaumont; Sir George Balfour; Lord Elcho; Peter Rylands	HC Deb, 23 Jun 1873, Vol 216(3rd), col 1264–1276 The Times, 24 Jun 1873
DEB163	Supreme Court of Judicature Bill Comment on delay in courts caused by patent cases	Debate: Sir George Jessel; Charles Lewis	HC Deb, 30 Jun 1873, Vol 216(3rd), col 1587 and 1591 The Times, 1 Jul 1873
DEB164	Whether the government accepts that the invention of [William] Hope is the same as [Edward] Boxer's –"Boxer Shrapnel"	Debate: Earl of Longford; Lord Napier and Ettrick; Marquess of Lansdowne	HL Deb, 25 Jul 1873, Vol 217(3rd), col 966–970 The Times, 26 Jul 1873
DEB165	Supply: Patent Office £301 16s 10d	No debate	HC Deb, 21 Mar 1874, Vol 218(3rd), col 206
DEB166	Supply: Patent Office £3500	No debate	HC Deb, 23 Mar 1874, Vol 218(3rd), col 251
DEB167	Supply: Patent Law £18,701 Debate on surplus and poor state of Patent Museum	Debate: Lewis Dillwyn John Whitwell; Thomas Earp; William H Smith	HC Deb, 17 Apr 1874, Vol 218(3rd), col 776–777 The Times, 18 Apr 1874
DEB168	[William] Hope's claim of being the inventor of [Edward] Boxer-Shrapnel's shell	Debate: Earl of Longford; Lord Napier and Ettrick; Earl of Pembroke; Marquess of Lansdowne	HL Deb, 12 Jun 1874, Vol 219(3rd), col 1492–1495 The Times, 13 Jun 1874
DEB169	Motion to refer petition of Leonard Edmunds to a Select Committee	Debate: Earl of Rosebery; Lord Selborne; Lord Redesdale; Marquis of Bath; Duke of Richmond; Lord Hatherley	HL Deb, 3 Jul 1874, Vol 220(3rd), col 1500–1516 The Times, 4 Jul 1874
DEB170	Need for patent reform	Speech out of Parliament: William Forster	The Times, 20 Jan 1875 (19 Jan 1875)
DEB171	Statement that intending to present Patent Bill	Comment: Earl Cairns	HL Deb, 5 Feb 1875, Vol 222(3rd), col 35–36 The Times, 6 Feb 1875
DEB172	Decision in *R v Feathers* (1865) 6 B & S 257 (122 ER 1191) and free use; Armstrong and Whitworth Committee	Debates: John Nolan; Lord Eustace Cecil	HC Deb, 5 Apr 1875, Vol 223(3rd), col 310–311 and 312 The Times, 6 Apr 1875

DEB173	Pollution of Rivers Bill Patent owners would make spurious claims to try to get their inventions worked to clean rivers	Comment: Duke of Somerset	HL Deb, 13 May 1875, Vol 224(3rd), col 555–556 The Times, 14 May 1875
DEB174	The need to develop a breech-loading rifle might be assisted by a reward to inventors	Comment: Wentworth Beaumont	HC Deb, 22 Jun 1875, Vol 225(3rd), col 344–345 The Times, 23 Jun 1875
DEB175	Supply: Patent Act £22,050	No debate	HC Deb, 25 Jun 1875, Vol 225(3rd), col 628 The Times, 26 Jun 1875
DEB176	Motion for a Select Committee to inquire into the petition of Charles Frederic Henwood relating to his developments in boat design	Motion: Marcus Beresford Debate: Edward Reed; Sir Edward Watkin; George Hunt; William Baxter; Sir John Hay; Joseph Samuda	HC Deb, 9 Jun 1876, Vol 229(3rd), col 1609–1619 The Times, 10 Jun 1876
DEB177	Discussion of receipts from Patent Office	Comment: William H Smith	HC Deb, 2 Apr 1877, Vol 233(3rd), col 654–655 The Times, 6 Apr 1877
DEB178	Supply: Inventors pay lots into economy and get little in return; Patent Museum full of scientific apparatus	Debate: Lyon Playfair; William H Smith; Sir Andrew Lusk	HC Deb, 31 May 1877, Vol 234(3rd), col 1167–1169 The Times, 1 Jun 1877
DEB179	Whether the government will consider giving John Clare compensation for his invention?	Comment: Joseph Biggar; George Hunt	HC Deb, 18 Jun 1877, Vol 234(3rd) col 1973–1974 and 1986 The Times, 19 Jun 1877
DEB180	Resolution: No further sums voted for the navy until John Clare's case considered	Motion: Joseph Biggar Debate: Marcus Beresford; Edward Reed; Algernon Egerton	HC Deb, 7 Aug 1877, Vol 236(3rd), col 543–545 The Times, 8 Aug 1877
DEB181	Observations: Claim of John Clare for compensation from the Board of Admiralty relating to metal shipbuilding	Debate: Joseph Biggar; Algernon Egerton; Marcus Beresford	HC Deb, 14 Mar 1878, Vol 238(3rd), col 1335–1336
DEB182	Supply: Patent Act £1229	No debate	HC Deb, 18 Mar 1878, Vol 238(3rd), col 1553 The Times, 19 Mar 1878
DEB183	Supply: £27,175; revenue £181,000; some help for poor inventors; office-keepers' fee should be omitted	Debate: Thomas Mellor; Alexander MacDonald; Sir Henry Selwin-Ibbetson; Sir Andrew Lusk; George Gregory; John Lush; Frank O'Donnell; Joseph Biggar; John Nolan; Thomas Cave; Charles Monk; Philip Muntz; Issac Bell	HC Deb, 13 May 1878, Vol 239(3rd), col 1764–1799 The Times, 14 May 1878
DEB184	Supply: Patent Office	No debate	HC Deb, 12 May 1879, Vol 246(3rd), col 135 The Times, 13 May 1879
DEB185	Observations: Claim of John Clare against Admiralty regarding iron shipbuilding	Debate: Joseph Biggar; Algernon Egerton; Charles Parnell	HC Deb, 13 Jun 1879, Vol 246(3rd), col 1872–1873 The Times, 14 Jun 1879
DEB186	Motion for Select Committee into Leonard Edmunds and Edmunds v Greenwood (26 Jun 1869)	Debate: Earl Redesdale; Earl Cairns; Earl of Camperdown; Earl Granville; Lord Stanley	HL Deb, 4 Jul 1879, Vol 247(3rd), col 1407–1414 The Times, 5 Jul 1879

(continued)

(continued)

DEB187	Patent law should be dealt with by Minister of Commerce, not Attorney-General	Debate: Sampson Lloyd; William Forster; Anthony Mundella; William Gladstone	HC Deb, 8 Jul 1879, Vol 247(3rd), col 1922, 1932–1933 and 1935 The Times, 9 Jul 1879
DEB188	Supply: Reduction of supply of the navy to call attention to the claim of John Clare	Motion: Joseph Biggar Debate: William Price; Edward Reed; Bedford Pim; Joseph Samuda; Algernon Egerton; Charles Parnell	HC Deb, 31 Jul 1879, Vol 248(3rd), col 1770–1776 The Times, 1 Aug 1879
DEB189	Supply: Patent Office £20,195	No debate	HC Deb, 28 May 1880, Vol 252(3rd), col 669
DEB190	No need for a judge hearing a patent case to have any scientific knowledge	Comment: Hugh Law	HC Deb, 22 Jul 1880, Vol 254(3rd), col 1143 The Times, 23 Jul 1880
DEB191	Employer's Liability Bill Attempt to immunise workmen against patent infringement	Amendment: Horace Davey Debate: John Dodson; Sir John Holker; Sir Henry James; William Biddell; Archibald Orr-Ewing; Charles Bradlaugh; John Gorst	HC Deb, 3 Aug 1880, Vol 255(3rd), col 127–132 The Times, 4 Aug 1880
DEB192	Lord Advocate's salary and its supplement by patent fees	Debate: Sir George Balfour; Lord Fredrick Cavendish	HC Deb, 16 Aug 1880, Vol 255(3rd), col 1274–1279
DEB193	Supply: Patent Office £4500	No debate	HC Deb, 16 Mar 1881, Vol 259(3rd), col 1210
DEB194	Debate on Technical Education Things can be made more cheaply in America and Belgium as they have more liberal patent laws; patent laws are odious and need reform	Comment: George Anderson; Anthony Mundella	HC Deb, 1 Apr 1881, Vol 260(3rd), col 529 and 537 The Times, 2 Apr 1881 (1 Apr)
DEB195	Hope the Board of Trade will deal with patent laws, as they need reform	Comment: Sir Baldwyn Leighton	HC Deb, 13 May 1881, Vol 261(3rd), col 461 The Times, 14 May 1881
DEB196	Supply: Patent Office £4500	No debate	HC Deb, 30 May 1881, Vol 261(3rd), col 1738
DEB197	Comment: Plant varieties are unprotected by patents	Comment: John Nolan	HC Deb, 31 May 1881, Vol 261(3rd), col 1843 The Times, 1 Jun 1881
DEB198	Supply: Patent Office £3000	No debate	HC Deb, 18 Jul 1881, Vol 263(3rd), col 1220
DEB199	Supply: Patent Office £17,438 Debate on Patent Museum	Debate: John Hinde Palmer; Sir Henry Holland; Charles Warton; Arthur O'Connor; Joseph Chamberlain; Lewis Dillwyn; Eugene Collins; William Craig	HC Deb, 2 Aug 1881, Vol 264(3rd), col 617–627 The Times, 3 Aug 1881
DEB200	French Commercial Treaty Whether it will address the requirement for local manufacturing of patent article?	Debate: Henry Jackson	HC Deb, 12 Aug 1881, Vol 264(3rd), col 1768–1769 The Times, 13 Aug 1881
DEB201	Discussion of motion for Select Committee into claims of John Clare and his patent for iron shipbuilding	Debate: Joseph Biggar; George Trevelyan	HC Deb, 13 Aug 1881, Vol 264(3rd), col 1856 and 1863–1865 The Times, 15 Aug 1881

DEB202	Leonard Edmunds' case should be reopened	Motion: Robert Fowler; Lord Frederick Cavendish; Sir John Hay; George Trevelyan	HC Deb, 16 Aug 1881, Vol 265(3rd), col 479 The Times, 17 Aug 1881 (16 Aug 1881)
DEB203	Speech at Retford: Patent laws a crime and injustice to inventors in the country	Speech: Anthony Mundella	The Times, 13 Jan 1882 (12 Jan 1882)
DEB204	Speech at Burton: Commercial men demand that patents should be cheaper	Speech: Sir Henry James; Sir William Harcourt	The Times, 23 Jan 1882 (21 Jan 1882)
DEB205	Supply: Patent Office £2500	No debate	HC Deb, 19 May 1882, Vol 269(3rd), col 1191
DEB206	Electric Lighting Bill Bill would reduce security of various patentees	Comment: Charles Warton	HC Deb, 15 Jul 1882, Vol 272(3rd), col 576 The Times, 17 Jul 1882
DEB207	Supply: Patent Office £20,849; comment on provisional patent museum	Debate: Arthur O'Connor	HC Deb, 28 Jul 1882, Vol 273(3rd), col 144 The Times, 29 Jul 1882
DEB208	Clare's invention in connection with iron shipbuilding	Comment: Joseph Biggar	HC Deb, 1 Aug 1882, Vol 273(3rd), col 481–482
DEB209	Inadequate nature of the Patent Museum	Debate: John Hinde Palmer; Joseph Chamberlain; Henry Broadhurst; Anthony Mundellea; Sir George Balfour	HC Deb, 10 Aug 1882, Vol 273(3rd), col 1401–1405 The Times, 11 Aug 1882
DEB210	Speech at Southwark: Grand Committee will enable patent reform	Speech: Arthur Cohen; James (Thorold) Rogers	The Times, 11 Dec 1882 (8 Dec 1882)
DEB211	Supply: Patent Office £5000	No debate	HC Deb, 15 Mar 1883, Vol 277(3rd), col 640
DEB212	Suggestion: Use patent office surplus to fund Patent Museum	Comment: George Anderson	HC Deb, 9 Apr 1883, Vol 277(3rd), col 1889 The Times, 10 Apr 1883
DEB213	Supply: Reducing vote to provide money towards improving Patent Museum	Debate: Bernard Molloy; George Shaw Lefevre; John Gorst; Sir Lyon Playfair; John Freke-Aylmer; Joseph Biggar; Joseph Chamberlain; Sir Henry Wolff; Viscount Folkestone	HC Deb, 21 May 1883, Vol 279(3rd), col 678–684 The Times, 22 May 1883
DEB214	Supply: Patent Office £3500	No debate	HC Deb, 31 May 1883, Vol 279(3rd), col 1413
DEB215	Professor Tyndall's resignation, as Trinity House trying to invalidate Wigham's patent	Debate: Earl of Dunraven; Lord Sudeley	HL Deb, 21 Jun 1883, Vol 280(3rd), col 1103–1112 The Times, 22 Jun 1883
DEB216	Navy has spent a fortune on patents for ordnance	Comment: Lord Eustace Cecil	The Times, 29 Jun 1883 (28 Jun 1883)
DEB217	Whether the House of Lords could consider the Patents Bill [PUBA14] before it completes passage through House of Commons?	Debate: Lord Redesdale	HC Deb, 10 Jul 1883, Vol 281(3rd), col 919–920
DEB218	Supply: £24,057 Debate on trade mark registry	No debate	HC Deb, 12 Jul 1883, Vol 281(3rd), col 1260

(continued)

(continued)

DEB219	Electric Lighting Provisional Orders Bill One company spent a fortune on useless patents last year	Comment: Viscount Bury	HL Deb, 3 Aug 1883, Vol 282(3rd), col 1449 The Times, 4 Aug 1883
DEB220	Patents for Invention Bill [PUBA14] Disposed of Bill in reasonable time, but has page and a half of amendments, so will not pass without opposition	Debate: William Tomlinson; Sir William Harcourt	HC Deb, 4 Aug 1883, Vol 282(3rd), col 1540 The Times, 6 Aug 1883
DEB221	Supply: Patent Office £1453 Comment on additional costs by new practice introduced at Patent Office	Comment: Leonard Courtney	HC Deb, 29 Feb 1884, Vol 285(3rd), col 245–246
DEB222	Supply: Patent Office £5000	No debate	HC Deb, 20 Mar 1884, Vol 286(3rd), col 389
DEB223	Royalties on telephones – Bell patent	Debate: Edmund Gray; John Slagg; Henry Fawcett	HC Deb. 22 May 1884, Vol 288(3rd), col 1052–1057
DEB224	Motion for Select Committee regarding the case of Lyndall Thomas, and the failure of the Admiralty to give him the payments promised	Proposed: Donald Macfarlane Debate: Robert Leake; John Nolan; Henry Brand; Sir George Balfour	HC Deb, 13 Jun 1884, Vol 289(3rd), col 310–316 The Times, 14 Jun 1884
DEB225	Supply: Discussion of increased pay for solicitor at Board of Trade	Debate: Joseph Chamberlain	HC Deb, 14 Jul 1884, Vol 290(3rd), col 1054 The Times, 15 Jul 1884
DEB226	Supply: Patent Office £23,178	No debate	HC Deb, 16 Jul 1884, Vol 290(3rd), col 1321 The Times, 17 Jul 1884
DEB227	Supply: Patent Office £6730 Discussion of patent fees and Irish Patent Library and expenses of International Bureau in Berne	Debate: Bernard Molloy; John Hibbert; Thomas Sexton; William Tomlinson	HC Deb, 20 Feb 1885, Vol 294(3rd), col 994–995 The Times, 21 Feb 1885
DEB228	£22,000 required to give rewards to inventors	Comment: Marquess of Hartington	HC Deb, 19 Mar 1885, Vol 295(3rd), col 1736
DEB229	Supply: Patent Office £7000	No debate	HC Deb, 18 May 1885, Vol 298(3rd), col 724
DEB230	Comments on complexity of patent proceedings	Debate: Henry Ince	HC Deb, 7 Jul 1885, Vol 298(3rd), col 1920
DEB231	Supply: Patent Office £9000	No debate	HC Deb, 18 Mar 1886, Vol 303(3rd), col 1287
DEB232	Levying of Income Tax, patent income	Comment: George Bartley	HC Deb, 11 May 1886, Vol 305(3rd), col 801–802 The Times, 12 May 1886
DEB233	Government of Ireland Bill Discussion of patent laws	Debate: Hugh Childers	HC Deb, 21 May 1886, Vol 305(3rd), col 1742–1743
DEB234	Supply: Patent Act £25,303 Debate on index of foreign patents; lack of novelty search; and high cost of fees; number of patents voided	Debate: Bernard Molloy; Baron Henry de Worms; Peter McDonald; William Tomlinson; Matthew Kenny; Thomas Power O'Connor; James Tuite; Sir Richard Webster; Michael Conway; Matthew Harris; Charles Tanner; Alexander Blane	HC Deb, 10 Sep 1886, Vol 309(3rd), col 120–131

DEB235	Supply: Brennan Torpedo and patent rights	Debate: Henry Labouchère; Sir William Crossman; Arthur O'Connor; Henry Northcoate; John Nolan; Samuel Story; John Heaton; George Shaw-Lefevre; Edward Stanhope; Sir Edward Reed; Alfred Illingworth; William H Smith; Joseph Dodds; James Lowther; Bernard Molloy; Charles Bradlaugh; Charles Tanner; William Caine	HC Deb, 10 Mar 1887, Vol 311(3rd), col 1849–1868
DEB236	Supply: Patent Office £9000 Money paid to Patent Office diverted to other purposes	Comment: Arthur O'Connor	HC Deb, 21 Mar 1887, Vol 312(3rd), col 1083–1084
DEB237	Supply: Patent Office £8000	No debate	HC Deb, 16 May 1887, Vol 315(3rd), col 136
DEB238	Customs and Inland Revenue Bill There should be some allowance for depreciation of a patent	Debate: George Bartley; Sir Charles Russell	HC Deb, 17 Jun 1887, Vol 316(3rd), col 521 The Times, 18 Jun 1887
DEB239	Supply: Patent Office £4000	No debate	HC Deb, 15 Jul 1887, Vol 317(3rd), col 959
DEB240	Supply: Patent Office £34,204 Minor debate	Debate: Louis Jennings; William Jackson	HC Deb, 8 Aug 1887, Vol 318(3rd), col 1559, 1566 and 1589
DEB241	Supply: Pay of Attorney-General and patent cases	Debate: Richard Webster; Sydney Buxton	HC Deb, 11 Aug 1887, Vol 319(3rd), col 122 and 126–127 The Times, 12 Aug 1887
DEB242	Criticism of the vote to buy torpedoes as described in a patent specification	Debate: George Shaw-Lefevre	HC Deb, 8 Sep 1887, Vol 320(3rd), col 1749–1752 and 1757 The Times, 9 Sep 1887
DEB243	Supply and comment on Patent Museum	Debate: Anthony Mundella	HC Deb, 6 Apr 1888, Vol 324(3rd), col 621–622 The Times, 7 Apr 1888
DEB244	Customs and Inland Revenue Bill The patent on saccharine has eight to ten years to run, so there is no risk to the beer industry	Comment: George Goschen	HC Deb, 27 Apr 1888, Vol 325(3rd), col 770 The Times, 28 Apr 1888
DEB245	Supply: No estimate for Patents Act	Debate: Charles Tanner	HC Deb, 5 Jul 1888, Vol 328(3rd), col 454
DEB246	Supply: Patent Office £13,000	No debate	HC Deb, 3 Aug 1888, Vol 329(3rd), col 1427
DEB247	Supply: Patent Office £23,305 Lack of court room for Comptroller; inadequacy of Patent Office buildings; arrears in abridgements	Debate: Bernard Molley; William Jackson; Sir Richard Webster; Charles Conybeare; George Bartley; John Heaton; Arthur O'Connor; Robert Hanbury; Charles Tanner; Joseph Biggar	HC Deb, 6 Nov 1888, Vol 330(3rd), col 560–567 The Times, 7 Nov 1888
DEB248	The exchange of papers between the British Patent Office and the American was not sufficient to supply our libraries	Comment: Henry Labouchère	HC Deb, 7 Nov 1888, Vol 330(3rd), col 620–621 The Times, 8 Nov 1888

(continued)

(continued)

DEB249	Supply: Patent Office £9000	No debate	HC Deb, 20 Mar 1889, Vol 334(3rd), col 257
DEB250	Supply: Patent Office £48,496 Need for foreign specification at Patent Office	Debate: Henry Labouchère; William Jackson; Handel Cossham	HC Deb, 10 May 1889, Vol 335(3rd), col 1743–1744
DEB251	Increase in costs of printing at Patent Office due to illustrated journal	Debate: William Jackson; Sir William Barttelot	HC Deb, 14 May 1889, Vol 336(3rd), col 38–39 and 40 The Times, 15 May 1889
DEB252	Motion on the amalgamation of the telephone companies; the fact the Post of Office should withhold consent and issues, including their patents	Motion: Duke of Marlbourgh; Debate: Lord Balfour; Marquess of Salisbury	HL Deb, 4 Jul 1889, Vol 337(3rd), col 1429 The Times, 5 Jul 1889
DEB253	Supply: Pensions for abolition of certain offices in Patent Office	Debate: Sir George Campbell; William Jackson	HC Deb, 17 Aug 1889, Vol 339(3rd), col 1597 The Times, 19 Aug 1889
DEB254	Discussion of whether Admiral [Philip] Colomb should be given some sort of reward for his signalling invention	Debate: Lord Sudeley; Earl of Clanwilliam; Earl of Northbrook; Earl of Ravensworth; Lord Elphinstone	HL Deb, 16 May 1890, Vol 344(3rd), col 1062–1078 The Times, 17 May 1890
DEB255	Comment: Sir William Palliser's patents	Debate: Henry Blundell; William Brodrick; Lord Hamilton	HC Deb, 16 May 1890, Vol 344(3rd), col 1172–1173, 1184–1185, 1190–1191 The Times, 17 May 1890
DEB256	Whether the government is in a position to state the reward to be given to Admiral Colomb for his signal invention (mention of numerous other payments)?	Debate: Lord Sudeley; Lord Elphinstone; Earl of Clanwilliam; Viscount Sidmouth	HL Deb, 27 Jun 1890, Vol 346(3rd), col 185–189 The Times, 28 Jun 1890
DEB257	Telephone companies should be able to obtain operating licences once the patents have expired	Debate: Duke of Marlbourgh; Earl of Jersey	HL Deb, 7 Jul 1890, Vol 346(3rd), col 903–913 The Times, 8 Jul 1890
DEB258	Motion to reduce Supply to Post Office due to failure to pay reward to Mr Cotton in relation to his invention of postal orders	Debate: Sir Stanley Northcote; Edward Norris; Henry Raikes	HC Deb, 23 Jul 1890, Vol 347(3rd), col 614 The Times, 24 Jul 1890
DEB259	Address for number and particulars of patents taken out by [Joseph] Speed in relation to the New Magazine Rifle	No debate	HC Deb, 23 Jan 1891, Vol 349(3rd), col 903 The Times, 24 Jan 1891
DEB260	Debate on New Magazine Rifle and the relevant patents	Debate: Edward Marjoribanks; Edward Stanhope; Robert Hanbury; William Brodrick; Frederick Rasch; John Nolan; Henry Seton-Karr; Sir Walter Barttelot; Henry Bowles; Elliot Lees; Henry Blundell; George Bethell	HC Deb, 3 Feb 1891, Vol 349(3rd), col 1631–1684 The Times, 4 Feb 1891
DEB261	Taxation of patent, but refusal of any sinking fund	Comment: George Bartley	HC Deb, 24 Feb 1891, Vol 350(3rd), col 1479–1480 The Times, 25 Feb 1891
DEB262	Comment on "profit" of £90,000 at Patent Office	Debate: Andrew Provand	HC Deb, 27 Feb 1891, Vol 350(3rd), col 1857

DEB263	Debate on reduction of patent fees	Debate: Sir William Harcourt; Sir Michael Hicks Beach; John Leng	HC Deb, 14 Jul 1891, Vol 355(3rd), col 1216–1230 The Times, 15 Jul 1891
DEB264	British patent policy more favourable to foreigners than foreign laws are to British inventors	Debate: Joseph Powell Williams; Sir George Campbell; Sir James Fergusson	HC Deb, 31 Jul 1891, Vol 356(3rd), col 1004–1006, 1008–1009 The Times, 1 Aug 1891
DEB265	Claim of [George] Jobson regarding the invention of time fuse	Debate: Robert Graham; Edward Stanhope	HC Deb, 31 Jul 1891, Vol 356(3rd), col 1036–1037
DEB266	Supply: Reduction of patent fees [See Political Notes, The Times, 12 Apr 1892]	Debate: John Leng; George Goschen; Hugh Watt	HC Deb, 18 Mar 1892, Vol 2(4th), col 1231–1234 The Times, 19 Mar 1892
DEB267	Supply: Telephone companies and patents	Debate: Charles Cameron; John Heaton; Sir Albert Rollit; Henry Labouchère	HC Deb, 29 Mar 1892, Vol 3(4th), col 169 and 179 The Times, 30 Mar 1892
DEB268	Comment on reduction of patent fees; and when new Patents Act will come into force?	Debate: George Goschen; Sir John Brunner	HC Deb, 11 Apr 1892, Vol 3(4th), col 1167–1168, 1175 and 1177
DEB269	Supply: Reduction of patent fees concession by Chancellor of Exchequer	Debate: John Leng; Alpheus Morton	HC Deb, 16 May 1892, Vol 4(4th), col 1049–1051
DEB270	Increase in printing costs at Patent Office	Comment: Sir John Hibbert	HC Deb, 14 Mar 1893, Vol 10(4th), col 58–59 The Times, 15 Mar 1893
DEB271	Appointment of clerk dealing with patent business for law officers	Debate: Sir Charles Russell; Robert Hanbury	HC Deb, 14 Mar 1893, Vol 10(4th), col 84–85 The Times, 15 Mar 1893
DEB272	Appointment of upper division clerks in the Patent Office	Debate: Sir John Hibbert	HC Deb, 1 May 1893, Vol 11(4th), col 1699 The Times, 2 May 1893
DEB273	Government of Ireland Bill Patent rights and legislative competence	Debate: George Bartley; Robert Hanbury; John Clancy; Sir John Rigby; Sir John Brunner; Anthony Mundella; Edmund Knox; Henry James; Arthur Balflour; Jesse Collings; Sir Francis Powell; Edmund Morel; Joseph Kenny	HC Deb, 12 Jun 1893, Vol 13(4th), col 831–838 The Times, 13 Jun 1893
DEB274	Army Estimates: Patenting by officials	Debate: Frederick Rasch; Robert Handbury; Henry Campbell-Bannerman	HC Deb, 27 Jun 1893, Vol 14(4th), col 184–185, 192–194, 205–206 The Times 28 Jun 1893
DEB275	Supply: What progress has been made with the Patent Office and patent fees?	Debate: Sir Michael Hicks Beach; Anthony Mundella; Joseph Chamberlain	HC Deb, 8 Sep 1893, Vol 17(4th), col 738–739, 742–744 The Times, 9 Feb 1893
DEB276	Debate on Cordite scandal and patents owned by officials	Debate: Robert Hanbury; Henry Campbell-Bannerman; William Field; Frederick Rasch; Thomas Cochrane; James Weir; Edward Stanhope; John Nolan; George Bartley; Thomas Gibson Bowles	HC Deb, 11 Sep 1894, Vol 17(4th), col 834–879 The Times, 12 Sep 1893
DEB277	Appointments to the Patent Office	Debate: Sir John Hibbert	HC Deb, 29 Mar 1894, Vol 22(4th), col 933

(continued)

(continued)

DEB278	Cost of patents and possible reduction of fees	Comment: James Weir	HC Deb, 18 Aug 1894, Vol 28(4th), col 1531–1532
			The Times, 20 Aug 1894
DEB279	Patent fees to law officers and the costs law officers meet from those fees	Comment: Sir Edward Clarke	HC Deb, 5 Mar 1895, Vol 31(4th), col 439–440
			The Times, 6 Mar 1895
DEB280	Select Committee on Telephone and Post Office Evidence as to the patent rights	Evidence	The Times, 16 Mar 1895 (14 Mar 1895)
DEB281	Select Committee on Telephone and Post Office Evidence as to the patent rights in telephones	Evidence	The Times, 23 Mar 1895 (22 Mar 1895)
DEB282	Notice of letter on stamping of patents	Letter to Mr Jackson	The Times, 28 Apr 1896 (27 Apr)
DEB283	Most motorcar patents are owned by foreigners	Comment: Henry Chaplin	HC Deb, 30 Jun 1896, Vol 42(4th), col 438
			The Times, 1 Jul 1896
DEB284	An increase in revenue due to patent stamps	Debate: Michael Hicks Beach	HC Deb, 29 Apr 1897, Vol 48(4th), col 1252
			The Times, 30 Apr 1897
DEB285	Patent Office: Criticised for granting patents which are not novel and taking fees	Debate: James Weir; Charles Ritchie; Victor Milward; John Denny; John Burns	HC Deb, 28 May 1897, Vol 49(4th), col 1564, 1573–1576
DEB286	Notice of giving a resolution on the state of patent law in the UK	Motion: John Briggs	HC Deb, 8 Mar 1898, Vol 54(4th), col 961
			The Times, 9 Mar 1898
DEB287	Debate on the National Telephone Company enterprise and patent rights	Debate: James Caldwell; Arthur Griffith-Boscawen; Ferdinand Begg	HC Deb, 1 Apr 1898, Vol 55(4th), col 1671–1737
			The Times, 2 Apr 1898
DEB288	Municipal Telephones: Government plan to buy up patent rights to increase availability	Evidence	The Times, 18 May 1898 (17 May)
DEB289	Treasury minute laid before House [HC/CL/JO/10/192/155] Minute states that law clerk in Patent Office requires a professional qualification not ordinarily acquired in the public service [Also see PPP99]	Noted	HC Deb, 27 Jun 1898, Vol 60(4th), col 191
DEB290	Patenting of aniline colours in England and German	Debate: Fredrick Cawley; James Bryce; Charles Ritchie	HC Deb, 29 Jul 1898, Vol 63(4th), col 547–549, 554, 565–566
			The Times, 30 Jul 1898
DEB291	A large number of coupler patents for railways have been granted	Comment: Charles Hopwood	The Times, 23 Feb 1899 (22 Feb 1899)
DEB292	Doubts that water-tube boiler patents valid; yet paid £146,000 in royalties	Comment: William Allan	HC Deb, 16 Mar 1899, Vol 68(4th), col 1003
			The Times, 17 Mar 1899
DEB293	Is it not a fact that the torpedoes, in respect of which £100,000 was paid in royalties, have been discarded?	Comment: Sir Edward Gourley	HC Deb, 22 Apr 1899, Vol 70(4th), col 291
			The Times, 22 Apr 1899

DEB294	Profit generated by Patent Office	Comment: James Weir	HC Deb, 12 May 1899, Vol 71(4th), col 56
DEB295	Additional Chancery Division judges and possibility of referring cases to referees	Debate: Llewellyn Atherley-Jones	HC Deb, 31 Jul 1899, Vol 75(4th), col 904–906 The Times, 1 Aug 1899
DEB296	Patents for rifles not bought by government, but allowed into foreign hands	Comments: Jasper Tully	HC Deb, 16 Feb 1900, Vol 79(4th), col 296–297
DEB297	Local authorities should be entitled to the patents of their employees	Comment: Sir Albert Rollit	HC Deb, 5 Apr 1900, Vol 81(4th), col 1349
DEB298	Railways (Prevention Accidents) Bill Proposed clause to allow Board of Trade to use patented safety inventions	Proposed: Sir Alfred Hickman; Sir Robert Finlay; William Bousfield; Sir Joseph Pease; Charles Ritchie	HC Deb, 28 May 1900, Vol 83(4th), col 1605–1608
DEB299	Municipal Trading Select Committee Comment: A great deal of industrial development arose out of patented inventions	Evidence	The Times, 28 Jun 1900 (26 Jun 1900)
DEB300	Cost of Patent Office extension	Debate: Henry Broadhurst; Aretas Akers-Douglas	HC Deb, 28 Feb 1901, Vol 90(4th), col 159–160, 166–167 The Times, 1 Mar 1901
DEB301	Supply: Cost of Patent Office extension and the need for a library	Debate: Sir Walter Foster; Sydney Buxton; Aretas Akers-Douglas	HC Deb, 1 Mar 1901, Vol 90(4th), col 213, 216, 218 The Times, 2 Mar 1902
DEB302	Administration of War Office and role of the Director-General of Ordnance in advising on patent matters	Comment: Lord Chelmsford	HC Deb, 5 Mar 1901, Vol 90(4th), col 519
DEB303	Supply: Cost of Patent Office extension and additional cost over-estimate	Debate: Aretas Akers-Douglas	HC Deb, 14 Mar 1901, Vol 90(4th), col 1675
DEB304	Royalty for manufacture of Maxim guns under patent agreed by the government to be fixed	Debate: Lord Stanley; Richard Haldane	HC Deb, 10 Mar 1902, Vol 104(4th), col 918–919 and 925 The Times, 11 Mar 1902
DEB305	Profit of UK Patent Office much higher than that of other patent offices around the world	Comment: Louis Sinclair	HC Deb, 3 Mar 1903, Vol 118(4th), col 1335
DEB306	Patent fees too high; and protection not sufficient	Comment: Louis Sinclar	HC Deb, 22 Apr 1903, Vol 121(4th), col 162 The Times, 23 Apr 1903
DEB307	Has anyone considered the validity of the Belleville boiler?	Comment: Sir William Allan	HC Deb, 14 May 1903, Vol 122(4th), col 758
DEB308	Tate and Lyle were not market leaders through patents, but business ability	Comment: John Fletcher Moulton	HC Deb, 28 Jul 1903, Vol 126(4th), col 662 The Times, 29 Jul 1903
DEB309	Inability of National Library of Dublin to take a free gift of American patent specifications	Comment: John Boland	HC Deb, 6 Aug 1903, Vol 127(4th), col 157
DEB310	Patentee of loom could not work it here, so had to dispose of the patent	Comment: John Crombie	HC Deb, 12 Feb 1904, Vol 129(4th), col 1226–1227 The Times, 13 Feb 1904

(continued)

(continued)

DEB311	List of telephone patents	Comments: Lord Stanley	The Times, 5 Mar 1904 (4 Mar)
DEB312	Weights and Measures Differing standards and patentee problems	Comment: Jesse Collings	HC Deb, 15 Apr 1904, Vol 133(4th), col 316
DEB313	Budget Speech Proper way to charge to Income Tax patent royalties	Comment: Austen Chamberlain	HC Deb, 19 Apr 1904, Vol 133(4th), col 560
DEB314	Promotion of clerks in Patent Office	No debate	The Times, 7 Jun 1904 (6 Jun)
DEB315	Supply – Board of Trade: The need for steps to be taken to require the working of a patent; German dyeing industry using British patents to enrich themselves; proposal of an Imperial patent; local working requirement	Debate: Louis Sinclair; Fredrick Cawley; Sir John Leng; Sir Joseph Lawrence	HC Deb, 16 Jun 1904, Vol 136(4th), col 296, 301, 342–344, 347 The Times, 17 Jun 1904
DEB316	Inadequacy of the law as to requiring local working of foreign patents	Debate on King's Speech Sir Edwin Durning-Lawrence	HC Deb, 16 Feb 1905, Vol 141(4th), col 360–368 The Times, 17 Feb 1905
DEB317	Novelty search of patent applications should be extended to cover foreign patents, not just British specifications	Comment: James Dalziel	HC Deb, 9 Jun 1905, Vol 147(4th), col 892–893
DEB318	Deputation to visit President of the Board of Trade arguing for a local working clause in the Patents Act	Note	The Times, 29 Mar 1906 (9 Apr 1906)
DEB319	Supply: Rewards to inventors at War Office	Deabte: Henry Forster; Richard Haldane; John Higham	HC Deb, 7 Jun 1906, Vol 158(4th), col 551–556 The Times, 8 Jun 1906
DEB320	Wireless Telegraphy Bill Comment on monopolies owned by Marconi and others in radio	Comment: James Dundas White	HC Deb, 13 Jul 1906, Vol 160(4th), col 1205–1206 The Times, 14 Jul 1906
DEB321	Comment: Criminal patent infringement	Comment: Arnold Lupton	HC Deb, 16 Jul 1906, Vol 160(4th), col 1455
DEB322	Patent Rights and the (Berlin) Radio-Telegraphic Convention Proposal for Select Committee	Debate: Sir Edward Sasson; John O'Connor; James Dundas White	HC Deb, 18 Dec 1906, Vol 167(4th), col 1296, 1304–1305 and 1307–1308 and 1327 The Times, 19 Dec 1906
DEB323	Patent Law reform and the need for it	Debate on King's Speech Comment: Earl of Chichester	HL Deb, 12 Feb 1907, Vol 169(4th), col 3 and 15
DEB324	Debate on King's Speech Patent Law reform and the need for it	Comment: Arthur Balfour	HC Deb, 12 Feb 1907, Vol 169(4th), col 73–74
DEB325	Debate on King's Speech Free trade does not exist in the minds of the promoters of the Patent Bill; contrary will promote new industries	Debate: Arthur Balfour; Austen Chamberlain; Theodore Talyor; John Burns	HC Deb, 20 Feb 1907, Vol 169(4th), col 871, 916, 941, 955 The Times, 21 Feb 1907
DEB326	Radio-Telegraphic Convention Select Committee There will be prejudice to patent rights by intercommunication	Summary	The Times, 18 Apr 1907 (19 Apr 1907)
DEB327	Treatment of patent income for taxation purposes	Comment: Austen Chamberlain	HC Deb, 22 Apr 1907, Vol 172(4th), col 1449 The Times, 23 Apr 1907

DEB328	Radio-Telegraphic Convention Select Committee Evidence relating to patent rights' connection to technology	Evidence	The Times, 27 Apr 1907 (23 Apr 1907)
DEB329	Radio-Telegraphic Convention Select Committee Evidence Marconi might refuse licence to use patents	Evidence	The Times, 1 May 1907 (30 Apr 1907)
DEB330	The need for a new patent judge	Comment: James Dundas White	HC Deb, 12 Jul 1907, Vol 178(4th), col 234 The Times, 13 Jul 1907
DEB331	Patent rights affected by Radio-Telegraphic Convention	Comment: Richard Haldane	HC Deb, 30 Jul 1907, Vol 179(4th), col 856 The Times, 31 Jul 1907
DEB332	Response to King's Speech Comments on effect of Patents and Designs Act 1907 [PUBA23]	Comment: Sir William Holland; Sir John Randles	HC Deb, 5 Feb 1908, Vol 183(4th), col 992–993, 995 and 1122
DEB333	The Patents Act [PUBA23] has prohibited all competition from outside certain trades and made possible tariffs; all that was wanted was to protect against unfair competition	Comment: Edward Goulding	The Times, 25 Mar 1908 (25 Mar 1908)
DEB334	Debate on Finance Bill Debate on the protective measures in Patents and Designs Act 1907 [PUBA23]	Debate: Bonar Law; David Lloyd-George; Winston Churchill; John Hills; Arthur Balfour; Herbert Asquith	HC Deb, 2 Jun 1908, Vol 189(4th), col 1740–1779 and 1787 The Times, 3 Jun 1908
DEB335	If capital movement is a good thing, what is the point of the protectionism of the Patents Act?	Comment: James Mason	HC Deb, 17 Mar 1909, Vol 2(5th), col 1156
DEB336	A patent has been taken out by a British firm to reduce the cost of manufacturing White Lead	Comment: Hugh Lea	HC Deb, 22 Mar 1909, Vol 2(5th), col 1450
DEB337	Debate on King's Address Patents and Designs Amendment Act 1907 [PUBA23], manufacturing clause and free trade	Debate: Samuel Storey; George Tryon; Herbert Spender Clay	HC Deb, 24 Feb 1910, Vol 14(5th), col 374, 381–382 and 424
DEB338	Foreign Tariffs and Home Industry The role of the Patents Act [PUBA23] and supporting local manufacture	Comment: Samuel Storey	HC Deb, 6 Apr 1910, Vol 16(5th), col 530–531
DEB339	Whether a patent should be treated as a wasting asset for tax purposes	Debate: Thomas Bowles; Ernest Pollock	HC Deb, 8 Jul 1910, Vol 18(5th), col 1994, 1997, 1998 and 2005
DEB340	Civil Service examinations at the Patent Office	Debate: Charles Hobhouse; Sir Laming Worthington-Evans; Sir William Anson; Leifchild Jones	HC Deb, 3 Mar 1911, Vol 22(5th), col 721, 725 and 727–728 and 779–780
DEB341	Whether the silk factory should get exemption under s 54 of the Factory Act 1901 when it was brought here by the Patents Act [PUBA23]?	Debate: Charles Bowerman; Charles Masterman	HC Deb, 24 May 1911, Vol 26(5th), col 391 and 392–394
DEB342	County Court Bill There is no reason why patent cases cannot be tried in County Court	Comment: Lord Alverstone	HL Deb, 12 Jul 1911, Vol 9(5th), col 416

(continued)

(continued)

DEB343	Advantages to the country from home manufacturing clause in the Patents Act	Comment: Basil Peto	HC Deb, 9 Aug 1911, Vol 29(5th), col 1301
DEB344	Debate on Finance Bill 1911 Effect of Patents and Designs Act 1907 [PUBA23] on employment	Debate: George Sandys; Sir Rufus Issacs	HC Deb, 12 Dec 1911, Vol 32(5th), col 2279 to 2282
DEB345	New Zealand has passed Act modelled on Patents Act [PUBA23] since Imperial Conference	Comment: Lewis Harcourt	HC Deb, 3 Apr 1912, Vol 36(5th), col 1220
DEB346	Consolidated Fund (Appropriation) Bill Proviso considered to exclude patents from provision relating to wasting assets	Debate: Ernest Pollock; Basil Peto	HC Deb, 2 Aug 1912, Vol 41(5th), col 2618 and 2622
DEB347	Report on Sinking of the Titanic Making wireless communication compulsory and patent rights	Comment: Richard Holt	HC Deb, 7 Oct 1912, Vol 42(5th), col 64
DEB348	Motion for a Select Committee into agreement with Marconi	Proposed: Herbert Samuel Debate: Sir Henry Norman; George Terrell; Martin Archer-Shee; Sir George Croydon Marks; Godfrey Collins; Sir Rufus Isaacs	HC Deb, 11 Oct 1912, Vol 42(5th), col 667–750
DEB349	Tariff Reform Debate Manufacturing clause in the Patents Act said by Chancellor of the Exchequer to lead to hundreds of thousands of jobs	Comment: George Tryon	HC Deb, 2 Apr 1913, Vol 51(5th), col 490
DEB350	Payment of £500 for a reward to Colonel [Bernard] Dietz, inventor of a method of signalling (by a disc)	Comment: Harold Tennant	HC Deb, 5 Jun 1913, Vol 53(5th), col 1147
DEB351	Proposal for an increase in supply to the Patent Office to improve examination; clarification of home manufacturing clause; administrative court to hear infringement actions	Debate: Alfred Bigland	HC Deb, 16 Jul 1913, Vol 55(5th), col 1320–1323
DEB352	Marconi patents and payment of royalties	Statement: Herbert Samuel Debate: Bonar Law; John O'Connor	HC Deb, 28 Jul 1913, Vol 56(5th), col 38–41
DEB353	Army Estimates Should reduce supply due to poor behaviour of War Office, which infringed Mr Holland's bullet	Motion: Rowland Hunt	HC Deb, 30 Jul 1913, Vol 56(5th), col 568–569
DEB354	Debate on New Marconi Agreement	Debate: Charles Masterman; Sir Henry Norman; Herbert Samuel; Sir George Croydon Marks; Lord Robert Cecil; Henry Terrell; William Redmond; James Falconer; Martin Archer-Shee; John Dennis; Bonar Law; Herbert Asquith	HC Deb, 8 Aug 1913, Vol 56(5th), col 1939–2031
DEB355	Supply – Royal Flying Corps: If patent laws don't allow airplane engines to made in the UK, they should be changed	Debate: James Dundas White	HC Deb, 25 Feb 1914, Vol 58(5th), col 1817

DEB356	An expert judge for patents is not necessary	Comment: Marquess of Salisbury	HL Deb, 25 May 1914, Vol 16(5th), col 300
DEB357	Patents in wireless have led to a monopoly for Marconi	Comment: Sir Henry Norman	HC Deb, 10 Jun 1914, Vol 63(5th), col 333–334
DEB358	Proposal for a reward for invention of automatic train coupling	Comment: Anderson Montague-Barlow	HC Deb, 9 Jul 1914, Vol 64(5th), col 1323
DEB359	Coal Mines Bill Proposed clause would compel use of patented invention	Comment: Reginald McKenna	HC Deb, 30 Jul 1914, Vol 65(5th), col 1681–1682
DEB360	The difficulty of working German inventions (calico and engineering) by reason of the burden of proof being on the person seeking revocation	Debate: Sir Arthur Markham; John Robertson	HC Deb, 10 Aug 1914, Vol 65(5th), col 2318–2319, 2332
DEB361	Trading with Enemy Act Why patent royalties not included in clause (which requires dividends etc. for enemies to be paid to public custodian)	Comment: William Watson Rutherford	HC Deb, 25 Nov 1914, Vol 68(5th), col 1178
DEB362	The Patents Act brought great works to this country, but decision of Parker J [probably Hatschek's Patent (1909) 26 RPC 228] undermined it	Comment: Sir Frederick Cawley	HC Deb, 27 Nov 1914, Vol 68(5th), col 1573–1574
DEB363	Patent royalties should be taken by public custodian	Comment: William Watson Rutherford	HC Deb, 30 Nov 1914, Vol 68(5th), col 710
DEB364	Dealing with patent royalties over the war; compulsory working powers; assimilation of patent laws to German laws; manufacturing clause	Comment: Walter Runciman; Sir Alfred Mond; Alfred Bigland; John Higham; Sir George Croydon Marks	HC Deb, 22 Feb 1915, Vol 70(5th), col 94, 114, 134, 135–136, 138, 141, 144–146
DEB365	Krupp's patent royalty	Comment: Sir Alfred Markham	HC Deb, 20 Jul 1915, Vol 73(5th), col 1414–1416
DEB366	Krupp patent fuse	Comment: Sir Alfred Markham	HC Deb, 21 Jul 1915, Vol 73(5th), col 1602–1603
DEB367	Proposal to add "patents and secret processes" to Finance (No 3) Bill	Debate: Thomas Lough; Edwin Montagu; John Dennis; Reginald McKenna; Sir Arthur Markham	HC Deb, 23 Nov 1915, Vol 76(5th), col 239–254
DEB368	After War Problems Need for patent law reform (and whether it encourages invention)	Statement: Lord Parker Response: Marquis of Crewe; Viscount Haldane	HL Deb, 14 Dec 1915, Vol 20(5th), col 615–621 and 623–627
DEB369	Allies' Co-operation Loosening patent working requirements; problems with chemical patents and issues about compulsory working in allied countries	Debate: Sir George Croydon Marks; Walter Runicman; Sir John Rees	HC Deb, 10 Jan 1916, Vol 77(5th), col 1344, 1361, 1375–1376
DEB370	Should not have allowed a German to patent Salvarsan [anti-syphilis drug]	Comment: Viscount Knutsford	HL Deb, 19 Jul 1916, Vol 22(5th), col 822
DEB371	Enemy Property Permission has been given to pay patent fees in enemy countries	Comment: Walter Runiman	HC Deb, 1 Nov 1916, Vol 86(5th), col 1717
DEB372	Non-Ferrous Metal Industry Bill Nothing in the Bill to preclude Germans working processes they have already worked	Comment: Thomas Lough	HC Deb, 11 Dec 1917, Vol 100(5th), col 1039

(continued)

(continued)

DEB373	Proposal of a reward of £250,000 to inventor who can solve issues of German U-boats sinking British ships	Debate: George Terrell; Bonar Law	HC Deb, 25 Feb 1918, Vol 103(5th), col 1094
DEB374	Finance Bill Whether a patent should be treated as a wasting asset	Debate: John Henderson	HC Deb, 3 Jun 1918, Vol 106(5th), col 1345–1346
DEB375	Debate on Aliens The approach taken to patent fees where owned by enemy aliens or not able to be worked	Debate: Sir George Cave	HC Deb, 11 Jul 1918, Vol 108(5th), col 534–535
DEB376	Rewards paid to serving officers in relation to inventions	Debate: Daniel Sheehan	HC Deb, 7 Aug 1918, Vol 109(5th), col 1501–1502
DEB377	£25,000 paid for rewards to inventors	Comment: William Wedgewood Benn	HC Deb, 15 Dec 1919, Vol 123(5th), col 126
DEB378	Small amount of money available for rewards to inventors	Debate: Joseph Kenworthy; James Hogge; Winston Churchill	HC Deb, 16 Dec 1919, Vol 123(5th), col 291–293, 297
DEB379	Larger awards to inventors are to be made by Royal Commission	Comment: George Tryon	HC Deb, 11 Mar 1920, Vol 126(5th), col 1589
DEB380	War Emergency Laws (Continuance) Bill Application to Island of Man – continuance of Patents, Designs, and Trade Marks (Temporary Rules) Act 1914 [PUBA28]	No debate	HC Deb, 29 Mar 1920, Vol 127(5th), col 1037–1046
DEB381	Finance Bill Clause (Exemption of Profits from Certain Profits)	Not moved	HC Deb, 16 Jul 1920, Vol 131(5th), col 2865
DEB382	Dyestuffs (Import Regulation) Bill German patents for dyes	Debate: Sir Edward Carson; Sir Robert Horne	HC Deb, 7 Dec 1920, Vol 135(5th), col 1964–1965
DEB383	Dyestuffs (Import Regulation) Bill German success in dyestuffs was largely achieved by subsidy; our patent laws handicap dye development; British Patent Office did not examine as well as German office	Debate: Lord Emmott; Lord Cawley	HL Deb, 21 Dec 1920, Vol 39(5th), col 716–717, 726–727
DEB384	Vote 3, various payments to inventors for war inventions by Air Ministry	Debate: Alfred Raperl	HC Deb, 21 Apr 1921, Vol 140(5th), col 2135–2136
DEB385	Hopes it will be the end of rewards for inventors	Debate: Alfred Raperl; Frederick Guest	HC Deb, 21 Mar 1922, Vol 152(5th), col 397, 412
DEB386	Supply – Air Ministry: What proportion of £500,000 is for rewards to inventors?	Debate: James Hogge; Frederick Guest; Mackenzie Wood	HC Deb, 23 Mar 1922, Vol 152(5th), col 776–778
DEB387	Wireless Broadcasting Invention found abroad can be patented here; foreigners restricted on patenting; local working	Debate: Frederick Kellaway; William Wedgwood Benn; Sir Frederick Hall	HC Deb, 4 Aug 1922, Vol 157(5th), col 1959–1960, 1964
DEB388	Supply – Board of Trade: Infringement of patents by Chinese traders; simplification of Patent Office practice; Patent Office cheapest in the world	Debate: Arthur Samuel; John Black; Sidney Webb	HC Deb, 19 Jun 1924, Vol 174(5th), col 2412–2415, 2441–2443 and 2451–2421

DEB389	Marconi patents and the working of the radio station	Debate: Vernon Hartshorn; John Moore-Brabazon	HC Deb, 1 Aug 1924, Vol 176(5th), col 2475–2578
DEB390	Ministry of Health should establish a research department	Comment: Walter Trevelyan Thomson	HC Deb, 16 Dec 1924, Vol 179(5th), col 928–929
DEB391	Patents not only improve employment, but increase its quality	Debate: James Kidd	HC Deb, 6 May 1925, Vol 183(5th), col 1036
DEB392	Finance Bill Clause (deduction in respect of royalties payable to persons not resident in the United Kingdom) – negatived	Proposed: Walter Forrest Debate: Douglas Hogg	HC Deb, 21 Jun 1926, Vol 197(5th), col 133–136
DEB393	What right does the Post Office have to acquire patents?	Comment: Sir George Hume	HC Deb, 15 Nov 1926, Vol 199(5th), col 1647–1648
DEB394	Government should get Bergius process for coal; obtaining patents in public interest	Debate: Duchess of Atholl; George Clayton; George Hardie	HC Deb, 11 May 1927, Vol 206(5th), col 489, 510–512, 515
DEB395	Tomlin J had 68 days on Royal Commission on Awards to Inventors	Comment: Sir Herbert Neild	HC Deb, 14 Feb 1928, Vol 213(5th), col 812
DEB396	Finance Bill Proposed clause to exempt awards to inventors from Royal Commission from Income Tax	Proposed: Sir Joseph Nall Debtate: Arthur Samuel; Thomas Shaw; John Moore-Brabazon; Winston Churchill; Cuthbert James; Robert Young; Robert Hudson; Chichester Crookshank	HC Deb, 3 Jul 1928, Vol 219(5th), col 1329–1337
DEB397	Appointment of Sir Charles Sargant to chair committee reviewing patent law [REP21]	Comment: Sir Philip Cunliffe-Lister	HC Deb, 6 May 1929, Vol 227(5th), col 1974–1975
DEB398	Very protectionist example of the Liberal government led to Patents and Designs Act 1907 [PUBA23]	Comment: Carlyon Bellairs	HC Deb, 9 Jul 1929, Vol 229(5th), col 803
DEB399	Amendment as to over-deductions and under-deductions of Income Tax	No debate	HC Deb,14 Apr 1930, Vol 237(5th), col 2688
DEB400	Resolution as to over-deductions and under-deductions of Income Tax	No debate	HC Deb, 30 Apr 1930, Vol 238(5th), col 205–206
DEB401	Dye manufacture and inadequacy of patent law	Debate: Lord Parmoor; Earl of Crawford; Lord Cawley	HL Deb, 15 Dec 1930, Vol 79(5th), col 554–556, 560–561, 568–570
DEB402	How can Germany with 11,000 patent processes be overtaken during the period of ten years?	Comment: Archibald Church	HC Deb, 17 Dec 1930, Vol 246(5th), col 1357–1358
DEB403	Airship Policy Those judging the proposed airships were often interested in the patents	Comment: Cecil Malone	HC Deb, 14 May 1931, Vol 252(5th), col 1450–1451
DEB404	Need for government support to make oil from coal	Debate: David Mason; Walter Runciman	HC Deb, 14 Apr 1932, Vol 264(5th), col 1115–1117
DEB405	British Museum Bill Legal deposit requirement does not apply to patent specifications	Debate: Viscount Snowden	HL Deb, 12 May 1932, Vol 84(5th), col 428
DEB406	How much has been paid to inventors by the Post Office award committee?	Comment: Viscount Wolmer	HC Deb, 24 Jul 1933, Vol 280(5th), col 2271

(continued)

(continued)

DEB407	British Hydrocarbon Oils Production Bill Imperial Chemical Industries have patent rights for making oil from coal	Debate: Joseph Batey; Sir William Wayland; Roland Robinson	HC Deb, 7 Mar 1934, Vol 286(5th), col 1013, 1918, 1920, 1921
DEB408	Inventors working secretly with own electricity; and rights of entry	Debate: Thomas Magnay; Arthur Reed; William O'Donovan	HC Deb, 4 May 1934, Vol 289(5th), col 671, 677, 690,
DEB409	Rewards to inventors by Air Minister of up to £1000	Comment: Sir Murray Sueter	HC Deb, 21 Mar 1935, Vol 299(5th), col 1459
DEB410	Arms Inquiry The Royal Commission should examine patent pooling agreements between the Electric Boat Company and Vickers, and Imperial Chemical Industries and DuPont	Comment: Lord Marley	HL Deb, 27 Mar 1935, Vol 96(5th), col 376
DEB411	Patent Office is a trading department, so the fees charged are assessed to pay for its running	Debate: William Morrison; Sir Percy Harris	HC Deb, 16 Jun 1936, Vol 313(5th), col 914–915
DEB412	The government should set up a new department to help patentees get their products to market	Comment: Frank Anderson	HC Deb, 9 Mar 1937, Vol 321(5th), col 1072
DEB413	An independent committee that makes awards to inventors at Post Office is the best system	Comment: George Tryon	HC Deb, 29 Jul 1937, Vol 326(5th), col 3451
DEB414	Whether the government is paying royalties on patents?	Comment: Austin Hopkinson; Robert Grant-Ferris; Sir Thomas Inskip	HC Deb, 15 Mar 1938, Vol 333(5th), col 273, 348, 362–363
DEB415	There should be an inquiry of the Patent Office to see how many patents could be unearthed which would increase production and employment	Comment: John Cartland	HC Deb, 14 Nov 1938, Vol 341(5th), col 618
DEB416	Those businesses which have pooled their patents have not showed any lack of initiative in the development of new processes	Comment: Viscount Swinton	HL Deb, 14 Feb 1939, Vol 111(5th), col 724
DEB417	British government paid £40,000 to Krupp's for use of patent during last war	Comment: Thomas Sexton	HC Deb, 26 Jun 1939, Vol 349(5th), col 147
DEB418	Rewards to inventions used during the war; probably set up a Royal Commission again	Comment: Lord Chatfield	HL Deb, 18 Jan 1940, Vol 115(5th), col 387
DEB419	Unofficial amended version of the Patents Act produced after the Act amended	Comment: Sir Herbert Williams	HC Deb, 30 Apr 1942, Vol 379(5th), col 1137–1138
DEB420	Finance Bill Patent royalties should not be treated as income	Debate: Viscount Bennett; Viscount Simon	HL Deb, 16 Jun 1942, Vol 123(5th), col 405–408
DEB421	Debate on United States federal indictment by chemical companies	Debate: Lord Strabolgi; Lord Melchett; Viscount Maugham; Lord Mcgowan; Viscount Simon	HL Deb, 15 Jul 1943, Vol 128(5th), col 585–603
DEB422	Patents not appropriate for lone inventors who look for fame; industrialists need patents; patent theory	Debate: Viscount Dawson; Viscount Bennett	HL Deb, 20 Jul 1943, Vol 128(5th), col 631–632, 649–651

DEB423	The government should buy the patent for quick food refrigeration	Comment: Francis Beattie	HC Deb, 3 Dec 1943, Vol 395(5th), col 727–728
DEB424	Penicillin patents pooled	Comment: Charles Peat	HC Deb, 2 Feb 1944, Vol 396(5th), col 1275–1276
DEB425	Research and development and need to reform patent law; smothering patents; failure of British industry in powder metallurgy and various other products	Debate: George Benson; William Helmore; David Owen Evans; James Wootton-Davies; Leonard Plugge	HC Deb, 19 Apr 1944, Vol 399(5th), col 235–237, 261, 274–277, 283
DEB426	Statement on the terms of reference and members of Inquiry Committee (Swann Committee) [REP22]	Debate: Hugh Dalton	HC Deb, 25 Apr 1944, Vol 399(5th), col 600–601
DEB427	Financial Statement (Budget) Lump sums for patents to be written off over life of patent	Debate: Sir John Anderson	HC Deb, 25 Apr 1944, Vol 399(5th), col 675–676
DEB428	Finance Bill Patent taxation; patents during the war and enemy patents; rewards to inventors for royalties	Debate: Alfred Edwards; Sir John Anderson; Sir Arnold Gridley; William Wavell Wakefield	HC Deb, 23 May 1944, Vol 400(5th), col 675–677, 682–683 and 691
DEB429	Finance Bill Whether private individual inventors should be on the same footing as corporations?	Debate: Viscount Bennett; Viscount Simon	HL Deb, 11 Jul 1944, Vol 132(5th), col 821–825
DEB430	Terms of reference of Swan Committee [REP22]; not saying when Bill will be introduced	Debate: Lord Woolton	HL Deb, 21 Mar 1945, Vol 135(5th), col 745–746
DEB431	Why has the power to vest enemy patents in the Custodian of Enemy Property not been used; such patents' future after the war; use of such patents by British industry; how many enemy secret patents are there at Patent Office?	Motion: Lord Vansittart Debate: Viscount Maugham	HL Deb, 22 Mar 1845, Vol 135(5th), col 761–783
DEB432	Debate on German war-related inventions	Motion: Lord Vansittart Debate: Lord Strabolgi; Lord Charwell	HL Deb, 29 May 1945, Vol 136(5th), col 246–259
DEB433	Price fixing, cartels and patents; suggestions of abolishing patents as too expensive to enforce	Debate: Dingle Foot; Oliver Lyttelton; Austin Hopkinson	HC Deb, 13 Jun 1945, Vol 411(5th), col 1707–1708, 1739–1731, 1742–1743
DEB434	Emergency Laws (Transitional Provisions) Bill Cl 7 extending Patents and Designs Act 1942[PUBA37]	Comment: George Oliver	HC deb, 20 Nov 1945, Vol 416(5th), col 246
DEB435	Debate on scientific resources Scientists evading patents, but not for purpose of scientific truth	Comment: Albert Blackburn; Herbert Morrison	HC Deb, 30 Nov 1945, Vol 416(5th), col 1842–1843, 1863–1864
DEB436	Two miners who have taken out patents are not keen on nationalisation of mines	Debate: Sir Cuthbert Headlam; James Murray	HC Deb, 29 Jan 1946, Vol 418(5th), col 745–746
DEB437	We have to stop people fiddling with patent law and get on with creating things	Comment: Ian Mikardo	HC Deb, 8 Aug 1947, Vol 441(5th), col 1858–1859

(continued)

(continued)

DEB438	Finance Bill Patent cost can be deducted from profits under Income Tax Act 1945	Comment: Sir Frank Soskice	HC Deb, 3 Dec 1947, Vol 445(5th), col 399–400
DEB439	Patent monopolies, patent pooling; research into patents	Debate: Harold Wilson; Sir David Maxwell Fyfe; Eric Fletcher; Elwyn Jones; George House; Oliver Lyttelton; Herbert Morrison	HC Deb, 22 Apr 1948, Vol 449(5th), col 2022–2025, 2052, 2055, 2095, 2097–2099, 2105–2106, 2110–2111, 2123–2124
DEB440	Selling a patent with payment annually is income	Debates: David Eccles; Sir Stafford Cripps	HC Deb, 3 Jun 1948, Vol 451(5th), col 1386 and 1389
DEB441	Gas Bill Cl 37 (foreign investment) Provisions' application to foreign patents	Debate: Hugh Gaitskell; Brendon Bracken	HC Deb, 10 Jun 1948, Vol 451(5th), col 2580–2581
DEB442	Monopoly (Inquiry and Control) Bill Accusations that patents have suppressed industry are without foundation; whether the position of patents under the Bill will be clarified?	Comment: Oliver Lyttelton Debate: William Shepherd	HC Deb, 29 Jun 1948, Vol 452(5th), col 2060–2061, 2159–2160
DEB443	Monopoly (Inquiry and Control) Bill Why provision is not necessary in relation to patents	Amendment: Viscount Bridgeman Debate: Viscount Maugham; Lord Chorley; Lord Balfour	HL Deb, 13 Jul 1948, Vol 157(5th), col 810–814
DEB444	[Marcel] Desoutter's patent taken over by government without reward; not same competition in the artificial limb market	Comment: Sir William Wavell Wakefield	HC Deb, 22 Jul 1948, Vol 454(5th), col 761
DEB445	Professor Williamson had patents for Bakelite and came back to England to exploit his patents	Comments: William Wells	HC Deb, 28 Jul 1948, Vol 454(5th), col 1392
DEB446	Export Guarantees Bill Whether the Bill would cover British-owned foreign patents, and royalties therefrom?	Debate: Frederick Erroll; Douglas Jay	HC Deb, 2 Feb 1949, Vol 460(5th), col 1700, 1714
DEB447	We have prevented Germany competing by investigating all their trade secrets and abolishing patent rights	Comment: John Hynd	HC Deb, 2 Mar 1949, Vol 462(5th), col 496
DEB448	Iron and Steel Bill Amendment dealing with transfer of patent rights and the development of new inventions	Proposed: Lord Balfour Debate: Lord Lucas; Viscount Swinton; Viscount Maugham; Viscount Ridley; Lord Kenilworth	HL Deb, 30 Jun 1949, Vol 163(5th), col 652–666
DEB449	Finance Bill – Avoidance of Transactions Clause would prohibit selling of patents without permission of the Treasury	Comment: David Eccles	HC Deb, 11 Jun 1951, Vol 488(5th), col 2186
DEB450	Professor Joliot-Curie handed over atomic patents to country (France); then hounded out in 1950	Comment: Stephen Davies	HC Deb, 17 Jul 1951, Vol 490(5th), col 1199–1200
DEB451	Paris Convention will come back into force in Japan upon signing of Peace Treaty	Comment: Arthur Colegate	HC Deb, 25 Jul 1951, Vol 491(5th), col 563–564

DEB452	Japan agreed to adhere to treaties on industrial property	Comment: Robert Hudson	HC Deb, 26 Jul 1951, Vol 491(5th), col 619–620
DEB453	Electric Lamp Manufacturers Association's patent policies	Debate: Peter Thorneycraft	HC Deb, 13 Nov 1951, Vol 493(5th), col 21W
DEB454	Japanese Peace Treaty Requiring respect for patents and copyright	Debate: Walter Fletcher	HC Deb, 26 Nov 1951, Vol 494(5th), col 900 and 901
DEB455	Monopolies Commission Report Electric Lamp Industry, recommendation (i)	Debate: Duncan Sandys	HC Deb, 19 May 1952, Vol 501(5th), col 11–12W
DEB456	Patent law analogy with televising of sporting events and copyright	Debate: Lord Lucas	HL Deb, 25 Jun 1952, Vol 177(5th), col 436–437
DEB457	Pooled patent and Electric Lamp Manufacturers Association	Debate: Frank Tomney; George Darling; Henry Strauss	HC Deb, 23 Jul 1952, Vol 504(5th), col 571–573, 615 and 662
DEB458	Printing of specifications cost Patent Office £70,000	Comment: John Boyd-Carpenter	HC Deb, 18 Mar 1953, Vol 513(5th), col 151
DEB459	William Newton campaigned against bad patent law in 1852	Comment: Charles Pannell	HC Deb, 20 Jul 1953, Vol 518(5th), col 107
DEB460	Discussion of European Patent Office with Spain (why Yugoslavia not invited)	Debate: Geoffrey de Freitas; Anthony Nutting	HC Deb, 23 Oct 1953, Vol 518(5th), col 2383, 2389
DEB461	Atomic Energy (Anglo-US Agreement) licensing of patent rights	Statement: Sir Anthony Eden	HC Deb, 20 Jun 1955, Vol 542(5th), col 1034–1038
DEB462	Abuse of monopoly in relation to patents should be applied to trade marks	Comment: Sir Lionel Heald	HC Deb, 13 Jul 1955, Vol 543(5th), col 1972
DEB463	Patent Office, and library, needs to expand with properly trained staff	Debate: Austen Albu	HC Deb, 21 Jul 1955, Vol 544(5th), col 581–582
DEB464	Board of Trade responsible for patent law	Comment: Arthur Bottomley	HC Deb, 27 Oct 1955, Vol 545(5th), col 505
DEB465	Companies with suggested schemes and patentable inventions; use of patented inventions abroad	Debate: Graham Page; Robert Edwards; Frederick Lee; John Hall	HC Deb, 24 Feb 1956, Vol 549(5th), col 705–706, 712, 726, 739
DEB466	Patents owned by Atomic Energy Authority should be licensed on commercial basis	Statement: Rab Butler	HC Deb, 14 Mar 1956, Vol 550(5th), col 377–378
DEB467	Will the government amend the law to make plants patentable subject matter?	Motion: Lord Lucas Debate: Earl St Aldwyn; Viscount Elibank; Earl of Swinton	HL Deb, 19 Feb 1957, Vol 201(5th), col 987–989
DEB468	Sir Frank Whittle's patenting of the jet engine	Comment: Lord Ogmore	HL Deb, 11 Dec 1957, Vol 206(5th), col 1036
DEB469	Obtaining drugs from the United States incurs royalty costs which would not be incurred if they were made in this country	Comment: Arthur Blenkinsop	HC Deb, 17 Mar 1958, Vol 584(5th), col 1012
DEB470	Tribunal and Inquiries Bill Removal of the Comptroller by the Lord Chancellor not appropriate due to administrative functions	Comment: Viscount Kilmuir	HL Deb, 1 Apr 1958, Vol 208(5th), col 591

(continued)

(continued)

DEB471	Why should we tolerate a semi-monopoly in poliomyelitis vaccine when all drugs companies should co-operate to produce it?	Comment: Maurice Edelman	HC Deb, 12 May 1958, Vol 588(5th), col 10
DEB472	Whether the regulation of trade marks, designs and patent infringement should be standardised?	Motion: Lord Shepherd Debate: Lord Mancroft; Lord Lucas; Viscount Elibank	HL Deb, 3 Jul 1958, Vol 210(5th), col 524–527
DEB473	Appointment of a Comptroller with no scientific qualifications	Comment: Frederick Willey	HC Deb, 18 Dec 1958, Vol 597(5th), col 1330–1331
DEB474	Suggests off-patent drugs are substandard; small percentage of drugs' price is paid towards research; paying for patent rights outside this country for research done here; s 41 of the Patents Act 1949 [PUBA40]	Debate: Julian Snow; Richard Thompson	HC Deb, 12 Mar 1959, Vol 601(5th), col 1516, 1517–1519, 1531
DEB475	Resumption of industrial property protection in Anglo-Egyptian relations	Comment: Derick Heathcoat Amory	HC Deb, 16 Mar 1959, Vol. 602(5th), col 40
DEB476	Trade deal with Russia held up by United States patent rights	Comments: Harold Wilson; Sir David Eccles	HC Deb, 9 Apr 1959, Vol 603(5th), col 390–391
DEB477	Jet engine patent lapsed because Air Ministry would not pay £5 renewal fee	Comment: Lord Ogmore	HL Deb, 20 Jul 1959, Vol 218(5th), col 241
DEB478	Businesses wondering whether goods made under British licence can be sold in the Common Tariff area	Comment: Harold Wilson	HC Deb, 14 Dec 1959, Vol 615(5th), col 1159–1160
DEB479	One Chancery judge fully engaged with patent work	Comment: Viscount Kilmuir	HL Deb, 28 Nov 1960, Vol 226(5th), col 961
DEB480	Clash between Massey Ferguson and a United States firm over tractor patents	Comment: John Morris	HC Deb, 6 Feb 1961, Vol 634(5th), col 132
DEB481	Why does the government refuse to allow hospitals to make use of patent rights available to other Crown services?	Comment: George Brown; Harold Wilson	HC Deb, 8 Feb 1961, Vol 634(5th), col 419 and 430
DEB482	Cost of drugs to National Health Service; Patents Act 1949, s 41 [PUBA40]	Debate: John Arbuthnot; Barnett Stross; Julian Snow	HC Deb, 15 Feb 1961, Vol 634(5th), col 1456–1457, 1539–1540, 1543, 1574
DEB483	Debate on Patent Office Library and National Reference Library for Science and Innovation	Motion: Austen Albu Debate: Denzil Freeth; Frederick Peart	HC Deb, 14 Mar 1961, Vol 636(5th), col 1355–1368
DEB484	Fees to Patent Office not directed to be paid to Exchequer	Comment: Sir Edward Boyle	HC Deb, 25 Apr 1961, Vol 639(5th), col 380
DEB485	National Research Development Corporation should set up industries to exploit inventions; Patent Office development on South Bank	Debate: Judith Hart; Arthur Skeffington	HC Deb, 10 Jul 1961, Vol 644(5th), col 126–127, 150–151
DEB486	Commending decision to use s 46 of the Patents Act 1949 [PUBA40] to purchase drugs	Debate: Kenneth Robinson; Enoch Powell	HC Deb, 11 Jul 1961, Vol 644(5th), col 234 and 241
DEB487	Russian inventors have learnt not to apply for patents	Comment: Earl of Halsbury	HL Deb, 15 Nov 1961, Vol 235(5th), col 696–697

DEB488	Public purse and buying drugs; public interest in patents; pharmaceutical patents in Europe; Patents Act 1949, s 41 [PUBA40]; term of patents	Debate: Harold Wilson; John Arbuthnot; Jeremy Thorpe; Cledwyn Hughes	HC Deb, 30 Nov 1961, Vol 650(5th), col 649–650, 670–671, 672–673, 697–699, 701–702, 713, 754–755
DEB489	Patent licensing of ICI and Courtaulds seriously limits competition; likewise, international patent agreements; expiry of Courtaulds' patent	Comment: Douglas Jay; Robert Edwards; William Wikins	HC Deb, 14 Feb 1962, Vol 653(5th), col 1329, 1332, 1383, 1407
DEB490	Reference to case where agreement related to patent not registerable	Comment: Sir Lionel Heald	HC Deb, 24 Jul 1962, Vol 663(5th), col 1367
DEB491	Dissemination and compulsory licences under Euratom	Comment: Peter Thomas	HC Deb, 3 Aug 1962, Vol 664(5th), col 1001–1002
DEB492	Outrage at how Japanese have abused our patent law	Comment: Maurice Edelman	HC Deb, 5 Dec 1962, Vol 668(5th), col 1407
DEB493	Patents Act 1949, s 41 [PUBA40]; drugs are patented; drugs at lower price	Debate: Laurie Pavitt; Anthony Barber	HC Deb, 6 Dec 1962, Vol 668(5th), col 1555–1556, 1584–1585, 1589
DEB494	British Library serves purpose of being the library for the Patent Office; separation of roles	Comment: Austen Albu	HC Deb, 20 Dec 1962, Vol 669(5th), col 1522
DEB495	Urgent need for office space for Patent Office (three years ago)	Comment: Sir Colin Thornton-Kemsley	HC Deb, 12 Mar 1963, Vol 673(5th), col 1209
DEB496	System of communication satellites built on patent rights would undermine co-operation	Comment: Charles Leslie Hale; Frederick Lee	HC Deb, 29 Mar 1963, Vol 674(5th), col 1716, 1745
DEB497	Whenever the Japanese hear about a new patent, they apply for licences	Comment: Hervey Rhodes	HC Deb, 4 Apr 1963, Vol 675(5th), col 683
DEB498	National Reference Library of Science to be built next year and include Patent Office Library	Comment: Earl of Dundee	HL Deb, 9 Apr 1963, Vol 248(5th), col 929
DEB499	British Museum Bill Patent Office Library	Debate: Lord Chorley; Baroness Wootton; Viscount Eccles; Earl of Dundee	HL Deb, 6 May 1963, Vol 249(5th), col 453–454 and 457–459, 463, 465, 467–468
DEB500	Do Scottish chemists pay retail price for drugs, or do they rely on s 46 of the Patents Act 1949 [PUBA40]?	Comment: Jesse Dickson Mabon; Michael Noble	HC Deb, 8 May 1963, Vol 677(5th), col 539, 554
DEB501	National Research Development Corporation giving loans (to hovercraft) to raise money from patents	Comment: Roger Cooke	HC Deb, 2 Aug 1963, Vol 682(5th), col 868
DEB502	Does the Prime Minister think that the National Research Development Corporation is the destruction of personal freedom? When drug patents were busted, Minister of Aviation negotiated; large number of patents taken out in Germany for patents	Comments: Harold Wilson; David Ginsburg	HC Deb, 19 Nov 1963, Vol 684(5th), col 825, 829, 903
DEB503	Patent arrangements between Atomic Energy Authority and industry are extraordinary	Comment: Earl Alexander	HL Deb, 16 Mar 1964, Vol 256(5th), col 691–692

(continued)

(continued)

DEB504	UN Development Decade Surrender of patents to assist developing countries	Comment: Earl of Iddesleigh; Lord Drumalbyn	HL Deb, 24 Jun 1964, Vol 259(5th), col 206 and 254
DEB505	Jurisdiction over contract *British Nylon v ICI* [1953] Ch 19 and assignment of patent	Comment: Sir John Hobson	HC Deb, 15 Jul 1964, Vol 698(5th), col 1276
DEB506	Hope government will grant compulsory licences so patents which have been abused can face healthy competition	Comment: Jeremy Thorpe	HC Deb, 2 Dec 1964, Vol 703(5th), col 634
DEB507	British patent rights should be supported in this country, but also abroad	Comment: Lord Ferrier	HL Deb, 11 Feb 1965, Vol 263(5th), col 358
DEB508	Russian views have changed; now signed Paris Convention.	Comment: Tam Dalyell	HC Deb, 13 Apr 1965, Vol 710(5th), col 1263–1264
DEB509	Finance Bill (Valuation Purchase Tax goods containing copyright material) Explains how patent clause works	Debate: Graham Page; Dingle Foot	HC Deb, 17 May 1965, Vol 712(5th), col 1163–1168
DEB510	Finance Bill Payment within close company, limiting patent royalties to reasonable amount	Comment: William Stratton Mills; John Diamond	HC Deb, 22 Jun 1965, Vol 714(5th), col 1638, 1641
DEB511	Finance Bill Extending meaning of "distribution" to include patents	Proposed: Sir Lionel Heald Debate: Patrick Jenkin; Robert Cooke; Anthony Barber; Edward Short	HC Deb, 12 Jul 1965, Vol 716(5th), col 202–210
DEB512	Ministry of Technology, patent system; encouraging applications from government; removal of Patent Office from London	Debate: Frank Cousins; Sir Lionel Heald; Richard Marsh; Jeremy Bray; Robert Brown; Robert Shelon; Eric Lubbock	HC Deb, 14 Jul 1965, Vol 716(5th), col 523, 555–563, 609
DEB513	Work of Lady Lovelace's book about computers written in 1830s invalidates many modern patents	Comment: Lord Bowden	HL Deb, 2 Mar 1966, Vol 273(5th), col 715–716
DEB514	Spreads income over years for patent royalties	Comment: Peter Hordern	HC Deb, 20 Jun 1966, Vol 730(5th), col 203 and 223
DEB515	Finance Bill Proposed amendment to restrict patent royalties to reasonable consideration	Proposed: Patrick Jenkin Debate: Joel Barnett; Raymond Gower; Sir Lionel Heald; Norman St John-Stevas; Sir Eric Errington; William Stratton Mills; Ian Percival; Eric Lubbock	HC Deb, 21 Jun 1966, Vol 730(5th), col 373–401
DEB516	Double Taxation Agreement USA The agreement puts British inventors in the USA at a disadvantage to United States ones here	Comment: Peter Bessell	HC Deb, 23 Jun 1966, Vol 730(5th), col 1089
DEB517	If patent rights are treated as capital assets, why does Capital Gains Tax not apply?	Debate: Niall MacDermot	HC Deb, 12 Jul 1966, Vol 731(5th), col 1247–1248
DEB518	Finance Bill Proposed amendment to restrict patent royalties to reasonable consideration [See also DEB486]	Proposed: Sir Lionel Heald Debate: John Diamond; Harold Lever; Terrence Higgins	HC Deb, 13 Jul 1966, Vol 731(5th), col 1631–1641

DEB519	Government in negotiations with the inventor to make the Possum (for paralysed persons) available	Comment: Charles Loughlin	HC Deb, 8 Aug 1966, Vol 733(5th), col 1179
DEB520	Double Taxation Relief Switzerland Convention requires accepted price for patents	Debate: Patrick Jenkin	HC Deb, 7 Nov 1966, Vol 735(5th), col 1094
DEB521	National Research Development Corporation has had difficulty spending its budget because all good inventions are taken up by industry	Comment: Lord Erroll	HL Deb, 1 Dec 1966, Vol 278(5th), col 861
DEB522	Best newspaper packing invention in world a British patent, but not available here	Comment: Lord Ferrier	HL Deb, 25 Jan 1967, Vol 279(5th), col 649
DEB523	Scheme for single European patent	Comment: George Darling	HC Deb, 1 Feb 1967, Vol 740(5th), col 497–471
DEB524	With all the organisations advising inventors, there is almost too much advice	Comment: Bernard Weatherill	HC Deb, 10 Feb 1967, Vol 740(5th), col 1962
DEB525	Difficulty of Admiralty Research Laboratory selling the invention for cavitation corrosion in diesel-engine pistons	Comment: Roy Mason	HC Deb, 15 Mar 1967, Vol 743(5th), col 619–620
DEB526	European patent will be a substantial change for technical producers	Comment: Lord Erroll	HL Deb, 9 May 1967, Vol 282(5th), col 1370
DEB527	Soviet Union taking part in discussions in Council of Europe on patent law	Comment: Sir Geoffrey de Freitas	HC Deb, 10 May 1967, Vol 746(5th), col 1549–1550
DEB528	Finance Bill Copyright owners put in same position as patentees	Debate: Sir Edward Boyle	HC Deb, 7 Jun 1967, Vol 747(5th), col 1144
DEB529	Suggestion of technology transfer from universities	Comment: Lord Sherfield	HL Deb, 14 Jun 1967, Vol 283(5th), col 975
DEB530	Finance Bill Expenditure on know-how clause debate	Proposed: Patrick Jenkin Debate: John Diamond; Iain Macleod	HC Deb, 15 Jun 1967, Vol 748(5th), col 905–916
DEB531	Finance Bill Group of companies' taxation; problems with know-how clause	Comment: Patrick Jenkin	HC Deb, 27 Jun 1967, Vol 749(5th), col 349–350
DEB532	No action by Board of Trade to harmonise patent law with Europe	Comment: Lord Balniel	HC Deb, 20 Jul 1967, Vol 750(5th), col 2599
DEB533	Need for collaboration over patent law	Comment: Eric Moonman	HC Deb, 24 Jul 1967, Vol 751(5th), col 286
DEB534	It is undesirable that National Reference Library for Science and Invention separated from Patent Library	Comment: Lord Douglas; Lord Winterbottom	HL Deb, 28 Nov 1967, Vol 287(5th), col 3
DEB535	British Library delay in housing Patent Office Library; National Library for Science and Innovation part of British Library; failure of Patent Office being moved to South Bank; separating Patent Library material from rest	Debate: Viscount Eccles; Baroness Phillips; Viscount Radcliffe; Earl of Cranbrook; Viscount Boyd	HL Deb, 13 Dec 1967, Vol 287(5th), cols 1116–1117, 1123–1124, 1139–1140, 1196, 1225–1226

(continued)

(continued)

DEB536	Clinical trials are rushed to get patents and drugs to market	Comment: Baroness Summerskill	HL Deb, 20 Dec 1967, Vol 287(5th), col 1510
DEB537	Need for patent harmonisation if there is a Free Trade Agreement	Comment: Peter Kirk	HC Deb, 24 Jan 1968, Vol 757(5th), col 464–465
DEB538	Is there is an organisation for dealing with patents and their exploitation for the nationalised industries?	Comment: Lord Arwyn	HL Deb, 31 Jan 1968, Vol 288(5th), col 826–827
DEB539	Medicines Bill Criticism of Sainsbury Committee [PPP105]; patenting of drugs in public interest; regulations creating patent infringement defence	Debate: Nigel Fisher; Michael English; Laurie Pavitt	HC Deb, 15 Feb 1968, Vol 758(5th), col 1653, 1675, 1683, 1693– 1694
DEB540	Ownership of hovercraft patents	Earl of Kinnoull; Lord Granville; Earl of Bessborough	HL Deb, 26 Mar 1968, Vol 290(5th), col 959–961, 967, 969–970
DEB541	What progress has been made on the formation of the European Centre for Technology?	Debate: Lord Chalfont; Earl of Bessborough; Lord Mitchinson; Lord Sherfield	HL Deb, 10 Apr 1968, Vol 291(5th), col 327–329
DEB542	There needs to be a way of exploiting inventions in nationalised industries	Comment: Lord Arwyn; Lord Shackleton	HL Deb, 2 May 1968, Vol 291(5th), col 1228–1232, 1256–1257
DEB543	Sainsbury Report Not wanting to prejudice statement in House on s 46 of the Patents Act 1949 [PUBA40]	Debate: Lord Kennett; Lord Newton	HL Deb, 24 Jun 1968, Vol 293(5th), col 1127–1131
DEB544	Statement on Sainsbury Report, including patent rights	Statement: Kenneth Robinson; Maurice Macmillan; Shirley Summerskill; Dudley Smith; John Dunwoody; David Crouch; Laurie Pavitt; Tim Fortescue; Lord Balniel	HC Deb, 24 Jun 1968, Vol 767(5th), col 43–45
DEB545	Customs (Import Deposit) Bill Proposal that deposit not required where patented	Proposed: John Bruce-Gardyn Debate: John Hall; George Drayson; Sir Henry Legge-Bourke; David Mitchell; John Biffen; Richard Taverne	HC Deb, 3 Dec 1968, Vol 774(5th), col 1443–1453
DEB546	Tax laws should be more in favour of patentees	Comment: Lord Arwyn	HL Deb, 11 Dec 1968, Vol 298(5th), col 604–605
DEB547	Industrial Information Bill Definition of information, and "incomplete patent" etc.	Debate: Edmund Dell	HC Deb, 13 Dec 1968, Vol 775(5th), col 808, 821, 823
DEB548	Patenting of CS gas	Comment: Lord Brockway; Lord Shepherd	HL Deb, 5 Feb 1969, Vol 299(5th), col 182 and 192
DEB549	Community Patent Convention Government's desire to harmonise patent law – welcome news	Debate: Lord Chalfont; Lord Merrivale; Lord Kings Norton; Lord Arwyn	HL Deb, 12 Mar 1969, Vol 300(5th), col 489, 525, 528, 538–540
DEB550	Uniformity of patent law would make technology exchange easier	Comment: Lord Energlyn	HL Deb, 19 Mar 1969, Vol 300(5th), col 971
DEB551	Conflict of interests between National Research Development Councils and patentees working for them	Comment: Lord Balogh	HL Deb, 5 Feb 1970, Vol 307(5th), col 776–777

DEB552	Double Taxation Relief (Trinidad and Tobago)	Motion: Richard Taverne Debate: John Nott	HC Deb, 26 Feb 1970, Vol 796(5th), col 1521–1525
DEB553	Statement on National Libraries; government understands importance of having Patent Office near combined libraries	Comment: Edward Short	HC Deb, 7 Apr 1970, Vol 799(5th), col 248
DEB554	Coal Industry Bill Ownership of certain patents, including by employees	Debate: Patrick Cormack	HC Deb, 3 Dec 1970, Vol 807(5th), col 1537–1538
DEB555	Atomic Energy Authority Bill Clause excluding from transfer patent rights	Debate: Airey Neave; Sir Henry Legge-Bouke; Nicholas Ridley; Tony Benn	HC Deb, 15 Jan 1971, Vol 809(5th), col 389–394
DEB556	Whether the United States liquidator will seize Rolls-Royce's patents	Debate: Phillip Whitehead	HC Deb, 26 Feb 1971, Vol 812(5th), col 1082–1083
DEB557	British Library Science Reference Library from 1978	Comment: Viscount Eccles	HL Deb, 2 Mar 1971, Vol 315(4th), Col 1278
DEB558	Government acquisition of Rolls-Royce patents	Debate: Frederick Corfield; James Scott-Hopkins; William Whitelaw; Peter Rost; Phillip Whitehead	HC Deb, 11 Mar 1971, Vol 813(5th), col 624, 628, 629, 641–642, 666–667
DEB559	Employee inventions at Royal Dockyards	Comment: Dame Joan Vickers	HC Deb, 27 Jul 1971, Vol 822(5th), col 481
DEB560	EEC law will only affect limited area of domestic law, including patents	Comment: Lord Lloyd	HL Deb, 27 Jul 1971, Vol 323(5th), col 369
DEB561	The difficulty of harmonising British patent law with that on Continent	Comment: Philip Goodhart	HC Deb, 25 Oct 1971, Vol 823(5th), col 1267–1268
DEB562	Purchase by government of Rolls-Royce patents	Debate: Tam Dalyell; Bruce Millan; Frederick Corfield	HC Deb, 29 Feb 1972, Vol 832(5th), col 323–325, 343, 351
DEB563	European Communities Bill Debate on Euratom Treaty and patents	Debate: Tony Benn; Trevor Skeet; Peter Emery	HC Deb, 4 Jul 1972, Vol 840(5th), col 310–311, 328–329, 333–334
DEB564	European Communities Bill Patents and licensing and rules in France	Comment: Lord Brown	HL Deb, 25 Jul 1972, Vol 333(5th), col 1319
DEB565	Atomic Energy Authority (Weapons Group) Bill Cl 1 and 5 (transfer of patents and information)	Debate: Ian Gilmour	HC Deb, 30 Jan 1973, Vol 849(5th), col 1167 and 1170
DEB566	Rolls-Royce and government acquiring patents	Debate: Tam Dalyell; Cranley Onslow	HC Deb, 13 Feb 1973, Vol 850(5th), col 1235–1236 and 1238
DEB567	Monopolies Commission Report shows best and worst of patent law; Common Market and patent policy; retention of the Patents Act 1949, s 46 [PUBA40]; repeal of s 41; pending expiry of patent	Debate: Shirley Summerskill; Laurie Pavitt; Peter Emery	HC Deb, 3 May 1973, Vol 855(5th), col 1611–1612, 1617, 1624–1626
DEB568	What is position of Italians on patent law?	Comment: Lord Harvey	HL Deb, 16 May 1973, Vol 342(5th), col 871

(continued)

(continued)

DEB569	Government Trading Funds Bill Patent Office could become trading fund	Comment: Nicholas Ridley	HC Deb, 19 Jun 1973, Vol 858(5th), col 635
DEB570	Regulation of Prices (Tranquillizing Drugs) (No 2) Order 1973 Patents Act 1949 [PUBA40], s 41 licence did not affect Roche market share; monopoly purchaser NHS; repeal of s 41; burden of proof on Roche; pharmaceutical industry and patent reform; s 46	Debate: Lord Stow Hill; Lord Reay; Lord Sainsbury; Lord Brown; Lord Ferrier	HL Deb, 22 Jun 1973, Vol 343(5th), col 1604, 1620–1621, 1626, 1647, 1656–1658
DEB571	Whether s 41 and 46 of the Patents Act 1949 [PUBA40] are being used to purchase drugs from alternative sources is approriate? Patentees need to get some reward for research	Debate: Laurie Pavitt; Michael English; Sir Geoffrey Howe	HC Deb, 27 Jun 1973, Vol 858(5th), col 1532–1533, 1534
DEB572	Regulation of Prices (Tranquillizing Drugs) (No 3) Order 1973 What is the point of a patent if price-fixed; drugs are very cheap?	Comment: Nicholas Ridley	HC Deb, 4 Jul 1973, Vol 859(5th), col 653–654
DEB573	Regulation of Prices (Tranquillizing Drugs) (No 3) Order 1973 Use of the Patents Act 1949 [PUBA40], s 46 instead of buying from Roche; banks and repeal of s 41	Debate: Lord Todd; Lord Ferrier; Earl of Limerick	HL Deb, 5 Jul 1973, Vol 344(5th), col 444–445, 451–452, 463
DEB574	Debate on the effect on British Patent Office caused by European Patents Convention	Debate: Ronald Bell; Peter Emery	HC Deb, 19 Jul 1973, Vol 860(5th), col 887–897
DEB575	International Organisations Land Bill Disappointment at European Patent Office not coming to the United Kingdom	Debate: Reginald Eyre; Reginald Freeson	HC Deb, 19 Dec 1973, Vol 866(5th), col 1563–1565
DEB576	Finance Bill Debate on patent royalties amendment	Debate: Peter Hordern; John Gilbert	HC Deb, 21 Jan 1975, Vol 884(5th), col 1343–1344 and 1346
DEB577	Industry Bill Patent-related amendment	No debate	HC Deb, 2 Jul 1975, Vol 894(5th), col 1628
DEB578	North Sea Oil Government taking patent rights	Debate: Lord Lloyd	HL Deb, 25 Sep 1975, Vol 364(5th), col 563–564
DEB579	When will patent law be reformed?	Debate: Patrick Jenkin	HC Deb, 25 Nov 1976, Vol 921(5th), col 309–310

Index of inventors

Redmund, David (steam engines), 423 (PRVB107), 434 (PRVB125)

Reece, Rees (peat), 440 (PRVB134)

Reith, Buchanan (hatch fitting), 742 (Q755, Q760), 743 (Q764)

Rettie, Robert (signalling), 597 (PPP24), 599 (PPP38, PPP39), 640 (PET153), 650 (PET216)

Reverley, Henry (ordnance), 655 (PET263)

Rhan, George (fire proof cement), 637 (PET130)

Richards, Laurence (low carbon retort), 723 (Q496)

Richardson, Henry (life boat), 599 (PPP41)

Richmond, Vincent (Lt Col) (airships), 734 (Q640)

Roberts, William (anatomy), 630 (PET49, PET51), 632 (PET73), 635 (PET107, PET109, PET111)

Robey, James (deodorising), 313 (PRVA88)

Rodgers, James (tyres), 344 (PRVA117)

Roe, John (shipping coal), 343 (PRVA116)

Rome, Thomas (smelting), 481 (SCOT29)

Rose, Thomas (and Charles) (small pox), 652 (PET233), 656 (PET270)

Rowcett, William (telegraph), 660 (PET312)

Sabatier, William (textile), 240 (PRVA30), 371 (PRVB29)

Savery, Thomas (steam engine), 223 (PRVA13), 482 (SCOT31)

Sayer, George (Captain) (life boat), 690 (Q49), 691 (Q65)

Scoffern, John (Dr) (sugar), 598 (PPP29)

Scott, George (furnace), 652 (PET235)

Scott, George (Sq Ldr) (airships), 734 (Q640)

Scott, James (assorted), 476 (SCOT17), 477 (SCOT18)

Scott, Percy (Captain) (gunnery), 564 (PRZA45)

Sealy, Edward (leather), 387 (PRVB52)

Sharpnel, Henry (Lt Gen) (shells, shrapnel), 639 (PET145), 640 (PET146, PET147, PET149), 642 (PET165), 646 (PET184), 658 (PET290), 659 (PET300, PET301)

Shaw, William (lead pipes), 446 (PRVB142)

Shepard, William (rubber), 443 (PRVB138)

Shepherd, George (naval), 652 (PET232)

Sievier, Robert (rubber/cables), 252 (PRVA41), 410 (PRVB86)

Sillar, George and William (sewage), 310 (PRVA85)

Simpson, James (perambulators), 337 (PRVA111)

Sinclair, Daniel (railways), 449 (PRVB146)

Skrivanow, Gregory (electricity), 450 (PRVB147)

Slade, C.G (Colonel) (webbing), 700 (Q191)

Sleigh, Adderley Willocks (breakwater), 638 (PET133), 653 (PET246), 654 (PET257)

Smith, Christopher (indigo), 447 (PRVB143)

Smith, Francis Pettit (propeller), 262 (PRVA47)

Smith, Gavin (pumps), 472 (SCOT5)

Smith, James (furnace), 315 (PRVA90)

Smith, James (steam engine), 482 (SCOT31)

Smith, William (candle), 276 (PRVA58)

Smyth, James Carmichael (nitric fumigation), 550 (PRZA29)

Smyth, William (soles/shoes), 322 (PRVA97)

Snider, John Vaughan (rifle), 658 (PET291), 775 (DEB117)

Snooke, John (life boat/lighting at sea), 637 (PET126), 641 (PET155)

Speed, Joseph (rifle), 604 (PPP98), 701 (Q203), 784 (DEB259)

Spencer, John (steam engine), 445 (PRVB140)

Stafford, Daniel (carriages), 416 (PRVB93), 418 (PRVB97)

Stead, David (paving), 269 (PRVA53), 419 (PRVB98)

Stephens, Joanna (curing stone), 528 (PRZA2)

Stephens, Thomas (pot ash), 530 (PRZA5)

Stevens, John Lee (steamships), 600 (PPP58)

Storer, William (optical), 567 (PRZC4)

Stratham, W (pit props), 709 (Q301)

Stuckey, William (pneumatic engine/filtering water), 428 (PRVB114), 429 (PRVB115), 637 (PET128, PET129)

Swain, Sampson (metal working), 374 (PRVB35)

Taylor, Elizabeth (block apparatus), 230 (PRVA21)

Taylor, William Hannis (carrying oil/paving), 449 (PRVB145), 422 (PRVB105), 425 (PRVB109), 426 (PRVB111)

Terry, Charles (sugar), 258 (PRVA44)

Terry, Victor (working in Italy), 735 (Q656)

Thomas, Lynal (Lyndall) (explosives/guns), 697 (Q151), 782 (DEB224)

Thompson, Simeon (cranes), 403 (PRVB77)

Thomson, Robert (roadsteamer), 602 (PPP76)

Thrackton, Edward (life boat), 624 (PET1)

Tilloch, Alexander (anti-forgery), 624 (PET4)

Tilt, Joseph (salt pans), 404 (PRVB79)

Torassa, John Bapiste (painting), 259 (PRVA45)

Tosswill, Charles Speare (fire proof cement), 637 (PET130)

Trengrouse, Henry (preservation of life at sea), 578 (PRZC18)

Trueman, Albert (metal/copper), 441 (PRVB135)

Truss, Thomas (submarine air-lock), 718 (Q426)

Tuite, John (pumps), 370 (PRVB27, PRVB28)

Turner, James (dyes), 236 (PRVA26), 379 (PRVB43)

Tweeddale, George (Marquis) (bricks), 263 (PRVA48)

Tyndale, William Clifford (drain pipes), 704 (Q246)

Vancouver, John (painting), 395 (PRVB64)

Vardy, James (metal), 268 (PRVA52)

Vauclain, Samuel (steam locomotive), 350 (PRVA122)

Index of companies

Index of inventions/products

davit, 725 (Q520)

death ray, 730 (Q582)

desalination (salt water fresh), 221 (PRVA11), 360 (PRVB11), 361 (PRVB13), 362 (PRVB15), 364 (PRVB18), 365 (PRVB19), 429 (PRVB115), 531 (PRZA6), 574 (PRZA13), 600 (PPP55)

drainage, 544 (PRZA23), 704 (Q246)

dredging, 226 (PRVA17), 265 (PRVA49), 371 (PRVB30)

drugs (particular): ampicillin, 761 (Q1032); anti-malaria drugs, 738 (Q700); anti-toxin patent, 705 (Q258); aspirin, 748 (Q844); chloramphenicol, 750 (Q867); chlorothiazide, 750 (Q867); penicillin, 744 (Q779), 749 (Q853), 795 (DEB424); poliomyelitis vaccine, 798 (DEB471); potassium cyanide, 705 (Q254); salvarsan (antisyphilitic) payments relating to 723 (Q493), 791 (DEB370); small pox, cure, 652 (PET233), 656 (PET270); stone, cure for, 528 (PRZA2); tetracycline, 750 (Q867), 752 (Q904), 755 (Q942); tetralysal, 752 (Q901); vaccination, 548 (PRZA28), 551 (PRZA30); vitamins, 739 (Q713, Q714, Q716)

drugs, animal, 757 (Q977)

drugs, 751 (Q881), 752 (Q905), 754 (Q925, Q928), 759 (Q1005), 797 (DEB469), 802 (DEB539); balance of payment, 762 (Q1052); clinical trials, 802 (DEB536); drugs royalties, 750 (Q870, Q871); extension, 762 (Q1053); law reform and White Paper, 765 (Q1105); Percentage of patents relate to, 759 (Q1004); prices, 748 (Q842), 749 (Q860, Q861), 750 (Q868, Q869, Q872); profit, 758 (Q988) harmonising law relating to, 762 (Q1058), quality, 798 (DEB474); restriction on patenting introduced, 56 (PUBA31); US, 747 (Q824); see Patents Act 1949, ss 41 and 46

dyes, 234 (PRVA24), 236 (PRVA26), 367 (PRVB23), 373 (PRVB33), 378 (PRVB42), 379 (PRVB43), 382 (PRVB45), 388 (PRVB53), 447 (PRVB143), 537 (PRZA14), 540 (PRZA17, PRZA18), 541 (PRZA19), 542 (PRZA21), 731 (Q601), 793 (DEB401); aniline 786 (DEB290); German industry, 788 (DEB315); see Dyestuff (Import Regulation) Bill

electricity, 450 (PRVB147), 453 (PRVB150)

engines: diesel, 801 (DEB525); rotary, 434 (PRVB124)

explosives, 602 (PPP74), 692 (Q74, Q80), 697 (Q151), 704 (Q242), 776 (DEB141), 778 (DEB164, DEB168), 782 (DEB224); EXE powder, 704 (Q242); fuses, 658 (PET295, PET297), 693 (Q89), 700 (Q187, Q189, Q190), 701 (Q195, Q200), 785 (DEB265); see cordite

fabrics: baize, 478 (SCOT21, SCOT22), 486 (SCOT63), 487 (SCOT68); cloth, 492 (SCOT125); fur, 282 (PRVA62); lace, 403 (PRVB76); linen, 485 (SCOT40), 487 (SCOT65, SCOT67, SCOT68, SCOT73); lustrings, 221 (PRVA12); seal hair, 571 (PRZC9), 574 (PRZC12), 576 (PRZC15); silk, 488 (SCOT86), 492 (SCOT124); wool, 486 (SCOT51), 487 (SCOT66, SCOT68), 488 (SCOT80, SCOT87 to SCOT89), 490 (SCOT99, SCOT103, SCOT104, SCOT110), 492 (SCOT119, SCOT122), 493 (SCOT126, SCOT127); worsted, 490 (SCOT108); see also leather

filtration, 261 (PRVA46), 313 (PRVA88), 429 (PRVB115), 637 (PET128, PET129), 697 (Q149)

fire proof, Acts 232 (PRVA23), 341 (PRVA114); cement, 637 (PET130); Patent Office, fireproofing of 708 (Q292); rewards, 539 (PRZA16)

fish: rights, 486 (SCOT54); salt, 213 (PRVA2), 355 (PRVB1); transporting of 532 (PRZA8)

flax, 246 (PRVA35), 294 (PRVA71), 296 (PRVA72), 396 (PRVB65), 421 (PRVB102), 442 (PRVB136), 627 (PET25), 628 (PET36)

food: bread, 635 (PET110); butter, 140 (PUBB3); milk, frozen, 746 (Q816), 747 (Q820); potatoes, 314 (PRVA89); production, 331 (PRVA105), 107 (PUBA71), 110 (PUBA73), 111 (PUBA74); saccharine, 783 (DEB244); spelter, 371 (PRVB29); vinegar, 407 (PRVB83), 489 (SCOT98), 490 (SCOT101); see also fish, sugar

fortifications, 654 (PET249)

friction reduction, 390 (PRVB55)

furnaces, 315 (PRVA90), 317 (PRVA92), 332 (PRVA106), 334 (PRVA108), 374 (PRVB35), 574 (PRZC13), 652 (PET235), 653 (PET238, PET239); smelting, 481 (SCOT29)

furniture: baths, 356 (PRVB3); cabinet maker, 491 (SCOT114)

gas, 255 (PRVA42), 276 (PRVA58), 417 (PRVB95), 743 (Q774); coal, 400 (PRVB71); CS gas, 758 (Q986, Q987, Q992), 802 (DEB548); nerve gas, sales abroad, 758 (Q991); poison, 638 (PET136), 639 (PET140), 652 (PET228); purification, 603 (PPP86), 695 (Q113); VX Gas, 764 (Q1083, Q1084)

glass, 332 (PRVA106), 357–9 (PRVB6 to PRVB8), 411 (PRVB88), 474 (SCOT9), 480 (SCOT27), 481 (SCOT28), 489 (SCOT91 to SCOT94, SCOT97), 769 (DEB40)

gun, 602 (PPP77), 655 (PET261), 687 (Q5), 693 (Q88), 697 (Q151), 778 (DEB162), 782 (DEB224); Bren, 738 (Q699, Q703); experimental, 603 (PPP89); gun with 100m range, 725 (Q523); loading, 697 (Q152), 727

Index of parliamentarians

Bridgeman, William (1864–1935), 724 (Q503, Q504, Q505, Q507, Q509, Q510, Q512, Q513), 725 (Q517, Q518), 726 (Q527, Q531)

Bridgewater, (3rd) Earl of (John Egerton) (1646–1701), 221 (PRVA11)

Bright, John (1811–1889), 692 (Q77, Q78), 770 (DEB43)

Brittain, Sir Harry (1873–1974), 727 (Q550), 731 (Q595)

Broadhurst, Henry (1840–1911), 179 (PUBB36), 180 (PUBB37), 181 (PUBB38), 186 (PUBB41), 700 (Q188), 781 (DEB209), 787 (DEB300)

Brockway, (Archibald) Fenner (Lord) (1888–1988), 750 (Q875), 751 (Q887), 802 (DEB548)

Brodrick, William (1856–1942), 700 (Q191), 701 (Q196), 702 (Q217, Q218, Q220), 709 (Q312), 784 (DEB255, DEB260)

Brogden, James (1765–1842), 559 (PRZA39)

Brooke, Henry (1903–1984), 750 (Q874)

Brooke-Pechell, George (1789–1860), 768 (DEB25)

Brooks, Edwin (1929-), 760 (Q1025)

Brotherton, Joseph (1783–1857), 272 (PRVA55), 274 (PRVA56), 286 (PRVA65), 289 (PRVA67), 293 (PRVA70), 294 (PRVA71), 297 (PRVA73), 298 (PRVA74), 435 (PRVB127), 438 (PRVB132), 439 (PRVB133), 440 (PRVB134), 768 (DEB17, DEB25, DEB27), 769 (DEB29, DEB30)

Brougham and Vaux, Lord (Henry) (1778–1868), 12 (PUBA2), 15 (PUBA3), 80 (PUBA44), 156 (PUBB18, PUBB19), 157 (PUBB20), 162 (PUBB23), 687 (Q9), 768 (DEB16), 771 (DEB64)

Brown, Alexander (1844–1922), 174 (PUBB32), 175 (PUBB33), 178 (PUBB35), 179 (PUBB36), 180 (PUBB37), 181 (PUBB38), 186 (PUBB41), 695 (Q121)

Brown, Charles (1884–1940), 195 (PUBB50)

Brown, Douglas Clifton (1879–1958), 62 (PUBA34), 65 (PUBA36)

Brown, Ernest (1881–1962), 737 (Q679, Q682)

Brown, George (Lord) (1914–1985), 745 (Q802), 748 (Q840), 798 (DEB481), 803 (DEB564), 804 (DEB570)

Brown, Robert (1912–1996), 800 (DEB512)

Browne, Issac Hawkins (1745–1818), 551 (PRZA31)

Bruce, Henry (1815–1895), 778 (DEB160)

Bruce-Gardyne, John (Jock) (1930–1990), 758 (Q982), 802 (DEB545)

Brunner, Sir John (1842–1919), 702 (Q216), 709 (Q303), 785 (DEB268, DEB273)

Bryce, James (1838–1922), 705 (Q256, Q257, Q258, Q259), 786 (DEB290)

Buchanan, George (1890–1955), 736 (Q668)

Buckingham and Chandos, (3rd) Duke of (Richard Temple-Nugent-Brydges-Chandos-Grenville)

(1823–1889), 34 (PUBA17), 332 (PRVA106), 449–51 (PRVB146 to PRVB148)

Buckley, Albert (1877–1965), 728 (Q566)

Bull, Sir William (1863–1931), 715 (Q381, Q387), 720 (Q457), 729 (Q574), 731 (Q609)

Buller, Sir John Yarde (1771–1849), 262 (PRVA47)

Bulwer, Henry Lyton (1801–1872), 146 (PUBB10)

Burden, Thomas (1885–1970), 67 (PUBA38)

Burdett, Sir Francis (1770–1844), 768 (DEB25)

Burdon, Rowland (1757–1838), 382 (PRVB46), 547 (PRZA27)

Burgin, (Leslie) Edward (1887–1945), 736 (Q670, Q671, Q676), 737 (Q688)

Burke, Edmund (1730–1797), 567 (PRZC5)

Burke, Wilfred (1889–1968), 740 (Q730)

Burnet, Gilbert (1643–1715) (Bishop of Salisbury), 219 (PRVA10)

Burns, John (1858–1943), 705 (Q259), 718 (Q422), 786 (DEB285), 788 (DEB325)

Burrell, Sir Charles (1774–1862), 290 (PRVA68), 434 (PRVB126)

Burt, Thomas (1837–1922), 703 (Q234), 705 (Q253)

Bury, Viscount (Arnold Keppel) (1858–1942), 782 (DEB219)

Butcher, Herbert (1901–1966), 99 (PUBA63)

Butcher, Sir John (1853–1935), 721 (Q466)

Butler, (Richard) Rab (1902–1982), 104 (PUBA68), 112 (PUBA75), 746 (Q805, Q811), 748 (Q840), 797 (DEB466)

Butler, Joyce (1910–1992), 132 (PUBA91)

Butler, Sir George (1887–1929), 733 (Q630)

Buxton, Sydney (1853–1934), 699 (Q168), 705 (Q254), 712 (Q343), 716 (Q392, Q394, Q398, Q400), 717 (Q402 to Q406, Q411), 783 (DEB241), 787 (DEB301)

Byrne, Edmund (1844–1904), 189 (PUBB43)

Caine, William (1842–1903), 783 (DEB235)

Cairns, John (1859–1923), 725 (Q522)

Cairns, Lord (Hugh) (1819–1885), 167 (PUBB29), 170 (PUBB30), 307–10 (PRVA82 to PRVA85), 696 (Q128), 771 (DEB61), 778 (DEB171), 779 (DEB186)

Caldwell, James (1839–1925), 45 (PUBA23), 50 (PUBA25), 786 (DEB287)

Callaghan, James (1912–2005), 747 (Q821)

Cameron, Charles (1841–1924), 701 (Q201, Q208), 785 (DEB267)

Campbell, Edward (1879–1945), 732 (Q620)

Campbell, Henry (1856–1924), 701 (Q209)

Campbell, Lord (John) (1779–1861), 769 (DEB28)

Campbell, Lord Frederick (1729–1816), 239 (PRVA29)

Campbell, Sir David (1891–1963), 746 (Q808, Q810, Q812, Q813)

Rigby, Sir John (1834–1903), 705 (Q250)

Rigg, Richard (1877–1924), 711 (Q327)

Rippon, Geoffrey (1924–1997), 750 (Q871)

Ritchie, Charles (1838–1906), 32 (PUBA15), 705 (Q260), 706 (Q261, Q263, Q264, Q265, Q266, Q273), 707 (Q274), 707–708 (Q275 to Q289), 708 (Q291, Q293, Q296, Q298), 710 (Q322), 786 (DEB285, DEB290), 787 (DEB298)

Robert, Emrys (1910–1990), 742 (Q759)

Roberts, Albert (1908–2000), 761 (Q1031)

Roberts, George (1868–1928), 720 (Q454 to Q456, Q458), 721 (Q459, Q462, Q463)

Roberts, Goronwy (1913–1981), 755 (Q948)

Roberts, Gwilym (1928-), 756 (Q953)

Roberts, Samuel (1852–1926), 713 (Q354)

Robertson, John (1856–1933), 53 (PUBA27), 718 (Q425), 791 (DEB360)

Robertson, John (1913–1987), 757 (Q971)

Robinson, Kenneth (1911–1996), 123 (PUBA84), 750 (Q869, Q870, Q877), 751 (Q878, Q883, Q889, Q891), 752 (Q892), 753 (Q911, Q914, Q915, Q918, Q919), 754 (Q921, Q922, Q924, Q925, Q928), 755 (Q942), 758 (Q988, Q989), 798 (DEB486), 802 (DEB544)

Robinson, Roland (1907–1989), 794 (DEB407)

Rochester, Earl of (Laurence Hyde) (1642–1711), 218 (PRVA9)

Rodgers, George (1925–2000), 765 (Q1097)

Rodgers, Sir John (1906–1993), 749 (Q847, Q853), 756 (Q956), 762 (Q1050)

Rodgers, William (1928-), 764–765 (Q1083 to Q1085)

Roebuck, John (1801–1879), 427 (PRVB112)

Roebuck, Rory (1929-), 758 (Q994)

Rogers, James (Thorold) (1823–1890), 781 (DEB210)

Rollit, Sir Albert (1842–1922), 187 (PUBB42), 190 (PUBB44), 785 (DEB267), 787 (DEB297)

Rolt, Peter (1798–1882), 772 (DEB78)

Romilly, Sir John (1802–1874), 81 (PUBA45), 82 (PUBA46)

Rooker, Jeff (1941-), 765 (Q1101)

Roolfe, Robert (1790–1868), 15 (PUBA3)

Roscoe, Sir Henry (1833–1915), 699 (Q172)

Rose, Frank (1857–1928), 732 (Q617)

Rose, George (1744–1818), 557 (PRZA37)

Rosebery, (5th) Earl (Archibald Primrose) (1847–1927), 778 (DEB169)

Rosse, (3rd) Earl of (William Parsons) (1800–1867), 769 (DEB39)

Rost, Peter (1930-), 803 (DEB558)

Rowlands, James (1851–1920), 721 (Q463), 722 (Q482), 724 (Q506, Q513), 725 (Q519)

Runciman, Walter (1870–1949), 55 (PUBA28, PUBA29), 718 (Q429), 719 (Q430, Q438, Q442, Q444), 720 (Q445, Q446, Q451), 736 (Q674), 737 (Q677, Q685, Q690), 738 (Q692), 791 (DEB364, DEB369, DEB371), 793 (DEB404)

Russell, Alexander West (1879–1961), 195 (PUBB50), 734 (Q641)

Russell, Lord John (1792–1878), 687 (Q6, Q7), 769 (DEB30), 770 (DEB47)

Russell, Sir Charles (1832–1900), 783 (DEB238), 785 (DEB271)

Russell, Sir Ronald (1904–1974), 129 (PUBA89), 756 (Q959), 760 (Q1015)

Russell, Sir Thomas (1841–1920), 715 (Q380, Q386)

Rutherford, William Watson, 791 (DEB361, DEB363, DEB364, DEB371)

Ryder, Dudley (1762–1847), 387 (PRVB52)

Rylands, Peter (1820–1887), 777 (DEB146), 778 (DEB162)

Sainsbury, Lord (John) (1927-), 804 (DEB570)

Salisbury, (3rd) Marquess of (Robert Gascoyne-Cecil) (1830–1903), 784 (DEB252)

Salisbury, (4th) Marquess of (James Gascoyne-Cecil) (1861–1947), 791 (DEB356)

Salt, Edward (1881–1970), 741 (Q742)

Salter, Sir Arthur (1859–1928), 739 (Q708)

Samuda, Joseph (1813–1885), 775 (DEB121), 776 (DEB126, DEB133), 779 (DEB175), 780 (DEB188)

Samuel, Arthur (1872–1942), 730 (Q586), 731 (Q595) 732 (Q615, Q616, Q618 to Q620, Q622), 733 (Q633), 734 (Q644), 735 (Q659), 792 (DEB388), 793 (DEB396)

Samuel, Herbert (1870–1963), 717 (Q407), 718 (Q415, Q416, Q418, Q419, Q421), 790 (DEB348, DEB352, DEB354)

Samuelson, Henry (1845–1937), 695 (Q114)

Samuelson, Sir Bernard (1820–1905), 696 (Q134, Q135), 697 (Q153), 698 (Q154, Q155), 699 (Q176), 704 (Q240)

Sandeman Allen, John (1892–1949), 731 (Q601)

Sandon, Viscount (Dudley Ryder) (1831–1900), 695 (Q117)

Sandon, Viscount (Dudley Ryder) (1798–1882), 250 (PRVA39), 768 (DEB21)

Sandys, Duncan (1908–1987), 746 (Q809, Q814), 797 (DEB455)

Sandys, George (1875–1937), 790 (DEB344)

Sasson, Sir Edward (1856–1912), 788 (DEB322)

Saville, Sir George (1678–1743), 232 (PRVA23)

Saye and Sele, (13th) Lord (Thomas Twistleton) (c1735-1788), 230 (PRVA21)

Scarsdale, Lord (Nathaniel Curzon) (1726–1804), 228 (PRVA19), 231–235 (PRVA22 to PRVA25)

Index of legislation

Index of cases

General index

drugs from abroad, 750 (Q873); profit on sale, 758 (Q990); return on drug patents, 763 (Q1064); royalty payments, 749 (Q861); voluntary scheme, 749 (Q861), 751 (Q881), 753 (Q907)

Edmunds, Leonard, accounts 660 (PET313), 693 (Q94), 777 (DEB155); appointment, 690 (Q57); arrest, 692 (Q81, Q83), 777 (DEB143); case, his, 680 (PET571), 774 (DEB109), 775 (DEB112), 776 (DEB130), 781 (DEB202); censure, 775 (DEB112); grievances, 660 (PET309, PET310); his paper, 692 (Q76); inquiry, 657 (PET289), 659 (PET302), 660 (PET314, PET315), 690 (Q51); misconduct/holding money, 690 (Q54, Q56); pension, 657 (PET285); recovery of lost funds/ proceedings, 691 (Q61, Q62); refer to auditor, 693 (Q94), 777 (DEB155), 778 (DEB161); refer to Select Committee, 778 (DEB169), 779 (DEB186); report of inquiry 690 (Q53); report on affair, 587 (REP10, REP11)

Egypt, effectiveness of patent law, 777 (DEB153); industrial property law, 798 (DEB475)

Elizabeth I, "Golden Speech", 767 (DEB4)

emergency legislation, extension, 795 (DEB434)

Empire patent, 620–621 (EMP1 to EMP16), 629 (PET44), 645 (PET180), 710 (Q315), 716 (Q393), 731 (Q599)

employee (infringement), exemption, 792 (DEB388), immunity, 780 (DEB191)

employee (inventions), government intention to change law, 760 (Q1029); local authority employees, 787 (DEB297); Patents Act 1949, s 56, 765 (Q1101); Royal dockyards, 803 (DEB559); transfer of patents, 700 (Q188)

enemy patents (WWI), correspondence with patentee, 723 (Q486); German patents, 719 (Q430, Q434, Q438), 720 (Q453), 721 (Q460), 723 (Q494); number granted, 720 (Q458), 721 (Q460), 722 (Q481), 723 (Q497); policy, 724 (Q502); renewal of, 791 (DEB371)

enemy patents (WWII), 739 (Q719, Q720), 740 (Q734), 743 (Q776), 744 (Q782, Q785); applications for, 739 (Q709); inventions by enemies, 795 (DEB432); Max Burg, 722 (Q485); used before, 741 (Q736); value of seized patents, 743 (Q774); worked by government, 739 (Q711); see also Public Custodian

Euratom, compulsory licences, 799 (DEB494); disclosure obligations, 751 (Q884), 751 (Q887), 799 (DEB491); see also European Communities Act 1972

European Centre for Technology, 802 (DEB541)

European Free Trade Association (EFTA), harmonisation, 802 (DEB537); meeting of, 759 (Q1003), 760 (Q1014, Q1026)

European Patent Convention: conclusion of negotiations, 759 (Q1002), 763 (Q1077); deposit copy, 761 (Q1033); Diplomatic conference, 763 (Q1071); European Commission, Question 135/74 (link to Community Patent Convention), 764 (Q1086); intentions in respect of, 759 (Q1002); modifications sought by UK, 762 (Q1057), 763 (Q1066); prospects, 761 (Q1043); ratification, 763 (Q1064, Q1066, Q1071), 765 (Q1096, Q1106, Q1108), 766 (Q1110); see also European patent law; European Patent Office

European patent law, collaboration, 801 (DEB533); difficult of harmonising, 803 (DEB561); involvement of Yugoslavia, 797 (DEB460); harmonisation, 749 (Q858), 762 (Q1058), 801 (DEB532), 802 (DEB537, DEB549); involvement of Soviet Union, 801 (DEB527); technical producers, 801 (DEB526); Tookey Committee, 752 (Q899)

European Patent Office, effect on UK Patent Office, 762 (Q1049), 763 (Q1068), 804 (DEB574); location, 762 (Q1047, Q1050, Q1051), 764 (Q1079, Q1081), 804 (DEB575); representation made by UK, 763 (Q1070); statement, 763 (Q1067)

European Technological Committee, staff involved, 758 (Q984)

expired patents, 729 (Q570); full term, 729 (Q572); royalty on 719 (Q439); trade marks and, 722 (Q472)

Explosives Committee, 704 (Q243, Q244), 709 (Q312)

export of machinery, restriction, 635–637 (PET112 to PET123)

Export Order, delay, 758 (Q982)

extension of term (generally), 713 (Q360, Q361); see also prolongation

extensions of time under patents laws, 673 (PET475), 746 (Q810); applications to Lord Chancellor, 600 (PPP52, PPP53); cost of processing application, 757 (Q976)

Financial Statement, entries 1921, 726 (Q540); receipts: 1922, 727 (Q547); 1928, 732 (Q618)

foreign earnings, currency for royalties, 747 (Q828); patents, 746 (Q805); US patents, 746 (Q811)

foreign law, patents, 603 (PPP81)

foreigners, patents granted to, 711 (Q333)

France, automatic expiry of patent, 708 (Q287, Q291); importation / manufacture patented articles, 697 (Q142); number of applications, 715 (Q388), 716 (Q390)

Fry Committee (1901) [REP17], implementation, 709 (Q307), 710 (Q313, Q318); publication of report, 709 (Q306), 710 (Q318)

Germany, abolition of patents, 796 (DEB447); automatic expiry of patents, 708 (Q287, Q291); German Patent Office, 744 (Q782); number of applications, 715 (Q388), 716 (Q390); number of patents granted, 793 (DEB402), 799 (DEB502); patent legislation of, 603 (PPP88); translation of patent law, 695 (Q124)

gift to nation, 637 (PET129, PET130), 652 (PET233)

government held patents, vested in single body, 743 (Q771)

Great Exhibition 1851 [EXB1], 641 (PET156), 642 (PET162), 643 (PET170)

Great London Exhibition (1862), mining illustrations, 697 (Q141); purchase of buildings, 773 (DEB88)

harmonising (patent) law, 706 (Q265), 729 (Q578), 802 (DEB537, DEB549); assimilate across Europe, 749 (Q858), 801 (DEB532), 803 (DEB561); assimilate law to France, 710 (Q317); assimilate law to Germany, 710 (Q317), 791 (DEB364); assimilate law to USA, 703 (Q226); assimilate with trade marks, designs, 729 (Q578), 798 (DEB472); correspondence on, 603 (PPP82); difficulty, 803 (DEB561); drug laws, 762 (Q1058); others laws more favourable than British, 785 (DEB263)

Herschell Committee (1887–8) [REP14], correspondence since, 602 (PPP79); all evidence printed, 699 (Q167); implementation, 699 (Q171)

home manufacture (working) rule, 1907 Bill, 712 (Q351, Q353), 713 (Q361); advantages of, 790 (DEB344); amendment of 1907 Act, 718 (Q422); burden of proof for revocation, 791 (DEB360, DEB364); clarification, 790 (DEB355); effect of 1907 Act, 713 (Q362, Q364), 714 (Q368, Q369, Q372, Q373, Q374), 715 (Q386), 716 (Q392, Q398, Q404, Q405), 789 (DEB332 to DEB335, DEB338, DEB341), 791 (DEB369); employment, 790 (DEB344, DEB349); extension of one year period, 714 (Q371, Q372); Factory Act 1901 exemption, 789 (DEB341); France, 780 (DEB200); free trade (anti), 788 (DEB325), 789 (DEB333, DEB337), 793 (DEB398); German-American, 714 (Q368), 716 (Q389); Germany, 716 (Q389); introduction in UK, 710 (Q320), 788 (DEB316, DEB318); Ireland, working in, 714 (Q375), 715 (Q380, Q386); Italy, 735 (Q655, Q656, Q658); representations to/from other countries, 713 (Q364), 714 (Q373, Q374); royalties received, 717 (Q404); Tunbridge Wells Drill Hall, use of foreign tile, 716 (Q397); UK only country without, 706 (Q263)

Hopwood Committee (1900) [REP16]

Howitt Committee (1956) [REP23], report, 747 (Q827)

impeachment, 209 (PRVA1)

income tax, 605 (PPP103), 782 (DEB232), 788 (DEB313), 794 (DEB420); abolition on patent sales, 744 (Q778), 796 (DEB440); collection in Scotland, 711 (Q335); difficulties during war, 719 (Q437), 795 (DEB428); German patents during WWI, 719 (Q434); income tax on awards by Royal Commission, 727 (Q546), 731 (Q604, Q607), 732 (Q616, Q619, Q622), 793 (DEB396)

India, disadvantages to residents, 702 (Q212); extension to India of patent law, 688 (Q21)

industrial conference, Madrid, 700 (Q194)

industrial development, patent law, 787 (DEB299)

injunctions, commons law courts, 18 (PUBA6); patents cases 772 (DEB78)

inquiries into particular inventions, 627 (PET28, PET30), 628 (PET36), 629 (PET48), 630 (PET50, PET56), 631 (PET68, PET71), 633 (PET84, PET85), 635 (PET105, PET106, PET108 to PET111), 637 (PET124, PET126 to PET128), 638 (PET134, PET137), 639 (PET139, PET140, PET142), 640 (PET150, PET153), 641 (PET155, PET157 to PET160), 648 (PET199), 650 (PET216), 651 (PET217), 652 (PET228 to PET231), 653 (PET242 to PET246), 654 (PET248, PET249, PET251, PET253, PET254, PET256 to PET259), 655 (PET263, PET266), 656–657 (PET269 to PET284), 658 (PET295, PET297), 660 (PET308), 665 (PET374, PET376), 666 (PET379 to PET381), 669 (PET420, PET422), 676 (PET510, PET511)

International Congress, 736 (Q666)

International arrangements, 166 (PUBB28)

international exhibitions, 16 (PUBA4), 17 (PUBA5), 24 (PUBA10), 25 (PUBA11), 26 (PUBA12), 27 (PUBA13), 163 (PUBB24), 659 (PET307), 690 (Q47), 697 (Q153), 698 (Q157); *see also* Great Exhibition (1851), Great London Exhibition (1862), Philadelphia Exhibition (1876); Paris Exhibition (1900); *generally see* Chapter 6, Part 4

International Patent Office, government position, 757 (Q974)

Inventions from Public Funds (1922) [REP19]

inventors, assistance to, 760 (Q1021); Inventors' Association, 442 (PRVB137); small return to, 779 (DEB178); too much advice given to, 801 (DEB524)

Ireland, adoption of patent regulation, 767 (DEB5); *see also* Government of Ireland Bills 1886 and 1893

Irish Free State, British patents not valid, 731 (Q600); patents after division, 728 (Q562, Q566), 729 (Q572), 731 (Q599)

Italy, patent law, 803 (DEB568); Hague Conference (Paris Convention) amendments, 735 (Q655, Q656), 735 (Q658)

Statutory Instruments: consolidation, 756 (Q962); included in Parliamentary Papers, 708 (Q288); Patent Rules 1905 annulment, 711 (Q340); purchase in Ireland, 709 (Q305); *see also* Part 4 and Part 6, Chapter 3

statutory tribunals, 749 (Q857), 797 (DEB470)

stimulating industry, 753 (Q907, Q908)

Strasbourg Convention, changes in law required by, 605 (PPP104); report of Patent Liaison Group, 755 (Q943); unratified conventions, 756 (Q960)

Supply Memorandum, 731 (Q605); non-defence research, 759 (Q999); Patent Office estimate, 601 (PPP67), 730 (Q593), 773 (DEB93); printing patents, 770 (DEB50), 771 (DEB55, DEB58, DEB59), 772 (DEB76), 773 (DEB86), 784 (DEB251), 785 (DEB270)

surplus, Patent Office, amount, 705 (Q252), 711 (Q329), 713 (Q360), 733 (Q624, Q628, Q629), 735 (Q652), 784 (DEB262), 787 (DEB305); diverted, 783 (DEB236); publication of, 706 (Q264); related to which type of right, 706 (Q264); status of, 736 (Q667); use: grant rewards to inventors, 653 (PET247), 777 (DEB148); improve buildings, 708 (Q294), 771 (DEB60); museum, 658 (PET292), 662 (PET334, PET335), 694 (Q103), 778 (DEB167), 781 (DEB212); novelty exam, 707 (Q284); reduce fees, 652 (PET234), 701 (Q202), 702 (Q210), 708 (Q294), 710 (Q324), 729 (Q575)

Swann Committee (1945–7) [REP22], constitution, 744 (Q788); implementation, 742 (Q756), 743 (Q772): terms of reference, 741 (Q742, Q745), 795 (DEB426), 795 (DEB430);

taxation (deductions), 717 (Q410), 741 (Q738), 793 (DEB396), 796 (DEB438); development costs, 741 (Q739); overseas royalties, 793 (DEB392); industrial research, tax relief, 740 (Q733); lump sum, 795 (DEB427); over-deduction, 793 (DEB399, DEB400); wasting asset, 789 (DEB339)

taxation (France), 744 (Q784)

taxation policy, 802 (DEB546); adequate for inventors, 758 (Q997); comparison with copyright, 800 (DEB509); whether encourage local development of inventions, 747 (Q832), 748 (Q834)

taxation (depreciation), 783 (DEB238), 789 (DEB339), 790 (DEB346), 792 (DEB374)

taxation (double), 800 (DEB516), 801 (DEB520), 803 (DEB552)

taxation (know-how), 801 (DEB530, DEB531)

taxation, 741 (Q737), 782 (DEB232), 784 (DEB261), 788 (DEB327); legislation, 84 (PUBA48), 86 (PUBA49), 88 (PUBA52), 90–94 (PUBA54 to PUBA58), 98 (PUBA62), 101–103 (PUBA65 to PUBA67), 114 (PUBA76), 115 (PUBA78), 120 (PUBA82), 124 (PUBA85), 126 (PUBA87), 130 (PUBA90), 133 (PUBA92); Selective Employment Tax, 757 (Q967), 760 (Q1018)

taxation (royalties), 715 (Q379), 788 (DEB313), 791 (DEB363, DEB364), 793 (DEB392), 794 (DEB414, DEB420), 795 (DEB428), 796 (DEB446), 800 (DEB510, DEB514, DEB515, DEB518)

threats, groundless, 28 (PUBA14)

Transvaal, British patent rights, 709 (Q303)

Treasury Committees, Privy Seal Office, 585 (REP5)

Treaty of Rome (EEC), Article 85 (TFEU, art 101), 763 (Q1063); joining, effect on patent law, 762 (Q1059), 763 (Q1064); patent law, 750 (Q873), 803 (DEB560); *see also* Community (EEC) Patent Convention

UN Development Decade, proposal to surrender patents to support, 800 (DEB504)

United States: Anglo-American Agreement, 740 (Q727); assimilate law, 703 (Q226); automatic expiry of patent, 708 (Q287); brain drain, 756 (Q957); compact prosecution, 754 (Q930); copies of specifications declined, 709 (Q309, Q311), 710 (Q314); difference from UK, 701 (Q205), 702 (Q222), 711 (Q326); fees, repaid by US government during war, 728 (Q559); infringement by US government, 736 (Q675); number of applications, 715 (Q388), 716 (Q390); number obtained by Englishmen, 702 (Q219); royalties, 758 (Q996); specifications, not sent, 701 (Q205); specifications, number increased 703 (Q224); treaties, 615 (TRE3, TRE10), 616 (TRE26), 617 (TRE38, TRE42), 618 (TRE48, TRE50); term of protection, 734 (Q642); Weekly Gazette 696 (Q137)

unity of invention, 28 (PUBA14), 498 (SI)

universities, technology transfer, 801 (DEB529)

unpatented inventions for defence purposes, report, 593 (REP23), 747 (Q827)

Value Added Tax (VAT), 800 (DEB509)

vanity patents, 794 (DEB422)

vessels, foreign (infringement), 18 (PUBA6), 89 (PUBA53), 96 (PUBA60), 100 (PUBA64)

Vienna Exhibition 1873 [EXB5]: attendance of Thomas Webster, 694 (Q101, Q102), grants to exhibit, 693 (Q92, Q97)

vote on supply to Patent Office: 1854, 770 (DEB47); 1855, 770 (DEB54); 1856, 771 (DEB56); 1857, 771 (DEB60); 1858, 771 (DEB61); 1859, 771 (DEB66); 1860, 772 (DEB72); 1861, 772 (DEB77); 1863, 773 (DEB89); 1864, 773 (DEB93, DEB95), 774 (DEB102); 1865, 774